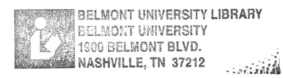

# International Directory of
## COMPANY
## HISTORIES

# International Directory of

# COMPANY HISTORIES

## VOLUME 16

*Editor*
**Tina Grant**

## St. James Press
AN IMPRINT OF GALE

Detroit · New York · Toronto · London

## STAFF

Tina Grant, *Editor*

Miranda H. Ferrara, *Project Manager*
Michael J. Tyrkus, *Contributing Editor*
Peter M. Gareffa, *Managing Editor, St. James Press*

The paper used in this publication meets the minimum
requirements of American National Standard for Information Sciences—
Permanence Paper for Printed Library Materials, ANSI Z39.48-1984.

This book is printed on recycled paper that meets Environmental Protection Agency Standards.

**Library of Congress Catalog Number: 89-190943**

**British Library Cataloguing in Publication Data**

International directory of company histories. Vol. 16
I. Tina Grant
338.7409

ISBN 1-55862-219-5

Printed in the United States of America

St. James Press is an imprint of Gale

Cover photograph courtesy of the New York Stock Exchange

10 9 8 7 6 5 4 3 2 1

# CONTENTS

## Company Histories

# PREFACE

The St. James Press series *The International Directory of Company Histories (IDCH)* is intended for reference use by students, business people, librarians, historians, economists, investors, job candidates, and others who seek to learn more about the historical development of the world's most important companies. To date, *IDCH* has covered over 2,650 companies in sixteen volumes.

## Inclusion Criteria

Most companies chosen for inclusion in *IDCH* have achieved a minimum of US$100 million in annual sales and are leading influences in their industries or geographical locations. Companies may be publicly held, private, or non-profit. State-owned companies that are important in their industries and that may operate much like public or private companies also are included. Wholly owned subsidiaries and divisions are presented if they meet the requirements for inclusion.

Entries on companies that have had major changes since they were last profiled may be selected for updating.

The *IDCH* series highlights 10% private and non-profit companies, and features updated entries on approximately 25 companies per volume.

## Entry Format

Each entry begins with the company's legal name, the address of its headquarters, its telephone number and fax number and a statement of public, private, state, or parent ownership. A company with a legal name in both English and the language of its headquarters country is listed by the English name, with the native-language name in parentheses.

Also provided are the company's founding or earliest incorporation date, the number of employees, and the most recent sales figures available. Sales figures are given in local currencies with equivalents in U.S. dollars. For some private companies, sales figures are estimates. The entry lists the exchanges on which a company's stock is traded, as well as the company's principal Standard Industrial Classification codes. American spelling is used throughout, and the word "billion" is used in its U.S. sense of one thousand million.

## Sources

The histories were compiled from publicly accessible sources such as general and academic periodicals, books, annual reports, and material supplied by the companies themselves.

## Cumulative Indexes

Following the entries are two indexes: the **Index to Companies**, which provides an alphabetical index to companies discussed in the text as well as companies profiled, and the **Index to Industries**, which allows researchers to locate companies by their principal industry. Both indexes are cumulative and specific instructions for using the indexes are found immediately preceding each index.

## New Series Features

Beginning with Volume 16 *IDCH* features include:

- A **Company Perspectives** box which provides a short summary of the company's mission, goals, and ideals

- Bold **Paragraph Headings** which allow users to scan entries to find topics or time periods of interest to them

## Suggestions Welcome

Comments and suggestions from users of *IDCH* on any aspect of the product as well as suggestions for companies to be included or updated are cordially invited. Please write:

The Editor
*International Directory of Company Histories*
St. James Press
835 Penobscot Building
Detroit, Michigan 48226-4094

## ABBREVIATIONS FOR FORMS OF COMPANY INCORPORATION

| A.B. | Aktiebolaget (Sweden) |
|------|------------------------|
| A.G. | Aktiengesellschaft (Germany, Switzerland) |
| A.S. | Atieselskab (Denmark) |
| A.S. | Aksjeselskap (Denmark, Norway) |
| A.Ş. | Anomin Şirket (Turkey) |
| B.V. | Besloten Vennootschap met beperkte, Aansprakelijkheid (The Netherlands) |
| Co. | Company (United Kingdom, United States) |
| Corp. | Corporation (United States) |
| G.I.E. | Groupement d'Intérêt Economique (France) |
| GmbH | Gesellschaft mit beschränkter Haftung (Germany) |
| H.B. | Handelsbolaget (Sweden) |
| Inc. | Incorporated (United States) |
| KGaA | Kommanditgesellschaft auf Aktien (Germany) |
| K.K. | Kabushiki Kaisha (Japan) |
| LLC | Limited Liability Company (Middle East) |
| Ltd. | Limited (Canada, Japan, United Kingdom, United States) |
| N.V. | Naamloze Vennootschap (The Netherlands) |
| OY | Osakeyhtiöt (Finland) |
| PLC | Public Limited Company (United Kingdom) |
| PTY. | Proprietary (Australia, Hong Kong, South Africa) |
| S.A. | Société Anonyme (Belgium, France, Switzerland) |
| SpA | Società per Azioni (Italy) |

## ABBREVIATIONS FOR CURRENCY

| DA | Algerian dinar | Dfl | Netherlands florin |
|----|----------------|-----|--------------------|
| A$ | Australian dollar | NZ$ | New Zealand dollar |
| Sch | Austrian schilling | N | Nigerian naira |
| BFr | Belgian franc | NKr | Norwegian krone |
| Cr | Brazilian cruzado | RO | Omani rial |
| C$ | Canadian dollar | P | Philippine peso |
| DKr | Danish krone | Esc | Portuguese escudo |
| E£ | Egyptian pound | SRls | Saudi Arabian riyal |
| Fmk | Finnish markka | S$ | Singapore dollar |
| FFr | French franc | R | South African rand |
| DM | German mark | W | South Korean won |
| HK$ | Hong Kong dollar | Pta | Spanish peseta |
| Rs | Indian rupee | SKr | Swedish krona |
| Rp | Indonesian rupiah | SFr | Swiss franc |
| IR£ | Irish pound | NT$ | Taiwanese dollar |
| L | Italian lira | B | Thai baht |
| ¥ | Japanese yen | £ | United Kingdom pound |
| W | Korean won | $ | United States dollar |
| KD | Kuwaiti dinar | B | Venezuelan bolivar |
| LuxFr | Luxembourgian franc | K | Zambian kwacha |
| M$ | Malaysian ringgit | | |

# International Directory of
# COMPANY
# HISTORIES

# ACER

## Acer Inc.

6F, 156 Min Sheng E. Road Sec.3
Taipei 105 R.O.C.
Taiwan
(886) 2-545-5288
Fax: (886) 2-545-5308

*Public Company*
*Incorporated:* 1976
*Employees:* 11,000
*Sales:* NT $63.02 billion (US $3.2 billion) (1994)
*Stock Exchanges:* Taiwan
*SICs:* 3571 Electronic Computers: 3577 Computer
    Peripheral Equipment, Not Elsewhere Classified

Called "the region's most impressive technology company" in a 1996 article in *The Economist,* Acer Inc. is Taiwan's leading exporter and the world's seventh-largest personal computer brand. The company also ranks among the world's ten biggest manufacturers of individual components like keyboards, monitors, and CD-ROM drives, and is America's ninth-largest personal computer producer. By 1995, the company was producing four million PCs annually, 25 percent of them OEMs (products sold under other companies' labels). Under the guidance of Chairman and CEO Stan Shih, Acer used groundbreaking strategies to bounce back from a US $22.7 million loss in 1991, earning US $205 million on sales of US $3.2 billion in 1994. Shih hoped to increase Acer's global sales to US $15 billion by 1999, by which time the company would operate as a "federation" of local manufacturing, assembly, and marketing units.

### Business Origins

Acer's founder was born Shih Chen Jung in 1945. A shy youth, Shih blossomed at National Chiao Tung University, where his natural math aptitude helped him graduate at the top of his class. Shih, who later westernized his given name to Stan, earned a master's degree in 1972 and went to work as a design engineer at Qualitron Industrial Corp.

It was not long, however, before the entrepreneurial bug bit Shih; in 1976, he and several friends founded Multitech International with a $25,000 initial investment. The new firm started by designing hand-held electronic games, then expanded into the distribution of imported semiconductors. Shih renamed his company Acer Inc. in 1981. The name was derived from the Latin word for acute or sharp.

The company enjoyed its first international success that year with the launch of MicroProfessor, a teaching tool. The company began manufacturing PC clones—computers and components that were sold to larger companies with strong brand names—in 1983. Acer diversified vertically in the late 1980s, soon becoming "one of the most vertically integrated microcomputer manufacturers in the world," according to *Los Angeles Business Journal.*

In 1995, *Fortune*'s Louis Kraar called Stan Shih "a fascinating combination of engineering nerd, traditional Chinese businessman, avant-garde manager, and international entrepreneur, with an outsize ambition and vision to match." The young CEO applied all of these talents to his young enterprise. In stark contrast to the micromanagement, nepotism, and profit-taking typical of Taiwanese companies, Shih established a modern, progressive corporate culture. Although Shih's wife, Carolyn Yeh, served as the company's first bookkeeper, the founder vowed that his three children would have to look for jobs elsewhere. Time clocks were anathema, even in production plants. In 1984 he established Taiwan's first stock incentive program. Within four years, 3,000 of Acer's employees were also stockholders.

In 1981, Acer hinted at a sweeping change in strategy with the establishment of Third Wave Publishing Corp. The term "third wave" referred to the most recent phase of the history of Taiwan's computer industry: the first was characterized by trademark and patent piracy, the second by clonemaking, and the third by technological innovation. Instead of simply churning out other companies' designs, Acer began to set itself apart from most of its Taiwanese competitors by doing its own research and development. For example, the company developed one of the world's first Chinese language computer sys-

3

tems. In 1986, Acer was second only to Compaq to introduce a 32-bit PC with an Intel 386 microprocessor.

Acer went public in 1988, having chalked up average annual growth of 100 percent from 1976 to 1988. In 1988, net profits totaled more than US $25 million.

### Early 1990s Setbacks

The late 1980s brought internal and external changes that had a devastating effect on Acer. The internal problems were completely unexpected. In 1989, Shih hired Leonard Liu away from a 20-year career with International Business Machines Corp. (IBM), making him president of the Acer group and chairman and chief executive officer of Acer America Corp. Described in an October 1995 *Fortune* article as "a cerebral Ph.D. in computer science from Princeton," Liu had previously been the "highest-ranking Chinese American executive" at IBM. Liu's managerial style reflected his experience at "Big Blue": in contrast with Shih's traditionally progressive corporate culture, Liu tried to centralize control of Acer. His off-putting approach has been blamed for a management exodus in the early 1990s.

At the same time, the computer industry quickly matured, shifting from a high profit margin business to a low margin commodity practically overnight. Price wars pushed component prices down so rapidly, and a strong New Taiwan dollar made the country's goods so expensive, that it became difficult to make a profit on the finished product.

Acer's sales rose from US $530.9 million in 1988 to US $977 million by 1990, but its profits dropped from US $26.5 million to US $3.6 million during the same period. In 1991, Acer posted its first ever annual loss, US $22.7 million. More than US $20 million of that shortfall came from Acer America, which had struggled since its inception. Acer's stock dropped to 50 percent of its initial public offering price. Shih had to sell Acer's headquarters to make a profit in 1992.

These difficulties, however, did not deter Shih from making several expensive, and oft-criticized, expenditures during the late 1980s and early 1990s. In 1989, Acer invested US $240 million in a joint venture with Texas Instruments and China Development Corporation, a Taiwanese development bank. The cooperative enterprise built Taiwan's first DRAM (dynamic random access memory) factory. Half of its output was sold to Acer, and the other half was sold on the world market. Some industry observers ballyhooed the project, noting a glut in the global DRAM market. Acer also expanded production capacity at its main plant, spent US $36 million on a global marketing campaign, and made questionable acquisitions in the United States and Germany. *Financial World*'s Jagannath Dubashi was skeptical that the company's investments would pay off, noting in her July 1991 coverage of the company that "this new aggressiveness seems both poorly timed and unrealistic." She even characterized the company's bold moves as "a desperate gamble."

At the time, Shih would have been the first to agree with such an assessment. In January 1992, he offered to resign from the company he had founded. Acer's board of directors turned

down Shih's resignation, but accepted Leonard Liu's withdrawal three months later. By mid-year, Shih had resumed day-to-day administration of Acer and its American subsidiary.

Instead of being cowed by the setback, Shih was determined to cement Acer's future in the PC industry by transforming it from just another OEM into one of the world's leading computer brands. He would achieve this goal via several revolutionary strategies.

### New Methods Pace Mid-1990s Turnaround

In a 1995 *Financial World* article, Shih compared Taiwanese computer manufacturing to Chinese restaurants, saying that "Chinese food is good, and it is everywhere, but it has no uniform global image or consistent quality." The same was true of personal computers; although most were made in Taiwan, they were sold under several (primarily American and Japanese) brands, with varying levels of quality. Shih wanted Acer to be more like McDonald's, the quintessential fast food restaurant that boasted a strong brand image and strict quality standards.

This unique paradigm shift required a complete overhaul of Acer's production and distribution scheme. Instead of assembling computers in Taiwan, as it had done for more than a decade, the company began to ship components to 32 locations around the world for assembly. Shih compared computer components like casings, keyboards, and mice to staples like ketchup and mustard that could be shipped slowly and stored indefinitely. He likened the motherboard, which had to have the "freshest" technology possible, to the meat in a sandwich. It was shipped by air from Taiwan to each assembly operation. And finally, Shih compared the CPU and hard drive to "very expensive cheese: we try to source them locally." Shih's adoption of this unique strategy earned him the nickname "the Ray Kroc of the PC business."

This production scheme saved on shipping costs and enabled Acer to include the most up-to-date (Shih liked to call it the "freshest") technology available. In Acer-speak, "fresh" meant innovative. Not content to rely on low-end knockoffs of other companies' technology, Acer stayed abreast of the industry's latest developments. In 1992, it launched a multi-user UNIX system as well as 386- and 4865x-based PCs. That year also saw the introduction of an international service and support network, a vital element of any successful PC business in the 1990s. In 1993, Acer unveiled a new PC that came equipped with a RISC (reduced instruction-set computing) chip and Microsoft Corp.'s most recent version of the Windows operating system.

Shih hoped to bring the "fast food" concept all the way to the retail level, so that customers could custom-order computers with peripherals and memory capacity specifically suited to their needs. Acer tested this concept at a company-owned retail store in Taipei. It seemed to be as close as Acer could come to McDonald's-style service: only two hours passed from the time a system was ordered to the time it was booted.

Shih's "global brand, local touch" strategy was closely related to the "fast food" distribution concept. Instead of creating a series of centrally controlled foreign subsidiaries, Acer established a network of virtually autonomous affiliates, much like a fast food franchise system. Each of these affiliates was managed by a group of locals who determined product configurations, pricing strategies, and promotional programs based on national or regional preferences. The affiliate would usually have just one Taiwanese person on staff to facilitate interorganizational communications. *Sales & Marketing Management* characterized the system as a "revolutionary departure from the traditional hierarchical model of worldwide branches and subsidiaries reporting to a head office." Instead, it was "a commonwealth of independent companies, united only in their commitment to a common brand name and logo."

This strategy gave each Acer affiliate the semblance of a local company, an image that carried with it several benefits. Perhaps most important, it helped to downplay Acer's Taiwanese roots. Despite the country's large strides in the area of quality, "made in Taiwan" continued to carry negative connotations in the minds of many consumers. While Shih was proud of his company's heritage, individual affiliates often found it efficacious to de-emphasize that aspect of the business.

Globalization at Acer employed a third strategy adapted from an Asian chess-like game called "Go." Instead of jumping directly into the world's largest and most important computer markets, Acer conquered the surrounding markets before entering the United States. For example, Acer established itself as the leader in less hotly contested markets in Latin America, Southeast Asia, and the Middle East. By 1995, it was the top-selling computer brand in Mexico, Bolivia, Chile, Panama, Uruguay, Thailand, and the Philippines, not to mention Taiwan.

This combination of tactics worked quickly and well, vindicating many of Acer's previously criticized moves. In 1993, Acer posted record profits of US $75 million; 43 percent of that year's net was generated by the DRAM joint venture, considered "the most efficient in the DRAM industry" by some observers. From 1994 to 1995, Acer advanced from fourteenth to ninth among the world's largest computer manufacturers, surpassing Hewlett-Packard, Dell, and Toshiba. Total sales grew to US $3.2 billion in 1994, and net income increased to US $205 million, as Acer America turned its first annual profit in the 1990s.

### Strategies for the Mid-1990s and Beyond

In the mid-1990s, Acer began to globalize production as well as assembly, building a keyboard and monitor plant in Malaysia in 1994. The company planned a motherboard and CD-ROM factory for the Philippines and hoped to set up production in Argentina, Chile, Thailand, Dubai, South Africa, Brazil, India, the People's Republic of China, and the former Soviet Union.

In 1994, Shih unveiled a plan to "deconstruct" Acer into 21 publicly traded business units by the end of the 20th century. Acer Inc. would continue to own anywhere from 19 percent to 40 percent of the firms' stock, but Shih hoped that their independent status would enable the individual units to compete more effectively by facilitating entrepreneurship, inspiring research and development, and allowing for corporate fundraising through stock and bond offerings. Michael Zimmerman of *PC Week* speculated on another possible motivation behind the plan, known internally as "21-in-21." His June 1994 piece on Acer noted that "Separating the divisions will also clear a path for Shih to retire and, as one observer said, 'to leave his legacy intact' by not risking the future of his brainchild to a successor." In fact, Shih told *PC Week* that he "expects to withdraw from Acer and the workforce" by 1999.

Acer Computer International, the company's Asia-Pacific distributor, had its initial public offering in September 1994. The approximately US $55 million floatation was oversubscribed by about 20 times. Spin-offs of Acer Peripherals, the corporation's manufacturer of keyboards and monitors, and Acer Sertek, the Taiwanese distribution operation, were planned for 1996. Stock in Acer America and certain Latin American operations was slated to go on the auction block by 1997.

*The Economist* reported that Acer's revenues had increased by 75 percent from US $3.2 billion in 1994 to US $5.7 billion and that Shih hoped to increase that figure to US $15 billion by 1999 via expansion into consumer electronics like televisions and fax machines. The article also emphasized that "Given the computer industry's history of wild swings, Mr. Shih's success may not last forever; but his company is one of the few large ones in developing Asia that may be able to teach western businesses more than it can learn from them."

### Principal Subsidiaries

Hsiang Chih Technology Corp. (99.7%); Yang Chih Technology Corp. (74.98%); Hsin Chi Technology Corp. (85.68%); Li Chi International Corp. (51.5%); Acer America Corp. (United States); Acer Sales & Distribution (Hong Kong; 85%); Acer Japan Corp. (Japan; 83.34%); Acer Latin America, Inc. (United States; 85%); Acer Computer Australia Pty. Ltd. (Australia; 85%); Acer Sales and Service Sdn Bhd (Malaysia; 85%); Acer Computer (South Asia) Pte. Ltd. (Singapore; 85%); Acer Computer (Far East) Ltd. (Hong Kong; 72.3%); Fora Worldwide Corp. (United States; 63%); Acer Computer France (France); Acer Computer B.V. (Holland); Acer U.K. Ltd.; Acer Italy S.R.L. (Italy); Acer Computer GmbH (Germany); Acer Scandinavia A/S (Denmark); Acer Computer Vienna (Austria); Acer Market Services Ltd. (Hong Kong; 67.36%); Multiventure Investment Inc. (99.98%); Chun Chi Investment Corp. (99.99%); Acer Worldwide Inc.; Acer European Holdings Acer Holding International Inc. (85%); Acer Computer International Pte. Ltd. (Singapore; 85%); Long Hsien International Co., Ltd. (99.99%); Long Chen International Co., Ltd. (99.99%); The Third Wave Publishing Corp. (99.99%); Hoison Ltd. (99.99%); Chien Chi Technology Management Consulting Co., Ltd. (99.94%); Te Chi Semiconductor Corp. (67.98%).

### Principal Divisions

Acer Peripherals, Inc. (46.35%); Acer Sertek Inc. (48.99%); Kuo Chi Electrical Co., Ltd. (49.99%); Acer Argentina S.A. (Argentina; 42%); SV-Acer Co., Ltd. (49%); Acer Africa Pty. Ltd. (50%).

### *Further Reading*

"The Acer Group," *Los Angeles Business Journal,* September 2, 1991, p. S10.

"Bits and Bytes," *The Economist,* March 9, 1996, p. S20.

Brennan, Laura, "High-Tech Union Shatters Merger Myth: Acer, Altos Upbeat on Profits, Channels," *PC Week,* March 4, 1991, p. 123.

Carlton, Jim, "Compaq and Acer Are Slashing Prices on Entry-Level PCs To Expand Market," *Wall Street Journal,* November 17, 1995, p. A3.

DiCarlo, Lisa, "Acer To Expand Beyond PCs," *PC Week,* April 22, 1996, p. 125.

Dubashi, Jagannath, "The Dragon's Curse: Why Taiwan's $1 billion Acer Group Is Betting the Store on PCs," *Financial World,* July 23, 1991, p. 46.

Engardio, Pete, "For Acer, Breaking Up Is Smart To Do," *Business Week,* July 4, 1994, p. 82.

Engardio, Pete, and Neil Gross, "Acer: Up from Clones—and Then Some," *Business Week,* June 28, 1993, p. 54.

Hamm, Steve, "Ace in the Hole," *PC Week,* June 13, 1994, p. A1.

Huang, Charlene, "Acer Group Plans Major Leap in PC Market," *Electronics,* January 23, 1995, p. 13.

——, "Acer Aims at Latin America PC Market," *Electronics,* July 25, 1994, p. 14.

"Inferiority Complex," *The Economist,* February 1, 1992, p. 78.

Kraar, Louis, "Acer's Edge: PCs To Go," *Fortune,* October 30, 1995, p. 186.

Lazlo, J. J., "Electronics Industry 1995 Far East Review," *PaineWebber Inc.,* January 2, 1996.

Mantel, Kimberly, and Wei, Carol, "The Datamation 100: Acer Inc.," *Datamation,* September 1, 1992, p. 89.

Morris, Kathleen, "The Disintegration Model," *Financial World,* June 20, 1995, p. 32.

Shapiro, Don, "Ronald McDonald, Meet Stan Shih," *Sales & Marketing Management,* November 1995, p. 85.

Tanzer, Andrew, "Made in Taiwan," *Forbes,* February 26, 1996, p. 134.

——, "The Great Leap Forward," *Forbes,* April 15, 1991, p. 108.

"TI Enters Taiwan Venture To Make DRAMs," *Electronic News,* May 15, 1989, p. 1.

Whiting, Rick, "Getting Acer Back on Track," *Electronic Business,* February 1993, p. 76.

Zimmerman, Michael R., "Acer To Divest into 21 Public Businesses: Growth Plan To Be Complete by Year 2000," *PC Week,* June 20, 1994, p. 109.

—April Dougal Gasbarre

# Aeroquip Corporation

**3000 Strayer Road**
**Maumee, Ohio 43537**
**U.S.A.**
**(419) 867-2200**
**Fax: (419) 867-2390**

*Wholly Owned Subsidiary of TRINOVA Corp.*
*Incorporated:* 1940
*Employees:* 8,368
*Sales:* $1.1 billion (1995 est.)
*SICs:* 3089 Plastics Products, Not Elsewhere Classified;
3052 Rubber & Plastics Hose & Belting; 3061
Mechanical Rubber Goods

With operations on five continents, Aeroquip Corporation ranks among the world's largest producers of industrial hoses, fittings and clamps. Over the course of its more than fifty years in business, Aeroquip's product line has expanded from a limited number of proprietary hoses and fittings for aircraft to include hundreds of products used in applications ranging from automobiles to spacecraft. The company was acquired by Libbey-Owens-Ford Glass Company in a friendly merger in 1968 and moved its headquarters to Maumee, Ohio, a suburb of Toledo. When Libbey-Owens-Ford sold its historic name and glassmaking capacity to Pilkington PLC in 1986, the parent gave the remaining companies (including Aeroquip) the collective name "TRINOVA." By the mid-1990s, Aeroquip's markets included: automotive, off-highway equipment, industrial machinery, air conditioning and refrigeration, commercial and military aircraft, marine equipment, machine tool manufacture, material handling, and even amusement parks.

### Early History

Aeroquip was founded by Peter F. Hurst, who emigrated from Germany to the United States in 1939. Trained as an engineer, Hurst had begun his postgraduate career with the Berlin-based Argus Motor Company's British aircraft operations in 1934. Before long the 24-year-old Hurst was placed in charge of Rotadisk, a subsidiary that designed and made aircraft brakes. Under contract with German aircraft manufacturer Focke-Wulf, Hurst and Rotadisk undertook a thorough overhaul of the airplanes' wheels and hydraulic brakes. The braking system's hoses came under particular scrutiny. Up to this point, hoses were permanently attached to the systems they served. When they wore out, the entire brake mechanism had to be replaced. Hurst's team came up with a detachable, reusable hose fitting that allowed the less durable hoses to be replaced without having to go through the tedious and time-consuming process of draining the entire system. This relatively simple device reduced the weight of the hydraulic brakes, simplified repair, and helped increase the aircraft's fuel efficiency. It also became the foundation of Hurst's lifelong work.

The inexorable build-up to World War II brought profound changes to Hurst's life and career. In 1939, Argus sent the young engineer to America in the hopes of setting up a U.S. subsidiary. Hurst had barely spent a week in the United States when Germany invaded Poland. Loath to return to his homeland, Hurst got an extension of his original three-month visa and stayed stateside. Hurst licensed the patents for the hydraulic devices from Argus and began negotiating a licensing and manufacturing agreement of his own with Hayes Industries Inc. of Jackson, Michigan. When that plan fell through, he decided instead to form his own manufacturing concern. Hurst enlisted the financial and managerial backing of some of Jackson's most prominent businessmen, among them: Charles Hollerith, Don T. McKone, Sr., Stuart M. Schram, Donald M. Teer, and F. F. Ingram. Hurst convinced these five and five others to invest $1,000 each in the new venture. They called their company Aeroquip—a contraction of aeronautical and equipment. Before that first year was out, the new company's stakeholders chipped in another $10,000 each to purchase an abandoned milk processing plant and manufacturing equipment. Within two years, the company's employee roster had burgeoned to 100.

### Contributions to U.S. Military Effort during World War II

Aeroquip's hydraulic devices caught the attention of American military leaders, and their eagerness to outfit U.S. warplanes with the new system got Aeroquip off to a healthy start. In fact, company publications proudly note that "Aeroquip hoses and fittings became the U.S. standard for military aircraft use." Wartime demand ran so high that at times the company struggled to meet it.

However, war brought other, less welcome changes to the company. By virtue of his German citizenship, Hurst was compelled to relinquish his position as general manager at Aeroquip when America joined its European allies in declaring war on the Axis countries. (Since Hurst had not yet attained full citizenship, he had been classified as a "consultant" with the title of general manager at Aeroquip. Founding investor Don T. McKone held the title of president from the company's inception until 1948.) Hurst's pragmatic acquiescence to what must have been a rather insulting order—as an "enemy alien," he wasn't even allowed to enter Aeroquip's plant—enabled the company to maintain is lucrative military contracts. After a 21-month hiatus (during which the indomitable immigrant started a thoroughly patriotic recycling company), Hurst was permitted to return to Aeroquip's executive ranks. He became an American citizen in 1945 and went on to serve the company as president and later CEO and chairman from 1948 until he suffered a stroke and died in 1969 at the age of 58.

Wartime sales peaked at over $6.2 million in 1944, then plunged to less than $1 million in 1946 with the loss of military demand. Aeroquip began to shift its emphasis from military to commercial aircraft but encountered many difficulties in the immediate postwar era. In the midst of these financial problems, a two-month strike that the company itself described as "bitter" marred 1948.

### Growth through Acquisitions during the 1950s and 1960s

Aeroquip went public with the sale of over 150,000 shares at $4 each in July 1950. The proceeds went primarily to the original stockholders, but the company itself cleared about $65,000 to fund the ambitious acquisition plan that helped develop Aeroquip's new commercial interests. From 1948 to 1959, Aeroquip acquired four domestic manufacturers of hydraulic systems components. The 1955 acquisition of Marman Products Company was a highlight of the decade. Originally founded by Herbert "Zeppo" Marx of the Marx Brothers, by the mid-1950s this company specialized in clamps couplings and straps for airplanes. Aeroquip even expanded internationally, acquiring its Canadian licensee in 1955 and establishing two plants in Germany in 1959. Sales grew rapidly in concert with the pace of acquisitions. Annual revenues increased about 45 percent, from $33.4 million in 1956 to $48.23 million by 1959, and profits kept pace, growing by 50 percent, from $1.8 million to $2.7 million.

The 1960s brought more acquisitions, fueling vertical integration and furthering geographic expansion. Barco Manufacturing Co. of Illinois, a producer of ball, swivel and rotary joints, was brought on board in 1962. Aeroquip added the capacity to manufacture its own hoses with the 1963 purchase of Republic Rubber Division of Lee Rubber and Tire Corp. Domestic acquisitions for the decade wrapped up with the additions of Robot Manufacturing Co. in 1964; Kennedy Automatic

Products Co. in 1966; and Oil Equipment Manufacturing Company in 1969. Aeroquip created two foreign affiliates—a joint venture in Mexico and a Brazilian subsidiary—in 1965.

### Merger with Libbey-Owens-Ford: 1968 and After

Aeroquip's multi-decade string of acquisitions helped it break the $100 million sales threshold in 1966. By 1968, the company had 4,480 employees, sales of $123.4 million, over $4.4 million profits, and a presence in six countries. But President Hurst foresaw an even bigger future for Aeroquip and began to seek affiliation with a larger company that could provide his firm with sufficient financial backing to continue its global expansion. When negotiations with the first candidate, Westinghouse, failed, Hurst successfully merged Aeroquip with the Libbey-Owens-Ford Glass Company (LOF) in 1968 through an exchange of the two companies' shares. The new parent provided Aeroquip with the funding it needed to continue to increase manufacturing capacity, penetrate new markets, and create new products. Don T. McKone, son of founding president Don Townsend McKone, succeeded Hurst as president in 1968, when Hurst briefly assumed the titles of chairman and CEO. The new president had started his career at Aeroquip in 1949, working his way through the ranks at the Van Wert and Los Angeles plants before becoming an executive in 1961.

Overseas expansion via acquisition and internal growth was emphasized during the 1970s. Aeroquip acquired its "largest and oldest licensee," Britain's Super Oil Seals & Gaskets Ltd., and merged it with the concurrently purchased Yates-Barco Ltd. to form Aeroquip (U.K.) Ltd. in 1970. The company established a strong presence in France, acquiring one company and creating two others by 1978. By the end of the decade, Aeroquip also had a presence in Sweden, Japan, Belgium, Spain and Italy.

Aeroquip pursued domestic as well as overseas expansion during the 1970s. In 1974, the company acquired the Gustin-Bacon Group, a manufacturer of pipe joints, from Certain-teed Products Corporation and made it a division. Aeroquip created the Aerospace division one year later. Contrary to its rather restrictive name, this segment of the company made components for race cars and military helicopters, for example. Before the decade was out, Aeroquip added the Tomkins-Johnson Company, a manufacturer of industrial cylinders, in Jackson, Michigan. By 1978, Aeroquip's sales exceeded $340.8 million.

The company carried on its tradition of promotion from within in the 1970s and 1980s. In 1976, Frederick Schwier succeeded Don McKone to become the company's fourth president. Schwier had joined the company in 1951 and advanced through the sales department. When Schwier was promoted to president and chief operating officer of LOF in 1980, Harry A. Bancroft assumed Aeroquip's top spot. Trained as an engineer, Bancroft was already a 30-year veteran at the company by the time he was promoted to its presidency.

Aeroquip continued to expand its global manufacturing and distribution network throughout the 1980s, but the most significant event of the decade concerned its corporate structure.

### Formation of TRINOVA: 1980s and 1990s

By the mid-1980s, LOF's diversifications into fluid power and plastics—among them Aeroquip—had grown to exceed annual glass sales. The parent company sold its historic name and glassmaking operations to Britain's largest glassmaker, Pilkington Brothers PLC, in 1986. TRINOVA was formed through the amalgamation of the businesses that remained: Aeroquip, Vickers (another fluid power firm acquired by LOF in 1984), and Sterling Plastics Inc. (acquired by LOF in 1985). According to a 1990 company history, "the TRINOVA name was counted by combining 'tri' (meaning three) with 'nova' (a bright new star)."

G. William Moody, who succeeded Harry Bancroft as Aeroquip's president in 1985, guided the company through this period of transition. After having logged over two decades with the company, Moody's presidency was rather brief but undoubtedly eventful: he retired at the end of 1988. With more than 25 years' experience at Aeroquip, Howard M. Selland was promoted to the company's leading role in 1989 and oversaw what a corporate profile described as "the most extensive reorganization in the company's history": the 1989 merger of Aeroquip and its "sister TRINOVA company," Sterling Engineered Products. The union added plastic molding capacity to Aeroquip's core hydraulic components and systems. The rationalization of operations that followed brought a flurry of corporate divestments in an effort to "streamline operations and blend core competencies."

While parent company TRINOVA no longer breaks out Aeroquip's annual sales and profits, instead delineating sales by market category, Aeroquip appeared to contribute over half the business's turnover in the early 1990s. TRINOVA struggled in the early 1990s, recording multimillion-dollar net losses in 1992 and 1994, but it appeared to have recovered by 1995, recording a $94.9 million profit on $1.88 billion in sales. The parent expected new product development, strategic alliances, and the continuous pursuit of efficiency to continue this positive trend.

For its part, Aeroquip launched a unique sales concept in 1995, opening an industrial retail store in Toledo, Ohio. Open 24 hours a day, the shop caters to the construction, transportation and agricultural markets. The company expected its distributors to launch 140 such outlets in 1996. Under the continuing guidance of President Howard Selland, Aeroquip hoped to drive continuous growth through innovation.

### Principal Operating Units

Industrial Americas Group; International Group; Automotive Group; Aerospace Marine Group.

### Principal Divisions

Industrial Connectors Division; Air Conditioning & Refrigeration Products Division; Aeroquip European Industrial Division; Asian Division; Fluid Connectors Division; Exterior Trim Division; Molded Products Division; Interior Display Division; Hose Products Division; Marine Products Division; Coupling Products Division; Clamp Products Division; European Aerospace Operations.

### Further Reading

*The Flying A: 50th Anniversary.* Maumee, Ohio: Aeroquip Corp., 1990.

Shaw, David, "Aeroquip Is Booming," *European Rubber Journal,* July 1993, p. 17.

*TRINOVA Fact Book.* Maumee, Ohio: TRINOVA, 1995.

Weil, Michael S., "Reusable Hose Fittings for Aviation Markets Launched Aeroquip," *Hydraulics & Pneumatics,* August 1982, p. 78.

"Yokohama Aeroquip Stake to be Sold for $34 Million," *The Wall Street Journal,* March 4, 1996, p. 4B(E).

—April Dougal Gasbarre

# Alberta Energy Company Ltd.

<table>
<tr><td>

**#3900, 421 - 7 Avenue S.W.**
**Calgary, Alberta T2P 4K9**
**Canada**
**(403) 266-8111**
**Fax: (403) 231-3687**

*Public Company*
*Incorporated:* 1973
*Employees:* 700
*Sales:* US $664 million (1995)
*Stock Exchanges:* Toronto Montreal New York
*SICs:* 1382 Oil & Gas Exploration and Production; 1389
    Pipelining; 5052 Petrochemicals

</td></tr>
</table>

Alberta Energy Company Ltd. is the second largest oil and gas producer in Canada. The company's primary activities involve oil and natural gas exploration, development and production, and the ownership and operation of petroleum pipeline systems. In December of 1995, Alberta Energy Company Ltd. paid $1.1 billion to acquire Conwest Exploration Company Ltd., one of the most prominent oil and gas exploration firms in North America. The transaction immediately propelled Alberta Energy to the top of the oil and gas industry, increasing its market capitalization to $2.2 billion. The merger was a boon to Alberta Energy, and increased its exploration land by 56 percent, natural gas reserves by 49 percent, conventional oil reserves by 84 percent, gas production by 55 percent, and conventional oil production by 96 percent. In addition to its expansion on the North American continent, Alberta Energy has made a commitment to pursue exploration and development opportunities in the Neuquen Basin of Argentina, an area with a high potential for significant oil and gas revenues.

## Early History

At the height of the OPEC oil embargo during the early 1970s, the government of the province of Alberta, Canada, decided to initiate a capital investment program to lessen the dependence on foreign oil. The government organized a group of managers and executives from the oil and gas exploration industry and proposed to form a new company that would be operated on a for-profit basis by nongovernment personnel. The concept of forming a new oil and gas exploration firm was attractive to a number of the businessmen approached by the Alberta provincial government, and they agreed to organize and manage the company, despite some reservations expressed regarding the volatility of the industry at that time. In September of 1973, the Alberta Energy Company Ltd. was incorporated, and in just two years the firm was fully operational.

Initially, Alberta Energy focused on gas exploration and production as well as conventional oil exploration and production. Operating almost exclusively in the province of Alberta, the company purchased extensive tracts of land in the Berland River area of west-central Alberta and the region around East Peace River Arch, both with potentially high reserves of oil and gas. During the mid- and late 1970s, management decided to diversify its activities to provide a more stable cash flow for company operations, and the company entered the lumber industry to produce fiberboard for the commercial market.

In the early 1980s, however, with the fear of another oil embargo receding into the past, the deregulation of the natural gas industry in Canada, and the highly protectionist attitude of the United States in the area of forest products, the company's revenues began to plummet. Yet the talent and dogged persistence of the company's management team guided it through these trying years. Management successfully renegotiated Alberta Energy Company's gas contracts, established more sensitive market pricing, and confirmed long-term purchasing agreements. As the price for a barrel of crude oil fell, it was offset by the concurrent lower price for petroleum land purchase, and company management began to acquire ever-larger tracts of land in Alberta for exploration and development. In addition, the provincial government of Alberta declared a royalty holiday for new oil production, thereby boosting the profits of new oil discovered by the company during this time. Finally, management implemented a restructuring program that reduced the company's operating expenses by consolidating the responsibilities of staff members, requiring longer work hours of its employees, and initiating a cost-cutting strategy for all oil and gas exploration.

### Growth and Expansion in the Late 1980s

The restructuring strategy implemented by Alberta Energy Company's management team was successful beyond its expectations. From 1982 to 1986, the average daily western Canadian gas production at the company increased from 193 to 252 million cubic feet. The average daily western Canadian conventional oil production from 1982 to 1986 increased from 346 to 4,613 barrels. And the company oil and natural gas landholdings during the same time shot up from 2.8 million to 3.2 million acres. By 1986, the company held interest in 2,960 producing gas wells and 265 producing oil wells, almost all of them located in Alberta. During this time, the company acquired the following: Chieftain Development Company, Ltd., a firm involved in the international gas and oil exploration industry; Pan-Alberta Gas Ltd., one of Canada's leading natural gas marketers; and Blue Ridge Lumber Ltd., a softwood lumber plant that Alberta Energy management turned into a leading medium density fiberboard manufacturing operation.

In 1986, the company established a separate operating division for its burgeoning pipeline operation. Earlier, the company had commissioned the building of the Alberta Sands Oil Pipeline, a 270-mile pipeline that delivered oil from a plant located at Fort McMurray to the Edmonton area, where it was distributed to local refineries. Another pipeline, the Cold Lake Heavy Oil Pipeline, provided a transportation network for heavy oil blends from the Primrose/Cold Lake area to Edmonton. The final system to be incorporated into the company's pipeline operating division was the Alberta ethane gathering network, which collected ethane from natural gas processing plants within Alberta and transported it to storage caverns located near Fort Saskatchewan.

By 1989, Albert Energy Company owned more than six million acres of exploratory and development landholdings in Alberta, Saskatchewan, British Columbia, and Beaufort, and ranked as one of the top ten companies in total reserves and in oil and gas production levels in the Western Canadian Sedimentary Basin. One of the major areas of exploration during this time was the Waskahigan/Karr/Gold Creek in west-central Alberta. The company held 330,000 acres of land in the area, which included four exploratory wells and ten development wells. Alberta Energy Company reported 100 billion cubic feet of natural gas reserves and 3.6 million barrels of oil and natural gas liquids in its landholdings. Within one year, management projected that production levels would surpass 18 million cubic feet of gas and 600 barrels of natural gas liquids. Although prices for gas declined by four percent, sales of synthetic and conventional oil increased by more than 20 percent and production was at record levels.

During the same year, Alberta Energy Company, through its 50 percent share in the Pacific Coast Energy Corporation, successfully negotiated with both the Canadian government and the British Columbia provincial government to begin construction of the Vancouver Island Natural Gas Pipeline. With a price tag of more than $280 million, the pipeline would deliver natural gas to Vancouver Island and southwestern British Columbia. Alberta Energy also had an interest in the Iroquois Gas Transmission System, which stretched from Iroquois, Ontario to Long Island, New York. In addition to these new developments, the company completed a major renovation and expansion of its Cold Lake Heavy Oil Pipeline, which operated from northeastern Alberta to Edmonton. One of the innovative aspects of this renovation program included state-of-the-art variable speed pump technology. The company's operation of all the pipeline systems under its control was one of the safest in Canada, and for the third straight year there had been no lost-time mishap.

In the two other sectors of the company's activities, development occurred rapidly. The Blue Ridge Lumber operation reported record shipments of both lumber and medium density fiberboard in 1989, with a high volume of chips sales adding to the firm's profitability. Under Alberta Energy management, Blue Ridge Lumber Ltd. was committed to extensive and continuous reforestation programs, resulting in nearly 8,000 acres of the company's landholdings being seeded for regeneration. The company's petrochemicals divisions, having experienced a short period of depressed prices for nitrogen fertilizer at the beginning of the year, began to see prices rise as the year went on. In its first full year of operating within the continental United States, Alberta Energy Company had established ammonium nitrate subsidiaries in Borger, Texas, in Beatrice, Nebraska, in Early, Iowa, and in Leal, North Dakota.

### Development During the 1990s

In the early 1990s, a severe and widespread economic downturn spread throughout Canada, yet Alberta Energy Company weathered these conditions with remarkable success. In 1992, natural gas sales, measured in cubic feet per day, increased by ten percent, and oil and natural gas liquid sales increased by 12 percent. Because of the company's astute management, especially in the areas of oil and gas production and lumber operations, net earnings rose an impressive 206 percent. Much of this increase was due to strict cost controls, which resulted in a nominal increase of only one percent in operating expenses for 1992. For example, the company's funding and development costs were drastically reduced during the early 1990s. From 1988 to 1990, exploration and development costs amounted to $15.20 per barrel; by 1992, exploration and development costs amounted to $6.40 per barrel.

In 1992, the sources of Alberta Energy Company's operating income were a combination of natural gas, conventional oil, lumber, and pipeline revenues. Surprisingly, during this time, the largest generator of revenue was the company's strong pipeline operation. In 1992, Alberta Energy Company wholly owned and operated approximately 820 miles of crude oil pipelines and had a one-third interest in a highly successful 550-mile ethane gathering system in the province of Alberta. In addition, the company still owned a one-half interest in a natural gas pipeline to Vancouver Island. To expand its activities in this area and continue to reduce operating costs, the company began negotiating with a potential Japanese partner to commercialize its "transoil" technology, an innovative technique that uses water to pipeline heavy oil, rather than the traditional oil-based diluent.

1995 was one of the best years for Alberta Energy Company. The company's exploration and development program, the largest to date in more than ten years, resulted in 235 new wells, including 44 that were explorational and 191 that were developmental, with an astounding success rate of 84 percent. Conventional oil production during 1995 increased by 36 percent, primarily as a result of new drilling successes at the company's Suffield and Ogsten sites. Total liquids production increased by a total of 15 percent, more than 42,000 barrels per day. Although the company maintained and expanded its pipeline network throughout Alberta, as well as other smaller investments, management decided to sell the forest products and lumber operation and its associated fiberboard manufacturing facilities. This allowed Alberta Energy Company to lessen its debt and to garner its financial resources for long-range opportunities.

One of these opportunities involved the expansion of exploration and development operations into South America. During 1995, the company invested $16 million in the acquisition of properties near the undeveloped Neuquen Basin of Argentina. This brought Alberta Energy Company's holding in that country to nearly 500,000 acres, with a 23-square mile region high in potential for oil and gas recovery. Because of lack of investment capital over the years, oil and gas exploration and development in Argentina lagged 20 to 30 years behind the rest of the world. As a result, management at Alberta Energy Company made a commitment to devote up to ten percent of its total budget for oil and gas exploration and development to its Argentinean endeavor. One of the new technologies that the company hoped would yield large tracts of oil was the horizontal drilling method used so successfully in Western Canada.

The most important transaction in the company's history, however, involved the acquisition of Conwest Exploration Company Limited for $1.1 billion. One of the most prominent and successful oil and gas exploration companies in North America, Conwest was primarily operating in the West Peace River Arch region of Alberta province. The merger, a friendly transaction, created the second largest publicly traded oil and gas exploration company on the Canadian stock exchanges.

More important, the merger dramatically increased Alberta Energy Company's exploration land, natural gas reserves, conventional oil reserves, gas production, and conventional oil production. With the acquisition of Conwest, the company's stock price shot up 22 percent during 1995.

Given the volatility of the oil and gas exploration industry, Alberta Energy Company's purchase of Conwest and its assets provided the long-term stability that management sought. Having sold all of its non-oil and gas business, the company was ready, and possessed the resources, to focus exclusively on oil and gas exploration.

### Principal Subsidiaries

A.E.C. Argentina S.A.; AEC Energy Resources Ltd.; AEC Power Ltd. (66.7%); Alberta Oil Sands Pipeline Ltd.; Alenco Gas Services Inc.; Alenco Inc.; Alenco Iroquois Pipelines Inc.; Alenco Pipelines Inc.; Alenco Resources Inc.; Conwest Exploration Company Limited; Express Pipeline Inc.; Express Pipeline Ltd. (50%); Pan-Alberta Resources Inc. (49.9%); Stealth Resources Limited.

### Further Reading

"Alberta Energy Company," *Energy Line: Company Newsletter,* Alberta Energy Company, September 1995, p. 1.
"Alberta Energy Company TransCanada Revives Plan for Pipeline to U.S." *The Wall Street Journal,* June 12, 1995, p. C15(E).
"Alberta Energy Gets Financial Assurances for Empress Pipeline," *The Wall Street Journal,* December 18, 1995, p. B4(E).
Morton, Peter, "Alberta Energy Boosts Gas Reserves as Part of Broader Strategy," *The Oil Daily,* February 14, 1994, p. 5.
——, "Alberta Energy Plans To Boost Reserves, Capture New Markets," *The Oil Daily,* April 11, 1994, p. 6.
——, "Alberta Energy Takes 1st Step in Argentina," *The Oil Daily,* October 5, 1994, p. 4.
Wallack, William, "Four Firms Sign Up with Nymex, EnerSoft To Join Channel 4," *The Oil Daily,* May 10, 1994, p. 3.

—Thomas Derdak

# Allied Irish Banks, plc

**Bank Centre**
**P.O. Box 452**
**Ballsbridge**
**Dublin 4**
**Ireland**
**(353) 1-660-0311**
**Fax: (353) 1-660-1474**

*Public Company*
*Incorporated:* 1966 as Allied Irish Banks Limited
*Employees:* 15,105
*Sales:* IR £1.20 billion (1995)
*Stock Exchanges:* Dublin London New York
*SICs:* 6000 Depository Institutions; 6020 Commercial
    Banks

Allied Irish Banks, plc (AIB) is the largest bank in Ireland, and its significant investments in the United States, Great Britain, and Europe make it important internationally. As the largest private sector employer in Ireland and the second largest public company, it is difficult to overstate AIB's importance on its home turf: 40 percent of the banked population there are customers. The company's assets are valued at IR £21.8 billion, making it one of the world's 200 largest banks and placing it mid-list in the *Financial Times* ranking of Europe's 500 largest companies.

## *Origins*

As the three points in the company's old logo suggest, Allied Irish Banks Limited was formed in 1966 as an amalgamation of three banks: the Royal Bank of Ireland Ltd. (founded 1836), the Provincial Bank of Ireland Ltd. (founded 1825), and the Cork-based Munster and Leinster Bank Ltd. (founded in 1885 to take over the failed Munster Bank), the largest of the three independent banks remaining in Ireland, which contributed more than half of the shares of the new holding company. (The heritage of these banks could be traced back even further; Munster and

Leinster's holdings included those of a private bank dating to the days of William of Orange.) The banks, when combined, provided thorough coverage of the island, both geographically and economically. Altogether, their combined assets were worth £250 million. After operating in a type of loose "Trinity" arrangement, in 1968 the banks began to trade as one company; this integration was fully completed in 1972.

Many industries in the British Isles faced consolidation during the 1960s; for the Irish banking industry, this reduction in numbers first affected the numerous private banks of the 17th century until the Central Bank Act of 1942 left the country with eight major banks. Earlier in 1966, the Bank of Ireland (not to be confused with the Royal Bank) had bought the Irish interests of the National Bank. In the mid-1960s, *The Economist* reported the island had a thousand branch offices to serve less than five million people; it was felt that fewer, larger banks would be able to provide more modern and efficient service (the bank employees union, which had held a strike just before AIB's creation, was another factor).

Both Allied Irish Banks and its slightly larger rival, the Bank of Ireland, entered this phase of consolidation under pressure from North American competitors, which first entered the Irish market in 1965, beginning with First National City Bank. Both the Bank of Ireland and AIB began offering new services and forming international strategic alliances; AIB showed itself to be more dedicated to merchant and industrial banking. In a March 1968 company statement, Chairman Edmond M. R. O'Driscoll reported on a newly formed alliance between AIB and Toronto-Dominion Bank, strengthening AIB's international stance. At the same time, a recently devalued pound stimulated growth on the home front.

AIB continued to standardize its three families of branch offices, which in 1971 numbered 281 in the Irish Republic and 46 in Northern Ireland; only 11 branches had been closed after the merger. During this time, several subsidiaries specialized in various areas of business finance: the Hire-Purchase Company of Ireland and its Northern Ireland counterpart (brought to the group by the Munster and Leinster Bank); Mercantile Credit Co. of Ireland (a hire-purchase bank in which Provincial Bank had a 40 percent stake); Allied Irish Leasing Ltd., which fi-

**Company Perspectives:**

*AIB, wherever we operate, will be the leading Irish banking group, creating superior value for our customers and shareholders. Our success will be determined by: the level of customer satisfaction; the return to our shareholders; the contribution of individuals and teams; our performance as a good corporate citizen.*

nanced industrial expansion; and the Allied Irish Investment Corporation, a merchant bank formed in association with Hambros Bank, Toronto-Dominion, and the Irish Life Assurance Company. In 1967, the group boasted assets of £318 million. The late 1960s were booming years for Irish industry, one of the fastest growing in Europe, and for AIB.

### Changes in the 1970s

In the early 1970s, Allied Irish Banks, which formerly derived income only from interest on loans, began charging fees for services, such as 5p per transaction and 5p per £100 withdrawal of cash. The competitive situation inspired the new way of doing business.

Wages accounted for three-fourths of a bank's costs; in the 1970s, bank employees, among the most highly paid workers in the country, lobbied for increases in salaries. The Irish Bank Officials Association, spurred by staff alienation after the merger, called a devastating, eight-month strike in 1970, which sent customers scrambling to the smaller, nonassociated banks. Two other strikes were called during the decade. As Mary Campbell reported in *The Banker,* ''[The Union's] strength is reflected . . . in the incredible facts that these banks cannot employ married women or take on new staff (except in certain specialized cases) who are 21 years of age; starting salaries are the same at all ages.'' To make matters more expensive, the banks often sent promising staff members to earn an M.B.A. Both AIB and the Bank of Ireland succeeded in reforming staff grades in 1989, resulting in some cost savings and better utilization of specially skilled employees without significant layoffs. As AIB Chief Executive Gerald Scanlan told *The Banker:* ''We're no longer paying people IR £24,000 for an IR £8,000 job.'' At the same time, AIB continued to fight for longer hours; its Irish branches were open only half the hours of its American ones.

A common language and a history of Irish immigration made America an attractive overseas market. AIB's first New York branch opened in 1978, specializing in serving companies from the British Isles. In 1983, AIB Group invested in a 43 percent share of America's First Maryland Bancorp, with its 1820s roots making it even more venerable than the original three Allied Irish Banks. After increasing its stake in First Maryland to 49.7 percent in 1988, AIB offered to buy the rest of the shares and, by March 1989, the company had, for a total investment of US $522 million. At the end of 1991, AIB's subsidiary First Maryland Bancorp bought The York Bank and Trust Company, entering AIB in the southern Pennsylvania

market. First Maryland Bancorp offered credit cards through another subsidiary, First Omni Bank NA.

AIB restructured itself in 1986. It became a stockbroker in 1987 with the opening of Allied Irish Securities, a few weeks before the market collapsed on infamous Black Monday. Two years later, after agreeing to buy Ireland's second largest stockbroker, Goodbody James Capel (the Bank of Ireland owned 49 percent of the largest, J&E Davy), it formed the Capital Markets division to manage all of its treasury, international, corporate banking, and investment banking operations. Insurance and stock brokering interested both AIB and its chief rival.

### Expansion in the 1990s

Early in 1991, AIB merged with TSB Northern Ireland plc. The company's operations in Northern Ireland, known as First Trust Bank, numbered nearly 100 branches with 1,400 employees. Although AIB spent much effort in developing its successful overseas business, it (like the Bank of Ireland) seemed to fare best in its home territory. This is largely because of the Irish economy, which performed relatively well, with a less intense downturn early in the 1990s than that of Britain, where AIB also had a long-established presence. In 1992, Allied Irish lost IR £26 million in Britain; the next year it succeeded in reclaiming a profit of IR £7 million. Unfortunately, Ireland, quite dependent on England for trade, suffered its own recession a couple of years later, enduring high unemployment and high interest rates.

In the mid-1990s, Ireland accounted for just under half of the group's income and the United States accounted for about 30 percent. Besides its subsidiary First Maryland Bancorp, the group maintained an AIB branch in New York City. Other locations included Brussels, the Cayman Islands, the Channel Islands, Frankfurt, and the Isle of Man. In addition, the company obtained a 16.3 percent shareholding (worth about IR £13 million) in the Polish bank Wielkopolski Bank Kredytowy. AIB had been advising the 63-branch bank since 1991. Neither AIB nor the Bank of Ireland appeared especially optimistic about continental prospects, with the exception of Eastern Europe. In 1994, AIB bid for the state-owned Budapest Bank.

The Pacific Rim was also an important venue. By the late-1980s, offices were operational in Singapore, Sidney, and Tokyo. In 1995, the company's partnership with Phillip Securities in Singapore was mirrored by a new Malaysian partnership involving both Phillip and Grand Care. Both ventures shared the name Allied Phillip Capital Management and offered investment management services in the emerging Pacific market.

AIB earned admiration for its innovative management and quality assurance practices. In the late 1980s, it implemented an ''action learning'' program to set management priorities in the large and evolving market in Great Britain. Although Ireland, with a population (3.5 million) not much larger than South Carolina's, seemed to provide only limited opportunities for growth, Allied Irish Banks was one of the few foreign banks to expand successfully into the United States. Its conservative approach, cultivated in light of its size and regional origins, seemed sure to offer similar returns in the future.

## Principal Subsidiaries

AIB Capital Markets-Corporate Finance Ltd.; AIB Custodial Services; AIB European Investments Ltd.; AIB Finance & Leasing; AIB Fund Management Ltd.; AIB International Consultants Ltd.; AIB International Financial Services Ltd.; AIB Investment Services Ltd.; AIB Securities Services Ltd.; Allied Irish Capital Management Ltd.; Ark Life Assurance Company Ltd.; CICM (Ireland) Ltd.; Goodbody Stockbrokers; AIB Bank Ltd. (Great Britain); AIB Bank (Channel Islands) Ltd. (Great Britain); AIB Bank (Isle of Man) Ltd. (Great Britain); AIB Fund Managers (Channel Islands) Ltd. (Great Britain); AIB Investment Managers Ltd. (Great Britain); AIB Trust Company (Isle of Man) Ltd. (Great Britain); AIB Trust Company (Jersey) Ltd. (Great Britain); AIB Unit Trust Managers Ltd. (Great Britain); AIB Investment Managers Ltd. (Northern Ireland); First Trust Bank (Northern Ireland); AIB Bank Ltd. (Belgium); AIB Bank Ltd. (Germany); Allied Phillip Capital Management Sdh Bhd (Malaysia); Wielkopolski Bank Kredytowy SA (Poland; 16.3%); AIB Bank Ltd. (Singapore); Allied Phillip Capital Management Ltd. (Singapore); Allied Irish Banks (United States); First Maryland Bancorp; First National Bank of Maryland (United States); First National Bank of Maryland DC (United States); First Omni Bank NA (United States); The York Bank and Trust Company (United States).

## Principal Divisions

AIB Bank; USA Division; AIB Capital Markets.

## Principal Operating Units

Republic of Ireland; Northern Ireland; Britain; Group Treasury & International; Investment Banking; Corporate Banking.

## Further Reading

AIB Group Public Affairs, *The AIB Group,* Dublin: AIB Group, September 1995.

"Banks Face Squeeze on Profits," *The Banker,* February 1979, pp. 87–92.

Barrow, G. L., *The Emergence of the Irish Banking System 1820–1845,* New York: Gill and Macmillan, 1975.

Bee, Robert N., "Buying into a US Bank: The Allied Irish Experience," *The Banker,* July 1986, pp. 32–35.

Blanden, Michael, "Back to the Home Turf," *The Banker,* February 1990, pp. 61–62.

——, "Celtic Tiger on the Prowl," *The Banker,* February 1995, pp. 35–38.

——, "Green, Green Grass of Home," *The Banker,* February 1992, pp. 19+.

Bourke, Kevin J., "Implementing a Marketing Action: A Programme for AIB Group," *Long Range Planning,* December 1992.

Bray, Nicholas, "Allied Irish Banks Looking To Resume International Expansion Begun in '80s," *The Wall Street Journal,* February 3, 1995, p. B6.

——, "Analysts Point to Bank of Ireland, A.I.B. as Top Choices Among European Stocks," *The Wall Street Journal,* May 16, 1994, p. A11.

Campbell, Mary, "Irish Banking Today," *The Banker,* November 1972, pp. 1,388–1,394.

Gilbart, James William, *The History of Banking in Ireland,* London: Longman, 1836.

Kimbell, Lucy, and Smosarski, Grog, "Wielkopolski Grows with Polish Economy," *Central European,* April 1994, p. 37.

McRae, Hamish, "Irish Banks Consolidate," *The Banker,* August 1968, pp. 707–13.

Murphy, Paul, "Gloves Off and Come Out Fighting," *The Banker,* February 1989, pp. 43–48.

——, "Seconds Out, Round One," *The Banker,* February 1988, pp. 42–49.

"New Head Sought for WBK," *Finance East Europe,* May 12, 1995, p. 8.

O'Hara, Terrence H., "Perpetual To Sell Credit Card Unit to Irish Bankers," *Washington Business Journal,* April 1, 1991, p. 4.

Panday, Mark, "Irish Banks Set Priority Markets," *Euromoney,* July 1989, pp. 99–100.

"Ready for a New Brew," *The Banker,* February 1993, pp. 13–16.

"The Second Group," *The Economist,* August 27, 1966, pp. 848–49.

Seekings, David, "Allied Irish Banks in Britain: Organisational and Business Development Through Action Learning," *Leadership and Organization Development Journal,* 1987, pp. 26–31.

Shapiro, Stacy, "Irish Government Takes Control of Insurer," *Business Insurance,* March 25, 1985.

"Small Is Beautiful," *Euromoney,* January 1990, pp. 29, 32.

Spender, Barnabas, "De Buitleir Sees an Allied Vision," *International Tax Review,* July/August 1993, pp. 44–46.

Stewart, Kathryn, "Corporate Identity: A Strategic Marketing Issue," *International Journal of Bank Marketing,* 1991, pp. 32–39.

Thackray, John, "Curate's Egg for Foreign Bankers," *Euromoney,* November 1989, pp. 121–37.

Wills, Gordon, "What Manager Doesn't Study at Home?" *European Journal of Marketing,* 25, no. 4, 1991, pp. 128–132.

Wilson, Brian, "Organisation and Business Development Through Action Learning," *International Journal of Bank Marketing,* 1988, pp. 57–66.

—Frederick C. Ingram

# American Biltrite Inc.

**57 River Street**
**Wellesley Hills, Massachusetts 02181**
**U.S.A.**
**(617) 237-6655**
**Fax: (617) 237-6880**

*Public Company*
*Incorporated:* 1954 as American Biltrite Rubber
    Company
*Employees:* 600
*Sales:* $106.1 million (1994)
*Stock Exchanges:* American
*SICs:* 3253 Ceramic Wall & Floor Tile; 3069 Fabricated
    Rubber Products, Not Elsewhere Classified; 2672
    Coated & Laminated Paper, Not Elsewhere Classified

A leader in its field, American Biltrite Inc. produces adhesive-coated, pressure-sensitive papers and films, pressure-sensitive tapes and adhesive products, and floor coverings. During the mid-1990s, American Biltrite operated through five plants located in the United States, Europe, Canada, and the Far East, marketing its products to a wide range of industries.

American Biltrite began as a small family-owned enterprise when Miah Marcus and Frank Bernstein jointly founded the Ewell Rubber Company in 1908. The business partnership established between Marcus and Bernstein that year marked the beginning of a close association between their two families, one that would unite generations of their descendants for decades to come. Together, the Marcus and Bernstein families led the company through its formative decades and into maturity, developing it into a recognized world leader in its field through expansion and diversification, as each successive generation assumed the reins of command first held by Miah Marcus and Frank Bernstein. The legacy of Marcus-Bernstein leadership lasted 74 years, spanning two world wars, a decade-long depression, and sweeping technological advancements in the industry. Then, after the two families decided to go their separate ways, their dissociation gave birth to an entirely new company, American Biltrite Inc. of the 1990s. For the Marcus family, who continued to control American Biltrite during the 1990s, much was owed to the early efforts of their forefather, Miah Marcus, and his business associate, Frank Bernstein.

## The First Fifty Years

When Miah Marcus and Frank Bernstein started Ewell Rubber in 1908, they joined one of the oldest industries in the United States, a business that traced its roots to the first shoemakers in the American Colonies. Although Marcus and Bernstein were not cobblers, they were closely involved with the cobblers of their time, having established Ewell Rubber as a manufacturer of rubber heels and soles for the shoe rebuilding industry. In this business, Ewell Rubber and its descendant companies would remain for the decades to follow, developing into the largest producer of its kind in the world.

The company did not take long to begin its long climb to the top of its industry, recording encouraging success from the beginning of its corporate life. By 1910, two years after its founding, Ewell Rubber's business was brisk enough to warrant the addition of a second manufacturing facility, known as Panther Rubber Mfg. Co., in Stoughton, Massachusetts. The company's next defining move occurred in 1913, when Marcus and Bernstein established a Canadian division. The foray into Canada marked a signal year in the young company's development, extending its presence beyond U.S. borders for the first time and securing a foothold in markets that would contribute revenue for the remainder of the century. Next, another manufacturing facility was established in Chelsea, Massachusetts in 1917, adding a fourth facet to the company's scope of operations as it neared the conclusion of its first decade of existence. The division in Chelsea, originally named the Panco Rubber Company, was dedicated to the production of heels and soles, as were the other two U.S. facilities in Stoughton and Trenton. In 1932, the Chelsea and the Stoughton operations were renamed the Panther Panco Rubber Company, a corporate title that would endure until 1951, when the company became known as American Biltrite Rubber Company.

During these first decades of growth, the company entered into a new business, that of flooring materials, which, along with rubber heel and sole production, established its existence during the years of Marcus-Bernstein leadership and constituted the basis of American Biltrite's business after the departure of the Bernstein family. In 1917, when the Chelsea plant was built, the production facility at Trenton, the birthplace of the company, was expanded and revamped to produce Amtico Rubber Flooring, giving birth to the American Tile and Rubber Company. From the production of rubber floorings, the company later established additional facilities to manufacture vinyl floorings, eventually becoming the world's largest producer of floorings made with both materials. Driven by the business generated by its two product lines, footwear materials and flooring materials, the company persevered through the 1930s, withstanding the debilitative effects of the Depression, and entered the 1940s, as the United States geared itself for the entry into the Second World War.

During the war, the Amtico manufacturing facilities were converted to produce shoe soles for the U.S. Marine Corps and the U.S. Navy. The production plants at Chelsea and Stoughton also did their part to aid in the prosecution of the war effort, supplying the armed forces with heels, soles, and raincoats, for which the company received Certificates of Appreciation in recognition of its valuable contributions.

The conclusion of international hostilities and the beginning of the 1950s ushered in a decade of prolific, unprecedented growth for the Marcus-Bernstein-controlled company, the last decade in which the concern operated out of the public spotlight. As if to signal the arrival of exponential growth and the ascension to global leadership in its markets, the company changed its name in 1951, adopting the corporate title, "American Biltrite Rubber Company." Under this banner, American Biltrite moved forward during the 1950s, recording resolute growth as the postwar rebirth of the nation's economy invigorated manufacturing industries across the country. Between 1954 and 1959, American Biltrite enjoyed uninterrupted sales and earnings growth, recording during the six-year period a 151 percent increase in annual sales and a prodigious 745 percent leap in net income. On the heels of this impressive upswing in sales and earnings, American Biltrite became a publicly traded company, making its initial stock offering in April 1959 as it concluded its first 50 years of business and moved forward under the scrutiny of the public eye.

### 1960s Expansion

The energetic climb of sales and earnings came to a halt in 1960, but the setback was only temporary, engendered by start-up costs incurred from an ambitious expansion program launched by the company as the decade began. The expansion program became the largest in American Biltrite's history by the time it was concluded, bolstering the company's already solid and world-recognized market position. Before the benefits of the expansion program were realized, American Biltrite's annual sales volume exceeded $70 million and its market dominance already had been established. The company ranked as the largest producer of rubber soling material in the world, one of the four largest manufacturers of rubber heels, and one of the two largest producers of solid vinyl and rubber floor coverings. Footwear and floorings, however, only represented part of American Biltrite's manufacturing scope. Buttressing its stalwart market leadership in these two business areas was the company's involvement in a host of other markets, giving it a balanced customer base. Of

American Biltrite's total sales volume at the beginning of the 1960s, 40 percent was generated by the company's industrial rubber and miscellaneous products division, which manufactured a variety of products for the oil and automotive industries. Another 25 percent of sales was derived from the production of transmission and conveyor belts for the construction, mining, textile, automotive, air conditioning, agricultural, and aviation industries. All told, the company was registering enviable success in each of its business areas as the 1960s began. Moreover, as the decade unfolded American Biltrite improved itself on all fronts, strengthening each segment of its operations through aggressive expansion and strategic acquisitions.

The expansion program of the early 1960s began in 1960 with the acquisition of National Shoe Products Corp., a distributor of shoe supplies to manufacturers. With the distribution area of its Biltrite footwear products line broadened by the addition of National Shoe Products, American Biltrite next strengthened its floor coverings business, acquiring a vinyl-asbestos and asphalt coverings manufacturer, Bonafide Mills, Inc., in 1961 and doubling the production capacity of its Amtico Rubber Flooring division in Trenton, New Jersey in 1962. Two new manufacturing plants began operation in 1962 as well, a shoe and heel facility in Ripley, Mississippi and a pressure hose manufacturing facility in Hohenwald, Tennessee. Additional expansion efforts were completed at the company's chemical production plant in Wilmington, Massachusetts and its Sherbrooke plant in Quebec, which provided American Biltrite with its first Canadian facilities for manufacturing vinyl asbestos and asphalt tile. By the end of 1963, manufacturing square footage had been increased roughly 50 percent. Growth continued in the years following, making the 1960s as productive a decade as the 1950s.

By 1967, sales had nearly doubled from the total recorded at the beginning of the decade, reaching $142 million. Of total sales during the late 1960s, one-third was generated by Amtico Rubber Flooring and the solid vinyl and asbestos tile flooring it manufactured. Still a leader in its field, Amtico Rubber Flooring's product line was broadened in 1967 with the acquisition of Dalton, Georgia-based Noxon Mills, Inc., a manufacturer of various types of carpeting. Montreal-based Consolidated Carpet Mfg., Ltd. was purchased the following year, adding another carpeting concern to the company's fold and aiding in its push to become a major carpet producer. Two other divisions rounded out the rest of American Biltrite's operations: Biltrite Footwear, the world's largest producer of shoe soling materials, which widened its lead in 1967 with the acquisition of Cat's Paw Rubber Company, and a relatively new division, Boston Woven Hose & Rubber.

Boston Woven Hose & Rubber had been acquired in 1956, midway through American Biltrite's six-year period of vigorous growth during the decade, ranking the company as a leader in the production of industrial rubber products such as rubber and plastic bases, conveyor belts, and transmission belts. Within this division was the synthetic turf and sports surface department, which was regarded by industry observers as perhaps the most promising area of American Biltrite's business during the late 1960s. Two new products introduced during the late 1960s by this department, Uni-Turf and Poly-Turf, were marketed in relatively new niches in the broadly defined flooring materials market. Uni-Turf, soon after its introduction, had been used at several major tennis tournaments, and Poly-Turf, a synthetic grass that could withstand cleated shoes, had scored encouraging initial success as a surface for outdoor playgrounds and baseball and football stadiums.

### 1982 Reorganization

The wide-ranging business interests that composed American Biltrite's operations provided steady, consistent growth as the company entered the 1970s, the last decade of Marcus-Bernstein leadership and the last decade the company's business mix would be as diverse. In 1982, the Marcus and Bernstein families, who each owned 37.5 percent of American Biltrite, signed a definitive agreement to divide into two separate corporations. At the time they declined to provide a reason for the split. From 1982 forward, there would be two companies that shared the roots of American Biltrite: Biltrite Corporation, which comprised the domestic footwear business formerly belonging to American Biltrite, and American Biltrite Inc., consisting of the floor covering, tape products, and Canadian businesses formerly owned by American Biltrite. After seven decades of close cooperation, the two families had severed the ties that linked them together, with the Bernsteins assuming 75 percent control of Biltrite Corporation and the Marcuses controlling 75 percent of American Biltrite Inc. The remaining 25 percent of each company was sold to the public.

In the wake of the 1982 spin-off, American Biltrite underwent several years of dramatic change, quickly assuming the attributes that would characterize the company during the 1990s. In June 1983, Marcus-led management steered American Biltrite in a new direction, acquiring 50 percent interest in K&M Associates, a national jewelry supplier that sold costume jewelry to large retail chains such as Sears and Wal-Mart. Although the acquisition of a jewelry supplier took the company in a decidedly different direction, the 50 percent stake in K&M Associates proved to be a boon to American Biltrite's profitability. By 1985, the profits gleaned from K&M Associates' business activities were contributing more than half of American Biltrite's total earnings, buoying the company's stature as it sought to redefine itself following the 1982 reorganization.

In addition to developing entirely new business interests, American Biltrite also focused on strengthening its more traditional business interests, such as building a $4 million vinyl floor tile manufacturing facility at its Amtico Rubber Flooring division's plant in Trenton, New Jersey in late 1985. The following year, the company completed its most defining move in its new, modern era, acquiring Ideal Tape Co. from Chelsea Industries for $9.3 million. A manufacturer of pressure-sensitive tape for the footwear, computer, and heating, ventilating, and air conditioning (HVAC) industries, Ideal Tape would become one of the primary engines driving American Biltrite's growth during the late 1980s and into the 1990s. With manufacturing plants in Lowell, Massachusetts, St. Louis, Missouri, and Renaix, Belgium, Ideal Tape also increased American Biltrite's global presence and, combined with the marketing strength of the company's Canadian footwear division, enabled American Biltrite to secure a more entrenched position in Canada in particular.

In the four years since the Bernsteins and Marcuses had divided their assets, by the end of 1986, American Biltrite had made tremendous strides. Revenues had more than doubled since the 1982 split, rising to $110.1 million, and the company's earnings had recorded a robust jump, soaring to $3.1 million from a deficit in 1982. American Biltrite continued to expand its customer base and product lines during the late 1980s and into the 1990s, building its growth on the development of its pressure-sensitive and adhesive tape products. In 1993, the company completed the formation of a joint venture with Congoleum Corporation that combined its floor tile business with Congoleum's principal business of producing sheet vinyl flooring, creating an entity that retained the name Congoleum Corporation yet was 44 percent owned by American Biltrite.

As American Biltrite entered the mid-1990s, the company was enjoying substantial growth, with its two primary divisions achieving high levels of performance. In 1994, American Biltrite's tape products division recorded a 28 percent increase in sales, the largest in the division's history. The company's Ideal Tape division also recorded a banner year, increasing its sales 18 percent, the biggest gain in its history. As American Biltrite prepared for the late 1990s and the future, its international business was growing rapidly, particularly in the Far East and in Australia, where the company served markets through its Singapore-based operation, American Biltrite Far East, Inc. With both its domestic and foreign businesses performing encouragingly well, American Biltrite's expectations for future growth were justifiably optimistic, as another generation of the Marcus family guided the company toward its second century of business.

### Principal Subsidiaries

American Biltrite (Canada), Ltd.; American Biltrite International, Inc.; American Biltrite Far East, Inc. (Singapore); American Biltrite Sales Corporation; Ideal Tape Co., Inc.; American Biltrite Intellectual Properties, Inc.; K&M Trading (H.K.) Limited (Hong Kong); Congoleum Corporation.

### Principal Divisions

Tape Products; Ideal Tape Co.

### Further Reading

"American Biltrite," *Rubber World,* July 1986, p. 5.

"American Biltrite Board Clears Accord To Split Firm into 2 Companies," *Wall Street Journal,* May 26, 1982, p. 41.

"American Biltrite Closing Two Plants," *Barron's,* November 17, 1980, p. 51.

"American Biltrite Rubber," *Financial World,* December 27, 1972, p. 16.

"American Biltrite Rubber," *Wall Street Transcript,* July 8, 1968, p. 13,793.

"American Biltrite Rubber Results Snap Back from a Modest Decline," *Barron's,* September 30, 1963, p. 22.

"American Biltrite Signs Accord To Split into Two Concerns," *Wall Street Journal,* August 12, 1982, p. 5.

"Flashier Than It Looks," *Forbes,* September 9, 1985, p. 158.

Maturi, Richard J., "Tape Measure," *Barron's,* May 11, 1987, p. 64.

Nicholson, Sy, "American Biltrite Has Many Facets for Continued Growth," *Investment Dealers' Digest,* 1961, p. 32.

Rolland, Louis J., "Biltrite on the Amex," *Financial World,* December 11, 1963, p. 21.

—Jeffrey L. Covell

# American Tourister, Inc.

**91 Main Street**
**Warren, Rhode Island 02885**
**U.S.A.**
**(401) 245-2100**
**Fax: (401) 247-0988**

*Wholly Owned Subsidiary of Samsonite Corp.*
*Incorporated:* 1933 as American Luggage Works
*Employees:* 1,000
*Sales:* $140 million (1993 est.)
*SICs:* 3161 Luggage

American Tourister, Inc., is one of the oldest and best-known luggage brands in the United States. Its commitment to selling durable and affordable luggage, which began with the company's founding in the 1930s, continued into the 1990s. Despite several changes in parent companies in the 1970s, 1980s, and 1990s, American Tourister retained its brand recognition with the public, particularly through its association with luggage-abusing gorillas featured in its famous advertising campaign.

Sol Koffler, founder of American Tourister, was introduced to the luggage industry in the 1920s. A recent immigrant to the United States, Koffler worked in a plant that manufactured steamer trunks and in a pocketbook factory. The methods of luggage construction that Koffler learned were typical of the industry; thin strips of wood and plywood were glued together and then covered with either paper or cloth for inexpensive luggage or with leather for expensive luggage. Koffler set out on his own, determined to produce a more durable product.

### Early History

In 1933 Koffler founded American Luggage Works by opening a shop in a vacant grocery store in Providence, Rhode Island. Although his first luggage did not revolutionize luggage design, Koffler was sure he had created a significantly more durable product than any competitor's in the same price range. The suitcase sold for one dollar, and, in the first year of opera-

tion, American Luggage Works sold 5,000 suitcases. As the company's only employee, Koffler handled all aspects of the business himself that year. Within two years, Koffler had hired several employees, although he himself continued to handle the luggage design and the company's sales. The company's product line had expanded to include two sizes, which sold for two and three dollars. Each size was produced in two colors, black or brown. Retailers throughout the Providence-Boston area carried the line.

The company's major breakthrough came soon after its founding. Koffler adapted machinery used to make plywood radio cases so that it would bend materials to make his luggage. The new equipment enabled him to simplify suitcase design significantly and still increase its durability. Typical luggage of the time was constructed of numerous pieces, making a squat and unwieldy suitcase that tended to split and crack. Koffler's new design was slim and round-cornered but still provided more room than other suitcases did. Other new features, such as linings and zippered pockets, enhanced the product's appeal. To distinguish this line from the previous ones, Koffler named it American Tourister.

The new line was a resounding success and set a new standard for the industry. American Luggage Works grew rapidly as a result; by the beginning of World War II the company enjoyed revenues of more than $100,000. The company's product line had expanded as well, with four colors, four styles, and eight sizes being offered by the early 1940s. The war diverted the company's attention from luggage, however, as it helped with the war effort. At the war's conclusion, American Luggage Works reentered the luggage industry poised to become a national concern.

In 1945, despite its rapid growth in the previous decade, American Luggage Works remained a regional firm. Aiming for sales across the United States, Koffler decided to spread awareness of the American Tourister brand. He apportioned $12,000 for a national advertising campaign, the first ever undertaken on behalf of the company. An amount unusually large for the time, that first national advertising budget set the stage for the company's continued commitment to large-scale advertising in future years.

### Pioneering New Materials

Innovation helped propel the company forward during the next two decades. The first luggage manufacturer to make an all-vinyl case, American Luggage Works went on to produce the industry's sleekest and smoothest cases from molded ply- wood veneer. The year that particular line was introduced, the company records that it sold its entire year's production of leather and vinyl cases in the first two hours of that year's national trade show. One of the first to see the benefits of a revolutionary new material developed during the war, Koffler made sure American Luggage Works introduced molded plastic luggage before anyone else did. Koffler met Don Hawley of Hawley Products at that same trade show and discussed the aqueous plastic material Hawley had first produced for use in shell casings and pith helmets during the war. Koffler recog- nized that the composition's lightness, malleability, and tensile strength made it a prime material for luggage production. De- spite the company's success with its current products and the need to retool production completely to use the new material, Koffler wholeheartedly entered into the new venture, even mortgaging his house to help finance it.

Once again the new line of American Tourister hard-sided luggage introduced a new standard of durability and economy to the luggage industry. Customers immediately responded well to the product. The company improved the chemical composi- tion further in 1954, resulting in a case that was virtually indestructible. When the company started to receive reports of American Tourister luggage surviving incredible accidents, Koffler used them in advertisements to promote the luggage's durability. One true-life account reported that an American Tourister suitcase fell off a car traveling 60 miles per hour and was run over by another car. Other than a few scuff marks on the outer surface, the case was undamaged.

### Testimonials and Gorilla Advertisements

These true-life accounts inspired the company's famous gorilla advertisements. Doyle Dane Bernbach agency created an award-winning print and television campaign that combined customer testimonials with photos or film of a ferocious-look- ing gorilla hurling and stomping on an American Tourister case in a zoo cage. Other advertisements demonstrated the luggage's durability even in unlikely luggage mishaps, such as a case being dropped from an airplane or a speeding train.

American Tourister continued to grow. By the 1970s, the company was one of the most popular manufacturers of mid- priced luggage in the United States. A general industry upswing in the 1970s helped the firm rise to a new peak in sales. Luggage owners replaced cases at a more rapid rate and leisure travel in general was on the rise. These trends and the company's en- trance into the growing market for business cases helped the company achieve record sales. In 1978 Koffler, who had re- mained involved in the operation of the business, sold his company to Hillenbrand Industries. A furniture manufacturer based in Indiana, Hillenbrand was attempting to expand and diversify by purchasing healthy market leaders.

American Tourister's first year as a Hillenbrand subsidiary marked a peak for the company. Sales in 1978 reached a record $83.8 million and operating profits amounted to a substantial $16.2 million. These figures may have simply reflected the market in general, however; *Industry Week* reported that the luggage industry was "enjoying a banner year." When the economy turned sour in 1980, American Tourister sales de- clined 7 percent and operating profits more than followed suit, dropping 60 percent in that year alone. The company tried to rally for its 50th anniversary in 1983, investing in prime time television commercials and print ads in such mainstream maga- zines as *Reader's Digest, Better Homes and Gardens,* and *People.* But the company was unable to regain the steady growth it had experienced throughout its history.

### Sold to Astrum International in the Early 1990s

Luggage sales did not revive, and in 1992 Hillenbrand an- nounced a $5 million operating loss for its durables segment, which comprised a security-lock manufacturer and American Tourister. The next year Hillenbrand sold American Tourister to Astrum International Corp., a sales and manufacturing holding company, for a reported $68 million. Astrum, formerly known as E-II Holdings Inc., had recently emerged from bankruptcy reorganization, which led to some speculation about the future of American Tourister.

Another factor influencing American Tourister's direction was Astrum's ownership of Samsonite Corp., a major competitor of American Tourister. Although at the time of the purchase Astrum said it would run American Tourister as a unit separate from Samsonite, it clearly planned some connection between the two. In 1994, Astrum named as president of American Tourister the former Samsonite vice-president of sales and marketing, Frank Steed. In a press release announcing this appointment, Astrum said, "With Steed at the helm . . . the two companies can establish product plans, marketing and advertising programs that will enhance both the American Tourister and Samsonite brand names. The combination of Samsonite's vast global resources and American Tourister's quality products will insure success as American Tourister enters the international marketplace, while enhancing the value of its name here in the United States."

In an attempt to distinguish American Tourister from Sam- sonite, Astrum initiated a major advertising campaign in early 1994. Capitalizing on the well-known gorilla ads from a decade before, the campaign featured a gorilla, a family of chimpan- zees, and an orangutan. The ads targeted family vacationers, a market clearly different from the business-oriented one pursued by Samsonite. The print ads ran in issues of *Parenting, Family Circle,* and *Ladies Home Journal* and used the tagline, "Ameri- can Tourister: Making travel less primitive."

### Spun Off as Subsidiary of Samsonite

In 1995 Astrum split into two public companies, Samsonite Corp. and Culligan Water Technologies Inc., with Samsonite taking Astrum's other luggage brands, Lark and American Tourister, with it. The split was designed to take advantage of the name recognition of Astrum's two largest brands. "Astrum. What's an Astrum?" the company's chief executive officer, Steven Green, said to *The Denver Post* in April 1995 when trying to explain the market confusion over Astrum's business focus. Green stayed on as chairman at Samsonite.

Although Samsonite was the world's largest luggage manufacturer and distributor in the early 1990s, Green saw much room for growth for it and its subsidiaries, especially overseas. In particular, he cited India and China as ripe for expansion. He also began moving the brands into new products, such as computer and camera cases, car-top carriers, and motorcycle saddlebags. These products required distribution channels that were unfamiliar to Samsonite and American Tourister, however, who relied mainly on luggage stores and luggage departments of mass merchandisers and department stores to sell their goods. Therefore, the focus was likely to remain on the businesses' traditional luggage market.

In February of 1996 Samsonite announced that it would be closing American Tourister facilities in Warren, Rhode Island and Jacksonville, Florida, resulting in the loss of 137 jobs. Hard-luggage production and important central office functions would be consolidated at Samsonite's Denver headquarters. American Tourister hard-sided luggage production from Florida would move to Denver, where the plant had extra manufacturing capacity. American Tourister's soft-sided luggage warehousing and distribution would remain in Jacksonville, however, because many of those products were made in the Dominican Republic. American Tourister's Rhode Island facilities would be split as well, with its finance, accounting, and information systems moving to Denver and its sales, marketing, and product design departments remaining in Warren. Although Samsonite planned to take a $2.4 million charge to cover the moves and integration, it hoped the consolidation would save the company about $3.3 million per year.

As American Tourister entered the late 1990s, its fate remained closely tied with its parent company. Samsonite was still hindered by its obligations to pay Astrum's reorganization debts. The three-year process of charging to earnings about $55 million per year in amortization of goodwill-type expenses was due to be completed in 1996. In addition, Samsonite's operating income fell $5 million in the nine months that ended October 31, 1995, compared with its operating income in the same period of 1994. Citing increased foreign competition and rising raw material costs as the culprits, Samsonite faced uncertain times ahead. Concerns for the company and its subsidiaries, however, were tempered by its brand recognition, its market dominance, and its long history.

### Further Reading

"Astrum To Buy Hillenbrand Unit," *Wall Street Journal,* August 31, 1993, p. B10.
"Hillenbrand Industries Inc.," *Wall Street Journal,* April 13, 1993, p. B4.
Kirk, Jim, "Tourister Back, Fury as Ever," *Brandweek,* April 25, 1994, p. 4.
Leib, Jeffrey, "Samsonite Consolidates in Denver," *The Denver Post,* February 7, 1996, pp. C1, 8.
——, "Samsonite Packed for Growth: New Products, Overseas Markets in Expansion," *The Denver Post,* October 23, 1995, pp. E1, 5.
——, "Samsonite To Go Independent: Astrum Sct To Spin Off Culligan," *The Denver Post,* April 25, 1995, p. C1.
Mahoney, Michelle, "Tourister Gorilla Reclaims Luggage-Mangler Title," *The Denver Post,* June 10, 1995, p. C1.

—Susan W. Brown

# Andreas Stihl

**Badstrasse 115**
**71336 Waiblingen**
**Baden-Wuerttemburg**
**Germany**
**7151 260**
**Fax: 7151 26 11 40**

*Private Company*
*Incorporated:* 1926
*Employees:* 5,500
*Sales:* $1.1 billion (1995)
*SICs:* 3546 Power Driven Handtools

Based in Waiblingen, Germany, Andreas Stihl manufactures the world's leading selling chain saws, as well as a variety of outdoor tools and equipment ranging from brushcutters, edgers, and trimmers to blowers, vacuum cleaners, and protective workwear. Stihl plants operate in Germany, Switzerland, Brazil, and in Virginia Beach, Virginia, while Stihl products are sold in approximately 130 countries by more than 16,000 dealer-servicers. Foreign sales accounted for about 80 percent of Stihl's $1.1 billion in 1995 revenues. Stihl's U.S. subsidiary, Stihl Inc., accounts for about one-third of the company's annual production.

### The Invention of the Chain Saw

An engineer, Andreas Stihl nonetheless began his career as a salesman for a German mill and industrial supply house during the 1920s. Stihl's work brought him in contact with loggers in the Black Forest, where the felling and bucking of trees were done with stationary saws or by hand, and the larger pieces of timber needed to be transported to saw mills for cutting. Stihl sought to introduce more modern methods to the logging trade.

In 1925, Stihl opened a small workshop in his home in Stuttgart and set to work designing a portable "tree-felling machine." The Stihl workshop manufactured a number of other products, including forehearths for steam boilers, in order to support these efforts. But by 1926, Stihl was ready with his first

prototype, a 140-pound electric "cross-cutting chain saw." The saw's bulk required it to be operated by two men, and its reliance on an electric motor limited its portability to areas where a power source was available. Stihl set to work creating a lighter, gasoline-driven saw. Nonetheless, the electric saw found its market, selling 50 in 1927. In that year, Stihl opened his first factory in Stuttgart. The following year, as sales of the electric saw reached 100, the company opened a sales office for northern Germany.

Stihl's gasoline saw was ready by 1929. This saw achieved a horsepower of 6; its weight of 101 pounds still required two men to operate it. Yet the saw was fully portable and would change the logging trade forever. In 1930, the saw was featured at the Leipzig trade fair, and sales of the saw soon spread beyond Germany into Holland, Belgium, Switzerland, and France. From the start, Stihl emphasized service along with the sale of his saws. Customers were trained in the operation, maintenance, and repair of Stihl's products. As international sales increased, Stihl trained specialists in each country, who provided customer instruction and service, along with sales. As one of Stihl's earliest salesmen wrote: "It won't do to sell saws to people without teaching, assisting and offering good service to users later."

Not everyone welcomed the chain saw. Many loggers resisted the new device, fearing the loss of their jobs, and often attacked Stihl's salesmen. But the rise of the chain saw became inevitable, and sales increased. By 1930, Stihl saws were being shipped to the United States. After a trip to the Soviet Union, Stihl received orders for several hundred of his saws. The Stihl factory moved to Bad Cannstatt, which later became part of Stuttgart, and during the 1930s the number of the company's employees swelled to 200.

Stihl continued to work on improving the saw's design. In 1931, Stihl introduced his second gas-powered saw, which weighed nearly 105 pounds—with a full gas tank—but achieved a horsepower of 8. Other improvements were made, such as an automatic chain lubrication system introduced in 1935. The following year, the company opened its first foreign sales and distribution office in Vienna. By 1937, Stihl managed to bring the weight of the chain saw down to 88 pounds. Stihl traveled to North America, broadening the saw's reach through the U.S. and into the Canadian market. Stihl also introduced courses in power saw technology in an effort to increase the chain saw's acceptance throughout the logging and forestry trades.

The Nazi rise to power encouraged Stihl's domestic growth but hampered its international development. In an effort to standardize production within industries, the Nazis' held competitions and Stihl's design became the authorized German chain saw. All other German chain saw manufacturers were required to license the Stihl design. But the outbreak of the World War II ended Stihl's international growth. During the war, the Bad Cannstatt plant was destroyed by bombs, and production was moved to Waiblingen. The German capitulation ending the European war also forced Stihl to a halt.

### Postwar Growth

By 1947, Stihl's factory reopened and was soon producing 90 chain saws each month. International sales also resumed; in the United States, Stihl bought out its former U.S. importer, and began assembling saws in the U.S. for the North American market. In 1948, the first Stihl Service Center was opened, offering a higher degree of customer service. Meanwhile, the company continued to improve the chain saw's design, with reducing the weight of the saw a primary concern. This concern led to the development of the one-man chain saw, which would revolutionize the chain saw industry by the end of the decade.

Stihl's first one-man saw was introduced in 1950. This saw was still too heavy for comfortable operation, but it led the way to the introduction of the Stihl BLK saw in 1954. At 31 pounds, with a horsepower of 4.5, the BLK was the first truly portable chain saw. Two years later, the BLK was chosen by the German army as its official chain saw; the BLK became the standard saw for many other military services and government organizations as well.

But the true revolution in chain saw technology—and the development that led to the worldwide acceptance of the chain saw—was the introduction of the Stihl Contra in 1959. The Contra, which featured a direct drive and diaphragm carburetor, weighed only 26.65 pounds, yet achieved a horsepower of 6. Stihl's sales boomed, and production rose from 104 saws per day to 500 saws per day by 1964. By then, the company was outgrowing its plant, and a second facility was built in Neustadt. The company's workforce grew to over 1,000. U.S. and Canadian demand surged with the introduction of the Stihl Lightning

saw, prompting the company to open its first North American warehouses.

In 1965, Stihl introduced an innovation in chain saw design with its anti-vibration system, which absorbed the impact of the saw's vibration, allowing steadier and less fatiguing control. This design change was quickly added by Stihl's competitors to their products as well. Three years later, Stihl added an electronic ignition system to its saws, improving their reliability. Other design changes included a more efficient chain lubrication system, an inertial chain braking system, which stopped the chain in the event of kickback, and a master control lever, which allowed the user to control the saws starting and stopping functions without releasing the saw's handle.

By 1971, Stihl's 2,000-strong workforce was producing 340,000 saws annually. In that year, Andreas Stihl's son, Hans Peter, took over as head of the company. Andreas Stihl died two years later. By then the company had added a new plant in Prüm, and a plant in Wiechs am Randen, near the Swiss border. The company's first overseas plant, Andreas Stihl Moto Serras LTDA in Sao Leopoldo, Brazil, began chain saw production in 1973. With 2,500 employees, Stihl's revenues topped DM 222 million.

The international oil crisis prompted by the Arab Oil Embargo of 1973 sent most industries into a recession. But in response to rising oil prices, the demand for wood as an alternative fuel skyrocketed, and with that demand came an increase in Stihl sales. The company increased its foreign manufacturing base, transferring chain production to a plant in Wil, Switzerland, and opening a U.S. plant in Virginia Beach, Virginia, in 1974. The company also established an assembly plant in Scoresby, Australia. By 1978, Stihl's revenues had more than doubled, to approximately DM 500 million (roughly $245 million). By the mid-1980s, about 50 percent of the company's production took place outside of Germany.

### Diversifying Products in the 1980s and 1990s

In 1980, worldwide chain saw sales reached a peak of 5.8 million units, with Stihl holding a commanding share of the market. But as oil prices leveled, and as the world entered the recession of the 1980s, sales slumped in the following years, dropping to 3.4 million units by 1984. Stihl's revenues continued to rise, from $355 million in 1981 to $489 million in 1986, increasing its share to 25 percent of the chain saw market; however, much of this revenue growth could be attributed to the falling value of the dollar against the German mark.

In response to the pressures on chain saw sales, the company began to diversify its product line in the 1980s. In 1986, the company began producing protective apparel and accessories, such as safety glasses, helmets, gloves, boots, and hearing protectors. Two years later, the company introduced specialized clearing saws for professional use, and in 1989 began production of trimmers and blowers.

Until the 1990s, most Stihl saws were designed exclusively for professional uses. Further improvements in design had decreased the weight of even the company's most powerful model to 20 pounds. Toward the middle of the decade, however, Stihl moved to tap into the small saw market—which represented about half of all chain saw sales—hitting below the $200 price point. Because the U.S. was the biggest market for small and nonprofessional chain saw purchases, the company moved production of all small saws to its Virginia Beach plant in 1994. By the following year, Stihl's U.S. facilities were producing more machines than its German plants for the first time in the company's history.

The diversification of the Stihl's product line helped drive the company's growth. Sales in 1995 topped $1 billion, with foreign sales accounting for roughly 80 percent. Stihl, which remained a family concern with the third generation entering the company, could be expected to maintain its world leadership in chain saws and other powered outdoor products.

## Principal Subsidiaries

Stihl KG (Germany); Andreas Stihl Moto Serras Ltda. (Brazil); Stihl Incorporated (U.S.); Stihl & Co. (Switzerland); Stihl Chain Saw (Aust.) Pty. Ltd. (Australia); Andreas Stihl Ltd. (U.K); Stihl Ges.mbH & Co. KG (Austria); Andreas Stihl Sarl (France); Stihl Ltd. (Canada); Stihl Chain Saw Ltd. (New Zealand); Andreas Stihl S.A. (Spain); Andreas Stihl N.V. (Belgium); Andreas Stihl B.V. (The Netherlands); Andreas Stihl AB (Sweden); Andreas Stihl A/S (Norway); Stihl Parts Inc. (U.S.)

## Further Reading

Bruce, Peter, ''Andreas Stihl Cuts Larger Overseas Niche,'' *Financial Times,* January 7, 1986, p. 21.
Tagliabue, John, ''Stihl: A Worldwide Family Business,'' *New York Times,* March 17, 1982, p. D4.
Wagner, Lon, ''Expansion Is Routine at Equipment Maker Stihl's U.S. Plant in Virginia,'' *Virginian Pilot,* November 13, 1995.

—M.L. Cohen

# Anglo American Corporation of South Africa Limited

44 Main Street
Johannesburg 2001
Republic of South Africa
(11) 638-9111
Fax: (11) 638-2455

*Public Company*
*Incorporated:* 1917
*Employees:* 250,000
*Sales:* R 3.37 billion (US $909.63 million) (1995)
*Stock Exchanges:* Johannesburg London Paris Brussels
    Antwerp Frankfurt Zürich Geneva Basel
*SICs:* 6719 Offices of Holding Companies, Not
    Elsewhere Classified

Formed in 1917 as South Africa's first home-based public limited company, the Anglo American Corporation of South Africa Limited (Anglo) has become a unique multinational group. It is the world's largest gold-mining organization and, through its 32.5 percent share in De Beers Consolidated Mines Limited and 29.4 percent share in De Beers Centenary AG, has a major interest in the distribution of some 80 percent of the world's rough-diamond production. At the same time, it dominates South Africa's domestic economy, with interests in an estimated 1,300 South African companies and control of at least one-quarter (and possibly as much as two-fifths) of the South African stock market. Its founding family, the Oppenheimers, has remained closely involved in the daily running of the group, although direct family control has become somewhat weakened. The group's corporate structure is based only in part on majority share ownership of subsidiary, associate, and other companies. Much of its control and influence lies in a complex web of connections based on family ties, friendships, and mutual business interests, although that interest is not infrequently accompanied by various forms of financial or commercial pressure.

The complexity of the connections is such that it is often difficult to distinguish between Anglo itself and the Anglo-De Beers group of companies or what might be referred to as the "Oppenheimer empire." The corporation has become in many respects a holding company, with diversified interests, such as gold-mining, being the formal responsibility of a group of associate companies. During the long period of apartheid, the Oppenheimers and the group itself were critical of various aspects of the apartheid system, while at the same time many of apartheid's opponents attacked Anglo on the grounds that it was profiting greatly from the system, and in practice was doing very little to change, or to mitigate, its effects. With apartheid's collapse in the early 1990s, Anglo has been preoccupied with protecting the empire it built up in the face of the pressures to nationalize some of its assets and to lessen its stranglehold on the South African economy.

## Early History

The roots of Anglo's history can be traced back to 1902, when Ernest Oppenheimer arrived in Kimberley representing diamond merchants A. Dunkelsbuhler & Co., a member of the Diamond Syndicate, the cartel that attempted to maintain prices for South African diamonds by regulating production. Working for Dunkelsbuhler and on his own account, Oppenheimer also became interested in gold and coal mining, and in 1905 acquired the Consolidated Mines Selection Company (CMS), originally formed in 1887, with properties on the Far East Rand gold field. By 1916, when that field's true value was more widely appreciated, Oppenheimer/CMS was in a stronger position there than any of the other Transvaal mining-finance groups.

CMS had a large number of German shareholders and directors, causing it to be rather unpopular during World War I. Oppenheimer was a naturalized British subject who identified strongly throughout his life with South Africa's British, against its Dutch Afrikaner community. Oppenheimer was nevertheless attacked because of his German origins. These points, coupled with the war-imposed restrictions on British capital exports, led him to seek U.S. financing to develop the field. An American connection in CMS introduced him to Herbert Hoover, through whom Newmont Mining Corporation, J.P. Morgan & Co., and Guaranty Trust became involved. With their support, Anglo was formed on December 25, 1917, with £2 million of autho-

**Company Perspectives:**

*The Corporation will continue to follow its successful strategy of geographic and business diversity, within the still relevant and appropriate mining finance house structure, to seek out and exploit opportunity wherever it is and ensure the continuation of superior long-term growth.*

rized capital, half of which was issued. Various political reasons have been advanced for the decision to locate the company in South Africa rather than Britain, but the primary reason was to avoid the possibility of double taxation problems.

Anglo joined the ranks of the mining-finance groups characteristic of South African mining. Cecil Rhodes and other early financiers concentrated ownership of individual mines in the hands of a few holding companies that provided basic financial, administrative, and technical services for the mines they owned. This process of concentration had begun with the diamond mines, initially because some claimholders had insufficient capital to continue exploitation as workings went deeper, and ultimately because ownership concentration meant more efficient production control. Gold-mining did not face oversupply problems, but given gold's fixed price and the highly speculative nature of mining investment, concentration of ownership meant more efficient use of technical and administrative resources. It also focused wealth and power in the hands of the relative few who sought it and were able to command the necessary capital. A system of interlocking directorships developed, creating a close, interdependent network. A relative latecomer to the field, Oppenheimer soon showed that he was more than a match for his predecessors, going on to absorb much of what they had built, and taking the concept of group control much further.

With a strong base in gold and access to U.S. capital, Oppenheimer was able to challenge the Diamond Syndicate and De Beers, the dominant producer. He was helped by influential British and German connections, and by contacts between Anglo director H. C. Hull, former finance minister of the Union of South Africa, and his former political colleague, Prime Minister Jan Smuts. Oppenheimer acquired most of the diamond mines in Namibia—then known as South West Africa—when the German companies operating them were encouraged to sell out to British interests. By the time De Beers and others learned of the negotiations, it was too late to prevent the sale to Anglo, and they initially welcomed the stability these acquisitions implied.

Anglo's Namibian mines were quickly brought under centralized control in Consolidated Diamond Mines of South West Africa (CDM). Initially CDM cooperated with the Diamond Syndicate, but in 1922 Anglo and Barnato Bros. reached a separate agreement for the purchase of the Belgian Congo's diamond output. In 1923 they acquired major interests in the Companhia de Diamantes de Angola, diamond mines in west Africa, and a share in British Guiana's diamond production. CDM subsequently became part of the De Beers group in 1930. More recently, CDM and Anglo have been cooperating with the

Namibian government in developing the country's gold resources.

In 1924, Anglo was given an 8 percent share in the Diamond Syndicate. The purchasing agreements Anglo had with non-South African producers, including the right to take up all of CDM's production, gave Anglo apparent control over such producers. This control was more apparent than real, but led smaller South African producers to look to Anglo as an alternative to the syndicate, with whom they were increasingly dissatisfied, owing to the prices they were offered. The principle of selling all of South Africa's diamonds through a single channel was seriously weakened. Anglo was asked to leave the syndicate, and established a rival organization joined by Dunkelsbuhler, Barnato Bros., and Johannesburg Consolidated Investments Ltd. (JCI), a group originally established by Barnato, and subsequently absorbed into Anglo's ambit.

The South African government was concerned about the implications for revenue of limited diamond production and a potentially disastrous price-cutting war between the two syndicates. The Diamond Control Act of 1925 gave the government sweeping powers to take over diamond production and distribution, and to prevent extreme behavior, namely price-cutting. As a member of Parliament, Oppenheimer had been able to introduce an amendment that required the government, if it enforced any provisions of the law, to give preference to South African-registered diamond purchasers; Anglo was the only one—while all the others were registered in London.

With Anglo continuing to grow financially stronger in the face of declining world diamond demand, the new syndicate was able to outbid the old in an offer to South African producers. On July 30, 1925, the new syndicate's offer was accepted and the old syndicate collapsed. Having gained effective control of distribution, Oppenheimer moved to control production as well. He became a De Beers director, while Anglo further strengthened its position by buying properties in two new South African fields and by consolidating and expanding its links with outside producers. Resistance was strong. Oppenheimer's bid, first made in May 1927, to take control of De Beers, only succeeded in December 1929 with the support of the Rothschilds, introduced through Morgan Grenfell. Oppenheimer became chairman of De Beers, clearing the way for the consolidation of production and distribution functions in one organization, the Diamond Corporation, formed in February 1930 under De Beers's and Oppenheimer's effective control.

Negotiations with Sir Chester Beatty and Sir Edmund Davis, which had led to agreements for purchasing west African, Angolan, and Congolese diamonds, also led Oppenheimer to participate in the development of the Northern Rhodesian—now Zambian—copperbelt and that country's lead and zinc mines. Although these rich deposits had been known to exist for several decades at least, technological difficulties had prevented exploitation. Progress in the use of flotation techniques opened up new possibilities after World War I. Anglo acted as engineering consultant to several companies formed to exploit these deposits, bringing some of them together in Rhodesian Anglo American Limited (Rhoanglo), formed in December 1928. American capital was also involved in this venture, as it was in the other group operating on the copperbelt, Beatty's Rhodesian Selection Trust.

Oppenheimer wanted to combine Morgan Grenfell, Beatty, and others in a syndicate to develop the Mount Isa lead mine in northwest Queensland, Australia. Initial surveys were not promising, and Anglo withdrew. Anglo subsequently became involved in various Australian undertakings, ultimately establishing an Australian subsidiary. Overall, however, the group's direct involvement in Australia has been rather limited.

### The 1930s through the 1980s

The 1930s saw further expansion of Anglo's holdings in the Far East Rand, in some cases in conjunction with New Consolidated Gold Fields. Anglo also began to move into the Orange Free State gold fields. The areas it acquired initially were generally unpromising. It was only by purchasing a stake in European and African Investments Ltd. in 1943, and subsequently gaining full ownership by acquiring most of the shares of its parent company, Lewis and Marks, in 1945, that Anglo laid the foundation for its subsequent domination of Free State gold-mining.

The 1930s and 1940s also saw the establishment of several subsidiary holding companies and the extension of the administration decentralization that characterizes Anglo. The precise extent to which effective Oppenheimer family control was maintained through E. Oppenheimer Sons, which absorbed A. Dunkelsbuhler & Co. in 1935, is unclear, but it is clear that personal influence remained strong. Anglo American Investment Trust (ANAMINT) took over Anglo's diamond interests in 1936, while West Rand Investment Trust (WRITS) took responsibility for gold mines in the Far West Rand field then opening up.

The decentralized structure was intended to allow, indeed to stimulate, on-the-spot decision-making, and to enable ideas to filter up from the people most directly involved in day-to-day operations. However, decentralization makes it extremely difficult to trace the details of financial connections within the group as the constituent companies remain separately incorporated. Effective control, or at least coordination by central management, has not been sacrificed; information is constantly exchanged, both formally and informally. Interlocking directorships, and the power to appoint directors, were augmented by personal contacts based on friendship and, more importantly, by family connections. Members of the Oppenheimer family held important positions in many of the companies. On another level, Anglo recruits people considered potentially high-powered, including a substantial number of former Rhodes scholars.

As the group developed, acquiring or establishing companies in various fields, the decentralized structure remained. Some companies became subsidiaries, with at least 50 percent of their shares held by Anglo. In other cases control mechanisms were more flexible, but just as effective. These included holding a greater number of shares than anyone else; the control of essential supplies, markets, or technology; and various financial links.

Between 1945 and 1960, Anglo became the world's largest gold-mining group, owing to expansion in the Orange Free State as well as the richer mines in the Far West Rand and Klerksdorp fields. Capital requirements were high, in part because the Free State gold deposits lay at considerably deeper levels than the Rand's. The 1946 African miners' strike, although rapidly repressed, was evidence of considerable upward pressure on African wages. Anglo decided to base Free State development on more capital-intensive techniques.

Building on its original financial concept, Anglo went further afield in its search for capital, securing about 27 percent of the £370 million raised from British sources; 23 percent from Switzerland, Germany, elsewhere in Europe, and the United States; and 43 percent from within the Anglo group itself. Most innovative, and significant in the longer term, was Anglo's drawing on surplus capital and nonmining savings generated within South Africa itself for 7 percent. The greater availability of domestic capital was a particularly important development after World War II, forming the basis for a measure of domestic financing of development which was associated in part with the expansion of Afrikaner, as opposed to British, capitalism. As internal savings increased over the following decades, they also laid the foundation for South Africa's ability to absorb a substantial portion of shares disposed of through disinvestment by foreign firms, although heavy reliance on foreign investment remained.

By 1960, Anglo had taken over the leadership of the gold-mining industry. It was also making heavy inroads into the country's industrial and service sectors. The difficulties of importing manufactured goods from Europe during World War I had stimulated interest in domestic industrialization. Increasingly powerful Afrikaner politicians were wary of mining interests prepared to finance industrial development, partly because of an underlying antipathy to capitalists, and partly because of their foreign, particularly British, identity. This led in 1928 to the formation of the Iron and Steel Corporation (ISCOR) as a nationalized basis for the country's iron and steel industry. As post-World War II mining developments generated more capital, pressure to create domestic investment opportunities led to increased, though often reluctant, cooperation between the government and the private sector which was increasingly dominated by Anglo.

Social and political considerations also became important, particularly after 1948 when the rationale for the apartheid system included the expectation that industries would be established along the borders of homeland territories, providing employment for the Africans increasingly forced to inhabit them. While that hope was never fulfilled, antagonism between British and Afrikaners began to diminish in the face of a perceived common threat from black Africans, and by the growth of Afrikaner involvement in business. The importance of Oppenheimer's and Anglo's financial strength also diminished some of the specific antagonism toward them. Despite the fact that Harry Oppenheimer, who succeeded his father as head of the group after World War II, often criticized the apartheid regime, it was widely accepted that he did not intend to attempt to destroy it, was prepared to work within it, and was pressing for changes that would improve the position of Africans primarily because it made good business sense.

In 1942 the government established the Industrial Development Corporation to promote and finance—through war taxes imposed on the mining industry—the expansion of ISCOR and a range of private industrial concerns. This was in some measure an attempt to create a counterweight to Anglo. Anglo's ability to draw on foreign capital sources, as well as foreign technology and other expertise, meant that the counterweight soon fell.

Initially, most of Anglo's industrial activity was directly related to mining. It had acquired African Explosive and Chemical Industries through its earlier investments in diamond interests. Its acquisition of Lewis and Marks brought it Union Steel and Vereeniging Refractories. In 1936 Anglo established Boart and Hard Metals, concerned with the use of industrial diamonds in mining and other drilling applications. In 1961 it created the Highveld Steel and Vanadium Corporation which, along with Steel Ceilings and Aluminum Works (SCAW), acquired in 1964, formed the basis of Anglo's control of South African specialized steel production, as well as created a strong foundation for heavy engineering. The merging of three construction companies— Lewis Construction, James Thompson, and Anglo American Construction—into LTA Ltd. created a construction giant.

Diversification also led Anglo into paper manufacturing (Mondi Paper Co., formed in 1967) and, through its 1960 takeover of Johannesburg Consolidated Investments, newspaper publishing (the Argus group and Times Media Limited). Building on motor vehicle distribution in the McCarthy group, it moved—by combining with Chrysler and then Ford—into automobile production as well. In freight services, in conjunction with Safmarine, it led the growth of containerized shipping in the country. Retail stores and large property holdings have also been acquired.

An important merger involving Anglo in the 1970s was between Rand Mines and Thomas Barlow. Rand Mines was a mining group that had not acquired interests in the Far West Rand and Orange Free State as its older Witwatersrand mines reached depletion. Seriously ailing, it came under Anglo control in the 1960s, but Anglo did little to revive it. Thomas Barlow had been a small engineering supply importer, which by 1970 controlled more than 70 companies manufacturing a wide variety of products. Barlow acquired all Rand Mines's issued shares in 1971. Anglo held 10 percent of Barlow Rand's shares directly. By 1972, after reorganization and expansion, the merged group controlled 131 subsidiaries and associates in nine countries. Although executive control remained in Barlow family hands, Anglo was not without influence in the firm.

At least as important as its industrial links was Anglo's involvement in the financial sector. In 1949, the South African government set up the National Finance Corporation (NFC) to receive large deposits—minimum £50,000—to be used for investment. Much of the NFC's funds came from and went back into mining. Anglo, for its part, formed a private merchant bank, Union Acceptances Ltd. (UAL), in 1955, supported by Lazard Freres and Barclays Bank. Offshoots and mergers followed, the most important mergers being those in the 1970s which brought UAL, Syfrets Trust Co., Old Mutual, and Nedbank together as Nedsual, providing commercial banking, insurance, and other financial services. Anglo went on to increase its holdings in insurance and other financial service institutions. Although Anglo disposed of its Nedbank holdings by the late 1970s, the merger with Nedbank was only one of the moves made by

Anglo that contributed strongly to the destruction of the barrier between British and Afrikaner capital.

Anglo did not merely compete with Barclays. The 1970s expansion saw Anglo's holdings in Barclays National Bank reach 17.5 percent of the total shares issued. In 1986, when Barclays International was forced by public pressure to complete its disinvestment in South Africa, Anglo acquired the greater part of the shares divested.

On the international scene, using many of the channels it had opened to bring capital into South Africa, Anglo also expanded its own holdings, primarily in mining, throughout the world. In London, Charter Consolidated, a 1965 merger of the British South Africa Company, Central Mining, and CMS, gave Anglo considerable investment opportunities in Africa, Europe, and Australasia.

Although diamonds replaced gold as Anglo's single most important source of profit in the 1980s, and despite wide-ranging diversification, gold remained at the heart of the group's activities. A substantial holding in the U.S. precious metals refiners Engelhard Corporation, along with a stake in the U.K.'s Johnson Matthey, gave Anglo access to important sources of highly profitable information about the world's gold trade.

Anglo's share in Engelhard was held by its subsidiary Minerals and Resources Corporation (Minorco), officially renamed Minorco in 1974. Minorco grew out of Rhoanglo. It was through Minorco that Anglo attempted to take over Consolidated Gold Fields (Consgold) in 1988. Anglo and Consgold had been closely associated—directly and indirectly—in many enterprises over the years, but relations between them were based at least as much on rivalry as on common interest, and the attempted takeover came as no surprise. Anglo acquired about 25 percent of Consgold. This attempt came up against U.S. antitrust legislation and Consgold was bought by Hanson Trust instead.

Anglo was at the center of political controversy in South Africa in the 1980s, not merely because of its economic strength, but because the Oppenheimers and the group itself took a public stand on the apartheid question. Politically active Ernest Oppenheimer and his son Harry were not in favor of black majority rule, but they did press for relaxation of certain aspects of the apartheid regime. Not surprisingly, they were particularly interested in decreasing dependence on migrant labor. A more settled, stable labor force was considered more productive and efficient. Although some stabilization of labor did occur, relatively little could be done in the face of government opposition. In 1987, along with some other mining groups, Anglo began to replace migrant workers' hostels with low-cost family accommodation. Like several other changes, this was seen by many as too little too late, and by others as merely a new method of social control. Anglo was not prepared to raise African wages sufficiently to allow workers effective freedom of housing choice.

In 1985, Anglo's chairman, Gavin Relly, and other senior Anglo personnel met representatives of the African National Congress (ANC) in exile. In April 1990 Anglo's Scenario Planning Team published proposals for South Africa's constitutional development. These placed great emphasis on federalism and devolution of power. More dispersed state power, Anglo has argued, will facilitate accommodation of divergent interest groups. This, along with a massive image-building campaign in the U.K. press has been part of Anglo's campaign to remain a major economic force in the country as its political structure changes inexorably.

### 1990s and Beyond

The rapid unraveling of the apartheid system in the early 1990s quickly changed forever the environment in which Anglo operated and gave rise to much speculation about Anglo's future as well as a great deal of maneuvering by Anglo to protect its interests. The major political events followed one after another: in 1990 the ban on the ANC was lifted and Nelson Mandela was released from prison; in 1991 the remaining apartheid laws were repealed; in 1992, an all-white referendum approved a new constitution that would lead to eventual free elections; and in 1994 the first nationwide free elections were held and were won by the ANC, with Mandela elected president.

Meanwhile, the 1990s started for Anglo with a change in leadership, as Julian Ogilvie Thompson, who at one time was Harry Oppenheimer's personal assistant, took over the chairmanship from the retiring Relly in 1990. At the same time, it was widely known that Oppenheimer's son Nicholas, then deputy chairman of Anglo and the head of De Beers's London-based diamond sales operation, was being groomed as the next chairman. The new leadership faced the consequences of Anglo's years of dealing with apartheid and the international boycotts and sanctions the system engendered. The company had been forced to reinvest its earnings within South Africa where it had no choice but to diversify in order to use all its excess cash. By the early 1990s Anglo had created, no doubt aided by the apartheid system itself, a powerfully diversified company with admitted control of 25 percent of the South African stock market, a figure that outside observers have placed as high as 40.5 percent. Threats to nationalize certain Anglo assets, notably its mines, and to break up the Anglo empire seemed quite real, although it eventually became apparent that Mandela had no intention of seizing the company's assets without compensation.

As part of a two-pronged defensive strategy, Anglo first moved to protect some of its assets from nationalization by increasing its overseas investments and by transferring assets into the control of subsidiaries and affiliated companies located outside South Africa, with Luxembourg-based Minorco the key affiliate. Minorco expanded its North American mining operations by acquiring the American firm Freeport-McMoRan Gold Company in 1990 (it was later renamed Independence Mining) and the Canadian-based Hudson Bay Mining & Smelting in 1991. In a 1993 $1.4 billion stock and asset swap, Minorco took over the South American, European, and Australian operations of both Anglo American and De Beers, which meant that all of Anglo's non-African, non-diamond assets were now consolidated within Minorco and out of the reach of nationalization.

Anglo's second strategy was a longer term one of making small concessions to the new political order over the course of several years, thus heading off the possibility that the country's

new government of national unity would force Anglo to make more dramatic changes. Essentially, this represented a revival of Anglo's strategy of co-option, previously used successfully with the Afrikaners, now being employed with the new group in power. Anglo sought to spin off some of its vast holdings to black South Africans, such as in the 1994 deal in which African Life was bought by a group of black businesspeople.

A more ambitious divestment began in 1995 when Anglo divided its Johannesburg Consolidated Investment Company, Limited (Johnnies) subsidiary into three separate companies: Anglo American Platinum Corporation Ltd. (Amplats), a trader of platinum and diamonds; JCI Ltd., an operator of gold, coal, ferro-chrome, and base metal mines; and Johnnies Industrial Corporation Ltd. (Johnnic), a holding company with industrial and real estate assets. Anglo intended to hold onto its minority stake in Amplats, but to sell its stakes in JCI and Johnnic to black South Africans. As of mid-1996 neither of the stakes had been sold, but a serious bid was developing for Johnnic, whose lucrative holdings included a 13.7 percent stake in South Africa's largest brewing company, South African Breweries; 27.8 percent of a beverages group, Premier; 26.4 percent in an automobile maker, Toyota SA Marketing; and 43.2 percent of a newspaper and magazine publisher, Omni Media. Little interest had been apparent for the JCI stake, with the *Economist* speculating that black South Africans' business inexperience made running a holding company more attractive than the messy business of mining.

Thus was Anglo slowly by the mid-1990s beginning to unbundle itself of its diverse and massive holdings in South Africa. The company's future was still clouded given the question of whether it was moving fast enough to suit those in the country wishing to see economic power transferred from white to black hands nearly as fast as political power had been transferred. And while Mandela's government seemed content with a go slow approach, the political situation was still unstable in the country, especially given Mandela's advanced age. Nevertheless, Anglo's moves to shelter more of its assets offshore made it much less likely that possible future government intervention in its affairs would prove devastating.

### Principal Subsidiaries

Abalyn Investment Holdings Limited; African and European Investment Company Limited; The Afrikander Lease Limited (53%); Anglo African Holdings Limited (Isle of Man); Anglo American Coal Corporation Limited (52%); Anglo American Corporation Botswana (Services) Limited; Anglo American Corporation (Central Africa) Limited (Zambia); Anglo American Corporation Services Limited (Zimbabwe); Anglo American Corporation Zimbabwe Limited (67%); Anglo American Gold Investment Company Limited (50%); Anglo American Investment Trust Limited (52%); Anglo American Properties Limited (66%); Anglo American Property Services (Pty) Limited; Anglo American Services (Netherlands) B.V.; Anglo American Ventures Limited (British Virgin Islands; 42%); Anglo European Holdings Limited (Isle of Man); Anmercosa Land and Estates Limited; A.R.H. Limited S.A. (Luxembourg); Aurora Holdings Limited (Liberia; 50%); Calina Investment Holdings Limited; Carlton Centre Limited (70%); Celltech Limited (Luxembourg; 95%); Centesis Investment Holdings Limited;

Delroy Investment Holdings Limited; Elandsrand Gold Mining Company Limited (55%); Erongo Holdings Limited (British Virgin Islands; 86%); Erongo Mining and Exploration Company Limited (Namibia; 58%); Ixion Investment Holdings Limited; Lagen Investment Holdings Limited; Lodestone Holdings Limited; Mainstraat Beleggings (1965) Beperk (60%); Marjoram Holdings Limited; Maudsley Holdings Limited; Minpress Investments Limited (British Virgin Islands); Morupule Colliery Limited (Botswana; 83%); Namakwa Sands Limited (76%); New Central Witwatersrand Areas Limited (50%); The New Era Consolidated Limited; Numitor Investment Holdings Limited; Pintail Investments Limited; Rand American Investments Limited; Rand Selection Corporation Limited; Randsel Investments Limited; RIL Limited (Zimbabwe); Runcorn Holdings Limited; South African Mines Selection Limited; South African Townships Mining and Finance Corporation Limited; Western Ultra Deep Levels Limited (75%); Zimro Limited.

### Further Reading

"Dancing Partners: Business in South Africa," *Economist,* April 27, 1996, pp. 70–71.

Fuhrman, Peter, "Harry Oppenheimer, African Empire Builder, Is Smiling Again," *Forbes,* September 16, 1991, pp. 130–37.

Gregory, Theodore, *Ernest Oppenheimer and the Economic Development of Southern Africa,* Cape Town: Oxford University Press, 1962.

Hocking, Anthony, *Oppenheimer and Son,* New York: McGraw-Hill, 1973.

Innes, Duncan, *Anglo American and the Rise of Modern South Africa,* London: Heinemann Educational Books, 1984.

Jessop, Edward, *Ernest Oppenheimer: A Study in Power,* London: Rex Collings, 1979.

Kanfer, Stefan, *The Last Empire: De Beers, Diamonds, and the World,* New York: Farrar Straus Giroux, 1993.

"A New Scramble," *Economist,* August 12, 1995, pp. 17–19.

"Not a Golden Titan, More Like a Pig in a Poke," *Economist,* October 7, 1995, pp. 67–68.

Pallister, David, Sarah Stewart, and Ian Lepper, *South Africa Inc.—The Oppenheimer Empire,* London: Simon & Schuster, rev. ed., 1987.

—Simon Katzenellenbogen
updated by David E. Salamie

# Arctco, Inc.

**600 Brooks Avenue South**
**Thief River Falls, Minnesota 56701**
**U.S.A.**
**(218) 681-8558**
Fax: (218) 681-3162

*Public Company*
*Incorporated:* 1983
*Employees:* 1,600
*Sales:* $367.1 million (1995)
*Stock Exchanges:* NASDAQ
*SICs:* 3799 Transportation Equipment, Not Elsewhere
    Classified; 2339 Women's/Misses' Outerwear, Not
    Elsewhere Classified; 2329 Men's/Boys' Clothing,
    Not Elsewhere Classified

One of the pioneers in its industry, Arctco, Inc. designs, manufactures, and sells Arctic Cat snowmobiles, Tigershark personal watercraft, and Bearcat all-terrain vehicles, as well as related parts, accessories, and garments. Based in Thief River Falls, Minnesota, Arctco was formed in 1983 to continue the legacy of snowmobile manufacture established by Arctic Enterprises, Inc., which went bankrupt in 1981. By the mid-1990s, Arctco had firmly established itself as a leading producer of snowmobiles and personal watercraft, having successfully resurrected the reputation and business of the defunct Arctic Enterprises. In early 1996, Arctco entered the market for all-terrain vehicles, a new area of business for a company enjoying strong growth in its traditional markets.

## Origins

When Edgar Hetteen saw his first snowmobile, his reaction was immediate, leaving no question about his feelings. "I wouldn't have anything to do with the thing at first," he later recalled, "I told my brother-in-law, David [Johnson], he had wasted our time and money building it and I wanted no more of it." For someone who would spend nearly every waking hour for the next ten years trying to arouse widespread enthusiasm in snowmobiles, Hetteen's words marked a decidedly chilly beginning to what would become a life-long love affair. Hetteen, who would go on to found the predecessor company to Arctco and, by doing so, position himself among the handful of pioneers in the U.S. snowmobile industry, was more concerned at the time about his farming equipment fabrication company than the curious sled that greeted him upon his arrival in Roseau, Minnesota. The year was 1955 and Hetteen had just returned from a sales trip, his latest effort at turning his company, Hetteen Hoist and Derrick, into a flourishing concern. It was proving to be a difficult task. Far removed from more populated, lucrative markets, Hetteen Hoist and Derrick was struggling in its eighth year of business, scoring only a modicum of success as a custom fabricator of specialized farm implements and tools. Hetteen's latest business trip had achieved lackluster results, and he was initially unimpressed with Johnson's snowmobile. Before long, however, one of the world's preeminent snowmobile manufacturers was established, spawning the creation of Arctic Cat snowmobiles and a new form of winter recreation for millions of people.

Johnson's initial design had been built at the request of a local resident, Pete Peterson, who asked the manufacturer to fabricate a "gas-powered sled." The proceeds from the sale of Peterson's snowmobile enabled Hetteen Hoist and Derrick to make payroll, tempering Hetteen's view considerably, and shortly thereafter another Roseau local placed an order for a gas-powered sled, as demand for the novel snow machines began to build. By the end of the winter of 1955–1956, Hetteen's company had constructed five snowmobiles; the following winter 75 machines were built, and during the winter of 1957–1958, more than 300 snowmobiles were produced by Hetteen and his workers. In the space of a few short years, the primary business of Hetteen's company had switched from fabricating farm equipment to building and testing machines designed for snow travel. Hetteen, by this point, was hooked.

For years, Hetteen had endeavored to sell the straw cutters, post setters, and other equipment his company made to markets outside Roseau, but had found little success. With snowmobiles, he sensed the opportunity to achieve the success that had eluded him with agricultural machinery. Early on he realized that in order to make his new product a success in distant markets it would have to be marketed as a recreational device, but during the late 1950s public interest in snowmobiles was essentially nonexistent, a hurdle Hetteen would overcome by launching an ambitious public relations campaign. In March 1960, Hetteen and three of his cohorts took their snowmobiles to Alaska and completed a 1,100-mile trek from Bethel to Fairbanks in 18 days, drawing the attention of newspaper reporters, magazine writers, and ham radio operators.

Hetteen returned to Roseau pleased by his success in piquing public interest in snowmobiles, but his arrival home did not meet with applause or congratulatory pats on the back. Hetteen Hoist and Derrick had since been renamed Polaris Industries, Inc. and capitalized by local investors, who were somewhat miffed that Hetteen had abandoned his duties at Polaris and gone to Alaska. As this dispute over the future course of the company was being played out, Hetteen was approached by a group of investors from Thief River Falls, Minnesota. Led by L. B. Hartz, a successful food broker and supermarket owner, the group offered to financially back Hetteen if he moved his company to Thief River Falls; Hetteen declined, and in May 1960, two months after completing his successful trek in Alaska, Hetteen sold his controlling interest in Polaris and returned to Alaska, where he hoped to start a new career as a bush pilot and frontiersman.

Hetteen's second visit to Alaska was not as successful as his first. After several months of working at isolated airstrips as a pilot and mechanic, Hetteen decided to accept Hartz's offer and renew his interest in designing, building, and testing snowmobiles. By the time Hetteen arrived in Thief River Falls at Christmas 1960, financial arrangements had already been made to provide him with a co-signed note for $10,000, which he used to rent an unused, 30-foot-by-70-foot grocery warehouse and to start his new business, Polar Manufacturing Company.

### 1962: Arctic Cat Is Born

Polar Manufacturing opened its doors on January 2, 1961 and initially manufactured electric steam cleaners and a device to kill insects called "Bug-O-Vac" in order to raise enough money to begin snowmobile production in earnest. The first snowmobile, the "New Polar 500," was completed by the end of the year and marketed as a utility model for use by forestry companies, power and light companies, telephone companies, and oil exploration companies. Although Hetteen had wanted to develop snowmobiles as a recreational product nearly from the outset of his involvement with the machines, he knew he needed to develop a need for snowmobiles before he could begin to develop a desire for them, but he would not have to wait long. In 1962, after its inaugural year of business, Polar Manufacturing was renamed Arctic Enterprises, Inc. and introduced the red-colored "Arctic Cat 100," the first front-engined sport sled in the United States, which Hetteen referred to as the "Tin Lizzie." Concurrent with the introduction of the Arctic Cat 100, a distribution network was established to carry the machine to distant markets, as Hetteen had always hoped. Although the New Polar 500 had been the first model produced, the Arctic Cat 100 represented the beginning of an era for both Arctic Enterprises and snowmobile enthusiasts across the country,

ushering in a new winter sport and launching the Arctic Cat tradition.

Distributor relationships were forged throughout a wide territory ranging from New York to Idaho, as the fledgling company sought to secure a foothold in distant markets. There were 19 distributors signed up for the 1963–1964 winter season and 13 Arctic Cat models, up from the six offered the previous year. During the first half of the decade, the company's sales climbed encouragingly, propelled by the increasing number of models produced each year and supported by a steadily growing distribution network, but annual profits were not demonstrating the same vibrancy. This inability to post consistent profit growth— the company lost $20,000 in 1964 on $750,000 in sales—was part of the reason Hetteen decided to step down from his leadership position in 1965 and hand the reins of command to Lowell Swenson. Hetteen, literally, had spent nearly all his time for the previous decade trying to make a successful snowmobile manufacturing company, and now as his company was on the brink of success he decided that a new leader was required to push Arctic Enterprises over the edge. Hetteen receded from the bustling activity pervading Arctic Enterprises, but he did not disappear altogether. Years later, Hetteen would return, but during the interim, Arctic Enterprises would grow into the flourishing concern he had long sought.

When Swenson became president of Arctic Enterprises in 1966 he made one goal of the company's future clear: "We [will] concentrate on one machine," he vowed, "and make it a damn good one." True to his word, Swenson spearheaded the effort toward designing a snowmobile that would carry the company into the future, putting to an end the era of the red Arctic Cats after the 1965–1966 winter season to make room for the black-colored "Panther." Debuting in 1966, the Panther possessed technological breakthroughs that would carry the company into the 1970s and drive its sales and, most important, its profits upward for the remainder of the 1960s.

In 1968, Arctic Enterprises generated $7.5 million in sales, three times the amount collected the year before, and posted $379,000 in net income or eight times the figure recorded in 1967, ending the nagging worries about profitability. In 1969, annual sales continued their exponential march upward, reaching $21.7 million, while net income eclipsed the $1 million plateau, climbing to $1.2 million. Business was booming, with the company holding a firm grip on nearly 12 percent of the U.S. market for snowmobiles, a percentage that perhaps could have been higher, but the two shifts working the production lines at the Thief River Falls facilities were not enough to satisfy the mounting demand for Panther snowmobiles. As the company prepared for the 1970s, it exited the 1960s with a full head of steam and high expectations for future growth. Production facilities were greatly expanded in anticipation of rising demand and a line of snowmobile clothing was introduced to give the company a more diversified footing in the rapidly expanding snowmobile industry.

### 1970s Collapse

The 1970s began as expected, with the company's annual sales soaring 113 percent to reach $46.5 million, its market share rising to 13 percent, and its net income jumping to $2.9

million. Prosperous times gave Arctic Enterprises the ability to diversify further, providing the financial means to acquire boat manufacturer Silverline, Inc. of Moorhead, Minnesota, the company's first major cross-seasonal acquisition, and to introduce mini-bikes on the market, both of which became part of the company's operations in 1970. The following year, Arctic Enterprises moved farther afield, acquiring lawn and garden manufacturer General Leisure, then, in 1973, introduced a line of French-made bicycles, but by this point the luster gleaming from Arctic Enterprises' operations had dulled considerably. The years of robust growth were over as quickly as they started.

The line of bicycles proved to be unsuccessful and General Leisure proved to be a costly mistake, leading to its divestiture in 1973, but these ancillary businesses were the least of Arctic Enterprises' problems. The demand for snowmobiles tapered off during the early years of the 1970s, beginning their downward climb in 1971 and causing Arctic Enterprises' most disastrous year in 1974. If it was any consolation for the employees and management in Thief River Falls, who in the space of a few months had watched their prolific rise screech to a halt, Arctic Enterprises was not alone in its downward free fall. Across the country, snowmobile manufacturers were reeling from the debilitative affects of depressed demand, with many going out of business. In 1970, when the snowmobile industry was thriving, there were more than 100 brands of snowmobiles on the market; by 1976, when the worst of the harsh economic times were over, the number of brands on the market had plunged precipitously to a mere 13.

As debilitative as waning snowmobile demand had been to Arctic Enterprises' business, however, conditions in the industry after the shake-out was completed placed the Thief River Falls concern in what could be regarded as a stronger position. Much of the competition in the United States had been weeded out, and Arctic Enterprises continued to reign as the largest producer of snowmobiles in the country. Recovery was quick in the late 1970s, sufficient enough to enable the company to finance the acquisition of its second boat manufacturer in 1977, when Arctic Enterprises purchased the Lund Boat Company and gained control of its manufacturing facilities in Minnesota, Wisconsin, and in Manitoba, Canada. Sales by the end of the year flirted with $100 million, reaching $99 million, while the company's market share had been bolstered by the departure of many of its competitors, rising to a whopping 25 percent. The following year, in 1979, sales soared 61 percent to $175 million, by which point the number of snowmobile manufacturers in the country had been whittled down to six. Once again business was booming, and the company was exiting the 1970s much as it had ended the 1960s, with its business interests moving forward on all fronts.

### 1980s: Reincarnation of Arctic Cat

To the chagrin of the workers and management at Thief River Falls, history continued to repeat itself in the decade ahead, as the early 1980s paralleled the early 1970s and rampant growth quickly disappeared. This time, however, the effects were much more devastating. Sales in 1980 climbed to $185 million, despite a decline in snowmobile sales throughout the country, but by far the most telling and most depressing finan-

cial figure for the year was the company's profit total. Arctic Enterprises lost $11.5 million during the year, a staggering blow that was followed by another $10 million loss the following year. As production totals in 1981 fell to their lowest levels since 1969, the bankers who had granted the company loans over the years became disgruntled and alarmed. Worried that the company would not be able to make good on its financial promises, the bankers called for the payment of $48.5 million in loans on February 6, 1981. Eleven days later, Arctic Enterprises filed for protection under Chapter 11 of the U.S. Bankruptcy Act. In a year that otherwise would have been celebrated as the company's 20th anniversary year, Arctic Enterprises was financially ruined.

The news could not have been worse, but even as steps were being taken to liquidate the snowmobile operations and the rest of the company was being sold piecemeal, there were some encouraging reports that at least seemed to underscore the strength of the Arctic Cat name in snowmobile circles across the country. Even though the company's production facilities had been shuttered, the demand for Arctic Enterprises' snowmobiles had increased. Remarkably, sales were up high enough for the company to capture 38 percent of the U.S. market one year after production had stopped, provided ample evidence that loyalty to and confidence in Arctic Enterprises' products remained high.

Dead but not forgotten, Arctic Enterprises was etched in the memories of its loyal customers, some of whom vowed never to ride a snowmobile again. The memory of the company was also etched in the hearts of its former employees, the pangs of which led a small group of former managers to attend the auction of Arctic Enterprises' various properties. Included in this group was Edgar Hetteen, who returned to witness the dismemberment of the company he had left nearly 20 years earlier; by the end of the day the group had acquired enough of Arctic Enterprises' properties to establish a new snowmobile manufacturing company, which was incorporated as Arctco, Inc. in 1983. As company advertisements would soon announce, the Cat was back, and for the legions of faithful customers the return of the popular Arctic Cat snowmobiles was welcome news.

After acquiring the production rights and the exclusive use of the Arctic Cat brand name, Arctco made preparations to get its product to market, beginning production of its snowmobiles in August 1983. The less than 3,000 snowmobiles made for the 1984 model year sold out quickly, enabling the company to generate $7.3 million in sales and post $600,000 in profit. All of Arctic Cat's trademarks, equipment, and manufacturing properties were subsequently acquired in 1986 and 1987, restoring much of the luster formerly radiated by Arctic Enterprises. Sales and profits rose energetically throughout the remainder of the decade, reaching an encouraging $138.8 million and $12.5 million, respectively, by the end of 1990, the year Arctco became a publicly-traded company.

During the first half of the 1990s, Arctco continued to enjoy impressive success, making its entry into the personal watercraft market and recording 21.5 percent annual growth in sales and 21.7 percent annual growth in net income. By 1994, when the company generated $268.1 million in sales, Arctco had surpassed the revenue volume recorded by Arctic Enterprises before its death knell had reverberated throughout Thief River Falls in 1981. As the company planned for the late 1990s and the new century ahead prospects for future growth were encouraging, bolstering confidence that the coming years would bring continued success to the thriving company. During the mid-1990s the North American snowmobile industry was expanding at a 20 percent annual clip, while the market for personal watercraft, the company's other primary business area, was recording annual gains in excess of 30 percent. Further opportunities for financial growth were opened to the company when it made its first foray into the market for all-terrain vehicles, a $1.2 billion industry during the mid-1990s that was recording nearly 20 percent annual growth. In January 1996, Arctco's first four-wheel-drive recreational and utility vehicle, the Bearcat 454, rolled off the company's production line, giving the company a diversified, cross-seasonal product line to drive its growth in the years ahead.

## Principal Subsidiaries

Arctco FSC, Inc. (U.S. Virgin Islands).

## Further Reading

"Arctco, Inc. Announces Plans for New Service Parts Distribution Center," *PR Newswire,* May 7, 1996, p. 5.

Autry, Ret, "Arctco," *Fortune,* November 19, 1990, p. 174.

Davis, Ricardo A., "Minnesota's Arctco Leaps into All-Terrain Vehicle Market," *Knight-Ridder/Tribune Business News,* April 9, 1996, p. 40.

"New Powder or Ice Ahead," *Business Week,* February 17, 1992, p. 123.

Ramstad, C. J., *Legend: Arctic Cat's First Quarter Century,* Deephaven, Minn.: PPM Books, 1987, 189 p.

—Jeffrey L. Covell

# Aris Industries, Inc.

**475 Fifth Avenue**
**New York, New York 10018**
**U.S.A.**
**(212) 686-5050**
**Fax: (212) 685-8281**

*Public Company*
*Incorporated:* 1947 as Uniroy of Hempstead, Inc.
*Employees:* 3,561
*Sales:* $188.1 million (1995)
*Stock Exchanges:* New York
*SICs:* 2311 Mens' & Boys' Suits, Coats & Overcoats;
2331 Women's, Misses' & Juniors' Blouses & Shirts;
2339 Women's, Misses' & Juniors' Outerwear, Not
Elsewhere Classified; 5136 Men's & Boys' Clothing
& Furnishings; 7389 Business Services, Not
Elsewhere Classified

During a checkered career the company known in the mid-1990s as Aris Industries, Inc. has occupied a precarious place in the apparel industry. After early success as a retailer named Unishops it fell into bankruptcy, emerging mainly as a manufacturer and importer called the Marcade Group that again went bankrupt. The company was renamed Aris Industries after returning to profitability in 1993.

Incorporated in 1947 as Uniroy of Hempstead, Inc., a retail menswear chain, the company was renamed United Shirt Shops, Inc. in 1953. It gradually evolved into a retailer of men's and boys' clothing in the leased departments of discount stores, specializing in moderate- and low-priced work clothes, shirts, socks, underwear, and sportswear. The number of units grew from seven in 1957, when it opened its first leased department, in Modell's Shoppers World in Lodi, New Jersey, to 19 in 1959 and 91 in 1962. The company was renamed Unishops, Inc. in 1961. Sales grew from about $500,000 in 1957 and $5 million in 1959 to $22.4 million in 1962, and income from $230,000 in 1959 to $890,000 in 1962. Company offices were in Jersey City,

with Bernard (Bud) Kessler as president and his brother Daniel as executive vice president.

### Rapid Growth in the 1960s

Unishops went public in 1962, offering 275,000 shares at $14 a share. By the end of 1963 there were 104 Unishops units; sales that year came to $27.4 million and income to $1.2 million. Unishops' stock became listed on the American Stock Exchange in 1964, when cash dividends were first paid out. The last conventional Unishops store closed in 1963. By late 1966, when Bud Kessler, now chairman, moved to Los Angeles, there were some 200 Unishops leased departments in stores from coast to coast, making the firm the largest in its field. Its landlords numbered 68, the largest of which was S.S. Kresge Co., operator of K-Mart, where Unishops had 48 units. Net sales reached $46.3 million and income $2.4 million in 1965, with an astonishing 31 percent return on net worth.

Unishops was able to grow rapidly because it cost only $16,000 for the company to open a new leased department, including the costs of fixtures, pre-opening payroll and advertising, and transportation of inventory to the new site. The $60,000 or so allotted to inventory was recoverable at the chain's other stores if a new unit failed. One cost-cutting technique was to use the firm's growing purchasing power to persuade manufacturers to store goods for Unishops until needed in the stores, thereby substantially reducing warehouse costs. Unishops was also rapidly developing its own private brands of merchandise; in 1966, goods sold under its label accounted for 79 percent of sales, compared to 40 percent five years earlier.

About three-fourths of all Unishops stores owned their own fixtures at this time. In most cases store operators provided central check-out services, with the Unishops leased department usually paid weekly, within 10 to 12 days after the sale. Rent was based on a percentage of sales, usually 8 to 11 percent. Unishops departments hired and supervised their own employees. Well over half of these units were unionized.

Unishops began expanding through acquisition as well as internally in 1966, when it purchased Clarkins, Inc., operator of a chain of three Ohio discount department stores. A fourth store in Dayton was added later in the year, and two more were opened in 1967. Between 1968 and 1971 the company also acquired J. Z. Sales Corp., operator of four leased departments selling housewares, hardware, outdoor supplies, and garden furniture; Mikemitch Realty Corp., operator of three Modell's Shoppers World discount department stores in the New York metropolitan area; Nescott, Inc., operator of 22 leased departments and 13 freestanding units selling prescription drugs and beauty aids; Star's Discount Department Stores, operator of three such stores in New York and three in Connecticut; Teril Stationers Inc., operator of leased stationery departments in 11 discount department stores; White Discount Department Stores of Massapequa, New York; Goldfine's Inc. of Duluth, Minnesota; and Perry's Shoes Inc. of New York. All these purchases were made for Unishops stock, enabling the company to avoid long-term debt.

Interviewed by the *New York Times* in 1969, Bernard Kessler said that while Unishops had expanded from selling men's and boys' wear to other specialties including hardware and beauty supplies, it was not trying "to be all things to all consumers." Accordingly, it was leasing out the supermarket food operation at Modell's and at Clarkins. He added that the company had gone upscale, raising both product quality and profit margins. A considerable amount of Unishops' goods were now being sold on credit, it was offering delivery service, and more personnel were being made available in order to assist customers in making their selections. The number of executives and division heads who had stock options was unusually high, according to Kessler, and, in keeping with the company's policy of allowing younger staff to share responsibility, the average age of its managers was 39.

Unishops' string of record sales and profits continued unabated into the early 1970s. It operated 277 leased departments in 35 states and 21 discount department stores in 1970, when net sales came to $183.8 million and net income to nearly $9 million. The dividend was increased for the sixth year in a row. Unishops stock reached as high as $89 a share before a two-for-one split in 1968 and as high as $70.50 before another two-for-one split in 1969. The company began taking over the operation of K-Mart stores, assuming, by the end of the year, the management of about 20 of the 56 units in which it had taken department leases. It also formed the Bobbie Sue division to operate leased ladies' and children's wear departments in 12 discount stores and apparel departments in certain company-owned units. Sales rose to $230 million in 1971, with net income of $7.6 million.

### Overexpansion and 1973 Bankruptcy

By this time Bernard Kessler was setting an objective of $1 billion in annual sales by 1980. The company's hectic pace of growth proved, however, to be unsustainable because of lagging consumer demand and increasing competition in discount retailing. In retrospect, moreover, it was found that the company had expanded without sufficient inventory controls, cash budgeting, or management depth. By the time Kessler died in 1972 at the age of only 50—his brother Daniel had died in 1969 at only 43—Unishops was in serious trouble. That year the company maintained 351 leased departments and sales volume reached a record $271 million, but it lost $4.5 million. In 1973 it lost

another $13.2 million, much of it due to the lagging Bobbie Sue division. In November 1973, when the company filed for Chapter 11 bankruptcy, there were 39 Unishops discount department stores, 37 specialty stores, and 281 leased departments in stores operated by others. Just prior to the bankruptcy petition, Unishops stock was trading for 50 cents a share.

Unishops responded to its plight with a major cost-cutting program. By January 1974 two-thirds of its freestanding stores and about 150 leased departments had been sold, otherwise disposed of, or were in the process of being eliminated. It sold some of the White and Nescott stores to other discounters in 1974 and disposed of all its Bobbie Sue departments. Star's and Modell's disappeared entirely. Sales fell to $145 million in 1973 and $111 million in 1974. In April 1975 a bankruptcy judge approved a company plan, covering 19 Unishops subsidiaries, which offered creditors about 42 cents on the dollar in cash (spread over five years) plus 34 percent of its stock. In all Unishops paid creditors $50 million on $91 million worth of debt, three-quarters of it in cash.

In mid 1975 Unishops was operating 13 Clarkins and Goldfine's discount department stores and about 200 leased departments. While most of them were confined to selling men's and boys' wear. Unishops also was operating Central Textile domestic goods and fabrics departments and Perry's Shoes departments. The number of employees had fallen from a high of 6,500 to 2,500. These stringent measures enabled the company to make a profit of about $2 million in both fiscal 1975 (ending January 25, 1975) and fiscal 1976. Net income in fiscal 1977 came to $1.5 million on sales of $117.8 million and in fiscal 1978 to $927,000 on sales of $127.3 million.

### 1977–1981: A Period of Restructuring

Under Herbert Wexler, Kessler's successor as president and chief executive officer, the company not only restored its standing with creditors but used some of its $61 million tax-loss carry-forward for acquisitions. In 1977 it purchased Paul Marshall Products Inc., a California-based importer of wicker and rattan home-furnishing accessories, for $5.5 million. In 1978 it purchased Youth Centre Inc., a New England group of 14 children's apparel stores, for $3 million. It acquired Marlene Industries Corp., a manufacturer of budget women's and infants' clothing, for $42 million in 1979. Unishops also shed some of its holdings during these and subsequent years, disposing of its Goldfine's stores in 1978 and discontinuing its Clarkins and Perry's Shoes stores, as well as the sale of men's and boys' wear, in 1981.

By these transactions Unishops became a completely different business, with Central Textile (which operated 44 leased departments in discount stores owned by others) as its only prior unit. Although the company retained some ties to specialty retailing, its major activities now were manufacturing apparel and importing furniture and giftware, with Marlene Industries accounting for more than three-quarters of Unishops sales and income in fiscal 1981, when it earned $3.4 million on volume of $201 million. Accordingly, the company changed its name to Marcade Group Inc. in 1981. Its long-term debt was $21 million.

### Red Ink Again in the 1980s

The restructured and redirected company failed to thrive, however. Hard hit by the severe recession of the early 1980s, Marcade fell into the red in fiscal 1983, losing $8.2 million on sales of $198.3 million. By the end of this period its short-term debt had risen to $29 million, requiring the company to go to its banks for a long-term revolving-loan agreement and short-term credit lines. Marcade lost $8.8 million in fiscal 1984 and $21.9 million on only $71.4 million in sales in fiscal 1985. By September 1985 it had $30 million in long-term debt and negative net worth.

In 1986 an investor group paid $4 million for a 40-percent stake in Marcade, with banks receiving $10 million in cash, notes, preferred stock, and 30 percent of the common stock in exchange for a restructuring of its debt. The investment partners were Charles Ramat, who became president, and Robert Lifton and Howard Weingrow, co-chairmen of the board. Ramat later became chairman as well as president and still held both posts in the mid 1990s. The new management moved corporate headquarters from Jersey City to Manhattan. Two years later, a private investor group headed by Alexander and James Goren acquired about 16.5 percent of the stock for $20 million.

The sharply higher price for Marcade shares reflected an impressive turnaround for the company. Ramat used tax-loss carry-forwards to purchase Booth Bay, Ltd., at the end of 1986 for more than $9 million; Perry Manufacturing Co. and Europe Craft Imports, Inc. in 1987 for $23.8 million and $32.1 million, respectively; and Above The Belt, Inc. and RJMJ, Inc. in 1989 for undisclosed sums. These undervalued companies enabled Marcade in fiscal 1989 to realize net income of $8.4 million on revenues of $286.7 million, and in fiscal 1990 it earned $13.4 million on revenues of $377.7 million. Marcade now was the 13th-largest apparel company in the nation.

### More Hard Times in the 1990s

These acquisitions, however, burdened the company with $80 million in debt. One of them, RJMJ, providing financing and servicing to apparel manufacturers, overextended itself and landed Marcade in deep trouble. Sales by Marlene Industries and Booth Bay declined dramatically during 1990, and the company ended the fiscal year losing no less than $66 million (of which restructuring expenses accounted for $42.5 million) on revenues of $365.6 million. In 1991 Marlene Industries, with trade liabilities of about $5.6 million, was liquidated, its creditors to receive 15 percent in cash and the rest over four years. Aris ended that fiscal year with a loss of $2.8 million on sales of $237.8 million.

By August 1992 Marcade had stripped itself of all units except Europe Craft Imports, selling Members Only men's outerwear and sportswear; Perry Manufacturing Co., maker of women's sportswear; and Above The Belt, a manufacturer of apparel for young men phased out the following year. A $52-million loan from its chief creditor, Heller Financial, Inc., was in default, and it was attempting to restructure about $25 million in junk-bond debt it had issued. When Heller declined to further extend a $31-million payment due October 31, 1992, Marcade

filed for Chapter 11 bankruptcy. It ended the fiscal year with a loss of $16.6 million on sales of $193.2 million.

Under a plan approved in June 1993, Marcade emerged from bankruptcy. Affiliates of Apollo Advisors L.P. acquired 48.8 percent of the company, which assumed the new name of Aris Industries Inc. It returned to profitability, earning $2 million on revenues of $192.6 million in fiscal 1994. After a special credit for debt forgiveness, the profits soared to $31.2 million. For fiscal 1995 Aris had net income of $2.2 million on sales of $188.1 million. For the first half of fiscal 1996, however, the company lost $2.7 million on net sales of $75.9 million. Long-term debt was $64.2 million in July 1995.

At the end of 1994 Aris Industries was engaged in the design, manufacture, import, and distribution of men's and young men's sportswear and outerwear and ladies' sportswear and other apparel. Perry Manufacturing was manufacturing and distributing moderately priced misses', women's, junior, and petite sportswear in knit and woven fabrics. It was a large supplier of private-label goods to national chain stores, including Hunt Club and Worthington for J.C. Penney and the Jaclyn Smith sportswear line for K-Mart. In addition, it was manufacturing goods for such large customers as Liz Claiborne and Lands End.

Europe Craft was importing and distributing men's outerwear, including cloth and leather jackets, and sportswear, including knit shirts, under the "Members Only" name. It had been granted licenses to manufacture and distribute men's outerwear and raincoats under the "Perry Ellis" name and was also designing, developing, sourcing and importing men's and boys' outerwear and sportswear product lines as an agent for various national store chains selling such products under the Europe Craft name or a private label. In addition, Europe Craft had granted licenses to licensees for men's dress and woven sport shirts, men's related active wear, boys' outerwear and sportswear, men's tailored suits and sports coats, and men's lounge and sleepwear. It also had granted exclusive distributorships in Canada, Mexico, and Central America. Europe Craft's products were being marketed nationally in department stores, specialty stores, and national retail chains. It also operated three stores located in factory outlet malls in Ohio, Virginia, and Tennessee.

Perry owned five manufacturing plants in Virginia and North Carolina, three in El Salvador, and one in Costa Rica. It also leased manufacturing and warehousing space in North Carolina, El Salvador, and Honduras. These facilities were producing the majority of the apparel it sold. The balance of its apparel was being produced by independent factories and contractors in the United States and Latin America. Perry was leasing sales offices in New York, Chicago, Dallas, and Miami.

Europe Craft's products were being manufactured overseas by independent factories, mostly in Hong Kong, South Korea, China, India, the Philippines, Bangladesh, Sri Lanka, Indonesia, and the United Arab Emirates. It was leasing a showroom in New York and offices in New York and New Jersey. Marlene Industries owned one remaining facility in Tennessee.

*Principal Subsidiaries*

Europe Craft Imports, Inc.; Perry Manufacturing Co.

*Further Reading*

Barmash, Isadore, "Chapter XI—The Story of Unishops' Recovery," *New York Times,* October 12, 1975, Sec. III, p. 16.

Furman, Phyllis, "Marcade Slips, Making One Deal Too Many," *Crain's New York Business,* December 10, 1990, p. 3.

"Marcade Files Chapter 11: Members Only Excluded," *Daily News Record,* November 4, 1992, p. 11.

"Marcade: Not Only a New Name, But a Total Overhaul of Unishops," *Business Week,* September 21, 1981, pp. 83, 87, 90.

Schifrin, Matthew, "Can't Get No Respect," *Forbes,* September 4, 1989, pp. 316–317.

"Unishops Asks for Protection under Chapter 11," *Wall Street Journal,* December 3, 1973, p. 3.

"Unishops Chain's Formula Puts 'People Idea' First," *New York Times,* August 24, 1969, Sec. III, p. 11.

"Unishops Comes Up Smiling with Brand New Stores," *Discount Merchandiser,* October 1976, pp. 29–32.

"Unishops—Growth Issue," *Financial World,* November 30, 1966, p. 11.

"Unishops—Higher Profits in Store," *Financial World,* February 7, 1971, p. 7.

"Unishops Moves Ahead," *Financial World,* March 5, 1969, pp. 13–14.

"Unishops Set to Rack Up New Peaks in Sales, Net," *Barron's,* April 10, 1967, p. 30.

—Robert Halasz

# Arkansas Best Corporation

3801 Old Greenwood Road
Fort Smith, Arkansas 72903
U.S.A.
(501) 785-6000
Fax: (501) 785-6009

*Public Company*
*Incorporated:* 1966 as Arkansas Best Corporation
*Employees:* 18,459
*Sales:* $1.43 billion (1995)
*Stock Exchanges:* NASDAQ
*SICs:* 6719 Holding Companies, Not Elsewhere
Classified; 4213 Trucking Except Local; 4731 Freight
Transportation Arrangement

Parent company of one of the leading truckers in the United States, Arkansas Best Corporation (ABC) ships general commodities both nationally and internationally through its motor carrier subsidiaries. During the mid-1990s, ABC operated as a less-than-truckload and truckload carrier, deriving nearly 70 percent of its annual revenues from its largest subsidiary, ABF Freight System, Inc. ABC was also involved in truck tire retreading and new truck tires sales through its 46 percent owned subsidiary, Treadco, Inc.

### 1966: A New Beginning

The formation of ABC in 1966 marked a new beginning of sorts for both the individual selected to lead the company and the 31-year-old trucking concern that spawned its creation. ABC, incorporated in May 1966, was organized to acquire Arkansas Best Freight System, Inc. (later renamed ABF Freight System, Inc.), a $32 million-a-year trucking concern based in Fort Smith, Arkansas that had been established in 1935 as Arkansas Motor Freight. Selected to lead the new parent company was the former finance director of the regional carrier, H. L. Hembree, who spent his childhood in Fort Smith growing up together, so to speak, with the company that would employ him as an adult. Hembree had joined the company in 1958,

seven years after his boss, Robert A. Young, Jr., had been named the company's chairman. By 1966, after Hembree had risen to the position of finance director, Young still served as the company's chairman, a position he would continue to hold when he directed the formation of ABC and named Hembree its president. Together, Young and Hembree, serving as chairman and president, respectively, composed the senior leadership of the new company formed in 1966 that, paradoxically, was already in the middle of its thirty-first year of business.

In the months leading up to the formation of ABC, Young and the rest of ABF Freight's management had decided to diversify into business areas other than trucking, resolving to acquire interests that would move the company into business areas not regulated by the Interstate Commerce Commission, the federal regulatory organization responsible for supervising the railroad and carrier industries. This the company quickly did, completing its first major acquisition seven months after ABC was incorporated. In December 1966, the company purchased Riverside Furniture Corporation and Twin Rivers Furniture Corporation, both of which had been established in 1946. The next acquisition moved ABC farther afield, both geographically and in business scope. In June 1968, ABC purchased a 64 percent stake in a Dallas, Texas-based financial institution, National Bank of Commerce, adding financial services to the company's widening roster of business interests. With these new additions rounding out ABC's major business interests, the company's management embarked on their new course, intent on applying their business skills to engender optimum profitability in the disparate business interests they maintained.

Within a few short years, ABC's management team had earned a solid reputation in the minds of analysts, drawing praise from nationally distributed publications that characterized the young cadre of managers as "ambitious, goal-oriented, and alert to opportunities for corporate growth." Heading this group and in charge of the day-to-day operations of the company was Hembree, who governed the company much like a former finance director would, with an emphasis on profitability and sound fiscal performance. "If you don't watch your costs," Hembree would explain later to a *Forbes* reporter about managing a trucking concern, "you can run up and down the highway with full loads and still go broke.'' Hembree, in the years ahead, would keep his eyes on costs, as they applied not only to ABF Freight, but to the three new additions as well. His was a perspective that placed a premium on profitability and gave ABC, which was described simply and accurately by industry pundits as a ''management company,'' the task of stewarding each of its business segments in the right direction.

By the time the dust had settled from the acquisition of the National Bank of Commerce in June 1968, ABC already was recording success in managing its new furniture business, having organized the Twin Rivers Furniture Corporation as a subsidiary of its Riverside Furniture subsidiary. By far the parent company's most important business, however, was its trucking concern ABF Freight. By the late 1960s, ABF Freight was covering 12,500 route miles, transporting food, textiles, apparel, furniture, appliances, chemicals, and machinery, along with a host of other goods, with no single type of commodity accounting for more than three percent of the company's total traffic. The nearly 40-year-old trucker hauled its freight through a 14-state area, servicing major commercial hubs throughout the Midwest and the southern United States, stopping throughout much of its service territory at company-owned terminals that were operated by another ABC subsidiary, Arkansas Bandag Corp., which also retreaded tires under a patented German process.

ABF Freight's service territory expanded before the end of the decade, moving into Pennsylvania and New York after ABC acquired Fast Freight, Inc. in November 1969. Although ABC collected roughly 80 percent of its annual revenues from its trucking business, the most promising segment of its business, at least in terms of financial growth, was its newly acquired furniture company. Riverside Furniture, which generated approximately 18 percent of its parent company's annual revenues during the late 1960s, manufactured popularly priced wood occasional tables, exposed wood living room furniture, and rocking chairs, marketing its products through the efforts of more than 50 salespeople. With roughly 5,000 wholesale and retail accounts and permanent showrooms in North Carolina, Los Angeles, San Francisco, and Seattle, Riverside Furniture ranked as one of the five largest table manufacturers in the United States, an enviable market position that was expected to grow stronger as the company benefited from the ''ambitious and goal-oriented'' management of ABC.

Early on, ABC's management was credited with staging two dramatic turnarounds, the reports of which educed financial analysts to recommend the company to prospective investors. Riverside Furniture recorded $9 million in annual sales in 1968, 26 percent more than the previous year's total. More impressive, however, was the growth achieved by National Bank of Commerce. Ranking as the fifth largest bank in Dallas County, Texas, National Bank of Commerce posted net operating earnings of nearly $850,000 in 1968, which represented an increase of 104 percent from the total recorded in 1967, giving senior management in Fort Smith every expectation that all three of their primary businesses would flourish during the decade ahead. As Hembree and the rest of his team prepared for the 1970s, plans were being made to bolster ABC's interests in each of its three major businesses, as the company searched for acquisitions in the transportation, consumer products, and financial services industries.

During the first few years of the 1970s, ABC followed through on its plans to grow through acquisitions, purchasing Flanders Manufacturing Co. and Coffey Furniture Industries, Inc., both of which were merged into Riverside Furniture's operations. The company also added to its trucking service territory by acquiring Youngblood Truck Lines, which extended ABF Freight's presence in the southeastern United States from 16 to 19 states. After this initial spurt of acquisition activity to start the decade, the company was enjoying encouraging success, with nearly every facet of its business demonstrating vibrant growth. By the end of 1973, ABC's furniture segment was accounting for roughly 30 percent of the company's total yearly sales, up from the 18 percent it contributed five years earlier, while the profits derived from furniture manufacturing had registered a greater leap, jumping from 12 percent to 32 percent during the five-year span. ABF Freight, meanwhile, had exhibited a vitality of its own, consistently ranking as one of the most profitable operations in the trucking industry. The thirty-first largest trucking concern in the country in terms of total revenues, ABF Freight now operated in a 19-state territory, bounded by Wisconsin, Ohio, Indiana, and New York on the north, Kansas, Oklahoma, and Texas on the west, Louisiana, Mississippi, and Georgia on the south, and North and South Carolina on the east.

Conspicuously absent from the series of acquisitions during the early 1970s were any additions to ABC's financial services segment. Despite increasing its net income two-and-a-half times in its first five years as a partly owned ABC subsidiary, National Bank of Commerce had proved to be an ill-advised acquisition. The bank, as one company observer noted, had ''serious collateral problems in its loan portfolio,'' but Hembree did not become aware of such problems until 1972, four years after he had invested in the bank. Once alerted to the problem, Hembree disposed of ABC's interest, explaining that ''autonomy was the problem with [National Bank of Commerce]. It was also the only subsidiary in which we had less than 100 percent interest.'' After writing off $22 million over a three-year period, Hembree had learned a valuable lesson, vowing ''we will never make that mistake again.''

### Change of Focus in the Mid-1970s

While the National Bank of Commerce was being divested, ABC continued to strengthen its trucking concern's business, completing a string of acquisitions during the mid-1970s that gave ABF Freight the operating authority to service a larger territory. By 1977, however, the value of gaining the operating authority to operate in additional territory was becoming questionable. The U.S. Congress was beginning to talk about deregulating interstate trucking, which would open routes to any interested trucking company and render ABF Freight's ever-growing portfolio of operating rights meaningless. Mindful that federal intervention would dramatically alter the dynamics of his company's mainstay business, Hembree knew a decision had to be made about the future course of ABF Freight and ABC if the government did indeed deregulate the trucking industry. For help, Hembree turned to his four full-time economic forecasters for advice on what the company should do in the event of deregulation.

Hembree's economic forecasters and their computers came up with three possible options: scale back expansion and become a regional trucker in the Midwest, sell the company to a larger competitor, or buy another trucking company and make a bid to become a major national carrier. In Hembree's mind, the first two options assured survival, but as he later explained to a *Forbes* reporter, "I didn't want to be just a survivor—makes it sound like you're going to a funeral. I wanted to achieve." Accordingly, he adopted the third option as the company's strategy, deciding that before deregulation opened the floodgates to the trucking industry ABF Freight would become a major national competitor.

The first step toward national prominence was taken in 1978, when Hembree authorized the acquisition of Denver-based Navaho Freight Line for roughly $15 million. The move immediately transformed ABF Freight from the country's 22nd largest trucking company into the eighth largest concern, representing a prodigious first step for the Fort Smith company. Next, the company acquired East Texas Motor Freight, Inc. in 1982, an acquisition that represented another important boost to ABC's stature. Once these acquisitions were fully digested, ABF Freight was a considerably larger company, serving nearly 90 percent of the nation's major metropolitan markets. Still the major engine driving ABC's growth, ABF Freight contributed the bulk of what its parent company declared in annual sales, a figure that had grown exponentially between the mid-1970s and mid-1980s, soaring from roughly $150 million to more than $500 million.

### Deregulation in the 1980s

The U.S. trucking industry, as expected, had become deregulated early in the decade, making the operating rights ABC had obtained through more than 30 acquisitions over a 45-year period essentially worthless. The passage of the 1980 Motor Carrier Act also precipitated another change in ABF Freight's business, one that would change the way in which the company operated and opened the doors to a flourishing segment of the carrier market. The number of licensed trucking companies doubled in the first few years after deregulation; then, just as quickly, a majority of the new entrants fell into financial ruin. The rising number of bankruptcies created more than $1 billion worth of extra business for those who survived, with the biggest profits going to those companies that operated as less-than-truckload (LTL) carriers. Aware of the shifting dynamics in its industry, ABC changed from being a truckload operator to an LTL carrier, ranking by the mid-1980s as one of the five leading competitors in the lucrative industry niche market.

Growth in the LTL segment pushed ABC forward throughout the remainder of the 1980s, as the company approached the $1 billion-in-annual-sales plateau. Despite the divestiture of its long-held furniture manufacturer, Riverside Furniture, which was sold in 1989, ABC was recording steady sales growth as it entered the 1990s. By the end of 1993, ABC could rightly call itself a $1 billion company, generating by year's end $1.009 billion in sales and posting more than $50 million in operating income.

With the addition of WorldWay Corporation, which was acquired in 1995, ABC was rapidly heading toward the $2 billion sales mark as it prepared for the late 1990s. Annual sales in 1995 reached $1.47 billion, but once WorldWay was fully absorbed by the company sales were expected to near $2 billion. As the company prepared for the late 1990s and the beginning of the 21st century, Robert A. Young III, the son of ABC's founding chairman, was leading the way as chief executive officer, hoping to continue the robust growth that had transformed the company's mainstay business from the 48 largest trucking company into the country's fourth largest.

### Principal Subsidiaries

ABC Treadco, Inc.; ABF Cartage, Inc.; ABF Farms, Inc.; ABF Freight System, Inc.; ABF Freight System Canada, Ltd.; ABF Freight System de Mexico, Ltd.; Advertising Counselors, Inc.; Arkansas Underwriters Corp.; Best Logistics, Inc.; Clover Insurance Co., Ltd.; Data-Tronics Corp. Integrated Distribution Systems, Inc; Land-Marine Cargo, Inc.; Treadco, Inc. (46%).

### Further Reading

"Arkansas Best Unit Acquisition," *Wall Street Journal,* December 29, 1978, p. 24.

Bagamery, Anne, " 'We Want To Achieve,' " *Forbes,* August 17, 1981, p. 58.

"Concern Concedes to Kelso, Drops Bid for Arkansas Best," *Wall Street Journal,* June 27, 1988, p. 17.

Mitchell, Ruth, "Truckin' On," *Arkansas Business,* July 15, 1991, p. 25.

Myers, Randy, "Growth Trucker," *Barron's,* November 11, 1985, p. 85.

Power, Christopher, "What Can You Buy with $116,325 and a Good Idea," *Business Week,* June 13, 1988, p. 38.

—Jeffrey L. Covell

# Armor All Products Corp.

**6 Liberty Drive**
**Aliso Viejo, California 92656**
**U.S.A.**
**(714) 362-0600**
**Fax: (714) 362-0619**

*Public Company*
*Incorporated:* 1972 as Very Important Products, Inc.
*Employees:* 150
*Sales:* $216.78 million (1995)
*Stock Exchanges:* NASDAQ
*SICs:* 2891 Adhesives & Sealants

Armor All Products Corp. develops and markets consumer chemical products that are used to protect and beautify automobiles and homes. Its brand names include Armor All, Rain Dance, Rally, E-Z Deck Wash, as well as others. Through its original Armor All Protectant, the company has established the Armor All brand name as one of the most recognized in the United States. In the 1990s, Armor All was parlaying that name recognition into sales growth from new lines of auto and home care products.

### 1970s Origins

The company that would become Armor All was started in 1972 by entrepreneur and marketing maestro Alan Rypinski. The chemical product upon which the company was based, though, had been under development since the early 1960s in a chemist's garage. That California polymer chemist and automobile aficionado had created the substance in an effort to develop a chemical treatment that would protect and prolong the life of the rubber parts of his new cars. What he developed was a treatment that prevented the harmful effects of ozone and ultraviolet rays from penetrating the surface of rubber and plastic parts, including tires and windshield wiper blades. A pleasing side effect of the chemical was that it left a clean, glossy finish that made even aged rubber and plastic appear new.

The milky substance that would one day become famous as Armor All Protectant languished in its creator's garage for five years before it was discovered. Rypinski came across the stuff in the late 1960s when he was trying to restore the interior of his vintage Jaguar. He was referred to a chemist that had developed a compound for just that purpose. Rypinski tried the treatment and liked it so much that he purchased the rights to license the product in 1967. In fact, the protectant had already moved out of its inventor's garage and into the market by the time Rypinski discovered it.

Armor All had first hit the shelves in 1966 under the name "Trid-on," or "no dirt" spelled backwards. Trid-on was sold by the owner of a specialty car shop in Southern California. He mixed Trid-on in 55-gallon drums in his back room and sold the brew in four-ounce plastic bottles to patrons of his store. By 1967 the substance had also made its way into the Briggs-Cunningham Automotive Museum as well as the Parnelli Jones new tire stores, where it was used to enhance tires and other rubber goods. Enter Rypinski. He took over licensing rights to the product and later purchased the marketing and manufacturing rights.

In 1972 Rypinski incorporated a company under the name Very Important Products, Inc., through which he began marketing Armor All Protectant. He began by hyping the substance as a sort of wonder product through a sales force that he dispersed across the country. Those regional sales managers worked out of motor homes, traveling to county fairs, trade shows, and shopping malls to demonstrate and sell Armor All. The public embraced Armor All. First-year sales hit $200,000 and Rypinski's new venture was up and running.

Rypinski spent seven years marketing Armor All Protectant. His savvy marketing blitz helped the product achieve significant name recognition in a relatively short span of time, particularly for a product that was virtually creating its own industry. Rypinski's basic goal was simple: get the product into the hands of the people. He knew from experience that if they tried Armor All they would most likely buy it again. He was right. By the late 1970s, demand for Armor All Protectant had soared and

**Company Perspectives:**

*We believe our strengths lie in our brands, our people and our financial resources, which underpin our ability to grow. The face of Armor All is changing, and we are positioned for the future.*

Rypinski's one-product company was generating millions in sales and profits.

### McKesson Acquires Armor All

Rypinski sold all of the rights to the Armor All brand name and protectant in 1979 to San Francisco-based consumer products company McKesson Corp. Rypinski, who was only 40 years old at the time, signed away his product in a deal that put $50 million into his pocket over a period of five years. McKesson's executives believed that Armor All was worth the huge payout. Indeed, they hoped to use their deep corporate pockets to market and distribute Armor All much more aggressively, not only in the United States but also abroad. Rypinski stayed with Armor All for five more years, using McKesson's fat bankroll to sustain his marketing push.

Under McKesson's corporate wing (McKesson spun Armor All off in 1986, but remained the majority shareholder of the publicly traded Armor All Products, Inc. into the mid-1990s) Armor All Protectant's sales surged to $70 million annually in 1984. Likewise, annual profits ballooned to an impressive $11.76 million. Still, although Armor All was a standout performer from a profit perspective, its total sales volume made it a relatively meager slice of the multibillion-dollar McKesson consumer products pie. In fact, McKesson executives were hoping to parlay the venerable Armor All brand name into much bigger returns. Holding them back during the early 1980s, though, was the huge amount of capital that was funneled to Rypinski as a result of the 1979 buyout agreement. The $50 million cash drain squelched, for example, plans to expand overseas.

Rypinski left Armor All in 1985 to pursue other entrepreneurial interests. Among other endeavors, as chief executive of Rypper Corp. (a worldwide marketer and distributor of auto wheels) he tried to market a newly patented wheel-cover system that bonded to a factory steel wheel. The product ultimately failed. He also became involved in an effort to market POGs— colorful, round, inch-and-a-half cardboard disks that once served as milk bottle cap linings—which were achieving fad status on Orange County, California playgrounds in the early 1990s. But Rypinski's management days at Armor All were not finished.

### New Directions in the 1980s

Stepping into the president slot at Armor All in 1984 was Jeffrey Sherman, who was only 35 years old at the time. Sherman had joined Armor All in 1978 as an accountant in the finance department. His reserved management style contrasted starkly with Rypinski's outgoing, entrepreneurial nature. Because Armor All had moved away from its "small company" roots and toward a more traditional corporate culture, however, Sherman's style seemed like a good fit. His goal was to use excess cash to broaden Armor All's product line and expand into foreign markets. That strategy reflected the fact that Armor All Protectant had matured, achieving an impressive one-third share of the entire $600 million automobile appearance market for waxes, polishes, and other specialty cleaners.

Recognizing the limited opportunities to increase sales of Armor All Protectant in the U.S. market, Sherman began looking overseas. Armor All entered Japan in 1984 and managed quickly to grab a 25 percent share of that rich market from a home-grown competitor. Armor All reached into West Germany in 1985 and enjoyed similar results. At home, Sherman began looking to penetrate untapped market segments. For example, the company began developing products and pitches to lure more women (Armor All's core market was males aged 18 to 49). Armor All also began distribution of a videotape to high school driver education programs; the tape equated a clean car with safe driving.

Importantly, Sherman also pioneered new products during the mid-1980s that exploited the famous Armor All name. By the late 1980s, in fact, Armor All was selling four products: the protectant, a cleaner, a car wax, and a car wash. The momentous strength of the Armor All name was evidenced by the success of Armor All Car Wax, which quickly surpassed Rain Dance car wax and was closing in on long-time industry leader Turtle Wax by the late 1980s. Armor All managed to achieve such gains with savvy marketing ideas. For example, it began pitching its car wax to women by way of an easy-to-use paste wax packaged similarly to mousse-style hair care products.

Armor All's sales surpassed $100 million in 1987 and profits increased to $17 million. Then, in 1988, Armor All purchased Borden Co.'s car care products line, which included well-known name brands Rain Dance, Rally, and No. 7. That acquisition brought a broad line of waxes, polishes, and additives to Armor All's offerings. The Borden purchase, combined with sales gains related to new product introductions, pushed the company's sales to $126 million in 1988 and then to $162 million in 1989. Unfortunately, profits failed to keep pace with revenue gains, evidencing underlying problems at Armor All. Indeed, after dominating much of the auto appearance products industry and posting successive sales and profit gains for nearly two decades, the company's performance was beginning to slip. Net income dropped to less than $20 million in 1990 and plunged to less than $7 million in 1991.

### Challenges in the 1990s

Armor All's problems going into the early 1990s were multi-fold. Although Sherman had achieved notable successes with Armor All's overseas push and product line expansion, the efforts had failed to produce the expected profits and had cost the company dearly in development and marketing expenses. Furthermore, Armor All's management team seemed unable to cope with the transition from a one-product company to a multiline marketing corporation. At the same time, Armor All was facing aggressive new competition. After years of buffeting more than 100 would-be competitors to its protectant, Armor All failed to quash a product introduced in the late 1980s by the STP division of First Brands Corp. Dubbed "Son of a Gun," the low-cost Armor All imitation product swept into the marketplace in the wake of a massive marketing campaign funded by First Brands. By 1990 Son of a Gun had stolen ten percent of Armor All's market share.

With Armor All's unblemished profit record at risk, Sherman resigned from the top post. After a short interim, he was replaced in 1991 by Kenneth Evans. Evans was a seasoned consumer products executive, having served as president of Thompson and Formby (paints and sealants) before working as a marketing executive and vice-president for the Do-It-Yourself division of Lehn & Fink. Evans quickly surmised that Armor All's operating strategy was obsolete given the rapidly shifting dynamics of the car care products industry. Armor All was still depending on its core protectant product for nearly three-quarters of its sales. Because that market niche had matured, Armor All would inevitably face lower profit margins and lower growth rates.

To overcome the company's dependence on its main product, Evans vowed in 1991 that within five years Armor All Products, Inc. would be generating less than 25 percent of its total revenue from Armor All Protectant. To that end, Armor All launched a series of new products beginning in the early 1990s. In 1992, for example, the company introduced Armor All Tire Foam Protectant, which was designed specifically to clean car tires. It followed that with Armor All QuickSilver Wheel Cleaner (which complemented its Armor All Car Wash), Spot & Wash Concentrate products, and wax products. In addition to diversifying, moreover, Evans initiated an aggressive effort to chase foreign market share. Late in 1991, for instance, Armor All agreed to have seasoned exporter S.C. Johnson handle its sales in foreign markets.

Evans also began cutting costs as part of an effort to help Armor All compete in an increasingly competitive market segment. Interestingly, he convinced Armor All's founder, Alan Rypinski, to rejoin the company in 1992 as chairman emeritus.

Evans hoped that Rypinski would be able to help him identify new markets and opportunities. To that end, in the mid-1990s Armor All branched out into the growing home care products arena with the purchase of E-Z Deck Wash brand name and business. It quickly broadened that popular product line to include several products (all bearing the Armor All brand name), including WaterProofing Sealer, Deck Protector, Vinyl & Plastic Protectant, Vinyl Siding Wash Kit, and Multi-Purpose Cleaner.

By 1995, earlier than expected, Armor All had achieved its corporate goal of reducing the portion of revenues contributed by Armor All Protectant to less than 25 percent. The result of that and other accomplishments was a surge in sales and a timely profit boost. Sales climbed from a 1990s low of $134 million in 1993 to $217 million in 1995 (fiscal year ended March 31, 1995), as net income climbed back toward $25 million. For the remainder of the decade, Armor All planned to ply the Armor All brand name to sustain international growth and add new products.

### Further Reading

"Armor All Founder Rypinski Rejoins Company," *Aftermarket Business,* December 1, 1992, p. 12.

Cook, Dan, "Armor All's New Boss Moves To Buff Up Its Image," *Orange County Business Journal,* February 24, 1992, p. 1.

Kennedy, Leslie, "Armor All Founder Alan Rypinski Rejoins Company," *Business Wire,* October 16, 1992.

O'Dell, John, "Chinks Develop in Armor All's Market Share," *Los Angeles Times,* March 25, 1990, p. D4.

Pool, Charles, "Corporate Profile for Armor All Products Corp.," *Business Wire,* October 30, 1992.

Schlax, Julie, "A Good Reason To Mess with Success," *Forbes,* September 19, 1988, p. 95.

Smith, Sara, "Armor All Products Corp.," *Fortune,* April 11, 1988, p. 71.

Sullivan, J. L., "Armor All Hawker Turns to Kid's Stuff," *Orange County Business Journal,* April 18, 1994, p. 1.

Warner, Fara, "Armor All Wants To Clean Some Son of a Gun's Clock: New Products, Global Brands and Niches Restore Lost Sheen," *Brandweek,* October 18, 1993, p. 32.

—Dave Mote

# Baker & Taylor, Inc.

2709 Water Ridge Parkway
Charlotte, North Carolina 28217
U.S.A.
(704) 357-3500
Fax: (704) 470-7860

*Private Company*
*Incorporated:* 1992 as Baker & Taylor, Inc.
*Employees:* 2,500
*Sales:* $900 million (1995 est.)
*SICs:* 5099 Durable Goods, Not Elsewhere Classified

A solid and respected leader in its field, Baker & Taylor, Inc., operates as the holding company for two companies involved in the entertainment and information services business, Baker & Taylor Books and Baker & Taylor Entertainment. During the mid-1990s, Baker & Taylor Books supplied books, spoken-word audiotapes, calendars, and related information services to more than 100,000 bookstores, schools, public, university, and special libraries, and government agencies worldwide, conducting its international business through Baker & Taylor International, Ltd. The other primary component of the holding company, Baker & Taylor Entertainment, supplied videocassettes, compact discs, audiocassettes, interactive games, CD-ROM, personal computer software, and related services and products to nearly 30,000 retailers and libraries in the United States.

When Baker & Taylor, Inc. was organized in 1992, Gerald G. Garbacz hailed its formation by proclaiming "the beginning of a new era" for the company. For those not familiar with the Baker & Taylor name, Garbacz's utterance seemed an obvious statement, considering that Baker & Taylor, Inc. was embarking on its inaugural year of business. But as chairman and chief executive officer of the newly formed company, Garbacz was intimately familiar with the Baker & Taylor name, having spent the previous 18 years working for Baker & Taylor Books, the nucleus of the fledgling holding company, Baker & Taylor, Inc. Throughout Garbacz's tenure at Baker & Taylor Books, the company and its sister distribution businesses, Baker & Taylor Video and Baker & Taylor SoftKat, had been owned by W. R. Grace & Co., a massive conglomerate with wide-ranging business interests, that, according to Garbacz and other senior executives, had been stewarding the Baker & Taylor businesses in aberrant directions. The years of frustration came to an end in 1992, however, when W. R. Grace & Co. sold the Baker & Taylor businesses, marking the beginning of what Garbacz and his management team hoped would be a new, more positive era in the company's history.

## 19th Century Origins

For Baker & Taylor Books, the change in ownership in 1992 represented the latest chapter in a corporate history that stretched back more than a century and a half before Garbacz took control of the company in the wake of W. R. Grace & Co.'s divestiture. The business had been founded by David Robinson and B. B. Barber in 1828, beginning its corporate life as a small bindery and subscription book publisher in Hartford, Connecticut. A short time later, Robinson and Barber opened a bookstore to distribute their own books and other publishers' books. After establishing a solid position in Hartford, the two businessmen moved their flourishing concern to New York City in 1835. During the ensuing years, the focus of the company's business shifted from publishing its own books, instead stressing the distribution of other publishers' books. The company was relying on this type of business to fuel its growth by the time its ownership was passed to the two men whose names would become synonymous with book distribution in the 20th century. In 1885, exactly 50 years after the relocation from Hartford to New York City, James S. Baker and Nelson Taylor purchased the company founded by Robinson and Barber, lending their surnames to a concern that would bear the Baker & Taylor name for more than the next century.

In terms of business focus, James Baker and Nelson Taylor did not alter the direction of the business they acquired from Robinson and Barber until 1912, when they abandoned publishing entirely and instead directed the company toward wholesaling. In the decades ahead, Baker & Taylor would establish itself as a prodigious competitor in its new business, becoming a familiar name to librarians and bookstore owners across the country who purchased books from the venerable wholesaler. In 1958, Baker & Taylor was purchased by *Parents Magazine,* remaining under its control until W. R. Grace & Co. acquired the company in 1970 and touched off a period in the company's history that insiders would later characterize as difficult years.

### *1970 Acquisition by W. R. Grace & Co.*

When Baker & Taylor joined the W. R. Grace & Co. fold, it joined a host of other businesses that operated under the expansive corporate umbrella of the diversified conglomerate. W. R. Grace & Co.'s corporate reach was broad, including a wide range of business interests that ran the gamut from Baker & Taylor's book wholesaling business, to the manufacture of oil rigs, to the marketing of bull semen. Positioned within this eclectic array of businesses, Baker & Taylor, to a certain degree, was lost in the wash. The company struggled to assert itself amid its parent company's diverse business interests, but as the years of W. R. Grace & Co.'s ownership wore on, its business began to suffer. Librarians, who had relied on and trusted the Baker & Taylor name for more than a century, began to reassess their opinion of the book wholesaler, and, as a result, the company gradually developed a reputation among its customers for inconsistent service. Changes were needed, but it would be years before Baker & Taylor's management could direct the company as they saw fit and enter into a new era without the influence of W. R. Grace & Co.

Garbacz witnessed the effects of W. R. Grace & Co.'s ownership of Baker & Taylor firsthand, joining the book wholesaler in 1974, four years after its acquisition by the diversified conglomerate. By 1980, Garbacz had risen to the position of president, a post that provided him with a revealing vantage point from which to evaluate the company's operation under W. R. Grace & Co. Garbacz would later say during an interview with *Library Journal* that W. R. Grace & Co.'s management "placed a great deal of emphasis on short-term financial performance with very little emphasis on the development of markets and human resources," chiding the parent company's approach to sustaining Baker & Taylor's long-term vitality. In spite of the damage done to the book wholesaler's reputation during the 1970s and 1980s, however, there were some positive aspects to W. R. Grace & Co.'s 22-year reign of control. It was while under the management of W. R. Grace & Co. that Baker & Taylor became a more diversified business, gaining, through acquisitions engineered by W. R. Grace & Co., two new facets to its long-established business of wholesaling all types of books. With the addition of these two sister distribution businesses, which extended the Baker & Taylor name into the computer software and videocassette distribution arenas, the foundation for the future Baker & Taylor, Inc. was created, engendering the well-rounded information and entertainment concern that existed in the 1990s.

The two companies that along with Baker & Taylor Books would compose Baker & Taylor, Inc.'s holdings during its inaugural year of business were Baker & Taylor Video and Baker & Taylor SoftKat, involved in videocassette distribution and computer software distribution, respectively. Baker & Taylor Video's roots extended back to 1975 when Chicago-based Sound Unlimited was founded. The company, which

lengthened its name in 1979 to Sound Video Unlimited, operated as a regional wholesaler of videocassettes, helping pioneer the distribution of videocassette programming in VHS and BETA formats before being acquired, along with another videocassette distribution company, VTR Incorporated, by W. R. Grace & Co. in 1986. Sound Video Unlimited and VTR were then merged, forming Baker & Taylor Video, the largest full-line videocassette distributor in the United States. The establishment of Baker & Taylor Video in 1986 coincided with the acquisition of another company by W. R. Grace & Co. that would later become an integral part of Baker & Taylor, Inc. when it emerged in 1992. In 1986, W. R. Grace & Co. acquired SoftKat, a computer software distribution firm founded in 1983 during the early years of the personal computer industry. Personal computers, in subsequent years, would become ubiquitous fixtures in homes and offices, while the demand for videocassettes would burgeon as well, giving Baker & Taylor Books two solid counterparts within W. R. Grace & Co.'s corporate structure.

The years spent under W. R. Grace & Co.'s management also strengthened Baker & Taylor's business in other areas, particularly in international markets. Although Baker & Taylor had crossed U.S. borders just before its acquisition by W. R. Grace & Co., operating its distribution activities in foreign countries through offices in Somerville, New Jersey, the company's international business was bolstered considerably while under the ownership of W. R. Grace & Co. Sales offices were opened in Australia and Japan in 1983 and 1986, respectively. Then, following the 1989 acquisition of Feffer & Simons, which operated as an international publishers' representative, Baker & Taylor International, Ltd. was formed, providing Baker & Taylor Books with a corporate conduit to extend its wholesaling services to international markets.

The formal establishment of an international division in 1989, coupled with the acquisition of videocassette and computer software distribution companies, made Baker & Taylor a diversified competitor in the distribution business, certainly more so than when the company was first acquired by W. R. Grace & Co. in 1970. But its diversity also educed the harshest criticism of W. R. Grace & Co.'s management by Baker & Taylor executives. Garbacz cited W. R. Grace & Co.'s central failure as the company's decision to operate the Baker & Taylor businesses as separate entities, reflecting to a *Library Journal* reporter that "there was a very large element of uncertainty under Grace; they didn't want the various units of B&T working together as closely as [Baker & Taylor management] wanted." This point was reiterated by another Baker & Taylor executive, who told *Publisher's Weekly,* "When we were owned by Grace, all three divisions operated as very separate, very independent companies with little or no interaction."

### *1992 W. R. Grace & Co. Divestiture*

For those disenchanted with the manner in which the Baker & Taylor businesses were managed under the auspices of W. R. Grace & Co., welcome news arrived in November 1991 when the diversified conglomerate announced its intention to sell its Baker & Taylor subsidiaries. Several months after the announcement, in early 1992, ownership of the Baker & Taylor businesses was passed to a group of Baker & Taylor management and The Carlyle Group, a private, Washington, D.C.-based merchant banking and investment firm whose specialty was acquiring businesses from large conglomerates. Like W. R. Grace & Co., Carlyle's business interests were diverse, including companies involved in real estate, airline catering, chemicals, aerospace, and commercial and military aircraft manufacturing. Unlike W. R. Grace & Co., however, Carlyle's management of the Baker & Taylor businesses met with the approval of Garbacz and his management team, ushering in the beginning of a new era for both Garbacz and Baker & Taylor.

The acquisition of the various Baker & Taylor businesses by Carlyle also engendered the formation of Baker & Taylor, Inc., which was organized in March 1992 as a holding company for Baker & Taylor Books, its distribution divisions, Video and SoftKat, and Baker & Taylor International, Ltd. Leading the newly formed Baker & Taylor, Inc. during its inaugural year of business was Garbacz, who was named chairman and chief executive officer of the company, in addition to his duties as the top executive of Baker & Taylor Books. Under Garbacz's stewardship, the Baker & Taylor units were governed in a decidedly more concerted manner than during the W. R. Grace & Co. years. The company's corporate culture was revamped and its focus was altered, transforming Baker & Taylor into an information and entertainment services firm rather than a company purely focused on distribution. As part of these changes, Baker & Taylor's software division, SoftKat, underwent a name change in 1992, becoming Baker & Taylor Software. The following year, Baker & Taylor Software, which dealt in educational and entertainment computer software, was combined with Baker & Taylor Video, a supplier of videocassettes and music recordings in both cassette and compact disc formats, to form Baker & Taylor Entertainment.

When Baker & Taylor employees reported for work on May 16, 1994, they heard surprising news. Chicago-based Follett Corp., a distributor of books, textbooks, and computer software to the school library market, had announced its intention to acquire Carlyle's 92 percent stake in Baker & Taylor, Inc., setting the stage for another new era in the company's history. With three divisions that operated in business areas similar to those of Baker & Taylor and another three divisions involved in markets not served by Baker & Taylor, Follett struck industry pundits as a good match for the units composing Baker & Taylor, Inc., an acquisition that would combine the $800 million in annual sales generated by Baker & Taylor, Inc. with Follett's $650 million in annual sales. Negotiations between family-owned Follett and Carlyle were conducted throughout

the rest of May, continuing on into June, but were called off in the middle of the month after several weeks of discussions failed to yield a final agreement between the two companies.

In the wake of the aborted sale, Carlyle announced that it would return to supporting Baker & Taylor's long-term strategy of upgrading its systems and achieving greater efficiencies through the consolidation of the company's operations, but the majority owner of the book, entertainment, and software distributor did make one important change. Slightly more than a week after the Follett deal fell through, Carlyle executives ordered sweeping changes in Baker & Taylor's top management, replacing Garbacz, who officially resigned as chairman and chief executive officer of the company, with three individuals, Patrick Gross, Joseph Wright, and Craig Richards. With Garbacz gone, it was up to Gross and Wright, who jointly served as the company's chairman, and Richards, who was named chief executive officer, to lead Baker & Taylor through its new era of business, as the venerable company moved toward its third century of business.

### Principal Subsidiaries

Baker & Taylor Books; Baker & Taylor Entertainment; Baker & Taylor International, Ltd.

### Further Reading

Annichiarico, Mark, "Baker & Taylor's Coup de Grace," *Library Journal*, September 15, 1993, p. 44.
"Climbing Quickly," *Business Journal of New Jersey*, September 1989, pp. 46, 53–54.
"Garbacz Departs as B&T Revamps Top Management," *Publisher's Weekly*, July 4, 1994, p. 10.
Millet, Jim, "Follett Corp. the Likely Buyer of Baker & Taylor," *Publisher's Weekly*, May 23, 1994, p. 26.
O'Brien, Maureen, "B&T Sale Finalized; Reorganized as Solo Corp.," *Publisher's Weekly*, March 30, 1992, p. 8.
Paige, Earl, "Baker & Taylor Settles in at Simi," *Billboard*, June 26, 1993, p. 67.
Peaff, George, "On the Fast Track," *Business Journal of New Jersey*, September 1989, p. 43.
"Projected Sales of Baker & Taylor to Follett Corp. Called Off," *Publisher's Weekly*, June 27, 1994, p. 13.
Seideman, Tony, "B&T To Simplify Ordering of Multimedia Products," *Publisher's Weekly*, August 1, 1994, p. 10.
St. Lifer, Evan, "Follett Ready To Finalize Deal for Baker & Taylor," *Library Journal*, June 15, 1994, p. 12.

—Jeffrey L. Covell

*Barrett Business Services, Inc.*

# Barrett Business Services, Inc.

4724 S.W. Macadam Avenue
Portland, Oregon 97201
U.S.A.
(503) 220-0988
Fax: (503) 220-6234

*Public Company*
*Incorporated:* 1965 as Barrett Business Services, Inc.
*Employees:* 11,480
*Sales:* $179.8 million (1995)
*Stock Exchanges:* NASDAQ
*SICs:* 7363 Help Supply Services

Barrett Business Services, Inc., ranked number 29 in *Forbes* magazine's *200 Best Small Companies in America* in 1995, provides professional employer services and temporary staffing to both small and large companies. Barrett, the largest company of its kind in Oregon, provided temporary employees to more than 5,000 businesses during the mid-1990s, generating roughly $100 million per year in sales from supplying clerical, technical, and light industrial workers on a temporary basis. The company's greatest success during that period, however, came from providing staff leasing services. By assuming responsibility for all personnel-related matters, including payroll and payroll taxes, employee benefits, health insurance and workers' compensation coverage, employee risk management, and other administrative tasks, Barrett moved to the forefront of its industry, recording substantial gains in sales and becoming a leading competitor in the U.S. temporary employment industry. The company provided its services through 16 branch offices, nine of which are located in Oregon, with the remainder located in Washington, California, Maryland, Idaho, and Delaware.

For more than 30 years, Barrett competed as a small, inconspicuous company, its presence in the U.S. temporary employment industry nearly indistinguishable from the myriad other small temporary employment companies scattered across the nation. The company spent this first era of its corporate history—one decidedly more prosaic than its second—quietly conducting its business and operating in the shadow of much larger companies, which, like Barrett, provided temporary workers to businesses whose permanent employees were either sick, vacationing, or of an insufficient number to complete a particular project. Although their business activities were similar, Barrett and industry stalwarts such as Manpower, Inc. and Kelly Girl Service, Inc., were in two different leagues financially speaking. Barrett generated a fraction of what larger companies in the industry collected in sales each year and, accordingly, received scant attention from industry observers for decades. By the late 1980s, however, Barrett's stature began to grow, thrusting the company into the national spotlight.

National recognition arrived quickly for the small Portland, Oregon-based company as the dynamics of the temporary employment industry changed during the mid- and late 1980s, providing it with new opportunities and new markets, which the company skillfully tapped to catapult itself toward prominence in the U.S. temporary employment industry. In the wake of the sweeping changes occurring in the industry, Barrett recorded an unprecedented surge of growth, increasing its annual revenue volume from $27 million in 1990 to $180 million by 1995 and its annual net income from $360,000 to $4.1 million. Although the company's traditional business of providing temporary employees to businesses grew resolutely during the first half of the 1990s, it was the prolific growth of a relatively new area of business, staff leasing services, which provided the definitive boost to Barrett's stature within the temporary employment industry.

Staff leasing, known variously as "employee leasing," or "co-employing," was the fastest growing sector within the broadly defined U.S. temporary employment industry during the 1980s and 1990s, providing an infusion of new business and new competitors for an American industry that traced its roots to the founding of the Pinkerton National Detective Agency in 1852. Although the security guards leased by Pinkerton marked the formal beginning of providing temporary workers as a business in the United States, the modern origins of the temporary employment industry date to the years immediately following World War II. The founding of Kelly Girl Service, Inc. in 1946 and Manpower, Inc. in 1948 heralded the beginning of the temporary employment industry as big business, ushering in several decades of vigorous growth, during which thousands of small companies entered the business of supplying employees to employers in need of temporary help.

### Origins

Barrett first opened its doors at the outset of this expansion of the temporary employment industry, decades before staff leasing services became a lucrative niche within the temporary employment industry. In 1951, Nancy Barrett founded the company, opening a small office in Baltimore, where she engaged in the business of supplying temporary help for the ensuing 20 years. Although Nancy Barrett's business provided the name for the Barrett Business Services of the 1990s and gave it its earliest founding date, the driving force behind the 1990s version of Barrett Business Services was Barry Temporary Services, a temporary employment company based 3,000 miles to the west of Nancy Barrett's Baltimore office.

Headed by Bill Sheretz, who would guide Barrett into the public spotlight during the 1990s, Barry Temporary Services operated one temporary employment office in Portland, Oregon when it merged with Barrett Business Services in 1971. Sheretz was named president of the merged companies, a position he would hold for more than 20 years. With Sheretz leading the way, Barrett continued its deliberate pace of growth for the next two decades, with the only appreciable expansion occurring in 1981 and 1984, when additional offices were opened in Seattle, Washington and Portland, respectively.

In the years spanning the 1971 merger and the vigorous growth recorded by Barrett during the first half of the 1990s, the temporary employment industry continued its robust expansion, albeit at a slower pace than during the 1950s and 1960s. More than 2,000 companies in the United States were supplying temporary workers to businesses during Barrett's first decade of business after the merger, their existence, like Barrett's, sustained by the simple need of businesses to maintain a sufficient work force in the face of temporarily departed employees and unexpected surges in business. The services provided by the industry became more comprehensive and, particularly for Barrett, more lucrative during the mid-1980s, when staff leasing services began to emerge as a more prominent aspect of the temporary employment industry.

For several decades before the 1980s, some businesses, particularly professional partnerships, had been using temporary employment services as a way to exclude clerical workers and other nonmanagement employees from retirement plans and from receiving other benefits. The Internal Revenue Service for years had attempted to put an end to this practice through the tax courts, achieving its greatest success with the Tax Reform Act of 1986, which effectively eliminated any pension plan advantages for businesses seeking them. Meanwhile, temporary employment companies that provided pension management services began looking for alternative sources of revenue, mindful that the future of pension management was in danger, and the direction the most progressive companies in the industry took was toward what had by then become known as "employee leasing." The ranks of temporary employment companies involved in providing employee or staff leasing services swelled; their numbers increased as the services supplied by the tempo-

rary employment industry became dramatically more complex and more comprehensive.

### Staff Leasing and Barrett During the 1980s

For businesses, particularly small and medium-sized companies, paying for staff leasing services made perfect business sense. Instead of simply providing workers on a temporary basis, staff leasing firms became the employer of record for the client company, leasing employees on a continuing rather than contingent basis and assuming the sundry administrative tasks associated with maintaining a work force. Generally, this business arrangement meant that the temporary employment company, the employer of record, was responsible for generating paychecks, providing health and workers' compensation insurance, and insuring that the client company was in compliance with legal and environmental regulations. In effect, the temporary employment company operated as an external human resources department for the client company. For smaller companies, which spent as much as 25 percent of their time handling employee-related paperwork, paying for staff leasing services eliminated time-consuming benefits administration and payroll chores, enabling them to devote their energies toward other, revenue-generating aspects of their business.

A trend within the U.S. temporary employment industry quickly emerged, as the popularity of staff leasing services swept throughout the country. In 1985 there were fewer than 100 firms employing a total of 10,000 workers under staff leasing arrangements. Over the course of the ensuing decade, the number of companies providing staff leasing services and the number of workers employed under such contracts skyrocketed, eclipsing 2,000 companies and two million individuals by 1995. To make conditions more favorable for temporary employment companies operating during the latter half of the 1980s and the first half of the 1990s, the traditional demand for temporary employees increased as well, as many businesses, both large and small, sought the work force flexibility and cost efficiencies realized from using temporary employment companies.

Conditions during this decade proved to be a boon for astutely managed companies that developed comprehensive staff leasing programs, and Barrett was one of them, positioning itself as a progressive competitor in the staff leasing arena by the beginning of the 1990s. The company introduced its staff leasing service in 1990 in its home state of Oregon, where three years earlier it had become a self-insured employer for workers' compensation coverage. At this point, as Barrett entered the staff leasing field, the company already had branched into another business area, seizing the opportunity to expand upon its self-insured employer status for workers' compensation by marketing its workplace safety program to small and medium-sized Oregon employers. Begun in the late 1980s, Barrett's safety program was designed to assist client companies in managing workplace injuries and reducing workers' compensation claims through on-site safety inspections, safety programs and training, and financial incentives to reward safe work practices.

### Energetic Growth in the 1990s

The marketing of Barrett's workplace safety program represented a harbinger of the diversification that would take place as the 1990s began, engendering dramatic growth in annual revenues during the first half of the decade and recasting the company as a decidedly more sophisticated competitor in the temporary employment industry. The inauguration of staff leasing services in Oregon in 1990 was followed by the introduction of identical services four years later to markets in Washington and Maryland. As the operating territory of the company's staff leasing services was being extended to include three states, Barrett completed moves to market itself as a self-insured employer outside of Oregon as well, obtaining self-insured employer status for workers' compensation in Maryland in November 1993 and in Washington in July 1994. Meanwhile, the company's traditional business of providing workers to fill clerical, technical, and light industrial positions on a temporary basis was growing steadily, adding to the sales gains achieved through the provision of staff leasing and workplace safety services.

In 1990, when Barrett's total sales amounted to $27 million, the company derived nearly all of its sales, $23.4 million, from providing temporary employees to businesses. Its staff leasing services accounted for $3.6 million of total sales. In 1994, when sales had soared to $140 million, the company generated $71 million from its temporary services business and $69 million from providing staff leasing services, more than doubling the size of its temporary services business and increasing its staff leasing business nearly twenty-fold. The gains were enormous, particularly the infusion of business gained from the company's quick advancement in the staff leasing field, which by the mid-1990s accounted for roughly half of Barrett's total sales. During this period of prodigious gain in sales, Barrett had become a publicly owned company, making its initial stock offering in June 1993. In the first three months after the public offering, Barrett's stock jumped 82 percent in value, then, aside from temporary fluctuations, increased steadily upward as the company entered the mid-1990s.

Energetic growth continued to reign following the dramatic gains recorded between 1990 and 1994. In 1995, Barrett's sales jumped to $180 million, exceeding the $175 million figure projected during the year. Net income rose from the $3.4 million posted in 1994 to $4.1 million, instilling confidence that the second half of the 1990s would be as successful as the first. As Barrett moved toward the future, the company was aggressively expanding into new markets, intent on securing new business in an industry that was growing at between 15 and 20 percent per year. Self-insured employer status for workers' compensation was obtained in Delaware in January 1995 and in California in March 1995. The following year, in April, Barrett acquired California-based StaffAmerica, Inc., a provider of both temporary staffing and staff leasing services with $6.7 million in 1995 revenues, and reached an agreement to acquire JobWorks Agency, Inc., a provider of temporary staffing and staff leasing services based in Oregon. Concurrent with these two moves toward expansion in April 1996, Barrett opened a new office in Boise, Idaho to provide staff leasing and temporary staffing services throughout southern Idaho. The company then set its sights on building upon the legacy of growth established during the early and mid-1990s, hoping to take its newfound prominence to new heights in the future.

### Further Reading

"Barrett Business Services, Inc. Announces California and Oregon Acquisitions and New Idaho Office," *PR Newswire,* April 1, 1996, p. 401SEM015.

Manning, Jeff, "New Public Companies Find Stock Market Capricious," *Business Journal—Portland,* September 20, 1993, p. 1.

Muoio, Peter, and Axelrod, Stuart, "Employee Leasing Continues To Expand," *Bankers Trust Research,* January 25, 1996, pp. 1–14.

—Jeffrey L. Covell

# Bell Sports Corporation

10601 N. Hayden Road, Suite 1-100
Scottsdale, Arizona 85260
U.S.A.
(602) 951-0033
Fax: (602) 951-0511

*Public Company*
*Incorporated:* 1953 as Bell Helmets
*Employees:* 1,000
*Sales:* $102.99 million (1995)
*Stock Exchanges:* NASDAQ
*SICs:* 3949 Sporting & Athletic Goods, Not Elsewhere
Classified

The Bell Sports Corporation is the leading manufacturer of bicycle helmets in the United States and one of the top producers of bicycle accessories in North America. The company, which pioneered the first hard shell bicycle helmet in the mid-1970s, is widely recognized for its long tradition of product innovation and safety. It sells a wide range of bicycle helmets for infants, youths, and adults under three brand names: Bell, BSI, and Bike Star. It also designs, manufactures, and markets a variety of bicycle accessories, such as bike carriers, child carriers, headlights, pumps, tires, and tubes, under the brand names Blackburn, Rhode Gear, VistaLite, SportsRack, and BSI. Although bicycle products are Bell's principal business, the company also manufactures auto racing helmets for drivers participating in races such as the Indianapolis 500. The only public company in the bicycle helmet industry, Bell Sports includes more than 50 companies and enjoys a greater than 50 percent share of the U.S. market, which has grown increasingly competitive since the passage of legislation in several states during the early 1990s requiring children to wear helmets.

### Early History

Although Bell Sports generates nearly all of its revenue from the bicycle helmet and accessories industry, its origins can be traced to the colorful helmets that have become a familiar part of the auto racing circuit and to the Los Angeles suburb of Bell,

a hotbed of high performance racing for more than 60 years. In 1953, three decades before bicycle helmets entered the mainstream, Roy Richter, a race car designer and driver whose Bell Auto Parts was at the forefront of the latest in high performance technology, began supplying his customers with a new type of fiberglass helmet. The innovative helmets were manufactured using a high-quality, hand-laminated process. They quickly gained favor with the racing community and were worn by such Indianapolis 500 stars as Bill Vukovich.

In 1957, though, an article appeared in *Sports Cars Illustrated*—the forerunner to *Car and Driver*—that would force Richter to redesign his product. According to the research of a Sacramento physician who had set up a small foundation in the name of his friend, Pete Snell, the victim of a fatal auto racing accident, most contemporary helmets, including the Bell ''500'' model, were useless; some, in fact, increased the trauma to the head during a crash by concentrating force on a single point of the skull. Richter immediately stopped production and, after acquiring the rights to a liner used by a rival company that had fared better in the tests, designed a new helmet, the Bell 500 TX, which became the first helmet to receive Snell Foundation approval. The innovative helmet would serve as the prototype for Bell's state-of-the-art helmets for years to come and would set a company standard for product safety.

At that time, helmets were made primarily of soft rubber. In 1963, however, two professors at the University of Southern California invented the process of using polystyrene, or foam, and Bell again had the forethought to purchase the rights to the more protective substance. The company then established a laboratory—the first of its kind in the United States—to conduct tests on the promising material and build its own foam machines at a cost of just $7,000 a piece. During the 1960s, the company found its niche manufacturing motorcycle helmets and evolved into the leader in the industry.

### Expansion in the 1970s

The demand for motorcycles exploded in the 1970s, and as many as 55 domestic companies began manufacturing helmets. But success for the vast majority of helmet producers was short-lived. As damages awarded in product liability cases skyrocketed, it became increasingly difficult for companies to obtain insurance. And distributors and dealers were hesitant to carry a product not covered by insurance. Although product liability concerns forced all but around 10 companies to stop manufacturing motorcycle helmets by the mid-1980s, Bell solidified its position in the market by establishing an unparalleled reputation for product safety. Although Bell, like its competitors, faced a number of lawsuits, it was forced to pay only one judgment, for $25,000 in 1977. That record of success, a benefit of having its own testing facilities, would continue well into the 1990s, as Bell won 27 straight cases over a 15-year period.

Although Bell focused its attention on motorcycle helmets during the remainder of the decade, it had enough vision to develop other aspects of its business. In 1975, the company quietly introduced a product that would later become its major source of revenue: the Bell Biker, the first hard shell bicycle helmet introduced onto the market. Prior to that introduction, cyclists wore leather helmets, if they wore any protection at all. At this time, though, efforts to market the high-end product were modest; Bell, the nation's largest manufacturer of motorcycle helmets through the early 1980s, attempted to take advantage of the continuing surge in the motorcycle industry.

Despite its preeminent position in this niche market, the $20 million company struggled to make a steady profit. In 1983, Phillip Matthews, a former executive at Wilson Sporting Goods, and two partners acquired Bell Sports. They enlisted the management services of Terry Lee, a Wilson executive in charge of sales and distribution, to help run the company. That same year, though, the motorcycle boom came to a halt and with it the demand for helmets. Matthews's partners wanted out of the deal, and Bell was forced to go into debt to buy back their shares. With nearly every penny of cash flow now going toward debt service, the company could no longer afford to produce new designs, the hallmark of the Bell reputation. What is more, quality slipped: some helmets even left the factory with crooked noses. A better financed Japanese competitor, Shoei, with its superior aerodynamic designs and venting technology at similar prices, began swallowing up some of Bell's U.S. market share.

### The New Focus of the 1980s

While the company's motorcycle helmet business was declining, though, bicycle riding suddenly grew in popularity, heightening the demand for helmets and creating an opportunity for the company to return to profitability. Although bicycle helmets comprised only 10 percent of revenues in 1984, sales started growing at 50 percent per year, thanks in part to the introduction of an infant bicycle helmet, the Li'l Bell Shell. Two years later, the company, now producing about 500,000 helmets a year, broadened its product line with the acquisition of its first bicycle accessory company and began manufacturing

such items as bicycle pumps, child seats, red flashing safety lights, and car racks. In 1988, Bell began marketing its products in Europe. That same year the company generated $24 million in revenues, while recording a modest profit, despite the continuing decline of its motorcycle helmet business.

Just before the close of the decade, the company underwent a major restructuring to prepare itself for the changing focus of its business. On November 16, 1989, a group of investors and lenders, including the former management and owners, took over ownership of the company through a leveraged buyout. The Bell Sports Holding Company, as it then became known, consisted of four related businesses engaged in the manufacture and marketing of motorcycle helmets, bicycle helmets, bicycle accessories, and auto racing products.

### The 1990s and Beyond

In 1991 Bell finally ended its 37-year involvement in the motorcycle helmet business, selling its manufacturing and licensing rights to an Italian competitor called Bieffe for an estimated $15 million. "We had to laser-focus on spending the scarce resources we had in the most effective way," Lee told *Forbes* magazine's Zina Moukheiber. Although the motorcycle market did rebound, Lee's strategy proved to be a success. Using the money generated from the sale to reduce debt, the company was now in better position to expand its most promising product lines. Bell, for instance, was now able to market its Li'l Bell Shell aggressively through advertisements in leading parents' magazines. By 1992, the company, with the help of strong expansion in its European markets, was generating $5 million in net profit on sales of $64.5 million, up 36 percent from the previous year.

In an attempt to reduce debt further and generate capital for continued expansion, Lee sold 52 percent of the company in an initial public offering made in April 1992. At that time the company changed its name to Bell Sports Corporation and was divided into four operating divisions: Bell, a Norwalk, California distributor of the company's premium brand of helmets; Rhode Gear, a Providence, Rhode Island distributor of entry- and mid-level helmets and non-helmet bicycle accessories; BSI, which markets helmets to discount stores and mass merchants such as Wal-Mart, Toys 'R' Us, and K-mart; and, finally, Bell Sports Manufacturing, a Rantoul, Illinois manufacturing and testing facility.

The same year that Bell went public it benefited from legislation that promised to create a boon in its principal market: New Jersey became the first state to require children under the age of 14 to wear bicycle helmets. New York, Connecticut, Georgia, Tennessee, Virginia, and Oregon quickly followed suit. A number of county and municipal governments across the country passed mandatory helmet laws as well. With California and other large states considering similar legislation, the small growth industry appeared ready to explode into a big business.

Bell controlled 50 percent of the bicycle helmet market at the time and, by virtue of its size, was the lowest-cost producer in the industry. The company was in a solid position to take advantage, having established relationships with a number of mass merchants, such as Wal-Mart and K-mart, as well as independent bike dealers. What is more, Bell was the only vertically integrated manufacturer in the industry, producing everything from the polystyrene inner lining to the glossy paint on the exterior of its helmets, enabling the company to minimize costs and to monitor product quality. As the only public company in the industry, Bell excited a number of investors on Wall Street; by late 1993 its stock had soared to $49 per share, an increase of more than 225 percent from its original offering of $15. Meanwhile, sales soared to a record $82.6 million and profits moved up to $7 million. Fiscal year 1994 proved to be another banner year as revenue jumped to $116 million and profits jumped to $10.4 million.

The meteoric rise of the company's stock, though, proved to be short-lived. Bell's success quickly attracted a host of competitors. There were few obstacles to entering the market, as bicycle helmets are not difficult to fabricate and plastic and foam are the only materials needed. What is more, the industry as a whole suffered from a slowdown in the passage of mandatory helmet legislation. Expectations for the market were exceedingly high, resulting in an inordinate growth in the market. For Bell, this represented an unprecedented drop in performance. Not only did stock prices fall below the $20 range, but revenue and profits declined. For the first time in four years, the company reported a loss as top competitors such as American Recreation, Troxel Cycling, and Giro Sport Designs encroached on Bell's marketing territory. And, for the first time in Bell Sports history, sales declined.

In an attempt to stay ahead of the competition—which quickly grew to about 50 companies—and regain the confidence of investors, Bell made several strategic moves. First, the company broadened its distribution network, making its BSI helmet, which was already being sold by Wal-Mart and K-mart, available to any store that wanted to carry the line. Whereas supplying discount stores with Bell products may have offended some of the company's regular bike shop customers, it was crucial for the company to further expand its control of the mass merchant market, which in 1994 was responsible for approximately 80 percent of all bicycle helmet sales, compared with only 20 percent three years earlier.

To support this full-scale movement into the mass market, Bell launched its most aggressive advertising campaign to date. The program included a national advertising and promotional campaign on television stations such as ESPN and MTV, as well as on other local and national spots, in magazines written for bicycle and sports/fitness enthusiasts, and in a few general publications. Bell's extensive advertising program was designed not only to promote the quality of the Bell brand name but to educate consumers on the importance of wearing bicycle helmets. Another segment of the company's marketing strategy was evident in its continued support of amateur and professional athletics. In 1994, for instance, the company sponsored more than 1,000 cyclists, triathletes, Indianapolis 500 racers, in-line skaters, and wheelchair racers, making the Bell name visible to millions of viewers, spectators, and potential purchasers. At the same time, the company strengthened its commitment to the National SAFE KIDS Campaign, which works to protect children from death and injury by promoting helmet use.

While trying to make the Bell name more visible in the United States, the company also attempted to strengthen its position in the global marketplace. The company began marketing its helmets in Europe in the late 1980s, opening its first European sales office, in Paris, in 1990 and its first European manufacturing facility, in southern France, later that same year. During the early 1990s, Bell also began developing a sales and distribution network in the Asia-Pacific region. The large amount of capital needed to initiate these endeavors, however, combined with the immaturity of these markets, prevented the international divisions of the company from making a substantial contribution to overall corporate profitability. In Canada, though, where mandatory helmet legislation passed in two Canadian provinces in 1995 (covering an estimated 13.4 million adults and children), Bell became the market leader.

In addition to more aggressive marketing and geographical expansion, Bell attempted to improve its performance through acquisitions. Chief among these purchases was the company's 1995 purchase of American Recreation Company Holdings, Inc., the nation's second-largest helmet manufacturer at the time, with a 22 percent market share. A distributor of bicycles and bicycle accessories through 2,500 retailers, American Recreation also marketed Mongoose and Pro Class mountain and road bikes for adults and children through 750 outlets at the time of the deal. The $75 million purchase represented Bell's largest acquisition to date and has promised to strengthen its leadership position in North America. Moreover, the combination of complementary products shared by the two companies represented the potential for significant economies of scale and lower production costs.

As Bell Sports entered the latter half of the decade, having moved its corporate headquarters to Scottsdale, Arizona, its ability to return to years of record sales depended largely on the efficient integration of its newest subsidiary. A $3 to $5 million reduction in operating expenses was expected once consolidation plans were completed. The actions of state and local legislators also promised to play a key role in the demand for bicycle helmets. In 1996, four additional U.S. states and two Canadian provinces passed mandatory helmet legislation, representing a potential market of more than 22 million adults and children. Bell Sports hoped to continue to take full advantage of this legislative trend.

### *Further Reading*

''Bell Sports: Hats Off?'' *Financial World,* August 2, 1994, pp. 14–15.

Cook, Anne, ''Bike-Safety Push a Boon to Rantoul Helmet Maker,'' *Champaign (Illinois) News-Gazette,* May 8, 1994.

Moukheiber, Zina, ''Mr. Lee, Meet Mr. Murphy,'' *Forbes,* February 13, 1995, p. 42.

Pressey, Debra, ''Bell Sports Hopeful After Lackluster '94,'' *Champaign (Illinois) News-Gazette,* March 26, 1995.

Tamaki, Julie, ''Heady Sales or Hogtied Business?: Motorcycle Helmet Law Runs Up Against Liability, Harley Riders,'' *Los Angeles Times,* October 28, 1991, p. D1.

Wiles, Russ, ''Bell Sports Gets OK to Buy Maker of Bikes, Accessories,'' *The Arizona Republic,* June 28, 1995, p. C2.

Yates, Brock, ''Reinventing the Wheel,'' *Car and Driver,* September 1993, pp. 107–112.

—Jason Gallman

# Bertucci's Inc.

**14 Audubon Road**
**Wakefield, Massachusetts 01880**
**U.S.A**
**(617) 246-6700**
**Fax: (617) 246-2224**

*Public Company*
*Incorporated:* 1984 as Bertucci's Inc.
*Employees:* 4,502
*Sales:* $120.2 million (1995)
*Stock Exchanges:* NASDAQ
*SICs:* 5812 Eating Places; 6719 Holding Companies, Not
Elsewhere Classified

Bertucci's Inc., a casual-dining chain, owns an ever-growing collection of full-service Italian restaurants that operate under the name "Bertucci's Brick Oven Pizzeria." During the mid-1990s there were roughly 80 Bertucci's restaurants scattered throughout 13 states in the eastern United States, each of which featured wood-fired brick ovens (which cook hotter than conventional pizza ovens) and served gourmet pizzas, salads, soups, and pasta dishes. Founded in suburban Boston, Bertucci's expanded quickly during the 1980s and 1990s, growing from a single restaurant in 1981 to the sprawling restaurant chain it had become by the mid-1990s.

By the time Joseph Crugnale decided to invest his time and energy into building a chain of Bertucci's Brick Oven Pizzeria restaurants, he had already amassed a substantial fortune, enough to warrant an early retirement for the Italian-born restaurateur. Remarkably, Crugnale had placed himself in this enviable position, sitting atop a $4.5 million fortune after less than a decade of work, by the time he was 31 years old. His greatest success, however, was still to come. Bertucci's would be Crugnale's crowning achievement, overshadowing by far what he had accomplished during his 20s and increasing his already sizable fortune considerably. From a single restaurant in 1981, Bertucci's developed into a chain that, during one five-year period, grew by 3,157 percent, quickly inundating the mid-

scale restaurant market surrounding the Boston area with a collection of full-service restaurants. As the chain grew, extending its presence outside of Massachusetts and then outside of New England, Crugnale's reputation grew, making both the founder and the company models of success in the U.S. restaurant industry.

Born in Sulmona, Italy, Crugnale landed his first job in the restaurant business after his family emigrated from their home country and settled in New England, where during his high school years Crugnale worked as a porter at the Sonesta Hotel in Cambridge, Massachusetts. Crugnale accumulated additional experience by working in restaurants in Massachusetts and Florida, gaining expertise in cooking from the chefs there, before making his entrepreneurial debut in 1974 when he opened his own ice cream stand. The following year, Crugnale refinanced his father's home and purchased Steve's Ice Cream from founder Steve Herrell, paying $80,000 for the enterprise that eight years later would make him a multimillionaire.

## Origins

Crugnale built Steve's Ice Cream into a lucrative national chain, establishing 26 stores through franchising agreements by the time he sold the concept to Integrated Resources in 1983 for $4.5 million. Under Crugnale's stewardship, Steve's Ice Cream had become wildly popular and it also indirectly spawned the creation of his signal success, Bertucci's. Two years before Crugnale divested himself of Steve's Ice Cream, he opened the first Bertucci's Brick Oven Pizzeria in his home town of Somerville, Massachusetts, establishing the Italian restaurant, with its wood-fired brick oven, two doors away from one of his Steve's Ice Cream stores. At the time, the reason for opening the Italian pizzeria was to eliminate the possibility of an ice cream competitor moving in; eventually, however, its existence would transcend any connection to forestalling the establishment of a competing ice cream shop.

The drive to secure prime real estate dictated Crugnale's actions after he sold Steve's Ice Cream, leading the Bertucci's founder into the real estate business. With the $4.5 million gleaned from the sale of his ice cream chain, Crugnale embarked on his new career in real estate. After less than two years, though, he became bored with malls and office buildings and reconsidered the potential of his pizzeria concept. Crugnale was convinced that Bertucci's, a name he had picked out of a magazine on a flight to New York, would work on a larger scale, with the restaurant's wood-fired brick oven and exotically topped pizzas providing the distinguishing characteristics for a chain of pizzerias. Crugnale made bold plans, resolving to open 20 Bertucci's Brick Oven Pizzerias during the ensuing five years, investing his future efforts wholly in achieving with pizza what he had previously accomplished with ice cream.

### Expansion Begins in Mid-1980s

Crugnale's ambitious expansion plans began with the opening of two restaurants in January and April 1985, each outfitted with an open-hearth brick oven fueled by hardwood logs and each serving specialty pizzas topped with an eclectic array of ingredients such as artichoke hearts and roasted eggplant. The wood-fired brick ovens, inspired by a visit to his grandmother's home in Italy, became the hallmark of Crugnale's restaurants as he expanded the chain during the mid- and late 1980s. He began by establishing units throughout the Boston metropolitan area, then moved outward in concentric circles, saturating white-collar markets in the region surrounding Bertucci's corporate headquarters in Woburn, Massachusetts. Crugnale endeavored to fulfill his objective of establishing 20 restaurant units by 1990, and he designed each restaurant differently, avoiding the presentation of Bertucci's as a chain. Crugnale also eschewed financing the expansion through franchising agreements, something he had been pressured into doing when he operated Steve's Ice Cream and for which he evidently had developed a distaste. "Franchising is a different business," Crugnale explained to *Restaurant Hospitality.* "You have to operate under a different set of rules, a set of rules I don't like."

No two Bertucci's were alike, yet each contributed profits to one company and that company was recording explosive growth as customers flocked to Crugnale's restaurants. Although Bertucci's was expanding at a rapid rate, little was spent on advertising to promote the chain's growth. Instead, the company relied nearly exclusively on word-of-mouth recommendations to compensate for the less than one percent of revenues that was spent on advertising. As the chain grew to 14 restaurants by the end of 1989, recommendations came not only from satisfied customers, but also from dining publications in the Boston area and from *USA Today,* which listed Bertucci's as one of America's top ten pizza restaurants in 1989. As the company entered the 1990s coming off its astounding 3,157 percent five-year growth rate, expectations for the future were justifiably bright, educing Crugnale to project that in the decade ahead Bertucci's would become a publicly traded company and would expand into a 100-unit chain with restaurants scattered throughout major metropolitan markets stretching between New England and Florida.

### Ambitious Plans for the 1990s

Again, Crugnale's expectations were decidedly ambitious, but the company was already moving resolutely toward becoming a pervasive fixture along the Atlantic seaboard by the beginning of the 1990s, having expanded its menu to include soups, salads, and an assortment of pasta dishes before moving into markets in Rhode Island and New Hampshire. To finance the realization of Crugnale's proclamation, Bertucci's became a publicly owned company in July 1991, when the company offered the 21 units composing the Bertucci's chain on the market for $13 per share. By the end of the year, after sales had increased 30 percent from the previous year to reach $37.4 million and net income had increased a gratifying 90 percent to surpass $3 million, Bertucci's stock price had nearly doubled, selling for $24.75 per share as the company continued to thrive despite the debilitative effects of a nationwide recession.

In 1992, when the number of Bertucci's restaurants increased from 26 to 36, Crugnale inaugurated delivery and take-out services, fueling sales growth further. The company's low food costs, which amounted to roughly 25 percent of sales, kept profitability high and rounded out what was proving to be a consistently successful enterprise on all fronts. The criteria for site selection during 1992 and in the years ahead were the same as the demographic factors that governed Bertucci's expansion during the 1980s: an area populated by white-collar professionals, 100,000 people within five miles of a Bertucci's unit, and average annual household incomes of $40,000.

### Falters in the 1990s

Adhering to these stipulations, Crugnale pushed the Bertucci's concept forward, rapidly pursuing his stated goal of establishing 100 restaurants by the end of the decade. The bigger the chain became, however, the more Crugnale and the rest of Bertucci's management had to navigate in unchartered waters, leaving the company exposed to the uncertain vagaries of operating in unfamiliar markets. For years, Bertucci's had expanded in concentric circles that rippled outward from the Boston area, but during the first half of the 1990s that strategy was abandoned to develop a more comprehensive geographic presence in the eastern United States. In 1994, when 18 new Bertucci's units opened their doors, the company moved into a host of new markets, including Orlando, Ocean Township, New Jersey, Atlanta, and Chicago, widening the chain's geographic scope substantially. The lack of familiarity with these and other new markets began to affect the company adversely. Sparking interest in some of the new units was proving to be more difficult than anticipated. By the end of 1994, when the company scaled back its expansion plans for 1995, announcing it planned to open between 10 and 12 units over the next two years instead of between 12 and 15 units in 1995 alone, the signs of wear and tear on the rapidly expanding chain were beginning to show.

Bertucci's difficulties were not made easier by a wrongful death lawsuit levied against the company the following year, in 1995. A year before the suit was filed, a New Hampshire woman, Janet Walker, had dined at a Bertucci's restaurant in Salem, New Hampshire and ordered a chicken pesto sandwich after reportedly asking the waitress whether or not the pesto sauce contained nuts, to which Walker was allergic. The waitress, according to the lawsuit, failed to mention that the pesto sauce did contain nuts, and as Janet Walker ate the sandwich she went into anaphylactic shock and then slipped into a coma. A week later, Walker died, prompting her family to file a $10.4 million lawsuit against Bertucci's in July 1995.

## Reassessment for the Future

The charges against Bertucci's came midway through the bleakest year in the company's history. Although sales increased 17 percent in 1995, eclipsing $120 million, and nine new restaurants were opened, the company's profits plunged 43 percent during the first fiscal quarter, followed by a $2.92 million loss in the fourth quarter. By the end of the year, Bertucci's was in the red, registering an $886,000 loss for all of 1995. The company that had spent all of its corporate life growing by leaps and bounds was now stumbling after its first decade of existence, reeling from the growing pains associated with what one industry observer characterized as a promising concept that tried to become a national power too fast. Crugnale conceded that there were problems hobbling the company as it entered 1996, but his comments characterized Bertucci's difficulties as nothing extraordinary. "What happened to us is typical of what happens to anybody," he related to *Restaurant Business* in January 1996. "You get beat up, you make mistakes, you stub your toe."

In 1996, Crugnale and the rest of his management team were intent on proving that Bertucci's difficulties merely represented a minor, temporary injury. Although the company expected to open eight new units during the year, the strategy for the future included a slower pace of expansion than recorded in the past, that is, opening smaller restaurants, renovating units more frequently, marketing more aggressively, and developing a greater presence in existing markets before entering new markets. Despite the signs of growing too fast, too soon, Bertucci's represented a powerful force as it entered the late 1990s, buoyed by sales that had grown exponentially during the course of its existence. Whether or not Crugnale and the rest of his management team could maintain a commensurate pace of growth in the future hinged on the success of the company's revamped strategy for the late 1990s and the continued popularity of Bertucci's Brick Oven Pizzeria restaurants.

## Principal Subsidiaries

Bertucci's Restaurant Corp.; Bertucci's Securities Corp.

## Further Reading

Allen, Robin Lee, "Bertucci's Reaches for a Bigger Slice of the Action," *Nation's Restaurant News,* October 23, 1995, p. 14.

——, "Bertucci's Inc. Served with $10.4M Wrongful-Death Suit," *Nation's Restaurant News,* August 21, 1995, p. 3.

"Bertucci's Loses $886K after $3.2M 4th-Q Charge," *Nation's Restaurant News,* March 11, 1996, p. 12.

"Bertucci's Opens Second Pizzeria," January 1, 1996, p. 63.

Casper, Carol, "Bertucci's: Making a Name for Itself," *Restaurant Business,* May 1, 1989, p. 242.

Coeyman, Marjorie, "Too Much, Too Soon," *Restaurant Business,* January 1, 1996, p. 30.

Keegan, Peter O., "Operations, Store Growth Fuel Boom at Bertucci's," *Nation's Restaurant News,* August 24, 1992, p. 14.

Mamis, Robert A., "Upper Crust: Bertucci's Inc.," *Inc.,* December 1989, p. 134.

Prewitt, Milford, "Newest 'Kids' on the Block Spark Analysts Interests," *Nation's Restaurant News,* March 30, 1992, p. 16.

——, "Bertucci's Brick Oven Pizza: A Slice above the Rest," *Nation's Restaurant News,* August 13, 1990, p. 12.

Neumeier, Shelley, "Bertucci's," *Fortune,* December 30, 1991, p. 121.

Soeder, John, "Local Boy Makes Good Pizza," *Restaurant Hospitality,* August 1992, p. 94.

"Three Italian Stallions," *Restaurant Hospitality,* August 1992, p. 85.

—Jeffrey L. Covell

# Beverly Enterprises, Inc.

155 Central Shopping Center
Fort Smith, Arkansas 72903
U.S.A.
(501) 452-6712
Fax: (501) 452-3760

*Public Company*
*Incorporated:* 1964
*Employees:* 82,000
*Sales:* $2.98 billion (1994)
*Stock Exchanges:* New York Pacific
*SICs:* 8051 Skilled Nursing Care Facilities; 8059 Nursing
& Personal Care, Not Elsewhere Classified; 8082
Home Health Care Services; 5122 Drugs,
Proprietaries & Sundries

Beverly Enterprises is the largest nursing home chain in the United States. Beverly operates more than 700 nursing homes and retirement centers across the United States, as well as seven retirement centers in Japan. Beverly also owns the nation's largest institutional pharmacy through its subsidiary, Pharmacy Corporation of America (PCA). PCA's 65 pharmacies provide services to patients in long-term care, home care, nursing homes, correctional institutions, assisted living facilities, and other managed health care facilities. Beverly operates eight acute long-term transitional hospitals and eight long-term care nursing facilities for patients who require extensive nursing for a month or more. Beverly also operates a small chain of hospices, to provide care for terminally ill patients.

## Early History

Formed in 1964, the company was clearly the industry leader by the mid-1980s after an aggressive acquisition campaign. At the time of its incorporation, the company consisted of three convalescent hospitals in the Pasadena region of southern California. The founder, Roy E. Christensen, was a Utah accountant. In its first decade, Beverly expanded into such things as plastics, printing, real estate development, and mirror manufacturing. As a result, the company was heavily leveraged and in the red by 1973. In 1971 Robert Van Tuyle was recruited as a director from his 40-year career in the chemical industry, and he immediately began to streamline Beverly, divesting the company of its unrelated interests and focusing on long-term health care.

In the late 1960s and early 1970s, the nursing home industry was experiencing a glut. The onset of Medicare and Medicaid in the mid-1960s had sparked a rush of new entrepreneurs in what had previously been a largely unprofitable industry. The too-rapid expansion stalled at about the time Van Tuyle joined Beverly, but he believed that the nursing home industry still had growth potential. Growth became Beverly's trademark beginning in 1977 when it purchased Leisure Lodges from its parent company, Stephens Inc., of Little Rock, Arkansas. Leisure Lodges was a chain of nursing homes. The purchase doubled Beverly's size, making it number two in the industry. David R. Banks, who had been chairman of the Leisure Lodges chain, joined Beverly as president and CEO in 1979.

Small chains and solo organizations were ripe for acquisition in the early 1980s because they were having trouble turning a profit on Medicaid reimbursements. Beverly's size and centralization, on the other hand, permitted economies of scale. Between 1976 and 1983, Beverly's revenues increased 12 times, primarily through acquisitions. The company grew from 47 homes in 1971 to 1,136 homes in 1985, when it had a presence in 45 states and Canada. By 1983 Beverly was the nation's largest operator of nursing homes. It had more than twice as many beds as the Hillhaven Corporation, its nearest competitor, and represented seven percent of the industry.

## Industry Changes and Challenges in the 1980s

A new "prospective payment plan," the result of federal legislation, promised to increase the flow of patients into convalescent centers by forcing hospitals to release them sooner. At the same time, the 1983 legislation changing Medicaid-Medicare reimbursement made the health care industry suddenly cost-conscious. These changes also meant that the industry was subjected to greater regulation by state and federal govern-

---

**Company Perspectives:**

*In a world where health care has made remarkable techno-logic advances, it is the human touch that makes the differ-ence. Today, we are being asked to consider innovative ways to deliver health care. For that, we formed strategic partner-ships to become a diversified, full-service company, the largest long-term care provider in the nation. We believe in providing quality care with compassion, kindness and re-spect for the individual needs of those who place their trust in us.*

---

ments. Beverly posted record profits in 1985. The company was less concerned by its growth-fueled debts and Medicaid cost-capping than by the industrywide labor problem with potential for a union battle. Turnover was high in the low-wage, high-stress work force of nursing homes.

Problems began to surface by 1986, as allegations of neglect prompted investigations by various state health officials. Be-tween 1985 and 1988, six Beverly facilities in Missouri were threatened with license revocation. In 1986, officials in Texas suspended Medicaid payments to 24 of Beverly's 134 nursing homes in that state, citing hazardous health deficiencies; the state revoked the license of one home. That same year, Beverly settled a legal battle with the state of California's department of health services by paying a record $724,000 in fines. The com-pany was accused of care so negligent that it contributed to or caused the death of nine patients in that state. Beverly agreed to pay the fines without admitting to the specific charges and was put on probation for two years. In 1987 health care officials in Maine and Washington, D.C. denied Beverly permission to open any new homes in their domains because of its poor patient-care record. In Michigan, the health department claimed that Beverly owned almost half of the facilities facing denial of Medicaid payments because of substandard care in 1987. Regu-lators in Minnesota asserted that eight deaths in Beverly homes there were related to neglect.

The sensational details of some of the specific charges—including rape and gangrene and amputation caused by infected bedsores—damaged Beverly's reputation and caused a drop in occupancy rates. The company lost $30.5 million on $2.1 billion in revenues in 1987. The same year, Beverly's top management tried an unsuccessful leveraged buyout of the company.

While occupancy rates were dropping and reimbursement problems worsened, labor expenses increased by between $90 and $120 million in 1987 when Beverly had to raise its wages. Nurse salaries were still less than competitive, and there was a shortage of nurses at this time. In addition, the expanding econ-omy was offering other options to unskilled workers. About 70 percent of the nursing home work force consisted of poorly paid, low-skilled nurses' aides. With its image and occupancy problems, Beverly was obliged to remedy its employee trou-bles. Violations of statutory requirements for staffing, training, and patient care were not unusual in an industry with labor costs

as its biggest expense. Labor costs accounted for 60 percent of Beverly's expenses. To combat the charges of chronic neglect, Beverly started a quality improvement program in 1988 and established a $5.7 million training center in Atlanta for nurses and administrators.

Beverly's $1.1 billion debt was beginning to pinch by 1988. The company considered filing for reorganization under bank-ruptcy court protection in that year. Instead, it began selling off properties. Beverly was fined another $124,000 after a reinspection of its Oak Meadows Nursing Center in Los Gatos, California, where negligence had contributed to four patient deaths in 1985. Officials found evidence of medical record falsifi-cation, medication errors, and neglect. The facility's license was revoked and Beverly sold the home in February 1988.

About the same time that Beverly was taken off probation in California late in 1988, Minnesota moved to revoke the license of all 42 of the company's nursing homes in that state. The National Labor Relations Board brought a case against Beverly, charging it with more than 200 labor violations in 36 homes in 6 states and accusing the company of engaging in a pattern of unfair labor practices. Management claimed that staff turnover, at 78 percent, not company policy, had precluded the formation of unions. At that time, about 11 percent of its staff was organized.

Troubles in California homes did not end with the probation. Beverly was fined more than $130,000 for patient neglect in its northern California Novato Convalescent Hospital, and the pro-bational status of another home was extended for two more years. In the first nine months of 1988, Beverly lost $12.3 million.

The occupancy rate at Beverly's more than 1,000 homes stabilized at 88 percent by 1989. Staff turnover had also been cut. At that time, the $40 billion nursing home industry, which served 1.5 million people in the United States, was in crisis. Although 63 percent of patient days were to be paid by Med-icaid, money from Medicaid only accounted for 41 percent of payments. The squeeze between rising costs and inadequate government reimbursement meant many companies were losing money. The average daily payment by Medicaid for a nursing home patient had risen an average of 4 percent between 1985 and 1988, but labor costs had risen 11 percent. Two-thirds of Beverly's staff were aides whose wages were only 50 cents an hour more than workers at fast food restaurants. High turnover contributed to the quality-of-care problems that plagued the industry.

### Late 1980s Reorganization

Beverly underwent extensive reorganization in 1989, includ-ing the elimination of three layers of management and a sub-stantial reduction in the number of its properties. Although there was an increase in revenues in 1989 over 1988, Beverly an-nounced a $120 million charge in the second quarter of 1989, a charge associated with the planned sales of 35 percent of its homes. Proceeds of the sale of 370 homes would help the company reduce its debt, as well as trim it of homes that did not fit into a new long-term strategy. Some of these planned sales, however, were not completed by the end of 1989.

Beverly sold 11.5 million shares of common stock in March 1990, netting about $45.7 million, to be used in refinancing debt. With about $470 million in debt to be restructured, the company made a public offering of $40 million of convertible debentures in mid 1990 and had plans to complete its debt refinancing by year's end.

Robert Van Tuyle stepped down as chairman of the board in May 1990, after 19 years of leadership. He was succeeded by David Banks. In summer 1990, the company moved its headquarters from Pasadena to Fort Smith, Arkansas. The move to new headquarters, in the back of a shopping center, was a cost-cutting measure, and it also put the company in closer proximity to its major shareholder, the Little Rock investment firm, Stephens Inc. Stephens owned 10 percent of Beverly's stock, and the firm had a keen interest in keeping Beverly financially sound. Stephens helped Beverly put through a sale of 41 of its Iowa nursing homes in 1990 to raise cash. The 41 homes were acquired by a nonprofit corporation called Mercy Health Initiatives (later known as Care Initiatives), financed by $86 million in tax-exempt revenue bonds. This deal became the subject of controversy when an Iowa Supreme Court judge found that Care Initiatives was a "shell" nonprofit controlled by a Texas banker, not truly a charitable institution. The banker had made a profit of at least $15 million. The story attracted more attention than it might have because the transaction had been handled by the Rose Law Firm, where First Lady Hillary Rodham Clinton worked, and two of the lawyers involved were close aides to President Clinton.

Beverly sold close to 200 of its homes by 1991, and the company's debt became more manageable. After having lost $160 million over the preceding three years, the company turned a profit in 1990 of $13 million. Beverly also worked to improve the quality of its care. The company instituted a continuing education program for its nurses, to expose them to the latest research in care for the elderly, and Beverly began to spend more on training its workers and on inspecting its facilities. Beverly needed to improve its image substantially to attract higher-income residents. In 1990, about 65 percent of Beverly's patients were paid for by Medicaid, which paid less than private insurers. Beverly aimed to bring down the proportion of Medicaid patients over the next few years to 50 percent. But the company still suffered allegations of patient abuse. And the company had trouble with its labor relations as well. In November 1990 a judge with the National Labor Relations Board cited Beverly in one case for illegally firing employees who were organizing a union, and more than a dozen similar complaints were being investigated.

Despite moves to contain costs and attract more profitable patients, Beverly did not perform as well in the 1990s as some of its competition. In response, the company began to move into higher-paying areas of patient care, such as rehabilitation therapy and subacute care. The company also made several acquisitions to bolster its pharmaceutical subsidiary, PCA. In 1994 Beverly paid about $112 million for Insta-Care Holdings Inc., the nation's fifth-largest institutional pharmacy business. In the same year, Beverly also acquired for PCA three drug distribution companies from Synetic, Inc. These acquisitions nearly doubled PCA's revenues, to more than $400 million.

Then in 1995 Beverly proposed to spin off PCA, selling 20 percent to the public and distributing the rest to shareholders. This move was seen by some analysts as an attempt to soothe investors, who felt they were not getting adequate returns from Beverly. The spin-off was announced in April, then abruptly canceled in June. Problems with pricing at PCA reportedly made the spin-off unadvisable, and management promised to pursue it in early 1996 instead. As that deadline approached, Beverly announced further cost-cutting measures and lower than expected earnings for the fourth quarter of 1995. The poor results were blamed on PCA's continuing trouble integrating its recent acquisitions. In January 1996 Robert Woltil, president of PCA, resigned. Chairman David Banks assured investors that Beverly was positioning itself well for the long term. But Beverly certainly faced a challenge in maintaining the delicate balance between keeping its costs down while providing quality care to its patients, and planning for growth while giving its stockholders adequate returns.

### Principal Subsidiaries

Affiliated Medical Center, Inc.; American Transitional Hospitals, Inc.; BESC, Inc.; Beverly Health and Rehabilitation Services, Inc.; Bonterra, Inc.; Brandywood, Inc.; Columbia-Valley Nursing Home, Inc.; Community Nursing Home, Inc.; Gulf States Pharmacies, Inc.; Hospice Preferred Choice, Inc.; Hospital Facilities Corp.; K-D Investment Co.; Liberty Nursing Homes, Inc.; Melrose Health Care Center, Inc.; Moderncare of Lumberton, Inc.; Northcrest Nursing Home, Inc.; Northgate Services, Inc.; Nursing Home Operators, Inc.; Oaks Nursing Home, Inc.; Pharmacy Corporation of America; Progressive Medical Group, Inc.; Retirement Communities of America; Sheltered Care Homes, Inc.; Sherman Oaks Convalescent Hospital, Inc.; South Alabama Nursing Home, Inc.; Spectra Health and Rehabilitation Services, Inc.; Tampa Health Care Center, Inc.

### Further Reading

"Beverly Enterprises To Pay $112 Million for Eckerd Subsidiary," *Wall Street Journal,* September 14, 1994, p. B7.

Feder, Barnaby, "What Ails a Nursing Home Empire," *The New York Times,* December 11, 1988.

Forest, Stephanie Anderson, "Might a New Doctor Cure Beverly," *Business Week,* August 7, 1995, pp. 68–70.

——, "TLC for Beverly—And Its Patients," *Business Week,* June 24, 1991, p. 122.

Hurst, John, "For Nursing Homes, Big Isn't Best," *Los Angeles Times,* April 7, 1988.

Jereski, Laura, "Beverly Enterprises' Spinoff Plan May Make Two Companies Worth Less on Their Own," *Wall Street Journal,* April 19, 1995, p. C2.

Miles, Gregory, "This Nursing Home Giant May Need Intensive Care," *Business Week,* November 7, 1988.

More, Thomas, "Way Out Front," *Fortune,* June 13, 1983.

Roos, Jonathan, "A Rose Law Firm Deal Revisited," *Wall Street Journal,* March 15, 1994, p. A20.

Schifrin, Matthew, "The White Knight's Black Eye," *Forbes,* June 11, 1990, pp. 44–48.

Taub, Stephen, "Beverly Enterprises' Latest Wrinkles," *Financial World,* June 30, 1987, p. 11.

—Carol I. Keeley
—updated by A. Woodward

# THE BON·TON

## The Bon-Ton Stores, Inc.

2801 East Market Street, P.O. Box 2821
York, Pennsylvania 17405
U.S.A.
(717) 757-7660
Fax: (717) 751-3198

*Public Company*
*Incorporated:* 1929 as S. Grumbacher & Son
*Employees:* 9,100
*Sales:* $607.4 million (1995)
*Stock Exchanges:* NASDAQ
*SICs:* 5311 Department Stores

The Bon Ton Stores, Inc. is a leading regional department store chain with sales in fiscal year 1995 of $607.4 million. The company concentrates on serving medium size communities, and as of April 1996, operated 67 stores in Pennsylvania, Maryland, New York, New Jersey, Georgia, and West Virginia. Bon-Ton stores are typically anchor stores in shopping malls and the primary department stores in their communities. They offer a wide assortment of moderately priced name brand and private label clothing, cosmetics, shoes, accessories, and home furnishings. The Grumbacher family controls 94 percent of the company's stock.

### Early History

Bon-Ton was started in 1898, when Max Grumbacher and his father, Samuel, opened S. Grumbacher & Son, a one-room millinery and dry goods store on Market Street in York, Pennsylvania. From the beginning, according to company material, the Grumbachers operated their business "with a close attention to detail and a conviction that business success would come to those who offered customers quality merchandise at a fair price with careful attention to their individual needs and wants."

As automobiles replaced horses and the country became more industrialized, through a world war and the Roaring Twenties, the Grumbachers continued to meet their customers'

needs. The store grew bigger and, in 1929, the company was incorporated as S. Grumbacher & Son. In 1931, Max's son, Max Samuel (M. S.), joined the company. When Max died in 1933, his widow, Daisy, and their two sons, M. S. and Richard, continued the business, forming a partnership in 1936. Following World War II, the family decided to expand operations. In 1946, a second Bon-Ton was opened, in Hanover, Pennsylvania. Two years later, the company moved outside Pennsylvania, acquiring Eyerly's in Hagerstown, Maryland, and in 1957 purchasing McMeen's in Lewistown, Pennsylvania. These early moves set Bon-Ton's policy of growing into adjacent areas by opening new stores and acquiring existing businesses.

### The 1960s, 1970s and 1980s: Years of Growth

The next three decades saw The Bon-Ton Stores continue to expand. In 1961, M. S.'s son, M. Thomas "Tim," entered the business, representing the fourth generation of Grumbachers. During the 1960s, the company opened new Eyerly's and Bon-Ton's in several Pennsylvania communities and one in West Virginia. They also started a discount chain, Mailman's, and, in 1969, retired the McMeen's name. During the 1970s, as the popularity of shopping centers began to grow, Bon-Ton opened eleven new stores in Pennsylvania and West Virginia.

The 1980s formed a period of rapid consolidation in the retail department store industry as major chains bought their competitors. The Bon-Ton Stores began the decade by opening more stores, establishing a new division, Maxwell's, and acquiring Fowler's department store in New York. When Tim Grumbacher was made CEO in 1985, the company operated 18 stores in four states. Two years later the company made a major move, buying the 11-store Pomeroy's chain from Allied Department Stores. That purchase made it possible for the company to move into seven new markets in Pennsylvania.

It also marked the beginning of a major shift in the company's marketing strategy and operations to concentrate on moderate-priced merchandise. The company discontinued the Mailman's discount chain, closed those stores, and eliminated the low margin product lines such as appliances and electronics at the Pomeroy's stores. It renamed all the remaining Eyerly's and Maxwell's either Bon-Ton or Pomeroy's and placed emphasis on providing a deep selection of brand name merchandise, such as Liz Claiborne, Levi Strauss, Alfred Dunner, Esprit, and Estee Lauder. The company also instituted its "Certified Value" program, which maintained value prices on a limited number of key items within each of its major product groups, such as turtlenecks, fleece, and denims.

With the increased income being generated from the Pomeroy acquisition, the company hired senior executives from national chains to strengthen its management and made significant investments to improve its operating and management information systems. In 1989, E. Herbert Ross, who had been with Federated Department Stores for 24 years, was named president and COO.

### The Early 1990s

The company began the decade by changing its logo in 1990 and completing the integration of the Pomeroy units. As those stores achieved the level of quality and style of the core stores, their name was changed to Bon-Ton. All stores carried apparel for the whole family, cosmetics, and accessories. Twenty-eight also carried home furnishings, such as china, linens, housewares, and gifts. Four offered bedding and furniture. All stores contained leased shoe departments, and many also had leased fine jewelry departments and leased beauty salons. Women's clothing was the largest merchandise category, representing 30.5 percent of net sales in fiscal year 1990. Net sales for 1990 increased 6.4 percent over 1989, with stores that had been open for 12 months or more (a common retail industry measurement) increasing their sales by 7.8 percent.

In 1991, the company, S. Grumbacher & Son, changed its own name to The Bon-Ton Stores, Inc. and went public, selling four and a half million shares on the NASDAQ market. At that time, Bon-Ton operated 33 stores, varying in size from approximately 30,000 to 160,000 square feet. Most were one of several anchor tenants in shopping malls in secondary markets; the others were located in or adjacent to strip shopping centers.

Prior to the initial public offering, the company developed a real estate strategic plan, identifying markets with similar demographic and competitive characteristics within or contiguous to its existing markets. Based on this plan, and despite the 1990–1992 recession which battered the department store industry, Bon-Ton continued to grow. It opened four new stores in New York and Pennsylvania and acquired the two-store Watt & Shand chain in Lancaster, Pennsylvania. In September 1992, President Herb Ross resigned and was replaced by Terrance Jarvis. In 1993, the company closed more stores than it opened and comparable store sales had a loss, a first for the company. However, net sales increased slightly, to $336.7 million from $333.7 million the year before.

The Bon-Ton Stores saw tremendous activity in 1994. In July, it acquired the Adam, Meldrum & Anderson Company (AM&A) for $2.1 million and the assumption of $40.6 million in AM&A's debt. The transaction added ten stores in and around Buffalo, New York. In September, it purchased 19 Hess Department Stores (Hess's), one of its major competitors in Pennsylvania, for $60 million. And in October, it acquired

certain assets of C.E. Chappell & Sons, Inc. (Chappell's), a six-unit department store company based in Syracuse, New York. These transactions doubled the company's size to 70, added 3.1 million square feet of retail space, and opened up three new markets—Buffalo and Syracuse, New York, and Allentown, Pennsylvania.

As Bon-Ton grew in the region, outlet stores for brand names such as Liz Claiborne and London Fog, and discount stores such as K-Mart and Wal-Mart, were becoming more popular. These stores offered customers, particularly those in suburban and secondary markets, shopping alternatives and low prices. The Bon-Ton Stores competed by concentrating on customer service, investing in its work force to do so. Sales associates received training in selling skills, customer service, and product knowledge. The company offered a liberal exchange and return policy, free gift wrapping, free shopping bags and special order capability. Selected stores also offered a personal shopper service. Associates were encouraged to keep notebooks of customers' names, clothing sizes, birthdays, and major purchases. In 1994 customers opened 250,000 new Bon-Ton credit card accounts, providing a customer database with over two million names.

The company also competed with its merchandise. To accomplish its goal of fashion leadership, Bon-Ton has been among the first in its markets to identify fashion trends, to advertise and stock new merchandise and to carry a full complement of sizes and colors of the items it sold. During 1994 the company added more name brands to its inventory, including Nautica, Tommy Hilfiger, Ralph Lauren Home, and Susan Bristol, and expanded its private label brands to ten percent of its sales.

The company ended the leasing of its shoe department and made it a company-owned business. This allowed Bon-Ton to offer footwear more in line with its apparel merchandise and resulted in a sales increase of 20 percent. The company also developed a Big and Tall Men's area. The concentration on customer service, more upscale fashion lines, and internal niche marketing led to an increase in comparable store sales of 6.1 percent for the year. Combined with the business from the 35 newly acquired stores, Bon-Ton's net sales for 1994 rose 47 percent to $494.9 million, and earnings soared to $1.23 per share or 55.3 percent.

### 1995 and Beyond

Nineteen ninety-five proved to be a difficult year for The Bon-Ton Stores as it integrated the AM&A, Hess's, and Chappell's stores into its operations. The company had net losses of 19 cents per share in the first quarter and 18 cents per share in the second quarter, but Wall Street analysts did not appear worried, since comparable-store sales increased 4.8 percent for the first half compared with 1994. As Peter Schaeffer, a stock analyst with Dillon, Read, & Co. told Susan Reda in an October 1995 *Stores* article, "Bon-Ton is a substantial company and this year's weak earnings do not connote a disaster in the making. The potential for this chain is great. I'm looking for a rebound next year."

The losses in the first half were due largely to poor sales performance at the AM&A and Chappell's stores. To bring the AM&A units in Buffalo into line with The Bon-Ton Stores' moderate-price apparel, the company had to eliminate the budget store business, which accounted for ten percent of AM&A's sales. In Syracuse, the company had to reduce Chappell's heavy emphasis on clothing and introduce its other merchandise offerings. Because the merchandise mix in the Hess's stores in Allentown was comparable with that of Bon-Ton, the change-over was less difficult, and sales performance was in line with expectations. During the year Bon-Ton acquired four vacant stores in Rochester, New York, giving the company locations in each of the four dominant malls serving that market. Late in 1995, Bon-Ton opened a 75,000 square foot store in Elmira, New York.

Another factor in the company's financial picture was the cost of its leadership change. In January, Terrance Jarvis resigned as president, and a search began for his successor. In August, the company named Heywood Wilansky president and CEO. Wilansky had held those positions at the Foley's division of May Department Stores Company, and May Company filed a breach of contract suit against him and The Bon-Ton Stores. Although the suit was settled in October, the litigation charges contributed to losses in the third quarter.

In addition, 1995 brought the company increased home furnishing business, including china, linens, housewares, and gifts. Ken McCartney was hired from Horne's to become Bon-Ton's first general merchandise manager. He added furniture in 19 stores and saw home furnishings increase from ten percent to 14 percent of the company's merchandise mix.

In January 1996, the end of its fourth quarter, the company closed three stores and announced plans to close five to seven underperforming stores, eliminating 700 positions. That restructuring represented the final steps in "digesting" its acquisitions. For its fiscal year 1995, The Bon-Ton Stores reported net sales of $607.4 million, a 22.7 percent increase from 1994. Because of fourth quarter restructuring charges of approximately $6 million, along with nonrecurring charges in the third quarter of $3.5 million, Bon-Ton had a net loss of $9.2 million for the year. Excluding those charges, net income for 1995 was $200,000 or $0.02 per share. Comparable-store sales for the year increased 0.2 percent.

By the mid-1990s the outlook for the department store industry was much brighter than it had been a few years earlier. "The shock and surprise of the mid-1990s is department stores' viability. Their bottom lines are a lot healthier than anyone would have forecast," retail consultant Alan Millstein said in a November 1995 *Business Week* article. Department stores were expected to slowly regain market share from outlet stores and discount retailers, according to a January 1996 *Business Week* article. As it entered the last half of the decade, however, The Bon-Ton Stores faced national competition (from May Depart-

ment Stores) in 13 of its 44 markets and the problem of catering to the economically-stretched middle-class customer. Ed Dravo, an investment analyst in San Francisco, recommended selling Bon-Ton shares in his column in the September 12, 1995 issue of *Financial World.* "Not only does Bon-Ton have economics playing against it, it is also in the retailing category that Wal-Mart likes to extinguish. Revenues are flat and earnings have disappeared."

However, the restructuring at the end of 1995, merchandise changes (including private brands and home furnishings), continued customer services, and centralized functions able to support a large store base appeared to place the company in a good position. Sales for February and March totalled $84.8 million, a 3.8 percent increase from the year before, despite the Blizzard of '96. Comparable-store sales increased 4.4 percent. Although Wilansky assumed the position of CEO, the Grumbacher family continued to be represented on the board of directors, with M. Thomas Grumbacher serving as chairman. Since the family held 94 percent of the stock and remained involved with the company, there appeared little likelihood of a takeover by a national department store chain.

### Principal Subsidiaries

The Bon-Ton Stores of Lancaster, Inc.; The Bon-Ton National Corp.; The Bon-Ton Trade Corp.; The Bon-Ton Receivables Corp.; Adam, Meldrum & Anderson Co., Inc.

### Further Reading

Chandler, Susan, "An Endangered Species Makes a Comeback," *Business Week,* November 27, 1995, p. 96.
——, "Gloomy Days Are Here Again," (Industry Outlook 1996: Services—Retailing), *Business Week,* January 8, 1996, p. 103.
"Charges Dip Bon-Ton Stores Deeper into Red," *Women's Wear Daily,* November 17, 1995, p. 9.
Dravo, Ed, "Short Takes," *Financial World,* September 12, 1995, p. 77.
Erlick, June Carolyn, "Bon-Ton Expands Home Goods," *HFN: The Weekly Newspaper for the Home Furnishing Network,* October 9, 1995, p. 11.
Kurtz, Mary, et al., "Reinventing the Store: How Smart Retailers Are Changing the Way We Shop," *Business Week,* November 27, 1995, pp. 84–91.
Pogoda, Dianne, "Bon-Ton Pumps Up Its Base," *Women's Wear Daily,* September 29, 1994, p. 3.
Pressler, Margaret Webb, and Steven Pearlstein, "Growing Out of Business: The Shakeout Has Just Begun in the Overbuilt Retail Industry," *The Washington Post,* February 22, 1996, p. 1A, 8A.
Reda, Susan, "The Bon-Ton Presses Regional Growth Plan," *Stores,* October 1995, pp. 22–23.
*Reuter,* "The Bon-Ton Stores, Inc. Said It Expects a Net Loss for the Fourth Quarter," February 5, 1996.
*Short History of the Company,* York, Penn.: The Bon-Ton Stores, Inc., 1995.

—Ellen D. Wernick

## BROOKSHIRE'S

# Brookshire Grocery Company

1600 West South West Loop 323
P.O. Box 1411
Tyler, Texas 75710
U.S.A.
(903) 534-3000
Fax: (903) 534-2206

*Private Company*
*Incorporated:* 1928
*Employees:* 3,700
*Sales:* $1 billion (1995 est.)
*SICs:* 5411 Grocery Stores

The Brookshire Grocery Company operates more than 100 supermarkets in Texas, Arkansas, and Louisiana. In addition to the standard fare of grocery items, company stores feature specialty departments including bakeries, delicatessens, floral shops, fresh fish and seafood counters, salad bars, and pharmacies. Long known for its concentration on customer service, the Texas-based company has two main operations: Brookshire Grocery, with its more than 80 full-service—and some say elegant—supermarkets, which average around 40,000 square feet; and Super 1 Stores, with its approximately 20 no-frills self-service stores, which range from 80,000 to 100,000 square feet. The billion-dollar company also boasts two distribution centers, two bakery plants, a dairy plant, and its own manufacturing complex. Founded during the late 1920s, the company is widely respected for its long tradition of friendly service, clean stores, and technological innovation.

### Early History

The humble origins of the Brookshire Grocery Company date back to 1928 and a 25 x 100-foot store in Tyler, Texas. The store was one of several stores in east Texas operated by the company's founder, Wood T. Brookshire, and his five brothers under the name Brookshire Brothers. The Brookshire brothers set out to build a local chain of grocery stores at a time when the chain store concept, which originated in the latter half of the nineteenth century with such grocery giants as the Atlantic & Pacific Tea Company (A & P) and the Kroger Company, had captured the imagination of many aspiring entrepreneurs. With mammoth chains such as A & P adding 10,000 stores during the decade, the Brookshire brothers attempted to build their own grocery empire by carving out a profitable niche in the east Texas market.

In keeping with the most progressive grocers of the era, the Brookshires adopted the self-service concept in their first stores. Customers, instead of first placing an order for a sales clerk to fill, made their own selections while following a more or less prescribed path designed to expose them to the appeal of the goods on the shelves. This innovative strategy, the forerunner to the modern supermarket, enabled grocers like the Brookshires to reduce operating expenses and, in turn, cut prices and build a strong customer base.

During the early 1930s, the supermarket gradually replaced the small grocery store. Like other grocers of the period, Brookshire operated its stores on a self-service basis and furnished its customers with larger displays of a wide variety of groceries as well as fresh meats, fruits, and vegetables. By dealing in a larger volume, the company was able to market its goods at aggressively low prices, while increasing profits and expanding its business.

In 1939, the Brookshire brothers dissolved their partnership, and Wood became the sole owner of three stores in Tyler, known by the trade name Brookshire's Food Stores, which later became the foundation for the 100-store company of the 1990s. Despite the economic hardships of the Great Depression, the company managed to expand its operations through the late 1930s: by the end of the decade, the fledgling grocery chain had opened its fourth store in the Tyler and Longview area, including the first air-conditioned store in east Texas.

### The Postwar Period

Growth continued through the World War II years and the rest of the 1940s as five more stores were added to the east

Texas area, in Winnsboro, Longview, Gladewater, and Kilgore. Like many businesses across the country, Brookshire's prospered during the favorable economic conditions of the postwar era; expansion continued at a steady rate.

The years following the war, however, also brought a new challenge to Brookshire Grocery and the rest of the industry. For more than a century, grocery stores were located on the Main Streets of the country and the downtown areas of large cities. As the population shifted from the cities to the suburbs following the war, though, serious parking problems arose in traditional shopping areas, creating the need for a new retail facility and a new grocery store location: the suburban shopping center. Not to be left behind by this change in the industry, Brookshire's constructed its first shopping center store before the close of the 1940s.

With the favorable economic conditions of the 1950s and the Eisenhower years, came further expansion for the company. To keep up with the growing demand from new stores in Corsicana, Marshall, Paris, Greenville and Mt. Pleasant, Brookshire's constructed its first grocery warehouse in 1953. With the onset of a new decade, the 17-store chain extended its operations beyond the Texas state line for the first time, venturing into the Louisiana market and opening stores in Bossier City and Natchitoches. New stores in Wills Point, Terrell, Palestine and Mineola, Texas, brought the total number of Brookshire stores to 31 by the end of the decade. In 1968, to better supply these existing stores and prepare for continued growth, the company erected a 175,000-square-foot distribution center in Tyler.

### Expansion in the 1970s and 1980s

The 1970s proved to be a decade of record growth for Brookshire Grocery. By 1975, despite the obstacles of a national energy crisis and a recessionary economy, the company had opened 13 new stores and made its way onto the *Chain Store Age* list of the fastest growing grocers. Two years later Brookshire's made its first appearance on the publication's list of the 100 largest food chains, recording an estimated $175 million in total revenue. During the remainder of the decade, revenue jumped more than 30 percent as the company inched its way up to number 76 on the list in a market dominated by such multibillion dollar giants as Safeway, Kroger, and A & P—despite operating in a comparatively small geographical area. While doubling its size to 62 supermarkets, Brookshire's did set up for business in a third state, opening three new stores in Arkansas as well as its first bakery plant.

This pattern of expansion continued into the early 1980s despite the recessionary conditions of the U.S. economy. In 1982, the company generated $350 million in revenue, having doubled its output in just seven years. By 1984, Brookshire's operated more than 70 stores and employed more than 4,000 people in its three-state region. In its home base of Tyler, with a population of 75,000, the company's eight stores enjoyed a 40 percent market share, despite the presence of at least 15 grocery stores in the area.

The strategy that enabled the company to experience such steady growth to this point was simple: beat the competition on strong and friendly service. As then president C. B. Hardin explained to Doug Harris of *Supermarket Business*, the company's strategy of "aggressive hospitality" demanded a strong commitment to service from its employees: "Our philosophy is when you come into one of our stores we want you to be greeted just as nice as if you were coming into our living room—because you're our guest, and the customer is our boss." With increasing competition from such mainstays as Kroger and newcomers as Tom Thumb-Page, Brookshire's fashioned its Southern hospitality into a well-orchestrated effort to please customers and stand out from the competition. With many of its stores located in oil-rich areas, the company attempted to out do the competition on service rather than price, making sure that customers were not only greeted at the door when they entered and at the checkout when they left but given heartfelt greetings from stockers and service counter employees as well. "We'd rather overdo it than underdo it," Hardin told *Supermarket Business*.

It would take more than friendly service, though, for Brookshire's to continue growing during the 1980s. As more and more competitors entered the scene, the company attempted to broaden its customer base by diversifying its operations and continuing its strategy of growth through geographical expansion. Chief among these developments was the company's opening of its first Super 1 Foods store in Alexandria, Louisiana, in 1984. In contrast to the traditional Brookshire store, with its elegant decor and state of the art technology, the new line of stores cut back on the frills so that it could offer the lowest prices possible.

Between 1984 and 1990, the company opened 11 Super 1 Foods stores in Louisiana and Texas. Unlike competitors in the wholesale foods market such as Sam's Wholesale Club, the Super 1 stores required no membership fees and were generally smaller in size. The new warehouse-type environment enabled customers to save money—usually around $15 a week—by purchasing in larger quantities and bagging their own groceries. Although the Super 1 Foods stores were designed to keep labor costs low, they retained the colorful decor and many of the specialty departments that had become a fixture at the full-service stores and, in this way, distinguished themselves from many other competitors in the wholesale market.

One of the money-saving innovations at the company's warehouse-style stores could be found at the checkout stand. While the full-service Brookshire's stores emphasized ambiance and an aesthetically pleasing checkout environment, the Super 1 units concentrated on getting customers through the checkout faster. To meet this goal, the company began installing triple belt checkstands in its 65,000-square-foot Super 1 units. The "Tri-Belt" system features an initial belt at the head of the checkstand that carries items to the scanner position and a second belt that moves each customer's scanned and paid-for order to a bagging station where the consumer bags his or her own order.

While diversifying its operations in the mid-1980s, the company also attempted to reduce costs by taking advantage of the latest computer technology. In 1984 the company replaced its mechanical time-clocks with microcomputer-based time accounting systems. With more than 4,000 employees in its 70 stores, the manual processing of weekly payroll had become a monstrous task for the 18 payroll clerks who had to recalculate and verify all time-cards in less than 24 hours. The short turn-around time prevented clerks from correcting overpunches and illegal punches—errors that were costing the company thousands of dollars weekly. Once the new computerized accounting system was installed, though, store managers were able to not only reduce such discrepancies but better monitor employee overtime as well. With payroll processing time cut in half, the front office was able to spend more time collecting on bad checks and handling other administrative duties. The bottom line, as then personnel administration supervisor Dan Adcock stated in *Chain Store Age Executive*, was a savings of about $500 per week per store.

### The 1990s and Beyond

One of the keys to Brookshire's continued success during the early 1990s was its traditional emphasis on serving the customer. Attracting shoppers to its Tyler stores in the face of an increasingly competitive market, however, required more than smiling cashiers and friendly stockers; it also meant responding to the cultural diversity and unique needs of its clientele. The transformation process for one Brookshire's store converted to a Super 1 Foods warehouse store, for instance, meant substantially increasing the Hispanic foods section to appeal to the area's small but rapidly expanding Hispanic population. By doubling the size of the Hispanic section through the addition of existing items and new foods such as corn tortilla mixes and sliced cactus and advertising in a local Hispanic paper, the store was able to attract customers from what had been, for the most part, an untapped market. By 1991, Hispanic shoppers represented nearly one-third of the store's total clientele.

Brookshire's transition into the discount foods market coincided with its move into the Dallas/Fort Worth area. New stores were opened in Allen, McKinney, and The Colony during the late 1980s. To keep pace with this steady expansion, the company added more than 250,000 square feet to its distribution center before the end of the decade, and in 1991, the company brought its first warehouse-type store to the area, opening a mammoth 100,000-square-foot Super 1 Foods in Plano. Two years later, Brookshire's increased its presence in the area's discount market, purchasing land for a new 70,000-square-foot Super 1 Foods in Garland. By 1995, the company had established a strong presence in the Dallas suburbs, with seven stores in operation.

The early and mid-1990s saw Brookshire's solidify its presence in existing markets and venture into new territory. The company's expansion to the east resulted in the construction of a second distribution center in 1992, located in Monroe, Louisiana. The state also became the site of Brookshire's 100th store, which opened in Marksville, in 1994. That same year the company, while boosting its total revenue to an estimated $700 million, acquired a 491,000-square-foot manufacturing facility near Tyler.

In addition to opening its own stores, Brookshire's sought to boost its share in various Texas markets by acquiring 16 stores from Thrift Mart, a $90 million, independent, family-run chain based in Granbury that got its start in the 1950s. Terms of the agreement were not released. The acquisition, which included stores in Fort Worth, Hurst, Aledo, and Granbury, represented the company's debut in the Fort Worth area and was heralded by company officials as a way to further increase the growing chain's buying power and offer its customers lower prices.

In an attempt to maintain its reputation for customer service excellence, Brookshire's entered into a multimillion dollar contract with the NCR Corporation for the latest in state-of-the art store automation technology. The installation plan, instituted in early 1996, called for an advanced checkout system that included an innovative, user-friendly, ATM-style interface designed to make checkouts faster and reduce employee training costs—by as much as 60 percent according to some estimates.

By improving the efficiency of its operations and by meeting the diverse needs of its customers through its upscale and warehouse stores, Brookshire's entered the late 1990s hoping to ward off the threat from a new competitor into the grocery market: the supercenter, a combination general merchandise and grocery market under one big roof. Having opened its first supercenter in Texas in 1992, Wal-Mart—which controlled 42 percent of the discount retail market in 1995 and employed one out of every 200 employed people in the United States—attempted to carve its own niche in the $390 billion grocery business, opening its 54th supercenter in Texas and its 230th nationwide in 1995. While the discount giant's increasing presence did not significantly affect Brookshire's larger markets, it did promise to threaten the company's market share in smaller communities where customers have to drive a greater distance to do their shopping and thus realize more benefits from the convenience of supercenters.

### Principal Operating Units

Brookshire Grocery Stores; Super 1 Food Stores.

### Further Reading

"Brookshire Finds a Better Way of Accounting for Its Time," *Chain Store Age Executive,* April 1985, pp. 67–68.
"Brookshire Grocery Covers All Bases," *Chain Store Age Executive,* December 1991, p. 28.
Garry, Michael, "Spicing up Sales," *Progressive Grocer,* April 1991, p. 34.
Halkias, Maria, "Wal-Mart, Kmart Set Sights on Small-Town Grocers' Turf," *Dallas Morning News,* July 7, 1995, p. 1D.

Harris, Doug, " 'Aggressive Hospitality' in Tyler, Texas," *Supermarket Business,* January 1984, pp. 39–40.

Lehbar, Godfrey M., *Chain Stores in America 1859–1962,* New York: Chain Store Publishing Corp., 1963.

Narayan, Chandrika, "Brookshire's Plans Plano Super Store," *Dallas Times Herald,* July 20, 1991, p. 1B.

"NCR Store Automation Solution Improves Customer Service and Reduces Training Costs for Brookshire's," *PR Newswire,* February 12, 1996, p. 212CLM008.

*A Proud Heritage of Serving Others,* Brookshire Grocery Corporation, 1994.

Scott, Dave, "Brookshire's, Venture Grab Garland Site for New Stores," *Dallas Business Journal,* January 7, 1994, p. 1.

Wren, Worth, "Tyler Grocery Firm Buys 16 Thrift Mart Stores," *Fort Worth Star-Telegram,* October 4, 1995, p. 1.

—Jason Gallman

# CAMBREX

# Cambrex Corporation

One Meadowlands Plaza
East Rutherford, New Jersey 07073
U.S.A.
(201) 804-3000
Fax: (201) 804-9852

*Public Company*
*Incorporated:* 1981 as CasChem, Inc.
*Employees:* 746
*Sales:* $350 million (1996 est.)
*Stock Exchanges:* American
*SICs:* 2869 Industrial Organic Chemicals; 2879
    Agricultural Chemicals

Cambrex Corporation is one of the most innovative manufacturers of specialty chemicals, fine chemicals, and commodity chemical intermediates in the United States. The company manufactures products for five specific area markets, including the following: health and pharmaceuticals, such as bulk active intermediates for generic drugs; specialty and fine chemicals, including high purity inorganic salts and customer-specified chemicals; agricultural intermediates and additives, used in herbicides and feed additives; performance chemicals, for use in electronics and biomedical applications; and coatings, made to enhance the performance of paints and coatings for various commercial, industrial, and retail applications.

## 1980s Origins

Cambrex Corporation was established through the efforts of two men, Cyril C. Baldwin, Jr. and Arthur Mendolia. These men had known each other for a long time, having become acquainted through their work in the chemical industry. Ambitious men in their own right, they decided to take advantage of what they perceived as unique opportunities in the specialty chemicals and fine chemicals markets, and they began searching for a company to purchase. In 1981, by means of a leveraged buyout, Baldwin and Mendolia purchased a castor oil company, which manufactured urethanes and castor oil derivatives, from

NL Industries. They renamed the company CasChem, Inc. and opened the firm's doors for business.

The strategy pursued by Baldwin and Mendolia involved pursuing and then carving out niche markets in the specialty chemical and fine chemical sectors where CasChem would develop proprietary technology, preferably through the creation of patents over the years. An essential element in this strategy included the acquisition of companies with the appropriate technology that CasChem could adapt and then develop for its own use. Baldwin and Mendolia assumed that making such acquisitions would reduce the time it took CasChem to develop the same technology in-house by at least ten years.

As the company began its business, CasChem was one of the largest purchasers of castor oil in the United States. The company used castor oil in the production of many of its products and, when the market was good, sold large quantities of castor oil derivatives in bulk to other companies within the United States. The purchase price of castor oil by the company was largely determined by the natural changes in weather that affect the castor bean crop. Fortunately, the price of castor oil had remained relatively stable during the early years of CasChem's operations. With China, India, and Brazil the largest commercial producers of castor oil in the world, CasChem bought directly from organizations in these countries and, as a result, initiated the beginnings of its foreign network.

## Acquisitions

The company's second acquisition, spearheaded by Baldwin and Mendolia, was EDT Technology. This company was involved in the manufacture of electronic plating chemicals and was widely regarded by industry analysts as one of the most promising firms in the area of specialty chemicals. Purchased in 1984, EDT Technology did not perform well from the start, but Baldwin and Mendolia decided to keep the company and judge its profitability within a span of three years. The company next acquired Spencer Kellogg, a manufacturer of castor oil derivatives. Bought in 1985, Spencer Kellogg fit in nicely with the already profitable operations at CasChem. During the same year, the company purchased Cosan, a producer of biocides and

---

**Company Perspectives:**

*Cambrex will be a leading specialty chemical company whose quality, innovation, and service exceeds the expectations of our customers. We will demonstrate an appreciation for our employees, respect for the environment, and concern for the communities in which we operate while providing a superior return to our owners.*

---

catalysts for the agricultural chemicals market. One year later, Nepera, Inc. was acquired, a manufacturer of specialty products for the pharmaceutical industry.

With the acquisition of Wickhen Products in 1987, a manufacturer of cosmetic intermediaries, CasChem counted a total of six companies under its management. The strategy of building a business through a process of acquisition led to the implementation of a decentralized management and organizational structure. The company operated each of its businesses as a distinctly separate subsidiary, with its own business manager. Each of the subsidiaries was in complete control of the resources for the manufacture of its products and, consequently, was also totally responsible for its profitability. A holding company, Cambrex Corporation, was set up to coordinate the supervision of all subsidiaries and to provide direct assistance whenever one of the companies was not performing satisfactorily. The holding company also provided services, such as pension and benefits management and advice, which was not directly associated with the financial performance of any of its subsidiaries.

Operating under this decentralized management structure, the company went public in 1987 to raise capital to continue its aggressive acquisitions campaign. At the same time, management decided to sell EDT Technology, admitting that it had misjudged the size of the niche market within which the firm's products were sold. Fortunately, the decentralized organization of the company began to produce results almost immediately. The close association between subsidiary companies and customers allowed Cambrex to meet the needs of the market with greater efficiency. Baldwin and Mendolia were convinced that this type of operating structure more than offset the additional costs incurred by employing duplicate staffs in the areas of research and development, sales, and general management.

In 1987, the Cambrex market mix included the following figures: coatings accounted for 28 percent of the company's business, health and drugs for 15 percent, performance chemicals for 21 percent, agricultural feed additives for 20 percent, and specialty fine chemicals for approximately 16 percent. One year later, however, the bottom fell out of almost all of these highly specialized markets. Competition from the growing number of small niche companies drove prices downward, and companies such as Cambrex, which had previously thrived on their manufacturing flexibility and ability to adapt to the specialized needs of customers, began to feel pressure from environmental regulations imposed by the federal government. As a result, Baldwin and Mendolia decided to pull the company out

of its aggressive acquisitions campaign and wait for a more opportune time to make new purchases.

After nearly two years, Cambrex restarted its acquisition campaign with the purchase of Heico Chemical, a manufacturer of inorganic chemicals based in Pennsylvania. Purchased from Humphrey Chemicals, Heico was supposed to propel Cambrex into the market for pharmaceutical intermediaries. Another reason for the purchase was that Heico was working closely with American Cyanamid Company to develop an intermediate for manufacturing a herbicide called *Persuit*. The collaboration looked like it would produce a certain success in the agricultural chemicals markets. After the purchase, however, management at Cambrex realized that the potential commercial value of the product was offset by the enormously high development expenditures. Consequently, the deal was abandoned and Cambrex was forced to write off the investment at a cost of $9.4 million. To compensate for this loss, in late 1989 Baldwin and Mendolia decided to purchase Heico's parent company, Humphrey Chemicals, to strengthen its base in the fine and specialty chemicals market.

By the late 1980s, Baldwin and Mendolia wanted to retire, and the two men realized that they needed to hire employees that could help them make the transition from an entrepreneurial management team to a professional management team. With this in mind, in 1990 James A. Mack was hired to assume the position of president and chief executive officer. Mack had previously worked as a vice-president at Olin Corporation, one of the largest and most influential manufacturers of chemical products and defense-related items in the United States. At the same time, Peter Tracey was brought in as chief financial officer. Tracey had an extensive background in financial supervision and management at a number of different firms, including Joyce International, Inc., an office products manufacturer, and Robotic Vision Systems, Inc., a maker of automation systems for industrial use.

Under the direction of Mack and Tracey, Cambrex immediately began to clarify its focus and to refine its long-standing acquisition policy. The two most important elements in the company's acquisition strategy included the continuing emphasis on fine chemicals and pharmaceutical intermediaries and the expansion overseas. The company's acquisition criteria were stringent: Mack and Tracey were looking for companies that had highly profitable niche market shares, ranged in size from $10 million to $30 million, did not require any substantial capital investment, and owned patents and proprietary technology that could be used by Cambrex in its already established markets. The two new management leaders thought the best place to look for acquisitions was in the animal health and pharmaceutical industries, where large multinational drug corporations intended to cease specialty chemicals production and focus more on research and end-product manufacturing.

There were two companies that met the criteria established by Mack and Tracey. Salsbury Chemicals was purchased from Solvay's Animal Health division in 1991. Salsbury specialized in the manufacture of bulk intermediates for photo chemicals and pharmaceuticals and conducted high-level research in nitration chemistry. The second company to meet management's strict acquisitions criteria was Zeeland Chemicals, a company that focused on specialty intermediates and on hydrogenation and resolution chemistry. The acquisition of these two companies significantly enhanced Cambrex's presence in the pharmaceutical and photo chemicals markets. Since both Salsbury and Zeeland supplied products for companies in the same market, they began to bring in customers for other companies under the Cambrex umbrella. For example, Polaroid, one of the major purchasers of ethylene maleic anhydride copolymer, a photo chemical made by Zeeland, soon began to transact business with the other companies within the Cambrex operational group.

As the market began to improve steadily for fine and specialty chemicals, Nepera, Inc., one of the Cambrex group companies that manufactured pyridine, began to increase its sales dramatically. Pyridine is used in the manufacture of many important pharmaceuticals and other intermediates such as animal vitamins, and Nepera was one of only four producers of pyridine throughout the world, and one of two manufacturers located in the United States. Nepera's export of 3-cyano-pyridine for the production of vitamin B3 shot up 36 percent from 1990 to 1991, largely because of purchases from customers in Taiwan and Korea. In addition, the company's feed-grade sales also increased rapidly, primarily because of the use of a pyridine-based vitamin that improves weight gain in the raising of poultry for customer consumption. By the end of 1992, more than 25 percent of total sales for the Cambrex group of companies were outside the United States, with Germany and China as the firm's largest export customers.

### The Mid-1990s and Beyond

As the company's operations grew, and sales throughout the world increased, Cambrex continued its growth by acquisition strategy. In January 1994, Cambrex purchased Hexcel Corporation, located in Middlesbrough, England, for a little less than $10 million. Renamed Seal Sands Chemicals, the company manufactured chemical intermediates used in the production of photographic, pharmaceutical, health care, plastics, and water treatment industries. In October of the same year, Cambrex made its most significant overseas acquisition. The company bought the Nobel/Profarmaco chemical business from Akzo Nobel, a large Swedish chemical producer, for just under $130 million. Nobel/Profarmaco was one of the European leaders in the manufacture of intermediates for pharmaceuticals and fine chemicals. The acquisition brought with it the entire operating facilities of Nobel Chemicals AB in Karlskoga, Sweden and Profarmaco Nobel S.r.l. in Milan, Italy, along with an extensive network of sales firms and offices located in the United States, England, and Germany.

These acquisitions, along with the improved performance of other companies in the Cambrex group, began to push revenues

upward. In 1994, sales of health care intermediates and pharmaceuticals jumped 34 percent over the previous year, while sales of specialty and fine chemicals shot up 36 percent. Sales of agricultural intermediates and additives increased an impressive 17 percent during this same period. Feed additives that were used to encourage poultry growth and reduce disease were up 25 percent from a year earlier, and sales of pyridine alone increased a hefty 12 percent.

By 1995, Cambrex had become well-known within the specialty and fine chemicals industry as a successful international company. Nearly 40 percent of all of the company's products were manufactured outside of the United States, and approximately 45 percent of all of its products were sold outside of the country where they were originally produced. With the acquisitions of firms in England and Sweden, Cambrex also increased its presence as a major supplier of bulk actives for the generic drug market.

In the mid-1990s, Cambrex management continued to search for companies to add to its impressive and growing list of products. Although sales of feed additives were increasing year after year, management focused on expanding its health and pharmaceuticals as well as specialty and fine chemicals businesses, which accounted for approximately 65 percent of total sales for the company.

### Principal Subsidiaries

CasChem, Inc.; Cosan Chemical Corporation; Heico Chemicals, Inc.; The Humphrey Chemical Company, Inc.; Nepera, Inc.; Nobel Chemicals AB; Profarmaco Nobel S.r.l.; Salsbury Chemicals, Inc.; Seal Sands Chemicals Limited; Zeeland Chemicals, Inc.; Cambrex Hong Kong Limited; Nobel Chemicals, Inc.; Nobel Chemicals GmbH; Nobel Chemicals Limited.

### Further Reading

"Akzo Nobel Sells Two Units To U.S., German Buyers," *Chemical and Engineering News,* September 26, 1994, p. 16.

"Cambrex Corporation," *The Wall Street Journal,* January 27, 1995, p. B2(E).

"Cambrex Corporation," *The Wall Street Journal,* July 19, 1995, p. C19(E).

"Cambrex Sees a Turnaround Starting in '92," *Chemical Marketing Reporter,* November 16, 1992, pp. 9–10.

Coeyman, Marjorie, "Fine and Custom Chemicals," *Chemical Week,* February 10, 1993, pp. 18–25.

Wood, Andrew, "Cambrex: Acquiring Expertise in Fine Chemical Intermediates," *Chemical Week,* April 5, 1995, pp. 52–54.

—Thomas Derdak

# CAMPBELL MITHUN ESTY

# Campbell-Mithun-Esty, Inc.

**222 South 9th Street**
**Minneapolis, Minnesota 55402**
**U.S.A.**
**(612) 347-1000**
**Fax: (612) 347-1515**

*Private Company*
*Incorporated:* 1933 as Campbell-Mithun Advertising, Inc.
*Employees:* 1,041
*Gross Billings:* $500 million (1995 est.)
*SICs:* 7311 Advertising Agencies

Campbell-Mithun-Esty, Inc. is one of the world's most renowned advertising agencies. Based in Minneapolis, Campbell-Mithun-Esty has worked on some of the most famous advertising campaigns in the industry, including Andersen Windowalls, Heileman's Old Style beer, Jockey For Her Underwear, 3M Disposable Masks, Granola Fruit Bars, Kohler Infinity Bath Whirlpool, Golden Grahams Cereal, Kmart, and a memorable host of others embedded in the American popular consciousness. With its headquarters in Minneapolis, the company has major offices in Chicago, Detroit, and New York, and in more than 20 smaller locations spread across the United States. Unfortunately, beginning with the late 1970s, the company has gone through a series of mergers and acquisitions, resulting in a dispersal of its creative energy and a decrease in worldwide billings. The recent 50–50 buyout between company management and The Interpublic Group of Companies, however, one of the world's largest advertising agencies, seems to have provided a new lease on life for Campbell-Mithun-Esty.

## *Early History*

The company opened in the midst of the Great Depression during a time of widespread business closings and bank failures. In 1933, Franklin Delano Roosevelt issued a nationwide Bank Holiday proclamation soon after his inauguration in March, closing all financial institutions to prevent further panic among the population. In April, Campbell-Mithun started its operations in the vacated offices of a failed bank in downtown Minneapolis. With a staff of five, including the two owners, the company began working on its first advertising campaign.

Ralph Campbell, one of the owners, had worked as a manager of the BBDO office in Minneapolis for years. Since it was the only office making money at the time, primarily because of Campbell's noncyclical foods accounts, he was ordered by the BBDO agency chief to relocate to New York and create a food division there. Campbell, nearing the age of 50, refused to move from his hometown. The head of BBDO regarded Campbell's decision as insubordination and promptly fired him. Campbell immediately decided to start a company of his own, using his contacts within the food industry as the basis for his first advertising campaigns. Knowing that he could not succeed on his own, Campbell asked Ray Mithun to be a partner in the undertaking. Mithun, a young man at 24 years of age, had grown up in Buffalo, Minnesota, just north of Minneapolis, graduated from the University of Minnesota, and held temporary jobs as a journalist and editor at various publications in the town. In 1930, Mithun was hired as a copywriter by Campbell at the BBDO office. Aware that Mithun was an excellent copywriter and talented adman, Campbell did not hesitate to ask the young man to join him as a full-fledged partner on equal terms.

The first three accounts of Campbell-Mithun included Andersen Corporation, Land O'Lakes, and Northwestern National Bank, all located in the greater metropolitan area of Minneapolis. In gaining newer and ever more prestigious accounts, the two partners developed a simple strategy. If they could not initially win the account that they wanted, the two men would arrange to work on one in the same category, demonstrate their agency's ability to develop good advertising for the company, and then go on to win the account that they really wanted. This strategy held true not only for the type of business, but for the size of the account as well. Good work on smaller accounts ultimately led to work on bigger ones. This strategy helped the fledgling company not only survive the Great Depression, but establish a name for itself as one of the most reliable and creative advertising firms west of the Mississippi.

## Company Perspectives:

*Strategic thinking matched with creativity and integrated communications resources are essential to succeeding in today's highly competitive marketplace. CME's mission is to create and execute innovative marketing communications programs that help its clients and their brands achieve dominance.*

### The War Years and Postwar Period

By the time America entered World War II in December of 1941, Campbell-Mithun was a well-established and thriving advertising agency. The company's accounts with Andersen Corporation, Land O'Lakes, and Northwestern National Bank continued to grow. But Ralph Campbell, who had a history of heart ailments, began to limit his time at the company's office. Mithun, as a result, began to take over more of the creative and administrative responsibilities. By the time Campbell died in the fall of 1949, during the halftime festivities of an Iowa-Minnesota football game, Ray Mithun had already assumed control of the firm's operations. One of the first decisions Mithun made after his partner's death was to hire Albert R. Whitman, a highly respected adman and top executive at Benton & Bowles in New York City.

Mithun and Whitman continued the strategy that the original two partners conceived to win new accounts. A good example of this strategy is illustrated by the story of winning the General Mills account. Although the Pillsbury Company was located in Campbell-Mithun's own backyard of Minneapolis, the advertising firm had an extremely difficult time landing the account. In 1951, management at Pillsbury finally handed Campbell-Mithun one of its subsidiary's accounts, the recently acquired Ballard Flour Company. Ballard Flour Company made biscuits, and Mithun immediately recognized the potential for a combination of television advertising and product demonstration. Soon the company was creating television advertisements proclaiming the delights of eating Ballard biscuits. To mix a metaphor, biscuits started selling like hotcakes, and Campbell-Mithun easily convinced Pillsbury not only to advertise its own biscuits but also to advertise other products under the company name. Within a few short years, the Pillsbury business grew into an $8 million account. A few years later, Mithun, who had always wanted to win the General Mills account, strode into that company's executive office in Minneapolis and announced that he had just resigned from the Pillsbury account and was ready to begin business with General Mills. Management at General Mills hesitated, but gave Campbell-Mithun some small product work. Needless to say, it grew into a full-fledged account not long afterward.

The manner in which Campbell-Mithun won or developed other accounts also became something of a legend within the advertising agency. During the firm's early years, it was contracted by the Gold Seal Company of Bismarck, North Dakota. Gold Seal, the manufacturer of Glass Wax window cleaner was constrained by a small budget, however. In spite of this limita-

tion, Campbell-Mithun created one of its most successful advertisements by encouraging the use of the window cleaner during the Christmas holidays. The ad campaign encouraged people to decorate their windows with festive holiday shapes such as reindeer, Santa Claus, sleds, and Christmas trees by spraying Glass Wax through stencils. When the product was sprayed on the window, it dried and created a white, powder-like residue. Upon removal of the stencils, the decorative holiday figures remained.

Another famous ad campaign involved the Northwestern National Bank of Minneapolis. Campbell-Mithun developed a weatherball for the company, a large sign that perched on one corner of the bank and was topped by a weatherball that changed colors according to fluctuations in the temperature. The weatherball turned white for cold weather, red for warm weather, green for no change in temperature and, in a burst of creativity by the company, was designed to blink when it was supposed to rain. For years, the weatherball was used by the bank in all its advertisements to unify the marketing campaign of its growing branch office network throughout Minnesota and neighboring states.

By the late 1950s and early 1960s, Campbell-Mithun was highly regarded within the advertising industry for its creative work. One of the ad campaigns that propelled the company to the front ranks of the industry was the ''Land of Sky Blue Waters'' television spot for Hamm's beer. The success of this campaign led to many other accounts across the country. Many people suggested to Ray Mithun that he relocate his agency to New York City, the heart of the advertising industry. Mithun wanted no part of the Big Apple, he said, and was determined to remain true to his Midwestern heritage. Campbell-Mithun did open an office in Chicago, however, which became one of the company's few permanent satellite locations. Offices were opened in other cities only when company staff had to work on an account there and, in accordance with Mithun's operating strategy, were closed when there was no longer any account to service or business to keep the office profitable.

### Growth and Transition During the 1970s and 1980s

Still active as a creative force within the company, in his late 60s Mithun was mindful of the fact that no advertising agency in Minneapolis had survived the first generation of leaders. Therefore, he did everything in his power to encourage staff members to become invested in the company. But when Mithun sold all of his stock back to the company in 1972, and then gradually withdrew from active participation in the agency before he retired in 1978, it was only one year later that management at Campbell-Mithun decided to accept an acquisition offer from New York-based Ted Bates, Inc., the fourth largest advertising agency in the world at the time. Campbell-Mithun had already surpassed the $100 million mark in billings and listed such prestigious clients as General Mills, Honeywell, 3M, Heileman Brewing Company, Land O'Lakes, International Dairy Queen, and Munsingwear. The largest acquisition in the history of the advertising industry, Bates added a highly renowned creative agency to help expand its growing list of accounts, while Campbell-Mithun gained access to the center of the advertising agency universe in New York City.

In 1986, Saatchi & Saatchi PLC, a London-based ad agency that was at the forefront of the acquisition and merger mania that shook the advertising industry during the 1980s, decided to purchase Ted Bates Worldwide and its subsidiaries, including Campbell-Mithun. In the late 1970s and early 1980s, Campbell-Mithun had experienced a difficult time procuring accounts outside of its Minneapolis and Chicago office locations; nonetheless, billings reached $250 million by 1983, making it the largest advertising agency west of the Mississippi River. The acquisition of Ted Bates Worldwide by Saatchi brought along with it another subsidiary, The William Esty Company. Formed in 1932, the New York-based William Esty Company, with billings of $563 million in 1983, held many of the automotive company accounts in Detroit, Michigan. Management at Saatchi, therefore, decided to merge Campbell-Mithun with Esty to create the most powerful ad agency in the midwestern United States. Named Campbell-Mithun-Esty (CME) in 1988, the new company had combined billings of $740.8 million and offices in Chicago, Detroit, Los Angeles, Minneapolis, New York, Toronto, and Windsor, Canada.

### The 1990s and Beyond

The combination of Campbell-Mithun with The William Esty Company appeared to be a good match. The number and prestige of accounts continued to increase, and Campbell-Mithun-Esty prospered accordingly. In January of 1992, CME acquired Goodwin, Dannenbaum, Littman & Wingfield. The oldest and largest independent advertising agency based in Houston, Texas, the purchase increased CME's billings to approximately $1 billion. In September of the same year, management at Campbell-Mithun-Esty announced the merger of CME and London-based KHBB to form a new international advertising agency network. CME-KHBB Advertising, Inc., with combined billings of $1.2 billion, was listed as the 17th largest ad agency in the world. The agency's offices were located not only in the United States and Canada, but also throughout Europe and Asia. The idea behind the merger, according to Saatchi & Saatchi management, was to create a network of small offices located in major cities around the world.

In February 1994, nearly two years after the formation of CME-KHBB Advertising Agency, management decided to return to the Campbell-Mithun-Esty moniker in North America to capitalize on the name recognition of its founders. Although the CME-KHBB name was retained in Britain and Continental Europe, to a certain extent the name reversal to Campbell-Mithun-Esty within the United States heightened the company's profile.

Unfortunately, not long afterward, Saatchi & Saatchi, which had changed its name to Cordiant, decided to dismantle CME-KHBB. The strategy behind the formation of CME-KHBB was not working and, with additional pressure on Cordiant from client Proctor & Gamble regarding the CME advertising campaigns for DowBrands, Campbell-Mithun-Esty was put up for sale. In April of 1995, Campbell-Mithun-Esty management and The Interpublic Group of Companies reached an agreement to enter into a joint ownership of the company. New York-based Interpublic, the second largest collection of advertising agencies in the world, purchased a 50 percent stake in Campbell-Mithun-Esty for an estimated $40 million, while CME management retained the other 50 percent interest.

In the mid-1990s, Campbell-Mithun-Esty had one of the most prestigious client lists in the advertising industry, including BASF, Borden, Century 21, Commerce Bancshares, ConAgra, DowBrands, Frigidaire, E. & J. Gallo, General Mills, Honeywell, International Dairy Queen, Kimberly-Clark, Kmart, Land O'Lakes, National Easter Seal Society, Northrup King, Pfizer, Pillsbury, Toro, and US WEST. Still headquartered in Minneapolis, Minnesota, the company had major offices in Chicago, Detroit, and New York City. Billings at the end of 1995 were reported to be $633.2 million and growing.

### Further Reading

"CME-KHBB Looks Back to Future for Name," *Advertising Age,* January 24, 1994, p. 2.
Elmquist, Marion, "Ray Mithun: Putting North at the Top of the Map," *Advertising Age,* August 8, 1983, pp. M4–M28.
Fitch, Ed, "Creative Focus," *Advertising Age,* October 24, 1995, p. 38.
Garfield, Bob, "Kmart Rises to Mediocrity, But Could Corner Greatness," *Advertising Age,* August 7, 1995, p. 33.
Kanner, Bernice, and Millman, Nancy F., "Bates Enters Midwest with C-M Buy," *Advertising Age,* November 6, 1978, pp. 1–101.
Lafayette, Jon, and Serafin, Raymond, "Saatchi Builds Its Third Major National Shop," *Advertising Age,* pp. 1–37.
Levin, Gary, "More CME Blues," *Advertising Age,* September 16, 1989, p. 6.
"Saatchi Expected To Put CME Up for Sale," *Advertising Age,* January 16, 1995, p. 2.
Selinger, Iris Cohen, "Geier's Deal-icious Week: Puris Rises at Interpublic, as Company Buys Half of CME," *Advertising Age,* April 10, 1995, p. 37.

—Thomas Derdak

# Campo Electronics, Appliances & Computers, Inc.

109 Northpark Boulevard
Fifth Floor
Covington, Louisiana 70433
U.S.A.
(504) 867-5000
Fax: (504) 867-5001

*Public Company*
*Incorporated:* 1972 as Giant TC, Inc.
*Employees:* 890
*Sales:* $294.62 million (1995)
*Stock Exchanges:* NASDAQ
*SICs:* 5731 Radio, Television & Electronics Stores; 5722
Household Appliance Stores

Campo Electronics, Appliances & Computers, Inc. is one of the most successful and fastest growing regional electronics and household appliance retailers in the United States. With headquarters in Covington, Louisiana, the company sells brand name consumer electronics equipment, major appliances, and home office technology in 31 stores across six states, including Louisiana, Texas, Mississippi, Alabama, Florida, and Tennessee. The company has a long history of selling its products in small and mid-sized towns across the Deep South and is beginning to compete with such large and well-established national retail chains as Sears & Roebuck, Circuit City, and Silo Electronics. From 1993 to 1995, Campo Electronics expanded from 22 to 31 stores, and net sales increased a whopping 189 percent, one of the most impressive returns ever recorded by a regional appliance and electronics retail company.

### Early History

The driving force behind Campo Electronics and the reason for its success is Anthony Campo, Jr., the president and chief executive officer of the company. Yet the firm started long before he was born. In 1927, Anthony's paternal grandfather, Anthony Campo, Sr., opened a general store in Harahan, Louisiana. During the late 1920s, the store sold dry goods and hardware to a small but loyal clientele from the rural areas surrounding the town, and sales remained just high enough to stay in business.

When the Great Depression swept across the United States after the stock market crash on Wall Street in the autumn of 1929, businesses throughout the country were threatened by financial hardship. Many firms and companies were forced into bankruptcy. Nowhere was this more evident than in the southern part of the United States, where severe drought during the early 1930s exacerbated the financial problems of the general populace. Retail stores were particularly hard hit, due to the impoverishment of many farming communities. General dry goods stores like the one owned by Anthony Campo, Sr. were able to scrape out a meager existence only by extending generous terms of credit to farmers and townspeople. It wasn't until the start of World War II that the economy of the Deep South began to improve, and the continued existence of the Campo general store became less precarious.

### The World War II Years

The advent of World War II dramatically altered the U.S. national economy, and with it the fortunes of retail stores across the country. As people returned to work in both the industrial and agricultural sectors of the economy, individuals had more purchasing power, and the Campo general store began to see an improvement in its financial status. Dry goods such as sewing materials were bought at premium prices by women making clothes for their families. Farmers, no longer constrained by their limited financial resources due to the government's encouragement and assistance in growing produce for U.S. service personnel, frequented the Campo general store with regularity, and purchased needed tools and small hardware items to keep their farms at maximum capacity. By the end of the war, the Campo general store was selling more hardware items such as nails, wrenches, hammers, and mechanical lubricants than at any previous time.

### The Postwar Period

During the late 1940s, and throughout the 1950s, the Campo general store was completely transformed by the postwar housing boom. As soldiers returned from overseas to marry their sweethearts, one of their most important goals was to settle down in a new house and raise a family. The GI Bill passed by Congress provided many veterans with the funds needed to finance a mortgage on a new house. Along with this increase in construction came the accompanying desire by many men to engage in home improvements of their own, and consequently there was a dramatic increase in demand for tools, nails, lumber, pipes, saws, and thousands of hardware items. The Campo general store did away with most of its dry goods merchandise and began to stock more hardware items. As demand continued to grow, the store responded by discontinuing all items except hardware supplies.

By the early 1960s, however, the housing boom in the United States had significantly slowed down. Businesses that had formerly thrived by providing supplies for the construction and housing industry began to feel the effects of the downturn in new home building. The Campo hardware store was also affected. Although farmers and rural communities still purchased hardware items from the store, sales crept lower and lower. Yet at the same time, there was a growing interest in consumer appliances and household electronic items such as radios, toasters, televisions, and record players.

Anthony Campo, Sr., although having grown older, was still an astute and enterprising businessman. He realized that the era of the general hardware store was quickly coming to its end and decided that more money could be made selling electronic appliances than selling nails and hammers. As a result, he closed his hardware store and opened the first Campo electronics store on the same site in 1967.

### Transition in the 1970s

Campo Appliance Company was successful from the day its doors opened for business. Selling such household appliance items as hi-fi stereos and electric mixers, the company made a name for itself in the area surrounding Harahan and in other small towns in the region. Anthony Campo, the son of Anthony Campo, Sr., inherited the store from his father and continued to emphasize the friendly customer service that had been a trademark of the business since the late 1920s. In 1972, in order to distinguish the company as an appliance retail store, and remove any lingering confusion with the general hardware business, Campo decided to change the name from Campo Appliance Company to Giant TC, Inc.

As the store continued to expand, and sales increased during the early and mid-1970s, a new family member joined the business. Anthony Campo, Jr. was cut from the same mold as his grandfather. Ambitious, headstrong, and impatient, but an astute businessman with a gift for recognizing trends within the electronics and retailing industries, Anthony Jr. graduated from high school with the intention of attending college in order to fulfill the requirements for a degree in business administration. Yet the young Campo became disenchanted with the prospect of having to take prerequisites in mathematics and biology before attending business courses. He changed schools four times before he ultimately dropped out, frustrated with what he thought were unnecessary obstacles to learning about business.

In 1975, the young Campo began working at his father's store as a salesman. Working his way from the ground up, Campo devoted six days a week to the family business. Campo not only worked in sales, but in marketing, personnel, operations, and finally management. By 1984, he had risen to the position of senior vice-president of the company and, in anticipation of what was to become one of his trademarks as an entrepreneur, immediately implemented an expansion program for his family's business. In 1985, under his direct supervision, the company purchased three Sound Trek stores, thus making a commitment to enter the burgeoning home stereo and car audio equipment market. Around the same time, Campo opened Mobile One, a cellular telephone dealership. By 1991, Anthony Campo, Jr. had succeeded his father as president and chairman of the board of directors, and in 1992 also assumed the title of chief executive officer. At the end of 1991, the new president and CEO thought a name change was appropriate, so he discarded the old name in favor of Campo Electronics, Appliances, and Computers, Inc.

### Acquisition, Expansion, and Innovation in the 1990s

One of the first moves Anthony Campo, Jr., made after succeeding his father, was to build upon what he had already conceived of and implemented—an unparalleled acquisitions and expansion policy. Almost immediately, Campo opened store after store across Louisiana and Mississippi. By the end of 1992, the company had grown from one store to a 13-store chain retailer, and sales had shot up to just under $75 million. During this time, Campo acquired Shreveport Refrigeration, a large, well-known consumer electronics retailer which operated nine "superstores" in northern Louisiana and northeastern Texas. For the fiscal year of 1992, Shreveport Refrigeration reported total sales of over $40 million. By the end of fiscal 1993, net sales for Campo Electronics had jumped to $101 million.

According to industry analysts, much of the success of Campo Electronics was due to the young president's innovative idea of a "concept" store. The "concept" store format became the model for all subsequent Campo stores and allowed customers to select from a broad range of consumer electronics, appliances, and home office products, including state-of-the-art computer technology. In the area of television and video, such brand names as GE, Magnavox, RCA, Samsung, Sony, and Zenith lined the stores' shelves, while in computer and home product items such brand names as Apple, Brother, Canon, Compaq, IBM, Packard Bell, and Panasonic were part of each store's floor stock. Each "concept" store was designed in such a way as to enable the customer to explore features of the products through hands-on displays. The design of the "concept" store is bright and open, almost glitzy, and contains 18,000 to 30,000 square feet of space.

One of the most successful aspects of the "concept" store has been to place a wide assortment of personal electronics products and items such as telephones, portable radios, and camcorders in the center of the floor in order to encourage impulse buying. This strategy has made personal electronics products the largest selling items in all of the company's stores. Another important aspect of the Campo "concept" store is to hire superb salespeople and train them to provide excellent customer service. It is the policy of Campo Electronics to require that each salesperson participate in a two-week training program when first hired, and to take part later in ongoing training seminars that keep them abreast of the latest developments in consumer electronics and appliances technology. Perhaps the most significant part of the success of the "concept" store has involved the ability of management to place each of the stores in high visibility locations such as strip shopping centers and free-standing formats to take advantage of major automotive thoroughfares.

Marketing has also played a large role in increasing sales at Campo "concept" stores. During the early 1990s, the company issued its own private label credit card to encourage repeat business and cultivate long-term relationships with customers. By the end of fiscal 1995, approximately 284,000 customers were holders of a Campo credit card, and 34 percent of all net sales involved purchases with these cards.

### The Mid-1990s and Beyond

By 1994, net sales for the company increased to over $194 million, and by the end of fiscal 1995 net sales had jumped to over $294 million. Much of the company's financial success is due to management's determination to develop and maintain a strong position in the electronics retail industry across the Mississippi Gulf Coast region. Focusing on small to medium-sized metropolitan markets, rather than on major cities, Campo Electronics has carved out a niche that is threatening the market share of such larger and better known national chain retailers as Sears, Circuit City, and Silo. The company opened 14 new stores in fiscal 1995 alone, in places such as Birmingham, Dothan, Huntsville, and Mobile, Alabama, Hattiesburg, Mississippi, Panama City and Pensacola, Florida, and Memphis and Chattanooga, Tennessee. These new openings brought the number of Campo stores to a total of 31 operating in six states, including Louisiana, Texas, Mississippi, Alabama, Tennessee, and Florida.

At the end of fiscal 1995, Anthony Campo, Jr. decided to temporarily halt the rapid expansion strategy of the early and mid-1990s in order to consolidate the company's gains and prepare for a new round of acquisition and expansion in the near future. Campo Electronics continues to attract new customers with its "concept" stores, and sales are increasing at a record pace. In less than five years, under the direction of a dynamic and visionary president, the company has grown from a one-store operation to a regional powerhouse in electronics retailing across the Deep South.

### Further Reading

"Campo Electronics, Appliances and Computers, Inc.," *HFD-The Weekly Home Furnishings Newspaper,* February 8, 1993, p. 56.
"Electronic Eye," *HFD-The Weekly Home Furnishings Newspaper,* April 26, 1993, p. 84.
Fox, Bruce, "Campo: Keeping Pace with Larger Rivals through Innovation," *Chain Store Age Executive,* July 1995, p. 27.
Hirsey, Peter, "Computers Fuel Campo Electronics' Gulf Coast Expansion," *Discount Store News,* April 17, 1995, p. C4(2).
McConville, James, A., "Dominating Dixieland: Campo Electronics, Appliances and Computers Boasts Market Leadership in New Orleans," *HFD-The Weekly Home Furnishings Newspaper,* April 5, 1993, p. 71.
"PCs, Home Office Items Now 13.6% of Campo Sales," *HFD-The Weekly Home Furnishings Newspaper,* November 28, 1994, p. 53.

—Thomas Derdak

# Canadair, Inc.

**400 Cote-Vertu Road**
**Dorval, Quebec H4S 1Y9**
**Canada**
**(514) 744-1511**
**Fax: (514) 744-6586**

*Wholly Owned Subsidiary of Bombardier, Inc.*
*Incorporated:* 1944
*Employees:* 6,200
*Sales:* $300 million (1995 est.)
*SICs:* 3721 Regional and Corporate Jets

Canadair, Inc. is one of the preeminent manufacturers of commercial and military aircraft in the world. Headquartered in Montreal, Canada, the company has built its fame on the ability to modify and improve upon existing designs and then customize aircraft to fit the specific needs of both domestic and foreign operators. Canadair is known for producing the CL-44 swing-tail cargo plane, one of the genuine workhorse transport aircraft used by NATO forces during the tense years of the Cold War in the 1950s, the CL-415 turboprop water bomber, designed to scoop up water from rivers and lakes and deliver it to areas besieged with forest fires, and the Global Express intercontinental business jet, one of the company's most successful aircraft designs.

### Early History

The history of Canadair starts in June of 1911. Vickers Sons & Maxim, a well-established and highly profitable British shipbuilder long associated with manufacturing ships of the line for the Royal Navy, decided to open a subsidiary in Canada to begin business with the Royal Canadian Navy. At its headquarters in Montreal, Canada, the company soon commenced large shipbuilding operations for the government and, during the First World War, built many ships used both by Canada and Britain to sustain the Allied war effort.

At the end of World War I, the management and engineers at the Canadian shipyard of Vickers Sons began to design and make

flying boats for use by the Royal Canadian police on the numerous lakes and inlets throughout Canada. In 1924, demand for the manufacture of flying boats was increasing at such a rate that management decided to hire and organize an aircraft design staff. The staff immediately went to work and designed a forestry patrol plane that became the staple of the Canadian forestry department. The Vedette, a three-seater flying boat with a powerful Rolls-Royce engine, made its maiden flight in November of 1924. Over the next six years, Vickers Sons designed and manufactured 60 of these flying boats for the Canadian government.

During the 1930s, the company naturally focused on the production of ships for both commercial and military use. Yet the small aircraft design staff was kept busy throughout this period. Most important, the staff was put to work on improving the designs of models from such famous companies as Fokker, Northrop, Avro, Bellanca, Fairchild, and Vickers-Supermarine in England. Under license from the companies to produce a variety of models, the aircraft design staff at Canadian Vickers Sons soon garnered a reputation for high quality work. Although the company produced only about 100 aircraft from 1930 to the beginning of World War II, the reputation of Vickers Sons as an airplane designer and manufacturer was acknowledged throughout the aviation industry.

### The World War II Period

When the Second World War started in September of 1939, an increased demand for aircraft production was made clear both by the British and Canadian governments. As a country in the Commonwealth, Canada supported the British resistance to the Nazi conquest of Europe. Vickers Sons, now commonly known as Canadian Vickers, began manufacturing large numbers of aircraft for the Royal Canadian Air Force (RCAF) and for the Royal Air Force (RAF) in England. When the United States entered the war in December of 1941, the U.S. Navy contracted Canadian Vickers to produce Consolidated PBY-5 amphibians, flying boats that were instrumental to the American war effort against the Japanese in the islands of the South Pacific.

With more and more contracts arriving for the manufacture of ships, and the Consolidated PBY-5 in the middle of its production

## Company Perspectives:

*Canadair has accumulated a wealth of experience in the design and development of complex aviation systems. Now as a member of Bombardier's aerospace group which includes de Havilland, Learjet, and Short Brothers, Canadair is committed to investing in its people, systems and facilities to remain competitive and at the leading edge of world aerospace.*

run, management at Canadian Vickers was forced to inform the Canadian, British, and American governments that the capital investment required to concentrate on shipbuilding was so large the company could not continue to build aircraft at the same time. Therefore, within a short period of time, Canadian Vickers would be forced to cease the manufacture of all aircraft. This decision was, of course, unacceptable to the Allied governments in the midst of fighting a global war against Japan and Germany. As a result, the American, Canadian, and British governments convinced Canadian Vickers to divest its division for aircraft design and production. On October 3, 1944, a new company, Canadair, was formed as a separate entity from Canadian Vickers. Under this arrangement, with funding provided by contracts from the Allied governments, Canadair was able to complete its production of military aircraft for the duration of the war.

### The Postwar Period

Before World War II ended, the Canadair factory supervisor traveled to Santa Monica, California to study the production techniques for the DC-4, a military transport plane made by the Douglas Aircraft Company. Canadair had already reached an agreement with Douglas to co-produce a modified version of the DC-4 for use in Canada. While at the Douglas plant, the supervisor discovered that Douglas was going to dispose of all the tooling and spare parts for the civilian DC-3 and the military C-47 and focus on the design and manufacture of a newer model once the war was over.

Presented with what he thought was a grand opportunity, the Canadair supervisor first convinced his superiors to purchase more than 600 railroad cars of spare parts and equipment from Douglas. He further advised them to acquire as many C-47 transport planes as possible. When the war ended, thanks to the foresight of one enterprising supervisor, the 9,000 employees at Canadair's plant in Montreal were doing a large volume of business supplying spare parts and modifying C-47 transport planes for the new demands of the military and civilian markets. The close working relationship with Douglas also helped Canadair reach an agreement with the American company to develop modified versions of the DC-4 for both the military and civilian markets in Canada. Designated the North Star, more than 70 of these aircraft were built by Canadair.

Canadair was purchased by the Electric Boat Company in 1947. The most famous manufacturer of submarines for the U.S. Navy during World War II, the Groton, Connecticut firm reorganized into a single corporate entity in 1952, calling itself

General Dynamics. Canadair thrived under the auspices of its new parent company. During the period from 1949 to 1958, the single most important aircraft design and development program at Canadair involved the production of North American F-86 Sabre Jets. The contract to design and build the Sabre Jet assured Canadair of a stable income for the entire decade of the 1950s, and many related subcontracts assisted other Canadian companies as well.

It is a well-known fact that Canadair's production of the Sabre F-86 made aviation history. In August of 1950, a company test pilot, Al Lilly, was the first man in Canada to surpass the speed of sound in an F-86. In 1952, Jacqueline Cochran, unsuccessful in convincing the United States Air Force to allow her use of an F-86 to become the first woman to break the sound barrier, finally persuaded the Royal Canadian Air Force to lend her one of its Sabre Jets. The only condition was that she become an employee of a Canadian firm. Canadair hired her as a consultant, and Ms. Cochran broke the sound barrier flying an F-86 in May of 1953, becoming the first woman in the world to achieve the feat. During the 10-year period of its contract, Canadair built 1,815 F-86 Sabre Jets, primarily for the American, Canadian, and British Air Forces.

Along with the modification and construction of military aircraft, Canadair built many commercial models as well during the 1950s. Canadair redesigned and manufactured the Bristol Britannia, transforming it from a highly successful commercial airliner into a military transport, the CL 44-Yukon. Another well-known redesign during this period was the maritime patrol/antisubmarine warfare aircraft, the CL-28 Argus. The reconfiguration of the Argus by Canadair involved a fully parallel AC electrical system and was revolutionary in the materials used for its construction, including for the very first time in aviation history the extensive use of titanium, metal-to-metal bonding, and a high-strength, extremely durable aluminum alloy. Although the CL 44-Yukon was initially designed exclusively for military use, after Canadair's redesign the aircraft gained a huge following from cargo airlines that resulted in numerous orders. The CL 44-Yukon was redesigned with a unique swing-tail cargo door, which allowed customers to load material straight in up to 87 feet in length. Canadair's policy of redesigning aircraft to meet the specific needs of its customers found expression in one of the CL 44-Yukons, which had its fuselage enlarged to transport Rolls-Royce engines from its plant in Britain to the production line at Lockheed's plant in California.

### Strategic Changes in the 1960s

During the 1960s, Canadair experienced one of the most successful periods in its history. The company completed the first aircraft design of its own in 1961, the CL-41 Tutor Jet trainer, which became famous for its agility in the air. The company manufactured more than 200 of these aircraft during the decade. The CL-41 remains in service at the Canadian Royal Air Force and is used by its precision flying team, the "Snowbirds." One of the most innovative designs to come out of Canadair at this time was the CL-84, tilt-wing aircraft. The CL-84 was the first airplane to make the transition from conventional to hovering flight in mid-air, which was revolutionary in the aviation industry. Although the CL-84 was extensively tested by the U.S. Navy, Canadair never received a contract for its production. Nonetheless, the design served as the precursor to Britain's famous Harrier Jump-Jet, the first military aircraft incorporating Canadair's "hover" technique to be produced.

During the mid-1960s, Canadair designed and manufactured the CL-215 water bomber, an aircraft made to scoop up thousands of gallons of water from rivers and lakes and then drop its load over forest fires. Many of these planes were built for the Canadian and U.S. forestry services to be used over the great expanses of woodlands in western North America. By the late 1960s, management had decided to reduce its reliance on contracts for military aircraft and to establish an extensive subcontracting business. Although the company continued to make parts for military aircraft used by the national air forces of such countries as Canada, Britain, and the United States, Canadair also began to make components for a variety of commercial airline manufacturers such as Boeing, McDonnell Douglas, and, later, the consortium known as Airbus. Canadair also produced remotely piloted vehicles and drones, which were used in the national space programs of the United States and a few Western European nations.

### Transition During the 1970s and 1980s

After nearly 30 years of reconfiguring aircraft for the military, as defense contracts declined the company was sold by General Dynamics to the Canadian government. Under new direction, management decided to make the bold move of entering the civilian aircraft market. In 1976, Canadair developed the Challenger 600, the first wide-bodied business jet. The Challenger 600 soon garnered a reputation within the aviation industry for its innovative design, including a revolutionary wide fuselage, a highly sophisticated airfoil, and high-bypass fanjet engines made by General Electric. The first Canadian civil jet to be produced, the Challenger 600 was an immediate success. During the late 1970s, at the request of the Canadian government, Canadair invested heavily in the manufacture of surveillance systems. One of the most influential designs of this kind included the CL-227 Sentinel, a rotary-winged remotely controlled vehicle system that could carry different types of payloads for either military or civilian use. The company also won major subcontracts for the Boeing 747SP and 767 aircrafts and for Lockheed's P-3C Orin antisubmarine airplane.

In spite of Canadair's ostensible success, the Canadian economy and the country's aviation industry experienced a downturn. As a result, the Canadian government decided to sell Canadair to Bombardier, Inc., a large, Montreal-based manufacturer specializing in transportation equipment and related products and services. With money invested by Bombardier, Canadair was able to establish a strong presence in the business jet market. New models of the Challenger corporate jet rolled off the production line and, at the same time, the company introduced the Canadair Regional Jet, a 50-passenger aircraft with state-of-the-art technology for the regional airline market. Additional subcontracts came from Airbus and, in an effort to take advantage again of the defense industry market, Canadair negotiated a contract with McDonnell Douglas to manufacture the nose barrel for the U.S. Navy's F/A-18A Hornet.

### The 1990s and Beyond

In 1991, Canadair brought out an updated and enhanced turboprop version of the CL-215 fire-fighting aircraft. The CL-415 amphibian could also be reconfigured and used for maritime research and rescue, personnel transport, and surveillance. The company also began working on the design of an intercontinental business jet, the Global Express. Powered by BMW Rolls-Royce engines, the Global Express corporate jet was able to transport eight passengers nonstop from Paris to Hong Kong or from Dallas to Moscow, establishing it as the intercontinental business jet with the longest range capability. When the Global Express was introduced in late 1995, Canadair was immediately overwhelmed by orders from around the world.

Well prepared for the future, and growing rapidly, Canadair has taken its place alongside such esteemed companies as de Havilland, Learjet, and Short Brothers as one of the firms in Bombardier's aerospace group. Supplied with the ample financial resources of its parent organization, Canadair will continue to build upon its experience by designing and manufacturing some of the most innovative aviation systems in the world.

### Further Reading

"Austria's Lauda Air Luftfahrt," *Aviation Week & Space Technology,* October 4, 1993, p. 19.

"Canadair Training Center Uses Advanced Technology," *Aviation Week & Space Technology,* September 20, 1993, p. 75.

"First RJ Corporate Version Delivered To Xerox," *Aviation Week & Space Technology,* February 8, 1993, p. 55.

Hughes, David, "BMW Rolls-Royce Wins Global Express Competition," *Aviation Week & Space Technology,* March 22, 1993, p. 58.

——, "Canadair Seeks Partner for Global Express Wing," *Aviation Week & Space Technology,* April 19, 1993, p. 52.

——, "New Tooling Scheme Used for CL-415," *Aviation Week & Space Technology,* March 8, 1993, p. 46.

Lavitt, Michael O., "Cockpit by Collins," *Aviation Week & Space Technology,"* July 26, 1993, p. 13.

Ott, James, "RJ Fuels Growth in Comair's Traffic," *Aviation Week & Space Technology,* December 12, 1994, p. 40.

Proctor, Paul, "Canadian Miser," *Aviation Week & Space Technology,* May 17, 1993, p. 21.

Searles, Robert, A., "Canadair: 50 Years of Finding a Niche," *Business & Commercial Aviation,* October 1994, pp. 128–134.

—Thomas Derdak

**CANSTAR**

# Canstar Sports Inc.

**5705 Ferrier Street**
**Suite 200**
**Ville Mont-Royal, Quebec H4P 1N3**
**Canada**
**(514) 738-3011**
**Fax: (514) 738-5178**

*Wholly Owned Subsidiary of Nike, Inc.*
*Incorporated:* 1969 as W.C.G. Sports Industries Ltd.
*Employees:* 1,830
*Sales:* C$201.59 million (1993)
*SICs:* 3949 Sporting and Athletic Goods, Not Elsewhere
Classified

Called the "Canadian king of hockey gear," Canstar Sports Inc. ranks as one of the world's leading ice skate manufacturers. According to an August 1994 *Forbes* article, the company's Bauer and Cooper brands are as widely recognized in Canada as Kleenex and Xerox are in the United States. Based in a suburb of Montreal, the company parlayed its strengths in hockey skates into a strong showing in the in-line skate market in the early 1990s. By that time, Canstar's stable of brands included Bauer, Micron, Lange, Mega, and Daoust ice skates; Flak and Cooper hockey equipment; and Bauer in-line skates. With U.S. sales of $36.4 million, the Bauer brand ranked fourth among in-line skate brands in 1993. Canstar was acquired by master marketer Nike, Inc. in the latter company's largest purchase ever, a $395 million transaction.

## Foundation and Corporate Development in the Mid-20th Century

The first pair of Bauer skates was hand-sewn in the early 1930s. By the mid-1950s, the Bauer line was the world's top seller of hockey skates, but was just one division of shoe-making conglomerate Greb Industries Ltd., best known as the first international licensee of Hush Puppies shoes. Greb also produced Kodiak boots and Collins safety shoes. Family-owned until 1974, Greb was acquired that year by Warrington Products

Ltd., which was in turn controlled by Cemp Investments Ltd. The transaction made Bauer a member of the Bronfman family holdings, whose Seagram's Co. was the world's biggest liquor company. ("Cemp" was an acronym for the Bronfman heirs: Charles, Edgar, Minda, and Phyllis.) Warrington had been incorporated in 1969 as W.C.G. Sports Industries Ltd. and went public under the new name two years later.

After an early 1970s surge, Bauer and its parent companies suffered through a severe contraction in the later years of the decade. From 1971 to 1982, Warrington chalked up five annual losses and its stock plummeted from $8.75 at its initial public offering to less than $1 by 1983. Bauer laid off more than one-third of its workforce and closed plants in Maine and Quebec. With the financial backing of Cemp, Warrington tried to diversify out of its free-fall, acquiring a match producer, a luggage company, an appliance maker, and a plastic pipe business.

## Sweeping Change Marks 1980s

The 1980s ushered in an era of sweeping change at the company. Although not yet affiliated with the firm, Icaro Olivieri was in many respects the orchestrator of its transformation. Born in 1940, this native of northern Italy apprenticed in his father's tool shop during the 1950s. Olivieri's work with hinges and springs inspired his 1964 design of an improved ski boot fastener. His buckle was quickly adopted in place of traditional laces. Without the benefit of formal training, Olivieri then invented injection molding equipment custom-made for the production of plastic ski boots. Within just a few years, the inventor's company had captured a commanding lead in the market for boot molds and metal buckles.

After touring Warrington's rather old-fashioned skate factory in 1975, Olivieri saw an opportunity to adapt his new technology to the hockey skate industry. The Italian founded a plant in Montreal and began churning out his Micron brand skates and Tyrol ski boots, the sleek, black plastic styling of which offered a significant challenge to Bauer's long-standing dominance of the market. Several years of intensifying competition culminated in the 1981 merger of the two competitors under the Canadian company's name with Olivieri as chairman.

The union created Canada's largest sporting goods firm and signaled Warrington's strategic refocus on that sector.

Given his own creative background, Olivieri sought to keep Canstar in the vanguard of design. Under his direction, the company consistently invested 2 percent to 3 percent of revenues in research and development. An intensive three-year study of hockey skates and skating culminated in the 1987 launch of the Micron Mega, a skate whose quality won Canstar the devotion of 70 percent of National Hockey League (NHL) pros. Even if they were not wearing Bauer or Micron, 90 percent of NHL players used Canstar's Tuuk or ICM blades. Commenting to *The New York Times,* analyst William J. Chisholm noted that Canstar's "sophisticated engineering, technology and research" gave it a decided edge over its competitors.

Warrington also augmented its line via an acquisition spree during this period. From 1981 to 1987, the company added Caper, Trappeur, Spalding, and Kerma brand ski equipment; Santana, Harvard, and (under Canadian license) Pony brand footwear; Helmetec brand helmets; and Flak brand hockey equipment to its family of sporting goods.

But this rapid diversification proved "a bust," in the words of *Forbes* magazine's Nina Monk. By 1987, Warrington wavered on the brink of disaster; it lost $34 million that year and was burdened with $90 million in debt. At the same time, intrafamilial differences among the Bronfmans precipitated the breakup of the Cemp investment group. That year, Warrington sold Greb Inc. and its line of fashion shoes, keeping Bauer and the sporting goods. In 1988, Olivieri and investment group Dynamic Capital Corp. stepped in to execute a leveraged buyout of the Bronfmans' 30 percent interest in Warrington. The chairman turned majority stakeholder renamed the firm Canstar Sports Inc. and brought in turnaround expert Gerald Wasserman.

Wasserman gave Nina Monk of *Forbes* magazine a curt evaluation of the company he joined, saying that it "had great brands but not much else." He divested Canstar's shoe and ski businesses to concentrate on hockey equipment, and, by 1989, the company was earning $8.7 million (US $6 million) on sales of $98.26 million (US $71 million). According to a 1991 article in *Financial Times of Canada,* Canstar sold nearly 50 percent, or 1.2 million pairs, of the 2.5 million ice skates sold around the world.

### Growth Through Focused Diversification in the 1990s

It was the perfect time to focus on skates. Ice hockey enjoyed unprecedented popularity in the early 1990s. Faye Landes, an analyst with Smith Barney (New York), told *Business Journal-Portland,* "Hockey is the hottest thing out there." Part of the resurgence was credited to the NHL, which achieved new heights of popularity under a more forward-looking team of leaders in the mid-1990s. Canstar's continued dedication to ice hockey was exemplified by its 1990 acquisition of Cooper Canada Ltd.'s hockey division. The country's premiere producer of protective hockey gear, Cooper offered a 1,700-item selection of pads, gloves, and helmets. Canstar acquired the Daoust ice skate business from A. Lambert International Inc. for

$30 million in 1992 and launched Canstar Apparel Inc., a manufacturer of hockey jerseys and socks, the following spring.

Given its substantial position in Canada's hockey skate market, Canstar cautiously sought new avenues for growth in the early 1990s, taking special aim at the burgeoning in-line skate market. Although ice hockey skates remained Canstar's core, accounting for more than one-third of annual sales in the mid-1990s, in-line skates were touted as the key to the company's future.

In-line skates are essentially a hockey-style boot with four roller skate-type wheels mounted in line from toe to heel. Although there's considerable debate over the origins of the in-line skate (some trace it to Yoshisada Horiuchi's 1969 development of a prototype, whereas others say it was first created in the 1800s), there is a general consensus that Minnesota's Scott Olson launched the modern industry in the early 1980s with his "Rollerblade" brand skate. Initially intended for hockey players to practice and keep in shape during the warm summer months, in-line skating soon spread to the general public. The sport's widespread popularity was credited to its combination of recreation, fitness, and competitive values.

From 1990 to 1994, the number of in-line skaters in North America increased from 2 million to nearly 20 million and wholesale revenues multiplied from $75 million in 1989 to $500 million in 1994, making in-line skating the fastest-growing sport in the United States. By 1995, the number of in-line skaters surpassed the number of participants in football, baseball, and soccer. Industry observers predicted that climb to continue, albeit at a slower pace, through the late 1990s.

Canstar got into the market in the late 1980s. In-line or off-ice skates grew from 2 percent of the firm's annual sales in 1990 to 18 percent by 1993. In 1992, the company became a founding sponsor of the 24-team professional Roller Hockey International League, as well as amateur leagues, in an effort to promote in-line skating. A 1995 brief in the *Chicago Sun Times* noted that roller hockey was the fastest-growing segment of the in-line market. The company also hoped to piggyback in-line skate sales on the growing popularity of the NHL, focusing especially on nontraditional skating areas in the southern United States, especially Florida, Texas, and California, where new team franchises were granted in the early 1990s.

In addition to its diversifications into related sporting goods, Canstar hoped that international expansion would provide a new avenue for growth. In 1993, the company acquired a controlling interest in Canstar Sverige AB and established an $8 million ice and in-line skate factory in Czechoslovakia. Canstar added British figure skate blade manufacturer Hatersley & Davidson to its roster of companies in 1994, thereby fulfilling two goals, diversification and geographic expansion, with one purchase. From 1990 to 1996, the geographic distribution of Canstar's revenues shifted from 70 percent domestic to about one-third indigenous.

In 1992, both Wasserman and President and Chief Operating Officer Donald C. MacMartin abruptly resigned. In 1994, Olivieri tapped Pierre Boivin, former president and CEO of Weider Sporting Goods and noted Wasserman follower, to become

Canstar's president. Despite the management upheaval, Canstar enjoyed rapidly rising sales and profits in the early 1990s. After declining from $105.9 million in 1988 to $98.26 million in 1989, sales more than doubled to $201.6 million in 1993. Profits increased from $3 million in 1988 to $15.33 million.

Rumors that the company was being targeted for acquisition by footwear giant Nike began to fly in mid-1994, when the latter company signed on to sponsor the National Hockey League. After months of denial from both parties, that December Nike announced that the two companies had come to an agreement. Icaro Olivieri would sell his 46 percent stake in Canstar to the American shoemaker. The $395 million purchase price paid by Nike to acquire Canstar made it Nike's largest acquisition to date.

The union promised benefits for both companies. Canstar gave Nike an instant, well-respected and well-established position in the fast-growing ice hockey and in-line skating markets. Canstar became part of a widely praised marketing and distribution powerhouse, but Nike president Philip Knight vowed that the US $4 billion giant would not interfere with its $200 million subsidiary's autonomy. Pierre Boivin praised the merger in a 1995 interview with Greg Pesky of *Sporting Goods Business,* saying, "I have seldom seen such a perfect marriage between two companies."

Boivin predicted that Canstar's sales would top $400 million and Bauer's share of the in-line market would increase from about 7 percent to 32 percent by the end of the 1990s. Having long enjoyed a dominant position in the hockey market, the company planned to focus its acquisition strategy on figure skating, apparel, and vertical integration. Boivin expected to target Eastern and Western Europe, South America, and Asia for geographic growth in the late 1990s.

### Principal Subsidiaries

Canstar Sports Group Inc.; Canstar Sports U.S.A., Inc.; Canstar Sports AG; Canstar Italia S.p.A.; Canstar Apparel Inc.; Canstar Sverige AB; Helmtec Industries Inc.; Helmtec U.S.A., Inc.

### Further Reading

"Bauer Named Sponsor of Pro In-Line League," *Sporting Goods Business,* July 1992, p. 24.

Best, Patricia, "A Dynasty Divided," *Maclean's,* May 18, 1987, p. 41.

Booth, Amy, "Snow Business Gives Company Something To Smile About," *Financial Post Magazine,* December 24, 1983, p. 36.

Dunn, Brian, "Canstar Rolling Its Way to Growth," *SportStyle,* June 14, 1993, p. 16.

Emerman, S. R., "Nike, Inc.—Company Report," Dean Witter Reynolds, *INVESTEXT,* July 7, 1995.

Ingram, Matthew, "Canstar Takes a Shot at New Game," *Financial Times of Canada,* September 30, 1991, p. 6.

"In-line Skating Still on a Roll: No Longer Considered a Fad, Sport Will Get Boost from Nike," *Chicago Sun Times,* February 9, 1995, p. 48.

King, Harriet, "Nike in Accord To Purchase Hockey Equipment Maker," *The New York Times,* December 15, 1994, p. D4.

Kryhul, Angela, "Quebec Firm Gets Canada Hush Puppies License," *Footwear News,* December 25, 1989, p. 20.

Lefton, Terry, "Nike Seeks To Ice Dance with Bauer Skates," *Brandweek,* October 3, 1994, p. 1.

Low, Kathleen, "Pony Canada Realigned in Multifaceted Deal," *Footwear News,* October 29, 1984, p. 2.

Marks, Anita, "Swoosh on Ice," *Business Journal-Portland,* October 21, 1994, p. 1.

——, "Nike Shells Out $395 Million for Canadian King of Hockey Gear, *Business Journal-Portland,* December 16, 1994, p. 1.

McDougall, Bruce, "Driven by Design," *Canadian Business,* January 1991, pp. 48–53.

Mills, Joshua, "Enthusiasm for Hockey Looks Like Good News for Skate Makers," *The New York Times,* February 22, 1994, p. C4.

Munk, Nina, "Hockey in the Sun," *Forbes,* August 15, 1994, p. 95.

Pesky, Greg, "Starting Line-Up," *Sporting Goods Business,* September 1994, p. 31.

——, "Pierre Boivin: President and CEO, Canstar Sports Inc.," *Sporting Goods Business,* January 1995, p. 46.

Robinson, Allan, "Warrington's Hush Puppies Have a Very Determined Daddy," *Financial Post Magazine,* July 15, 1978, p. 17.

Waters, Jennifer, "In-Line Skating Industry Is Still on a Big Roll," *Minneapolis-St. Paul City Business,* December 8, 1995, p. 1.

—April Dougal Gasbarre

# CASIO®

## Casio Computer Co., Ltd.

**Shinjuku-Sumitomo Building**
**2-6-1, Nishi-Shinjuku**
**Shinjuku-ku, Tokyo 163-01**
**Japan**
**(03) 3347-4803**
**Fax: (03) 3348-3629**

*Public Company*
*Incorporated:* 1957
*Employees:* 18,407
*Sales:* ¥401.67 billion (US$4.52 billion,1995)
*Stock Exchanges:* Tokyo Osaka Amsterdam Frankfurt
*SICs:* 3873 Watches, Clocks, Clockwork Operated Parts & Devices; 5065 Electronic Parts & Equipment, Wholesale; 3931 Musical Instruments; 3571 Electronic Computers; 3651 Household Audio & Video Equipment; 3579 Office Machines, Not Elsewhere Classified

Casio Computer Co., Ltd. manufactures desktop electronic calculators, digital and analog timepieces, digital notebooks and diaries, electronic musical instruments, audiovisual products, computers, and other consumer and industrial electronic products. Casio has developed a number of electronic products for consumers and businesses based on digital technology and the use of integrated circuits, such as digital cameras. The company also manufactures telecommunications products, including pagers and mobile phones. In 1969 Casio was among the first Japanese manufacturers to fully automate an assembly plant, and this sort of innovation has allowed the firm to remain cost-competitive with other larger electronic manufacturers. Much of Casio's success has been based not only on its technological and assembly innovations but also on its aggressive marketing and sales strategies. As a result of its assertive marketing, the company sells its diverse products in more than 140 countries.

### Early History

Casio Computer Company was founded in Tokyo in 1946 by the Kashio family. Four Kashio brothers—Toshio, Kazuo, Tadao, and Yukio—and their father founded a company that was to be managed under a "spirit of creation"; the company philosophy remains "creativity and contribution." The Kashio brothers still own about ten percent of all outstanding Casio stock, and the Kashio family retains effective financial control of the company. Other major holders of Casio stock are Japanese financial companies, none of which owns more than 4.29 percent. The Kashio brothers remain active in the management and operation of the company, as well: Toshio Kashio serves as chairman, and Kazuo Kashio is president.

The name Casio is an anglicized version of Kashio, demonstrating that from the beginning the company was acutely aware of the economic significance of international marketing. The Kashios believed that in the post–World War II environment a westernized name would render the company's consumer and business products more marketable, both domestically and internationally.

Casio was incorporated in 1957, following Toshio Kashio's invention of the first purely electric—as opposed to electromechanical—small calculator. The company capitalized on this invention and became the only Japanese manufacturer to specialize in electric calculators. After the introduction of semiconductors in the mid-1960s, electromechanical technology was replaced with electronic technology, and in 1965 Casio introduced the world's first desktop electronic calculator with a memory. Casio has consistently sought to expand its product line while relying upon calculators as its primary base of operations.

Prior to 1965 electromechanical calculators were large and expensive. Electromechanical calculators were literally desktop size, ranged in price from $400 to $1,000, and could complete only four functions—addition, subtraction, division, and multiplication. These earlier devices, limited in function and speed, were also prone to mechanical failure. The development of semiconductor and integrated-circuit technologies during the 1960s began to reduce the size and cost of electronic calculators dramatically and simultaneously enhanced their reliability. Electronic calculators were also easier to read, despite their smaller size, due to technical breakthroughs in light-emitting diodes (LED) and liquid crystal displays (LCD), and these new technologies required significantly less power to operate. Casio helped to develop LED and LCD technologies, and by the 1980s these technologies played an increasingly important role in the development of Casio's digital-timepiece and LCD-television markets.

## Company Perspectives:

*Casio's strategy is to popularize multimedia with innovative products that capitalize on new opportunities, that expand creativity for their users, and that can be used now—with existing infrastructure and new media—for reasonable prices. With unique functions and product concepts, we are expanding our product lineup for various lifestyles and consumer groups. We are also helping businesses increase creativity and productivity with advanced data and communications equipment. Our experience and exclusive technologies allow us to create personalized devices that are light, compact, and energy efficient.*

In 1964 the first transistorized, programmable, desktop calculators were introduced, and Japanese manufacturers, including Casio, began to assemble electronic calculators. The entire output from all Japanese electronic manufacturers in 1965 was only about 5,000 units. In 1969 Casio's Kofu factory became the first Japanese plant to mass produce electronic calculators. Very few of these early Japanese electronic calculators were destined for the U.S. market. In 1965 the United States imported just 69 electronic calculators from Japan, and in 1966 Japanese calculators accounted for less than one percent of the U.S. market. Casio did not begin to market its own products in the United States until 1970.

In the 1970s Japanese electronic products, particularly consumer electronics, began to capture a larger share of the ever-expanding U.S. market. By the mid-1970s Japanese electronic manufacturers came to dominate the U.S. electronic-calculator market. Japanese companies competed fiercely for market share, and eventually only Sharp and Casio were left. Casio aimed for the bottom of the market, selling small, low-cost calculators with a variety of novel functions.

The calculator division grew steadily, manufacturing standard electronic calculators, high-performance scientific calculators, pocket computers, and digital diary systems. Electronic notepads and digital diaries greatly expanded Casio's markets, particularly its domestic sales. The electronic-timepiece division also prospered, making a variety of digital and analog watches, many with built-in memory and storage features.

By the 1980s Japan had become the world's leading electronics exporter while the United States was the largest consumer of electronic products. While U.S. firms concentrated on military, industrial, and commercial products, Japanese firms emphasized consumer products.

### Expanding Product Lines in the 1980s

After years of market expansion during the 1970s and 1980s, however, Casio found that market demand in timepieces became stagnant. As a result of market saturation, Casio introduced a number of new timepieces to maintain market demand during the late 1980s, including such products as watches that measured altitude, depth, and barometric pressure; phone-dialing watches; and watches that could record caloric consumption or serve as a pedometer.

The electronic-musical-instrument division manufactured such products as electronic keyboards and digital synthesizers, guitar synthesizers, digital horns, and other sound generators. One of the Kashio brothers, Toshio, was responsible for the company's move into electronic instruments. He had been interested in mass-marketing musical instruments for a while, but manufacturing costs were too steep. However, new chip technology that was developed in the late 1970s made cheaper electronic instruments possible. Casio engineers began to develop electronic pianos at this time. They were marketed to amateur players who couldn't or wouldn't afford a traditional piano. Casio introduced electronic keyboards into the U.S. market in 1980.

U.S. sales began to take off in the mid-1980s. In 1983, the total number of electronic keyboards sold in the United States numbered less than 300,000. By 1987, American consumers bought close to five million. Most of these were low-end instruments, retailing for less than $300. By the end of the decade, Casio had captured roughly 55 percent of the electronic instrument market. Its pianos were principally low-cost products, but they provided lots of effects. With digital sampling and memory, keyboards could store dozens of sounds, songs, and patterns. Musical products suffered from potential market saturation, however, and the company lavished millions on advertising in order to keep its products fresh in consumers' minds. After an initial surge in sales, the company began to market enhanced or new lines of products to maintain market demand. During the late 1980s Casio began working to expand its musical markets by appealing to professional musicians and by developing sound products for use in live performances.

The electronic-office-equipment division manufactured such products as LCD televisions, TV/VCR combination units, office computers, electronic cash registers, point-of-sale scanning systems, and other audiovisual products. Casio hoped to build on its LCD technology to further expand its product lines and to ensure future growth and development.

In 1988 Casio introduced a new automated data-processing product line. An integrated business system designed to be used without costly programming, Casio referred to the product as an Active Data Processing System (ADPS). It included a processing unit which Casio hoped would create a universal business data format and a data-management system. Casio planned full-scale marketing of this new computer in early 1991 and strengthened its sales network. Casio hoped to use ADPS to strengthen and expand its role in business markets.

Since research and development plays a crucial role in the long-term viability of electronic manufacturers, Casio consistently devoted about four percent of its annual sales revenues to research and development. Among the more promising innovations pursued by Casio was COF (chip-on-film) technology, a method of mounting information on a computer chip that allows increased functional capabilities in lighter and thinner settings. The company adapted COF technology for use in electronic calculators, digital diaries, and printers. The company also began to incorporate this technology into smaller and lighter watches, LCD televisions, computers, and memory cards. In 1990 the company set up a subsidiary, Casio Electronic Devices, to promote the sale of its chip-on-film and LCD components.

### The 1990s

Casio attempted to expand its markets not only through technical enhancements and new product lines, but it also moved aggressively to increase the scope of its operations by expanding internationally. The company began to move some of its manufacturing facilities outside of Japan, to combat the expense of the strong Japanese yen. Casio first opened plants in nearby Taiwan and Hong Kong. Then in 1990, the company opened plants in California and in Mexico. Both Casio Manufacturing Corporation in San Diego and Casio Electromex in Tijuana were devoted to producing electronic musical instruments.

In 1991 Casio acquired an interest in the Asahi Corporation, a manufacturer of electronic appliances, calculators, and telephone answering machines, and began to diversify into new and promising product areas. It developed a "personal digital assistant" (PDA) with the Tandy Corporation, a small computer that could interface with traditional personal computers, as well as recognize handwriting and send e-mail. Casio's digital diaries became extremely popular with children in the mid-1990s. These hand-held devices combined traditional datebook functions—calendar, alarm clock, phone directory, memo pad—with functions of immense appeal to school-age consumers, including fortune-telling, secret passwords, a match-making adviser, and the "virtual pet." When the user pressed the "pet" button, a puppy would appear on the screen and do tricks. Casio's diaries were such a hit that production had to expand 20 percent in 1994 to keep up with demand. Later models had built-in infrared beam technology that allowed users to send messages to friends' diaries.

Sales of the diaries helped Casio increase its revenues in Japan in 1994, but the strong yen continued to cut into the profitability of the company's exports. Casio increased the amount of its manufacturing that was done overseas in order to combat this trend. While only 30 percent of Casio's production was overseas in 1993, two years later 80 percent of the company's products were made in foreign plants. By 1996 Casio had plants in Singapore, Malaysia, Thailand and Korea, in addition to its Hong Kong, Taiwan, and North American plants.

Casio began to expand into mainland China as well. In 1993, the company set up two joint ventures in China to manufacture pagers and other electronic devices, and in 1995 two more manufacturing and marketing joint ventures were established in China. Casio Electronics Co. in Zhongshan made electronic diaries and scientific calculators, and another company in Zhuhai produced electronic keyboards. This gave Casio another lower-cost Asian base for manufacturing and also gave the company a foothold in the Chinese consumer market, which was expected to grow markedly in the coming years. Casio also began marketing pagers in India, under a joint agreement with Mitsui and the Indian company Bharti Telecom, beginning in 1995.

Casio found a promising new market in the mid-1990s as a result of deregulation of telecommunications in Japan. Pagers had not been allowed for sale directly to consumers until March 1995. This changed as part of a liberalization of Japan's telecommunications industry, and Casio experienced record growth in its pager sales. In what seemed a typical move for Casio, which had enjoyed great success with kids' electronics in other areas, the company introduced a pager aimed at school children. Its "Bell-Me" pager translated telephone signals into text messages coupled with various happy or sad faces. Casio also developed a small mobile telephone it called the "personal handy-phone system" (PHS), which began commercial service in July 1995. This was similar to the digital mobile phones already in use in the United States. The PHS was tailored to the Japanese urban environment. It required an antenna within 100 to 300 meters, but it functioned ideally in Japan's densely populated cities.

Other telecommunications devices Casio marketed in the mid-1990s included the video phone. Previous video phones had been unsuitable for general consumers because of high cost and poor quality. Only large businesses with complex digital networks in place had been able to use video phones with success. Casio began marketing a home-use video phone in 1995 that was reasonably priced and worked well on regular analog telephone circuits. Consumers did not have to change their phone lines in order to use the new phones, and Casio hoped the new technology would become commonplace in the near future. Casio also introduced a low-cost digital camera in 1995. Like the video phone, the digital camera had been used in the corporate world but was previously not convenient for the general public. Casio introduced a moderately-priced, pocket-sized model that could be used by consumers with a personal computer.

Throughout the 1990s, Casio had shown its strength in translating new technology into desirable consumer items. Casio's genius was for making high-tech electronics into small, light, cheap and intriguing gadgets. It had done this with calculators, watches, keyboards and digital diaries. The company believed it was positioned for long-term growth using this strategy in the evolving telecommunications industry and in multimedia advancements to come.

### Principal Subsidiaries

Aichi Casio Co., Ltd.; Yamagata Casio Company; Casio Polymer Tec Co., Ltd.; Casio Electronic Manufacturing Co., Ltd. (71%); Casio Micronics Co., Ltd.; Casio Systems Co., Ltd.; Kofu Casio Co., Ltd.; Kochi Casio Co., Ltd.; The Casio Lease Company; Casio Electronic Devices Company, Ltd.; Asahi Corporation (65%); Casio Computer Company GmbH (Germany; 60%); Casio Computer Ltd. (Hong Kong); Casio Electronics Company, Ltd. (U.K.); Casio (Malaysia) Sdn. Bhd.; Casio Korea Company, Ltd.; Casio Taiwan Ltd.; Casio Asia Pte. Ltd. (Singapore); Asahi Electronics (Singapore) Pte., Ltd. (62.5%); Asahi Electronics (Thailand) Co., Ltd. (59%); Asahi Industries (Malaysia) Sdn. Bhd. (80%); Casio Inc. (USA; 60%); Casio Canada, Ltd.; Casio PhoneMate Inc. (USA); Casio Manufacturing Corporation (U.S.A.); Casio Electromex S.A. de C.V. (Mexico).

### Further Reading

Cignarella, Patricia, "Casio's Quest to Become the Pied Piper," *Adweek's Marketing Week,* January 16, 1989, p. 24.
Holyoke, Larry; Spindle, William; and Gross, Neil, "Doing the Unthinkable," *Business Week,* January 10, 1994, pp. 52–53.

—Timothy E. Sullivan
—updated by A. Woodward

# CDW®

## CDW Computer Centers, Inc.

1020 E. Lake Cook Road
Buffalo Grove, Illinois 60089
U.S.A.
(847) 465-6000
Fax: (847) 465-3838

*Public Company*
*Incorporated:* 1984 as Computer Discount Warehouse
*Employees:* 536
*Sales:* $628.72 million (1995)
*Stock Exchanges:* NASDAQ
*SICs:* 5045 Computers & Computer Peripheral
   Equipment & Software

CDW Computer Centers, Inc., is a leading seller of brand name microcomputer hardware and peripheral devices, including desktop and notebook computers, printers, video monitors, data storage devices, multimedia equipment, networking products, and software. CDW markets primarily through direct mail to end users, particularly business customers, in the United States.

### A New Industry Emerges

CDW was launched in 1984 by former used car salesman and Burger King franchise school dropout Michael Krasny. Krasny, a 1975 graduate of the University of Illinois, had taken a job after college selling used cars at his father's Toyota dealership in Chicago. He didn't like the work, but would later attribute much of his success to the simple truths he learned on his father's car lot. Bits of wisdom he would recall included: "Good luck many times comes disguised as hard work," "Pigs get fat, hogs get slaughtered," "Success means never being satisfied," and "People do business with people they like." Among other skills, he learned to negotiate. "Being that I was from the automobile business, I was good at negotiating," he said in the February 12, 1996, *Forbes.* "When I bought the machine [computer], I bought it right."

Krasny disliked car sales, but did enjoy trying to computerize the dealership's sales and finance departments. In 1982 he left the dealership, entered and then dropped out of Burger King's franchise school, and then decided to become a freelance computer programmer. The field was relatively young at the time—computers were just beginning to become common in homes and offices—and Krasny had trouble making ends meet. Frustrated and in need of cash, he decided to sell his computer system in 1984. He ran an advertisement in the Chicago Tribune classified section that read; "IBM PC 512K Memory— computer, color monitor, software, 2 disc drive, $1,500/best offer. Still in warranty."

To Krasny's surprise, he easily sold the system to the first person that responded to the ad. Furthermore, the second person that called to buy the computer offered to pay Krasny to set up a system for him. Cash-starved Krasny agreed. He bought a computer system, helped the person set it up, and charged a few hundred dollars for his services. Meanwhile, as people continued to call about buying his computer, Krasny developed a sales pitch designed to convince those prospects to let him set up a computer system for them. When some of them agreed, the venture that would become CDW (Computer Discount Warehouse) was born.

Krasny spent the next few years building a business of buying, selling, setting up, and repairing computer systems. Because personal computers were still relatively new, many people were intimidated by the technology. Thus, many of his customers were simply looking for someone who could tell them what to buy, how to set it up and turn it on, and how to keep it running. As computers became more user-friendly and buyers became more comfortable with PC technology, his emphasis shifted to sales. By 1985 Krasny found that he was selling many computer systems to a single buyer, a Chicago entrepreneur who simply resold them by mail at markups of about $300 per machine.

### Rapid Rise

Krasny recognized the potential of the Chicago entrepreneur's mail-order idea, and he knew that he was just as capable of selling his machines by mail. In November 1985 he published his first national advertisement in *PC World* magazine.

He hired a salesman to answer the phone, and never looked back. Krasny hired more salespeople and began running more and bigger advertisements in a number of national PC and computer-related publications. Sales shot past $10 million and would head toward $60 million annually by 1989.

While Krasny quickly discovered the power of direct marketing in the computer business, he also learned how to maximize the potential of that vast distribution channel. From the start, he decided to keep prices low and make money by shipping a high volume of units. While his nearby Chicago competitor tagged a $300 markup onto his gear, for example, Krasny charged only $25. He also maintained an intense focus on customer service, which became a hallmark of the CDW organization. The result was that CDW, unlike many of its competitors, managed to develop a loyal base of repeat customers—a valuable asset in the direct marketing business.

Thus, customer service and low prices became the foundation of CDW. "We have the right products at the right price due to our knowledge of what customers want and our close link with our vendors—distributors and manufacturers of computer products," Krasny said in the October 23, 1995, *HFN.* But CDW also prospered as a result of its savvy operational strategy. "Efficiency is the second vital ingredient for our competitive success," said Krasny. "Low overhead, high inventory turnover, and fast delivery to customers are the components of our cost-effective operating model. Third, we are dedicated to continuously improving everything we do."

The combination of a slick operating plan and a savvy marketing strategy helped make CDW one of the top two computer direct marketers by the early 1990s (the leader of the industry was Micro Warehouse). CDW's sales rose to $83 million before surpassing $100 million in 1991, and net income rose to $3.7 million in 1991. CDW's gains in 1991 displayed the value of the company's formula for success. The personal computer business suffered an ugly downturn in that year that squelched sales by most retailers. In contrast, the direct marketing channel continued to grow. As overall personal computer shipments plummeted 14 percent in 1991, traditional retailers watched from the sidelines as direct marketers increased PC sales by a whopping 76 percent. "These guys [direct marketers] are really putting the squeeze on the personal computer dealers," said Owen Linderholm, senior editor of *PC World,* in the April 19, 1993, *Crain's Chicago Business.* "All they [dealers] have left to offer is more service."

### Changes in the 1990s

More service was exactly what the personal computer market needed less of as the 1990s progressed. Indeed, as computer makers scrambled to develop PCs and peripherals that were more user-friendly and the cost of computer systems dropped, direct marketers like CDW prospered. But CDW remained a step ahead of most of its competitors by continually employing new, shrewd tactics. For example, Krasny realized that many buyers were wary of purchasing expensive computers systems through the mail. To ease their fears, he established a storefront showroom that gave CDW more credibility. It also helped to boost sales, as about ten percent of CDW's revenue was garnered from its two Chicago stores by the early 1990s.

Krasny also boosted profits by adopting cutting-edge automation technology. For example, Krasny learned from a lawyer friend about the owner of a local company, United Stationers, that had an obsession with automation. Krasny followed that company's lead, automating its billing system and eventually other parts of the company. CDW had been processing 200 orders daily with 12 people in its billing department in the 1980s. By the early 1990s, after implementing new information systems, the same department was churning out 5,000 orders each day with only four workers. Nevertheless, Krasny continued to value his workers more than his technology, a trait he learned at his father's Toyota dealership. "My father asked people to work very hard, but gave them 150 percent of what they could earn somewhere else," Krasny said in the *Forbes* article. He paid CDW's employees with stock options and vacations, among other perks, and many of the company's salespeople earned well over $100,000 annually.

CDW continued to pursue its proven strategy in 1992 and 1993; it advertised its goods in PC trade publications and sold directly to customers via toll-free phone numbers. CDW targeted medium-size and larger companies, which often purchased large volumes of goods and became important repeat customers (business buyers accounted for roughly 80 percent of sales by the mid-1990s). The company also avoided manufacturing its own systems, a route that many of its competitors chose. Instead, CDW marketed a wide line of brand name computers and peripherals, focusing resources on its key strength of distribution. That simple strategy generated sales of $176 million in 1992 and $271 million in 1992, about $6.3 million and $13.55 million, respectively, of which was netted as income.

As CDW's bank account grew, so did Krasny's. Krasny took the company public in 1993 after changing the name from Computer Discount Warehouse to CDW Computer Centers. The initial public offering of stock brought expansion capital into CDW's war chest and provided Krasny just compensation for his efforts. (His profits from stock sales combined with his 43 percent ownership share gave the 40-plus-year-old entrepreneur a net worth of more than $350 million by the mid-1990s.) Investor excitement about CDW's prospects pushed the company's stock price from its offering price of $6.25 to more than $25 within a year. After two years, moreover, the stock was selling at a high of more than $60 per share.

CDW benefitted in the mid-1990s from numerous industry trends, including a proliferation of multimedia and other peripheral devices, booming computer replacement markets, and an uptick in capital spending by its core business clientele. Important to CDW's success were several big accounts that helped to dump millions of dollars worth of product into its distribution pipeline. CDW had much earlier landed a deal to sell computers for Compaq, the leading computer producer in the United States going into the mid-1990s. Then, in April 1994, computer mammoth IBM granted CDW permission to begin selling its units. Shortly thereafter, CDW also won permission to start selling a new Apple notebook computer.

CDW's success at landing major new vendors reflected the intensifying trend toward direct marketing, particularly to businesses, which was becoming a much more accepted means of saving money on computer purchases. In addition, CDW benefitted from an aggressive PC price war that broke out in 1994. Compaq initiated the contest when it slashed prices 11 percent to 22 percent on different models. IBM followed suit with a pugnacious 27 percent price cut. CDW's stock price rose immediately after each of the reductions as investors correctly anticipated big sales. CDW posted an impressive 52 percent gain in revenue in 1994 (to $413 million), and enjoyed record operating profits of $23 million.

### Sustained Growth

To the surprise of many analysts, CDW maintained rampant growth throughout 1995. With major electronics producers like Hewlett-Packard, Digital Equipment, Sony, Toshiba, and others clambering to get their goods into its distribution system, CDW tallied steady sales and profit gains. By 1995 CDW was marketing 20,000 items through its catalogs, had a 250-member sales force, and boasted a database of nearly one million customers and prospects. About 80 percent of its sales were to repeat customers, which confirmed the wisdom of the company's longtime focus on customer service. Sales for the year hit $629 million, about $20 million of which was netted as income.

CDW broadened its marketing effort in 1995 with the establishment of an "outbound" telemarketing department to contact and sell to prospects. That effort, combined with the 30-plus million catalogs it shipped out every year, was expected to boost 1996 sales. In addition, CDW was planning to diversify its product line to include numerous electronics products of interest to its core business customer base, including personal data assistants, digital cameras, and devices related to video transmission. CDW also planned to launch an Internet marketing program in 1996.

### Principal Subsidiaries

Northbrook Ad Agency, Inc.; Computer Discount Warehouse.

### Further Reading

Croghan, Lore, "Micro Warehouse CDW Computer Centers: The Endless Wave?" *Financial World,* June 20, 1995, p. 18.

King, Elliot, "PCs for Sale by Mail," *Target Marketing,* June 1992, p. 17.

Murphy, H. Lee, "Auspicious Beginnings for CDW, Shareholders," *Crain's Chicago Business,* May 2, 1994, p. 10.

Ryan, Ken, "CDW Enjoys Computing Success," *HFN: The Weekly Newspaper,* October 23, 1995, p. 102.

Samuels, Gary, "The Fine Art of Haggling: CDW Computer Centers' Founder Michael Krasny," *Forbes,* February 12, 1996, p. 70.

Veverka, Mark, "Direct Selling Computes for PC Retailer CDW," *Crain's Chicago Business,* April 19, 1993, p. 11.

——, "A Victor in Price Wars: IBM, Compaq Cuts Boost CDW's Sales Picture," *Crain's Chicago Business,* August 29, 1994, p. 70.

Wangensteen, Betsy, "Go-go Tech Issues Swing Like a Yo-yo," *Crain's Chicago Business,* January 1, 1996, p. 4.

—Dave Mote

# Celestial Seasonings, Inc.

**4600 Sleepytime Drive**
**Boulder, Colorado 80301**
**U.S.A.**
**(303) 530-5300**
**Fax: (303) 530-5969**

*Public Company*
*Incorporated:* 1972 as Celestial Seasonings, Inc.
*Employees:* 221
*Sales:* $70.1 million (1995)
*Stock Exchanges:* NASDAQ
*SICs:* 2099 Food Preparations, Not Elsewhere Classified

The largest manufacturer and marketer of herb teas in the United States, Celestial Seasonings, Inc. markets roughly 50 different tea varieties in the United States and abroad. Chiefly responsible for creating the herb tea industry in the United States, Celestial Seasonings was founded by Mo Siegel and Wyck Hay, who introduced the country's consumers to colorfully packaged, decaffeinated herb teas that offered "soothing teas for a nervous world." In 1984, the company was purchased by Kraft, Inc., then cut its ties to its parent company through a leveraged buyout in 1988 before going public in 1993. During the mid-1990s, Celestial Seasonings controlled an estimated 51 percent of the herb tea market.

### The Founding of Celestial Seasonings

The birth of the United States' largest manufacturer of herb teas begins in the canyons and forests of the Rocky Mountains, where 19-year old Morris "Mo" Siegel began gathering wild herbs in 1968. Despite its idyllic image of a teenager traipsing through meadows and harvesting what nature had to offer, the Rocky Mountain tableau, with 19 year-old Mo Siegel at its center, marked the beginning of what would in a short time become Celestial Seasonings, the pioneer of the herb tea industry in the United States and its leading competitor in the decades to come. What could have represented nothing more than a carefree excursion made during the "Summer of Love," or

perhaps another example of the 1960s generation "tuning in and dropping out" by returning to the simplicity of nature, represented instead the first stirrings of a powerful corporate enterprise, undoubtedly one of the anathemas of wild herb pluckers throughout the country. Though Mo Siegel's first herb harvesting trip touched off the creation of a new corporate force in the business world, the development of which was spearheaded by Siegel himself, the company's history did not betray the idyllic setting nor the revolutionary social movement from which it emerged. Celestial Seasonings, twenty years after it was created, continued to occupy a singular position in the corporate world, standing out as a unique enterprise that in many respects outlived and then carried forward the environmental and philosophical precepts engendering its birth. A colorful tale of corporate history was the result, a story played out during the company's formative decades that charted the rise, development, and maturity of Celestial Seasonings, building to the dominant market position it occupied during the 1990s.

Well before Mo Siegel traveled to the forested countryside neighboring Boulder, Colorado in 1968 to pick herbs, he demonstrated a penchant for using the yields of nature to make money. At age eight, Siegel picked wild berries and sold them to neighbors who used the berries to make jelly. Herbs, as the means to make tea, was another matter. In Europe and elsewhere, herb tea was a commonplace and sought after product, but in the United States herb tea was perceived generally as a medicinal beverage, a foul-tasting liquid imbibed by a select few and only when health concerns arose. Siegel was instrumental in changing the image and desirability of herb tea, helping create what would become a billion-dollar industry, but not until his soon-to-be partner joined him in 1970. That year, Wyck Hay, a pivotal figure in Celestial Seasonings' early development, and Siegel discovered a massive, naturally-grown crop of wild herbs. The pair enlisted the help of their friends, their wives and girlfriends, and picked the herbs, then used screen doors to sift them and a paper cutter to chop them. In the end, the team produced 500 pounds of their first blend of teas, then sold the quantity—amounting to 10,000 tea bags—to a local health-food store called the "Grainery", labeling the product somewhat mysteriously as "Mo's 36 Herb Tea."

## Company Perspectives:

*We remain committed to making the highest-quality, most inspiring, and most soul-satisfying specialty teas and good-for-you botanical products. In pursuing this passion, we remain dedicated to building shareholder value, to developing exciting, rewarding careers for Celestial employees and to contributing to our community and environment.*

The herb tea was packaged in hand-sewn muslin bags, the most inexpensive method available to the hopeful crew of entrepreneurs. Of these early days, Siegel later said, "We were so broke, we couldn't even afford to have ties to close the bags. So we went to Ma Bell and asked if we could have its telephone scrap wire. If you have ever opened a cable of telephone wire," Siegel explained further, "you see copper wire covered with multi-colored plastic. So we would slice the cable like that and slit it open, and there would be these cute little red and pink and blue wires. We would use those to close the tops of the bags."

### Growth in the 1970s

The beginnings of Celestial Seasonings were modest, to be sure, but prospects brightened somewhat with the arrival of Wyck Hay's brother, John Hay, in 1971. The more conventionally named Hay brought with him more fundamental needs for the meager tea-making venture, most notably money and a business degree, which neither Siegel or Wyck Hay possessed. Once settled from his trip from New York to Boulder, John Hay helped his brother and Siegel relocate from an old barn located outside Boulder and establish a larger base of operations in Boulder. Quickly, the business began to take shape. From delivering its tea to a local health-food store, the trio of entrepreneurs set their sights higher, expanding throughout Colorado, New Mexico, and as far away as the East Coast. Along with geographic expansion came the assemblage of a labor pool, as the aspirant tea producers gave up on the idea of picking all the herbs themselves and began buying the herbs. Gradually, a national herbal tea company began to emerge.

The following year, in 1972, the six employees who composed the venture were elevated to corporate legitimacy when Celestial Seasonings was incorporated, taking its name from the "flowername" of Wyck Hay's girlfriend, Lucinda Ziesing. That year also witnessed the introduction of one of the company's perennial best-selling products, Red Zinger Herb Tea, a mixture of hibiscus, rosehips, and lemon that made its debut in January 1972 and would be listed among Celestial Seasonings' leading sellers nearly 30 years later.

One year after incorporating his company, Mo Siegel began traveling around the globe, canvassing the world in search of herbs for Celestial Seasonings teas. As the 1970s progressed, the company steadily grew, making the leap from distributing its products to health-food stores to distributing its products to supermarkets, a move that greatly increased the familiarity and availability of Celestial Seasonings teas. Packaged in colorful boxes decorated with charging buffalos and dancing bears, the company's teas were embraced by consumers who were seeking "soothing teas for a nervous world," as the decaffeinated teas produced by Celestial Seasonings were marketed.

From a company whose exotic herb mixtures were labeled with whimsical names, such as "Red Zinger," "Sleepytime," and "Grandma's Tummy Mint," emerged a corporate culture that was unique, carefree, and casual. Among a list of milestones published by the company that highlighted Celestial Seasonings' history were pioneer events that pointed to the relaxed corporate atmosphere pervading the company's headquarters in Boulder: the inauguration of lunchtime volleyball in 1974, then lunchtime horseshoe in 1975, and the first non-vegetarian meal served at company headquarters in 1977. Despite the nonconformity of Mo Siegel, Wyck Hay and other executives, Celestial Seasonings, a decidedly non-corporate entity, flourished during the 1970s in the corporate world it refused to embrace, becoming the defining force in the herb tea industry.

Though lunchtime volleyball and the transportation of company executives on company bicycles rather than in company cars had their place in the development of Celestial Seasonings, there were other, more conventional events that described the company's rise during the 1970s. Sales eclipsed $1 million in 1974, Celestial Transport, a freight carrier, was established in 1976, and the distribution of teas to international markets began in 1977. By the beginning of the 1980s, the company was enjoying unblemished success, firmly positioned as the leader in a market that was growing rapidly and attracting an increasingly larger customer base comprised largely of coffee drinkers seeking a more salubrious alternative to hot, caffeinated beverages. Annual sales by 1983 were quickly approaching $30 million, up exponentially from the $1 million generated a decade earlier. With business booming and ambitious expansion plans on the table, including the purchase of 91 acres of land in Boulder in 1982 for the construction of future corporate offices, Siegel and his cohorts were ready to make a signal move into the public spotlight. An initial public offering (IPO) of the company's stock was slated for 1983, but before investors had the opportunity to purchase a stake in Celestial Seasonings disaster struck the company for the first time in its history.

In 1983, a Mississippi woman who was seeking some relief from a broken hip she was nursing, brewed a particularly strong batch of Celestial Seasonings' comfrey tea. Into one mug she steeped enough tea to make 18 servings, then drank the brew and subsequently complained of nausea and blurry vision. Researchers attributed her symptoms to a natural toxin called atropine that had mysteriously found its way into Celestial Seasonings' tea, which sent company officials scurrying about to somehow mitigate the damage to Celestial Seasonings' image. "It's been the worst week of my life," Siegel confided at the time, as preparations were made to recall 6,000 cases of comfrey tea and the plans for the $12 million IPO were scrapped. The damage done to the company's standing was not permanent, however, but in the wake of the aborted IPO, a new chapter in Celestial Seasonings' history began, one that would wed the informal Celestial Seasonings to the formality of a corporate giant.

### 1984 Acquisition by Kraft, Inc.

In 1984, Kraft, Inc. maker of "Miracle Whip" and "Velveeta" and a subsidiary of Dart & Kraft Inc., was orchestrating a diversification program that included entry into the beverage business, a move that was completed when the company acquired Celestial Seasonings and added the motley mix of people and products based in Boulder to its comparatively rigid and staid operations. Mo Siegel left the company the following year, but before his departure he selected his successor, Barnet M. Feinblum, Celestial Seasonings' treasurer for the previous four years. Upon taking the reins of command from Siegel, Feinblum appraised both his new responsibilities and the acquisition that had precipitated his rise, noting, "Kraft bought the best small company in America. The only thing I intend to change is the small."

During the ensuing years under Kraft's ownership, Feinblum's word's rang true, as the largest herb tea maker in the country before the acquisition became even larger after the acquisition. During the first four years of Kraft's ownership—the entire period the two companies would be united as it turned out—Celestial Seasonings blossomed, increasing its stature while under the sponsorship of its deep-pocketed corporate parent. Celestial Seasonings' advertising budget increased tenfold in the fours years of Kraft ownership, enabling the company to advertise for the first time on national television. Annual sales swelled from under $30 million in 1984 to $45 million by 1988, while diversification and international expansion picked up pace, as Celestial Seasonings benefitted from Kraft's distribution network and expertise.

The two companies were, however, complete opposites, and it was not long before their divergent corporate attitudes butted against each other. When Kraft's management ordered Feinblum to put an end to Celestial Seasoning's long-time practice of sponsoring and participating in bicycle races, Feinblum responded by signing Greg LeMond, America's preeminent road bicycle racer, to Celestial Seasonings' racing team, a deal both the public and Kraft management first learned about at a press conference after the agreement was reached. "If I'm going to be subordinate, I'm going to do it in a big way," Feinblum later admitted, but Kraft executives answered back by implanting an undercover agent at Celestial Seasonings' factory in 1987 after receiving anonymous letters that accused Celestial Seasonings' employees of using drugs.

What appeared to be the end of the increasingly strained relationship between Kraft and Celestial Seasonings occurred in 1988 when Kraft announced its was selling Celestial Seasonings to Thomas J. Lipton, informing Feinblum of the deal the day after the agreement was signed. The proposed combination of Celestial Seasonings and Lipton paved the way for a company that would control 81 percent of the tea market once Celestial Seasonings' 50 percent market share and Lipton's 31 percent market share were combined. Aside from the overwhelming market control the merger would engender, the union of Celestial Seasonings and Lipton also made sense on numerous other levels, providing a more suitable match for Celestial Seasonings than its four-year relationship with Kraft had produced. "Lipton are tea people," one Celestial Seasonings employee noted. "Kraft, they're cheese people."

### 1988 Leveraged Buyout

The merger never occurred, however, once Connecticut-based R.C. Bigelow, the maker of Constant Comment tea, raised objections and successfully blocked the merger on antitrust grounds. Family-owned R.C. Bigelow's intervention left Celestial Seasonings still under the ownership of Kraft, but before the year was out, the ties connecting the two companies were forever severed when Feinblum and Vestar Capital Partners, a New York investment firm, took Celestial Seasonings private in November 1988 through a leveraged buyout (LBO).

The LBO saddled the newly-independent Celestial Seasonings with $45 million of debt, an enormous load that required the company to double its revenues in the next five years and increase its operating margins from 15 percent to 20 percent of sales just to service its debt. To achieve this goal, the company's management, with Feinblum still leading the way, planned to launch new products and expand its loyal customer base, but after several years a new line of attack emerged, beginning with the return of one of the company's most pivotal personalities. Mo Siegel rejoined Celestial Seasonings in 1991 as chairman and chief executive officer, gaining a reported 25 percent interest in the company in exchange for his company, Earth Wise, Inc., a manufacturer of environmentally friendly products.

One year after Siegel's return from what amounted to a six-year hiatus, Celestial Seasonings continued to reign as the leader in the U.S. herb tea market, holding onto its enviable position by controlling half of the market for herb teas. By this point, in 1992, the company was generating more than $50 million in sales a year, but the debt incurred from the 1988 LBO still hobbled its ability to perform and expand as Celestial Seasonings' officials hoped. Relief from the pernicious influence of the debt on Celestial Seasonings' operations was sought in 1993, when the company once again prepared for an IPO. This time, as opposed to exactly ten years earlier, the public offering was completed, with 1.9 million shares of the company's stock entering the market in July 1993.

Celestial Seasonings raised $31 million from the IPO, a sum that helped whittle the company's debt significantly. Following the conversion to public ownership, Celestial Seasonings embarked on the course that would carry the company through the late 1990s. As company officials looked ahead to the future, they were attempting to broaden the range of Celestial Seasonings' products and contemplating several moves that would carry the company in new directions, including the possibility of opening Celestial Seasonings retail stores, which would serve hot and iced teas and stock the company's full line of tea products. With such developments possible in the future, Celestial Seasonings and its founder Mo Siegel moved ahead toward the late 1990s, beginning the next chapter in its unique corporate history.

### Principal Subsidiaries

Tea Direct, Inc.

### *Further Reading*

Atchinson, Sandra D., ''An Herbal Tea Party Gets a Bitter Response,'' *Business Week,* June 20, 1988, p. 52.

——, ''Kraft Is Celestial Seasonings' Cup of Tea,'' *Business Week,* July 28, 1986, p. 73.

——, ''Why Celestial Seasonings Wasn't Kraft's Cup of Tea,'' *Business Week,* May 8, 1989, p. 76.

''Hitting Bottom,'' *Inc.,* March 1994, p. 36.

Locke, Tom, ''A Taste for Success: Mo Siegel Trusts His Tastebuds in Running Celestial Seasonings,'' *Denver Business Journal,* July 30, 1993, p. 3A.

——, ''Celestial Seasonings Plans Public Offering,'' *Denver Business Journal,* June 4, 1993, p. 1.

Miller, Hilary S., ''Celestial Seasonings Takes Aim at RTD Tea—Again,'' *Supermarket News,* July 24, 1995, p. 30.

Nagle, Claire, ''It's High Time for Tea Tours,'' *Colorado Business Magazine,* March 1994, p. 66.

Steers, Stuart, ''Celestial Explores Retail: Herbal Tea Firm Seeks Partner,'' *Denver Business Journal,* May 5, 1995, p. 1A.

—Jeffrey L. Covell

**CERNER**

# Cerner Corporation

**2800 Rockcreek Parkway**
**Kansas City, Missouri 64117-2551**
**U.S.A.**
**(816) 221-1024**
**Fax: (816) 474-1742**

*Public Company*
*Incorporated:* 1980
*Employees:* 1,300
*Sales:* $186.9 million (1995)
*Stock Exchanges:* NASDAQ
*SICs:* 7375 Information Retrieval Services; 7371
  Computer Programming Services

Cerner Corporation is a leading supplier of information systems for the health care industry. Cerner designs, installs, and supports applications developed around a single architecture, called Health Network Architecture (HNA), which allows clinics, hospitals, HMOs, physicians, and integrated health organizations (IHOs) to share clinical and management data across multiple disciplines and facilities. Cerner's 12 major system applications, which are supported by more than 200 component applications, operate on the single HNA platform. This allows Cerner clients to purchase the entire HNA system, or to choose among the individual applications, adding applications as needed, while achieving a seamless flow of information across applications. These applications fit into four interrelated groups: clinical management, care management, repositories, and knowledge systems. With its products, Cerner has led the health care industry away from finance-driven information systems to a patient-centered system more appropriate for an increasingly integrated industry focused on managed care and cost-effective services. In addition to developing its own products, Cerner has forged several alliances to share technology and marketing activities with other companies. Cerner's goal is to automate the entire health management process, creating paperless patient records that the company calls the Electronic Medical Record (EMR), which can be accessed and shared by the full spectrum of medical and health professionals, as well as by the patient.

Cerner supports its products with eight regional offices in the United States and branch offices in Australia, Germany, Saudi Arabia, and England, providing technical and sales assistance to more than 1,330 client sites. Of these clients, more than 30 have implemented the full HNA system, and over 100 have linked multiple Cerner applications. As of the mid-1990s, Cerner's growth has come primarily from clients purchasing multiple applications. The majority of Cerner's clients are located in the United States; international growth is hampered somewhat by the need to translate its products into other languages, and international sales have been limited largely to countries with health care systems based on the U.S. and British models. Sales of Cerner applications, together with revenues from continued application support and add-on purchases, combined for $187 million, with a net profit of $22.5 million, in 1995. Cerner is led by chairman and CEO Neal Patterson, and president and COO Clifford Illig.

## The Beginnings

In 1979, Neal Patterson, Clifford Illig, and Paul Gorup left the management information systems consulting division of Arthur Anderson's Kansas City office to found Cerner as a developer of laboratory information systems. Cerner was incorporated in 1980, as the company worked to perfect its first product.

By 1984, Cerner was ready to roll out its first application, the PathNet laboratory information system. PathNet provided a comprehensive information system for laboratory clinicians, allowing laboratories to automate their processes. PathNet, which grew to combine applications for general laboratory information, microbiology, blood bank transfusion and blood bank donation, and anatomic pathology, broke away not only from the traditional paper-based sharing of information, but also from the prevailing financial focus of data gathering systems.

PathNet proved an early success. First year revenues were just under $2 million, with a net loss of $1.5 million. However, by the following year, Cerner turned a profit on $10.3 million in sales and was already establishing itself as a leading provider of laboratory information systems. By 1986 PathNet became the

## Company Perspectives:

*Cerner understands the challenges facing today's health systems to provide high quality care in a more efficient and effective manner. It is our belief that the key to success for the future of healthcare is the strategic use of an intrarelated information system. We provide our clients with the necessary technology to realize benefits today, and to achieve success in the health environment of tomorrow. At Cerner, we do not react to the past. Instead, we are helping to create the future.*

market leader, with more than 30 client site placements generating $17.5 million in revenues for a $2.3 million net profit. In that year, Patterson and Illig took Cerner public, offering one million shares at $16 per share.

Through the end of the decade, PathNet remained Cerner's primary source of revenue, but by 1985 the company had already begun to define what would become its Health Network Architecture. Cerner's goal was to automate the health care process, focusing the various aspects of the health care process—from registration to clinical care to pharmacy services to outcomes measurement—around the individual patient. By providing access across the continuum of a patient's care, the HNA system would achieve higher quality care, from prevention to treatment, as well as improved cost-effectiveness. Unlike paper-based medical charts, the medical records of a patient within Cerner's automated system could be made instantly available to each member of a health care network, including laboratory clinicians, nurses, general physicians, and such specialists as radiologists and surgeons, while also providing resources for patient input and information.

Cerner's vision of an HNA-based system would allow total management of a patient's care, including alerts and reminders to the patient of scheduled checkups, information to providers on patient clinical history, medication allergies, and the like, and a means to provide routine and emergency care based on information uploaded by the patient. In this, Cerner anticipated the changing focus of the health care system, from a fee-for-service system, to the largely managed care-based system of the 1990s. Equally, Cerner's vision anticipated the mid-1990s trend toward integration that would sweep the health care system, as more and more hospitals, clinics, and other providers moved toward providing vertically integrated, complete health care services.

Cerner's client base grew steadily in the late 1980s, reaching 70 sites in 1987, 120 sites in 1988, 170 sites in 1989, and reaching 250 sites in 1990. Installations were primarily of PathNet systems, and sales of systems made up the bulk of Cerner's revenues, which topped $57 million in 1990. However, recurring revenues, especially from support services and also from add-on applications sales, began to form an increasing share of Cerner's annual sales. Meanwhile, research and development spending grew from $4.2 million in 1987 to $10 million in 1990.

Cerner's R&D efforts began to show results as early as 1987, when it introduced two more components of its future HNA system: MedNet and Discern. MedNet joined PathNet in the clinical management family of Cerner products, offering support for pulmonary medicine, respiratory care, and other internal medicine departments. Discern formed the basis of Cerner's knowledge systems applications, offering retrospective and prospective databases and services that enabled providers to monitor patient care regimens and institute treatment and preventive protocols.

In 1988, Cerner added the next component of its clinical management systems, RadNet, which focused on automating radiology department functions. The following year, pharmacy support was added with the PharmNet application. As with PathNet, each new component was based on the same application architecture, allowing applications to be seamlessly combined to share information across applications.

The flexibility of Cerner's HNA set it apart from its competitors as well. Through the 1980s and into the 1990s, hospitals, clinics, and their various departments typically purchased "best of breed" applications, that is, individual products from many different vendors. As more and more hospitals and their departments began to forge the health care networks that slowly came to dominate the health care industry in the 1990s, they were faced with the task of forcing integration of their disparate information systems and products. This created not only confusion within each system but also the need to maintain costly support personnel to integrate the systems and maintain their functionality. By basing their applications around a single architecture, Cerner demonstrated a marked advantage for functionality as well as cost-effective operation.

### Into the 1990s

By 1990, more than 200 PathNet sites had been installed, solidifying Cerner's position as the leading maker of laboratory information systems. Cerner next moved to expand its product family beyond clinical management systems and into care management systems, with the introduction of its ProNet and CareNet products. ProNet provided automated support for patient management and registration, ordering, scheduling, and tracking processes. CareNet gave patient care planning, management, and measurement tools to nurses and other direct care providers. Care management was meant to play a central role in gathering information needed for the care process. With Cerner's care management tools, providers could more easily manage the many pieces of patient information, including demographic and financial data, health status, operations data such as treatment procedures and protocols, while linking this information to ordering, tracking, scheduling, and patient, case, and health records management.

By the end of 1991, Cerner's client base had expanded to 320 sites, producing revenues over $77 million and net earnings of $4.7 million. These sales still centered primarily around PathNet. Yet in 1991, Cerner moved closer to its goal of creating the paperless patient medical record with the acquisition of Intellimetrics Instrument Corporation of Massachusetts, and with the launch of its repository product line with the introduction of its Open Clinical Foundation (OCF). The OCF was an enterprisewide, relational database with multimedia capabilities, which captured the information generated by the various clinical and core systems to form a computer-based patient record, while also supporting data extraction capabilities for medical and outcomes research.

In 1991, Cerner also established its first international subsidiaries, in Australia and in the United Kingdom, marking the first implementation of its international strategy. In England, it took over service of PathNet systems originally installed in fifteen hospitals through a licensing agreement with McDonnell Douglas Information Systems. In Australia, agreement had been reached to install PathNet in the New South Wales Health System. With client sites already operating in Canada and Singapore, Cerner reached an agreement to install PathNet at the Riyadh Armed Forces Hospital in Saudi Arabia. International sales grew to $9 million by the end of 1991. By 1993, Cerner had established the first of its two German offices as well.

By the end of 1993, Cerner had completed the largest part of its product family, with the 1992 introduction of its SurgiNet and Open Management Foundation (OMF) products, and the 1993 introduction of its MRNet product. SurgiNet, part of Cerner's clinical management product line, offered information management support for operating room teams. OMF extended Cerner's repository line with tools for supporting management analysis and decision-making based on process-related information. MRNet functioned to link the OCF and OMF products in automating the chart management process for the medical records department. By 1993, Cerner's repository and care management products had begun to make significant contributions to the company's $120 million in revenues. Net earnings for 1993 reached $14.6 million.

In November 1993, Cerner acquired Megasource, Inc. in a stock-swap merger valued at approximately $6.7 million, creating the company's wholly owned Cerner Megasource Inc. subsidiary. The Megasource merger added an additional product to Cerner's clinical management group, MSMEDS, which added information management capabilities to pharmacy operations. This merger was significant in that roughly 80 percent of all physician orders, both in inpatient and outpatient areas, went for either laboratory or pharmacy services. With Megasource, Cerner filled out a significant presence in both services. During 1993, also, Cerner moved to expand its client support services, opening regional offices in Atlanta, Boston, Dallas, Kansas City, Los Angeles, and Washington, D.C., while providing 24-hour emergency support at its Kansas City headquarters.

### Forging Alliances in the 1990s

Strategic alliances had formed a part of Cerner's growth since the early 1990s. By 1991, Cerner had participated in a joint venture with Sony Corporation's medical electronics division to develop the Cerner Pathology PACS Workstation, which integrated Sony's color video capabilities with Cerner information technology. A second collaboration was formed with Beckman Instruments Inc. to introduce PathTrac, which

coupled parts of PathNet with Beckman's chemistry analyzer. A third alliance, with APACHE Medical Systems, Inc., gave PathNet, ProNet, and CareNet capabilities through APACHE workstations.

In 1994 Cerner extended its alliance strategy with the formation of the Cerner Alliance Program. Initial partners were SDK Health Care Information Systems of Boston, MEDIC Computer Systems of Raleigh, North Carolina, and Amisys Managed Care Information Systems of Rockville, Maryland. With these alliances, Cerner moved to add administrative and financial functions, based on HNA, that fell outside of its own development efforts. In addition to collaborating on engineering, the alliances also profited from some shared marketing activities.

By year-end 1994, more than 30 clients had contracted with Cerner for the broad implementation of the complete HNA system, including five contracts in the fourth quarter alone; another 100 clients had purchased multiple system components. The company rolled out support for the IBM RISC System/6000 processor and announced support for Microsoft's Windows interface. Revenues reached $156 million, and net earnings grew to $19.5 million, representing increases from 1990 of 217 percent and 686 percent, respectively. An important component of Cerner's success had been its aggressive R&D spending—more than $80 million in the first half of the 1990s, with plans to spend another $200 million by the year 2000.

In the mid-1990s, the trend toward consolidation and integration throughout the health care industry was evident. Increasing numbers of hospitals, clinics, physicians, and other providers were joining forces to create integrated health care organizations (IHOs). This trend would see a drop in the numbers of individual purchasers of information systems. Yet, the creation of large, regional health care systems would drive a resurgence in the need for automated information systems, with purchases of products and services expected to rise from $8.5 billion in 1995 to $13 billion by 1997. Cerner, with a mature product line centered around HNA raising $189.6 million in 1995 revenues, was positioned to continue its market leadership.

### Principal Subsidiaries

Cerner Megasource, Inc.; Cerner Corporation Pty., Ltd. (Australia); Cerner Deutschland GmbH (Germany); Cerner Arabia Co. Ltd. (Saudi Arabia); Cerner Limited (U.K.).

### Further Reading

*Electronic Medical Record: Supporting Lifetime Health Management.* Kansas City, Mo.: Cerner Corporation, 1995.
*Intrarelation: Characterizing Cerner's Health Network Architecture.* Kansas City, Mo.: Cerner Corporation, 1995.
Meyer, Gene, "Diagnoses on Cerner: More Growth Ahead," *Kansas City Star,* September 26, 1995, p. E20.
Tierney, Mary C., "Cerner Corporation," *Business Digest,* March 1996, p. 24.

—M. L. Cohen

# Checkers Drive-Up Restaurants Inc.

**600 Cleveland Street, Suite #1050**
**Clearwater, Florida 34615**
**U.S.A.**
**(813) 441-3500**
**Fax: (813) 443-7047**

*Public Company*
*Incorporated:* 1986
*Employees:* 8,000 (1995)
*Sales:* $200.9 million (1994)
*Stock Exchanges:* NASDAQ
*SICs:* 5812 Eating Places; 6794 Patent Owners & Lessors

With its distinctive black and white checkerboard squares surrounded by bright red and chrome, Checkers Drive-Up Restaurants Inc. took the fast food hamburger market by storm in the early 1990s. Quickly building hundreds of unique, vibrantly colored modular restaurants throughout the southeastern United States, Checkers' high volume double drive-through windows and low overhead allowed it to dominate the burger market, shocking the complacent Big Four (McDonald's, Burger King, Wendy's and Hardee's) and smaller regional hamburger chains. Checkers offered a simple menu with low-priced burgers and combination meals, and by 1993 the entire fast food industry was engaged in a ferocious price war with many fatalities. The consumer was the clear winner as burger chains and other fast food franchises opted to offer their own versions of "value"-priced items. Though 1994 and 1995 brought a slowdown and losses for Checkers and most of its double drive-through competitors, Checkers retrenched and continued to stake its claim in the ever-volatile burger industry.

### Birth of "The Champ," 1986–1988

Alabama native James E. Mattei, a successful real estate developer credited with renovating parts of downtown Mobile in the early 1980s to the tune of over $60 million, dabbled in the restaurant industry by building a few Wendy's franchises. When the restaurants didn't perform, Mattei ended up owning them and found that not only was half of the franchise's business from the drive-through window but the menu's most popular items were burger combination meals. To Mattei, the dining room, large parking lot, and extensive menu were an unnecessary drain on the restaurant. So why couldn't a pared down burger joint with an emphasis on faster service and a simple menu thrive where more cumbersome chains didn't? "That's how I ended up in this Checkers business," Mattei later told *Florida Trend* magazine in 1992.

Mattei, along with another real estate developer named Mark B. Reed, researched the hamburger market and culled ideas from several local and national chains. Six months before their first restaurant opened, a competitor named Rollo's debuted with drive-through windows on each side of a small, portable modular building in Mobile. The first Checkers (purportedly named after the ever-present Checker cabs) opened in April 1986 as a back-to-the-basics hamburger hut housed in a prefabricated modular building with no dining room or parking lot, but with two drive-throughs. Within months, Mattei and Reed opened three more Checkers, but their enthusiasm couldn't put the new chain into the black. When losses approached $20,000 per month, Mattei started looking for an additional partner. In 1987, he found Herbert G. Brown, a Florida businessman who developed shopping centers, mobile home parks, and a drug store chain he sold to Jack Eckerd back in 1970. Brown had also been chairman of his own furniture business for nearly 40 years.

When Brown came on board, Reed faded into the background. Mattei sold half of Checkers to Brown, and the two expanded into Tampa, Florida. Next came nearby Clearwater, a sort of last ditch effort, since Checkers was still losing money. Remarkably, the Clearwater restaurant raked in $70,000 in its first month and $100,000 in its second. The new Checkers location and a heavily touted grand opening helped put the company on the map. Mattei and Brown also improved their product, eschewing the segment leaders' premade sandwiches for made-to-order burgers. Checkers offered a sparse menu, good food, and fast service, advertised at 30 seconds or less. The chain's signature sandwich became the "Champ" burger, a fully dressed made-to-order quarter-pound of 100 percent ground beef for only 99 cents every day—this at a time when

---

similar sandwiches at McDonald's and Burger King went for double Checkers' price or more. The average ticket was $3.40, and with two drive-throughs, twice the number of customers were served in half the time.

### The Checkers Way, 1989–1991

Checkers was different from its competitors in several key aspects in addition to its shiny 1950s art deco-styled buildings and uniquely seasoned french fries. First, every restaurant began with a prefabricated 700-square-foot, 70,000-lb. modular unit produced by Champion Modular Restaurant Company, Inc. (a wholly owned subsidiary of the company bought in bankruptcy court for $650,000), which was then transported by truck directly to the new location. The slender modular units were cheaper to produce (selling for $230,000 to franchisees), could be relocated or recycled if necessary, were up and running in under three weeks rather than months, cut down on real estate costs, and Checkers was assured of quality and consistency as each unit was identical and came complete with all equipment (appliances, fixtures, grills, and computerized sales systems) and supplies. Start-up costs for a new Checkers restaurant, less land and franchise fees (which ran around $25,000), averaged less than $440,000.

Second, Checkers installed two drive-throughs as well as a walk-up window and small patio with tables to seat about 40 at each restaurant. Customers received their food more quickly, and the added expense of a large dining room and parking lot were eliminated. Third, Checkers concentrated on a limited menu of sandwiches (burgers as well as fish and chicken sandwiches), seasoned fries, soft drinks, and milk shakes which employees quickly learned to prepare. Prices were low, preparation was easy, and Checkers maintained its brief delivery time of 30 seconds or less to consumers.

By 1989 Checkers had doubled its size from 1988 and the partners (with Mattei as CEO and Brown as chairman) ruled over an ever-growing enterprise, finishing the year with total revenues of over $8.7 million and net earnings of $71,000. The next year Checkers was still going strong but the competition was heating up with its closest competitor, the Louisville, Kentucky-based Rally's franchise. Rally's was the double drive-through segment leader yet fell on hard times in 1990, giving Checkers an opportunity to surge in the market. In December, however, Taco Bell purchased a 77-unit burger chain called Hot 'n Now to join the double drive-through fray. Hot 'n Now's calling card was a burger combo meal (burger, fries and medium drink) for only $1.17, and though the bottom-of-the-barrel pricing attracted notice, neither Checkers nor Rally's paid much attention to the upstart despite the formidable clout of Taco

Bell's parent company, PepsiCo. Checkers ended 1990 with overall revenues of $25.3 million and net earnings over $1.5 million just as Rally's, under new management, readied for a comeback.

As Checkers gained prominence and drew customers away from other burger chains, analysts declared its formula a winner. Not only did Checkers save money with the Clearwater-based Champion producing its restaurant units, but cleared 10 percent or more for every modular restaurant sold to franchisees as well. Capable of producing over two dozen 14-by-28 foot buildings per month or 300-plus per year, Champion's sales brought in over $10 million or 24 percent of Checkers' overall revenue in 1991, and $1.4 million in earnings. On November 15, 1991 Checkers went public (under the ticker symbol CHKR) with shares priced at $16 each on a day when the Dow Jones fell 124 points. Nevertheless, Checkers' stock rose by 50 percent to $24.25 per share by the time the market closed, and the company realized proceeds of some $26 million. By the end of the year, Checkers had 119 restaurants (Rally's had 300), and total revenue climbed to $50.5 million with net earnings of $4 million. Despite the hoopla, a red flag was waving, as same-store sales had declined from $914,000 in 1990 to $894,000 in 1991, a little-noticed sign of trouble.

### The Big Four Fight Back, 1992–93

In February 1992, Checkers promoted its first combo meal (Champ burger, small fries, and medium drink) for $2.29, followed by a chicken sandwich combo for $2.99—both a healthy 15 percent lower than most competitors' combinations. Margins improved in the first quarter, with even same-store sales rising 9.5 percent (helped by a four-point fall in food costs and the new combos), and Checkers moved full-steam ahead with expansion. Eight new restaurants opened by the end of March alone, and 32 more were slated for the rest of the year. In May, Checkers returned to Wall Street for a second stock offering, raising $36 million for additional growth. Amid a flurry of expansion, Checkers (which now had over 161 units) announced in July that it expected to bring its South Florida units from 15 to 50 by year-end. By concentrating in an already established market, Checkers hoped to keep marketing and operational costs to a minimum. Yet the downside of clustering was saturation, and when coupled with stiff competition from the Big Four and Rally's produced a considerable risk. Next came plans to build a second Champion manufacturing facility in Kentucky, Indiana, or Ohio to slash transportation costs and increase modular unit production.

The company opened 106 new units in 1992 bringing the total number of Checkers to 225, or exactly half those of Rally's. In another competitive move, Rally's followed Checkers' lead and bought a modular restaurant producer, Beaman Inc., in North Carolina. Though Rally's was still the segment leader, in areas where Checkers penetrated the market first like Tampa and Orlando, Florida, and Mobile, Alabama, Checkers drove Rally's under in a relatively short time. Unfortunately, the reverse was true in areas heavily populated by Rally's, like New Orleans, where Checkers' units floundered. On average each Checkers restaurant systemwide brought in roughly $919,000 in 1992, which helped raise total revenues to just over $105.1 million and net earnings to $12.3 million for the year.

By 1993 the fast food hamburger market reached $25 billion or just over 31 percent of the total U.S. fast food market of $80 billion. The Big Four's restaurants numbered 25,000 across the country to a mere 1,200 double drive-throughs units nationwide. While the Big Four had already lowered prices to compete with Checkers and Rally's, McDonald's and Burger King were also testing back-to-basics hamburger shops with double drive-throughs—the former with McDonald's Express and the latter with B.K. ExpressWay. Checkers' expansion continued with 181 new units, predominantly in the southeastern portion of the United States (as far west as Texas and easterly up to Pennsylvania), along with several developing markets in the Midwest. "Our first plan was to become a regional presence, then a national chain and in time, an international force," Brown told the *Tampa Bay Business Journal* in May. The company had certainly accomplished the regional presence and was well on its way to becoming a nationally known outfit.

By the third quarter of 1993, Checkers' revenues increased by 81 percent to $49 million and net earnings were strong at $4.1 million, a leap of 32 percent from the same period in 1992. Yet same-store sales dropped 5.3 percent systemwide from slower traffic and competition from both its own stores and others. Undeterred, Checkers continued to expand in Florida and elsewhere, including the InnerCity Foods Joint Venture Company (75 percent Checkers) with former Chicagoan La-Van Hawkins. Hawkins, who had previously owned 13 Checkers in Philadelphia and Atlanta, had recently sold them back to the company for $13 million in stock. The new joint venture began again in Philadelphia and Atlanta, with 11 Checkers restaurants in economically-depressed communities. The new stores provided 700 jobs while taking advantage of a largely untapped market. InnerCity and Checkers had plans to open as many as 35 additional units before the end of 1994.

Checkers also worked on an extensive advertising campaign to offset the gains of Burger King, McDonald's, and Wendy's, who reported strong sales from value-priced sandwiches and combo meals. Since Checkers had doubled its size annually for four straight years, all proceeds from the first and second stock offerings were depleted. Management considered a third offering, but decided instead to seek financing and utilize an existing credit line. At year-end, Checkers had opened 181 new stores for a total of 404 (227 company-operated and 177 franchised) in 20 states, including 163 restaurants located in Florida. While overall revenue for 1993 topped $189.5 million with net earnings of $15 million, the warning flags were again unfurled as the fourth quarter figures brought another decrease in same-store sales, this time to 10 percent systemwide.

### The New Era, 1994–1996

The dawn of 1994 found Checkers and its two chief competitors (Rally's and Hot 'n Now) faced with sagging sales, the triumph of the Big Four's value-pricing, and the successful emergence of several smaller regional burger chains. Faced with a declining and saturated marketplace, Rally's and Checkers struck a $2 million deal to eliminate direct competition by granting one another exclusive dominions in some

Southern cities. Checkers bought nine Rally's in Atlanta and another nine in Miami; Rally's took over 18 Checkers units in Memphis, Raleigh, North Carolina, and Columbia, South Carolina, and three other areas. Hot 'n Now, however, no longer seemed a threat since Taco Bell "temporarily" closed some 40 restaurants in March. Also in March came the retirement of president and CEO Mattei, who was replaced by James F. White, Jr. as vice chairman and CEO. In August, Richard C. Postle, formerly of Kentucky Fried Chicken and Wendy's, joined Checkers as president and COO along with several second tier managers to help guide the company through its increasing difficulties. Brown, White, and Postle hoped to get through the transition by reducing operational costs, introducing new products, and concentrating on existing core markets.

At the end of the year, despite plans to open as many as 200 additional restaurants, the cost of too-rapid expansion and over-clustering caught up with Checkers. Faced with lawsuits by disgruntled shareholders over accounting practices, and another from franchisees who said the company blocked their plans to offer their own stock, Checkers reported revenues of $221 million and a net loss of $6.7 million, with same-store sales falling 14 percent systemwide. Segment leader Rally's suffered further losses in both 1993 ($10.1 million) and 1994 ($19.3 million). Yet a slight turnaround for Checkers had already begun with the continued success of the InnerCity Joint Venture with La-Van Hawkins and the introduction of the Monster Value Menu (featuring a myriad of food items for 99 cents), kids' meals, and a honey-grilled chicken sandwich. Rally's also tried something new, a third-pound burger called the Big Buford, and hoped the large sandwich's debut would help pull the company out of the red.

By January 1995 there were 496 Checkers restaurants (261 company-owned and operated and 235 franchises) in 23 states and the District of Columbia. Rumors swirled that the company might merge with former foe Rally's (whose stores numbered 526), seen as a natural progression by some considering both double drive-through chains still suffered same-store slumps and heightened competition from the Big Four. Instead, both chains turned to Mexican food: Rally's unveiled a cobranding marketing ploy with Green Burrito while Checkers experimented with L.A. Mex, its own in-house variety of Mexican fare. Priced from 99 cents to $2.99, L.A. Mex sold burritos, fajitas, nachos, tacos, and grilled chicken salads alongside its standard sandwiches and fries. The first Checkers/L.A. Mex prototype opened in July 1995 and immediately produced a double-digit sales increase at the location. Another 50 combination restaurants in the Tampa, St. Petersburg, and Sarasota (Florida) markets were planned by the end of January 1996. Additionally, Checkers started negotiating with another fast food chain (with a strong breakfast presence) about sharing space and menu items.

Mid-year Checkers again shuffled its top executives when Rick Postle departed and was replaced by Albert J. DiMarco as CEO. Rumors reported that White, too, was stepping down as vice chairman. While little was constant in the fast food industry, Checkers' continuing survival was contingent on a few key factors: to stop cannibalization of its own markets and proceed carefully with expansion plans; to maintain its identity amid so many competitors; and to keep making and selling what Brown deemed the "best burger" in the marketplace—the award-winning, fully dressed Champ Burger.

### Principal Subsidiaries

Champion Modular Restaurant Company, Inc.; InnerCity Foods Joint Venture Company.

### Further Reading

"Checkers Drive-in Restaurants," *Barron's,* November 9, 1992, pp. 35–36.

De Lisser, Eleena, "Fast-Food Drive-Throughs Lose Speed," *Wall Street Journal,* October 27, 1994, pp. 1B, 7B.

Green-Bishop, Joseph, "Minority Business: Special Report," *Baltimore·Business Journal,* September 16–22, 1994, pp. 29–30, 35.

Hagy, James R., "After Fast Growth, What's the Next Move?," *Florida Trend,* November 1992, pp. 40–45.

Hayes, Jack, "Drive-Thru Concepts Fight Back in Burger Price War," *Nation's Restaurant News,* April 3, 1995, pp. 1, 94.

Howard, Theresa, "Big 3 Shift Gears to Stay on Course," *Nation's Restaurant News,* April 11, 1994, pp. 1, 37, 40, 42.

——, "Checkers 3rd-Q Net Jumps While Same-Store Sales Drop," *Nation's Restaurant News,* November 8, 1993, pp. 14, 101.

"In the Shop," *Restaurant Business,* October 10, 1995, pp. 70–76.

Liddle, Alan, "Checkers Sees 1st Q Jump in Operating Income," *Nation's Restaurant News,* April 27, 1992, p. 14.

Mullins, Betsy, "Fast-Moving Checkers Builds South Florida Base," *South Florida Business Journal,* July 6, 1992, pp. 1, 20.

Ossorio, Sonia, "Prefabs Help Grease Burger Bottom Line," *Orlando Business Journal,* June 12, 1992, pp. 1, 38.

——, "Checkers vs. Rally's for No. 1," *Tampa Bay Business Journal,* April 30, 1993, pp. 1, 12–13.

Smith, Katherine Snow, "Checkers' Newest Market: The Nation's Inner Cities," *Tampa Bay Business,* January 21, 1994, pp. 1, 12.

——, "Welcome to 99-Cent Land" and "Checkers' Midwest Modular Site to Save Money, Fuel Growth," *Tampa Bay Business,* September 3, 1993, pp. 1, 36, 37.

—Taryn Benbow-Pfalzgraf

# Chemi-Trol Chemical Co.

**2776 County Road 69**
**Gibsonburg, Ohio 43431**
**U.S.A.**
**(419) 665-2367**
**Fax: (419) 334-5285**

*Public Company*
*Incorporated:* 1952
*Employees:* 284 full-time, 117 seasonal
*Sales:* $71.05 million (1995)
*Stock Exchanges:* NASDAQ
*SICs:* 3443 Fabricated Plate Work (Boiler Shops); 3423
   Hand & Edge Tools, Not Elsewhere Classified; 7389
   Business Services, Not Elsewhere Classified; 5191
   Farm Supplies; 5083 Farm & Garden Machinery;
   3546 Power-Driven Handtools; 1721 Painting & Paper
   Hanging

Headquartered in a small, northwest Ohio community of 2,500 people, Chemi-Trol Chemical Co. is one of America's biggest providers of pavement marking services, with operations in Ohio, Indiana, Michigan, and Kentucky. This diversified manufacturer, distributor, and service company is organized into four divisions. The Chemical Group is the historic core of the business, contributing about 20 percent of annual sales. It makes and operates herbicide spraying equipment used to control weeds along roadsides. By the mid-1990s, the business had diversified and grown to the point that the Tank Division, which produces liquid propane gas storage tanks, was Chemi-Trol's primary revenue generator. Chemi-Trol's Cal-Van Tools Division manufactures and distributes specialty automotive tools, and it contributed 22 percent of yearly turnover. The firm's fourth and smallest division, Cory Orchard and Turf, supplies pesticides and herbicides to golf courses and orchards. It generated less than 10 percent of Chemi-Trol's annual sales in the mid-1990s. Chemi-Trol has enjoyed a consistent succession of management, having had only three chief executives over the course of its four-decade history.

## Postwar Genesis

Chemi-Trol was founded by Fred W. Karlovetz, a busy northwest Ohio farmer. When he was not working his fields or managing the farm, Karlovetz supplemented his cash flow with a night job at a local sugar beet processing plant. He also operated a home-based agricultural chemical sales business called Commercial Chemical Company. In the summers the ingenious entrepreneur mixed whitewash with insecticide, then traveled the area selling the combined service to his fellow farmers.

Karlovetz's home-based chemical business dealt primarily in products from Dow Chemical Company, and Dow's 2-4D herbicide was the catalyst that brought Chemi-Trol to life. Merging his spraying business with his chemical sales operation, the inventive farmer started using Dow's new product to eradicate the poison ivy that had overtaken many local roadsides. Karlovetz soon began offering his services to local government officials, who found that the herbicides were cheaper and more efficient than mowing. It was not long before Karlovetz's brother-in-law, Clyde Claypool, bought his own equipment and undertook spraying as a supplementary occupation.

In 1952, Karlovetz invited a business associate, Arthur Doust, to join him and his brother-in-law in the incorporation of Chemi-Trol. Doust, who had a degree in agricultural chemistry and horticulture from Ohio State University, left his job as a sales representative with Dow Chemical Company to take a chance on the new venture. Karlovetz, Claypool, and Doust, along with local banker William J. Dudley, formed the core of Chemi-Trol's first three decades of management.

With the mechanical expertise of a resourceful neighbor, Dale Zimmerman, Chemi-Trol began building the specialized tanks and sprayers used to apply herbicide along local roadways. Operating from Karlovetz's barn (which continued to be part of Chemi-Trol's headquarters complex through the early 1990s), they sold equipment, chemicals, and services to county commissioners throughout northwest Ohio. Before the end of the 1950s, these fledgling executives convinced the state of Ohio's chief landscape architect, as well as other government road and highway officials, that spraying roadsides with weed killer was more economical than mowing.

Chemi-Trol also diversified into edgeline pavement marking during the 1950s. Before 1956, only New Jersey had a policy of painting edgelines on its paved roads. When Ohio's governor contracted for 5,000 miles of highway edgelines that year, Chemi-Trol seized the opportunity to adapt its herbicide sprayers to apply paint. The company's unique expertise won it several lucrative contracts and helped fuel a dramatic expansion of Chemi-Trol's work force. It proved a well-timed diversification: the company's growth mirrored that of the new highways that began to crisscross the state with the support of the 1956 federal interstate highway construction act. The little northwest Ohio business's sales grew quickly in these early years, surpassing $1 million in 1958 and $2 million by 1961.

### Growth Through Acquisition and Diversification in the 1960s and 1970s

As Chemi-Trol matured from a sideline into a full-fledged business, several of its core functions were reorganized into individual divisions. The Chemical Group merged pavement marking and vegetation management (the Contracting Division) with sales of herbicides and chemical delivery systems (the CADCO division, established 1987). As pavement marking technology evolved in the 1970s, Chemi-Trol expanded into thermoplastic markers and traffic engineering. By the end of that decade, Chemi-Trol trucks could be spotted treating weeds and marking roads throughout the Midwest. Although this aspect of the business grew vigorously, it was seasonal, with activity focused almost exclusively from April to November. Chemi-Trol needed other business interests to even out its cyclical cash flow.

Chemi-Trol's manufacture of its own equipment spawned two separate business segments: the Cal-Van Tools Division and the Tanks Division. In 1963, the company acquired Electronic Tool Company (ETCO), a New York firm that made specialty hand tools for the automotive aftermarket. Over the next few years, Chemi-Trol acquired and merged six other toolmakers into this division. In 1964, Cal-Van expanded into the production of bronze grave markers for military veterans. Renamed Cal-Van Tools in 1966, this business segment was later relocated to a small town in northwest Ohio, where it distributed other manufacturers' equipment as well. By the late 1970s, Cal-Van brand tools were distributed worldwide.

The Tank Division likely evolved from Chemi-Trol's manufacture of its own specialty vessels for its mobile herbicide sprayers. Corporate lore recounts that it originated in the mid-1950s, when Fred Karlovetz discovered that his own home's propane tank had traveled all the way from Oklahoma. In 1957, Chemi-Trol acquired an abandoned steel fabrication plant in northwest Ohio and adapted it for production of "steel pressure tanks," most of which are used for above-ground and underground storage of liquefied petroleum gas. Used primarily for rural residential heating systems, the tanks range in size from 124 gallon capacity to nearly 2,000 gallon capacity. In 1978, the company formalized a previously sporadic tank financing program as its Leasing and Finance Division. Within five years, about 20 percent of Chemi-Trol's tank customers took advan-

tage of one or the other of these payment plans. By the early 1990s, the Tank Division was Chemi-Trol's largest, contributing 45 percent to 50 percent of annual sales.

Chemi-Trol rounded out its roster of divisions with the 1966 acquisition of Indiana's Cory Orchard and Turf, a full-line distributor of tools, equipment, and chemicals used by fruit and nut growers. This division expanded into Kentucky in 1984 and branched out into golf course turf maintenance in 1990.

Karlovetz supervised the day-to-day operations at Chemi-Trol from 1952 until 1969, when he advanced to the honorary position of chairman and chief executive officer. By the time he went into semiretirement, Karlovetz's little service company had more than $5 million in sales.

Arthur Doust succeeded his friend as president that year. Chemi-Trol enjoyed its most energetic period of growth during the early years of his term in office. Sales quadrupled from about $5 million in 1968 to more than $20 million in 1976, the year that Chemi-Trol acquired the Karlovetz farm. By the time it celebrated its 25th anniversary in 1977, the company claimed to be "the largest contract applicator of pavement marking and vegetation control in the United States," with 42 roadside sprayers and 10 stripe-painting trucks. Doust also oversaw the publication of Chemi-Trol's first formal annual report and the creation of an employee stock option plan in the 1980s.

Revenues increased 38 percent from $27.6 million in 1980 to $38.8 million in 1985. Net income declined during the early 1980s recession, then rebounded for a net increase of 15 percent, to $1.2 million, during that same period.

### Management Shakeup in the Mid-1980s

The 1985 death of company founder Fred Karlovetz alerted management to the aging of its top leaders and was one impetus behind a fairly comprehensive "changing of the guard" in the latter years of the decade. In 1987, the leaders of the Tank, Cory Orchard Supply, and Cal-Van Tools divisions all retired, either fully or partially, to be replaced by a new generation of managers. Arthur Doust also turned over direction of the business to Robert W. Woolf at the end of that year, advancing to chairman and CEO. Former Vice-President Woolf was a 15-year veteran of Chemi-Trol's corporate office. Doust continued to work daily into the 1990s and was honored for his dedication with the 1991 Northwest Ohio Entrepreneur of the Year award for manufacturing.

The management shakeup, not to mention a health economy, helped boost Chemi-Trol's sales and profitability in the late 1980s. Sales increased 65 percent, from $38.8 million in 1985 to $64 million in 1990, and net income nearly doubled to its highest level ever, $2.4 million.

Chemi-Trol's management took great pride in its employee perks, which included recreational facilities (a swimming pool and tennis court) and an employee stock option plan that totaled $10 million by the early 1990s.

## The 1990s and Beyond

Although Chemi-Trol's productivity rose appreciably in the early 1990s, other issues affected the bottom line. The number of employees (weighted to account for seasonal workers) per $1 million in sales was driven down from 6.1 in 1991 to 5.4 in 1995. During the same period, revenues slid 13 percent from 1990 to 1991, then rose to a historic high of $71 million by 1995. By contrast, profitability was rather anemic, sliding to a low of $897,000 in 1993 before rising to $1.5 million in 1994. Chemi-Trol blamed its uneven performance on heavy price competition, rising raw materials prices, and high capital investments in plant, automation, and marketing. Company executives hoped that the "dues" they paid in the early 1990s would yield bigger returns in the late 1990s and into the 21st century.

## Principal Divisions

Cal-Van Tools Division; Cory Orchard Supply Division; Chemical Division; Tank Division; Leasing and Finance Division.

## Further Reading

*Chemi-Trol Chemical Company: 25 Years of Progress,* Gibsonburg, OH: Chemi-Trol Chemical Company, 1977.

Iverson, Doug, "It All Began in a Barn," *The Blade,* July 11, 1991, p. 37.

"Sandusky County: We're Open for Business," *The News-Messenger,* November 20, 1993 (special section).

"There's No Stunting Chemi-Trol's Growth," *The Blade,* March 23, 1992, p. 20.

—April Dougal Gasbarre

# Cincinnati Financial Corporation

P.O. Box 145496
Cincinnati, Ohio 45250-5496
U.S.A.
(513) 870-2000
Fax: (513) 870-0609

*Public Company*
*Incorporated:* 1950 as The Cincinnati Insurance
    Company
*Employees:* 2,289
*Total Assets:* $6.10 billion (1995)
*Stock Exchanges:* NASDAQ
*SICs:* 6331 Fire, Marine & Casualty Insurance; 6311 Life
    Insurance; 6321 Accident & Health Insurance; 6719
    Holding Companies, Not Elsewhere Classified

With assets of over $6 billion, Cincinnati Financial Corporation ranks among America's 20 most profitable publicly-traded property-casualty insurance companies. This holding company—known in some circles as "Cin-Fin"—controls three property and casualty insurers, a life insurance subsidiary, and a leasing firm. Within the property-casualty field, Cincinnati Financial Corp. specializes in personal policies for auto and home owners as well as commercial insurance for small businesses. All of the company's insurance products are sold and serviced through a network of fewer than 1,000 independent insurance agents. Although the firm writes insurance policies in 26 midwestern and southeastern states, home state Ohio remained its largest single market in the mid-1990s.

Throughout its history Cincinnati Financial's low cost structure, conservative investment strategy, and strong network of agents have enabled it to consistently outperform property and casualty insurance industry averages. In fact, *Barron's* analyst Harlan S. Byrne has characterized Cin-Fin as "one of the best-performing of property-casualty insurance companies." Its revenues increased from $1.05 billion in 1990 to $1.74 billion in 1995, and net income grew from $128.96 million to $227.35

million during the same period. The 45-year-old company celebrated its 35th consecutive year of dividend increases in 1995. At that time, independent agent and co-founder John J. Schiff continued to chair Cincinnati Financial's executive committee, while his son, John J. Schiff, Jr., served as company chairman. Robert Morgan started his 13th year as Cin-Fin's president and CEO that year.

### Postwar Origins

The business was chartered as The Cincinnati Insurance Company in 1950 by two brothers, John ("Jack") and Robert Schiff. Jack, the elder of the two, had graduated from Ohio State University in 1938 and started working with Travelers Insurance Company that same year. After serving in the military during World War II, Jack launched an independent insurance agency. His independent insurance agency did not represent any single firm and could therefore sell policies from any number of companies. Robert joined his brother's business in 1946, when he graduated from Ohio State.

It wasn't long before Jack conceived of a new insurance company, one created, owned, and operated by insurance agents themselves. A 1949 meeting with family friend and respected colleague Chester T. Field helped bring the idea to life in 1950. Field and the Schiffs persuaded several local independent agents to join them, including Harry Turner, who became the company's first president. Robert Schiff was the company's first vice-president, while Jack Schiff was named secretary-treasurer, and Chester Field served as a board member. The board raised $200,000 in initial investments and enlisted several independent agents from around the state to begin promoting Cincinnati Insurance Company's fire, auto, and later marine and theft insurance.

The Cincinnati Insurance Company (CIC) was founded on several key concepts, including a conservative investment and growth strategy, low expenses, and a strong agent network. The company kept costs low by hiring agents who either had their own offices or worked out of their homes. This strategy would continue throughout CIC's history; in the early 1990s, expenses were only about ten percent of annual premiums, one of the

## Company Perspectives:

*Our mission is to provide local independent agents with competitive insurance products, superior service and market stability, enhancing their ability to deliver quality financial protection to businesses and individuals in their communities.*

lowest rates in the industry. The company also kept costs low by carefully choosing its clients as well as its agents, making sure that both were "cream of the crop."

The firm had two primary constituencies: the independent agents to whom it offered insurance products, and the clients to whom independent agents sold the individual policies. CIC forged strong relationships with its agents by paying high commissions (up to 20 percent of premiums); providing responsive claims service, and encouraging agents to own company stock. In a 1990 *Financial World* article, McDonald & Co. analyst Nancy Benacci noted that Cin-Fin had "a claims person in every town and ⌊made⌋ payments and adjustments fast." A newspaper article written around the time of the company's formation called CIC "the first company owned exclusively by Ohio insurance agents and Cincinnati businessmen." By the early 1990s, company agents owned about one-fifth of its equity. *Financial World's* Adrienne Linsenmeyer noted that in 1990 "70 percent of Cin-Fin's independent agents rate the company tops and book their best business with the company." CIC won over customers by offering guaranteed rates; policies with premiums that did not increase for up to five years. These factors laid a solid foundation upon which the Schiff brothers and their colleagues built a prosperous business.

### Solid Growth in the 1950s and 1960s

Insurance companies typically have two possible profit centers: underwriting (or selling insurance policies) and investing. An underwriting profit is expressed in industry parlance as the "underwriting margin" or "combined ratio." The combined operating ratio compares claims and overhead to premiums collected. A combined operating ratio of 100 or more indicates that a company's expenses equaled or exceeded the premiums that it collected. A ratio of 105, for example, indicates that a company suffered a loss of five percent on underwriting; premiums collected fell short of claims and operating expenses. Beginning in the 1960s, property and casualty insurers in general did not make money on underwriting. Consequently, any profits made were usually generated through shrewd investment of premiums.

CIC consistently achieved underwriting profits throughout the 1950s and 1960s. By 1955, CIC's roster of products included homeowner's and commercial all-risk plans. From the outset, the firm tailored its policies to small businesses across the Midwest. CIC expanded geographically during its first five years in business, hiring agents in Kentucky in 1955 and Indiana the following year. Gross annual premiums multiplied from $92,000 in 1951 to $928,000 in 1956.

From 1956 to 1971 the company averaged a 9.2 percent annual profit on underwriting. During this period of CIC's history, the company conservatively invested its surplus in government bonds, one of the most low-risk vehicles available. From 1956 to 1968, CIC expanded its reach into six new, primarily Midwestern, states: Michigan, Pennsylvania, Florida, Georgia, Alabama, and Tennessee. The company also broadened the types of coverage it offered during this period, adding earthquake, automobile comprehensive and collision, burglary, and robbery options. By 1967, CIC offered 13 types of insurance. Harry Turner served as president until 1963, providing the young company's first decade with what successor Jack Schiff called "wise, conservative management."

### Reorganization Brings New Era of Growth

As president of CIC from 1963 to 1975, Jack Schiff ushered in a more aggressive era. In line with a trend that swept the insurance industry in the 1960s, CIC established Cincinnati Financial Corp. as a holding company in 1968. Harry Turner served as the new entity's chairman, while Jack Schiff was president and, starting in 1973, chief executive officer.

The corporate reorganization signaled a period of diversification and rapid growth in revenues and net income. In 1970, Cin-Fin created CFC Investment Company. This segment of Cin-Fin bought and sold commercial real estate for investment purposes. It also provided low cost loans to agents and offered vehicle leases and loans for the agents and their customers.

Public stock floatations in 1971 and 1972 raised about $14 million, $3.5 million of which was used for debt reduction. The remainder went into a fund used in 1972 to acquire The Life Insurance Company of Cincinnati and Queen City Indemnity, a property/casualty firm. Cin-Fin made its biggest purchase ever the following year, merging with Inter-Ocean Corporation, another Cincinnati company and life insurer. The transaction increased Cin-Fin's asset based by almost 60 percent, to $161 million, by the end of 1973. Inter-Ocean Chairman W.G. Alpaugh, Jr. replaced the retiring Harry Turner as Cin-Fin chairman in 1973.

This string of acquisitions helped increase Cincinnati Financial's revenues dramatically, from $19.7 million in 1968 to $96.7 million in 1973, while its net income shot from $1.1 million to $9.8 million. During this time, Cin-Fin's primary profit center shifted from underwriting to investing. From the 1970s through the early 1990s, the insurance industry overall averaged a seven percent annual loss on underwriting. Cincinnati Financial's insurance businesses were more profitable than most, but they still only broke even on average, bringing an increased emphasis on investing.

In 1972, the company hired James Miller as its first full-time investment department employee. According to a late 1995 article in *Forbes* magazine, Miller and Cin-Fin demanded the same performance of its investments that it expected of its own stock: "We want dividends and companies that will increase their dividends." For all its conservatism, by the early 1990s, about half of the insurer's investment portfolio was in common stocks. In fact, nearly 43 percent of the fund was tied up in just two stocks: Fifth Third Bancorp and Alltel, both based in Ohio.

In spite of this fundamental change in its business, Cin-Fin's growth continued unabated through the remainder of the decade. Revenues expanded from less than $100 million in 1973 to over $330 million by 1980, and profits jumped from $9.8 million to $33.4 million during the same period.

### *"Weathering the Storms" of the 1980s*

Robert Morgan succeeded co-founder Jack Schiff as CEO in 1982. Morgan—who had joined Cincinnati Insurance in 1966, advanced to vice-president and general manager in 1972, and became president in 1976—oversaw a relatively difficult decade for Cin-Fin and other property-casualty insurers. A string of natural disasters highlighted by Hurricane Hugo battered underwriting results, and investment pitfalls including commercial real estate and junk bonds led to the downfall of several insurers. Cin-Fin suffered the effects of both these trends, though not nearly as severely as some of its rivals.

The company experienced its first-ever decline in profits from $68.7 million on $490.6 million revenues in 1984 to $55 million on $596.5 million in 1985. During the mid-1980s, property-casualty insurers averaged a combined ration of 116, but in the latter years of the decade, Cin-Fin managed to keep its combined ratio under 100. Revenues increased to $974.4 million and net grew to $111.5 million by 1989, and the dividend nearly doubled from 1986 to 1990.

Cin-Fin's performance won it increased attention from business analysts in the early 1990s, but not necessarily for its insurance activities. To be sure, such observers as *Barron's* Harlan S. Byrne praised the company's "better than average" underwriting results and "tight-fisted control of expenses." But others, including *Forbes'* Thomas Easton, admired the company as "a well-run insurer coupled to a closed-end fund with a superb performance record." Easton noted that the insurer's investment returns had beaten the Standard & Poor's 500 by four percentage points from 1985 to 1995, for example. Cincinnati Financial Corp.'s bottom line bore out these accolades. Having broken the $1 billion revenue mark in 1990, Cincinnati Financial Corp. approached $2 billion in 1995. Net income increased from $128.9 million to $227.4 million during the same period.

### *Principal Subsidiaries*

The Cincinnati Insurance Company; The Cincinnati Casualty Company; The Cincinnati Indemnity Company; The Cincinnati Life Insurance Company; CFC Investment Company.

### *Further Reading*

Byrne, Harlan S., "Cincinnati Financial Corp.," *Barron's,* January 21, 1991, p. 49.

——, "Cincinnati Financial: Weathering the Storms, Feathering Its Profits," *Barron's,* May 31, 1993, p. 33.

Calise, Angela K., "Cincinnati Financial Moves to Relieve Investor Fears," *National Underwriter Property & Casualty-Risk & Benefits Management,* October 15, 1990, p. 63.

Curry, Robert P., *Prospectus Fulfilled: The Evolution of the Cincinnati Financial Corporation,* Cincinnati: The Cincinnati Financial Corporation, 1984.

Easton, Thomas, "What's in a Name?" *Forbes,* December 18, 1995, p. 294.

Geer, Carolyn T., "Its Agents Do Their Homework," *Forbes,* January 4, 1993, p. 166.

Linsenmeyer, Adrienne, "Cincinnati Financial: Bucking the Trend," *Financial World,* December 11, 1990, p. 14.

Weinstein, Marc, "Property and Casualty firms Expected to See Brighter '86; Local Insurers to Follow Industry Trend," *Cincinnati Business Courier,* August 11, 1986, p. 15.

—April Dougal Gasbarre

# CitFed Bancorp, Inc.

**One Citizens Federal Center**
**Dayton, Ohio 46402**
**U.S.A.**
**(513) 223-4234**
**Fax: (513) 223-4238**

*Public Company*
*Incorporated:* 1991
*Employees:* 602
*Total Assets:* $2.1 billion (1995)
*Stock Exchanges:* NASDAQ
*SICs:* 6035 Savings Institutions Federal Charter

CitFed Bancorp, Inc., is the holding company for Citizens Federal Bank, F.S.B., one of the oldest savings and loan associations in the state of Ohio. Citizens Federal has had few presidents since its founding in 1934, yet those individuals have managed the bank remarkably well. In 1981, for example, Citizens Federal was the 14th largest savings association in Ohio, with 13 offices and approximately $500 million in assets. By the end of fiscal 1983, Citizens Bank had developed into one of the largest savings associations in the state, with over 50 branch offices and $1.5 billion in assets. Astute and talented management continues to guide Citizens Federal Bank, and its operations are not only highly efficient and customer friendly, but still expanding within the state of Ohio.

## Bold Beginnings in the Great Depression

Citizens Federal Savings and Loan Association opened its doors for business on August 6, 1934. This was a remarkable feat, considering the fact that the Great Depression had taken hold of the entire United States five years earlier. By 1933 40 percent of all home mortgage loans in the United States, amounting to a total of $20 billion, had defaulted. The result was a disastrous rate of foreclosures running at an astounding 26,000 per month. Nearly 2,000 savings and loan associations had gone bankrupt, with depositors losing over $200,000.

Part of Franklin Delano Roosevelt's New Deal involved the passage of the Home Owners Loan Act. This legislation established a system of federal charters for the troubled savings and loan associations, and created the Home Owners Loan Corporation. Under the auspices of the new law, already existing savings and loan associations were allowed to exchange mortgages that had defaulted for bonds issued by the Home Owners Loan Corporation. The West Side Building and Loan, located in Dayton, Ohio, was the first such organization in Ohio to take advantage of the new federal legislation. Changing its name to Citizens Federal Savings & Loan Association of Dayton, the company opened with approximately $800,000 in assets for lending to customers.

Citizens Federal Savings & Loan Association was successful from the start of its operations, primarily because the company maintained a conservative financial loan policy that was extremely effective, especially during the latter part of the Great Depression. Management decided to avoid any speculative investments, establishing a strict lending policy whereby loans were provided to customers only when they were guaranteed by homes or business holdings. In addition, there were very stringent limitations placed on loans that were provided by the firm to its own corporate officers. Most importantly, however, all customer deposits were insured, and, in a striking innovation for the 1930s, depositors also received a fixed rate of interest on their money. Finally, loans were amortized, so that all the firm's customers would know the exact amount of each monthly payment and precisely when the amount of the loan would be paid in full.

By 1937 Citizens Federal Savings & Loan Association had increased deposits to six times the amount the firm had started with—and funding for mortgages had been provided to more than 2,000 customers. Having always considered its mission to emphasize the importance of individual home ownership, Citizens Federal established a unique customer service information center called the "Homeowners Library." This center included an impressive up-to-date collection of information on building and modeling homes, so that individuals could study various materials such as architectural drawings and interior design books to help them create their own dwellings. At no cost or charge, the Homeowners Library was a phenomenal success, with numerous customers drawing on the wealth of information at the center. By 1940 Citizens Federal was growing at a rapid pace, and reported over $10 million in assets.

When the United States entered World War II in December 1941, Citizens Federal's primary function, loaning money for mortgages, came to an abrupt halt. All civilian construction was brought to an immediate stop, and was not resumed until after the war ended. In spite of this obstacle, Citizens Federal enthusiastically supported and sold war bonds for the United States government and the war effort. In one memorable occurrence, Citizens Federal built a ''Victory War Bond Wagon'' that toured the streets of downtown Dayton selling war bonds six days a week. From August 1942 through December of the same year, the firm jumped from 21st to first of all savings and loan associations selling war bonds. By the end of the war, the company reported an astounding 292,000 separate transactions for the sale of war bonds, and had accumulated nearly $20 million in total war bond sales.

### Postwar Prosperity

When World War II ended, millions of soldiers who had fought overseas returned home and married, and one of their foremost goals was building a home. Citizens Federal picked up where it had left off before the war, and made the first GI Bill mortgage loan in the state of Ohio. With more and more soldiers taking advantage of the bill, the value of first home mortgages made by Citizens Federal shot up from $8.5 million in 1946 to over $29 million in 1956. Along with the increased construction activity throughout the state of Ohio, many people were moving from cities to suburbs, especially in the Dayton area. In order to continue providing its customers with highly efficient service, Citizens Federal opened offices in major suburban shopping centers, including Town & Country, Northtown, and Eastown. By extending hours of service to 8:00 in the evening at its suburban locations, the company brought in many new customers.

During the 1950s, Citizens Federal continued to expand its office locations and improve upon its customer service. Although growth was important to the company's management, of greater significance was the firm's earnings. As Citizens Federal's net worth continued to increase during the decade, man-

agement decided that it was not worth pursuing growth for its own sake. Consequently, even though a number of offices were opened in suburban locations for the convenience of its customers, Citizens Federal did not pursue an aggressive growth strategy until well into the 1980s.

### Technological and Regulatory Changes, 1960s and 1970s

The 1960s ushered in major changes for the company. One of the biggest influences on the financial community was the development of the computer. During this decade, Citizens Federal was the second savings and loan company in the nation to install its own online computer system within existing company facilities. Installing such a system meant a dramatic change for both financial institutions and their customers: Citizens Federal could now produce highly accurate daily statements of all financial transactions and operations, while customers could begin earning interest almost immediately with their deposits. In 1964 Citizens Federal merged with Lincoln Federal Savings, another large savings and loan association in the Dayton area. The merger resulted in an institution with over $100 million in assets. One year later, the total assets of Citizens Federal had increased to $113 million.

The decade of the 1970s was a watershed for the company. The financial community was changing rapidly, as were longtime federal regulations, and Citizens Federal took advantage of the changes. Since their inception, savings and loan associations were the primary lenders to individual homeowners for their very first mortgage, while commercial banks were involved in underwriting land developments. With new federal legislation passed by Congress during the early 1970s, savings and loan associations were allowed to create subsidiary companies to engage in land development. In 1971 Citizens Federal established its own land development company, Dayton Financial Services, and the new subsidiary immediately undertook three major projects south of the city of Dayton, including Quail Run, Woodland Greens, and Pebble Creek. By the end of fiscal 1972, the assets of Citizens Federal had grown to over $200 million. Management devoted the remainder of the decade to expanding its services, taking advantage of the enormous technological changes within the financial services industry, and improving upon the company's ever-growing assets.

### Regional Expansion, 1980s and 1990s

In 1980 Citizens Federal posted $471 million in assets. Yet management was determined to surpass the $1 billion mark and to expand the company from a local savings and loan association in Dayton, Ohio, into a regional financial network. Management decided the only way to accomplish this goal in a relatively short period was to pursue an extremely aggressive acquisition strategy. In 1981 Citizens Federal purchased the Columbus Savings & Loan, a $32 million savings and loan association with three offices. During the same year, the company acquired Home Savings of Dayton, another savings and loan association with approximately $125 million in assets. In 1982 Citizens Federal bought the 12 offices of Cardinal Federal Savings and Loan Association. The offices, located in Columbus, Ohio, contributed an additional $200 million to the company's asset base. Not long afterward, Citizens Federal acquired the Ohio State Federal Savings & Loan, adding another $276 million to its assets, and a total of 16 offices located in Columbus and Chillicothe, Ohio. The Liberal Savings and Loan Association was also acquired during the same year, and brought with it offices located in Lebanon, Wilmington, and Cincinnati. At the end of its two-year whirlwind buying spree, Citizens Federal had achieved both of the goals it had set for itself: the company had grown by acquisition into a major regional financial services network, and had rapidly increased its total asset base to $1.5 billion.

During the mid and late 1980s, Citizens Federal maintained its commitment to providing mortgage loans to first-time homeowners. In the interests of its customers, the company dropped its loan interest rate two full percentage points during this period, resulting in many new mortgage loans throughout the savings and loan's territory. Concurrently, Citizens Federal continued to expand by either acquiring or building new offices in the Columbus, Cincinnati, and Dayton metropolitan areas.

In January 1991, management decided to create a bank holding company to further strengthen and coordinate the growing financial services that Citizens Federal was providing. CitFed Bancorp, Inc., was the name chosen to incorporate all the financial activities of Citizens Federal, CitFed Mortgage Corporation of America, and Dayton Financial Services Corporation. As CitFed grew during the early 1990s, the firm continued to acquire new offices and offer more financial services to its customers throughout the region within which it was operating. In 1994 CitFed benefitted from the withdrawal of Union Federal Savings Bank from the southwestern Ohio region. Union Federal, a privately operated savings and loan based in Indianapolis, Indiana, decided to sell its six southwestern Ohio offices to CitFed, primarily because of the rising costs associated with operating in diverse markets, and because of its inability to compete with CitFed's aggressive pricing structure for customer services.

During 1995 CitFed continued its growth through acquisition strategy. In March of that year management reached an agreement with PSB Holding Company, located in Xenia, Ohio, and formed as the holding company for Peoples Savings Bank, to merge its operations with CitFed. The merger resulted in the acquisition of six additional offices, including locations in Greene County, Warren County, and Montgomery County. The

purchase of the offices in Greene County was especially important, since the area was projected to be one of the fastest growing counties in the state, with major employers such as Wright-Patterson Air Force Base, the Air Force Institute of Technology, and Wright State University. Management at CitFed was anticipating significant income producing value from Greene County alone within five years.

In 1995 CitFed reported an overall gain in new accounts of 32,000. Largely due to this surge in new customers, the company's branch offices generated a hefty $6.9 million in service fees, a jump of 27.3 percent over the previous year. During the same year, savings deposits at the bank grew by $209 million, while certificates of deposit grew by $115 million. From fiscal 1994 to the end of fiscal 1995, CitFed's total assets grew from $1.8 billion to $2.1 billion, an impressive increase by any standard.

CitFed operates 28 Citizens Federal Bank, F.S.B., branch offices throughout the six counties in the greater Dayton metropolitan area, and a total of 11 CitFed Mortgage loan offices in Ohio, Kentucky, North Carolina, and Virginia. Management at CitFed is committed to providing more extensive and efficient services for its customers, while it pursues an aggressive strategy of growth through acquisition.

### Principal Subsidiaries

Citizens Mortgage Corporation of America; Dayton Financial Services, Inc.; CitFed Properties, Inc.

### Further Reading

Bronstien, Barbara, "Union Federal to Focus Its Energy Back Home in Indiana," *American Banker,* December 2, 1994, p. 7.
"CitFed Bancorp Acquisition," *Wall Street Journal,* February 1, 1995, p. A14(E).
"CitFed to Call Euronotes," *American Banker,* July 30, 1993, p. 22.
"Citizens Federal Bank," *American Banker,* May 19, 1994, p. 7.
Cline, Kenneth, "Costlier Deposits May Put Squeeze on Margins," *American Banker,* January 6, 1995, p. 6.
Kirby, Jerry, *The Story of Citizens Federal Savings and Loan Association of Dayton,* Newcomen Society: New York, 1984.
Morris, Edward L., "Congress Must End the Terror Stalking Innocent S&L Officers," *American Banker,* July 30, 1993, p. 4.

—Thomas Derdak

# Cobra Golf Inc.

**1812 Aston Avenue**
**Carlsbad, California 92008-7306**
**U.S.A.**
**(619) 929-0377**
**Fax: (619) 929-0372**

*Wholly Owned Subsidiary of American Brands Inc.*
*Incorporated:* 1978 as Cobra Golf Inc. II
*Employees:* 668
*Sales:* $175 million (1995 est.)
*SICs:* 3949 Sporting & Athletic Goods, Not Elsewhere
    Classified; 5091 Sporting and Recreational Goods &
    Supplies

Cobra Golf Inc. is a leading designer, manufacturer, and marketer of high-quality golf clubs. Its clubs are targeted at the premium-priced market, with features like oversized heads and graphite shafts. The company also markets golf bags and other accessories that are manufactured by third parties. Cobra was a public company until it was purchased in January 1996 by conglomerate American Brands Inc.

## 1970s Founding

Cobra was inspired in 1973 by Australian Thomas L. Crow. Crow, the winner of the 1961 Australian amateur golf championship, had decided to channel his passion for the game of golf into designing clubs. The idea that sparked Cobra came to Crow in the early 1970s, when he noticed that many American golfers purchased golf clubs individually; they often purchased individual clubs on impulse, hoping that the new devices would improve their golf game. In an effort to tap that high-end market, Crow rounded up $150,000 in venture capital and started a small custom club business. He designed what became known as the "Baffler" wood, a specialized club with a patented soleplate that helped move the ball out of difficult lies on the golf course. Importantly, Crow's clubs were designed to reduce drag during the swing and to increase the lift of the ball.

Crow's company began to experience rapid growth after it was incorporated as Cobra Golf Inc. II in 1978. In that year, Crow was joined by Gary Biszantz, a former San Diego Ford car dealer and an early investor in the company. Crow and Biszantz introduced the company's first product in 1980: the Baffler wood, which integrated the design advantages developed earlier by Crow. Through an aggressive mass marketing effort, the company was able to generate big demand for its Baffler clubs and to increase sales rapidly. Indeed, by 1985 Cobra was selling about $4.5 million worth of its Baffler clubs annually.

## Product Line Expansion in the 1980s

While riding a surging wave of demand for its Baffler clubs, Cobra began developing a new line of improved clubs in the early 1980s. In 1985 it introduced the new line of Cobra clubs, which were eventually a huge success. The clubs differed from others on the market because they sported lightweight graphite shafts. The lighter clubs allowed golfers, especially older players and women, to swing the club faster and hit the ball farther. The innovation was important, because it appealed to the fastest growing and most lucrative segments of the market, women golfers and seniors, the latter of whom spent much more on golf equipment than younger golfers. Cobra was one of the first companies to offer graphite shafts for entire sets of clubs, including woods and irons.

Cobra's new line of clubs reflected an emphasis on design continually nourished by its founder and sustained by new management, which pursued a "golf through science" approach to design. In the late 1980s and early 1990s Cobra continued to adopt leading edge technologies that it believed helped it to create the most advanced clubs on the market. It used the most recent computer-aided design technologies, for example, as well as laser modeling, high-speed cameras, and robotic testing. Its research and development team also experimented with lightweight aerospace materials in its pursuit of the optimal club. "We believe we have the foundation laid to come out with whatever product we need to come out with," said Dave Schaefer, chief operating officer, in the November 28, 1994 issue of *San Diego Business Journal.* "You have a product that

## Company Perspectives:

*From the very beginning with our first product, the Baffler, which grew to be a tremendously popular line of utility clubs, Cobra has always believed in the following fundamental principals: We have always been dedicated to building the highest quality golf equipment possible. We have consistently sought to provide the functionality players seek. Since our founding, our intent has been to make the game easier and more enjoyable to play and we have always offered our products at a fair price.*

you're advertising and people buy it—you better make sure your testing backs up what you're producing.''

Augmenting Cobra's management team during the mid-1980s was Mark McClure, a former ski instructor and golf pro who became Cobra's marketing mastermind. Among other moves, McClure borrowed a trick that he had seen ski manufacturers use to market their new products—giving them away. He began to send Cobra clubs to pro shops with requests that the pros try them and to lend them to customers. "Like ski instructors, club pros command quite a bit of respect, and that is the strongest possible advertising," McClure said in the November 7, 1994 issue of *Forbes*. After using the clubs for a year, the pro shops were allowed to buy them at a significant discount or to return them. Returned clubs were simply reconditioned and sold.

Spurred by the success of its high-quality graphite-shaft clubs, Cobra's revenues were approaching $20 million annually by the late 1980s. Cobra had become a leading name in golf equipment throughout the world, with distributorships in Canada, Japan, Europe, and Australia (Australia accounted for roughly 20 percent of Cobra's sales in 1989). But Cobra's greatest period of growth was yet to come. In fact, between 1989 and 1993 Cobra's sales lurched from barely more than $20 million annually to about $56 million. The reasons for the expansion were multifold, but were largely the result of a savvy marketing strategy devised mostly by McClure. McClure was rewarded in 1990 with a promotion to chief executive of the company; founders Crow and Biszantz assumed the roles of vice-chairman/chief designer and chairman, respectively.

Among McClure's greatest marketing coups was his signing of top-ranked endorsers, including respected golf professionals Hale Irwin, Beth Daniel, and Greg Norman (also known as The Shark). Greg Norman's endorsement was the biggest feather in Cobra's cap, because he was among the top-ranked players on the circuit when he signed on with the company. McClure knew that Cobra could not afford Norman's multimillion-dollar endorsement price. Instead, he offered him a package that included an equity stake in the company, a chance to help design Cobra's clubs, and the opportunity to own, eventually, the Cobra distribution system in Norman's homeland of Australia. Norman, a long-time friend of Cobra's original founder and fellow Aussie, Tom Crow, accepted the offer. The arrangement

was ultimately a success, as Norman went on to become the number two ranked player in the next few years.

At least as important to Cobra's success as its marketing program during the early and mid-1990s was the introduction of its third, and most profitable, product line: King Cobra. The King Cobra line was inspired by the success of competitor Callaway Golf Co.'s Big Bertha clubs, which Callaway introduced in 1991. Big Berthas were oversized woods that sported larger sweet spots, thus enabling classic duffers to drive the ball farther and straighter even when they hit the ball off-center. Furthermore, the clubs allowed better golfers to swing harder, knowing that the effect of a slight error in their swing would be minimized.

Cobra was intrigued by the huge success of the Big Bertha woods, which quickly snapped up a fat 30 percent of the entire $500-million-plus wholesale market for woods. Eager to tap into the profitable new market niche, Cobra began designing its own oversized clubs. But while Callaway remained focused on its oversized drivers, Cobra decided to broaden the oversized market with a set of oversized irons. Cobra invested $2 million to develop a line of high-end irons that sported oversized heads and graphite shafts. It introduced the King Cobra line in 1993, selling the clubs in sets at a retail price of about $1,000.

The King Cobra men's clubs were a huge success, representing about 75 percent of the company's sales within one year after their introduction. Cobra followed up with an equally popular line of King Cobra clubs for seniors and women. To help launch the King Cobra line, Cobra went public in September 1993 with a stock sale that raised $38.5 million. The cash was used to launch an advertising blitz, among other initiatives. In the summer of 1994 Cobra initiated a $5 million television network advertising campaign featuring Greg Norman and its King Cobra line. Augmenting such advertising efforts was Cobra's existing national network of 4,200 on-course golf pro shops and 900 accounts with off-course specialty stores.

Cobra drew on its cash surplus to pursue other avenues to growth. For example, in April of 1994 Cobra paid about $1 million for Cumo Sports, a manufacturer and marketer of apparel, including men's and women's golf and resort clothing imported from Italy. Cobra hoped to use the company to help develop its own apparel and related goods using the respected Cobra name. In addition to branching into apparel, Cobra, in 1991, had become the only U.S. golf equipment manufacturer in the United States to manufacture its own graphite shafts. The vertical integration allowed the company to achieve economies of scale and greater quality control and was credited with helping Cobra to achieve profit margins about six percent higher than its closest competitors.

High profit margins, huge demand for its oversized King Cobra clubs, and healthy sales of its existing products allowed Cobra to post big sales and profit gains in the mid-1990s. Incredibly, Cobra increased revenues more than 100 percent in 1994 to $124 million, and net income doubled to nearly $23 million. In addition to its various King Cobra club lines, Cobra was still generating revenue from its Baffler woods and traditional Cobra irons and woods. It had also introduced lines of specialty clubs, such as its computer-milled and King Cobra Mallet putters, and was marketing various apparel and accessory items. Furthermore, by late 1995 Cobra had expanded its distribution network to include about 7,500 on- and off-course shops.

### Acquisition in the Mid-1990s

After boosting sales toward the $200 million mark in 1995, Cobra Golf was purchased by diversified, $11.6 billion conglomerate American Brands Inc., of Greenwich, Connecticut. In late January 1996, American Brands purchased the Carlsbad, California-based golf equipment company in a transaction valued at about $700 million. American Brands was known as the owner of name brands including Jim Beam bourbons, Master Locks, Swing office supplies, Benson & Hedges cigarettes, and Moen faucets. But it had also started buying what was becoming a venerable group of golf equipment holdings. In addition to Cobra, American owned well-known Foot-Joy Golf Shoes and gloves as well as the respected Titleist Golf Ball name.

Cobra entered 1996 as the leading manufacturer of oversized irons and one of a few brand names that together controlled more than 75 percent of the entire golf club market. It was banking on new technology to carry it into the 21st century, including the use of titanium to make its clubs, which would allow it to profit from the replacement market inevitably created by technological breakthroughs like graphite shafts and oversized club heads.

### Principal Subsidiaries

Cumo Sports; Cobra Golf Australia.

### Principal Divisions

Cobra Golf Sales Group; Cobra Golf Production Group; The Technical Services Group; Customer Service Group.

### Further Reading

Acello, Richard, "American Brands Puts Cobra Golf into Its Corporate Bag," *San Diego Daily Transcript,* December 19, 1995, p. 1.

"American Brands Buys Cobra," *The Wall Street Journal,* January 30, 1996, p. B2.

Biberman, Thor Kamban, "Cobra Golf's Acquisition by American Brands Is Official," *San Diego Daily Transcript,* January 25, 1996, p. 1.

*Cobra Golf, Inc.,* Carlsbad, Calif.: Cobra Golf Inc., 1995, company document.

"Corporate Profiles 1995: A Superior Equipment Maker, Cobra Had To Go Out and Buy Clothing," *San Diego Daily Transcript,* January 23, 1995, Section S, p. 62.

Darlin, Damon, "Borrow From Thy Neighbor," *Forbes,* November 7, 1994, p. 214.

Jenks, Alison, "Corporate Profile for Cobra Golf Inc.," *Business Wire,* October 20, 1995.

Kleske, Andrew, "Cobra Golf Is Seeking To Join Its San Diego Brethren in IPO Club," *San Diego Daily Transcript,* August 2, 1993, p. 1.

McClure, Mark, "Greg Norman Signs Worldwide Agreement To Represent Cobra Both on Golf Course and in Boardroom," *Business Wire,* August 14, 1990.

"Offer for Cobra Golf Incorporated by American Brands Completed," *PR Newswire,* January 24, 1996.

Schwab, Dave, "Cobra Putting Snake Bite on Its Competition," *San Diego Business Journal,* November 28, 1994, p. 30.

—Dave Mote

# Cold Spring Granite Company

**202 S. Third Avenue**
**Cold Spring, Minnesota 56320**
**U.S.A.**
**(320) 685-3621**
**Fax: (320) 685-8490**

*Private Company*
*Incorporated:* 1920 as Rockville Granite Company
*Sales:* $100 million (1995 est.)
*Employees:* 1200
*SICs:* 1411 Dimension Stone; 3281 Cut Stone & Stone
    Products

Cold Spring Granite Company claims to be the largest granite quarrier and fabricator in the world based on number of quarries, sales volume, and the unparalleled number of granite colors offered to customers. The small-town business has earned the respect of architects and gained an international reputation on its ability to provide a complete array of services from mining and finishing to installation. Product lines include architectural and monumental granites with interior, landscape, and industrial applications, and bronze memorials. The privately held company has been led by three generations of the same family.

### The Early Years in Rockville

Henry Nair Alexander worked in the granite and slate quarries of his native Scotland alongside his father and brothers. In 1880, he and two of his brothers emigrated to the United States and cut stone in Portland, Maine. He returned to Scotland two years later in order to finish a contract for granite barns. While back home he met and married Maggie Milne.

The American granite industry started to develop west of Chicago just as the second half of the 19th century began. Alexander decided to follow other Scotsmen to the massive granite fields in central Minnesota. In 1889 he and seven other men working for the Breen and Young quarry struck out on their own to form the Rockville Granite Company. Their first big contract—eight large columns—was for the Minnesota State Capitol in St. Paul.

Alexander bought out his partners on September 29, 1898, and became sole owner of Rockville Granite Company. He then moved the business to a quarry location closer to the Great Northern Railroad right-of-way and began modernizing his equipment. He also purchased a farm in the Rockville area to help support his growing family. Carrying on the family tradition Henry's sons started working in the quarry at a young age. A daughter received business training and took over the bookkeeping. In general, Alexander believed a family was a stabilizing influence on his workers, and that belief would come to influence the philosophy of the business, then and in the future.

Rockville Granite Company faced stiff competition when a larger concern, the Clark and McCormick Granite Company, set up shop in 1907 and began quarrying the gray granite which was so plentiful in the area. Alexander kept the business going with projects such as Chicago's Iroquois Theatre and the Minneapolis disposal system. When Henry became ill from pneumonia in 1912, 22-year-old Patrick Alexander, who had left home to work in quarries around the country and in Canada, came home and took over management of the company. Fourteen-year-old John Alexander also helped out at the plant, but their brother William Alexander continued to farm.

When Henry died in 1913, Maggie Alexander decided to try to sell the business to the Clark and McCormick quarry. Unable to get what she felt was a fair price she kept the business, and Patrick became the youngest granite company manager in the country. John, a high school student, helped on weekends, and William assisted with blacksmith work when needed. Maggie died in 1916, and Patrick and John became the owners of Rockville Granite Company, which was valued at about $6,000 including plant, equipment, and property.

John was intent on getting a college education, but that changed when Patrick was called to serve in World War I. John had to return home to help run the plant. By the end of the war the amount of work coming into the plant was on the rise, but business was good for the company's competitor, too. The

Clark and McCormick Quarry had acquired practically all the gray granite outcroppings in the area to supply granite for the cathedral being built in St. Paul. Rockville Granite Company had to find a new site in order to keep running. John gave up his plans to return to college and helped Patrick look for a new location for the company.

### The Move to Cold Spring

The site of a burned down flourmill, just west of Rockville in Cold Spring, looked like a promising location. It was on a river with a dam for supplying power, and the town needed new businesses. The loss of the mill had cost jobs, and the other big employer, Cold Spring Brewing Company, was suffering because of prohibition. Cold Spring banker Fred Stein and Cold Spring Brewing Company owner Ferdinand Peters recruited several other businessmen to help bring the quarry company to town.

On October 5, 1920, Rockville Granite Company was incorporated with Peters as president, Patrick Alexander as second vice-president, John Alexander as secretary, and Fred Stein as treasurer. The mill purchase price was $30,000. The company made a $200,000 stock offering and quickly sold over 40 percent of that and then borrowed additional cash to finance the startup costs. The new plant began operation in the spring of 1921. The Alexander brothers, as managers of the newly incorporated company, searched for new granite outcroppings to supply material for the plant. The stone they found had a pink tinge and was used to supply their first major job, the Stearns County Court House in St. Cloud.

The Rockville Granite Company was now on solid financial ground, and the company could begin growing. A full-time draftsman and later drafting assistants were hired and concentrated on architectural projects. A sales force was formed and opened offices near large building construction sites in Minneapolis, Chicago, St. Louis, and Philadelphia. New equipment was purchased and quarry and plant operations were revamped to cut down waste and increase efficiency. By 1923 the company could retire its debts and pay interest on its stock. Well-established in its new location, with an expanded physical plant and about 75 full-time employees, the company was ready for a name change. In 1924 Rockville Granite Company became Cold Spring Granite Company.

Growth created its share of problems for Cold Spring Granite. The company, which had operated a union, or closed, shop for many years, was struck when a contract was made to deliver granite to an open shop on the West Coast. The labor movement was in its formative years and working to gain strength and momentum; a compromise which would have allowed Cold Spring to fill its contract could not be negotiated. The closed shop policy was ended, and about one-quarter of the men left the company. But due to relatively high wages the vacancies were quickly filled. Many of the men hired then later moved to supervisory positions. And others who joined on at the time were to be the first in a line of family members stretching for several generations that worked for the company.

According to John Dominik, author of *Cold Spring Granite: A History,* the company found early success due to the experience of the employees and their ability to innovate. Men with

expertise in the industry were drawn on board, and Patrick Alexander strove to introduce production techniques that enhanced their competitiveness. Together they adapted equipment from other heavy industries for use with granite and became leaders in the field.

### The Depression and War Years

The economic depression of the 1930s dried up the architectural work Cold Spring Granite had depended on in its early years, and the company had to temporarily shut down. After resuming operations the company responded by shifting to monument work and by becoming increasingly self-sufficient. Employees painstakingly built their own surfacing wheels, which were needed to finish the stone, and when the cost of the steel shot used in the cutting process rose dramatically, they made that, too.

During the Depression, John Alexander took over the management of monument sales. In order to keep the plant running in the winter months he offered incentives to monument dealers who placed off-season orders. Promotional materials with drawings and photographs of the monuments and mausoleums were also generated. After the economy improved and architectural work increased monument sales continued to hold an important position in the company.

Transportation was a large part of the expense of granite production. Cold Spring Granite had persistent difficulties relating to delivery of its unwieldy product. Most shipments were made by rail: breakage and long delays were common. In the mid-1930s, a trucker who hauled the company's granite from the plant to the railroad proposed that finished granite could be shipped directly to work sites on semi-trailer trucks. Consequently, Cold Spring shifted away from rail to truck transportation, ending its dependence on railroad schedules and routes, cutting shipping costs, and lessening the risk of damage which occurred during the transfer of stone from truck to train to truck.

The company suffered an important loss in 1938 with the death of its president. Ferdinand Peters had guided the company through its incorporation and managed the financial aspects of Cold Spring Granite while the Alexanders concentrated on production. With Peters's death, Patrick Alexander once again headed the company his father had founded. He soon faced another crisis.

When the United States entered World War II architectural steel manufacturers diverted their efforts to military production: construction jobs became scarce. But Cold Spring Granite had the experience and equipment for handling large, heavy material. John Alexander pursued war contracts and then managed production. The plants were converted to handle steel instead of stone and manufactured—among other things—ships bottoms and hull sections. Men who had been quarriers learned to be welders.

With the end of the war came a flood of structural granite orders. But the quarries had been nearly idle for four years, and experienced men had been lost to the war. Cold Spring fell behind in production. To ease the burden the Royal Granite Company in St. Cloud was purchased. The monument end of the business also needed some attention, for consumer preferences had changed. Flat markers—which allowed for easier care of cemetery land and created a parklike look—had cut into the market. Ferdinand "Frosty" Peters, son of the late Cold Spring president, promoted a line of bronze markers anchored in granite, and a wholly owned subsidiary, Granit-Bronz, Inc., was established. During this time of change the company again lost its president when Patrick Alexander died in 1948 and was succeeded by his brother.

### Time of Expansion

"John Alexander's tenure as president of Cold Spring Granite Company was marked by unprecedented expansion," wrote John Dominik. It was through those acquisitions that the company "became the largest granite concern in the world." Prior to World War II Cold Spring Granite had already obtained quarries that allowed it to supply a rich variety of colors to its market: "black" Canadian granite; South Dakota Ruby Red granite; and Minnesota Rainbow granite. During the war the company purchased the quarries situated in the original Rockville location. The postwar expansion began with Royal Granite and was followed by the purchase of the Texas Granite Company of Marble Falls; a Purple Crystal granite quarry near Rockville; a quarry and a small plant in Raymond, California; the Lake Placid Granite Company in New York; and still more quarries in Minnesota, South Dakota, California, and Canada. The quarries and plants purchased during the 1950s and 1960s benefited the company in terms of proximity to desirable market areas or job sites and with the added expertise of the new employees.

As the company expanded Cold Spring Granite won larger architectural contracts. In 1957, the company was chosen as granite supplier for the new Air Force Academy in Colorado Springs, Colorado. Rockville granite was used for fortress walls, building facing, walkway steps, and the plaza. The million-dollar project was the beginning of a push to convince architectural firms to use their granite in large construction projects.

Just as the combined talent of the Cold Spring crew had solved production problems in the past, they came together to meet the architectural challenges of the 1960s. New techniques were developed in order to apply granite to modern office towers such as the 54-story Bank of America building in San Francisco. After completing several skyscraper projects, the company shifted its focus to large plazas including those at the Atlanta International Headquarters of Coca Cola Company, the Chicago Civic Center, and the Twenty State Street Mall in Boston.

Even though the architecture of the 1960s and 1970s was dominated by modernism—more large commercial buildings were faced with glass, metal, and precast concrete than with stone—Cold Spring grew. Between 1975 and 1980 sales increased by $5 million per year, with sales topping $50 million in 1980. By the early 1980s builders had begun to move away from modernism and emphasized the color and tradition found in stone. Cold Spring Granite Company rode with that resurgence.

### A Third Generation of Alexander Family Leadership

The leadership of Cold Spring Granite had passed on to a third generation by this time. Thomas Alexander, Patrick's middle son, was made president in 1968. Like his father and uncle before him, his involvement in the company started at an early age, first with small jobs around the office and then work in the plant. An experienced pilot, Thomas nearly left the granite business, but his uncle, John Alexander, brought him on as his assistant. Through doing the company's production cost accounting Thomas became familiar with every aspect of the company, which enabled him to guide the development of new products and production methods.

In 1983 Patrick Alexander, the namesake of his uncle, became the fifth Alexander to lead the company. He had followed in their footsteps and learned the business from the ground up. He worked in the quarries and the precasting plant while still in high school. After graduating from St. Edward's College in Austin, Texas, he went on to the Marble Falls plant. Eventually Patrick took over supervision of operations at Raymond, Lake Placid, Texas, and Cold Spring Granite of Canada, Ltd.

The first five years of Patrick Alexander's term as president were marked by rapid growth. The number of employees increased from 700 to 1700, annual revenues rose to more than $110 million, and the company spent $40 million for quarry and plant improvements. But it also was a time marked by uncertainty. In the mid-1980s the granite industry was hit by high building vacancy rates and apprehension about federal tax law revision: the result was a slowdown of office and apartment construction. Foreign competitors were also an issue of concern for the American granite industry. Italy held 70 percent of the total structural granite market, compared with Cold Spring's 15 percent.

In 1987 Cold Spring along with two other American granite companies filed a suit with the International Trade Commission (ITC) against Italian and Spanish granite firms. They claimed that government subsidies were allowing the foreign companies to sell granite below cost. Patrick Alexander was quoted in the *Star Tribune* as saying that the Italian and Spanish firms "are slowly but surely driving otherwise competitive U.S. companies out of business." The companies were seeking penalty duties on foreign granite. Even though the commission initially found that there was a "reasonable indication" that U.S. granite firms were being hurt, ultimately it ruled against them.

Although the purchase of new granite and plant sites had slowed in the 1970s and 1980s it had not ceased entirely. Cold Spring acquired Capitol Marble and Granite Company, Inc., Granite Falls, Texas, in 1988. With Capitol's annual revenues of $20 million, the investment was expected to boost Cold Spring's sales to $130 million.

In 1989, *Corporate Report Minnesota* reported that Cold Spring Granite controlled 30 percent of the $500 million domestic market for granite, employed 1900 workers, and operated 31 quarries. Structural granite still provided its greatest source of revenue, but one-third of its business came from tombstones and mausoleums, and another ten percent from a new commercial line of highly polished granite tiles and countertops.

### The 1990s and Beyond

Cold Spring Granite laid off over 400 employees in 1991 in response to a severe downturn in the construction business. To help boost sales it introduced a line of unfinished granite slabs targeted for sale to international granite fabricators. Continued diversification resulted in a drop of architectural sales to about 28 percent of business by 1995. With a long history of successful adaptation to rapidly changing circumstances, a powerful legacy in itself, Cold Spring Granite nonetheless appeared solidly positioned in the industry as it prepared to enter its second century in business.

### Principal Subsidiaries

Granit-Bronz C.S.G Inc.; Texas Granite Corp.

### Further Reading

"Cold Spring Granite Acquires Texas Firm," *Star Tribune* (Minneapolis), November 22, 1988, p. 8D.

Dominik, John, *Cold Spring Granite: A History,* Cold Spring, Minn.: Cold Spring Granite Company, 1982.

Kahn, Aron, "Granite Firm Stonewalled by Economy," *St. Paul Pioneer Press,* September 13, 1991.

Klobuchar, Jim, "Firm Will Help You Say It with Granite," *Star Tribune* (Minneapolis), November 1, 1988, p. 1B.

McDonnell, Lynda, "Trade Deficit Keeps Rising; Hits at Home," *St. Paul Pioneer Press and Dispatch,* September 15, 1986, p. 1.

"Minnesota Shares in Stone Revival," *St. Paul Pioneer Press and Dispatch,* October 19, 1986, p. 1D.

"1995 CEOs of Minnesota," *Corporate Report Minnesota,* July 1995, p. 35.

Phelps, David, "Granite Firms Charge Unfair Competition by Europeans," *Star Tribune* (Minneapolis), July 29, 1987, p. 1M.

——, "Business Visas to Japan Called Hard to Get," *Star Tribune* (Minneapolis) February 29, 1988, p. 5D.

Rosengren, John, "Ground-Breaking Growth," *Corporate Report Minnesota,* July 1989, pp. 60–63.

Sundstrom, Ingrid, "Business Is Solid at Cold Spring Granite," *Star Tribune* (Minneapolis), October 9, 1988, p. 1D.

Thomma, Steven, "Panel Acts to Bolster Granite Firm," *St. Paul Pioneer Press and Dispatch,* September 10, 1987.

Weinberger, Betsy, "Cold Spring Granite Wants Out of Carlson Center Lease," *Minneapolis/St. Paul City Business,* August 14, 1992.

Wickland, John A., "Saws Scream Night and Day at Big Granite Works," *Minneapolis Tribune,* September 5, 1954.

—Kathleen Peippo

# The Columbia Gas System, Inc.

20 Montchanin Road
Wilmington, Delaware 19807
U.S.A.
(302) 429-5000
Fax: (302) 429-5461

*Public Company*
*Incorporated:* 1926 as Columbia Gas & Electric
 Corporation
*Employees:* 9,895
*Sales:* $2.6 billion (1995)
*Stock Exchanges:* New York
*SICs:* 1311 Crude Petroleum & Natural Gas; 4923 Gas
 Transmission & Distribution; 6719 Holding
 Companies, Not Elsewhere Classified

The Columbia Gas System, Inc., is one of the largest integrated natural gas systems in the United States. Columbia has two production subsidiaries that explore for and produce natural gas at numerous sites throughout North America. The company also operates five distribution subsidiaries that serve more than 1.9 million customers—residential, commercial, and industrial—in Ohio, Kentucky, Pennsylvania, Virginia, and Maryland. Columbia also provides wholesale service to other gas distributors. The company operates two interstate gas transmission subsidiaries, Columbia Transmission and Columbia Gulf. These two companies operate a network of 23,000 miles of pipeline. Columbia Transmission transports and stores gas throughout the Northeastern and Mid-Atlantic states, as well as portions of the Midwest. Columbia Gulf transports gas through its pipeline from the Gulf of Mexico to West Virginia, as well as within the Gulf Coast area. Columbia also operates a marketing subsidiary to oversee its own natural gas marketing efforts, and to provide supply and fuel management services to natural gas distribution companies and independent producers. Columbia also owns the largest liquefied natural gas receiving and regasification facility in North America, at Cove Point, Maryland. The company, through two subsidiaries, also sells propane wholesale and retail to more than 68,000 customers.

## Strong Foundation: 1906–1960

Columbia Corporation, formed in 1906 in Huntington, West Virginia, produced natural gas in that state and eastern Kentucky for delivery to Cincinnati, Ohio. Later renamed Columbia Gas & Electric Company, it doubled in size with the acquisition of Ohio Fuel Corporation in 1926. The resulting company was incorporated in Delaware as Columbia Gas & Electric Corporation.

The addition of Ohio Fuel greatly increased the volume of gas that the company sold. Natural gas had rapidly decreased in price as gathering and transmission systems improved and usage increased. Columbia's electricity sales, although still significant, were flattening. By the late 1920s it was clear that natural gas held the key to the company's growth. Oil was a companion product that Columbia Gas & Electric exploited.

The arrival of high-pressure pipelines in the late 1920s broadened the company's growth potential; natural gas then could be transported vast distances from the fields where it originated. Columbia pushed its lines eastward throughout Pennsylvania, and into New Jersey and New York state. In 1930 the acquisition of a 50 percent interest in Panhandle Eastern Pipe Line Company allowed Columbia to connect its eastern lines with natural gas fields in Texas. Meanwhile, Columbia Gas & Electric had gained control of virtually all the important reserves in northern Appalachia.

The greater availability of natural gas during the 1930s resulted in an increase in its utilization by industry. Natural gas burns almost twice as hot as manufactured gas and burns more cleanly. As its price fell, demand rose. At the same time that industry was discovering natural gas, however, industrial output was being curtailed due to the Great Depression. As a result, Columbia's earnings declined steadily from 1929 until 1935. In 1935, however, rebounding earnings doubled those of the previous year.

In 1935 the Public Utility Holding Company Act brought Columbia Gas & Electric under federal regulation. Antitrust litigation forced the company to divest Columbia Oil & Gasoline, the subsidiary that controlled Panhandle Eastern Pipe Line

---

**Company Perspectives:**

*The Columbia Gas System, Inc., through its subsidiaries, is active in pursuing opportunities in all segments of the natural gas industry and in related energy resource development. Exemplified by Columbia's three-star logo, these separately managed companies strive to benefit: system shareholders, through enhancing the value of their investments; customers, through efficient, safe, reliable services; and employees, through challenging and rewarding careers.*

---

Company. In 1936 Detroit, Michigan, was linked with the Columbia system, and natural gas was transmitted directly from Columbia's Texas fields. The connection helped Columbia reach new heights in sales and earnings for 1936.

In 1938 the Justice Department filed an antitrust suit against Columbia Gas & Electric, citing restraint of trade in the natural gas industry, and antitrust suits plagued Columbia for the next few years. In 1946 the company was forced to sell off the last of its electrical subsidiaries, a process that had been underway for several years. The company changed its name to the Columbia Gas System, Inc., in 1948 to reflect this change. Columbia was now almost exclusively in the natural gas business, although oil remained a part of these operations because the two resources were usually found together. During World War II demand for fuel was such that many turned to natural gas. The popularity of natural gas as a fuel was so great by the end of World War II that suppliers could not keep up with demand, and Columbia had to turn down new requests for service. Gas shortages continued until the early 1950s, when pipelines connected Columbia with gas fields in the Southwest and the Gulf of Mexico.

The Columbia Gas System grew in the 1950s through acquisitions in and around the company's chief operating region—northern Appalachia. In 1956 the company began a corporate simplification process aimed at reducing the number of subsidiaries subject to both federal and state regulation. The consolidation was completed in 1971.

### Shortages and Other Challenges, 1960s and 1970s

Throughout the 1960s Columbia performed very well. Revenues increased an average of 5.9 percent each year between 1961 and 1971. By 1967 Columbia was the largest integrated natural gas system in the United States. Demand for natural gas had doubled between 1956 and 1970, and throughout the 1970s demand for natural gas heavily outweighed supply. Columbia blamed U.S. regulation of interstate gas prices for this situation.

Columbia reacted to shortages by broadening its search for gas. Drilling efforts increased in Appalachia, offshore Louisiana, and Alaska. Columbia looked to liquefied natural gas (LNG) imports to help fill the gap between supply and demand. LNG was shipped from Algeria to a new regasification plant in Maryland. Although the price of natural gas was climbing, it still remained a relatively cheap form of energy in the early 1970s. In Columbus, Ohio, for example, the cost of heating a

home by gas was about half that of using heating oil. Columbia's gas sales reached a new peak in 1972. The relative economy of natural gas continued to grow in 1973 and 1974, when the OPEC oil embargo sent the price of oil to new heights.

By 1974 the natural gas shortage was becoming critical. Regulators were reluctant to grant rate increases, causing Columbia's funds earmarked for new exploration to remain limited. Columbia curtailed delivery of gas, and no new customers were accepted.

In April 1974 Columbia began producing synthetic natural gas from oil at high cost. The company was capable of synthesizing four percent of its needs from a single plant. Natural gas supplies continued to fall far short of demand, and in 1976 25 percent less gas was sold than at the company's peak in 1972.

The severe winter of 1976–77 was devastating for Columbia. Caught without adequate reserves after selling gas it projected would be in excess of demand, the company cut service. Factories and schools closed for weeks in some of the company's operating areas, and public outrage focused on Columbia. Columbia Gas System, then selling seven percent of all natural gas sold in the United States, attempted to remedy the situation by signing long-term contracts to buy gas from producers.

Utility regulators tried to remedy the shortage problem in the late 1970s by allowing rate increases that afforded Columbia improved earnings despite the low volume. Earnings in 1978 were up sharply over 1977.

Legislation was passed in 1978 that effectively deregulated the prices gas producers could charge at the wellhead. Intended to give incentive to producers to drill new wells, it resulted in very rich, long-term deals at guaranteed rates for producers. Hoping to ensure that it would never again experience shortages like those of 1976–77, Columbia Gas System entered into long-term contracts with producers at fixed rates during the late 1970s. It was a seller's market, and producers required pipelines like Columbia to accept take-or-pay clauses, which ensured that any gas the producers tapped would be purchased no matter what the market conditions were.

Columbia then had assured supply. The company's higher prices were more easily passed on to customers since regulation had become less stringent. Problems arose, however, because regulatory approval was required on rate increases or decreases. Once Columbia's price went up, it stayed up until regulatory commissions allowed it to drop. Columbia's gas was actually priced 28 percent above the national average in 1980. In response, Columbia's industrial customers, already annoyed by the interrupted service of the 1970s, defected to cheaper energy sources. In 1982 Columbia's largest single industrial customer, the Sohio Chemical anhydrous-ammonia plant in Lima, Ohio, quit Columbia altogether. The plant had previously bought nearly two percent of Columbia's total output. By the time rate reductions came through, many of Columbia's industrial customers had deserted the company.

### Recession, 1980s

The recession of the early 1980s hit Columbia's remaining industrial users hard, causing demand to fall. At the same time, energy prices worldwide collapsed. Columbia still had long-term contracts with producers to buy natural gas at the high prices of the late 1970s—gas it had to buy whether or not it could be sold.

In 1982 the company tried to cancel all its contracts, claiming that the catastrophic effects of the recession on Columbia's customers constituted a force majeure, nullifying the contracts. Producers and other pipelines serving Columbia refused, offering only to renegotiate. Major lawsuits followed in 1983, and, although gas producers eventually did renegotiate with other pipelines and distributors owing to the difficult economic times, Columbia was dealt with less cordially.

In 1985 Columbia faced possible bankruptcy. Still bound to long-term contracts, the company offered its major suppliers $800 million to settle the take-or-pay contracts. Faced with little choice, the producers took the deal. Columbia reduced prices and sold its gas at a total of $1 billion below cost over the next two years.

In the mid-1980s, new Federal Energy Regulatory Commission rules required pipelines to ship other distributors' gas. Columbia entered this business heavily. By 1989 only 30 percent of the natural gas moving through Columbia's pipelines was owned by the company, compared with 90 percent a decade earlier. By 1990 Columbia's share was down to six percent. In the late 1980s Columbia announced it intended to resume shipping its own gas—an activity that was riskier but also more profitable.

Losses plagued the company throughout the later 1980s, as it continued to fulfill its long-term contracts. Columbia continued to write off millions of dollars each year, and expected to continue to do so through 1995. Up to $40 million in losses would be recovered annually through rate increases, but the rest was a certain loss.

### Financial Challenges, 1990s

In 1990 unusually warm weather caused gas prices on the spot (short-term) market to remain much lower than expected. Customers began to buy low-cost gas on the spot market, while Columbia was still obligated to buy at the high prices specified in its long-term contracts signed with gas producers in the 1980s and even earlier. The company was again in serious financial straits. The company began negotiations to break some of its long-term contracts, in exchange for a $600 million settlement. But the issues were complicated, and could not be resolved quickly. Columbia suspended its dividend payment in June 1991, and Columbia and a subsidiary, Columbia Gas Transmission, filed for protection from creditors under Chapter 11 of the U.S. Bankruptcy Code in July. Both companies were granted debtor-in-possession status, allowing them to continue normal business operations.

Columbia's management expected the company to be in bankruptcy for only a short time, as the company's business was basically sound, and Columbia simply needed to reach an agreement with the holders of its crippling contracts. However, sorting out how much the contracts came to was not an easy job. The company claimed that it had contractual obligations totalling $1 billion, while the gas producers it had contracted with claimed in court they were owed $13 billion. There were other complicating factors as well. The Internal Revenue Service filed a $530 million claim against Columbia Gas Transmission, and Transmission customers collectively filed a suit for a refund of $350 million. At issue as well were various transfers of funds between Columbia Gas System and Columbia Transmission and another subsidiary.

While the bankruptcy negotiations dragged on, Columbia took steps to improve its financial position. In 1993 Columbia Transmission got out of the onerous business of selling Columbia's gas, and became principally a storer and transporter. And while Columbia's more than 4,800 gas purchase contracts were up in the air in bankruptcy court, the company was able to begin buying gas at lower market prices. Columbia also invested hundreds of millions of dollars to upgrade its existing pipeline system and expanded its capacity to deliver gas in the eastern part of its service area. The company's income began to rise with these moves, and by 1994 Columbia's net income had reached more than $240 million.

The bankruptcy proceedings remained deadlocked until early 1995. In April, Columbia Gas and its subsidiary Columbia Transmission offered bankruptcy reorganization plans that were acceptable to the companies' creditors. Columbia Gas named a new chairman, Oliver G. Richard 3d, in April as well. The previous chairman, John H. Croom, had said in 1992 that he would retire as soon as Columbia emerged from Chapter 11. The reorganization plans were approved by a judge in November. Columbia agreed to distribute approximately $3.6 billion to its creditors—more than the company had initially claimed it owed, but far less than the $13 billion its creditors had claimed. Columbia Transmission agreed to pay about $1.2 billion to gas producers to settle its contracts, and $2.2 billion to its parent to settle a debt from 1991.

### Looking Forward

Columbia's new chairman was able to announce good news shortly after he took office. In March 1996, the company paid its first dividends since it had filed for bankruptcy in 1991. Columbia also made a public offering of five million shares of common stock in March to cover short-term debts. The company anticipated strong earnings in 1996, when it could begin to put its era of bankruptcy behind it.

### Principal Subsidiaries

Columbia Gas Development Corporation; Columbia Natural Resources, Inc.; Columbia Gas Transmission Corporation; Columbia Gulf Transmission Company; Columbia LNG Corporation; Columbia Gas of Kentucky, Inc.; Columbia Gas of Ohio, Inc.; Columbia Gas of Maryland, Inc.; Columbia Gas of Pennsylvania, Inc.; Commonwealth Gas Services, Inc.; Columbia Atlantic Trading Corporation; Columbia Coal Gasification Corporation; Columbia Propane Corporation; Commonwealth Propane, Inc.; TriStar Capital Corporation; TriStar Ventures Corporation.

### Further Reading

Baldwin, William, "Paying the Piper," *Forbes,* November 22, 1982.
"Columbia Gas Picks Chairman," *New York Times,* March 16, 1995, p. D10.

"Columbia Gas—Sound Income Issue," *Financial World,* August 23, 1972.

Cook, James, "The Uses of Adversity," *Forbes,* November 27, 1989, pp. 60–64.

Egan, John, "Chapter and Purse," *Financial World,* October 1, 1991, pp. 28–29.

Goldner, Diane, "Columbia Gas Is Hot on Wall Street This Year. Much Too Hot to Handle," *Financial World,* October 12, 1993, pp. 59–61.

Ivey, Mark, "Will This Bubble Ever Burst?" *Business Week,* July 15, 1991, p. 35.

Jereski, Laura, "Columbia Gas's Reorganization Plan Provides Pipe Dream for Some, Long Wait for Skeptics," *Wall Street Journal,* January 24, 1994, p. C2.

Pomroy, John, "Recent Merger Aids Earning Power of Columbia Gas & Electric," *Magazine of Wall Street,* January 29, 1927.

Rogers, Michael, "Brinkmanship Wins for Columbia Gas," *Fortune,* November 25, 1985, p. 57.

Salpukas, Agis, "Columbia Gas Moves to Break Its Bankruptcy Deadlock," *New York Times,* April 18, 1995, p. D7.

—Thomas M. Tucker
—updated by A. Woodward

# SAINT-GOBAIN

# Compagnie de Saint-Gobain S.A.

Les Miroirs
F - 92096 La Defense Cedex
France
(33) (1) 47 62 30 00
Fax: (33) (1) 47 78 45 03

*Public Company*
*Incorporated:* 1665 as Compagnie des Glaces
*Employees:* 80,909
*Sales:* FFr74.5 billion (1994)
*Stock Exchanges:* Paris
*SICs:* 3211 Flat Glass; 3086 Plastics Foam Products;
2657 Folding Paperboard Boxes, Including Sanitary;
3296 Mineral Wool; 3241 Cement, Hydraulic; 3494
Valves & Pipe Fittings, Not Elsewhere Classified

Compagnie de Saint-Gobain S.A. came into existence more than 300 years ago, in 1665, as the royal glassmakers to Louis XIV, the Sun King of France. Today it is a multinational group of 292 companies in 37 countries worldwide but still retains a strong French identity, having survived both nationalization and reprivatization in the 1980s virtually unscathed. Saint-Gobain is one of the leading 10 French industrial groups and in the world's top 100 in sales. The company's subsidiaries fall into six main divisions: flat glass; containers, insulation and reinforcement; pipe; building materials; and industrial ceramics and abrasives. In each of these divisions, Saint-Gobain operates across Europe and in South America and Asia as well. Principal products include flat glass for buildings; glass bottles; automotive glass; grinding wheels; insulation; glass and rock wool; industrial ceramics; fiber reinforcements for automobile body parts, electrical insulation and printed circuit boards; cast iron pipes and fittings; drain pipes; water pipes; concrete pipes; roofing materials, and many others.

From its original base of flat glass manufacture in the 17th century using traditional methods, the company rapidly began to organize production on an industrial basis, establishing a strong European presence during the 19th century. It diversified into the chemical sector as well as other glass-based products. It has operated in Brazil since the 1930s, and in the United States since 1974. Following an attempted takeover bid by a much smaller French glass concern in 1969, Saint-Gobain merged with Pont-à-Mousson—founded in 1854—which makes products for the construction industry and is famous for its cast-iron pipes. The group then took its present form. In addition to flat glass, a large range of glass products, including bottles and containers, glass fibers, and wool, now account for about half of group sales. The merger with Pont-à-Mousson made Saint-Gobain the world's leading manufacturer of ductile cast-iron piping for water supply systems.

## Early History

Saint-Gobain is the only survivor of a group of private manufacturers founded in 1665 as part of the economic revival of France planned by Jean Baptiste Colbert, chief minister of Louis XIV. The letters patent which created the Compagnie des Glaces granted the company a monopoly on production and sale of glass in France. The original name of the company was Dunoyer, after the individual to whom these privileges were accorded. A group of Venetian glass-workers was persuaded to come to Paris, and production began in the Faubourg Saint-Antoine. However, disputes and difficulties arose with the Venetian authorities and workers, and they returned to Venice after two years. The company then formed an association with Richard Lucas de Nehou, proprietor of a glassworks at Tourlaville, near Cherbourg. Glass produced there was sent to Paris for the finishing process of grinding and polishing. In around 1680, Richard's nephew Louis was responsible for an invention that transformed the manufacture of glass and that remained in use until 1920; glass could now be rolled out on a flat surface, allowing much larger sheets to be produced. After Colbert's death in 1683, his successor Louvois allowed the establishment of rival companies and restricted the original company to the production of blown glass. This led to the establishment in 1692 of a new factory at the village of Saint-Gobain, which lay nearer Paris and was designed for the new process.

Following the death of Louvois, the newly created companies were united with Dunoyer under the name of Plastrier, but prob-

---

### Company Perspectives:

*Saint-Gobain is a worldwide leader in engineered materials. We transform materials in which we have a long history of experience: glass, cast iron piping, fibre reinforcements, ceramics . . . adding our technological know-how in order to respond to increasingly diverse customer needs worldwide.*

---

lems continued, and by 1702 Plastrier was declared bankrupt. Rescue came in the surprising form of the Geneva bank of Antoine Saladin. After complex negotiations, Saladin purchased the company, now to be called Dagincourt. The influence of the Swiss bank was to be felt throughout the 18th century.

The company now possessed a more entrepreneurial spirit and was able to exploit the new technique of rolled glass, benefiting from 18th-century prosperity and the numerous new uses for glass, especially mirrors. Technical expertise was brought in from 1740, to supplement the aristocratic element always prevalent in the company. Various rationalizations and reforms took place from 1755 to 1760 in response to the expansion of the market.

The company ceased glassblowing in 1763, and the ovens were improved. At the village of Saint-Gobain itself, a separate workers' enclave was established in 1775, partly as a solution to rivalry between the workers and other villagers.

The French Revolution of 1789 and its aftermath caused serious disruption, and it took 40 years to restore sales to the level of the best years of the Ancien Régime. In 1806 the first attempts at diversification took place, with the implementation of the Leblanc process for producing soda ash, an important ingredient for glass and later for many other industrial materials. This activity was transferred to new works at Chauny in 1822. The Tourlaville glass works closed in 1824, and production was concentrated at Saint-Gobain. In 1830 the company was incorporated as a société anonyme. The revolution had ended its monopoly, and there was a threat of competition from English glassworks—Ravenhead had been started by ex-Saint-Gobain workers—and several new French glass factories established during the 1820s, notably Saint-Quirin. The distribution of shares in the new company still reflected an aristocratic bias not suited to the world of 19th-century industry. Nevertheless, rationalization was taking place during this period, led by directors recruited from among technical university graduates. The process of mechanization had begun at the turn of the century.

With the boom in public building, the middle of the 19th century was a turning point for Saint-Gobain, heralding a golden age under the long presidency of the Duc de Broglie from 1866 to 1901.

Foreign ventures began with the lease of a factory at Stolberg in Germany in 1857, and in the following year a merger with its principal French rival Saint-Quirin gave Saint-Gobain a second presence in Germany—the glassworks built in 1853 at Mannheim, which was also to be the site of a French workers' city. Two other younger French rivals, Commentry and

Prémontré, had been acquired jointly before the merger. These moves were prompted by the growing threat of competition from Belgium, as well as the expanding English glassworks. Broglie's predecessor as president, Antoine-Pierre Hély D'Oissel, recruited Hector Biver, an Englishman who had also worked in Belgium. Following its 1858 merger, the company became the Société Anonyme de la Manufactures des Glaces et Produits Chimiques de Saint-Gobain, Chauny et Cirey. On the chemical side, the company benefitted from the presence of the famous chemist Joseph Louis Gay-Lussac, who had been president from 1844 to 1850, and who perfected his method of sulfuric acid production at Chauny. Considerable effort was devoted to improving the social and educational conditions of the workers, with the provision of schools, chapels, orphanages, savings and pension schemes, and even philharmonic and shooting societies. The image of aristocratic incompetence was largely dispelled during the second half of the 19th century.

### Entering the Modern Era

After 200 years, a fundamental shift occurred as a result of the merger with the firm of Perret-Olivier in 1874. The company consequently comprised nine chemical works compared with eleven, including three overseas, for glass: the turnover was almost equal in both sectors. Continuing strong Belgian and U.K. competitors in the glass industry were now joined by the United States and Germany, reducing Saint-Gobain's share of an expanding market. Pittsburgh Plate Glass, founded in 1883, attained the size of Saint-Gobain in only six years. The company responded by improving production methods and constructing further production sites in Europe: at Pisa, Italy, in 1889, and at Franière, Belgium, between 1898 and 1900. Subsidiaries were acquired in Holland, Spain, and Germany. Turnover increased from FFr18 million in 1890 to FFr47 million in 1913. Saint-Gobain was now Europe's leading glass producer, with 26.8 percent of the market, followed by Belgium with 23.3 percent and Pilkington with 22 percent. Engineers played a growing role in a centralized administration in this period, but provisions continued to be made for the workers: at Pisa there was a children's home, dispensary, and school, and training in housework was provided.

The early 1900s also saw the introduction of highly significant technical developments in glassmaking, including the Bicheroux and Fourcault processes, which allowed continuous sheets to be produced. A joint venture undertaken with Pilkington to exploit the American Window Glass process, although not a technical success, helped in the forging of a commercial treaty between the glassmakers of Belgium, France, and the United Kingdom, which lasted until World War II. The end of the 19th century also saw a radical change in the chemical division, where new processes resulted in the conversion of plants to superphosphate fertilizer production, for which Saint-Gobain was to remain famous in France until the abandonment of all its chemical interests in 1970.

The presence of French aristocrats and Genevan families still exerted considerable influence on the company, but with the quotation on the French Bourse in 1907 came greater dispersion of capital. From 1893, a new administrator, the archeologist and diplomat Melchior de Vogüé, accelerated administrative reform, giving more power to the divisions and creating the new posts of secretary-general and inspector of finances. He was president from 1901 to 1916. New headquarters were constructed in Paris between 1899 and 1902. Moves were made toward a more open management, with the consensus of shareholders, but capital ventures continued to be financed on an internal basis.

At the beginning of the 20th century, key factors in the company's development were the growth of U.S. competition, further technical developments in glassmaking, and extensions of its use. In addition to new types of continuous processes and improved furnaces, there were innovations in grinding and polishing techniques and, perhaps most significant, the discovery of tempering to produce security glass and allow its shaping. This discovery opened the way for expansion into the automobile market as well as the structural and artistic markets. Security glass was developed and patented by Saint-Gobain, and manufacturing on a production line for Citroën began in 1929. A new factory had been opened in 1920 at Chantereine to exploit the new processes.

International relations were important in the late 1920s; various accords led to stabilization of the industry between manufacturers in the United States, United Kingdom, and France. Saint-Gobain chose the Pittsburgh process for window glass as technically superior to its competitors. Surprisingly, glass bottles and flagons were still being manufactured at this time by the traditional glassblowing method, usually by small family enterprises scattered throughout France, Spain, and Italy. Saint-Gobain gradually absorbed these firms, as the increasing pace of mechanization rendered them uncompetitive. The 1930s witnessed perhaps the most important strategic move in the recent history of the company: diversification into glass fiber. Known by 18th-century English nobles, whose wigs had to be fireproof because of candles, glass fiber was also said to have been used in the Empress Josephine's coronation dress. Saint-Gobain, convinced by its U.S. contacts of the potential market for this product, obtained the necessary licenses, formed a new company, Isover, and acquired Balzaretti-Modigliani in Italy. However, production did not begin on an industrial scale until after World War II. Considerable research into improvements followed, which led to the intervention of the TEL and SUPERTEL processes for insulating materials, licensed by Saint-Gobain throughout the world.

Meanwhile the chemical side of the business had continued to decline, partly because of unsuccessful diversifications in this area. Of various diversifications attempted, including petroleum refining, one proved to be a long-term success: cellulose production. This began in 1920 and is the only process surviving from this period. An association with Papeteries Navarre in 1924 led to the formation of Cellulose du Pin and construction of a works at Facture in the Landes in 1928. It was planned at first to produce fibers for paper-based artificial textiles, but their decline after the war led to a switch to Kraft paper and bags.

The rest of the chemical side continued to be dangerously exposed. Saint-Gobain had refused an offer from Solvay for a merger in 1927 and 1928, which would have created a Franco-Belgian group on a par with ICI or I.G. Farben. Another proposal, from Kuhlmann for a French chemical union, was also turned down. These negative responses may have sprung from the desire by management to cling to the old regime. Management reforms in the 1920s and 1930s had been only tentative, and it was not until the presidency of Pierre Hély D'Oissel from 1936 to 1953 that fundamental changes in management and structure were initiated, heralding the new models of management of the 1950s and 1960s.

### Postwar Changes

The period from 1950 which led up to the merger of the two very dissimilar firms of Saint-Gobain and Pont-à-Mousson in 1970 was characterized by the growing power of the state in the French economy, begun during World War II under the Vichy regime. Senior officials of government were closely involved in the management of a planned economy and saw much of French industry as archaic and fragmented. The glass industry continued to flourish, and Saint-Gobain acquired a stake in its famous Belgian rival, Glaceries de Saint-Roch. Overseas expansion in glass fiber was dramatic, and the development of a presence in Brazil from 1960 supplemented solid bases in Belgium, Germany, Italy, Switzerland, and Spain. The TEL process was proving successful in the United States, and led to the acquisition of interests in the CertainTeed Corporation and the conversion of three old factories, which gave the company 10 percent to 15 percent of the U.S. market. However, another U.S. venture went wrong. A new subsidiary, American Saint-Gobain, founded in 1959, having already acquired four glassworks, then designed a new one in Greenland, Tennessee, intended to exploit the latest techniques in grinding and polishing. Disastrously, this factory did not open until 1962, after the invention of float glass by Pilkington. This revolutionary technique obviated the need for lengthy finishing processes. To compound the problem, the United States reacted strongly to the French invasion by an increase in tariffs of 30 percent.

Although the invention of float glass effectively killed off American Saint-Gobain, the parent company did not take the new process seriously until 1965, when it had to be acquired on much less favorable terms than were available just after the invention in the 1950s. Saint-Gobain, however, made up for lost time by rapidly modernizing all of its factories, starting with those overseas, thus helping amortize the old installations.

The 1960s also witnessed unsatisfactory alliances during the company's last attempts to revive its chemical operations, notably the creation of Péchiney-Saint-Gobain to develop organic chemicals, in particular the new plastics materials. Due to the instability of this sector, a government commission recommended a fundamental regrouping. However, before these recommendations could be acted upon, Rhône-Poulenc preempted them by acquiring Péchiney-Saint-Gobain. Péchiney itself did not want the chemical interests, and Saint-Gobain could not afford to buy them.

### Merger Negotiations in the 1960s

During this period the company raised capital to fund various ill-fated ventures. The increasing deficit caused further recourse to the banks, much against the Saint-Gobain tradition. At the end of 1968 came a major turning point: the dramatic offensive by Boussois Souchon Neuvesel (BSN) with a public offer for exchange to acquire 30 percent of Saint-Gobain, following tentative negotiations, which Saint-Gobain had rebuffed. BSN, a small but ambitious glass producer with an annual turnover of just under FFr600 million, had set its sights on a company with consolidated funds of more than FFr5 billion. BSN had chosen the moment when Saint-Gobain was suffering from the effects of the chemical restructuring as well as internal management struggles; these difficulties were reflected in the low price of the shares at the time. The offensive was a technical failure, securing only seven percent of Saint-Gobain's capital, one million shares out of the minimum 3.4 million required. A vigorous rescue bid had to be mounted by a consortium of banks led by the Compagnie de Suez, and 40 percent of the shares changed hands during the battle. This shift left the company badly shaken and with diminished funds. As a direct consequence of this affair, the bankers took the initiative in arranging the merger with Pont-à-Mousson, which they saw as a means of securing Saint-Gobain against further attacks of this nature. Arnaud de Vogüé, president since 1952, was initially reluctant but eventually recognized the end of the grand liberal regime of Saint-Gobain and the beginning of a new era.

One-third of the size of Saint-Gobain, Pont-à-Mousson, founded in the 1850s, had begun to detach itself from its coal and metallurgical interests during the 1960s. Originally founded by local coal merchants in the Lorraine after the discovery of new iron-ore deposits, the little town of Pont-à-Mousson between Metz and Nancy was chosen as the site of the first blast furnace in 1860. The company began to pursue a strategy of vertical integration, with the control of mines, ironworks, and end products, a policy continued right up until the 1960s. In 1866 it made the key decision to specialize in the production of cast-iron pipes. The invention in Brazil in 1915 of an improved technique of casting pipes using centrifugal force led to the company's establishing production in Brazil in 1937. After World War II, a new importance was given to cast iron by the ductile iron process, discovered by researchers at International Nickel in Canada during the 1940s. Pont-à-Mousson quickly obtained a license from a U.K. subsidiary of International Nickel, and began production in 1950. Even so, the old type of cast-iron pipe remained in production until the end of the 1960s.

In contrast to Saint-Gobain, the dominant personalities in the history of Pont-à-Mousson were engineers, notably Camille Cavallier, sole administrator from 1900 to 1917 and president from 1917 to 1926. In 1970, following the merger, a provisional organizational structure was adopted, based on the Pont-à-Mousson model, and it was Pont-à-Mousson's director, Roger Martin, who succeeded Arnaud de Vogüé as the head of the new group. A gradual process of rationalization then took place, involving decentralization, the establishment of a management structure, and the creation of product-based departments. In 1978, following a convention of all 41 directors, more fundamental reorganization of the new group led to the replacement of the six market departments by ten production-oriented branches. The 1970s also witnessed the jettisoning of the remaining chemical and petroleum investments, as well as the iron and steel interests inherited with Pont-à-Mousson. A brief flirtation with the products for nuclear reactors in 1972 was abandoned for political reasons. In glass fiber, the U.S. presence was reinforced by control of CertainTeed, and in France a new factory for insulation products was built at Orange. The energy

crisis helped here: between 1973 and 1975 Saint-Gobain doubled its European production of glass fiber. Significant investments were also made in float glass, with Saint-Gobain building ten out of the 17 new plants constructed in Europe during 1976.

The new strength of the combined companies was illustrated by their ability to weather the crises of this period, including heavy losses in brassware and machinery during 1977 and 1978, and a sudden downturn in the insulation market in 1981, resulting in massive overproduction.

### The 1980s and 1990s

After the 1978 reorganization, a search for further diversification led to the decision to enter the information technology sector. A joint subsidiary, Eurotechnique, was set up with National Semiconductor to produce electronic components, a partnership established with Cii-HB, and 30 percent of the capital of Olivetti acquired. However, before this venture could get off the ground, Saint-Gobain was nationalized by the new government of 1981 and forced to liquidate these holdings between 1982 and 1983. Yet Saint-Gobain was the only nationalized company to retain its top management, who continued to pursue their vigorous investment strategy and maintain a high level of industrial activity. The result was increased debt, countered by such austerity measures as plant rationalization. The group had to be slimmed down further with approaching reprivatization in 1986. The effect of these policies was spectacular; global profits increased by a factor of seven in six years.

The company made several important acquisitions in the early 1990s. In 1990 Saint-Gobain acquired the U.S. company Norton, which was the world's leader in abrasives. The company paid $1.9 billion for Norton, one of the biggest French takeovers of an American company. The deal with Saint-Gobain rescued Norton from a hostile takeover by a British conglomerate, and Norton was a valuable asset. Norton was the only world producer of all three leading kinds of industrial abrasives—grinding wheels for machining metals, coated abrasives for polishing wood and glass, and "super-abrasives" with a diamond or boron nitride base. Norton had a strong reputation for quality, and its purchase gave Saint-Gobain a firm presence in the North American market. Saint-Gobain also acquired two German glassmakers in 1991, GIAG and Oberland. By 1992, Saint-Gobain had become the world's leading manufacturer of glass.

However, sales began to slump by 1992, and net income fell precipitously. Despite sales of over FFr 70 billion each year from 1991 through 1993, the company was beset by a downturn in the industrial cycle that it could do little to control. Demand for its products was low across Europe, and the company's activities in Asia were not vigorous enough to offset the lull in its home economy. In 1993, Saint-Gobain's profits plunged 45 percent. The company struggled to rein in costs and reduce its debt. The next year, Saint-Gobain took a major step to strengthen its core business by selling off its paper, pulp and packaging unit. The company raised FFr5.63 billion ($1.07 billion) by selling its paper subsidiary La Cellulose du Pin to an Irish company, Jefferson Smurfit Group PLC. Saint-Gobain had been involved in the paper industry for 70 years, but the company's chairman, Jean-Louis Beffa, called La Cellulose du Pin "too small and too French" to be a global player like the rest of

Saint-Gobain's divisions. The loss of the paper business was expected to cut Saint-Gobain's sales by 10 percent, but the injection of cash was badly needed.

The next year, the recession in Europe seemed to be ending. Sales volume rose, although prices were still slack. Saint-Gobain did very well in North America in 1994, which improved the company's overall performance, and Saint-Gobain announced that it was ready to resume acquisitions, now that sales and profits were back to manageable levels. In June 1995 the company announced a complex deal with two companies that would effectively make Saint-Gobain the largest glass-packaging manufacturer in the world. Saint-Gobain spent $1 billion for management control of a joint venture with Ball Corp., an American manufacturer. The joint venture bought up Ball Glass Container Corp. and another U.S. glass container manufacturer, Foster Forbes, giving Saint-Gobain control of 22 U.S. plants. The deal put Saint-Gobain second only to Owens-Illinois in the U.S. glass-packaging market. Saint-Gobain was already the leader in the European glass-packaging market, and it was important to the company to expand into the North American market. The deal with Ball Corp. seemed indicative of the company's future plans, to increase Saint-Gobain's presence in markets far from Europe.

### Principal Subsidiaries

Saint-Gobain Vitrage; Saint-Gobain Emballage; Saint-Gobain Desjonquères; Pont-à-Mousson SA (99%); Everite; Isover Saint-Gobain; Socar; Société Européenne des Produits Réfractaires; Vetrotex Saint-Gobain; Glaceries de Saint-Roch (Belgium, 98%); Barbará (Brazil, 60%); Brasilit (Brazil, 86%); Scan-Gobain Glass A/S (Denmark, 81%); Vegla GmbH (Germany, 99%); Halbergerhütte GmbH (Germany); Fabrica Pisana (Italy); Balzaretti Modigliani (Italy, 87%); Vetri (Italy, 73%); Cristaleria Española (Spain, 73%); Gullfiber AB (Sweden, 99%); Stanton PLC (U.K., 99%); TSL Group (U.K., 99%); CertainTeed Corporation (U.S.A.); Norton Company (U.S.A.).

### Further Reading

Comcs, Frank J., "The Yuppie Who's Rewriting the Socialist Agenda," *Business Week,* May 13, 1985, p. 46.
"France's Saint-Gobain Says It Expects Drop in Net Profit for 1993," *Wall Street Journal,* April 2, 1993, p. A4B.
Hamon, Maurice, *Saint-Gobain (1665–1990): The Making of a French Multinational,* Editions Jean-Claude Lattès, 1990.
Kamm, Thomas, "Gobain in Deal to Establish a Bottle Giant," *Wall Street Journal,* June 28, 1995, p. 10A.
——, "Transaction Gives Saint-Gobain New Growth Potential," *Wall Street Journal,* August 23, 1994, p. 4B.
Truell, Peter, "Scandals Crimp Business for French Firms," *Wall Street Journal,* October 20, 1994, p. 10A.

—Peter W. Miller
—updated by A. Woodward

# Concord Fabrics, Inc.

1359 Broadway
New York, New York 10018
U.S.A.
(212) 760-0300
Fax: (212) 967-7025

*Public Company*
*Incorporated:* 1958
*Employees:* 435
*Sales:* $180.2 million (fiscal 1995)
*Stock Exchanges:* American
*SICs:* 2259 Knitting Mills, Not Elsewhere Classified;
    2299 Textile Goods, Not Elsewhere Classified

Concord Fabrics, Inc. designs and produces knit fabrics and designs woven fabrics from both natural and synthetic fibers, in a wide variety of colors and patterns. Most of its output is sold to manufacturers, chiefly of women's apparel. The company also sells its products to chain, department, and fabric stores for retail sale to customers who sew at home. The Weinstein family has held a controlling interest in the firm since its inception.

## Concord Fabrics in the 1960s

Based in New York City, Concord Fabrics was incorporated in 1958 as the successor to a business that began in 1920 as a staple converter for small apparel manufacturers. It went public in 1968, when 300,000 of its shares were offered for $15 per share. The following year 200,000 more shares were offered at $20 per share. The rest of the stock (about 70 percent) was held by the Weinsteins. At that time the company was a fabric designer and merchandiser with no production facilities. Its net sales had risen from $22.2 million in 1963 to $41.3 million in 1967, and its net income had increased from $485,000 to $1.3 million in that time. Alvin Weinstein was chairman of the company, and his brother Frank was president.

Concord Fabrics was developing, designing, and styling fabrics from woven and knitted greige (unfinished) goods bought from outside sources. Independent plants then printed, dyed, and finished the goods with designs, colors, and combinations specified by Concord Fabrics. At this time the company was producing about 20 types of woven fabrics in a wide range of solid colors. These were coordinated with about 75 plaids and 100 prints. Knit fabrics, introduced in 1967, were available in five fabric types and about 30 patterns. Designs were contemporary and intended for a youthful market. The company leased space in Manhattan's garment district for its main offices and showroom and for warehousing and distribution. For a time it also leased an office and showroom in Los Angeles.

About 72 percent of the output of Concord Fabrics in 1968 was going to manufacturers of young women's moderately priced casual clothing. The rest was being sold to department stores and other retailers as piece goods for sewing at home. This market, which indicated growing interest by young women in sewing, had grown to 28 percent of company output from only 11 percent in 1965. In all, about 3,000 customers were being served by 50 commissioned salesmen handling Concord's goods exclusively and 44 agents who also handled competing lines.

## Entering Manufacturing in the 1970s

Sales and profits increased in the following years for Concord Fabrics, which continued to benefit from the growth of the home sewing market. Annual sales increased from $53.3 million in 1968 to $82.2 million in fiscal 1975 (ending August 31, 1975), and net income rose from $2.2 million to $3.7 million. No dividends were distributed after 1970, however. Leonard Machinery Corp., a subsidiary of Concord Fabrics, was sold in 1972. In 1971 the company opened its first production facility, a 110,000-square-foot knitting mill constructed on 60 acres of land purchased in Milledgeville, Georgia.

Majority ownership of Concord Fabrics was held at this time by AFW Fabric Corp., which in turn was owned by Alvin Weinstein, Frank Weinstein, and several Weinstein family trusts. When a merger of the two companies was proposed, other holders of Concord Fabrics stock complained that the $3 per share offered them was inadequate, even though the stock was trading for less than that amount when the plan was announced. Five lawsuits were filed to halt the merger, one of them by the attorney general of New York, who was granted a temporary injunction blocking the action by a state court in June 1975. The merger plan was dropped in February 1976, by which time Concord Fabrics stock was trading at $9.50 per share.

Concord Fabrics broadened its scope in 1976 by leasing a 140,000-square-foot dyeing and finishing mill for woven goods in Washington, Georgia. (This plant was purchased in 1986.) But the late 1970s were difficult years for the company, which lost $164,514 in fiscal 1977 on sales of $78.3 million. Sales rose to $93.8 million in fiscal 1978, but net income amounted to only $472,000. During the next two years, as Concord Fabrics directed its efforts toward the more profitable women's fashion apparel market, sales slumped and the company fell into the red. Long-term debt was nearly $8 million in 1980.

### Acquisitions in the 1980s

By fiscal 1983 Concord Fabrics was back on track, economies enabling it to earn $1.2 million on sales of $84.3 million. The following year the company earned $3.1 million on a sales volume of $116.2 million. In 1984 it acquired, for $825,000 in cash, Eastern Software Distributors, Inc., a microcomputer software and paper products distributor with annual sales of about $4 million. Established as a subsidiary of Concord Fabrics, Eastern Software, based in a suburb of Baltimore, was "intended to provide a vehicle for growth in an expanding field," according to Alvin Weinstein. It proved not to be profitable, however, and soon was disposed of by the parent company.

Concord Fabrics formed a new heat transfer print unit, called the Printed Knit Division, in 1985. A company spokesman said the new division would function as a converter, buying both the transfer print paper and the knitted fabric to style and sell these prints. The new division was to complement and capitalize on the capabilities of the company's existing print work. In 1987 Concord Fabrics acquired Trilogy Fabrics, Inc., a New York print converter, and hired its principals to run its print fabrics division. Subsequently, however, Concord Fabrics contracted out all of its print requirements. A dyeing and finishing plant in Chino, California, was purchased in 1987. The machinery and equipment were sold in 1994 for $2 million to another company, and the building was leased.

After earning only $76,000 in fiscal 1985 and $463,000 in fiscal 1986, Concord Fabrics had a net income of $2.2 million on sales of $138 million in fiscal 1987. In fiscal 1988, however, it lost $3.6 million on sales of $139.1 million. That year, even though the Weinstein family held about 62 percent of the company's stock, shareholders approved an antitakeover measure creating two classes of stock. For each current share, stockholders received one Class A and one Class B share, with each Class B share having 10 votes, compared with only one for each Class A share. The change, said Alvin Weinstein, "will help the current management retain control of the company and let them worry about something longer than three months ahead."

### Mixed Results in the 1990s

Concord Fabrics returned to profitability in fiscal 1989, when it earned $3.6 million on $174.4 million in net sales. The following year it had net earnings of $4.3 million on sales of $195 million. Sales ranged between $197 million and $201.7 million during the next four fiscal years. Net income was below $1 million in 1991 and 1992, but it rose to $4.6 million in 1993 and a record $6.4 million in 1994.

Concord Fabrics launched two new fabric lines for home furnishings in 1991. The company, in 1994, purchased Kat-Em International Inc., a Los Angeles importer and distributor of woven and knitted fabrics with annual sales of about $25 million, for $1.15 million. It believed this purchase would enhance its ability to buy fabric and sell its output overseas.

In fiscal 1995 Concord Fabrics again fell into the red, losing almost $3 million on sales of $180.2 million. This outcome reflected a deficit by Kat-Em International (which accounted for about 13 percent of consolidated sales) as well as the fluctuating and highly competitive nature of the textile and apparel industries. Historically, Concord's sales had been affected not only by general economic conditions but also by the degree of public acceptance of its fabrics and designs.

Concord Fabrics closed its Washington plant in 1995 because of poor business. By the end of the year its only remaining production facility was the knitting and finishing plant in Milledgeville, which now occupied 130,000 square feet. The company believed this facility would provide substantially all of its requirements for the knitting, dyeing, and finishing of knitted fabrics. Its requirements for the finishing and printing of woven goods to its specifications would be contracted to outside finishers, who were doing the bulk of this work even before the Washington plant was closed.

In fiscal 1995 woven fabrics accounted for 69 percent of the company's fabric sales. The unfinished goods were obtained from about 85 suppliers and designed by the Concord Fabrics staff to meet current and developing styles. Knitted fabrics accounted for the other 31 percent of fabric sales. Yarn for knitting was being purchased from 13 suppliers in fiscal 1995. The company generally produced knitted fabrics to meet orders received in advance and, as a result, these fabrics usually were not being styled with a view to anticipating fashion trends. During the year 88 percent of the yarn purchased by Concord Fabrics was knitted at the Milledgeville plant.

Sales of Concord's finished products were being made both by company salesmen and independent sales agents. In fiscal 1995, 68 percent of the company's fabric sales were to manufacturers and 32 percent to retail stores. Sales were made primarily to manufacturers of budget- and moderate-priced women's apparel, but also to manufacturers of men's wear, to the home furnishings industry, and for resale to the home sewing market. Of about 4,100 customers in fiscal 1995, the largest, a retail chain store, accounted for about 3 percent of sales, and the 20 largest accounted for 27 percent of sales. The New York metropolitan area was the principal sales market.

Alvin Weinstein was still chairman of Concord Fabrics in 1995. His brother Frank was vice-chairman. Earl Kramer had been president of the company since 1979. Company headquarters remained in Manhattan's garment district, where Concord also continued to maintain a showroom. The company's long-term debt was $20 million in May 1995.

### *Principal Subsidiaries*

Concord FSC, Inc.; Kat-Em International Inc.; Trilogy Fabrics, Inc.

### *Further Reading*

"Agreement Is Set To Purchase Kat-Em International Stock," *Wall Street Journal,* February 22, 1994, p. A4.

"Concord Acquires Trilogy," *WWD,* July 20, 1987, p. 11.

"Concord Fabrics Fashions Growth Pattern Via Innovative Stress," *Barron's,* December 16, 1968, p. 37.

"Concord Fabrics Forms Printed Knit Division," *Daily News Record,* August 27, 1985, p. 8.

"Concord Fabrics Inc., AFW Fabric Abandon Proposal To Merge," *Wall Street Journal,* February 11, 1976, p. 21.

"Concord Fabrics Inc. Merger with AFW Is Blocked by a New York State Court," *Wall Street Journal,* June 13, 1975, p. 19.

Luther, Michael, "Concord's Caplan: Converters Facing 'Era of Hard Sell,' " *Daily News Record,* January 10, 1979, p. 17.

"Shareholders Ratify Measure Creating 2 Classes of Stock," *Wall Street Journal,* April 5, 1968, p. 8.

—Robert Halasz

a Du Pont company

# Conoco Inc.

600 North Dairy Ashford Road
Houston, Texas 77079
U.S.A.
(713) 293-1000
Fax: (713) 293-1058

*Wholly Owned Subsidiary of E.I. du Pont de Nemours
and Company*
*Incorporated:* 1920
*Employees:* 17,000
*Sales:* $17.66 billion (1995)
*SICs:* 1311 Crude Petroleum & Natural Gas; 2911
Petroleum Refining

Conoco Inc. is a fully integrated and broadly based oil and gas company, involved in all aspects of the petroleum business on an international scale. Since its acquisition by Du Pont in 1981, Conoco has moved toward a renewed concentration on petroleum, as well as specialty petroleum and commodity products that play an integral part in Du Pont's other industrial operations. Upstream operations mainly located in North America, the North Sea, Dubai, and Indonesia produce more than 430,000 barrels of crude oil and 1.3 billion cubic feet of gas per day. Downstream operations process about 700,000 barrels of crude oil and other feedstock each day at four refineries in the United States, one in the United Kingdom, and one in Germany in which Conoco holds a 25 percent stake. Conoco's marketing operations include more than 7,000 retail outlets in the United States, Europe, and the Asia-Pacific region selling petroleum products under the Conoco, Jet, and Seca brand names. The company's transportation assets include eight oceangoing tankers and full or part-ownership in 8,000 miles of pipelines. Conoco is also the worldwide leader in supplying graphite coke to the steel industry. Conoco is Du Pont's largest subsidiary, accounting for about 42 percent of the parent company's annual revenues.

## Early History as Continental Oil

Conoco's earliest predecessor, Continental Oil & Transportation Company (CO&T), was founded in Ogden, Utah, in 1875 by Isaac Elder Blake to transport petroleum products from the East Coast for sale in Utah, Idaho, Montana, and Nevada. Operations were later expanded to include Denver and San Francisco, and in 1877 the company was reincorporated in California.

Blake's pioneering use of railroad tank cars to transport oil contributed to CO&T's quick success. By the early 1880s, CO&T was sending modest shipments to Mexico, Canada, the Hawaiian islands, the Samoan islands, and Japan. In the western United States it was competing with Standard Oil.

In 1884 CO&T agreed to become a Standard affiliate. The following year CO&T merged with Standard's Rocky Mountain operations, and the company was reincorporated in Colorado as the Continental Oil Company. Blake was named president of the new concern, and headquarters were established in Denver. Continental continued to function much as CO&T had, although operations were consolidated with Standard's in Colorado, New Mexico, Wyoming, Montana, and Utah.

Continental products were purchased from Standard and other providers in the East and included kerosene refined for lamp oil, lubricating oils, heavy oil for heating fuel, and paraffin used in candlemaking. In 1888 Continental eliminated the need for transporting products from the East Coast by acquiring a minority interest in United Oil Company with production and refining interests in Colorado.

In 1893 Blake resigned, having become bogged down in personal debt due to heavy investments in railroads and other ventures. For the next 14 years, Henry Morgan Tilford served as president. By 1900, Continental was heavily involved in the marketing of kerosene, although its product line had been expanded to include lamps, cooking stoves, ovens, and a variety of household and industrial oils.

Continental continued to grow in its own market under Tilford but did not venture outside of the Rocky Mountain area, where it became the Standard affiliate most closely resembling a monopoly. In 1906 Continental took over Standard bulk stations in Idaho and Montana, and by the end of the year controlled better than 98 percent of the western market.

In 1907 Continental purchased the Denver office building that housed its sixth-floor headquarters and renamed it the Continental Oil Building. That same year, Edward T. Wilson, who had worked his way up from junior clerk, was named president.

In 1911 the U.S. Supreme Court ordered Standard Oil to divest some of its holdings. Two years later Continental Oil Company became one of 34 independent oil companies formed as a result of the court's antitrust ruling. Continental tapped into the growing market for automobile gasoline in 1914 and built its first service station. Two years later Continental bought out United Oil and officially entered the oil production business.

During World War I Continental worked under the direction of the oil division of the U.S. Fuel Administration, producing airplane fuel for pioneer aircraft and training planes. In 1919 the company adopted a new trademark, a circular emblem with a soldier standing below the word Conoco.

In 1924 C. E. Strong, who had worked his way up through the Continental accounting department, was elected president and chief executive officer. Continental became a fully integrated oil company later that year when it merged with Mutual Oil Company, owning assets in production, refining, and distribution.

By 1926 Continental's assets topped $80 million, including 530 miles of pipeline, six refineries, and marketing operations ranging through 15 states. That year, sales surpassed $50 million for the first time. The following year the company moved into its new $1 million Denver headquarters, and S. H. Keoughan, a former president of Mutual Oil, was named president and chief executive officer of Continental.

In 1929 Continental merged with Marland Oil Company. The Marland Oil Company had been incorporated in 1920 to combine assets of the Marland Refining Company and Kay County Gas Company, all under the direction of Ernest Whitworth Marland. E. W. Marland, a Pittsburgh attorney turned oil wildcatter, had come to Oklahoma in 1908 and a year later discovered oil on Indian burial grounds near Ponca City. Marland later assembled a staff of geologists who led him to one strike after another, while his young companies paced development of the Oklahoma oil industry and the new group of independent oil concerns. Marland's interests in exploration extended outside of Oklahoma, leaving him in need of additional financing. In 1923, that financing approached Marland when John Pierpont Morgan of J.P. Morgan & Co. offered to become Marland Oil's banker. E. W. Marland agreed and sold Morgan $90 million in company stock.

By 1926 the company owned or controlled 5,000 tank cars emblazoned with Marland Oil's red triangle, operated more than 600 service stations in the Midwest, and was marketing products in every state as well as in 17 foreign countries. Employees shared in the success, receiving high salaries, free medical and dental care, and company loans to buy homes. In 1926 Marland negotiated the right to explore for oil in Canada on land concessions owned by the Hudson's Bay Company of Canada.

However, while Marland had expanded rapidly, so had its liabilities, which had grown to more than $8 million by the end of the year. Marland blamed the company's increasing liabilities on Morgan's bankers, who had forced him to sell oil to Standard, vetoed pipeline plans, and stymied expansion during the mid-1920s. By 1928 those bankers had gained increasing power on the company's board. During an executive committee meeting that year Marland was informed that he would be replaced as president by Dan Moran, former vice-president of the Texas Company. Marland was offered the chairmanship of the company and a pension but was told he would have to leave Ponca City. Marland promptly resigned and left the oil industry altogether shortly thereafter. He was later elected Oklahoma governor and became instrumental in leasing state capital grounds for oil production.

In January 1929 Marland Oil acquired the Prudential Refining Company with a large refinery in Baltimore, Maryland. In June of that year Morgan bankers fostered a merger agreement between Marland Oil and Continental, under which Marland agreed to purchase Continental while the Continental name would be retained. Moran was named president and chief executive officer, Edward Wilson chairman of the board, and Keoughan chairman of the executive committee.

Shortly after the new Continental moved its headquarters from Denver to Ponca City in 1929, the stock market crashed with the company holding a $43 million debt load. During the first full year of the ensuing Depression, Continental lost nearly $11 million. While losses were mounting that year, Moran devised a scheme for a pipeline that would run from Ponca City to Chicago and Minnesota and greatly reduce transportation costs. A partnership was formed called the Great Lakes Pipe Line Company, and Continental subscribed to a 31 percent stake.

### The 1930s and 1940s

In 1932 Continental entered the Midwest through the acquisition of 119 service stations and 43 bulk plants. Meanwhile an emphasis on research resulted in the development of new products, which included Germ Processed Motor Oil and Bronze Gasoline, touted as a high-performance fuel. To reduce company debt, Moran focused the company's attention on domestic operations. In 1933 the Sealand Petroleum Company in the United Kingdom, formed seven years earlier by Marland, was sold and the following year Hudson's Bay operations were shut down. Continental also withdrew from northeastern states but maintained production at the Baltimore refinery to serve southern markets. By 1937 Continental had eliminated its debt load, and in December of that year 5,000 bonus checks worth a total of $770,000 were awarded to employees.

During the late 1930s Continental expanded its pipeline system by purchasing majority interests in the Rocky Mountain Pipe Line Company and the Crude Oil Pipe Line Company. Refinery operations were expanded in 1941 and a new $4.5 million refinery was opened in Lake Charles, Louisiana. In June of that year, Continental introduced its new lubricant, Conoco Nth Motor Oil, to meet the demand for heavy fuel oils.

During World War II the U.S. government constructed a 100-octane refinery in Ponca City, and Continental's vice-president of manufacturing, Walter Miller, was named to supervise operations. The plant went online in mid-1943 and began producing high-octane jet gasoline. Following the war, Continental focused on areas in which it was fully integrated, namely Texas, Colorado, Oklahoma, Illinois, Kansas, Missouri, and Iowa.

In 1946 a new era of oil exploration was launched when Continental joined with three other oil companies in developing Laniscot I, the world's pioneer offshore exploration boat. The following year Dan Moran resigned because of ill health, and Leonard F. McCollum left Standard Oil Company of New Jersey to become president and chief executive officer at Continental. McCollum's aggressive exploration program soon led to the 1947 acquisition of oil leases for 209,000 acres in the Gulf of Mexico. Hudson's Bay Oil and Gas Company (HBOG) was reactivated about the same time, after oil was discovered in Alberta, Canada. In 1948 Continental joined Ohio Oil Company and Amerada Petroleum Corporation in forming Conorada Petroleum Corporation to explore for oil outside North America.

Continental also initiated a refinery modernization and construction program in the late 1940s, leading to enlarged refineries in Denver and Ponca City and a new refinery in Billings, Montana. Meanwhile, production efforts in Kansas were reduced as the company focused on Texas, Kansas, California, and Wyoming.

### Exploration and Diversification in the 1950s and 1960s

Continental celebrated its 75th anniversary in 1950 by breaking ground for a $2.25 million Ponca City research laboratory and relocating its headquarters from Ponca City to Houston. The company also broke into new business fields during the early 1950s. A synthetic detergent plant was acquired, and Continental Oil Black Company was formed to produce carbon black, used in the production of synthetic rubber.

In 1952 Continental acquired interests in 1,390 miles of pipeline, including the new 1,080-mile line from Wyoming oil fields to an important refining center in Wood River, Illinois. Four years later offshore exploration was revolutionized when Continental, along with the Union, Shell, and Superior oil groups, launched CUSS I, the world's first drill ship.

Continental's interest in overseas exploration grew throughout the decade, and by 1957 the company held exploratory concessions for nearly 50 million acres outside the United States, including land in Libya, Guatemala, and Italian Somaliland. Hudson's Bay Oil and Gas Company (HBOG), by 1957, had rights to a total of 700,000 acres in Egypt, Libya, Somalia, British Somaliland, Venezuela, and Guatemala.

During the 1960s, Continental purchased several independent gasoline station chains in Europe to provide a market for its newly found Libyan oil. Included in a string of acquisitions were SOPI, with more than 400 stations in West Germany and Austria; Jet Petroleum, Ltd., with more than 400 stations in the United Kingdom; SECA, with stations in Belgium; Arrow Oil Company, with 70 retail outlets in eastern Ireland; and the U.K. Georg Von Opel chain of 155 stations in West Germany.

Continental also strengthened its European presence in the carbon black market by establishing production facilities in Italy, the Netherlands, France, and Japan. The company's presence in North and South America also grew with an expansion of its Montana pipeline system and purchase of the Douglas Oil Company, operating three southern California refineries and more than 300 stations. Continental opened a new refinery near the Atlantic Ocean entrance to the Panama Canal and acquired Mexofina, S.A. de C.V., with exploratory rights in Mexico.

Annual sales topped $1 billion in 1962 and diversification moves followed. In 1963, Continental acquired American Agricultural Chemical Company (Agrico), a major manufacturer of plant foods and agricultural chemicals. About the same time Continental became involved in the production of biodegradable detergents and plastic piping.

In 1964 Andrew W. Tarkington, a former executive vice-president, was named president of Continental. McCollum remained chief executive and was named to the additional post of chairman. By that time, Continental was pumping more crude out of Libya, Canada, Venezuela, and Iran than it was producing in the United States, with Libyan oil having almost by itself made Continental an international dealer. Exploration and production teams also were operating in the Middle East, Mexico, Panama, Argentina, Pakistan, New Guinea, and Australia. With its worldwide presence growing, Continental moved its headquarters from Houston to New York that same year.

In 1966 Continental diversified into minerals and acquired Consolidation Coal Company (Consol), the second largest U.S. coal-producing company. During the late 1960s expansion and diversification continued as the company purchased the Australia pesticides distributor Amalgamated Chemicals, Ltd. as well as Vinyl Maid, Inc., a manufacturer of polyvinyl chloride containers. Continental also entered joint agreements to build a calcined-petroleum coke plant in Japan, a polyvinyl chloride resin plant in the United Kingdom, and Spain's first biodegradable detergent plant.

In 1967 Tarkington assumed the additional duties of chief executive officer while McCollum remained chairman. During the next two years Tarkington spearheaded consolidation efforts and established new policies for gauging financial risks. John G. McLean, another former executive vice-president, was named president and chief executive officer in 1969, replacing Tarkington, who was named vice-chairman of the board.

## New Leadership and a New Name in the 1970s

McLean reorganized administrative levels and created a management team with four divisions—Western Hemisphere petroleum, Eastern Hemisphere petroleum, Conoco Chemicals, and Consol. In 1972 he replaced McCollum, who had retired as company chairman. Under McLean's leadership, the company established a policy of focusing on its new mix of natural resources, including coal, uranium, and copper. During the early 1970s the company sold its plastic pipe manufacturing business and interest in Amalgamated Chemicals and closed a petroleum sulfonates plant. Continental stepped up its mineral production during the same period, entering joint ventures to develop uranium prospects in Texas and France. With the onset of the 1973 oil crisis, Continental accelerated its search for oil outside the Middle East, and during the next two years made significant discoveries in the North Sea.

In March 1974, Howard W. Blauvelt was named to fill the post of president, which McLean had left vacant when he assumed the chairmanship. Within two months, however, the responsibilities of chairman and chief executive were also thrust upon Blauvelt, following the untimely death of McLean. During this time of upheaval, John Kircher was named president.

Conoco Coal Development Company, a wholly owned subsidiary, was formed in 1974 to coordinate research and long-range planning for the production of synthetic fuels made from coal. That same year the company signed a ten-year contract for oil and gas exploration for over two million acres in Egypt.

In 1979 Continental changed its name to Conoco Inc. That year, Ralph E. Bailey was named president, replacing Kircher who remained deputy chairman, a post to which he had been appointed in 1975.

During the late 1970s Conoco entered three major joint ventures, combining with Monsanto Company to manufacture ethylene and related products, with Du Pont in a $130 million oil and natural gas exploratory program, and with Wyoming Mineral Corporation, a subsidiary of Westinghouse Electric Corporation, to develop a Conoco uranium deposit in New Mexico. Blauvelt resigned as chairman and chief executive officer in 1979 and was replaced by Bailey in both positions.

## The 1980s: Takeover by Du Pont

Conoco began the 1980s as the ninth largest oil company in the United States with $2 billion dedicated to capital outlays. In 1980 Conoco purchased Globe Petroleum Ltd., with 220 retail outlets in the United Kingdom, and entered into a second exploration venture with Du Pont. A facility expansion program was also initiated early in the decade, including a $2 billion upgrade of the Lake Charles refinery, additions to the Lake Charles coke-manufacturing plant, and construction of a Lake Charles detergent chemical plant as well as a St. Louis-based lube-oil plant. In 1981 the company announced it would build a new world headquarters in Houston for its petroleum and chemical operations.

In May 1981, Dome Petroleum, Ltd. of Canada offered to buy 13 percent of Conoco's common stock for $910 million, in hopes of exchanging the stock for Conoco's 53 percent stake in HBOG. A month later a deal was consummated giving Dome a 20 percent interest in Conoco, which was traded along with $245 million for Conoco's stake in HBOG. The transaction sent a message that Conoco was ripe for a takeover, and a bidding war for the company ensued with Seagram Company and Mobil Corporation participating. With threats of a hostile takeover looming, Conoco went in search of a white knight—a friendly acquirer—and found Du Pont a willing participant. By August 1981, Du Pont had acquired Conoco for $6.8 billion in the most expensive merger to that date.

Following the takeover, Du Pont consolidated Conoco operations and began selling the oil company's interests to reduce a $3.9 billion debt incurred in the purchase. During the first three years after the takeover Du Pont closed down some oil and chemical facilities and sold better than $1.5 billion in Conoco assets, including Continental Carbon Company and a variety of chemical, mineral, oil and gas assets. Conoco Chemicals was absorbed by Du Pont's larger petrochemicals departments. Du Pont also began utilizing some of Conoco's former chemical assets, including its ethylene business. By 1983 Du Pont had increased its output of ethylene, a petrochemical feedstock used in making polyethylene, from 850 million pounds annually to three billion pounds.

In 1983 Constantine S. Nicandros was named president of Conoco. In the following years, Conoco stepped up offshore exploration and production efforts in the Gulf of Mexico and the North Sea. In 1984 the company began operating the world's first tension leg well platform for deep-sea oil exploration in the North Sea, with capabilities of producing oil under 2,000 feet of water.

During the mid-1980s, Conoco also expanded its oil and gas activities in Canada and Egypt. In January 1985 Conoco joined four other oil companies in a $312 million partnership to produce oil in Alaska. However, two years later Conoco pulled out of the partnership, after the price of crude oil dropped.

In 1987 Bailey retired as chairman and his position was eliminated. Edgar S. Woolard was named president of Du Pont, with duties to include overseeing Conoco operations. At the same time, Nicandros assumed the additional duties of chief executive officer.

During the late 1980s Conoco made significant oil discoveries in Norway, the United Kingdom, Indonesia, Ecuador, and the United States. In 1989, after a two-year lapse, Conoco reopened its oil fields in Alaska. That same year 64 service stations were purchased in the Denver area in an effort to boost name recognition and sales by branded outlets. In an early 1990 joint venture, Conoco and Calcined Coke Corporation formed a company called Venco to enhance Conoco's ability to meet Du Pont's needs for specialty coke products.

## The 1990s and Beyond

Nicandros would head Conoco from the early 1990s until 1996, a period in which he became widely known both within and outside the international oil industry because of his commitment to the environment and his company's penchant for prospecting in high-risk areas. In 1990 he issued his "nine points for environmental excellence" program as a guide for Conoco's future development in an "earth-friendly" manner. Hailed by environmentalists and anticipative of future U.S. Congressional mandates, the program's most striking commitment was to construct only doubled-hulled tankers in the future in order to prevent oil spills at sea. Industry experts estimated that adherence to the program cost Conoco $50 million a year.

Conoco began the 1990s with exploration teams in 21 countries, and under Nicandros the company aggressively sought new areas of exploration in the early 1990s. With the huge oil fields of North America and the North Sea continuing to be drained, Conoco more than any other oil company reached out to high-risk areas as a long-term strategy of keeping its reserves at an acceptable level. In 1991 the company formed a joint venture in Russia—in that country's largest oil investment by a foreign country to date—to drill oil in the Russian Arctic. By fall 1994, the Ardalin oil complex began producing crude oil out of its field of 110 million barrels of recoverable oil beneath the frozen tundra. Conoco also began to see results in 1995 from its 18 percent interest in a $3.9 billion project in the Norwegian Sea, which involved a 288,000-ton tension leg platform installed at a water depth of 1,150 feet through a combined 30 million person-hours of work over a four-year period.

However, a few of the company's exploration efforts met with some challenges. In March 1995, for example, after three years of negotiations, a $1 billion deal to produce oil in Iran was blocked by the Clinton administration as part of increasingly hostile relations between the United States and Iran. Moreover, in January 1996 a consortium led by Conoco proposed to develop a natural gas field in northern Mexico, a country highly protective of its petroleum industry. Two months later Conoco signed a deal with the state oil company of Taiwan to explore for oil and gas in the Taiwan Strait, an area that had recently been the site of Chinese war games. In April Vietnam's state-owned Petro-Vietnam awarded Conoco rights to develop three million acres of the South China Sea, an area whose sovereignty was in dispute between Vietnam, China, and other southeast Asian countries. China, which had already granted rights to an overlapping area to Denver-based Crestone Energy Corp., issued a warning to Conoco not to proceed, with the company responding that it would leave the issue up to the involved governments.

Meanwhile, also in Asia, Conoco began in 1993 to develop refining and marketing operations as a start toward capturing part of the region's fast-growing petroleum market. That year, the company began by building gas stations in Thailand under the Jet brand name, with a goal of having 260 retail outlets in place by the year 2004. Then in 1994 Conoco entered a joint venture (holding a 40 percent stake) with Petronas, the national oil company in Malaysia, and Statoil of Norway to construct a 100,000 barrel per day, $1.1 billion refinery in Malaysia. This represented Conoco's largest investment outside the United States. Future plans were to spend more than $2.5 billion in Malaysia through 2005, with plans for more than 200 retail outlets in the country. Overall, from 1996 to 1998, Conoco planned to spend ten to 15 percent of its $2.5 billion capital spending budget in Asia.

Conoco's overall operating results stagnated during the early 1990s under the pressure of heavy competition. The after-tax operating income as a percentage of sales mark of 6.7 percent in 1990 represented the high level through 1996. A three-year restructuring program that Nicandros initiated helped the company post better results than it would have otherwise. In addition to its exploration efforts and entrance into Asia, neither of which helped in the short term, Nicandros also sought new areas for growth within the broader energy sector, notably the establishment of a Conoco Power business unit which would pursue projects in the worldwide electrical power market. One possible shorter-term aid to company profitability arose in the talks between Conoco and Phillips Petroleum Co. started in late 1995 regarding the combination of the companies' domestic marketing, refinery, and pipeline operations in a 50–50 venture. This would have created the sixth-largest refiner of crude oil in the United States and the second-largest chain of U.S. gas stations, but talks broke off in June 1996 when the two sides could not reach agreement on "significant commercial issues."

During the 14 years since the Du Pont takeover, the parent company's shareholders had not always benefited from the Conoco acquisition, according to some observers. Although about 42 percent of Du Pont's revenues were derived from Conoco operations, Conoco contributed only about 17 percent of after-tax operating income to Du Pont's overall total. Following the takeover, Du Pont had been left with Seagram holding 24 percent of its common stock and a seat on Du Pont's board. In the spring of 1995, Du Pont paid $8.8 billion to repurchase all the shares Seagram then held, leaving a huge debt load behind. At the same time Du Pont announced plans to sell $650 million in Conoco assets. Speculation then arose about the possibility that Du Pont would divest itself of Conoco, in particular after Jack Krol replaced Edgar Woolard as chief executive of the parent company.

It was in these difficult and uncertain circumstances that Archie W. Dunham succeeded Nicandros as Conoco chairman, president, and chief executive at the beginning of 1996. Dunham's term at the helm was certain to be a critical one for the future of a troubled giant of the oil industry.

### *Principal Subsidiaries*

Conoco Asia Pacific Ltd.; Conoco Canada Limited; Conoco Europe Gas Limited; Conoco Exploration Production Europe Limited; Conoco France Hydrocarbures; Conoco Indonesia Inc.; Conoco International Petroleum Company (Russia); Conoco Middle East Ltd.; Conoco Norway Inc.; Conoco Overseas Oil Company; Conoco Trinidad Inc.; Conoco (U.K.) Limited; Continental Europe Energy Company; Continental Netherlands Oil Company; Dubai Petroleum Company; DuPont Nigeria Ltd.; DuPont Services B.V. (The Netherlands); Conoco Power; Conoco Asia Pacific Sdn. Bhd.; Conoco International Singapore; Conoco Ireland Limited; Conoco Jet Malaysia Sdn. Bhd.; Conoco Limited (United Kingdom); Conoco Mineraloel GmbH (Germany); Conoco Thailand Ltd.; DuPont Scandinavia AB (Sweden); Société Européenne Des Carburants (SECA, Belgium).

### *Further Reading*

Brauchli, Marcus W., "China, in Sharp Rebuke, Warns Conoco about Plans to Seek Oil with Vietnam," *Wall Street Journal,* April 23, 1996, p. A15(W), A18(E).

*Conoco: The First One Hundred Years,* New York: Dell Publishing Co., Inc., 1975, 238 p.

de Rouffignac, Ann, "Conoco Goes Through a Changing of the Guard," *Houston Business Journal,* December 1, 1995, p. 16.

Fritsch, Peter, "Conoco Proposes to Develop Gas Field in Mexican Sector Closed to Foreigners," *Wall Street Journal,* January 9, 1996, p. A4.

Holloway, Nigel, "Conoco Discovers Asia," *Far Eastern Economic Review,* October 26, 1995, p. 78.

Kelly, Kevin, "You Got Trouble Right Here in Ponca City: A Bitter Dispute over Whether Its Conoco Refinery Is a Toxic Hazard," *Business Week,* June 27, 1988, p. 38.

Knowles, Ruth Sheldon, *The Greatest Gamblers: The Epic of American Oil Exploration,* Norman: University of Oklahoma Press, 1978, 376 p.

Mathews, John Joseph, *Life and Death of an Oilman: The Career of E. W. Marland,* Norman: University of Oklahoma Press, 1951, 259 p.

McWilliams, Gary, Joseph Weber, and Susan Garland, "Why Didn't Conoco See This One Coming?: Washington's Signals on Iran May Have Been Too Subtle," *Business Week,* March 27, 1995, pp. 40–41.

Plishner, Emily S., "The Dilemma: Will DuPont's New CEO Spin Off Conoco?," *Financial World,* December 5, 1995, p. 34.

"Risk and Return," *Economist,* April 27, 1996, p. 66.

Rosett, Claudia, and Allanna Sullivan, "Conoco Tests the Tundra for Oil Profits," *Wall Street Journal,* September 1, 1994, p. A6.

—Roger W. Rouland
—updated by David E. Salamie

# Countrywide®

# Countrywide Credit Industries, Inc.

155 North Lake Avenue
Pasadena, California 91109-1857
U.S.A.
(818) 304-8400
Fax: (805) 520-5414

*Public Company*
*Incorporated:* 1969
*Employees:* 4,900
*Sales:* $860.7 million (1996)
*Stock Exchanges:* New York
*SICs:* 6162 Mortgage Bankers & Correspondents; 6719
    Holding Companies, Not Elsewhere Classified

Countrywide Credit Industries, Inc. is the nation's leading independent residential mortgage lender, with approximately five percent of the residential mortgage writing business. The company, with more than 330 offices located throughout the United States, is also the market leader in loan servicing—the collection of payments and the handling of paperwork involved with loans. Known for keeping operating costs down and improving efficiency through the use of state-of-the-art technology, the company commonly known as "the McDonald's of mortgage banking" has received widespread attention from the national media for its discounted loan fees, rapid growth, and development of affordable lending programs designed to reach low- and moderate-income home buyers.

### Early History

Countrywide was founded in 1969 by David Loeb, a New Yorker who had moved to Virginia to expand his fledgling mortgage banking business, United Mortgage Servicing, and his top-notch young salesman, Angelo Mozilo, a native of the Bronx who began processing loans at the age of 16. After Loeb was forced to relinquish his original 50 percent stake in United due to pressure from corporate raiders, the two set out to build a new mortgage company they ambitiously named Countrywide. They opened their first office in Anaheim, California. While

Mozilo, known for his self-confidence and survival instincts, served as the loan officer, Loeb, whose strength was in holding down costs, performed the underwriting duties from an office in New York City.

In an attempt to speed their progress toward becoming a nationwide company, the partners quickly went public—an unusual move in the industry. Their stock offering, however, proved initially to be a mistake: in exchange for a smaller portion of ownership and an assortment of lawyers, directors, and shareholders to answer to, the founders received only a small portion of new capital, $800,000—not enough to see the company through its first years. To keep Countrywide afloat, Mozilo hit the streets of Los Angeles selling loans, while his wife and their three children stayed with relatives back East. Loeb, meanwhile, closed the New York office and moved to Los Angeles.

### The "1974 Equation"

During the early 1970s, the company managed to stay in business despite the onset of inflation and high interest rates. By 1974, the firm had expanded to eight branch offices, but it was nowhere near realizing its dream of becoming a nationwide company and, more important, it was barely making enough money to survive. It appeared that while the firm's eight offices were doing quite well, Countrywide itself, which bore nearly all the risks of the operation, was not.

Realizing that a drastic change had to be made for the company to prosper, Loeb developed a radical idea: fire all of the salesmen and rebuild the corporation under a new philosophy. Like other mortgage companies, Countrywide employed a highly paid, commissioned sales force. This conventional approach, Loeb reasoned, placed more emphasis on the sales team than on the product itself, and Countrywide's "product," he continued, should be its price—the combination of interest rates and points that would provide the home buyer with the best value. In order to achieve this goal, Loeb planned to convert the branch offices into uniform loan processors, with the central office taking care of sales by mailing out notices to realtors.

Although Mozilo, who had developed a reputation for forming close relationships with employees, initially balked at such draconian measures, he eventually came to accept his partner's "product driven" philosophy. "Interest rates are the very fiber of what this country is all about," he stated in *Mortgage Banking*. "The success or failure of capitalism rides with interest rates—it's where the tar hits the road." Rather than making the change gradually, Mozilo painfully agreed to fire 92 of the company's 95 employees and shut down all of the branch offices at once, retaining the services of only a single secretary to help him and Loeb put together the first mailings to realtors.

The product that Countrywide made available was attractive. Not only were their interest rates lower than the competition's, but they offered an unprecedented guarantee to lock in the rate quoted at the time of origination through the 60 to 90 days it takes to close a transaction on a home. Nevertheless, few realtors were impressed; Mozilo was again forced to hit the pavement to keep the company afloat. This time his job was to convince realtors that they could benefit from his company's new idea.

Mozilo finally persuaded enough realtors to necessitate the reopening of the first Countrywide branch office in Whittier, California. The office was so successful that it nearly collapsed from the volume of new loans to be processed. New offices were soon needed to handle the ever-increasing demand. Although Countrywide handled a large amount of loans, it was able to maintain its high standards for approval because its loan processors were no longer motivated to take a chance on a questionable loan just to get a sales commission. Despite the ominous presence of stagflation and 17.5 percent interest rates strangling the real estate market, Countrywide rebuilt itself into a profitable company by 1978.

### Consistent Growth in the 1980s

While discounted prices created the demand that fueled the company's early growth, uniformity was the key to maintaining effective management. Each new Countrywide office that opened shared the characteristics of its predecessors: a shopping center or Main Street storefront, approximately 1,000 square feet of office space with a private area for meetings with applicants, and no more than two full-time employees. While a few offices were decorated with elegant furnishings, most conformed to the standard, no-frills company look. By standardizing everything from loan processing to floor coverings, Coun-

trywide was able to keep costs down and improve efficiency. Not only did this strategy boost loan quality, it lowered the cost of loan originations below the one percent allowed by the Federal Housing Administration (FHA). Other mortgage bankers, in contrast, were losing money on originations and had to raise servicing fees to make up the difference.

Countrywide's unconventional discounting and standardization policies were not the only factors that contributed to its rise to the top of the mortgage banking industry. The ability to skillfully read—or some would say fortuitously guess—when interest rates would fall also played a major role. In the early 1980s, while rates were still high, the company began selling off its servicing business to maintain profitability. While critics believed such a move was the equivalent of trading in valuable assets for short-term gain, Mozilo, who expected the record-high rates to fall, reasoned that what appeared to be assets would quickly become liabilities once rates fell and throngs of homeowners began refinancing their homes.

Mozilo's gamble paid off. Interest rates plummeted, creating a boom in the refinancing business. Countrywide, having gained wider access to capital markets through its growing profitability, was prepared to meet the new demand, and, with the lowest originating fees and interest rates in the industry, Countrywide was able to take full advantage. By the mid-1980s, the company had expanded to 104 offices in 26 states, providing itself with the facilities to make the most of the boom years of 1984 and 1986. The firm also increased its loan production by initiating a registry program, agreeing to sell mortgages originated by small Savings and Loans and guaranteeing a loan rate to mortgage applicants. As a result of such strategies and market conditions, the company was able to process more than $3.2 billion in originations by the middle of the decade.

In the midst of the boom in loan originations, Countrywide had the wisdom to realize that such favorable conditions would not last forever. A plan for maintaining profitability when interest rates rise had to be developed; otherwise, the completion of a natural business cycle would seriously threaten the company. Again, the company chose the unconventional route. Just as it had earlier sold off many of its loan servicing contracts to raise capital, it now decided to build that business to buffer changes in the market. The balanced strategy, which the company calls the "macro hedge," has helped to make the company's bottom line less sensitive to changes in interest rates. By holding on to the servicing rights of its loans and aggressively purchasing the rights to service mortgages originated by other lenders, the company has been able to sustain earnings when a rise in interest rates causes a decline in loan originations. As the decade progressed, the company's servicing portfolio played an increasingly important role, reaching the $1 billion mark in 1984, only to increase tenfold over the next four years. In 1988, the company founded a new subsidiary, Countrywide Servicing Exchange, to act as a broker for buyers and sellers of servicing rights.

### Explosive Growth in the Late 1980s and Early 1990s

While Countrywide grew steadily through its first two decades, it was at the turn of the decade that revenues and profits began to soar. One of the principal factors behind the arrival of the company was the unforeseen collapse of the Savings and

Loan industry, the mortgage bank's chief rival. Most mortgage banks, however, were unable to keep up with the demand that rushed their way because they depended on commercial banks, which had tightened their purse strings as a result of the S & L scandal, for the money they lent out. While most mortgage banks were set back by the limits of the banks' willingness to lend, Countrywide had no such problem. One of the few public companies in the industry, it already had access to capital. With a proven track record of efficient management and favorable market conditions, Countrywide was a safe bet for investors, who eagerly put up $409 million for new issues of stock between 1987 and 1992.

Countrywide was able to handle the wave of new business without being overwhelmed largely because of its commitment to technology back in the 1970s. Having invested heavily in computerized loan processing at a time when other mortgage bankers were not buying technology, the company further stood out from the competition through its ability to accommodate the surge of new employees and offices needed to handle the added demand. With such a solid technological infrastructure in place, the cost and time needed to train new loan production employees was reduced, making it easier for the company to maintain profitability despite fluctuations in the market. During refinancing booms, for instance, the company has been able to hire temporary employees to meet the immediate demand, sometimes letting them go when conditions change.

In addition to giving Countrywide the flexibility to meet the ever changing demands of the volatile housing market, technological innovation has enabled the company to reduce the time and cost associated with loan processing and funding. In 1990, for instance, the company introduced its own state-of-the-art loan origination service, EDGE, which was designed to reduce the risks of deficient loans and guarantee pricing. The system was able to significantly reduce origination and processing costs, while accelerating funding time to less than 30 days on conventional loans, by enabling loan representatives to enter customer information only once. Common information can then be copied to other files automatically; figures such as loan rates and discount points can be downloaded as well. EDGE then prints out completed legal copies of all documents on a laser printer, eliminating the need for preprinted loan forms and saving the company $1 million a year.

### The 1990s and Beyond

By 1992 Countrywide began to realize the full benefits of the strategy it conceived in the 1970s and refined over the next two decades. Largely as a result of its continued commitment to technology, its balanced marketing strategy, and its unmatched aggressive pricing, the company emerged as the nation's top mortgage banker. Taking full advantage of a 19-year low in interest rates, Countrywide originated more than $30 billion in mortgages, moving past such perennial powers as Prudential Insurance Co. and Norwest Corp., while enjoying $246 million in total revenue and profits of $60.2 million—a 170 percent jump from the previous year.

In an attempt to further reduce origination costs and extend its lead over the competition, Countrywide made another landmark advance in the field of artificial-intelligence underwriting systems the following year, through its introduction of the Countrywide Loan Underwriting Expert System (CLUES). The state-of-the-art system was developed to expedite loan processing by handling most routine cases automatically. Able to not only approve an application—in less than a minute in routine cases—but to underwrite all types of mortgage loans, the system has helped Countrywide's underwriters spend more time on difficult or exceptional cases. With CLUES handling more than 7,000 loans per month, nearly 85 percent, underwriters have been able to increase production and attract more customers.

As Countrywide entered the mid-1990s, it directed much of its attention to a market that has been traditionally underserved by banks and mortgage companies alike: the low- and moderate-income population. In 1992, the company launched the "House America" program, to attend to this need. Designed to make the American Dream of home ownership a reality for those who lacked the finances, the credit history, or the stable employment necessary to qualify for a loan an opportunity to do so, House America represented an unprecedented move in the industry. Under the flexible underwriting program, customers have been approved for mortgages with a down payment of as low as three percent of the sale price. The program has also provided financial counseling and education to thousands, helping individuals with high student loan payments and unstable employment alike to find ways to better manage their money. Countrywide supported its commitment to this goal by pledging to sell $5 billion in House-America type loans to the nation's two largest mortgage lenders, the Federal National Mortgage Association, "Fannie Mae," and the Federal Home Loan Mortgage Corp., "Freddie Mac," both of which were established by Congress to ensure that lenders have a constant source of money for mortgages.

According to Mozilo, House America, as its mission statement reads, was designed for the purpose of creating an "equality paradigm . . . which will positively impact the revitalization of local communities and economies through home ownership." Accordingly, Countrywide has taken unprecedented measures to give minority populations greater access to loans. The company's field officers, in fact, do not have the authority to deny loans to minority applicants; officials from central headquarters, including Mozilo, must first review the applications.

While Countrywide's commitment to equal housing has drawn widespread praise, it also promises to be good business. With the nation's population growth occurring fastest among immigrant populations, minority and low-income groups represent perhaps the area of greatest potential to the company. According to a *USA Today* survey, only 43 percent of African American and 40 percent of Hispanic families—compared to 70 percent of white families—own their own home. Countrywide's continued success may depend largely on its ability to reduce this disparity. Plans to market no-load mutual funds, stocks, annuities and money market funds in 1996 may also contribute to the company's predicted annual earnings of more than $300 million by the end of the decade.

### Principal Subsidiaries

Countrywide Home Loans, Inc.; Countrywide Financial Planning Services, Inc.; Countrywide Capital Markets, Inc.; Countrywide Securities Corp.; Countrywide Servicing Exchange; CTC Foreclosure Services Corp.; LandSafe, Inc.; Countrywide Investments, Inc.; Countrywide Agency, Inc.

### *Further Reading*

Barrett, Amy, ''Countrywide's Home Sweet Loans,'' *Business Week,* September 14, 1992.

Cocheo, Steve, ''Mortgage Machine,'' *American Banking Association Banking Journal,* October 1995.

Collett, Wayne C., ''Homeward Bound,'' *Mortgage Banking,* January 1995, pp. 1–6.

Darlin, Damon, ''Desensitizing,'' *Forbes,* September 14, 1996, pp. 60–61.

Hill, Christian, and Carlton, Jim, ''Countrywide Credit Takes Mortgage Market by Storm,'' *The Wall Street Journal,* September 4, 1992.

Kulkosky, Edward, ''Mozilo's Countrywide Still in the Fast Lane,'' *American Banker,* June 11, 1993.

Magnet, Myron, ''Countrywide Credit Industries: Be Ready to Push Your Luck,'' *Fortune,* April 4, 1994.

Willette, Anne, ''New Rules Help More People Qualify,'' *USA Today,* November 15, 1994.

—Jason Gallman

# Cray Research, Inc.

**655A Lone Oak Drive**
**Eagan, Minnesota 55121**
**U.S.A.**
**(612) 683-7100**
**Fax: (612) 683-7198**

*Wholly Owned Subsidiary of Silicon Graphics, Inc.*
*Incorporated:* 1972
*Employees:* 4,840
*Sales:* $676.24 million (1995)
*SICs:* 3571 Electronic Computers

Cray Research, Inc. is the world's premier producer of supercomputers—high-performance computer systems that can handle a large number of calculations in a very brief time. Through an aggressive new product development program, Cray introduced in the mid-1990s a full range of systems from low to high end. The last of the independent supercomputing firms, Cray accepted a takeover offer from Silicon Graphics, Inc. in early 1996.

## Early History

Cray Research was formed through the efforts of Seymour Cray, a recognized genius in the design of supercomputers. Cray was born in 1925 in Chippewa Falls, Wisconsin, and spent a boyhood devoted to tinkering with electronic gear. After service in World War II working as a radio operator and then functioning as a specialist in breaking Japanese codes, he attended the University of Minnesota, earning a bachelor of science degree in electrical engineering and another in applied mathematics, both in 1950. He decided to enter the computer industry and took a job with Engineering Research Associates, founded by William C. Norris. Through a series of mergers, Engineering Research Associates was brought under the control of Sperry Rand Corporation. Norris left Engineering Research Associates and established Control Data Corporation in 1957. Cray soon followed him to the new company. Among his early projects at Control Data, Cray developed the 1604, one of the first computers to use transistors in place of vacuum tubes.

Control Data shared in the booming computer industry of the 1960s, experiencing a period of rapid growth. Cray became disenchanted with the bureaucracy that this growth created and insisted that the company build him a separate research facility in his home town of Chippewa Falls. In this new facility, he came up with the CDC 6600, the first commercial computer capable of handling three million program instructions per second. Cray's special talent was in putting the circuits of a computer very close together, reducing the time taken for electric signals to pass between them. This closeness, however, increased the heat generated by the circuits. Cray was able to introduce innovative ways of removing this heat.

Cray's success at Control Data eventually hit a stumbling block. In 1972, top management at the corporation halted his plans for a new computer, telling him he could continue working on it only after another computer project was completed.

Instead of waiting, Cray and a group of followers left Control Data to set up Cray Research. Their purpose in starting the new company was to design the first supercomputer, which they ultimately named the CRAY-1. Cray Research was initially situated in Cray's laboratory in Chippewa Falls. After several years of work on the supercomputer project, in March 1976, the company delivered its first computer to the National Center for Atmospheric Research. This sale enabled it to earn back its original investment.

The CRAY-1 was the fastest computer then available. It used the technique of vector processing, which employs a system wherein a series of operations are manipulated at once as opposed to scalar processing where operations take place one at a time. The CRAY-1 could execute 32 operations simultaneously, making it able to complete ten times the work of some larger systems. While it was delivering its first sale, the company also made its first public offering of stock. The company complemented its supercomputers with software programs, releasing its Cray Operating System (COS) and Cray Fortran Compiler in 1977.

During its early years of operation, Cray Research sold its supercomputers to government laboratories and agencies. The main application of supercomputers was in physical simulation, wherein computer models were used to analyze and forecast the response pattern likely to take place in a system composed of physical variables. Early applications of these models were in gauging the effects of nuclear weapons and in meteorology. Since these types of applications were performed under the aegis of the government, it was felt that the market for supercomputers would be very limited. In 1978, however, Cray Research was given its first order from a commercial organization.

### Second Generation Systems—Early 1980s

The CRAY-1 system became the CRAY-1/S and the CRAY-1/M systems. As the 1980s began, the company decided to begin development of the next generation of supercomputers. To concentrate his efforts on that development, Seymour Cray resigned as CEO in 1980, and in 1981 he stepped down as chairman. John Rollwagen became CEO in 1980 and chairman in 1981. Cray retained his ties with the company as an independent contractor and as a member of the board of directors. The new project called for the design and development of the CRAY-2, intended to be the first computer on the market that used chips made of gallium arsenide. When the gallium arsenide chips were not available, Cray returned to silicon. The CRAY-2 system was completed in 1985, achieving a performance level ten times that of the CRAY-1.

Because the CRAY-2 project contained an element of risk due to its innovative technology, Rollwagen had the company initiate a second project based on a further upgrade of the CRAY-1 technology. Under the direction of Steve S. Chen, the CRAY X-MP system was devised. This system marked the first use of multiprocessors, where a number of microprocessors are linked together to take on bigger jobs. Introduced in 1982, the CRAY X-MP was originally a dual processor, with a speed three times that of the CRAY-1.

As had been done with the CRAY-1, both the CRAY-2 and the CRAY X-MP supercomputers evolved into more sophisticated systems. The CRAY X-MP served as the basis for a series that consisted of 11 models. The more innovative CRAY-2 design had three-dimensional circuit interconnections linking circuit boards within a module. Software enhancements were also made available, with the 1986 introduction of a new operating system, UNICOS, which combined the COS system with the AT&T UNIX System V. This advance was especially important because UNIX was well established as the industry standard, especially in areas of scientific application, where supercomputing has been so useful; meanwhile an advanced Cray Fortran Compiler, named CF77, was also made available.

### Third Generation Systems—Late 1980s

By the mid-1980s Cray Research embarked on producing another generation of supercomputers, again following several paths. In 1986, Chen began working on a new system of highly innovative design, relying on significant technological advances in five different areas. After spending nearly $50 million on the project, the company decided to discontinue it. Chen left the company in 1987, taking 45 engineers from Cray Research, to form Supercomputer Systems, Inc., with plans to build a supercomputer using as many as 256 microprocessors.

Seymour Cray completed design work on the CRAY-3 supercomputer system in 1987. The CRAY-3 marked another effort to use gallium arsenide chips, a prospect made more feasible by the production of the first of the new type of chips suitable for computer production in the 1980s. While awaiting the CRAY-3, the company developed and introduced the CRAY Y-MP system, which combined the power of eight central processing units to give it 30 times the power of the original CRAY-1.

Cray Research passed two important milestones in 1987. First, it delivered its 200th computer system, especially noteworthy since it had taken from 1976 to 1985 to reach a total of 100 computer shipments. This rapid expansion made possible the second milestone, the inclusion of Cray Research among the nation's largest companies, listed in the *Fortune 500*. This period of rapid expansion was possible because the company was able to market its supercomputer systems to commercial corporations engaged in petroleum exploration, automobile production, and the aerospace industry.

Cray Research underwent a major restructuring in 1989. Delays in the development of the CRAY-3 system were creating very high research costs, and the scheduled date for completing the project was reportedly postponed. In addition, the company had embarked on another project, the C-90, as a new stage in the CRAY Y-MP product line. Rather than discontinue one of the projects, Rollwagen decided to create a new company, Cray Computer Corporation, to be headed by Seymour Cray. Located in Colorado Springs, Colorado, Cray Computer would continue the development of the CRAY-3 supercomputer. On November 15, 1989, Cray Research issued shares of Cray Computer to its stockholders, retaining a 10 percent ownership in the new company (which it later sold). Seymour Cray resigned from the board of directors of Cray Research, severing formal connections with the company he had formed, although he remained a stockholder.

Even after this spinoff Cray Research retained a solid position as the leading company in the production of supercomputers, with about two-thirds of the world market. In 1989, it phased out the CRAY-2 and CRAY X-MP as new models of the CRAY Y-MP were coming on line. There were continuing plans for development of the C-90 project, which was renamed the CRAY Y-MP/16. The company also began development of enhanced systems for supercomputer networking to facilitate scientists' access to Cray supercomputers from a variety of other types and brands of computers. In addition, there were plans to bring to the market an entry-level supercomputer, which would use the technology of the CRAY Y-MP, but would have a much lower price with reduced installation and operating costs.

As the market for supercomputers expanded, Cray Research diversified its sales efforts both in terms of type of customers and geographic region. In 1989 governments remained the largest customers, buying 31 percent of Cray Research's output; other important purchasers of Cray machines included universities, aerospace, petroleum, and automotive companies, energy producers, and weather and environment analysts. Sales in North America that year were 61 percent of the total. Approximately 75 percent of revenue between 1987 and 1989 was derived from sales of computer systems, with remaining income from leased systems and service fees.

Cray Research also took measures to provide for better distribution of its products. It entered into an arrangement with Control Data to make Cray supercomputers available to Control Data's customers, using Cray products to replace Control Data's line of supercomputers that was discontinued in 1989. Marcelo Gumucio, who directed Cray Research's marketing operation, was named president and chief operating officer in 1988. By placing more emphasis on the marketing of its products, with less attention paid to product development, Cray Research anticipated that it would be better able to meet the challenges of international competition in the supercomputer industry.

### 1990s and Beyond

The early 1990s were a shakedown period in the industry, particularly for independent firms in the United States, and for a time Cray itself seemed very vulnerable. Increasing competition from Japanese computer giants—Fujitsu, Hitachi, and NEC— and from U.S. giant Intel had by 1990 already cut Cray's market share to about 65 percent; this compared to the 80 percent level for the number of installed supercomputers that were Cray models. Looming on the horizon were several upstart companies seeking to build less-expensive but still very powerful models—such companies as Alliant, Convex Computer, Kendall Square Research, nCube, Supercomputer Systems, and Thinking Machines—or create high-end models such as Seymour Cray's Cray Computer. At the same time, Cray Research faced the decline of its core market—government agencies and laboratories, the military, and government-supported entities such as universities and research centers—with the end of the Cold War and cutbacks or slowdowns in government spending worldwide.

Facing these threats, Rollwagen reportedly realized in 1990 that he had put the wrong man in charge in the person of Gumucio. Just when Cray needed more than ever to tap into its engineers' expertise, Gumucio's formal management style—he increased reports and procedures required of employees for the purpose of setting specific goals—stifled their creativity and dampened morale. The more inspiring figure of Rollwagen resumed operating responsibilities.

At the end of 1990, Cray's install base stood at 262 systems in 20 countries. With little chance to expand within its core governmental market, Rollwagen knew that future growth would have to come from the commercial sector, notably the aerospace, automotive, financial, health care, and telecommunications industries; and that, in order to penetrate these new markets, Cray itself would have to start offering lower-priced models.

Initially, Cray moved into the low-end supercomputer market through acquisitions. In early 1990 it made its first move by acquiring Supertek Computers, Inc., a troubled California-based maker of Cray-compatible minisupercomputers— general-purpose scientific computers that are not as powerful as standard supercomputers. Since minisupercomputers sold for as little as $250,000, Cray viewed them in part as an entry level for new customers who might later be tempted to invest in a multimillion-dollar supercomputer. Also on the low end was the 1991 purchase of superserver—high-end servers within a client-server environment—assets of the bankrupt Floating Point Systems, which became Cray Research Superservers, Inc. The following year this new subsidiary introduced its first product, the Cray S-MP, which was designed for the widely used Sun Microsystems' SPARC processor client-server environment.

Meanwhile, Cray's newly energized product development program produced results on both the low and high end. Within one month in late 1991, Cray introduced an entry-level system priced at about $340,000 called the Y-MP EL and its fastest vector supercomputer to date, the C90, with operational speed four times that of its previous fastest model. Cray had also begun work on a new type of supercomputer (at least for Cray), a massively parallel processing (MPP) system. Long touted by some analysts as the inevitable successor to the vector systems pioneered by Cray, MPP systems linked a number of standard microprocessors to create a virtual supercomputer at a potentially much lower cost than vector systems. MPP systems were the type that the upstart supercomputer companies were developing.

In 1992, even though its entry-level system resulted in 70 new customers and exceeded the company's sales projections, Cray posted a net loss of $14.86 million. Its new products and acquisitions not yet paying off in full, the firm had to take a $42.8 million restructuring charge late in the year to cut costs— it closed one plant and eliminated 650 jobs, or one-eighth of the work force.

Early in 1993, Rollwagen resigned to join the Clinton administration and was replaced by John F. Carlson, a 16-year Cray veteran. Later that year, Cray's first MPP system was rolled out, the T3D. Although scoffed at by rivals because it had to be linked to a standard Cray vector system, the T3D outperformed other MPP systems and helped put a number of the upstart firms out of business (such as Thinking Machines and Kendall Square Research) or into the arms of larger firms (such as Convex Computer which was acquired by Hewlett-Packard in 1995).

Although Cray returned to profitability in 1993, additional restructuring was needed to improve the company's operations. In 1994, which saw the resignation of Carlson, an $8.3 million charge was incurred, while in 1995, when former vice-chairman of Eastman Kodak and former president of Sun Microsystems J. Phillip Samper became chairman, $187.7 million in charges were booked. The 1995 charges contributed to a full-year loss of $226.4 million, but were incurred within a critical year in which three major new products were introduced: a new low-end J90 series; a new high-end vector system, the T90 series (touted as the first wireless supercomputer and five times faster than its predecessor, the C90 series); and Cray's second-generation MPP system, the T3E. The last of these, unlike its predecessor, did not need to be connected to a traditional vector supercomputer and had a top theoretical speed of one teraflops (one trillion operations per second), a long-sought-after speed level. On the basis of these introductions, Cray built up by year-end 1995 a $437-million order backlog. Even without having filled the backlogged orders, Cray could still boast of having increased its installed base to 758 systems in 37 countries (nearly three times the level of 1990).

By early 1996, Cray Research was the only independent supercomputing firm left. Among the victims was Cray Computer, which declared bankruptcy early in 1995. Cray Research had survived and now had a range of products to offer from lower-end superservers and minisupercomputers to entry-level supercomputers to high-end vector and MPP supercomputer systems. But it now competed directly with several firms with much deeper pockets—the Japanese computer giants and Intel on the high end and Hewlett-Packard, IBM, Sun Microsystems, and Silicon Graphics, Inc. (SGI) on the lower workstation end. So when SGI, a leader in high-powered workstations with a particular emphasis on graphics-oriented systems, made a friendly takeover offer early in 1996, Samper and other Cray executives decided to accept the offer rather than attempt to continue to compete against such giants. The $739.2 million deal bolstered SGI's position in the technical-computing arena and simultaneously ended the era of independent supercomputer companies.

Although no longer independent, Cray Research had survived the early 1990s and could now tap into SGI's deep pockets to develop future systems. It would have to do so without Samper, who resigned shortly after the takeover and who had been credited with turning Cray around in his brief tenure to the point that it was desired by SGI. Robert H. Ewald was to continue as Cray's president and CEO and handle day-to-day operations.

### Principal Subsidiaries

Cray Research France S.A.; Cray Research GmbH (Germany); Cray Research Japan, Ltd.; Cray Research Superservers, Inc.; Cray Research (UK) Ltd.

### Further Reading

Basil, Richard, "The Origin of PCs (and Descent of Cray)," *PC Magazine,* May 15, 1984, p. 128.

Bulkeley, William M., "Pact to Buy Cray Marks 'End of an Era' of Independent Supercomputing Firms," *Wall Street Journal,* February 27, 1996, p. B9.

Churbuck, David, "Cray Versus Japan Inc.," *Forbes,* September 4, 1989, pp. 118–19.

Cook, James, "War Games," *Forbes,* September 12, 1983, p. 108.

Donlan, Thomas G., "Not So Super Outlook: For Cray Research, Competition Looms," *Barron's,* February 5, 1990, p. 39.

Finley, Michael, "Cray's New Way," *PC Week,* September 18, 1995, p. A5.

Johnson, Jan, "A Look Inside Cray," *Datamation,* May 1982, p. 57.

"Jurassic Pact," *Economist,* March 2, 1996, pp. 58–59.

"Megaflopolis: Supercomputers," *Economist,* November 28, 1992, p. 79.

Mitchell, Russell, "Can Cray Reprogram Itself for Creativity?," *Business Week,* August 20, 1990, p. 86.

——, "The Genius: Meet Seymour Cray, Father of the Supercomputer," *Business Week,* April 30, 1990.

——, "Now Cray Faces Life Without Cray," *Business Week,* May 29, 1989, p. 31.

——, "What? Cray Computers Eating Dust?," *Business Week,* November 25, 1991, p. 88.

Mitchell, Russell, and Gary McWilliams, "Cray Eats Crow," *Business Week,* October 4, 1993, p. 108.

Murray, Charles J., "The Ultimate Team Player: Lester T. Davis, Winner of the *Design News* Special Achiever Award, Supplied the Technical Vision That Helped Cray Research Dominate the Supercomputer Industry," *Design News,* March 6, 1995, pp. 88–95.

Murray, Chuck, "Changing Customers Fuel Supercomputing Shifts, *Chicago Tribune,* December 18, 1994.

"Perilous Descent: Cray and Supercomputers," *Economist,* April 21, 1990, pp. 81–82.

"The Race Is Not Always to the Gigafloppiest," *Economist,* April 15, 1989.

Rigdon, Joan E., and William M. Bulkeley, "Silicon Graphics Inc. Agrees to Acquire Cray Research in $739.2 Million Deal," *Wall Street Journal,* February 27, 1996, pp. A3, A4.

Schatz, Willie, "Who's Winning the Supercomputer Race?," *Datamation,* July 15, 1989.

Stedman, Craig, "Cray Fights for New Users," *Computerworld,* March 6, 1995.

—Donald R. Stabile
updated by David E. Salamie

# Crown Crafts, Inc.

**1600 Riveredge Parkway, Suite 200**
**Atlanta, Georgia 30328**
**U.S.A.**
**(770) 644-6400**
**Fax: (770) 644-6410**

*Public Company*
*Incorporated:* 1957 as Janyjo, Inc.
*Employees:* 2,148
*Sales:* $211 million (1995)
*Stock Exchanges:* New York
*SICs:* 2211 Broadwoven Fabric Mills, Cotton; 2221
    Broadwoven Fabric Mills, Manmade Fiber & Silk;
    2392 House Furnishings, Not Elsewhere Classified

Crown Crafts, Inc. designs, manufactures, and sells bed covering products and related accessories, including comforters and various jacquard-woven and other textile goods. Its products are marketed under several brand names including Crown Crafts, Goodwin Weavers, Royal Sateen, Ungaro, Bob Timberlake, Perry Ellis, and Colonial Williamsburg. Crown Crafts operated for several years as a relatively small manufacturer of bedspreads and crushed velvet products until the mid-1980s, when it began acquiring other companies.

## Modest 1950s Beginnings

The company that would become Crown Crafts started out in 1957 as a small manufacturer of bedspreads. Incorporated as Janyjo—the company would change its name to Crown Crafts in 1968—the enterprise became one of many textile producers based in and around the Calhoun, Georgia, area. Janyjo was moderately successful during most of the 1960s as a small but profitable maker of tufted bedspreads, and gradually expanded into other textiles and accessories. In 1967, for example, it added jacquard-woven bedspreads to its product line. Jacquard-woven products, weaved on a special "Jacquard" loom, could allow for more intricate patterns in the fabric, and Crown Crafts' jacquard-woven line would later prove pivotal to the company's growth.

## Growth and Diversification in the 1970s

Even more important to the company during the 1970s, however, was its line of crushed velvet goods. Indeed, flocked (crushed velvet) fabrics became hugely popular during the 1970s, and Crown Crafts aggressively targeted that growth market, investing heavily in equipment necessary to manufacture velvet bedspreads, draperies, and related goods. Crown Crafts became a leader in its niche, and its tufted and jacquard-woven goods became secondary to its core of flocked product lines. To fund expansion, Crown Crafts borrowed about $4.5 million in the mid-1970s from Prudential and used the cash to expand its production capacity. As sales of its then-popular crushed velvet materials soared, Crown Crafts' revenues grew. By the early 1980s the company was generating more than $20 million in annual sales.

## Economic Downturn and Recovery

Crown Crafts' sales peaked at $22.9 million in 1982. Guided by savvy management since its inception, the company had never posted a loss and its future looked bright. Unfortunately, the market for flocked goods began to wane in 1982 before plunging in 1983. Within a few years, in fact, the flocked goods market withered to almost nothing. Crown Crafts was left reeling by the sudden shift in consumer tastes. The company suddenly found itself a leader in a market for a product that had, like the leisure suit, become an amusing relic of 1970s fashion. The company's revenues dropped more than 20 percent in 1983, to just $18.3 million, and Crown Crafts was forced to post its first loss, of $338,000.

Crown Crafts was in financial trouble by 1983. With both profits and cash flow in rapid decline, management feared that the company would be unable to cover its debt obligations. Rather than force Crown Crafts to liquidate assets to pay of its loan, however, Prudential agreed to loan $4 million more to Crown Crafts to help it shift into a new line of business. Crown Crafts had already identified bed comforters as a potential growth market for the 1980s. To that end, in 1982 it had started to sell a line of tufted chenille comforter products as part of an effort to supplant lagging velvet sales. The comforters were manufactured for Crown Crafts by Decorator Comforters, a Roxboro, North Carolina-based producer of padded quilts used as bedspreads. In 1984, Crown Crafts used cash from the $4 million loan to purchase Decorator Comforters Inc.

Crown Crafts' move into the emerging market for comforters and related products was shrewd. Demand surged beginning in the early 1980s and strengthened throughout the 1980s. Crown Crafts quickly added a full line of print and solid-color comforters with matching pillow shams, dust ruffles, and window treatments. In 1986 it became one of the first companies to combine those elements in efficient, matching sets. "We pioneered the concept of a comforter set, with the comforter, shams, and ruffle in one package, because it's profitable to the retailer," remarked Randolph Schmatz, vice-president of sales and marketing, in the March 13, 1989 *Atlanta Business Chronicle*. "Retailers don't employ as many sales people and this eliminates the need of running around the store looking for matched sets," he added.

Crown Crafts capitalized on market growth by asserting itself as a leader in the comforter market. For the first time, the company began selling its comforter sets in major department stores under the Crown Crafts brand name. The strategy was a success, and by 1989 Crown Crafts was known as the leading supplier of comforter products to department stores. Crown Crafts' emphasis on comforters and accessories, particularly packaged sets, not only helped it to avert financial distress, but allowed it to sustain the rapid growth it had achieved during much of the 1970s. Sales grew at an average pace of about 30 percent during much of the 1980s, and profits rose accordingly. The company posted a $350 million deficit in 1985 but was generating steady profits by 1986 and would continue to grow both sales and net income into the mid-1990s.

Crown Crafts' sales grew rapidly to $33.6 million in 1985 before rising nearly threefold to $91.39 million in 1989. Based primarily on the success of its comforters, the company had grown from a relatively small textile and fabrics manufacturer to a nearly $100 million retail supplier. Augmenting gains with comforters, however, were other product lines. Of import was the evolution of Crown Crafts' jacquard-woven products, which were basically soft, cotton, blanket-like fabrics with intricately woven colors and fabric patterns. Since the late 1960s, Crown Crafts had been producing commodity-type bedspreads and blankets at its Georgia finishing plants, but it wasn't until the late 1980s that its jacquard-woven effort came to fruition.

Recognizing the slowly increasing popularity of jacquard-woven goods, Crown Crafts had started distributing imported acrylic jacquard-woven throws in 1984. The effort was stymied, however, by consumer preference for natural fibers. So in 1987 Crown Crafts began weaving its own jacquard-woven "throws" (or light blankets) using cotton yarns in its Georgia mill. The throws were an immediate success on the market. The company boosted production and began to aggressively market the throws throughout its North American distribution channels. The company gradually added a number of new patterns, including Oriental, holiday, and floral designs, among others. In fact, Crown Crafts developed one of the most technologically advanced design centers in the world for woven fabrics.

### New Directions in the 1990s

By 1990 Crown Crafts was generating sales of more than $100 million annually and netting income of about $6.7 million. It made most of that money through the sale of bedroom furnishings—comforters, bedspreads, and throws—which it sold through department stores and some national discount retailers. Beginning in the early 1990s, however, management began to take the company in a new direction. Rather than just expanding internally with add-on products and new distributors, the company began a growth program that included acquisitions and the addition of entirely new products. That initiative would be credited with more than doubling Crown Crafts' revenue base within five years and changing the company from a textile manufacturer to a diversified home products supplier.

The effort to expand its market reach was signaled by the 1989 introduction of the Royal Santeen brand, which Crown Crafts developed in cooperation with Kita Consolidated, Ltd. of Israel. Crown Crafts used the brand to enter the high-end luxury market for bed sheets, but also comforters and accessories. Crown Crafts would eventually enter into several agreements that allowed it to market various products under brand names including Ungaro Paris and The Lang Collection. Crown Crafts' first major acquisition came in 1991, when it purchased Goodwin Weavers. That buyout pushed Crown Crafts' sales past $120 million in 1991 and gave the company an important toehold in the rapidly growing market for high-end cotton jacquard-woven throws.

Interestingly, Goodwin Weavers' history dated back to 1812 and an English silkweaving enterprise. The founder's son, James Goodwin, moved to the United States in 1837 and started weaving wool. The business was passed down for generations, along the way developing a venerable reputation as a maker of high-quality textiles. In the 1980s the company began making high-end cotton afghans, which became very popular in the late 1980s and 1990s. Crown Crafts purchased the company as a way to increase its exposure in the surging cotton throw market and to expand production capacity. The buyout was mutually beneficial, as the Goodwin family benefitted from access to Crown Crafts' capital resources and its advanced design facility in Georgia. Moreover, the subsidiary was allowed to continue operating relatively autonomously.

Despite activities related to its throws and other jacquard-woven goods, Crown Crafts continued to derive most of its income from its still-growing core lineup of comforters and accessories. Competition from low-cost foreign manufacturers hurt many of its American counterparts, but Crown Crafts managed to increase market share in the comforter segment and boost sales with its highly efficient manufacturing operations and savvy marketing strategy. Meanwhile, it enjoyed solid gains in the jacquard cotton throw arena. Jacquard products made up less than three percent of the total beddings market when Crown Crafts decided to target the niche. By the mid-1990s, however, jacquards were accounting for roughly 20 percent of the total market. Because Crown Crafts was among the first companies to recognize the trend, it profited from the market growth.

Spurred by sales gains in both its comforter and jacquard product lines, Crown Crafts' revenues climbed to $151 million in 1993 and then to $187.34 million in 1994. Meanwhile, net income inched up steadily to more than $9 million annually. Gains in the comforter division were squelched in 1995, however, as market tastes again shifted, similar to the move away from crushed velvet in the early 1980s. In mid-1995, in fact, Crown Crafts reported a 63 percent drop in its first quarter profits. The decline was attributable to slow comforter sales. Fortunately, Crown Crafts was better prepared to deal with the slowdown in that core product segment because of the strength of its jacquard-woven division. Shortly before the comforter market slowdown, in fact, Crown Crafts had purchased a North Carolina company that operated 16 jacquard looms.

Crown Crafts was emphasizing the surging jacquard business going into the mid-1990s. Early in 1995, for example, the company had reached a potentially lucrative agreement with Walt Disney Co. to produce and sell jacquard-woven cotton throws featuring designs with Disney characters. Buoyed by overall gains in the jacquard segment, Crown Crafts managed to boost 1995 sales to $211 million, about $11 million of which was netted as income. Going into 1996, Crown Crafts was moving to establish itself as a diversified supplier of home accessories, including not only textiles but also various gift and decorative items. To that end, it created a new division dubbed Crown Home & Gift, which purchased two infant and juvenile goods suppliers—Red Calliope and Pillow Buddies—as well as another luxury throw supplier named Churchill Weavers.

For the mid- and late 1990s, Crown Crafts planned to evolve from a manufacturer of basic bedding materials to a supplier of fashionable, contemporary home furnishings including carpeting, collectibles, and such thematic merchandise as the Disney cotton throws. It planned, for example, to boost sales from its new Crown Home & Gift division from about $35 million in 1996 to about $100 million by the late 1990s. Meanwhile, sales of its jacquard throws—Crown Crafts was the national leader in the jacquard-woven industry—and bedroom products continued to grow, surpassing in 1995 revenues from its comforter products.

### Principal Subsidiaries

Crown Crafts Home Furnishings, Inc.; Crown Crafts Home Furnishings of Illinois, Inc.; Crown Crafts Home Furnishings of California, Inc.; KKH Corporation; The Red Calliope & Associates, Inc.; Goodwin Weavers; Churchill Weavers, Inc.

### Further Reading

Abelson, Reed, "Crown Crafts," Fortune, June 19, 1989, p. 148.
Chestnut, E. Randall, "Crown Crafts, Inc. Becomes Disney Licenses," PR Newswire, June 2, 1995.
Frinton, Sandra, "Crown Open to Buy: Talking to Non-textile Accessory Firms," HFN—The Weekly Newspaper, January 22, 1996, p. 24(2).
Harte, Susan, "Bedding Market Awakens to Take on a New Texture," Atlanta Constitution, August 8, 1995, p. F3.
Morrison, Cindy, "Crown Crafts May Show Great Results . . . ," Atlanta Business Chronicle, March 13, 1989, p. A3.
Nellett, Michelle, "The Goodwins: A 75th Anniversary Feature Introducing Industry Families that Have Been Around for at Least Three Generations," Gifts & Decorative Accessories, November 1992, p. 96(4).
Schwartz, Donna Boyle, "The Dream Team: Crown Crafts' Bedding Goes From Sleepy to Sizzling Under Refocused Design Group," HFD—The Weekly Home Furnishings Newspaper, March 14, 1994, p. 31(2).

—Dave Mote

# CUC International Inc.

**707 Summer Street**
**Stamford, Connecticut 06901**
**U.S.A.**
**(203) 324-9261**
**Fax: (203) 997-8501**

*Public Company*
*Incorporated:* 1974 as Comp-U-Card of America, Inc.
*Employees:* 8,500
*Sales:* $1.42 billion (1996)
*Stock Exchanges:* New York
*SICs:* 7299 Miscellaneous Personal Services, Not Else-
where Classified; 7375 Information Retrieval Services

CUC International Inc. offers individual consumers access to various services and discounts related to shopping, travel, insurance, automobiles, dining, vacationing, credit card enhancement packages, and various discount and coupon programs. The company offers its services primarily through memberships to clubs and programs. Entering 1996, CUC had about 40 million members who paid $5 to $250 per year. The company was growing rapidly in the mid-1990s through acquisitions and internal expansion.

### An Idea ahead of Its Time: The 1970s

CUC started out in 1973 as Comp-U-Card (Comp-U-Card of America, Inc.), a company launched to deliver shopping services, including home shopping, using computers and credit cards. The glaring flaw in the strategy—one that the company's founder, Walter A. Forbes, acknowledged in retrospect—was that very few computers, particularly home computer systems, were accessible to shoppers at the time. Thus, Comp-U-Card, far ahead of its time, was destined to struggle in the dawning years of the information age, waiting for technology to catch up with its progenitor's stratagem. Indeed, CUC would languish for a full decade before gradually emerging as a force in electronic commerce.

"It was a silly investment at the time because there were no home computers," Forbes conceded in the April 24, 1995 *Forbes.* Nevertheless, he remained committed to the idea and continued to pour money into the flailing venture until its turnaround. Forbes was only 30 years old when he started Comp-U-Card. Only five years earlier he had graduated from the Harvard Business School before taking a comfortable job with a management consulting firm, helping other business owners and managers to run their companies. Shortly after going to work for that firm, he came up with his own business idea: electronic merchandising.

Specifically, Forbes became convinced that there had to be a better way to get merchandise from the factory floor to people's living rooms, rather than going through the traditional, torpid, costly distribution systems that incorporated numerous warehouses, retail stores, and brokers. He believed that computers could do the job much more efficiently. Buyers could simply place their order with a credit card using a computer terminal, which would immediately tell the factory or warehouse where to send the merchandise. Lower costs and lower prices, among other advantages of such a system, would effectively obsolete the traditional retail industry.

Forbes, with the help of several friends, launched Comp-U-Card in 1973 (they incorporated the business in 1974 as Comp-U-Card America, Inc.). For three years Forbes and the other investors dumped hundreds of thousands of dollars into the venture in an effort to create a sort of electronic retail store. Meanwhile, Forbes continued to toil at his job and help to manage Comp-U-Card on the side. Because few people had access to computers, Forbes decided to try the concept using television. He tried to create a home shopping network through which customers could view products, call in with a credit card number, and have the goods delivered. Forbes later tried in-store electronic kiosks, which featured pictures of items that passersby could order electronically. Both the television shopping and kiosk efforts ultimately failed.

By the late 1970s Forbes and his fellow investors had dumped about $2 million into Comp-U-Card. The company showed little promise of returning the investment anytime soon, if at all. Still, Forbes was convinced of the merit of his concept. In 1979, in fact, he surprised coworkers when he left his job to devote all of his energy to Comp-U-Card. Forbes was hoping that, by the early 1980s, the number of consumers who had access to home computers would constitute a viable market for his electronic shopping concept. To that end, in 1979 Comp-U-Card launched its first online home shopping service, Comp-U-Store Online.

### A New Strategy in the Early 1980s

Forbes was finally forced to accept the fact that the electronic shopping market still had not materialized. By 1982 Comp-U-Card was generating only a few million dollars in annual sales and still showed no signs of recovering the millions of dollars invested since the 1973 start-up. Still undeterred, Forbes decided to adopt a new strategy. After deciding to focus on telephone sales, he found that Comp-U-Card was uniquely positioned to capitalize on a related, emerging trend in the credit card business—"affinity" programs that offered credit card customers incentives like memberships in shopping clubs. Credit card companies, then, began offering memberships or discounts on memberships in Comp-U-Card's discount shopping services as a lure to attract new customers.

Comp-U-Card's first shopping service was dubbed "Shoppers Advantage." Shoppers Advantage members paid an annual fee (about $40 in the early 1990s), which gave them access to a toll-free number that they could dial to place orders for merchandise. Members could purchase brand name items and have the goods delivered directly to their home. Aside from the convenience, the service was designed to deliver lower prices in comparison to typical retail channels. Comp-U-Card paid the credit card companies a percentage of the membership fees it collected and benefitted from access to the credit card companies' mailing lists. Everybody involved benefitted, with the exception of competing retailers.

Comp-U-Card was able to offer low prices on its goods for several reasons. Aside from bypassing expensive brokers, Comp-U-Card took bids from numerous distributors. When a caller would phone in to purchase a pre-selected item, the Comp-U-Card representative would ply the database to find the lowest bid from hundreds of distributors on the particular item. Comp-U-Card would effectively award the sale to the lowest

bidder and add a mark-up of about five to ten percentage points to the price to cover its overhead (i.e. the toll-free phone call, shipping, and administrative costs). Many manufacturers initially refused to sell through Comp-U-Card for fear of irritating their retail customers, but Comp-U-Card was eventually able to convince most major manufacturers to use the channel, and the service grew to include more than 250,000 items by the early 1990s.

Thus, with its telephone shopping club marketed through credit card companies, Forbes had finally found a winning strategy for Comp-U-Card. Indeed, from about $4 million in 1983, Comp-U-Card's annual revenue rose past $50 million in 1985. Realizing the viability of the new strategy, Forbes changed the company's name to Comp-U-Card International in 1982 and in 1983 took it public to raise expansion capital. Comp-U-Card followed up with a second offering in 1984. Shortly before the first offering, moreover, Forbes sold licenses for its shopping clubs in Europe and Japan for about $6 million. The company's membership base exceeded one million in 1984, signaling the beginning of growth that would swell Comp-U-Card's membership ranks to 40 million by the mid-1990s.

By 1986 Comp-U-Card's sales had increased to nearly $90 million. More important, the company was showing healthy profits by then (net income totaled nearly $30 million between 1986 and 1988). Comp-U-Card's gains were also the result of complementary programs designed to piggy-back off of the success of the shopping club program. In 1985, for example, the company launched Travelers Advantage, a full-service travel club that guaranteed the lowest price for all travel arrangements to its members and returned five percent of every dollar spent through the service. Travelers Advantage eventually became an important profit center for the company.

### Diversifying in the Mid-1980s

As it expanded its membership programs, Comp-U-Card began diversifying in the mid-1980s as part of an overall strategy to create a multifaceted marketing organization that profited from technological changes in the marketplace. In 1986 the company acquired two companies: Benefit Consultants, Inc., a marketer of accidental death insurance through credit unions and banks, and Madison Financial Corp. (FISI*Madison), the nation's largest financial marketing organization and a provider of enhancement services (analogous to Comp-U-Card's shoppers club enhancement service) to more than 6,000 financial institutions. The acquisitions helped push Comp-U-Card's sales to $142 million in 1987 (fiscal year ended January 31, 1987), about $9 million of which was netted as income.

Reflecting its growing diversity, Comp-U-Card changed its name in 1987 to CUC International, Inc. It also launched another membership service, AutoVantage, which offered a variety of products and services for every phase of car ownership. Going into 1988, CUC was boasting about ten million members in all of its clubs combined. During that year, CUC bought a short-notice travel business and opened new satellite centers for its auto, travel, and shopping club services. Those efforts helped the company to boost sales to nearly $200 million in 1988, earning Walter Forbes a spot on the *Business Week* "CEO 1000" list. By the end of the 1980s the company was pulling in sales of close to $300 million and offering a growing diversity of discount products and services to its millions of members.

After rocketing throughout most of the mid- and late 1980s, CUC's stock price lurched downward in 1989, and shortsellers lined up to cash in on what many analysts expected would be a big drop in the company's value. The problem stemmed largely from questions about CUC's accounting methods, which seemed to artificially inflate earnings and emasculate cash flow. CUC executives acknowledged the problem and changed their accounting methods, adding credence to critics' claims that the company risked a downturn in profits if its customers didn't continue to resubscribe to its clubs. The critics had a point. If a significant portion of CUC's members did not resubscribe to its clubs, the company would have to incur huge marketing costs trying to replace them.

In fact, CUC achieved a membership renewal rate of about 70 percent that made it the envy of the industry. That meant that CUC, unlike many other subscriber services, could more easily profit from membership growth rather than maintaining an existing membership base. That benefit was reflected in sustained sales and profit gains; sales rose to $450 million in 1991 and $644 million in 1992, while net income climbed to $16 million annually. That growth was partly the result of more acquisitions and the start of new membership clubs. In 1989, for example, CUC launched Premier Dining, a national discount dining program. In 1991 the company started HealthSaver, which offered discounts on drugs, eyewear, and other health-related merchandise. Incredibly, by 1992 CUC was employing 5,000 workers and operating its network (mostly through licensees) in 36 countries.

### Expansion through Acquisitions in the Mid-1990s

During the early and mid-1990s CUC expanded greatly with significant acquisitions. In 1992, for instance, it acquired the venerable Entertainment Publications, the leading publisher of discount coupon books and promotions in North America. Similarly, in 1995 CUC bought Welcome Wagon International Inc. In addition, the company continued to add new services and membership clubs, including a new Home Shopping Travel Club and PrivacyGuard, which provided access to personal credit rating, driving, medical, and Social Security records. Furthermore, CUC entered into potentially lucrative partnerships to provide services with such big companies as Intel, Time Warner, and American Airlines.

Meanwhile, CUC continued to market its existing clubs geared mostly for shoppers, travelers, and other consumers. Indeed, by 1995 the company was sporting roughly 40 million members in its clubs and still achieving average resubscription rates of more than 60 percent. Interestingly, CUC returned to its roots in 1994 when it purchased the NetMarket Company, a leader in bringing commerce to the Internet. Finally, it appeared as though the interactive market for home shopping by computer was finally emerging as a viable distribution channel, just as Forbes had envisioned it more than 20 years earlier.

CUC sustained its blistering expansion drive into the mid-1990s, doubling revenues from $738 million in 1993 (fiscal year ended January 31, 1993) to $1.4 billion in 1996. During the same period, CUC's net income rose from $25 million to $163 million, making CUC a major force in its niche of the membership/electronic marketing industry. Signaling Forbes's intent to pursue his original dream of electronic commerce, CUC began pitching its clubs on the Internet and various online services in 1995. More important, early in 1996 CUC surprised observers when it announced a possible plan to pay a big $1.8 billion to acquire Sierra On-Line and Davidson & Associates, education and entertainment software manufacturers. CUC claimed that the purchase represented its first big move in a bid to become the biggest provider of online content in the world.

### Principal Subsidiaries

Benefit Consultants, Inc.; CUC Europe, Ltd. (United Kingdom); Entertainment Publications, Inc.; Essex Corporation; FISI Madison Financial Corporation; Interval International, Inc.; National Card Control, Inc.; The NetMarket Company; Welcome Wagon International, Inc.; Credit Card Sentinel Limited (United Kingdom); North American Outdoor Group, Inc.; GETKO Group Inc.

### Principal Divisions

Comp-U-Card Division.

### Further Reading

"CUC to Roll Out Shoppers Adventures," *ADWEEK Eastern Edition,* September 11, 1995, p. 12.
DePass, Dee, "Direct-Marketing Firm to Buy Outdoor Club," *Star Tribune-Minneapolis,* August 25, 1995, p. 3D.
Ellis, Junius, "These Internet Stocks Could Get You On-line for 70% Profits in a Year," *Money,* October 1995, p. 33.
"Entrepreneur of the Year," *Fairfield County Business Journal,* June 22, 1992, p. 7(2).
Hollifield, Ann, "CUC on the Move, Quietly Expanding Operations," *Business First-Columbus,* September 14, 1987, p. 3.
Lewis, Peter H., "CUC Will Buy Two Software Companies for $1.8 Billion," *The New York Times,* February 21, 1996, p. 1C.
Morgan, Sandra, "CUC International Acquires NetMarket Co.," *Business Wire,* November 15, 1994.
——, "CUC International Reports Record Year-End and Fourth Quarter Growth," *Business Wire,* March 21, 1995.
Oliver, Suzanne, "Virtual Retailer," *Forbes,* April 24, 1995, p. 126.
Plevyak, Laura, *CUC International Milestones.* Stamford, Conn.: CUC International, Inc., 1996.
Raphael, Steve, "Competitor Buys Entertainment Publishing," *Crain's Detroit Business,* October 21, 1991, p. 30.
Roberts, Jim, "Leguestar Deal Provides CUC with New Market," *Fairfield County Business Journal,* January 4, 1993, p. 1(1).

—Dave Mote

# Custom Chrome, Inc.

16100 Jacqueline Court
Morgan Hill, California 95037
U.S.A.
(408) 778-0500
Fax: (408) 778-7001

*Public Company*
*Incorporated:* 1970 as Custom Chrome
*Employees:* 369
*Sales:* $93.9 million (1996)
*Stock Exchanges:* NASDAQ
*SICs:* 5013 Motor Vehicle Supplies & New Parts

Custom Chrome, Inc. is the world's largest independent supplier of aftermarket parts and accessories for Harley-Davidson motorcycles. Controlling approximately 15 percent of the estimated $550 million aftermarket, the company is second only to Harley-Davidson itself. The approximately 13,000 products offered by the company include replacement parts, custom parts, and accessories and apparel, which are distributed to more than 4,700 dealers nationwide from warehouses in Louisville, Kentucky, in Harrisburg, Pennsylvania, and in Visalia, California. The company generates more than two-thirds of its annual revenue through the sale of its own products, ranging from transmissions to leather chaps, which are marketed under brand names such as RevTech, Premium, Dyno Power, and C.C. Raider. It also serves as a distributor of products offered by other manufacturers, such as Dunlop, Champion, Hastings, and Accel. The winner of several national advertising awards, Custom Chrome markets its products through a copyrighted 848-page catalog supported by a national telemarketing program, active participation in trade shows and consumer events, and advertising in magazines targeting the Harley-Davidson motorcycle market, which includes more than 1.2 million riders.

### Early History

Custom Chrome was founded in 1970 by Ignatius "Nace" Panzica, a 27-year-old mechanic who worked at a new car dealership and enjoyed racing and fixing up motorcycles. As an extension of his hobby, Panzica, along with three of his friends, opened a motorcycle accessory store in downtown San Jose, California. The new store, which they named Coast Motorcycle Accessories, was designed to meet the growing demand of the many riders they knew who customized their motorcycles with homemade parts not available on the market. The fledgling shop at that time had not yet limited itself to Harley-Davidson products; it carried parts and accessories for all brands of motorcycles. The company's first order, in fact, was for Honda motorcycle bars. The most popular requests in the early days of the small shop, though, were for 16-inch rear wheels and spoke kits.

Panzica's original plans were to operate the business as a one-person shop, with the other three working only part-time, around the schedule of their full-time jobs. As Vice-Chairman and co-founder Ty Cruze explained to *Business Journal's* Scott Hildula, "I just started at the shop as a part-time job and then bought in as an investor. It was just through us being enthusiasts that we found we could purchase things at prices better than most dealers could . . . and it just grew." The success of the business prompted Panzica to alter his plans. Two years later, he diversified his retail store operation into wholesale parts as well, becoming a distributor as the dealer industry grew. In an attempt to reach Harley riders outside of the California region, Panzica and his friends came up with the idea that would define the company's marketing strategy for the next 25 years. Working on a kitchen table in one of their homes, they created the first Custom Chrome catalog, publishing the first edition in 1973 and providing the advertising tool that made future growth possible.

### Expansion in the 1970s

By 1975, Panzica's modest expectations for his one-person motorcycle parts shop had been surpassed: that year the company generated one million dollars in sales. The original store could no longer hold the inventory his growing customer base demanded, and the company leased a 5,000-square-foot warehouse down the street to make room for a wholesale operation. As the population of Harley riders (who as a group are noted for their obsession with making their bikes distinctive) continued to grow, the need for further expansion arose. In 1978, the company again moved its operations, leasing a 10,000-square-foot building nearby, its first industrial-type warehouse. Before the end of the decade, the company again doubled its size by relocating its business to a new 20,000-square-foot building in east San Jose.

As Custom Chrome entered the 1980s, it benefited from the increasing popularity of Harley-Davidson motorcycles and worked to obtain a dominant position in the market by the middle of the decade, supplying 60 to 70 percent of all aftermarket Harley parts, excluding the motorcycle company's own aftermarket production. In 1982, Custom Chrome completed its fourth move in six years, opening in a 40,000-square-foot building in Morgan Hill, California. A combination of several factors contributed to such rapid growth. First, the company skillfully cultivated its relationship with Harley-Davidson, both the primary source of its business and its chief competitor, by promoting the image of individuality so much a part of the Harley mystique and the Harley Owners Group (HOG), the 250,000 member riders group. Taking advantage of the almost fanatical desire Harley riders have to personalize their bikes as a statement of their individuality, Custom Chrome became an easily accessible source for customizing parts, supplying aftermarket shops to which the manufacturer, with a network of only about 600 dealers, could not sell. At the same time, Custom Chrome was able to offer its customers prices ten to 15 percent lower than the competition, passing along the savings gained by manufacturing many of its parts in Taiwan. What is more, the company, which stocked parts for Harleys produced as early as 1936, was able to meet the unique needs of Harley enthusiasts who needed parts for their older bikes, ones that the manufacturer no longer carried.

Aggressive advertising also played a key role in the company's average annual sales growth during the early 1980s. Custom Chrome's marketing strategy at this time was carried out largely through its distinctive catalog, which not only provided attractive pictures of its product line, but supplied detailed information about the parts and offered suggestions for customizing and restoring as well. In 1982 the company's marketing department received its first Dealer's Choice "Best Catalog" award for its then 300-page publication, an award the company would receive again in 1983 and 1984.

Having emerged from the culture of Harley enthusiasts it now served, Custom Chrome knew firsthand the importance of customer service and the necessity of shipping orders as quickly and as inexpensively as possible. Accordingly, in 1985, the company introduced its "Eagle Express" freight program, enabling customers throughout the United States to receive their orders in three days by United Parcel Service (UPS) air shipment but at UPS ground shipment prices. As the company continued to develop its extensive warehousing system through technological upgrades and new buildings, rapid delivery time continued to set the company apart from the competition and contribute to sales growth.

### The Late 1980s: Blending Harley Values with Corporate Success

By 1986, Custom Chrome had developed into a 170-person company with sales in excess of $20 million. In addition, it now produced enough Harley parts to introduce a complete motorcycle kit. Although it had obviously come a long way from its origins as a small "biker hangout," it worked hard to project the unconventional image commonly associated with Harley-Davidson. Although Panzica and Cruze skillfully assembled a work force that included alumni from such companies as Hewlett-Packard Co. and Varian Associates Inc. and invested heavily in the latest computer technology to track inventory, they still ran the company with a laid-back attitude, preferring blue jeans and cowboy boots to pinstriped business suits, a strategy that managed to keep employee turnover lower. They decorated the walls of the corporate offices with Harley memorabilia rather than Ivy League degrees, underscoring the company's blue-collar roots and its commitment to its customers, many of whom were touring Harley-Davidson riders and Vietnam War veterans with a strong distaste for mainstream corporate values.

Maintaining this biker-friendly image and marketing strategy, however, did not prevent the company from building a state-of-the-art administration and 110,000-square-foot warehouse facility as its corporate headquarters in 1987. That same year, the company launched another first in the industry by organizing a Harley-Only Warehouse Dealer Show. Dubbed "The Greatest Show on Earth," the show was highly successful among Harley enthusiasts and vendors alike, setting the stage for what would become a mainstay in the Custom Chrome marketing strategy. Not only did the company make the show an annual event, but it began taking an active role in other consumer events for Harley-Davidson enthusiasts, such as the Black Hills Motorcycle Rally, a popular annual event held in Sturgis, South Dakota, and the annual Bike Week in Daytona, Florida. Participation in such events enabled the company to stay carefully attuned to the needs of its best customers and advertise its products at the same time.

As the decade drew to a close, business continued to prosper, especially in the eastern part of the United States. Harley-Davidson—in contrast to other domestic vehicle manufacturers such as Chrysler, Ford, and General Motors—managed to boost sales and market share in the face of increasingly strong foreign competition. To keep up with the increasing demand and improve upon its delivery time, the company again expanded its facilities, opening a new 85,000-square-foot building in Louisville, Kentucky in 1988. A year later Custom Chrome was awarded the Dealer's Choice Award for "Best Consumer Advertising," for the third time in a decade.

Although Custom Chrome benefited greatly from the success of Harley-Davidson during the 1980s, the relationship between the two companies has not been free of conflict. In 1989, the motorcycle manufacturer accused Custom Chrome of patent and trademark infringement, taking issue with its use of a brand name "Hawg," which closely resembled Harley's familiar trademark "Hog." At the same time, Custom Chrome brought a complaint against Harley-Davidson for packaging its products in a way that closely resembled the former's so-called "trade dress." A year later the two parties settled their differences: Custom Chrome agreed to stop using the "Hawg" name by 1992, and Harley-Davidson agreed to stop using the distinctive packaging style.

### Custom Chrome Goes Public in 1991

Although operating income continued to rise into the new decade, the company lacked the cash needed for further expansion and product research. A management-led leveraged buyout in 1989 by the Jordan Co. had resulted in the accumulation of enough debt to threaten the company's future growth. In 1991, after enduring two years of interest payments on the heavy debt load, Panzica took his 20-year-old company public to alleviate the debt burden. Having generated $39.6 million in revenues the previous year while consistently enjoying annual profit margins surpassing 40 percent for several years, the company hoped to raise enough capital to pay off the principal and accrued interest on loans and strengthen its credit line.

With its balance sheets stabilized, Custom Chrome was again ready to expand, creating the infrastructure for continued growth in the 1990s. A year after its initial public offering, the company opened a new 65,000-square-foot warehouse facility in Harrisburg, Pennsylvania. The new distribution facility made it possible for the company to provide one- to two-day delivery service for its customers in the entire New England area and on most of the East Coast.

### The 1990s and Beyond

The early 1990s proved to be years of strong growth for the company. Between 1991 and 1994, revenue jumped from $43.6 million to $74.9 million, while net income over the same period rose from a loss of $2.6 million to a profit of $6.4 million. Twice the size of its nearest independent competitor, the company enjoyed both the economies of scale and the financial strength to offer competitive prices and lead the industry in new product development at the same time. Despite such advantages, the company saw its market share decrease slightly in 1992 and 1993, primarily as a result of moves by small regional and national aftermarket competitors to undercut Custom Chrome's pricing on nonproprietary parts. In 1994, the company took several aggressive and highly publicized measures to ensure that its prices were indeed competitive. Such strategies included stamping the phrase "We Will Meet or Beat Any Printed Price" on its sales invoices and repositioning certain items within product lines in an attempt to make it easier for dealers to make comparisons with competitors' products. The intensive marketing program also stressed the company's record of superior performance and quick delivery time, qualities illustrated by three consecutive Dealer's Choice "Aftermarket Manufacturer of the Year" awards.

In October 1994, Custom Chrome was able to build upon its already strong reputation for customer service by constructing a new, and larger, 100,800-square-foot distribution facility in Visalia, California. The new site replaced Morgan Hill as the central distribution point for the company's markets throughout the western United States and was selected after talks with UPS confirmed that the Visalia location would improve the efficiency of Southern California deliveries, an important factor considering that the state accounted for 17 percent of the company's business. Once the company completed the monumental task of moving 13,000 part numbers to the new facility, it was able to guarantee one-day delivery to all of California and most of the western states.

As Custom Chrome entered the late 1990s, it sought to expand sales, first, by cultivating relationships with existing customers, realizing that repeat customers generate most of its revenue. In addition to bolstering its telemarketing program, the company increased its presence at motorcycle events throughout the country, transporting its newly assembled "mobile showroom"—a custom-built truck and 48-foot trailer housing six Harley-Davidson motorcycles outfitted with the latest in Custom Chrome parts—to several events each year. Attendance at trade shows and events enables the company to monitor customer satisfaction and introduce the more than 300 new products it usually develops each year.

Although Custom Chrome has traditionally derived most of its business from existing Harley-Davidson owners, its long-term growth prospects may be dependent upon future sales of new Harley-Davidson motorcycles. With an estimated 100,000 new bikes produced each year during the mid-1990s and both domestic and foreign demand on the rise, the company, according to most analysts, appeared to be in a favorable position.

### Principal Subsidiaries

CCI-Far East (Taiwan).

### Further Reading

Hayes, Mary, "Big 'Hog' Parts Seller Goes to Market," *The Business Journal-San Jose,* October 14, 1991, p. 10.

Hildula, Scott, "Morgan Hill Firm Rings $20 Million in Hog Outfit Sales," *The Business Journal,* October 27, 1986, pp. 1–2.

Jones, Danna M., " 'Nace' Panzica: Steers Motorcycle Parts Distributor to Public Success," *The Business Journal,* August 30, 1993, p. 12.

Kontzer, Tony, "Custom Chrome Confirms Moving Local Distribution to Visalia," *The Business Journal,* April 18, 1994, p. 7.

Labate, John, "Custom Chrome," *Fortune,* May 31, 1993, p. 99.

—Jason Gallman

Daimler-Benz
Aerospace

# Daimler-Benz Aerospace AG

Postfach 80 11 09
81611 Munich
Germany
+89 6 07-3 42 35
Fax: +89 6 07-3 42 39

*Public Company*
*Incorporated:* 1989
*Employees:* 50,784
*Sales:* DM 15.03 billion
*Stock Exchanges:* Munich
*SICs:* 3721 Aircraft; 3724 Aircraft Engines & Engine
Parts; 3728 Aircraft Parts & Equipment, Not
Elsewhere Classified; 3761 Guided Missiles & Space
Vehicles; 3764 Space Propulsion Units & Parts; 3669
Communications Equipment, Not Elsewhere Classified

With less than a decade under its belt, Daimler-Benz Aerospace AG has transformed the German aircraft industry from a bit player on the global scene into a leading star of the European aerospace industry. Commonly known as DASA, this affiliate of Germany's Daimler-Benz designs and manufactures both military and civilian aircraft, including missiles, helicopters, space, and commercial vehicles. DASA's Deutsche Airbus subsidiary is a lead partner in the pan-European Airbus consortium via a 37.9 percent share. Led by Group President Hartmut Mehdorn in the mid-1990s, DASA struggled to become consistently profitable. DASA was created in May 1989 through the merger of Messerschmitt-Böelkow-Blohm (MBB), Dornier GmbH, Motorenund Turbinen Union (MTU), and Telefunken System Technik (TST). The newly-formed conglomerate took a controlling (80 percent) interest in Deutsche Airbus that December.

## Background and Development of German Aerospace Industry

Although DASA wasn't formed until the late 1980s, its creation is intimately linked to several trends that characterized the German aerospace industry in the post-World War II era. Before the First World War, Germany had been an influential player in the aircraft industry. And afterwards, despite prohibitions against military development, German companies continued to create civilian and military aircraft. In fact, the country's build-up prior to World War II was distinguished by innovative technical and production capabilities.

After the Second World War, however, German aircraft companies were truly hamstrung. In his book *Airbus Industrie,* David Weldon Thornton noted that "after the defeat of the Third Reich Germany found itself prohibited from having an indigenous aviation capability." Although the advent of the Cold War helped revive the industry, at least in the Federal Republic of Germany (West Germany), the divided country's many aerospace companies continued to lag behind their contemporaries in Great Britain and France throughout the mid-20th century.

Regional rivalries within the German aviation industry exacerbated each company's inability to compete on a continental, let alone global, scale. Specifically, the German aircraft industry didn't start to consolidate until the mid-1960s, much later than did France, Britain, or most significantly, the United States. The pace of mergers quickened after 1968, when the West German parliament formally declared that it would use direct and indirect subsidies "to induce the enterprises to combine into larger, and thus competitive units."

But by that time, such American aerospace giants as Boeing Company, McDonnell Douglas Corporation, and Lockheed Corporation dominated the global market for commercial passenger aircraft. In order to compete more effectively, the federal governments and aerospace companies of France, Great Britain, and Germany began to investigate ways to pool their resources.

Four years of negotiations resulted in the December 1970 formation of G.I.E. Airbus Industrie, a consortium headquartered and incorporated in France. Founding members were France's Aérospatiale and Deutsche Airbus GmbH, a German joint venture created with contributions from five companies: Messerschmitt, Dornier, Blohm-Hamburger Flugzebau (HFB), Vereinigte Flugtechnische Werke (VFW), and Siebel. Each

## Company Perspectives:

*Because we are a company active in the field of high technology, the way we see the future determines our entrepreneurial activity. Decisions that we take today will affect every aspect of our lives in the 21st century. At Daimler-Benz Aerospace we are committed to securing the wellbeing of mankind in the world of tomorrow.*

took a 20 percent share in the Airbus affiliate, which was created in 1967.

Future DASA member MBB was formed through the union of Messerschmitt and Böelkow, two southern German interests that had themselves merged in the fall of 1968 with Blohm-Hamburger Flugzebau (HFB), a northern German manufacturer. By the late 1980s, only MBB and VFW still held stakes in Deutsche Airbus. Dornier, another major aircraft manufacturer and future DASA member located in southern Germany, was characterized as "jealously independent" in Thornton's 1995 study.

During the 1970s, German firms participated in several trans-European collaborations, but because of their small size German participants often had secondary roles and made most of the compromises.

### Formation of DASA in the Late 1980s

In 1987, German automaker Daimler-Benz had several reasons for acquiring and consolidating the German aerospace industry's largest players. First, Daimler-Benz leader Edzard Reuter hoped that DASA would help diversify his company from its core in luxury cars and heavy-duty trucks. He also believed that the aerospace business would complement the automotive operations by providing insights into new technologies and engineering. Perhaps more importantly, it was expected that the amalgamation would return Germany's aerospace industry to the position of leadership it had enjoyed in the early 20th century.

Daimler-Benz acquired controlling interests in MBB, Dornier, and MTU and merged them with its own Telefunken System-Technik (TST) electronics unit in May 1989. That December, the carmaker bought a controlling (80 percent) interest in Deutsche Airbus. The parent company organized these companies under Daimler-Benz Luftund Raumfahrt Holding (Daimler-Benz Aerospace Holding), a holding company 85 percent owned by Daimler-Benz and the rest by state and local governments. The carmaker also tried to add shipbuilding interests to the mix, but was prevented from doing so by the federal antitrust department.

Jürgen E. Schrempp, formerly a top executive with Mercedes' truck-building unit, was selected to lead the new company. Schrempp vowed to "wean Airbus from government subsidies" and "make DASA a bottom-line company," according to a May 1993 *Business Week* article. In 1990, he told *Aviation Week & Space Technology's* Michael Mecham that he wanted to transform DASA—and by extension the German

aerospace industry—from "a junior partner" to "an equal partner" in the European sphere.

But the amalgamation did not proceed as smoothly as Daimler-Benz might have planned. The hurdles were both political and cultural. Rivalries between the former competitors endured, despite their new alliance. Moreover, the Federal Cartel Office opposed Daimler-Benz's effort to bring Messerschitt-Beilkow-Blohm into the fold. The automaker had to bypass the ministry, applying directly to the Kohl administration to approve the merger. Critics in the German antitrust department, as well as remaining domestic aircraft manufacturers, worried about the concentration of power and government subsidies and contracts. Other more objective observers feared that Daimler-Benz had "overextended itself."

1990 was DASA's first year to operate as a fully consolidated corporation but it took until 1993 for the company to integrate all the member companies. Although Airbus Industrie made its first profit ever that year, Deutsche Airbus's loss heavily influenced DASA's DM135 million shortfall on DM12.5 million in revenues. Deutsche Airbus' 1991 profit helped carry its parent to a net income of DM50 million (US$31.25 million).

Profitability was fleeting, however, as a number of factors converged on the German aerospace industry. European economic unification influenced the consolidation of the continental market. The end of the Cold War and German reunification reduced military budgets and direct government subsidies in favor of economic restructuring and rebuilding the East German infrastructure. Military purchasing in Germany slashed 60 percent in the early 1990s, and civil markets also declined, as commercial airlines struggled to profit as well. The decline of these two major market segments demanded consolidation and intensified competition.

Company leader Schrempp employed several key strategies in the face of this difficult environment. First, he planned to forge joint ventures that would spread the costs, risks, and government subsidies among the partners, particularly in the development of new aircraft. The European Fighter Aircraft (EFA) project, for example, united the efforts of British, Italian, Spanish, and German manufacturers for what *Aviation Week & Space Technology* called "the continent's most ambitious program." The German government held a 33 percent stake in the project, but threatened several times to pull out and reduced its aircraft order from 250 to 200 in 1992. That same year, German defense minister Rühe announced that the country would abandon the EFA, but he was quickly forced to recant. Although CEO Schrempp wanted to reduce DASA's dependence on military contracts, he didn't want Germany to abandon the EFA. He was adamant that the country remain engaged, telling *Interavia/ Aerospace World's* Brian Davidson that abandoning the project "could mean the loss of 10,000 jobs and a severe loss from the technological standpoint." DASA and Germany were still participating when the EFA made its first test flight in 1994.

Outside of the EFA project, Schrempp sought to reduce DASA's dependence on the rapidly dwindling defense market from 45 percent of sales to 25 percent by 1997. He set out to accomplish that goal in a roundabout way, decreasing DASA's military emphasis by increasing its presence in civilian aircraft through the US$393 million acquisition of a controlling interest in Holland's Fokker in 1992. The purchase came after more than a year of negotiations with labor unions and politicians, during which DASA agreed to allow its newest affiliate to remain independent through 1995, when the Dutch government would sell its remaining 22 percent stake to the German company.

Fokker gave its new parent greater access to the American market via its strengths in the development of small (80- to 100-seat) regional aircraft. Although Fokker gained a much-needed infusion of capital, it lost US$77 million in 1993. Chairman Jan Nederkoorn, who had been in that post since 1988, resigned in the wake of that decline. In 1994, Fokker's board of management decided to begin the company's third major reorganization in as many years, cutting production by one-third and slashing the work force from 13,500 in 1990 to less than 9,000 by mid-decade.

It was a trend felt throughout the global aerospace industry. DASA reduced employment from 83,605 in 1991 to 81,872 in 1993 and expected to eliminate another 7,500 and close six plants by the end of 1994. While laudable, these efforts did not significantly improve DASA's position. The corporation lost a total of over DM1 billion (US$620 million) in 1992 and 1993, in spite of sales increases from DM12.4 billion (US$7.75 billion) in 1991 to DM18.6 billion (US$10.8 billion) in 1993. The new gush of red ink prompted a flurry of speculation that Daimler-Benz would end its airborne experiment. *Aviation Week & Space Technology's* Anthony Velocci noted that "Some aerospace analysts in the United States and Europe have been questioning Daimler's long-term commitment to DASA, and a few industry observers in Germany actually expect Daimler to sell its aerospace business within the next two years." But a sale wasn't forthcoming.

Schrempp and his mentor, Reuter, thought that an expansion of cooperative efforts would help turn DASA around, but Judy Bolinger, an analyst with Goldman Sach's London office, gave the corporation a threefold prescription for improved health in a 1993 *Aviation Week & Space Technology* article. She suggested that the company "improve MTU's weak market position" (it was then fifth among the world's eight aircraft engine manufacturers); downsize to fit its shrunken markets; and reduce its diversification to a few core competencies.

### Principal Subsidiaries

Daimler-Benz Aerospace Airbus GmbH; Dornier Luftfahrt GmbH (Germany); Eurocopter S.A. (France); Dornier Satellitensysteme GmbH (Germany); LFK-Lenkflugkorpersysteme GmbH; Dornier GmbH; Elekluft GmbH; E.S.T.-Entsorgungs- und Sanierungstechnik GmbH; Bayern-Chemie, Gesellschaft fur flugchemische Antriebe mbH; TDA Armements S.A.S.

(France); CMS Inc. (U.S.); The company also lists subsidiaries under the Daimler-Benz Aerospace name in Austria, France, Greece, Spain, Portugal, Italy, Mexico, China, South East Asia, Turkey, the United Arab Emerates, Belgium, Brazil, India, Japan, Korea, South Africa, and the United States.

### Further Reading

Banks, Howard, "Good-Bye to Cost-Plus," *Forbes,* November 23, 1992, p. 52.

"Consortiamania," *The Economist,* May 23, 1992, pp. 72–73.

Covault, Craig, "German Industry Confronts Crisis," *Aviation Week & Space Technology,* January 31, 1994, pp. 44–48.

Davidson, Brian, "Positioning DASA for the Future," *Interavia/Aerospace World,* June 1993, pp. 26, 28, 32.

Hill, Leonard, "Fokker/DASA: Finally A Deal," *Air Transport World,* June 1993, p. 26.

——, "Nederkoorn's Downfall," *Air Transport World,* April 1994, p. 58.

McIntyre, Ian, *Dogfight: the Transatlantic Battle Over Airbus,* London: Praeger, 1992.

Mecham, Michael, "Deutsche Aerospace Wants to Grow Out of Its 'Junior Partner' Role," *Aviation Week & Space Technology,* June 4, 1990, pp. 21–22.

——, "Deutsche Airbus Moves Into Black; DASA Makes $31 Million as Result," *Aviation Week & Space Technology,* June 8, 1992, p. 70.

——, "Deutsche Airbus Renamed; DASA Retires MBB Identity," *Aviation Week & Space Technology,* October 12, 1992, p. 64.

——, "Germany Weighs Cost of Unification as Deutsche Aerospace Seeks Expansion," *Aviation Week & Space Technology,* September 3, 1990, pp. 69, 73.

——, "Market Forcing Regionals to Think 'Consolidation'," *Aviation Week & Space Technology,* September 7, 1992, pp. 69–71.

Moorman, Robert W., "A Finger in Every Pie," *Air Transport World,* April 1994, p. 54.

"On the Runway," *The Economist,* April 8, 1989, pp. 72, 76.

Reed, Arthur, "Boeing & DASA: Sound, Fury and What?" *Air Transport World,* February 1993, p. 31.

——, "New Day Dawning in Deutschland," *Air Transport World,* March 1993, p. 82.

Sparaco, Pierre, "Facing Tough Times, DASA Looks Long Term," *Aviation Week & Space Technology,* May 31, 1993, p. 95.

Sutton, Oliver, "Restructuring DASA's Aircraft Group," *Interavia Business & Technology,* May 1994, p. 31.

Templeman, John, and Patrick Oster, "The Runway is Clear for Deutsche Aerospace," *Business Week,* May 10, 1993, pp. 39–40.

Thornton, David Weldon, *Airbus Industrie: The Politics of an International Industrial Collaboration,* New York: St. Martin's Press, 1995.

Velocci, Anthony L., Jr., "Daimler Stands By DASA Despite Mounting Losses," *Aviation Week & Space Technology,* November 1, 1993, pp. 61–62.

Verchere, Ian, "Can DASA Afford to Quit EFA?" *Interavia,* June 1992, p. 17.

——, "Germany Tempers Its Ambitions," *Interavia,* June 1992, p. 13.

—April Dougal Gasbarre

# Daniel Industries, Inc.

9753 Pine Lake Drive
P.O. Box 19097
Houston, Texas 77224
U.S.A.
(713) 467-6000
Fax: (713) 827-3880

*Public Company*
*Incorporated:* 1946 as the Daniel Orifice Fitting
    Company
*Employees:* 1,450
*Sales:* $168.56 million (1995)
*Stock Exchanges:* New York
*SICs:* 3824 Fluid Meters & Counting Devices; 3452
    Bolts, Nuts, Rivets & Washers; 3494 Valves & Pipe
    Fittings

Daniel Industries, Inc. is a leading manufacturer of energy measurement technology, including systems to measure the flow of gases, liquids, and steam. In addition, the company is a major international producer of high-technology equipment to transmit, distribute, and market oil, gas, and various other energy commodities. Having initiated a comprehensive reorganization strategy in early 1995, which focused on providing products for the natural gas industry, the development of technology involving liquid flow, and the expansion into specific sectors of the gas processing industry, the company was beginning to reap the rewards of its meticulous planning in the mid-1990s. Revenues increased dramatically, and sales offices were operating in such far flung locations as Calgary, Canada, Dammam, Saudi Arabia, Datchet, England, Falkirk, Scotland, Leiden, Holland, Moscow, Russia, Potsdam-Babelsberg, Germany, and Singapore.

### The Company's Founder Gets His Start in the Early 20th Century

Paul Daniel was born in Houston, Texas, on May 17, 1894. Educated in a one-room schoolhouse on the edge of the city, as a teenager Paul Daniel worked various odd jobs on the range in the burgeoning Texas metropolis. Yet as cattle raising became more and more modernized, and Houston began to lose its western "shoot 'em up" aura, the young man discovered that work was getting scarcer and scarcer. Finally, after much deliberation, and with guarded encouragement from his parents, the young man traveled to southern California in order to seek his fortune.

Arriving in California without money or prospects in 1915, Daniel found a job at the El Segundo Refinery operated by Standard Oil Company, one of the largest and most successful enterprises in the history of American business. During his time at the refinery, Daniel learned all he could about the oil industry, and the new technology that was designed to speed and control the flow of oil through pipelines running across miles of almost uninhabitable terrain. In just two years, the ambitious and knowledgeable man from Texas had been promoted to the prestigious position of Tank Gauger at the refinery, one of the most sought-after and respected jobs within the Standard Oil Company.

Daniel volunteered to serve in the U.S. Army when America entered World War I in 1917. Although most of the recorded history about American involvement in the First World War has focused on the European theatre, especially the fierce fighting around Belle Wood in the French countryside, American soldiers also fought against Germany in the Middle East and in Siberia. Daniel was assigned to the United States Army Siberian Expeditionary Force, which saw extensive action fighting alongside its Russian compatriots-in-arms. Daniel returned to the United States after two years of service, a wiser, stronger, and more determined man.

By 1920, Daniel was back in California working for the Pan-American Petroleum Company owned by an entrepreneur by the name of E.L. Dopheny. Under Dopheny's tutelage, Daniel learned more than ever about the oil industry and worked his way up the corporate ladder. Throughout the 1920s Daniel became acquainted with the intricacies of flow systems within the oil pipelines and, by 1928, he had risen to the position of assistant to the manager of the company's Natural Gas Division in Los Angeles, California.

The company was hard hit by the Great Depression in the early 1930s, and salaries were slashed dramatically. At first

## Company Perspectives:

*Integral to the Company's renewal and future are refocusing and redoubling efforts on natural gas markets. Daniel developed its well-earned reputation by providing high quality, technically advanced, reliable products and systems for natural gas markets. The Company's focus will be to augment its reputation with even higher quality products, systems and services to satisfy the needs of customers.*

Daniel didn't expect the economic hardships of the Depression to last very long, but when it became evident that no immediate relief was in sight, he grew worried about the security of his job. Indeed, during the height of the Great Depression in the early and mid-1930s, Daniel was slowly phased out of work at the company. Forced to scrap by for a living, he worked any job he could get. At the same time, however, he never gave up his hope of working for the oil industry once again, and he started designing an orifice fitting that would allow for the changing of plates within the oil pipeline system without interrupting the flow of the oil or allowing significant leakage. After a few years of work on his design, he was rewarded with a patent for the "senior orifice fitting," as he called it, a creation whose fundamental design remains the standard in the pipeline industry at the present.

### Daniel Starts a Business in the 1940s

With his patent in hand, and requests for the new device overwhelming him, Daniel decided to start his own business. The Daniel Orifice Fitting Company opened for business near the end of the Depression in Los Angeles, and began manufacturing orifice fittings, orifice plates, and meter tubes for the oil industry. Not long afterward, the company expanded its product line to include the manufacture of piston-controlled check-valves, orifice flanges, and Simplex plate holders. By the end of the decade, Daniel was head of a thriving business.

When America entered World War II in December 1941, the U.S. government contracted major oil companies to provide gas and oil to operate the tanks, jeeps, trucks, and various other motorized equipment used by soldiers in both the European and Pacific theatres. The major oil companies like Texaco and Standard Oil, in turn, contracted smaller firms to keep the flow of oil running smoothly. The Daniel Orifice Fitting Company benefitted directly from these contracts. In fact, business expanded so rapidly that the company opened a small plant in Houston, hometown of the founder and owner.

By the war's end, the Daniel Orifice Fitting Company had grown dramatically, and was poised to expand its manufacturing facilities and sales operations even further. Over the years, Paul Daniel had developed into a cautious but shrewd businessman, and he had grown to understand the value of expanding his company's operations in a slow but methodical manner. Gradually, throughout the 1950s, the company increased the number of its employees, built new manufacturing plants across the United States, and opened numerous sales and marketing offices, primarily in the western and southwestern regions of the country.

### Expansion During the 1960s and 1970s

By the mid-1960s, after Paul Daniel had left the active management of the company, the Daniel Orifice Fitting Company counted over 500 employees, five manufacturing plants located across the nation, ten sales offices, and 48 sales agency offices. In 1966, the board of directors decided to change the name of the company to Daniel Industries, Inc., in order to reflect the growing diversity of its product line and services.

The 1970s saw further expansion and growth for the company. Major acquisitions during this time included M&J Valve Company, an old and well-known firm that manufactured valves and gauges for the oil industry, and Oilfield Fabricating & Machine Company, one of the pre-eminent businesses in the supply of custom-made machine parts for oil and gas pipeline systems. In addition, management created a subsidiary named the Daniel Bolt Company, which was involved in the manufacture of products for oilfield machinery. Management also kept abreast of all the new developments in oilfield technology, and utilized innovations and new designs within the field to improve upon and expand the types of mechanical, electronic, and highly sophisticated computer-based products and systems the company was now producing. With the energy crisis at its peak during the mid- and late 1970s, and America determined to develop its own sources of energy in order to decrease dependence on foreign oil, Daniel Industries was at its high point.

### Downturn During the 1980s and a Return to Basics

The most profitable period in the company's history lasted for about ten years. When the energy crisis faded, and the price of oil went down drastically, the entire American oil industry was hit hard. By the end of the decade, energy companies in the gas and oil industry had lost over 370,000 jobs. Conservative estimates of job losses in the supporting industries were placed at over one million. Daniel Industries faced its first real crisis, and management decided to return to the basics. This meant liquidating inventories, reducing capacity, and eliminating jobs. At the same time, management rededicated itself to manufacturing fewer but higher quality products, streamlining manufacturing operations, encouraging innovative designs and product development, and improving customer service.

The most important development to come out of this difficult period was what became known as "partnership relationships" between Daniel Industries and both its customers and suppliers. A greater emphasis was placed on manufacturing quality products at competitive prices, with the common goal of minimizing total installation costs and operating expenses to the user. These partnership relationships were successful due to a number of strategic management innovations, including a material resource planning program, the use of computer numerical controlled machines and other highly specialized equipment, extensive employment of CAD/CAM systems, improved internal communications networks, and a new order-entry system.

### The 1990s and Beyond

By the early 1990s, Daniel Industries had developed three main core businesses: metering, electronics, and pipeline valves. The core metering business included manufacture of the industry's standard Senior Orifice Fitting, as well as gas turbine meters, and ultrasonic flow meters. As the company's focus has shifted from liquid metering to value-added gas metering, management believed that the ultrasonic flow meter was the meter of the future for all gas pipeline systems. The electronics division, which became a part of the company's metering business, focused on manufacturing items such as Daniel flow computers for the worldwide market. The company's flow control valve business retained its traditional manufacturing role of producing gate valves for liquid pipeline systems. By the mid-1990s, the company had added a line of ball valves, as well as specialty control valves for use in gas pipelines and gas and liquid storage facilities.

During the early and mid-1990s, Daniel Industries made a commitment to expand its marketing worldwide as well as to increase its customer service locations internationally. A sales and service office was opened in Singapore in order to take advantage of one of the world's fastest growing gas producing markets. A sales office was opened in Moscow with the purpose of cultivating the emerging natural gas markets in Russia. An office in London was established to provide direct communication links with customers and engineering companies conducting operations in the North Sea. A subsidiary was formed in Germany—Daniel Messtechnik GmbH—to provide the company with access to developing markets in Eastern Europe. Other major offices included locations in Saudi Arabia, Scotland, and The Netherlands.

In 1995, management at the company decided to implement a comprehensive reorganization strategy to make all of the company's operations more effective, and to increase shareholder value. As the restructuring program successfully progressed, all of the assets of the company were sold to an investor group headed by Russell Ginn, a Houston-based entrepreneur.

The change in ownership, however, did nothing to affect the expansion and growth of the company. In early 1996, the company purchased the Oilfield Fabricating & Machine Company and later in the year entered into an agreement with Framo Engineering AS of Norway to market and sell the Norwegian firm's highly innovative multiphase flow metering system. At the same time, the company acquired Spectra-Tek International, and concluded an agreement with Cooper Cameron Corporation to license worldwide that firm's geothermal gate valves and wellhead systems.

With its restructuring program completed, and with the financing to continue to develop new products and partnership arrangements, Daniel Industries was well poised to meet the challenges of the volatile oil and gas producing industry.

### *Principal Subsidiaries*

Daniel Automation Company; Daniel EN-FAB Systems, Inc.; Daniel Flow Products, Inc.; Daniel Industrial, Inc.; Daniel Valve Company; RBC Realty Inc.; Daniel Canada; Daniel Industries Ltd.; Daniel Messtechnik GmbH

### *Further Reading*

"Daniel Industries," *The Oil and Gas Journal,* August 7, 1995, p. 68.
"Daniel Industries," *The Wall Street Journal,* March 7, 1995, p. B2.
Fletcher, Sam, "Daniel Industries Sells Subsidiary," *The Oil Daily,* June 26, 1995, p. 6.
——, "Management Buys Daniel En-Fab Systems from Parent Company for Undisclosed Price," *The Oil Daily,* July 7, 1995, p. 2.
"Moorco Discloses Bid for Daniel Industries," *The Wall Street Journal,* March 9, 1995, p. C15.

—Thomas Derdak

# DARDEN
RESTAURANTS

# Darden Restaurants, Inc.

**5900 Lake Ellenor Drive**
**P.O. Box 593330**
**Orlando, Florida 32809-3330**
**U.S.A.**
**(407) 245-4000**
**Fax: (407) 245-5310**

*Public Company*
*Incorporated:* 1995
*Sales:* $3.16 billion (1995)
*Employees:* 124,730
*Stock Exchanges:* New York
*SICs:* 5812 Eating Places

Operating more than 1,200 units throughout the United States and Canada, Darden Restaurants, Inc. began its existence in 1995 as the world's largest full-service restaurant organization, occupying the casual-dining niche between fine-dining and quick-service restaurants. Specifically, the company was spun off from General Mills to its stockholders as an independent company, overseeing the restaurant chains Red Lobster, The Olive Garden, and, until late 1995, China Coast. Founded in 1968 and acquired by General Mills, Inc. in 1970, Red Lobster grew to become the nation's largest seafood and casual-dining restaurant chain. Launched in 1982, The Olive Garden became the largest chain of casual but full-service Italian restaurants. China Coast was an unsuccessful ethnic-restaurant chain that operated during the 1990s.

### The First Red Lobsters

William B. Darden, reared in Waycross, Georgia, opened, at the age of 19, a Depression-era Waycross lunch counter that he called "The Green Frog," promising "Service with a Hop." He went on to own some local motel and hotel properties and all or part of about 20 Howard Johnson restaurants. Inspired by the great popularity of seafood in two of his eight restaurants—one in Orlando and the other in Jacksonville—Darden opened his first Red Lobster restaurant in Lakeland, Florida, in 1968. Its manager was Joe R. Lee, a native Georgian who later became chief executive officer of Darden Restaurants.

Darden wanted to market a chain of moderately priced, family-style, full-service seafood restaurants. He chose to open in Lakeland because it was as far from the ocean as possible in Florida, and he wanted to test his concept outside of coastal areas. The first Red Lobster proved a booming success, so much so that Darden and his partners had to work full shifts to meet the objective of getting food to the table within ten minutes of the order.

By 1970, there were three Red Lobsters in operation, all in central Florida, and two more under construction. The three units, which despite their name specialized in the fried fish and hush puppies favored by southerners, averaged $800,000 each in annual sales, and earnings were solid, but the company lacked the cash to grow. For General Mills, a diversified food-products giant, acquiring Red Lobster Inns of America made sense because General Mills' fish sales accounted for about $80 million of revenue, or one-ninth of its total sales. Darden was hired to oversee the chain and open a restaurant headquarters in Orlando. He later became a General Mills vice-president and senior consultant, retired in 1984, and died in 1994.

General Mills upgraded Red Lobster into a midpriced seafood dinner house that was a model of corporate efficiency. Lee, who rose to become president of Red Lobster in 1975, carried a slide rule with him everywhere in the early 1970s to calculate prices and portion weights, and to quantify whatever else could be quantified. He also carried a thermometer in order to assure that entrees had been cooked to the proper temperature before being served. In 1971 Red Lobster established an in-house department for purchasing seafood on a worldwide scale. The company also established, long before the rest of the industry, a computerized point-of-purchase system to track how much of any given item was selling where.

### Rapid Growth in the 1970s

Red Lobster grew in each year of operation, and it grew rapidly. By the end of fiscal 1971 there were 24 restaurants with total sales of $9.1 million, and by the end of fiscal 1972 there were 47 with sales of $27.1 million. When Lee was named president of Red Lobster in 1975, there were 97 restaurants with 9,500 employees. In 1976 the General Mills subsidiary opened a microbiology laboratory in Orlando to ensure the quality of its products. Red Lobster ended that fiscal year with 174 units in 26 states and total sales of $174.1 million.

Because of higher costs, largely attributed to increased fuel bills for truck transportation and fishing boats caused by the Arab oil embargo of 1973–74, Red Lobster again felt the need to upgrade in the mid-1970s. It carpeted the floors, re-styled the interiors and added a few fresh dishes to its predominantly frozen menu, and it sharply jacked up prices to pay for the improvements. The strategy worked. By the end of 1980 Red Lobster, with 260 units and almost $400 million in annual sales, had reached ninth place among fast-food companies and accounted for more than half of total sales by seafood fast-food companies. Although a sit-down chain, frequently with lounges, it was considered "fast food" by some analysts because most entree items were delivered frozen.

Alternatively, however, by 1982 Red Lobster was rated as the nation's largest "dinner-house" restaurant chain, this being the name for a restaurant offering table service and a full lunch and dinner menu. With an average annual return on invested assets of 22.3 percent before taxes, it was one of the most profitable chains in its field, and its growth had come entirely without franchising.

### Wider Choices in the 1980s

Red Lobster provided General Mills with $75 million in operating earnings during fiscal 1982. By early 1983 there were 350 establishments in 36 states. The first of dozens of franchised Red Lobsters in Japan opened in Tokyo in 1982, and the first Canadian unit opened in 1983. Securities analysts attributed the chain's success largely to Red Lobster's position as the only nationwide seafood dinner chain and its extraordinary quality-control measures. According to one of its executives, while seafood could be 16 days old and still legally sold as fresh, Red Lobster's seafood, although frozen, was "fresh frozen" at five regional warehouses, each with a quality-control laboratory.

During 1982, however, Red Lobster decided to pursue a new direction. The chain's research, according to Lee, indicated that its customers resented waiting in line yet didn't like being hustled out, and wanted a more casual dining experience, with an atmosphere conducive to drinks, appetizers, and finger food to share instead of massive entrees. Accordingly, a prototype unit opened in Kissimmee, Florida, in 1984 was a grazer's delight, with a seafood bar serving up oysters, shrimp, clams, calamari, and other appetizers with drinks, and a glass-enclosed grill where fresh seafood was broiled over mesquite-wood flames. Red Lobster restaurants had deliberately been built without windows so that diners would not take up time seeking a table looking out, but the new unit had picturesque views. Waiters were instructed to relax instead of speeding diners through the dinner cycle.

In 1984, General Mills authorized a $104-million remodeling program for Red Lobster, the largest capital-spending item in the parent company's history. All 370 units were to be overhauled, with the menu 40 percent longer to include such items as seafood salads and pastas, and six or eight fresh-fish entrees available, twice as many as in the past. Dinner prices were lowered to draw more customers, with the expectation that patrons would make up for the difference by increased spending on appetizers and alcoholic beverages.

Red Lobster continued to reinvent itself and reward its parent company in subsequent years, passing $1 billion in North American sales during 1988. By then it was General Mills' second-largest revenue producer, trailing only the cereals division and accounting for about one-fifth of the parent company's business. A food-industry analyst told the *New York Times,* "They have a concept that works extremely well, but they also constantly refresh their franchise.... If Cajun food is hot, they'll put five Cajun entrees on the menu. Whatever's hot, they'll do it."

By this time Red Lobster was offering more than 100 seafood items every day. To supply its units it was buying about 58 million pounds of seafood every year, combing the world's oceans for the latest novelty. These included popcorn shrimp, caught off the shores of Brazil, slipper lobster from Thailand, and Pacific orange roughy, a whitefish, from New Zealand to supplement North American standbys from Florida stone crab and Maine flounder to Alaska salmon. By 1995 Red Lobster was purchasing seafood from 44 countries.

The array of options allowed the chain to draw in new customers by featuring bargain specials. Close contact between the chain's buyers and thousands of entrepreneurial fishing operations, and delivery by overnight air-express services, enabled much of the catch to reach units daily while still fresh. The price of Red Lobster dinner entrees ranged from about $7 to $19 in 1995. Lunch entrees ranged from about $4.30 to $7. Red Lobster also offered a lower-priced children's menu.

Questionnaires and focus groups also convinced Red Lobster of the importance of good service to securing follow-up trade. It held a four-day training course for servers before each restaurant opened and then required the staff to attend follow-up monthly classes. After 1986 waiters and waitresses were encouraged to display individuality in serving customers rather than relying on mechanical recitations of what the restaurant had to offer. The uniform of shirts and slacks was replaced by a maroon apron under which servers wore clothing of their own choice. They were also motivated by Red Lobster's reputation for good benefits, flexible hours, chances for advancement, and the hope of earning more than $100 in tips on good nights.

### The Olive Garden, 1982–1995

Fearing saturation in the seafood market, however, General Mills had decided years earlier to expand its restaurant group, which included York Steak House as well as Red Lobster. In 1982, following five years of painstaking research and about $28 million for development funds, the company opened the first Olive Garden restaurant in Orlando. By the end of 1985 there were eight such units, and by mid-1989 there were 145, making it General Mills' fastest-growing business and probably the fastest-growing major chain in the United States.

A 1991 *Forbes* article found the dinner portions, averaging only $10, enormous, but called the salad soggy with dressing, the chicken bland, and the fettucine alfredo like something out of a TV dinner. However, the public flocked to these outlets. Average sales per Olive Garden were $2.8 million that year, compared to $3 million for Red Lobster, and both were high for the industry. The Olive Garden ended fiscal 1992 with $808 million in sales and 341 outlets. It reached the $1-billion-a-year sales mark in 1993. The menu, in 1995, included not only Italian specialties such as veal piccata, baked lasagna, and chicken marsala but a variety of veal, beef, and seafood dishes. Dinner entree prices ranged from about $7 to $14.25, and lunch entree prices from about $4.25 to $8.75. A limited-menu Olive Garden Cafe concept in food-court settings at regional shopping malls was being tested. There were seven such units in late 1995.

### Ill-Fated China Coast, 1990–1995

The success of The Olive Garden encouraged General Mills to expand its ethnic-food format. After three years of development and test marketing the restaurant group launched China Coast in 1990 as the first national Chinese-food chain. This eatery opened with an eight-page menu, in *Newsweek's* words, "about as long as the list of emperors in the Ming Dynasty." The interiors were festooned with bamboo, paper lanterns, and Chinese-character wall scrolls, and the servers wore Chinese-style jackets. Eventually the China Coast chain grew to 51, but it failed to thrive and was ordered closed in 1995. During fiscal 1995 China Coast's sales came to only $71 million, and Wall Street analysts estimated it lost $20 million that year. Thirty China Coast restaurants were converted into Red Lobsters or Olive Gardens.

### Darden Restaurants

General Mills decided in 1995 to spin off its restaurant operations into a new company so that it could concentrate more on its consumer food products. Lee, the chairman and chief executive officer, named the new company Darden Restaurants in honor of his mentor and Red Lobster's founder. Stockholders received one share of Darden Restaurants common stock for each share of General Mills common stock they held. In their last fiscal year under General Mills' auspices, Darden Restaurants' constituent units had combined net income of $108.3 million.

Investors failed to rally around Darden Restaurants, whose stock ended its first day of trading on the New York Stock Exchange below the $12 to $13 a share expected by analysts. One securities analyst said that the restaurants had been accounting for only one-quarter of General Mills' operating profits while absorbing half of the company's capital spending for expansion and renovation. Nevertheless, its market capitalization of $1.8 billion made it second in size only to McDonald's among the nation's publicly traded restaurant companies.

Darden Restaurants indicated in early 1996 that the China Coast experience would not keep it from trying other ethnic formats. In March of that year it began test-marketing Bahama Breeze Caribbean Grille, with a menu drawn from Spanish, French, African, Dutch, Indian, and American influences. En-

trees, priced between $5 and $15, were to include Bahamian conch chowder, slow-roasted ribs, Caribbean paella, jerk chicken, and rum-glazed yellowtail dolphin, washed down with Caribbean-island beer and other drinks. Lee predicted that, whether Bahama Breeze went into operation or not, Darden Restaurants would add at least two chains to its repertoire by 1998.

Darden Restaurants executives expressed confidence that they were on the right track toward long-term robust growth. Casual dining, according to the company, was the fastest-growing segment of the full-service restaurant market, with sales increasing at more than twice the overall market's rate since 1988 and representing, in 1995, 32 percent of full-service restaurant sales, or $29 billion. The trend toward casual dining, it argued, was reflected in the less formal dress code in the work place and would continue in years to come. Moreover, the company noted that 40-to-60-year-olds were the most frequent visitors to casual-dining restaurants, and that the population aged 45 and older was expected to grow by 40 million through 2010.

At the end of fiscal 1995 Darden Restaurants was operating 1,250 restaurants in every state except Alaska. Seventy-three were in Canada. Red Lobster restaurants were being remodeled, with weathered wood accented by nautical artifacts for a wharfside effect, to be completed by the end of fiscal 1997. Of the company's units, 788 were on owned sites and 462 on leased sites. The company's long-term debt was $303.7 million in August 1995.

### Principal Subsidiaries

GMRI, Inc.

### Further Reading

Carlino, Bill, "Darden Gives Up on China Coast, Shutters Units," *Nation's Restaurant News,* September 4, 1995, pp. 1, 7.
——, "Darden Is Watching Which Way Bahama Breeze Blows," *Nation's Restaurant News,* January 29, 1996, pp. 1, 53.
——, "Jeffrey J. O'Hara," *Nation's Restaurant News,* October 9, 1995, pp. 176, 178.
——, "William Darden," *Nation's Restaurant News,* February 1996, p. 68.
Harris, John, "Dinnerhouse Technology," *Forbes,* July 8, 1991, pp. 98–99.
McGill, Douglas, "Why They Smile at Red Lobster," *New York Times,* April 23, 1989, Sec. 3, pp. 1, 6.
Miller, Annette, and Springen, Karen, "Egg Rolls for Peoria," *Newsweek,* October 12, 1992, pp. 59–60.
Papiernik, Richard, "New Stock Sparks Trades but No Wall Street Fireworks," *Nation's Restaurant News,* June 19, 1995, pp. 3–4.
Phalon, Richard, "Amicable Divorce," *Forbes,* May 8, 1995, pp. 70, 74.
Ponti, James, "A Guy Named Joe," *Orlando,* November 1995, pp. 32–39.
"Red Lobster Looking Abroad," *New York Times,* February 14, 1983, p. D3.
Romeo, Peter, and Norvell, Scott, "Looking Leeward," *Restaurant Business,* November 20, 1995, pp. 40, 44–46.
Saporito, Bill, "When Business Got So Good It Got Dangerous," *Fortune,* April 2, 1984, pp. 61–62, 64.

—Robert Halasz

# DART◎GROUP

# Dart Group Corporation

**3300 75th Avenue**
**Landover, Maryland 20785**
**U.S.A.**
**(301) 731-1200**
**Fax: (301) 731-1340**

*Public Company*
*Incorporated:* 1960
*Employees:* 10,700
*Sales:* $655.3 million (1995)
*Stock Exchanges:* NASDAQ
*SICs:* 5531 Automobile & Home Supply Stores; 5942
Book Stores; 5411 Grocery Stores; 6512
Nonresidential Building Operators

Dart Group Corporation, a pioneer in discount marketing and in the concept of "superstores," is a holding company for three chains of discount retail stores, a real estate company, and a financial business. At the beginning of 1996, Trak Auto, its discount auto parts chain, operated 276 stores in the metropolitan areas of Washington, D.C., Richmond, Virginia, Chicago, Pittsburgh, and Los Angeles. Crown Books, its discount book store chain, had 172 stores in California, Houston, Chicago, Seattle, and Washington, D.C. Total Beverage operated four discount beverage superstores in suburban Washington, D.C.

Dart Group also has three wholly owned subsidiaries. Cabot-Morgan owns shopping centers and other real estate. Dart Group Financial provides financing for inventory purchases by commercial businesses. Dart/SFW Corporation holds the company's 50 percent interest in Shoppers Food Warehouse, a 34-store discount grocery chain in the Washington, D.C., area. The Haft family of Washington, D.C., owns 100 percent of the company's voting stock.

### Early History: Discount Drug Stores

Dart Group was founded by Herbert Haft, who, with his wife, Gloria, opened his first drug store in the early 1950s, in the Cleveland Park area of Washington, D.C. The Hafts' store was a typical corner drug store of its time, offering prescriptions and drug-related merchandise at retail prices. In 1954, Herbert and Gloria opened the first Dart Drug store, in the Adams Morgan section of the city. With Dart Drug, Herbert Haft started a practice that eventually had a tremendous impact on merchandising—selling almost every product in his store below suggested retail prices.

Discount pricing was unheard of in Washington at that time and was illegal for items covered by "fair trade" laws, which required retailers to use the manufacturers' suggested prices. The low prices made Dart Drug popular with customers, but Haft faced over a hundred lawsuits from major pharmaceutical and supply companies trying to stop the practice.

Haft lost several rounds in the costly legal battle but took his case all the way to the Supreme Court, where the Justice Department sided with him. In 1960, the Court ruled against fixing wholesale prices, a decision critical to the growth of the discounting business.

The company was incorporated that year and grew as the Washington suburbs mushroomed during the decade. As a large discounter, the Dart Drug chain forced other drugstores in the area to lower prices in order to compete.

### The 1970s: Super Drugstores, Books, and Auto Parts

In the 1970s, Dart Drug took another marked departure from traditional drugstore operations, instituting "super" drugstores. The company began building outlets of up to 20,000 square feet, four times the size of corner drug stores. Haft filled the huge space with anything he could make a deal on. Soon his Super Darts were selling hardware, lumber, lawn chairs, coolers, and beer in addition to the usual health and beauty aids and drugs. Prescriptions, which accounted for 30 percent of sales in conventional drugstores, were only 15 percent of sales at Super Dart.

In 1977, elder son Robert joined his father's company and started Crown Books Corporation. The idea behind Crown Books was the subject of Robert's Harvard Business School thesis: books could be sold in discount format.

With the slogan, "You'll never have to pay full-price again," Robert discounted hardcover best-sellers 35 percent and paperback best-sellers 25 percent. The stores also offered remaindered books, paperbacks, magazines, and tapes at ten to 40 percent below publishers' suggested retail prices. Robert's approach initially alienated many publishers and competitors but proved to be only the first of several chains of discount booksellers. Robert, chairman and president of Crown Books Corporation, became president of Dart Group. Herbert remained as CEO of Dart Group, which owned 51 percent of the new company.

Robert followed his father's marketing strategies. Crown Books stores were clustered in certain metropolitan areas, which allowed the company to concentrate advertising and distribution costs. They were usually in strip shopping centers or downtown storefronts, saving rental costs over the mall locations favored by competitors. The layouts were identical— science fiction, travel, and cook books, for instance, were found in the same locations at each store. Store managers made local marketing decisions, concentrating on stocking books that moved. According to a 1987 *Fortune* article, Crown Books returned only 10 percent of its stock to publishers. Its competitors normally returned 30 to 60 percent.

In 1979, Herbert and Robert started Trak Auto Corporation, selling auto parts and accessories such as mufflers, batteries, pressure gauges, and seat cushions for 35 to 51 percent below suggested retail prices. The idea for Trak grew out of Robert's buying trips for Dart Drugs. "We would go to the Orient and buy tremendous amounts of automotive supplies for Dart Drug," Robert Haft told *Fortune*. Interested in the auto parts market because of the large volume, the Hafts discovered that mom-and-pop operations sold 80 percent of those types of products. National retailers such as Sears and Pep Boys— Manny, Moe & Jack, controlled most of the rest of the market, and the Hafts saw the opportunity for a national chain of discount stores for the car fanatic. Robert became president of Trak, and Herbert was chairman and CEO. Dart Group owned 68 percent of Trak.

The development of Trak followed the successful Haft formula. Stores were concentrated in the suburbs around major cities and located in strip shopping malls. These shopping centers often housed Crown Books and/or Dart Drug stores as well. Many of these malls in the Washington, D.C., area were owned by the Haft family's Combined Properties, Inc.

### The 1980s: Dart Drug Sale, Takeover Bids

In 1981, the Hafts began cutting costs at Dart Drug. One of their tactics was to delay paying bills so long that suppliers would offer a discount just to get paid. They also reduced the types of merchandise offered at the stores by 33 percent, downsized some stores, cut deliveries from the warehouse to once a week, and stopped giving cash refunds.

In 1984, after reducing costs by about $12 million a year, Dart Group sold the Dart Drug chain for $160 million to the stores' operating managers. That year, Dart Drugs, with 70 stores and assets of about $100 million, had sales of $283 million, and an after-tax return of 5.4 percent—twice the industry average. However, those profits had come about because of

cost-cutting. The stores were in such bad shape, the new owners took out advertisements in the *Washington Post* announcing that Dart Drugs is "no longer owned by the Haft family." Dart Group later paid $2.7 million to settle a Labor Department case alleging that the Hafts had failed to monitor the chain's pension fund, used as collateral in the sale.

The timing of the sale appeared good for Dart Group, as many major drugstore chains were soon reporting lower earnings. Major supermarkets had begun operating in-house pharmacies and they and mass retailers were stocking drugstore items. The Dart Drug chain, burdened by debt after the buy out, was later sold. It operated briefly as Fantle's Drug Stores, and went out of business in 1990.

With the profits from the sale of Dart Drug, plus $250 million raised later by selling bonds, the Hafts and Dart Group had the money to mount numerous takeover bids. In 1985 alone, they made bids for three companies. In its attempt to take over May Department Stores, Dart Group earned $1.4 million from selling back the more than $15 million worth of stock it had purchased. In its bid for Jack Eckerd Corp. of Florida, the second largest drugstore chain in the country, Dart Group earned $9 million by reselling a five percent stake it had purchased. Dart Group also bid $5.9 billion for Beatrice Cos. In 1986, the Hafts went after Stop & Shop and Safeway. In the Safeway attempt, Dart Group made a $97 million profit on its shares. The following year the company made a hostile takeover bid for Supermarkets General and gained $40 million when it sold its stock in the chain. To handle its investments, the company set up a new subsidiary, Dart Group Financial.

The takeover bids made the Hafts national business celebrities. While many retail specialists and Wall Street executives saw them as seeking quick windfall profits, they and their supporters pointed to their success with Dart Drug, Crown Books, and Trak Auto. No matter what the Hafts' objective was, the financial benefits of this strategy to Dart Group were obvious. The price of its stock went from $10.75 a share in 1982 to $152 in 1987.

The impact on the target companies was less positive. Safeway, with a $4.2 billion debt, had to sell off overseas divisions and close or sell 251 stores in the United States. After a $1.3 billion leveraged buy out, Stop & Shop had to sell 70 stores and cut 450 jobs, and in 1996 was sold to a Dutch company.

In 1983, Crown Books went public. In its six years of existence, it had grown into a chain with a market value of over $210 million. During the decade, however, the discount bookselling market was becoming more crowded. In 1985, Crown Books had an earnings high of 5.7 percent after taxes. The following year, Crown earned about $5.5 million on sales of $154, or about 3.6 percent after taxes, and was ranked fourth behind Waldenbooks Co., B. Dalton Bookseller, and Barnes & Noble. Trak Auto was having an even bumpier time. In 1986, it earned just $1.3 million on sales of $184 million.

### The Early 1990s: Beverages, Food, and a Family Feud

In March 1990, the company reached an agreement with the Securities and Exchange Commission (SEC), which had been investigating Dart Group since at least 1988, charging the company with operating more like an investment company than a corporation. Dart Group consented to the charges but did not admit or deny guilt. Under the settlement, the company agreed to open its books to more stringent SEC review for three years and not to violate investment company rules.

Dart Group continued to grow, expanding into the discount grocery business with Shoppers Food Warehouse Corporation, of which it owned 51 percent of the stock. The company also began applying the ''superstore'' concept to Crown Books and Trak Auto. By the end of 1992, Crown Books operated 250 stores. Generally, the stores were between 2,000 to 3,000 square feet, but 19 were in the new Super Crown format, ranging in size from 6,500 to 35,000 square feet.

The first Super Trak opened in 1992, with about three times the staff of a regular Trak store and twice the floor space. In October 1992, Herbert Haft kicked off the newest Dart Group concept, Total Beverage. The 25,000 square foot store in Chantilly, Virginia, was stocked with 4,000 wines, 500 beers, and more than 600 types of soda, juices, and water, all at discount prices.

The expansions resulted in increased sales, but company profits had been dropping for three years. In addition, many Wall Street analysts and investors thought the company's shares, which had hovered around $80 per share, could be worth as much as $150 or $200. ''The problem is that investors have had no idea what Herbert Haft was up to. It's an uncertainty that makes it hard for people to get excited about Dart,'' Robert Robotti of the New York brokerage firm Robotti & Eng told Kara Swisher of *The Washington Post.*

According to Swisher in her 1993 series on the Haft family, Robert Haft gradually moved away from his father's confrontational and secretive style and began to be more open and accessible to the local business community, Wall Street, and the press. As an example, he included more complete financial information in annual reports and other corporate statements. Robert also believed that Dart Group should acquire more retail chains and was working on deals to buy the Dollar Tree general merchandise stores and the Books A Million book chain. Herbert wanted to concentrate on real estate.

In March 1993, Robert asked Herbert to let him take over the leadership of the company. Although Robert had seemed destined to succeed his father, Herbert appeared to see the move as a grab for power. Herbert's first response was to use his 57 percent of Dart Group's voting stock to oust Gloria, Robert, and three other directors from the boards of Dart Group, Crown Books and Trak Auto. Then he fired Robert from the presidency of the Dart Group, the chairmanship of Crown Books, and other executive positions. He named son Ronald to the boards, made him president of Dart Group, and gave him stock options.

The family fight did not help the company or its subsidiaries. After posting profits since its founding, Crown Books reported a $200,000 loss for 1993, despite a 15 percent revenue rise. At Trak Auto, earnings fell 98 percent, to $81,000 for the year. The Dart Group explained that the losses were partly due to opening costs of superstores, but skeptics in Washington and on Wall Street thought Herbert was choosing to take the hits as a

strategy in his divorce suit with Gloria. The court intended to split property 50/50, and, according to a May 16, 1994 *Business Week* article, some people thought Herbert could buy Gloria out more cheaply by driving down the value of family holdings. In October, *Business Week* also reported that the stock options granted by Herbert to Ronald were also seen as a way for Herbert to make his assets less attractive in the divorce.

In May 1994, one of the other shareholders of Shoppers Food Warehouse exercised its right to reacquire one share of Shoppers Food Warehouse stock from Dart Group. This reduced Dart Group's ownership to exactly 50 percent.

That same month, Herbert settled with Gloria and Robert for $80 million and an agreement that they would leave Dart Group. By September, Herbert was at odds with younger son Ronald, his last family ally. Ronald accused his father of raiding company resources to pay the family settlement. Herbert said Ronald was trying to gain control of the company. An outside mediator was called in, and Ronald remained president of Dart Group. Meanwhile, Robert Haft sued Dart Group and Crown Books for breach of contract. After winning a jury award of $34 million, he promised never to be involved again with the family's real estate and retailing businesses.

In September, the board of Dart Group established an Executive Committee, made up of outside directors, to manage the company's affairs that related to the dispute between Herbert and Ronald. The boards of Crown Books, Trak Auto, and Total Beverage each established its own Executive Committee, made up of the same outside directors, with parallel authority.

For 1994, the company reported revenues of $967.4 million, down from $1.376 billion the year before. Part of the difference reflected the exclusion of Shoppers Food Warehouse sales as of May 1994, following the shift in ownership. Also contributing to the lower number were a $6.2 million charge related to restructuring and charges to Crown Books reserves related to the $34 million awarded to Robert Haft.

Dart Group's annual report indicated that results for 1994 ranged from dramatic improvements at Trak Auto to modest increases at Crown Books. Both Crown Books and Trak Auto continued to close or convert smaller stores, concentrating on opening larger superstores. During 1994, Trak Auto initiated the Super Trak Warehouse format, with approximately 40,000 square feet offering over 165,000 auto parts, and Crown Books increased its superstore format to 15,000 square feet.

### 1995: Board Control

During 1995, both Crown Books and Trak Auto continued their transition to larger stores. In October, the dispute between Herbert and Ronald was settled and Ronald received $37.9 million for his Dart holdings. He agreed to resign his presidency and other executive positions and to sell all his stock back to the company, with a trustee to be given voting rights to the stock.

In December, a Delaware judge gave the board of directors the power to manage and control day-to-day operations of Dart Group and its holdings without interference from the Hafts, until litigation involving the company and the family was resolved. Robert Marmon, senior vice-president and chief financial officer of the company told the *Washington Post,* "Now, however long it takes to settle the Haft-related litigation, it is clear that the executive committee is running the company." Later that month, Richard B. Stone, a former ambassador to Denmark and former chief operating officer of Washington-based Capital Bank N.A., was named voting trustee for Dart Group, to control 67.9 percent of the company's voting stock.

The board's control and Stone's appointment brought stability and direction to the management of Dart Group and its subsidiaries while the litigation among the Hafts continued. For example, in January 1996, Trak Auto moved into a new territory, Pittsburgh, with the acquisition of 14 auto parts stores which will be converted to Super Trak stores or Super Trak Warehouses. The shift in both chains to larger superstores should continue to pay off. Comparable sales for the newer formats increased during 1995.

### *Principal Subsidiaries*

Crown Books Corporation (51%); Trak Auto Corporation (68%); Total Beverage Corporation; Cabot-Morgan Real Estate Co.; Dart Group Financial Corporation; Dart/SFW Corporation.

### *Further Reading*

"Crown Books Reported Sales Decreased," *PRNewswire,* February 12, 1996.

"Dart Group Announces Settlement with Ronald Haft," Dart Group Press Release, October 6, 1995.

"Dart Group Corporation Announced Sales for Twelve Months," *PRNewswire,* February 12, 1996.

"Dart Group Corporation Announces Appointment of Voting Trustee," Dart Group Press Release, December 29, 1995.

DeWitt, Karen, "In Feud over Retail Empire, Family Splits in Public View," *New York Times,* August 29, 1993.

Lewyn, Mark, "Another Hair-Raiser at the Hafts," *Business Week,* May 16, 1994.

———, "All in the Haft Family," *Business Week,* September 12, 1994.

Meyers, Janet, "Hafts Don't Want to Be Have-Nots," *Advertising Age,* December 16, 1985.

Pressler, Margaret Webb, "Board Get Control Over Dart," *The Washington Post,* December 8, 1995.

———, "Dart Names Ex-Diplomat to Be Voting Trustee under Settlement," *The Washington Post,* December 30, 1995.

Robichaux, Mark, "Dart and Ronald Haft Reach Pact Seeking End to Bitter Legal Feud," *Wall Street Journal,* October 9, 1995.

Salwen, Kevin G., "Dart Group Violated Laws, SEC Charges," *The Wall Street Journal,* March 1, 1990.

Saporito, Bill, "The Most Feared Family in Retailing," *Fortune,* June 22, 1987.

Swisher, Kara, "The Hafts: A Retailing Family Feuds," two-part series, *The Washington Post,* July 25 and July 26, 1993.

———, "Haft Names Son Ronald to Boards," *The Washington Post,* July 30, 1993.

"Trak Auto Corporation Announced 14-Week and 53-Week Sales," *PRNewswire,* February 9, 1996.

Williams, Elisa, "Herbie Haft: D.C.'s Discount Man," *The Washington Times,* November 15, 1992.

———, "Offering Good Cheer for Cheap," *The Washington Times,* November 15, 1992.

—Ellen D. Wernick

# Deb Shops, Inc.

9401 Blue Grass Road
Philadelphia, Pennsylvania 19114
U.S.A.
(215) 676-6000
Fax: (215) 969-2830

*Public Company*
*Incorporated:* 1932
*Employees:* 2,600
*Sales:* $178.4 million (1995)
*Stock Exchanges:* NASDAQ
*SICs:* 5621 Women's Clothing Stores; 5632 Women's Accessory & Specialty Stores; 5611 Men's and Boy's Clothing Stores; 5942 Book Stores

Deb Shops, Inc. is a diversified company operating three chains of retail stores, with sales of $178.4 million in 1995. The largest chain, DEB, serves primarily junior-sized women between the ages of 13 and 40, offering coordinated sportswear, dresses, coats, shoes, lingerie, and accessories. As part of the company's 1996 reorganization, it added plus sizes to DEB's merchandise selection. At the beginning of 1996, the chain operated in 38 states, with most stores in the East and Midwest, and consisted of 292 DEB stores, one JOY store, and five CSO (Chain Store Outlet) stores.

The company also has two wholly owned subsidiaries. The Tops 'N Bottoms chain carries moderately priced apparel for both young men and women, much of it unisex. In January 1996, there were 10 Tops 'N Bottoms stores in four states. Atlantic Book Shops sells used books, publishers' overstocks, and hard-to-find titles at steep discounts. The chain, which Deb Shops purchased in 1995, consists of three book warehouses in Pennsylvania, New Jersey, and Delaware and 11 retail stores in resort areas in Delaware and New Jersey. Members of the company's founding families control about 75 percent of Deb Shops stock.

### Early History

In 1932, Philip Rounick and Aaron Weiner opened their first store in Philadelphia, Pennsylvania. JOY Hosiery offered cus-

tomers a wide variety of hosiery and foundations at reasonable prices. In 1939, nylon stockings came on the market and JOY Hosiery added them to its stock.

The 1940s saw the regulation of nylon use, as it was required for parachutes and other equipment for World War II. The government also regulated how much fabric could be used in clothing and banned the use of zippers and other metal fasteners. Despite nylon's limited availability, JOY Hosiery was able to obtain enough product to continue to stay in operation.

After the war and into the 1950s, JOY grew steadily, opening new stores in various Philadelphia neighborhoods. As restrictions were lifted on clothing manufacturing, a much wider selection became available. JOY reduced its offerings of lingerie and began selling moderately priced sportswear. The merchandise mix rapidly became 50/50, and remained so through the 1950s.

### 1960s and 70s: A New Focus

Marvin Rounick, Philip's son, joined the company in 1961. In 1965 Warren Weiner, Aaron's son, came on board. During the 1960s the suburbs around Philadelphia grew rapidly as families moved out of the core city. To serve their shopping needs, developers built malls and shopping centers. JOY tested those waters by opening suburban stores in shopping malls; their new concept provided a bigger store and a larger selection of merchandise. The 60s also saw the introduction of pantyhose, which eliminated the need for garter belts. With the growth of the women's movement, many young women stopped wearing girdles or bras. As a result, hose and lingerie became a smaller part of JOY's merchandise mix. It was also during this period that young people became a larger part of the consumer base, and the unisex look began to develop.

One thing that occurred during this time greatly influenced the company's financial strategy. "We had some financial problems," President and CEO Marvin Rounick recalled in a 1986 article in *Chain Store Age Executive*. "And the banker who handled us retired and a new banker came in to replace him. We went to him for money and he told us we weren't a good credit risk." When the company nearly folded after their bank dropped them, Rounick vowed to keep the company debt free. That policy never changed.

## Company Perspectives:

*Our basic merchandising philosophy is to provide our customers with the latest, updated, fashionable merchandise at the most competitive prices possible.*

In the early 1970s the younger Rounick and Weiner took a more active role in the company's management and made three decisions that changed the company completely. First, they closed most of the original neighborhood stores and quickly opened larger units in shopping malls. Second, they concentrated on sportswear and dresses for the junior customer and eliminated merchandise in other sizes. Finally, to reflect the company's new emphasis, they changed the name of their stores to DEB. Merchandise ranged from peasant tops and skirts in the early 70s to the ''Annie Hall'' look of men's suits and ties. By 1975, the company had sales of $9.5 million and earnings of $400,000. In 1979, Marvin Rounick was named president and chief executive officer.

### The 1980s

Deb Shops began the 1980s with 59 stores. Within two years, it had 121 stores, sales were more than $70 million, and earnings were up to $5.5 million. Warren Weiner rejoined the company in 1982, having left in 1975, and was named executive vice president and treasurer. The following year the company went public, raising nearly $27 million. According to a 1983 *Forbes* article, the funds went for spending money for Rounick, his brother Jack, and Weiner, the major shareholders in the company. ''We were wealthy before,'' Rounick said in the article. ''It's just that now we can spend it.'' Deb Shops had no debt and expansion continued to be paid for from its working capital.

The company's target was primarily young women, 13 to 21 years old, with a small number of customers in their 20s and 30s. Rounick was successful because of his pricing strategy and tight inventory. He sold his dresses and other apparel at low-to-mid prices, below those of more upscale, designer clothing, and cut the prices immediately if an item was not selling after two weeks. If the sale prices didn't move the item, he shipped it to one of the company's CSO (Chain Store Outlet) stores where it was sold at a steep discount. The fast movement of the stock meant customers could expect up-to-date, trendy merchandise. That freshness, combined with inexpensive prices, attracted young shoppers.

Despite the company's success, Rounick realized he had to make some adjustments to his marketing strategy in response to changing demographics: predictions forecast that by 1990, there would be 14 to 15 percent fewer women aged 14 to 24. Unlike many of its competitors, Deb did not abandon its specialization in junior customers looking for moderately priced clothes. Rounick's answer was to market junior as a size, not an age group. Under this strategy, the company would follow customers as they grew up, serving both teens and their mothers.

Accordingly, in 1983 the company started selling basic as well as trendy junior clothing.

In addition to offering a wider variety of styles, the company made some decorating changes to attract older shoppers: its green, white, and purple color combination became purple, raspberry, and white; and lower pile purple carpeting replaced the stores' purple shag. Gone, too, were the enclosed storefronts. Instead windows were installed to show the merchandise and draw customers in.

Another part of Rounick's marketing strategy was to encourage add-on shopping by selecting merchandise that was coordinated with something else in the store. DEB displayed its merchandise in coordinated, layered groupings, complete with accessories. As Willard Brown, an analyst with First Albany, told *Chain Store Age Executive* in a 1986 article, ''Every top is coordinated with every pair of pants; and if you buy the top and pants, then they have a handbag that goes with them, too. So every time Rounick sells one piece of merchandise, he's put himself into the position to sell another piece.''

The marketing changes worked. Within two years, customers at DEB stores, while still concentrated in a 13 to 25 age group, ranged in age up to 40, and sales in 1985 increased to $147.1 million.

The company was opening between 30 and 40 new stores a year, with most in regional shopping centers in major metropolitan areas. As these malls increased their rents, however, Deb began looking to mid-size markets and secondary markets adjacent to a major town. The company also started opening stores in less expensive strip shopping centers. ''They [strip center stores] are not doing the same business as the malls,'' Rounick explained in the *Chain Store Age Executive* article, ''but because of the reduced costs we found we can make money in the first year.'' By 1989 the company had stores in 67 strip centers. Stores ranged in size from 5,000 to 10,000 square feet, with the average store occupying 6,000 square feet.

The movement into strip centers was only one cost cutting effort the company initiated during the last part of the 1980s. The women's clothing business in general softened, and sales dropped. The reason appeared to be customer dissatisfaction with what the designers offered them. In 1987, Deb's profit margin dropped as customers waited for markdowns and sales before buying.

Rounick's response was to improve inventory control in order to cut costs and to sell more clothes at full price. In 1988, Deb expanded its warehouse space to 280,000 square feet and installed a computer-controlled sorting and distribution system. The new distribution system and the company's point of sale merchandise data system helped managers analyze and respond to what customers were buying. Inventories arrived at the stores twice a week and store displays were changed each week. While the company continued to mark down slow-moving merchandise, there was less of it. As a result of cost-cutting, although sales for 1988 were down 2 percent to $194 million, earnings increased 15 percent to $13.7 million. During 1988, Deb expanded beyond the Midwest, opening stores in Washington,

Oregon, and California, and ended the year with 316 stores in operation.

In 1989, the company continued to expand, using its own capital to open 31 new stores. It also began increasing its private-label business in order to improve its profit margins. Its profitability and $71 million in equity was very attractive. According to an August 14, 1989 article in *Barron's,* there were rumors that Milton Petrie, who owned the competing Petrie Stores, Inc. and more than 15 percent of Deb stock, might attempt a hostile takeover of Deb. Nothing came of it. For the year, the company set record net sales of $202 million and reached its peak earnings of $17.6 million.

### The 1990s and Beyond

During the early part of the decade, Deb continued to expand, opening DEB stores in Colorado, Idaho, New Mexico, Oklahoma, and Texas. The company also acquired Tops N' Bottoms, a New York chain selling name-brand clothing for young men and women at moderate prices. In addition to the smaller (2,300 to 3,400 square feet) stand-alone stores in the chain, the company opened Tops N' Bottom departments in several DEB stores. The number of stores operated by the company peaked in fiscal year 1992, with 373 open as of January 31, 1993. That year also saw the company's highest sales, $229.5 million. But earnings fell by 18 percent.

In 1993, Deb introduced its private label credit card, which also served as a mechanism to contact customers by direct mail. The company opened 11 new stores, but saw sales decline by four percent. Sales continued to decline, even with reduced costs as underperforming stores were closed. In 1994 the company opened eight new stores and had a net loss for the first time. In April that year, management spent $16.8 million in cash to buy back the block of stock owned by Petrie Stores Corporation. With that acquisition, insiders, including Martin and Jack Rounick and Warren Weiner, owned 75 percent of the company stock.

Sales continued to drop in 1995 and the company opened only one new store while closing 33 DEB units and one Tops N' Bottoms store. Rounick introduced shoes into 200 DEB stores to generate new business and stimulate sales. That move added approximately $4.6 million to sales for the year, but continued customer resistance to offerings in women's clothing resulted in total sales of only $176.7 million and an earnings loss of $4.2 million.

On October 20, 1995, the company bought Atlantic Book Stores for $4.47 million. ''The apparel industry has seen a downturn in the last three to five years, and one of the strategies to stem the tide of our decline is to diversify,'' Deb's chief financial officer Lewis Lyon told *The Philadelphia Inquirer.*

Martin Simon, who was 72 when he sold his company to Deb, began his book business by selling used books to department stores. At the time of the sale, the Atlantic Books chain consisted of 14 stores. Three were full-service warehouse stores, between 12,000 and 26,000 square feet large. These specialized in remainder books at greatly discounted prices while also offering bestsellers, new titles, and magazines. The Atlantic Book Warehouse stores were located in Montgomeryville, Pennsylvania; Cherry Hill, New Jersey; and Dover, Delaware. The other 11 stores were located in resort towns along the coasts of New Jersey and Delaware. These units were much smaller, between 1,000 and 2,000 square feet, and sold primarily remainder books and some new titles.

Deb indicated it planned to expand the chain by adding warehouse stores in high traffic areas. Because of the warehouse concept, the company did not anticipate any direct competition with other discount chains such as Waldenbooks, Barnes & Noble, and Borders.

In its apparel business, Deb announced it was shifting from its all-junior concentration. By April 1996, the company expected to introduce plus sizes into one-third of their stores. Up to 19 DEB stores were to be converted to plus size stores called DEB PLUS and about half of the Tops N' Bottoms departments in DEB stores would become plus size departments.

Deb Shops' diversification efforts appeared to build on the company's responsiveness to demographic changes and its retail operations and distribution expertise. The fact that the company was debt-free and had over $51 million in cash at the beginning of 1996 gave it some measure of flexibility and staying power as it made its changes.

### Principal Subsidiaries

Atlantic Book Shops, Inc.; Tops 'N Bottoms, Inc.

### Further Reading

Angrist, Stanley W. ''So Far, So Good,'' *Forbes,* October 24, 1983, p. 144.

Brammer, Rhonda, ''Sizing Up Small Caps: Down, But Not Out,'' *Barron's,* January 30, 1995, p. 19.

''Bubble Gum By Night, Apple Pie By Day,'' *Chain Store Age Executive,* May 1986, pp. 35–39.

Byrd, Jerry W., ''Philadelphia's Deb Shops to Buy Atlantic Book Shops, Inc.,'' *The Philadelphia Inquirer,* October 23, 1995.

Slovak, Julianne, ''Companies to Watch,'' *Fortune,* January 1, 1990, p. 89.

Wyatt, Edward A., ''Looking Good: Deb Shop Fashions a Neat Gain in Earnings,'' *Barron's,* August 14, 1989, pp. 15, 17.

—Ellen D. Wernick

# Dentsu Inc.

**11-1, Tsukiji**
**Chou-ku, Tokyo 104**
**Japan**
**(03) 5551-5111**
**Fax: (03) 5551-2013**

*Private Company*
*Incorporated:* 1901
*Employees:* 5,910
*Gross Billings:* $13.74 billion (1995)
*SICs:* 7311 Advertising Agencies; 4899 Communication
    Services, Not Elsewhere Classified

Dentsu Inc. is the largest advertising company in the world, with the highest gross billings among all advertising firms worldwide for more than 20 years. Dentsu has 32 offices in Japan and affiliates or subsidiaries in 35 countries. It is the leading advertising firm in Asia, with branches or affiliates in 11 countries including China, India, Korea, Thailand and Malaysia. Dentsu also operates affiliates in Australia and New Zealand, in nine countries in the Middle East, and in Europe. Dentsu also maintains a presence in the United States through a joint venture with Young & Rubicam that comprises seven subsidiaries in New York, Atlanta, Los Angeles and New Jersey. Dentsu works with a "total communication" strategy that extends beyond the traditional parameters of the advertising business. As well as designing print and broadcast media advertising, the company does market research, including new product planning and corporate image design; it also handles publicity campaigns for such prominent events as sports contests and science expos, for which Dentsu may design everything from the opening ceremonies to personnel uniform design. Dentsu owns stock in some of Japan's largest newspapers and television networks, and the company itself is partially owned (48 percent of available shares) by Japan's two leading news services, Kyodo and Jiji.

## Early History

Dentsu was founded in 1901 by Hoshiro Mitsunaga, a journalist from Osaka. Mitsunaga actually founded two closely related companies: his Telegraphic Service Company was an international news wire service, and his Japan Advertising Ltd. brokered advertising space. Mitsunaga often took payment for his wire service in the form of ad space in newspapers, then resold the ad space to his clients. The two companies merged in 1907, under the name Japan Telegraphic Communication Company (Nihon Denpo-Tsushin Sha). This compound name became shortened to Dentsu. Dentsu secured monopoly rights to distribute the United Press wire service in Japan, giving the company unique leverage over the newspapers it serviced. Dentsu was able to use its influence to get favorable rates for advertising space, and as early as 1908, the company was the acknowledged leader in Japan's communications industry. Dentsu began collecting and publishing statistics on advertising volume in 1909, the first to do so in Japan, and by 1912, the company had headquarters in Tokyo's fashionable Ginza district.

Dentsu was the largest broker of advertising space in Japan almost from its inception. However, the agency was practically dismantled in the prewar years. In 1936, the Japanese government formed its own news service, Domei, and Dentsu had to surrender its wire service. Then in 1943, the government consolidated all existing advertising agencies into 12 entities. Dentsu controlled four of the 12 agencies, but because of the war, business dwindled. Founder Mitsunaga died in 1945. There were two intervening presidents, and then the company began to rebuild under the leadership of the remarkable Hideo Yoshida. Yoshida had worked for Dentsu through the war, and he took the presidency in 1947.

## Postwar Ascendence

Yoshida was known as "the big demon," and Dentsu's ad men were "little demons" for their frantic hard work. Yoshida expected Dentsu's executives to report to work one hour earlier than the rest of the staff, and required daily written reports from department heads for his personal perusal. The staff yearly tested its strength with an overnight trip to climb Mount Fuji, but Yoshida showed his management skill as much in who he hired as in what he had them do. Immediately after the war, Dentsu hired dozens of former government and military officials. Dentsu also made it a practice to recruit sons of officials and prominent businessmen, so that the company soon had a wealth of personal contacts with its corporate and government clients. Beyond this, Yoshida's most prescient step was to invest in Japanese radio and television.

Dentsu is credited with founding commercial radio in Japan. The agency submitted the first application for a commercial radio station in the country just months after the war ended, and Yoshida spoke before the Japanese Diet in 1950 on the importance of commercial broadcasting. The company invested in what later became Tokyo Broadcasting System, one of five major commercial radio networks in Japan. Dentsu invested heavily in television as well. Dentsu loaned start-up funds to local stations, found them crucial advertising sponsors, and even provided personnel to manage them. Dentsu's patronage basically made television possible in the postwar years. As a result, as radio and television grew into a modern industry, Dentsu grew too. Because of the company's complex personal and financial ties, Dentsu was given the lion's share of advertising time. Dentsu was able to set aside huge blocks of prime time television for itself—as much as 60 percent of lucrative prime time advertising slots. Thus the company was virtually guaranteed clients. Companies had to come to Dentsu if they wanted the best advertising exposure. Dentsu also had a similar "block buying" arrangement with major newspapers, buying from 30 percent to 50 percent of space in national dailies. Dentsu was an investor in the major daily *Mainichi Shimbun,* as well as in a dozen other newspapers. Overall, its position with the media was unparalleled. No other agency had anything like the access that Dentsu had to all Japan's major advertising venues. By 1957, there were close to 800 advertising agencies in Japan, and Dentsu's billings alone made up more than a quarter of the industry total.

The Japanese economy grew in double digits in the 1960s and 1970s, carrying Dentsu with it. By 1968, Dentsu's billings were just behind the leading American firms J. Walter Thompson, Young & Rubicam and Interpublic. The company had 5,000 accounts, including the biggest Japanese firms and the Japanese business of some American companies. Dentsu had made it standard practice to accept the accounts of competitive companies, for example doing advertising for both carmakers Honda and Nissan, and for rival electronics firms Matsushita and Toshiba. Dentsu handled competing accounts in separate buildings, or, if that was not possible, at least on separate floors. This arrangement seemed to work well, and it was one more way that Dentsu dominated Japanese advertising. With its enormous media clout, and its willingness to serve everyone, Dentsu surpassed every other agency in the country by a wide margin.

In 1974, Dentsu overtook J. Walter Thompson and became the largest advertising agency in the world.

At least 95 percent of Dentsu's billings came from within Japan. Dentsu had opened offices in New York, Bangkok, Chicago, Los Angeles, Paris, Melbourne, Taiwan, Singapore and Hong Kong in the 1960s, but only three of these actually offered advertising services. The company was cautious about expanding abroad, even though by the late 1970s this was clearly the agency's next step. Differences between Japanese and American or European advertising style made it difficult for Dentsu to go abroad, and the company was built on Japanese-style personnel management, which included at that time lifetime guarantees of employment in exchange for corporate loyalty. In an interview with *Advertising Age* in 1977, Dentsu's then-president Hideharu Tamaru noted that these factors would constitute a difficulty if Dentsu were to acquire a foreign agency. Tamaru suggested that Dentsu would initiate a joint venture with an international agency in order to expand overseas.

### Expansion in the 1980s

However, the international link was slow in coming. Dentsu found new ways to extend its market in Japan, designing huge events like the celebration of America's bicentennial in Japan, an International Ocean Exposition, and completing a government commission for a new museum of telecommunications. Dentsu worked on the design of shopping centers, specializing in aspects like people movement patterns. It worked with the government, compiling information on leisure time, doing public opinion surveys, and working for such government agencies as the National Railways. The domestic market still was not big enough for Dentsu, however, and by the end of the 1970s, advertising spending began to dip in Japan. The proportion of Dentsu's billings from television advertising began to decline, while the company increased its billings from sports and other large promotions. Without the high earnings from television, Dentsu's overall profitability began to sink.

It was clear that Dentsu had to move beyond Japan to tap more lucrative markets. One result of Dentsu's effective lock on domestic advertising was that its competitors had already established international partnerships. Japan's number two agency, Hakuhodo, had been involved in a joint venture with the American firm McCann-Erickson since 1960, and a dozen other Japanese ad agencies had similar partnerships by 1980. In 1981, Dentsu finally made its move and announced a joint venture with Young & Rubicam. The arrangement, called DYR, gave Young & Rubicam entry into Japan and let Dentsu access Young & Rubicam's expertise in the American and European markets. Initial billings were $70 million, but this had grown to $246 million within four years. Dentsu also opened a Shanghai office in 1981. China was not seen as a particularly promising market at that time, but Dentsu saw growth potential. The company worked patiently to make itself known in China. It planned and promoted a huge "popular concert for youth," televised in both China and Japan, with 300 Japanese musicians performing for a crowd of 30,000 young Chinese in Beijing.

Dentsu used its contacts with Young & Rubicam to enter the American and European markets. It established Young & Rubicam-Dentsu offices in New York and Los Angeles in 1983, and in 1984 formed DYR S.A., a joint management company to administer the company's international sales network. Dentsu opened its own subsidiaries in France and Great Britain in the next few years. In spite of this, the company's profits fell in the mid-1980s. Though still leading the world in billings, by 1984, Dentsu's profits had fallen behind that of Young & Rubicam. Despite all its efforts, in 1984 still less than five percent of Dentsu's billing was from export advertising. Japanese companies were spending billions of yen on advertising abroad, but it was mostly placed through foreign agencies. Dentsu got a new president in 1985, Gohei Kogure, and he reaffirmed the agency's commitment to international expansion. He resolved to cut costs at home by reducing staff, and he engineered a new image for Dentsu, with the slogan, in English, ''Communications Excellence Dentsu.''

In 1987, Dentsu and Young & Rubicam retooled their earlier link, teaming up also with Eurocom France, Europe's leading ad agency. The new, three-way partnership was called HDM Worldwide. The new company linked 39 cities in Asia, Europe and the United States. Dentsu hoped to win new clients, and to increase its percentage of overseas billings to 20 percent. Dentsu also opened another subsidiary in the United States in 1987, DCA Advertising, and established offices in Germany and the Netherlands.

While Dentsu looked abroad for new, profitable markets, the company also changed the way it did business in Japan. In 1987, Dentsu premiered the first comparison ad on Japanese television. Advertising in which one product is directly compared to a rival had not been done in Japan, as it was considered in poor taste. A Japanese Fair Trade Commission issued guidelines in 1986 stating that comparative advertising was allowable, and Dentsu was the first to try it out. In a $1 million campaign for All Nippon Airways, Dentsu's ads claimed that All Nippon's seating was more comfortable than that of unnamed ''others.'' Mild by American standards, the ad nevertheless demonstrated that Dentsu was willing to explore new techniques. The agency did well in the late 1980s, riding a boom in consumption in Japan.

### The 1990s

Eurocom left the three-way joint venture HDM in 1990. The venture was renamed Dentsu, Young & Rubicam Partnerships, concentrating on Asia, America, and Australia and New Zealand. To make up for the loss of its European partner, Dentsu invested in another European advertising network, the London-based Collett Dickinson Pearce International Group. Dentsu then began a streak of acquisitions and investment partnerships, buying part or all of nine agencies in Europe between March 1990 and September 1992. Only a week apart in September 1992, Dentsu acquired 100 percent of BLD Europe, a Brussels firm, and a minority stake in another firm called Publi-Graphics. Publi-Graphics was based in Paris but handled advertising primarily in the Middle East, with such large clients as Johnson & Johnson, Seiko, Nintendo, Eastman Kodak, and Nestle.

Two years later, Dentsu's international expansion plans changed direction. Many multinational companies had initially expanded to Asia because of low-cost manufacturing, but by the mid-1990s, the consumer markets in Asian countries were also attracting interest. Dentsu began investing in Asian advertising

agencies and expanding its own offices to Asian cities in order to capitalize on this trend. In 1994, Dentsu formed a joint-venture in China with two advertising firms there. The joint-venture was named Beijing Dentsu, with offices in Beijing and Shanghai. The company began with only one client, a personal products company called Kao Corp., but Beijing Dentsu expected to bill $10 million in its first year, and grow by 15 percent to 20 percent annually. Dentsu also invested in ventures in Singapore and Malaysia.

Besides looking to Asia for new growth, Dentsu turned to new technologies as a source of future income. In 1996 Dentsu launched a new subsidiary in Japan, called Dentsu Tec Inc., with the Tec standing for ''*Technology* for *Exciting* *Communication*.'' This company aimed to develop new promotional opportunities using digital and networking technologies. Dentsu also founded Japan's first firm specializing in Internet advertising. The joint venture with Tokyo's Softbank Corporation was called Cyber Communications Inc., or CCI. CCI planned to buy and resell advertising space on the Internet and to help develop and deploy Internet technology in Japan.

### Principal Subsidiaries

Dentsu Inc. Kansai; Dentsu Inc. Chubu; Dentsu East Japan Inc.; Dentsu West Japan Inc.; Dentsu Inc. Fukuoka; Dentsu Inc. Hokkaido; Dentsu Tohoku Inc.; Ad Dentsu Tokyo Inc.; Dentsu Tec Inc.; Dentsu, Young & Rubicam Inc.; Dentsu USA Inc.; Dentsu Europe Ltd.; Dentsu Holdings B.V. (The Netherlands); Dentsu (Thailand) Ltd.; Taiwan Advertising Co., Ltd.; Kuohua Inc. (Taiwan); Beijing Dentsu Advertising Co., Ltd.; Dentsu Mandate (Malaysia) Sdn. Bhd.; Pt. Inter Admark (Indonesia); DCA Advertising (USA); Nova Promotion Group Inc. (USA); Dentsu Burson-Marsteller Inc. (USA); Travis-Sennett-Sully-Ross Ltd. (England); BLD Europe S.A. (Belgium); CCP Positioning S.R.L. (Italy); Schuster & Partner Gmbh (Germany); NAP-TV Kft. (Hungary); ISL Marketing AG (Switzerland); Dentsu Oceania Pty. Ltd. (Australia); SSB Advertising Pty. Ltd. (Australia).

### Further Reading

Bechtos, Ramona, ''Dentsu Gives Itself a Broader Label: Consultants on Life Styles and Society,'' *Advertising Age,* August 23, 1976, pp. 22–25.

''Big Demon Adman,'' *Fortune,* October 1958, p. 92.

Burton, Jack, '' 'Dark Horse' Will Keep Dentsu on Global Path,'' *Advertising Age,* June 10, 1985, pp. 3, 100.

——, ''Media Clout Is Source of Dentsu Power,'' *Advertising Age,* October 24, 1983, pp. M11, M14.

Chase, Dennis, ''Y&R, Dentsu Eyeing Worldwide Linkup,'' *Advertising Age,* May 25, 1981, pp. 1, 78.

''The Demons of Dentsu,'' *Newsweek,* March 24, 1969, p. 75.

''Diverse Dentsu Nudges Aside JWT for Global No. 1 Status,'' *Advertising Age,* January 21, 1974, pp. 3, 60.

Holden, Ted, and Dunkin, Amy, ''Japan Is Getting Too Small for Dentsu,'' *Business Week,* October 26, 1987, pp. 62–66.

Kilburn, David, ''Comparison Ads Make First Flight in Japan,'' *Advertising Age,* June 8, 1987, p. 61.

——, ''Dentsu Concentrates on Growing in Asia,'' *Advertising Age,* May 23, 1994, p. 54.

——, ''Dentsu Expanding to Mideast, Europe,'' *Advertising Age,* September 7, 1992, p. 4.

——, "Dentsu Looks Inward," *Advertising Age,* April 20, 1987, p. 63.

——, "Dentsu Opening U.S. Promo Shop," *Advertising Age,* July 8, 1991, pp. 3, 34.

——, "How Dentsu's New President Fights Recession," *Advertising Age,* June 21, 1993, pp. 4, 48.

Link, Luther, "Dentsu Critic Calls It 'Public Menace'," *Advertising Age,* January 21, 1974, pp. 69–70.

Matsuda, Mat, "Dentsu Eases through Open Door," *Advertising Age,* December 14, 1981, p. S9.

——, "Dentsu's Tamaru: 'Bridging the 21st Century'," *Advertising Age,* November 9, 1981, pp. 74–78.

Phalon, Richard, "A Japanese Setback," *Forbes,* October 7, 1985, pp. 110–114.

Thompson, John R., "International Growth a Main Priority for No. 1 Dentsu Shop," *Advertising Age,* October 10, 1977, pp. 26–27.

—A. Woodward

# dick clark productions, inc.

**3003 W. Olive Avenue**
**Burbank, California 91505**
**U.S.A.**
**(818) 841-3003**
**Fax: (818) 954-8609**

*Public Company*
*Incorporated:* 1977
*Employees:* 525 (est.)
*Sales:* $46.64 million (1995)
*Stock Exchanges:* NASDAQ
*SICs:* 7812 Motion Picture & Video Production; 7389
  Business Services, Not Elsewhere Classified; 5812
  Eating Places; 5122 Drugs, Proprietaries & Sundries

Inextricably wed to the fame of its founder, dick clark productions, inc. operates as an entertainment company with its business interests organized in three segments: television production, corporate communications, and entertainment-themed restaurants. Established by Dick Clark in 1957, dick clark productions was built on the success of its founder's near four-decade reign as the host of the widely popular "American Bandstand." From the popularity of this television program, Dick Clark, the company's chairman and chief executive officer, assembled a multifaceted corporation that rivaled his storied career as the host of numerous radio and television programs and specials. In 1995, Dick Clark's dick clark productions generated $46.6 million in sales.

Referred to for decades as "America's oldest teenager," Richard W. Clark got his start in the entertainment business during his teenage years, beginning a career that would flourish for more than a half century. The son of a Mount Vernon, New York, commodities broker who would go on to own a cosmetics firm and a radio station, Richard "Dick" Clark landed his first job in the industry at age 17 when he began working at WRUN radio in Utica, New York. By the time Clark enrolled at Syra-

cuse University in 1947, he knew he wanted to make a living in the radio business, deciding early on in his adulthood that working in the entertainment industry was his calling. After he was graduated from Syracuse with a Bachelor of Science degree in business administration, Clark made the jump to television, serving as the news anchorman at television station WKTV. After a short stint there, Clark moved to Philadelphia in 1952 to work for WFIL radio and television.

### "American Bandstand" Created in 1957

The move to Philadelphia providentially placed Clark in the right location at the right time, though it would be another four years before the opportunity arrived that would launch the young Clark toward fame and wealth. When Clark joined WFIL in 1952, a television show at the station called "Bandstand" began airing to a regional audience. Four years later, in 1956, Clark was named host of the program, starting out, as he would later write in his autobiography, when, "I don't think I knew more than one or two tunes on the music list. I listened to the kids and let them tell me what they liked." Clark explained further, "I knew that if I could tune into them and keep myself on the show, I could make a great deal of money."

More than the host of a music show, Clark was already demonstrating a predisposition to the business side of the entertainment industry, a perspective fostered, no doubt, during his years at Syracuse University. Clark did not strike out to become a radio or television star; his aspirations were comparatively modest. Clark was interested in a career, either on-air or behind the scenes, knowing that the latter offered the greatest chance of a stable working life. Nevertheless, he threw himself into his new job as the host of "Bandstand," giving himself the opportunity to use his on-screen fame to assemble a corporate empire, the foundation of which rested firmly on the success of the new show he took over in 1956.

In 1956, however, Clark was neither famous nor was "Bandstand" a television show that could support a corporate empire. This would change quickly. Clark made an enormous leap toward elevating the popularity of his show and the familiarity of his name one year after he became host. In 1957, Clark persuaded the ABC network to broadcast ''Bandstand'' nationally, which ABC did in August 1957, airing the show—which was renamed ''American Bandstand'' to reflect its national audience—five afternoons a week.

So began a national institution, a television show that would propel largely unknown musicians toward stardom and dictate fashion and musical tastes for decades to come. Built around a format that included musical performances by the legendary and the yet-to-be discovered, ''American Bandstand'' proved to be a smashing success, winning the hearts of teenagers throughout the country. For those lucky few who gained admittance as audience members (then took the stage and danced to the week's hottest hits, offering commentary on the music in between their renditions of the ''Twist'', ''The Cha-Lypso,'' and the ''Locomotion,'') ''American Bandstand'' offered the chance to listen and hear the latest entertainment phenoms, an opportunity not lost on television viewers throughout the United States. Within a few short weeks after Clark convinced ABC to carry the program nationwide, ''American Bandstand'' eclipsed the popularity of all its rival television shows, quickly becoming the country's highest-rated daytime show.

After those first few weeks, ''American Bandstand'' went on to achieve unparalleled success, beginning a run that would span 37 years, making the show the longest-running music/variety program in television history. ''American Bandstand'' viewers and audience members witnessed the debut performances of Frankie Avalon, the Everly Brothers, and Chubby Checker during the 1950s, were there to see The Doors, Aretha Franklin, and Little Stevie Wonder during the 1960s, the Carpenters and the Jackson Five during the 1970s, and rising stars Madonna and Prince during the 1980s. In the end, ''American Bandstand'' did indeed represent a more than adequate foundation upon which to build a corporate empire, but Clark did not wait for his later success to spur him toward distinction in the business world. Clark formed his company in 1957, the same year he approached ABC executives about turning ''Bandstand'' into a nationally broadcast program, naming his corporate entity ''Click.''

Before ''American Bandstand'' vaulted itself into television history, Richard W. Clark, the businessman, was orchestrating the assemblage of a business that could compensate for the caprice of stardom. ''The one thing I did know very early in the game,'' Clark later confided to the *Los Angeles Business Journal*, ''was that being a performer does not necessarily carry with it a lot of longevity. That's why I became a producer.'' Despite the fact that the popularity of ''American Bandstand'' was exceeding even the most optimistic expectations, Clark did not limit his activities to hosting a five-day-a-week television program. Instead, he devoted his off-hours to assembling and then acting as disk jockey at sock hops in the Philadelphia area, charging teenagers 75 cents each to dance to the latest music hits, much like his ''day job'' as the host of the increasingly popular ''American Bandstand.''

By the end of the 1950s, as ''American Bandstand'' was capturing the country's attention, Clark, according to his estimates, was netting $50,000 a year from the sock hops alone. To this prodigious sum he would add the money gleaned from his ownership of record companies, music-publishing companies, a record distributor, and a record-pressing plant. In addition to these business activities, Clark and another WFIL employee were entirely responsible for producing ''American Bandstand,'' spending countless hours in the stark offices of WFIL, superintending the creation and organization of the most popular music television program in the United States.

The corporate organization for all of Clark's variegated business interests was dick clark productions, inc., the successor to Click, a company whose corporate title was not capitalized, yet served as a corporate repository of sorts for an entertainment personality whose career spelled success in capital letters. Eventually, dick clark productions would be responsible for more than 7,500 hours of entertainment programming, more than 250 television specials, and more than 20 theatrical and television movies, while its chairman and chief executive officer, Dick Clark, would expand upon the recognition he earned as the never-aging host of ''American Bandstand'' to become a ubiquitous presence on U.S. television and radio. While watching the whimsical cavalcade of fashion pass from year to year from his sentinel position as host of ''American Bandstand,'' Clark took on other assignments with relish, serving as host for ''Dick Clark's New Year's Rockin' Eve,'' the highest-rated New Year special, hosting ''TV's Bloopers and Practical Jokes,'' and hosting an assortment of game shows, most notably the ''$25,000 Pyramid.'' Clark wrote books, emceed beauty pageants, and talked over the airwaves as host of two nationally syndicated radio shows. In an industry where longevity was the exception, Clark built a before-the-scenes career that was unique, becoming the only person to host top-rated series on all three networks and in syndication at the same time.

Remarkably, amid the television and radio appearances that made Clark's youthful face famous, Clark was as active behind the camera and microphone as he was in front of it, living out, in effect, a separate life as Richard W. Clark, chairman and chief executive officer of dick clark productions. Clark, as a businessman, became known for his focus on the bottom line and for his attention to producing a program on time and on budget. Clark was also known for his strict scheduling, belying the easygoing nature that characterized his public persona. It was not uncommon for Clark to schedule a 12-minute meeting, or to arrange meetings to begin at precisely 17 minutes after the hour. "Dick is not the kind of guy who will sit for hours swapping stories over a cup of coffee," a network executive once noted. Instead, Clark pursued his business interests with the same energy he devoted to his entertainment career. For Clark and dick clark productions, the marriage of affable host and focused businessman proved to be a lucrative mix.

### Company Moves to Los Angeles in the 1960s

Dick clark productions moved West in 1964, intent on expanding its entertainment business. The company opened an office on Sunset Boulevard and began producing not only "American Bandstand," but other pop-music shows and several low-budget movies. Clark was clear with his intentions for his company, later framing his corporate desires succinctly to a reporter from the *Los Angeles Business Journal.* "We want to do anything," Clark said, "of a recurring nature, anything that's on regularly, whether it be once a year, once a month, five days a week, or once a week. Anything that's on regularly gives you financial stability, and that's what we're seeking." Once established in Los Angeles, dick clark productions would go on to become a leading independent producer of a wide range of television programming for major television networks, cable networks, syndications, and advertisers, producing award shows, entertainment specials, comedy specials, talk show series, and television movies. As the resume of Dick Clark grew, so did his company, becoming, by itself a fixture within the entertainment industry.

In 1972, dick clark productions entered the field of prime-time television programming, producing the first "American Music Awards" program of many to follow. Six years later, in 1978, the company signed a multi-million dollar development and production agreement with NBC. The contract represented one of the largest ever signed at the time, and gave dick clark productions the mandate to produce movies, specials, and series for television.

### Public Offering in the 1980s

In the wake of this mega-deal, annual revenues and net income for dick clark productions tripled between 1982 and 1986, the last year the company would operate as a privately-owned concern. In 1987, when dick clark productions became a publicly-traded corporation, the company was coming off a year during which it had generated $32.3 million in sales and more than $4 million in profit, sizeable financial totals to be sure, but the company needed greater financial resources to continue the legacy of growth established during the previous 30 years. Hoping to gain "a little more ability to spend money on more people and develop more projects," Clark took his company public in January 1987, offering dick clark productions common stock in an initial public offering that collected roughly $8 million.

Two years after the public offering that ceded 15 percent ownership in dick clark productions, the company formed a booking division, establishing the dick clark agency in Burbank, California, as a full-service concert tour and club booking

enterprise to widen the scope of Clark's entertainment business interests. In 1991, another subsidiary was formed, dick clark corporate productions, which operated as a production services firm for numerous corporate events. Through dick clark corporate productions, the parent organized sales presentations, trade shows, and new product introductions, among other events, for stalwart companies such as Apple Computer, AT&T, BMW, Boeing, Honda, IBM, Intel, and Wendy's.

### 1990s Diversification

The range of dick clark productions' business interests continued to broaden as the 1990s progressed, including the 1992 establishment of a subsidiary named Dick Clark's American Bandstand Grill. For those familiar with the chain of Hard Rock Cafe's dotting the globe, Dick Clark's American Bandstand Grill echoed a familiar refrain, embodying a restaurant concept that strove to wed four decades of "American Bandstand" memorabilia and lore with food to create an entertainment-themed restaurant chain. The first unit opened in 1992 in Overland Park, Kansas, followed by a dance-club version that opened its doors in Reno, Nevada. Two years later, another two units were opened, one in Columbus, Ohio, and another in Indianapolis, with the fifth unit in Cincinnati greeting the expected public in early 1995.

As Dick Clark's American Bandstand Grill developed into a chain, the subsidiary's parent company, dick clark productions, was paving new ground elsewhere. In 1993, the company established a direct television marketing business that touted a propriety line of skin care products sold under the "geviderm" label, then formed CLICK Records in 1994 as a new record label, using the name of the company Dick Clark had originally established in 1957.

CLICK Records was organized in association with Sony Music, enabling dick clark productions to distribute its recordings globally. The addition of this new venture along with the other business interests held by dick clark productions made for a well-rounded and stable company that stood poised during the mid-1990s for growth in the future. As the company prepared for the late 1990s, its stature was reinforced by two television series commitments, one for a syndicated talk show starring television actress Tempestt Bledsoe and another for a 90-minute, weekday talk/variety series for TNN. With these two shows and the bevy of other programs it had produced providing momentum, dick clark productions moved toward the future, its inseparable tie to its founder casting a youthful and energetic light to lead the company forward.

### Principal Subsidiaries

The Dick Clark Film Group, Inc.; Dick Clark Features, Inc.; Dick Clark Presentations, Inc.; Dick Clark Media Archives, Inc.; Dick Clark Company Music, Inc.; Dick Clark Restaurants, Inc.; C&C Joint Venture; Match Productions; Dick Clark Productions, Inc.; The dick clark agency, Inc.; Broadcast Arts Joint Venture; Geviderm, Inc., Metcalf Restaurants, Inc.; Reno Entertainment, Inc.; Dick Clark's American Bandstand Club; Buckeye Entertainment, Inc.; Hossier Entertainment, Inc.

### *Further Reading*

Bannon, Lisa, "Dick Clark Productions to Hit Charts with a 48% Rise in Quarterly Profit," *Wall Street Journal,* May 13, 1996, p. B4H.

Barrier, Michael, "American Handstand," *Nation's Business,* October 1987, p. 89.

Frook, John Evan, "Dick Clark Hopes for a Hit with Restaurant Featuring a Slice of American Bandstand," *Los Angeles Business Journal,* March 12, 1990, p. 28.

Howard, Bob, "Dick Clark Means Business When He Talks Show Business," *Los Angeles Business Journal,* July 27, 1987, p. 1.

Maycumber, S. Gray, "Dick Clark Productions Licenses 20–20 Sports," *Daily News Record,* May 22, 1986, p. 7.

Shepardson, Monty, "dick clark productions inc.," *Los Angeles Business Journal,* November 11, 1991, p. 33.

Waddell, Ray, "Dick Clark Prods. Forms Booking Division," *Amusement Business,* July 1, 1989, p. 6.

—Jeffrey L. Covell

# Dillard Department Stores, Inc.

1600 Cantrell Road
Little Rock, Arkansas 72201
U.S.A.
(501) 376-5200
Fax: (501) 376-5917

*Public Company*
*Incorporated:* 1964
*Employees:* 40,312
*Sales:* $5.92 billion (1995)
*Stock Exchanges:* New York
*SICs:* 5311 Department Stores

Based in Little Rock, Arkansas, and located throughout suburbs and secondary markets in 24 states in the South, Southwest, and Midwest, Dillard Department Stores, Inc., operates 245 stores selling brand-name goods in the middle to upper-middle price ranges. Key product lines include home furnishings and fashionable clothing. Dillard's stores rarely run discount promotions, preferring an everyday pricing strategy based on local competition, aided by a sophisticated computerized inventory and sales system.

### Early 20th Century Beginnings

The company was founded—and in the mid-1990s was still headed—by William Dillard. Born in 1914, Dillard was raised in a merchandising family in tiny Mineral Springs, Arkansas. He worked in his father's hardware store and later studied at the University of Arkansas and the Columbia University School of Business. After earning his master's degree at Columbia and completing a Sears training program, Dillard borrowed $8,000 from his father and in February 1938 opened T.J. Dillard's in Nashville, Arkansas, near his home town.

From the first, business was good. His father's wholesalers extended him credit, and customers reacted positively to his well-known father's name, "T.J." Dillard and his wife, Alexa, stocked the store with name-brand merchandise they had bought at low prices. With heavy advertising, first-year sales reached $42,000.

At the onset of World War II, Dillard volunteered for service in the Navy. He sold his merchandise to another store, but kept his store open to collect on credit accounts. While Dillard was waiting for his naval commission, his father died. Family responsibilities called him home, and when the commission came through, he declined it.

In 1944 Dillard and his wife reopened their store. Despite the war, retail sales hit $300,000 in 1945. Business was so good, in fact, that in 1946, Dillard added an 80-foot-long addition. Considering the following year's $340,000 in sales an absolute maximum, Dillard sought new opportunities elsewhere. He invested $50,000 in the proposed expansion of Wooten's Department Store in Texarkana, a town split down the middle by the Texas-Arkansas border. After commuting between Nashville and Texarkana for six months he decided to settle in Texarkana. In March 1948, Dillard sold T.J. Dillard's and upped his stake in Wooten's to 40 percent, changing its name to Wooten & Dillard Inc.

With Wooten's consent, Dillard decided that, instead of expanding the existing store, Wooten & Dillard should open a new store featuring name brands and revolving credit. Despite strong sales, Wooten & Dillard lost money during its first six months, and Wooten asked Dillard to buy him out. To assemble the needed $100,000 in capital, Dillard collected investors and obtained a loan from the Federal Reconstruction Finance Corporation. By March 1949, he controlled the company. Dillard then began a massive newspaper advertising campaign, developing a relationship with the media that was to become his trademark. Within three months the store was profitable.

### Expansion in 1950s and 1960s

Ready to expand again in 1955, Dillard bought a 7,500-square-foot Magnolia, Arkansas, store from a family friend. Magnolia, a town of 7,000 located 55 miles from Texarkana, proved a lucrative market. The following February Dillard added appliances and furniture to his line of products.

## Company Perspectives:

*At Dillard's, respect for our customers is paramount. Building enduring relationships with customers has, in large measure, accounted for our steady growth and continued financial success. Experience has shown that we can best earn their trust by always emphasizing value.*

His next opportunity came in 1956. Mayer & Schmidt had long been Tyler, Texas's most successful store. A failed attempt at expansion, however, had left it financially vulnerable. In April 1956 Dillard and a group of investors bought it. Dillard completely remodeled the place, expanding into the basement and leasing some departments. When he reopened in September, he advertised heavily in the local papers; the store soon set records for one-day sales.

Dillard's astute financing and smooth turnarounds caught the attention of the region's bankers. In 1959 Fred Eisman, a director of the First National Bank of St. Louis, asked Dillard to buy a failing Tulsa, Oklahoma, department store, Brown-Dunkin. Dillard jumped at the idea. Tulsa was bigger than Tyler, and Brown-Dunkin was bigger than Mayer & Schmidt. With the help of friends, bankers, and other investors, Dillard raised $325,000 and in February 1960 bought the store.

Turning Brown-Dunkin around was difficult. Within 24 hours of the purchase, disgruntled union members began picketing the store, protesting a previous dismissal of maids and elevator operators. A week later Dillard discovered a cigar box filled with $150,000 in unpaid bills. Struggling with the situation, Dillard sold his Texarkana and Magnolia stores to Alden's for $775,000. In three months, the union gave up picketing, and with a loan from the National Bank of Tulsa, Dillard paid off Brown-Dunkin's debts. Finally he launched a newspaper campaign and got the store into the black.

In 1961, as Dillard was consolidating Brown-Dunkin, he formed Dillard Investment Company, Inc. With bank loans, Dillard Investment bought Dillard's credit accounts. As customers paid their bills, the subsidiary repaid the banks. This gave Dillard stores the benefit of credit sales while remaining free of debts.

In 1962 Dillard wanted to return with his family to Arkansas. At the time, there were two leading stores in Little Rock, the Gus Blass Department Store and the Joseph Pfeifer Department Store. Rebuffed in his bid for Blass, Dillard turned to Pfeifer. After extensive negotiations, Pfeifer president Sam Strauss accepted Dillard's bid of more than $3 million.

Dillard was again creative with capital. He collected investors, sold $325,000 worth of stock to Mayer & Schmidt shareholders, and convinced Sperry & Hutchinson, makers of S & H Green Stamps, to invest $1.5 million in exchange for issuing its stamps in his stores. In the fall of 1963, the Mayer & Schmidt store bought the Pfeifer store.

In January 1964, shareholders reincorporated Mayer & Schmidt in Delaware, where laws were more favorable. They changed the name of the company to Dillard Department Stores, Inc., but retained the names of the individual stores until 1974.

In February 1964, Gus Blass Co. allowed Dillard to buy the 192,000-square-foot Little Rock store and a 61,000-square-foot store at Pine Bluff, Arkansas. Since the main Blass store was just two blocks from Pfeifer, Dillard concentrated on remodeling the Pine Bluff store. By year's end, total corporate sales reached $41.2 million.

Two other key events occurred in 1964: the company installed its first computer system and it opened its first mall store. The computers were the start of one of the industry's most advanced tracking systems. The mall store, on the west edge of Little Rock, marked the beginning of a move to the suburbs. Under various names, Dillard opened six more mall stores during the years from 1964 to 1968.

The year 1968 also marked the next turning point in corporate organization. For better administration, Dillard divided his 15 stores into three divisions: Arkansas, Oklahoma, and Texas. He also formed Construction Developers, Inc., a wholly owned subsidiary, to manage the company's real estate holdings.

In 1969 Dillard turned to the stock market. He divided the stock into two classes. Class A would raise money. Class B, the voting stock, would remain under Dillard's control. Listed on the American Stock Exchange, the first offering sold 242,430 shares worth $4 million.

### Acquisitions in the 1970s and 1980s

Dillard opened three mall stores in 1970, and in August 1971, he purchased five Fedway stores from Federated Department Stores. Though not unprofitable, Federated considered the Fedway stores less than successful. After restocking the stores with name brands, Dillard renamed the stores Dillard's in 1972. By the end of that year, Dillard had 22 stores and sales of more than $100 million. Three of that year's four new stores had a regional rather than metropolitan focus. As such, they were placed at the convergence of major highways.

The year 1973 marked the beginning of Dillard's border operations. To attract the inhabitants of nearby Matamoros, Mexico, the recently opened Brownsville store accepted the peso and extended credit to Mexican citizens.

The following year, Dillard bought five Leonard's stores from the Tandy Corporation for stock and cash. Leonard's provided an instant saturation of the Dallas-Fort Worth market. Saturation was an important factor as it allowed the company to spread advertising costs over many stores. By year's end, company-wide sales reached $173.4 million. More mall stores opened through the mid-1970s. Two stores came on line in 1975, including the first in Kansas, and in 1976 Dillard opened a record six stores in Texas, Oklahoma, and Louisiana.

In 1977 William (Bill) Dillard II, William Dillard's son, was named president and chief operating officer. William Dillard remained chief executive officer and chairman of the board, while E. Ray Kemp was named vice-chairman and chief administrative officer. By year's end, there were 38 Dillard's with sales of $269 million.

While sales had doubled from 1973 to 1977, debts had also doubled. By the end of 1977, the company lacked expansion capital. Searching for money, William Dillard met A. C. R. Dreesmann, chief executive officer of Vroom en Dreesmann B.V., the Netherlands' largest retail company. Dreesmann agreed to become Dillard's largest stockholder and to stay out of management. In February 1978, the board approved the sale of $24 million worth of Class A stock to Vroom en Dreesmann's subsidiary, Vendamerica B.V. The sale took place in three annual installments and gave Vendamerica 55 percent of the Class A shares. In 1979 Dillard used Vendamerica's first installment to build four new stores and remodel several older ones.

In 1980 rising interest rates checked Dillard's profits growth. Higher rates meant bigger payments on borrowed money and also hurt Dillard's own credit sales. Nevertheless, in 1980, Dillard added six stores in Texas and Oklahoma.

By contrast, 1981 was a banner year. The booming oil industry fueled sales growth, and management shifted its emphasis toward fast moving soft goods and away from less profitable home furnishings. Sales increased 26 percent to $470.7 million, profits vaulted 91 percent to $16.3 million, and earnings per share surged 85 percent to $5.35.

In 1982 new Dillard's stores opened in Dallas and Memphis. The success of the Memphis store prompted Dillard to lease three former Lowenstein stores and saturate the Memphis market. The three Memphis stores were a part of the record 11 new Dillard's opened in 1982. In the early 1980s, Dillard's grew at twice the department store average. Although the devaluation of the peso had a negative effect on border operations, 1982 profits still rose to $21.95 million.

As profits skyrocketed, so did stock prices. High stock prices reduced the company's financial flexibility, and in 1983 it embarked on a series of stock splits. With new capital available, Dillard acquired 12 St. Louis-area Stix, Baer & Fuller stores from Associated Dry Goods. The purchase came about through a chance meeting. While waiting for a flight at New York's LaGuardia Airport, William and Bill Dillard spotted mall developer Ed DeBartolo's corporate jet. They stopped for a visit and by chance met Bill Arnold, Associated's chairman. Arnold mentioned the possibility of selling Stix, Baer & Fuller, and months later, when new mall space became difficult to find, Dillard bought the stores.

The company had yet another year of massive expansion in 1984. In August Dillard agreed to pay the Dayton Hudson Corporation $140 million for 18 John A. Brown stores and 12 Diamond stores in the southwestern United States. Though not unprofitable, the stores performed below the Dayton Hudson average. Dillard immediately changed the John A. Brown stores to Dillard's. The Diamond stores went through a longer process in order to acquire the Dillard's name. In response to the needs of these western stores, Dillard added a new division based in Phoenix.

By the end of 1984, Dillard's sales had increased 50.7 percent to $1.27 billion. Net profit had jumped $15 million to

$49.5 million, and the number of stores had increased from 66 to 93. Indeed, the only stain in the company's performance that year came through some poor publicity generated when Dillard's failed to feature any minority models in a major advertising supplement. The National Association for the Advancement of Colored People (NAACP) complained and the next year protested the company's treatment of minorities, announcing a boycott of the stores. In 1986 William Dillard agreed to hire more African Americans and include more of them in management, a move that resolved the dispute.

The middle and late 1980s were marked by a shrewd reading of other department stores' finances. In 1985, after a management-led buyout of the R.H. Macy Company, Dillard went to New York, hoping that Macy's management would sell stores for needed capital. Within three months he closed a $100 million deal for 12 Macy's stores in Kansas City, Missouri, and Topeka and Wichita, Kansas.

Also during this time, Campeau Corp., a Canadian company that had acquired Allied Stores Corp., needed cash to defray expenses. For $225 million, Campeau sold Dillard's 27 Joske's department stores and three Cain-Sloan department stores in 1987. Joske's gave Dillard what some described as a monopoly in Texas and pushed the retailer into the Houston market, while Cain-Sloan gave Dillard's a presence in Nashville, Tennessee. In 1989, in a joint venture with The Edward J. DeBartolo Corporation, Dillard's acquired the Higbee Company, a chain of 12 Ohio department and specialty stores, in a $165 million deal.

While continuing to open new stores in Missouri, Oklahoma, and Texas, Dillard's 1989 focus was again on acquisitions. Dillard acquired New Orleans-based D.H. Holmes Company, a chain of 17 stores located in Louisiana, Mississippi, Alabama, and Florida. Although Holmes was a consistent money-loser, Dillard was confident of a turnaround and was hungry for Holmes's New Orleans and Baton Rouge properties. In 1989 Dillard also moved its stock listing to the New York Stock Exchange and offered two million shares of Class A common stock as well as two sets of debentures.

### 1990s and Beyond

Dillard's continued its acquisition campaign in 1990, paying BAT Industries $110 million for J. B. Ivey & Company's 23 stores in the Carolinas and Florida. The price of $109 million, or one-third of annual sales, compared favorably with rates others were paying for BAT assets. The purchase also provided Dillard's a base from which to expand in such lucrative markets as Jacksonville and Daytona Beach, Florida, and Raleigh-Durham, North Carolina.

While for many retailers, 1990 was a disastrous year, Dillard's experienced some unique gains. Some estimated that Dillard's enjoyed an 18 percent same-store sales gain over 1989. In 1990 every expense item on the company's income statement dropped as a percentage of sales. Because the company's ratio of debt to capital is lower than that of competitors, interest was less of a problem for Dillard's than for its competition.

By 1992, Dillard's acquisitions program was winding down. In 1991, the company gained eight Maison Blanche Department

Stores located in central and western Florida. The following year the company bought four more stores in Ohio from Joseph Horne Co. to add to its Higbee's chain, but only after Horne sued Dillard's over its backing out of a deal to acquire Horne in the late 1980s; Horne officials claimed the failed deal ruined the company's finances by disrupting its operations and leading to the departure of key executives. Dillard's received the first significant battering of its clean reputation as a result, but seemed to emerge otherwise unscathed. Also in 1991, Vendamerica sold all of its shares in Dillard's in a public offering.

By 1992, Dillard's had failed to turn around the Higbee's stores in Ohio, but nonetheless increased its exposure by buying out its partner, DeBartolo, for about $90 million. The company also announced that year that it would enter the Mexican market through the development of Dillard's anchors for five planned regional department stores. By mid-1996, the venture had not borne fruit, the apparent victim of the Mexican economic crisis of 1994.

Starting in 1991, the company significantly increased the number of new stores it was opening each year—ten added in 1991 and 11 the following year. Indeed, 1993 saw the beginning of an official shift in the company's growth strategy away from acquisitions and to the opening of new stores. From 1993 to 1995, 26 new stores were opened, while none were added through acquisition. A record 16 new stores were planned for 1996. One advantage of this growth strategy was that Dillard's could carefully choose the locations for its new stores, and it moved into such desirable areas as Louisville, Atlanta, Denver, and Colorado Springs.

By 1993, sales at Dillard's had grown to $5.13 billion, a sixfold increase over a ten-year period, while profits were also multiplying from $34.1 million to $241.1 million. Signs of a downturn, however, were evident even in the 1993 results as sales increased only nine percent, following year after year of growth in the 12 to 19 percent range. Profits, meanwhile, had increased only two percent over 1992. This slowdown continued through 1995 as sales increased eight percent in 1994 and seven percent in 1995, while profits increased only slightly to $251.8 million in 1994 before falling dramatically to $167 million in 1995 (which even without a $78.5 million charge for impairment of long-lived assets would still have totaled only $245.6 million).

Analysts reasoned that Dillard's was in part a victim of weak sales of women's apparel industrywide, which could be devastating for a company that generated about 40 percent of its sales from this sector. But the company's marketing strategies were also identified as contributing to the difficulties, in particular its longstanding everyday pricing policy; some observers noted that Dillard's lack of promotions caused it to lose customers to other department stores, which lured people through their doors by running sales on an almost constant basis.

Although it was sticking with its marketing policies as of mid-1996, Dillard's reorganized its operating divisions along geographic and climatic lines in March 1996 in order to improve operating results. The company's Cleveland and San Antonio divisions were merged into the company's other divisions, leaving the company with a more streamlined operation with five divisional buying offices.

From a small department store in Arkansas, William Dillard built one of the fastest growing department store chains in the United States. Expanding first by acquisition and later by placing stores in suburban malls and buying underperforming assets from debt-burdened competitors, Dillard's has grown without burdening itself with crushing debt. Heading into the end of the century, the question facing Dillard's was whether it could turn itself around from the difficult period of the mid-1990s and reestablish its formerly lofty position, which just a few years earlier had it placed at the forefront of the department store industry.

## *Principal Subsidiaries*

Cain Sloan, Inc.; Construction Developers Inc.; Dillard Investment Co. Inc.; Dillard National Bank; Dillard Travel, Inc.; D.H. Holmes Company, Limited; J.B. Ivey & Company.

## *Further Reading*

Brown, Susan, "Dillard: Acquiring for the Future," *Financial World,* October 30, 1990, p. 19.

Caminiti, Susan, "A Quiet Superstar Rises in Retailing," *Fortune,* October 23, 1989, pp. 167–69.

——, "The New Champs of Retailing," *Fortune,* September 24, 1990, pp. 85–100.

Fisher, Christy, and Laura Loro, "May, Dillard Hot, but All Watch Specialty Inroads," *Advertising Age,* January 28, 1991, p. 23.

Forest, Stephanie Anderson, "Dillard's Has a Dilly of a Headache," *Business Week,* October 3, 1994, pp. 85–86.

Morgenson, Gretchen, "A Midas Touch," *Forbes,* February 4, 1991, p. 42.

Rosenberg, Leon Joseph, *Dillard's: The First Fifty Years,* Fayetteville: The University of Arkansas Press, 1988, 141 p.

Schroeder, Michael, and Wendy Zellner, "Hell Hath No Fury Like a Big Store Scorned: Horne's Department Store Is Suing Dillard, the Suitor that Balked," *Business Week,* September 23, 1991, pp. 39–40.

Sutor, Ruthanne, "The Friends of Bill Dillard," *Financial World,* September 6, 1988, p. 22.

—Jordan Wankoff
—updated by David E. Salamie

# Donaldson

## Donaldson Co. Inc.

**1400 West 94th Street**
**Minneapolis, Minnesota 55431-2370**
**U.S.A.**
**(612) 887-3131**

*Public Company*
*Incorporated:* 1936
*Employees:* 5,038
*Sales:* $703.96 million (1995)
*Stock Exchanges:* New York
*SICs:* 3569 General Industrial Machinery, Not Elsewhere
   Classified

With operations in North and South America, Europe and Asia, Donaldson Co. Inc. is one of the world's largest manufacturers of specialty air and liquid filters. Donaldson's products are used in applications ranging from whole factory air filters to tractors and construction equipment, to computer disk drives. After suffering its first and only net loss in 1983, the company that *Money* magazine has characterized as a "baby blue chip" made a long, difficult comeback. Having made the shift from its mature, cyclical core business, Donaldson chalked up six consecutive earnings records and average annual sales increases of 10.7 percent from 1990 to 1995.

### Pre-World War I Foundation

Founder and company namesake Frank Donaldson was born and raised in southern Minnesota. After earning a degree in engineering from the University of Minnesota in 1912, he went to work as the western U.S. sales representative of Bull Tractor Company in Minneapolis. Donaldson found that one unhappy customer in Utah was having a great deal of difficulty keeping his new Bull tractor running. Donaldson had the dust-choked vehicle completely refurbished, but within a few days it was again out of commission. Taking matters into his own hands, Donaldson improvised a filter from a wire cage, eiderdown cloth, and an eight-foot-long pipe. When the enterprising young salesman proudly told his supervisors of his "modification," he was promptly fired for pointing up Bull's flaws.

Donaldson realized that although he was out of a job, he had something better: an invention that could be sold to tractor companies throughout the farm belt. With some help from his father W.H.L. Donaldson, who owned a St. Paul hardware store, and his brother Bob, a sheetmetal fabricator, Frank designed a filter he called the "Twister." The conical device used centrifugal force to spin dirt out of the air before it passed into the engine. In 1916, Frank and his father each made an initial $200 investment in the new enterprise and named it Donaldson Engineering Company. Frank began demonstrating prototypes to former employer Bull Tractor, as well as other major midwestern equipment manufacturers.

External and internal pressures made Donaldson's early years a bumpy roller coaster ride. Sales were rather slow that first year, but in 1917 the company won a contract to manufacture air cleaners for artillery tractors used in World War I. Before the year was through, Frank was drafted into the Army Corps of Engineers, leaving his father to run the fast-growing business. Overwhelmed, W.H.L. brought Bob into the firm at a salary of $150 per month and 25 percent of the company's profits (or half of W.H.L.'s stake). But when a competing filter company, Wilcox-Bennet, brought a potentially expensive patent infringement suit against Donaldson later that same year, the patriarch went back on his employment agreement with Bob, applying the funds he saved to the company's legal defense. Bob withheld access to his machine shop in retribution, throwing the business further into chaos. Worse yet, W.H.L. began claiming sole ownership of the busy company that Frank had founded.

### Interwar Reorganization and Early Growth

Months of infighting followed Frank's postwar homecoming. In the fall of 1918, the family settled its disagreement by incorporating the business as Donaldson Co., Inc. Frank owned 45 percent of the new corporate entity, Bob got 25 percent, their sisters Amanda and Mae each owned 12.5 percent, and mother Lottie held 5 percent. W.H.L. relinquished corporate ownership, settling instead for a royalty on any air filter he invented. Since he never came up with a product for Donaldson, the company's incorporation marked his final formal involvement in the firm. (Lottie gave Frank her shares upon W.H.L.'s death in 1926.) The lawsuit that precipitated this ownership crisis

## Company Perspectives:

*We believe all of the people of Donaldson Company should strive to conduct themselves in such a manner that the Company and those associated with it will stand for: Integrity in our dealings with customers, employees, shareholders, government authorities, suppliers, neighbors and the public; Quality in our products and services, in our manufacturing methods and general management; Technology in our particular fields of research, product development, engineering, and manufacturing; Growth in sales profits and strength within our areas of special interest and competence; Progress toward an environment where our people have increasing opportunities for contribution, fulfillment and reward.*

remained unsettled until 1919, when Donaldson agreed to purchase a U.S. license for Wilcox-Bennet air filters for $15,000 and a royalty on each unit.

The 1920s brought stability, new products, and increased prosperity. In 1920, Donaldson launched a second type and brand of filter, the Simplex. This air cleaner used oil-soaked moss to trap dust before it could enter a motor or engine and cause damage. The company combined characteristics of both its filters with the introduction of the patented Duplex that same year. Donaldson also forged its first contract with the John Deere Tractor Company during the 1920s. John Deere would become a major customer, accounting for one-third of annual sales by the end of the decade. After suffering a $4,000 loss in 1921, the company's sales multiplied from $19,554 in 1924 to $204,667 by 1928. By 1929, Donaldson was selling 200,000 units per year.

In addition to new product development, Donaldson sought close involvement with its customers' design processes so that their filters would work as well as possible in each manufacturer's tractors. In fact, the company began producing oil-bath type air cleaners in response to customer demand. In 1929, the corporation hired William Lowther to design a proprietary oil-washed air cleaner. His N.S. Filter was patented in 1932, but by that time the company would be scrambling to come up with the funds needed to begin manufacturing the new product.

Donaldson also diversified into tractor seats and spark-arresting mufflers in the late 1920s. The company had hoped to use a stock offering to fund the launch of an aftermarket car heater during this period as well, but the stock market's 1929 crash postponed that first public equity flotation.

Nature conspired with the worsening economy, wreaking havoc on America's farmers and the industries that served them. A five-year drought and grasshopper plagues denuded the midwestern landscape, turning the heartland into a dust bowl. When farmers hurt, tractor companies hurt and so did Donaldson. During the 1930s, the Minnesota manufacturer slashed its payroll by 70 percent, from 40 to 12, and its chief executives halved their own salaries and borrowed against life insurance policies to keep their business afloat. In 1934, Donaldson defaulted on payments to several suppliers.

It was then that Frank Donaldson and corporate attorney Ken Owen devised a plan to get the company's new oil-washed air cleaner into production and revive its cash flow. They sold the device's patent for $4,000 to a group of investors composed primarily of Donaldson stockholders. In exchange for a small royalty on each unit sold, the new owners licensed rights to produce the filter back to the company. Ford Motor Company started testing the filter mid-year and soon found that the device served its purpose well without sacrificing speed or efficiency. The contract that resulted took Donaldson from famine back to feast within months. Sales to Caterpillar, John Deere, Cummins Engine, and many other manufacturers of heavy vehicles boosted sales to $465,000 and profits to $88,000 by 1935.

By the end of this traumatic decade, annual sales hovered near $1 million, and the company's 200 employees manufactured 300,000 air cleaners each year. With a dominant 90 percent share of the market for farm and construction engine air cleaners, Donaldson sought growth through exports to Great Britain, Sweden, New Zealand, and Australia.

### World War II and Beyond

During World War II, Donaldson manufactured bomber gun sights, bayonet holders, crankcase valves for tanks, and, most important, air cleaners for tanks used in the difficult and dusty conditions of the North African desert.

The early 1940s brought a management shakeup as well. After Frank Donaldson suffered a stroke in 1942, brother Bob retired from day-to-day oversight of the company to become chairman. While Frank Donaldson continued as president, John Enblom was promoted from acting general manager to executive vice-president with effective control. This administrative arrangement lasted only two years. When Frank died of heart failure in 1945, John Enblom advanced to the presidency. Upon his return from World War II service, Frank Donaldson, Jr. assumed the title of vice-president.

In spite of this unexpected leadership transition and a month-long strike, Donaldson did well during the early 1940s. Having established its first branch office in Milwaukee, Wisconsin in 1938, the company added satellite offices in Cleveland, Chicago, and Detroit, and launched its first international production facility in Canada. Sales multiplied from less than $1 million in 1939 to $3.5 million by 1947, with profits topping $359,000.

But in the late 1940s, the Internal Revenue Service began to question the royalty plan that had saved Donaldson from bankruptcy during the Great Depression. The government agency charged that the royalties were "dividends in disguise," and that the company owed back and current taxes on these diverted profits. The IRS contended that royalties are paid before taxes and, therefore, are considered a tax-deductible business expense and that dividends are paid out of after-tax profits. By paying "royalties" to what was essentially a group of shareholders, the company had avoided $1.3 million in taxes in the process. Donaldson, which was only worth $1.27 million at the time, struggled to reach a lower settlement with the IRS over the next two years, but finally had to go to court.

The legal crisis brought on a mutiny of sorts at Donaldson. President John Enblom, along with pivotal employees Bill Lowther and Roger Cresswell, all members of the executive committee, issued an ultimatum: either Frank Jr. sold them 51 percent of the company for $200,000, or they would all quit and start a competing company. Frank Jr. marshaled the Donaldson family—which still owned the vast majority of the company's equity—and they agreed not to sell.

True to their word, the three executives quit to form Crenlo Corp. in 1951. At the age of 31, Frank Jr. became president of a company with $5.5 million in annual sales. Although he had a degree in engineering from Harvard, where he minored in economics and graduated cum laude, his lack of day-to-day experience made the early 1950s a difficult period of transition for the business.

Frank Jr.'s first order of business was to replenish the "brain trust." He sought management help from his cousin, Dick Donaldson, who became vice-president of sales and engineering. The new president established the company's first formal research and development department in 1951 and brought in consultants from the Stanford Research Institute the following year. Seven years of research and testing resulted in the 1959 launch of the "Donaclone," the first heavy-duty air cleaner to use a paper filter. The brand name combined Donaldson and cyclone, and the device harked back to the company's original Twister brand filter. It used a series of "cyclone tubes" to spin dirt out of the air. The Duralife paper filter served as a final dirt trap. The new product was such a success that, during its first year, it accounted for 20 percent of Donaldson's annual sales.

In the meantime, Donaldson had gone public with a modest $124,000 offering. Frank Jr.'s first decade in office was incredibly successful. Sales nearly doubled, from $5.5 million in 1950 to a record $10.1 million in 1959, and profits more than doubled, from $315,000 to $669,000 during the same period.

But this was only the beginning of what a company history dubbed "the age of the Donaclone." Sales tripled over the course of the 1960s, to $35.9 million in 1969, as clients ranging from Caterpillar to the U.S. Army adopted the new filter for their heavy-duty machinery. Geographic expansion also contributed to this growth, as Donaldson established joint ventures and licensing agreements with businesses in Britain, France, Germany, Brazil, and Australia. By the end of the decade, it had wholly owned subsidiaries in Germany, Belgium, and South Africa as well. Formalized in 1963, the International Division grew 30-fold from 1963 to 1970.

Frank Donaldson, Jr. advanced to chairman and CEO in 1973. In a departure from the traditional promotion from within, Donaldson hired William Hodder, formerly president of Target Stores and a director of Donaldson for just four years, to succeed the founder's son. Hodder took the company on something of an acquisition spree, merging with St. Paul, Minnesota's Torit Corp. and acquiring Majac, Inc. and Kittell Muffler and Engineering in rapid succession. The new affiliates helped diversify Donaldson from its core. Torit added dust collectors that could clear the air in whole factories, while Majac specialized in making dust (it disintegrated materials to specifically sized bits) and Kittell produced heavy-duty sound controllers.

Donaldson also diversified from within, establishing a hydraulic fluid filter division in 1975.

In spite of inflation and the energy crunch, Donaldson's strategy of "focused diversification" kept the company's sales and earnings on a counter-cyclical rise throughout the decade. Sales broke both the $100 million and $200 million thresholds over the course of the decade, and net income more than doubled from $6 million to $14.2 million. In 1979, the company was listed on the New York Stock Exchange.

### Reorganization and Retrenchment in the 1980s

After this stellar decade, however, "stagflation" hit Donaldson's core constituencies hard in the early 1980s. Two prominent examples of the recession in the heavy machinery industry were International Harvester, which lost $3 billion, and John Deere, whose plants came to a standstill for two months during the early 1980s. Donaldson's sales skidded from $264 million in 1981 to $203 million by 1983, when the company suffered its first-ever annual loss, a $3.5 million shortfall. Blaming its difficulties in part on overexpansion in the late 1970s, the company closed two plants and scaled back the remaining U.S. production to 50 percent of capacity. Employment was reduced by more than 25 percent from 1980 to 1985. Administrative personnel accepted mandatory unpaid leave and a salary freeze. Sales and profits began to recover in 1984, the same year that Frank Donaldson, Jr. announced his retirement.

But perhaps most important, the early 1980s crisis highlighted Donaldson's dependence on a mature market and precipitated a more thorough diversification. From 1984 to 1990, the company poured $40 million into acquisitions and joint ventures and plowed another $50 million into research and development. Hoping to eliminate duplication of effort and gain efficiencies, top executives reorganized the company into five groups: Industrial; International; Original Equipment; Aftermarket; and Worldwide Support. Having focused almost exclusively on the original equipment market throughout its history, the company began to target the filter aftermarket. Research and development efforts paid off in the form of new products for industries ranging from computers to passenger autos to pharmaceuticals. Sales in nontraditional markets grew to $129.5 million by 1990, almost one-third of annual sales.

It took most of the 1980s for these new strategies to come to full fruition, but the geographic, product, and market diversification helped even out Donaldson's cyclical performance. The budding conglomerate began to realize its goal of steady growth in profitability in the early 1990s, when rising net sales combined with an annual return on sales of more than 5 percent. Revenues increased from $422.89 million in 1990 to $703.96 million in 1995, and net income jumped from $21.03 million to $38.54 million.

With Chairman and CEO William Hodder nearing mandatory retirement, Donaldson settled the question of succession. In 1994, William Van Dyke capped a more than 20-year career at the company with his appointment to the positions of president and chief operating officer. He was expected to advance to the chief executive office in 1996. The company planned to achieve double-digit annual earnings per share increases by developing air filters for passenger cars, forging strategic alliances, and maintaining its long-standing clients.

### Principal Subsidiaries

ENV Services, Inc.; Donaldson Europe, N.V. (Belgium); Donaldson Coordination Center, N.V. (Belgium); Donaldson Gesellschaft m.b.H. (Germany); Donaldson Filter Components, Ltd. (England); Donaldson Torit, B.V. (Netherlands); Donaldson France, S.A.; Donaldson Italia s.r.l.; Nippon Donaldson, Ltd. (Japan); Donaldson Far East Limited (Hong Kong); Donaldson Australasia (Pty.) Ltd. (Australia); Donaldson Filtration Systems (Pty.) Ltd. (South Africa); Donaldson, S.A. de C.V.; Donaldson do Brasil Ltda. (Brazil).

### Further Reading

Abelson, Reed, "Exhausting the Possibilities," *Forbes,* May 25, 1992, p. 260.

Croghan, Lore, "Don't Look Back," *Financial World,* July 18, 1995, p. 50.

Goodman, Jordan E., "These Baby Blue Chips Promise To Become Grown-up Champs," *Money,* May 1991, p. 65.

Jaffe, Thomas, "Cleaner Air Company," *Forbes,* September 14, 1992, p. 562.

Keenan, Tim, "Let's Clear the Air: Donaldson, Hoechst Celanese Develop New Filter," *Ward's Auto World,* September 1995, p. 85.

Martin, Norman, Sawyer, Christopher A., and Sorge, Marjorie, "The Ultimate in Air Fresheners," *Automotive Industries,* February 1996, p. 173.

Morais, Richard C., "Hong Kong Is Just Around the Corner," *Forbes,* October 12, 1992, p. 50.

Peterson, Susan E., "Van Dyke Heir Apparent To Take Over Donaldson," *Star Tribune,* August 11, 1994, p. 3D.

"Salesman's Solution to Tractor-Choking Dust Leads to Founding of Filter Manufacturing Company," *Hydraulics & Pneumatics,* May 1983, p. 80.

*Toward a Cleaner, Quieter World: History of the Donaldson Company, 1915–1985,* Minneapolis, Minn.: Donaldson Co., Inc., 1985.

Youngblood, Dick, "Diversified Firm Yields Dividends," *Star Tribune,* February 4, 1991, p. 1D.

—April Dougal Gasbarre

# Douglas & Lomason Company

24600 Hallwood Court
Farmington Hills, Michigan, 48335-1671
U.S.A.
(810) 478-7800
Fax: (810) 478-5189

*Public Company*
*Incorporated:* 1902
*Employees:* 5,900
*Sales:* $561.18 million (1995)
*Stock Exchanges:* NASDAQ
*SICs:* 3465 Automotive Stampings; 3535 Conveyors and
     Conveying Equipment; 2531 Public Building and
     Related Furniture; 3713 Truck and Bus Bodies

The Douglas and Lomason Company is a leading worldwide supplier of automotive seating systems. Founded in 1902 as a manufacturer of decorative trim for carriages and sleighs, Douglas and Lomason is one of the oldest continuous suppliers of parts to the moving vehicle industry. Through the company's Bestop subsidiary and Chartland division, Douglas and Lomason also manufactures soft tops and accessories for sport utility vehicles as well as a variety of material handling equipment for industrial customers.

### Company Origins

Douglas and Lomason was founded in Detroit in 1902 as a manufacturer of carriage accessories by Alexander G. Douglas, Harry A. Lomason, and Albert J. Cloutier. Douglas and Lomason were to contribute their knowledge of the carriage hardware trade to the enterprise, while Cloutier, a tailor by profession, was to provide the capital. Douglas was named the company's first president, and Lomason became company secretary and treasurer. The company's first products were carriage and sleigh rails, handles, and name plates but by 1909 more luxurious carriage accessories such as footmen's loops and flower vases were added to the company's line.

In 1905 came the company's first recognition that the horse-less carriage might be the vehicle of the future and Brass Automobile Rails were introduced to the list of Douglas and Lomason products. Set up in a new factory on Brooklyn Avenue in Detroit that was to remain the company headquarters into the 1970s, Douglas and Lomason became one of the leading manufacturers of plated trim for carriages and automobiles.

World War I brought a brief hiatus to the company's rapid expansion into the automobile industry as wartime production of machine gun components replaced the more frivolous metal trim in the Brooklyn Avenue factory, but the postwar boom saw a growing demand for Douglas and Lomason products to serve the new American obsession, the automobile.

By the 1920s elaborate horse-drawn carriages and sleighs had become relics of a bygone era, and Douglas and Lomason had fully entered the automobile supply industry. The firm produced metal automobile components of all types including running boards, windshields (then optional), hinges, and locks. However, decorative moldings and trim were to become their stock in trade. The Brooklyn Avenue factory, which had by this time been expanded several times, was now refitted to accommodate new metallurgical techniques and materials. Traditional forging and casting was quickly being replaced by steel stamping and rolling, and Douglas and Lomason not only adopted these new technologies but actually manufactured much of the necessary machinery. By the mid-1920s the American automobile industry was producing about four million cars a year, with Douglas and Lomason supplying parts to all of the major manufacturers. By 1927 annual sales for the company had climbed to $728,000.

### Depression and Recovery

Like most American businesses Douglas and Lomason suffered major setbacks during the Great Depression of the 1930s. With sales dropping to only $300,000 in 1932, the company was forced to lay-off scores of workers and to cut back production to only two days a week. The company's first president, Alexander Douglas, retired amidst this decline, and company founder and treasurer Harry A. Lomason took over the presidency of the troubled firm in 1932.

Harry was the first in a series of Lomason family members who were to manage the company throughout the rest of the century. Although the Douglas name would be retained by the company for the sake of continuity, Douglas sold out all his interest in the auto parts firm at the time of his retirement.

Douglas and Lomason founded its recovery from the Depression in large part on the development of stainless steel trim for the new streamlined automobile designs. Stainless steel provided protection from corrosion for the speed lines and accents that were included in the new designs. The new material also allowed for a corrosion-free seal for the new permanent windshields that were a major part of the streamlined automobile. In fact, Douglas and Lomason were pioneers in the use of stainless for these applications, and costly experimentation with the new material paid off for the company in 1935 when sales once again soared to almost $1.4 million and continued to climb through the decade, topping $4 million by 1940.

### World War II and the Postwar Boom

World War II saw Douglas and Lomason once again dropping all civilian production in order to supply defense materials ranging from bombs to military vehicle parts for the U.S. army and navy. When peace returned, the soaring postwar demand for cars created a boom for the entire auto parts industry. Douglas and Lomason took advantage of growing demand to enter a new automotive parts market that would prove to dominate the company's future, automotive seating. The double product line of ornamentation and seating allowed the company more flexibility to respond to ever-changing trends in automobile design. The postwar boom caused sales to multiply five times over the five-year period from 1945 to 1950, rising from $2.3 million to $15.8 million in 1950.

The 1950s were a time of change and expansion for Douglas and Lomason. When president Harry A. Lomason died in 1950, his son William K. Lomason succeeded him as president and undertook a process of regional expansion and product diversification. As Douglas and Lomason increased production, the Detroit plant (which had undergone numerous expansions and additions since its construction in 1912) became unable to

accommodate further growth. In addition, labor unrest had begun to plague Detroit area automobile manufacturers as workers demanded a larger share in the surging profits of the industry. In fact, Douglas and Lomason was the subject of a protracted and bitter strike in the mid-1950s that left the company with a 51 percent decline in sales.

By opening manufacturing plants in other states, the company hoped not only to expand its capacity but also to reduce labor strife and costs. In 1955 Douglas and Lomason opened two new plants in the Georgia towns of Carrollton and Newnan to manufacture stretch bent moldings for use as automotive trim. These openings were followed in 1958 by the founding of a new subsidiary in Carrollton called the Douglas and Lomason Plating Corp. This subsidiary would manufacture anodized aluminum, a new and lightweight alternative to steel that was to be used by Douglas and Lomason to produce automotive moldings and grilles.

Douglas and Lomason's geographic expansion accelerated in the 1960s and, with sales reaching $30 million, the company opened new plants in Arkansas, Mississippi, Nebraska, Iowa, and Georgia. Lightweight and attractive, anodized aluminum trim became an important new product in the automotive industry, and Douglas and Lomason began to expand their aluminum trim manufacturing facilities in Georgia and Mississippi. New plants in Arkansas and Nebraska concentrated on the manufacture of automotive seat frames, the company's growing secondary product line.

Most significantly, the 1960s saw Douglas and Lomason entering nonautomotive product lines through the acquisition of other companies. In 1962 Douglas and Lomason purchased Superior Atlanta Manufacturing Inc. along with its subsidiary Cen-Tennial Cotton Gin Co. (later renamed Centennial Industries). Although the production of cotton gin machinery was discontinued by the mid-1960s, under Douglas and Lomason Centennial now also began manufacturing special truck bodies for the beverage industry. The specialized truck body industry, expanded through a series of acquisitions through the 1960s and 1970s, was to remain a significant source of revenues for the company into the 1990s.

Also acquired during this period was the Chantland Company of Humboldt, Iowa, a maker of conveyors and pulleys for the material handling industry which was likewise to become an important part of Douglas and Lomason's product mix. A much shorter-lived excursion outside of the auto parts industry came in 1968 with the establishment by Douglas and Lomason of Shamrock Air Lines, a custom contract air cargo carrier run out of Willow Run Airport in Ypsilanti, Michigan. Although this new venture would enjoy initial success with offices in Atlanta, Georgia, and San Juan, Puerto Rico, by 1976 the spiralling cost of fuel forced the closure of the small airline.

### Consolidation and Reorganization in the 70s and 80s

The company's prior rate of expansion was slowed in the 1970s, a decade of consolidation and reorganization for Douglas and Lomason. The Douglas and Lomason Plating Corporation was dissolved and the aluminum anodizing processing works were moved to the Carrollton plant. The production of tools, dies, and jigs for Douglas and Lomason manufacturing machinery was now centralized at the Carrollton location with the establishment of a new company division called the Trojan Tool Division. All material handling equipment manufacture which had previously been spread out at a number of plants was also centralized at the Chantland division in Humboldt, Iowa. Most significantly, in 1976 the Detroit plant that had served as the Douglas and Lomason headquarters for 65 years was closed and new corporate offices were established in suburban Farmington Hills, Michigan. In the same year, W.K. Lomason who had been the company president since 1950, retired from the position and was succeeded by his son Harry A. Lomason II.

The 1980s were a difficult time for the U.S. domestic auto industry as foreign imports began to make serious inroads into the American auto market. Suppliers like Douglas and Lomason were forced to reorganize production and engineering processes in order to succeed in this new and highly competitive environment. The big automakers were demanding more flexibility from their parts suppliers to avoid the backlogs of unpopular cars that had caused huge losses in the late 1970s and early 1980s.

The "Just-in-Time" (JIT) system of delivery that had parts manufactured only as increased demand warranted became the standard industry practice by the mid1980s. In 1986 Douglas and Lomason opened a new state of the art facility in Richmond, Michigan, to manufacture complete seat assemblies on a JIT basis and began plans for a new facility at Havre de Grace, Maryland which would produce JIT delivery seating for Chrysler beginning in 1988.

Meanwhile, the anodized aluminum trim that had been the mainstay of the company's decorative trim operations began to fall out of favor with consumers. In addition, aluminum supplies were becoming problematic as it became more and more difficult to obtain the high quality raw material required by the fabrication process and yet keep prices at a level that would satisfy the big automakers. Profit margins for the company's aluminum trim operations started to dwindle at an alarming rate and Douglas and Lomason began to look towards plastic as the new material for exterior decorative trim.

In 1988, the company opened a facility in La Grange, Georgia, to produce plastic bi-laminate and extruded moldings. Although initially successful, even these efforts would not achieve the kinds of sales that had driven aluminum trim production in the 1960s and 1970s and, by 1996, with the auto industry moving increasingly towards large molded plastic for exterior decorative trim, Douglas and Lomason would discontinue the decorative trim production that had been the company's stock in trade since 1902.

### Trouble and Recovery in the 1980s and 1990s

By the late 1980s the re-tooling and reorganization required by the new demands of the domestic auto industry had begun to take their toll on Douglas and Lomason's bottom line. In 1988 and 1989, in spite of sales of about $400 million, the company posted a $3 million net loss for two years running. While most of this loss could be attributed to higher than expected start-up costs at the Havre de Grace and La Grange plants, the company

also experienced high engineering costs in the design of the new products demanded by the highly competitive parts industry. Increasingly, automakers were relying on parts suppliers to provide the innovative engineering required by new car designs instead of merely placing orders for parts designed by the automakers themselves. This additional burden forced Douglas and Lomason to reorganize and update its entire engineering and design facilities at substantial cost to the company's net earnings.

In spite of these new efforts to revamp its engineering capabilities, in the early 1990s the company lost an important contract for seating for Chrysler midsize cars to larger rival Johnson Controls forcing the closure of the Havre de Grace plant. Although the company recovered its profitable position from 1990 to 1992, plant closings once again saw Douglas and Lomason posting a net loss of $7 million in 1993 in spite of sales of almost $425 million.

In the early 1990s, Douglas and Lomason began to look to foreign partnerships both in order to serve foreign markets as well as to demonstrate the company's global capabilities to the large American auto firms. In 1995 the company established a joint venture with Shanghai Traffic Machinery Factory in China called the Shanghai Lomason Automotive Seating Systems Company that would produce seat frames for the Volkswagen Santana. Later that year Douglas and Lomason entered into a joint venture, to be called Euro American Seating, with German firm Kieper Recaro, Europe's premier seating supplier. These two joint ventures along with a previously established partnership with Namba Press Works of Japan would provide the company with an important global presence as it entered the last years of the century.

After a series of poor years, the reorganization and consolidation of company operations began to pay off, and in 1995 Douglas and Lomason reported a net profit of $4 million on sales of $561 million. The acquisition of Bestop Inc., a maker of soft tops and accessories for sport utility vehicles, contributed to this recovery as did growing sales at the company's Chantland Division, which had continued to manufacture material handling equipment for a variety of industrial applications. Although the worldwide automobile industry was still undergoing tumultuous changes, it appeared from the vantage of the late 1990s that Douglas and Lomason would be in a position to adapt to these changes and enter its second century of auto parts manufacture.

### Principal Subsidiaries

Bestop, Inc.

### Principal Divisions

The Chantland Company; Douglas and Lomason Company Truck Body Division.

### Further Reading

Darling, Ed, "A Company is Known by the People it Keeps: Douglas and Lomason Company 75th Anniversary," *Douglas and Lomason Company Staff Nooz,* April 1977, pp. 1–8.

Byrne, Harlan S., ''Douglas and Lomason Co.: If Profits are Climbing Can a Rise in Sales be Far Behind?'' *Barron's,* November 30, 1992, pp. 53–54.

Ramirez, Charles, ''Seat-Maker Plants Spared,'' *Crain's Detroit Business,* May 23, 1994, p. 27.

''Seat Makers Not Sitting Tight: Farmington Hills Firm Sees Potential in Asian Markets,'' *Detroit News,* February 17, 1995, p. E1.

Sherefkin, Robert, ''Chrysler Cuts Douglas and Lomason from Tier One,'' *Crain's Detroit Business,* January 30, 1995 p. 1.

Templin, Neal, and Jeff Cole, ''Working Together: Manufacturers Use Suppliers to Help Them Develop New Products,'' *The Wall Street Journal,* December 19, 1994, p. A1.

—Hilary Gopnik

# Eagle Hardware & Garden, Inc.

**981 Powell Avenue Southwest**
**Renton, Washington 98055**
**U.S.A.**
**(206) 227-5740**
**Fax: (206) 204-5169**

*Public Company*
*Incorporated:* 1989 as Eagle Home & Garden, Inc.
*Employees:* 3,850
*Sales:* $615.6 million (1995)
*Stock Exchanges:* NASDAQ
*SICs:* 5251 Hardware Stores

A leading competitor in the home improvement industry, Eagle Hardware & Garden, Inc. operates a chain of enormous stores in the western United States that offer a wide selection of merchandise. During the mid-1990s, 24 stores composed the Eagle chain, each averaging roughly 120,000 square feet of space. Although the company did not open its first store until late 1990, it quickly expanded to become one of the dominant retailers in its industry by the mid-1990s, with stores in the Pacific Northwest, Utah, Colorado, Montana, and Hawaii.

When David J. Heerensperger relinquished his posts as chairman and chief executive officer of Pay 'N Pak Stores, Inc. in August 1989, the end, it would seem, had come to what had been an illustrious career in the home building industry. In his early 50s at the time, Heerensperger had been actively involved in the retail sale of hardware products for the previous 35 years, achieving remarkable success during his years of service, most notably by turning Pay 'N Pak, a home building retail chain, into a regional powerhouse. When Heerensperger joined Pay 'N Pak it was a $15 million-a-year company making its way through its first decade of business. By the time the reins of command were passed to Heerensperger's successor exactly 20 years later, Pay 'N Pak had grown enormously, collecting more than $400 million in sales each year. Not surprisingly, Heerensperger had benefited financially from his years at the helm of Pay 'N Pak, reaping the rewards from what was widely regarded as astute, prescient, and enterprising leadership. Heerensperger left the $400 million company he had built owning roughly 12 percent of it, enough to finance his retirement one hundred times over and spend his days reflecting on his distinguished career. Instead, Heerensperger began anew, creating Eagle Hardware & Garden almost immediately after leaving Pay 'N Pak, opting to forego retirement to orchestrate another assault on his competitors and jump once again into the home building retail market. In less than three years, Pay 'N Pak would sink into financial ruin, collapsing just as Heerensperger was in the process of achieving the greatest success of his professional life.

## Founder's Early Years

The path toward Heerensperger's success with Eagle Hardware & Garden began in 1954 when, at age 17, he was hired to do inventory for a hardware store in Longview, Washington. Five years later, the man who had hired Heerensperger was impressed enough with his work that he loaned Heerensperger $4,000 to open his own hardware store in Spokane, Washington called Eagle Electric & Plumbing Supply. Another store was added later, as the young entrepreneur enjoyed early success. Then in 1969 the definitive moment in his career arrived when his company and Buzzard Electrical & Plumbing merged with a 19-store plumbing and electrical supply chain named Pay 'N Pak, which had been formed eight years earlier. Heerensperger became the new leader of the merged entities and quickly made his presence known, initiating several important changes that would make the Seattle-based chain the success it would later become and offered glimpses into the way Eagle Hardware & Garden would later operate.

In addition to other changes that were peculiar to Pay 'N Pak's condition at the time, Heerensperger took the company public following the merger and dramatically enlarged the size of Pay 'N Pak stores. Within a few short years, square footage was increased by 70 percent, transforming 18,000-square-foot stores into 33,000-square-foot super stores, well before such massive retail outlets became the norm in the retail industry. A greater emphasis on customer service was inculcated, including the employment of a training director charged with developing an instructional program stressing product knowledge and vari-

## Company Perspectives:

*Eagle Hardware & Garden believes that its unique merchandising concept differentiates the Company from its competitors by combining a customer-friendly store with a "More of Everything" merchandising strategy, outstanding customer service, everyday low pricing and convenient store locations.*

ous installation techniques for products sold by Pay 'N Pak stores. Strengthened by enhanced service and store size, Pay 'N Pak flourished, establishing an enviable record of sales and profit growth, as well as a robust rate of expansion.

During the last decade of Heerensperger's reign over the fortunes of Pay 'N Pak, the retail chain began to reel from heavy debt and competition, as the company gradually began to suffer from the growing presence of home building retailers such as Kmart Co.'s Builders Square, Home Depot Inc., and Homeclub. Eyeing the coming storm, Heerensperger vowed in 1984 to maintain Pay 'N Pak's market share, no matter the cost. Before long, a price war flared up and Pay 'N Pak joined the fray, slashing its prices to keep pace with its deeper-pocketed competitors. By 1986, the struggle to maintain market share was beginning to wear on the company, as its earnings began to slip. Then, in 1987, Pay 'N Pak's shaky health was aggravated further by a hostile takeover attempt led by corporate raider Paul Bilzerian, who failed in his attempt but only after a management-led buyout of the company rebuffed his advances.

The leveraged buyout saddled Pay 'N Pak with debt, the last thing the company needed as it waged a price war and attempted to service that debt with dwindling profits. By 1989 (Heerensperger's last year as chairman and chief executive officer), Pay 'N Pak was headed toward serious trouble, igniting disputes between Heerensperger and outside directors of the company who emerged on the scene after the 1987 buyout. Relations between Heerensperger and Pay 'N Pak's outside directors quickly soured. Heerensperger was annoyed by the intrusion of the outside directors, while the outside directors grew increasingly anxious about the future state of the company, creating an uneasy tension that lingered until Heerensperger left the company in August, holding stock and cash that amounted to $13 million.

### Eagle's Origins

Although his tenure at Pay 'N Pak had ended on a decidedly sour note, Heerensperger's achievements during his 20-year control over the company were numerous and widely praised by those within the home building retail industry. Rather than gloat about his distinguished career, Heerensperger moved forward with his new plans with remarkable speed. In November 1989, two short months after resigning from Pay 'N Pak, Heerensperger incorporated his new company and named it Eagle Hardware & Garden, Inc., resurrecting the name of the electric and plumbing supply store he had founded in Spokane in 1959. Heerensperger's intentions were clear from the start: He would

establish a home building supply retail chain that would offer "the most complete selection of hardware, garden, and building materials in the region," as he announced in the *Puget Sound Business Journal.* In formulating plans for his new retail concept, Heerensperger would include several of the defining characteristics that had enabled him to record the success he achieved with Pay 'N Pak, but on a much larger scale. Eagle Hardware stores would be considerably larger than Pay 'N Pak stores and offer a much broader and deeper selection of merchandise. Fittingly, the chain's motto would be "More of everything," a phrase that succinctly described the massive stores to come in the next few years.

In what would be his final annual meeting at Pay 'N Pak in 1988, Heerensperger declared to those in attendance that "there will never be a day that I won't be proud of what we've done. . . . Every time I see a big Pay 'N Pak truck going up the street, I'll be really happy." As he busied himself with "getting blueprints going and leases signed" in early 1990, however, Heerensperger was gambling his own money and reputation on beating home improvement chains, Pay 'N Pak included, and carving a lasting position for his new company in already crowded markets.

Heerensperger invested $4 million of his own money in his new venture, then gained an additional $4.5 million from primarily local investors, who purchased an interest in the company at $2.75 per share in a private placement in June 1990. The first Eagle Hardware store, a sprawling building measuring more than 100,000 square feet inside, opened its doors in November 1990, with the company's motto, "More of everything," triumphantly emblazoned across the front. Located in Spokane, where Heerensperger had cut his teeth in the retail business with the first of his Eagle Electric & Plumbing Supply stores in the late 1950s, Eagle's maiden store contained more than 50,000 items, including 150 types of hammers, a lighting section with 1,400 fixtures, and a customer lounge. The Spokane store represented retailing on an enormous scale, easily larger than Pay 'N Pak's stores and larger even than Home Depot's stores, the ranking king of the heap. Inside the store, friendly, helpful service was the rule, much as it had been once Heerensperger assumed control over Pay 'N Pak. In fact, Heerensperger hired 50 former Pay 'N Pak employees to provide such service at his first store.

By June of 1991, Heerensperger had secured additional financial help, raising $10 million in another private placement to help fund the company's expansion. At the time, there was supposed to be another store already established, but construction and permitting delays had slowed progress. The unexpected delays did not keep the company at a standstill, however, and by August another store had opened for business, this time in Tukwila, Washington, a suburban community near Tacoma that would serve as Eagle's headquarters. Two more stores were established in November, one in Seattle and another in Bremerton, Washington, each averaging 120,000 square feet in size. Now with four stores in operation, Heerensperger began the push to develop Eagle into a strong regional chain, confiding to a reporter for the *Puget Sound Business Journal,* "These stores are tough to operate. I don't expect we'll have more than 30 or 40 of them." For the year, Eagle generated $51 million, but Heerensperger was already looking toward the day when, considering his projected ceiling of growth, Eagle would be pulling in $1 billion in sales per year.

### Eagle Goes Public in 1992

Few could doubt he might reach such a total, particularly after the events of 1992 were played out, when three more stores were added to the company's fold. A Seattle store opened in August, followed by the establishment of a store in Federal Way, Washington the next month, when Pay 'N Pak finally caved in under the weight of debt and closed its doors forever. The third store, which began business in October, extended the company's presence beyond Washington's borders for the first time and into Alaska, where a 168,000-square-foot store was opened in Anchorage. The opening of these three stores during a three-month span had been aided in part by the company's initial public offering in July, when Eagle's stock sold for $14 per share. By October, when the Anchorage store opened, Eagle's stock had soared, jumping to $31.25 at one point during the month, instilling confidence that Eagle in the years ahead would become a dominant force in the hotly contested home improvement market.

Like Pay 'N Pak, Eagle had become a publicly traded company under Heerensperger's control, and like Pay 'N Pak, Eagle was demonstrating exponential sales growth under the stewardship of its founder. Sales for 1992 had nearly trebled from the previous year's total, leaping to $147 million, while the company's net income had increased to nearly four times the figure recorded for 1991, eclipsing $4 million. As the company entered 1993, plans called for opening six new stores in the coming 12 months, a goal Heerensperger and his management team fell short of by one store. Still, the addition of five stores in one calendar year represented a prodigious achievement, shoring up the company's presence in its home state of Washington, where four of the new stores were located, and expanding its geographic scope once again with the establishment of a store in Waipahu, Hawaii.

By mid-1993, when ten stores composed the Eagle chain, expansion was taking place at a rapid clip, while the existing stores, each of which averaged $29 million in sales per year, were flourishing. Looking ahead, the company was planning to open five to seven stores per year for at least the next several years, which would soon make the Eagle chain one of the dominant home improvement retailers in the western United States. With two more stores slated to open before the end of the year, Eagle was moving forward resolutely, achieving results that drew national attention and distinction. In 1993, the trade publication *Building Supply Home Centers* named Eagle its 1993 retailer of the year and Heerensperger its "master entrepreneur" of the year. Still more recognition came from *Fortune* magazine, which ranked Eagle as the second fastest growing company in the country. When the year was concluded, the financial figures were announced and, as expected, the company continued to record energetic growth. Annual sales had more than doubled, reaching $322.9 million, a gain mirrored by profits for the year, which rose to $10.7 million.

Eagle completed its third round of public financing in March 1994, raising $86 million from the offering, but aside from the welcome infusion of cash, the company's management would look back on 1994 as the toughest year in Eagle's short history.

Home Depot, the undisputed giant in the home improvement industry, had opened five stores in the Puget Sound area over the past several years, encroaching on Eagle's home territory and intensifying the competition in what already had been a heavily contested market. To make matters worse, the company stumbled for the first time, shaking investor confidence in Eagle's future growth. Earlier, the company had established a Canadian subsidiary to superintend the operation of Eagle stores in Edmonton, Alberta, but a little more than a year later the foray into Canada had proved to be an unsuccessful venture. The closing of the Canadian subsidiary in 1994 caused Eagle's year-end earnings to fall considerably, despite a 61 percent gain in sales. For the year, the company collected $518.7 million in sales, but recorded its first loss, registering a staggering $6.3 million deficit.

In January 1995, Eagle opened its first store in Montana, a 142,000-square-foot establishment in Billings, and its third store in Utah, having entered the state for the first time in May 1994, when Eagle outlets were opened in Murray and Sandy. Attracted by Utah's fast-growing economy, several of the country's largest home improvement chains were moving into the state, Home Depot included, and Eagle moved quickly to establish a solid footing in the state. The company upped its ante in May 1995, establishing its fourth Utah store in Orem, concurrent with the opening of two more stores in Washington, which became the company's thirteenth and fourteenth stores in its home state. The three stores opened in May represented the greatest number established in one month. On the heels of this unprecedented spurt of growth, however, the company announced it would scale back its expansion in the future. Instead of opening five to seven stores a year, as company officials had announced in 1993, projections for the years ahead called for the establishment of between three and five stores a year.

At the end of 1995, a year in which Eagle generated $615.6 million in sales and posted $11.3 million in net income, eclipsing the total recorded before the company's Canadian subsidiary was closed, competition was continuing to intensify. Many of Eagle's stores were matched against Home Depot stores located within throwing distance, setting the stage for what promised to be a battle that would reach a definitive conclusion, with either Eagle or Home Depot coming out the winner and the loser sent packing. As Eagle prepared to open its third and fourth stores in Colorado in 1996 and another in Wenatchee, Washington, Heerensperger was keenly aware of the importance the late 1990s would represent for his chain. "This is war," he flatly explained to a *Forbes* reporter, referring to Eagle's rivalry with Home Depot. "They are aiming for us, but we're a thorn in the side," he continued, "Eagle is the first home center they haven't completely run over." As Eagle, with Heerensperger at the helm, headed into the late 1990s, all efforts were being devoted to keep Home Depot at bay and to continue the remarkable progress that had taken what was only an idea in 1990 and turned it into a flourishing, $600 million-a-year company.

### Further Reading

"Eagle Hardware Continues To Expand," *Do-It-Yourself Retailing,* August 1992, p. 31.

"Eagle Hardware Opens Another Three Stores," *Building Supply Home Centers,* July 1995, p. 1.

"Eagle Opens Second Store," *Do-It-Yourself Retailing,* August 1991, p. 29.

"Eagle Quits Canada; Small Stores on Tap," *Building Supply Home Centers,* December 1994, p. 1.

"Eagle Reports Strong Third Quarter," *Do-It-Yourself Retailing,* January 1996, p. 19.

La Franco, Robert, "Comeuppance?," *Forbes,* December 4, 1995, p. 74.

Oberbeck, Steven, "Home-Improvement Retailers Follow Housing Boom into Utah," *Knight-Ridder/Tribune Business News,* February 5, 1995, p. 2.

Prinzing, Debra, "Eagle Hardware Nails Down $10 Mil.," *Puget Sound Business Journal,* June 24, 1991, p. 1.

——, "Hardware Chains Revisit Old Grudges," *Puget Sound Business Journal,* August 19, 1991, p. 1.

——, "Heerensperger: Priming Eagle for a Steep Climb in Growth," *Puget Sound Business Journal,* December 25, 1992, p. 12.

——, "Inventory Woes Shoot Down Eagle," *Puget Sound Business Journal,* December 11, 1992, p. 1.

——, "IPO for Eagle Expected Shortly," *Puget Sound Business Journal,* January 24, 1992, p. 1.

——, "Seattle Entrepreneur Sprouts New Venture," *Business Journal-Portland,* January 29, 1990, p. 8.

Schober, William, "1994 Giants: Poised for Aggressive Growth," *Building Supply Home Centers,* February 1994, p. 40.

Szymanski, Jim, "Tukwila, Wash.-Based Eagle Hardware Scales Back Expansion Plans," *Knight-Ridder/Tribune Business News,* May 30, 1995, p. 53.

—Jeffrey L. Covell

# Ekco Group, Inc.

**98 Spit Brook Road**
**Nashua, New Hampshire 03062**
**U.S.A.**
**(603) 888-1212**
**Fax: (603) 888-1427**

*Public Company*
*Incorporated:* 1903 as Edward Katzinger Co.
*Employees:* 1,225
*Sales:* $277.1 million (1995)
*Stock Exchanges:* New York
*SICs:* 2879 Agricultural Chemicals, Not Elsewhere
Classified; 2392 House Furnishings, Except Curtains
and Draperies; 3089 Plastic Products, Not Elsewhere
Classified; 3469 Metal Stampings, Not Elsewhere
Classified; 3496 Miscellaneous Fabricated Wire
Products; 3991 Brooms and Brushes; 5023 House
Furnishings

Ekco Group, Inc. manufactures and markets a broad line of household products, including kitchenware and bakeware, molded plastic products, and pest-control and animal-care products, under the Ekco and other brand names. In the mid-1990s, Ekco billed itself the leading supplier of metal bakeware in the United States and the largest supplier of kitchen tools and gadgets in the United States.

## Family Enterprise Until 1945

Ekco was founded by Edward Katzinger, a journeyman tinsmith who emigrated from Austria to New York City in 1881 at the age of 18. He left his secure $25-a-week job as a master mechanic in a New York tinsmith shop to open a business in Chicago in 1888. Named the Edward Katzinger Co., this concern manufactured tin pans for commercial bakeries. By 1899 the company, which was always profitable, had a product line that included equipment for confectioners and ice cream manu-

facturers as well as bakeries. A five-story factory went up in 1906 and a seven-story addition in 1913.

Born over the shop in 1894, Edward Katzinger's son Arthur was an unruly child expelled from high school. He was packed off to a military school and returned, reformed, to become a 12-letter athlete and captain of the football, basketball, and track teams at Armour Institute (later the Illinois Institute of Technology), from where he graduated with a degree in mechanical engineering in 1916. He then joined his father's company as plant manager. He later said that, after the death of an older brother in 1919, his father "took me out of the factory and told me to run the company."

In 1923 the Katzingers built a new, up-to-date two-story factory on Chicago's Northwest Side. The first of 35 acquisitions in the next 35 years—that would make Ekco the world's largest manufacturer of nonelectric housewares—took place in 1927, when the Katzingers purchased the August Maag Co., a small Baltimore bakeware manufacturing firm. Two years later the company entered the kitchenware business when it purchased the A & J Manufacturing Co. of Binghamton, New York, the largest producer of kitchen tools. During the next three years—the first three years of the Great Depression—Ekco expanded its Chicago manufacturing complex and moved the A & J facility there, replaced the Baltimore plant with a replica of the Chicago one, and tripled its earnings. When Edward Katzinger died in 1939, Arthur Katzinger assumed the presidency. By the time the company went public in 1945 under the name Ekco Products Co., using the initials of the founder, the founder's son had changed his last name to Keating and had assumed position as chairman of the board.

Ekco continued to grow by acquisition during these years. It purchased Geneva Cutlery Co. of Geneva, New York, in 1934 and formed a 69 percent Ekco-owned English subsidiary called Platers and Stampers, Ltd. in 1937 to make a line of housewares there. Ekco purchased Sta-Bright Products Corp., a New Haven, Connecticut, producer of stainless-steel cutlery, in 1943; E.L. Tebbets Spool Co., a manufacturer of wooden handles, rolling pins, spools, and toy parts in Locke Mills, Maine, in 1945; and Massillon Aluminum Co., an Ohio manufacturer of cooking utensils, in 1945. Net sales rose from $5.4 million in 1938 to $19.5 million in 1944 and net income from $357,000 to $1.06 million over this period.

### Ekco Products Co. 1945–1965

Armed with funds raised by the sale of stock to the public, Ekco Products made acquisitions at an even more rapid pace in the decade following the end of World War II. Among the companies purchased were Murdock Metal Products of Chicago; Byesville Products Co. of Byesville, Ohio; Bergen Forge Co. of Bergen, New Jersey; Diamond Silver Co. of Lambertville, New Jersey; Minute Mop Co. of Chicago; Republic Stamping and Enameling Co. of Canton, Ohio; Adams Plastic Co. of Holyoke, Massachusetts; Autoyre Co. of Oakville, Connecticut; and Shore Machine Corp. of New York City. A Canadian subsidiary was established in 1947 and a Mexican one in 1948. In 1949 Ekco organized the National Glaco Chemical Co. to handle the treatment and coating of commercial baking pans under a new process. Prudential Housewares, Inc., a house-to-house selling organization later renamed Ekco Home Products, was created in 1947. By the late 1950s it was said that Ekco produced some 65 percent of all kitchen tools and 40 percent of all kitchen and table cutlery.

By 1960 Ekco Products, including its subsidiaries, was manufacturing and selling a wide variety of housewares and builders' hardware items, commercial baking pans, and industrial food-handling equipment. Principal trade names were Ekco, Ekco Eterna, Ekcoloy, Ekco-Autoyre, Flint, Geneva Forge, Waverly Edge, Berkeley, Kennatrack, Worley, McClintock, and Pakkawood. The company's divisions alone had 11 factories in the United States. Among subsidiaries, National Glaco alone had 15 manufacturing plants. The English subsidiary, renamed Prestige Group Ltd. in 1956, not only operated five factories in England but two in Germany. Other foreign subsidiaries had plants in Toronto, Mexico City, and Sydney, Australia. Net sales rose from $31.5 million in 1950 to $85.2 million in 1960; net income increased from $2.9 million to $4.8 million in that period.

Ekco also entered new fields during these years. With the Aluminum Co. of America (Alcoa) it formed Ekco-Alcoa Containers, Inc. in 1955 to supply rigid aluminum-foil containers, particularly to processors of frozen foods and for TV dinners. Ekco purchased its partner's interest in 1962 and changed the company's name to Ekco Containers, Inc. In 1963 Ekco formed a joint venture with Haustrups Fabriker Co. to establish an aluminum-foil container company in Denmark. The following year Prestige established a joint venture with McGraw-Edison to manufacture and sell small appliances in England and export them to the rest of the world outside North America. Also in 1964, Ekco Products Imports Co. was created to sell cordless electric toothbrushes, shoe polishers, and other goods manufactured in Europe and the Far East to distributors in the United States.

Ekco containers accounted for 13 percent of overall company sales in 1964. The builders and industrial division accounted for 14 percent, and the bakery and chemicals division for 11 percent. A 1964 *Financial World* study reported that while each major Ekco domestic and international division was

doing well, the international operations were showing greater growth than the domestic divisions. Ekco had record sales and earnings of $117 million and $7.6 million, respectively, that year, with an excellent 17 percent return on shareholders' equity. However, the company was running out of other firms to acquire without the likely prospect of antitrust suits. In 1965 it agreed to be purchased by American Home Products Corp. for an estimated $145 million worth of stock.

### Under American Home Products 1965–1984

In becoming the Ekco Housewares division of American Home Products, the former Ekco Products entered into a very different corporate culture from its own. This giant conglomerate was, in theory, highly decentralized, with 11 autonomous subsidiaries in 1970 and a tiny corporate staff. But almost all non-budgeted expenditures of $250 or more had to be explained in a special report to headquarters, examined by a corporate finance committee, and personally approved by the company's chairman and president. According to a later account of the housewares division under American Home Products, "a series of presidents and other executives came and went before they could even find the executive washroom." In 1967 the housewares division's $124.8 million in sales was 12 percent of American Home's total.

By 1972 the housewares division had been divided into three operations: Ekco Products Inc., Ekco Housewares Co., and The Prestige Group Limited. Ekco Products provided commercial baking pans and service, aluminum containers, food-handling systems, and industrial coatings and closing machinery. Ekco Housewares marketed cookware, cutlery, kitchen tools, tableware, and accessories under a number of brand names, such as Ekco, Flint, Granny, Criteria, Geneva Forge, and Berkeley. Prestige Group was the largest nonelectrical housewares manufacturer outside of the United States. Combined net sales for these units was estimated at $186 million in 1971, or 13 percent of the parent company's total and 22 percent of its sales outside the United States.

### Privately Held 1984–1987

American Home Products sold its housewares operations in 1984 to concentrate on its prescription-drug business. Its 73 percent stake in Prestige Group was sold for about $51 million to Gallaher Ltd., a British-based unit of American Brands Inc. Ekco Products was sold to the Packaging Corp. of America, a unit of Tenneco Inc. Ekco Housewares was sold for $120 million to a group led by Gibbons, Green, Van Amerongen Ltd., a New York investment-banking firm specializing in leveraged buyouts that retained a 15 percent interest in the firm. Ekco Products and Ekco Housewares had combined sales of $330 million and pretax profits of about $55 million in 1983.

Ekco Housewares Co., with about $200 million in annual sales at this time, had many strengths. The company held 40 percent of the U.S. market in bakeware and more than 20 percent in kitchen utensils, which almost certainly ranked it tops in this field. Its market segment was far lower in cookware, cutlery, and flatware, which it mostly marketed door to door in the United States or sold to overseas outlets. Based in Franklin Park, Illinois, a suburb of Chicago, it was placed under the direction of Finn Schjorring, a Dane with Canadian citizenship who vowed to "reestablish the company to its former glory." Interviewed by *HFD*, Schjorring, a former American Home Products manager who had joined Ekco Housewares in 1983 as a consultant, said, "I feel that American housewares [manufacturers] have ignored the proper presentation of merchandise to the consumers to entice them to want to buy. We simply have not been entrepreneurial nor creative enough in our approach. . . . Food-preparation products should be aesthetically pleasing, and we want to bring contemporary concepts in the way of design. Europe is where the trends are born, and we will bring some of that innovation over here."

A year later, in another *HFD* interview, Schjorring was even more outspoken. "It's hard to believe," he said, "but the products Ekco and other American manufacturers are turning out today aren't much different from what we were making a century ago. In kitchen tools and other products, the U.S. market is hopelessly old-fashioned, uninteresting, and unimaginative. As a result, all of our businesses here are underdeveloped." In less than a year's time he installed a new management team with an equity stake in the firm, designed several new product lines, and moved aggressively to step up advertising and marketing. He cut back the sales force, signing distribution agreements with 68 food brokers to serve the U.S. grocery-store trade, which accounted for about half of company sales, in order to devote more attention to the other accounts. He also sold the company's home-security division. The Chicago plant, among the largest of Ekco's seven factories, was closed in 1986.

New products launched by Schjorring included bakeware with a coating 70 percent "slipperier" than the old one to release food better and clean easier, a nonstick broiler pan, and a Nova line of European-styled kitchen tools in bright primary colors. He indicated that Ekco would become more prominent in department stores and other better retail channels as new lines of cookware and cutlery were developed. "There is no reason kitchen utensils should be stuck away in a drawer," he told *HFD*. "They can hang on a wall and enhance the decor of a home."

### Sold Again in 1987

Schjorring did not have a chance to realize his ambitions, however, for Ekco Housewares was sold in 1987 for about $124 million. The buyer was Centronics Corp., a shell corporation formerly known as Centronics Data Computer Corp., a manufacturer of computer printers that used the proceeds of about $85 million from the sale of this business to buy Ekco Housewares. In 1988 Centronics, based in Nashua, New Hampshire, changed its name to Ekco Group, Inc. Later that year Ekco Group sold its Canadian industrial container business to Packaging Corp. of America for about $12 million.

The new owners almost immediately faced a challenge from a group, including Sonar Partners, L.P., that held more than eight percent of the shares and wanted to sell the company, distributing the proceeds to the shareholders. Management tightened its defenses against a possible takeover and bought out the dissidents in March 1989, paying $5.4 million for their shares.

Ekco Group consisted, in 1988, of Ekco Housewares and Ekco Canada, with annual sales of $130 million, of which the latter accounted for 21 percent. Ekco Housewares, the leading nonstick bakeware supplier, was best known for its Baker's Secret brand and did more than half its business in bakeware, although also selling kitchen tools and gadgets. Robert Stein, president and chief executive officer of Ekco Group, said that a new emphasis had been placed on improving on-time delivery rates. In early 1989 Ekco Group acquired Woodstream Corp., a manufacturer and distributor of plastic storage cases such as fishing-tackle boxes, tool boxes, and gun cases for about $25.7 million. Later in the year it bought the Victor mouse- and rat-trap line from McGill Metal Products Co.

The acquisition of Woodstream enabled Ekco Group's revenues to rise from $135 million in 1988 to $166 million in 1989, and net income from $3.1 million to $4.1 million. In 1990 revenues fell to $162 million and net income to $1.8 million. However, the fall in income reflected a restructuring charge of $3.6 million, and the company managed to lower its debt from about $100 million to below $90 million. Revenues rose to $166.7 million in 1991, and net income to a record $10.1 million.

Under Stein's direction, Ekco Group closed six plants and reduced the work force by 60 percent. He realigned the sales force from being organized by product division to organization by distribution channel. One group was assigned to supermarkets, a second to hardware and mass-market outlets like Kmart and Wal-Mart, and the third to export markets. A number of studies on consumer attitudes were conducted on a spectrum of issues from quality to value, with the object, Stein said, to "be the total service-leader-supplier, so that price is not the only difference." Employees were, at every level, faced with a much greater amount of both responsibility and accountability, with top executives limited to decisions purely strategic in nature.

Ekco Group acquired the animal-care products division of Beacon Industries, Inc. in December 1991. A month later it completed the acquisition of Frem Corp., a manufacturer of molded-plastic storage components, for $18.6 million in cash and stock. In 1993 it purchased Kellogg Brush Manufacturing Co., maker of brooms, brushes, and mops, for $33.9 million in cash and stock. Ekco also assumed $13.1 million of Kellogg's debts. The management of both Frem and Kellogg was retained.

Ekco Group's net revenues reached $206.6 million in 1992. Net income that year was $8.6 million. In 1993 net revenues, enhanced by the Kellogg acquisition, rose to $246.4 million, but after a $3.2-million accounting charge for postretirement and employee benefits, the company incurred a deficit of $988,000. The restructuring included a cut of about ten percent in the company's work force, most of it in the Ekco Housewares division. In 1994 net revenues rose to $267 million, and net income was a record $11.4 million. For 1995 the figures were $277.1 million and $8 million, respectively. The long-term debt was $132.7 million at end of September 1995.

In 1995 Ekco Group was manufacturing and marketing a broad line of metal bakeware for home use under the Baker's Secret and Ekco trademarks. It was selling over 1,000 kitchen tools and gadgets under the Ekco and Ekco Pro trademarks and also was marketing stainless-steel and carbon-steel cutlery and stainless-steel flatware, mixing bowls, and colanders. Some of these kitchenware products also were being manufactured and assembled by Ekco. Ekco also was manufacturing and marketing a broad line of cleaning products and nontoxic pest-control and small animal-care and -control products. It was also manufacturing and marketing injection-molded plastic housewares, office, and juvenile products. Its customers included the 30 largest mass merchandisers in the United States, including Wal-Mart and Kmart—its biggest clients—and more than 90 percent of all U.S. supermarkets.

Bakeware accounted for 29 percent of Ekco's sales in 1995. Kitchenware followed, with 26 percent; cleaning products came to 19.5 percent; pest- and animal-control products to 12 percent; molded plastics to ten percent; and VIA, an international housewares subsidiary formed in 1994, accounted for the remaining 3.5 percent.

In 1995 Ekco owned seven manufacturing and distribution plants in the United States and an office and distribution facility in Canada. It was leasing eight facilities, including executive offices in Nashua, New Hampshire, administrative offices for the housewares division in Franklin Park, Illinois, a manufacturing plant in Mexico, and offices in Great Britain.

### Principal Subsidiaries

Ecko Housewares, Inc.; Ekco Canada, Inc.; Frem Corporation; Kellogg Brush Manufacturing Co.; Woodstream Corp.; Cleaning Specialty Company; Wright-Bernet, Inc.; B. VIA International Housewares, Inc.; Ekco Consumer Products Ltd. (U.K.).

### Further Reading

"American Home: A Reticent Giant," *Business Week,* March 21, 1970, pp. 76, 82.

"American Home, Ekco Directors Agree on Merger," *Wall Street Journal,* July 30, 1965, p. 5.

"Arthur Keating of Ekco Is Dead," *New York Times,* December 14, 1967, p. 47.

Bedingfield, Robert E., "Personality: Executive from Old School," *New York Times,* July 30, 1961, Sec. 3, p. 3.

Benson, Tracy, "EKCO Caters to Customers," *Industry Week,* June 3, 1991, pp. 11–12.

Byrne, Harlan S., "Ekco Group," *Barron's,* May 6, 1991, pp. 42–43.

Casey, Lisa Ann, "Ekco Group to Continue Acquiring in Addition to Improving Internally," *HFD,* January 30, 1989, p. 96.

*Ekco Housewares Company,* Franklin Park, Ill.: Ekco Housewares Co., company document.

"Ekco's Electrical Enterprise," *Forbes,* March 15, 1965, p. 46.

Murphy, H. Lee, "Ekco's New European Flair," *HFD,* July 22, 1985, pp. 50, 52.

Troy, Terry, "Ekco Aims to Purchase Kellogg," *HFD,* January 4, 1993, p. 74.

——, "Ekco-ing SUCCESS," *HFD,* February 24, 1992, pp. 60, 64–65.

Waldholz, Michael, "American Home Expects to Complete Sale of Ekco Units," *Wall Street Journal,* May 3, 1984, p. 14.

Zapfel, Dolph, "CEO's Quest: Making Ekco Sound Again," *HFD,* December 21, 1984, p. 37.

—Robert Halasz

# Everex Systems, Inc.

48431 Milmont Drive
Fremont, California 94538
U.S.A.
(510) 498-1111
Fax: (510) 651-0728

*Wholly Owned Subsidiary of Formosa Plastics Group (Taiwan)*
*Incorporated:* 1983 as Everex Systems, Inc.
*Employees:* 900
*Sales:* $503 million (1992; purchased by Formosa in 1993)
*SICs:* 3571 Electronic Computers; 3577 Computer Peripheral Equipment, Not Elsewhere Classified

Headquartered in Fremont, California, Everex Systems Inc. designs and manufactures Pentium-based computer systems, multimedia systems, and related peripheral devices. Everex grew quickly during the late 1980s before filing for bankruptcy in the early 1990s. The company was purchased in 1993 by Formosa Plastics Group, the $14 billion multinational conglomerate controlled by Taiwan's Wang family.

## Seeds of Success: The Young Founder

Everex was created by Steve Hui (pronounced hoy), an engineer, entrepreneur, and son of a former Chinese peasant. It was Hui's father, P. S., who gave him the determination to succeed. P. S. Hui had left his small village when he was 13 years old because his parents could no longer afford to support him and his brother. The brothers were sent to a city, where they eked out a living washing clothes and became involved in the Seventh Day Adventist Church. P. S. struggled to qualify for one of the handful of scholarships offered by the church, and was able to attend a Chinese university. He became a surgeon and, because of exemplary service during the Korean War, was one of the few Chinese allowed to relocate to Hong Kong after the conflict.

Steve Hui would later attribute his discipline and drive to the example set by his father. Hui was able to attend college in the United States, where he earned his mechanical engineering degree at the University of Texas. He worked in the oil-testing division of Schlumberger for a few years before moving back to Hong Kong, where he married his high school sweetheart and took a job with a Chinese electronics company. A few years later he won a scholarship to the University of California Berkeley. He moved back to the United States to get a bachelors degree in electrical engineering and a masters degree in mechanical engineering. To make ends meet during school, his wife sold some of her family heirlooms. After graduating, he worked a few years at Amdahl Corp. and Storage Technology Computer Research before deciding in the early 1980s to strike out on his own.

Hui was determined to make his mark, and he believed that building his own electronics company was the way to do it. Specifically, he believed that the burgeoning personal computer (PC) industry offered much potential and complemented his background. Desktop personal computers were just beginning to penetrate the mass market at the time, and sales of IBM-compatible machines were growing. So Hui designed, built, and began to market his own IBM-compatible PC, a clone of the popular IBM AT computer. PC sales soared during the mid-1980s and Hui emerged as one of the leading producers of IBM-compatible PCs in the United States.

Hui's early efforts were funded through contacts in his native Hong Kong. While working for the Chinese electronics firm during the mid-1970s he had sold an automatic printing circuit board etching system to a mid-size Hong Kong electronics firm. The company was owned by the Wong family. The sale was important because it was one of the first systems of its type to be installed in the country. Hui initially had trouble getting the system to operate, but he parlayed the problems into a positive relationship with the Wongs. "We couldn't get it to run properly. By the second week I felt so terrible. And it got worse," Hui recalled in the *Business Journal-San Jose.* "The old man of the Wong family was so nice to me." In fact, the Wongs offered Hui a job after he installed the system.

## The Startup

It was to the Wongs that Hui turned for help in getting his company started. With their assistance, he was able to round up about $300,000 in startup capital. He used that cash to develop and start marketing his first PC. Hui incorporated the venture in 1983 as Everex Systems, Inc., choosing the name Everex to indicate "forever excellent". He was joined by cofounders John Lee and Wayne Cheung. The company initially found success selling its computers to resellers, which marketed the systems primarily through mail-order channels under their own brand name. Sales quickly climbed into the tens of millions of dollars. Hui drew from that success to branch out into the sale of peripheral devices that integrated Everex's proprietary controller boards, which acted as the brains of the devices. By 1986 the company was generating revenues of $63 million annually, about $3.6 million of which was netted as income.

From the start, Hui chose to model his venture after successful U.S. companies. For example, he had learned from his American classmates that they didn't like to work for Chinese-run businesses because they were typically family-oriented. So Hui chose not to hire any family members to help him manage the company. He also styled the company's headquarters after those of early Silicon Valley enterprises; the office was basically one giant room without walls, with desks pushed close together and the top executives, including Hui, sitting with the rest of the employees. The goal was to create an atmosphere of open communication, teamwork, and excitement. That atmosphere became increasingly important as the company's work force swelled, from less than 300 in 1985 to more than 1,000 in 1987, and later to more than 2,000.

Hui's savvy management strategy combined with a surging PC market propelled rampant growth at Everex throughout the mid-1980s and into the late 1980s. By mid-1987 Everex was selling its IBM-compatible PC systems through a network of "satellite" retailers that marketed the systems through mail order under a dozen different brand names. Those retailers were shipping thousands of computers every week. Furthermore, Hui had carved a profitable niche in the expanding peripherals market, selling a broad line of computer peripherals that incorporated Everex's controllers. Going into 1988, Everex was selling a total of more than 30 different products, including tape-backup systems and hard disks. In tape back-up systems, in fact, Everex had become the global leader with more than 50 percent of the world market.

Because its products were marketed under different brand names, Everex, despite its notable presence in the PC industry, was relatively unknown to most consumers. Importantly, though, Everex had become a respected name in financial markets. Indeed, in 1986 Everex attracted a fat $18 million in investment capital with the help of investment banking firm Goldman, Sachs; it was the largest private placement of funds in the nation that year. Early in 1987, moreover, Merrill Lynch's

venture fund contributed another $750,000. That left the Wong family and its Wong International Holdings with a stake in Everex of roughly 38 percent.

### Rise and Fall

Hui used the cash to develop new products, but also to purchase other companies and technology. Early in 1987, for example, Everex bought Signet Communications Corp., a vendor of computer networking products. Hui also set up a subsidiary called Joy Systems Inc., which customized the company's computers for mail-order sale under the Joy brand name. New products and ongoing market growth helped Everex to more than double sales in 1987 to about $160 million, about $8.6 million of which was netted as income. Those figures climbed to $267 million and $10.5 million, respectively, in 1988. In 1989, moreover, Everex pushed worldwide sales to $377 million as profit surpassed $21 million, making Everex an emerging leader in the IBM-compatible PC business.

Everex kept a relatively low public profile during the 1980s, but decided in 1990 to start boosting its exposure. "I don't know why, but it just seems like whenever I'd start reading about a company in the papers, that company was at its peak and on the way down," Hui told the *Business Journal-San Jose*. "I certainly hope that's not the case here." Those prophetic words signaled a PC industry shakeout that would soon leave Everex and many of its competitors gasping. Although Everex continued to post sales and profit gains into the new decade, the dynamics of the PC industry were changing in a way that did not complement the company's strategy. In fact, Everex's days of prosperity were numbered.

Despite sales and profit gains, Hui and fellow executives realized that Everex faced an uphill battle going into the 1990s. PC sales were slowing and major computer manufacturers were slashing prices and willing to exact minute profit margins in return for market share. Industry consolidation would be the result, and it was clear that only the largest, most efficient competitors would prosper in what had effectively become a commodity business. Late in 1990, Chief Executive Hui and Executive Vice-president Lee decided to take a 25 percent pay cut for the 1991 year, while other Everex executives agreed to a ten percent pay reduction. Those reductions were a prelude to big labor cutbacks—Everex's work force had swelled to 2,500 by 1990—and cost reduction efforts throughout the early 1990s.

Although Everex's problems were partly attributable to PC industry turbulence, they were also the result of a weak market strategy. Critics believed that the company had lost focus, moving too quickly from its core PC business to chase a variety of related niches such as networking and peripherals. Among other far-flung projects, Everex was working to develop an advanced computerized drafting table, clones for Apple Macintosh and Sun Microsystems workstations, and its own microprocessor. Announcing his ambition, Hui told a *Forbes* reporter in 1989 that "In the next five years many pages will be written in the history of the computer industry, and more than a few of them will be written about Everex."

As it shifted emphasis to other numerous projects, Everex's PC clone business lagged and fell prey to more focused competitors like Dell and Compaq. When competition in the PC business intensified, Everex's clone business stumbled and cash flow from its other businesses was insufficient to support the entire enterprise. After posting sales and profits of $437 million and $24.5 million in 1990, Everex's revenue leveled and the company suffered an embarrassing $48 million net loss for the 1991 fiscal year ending in August 1991. And sales and profits were slipping going into 1992.

Realizing the urgency of the situation, Everex's board of directors decided early in 1991 to hire Harold Clark to assist Hui in managing the company. Clark, who was appointed president and chief operating officer, was experienced in turning around troubled companies. Under Clark's direction, Everex eliminated projects that were draining cash and aggressively restructured, shedding all but 900 of its workers by late 1992. In addition, Clark tried to engineer the acquisition of PC maker Northgate Computer Corp., which would have given Everex a ready made mail-order distribution channel for its PCs. The effort ultimately failed, however, as Everex's balance sheet worsened. For the 1992 year, in fact, Everex suffered a loss of roughly $100 million on sales of about $433 million.

Everex's situation continued to deteriorate. Both Hui and Clark resigned in December of 1992, and Everex's board hired Jack Kenney, an executive experienced in high-tech turnarounds, to head the failing enterprise. Less than one month later, Everex, unable to meet its debt obligations, filed for Chapter 11 bankruptcy protection from its creditors. Kenney then went to work trying to restructure the company's debt and renew its solvency. He shed many of the company's remaining product lines, including printers, scanners, and Macintosh products, and focused Everex on its core line of 486-microprocessor PCs. He also continued to cut unnecessary costs and eliminate workers.

### New Ownership in the 1990s

Before Kenney could complete the turnaround, Everex was bought out by a consortium of Taiwanese companies. In November of 1993 the Yside Investment Group, a subsidiary of the Formosa Plastics Group, purchased the company and all of its patents, products, and trade names. Yside changed its name to Everex, and Everex became one of several high-tech holdings in the portfolio of Taiwan's vaunted Wang family. The Wang family had built a $10 billion multinational conglomerate by 1993, which had started years earlier with Chairman Y. C. Wang's Formosa Plastics concern. Y. C.'s daughter, Charlene, had started a PC company in the mid-1980s that had become a $600 million manufacturer by 1993. That success prompted the Wang family to begin assembling a portfolio of high-technology companies.

Everex made a nice addition to the Wangs' group of companies, because, for only $2.3 million, it gave the Wang's an immediate presence in the United States. Although Everex's revenue base had eroded to about $150 million annually by the time Formosa bought it, the company was still under contract to supply about $2 billion worth of equipment to the U.S. Government. Furthermore, Everex possessed certain technologies that were of interest to other Wang companies. Y. C. Wang appointed his 36-year-old daughter, Cher, to the company's helm. The Wangs' long-term goal was to make their high-tech group of companies a global leader in information processing.

Under the wing of its new, well-heeled owner, Everex's managers whipped the company's product line into shape during the mid-1990s, shedding antiquated and unprofitable products and emphasizing a newly developed line of computer systems and servers based on new Pentium-processor technology. Going into 1996, those products included its new DX4 PC systems, Pentium-processor notebooks, and STEP multimedia systems. The company had also developed a line of networking products and systems. Most of the Everex's products were still being sold through resellers and other nonretail distribution channels.

### Further Reading

Aragon, Lawrence, "Everex Announces New Chief Executive Officer and Chief Financial Officer," *Business Journal-San Jose,* December 14, 1992.

Aragon, Lawrence, with David Barry and Pete Barlas, "Everex Files 11, Drops Space, Hits Valley Creditors," *Business Journal-San Jose,* January 11, 1993, p. 9.

"Asian Conglomerate Purchases Embattled Everex," *PC Week,* October 18, 1993, p. 154.

Carlsen, Clifford, "Everex Proposal Crashes, Burns," *San Francisco Business Times,* July 10, 1992, p. 1.

——, "Everex Systems Seeks $40 Million in Stock Offering," *San Francisco Business Times,* June 29, 1987, p. 1.

Davis, Joe, "Everex Systems Inc. Becomes Subsidiary of Formosa Plastics Group," *Business Wire,* November 11, 1993.

Engardio, Pete, and Margaret Dawson, "A New High-Tech Dynasty?," *Business Week,* August 15, 1994, pp. 90–91.

*Everex Corporate Profile,* Fremont, Calif.: Everex Corp., May 7, 1996.

Glitman, Russell, "Everex Systems Gain Fortune without Fame," *PC Week,* June 2, 1987, p. 167.

Goldman, James S., and Michael Krey, "Everex, with Its Sales Slowing, Plans 250 Layoffs," *Business Journal-San Jose,* January 14, 1991, p. 11.

Krey, Michael, "Executives at Everex Slash Their Own Salaries," *Business Journal-San Jose,* December 17, 1990, p. 4.

——, "Steve Hui: His Quest to Be a Major Force in Business Was Honed by Father's Example," *Business Journal-San Jose,* February 5, 1990, p. 12.

Moore, Mark, "New CEO Kenney Charts Recovery Course for Everex," *PC Week,* May 17, 1993, p. 117.

Pitta, Julie, "Deserted by Destiny," *Forbes,* February 1, 1993, p. 75.

Whalen, Michael, "Everex Announces New Chief Executive Officer and Chief Financial Officer," *PR Newswire,* December 28, 1992.

—Dave Mote

# Fabri-Centers of America Inc.

**5555 Darrow Road**
**Hudson, Ohio 44236-4054**
**U.S.A.**
**(216) 656-2600**
**Fax: (216) 463-6675**

*Public Company*
*Incorporated:* 1951 as Cleveland Fabric Shops, Inc.
*Employees:* 17,600
*Sales:* $677.28 million (1995)
*Stock Exchanges:* New York
*SICs:* 5949 Sewing, Needlework & Piece Goods

With sales of $677.28 million, nearly 1,000 fabric stores in 48 states, and an estimated 18 percent of the retail fabric market, Fabri-Centers of America Inc. is the country's largest fabric retailer. The company's Jo-Ann Fabrics and Crafts, Cloth World, and New York Fabrics and Crafts superstores carry wide selections of fabric, notions, and craft goods. The chain boasts nearly double the sales and locations of its nearest competitor, Hancock Fabrics. Led by third-generation president and CEO Alan Rosskamm, descendants of the founding families continued to own about one-fourth of the publicly-traded firm's stock into the mid-1990s. Having survived a dramatic shakeout in the retail fabric industry, Fabri-Centers set its sights on becoming a "category killer" in the late 1990s.

## Founding and Early Development

The chain was founded in 1943 by two German immigrant families, the Rohrbachs and the Reichs. The Reichs had an importing business dealing in Swiss cheese, anchovy paste and pickles, and they invited their friends to start selling fabric in their suburban Cleveland storefront. When Berthold Rohrbach died that same year, his 30-year-old daughter, Alma Zimmerman, went to work full-time at the store with Hilda Reich. Hilda's daughter, Betty, joined the family affair in 1947, and she and Alma opened the chain's second store in Cleveland soon thereafter.

Betty married Martin Rosskamm in 1948, and he quit his upper-level management position at a knitting mill to join the fabric company. Cofounder Hilda Reich continued to supervise a Fabri-Center store until her death at the age of 87 in 1986. Alma, her husband, Freddy, and Betty continued to serve on the board of directors into the mid-1990s, but it was Martin Rosskamm who became a driving force behind the chain's continuous expansion throughout the Midwest. Seeking a less geographically exclusive name to take the chain into the Pittsburgh area, the families created Jo-Ann by merging two of their children's names: Jo from Joan Zimmerman and Ann from Jackie Ann Rosskamm. Fabri-Centers' small specialty stores, which were often located in the regional shopping malls that sprung up in the postwar era, competed well with the fabric departments of larger general merchandise stores. The chain incorporated as Cleveland Fabric Centers, Inc. in February 1951, changing its name to Fabri-Centers of America, Inc. in 1968 and going public the following year.

## Facing a Changing Market in the 1970s and 1980s

The retail fabric market began to decline in the 1970s, as more women went to work outside the home, and home sewing declined. At the same time, however, department stores and mass merchandisers were eliminating their fabric and notions departments, reducing the net number of retail fabric outlets by almost half from 1977 to 1983. This market contraction allowed Fabri-Centers and other leading specialty chains to continue to capture sales and share despite the overall market reduction. Top executives would look back on the 1970s as "glory days," when growth was relatively easy and profitable. By 1983, Fabri-Centers boasted over 600 stores under the Jo-Ann, Showcase of Fine Fabrics, and House of Fine Fabrics names in 33 states. As president and CEO through 1985, Martin Rosskamm guided a doubling of Fabri-Centers' annual sales, from $120.9 million in fiscal 1979 (ended January 31 of that year) to $226.9 million in fiscal 1985. Profits increased robustly during that period as well, from $4 million to $7.2 million, and the chain's share of the national retail fabric market increased to over 5.5 percent as it advanced to the number-two rank.

This period lulled the chain into a false sense of security that would come back to haunt it in the mid- and late-1980s. In a 1995 interview with *Financial World*'s Lore Croghan, Martin's son Alan Rosskamm acknowledged that "We were out-

**Company Perspectives:**

*We will not be satisfied to rest on our accomplishments. Our mission is to provide our customers with the fabric and craft-related products they need to fulfill their creative ambitions. Our goal is to be the leader in our industry.*

assorted, outpromoted and undersold. . . . There were fundamental industry changes that we had been slow to recognize.''

That's when the company found its profit margins squeezed by rising costs and a maturing market. Fabric retailers had historically been recession-resistant—stung by the high cost of retail clothing, many women flocked to fabric stores to make their own clothes during economic downturns—but when the economy went sour in the early 1980s, manufacturers of ready-to-wear apparel slashed their own prices, eradicating any ''homemade'' savings and taking the wind out of fabric retailers' sails. Rampant price-cutting in the retail fabric industry exacerbated the effects of the early 1980s recession. When Alan Rosskamm succeeded his father as president and CEO of the company in 1985, Fabri-Centers' net profit margin was less than .5 percent. While sales continued to rise, from $209.4 million in fiscal 1984 to $239.4 million in fiscal 1987, net income declined from $4.5 million to $1.7 million. The slide culminated in a net loss of $4.9 million on $266.7 million sales in fiscal 1988. It was the first loss in the chain's 45-year history. The new president admitted to Delinda Karle of the *Cleveland Plain Dealer* in May 1988 that ''All of a sudden, our business started shrinking and our expenses started rising.''

### Transformation and Diversification in the 1990s

Rosskamm launched a multifaceted turnaround plan that year. His was a risky proposition attempted by many of his rivals with varying degrees of success in the late 1980s and early 1990s. A key to the strategy was a wholesale move of its stores from high-rent, relatively small shops in malls to large ''superstores'' in strip malls. In fiscal 1992 alone, Fabri-Centers opened 121 superstores (with up to 15,000 square feet of space) and closed 108 outmoded locations.

However, Fabri-Centers wasn't the only chain with growth on its mind—its six major competitors were also adding dozens of big stores, leading inexorably to a glut of the mature market. Casualties of these hard-fought ''fabric wars'' began to mount: by the mid-1990s, only Fabri-Centers and Hancock Fabrics were left standing. Both House of Fabrics and Piece Goods Shops were mired in bankruptcy, and many of the other former leaders were either bought out or liquidated.

Fabri-Centers came out on top but not without its share of bruises and scars. In an effort to diversify from the stagnant fabric market, which stood at about $4 billion throughout the late 1980s and early 1990s, the company launched Cargo Express, a chain of specialty housewares, in 1984. Spearheaded by Alan Rosskamm, this discount chain sold cutlery, stemware, glassware and other tableware in 18 stores by 1988. In spite of

its growth, the concept didn't record an annual profit until fiscal 1990, and Rosskamm characterized the business as ''a break-even venture'' accounting for less than 3 percent of Fabri-Centers' overall sales in 1992. Heavy discounting and intense competition in the category forced Fabri-Centers to put the 41-store operation on the selling block in 1993. Unable to find a buyer, the executives liquidated the inventory and closed the stores in 1994, taking a $5.2 million loss on the transaction.

Cargo Express' protracted failure (combined with the generally poor condition of the retail fabric industry) contributed to a sharp and rapid decline in Fabri-Centers' stock price. The company's stock fell from a high of $47.25 in January 1992, when Fabri-Centers announced record high earnings of $17.5 million, down to less than $13 by that July. Before the year was out, Standard & Poor's had lowered its rating of Fabri-Centers' paper to junk bond status.

CEO Rosskamm reacted quickly, cutting salaries on a sliding scale and eliminating some administrative staffers. Other more fundamental changes that had already been instituted as part of the turnaround program of the late 1980s would be the factors that kept Fabri-Centers at the top of the fabric game in the mid-1990s. Efficiency efforts included construction of a new distribution center and creation of a state-of-the-art computer system that linked operations from the point of sale to the warehouse. From 1987 to 1990, these efforts helped reduce overhead by 20 percent, from 48 percent of sales to 40 percent of sales. The chain also experimented with deep discount Best Fabric Outlets, aired its first television commercials, and launched a custom drapery business.

Fabri-Centers also found a profitable and logical diversification niche in the crafting boom of the 1990s. The craft segment, encompassing everything from seasonal and holiday decorations to home decor, multiplied from $2 billion in 1990 to more than $10 billion by 1995. Along with several other industry observers, CEO Rosskamm attributed the boom to the ''cocooning'' trend that found families spending more time at home. Craft goods contributed nearly one-third of Fabri-Centers' annual sales by that time.

### The Rise to the Top

Fabri-Centers solidified its position at the top of the retail fabric heap with the 1994 acquisition of fourth-ranking Cloth World's 343 stores from Brown Group Inc. The $100 million cash purchase fleshed out Fabri-Centers' presence in the southern United States, bringing it to 48 states. The transaction increased the chain's debt (and brought a revisitation of Standard & Poor's ire), but it also positioned Fabri-Centers to become a ''category killer:'' a destination store whose enormous selection and low prices draws customers. The chain expected to spend 18 months and up to $45 million to convert the Cloth World stores to the Fabri-Centers format (although they kept their well-established name). CEO Rosskamm called the deal ''an enormous growth opportunity for Fabri-Centers.''

The chain emerged from its industry's shakeout in relatively good health. Over the course of the early 1990s, Fabri-Centers' sales increased 83.3 percent, from $368.6 million in fiscal 1991 to $677.3 million in fiscal 1995. Profits, meanwhile, had not yet regained the $17.5 million record set in fiscal 1991, slipping to a low of $2.2 million in fiscal 1994 and amounting to $11.7 million in fiscal 1995. While Fabri-Centers was considerably larger than second-ranking Hancock Fabrics, according to a February 1995 article in *Barron's,* the Cleveland based chain had a higher debt load, lower market value, and lower profitability, proving that bigger is not always better. Alan Rosskamm, who was in his mid-40s in the mid-1990s, hoped to turn that adage on its ear in the latter years of the decade.

### Principal Subsidiaries

FCA Financial, Inc.; Fabri-Centers of South Dakota, Inc.; Fabri-Centers of California, Inc.; FCA of Ohio, Inc.

### Further Reading

Barnes, Jon, "Fabri-Centers' Turnaround Earns It Spot on Picks List," *Crain's Cleveland Business,* December 19, 1988, p. 23.

Brammer, Rhonda, "A Great Notion?" *Barron's,* February 13, 1995, p. 20.

Canedy, Dana, "Sewing Up the Market," *Cleveland Plain Dealer,* February 19, 1995, p. 1H.

Clark, Sandra. "Superstores Help Boost Net Sales at Fabric Chain," *Cleveland Plain Dealer,* May 19, 1992, p. 5G.

——, "Fabri-Centers to Expand Cargo Express Unit," *Cleveland Plain Dealer,* May 22, 1992, p. 2F.

——, "Fabri-Centers," *Cleveland Plain Dealer,* June 1, 1992, p. 28F.

——, "Fabri-Centers to Cut Staff, Salaries," *Cleveland Plain Dealer,* July 15, 1992, p. 1E.

——, "Fabric Chain Tries New Marketing Strategy," *Cleveland Plain Dealer,* September 2, 1992, p. 2H.

"Craft Industry Implemented Strong 1992 Sales Gains," *Discount Store News,* July 5, 1993, p. 86.

Croghan, Lore, "Shakeout at the Strip Mall," *Financial World,* May 23, 1995, p. 48.

Gerdel, Thomas W., "Fabri-Centers to Open Tableware Stores Here," *Cleveland Plain Dealer,* April 6, 1984, p. 6E.

——, "Fabri-Centers Led by Rosskamm Son," *Cleveland Plain Dealer,* June 4, 1985, p. 1D.

——, "Fabri-Centers Buying Cloth World Chain," *Cleveland Plain Dealer,* August 26, 1994, p. 1C.

Gleisser, Marcus, "Fabric Firm Adds Sewing Machines," *Cleveland Plain Dealer,* June 7, 1983, p. 3C.

——, "Fabri-Centers Moving into Tableware Sales," *Cleveland Plain Dealer,* December 1, 1984, p. 3B.

——, "Fabri-Centers Cuts 80 Jobs, Closes 8 Stores," *Cleveland Plain Dealer,* June 7, 1988, p. 6D.

——, "Store Expansions Aid Fabri-Centers Sales," *Cleveland Plain Dealer,* May 21, 1991, p. 2F.

——, "Softer Sales Hit Stock of Fabri-Centers," *Cleveland Plain Dealer,* June 4, 1992, p. 1D.

——, "Firms' Chief Downplays Stock Declines," *Cleveland Plain Dealer,* June 10, 1992, p. 2F.

Gordon, Mitchell, "A Special Place: Fabri-Centers Sees Bright Future as Department Stores Leave the Fold," *Barron's,* April 18, 1983, p. 59.

Hass, Nancy, "Fabri-Centers: Sewing Up the Market," *FW,* March 17, 1992, p. 18.

Hill, Miriam, "Fabri-Centers Wants to Unload Money-Losing Cargo Express," *Cleveland Plan Dealer,* March 9, 1993, p. 1F.

——, "Fabri-Centers President Unexpectedly Resigns Post," *Cleveland Plain Dealer,* April 6, 1993, p. 1F.

——, "Analysts Applaud Fabri-Centers' Move," *Cleveland Plain Dealer,* December 22, 1993, p. 2F.

Karle, Delinda, "Fabri Centers Patching Its Financial Quilt," *Cleveland Plain Dealer,* May 2, 1988, p. 6C.

Kuhn, Susan E., "Companies to Watch: Fabri-Centers of America," *Fortune,* July 30, 1990, p. 132.

Phillips, Stephen, "SEC Finds Fault with Fabri-Centers," *Cleveland Plain Dealer,* November 16, 1995, p. 1C.

——, "Store Crafting a Winning Strategy," *Cleveland Plain Dealer,* November 17, 1995, p. 1C.

Yerak, Rebecca, "Fabri-Centers Is Pleased with Cargo Express," *Cleveland Plain Dealer,* June 5, 1990, p. 8D.

——, "Superstores Hike Sales at Fabri-Centers," *Cleveland Plain Dealer,* May 17, 1991, p. 1E.

—April Dougal Gasbarre

# Fender Musical Instruments Company

**7975 North Hayden Road**
**Scottsdale, Arizona 85258**
**U.S.A.**
**(602) 596-9690**
**Fax: (602) 596-1384**

*Private Company*
*Incorporated:* 1959
*Employees:* 600
*Sales:* $160 million (1995)
*SICs:* 3931 Musical Instruments

In 1996, Fender Musical Instruments Company was the leading maker of solidbody electric guitars with an estimated 50 percent of the U.S. market. The company, which marketed products under several brand names, including Fender, Guild, Sunn, Floyd Rose, Rodriguez and Squier, produced an estimated 1,000 guitars a day in more than 100 different colors and finishes.

Clarence Leo Fender, born in 1909 near Anaheim, California, never learned to play the guitar, but the company he started in 1943, which would become the Fender Musical Instruments Company, and the guitars and amplifiers he designed changed the course of popular music. Fender's reputation for producing quality amplifiers and electric guitars was already established in country music when rock and roll began to sweep the nation in the late 1950s and early 1960s. When early rock stars, including Buddy Holly, Jimi Hendrix, Eric Clapton and The Beatles, began playing Fender's brightly-colored guitars and basses, the company's success was ensured.

### The Early Years

Fender began tinkering with radios in 1922, and by the time he graduated from high school in 1928, he was operating an amateur "ham" radio station. He was also building amplifiers and public-address systems, and from 1930 until 1938, he supplemented his income as a California civil-service accountant by renting his homemade equipment for dances, political rallies, and baseball games. In 1938, he opened a repair shop, Fender's Radio Service, in Fullerton, California. The shop also sold phonographs and repaired amplifiers.

In the early 1940s, Fender teamed up with Clayton "Doc" Kauffman, then a professional violinist and lap-steel guitarist, to design a phonograph record-changer. They sold their design for $5,000 and formed K&F Manufacturing. In 1943, K&F Manufacturing developed a new pickup for electric guitars in which the strings passed through the magnetic coil. K&F filed for a patent on the pickup in 1944, which was granted in 1948. Fender later said that K&F built its first guitar to test the new pickup.

By 1945, Fender and Kauffman, working out of a shack behind the radio-repair shop, were manufacturing amplifiers and lap-model Hawaiian steel guitars, which were sold as sets. Fender wanted to expand the business, taking advantage of the fact that many musical instrument companies had gone out of business during World War II, but Kauffman was worried about going into debt.

Fender told *BAM* magazine, "It cost a lot of money to get into large scale production, and the 1930s depression was still fresh in Kauffman's mind, so he didn't want to get involved. He had a ranch or farm in Oklahoma, and he was afraid if we got overextended on credit he might lose it. He thought he'd better pull out while he had a full skin." Kauffman told much the same story to *Guitar Player* magazine: "I got scared of the business.... I didn't have much faith in guitars, and I asked Leo to buy out my half of the business." Fender agreed to trade Kauffman a small press punch for his share of K&F Manufacturing.

In 1946, Fender renamed the business the Fender Electric Instruments Company. That same year, he signed an agreement with Radio & Television Equipment Company (Radio-Tel) of Santa Ana, California, which had been supplying parts for his repair shop, to be sole distributor for Fender amps and guitars. Fender also turned over operation of his repair shop to Dale Hyatt, so he could concentrate on making musical instruments. By 1949, Fender amps and guitars were firmly entrenched in the country music industry.

### The 1950s Telecaster

In the spring of 1950, the Fender Electric Instruments Company introduced a single-pickup, solidbody electric guitar, which it called the Esquire. The company started taking orders for the Esquire, but before Fender could start full production, the guitar had been redesigned as a dual-pickup solidbody called the Broadcaster. The Broadcaster was renamed the Telecaster in 1951 because of a conflict with Gretsch Broadkaster drums. Although it was sometimes derided as a "canoe paddle," because of its plain solid-ash body and screwed-on fretted maple neck, the Telecaster became the first commercially successful solidbody electric guitar.

Other guitar makers had created solidbody electric guitars as early as the mid-1930s, and in his book, *Fender: The Inside Story,* Forrest White, former vice-president and production manager for the Fender Electric Instruments Company, traces the concept of the Telecaster to a guitar that a part-time guitar maker in southern California, Paul Bigsby, created in 1947 for Merle Travis.

Fender supplied amplifiers for the Saturday night "Cliffe Stone Show" in Placentia, California, and there seems little doubt that Fender would have seen Travis play his custom-designed electric guitar on the show. In 1979, Travis wrote in the *JEMF Quarterly* that he loaned his guitar to Fender for a week to make a copy, and he argued for years that he, not Fender, should be considered the father of the solidbody electric guitar.

Regardless, in 1951, Fender received a patent for "a new, original, and ornamental Design for a Guitar," and it was Fender who popularized the electric, solidbody guitar. In *American Guitars, An Illustrated History,* Tom Wheeler, former consulting editor for *Guitar Player* magazine, calls Fender "the Henry Ford of electric guitars and the Telecaster . . . his Model T." With the success of the Telecaster, which sold for $189.50, Fender closed his repair shop to devote all his energy to designing and manufacturing musical instruments, which by late 1951 also included the first electric bass.

Before long, however, Leo Fender became unhappy with his distribution arrangement with Radio-Tel, which seemed content to focus its marketing efforts on Fender's amplifiers and lap-steel guitars. In his book, White quotes his former employer: "During this time, they (Radio-Tel) didn't sell hardly any of our (solidbody) guitars. [The guitars] just sat there in this garage, and termites got into them and ate through the bodies. We never found out about the termites until dealers started calling us about holes in the guitars. We ended up taking back 500 guitars and had to burn them all."

In 1953, Leo Fender formed Fender Sales, Inc., to take over distribution from Radio-Tel. Surprisingly, his partners in the venture were, or had been affiliated with Radio-Tel, including Donald Randall, former sales manager who became president of the distribution company, and Charles Hayes, a former salesman. The third partner was F. C. Hall, who owned Radio-Tel. Later that year, Hall purchased the Electro String Instrument Corporation from founder Adolph Rickenbacker, putting himself in the position of being both Fender's competitor and partner. When Hayes died in an automobile accident in 1955, Fender and Randall bought his interest in Fender Sales from his widow and ousted Hall. Fender and Randall each then owned 50 percent of the distribution company, although Fender continued to own 100 percent of Fender Electric Instruments.

In 1954, Fender Electric Instruments introduced the Stratocaster. While the Telecaster may have looked like a canoe paddle, Tony Bacon and Paul Day, authors of *The Fender Book,* describe the Stratocaster as "in some ways [owing] more to contemporary automobile design than traditional guitar forms, especially in the flowing, sensual curves of that beautifully proportioned, timeless body." The Stratocaster also included a built-in vibrato and came in a variety of Du Pont car colors. It became the most popular and most copied solidbody electric guitar ever made. It was also the guitar that would make Fender Electric Instruments worth millions of dollars and make Leo Fender an icon among rock musicians.

Building on the phenomenal success of the Stratocaster, Fender Electric Instruments introduced a line of less expensive guitars and amplifiers in 1955. The "studio instruments" were branded with the name "White," a tribute to Fender's production manager, Forrest White. The company also introduced a three-quarters sized solidbody guitar in 1955, an electric mandolin in 1957, a short-lived electric violin in 1958, and its first acoustic guitars in 1964. Fender dabbled briefly with brass instruments, buying a horn company and introducing the Hayes brand in 1954. However, the horn business, like the White brand, was abandoned a year later. Fender Electric Instruments, which had fewer than 15 employees in 1947, had more than 100 employees by the time it incorporated in 1959.

### The CBS Years

In 1964, Leo Fender, then 55, became ill and offered to sell Fender Electric Instruments to Randall, still his partner in Fender Sales, for $1.5 million. At the time, the company was producing 1,500 amplifiers, electric guitars, acoustic guitars, and other instruments per week, and was the largest exporter of musical instruments in the United States. Fender Electric Instruments employed 600 people, 500 of them in manufacturing.

Randall didn't have the resources to purchase the company himself but agreed to find another buyer. After talking with several companies, including the Baldwin Piano & Organ Co., Randall negotiated a deal with the Columbia Broadcasting System. On Jan. 5, 1965, CBS announced that a subsidiary, Columbia Records Distribution Corp., had purchased Fender Electric Instruments and Fender Sales for $13 million. The press release noted, "The Fender guitar is considered the outstanding instrument of its type by both professional musicians and amateurs." The new Columbia Records division was known initially as Fender CBS, but that was changed to CBS Musical Instruments in 1966, as it acquired other companies, including Steinway & Sons and flute maker Gemeinhardt Co.

CBS began making changes almost immediately. Fender Electric Instruments had expanded haphazardly over the past 20 years until it occupied 29 buildings scattered throughout Fullerton. To consolidate operations, CBS announced plans to build a 120,000-square-foot, $1.3 million facility, complete with a dust-free air-filtering system. The building was completed in 1966. CBS also began sending efficiency experts to Fullerton to analyze how the former Fender Electric Instruments Company operated. White, who had been responsible for production since 1954, commented in his book, "We had been invaded by a horde of 'know-it-all CBS experts' at both Fender Sales and the factory."

Demoted from vice-president to plant manager with the takeover, White quit less than two years later in a dispute over the quality of an amplifier that CBS planned to introduce. He wrote, "I asked all of my key personnel to come to the conference room. I told them that I had too much respect for Leo to have any part in building something that was not worthy of having his name associated with it."

Many other longtime Fender employees also believed that quality was declining, as CBS cut back on product lines and produced few new models. Randall, who had become vice-president and general manager under CBS, left the company in 1969 but apparently more because of corporate politics than a concern over quality. White quotes him as saying, "Everybody at CBS was climbing the corporate ladder, stepping on everyone else's fingers as they climbed up. There was a tremendous amount of infighting." However, despite the management upheaval and concerns over quality, sales at CBS Musical Instruments almost tripled from $20 million in 1971 to nearly $60 million in 1981.

Meanwhile, Leo Fender had been retained by CBS as a consultant in research and development from 1965 until 1970, although according to White, CBS executives made fun of his ideas. In 1972, Fender's consulting business, CLF Research, began manufacturing stringed instruments for Tri-Sonics, Inc., a company formed by White and Tom Walker, a former district manager at Fender Sales. Tri-Sonics changed its name briefly to Musitek, short for Music Technology, before finally settling on Music Man, Inc., in 1974. Fender was named vice-president in 1974 and became president in 1975. The company was sold in 1984.

In 1980, Leo Fender and George Fullerton, another longtime Fender Musical Instruments employee who quit CBS, formed G&L Inc. to market instruments made by CLF. G&L originally stood for George and Leo, but when Fullerton sold out in 1986, receptionists began answering the telephone, "Guitars by Leo." The company was sold after Fender's death in 1991.

## Post-CBS

By the early 1980s, Japanese competition was beginning to affect the bottom line at CBS Musical Instruments. CBS tried shifting some of its manufacturing to Korea to reduce tooling costs, but that experiment was abandoned by the end of the year because of poor quality. CBS also recruited three top executives from Yamaha Musical Instruments. John McLaren was brought in to head up CBS Musical Instruments, William Schultz was hired as president of the Fender division, and Dan Smith was named director of marketing for electric guitars.

In *The Fender Book,* Tony Bacon and Paul Day, quote Smith: "We were brought in to kind of turn the reputation of Fender around, and to get it so it was making money again. It was starting to lose money, and at that point in time everybody hated Fender. We thought we knew how bad it was. We took for granted that they could make Stratocasters and Telecasters the way they used to make them, but we were wrong. So many things had changed in the plant."

In 1982, Schultz virtually shut down U.S. production of Fender guitars, focusing instead on re-issuing limited editions of top-of-the-line, "classic" Fender guitars from pre-CBS days. Schultz also formed a joint venture, Fender Japan, with two Japanese distributors, Kanda Shokai and Yamano Music. Fuji Gen-Gakki, which made Ibanez brand instruments, was licensed to manufacture Fender guitars, which were sold only in Japan. Fuji Gen-Gakki also manufactured lower-priced, vintage Fender guitars under the Squire Series brand name. The Squire Series originally was intended for the Japanese and European market, but export to the U.S. market began in 1983.

A year later, with CBS a potential takeover target, the company began soliciting offers for its Fender musical instruments division. Among the companies expressing interest were the International Music Co. and Kaman Music Corporation, which manufactured Ovation guitars. In the end, however, CBS offered to sell to a management group headed by Schultz for $12.5 million. The sale was completed in March 1985, and the company name was changed to Fender Musical Instruments.

According to *Forbes,* the management group borrowed $9 million and CBS took back a note for $2.5 million, which gave Fender Musical Instruments about $11 in debt for every $1 in equity. Making matters worse, the sale did not include the production facilities in Fullerton, which CBS sold separately. As a result, Schultz, chairman of the company, was forced to halt all U.S. production of Fender guitars, and only Japanese-made instruments were listed in the 1985 catalog. Schultz also slashed employment at Fender Musical Instruments from 800 to about 90 workers, mostly in research and design.

To begin rebuilding the company, Schultz created the Fender Custom Shop in Corona, California, which produced about five models for a Vintage reissue series and began offering free or discounted guitars to rock music stars. In return, the musicians agreed to appear in Fender Musical Instruments advertisements. In 1986, Fender Musical Instruments introduced the American Standards model Stratocasters and Telecaster guitars. By 1996, the Corona plant, which also produced the company's amplifiers and speakers, employed about 600. Schultz, who moved company headquarters to Scottsdale, Arizona, in 1991, also opened guitar-manufacturing facilities in Mexico, China and Korea. By the mid-1990s, production was estimated at 50,000 guitars a year. William Mendello, then president of Fender Musical Instruments, told *Forbes* in 1996 that he estimated the value of the company at about $250 million if it went public. Revenues for the closely-held company were estimated at $160 million.

### Further Reading

Bacon, Tony, and Paul Day, *The Fender Book,* San Francisco: Miller Freeman, Inc., 1992.
Matzer, Marla, "Playing Solo," *Forbes,* March 25, 1996, pp. 80–81.
Smith, Richard, "Fifty Years of Fender, 1946–1996," Fender Musical Instruments (press release), 1996.
Wheeler, Tom, *American Guitars: An Illustrated History,* New York: Harper Perennial, 1992.
White, Forrest, *Fender: The Inside Story,* San Francisco: Miller Freeman, Inc., 1994.

—Dean Boyer

# Fibreboard Corporation

2121 North California Boulevard, Suite 560
Walnut Creek, California 94596
U.S.A.
(510) 274-0700
Fax: (510) 274-0715

*Public Company*
*Incorporated:* 1911
*Employees:* 3,500 (est.)
*Sales:* $380.8 million (1995)
*Stock Exchanges:* American
*SICs:* 2491 Wood Preserving; 3292 Asbestos Products;
7011 Hotels & Motels

A venerable company with an eclectic array of business interests, Fibreboard Corporation operates in three primary business segments: vinyl siding manufacture, resort operations, and industrial insulation. During the mid-1990s, Fibreboard owned and operated Sierra-at-Tahoe and Northstar-at-Tahoe, two ski resorts in Lake Tahoe, California, a vinyl siding manufacturing and distribution business based in Ohio, and industrial insulation manufacturing facilities.

In the mid-1990s, Fibreboard derived the bulk of its sales from businesses acquired during the previous five years. While this could be said of thousands of American companies operating midway through the decade, in Fibreboard's case the statement had special meaning, considering the company had been founded in 1884, more than a century before the sweeping changes that would redefine the company in the 1990s. The 1990s would prove to be Fibreboard's signal decade, a period that saw the company recover from near financial ruin and managerial chaos and quickly emerge, reshaped and invigorated, as one of Wall Street's hottest prospects. Though Fibreboard's business was predicated on more than a century of existence as it entered the 1990s, the events following its most tumultuous year in 1991 extensively transformed the company, creating a corporate entity that increasingly bore less and less resemblance to the Fibreboard of the previous 100 years.

## Origins

During the years leading up to the most significant decade in its history, Fibreboard lived a comparatively serene corporate life. The company established its first industrial insulation plant in Emeryville, California, in 1884, beginning a 112-year tenure in the East Bay area of San Francisco that included its acquisition by Louisiana-Pacific Corporation in 1976 and then its divestiture by the giant, Oregon-based forest products company slightly more than a decade later. After Fibreboard was cut loose from the aegis of Louisiana-Pacific Corporation in 1988, the company not only owned sizeable timberland and operated a wood products division but also oversaw Northstar-at-Tahoe, a ski resort in northern California developed during the 1970s on company acreage. With these primary businesses supporting the company in its newfound freedom as a spinoff from Louisiana-Pacific Corporation, Fibreboard recorded moderate success for several years under the stewardship of chairman and CEO Lawrence Hart. The company's profitability, however, quickly began a downward spiral, raising concern among all those involved with Fibreboard about the company's future.

In 1989, the first full year after the Louisiana-Pacific Corporation spinoff, Fibreboard posted $5.3 million in profit. The following year earnings slipped alarmingly to $1.3 million, then in 1991 the hammer fell, leaving the company with a staggering $43.9 million loss that threatened to bring to an end Fibreboard's more than century-old business. The company's waning profitability and its massive loss in 1991 were blamed on the acquisition of inefficient sawmills, ill-timed and ill-advised investments in experimental new ventures, and a managerial and administrative force that had become bloated. In the midst of this turmoil, Lawrence Hart relinquished his posts, with no individual immediately named to succeed him, creating a leadership void that fomented shareholder anxiety and exacerbated concerns about Fibreboard's future. On top of these problems was heaped the most portentous issue facing Fibreboard, an ominous legal problem that had been threatening the company's fortunes for decades. Although Fibreboard had abandoned the asbestos business in 1972, the company was facing as many as 80,000 individual claims of health damage from the fire retardant at the time of the disastrous loss in 1991. A legal ruling on the lawsuits filed against the company was pending as Fibreboard struggled with its financial woes, leading observers to predict the company's imminent demise. Those who prognosticated the financial ruin of the company, however, were to be proven wrong in the years ahead.

### Arrival of John Roach in the 1990s

With Lawrence Hart gone and the company on the brink of bankruptcy, Fibreboard was facing a host of problems, its future questionable at best. The company's shareholders staged a revolt, clearly unhappy with the way things were going, and to their chagrin company officials named a successor to Lawrence Hart that met with their disapproval. Dissident shareholders wanted to bring in a professional turnaround expert to steer the company toward recovery, but instead John Roach, an industrial management graduate from the Massachusetts Institute of Technology, was selected. Roach, who joined Fibreboard in July 1991 after leaving insulation manufacturer, Manville Corp., assumed his duties despite shareholder objections, with full confidence in himself and his ability to turn an essentially worthless company, as one analyst described Fibreboard, into a flourishing concern once again.

From the outset, Roach viewed the problems riddling Fibreboard as a general would face a battle. As he later reflected, his plan for recovery was precise and comprehensive. "My assessment of Fibreboard and my own due diligence in 1991," Roach explained in 1994, "was based on the core business and the potential of a settlement. My initial course of action was to move on three fronts: one, to demonstrate the highest potential of existing assets; two, to settle litigation; and three, rapid expansion." Once his management team was assembled, Roach, as Fibreboard's new chief executive officer and chairman, quickly moved to check the company's plunging profits, consolidating Fibreboard's six separate wood products businesses, which together generated more than 70 percent of the company's total sales, into one. The consolidation began a little more than a month after Roach joined the company, and in the months ahead Roach continued to make his presence known by closing costly operations and cutting costs wherever he could.

By the end of 1992, positive results were already evident. Following the mammoth $44 million loss in 1991, Fibreboard generated $239 million in sales and posted $9.4 million in profit in 1992, quickly jumping out of the red to record a mercurial rise in net income. Once the company was operating efficiently, Roach moved to expand the company's operations, hoping to build Fibreboard into a billion-dollar company by the end of the 1990s. To achieve this ambitious goal, Roach intended to boost Fibreboard's financial stature through internal growth, diversification, and through acquisitions. In April 1993, Roach made his first major move, signing a letter of intent to purchase Sierra Ski Ranch, one of Lake Tahoe's largest ski areas, a 2,000-acre facility owned and operated by the Sprock family since 1955.

The acquisition of Sierra Ski Ranch, which was subsequently renamed Sierra-at-Tahoe, bolstered Fibreboard's involvement in resort operations, complementing the vested interest it held in running Northstar-at-Tahoe, but in terms of financial importance there were other facets to Fibreboard's

business that held greater meaning. Resort operations contributed less than 10 percent of Fibreboard's total annual revenue, while the two other business segments, industrial insulation and wood products, accounted for the balance. The company's industrial insulation products group, a business segment that Roach referred to as "a little jewel," operated as a low-cost producer of highly specialized pipe insulation for the petrochemical industry, while Fibreboard's wood products business contributed 72 percent of the company's total revenue.

The composition of Fibreboard's operations would soon change after 1993, but before the year was through a pernicious chapter in the company's history was closed. In September 1993, the company agreed to pay $3 billion to current and potential victims of the asbestos products it had manufactured, bringing to an end four decades of asbestos liability problems. The settlement figure was enormous, certainly more than a company of Fibreboard's size could be expected to pay, but thanks to two insurance policies purchased decades earlier by company managers, all the money was paid by Fibreboard's liability insurers, Continental Casualty Co. and Pacific Indemnity Co.

### 1994 Acquisition of Norandex

Once free from the worries and potentially devastating affect its asbestos litigation problems posed, Fibreboard began redefining itself for the future ahead, with Roach leading the way. Financially, 1993 had been another year of positive growth, with the company collecting $265.2 million in revenue and recording $11.7 million in profit, an encouraging gain from the total registered the year before. In response to the company's sustained financial growth, investors expressed their confidence in the company and its new management, marking a banner year for Fibreboard on the American Stock Exchange, a year during which the company's stock price rose an eye-catching 404 percent, the second-largest gain by any company in 1993 on the exchange. Attempting to build on this success, Roach and his management team embarked on a plan to greatly alter and enlarge Fibreboard's operations, acquiring Ohio-based Norandex in July 1994 for $120 million. The acquisition of Norandex, a leading manufacturer of vinyl siding for homes, nearly doubled Fibreboard's sales volume, bringing the company into a new business area that was expected to support its growth in the coming years. In the wake of this pivotal acquisition, Fibreboard shored up its new involvement in the vinyl siding business by spending roughly $22 million during the year following the purchase of Norandex to acquire 22 vinyl siding distribution centers scattered across the country, thereby strengthening the new engine that would drive its growth.

For Fibreboard, the developments in 1995 would be no less determinative than the developments in 1994. Roach not too subtly hinted at what would unfold in 1995 during an interview with Walnut Creek, California's *Contra Costa Times*. The subject of the interview was Fibreboard's wood products business and its future with the company, which Roach was quite clear about, saying, "A divestiture would allow us to redeploy our financial resources and take advantage of a number of strategic opportunities which we believe may better complement our rapidly expanding franchise in the building products industry." Roach reiterated his position regarding the wood products division, stating, ''We would move forward with such a transaction if the wood products operations prove to have greater strategic value to a party other than Fibreboard.'' For the wood products business, the writing was on the wall.

Before the year was through, Fibreboard had divested itself of the wood products division, selling the business for $239 million. With the proceeds from the sale, Roach paid off some of the debt the company had incurred from the acquisition of Sierra Ski Ranch and Norandex, saving the balance to fund further acquisitions as the company prepared to enter the late 1990s. For the future, Roach and his management team planned to keep expanding Fibreboard's operations through diversification and acquisitions, but they would do so from a new headquarters location. In April 1996, the company announced its intentions to relocate in August from the San Francisco area to Dallas, where top executives would be closer to Fiberboard's biggest businesses, which were primarily located east of the Rocky Mountains. As the company prepared to move to Texas, it was also embarking on a new era in Fibreboard's lengthy history, reshaping itself as an aggressive, growth-oriented company for the 21st century.

### Principal Subsidiaries

Norandex Inc.; Pabco Metals Corporation.

### Principal Divisions

Norandex; Northstar-at-Tahoe; PABCO Insulation.

### Further Reading

Burstiner, Marcy, ''Fibreboard Looks Abroad for Way Out of the Woods,'' *San Francisco Business Times,* May 20, 1994, p. 3.

Carlsen, Clifford, ''Branching Out of Timber Business,'' *San Francisco Business Times,* July 29, 1994, p. 6A.

——, ''Fibreboard Head Plans to Leave Timber Company,'' *San Francisco Business Times,* April 15, 1991, p. 8.

''Double Indemnity,'' *Forbes,* September 13, p. 246.

''Fibreboard Reorganizes Wood Products Business,'' *Forest Industries,* September 1991, p. 6.

''John D.C. Roach,'' *Forest Industries,* September 1991, p. 51.

Levander, Michelle, ''Calif's Fibreboard Agrees to Settlement of Record $3 Billion in Asbestos Suit,'' *Journal of Commerce and Commercial,* December 29, 1993, p. 7A.

Liedtke, Michael, ''Fibreboard Corp. To Relocate from California to Texas,'' *Knight-Ridder/Tribune Business News,* April 26, 1996, p. 42.

——, ''Purchase Makes Fibreboard California's Largest Ski Resort,'' *Knight-Ridder/Tribune Business News,* August 31, 1994, p. 83.

McLean, Herbert E., ''High Stakes, Gentle Touches,'' *American Forests,* July/August 1994, p. 17.

Wozencraft, Ann, ''Fibreboard Corp. to Buy Back Up to $20 Million of Common Stock,'' *Knight-Ridder/Tribune Business News,* June 7, 1995, p. 60.

—Jeffrey L. Covell

# Finlay Enterprises, Inc.

**521 Fifth Avenue**
**New York, New York 10175**
**U.S.A.**
**(212) 808-2060**
**Fax: (212) 557-3848**

*Public Company*
*Incorporated:* 1911 as Seligman & Latz
*Employees:* 6,250
*Sales:* $654.5 million (1995)
*Stock Exchanges:* NASDAQ
*SICs:* 5944 Jewelry Stores; 6719 Holding Companies,
    Not Elsewhere Classified

Finlay Enterprises, Inc. is one of the leading jewelry retailers in the United States, with sales of $654.5 million in 1995. Unlike competitors such as Zale Corp., Finlay operates few self-standing retail locations. Instead, the company operates fine jewelry departments in leased spaces in stores owned by 26 major and independent host store groups. The largest share of Finlay's 827 U.S. departments are located in stores in The May Department Stores group, including stores such as Filene's, Kaufmann's, and Lord & Taylor, which acts as host to 343 Finlay departments. Another top Finlay host is Federated Department Stores, Inc., which owns stores such as Rich's, Sterns, and Burdines, and which hosts 153 Finlay departments. Independent store groups featuring Finlay Fine Jewelry departments include Belk, Carson Pirie Scott, Liberty House, Dillard's, Steinbach, and others, bringing Finlay into 43 states and Washington, D.C. Finlay is the largest operator of leased jewelry departments in the United States.

## Business Organization and Relationships

The practice of leasing jewelry departments is widespread in the department store industry, a relationship that provides benefits to both lessor and lessee. Jewelry is a specialized industry with costs and factors that lie outside of the typical department store's core base of clothing and home furnishings. Department stores are able to avoid the high costs associated with retail jewelry, such as slow, typically one-year inventory turns and expensive inventory maintenance. Lessees such as Finlay provide management expertise, marketing, merchandising, purchasing, employee hiring, training and payroll, inventory control, and security, as well as specialized relationships within the fragmented jewelry industry, while providing department store customers with the attraction of a fine jewelry department.

Finlay and other jewelry department lessees benefited from this relationship by avoiding the high investment costs of establishing and maintaining company-owned retail locations. By avoiding stand-alone formats, new Finlay departments were generally profitable within one year of opening. Finlay departments also enjoyed the enhanced reputation and customer traffic of a department store, and marketing could be tied in with the host's storewide promotions. Finlay also benefited from a reduced credit risk, as department stores generally assumed the risk of extending and collecting the credit for Finlay sales. Net sales usually were remitted to Finlay on a monthly basis, whether or not the host store had collected on the sale.

Finlay's leases ranged from one to five years and provided for rents based on the level of sales; rents typically ranged from 10 to 15 percent of sales. Finlay enjoyed long-term relationships with most of its host stores; 19 of its 26 store groups leased Finlay departments for more than five years, representing nearly 80 percent of Finlay annual sales, and 13 had relationships with Finlay lasting longer than ten years, representing nearly 65 percent of Finlay's revenue. Part of Finlay's growth was tied into the expansion of its host store groups. In the period from 1990 to 1995, for example, Finlay added 121 departments through the opening of new stores in its host groups' chains. Consolidation trends in the department store industry also aided Finlay's growth. As department stores featuring jewelry departments of Finlay's competitors were absorbed by industry giants such as May and Federated, Finlay's relationships with these groups often allowed the Finlay department to take over as lessee.

These lease relationships, however, exposed Finlay to certain risks. The closing of a department store meant the loss of Finlay's leased location and a corresponding loss of revenue. Consolidation—such as Federated's acquisition of R.H. Macy & Co. in 1994, which operated its own department stores—could lead to the termination of Finlay's leases. Finlay also faced the risk that a department store group would decide to assume operation of their own jewelry departments. Finally, Finlay remained exposed to losses presented by the bankruptcy of its host chains.

In addition to its domestic leased jewelry department business, Finlay operated France's largest leased jewelry operations since its 1994 acquisition of Société Nouvelle d'Achat de Bijouterie (Sonab), which included 104 locations in such leading French stores as Galeries Lafayette and Nouvelles Galeries. In 1994, Finlay also began test operations of a chain of company-owned outlet stores, called New York Jewelry operations, which had grown to seven locations by 1996.

### A Giant Without a Name

Founded in 1911 as Seligman & Latz, the company's original focus was the operation of beauty salons, also under a lease arrangement with department and specialty stores. Jewelry sales were soon added to the company's portfolio, and by 1942, the company opened its first leased Finlay Fine Jewelry department. By 1960, Seligman & Latz operated in more than 50 locations, generating nearly $170 million in revenues.

Yet the company remained essentially nameless with the general public, which tended to identify the company's beauty salons and jewelry departments with the stores in which they operated. For much of its history, the company's emphasis was on its beauty salons and products, which later included the Adrien Arpel line of cosmetics, skin care, and related products. Toward the mid-1970s, with annual revenues shrinking to $160 million, the company's focus began to shift. Jewelry sales began to represent the fastest growing share of revenues.

In 1978, jewelry provided less than $75 million of Seligman & Latz's $208 million in revenues. Four years later, Seligman & Latz's revenues swelled to $304 million; much of this growth was provided by the company's Finlay division, which had doubled in size, to $145 million in sales. The beauty division, meanwhile, had grown more slowly during this period, from $133 million in 1978 to $159 million in 1982. Together, the two divisions operated in more than 100 leading department store and specialty groups in ten countries, with Macy's providing the largest—13.8 percent—of the company's revenues, closely followed by Associated Dry Goods, May, and Gimbel Bros. Profits, however, had been shrinking. Net income, which had neared $5 million in the mid-1970s, slipped to barely more than $1.5 million by 1980.

Despite its low profile, in stark contrast to its luxury goods-oriented business (for example, the company's annual reports during the time offered little more than a reproduction of the company's SEC filing), Seligman & Latz began to attract the attention of investors. The company seemed ripe for a takeover, in fitting with the flurry of corporate takeovers that marked the 1980s.

### Leveraged Buyouts and an Initial Public Offering in the 1980s

In February 1984, Seligman & Latz reached agreement with City Stores Company and its subsidiary, Diversified Investments, Inc., which would merge the two companies under the Seligman & Latz name. The company faced a difficult year, stemming from a conversion to a new inventory system that forced Seligman & Latz to stop shipments for a full year, an increase in shrinkage from theft, and the loss of several key managers. At the same time, Seligman & Latz had fallen behind the industry in sales per square foot. Underfinanced, the company was having difficulty maintaining inventory in an industry where broad selection played a key role in sales. The company's problems were further exacerbated by a general slump in the jewelry industry and its slow recovery from the recession of the early 1980s. When Seligman & Latz, despite revenue gains to $342 million, posted a loss of $2.2 million for the year, City Stores balked on the merger agreement.

Yet the company had already attracted the attention of another group of investors. As early as 1982, Harold Geneen, former chairman of ITT, had presented David Cornstein with Seligman & Latz's annual report and asked Cornstein how he would run the company. Cornstein, whose involvement in the leased jewelry business reached back more than 20 years, and whose Tru-Run Inc., a jewelry and watch repair company, had outlets in 80 stores, identified many of Seligman & Latz's key problems.

Geneen and Cornstein began to seek financing and in 1985 structured a leveraged buyout (LBO) of Seligman & Latz for $42 million, including $1 million of Geneen's private funds. A chief investor in the LBO was Transcontinental Services Group N.V., with financing arranged through Manufacturer's Hanover Trust, Phoenix Mutual Life Insurance, and Banker's Life and Casualty. The new owners took Seligman & Latz private.

Under President and CEO Cornstein, the company was restructured as a holding company, SL Holdings, which now included Tru-Run Inc. The new management posted rapid improvements in the Finlay division, doubling store sales to $1,000 per square foot and boosting Finlay's annual revenues to $265 million in 1987 and to $315 million in 1988. The number of Finlay outlets also grew, from 460 in 1985 to 525 in 1988. Meanwhile, the beauty division, which had grown to nearly 1,000 locations, continued posting $5 million annual losses.

In 1988, Cornstein and Geneen engineered a buyout of the company's jewelry division, in a deal worth $217 million, with financing arranged through Westinghouse Credit Corp. As part of the restructuring, Seligman & Latz's beauty division, including Adrien Arpel, was sold to Regis Corp. in Minneapolis for $17 million. The company, now specialized in jewelry, was renamed Finlay Enterprises, Inc.

By the start of the 1990s, Cornstein and Geneen began to make plans to take Finlay public, in part to help ease the debt load carried over from the buyout. In 1991, Finlay attempted an initial public offering (IPO) of five million shares, including one million shares of stock held by company principals, to raise up to $125 million. But the recession of the period and steep sales drops across the industry, coupled with Cornstein's and Geneen's sale of their own stock, scared off investors. The company was forced to back down from the IPO. Shortly afterward, Geneen retired from the company.

In an effort to recapitalize the company after Westinghouse exited the financial services market, Cornstein approached Thomas H. Lee, whose Boston investment company had funded the growth of Snapple. In 1993, Lee organized a buyout of Finlay, taking 28 percent of the company, and, with Desai Capital Management Inc.'s 32 percent share, gaining control of Finlay Enterprises.

The new owners moved to expand the company, acquiring Sonab in 1994 from Galeries Lafayette and launching the first test location of New York Jewelry Outlet. The following year, Lee and Desai took Finlay public, selling 2.62 million shares for a net of $30 million. By then, Finlay operated nearly 800 locations, including its French stores, for 1994 revenues of $552 million. With its strong French base, the company began to look toward a deeper penetration of the European market. In March 1996, Finlay signed an agreement to lease seven departments in the 89-store, United Kingdom-based Debenhams department store chain. Expansion into other countries was expected to follow. Finlay's future plans also called for expanding its New York Jewelry Outlet chain to as many as 60 stores. With its long-term lease relationships with leading department store chains, strengthening promotions, and rising revenues, Finlay was likely to maintain its glittering position in the U.S. jewelry industry and make a name for itself as well.

### Principal Subsidiaries

Finlay Fine Jewelry Corporation; Société Nouvelle d'Achat de Bijouterie (France).

### Further Reading

Furman, Phyllis "Glittering Jeweler Re-emerges in Big IPO," *Crain's New York Business,* September 16, 1991, p. 3.

——, "No-Name Jeweler Now Pursuing the Spotlight," *Crain's New York Business,* June 12, 1995, p. 1.

Grant, Peter, "Geneen and Friend Shine with Gold," *Crain's New York Business,* December 19, 1988, p. 1.

Metz, Robert, "A Low-Keyed Concessionaire?," *New York Times,* March 26, 1981, p. D6.

Springsteel, Ian, "Diamonds in the Rough," *CFO: The Magazine for Senior Financial Executives,* September 1995, p. 29.

Trachtenberg, Jeffrey A., "Good as Gold?," *Forbes,* May 20, 1985, p. 62.

—M.L. Cohen

# Forest City Enterprises, Inc.

10800 Brookpark Road
Cleveland, Ohio 44130
U.S.A.
(216) 267-1200
Fax: (216)433-1827

*Public Company*
*Incorporated:* 1960
*Employees:* 3,287
*Operating Revenues:* $506.89 million (fiscal 1996)
*Stock Exchanges:* American
*SICs:* 6513 Apartment Building Operators; 6512
    Nonresidential Building Operators

With properties in 25 states worth a total of $2.6 billion, Forest City Enterprises, Inc. is a developer and manager of commercial and multifamily residential real estate. By the mid-1990s, Forest City's apartment division ranked among America's 20 largest owners of multifamily developments. The firm's real estate portfolio nearly quadrupled from $434 million in 1985 to $2.4 billion in 1995, as it concentrated on larger, more ambitious projects. In addition to its real estate interests, the 75-year-old company operates North America's second largest lumber wholesaler. In 1996, descendants of the founding Ratner family continued to own a controlling interest in the company. President and Chief Executive Officer Charles A. Ratner appeared poised to lead the corporation into the 21st century.

## Foundation and Development in Early 20th Century

The family affair began in 1905, when members of the Ratner clan began to emigrate to the United States from their native Poland in 1905. Charles, the eldest and first to arrive in Cleveland, Ohio, founded Forest City Lumberyard in 1922. Upon their arrival, Leonard and younger siblings Max, Fannye, and Dora borrowed money to start a small creamery offering milk, butter and eggs. Trained as a weaver, Leonard joined his older brother in the lumber business mid-decade, opening Buckeye Lumber in 1924. Two years later, the Ratners sold their creameries to focus on the lumber and building materials market. In the late 1920s, Leonard and Charles turned the lumberyard over to brother Max, who had just earned a law degree from Case Western Reserve's John Marshall Law School. Fannye's husband, Nathan Shafran, came into the lumber business around this same time. Leonard and Charles founded B & F Building Co., which constructed single-family homes on Cleveland's east side. Leonard rejoined the family lumber firm in 1934, bringing with him his expertise in residential construction.

Although the company sold construction materials primarily to contractors in the 1920s, 1930s and 1940s, it also reached out to the general public during the Great Depression. At this time, Forest City Lumber started a lending program that enabled homeless people to borrow $549 toward the purchase of building materials. By investing their own "sweat equity," these struggling individuals could build a very inexpensive home.

Forest City made its first forays into the real estate business during the 1930s and 1940s by acquiring inexpensive land that had been repossessed by banks and other institutions. Some lots were purchased as cheaply as $10 each. During the interwar period, the company lent land and building materials to local builders with the understanding that they would pay for both when they sold the homes. Forest City became a pioneer in the construction of prefabricated homes in 1941, but this activity was interrupted by World War II, during which the company made wooden munitions boxes.

Sam Miller, who joined the company in 1947, has been credited with launching Sunrise Land Co., the land development arm of the business. Miller became a full-fledged member of the family shortly thereafter, when he married Leonard's daughter Ruth. Envisioning an opportunity for growth in the postwar housing shortage, the Ratners entered residential construction, and was a key developer of some of Cleveland's largest suburbs. The group also began to develop its extensive landholdings into apartments and shopping centers. This new focus on consumers may have lead the company to begin converting its lumberyards into do-it-yourself home stores in 1955. Forest City's early entry into this important market

---

**Company Perspectives:**

*Forest City Enterprises is a national owner and developer of real estate, committed to building superior, long term value for its shareholders and customers. We accomplish this through the operation, acquisition and development of commercial, rental housing, urban entertainment and land development projects. We operate by developing meaningful relationships and leveraging our unparalleled entrepreneurial capabilities with creative talent in a fully integrated real estate organization.*

---

helped make it Ohio's biggest building materials company by the end of the decade.

### Incorporation Signals Transition

Forest City Enterprises was incorporated in 1960 with Leonard Ratner as chairman and Max Ratner as president. The company made an initial public stock offering that same year, selling a 19.5 percent stake at a face value of $4.5 million. Forest City's stock was listed on the American Stock Exchange by 1965. Although the company continued to develop its retail and wholesale lumber businesses during the 1960s and 1970s, this corporate reorganization represented a turning point for the company, when real estate came to the fore.

Under the direction of Max Ratner's son, Charles, beginning in 1966, Forest City's building materials chain grew from $12 million in annual sales to nearly $200 million over the next two decades. The division added one of America's largest lumber distributors, an Oregon company, to its portfolio in 1969. Over the course of the 1960s and 1970s, it opened stores in Detroit, Chicago and Akron. By the late 1970s, the chain boasted 20 do-it-yourself centers.

Forest City's real estate developments took several forms. The company built, owned and operated shopping centers, malls, office buildings, industrial parks and hotels. It also acquired Akron's Thomas J. Dillon & Co., Inc., a construction company in 1968. Under the guidance of Nathan Shafran, Forest City applied its patented method of modular high-rise housing construction to this new subsidiary. The firm's "Operation Breakthrough" program erected nearly 60,000 units of low-cost housing for the elderly over the next 30 years. By the end of the 1970s, Forest City owned 17 shopping centers and 39 apartment buildings with a combined total of 10,800 housing units. The company had also diversified into mortgage banking, property leasing, and property management, as well as petroleum and natural gas development.

Albert B. Ratner advanced to the presidency in 1973, when Max assumed the chairmanship and Leonard took the title of founder chairman. Corporate revenues increased from $32 million in 1963 to $235.3 million by 1979, but net income only grew from $1 million to $1.4 million.

### Major Urban Projects Characterize 1980s

At the dawn of the 1980s, Forest City began to phase out its smaller ventures and concentrate its resources on larger urban developments. The most significant divestment of this transition came in 1987, when the company sold its Forest City Materials chain to Handy Andy Home Improvement Centers, Inc. Forest City had dominated the local home improvement market until the early 1980s, when DIY Home Warehouse and Kmart Corp.'s Builders Square infiltrated Cleveland. Forest City tried to match the competition with deep discounts and a switch to a warehouse format, but soon realized that it needed more volume and more buying power to compete with these large, well-financed national chains. This dramatic break with the company's traditional business freed it to focus on the mega-projects for which it would become nationally known in the 1980s and 1990s.

Forest City played a key role in the revitalization of downtown Cleveland, then applied the skills it had gained to urban projects throughout the United States. In 1980, the company bought Cleveland's Terminal Tower, a passenger rail terminal originally built before the Great Depression. Although the $250 million project endured several fits and starts, it would become a cornerstone of the city's rebirth. When completed in 1990, the three million square foot, multi-use urban renewal redevelopment featured hotels, a mall, and offices. Renamed Tower City, the project helped push Forest City's real estate portfolio over the $2 billion mark in 1991. Major retail and commercial projects in Boston, Pittsburgh, Brooklyn, Los Angeles, Tucson, San Francisco, Chicago, and elsewhere echoed the scale and impact of Tower City in Cleveland. Forest City also continued to pursue residential developments throughout this period, creating everything from single-family inner-city projects to luxury apartments and condominiums.

Although Forest City sailed through the late 1980s, early 1990s credit crunch better than many of its competitors, it was compelled to eliminate its quarterly dividend in 1991 and put the brakes on 17 projects in 1992.

### Foreign Investment and Casinos Carry Forest City into 21st Century

Having specialized in large urban redevelopments for about a decade, a confident Forest City wagered future prosperity on international projects and gambling houses. The company made its first international foray via a 1993 joint venture with Mexico's Grupo Protexa. Ian Bacon, the executive in charge of this endeavor, compared Mexico to the United States of the 1950s and 1960s: a market ripe for the development of regional malls and shopping centers.

The developer became increasingly involved in the construction and management of casinos—euphemistically dubbed "urban entertainment" in the industry—in the mid-1990s. Projects in Pittsburgh, Las Vegas, and Atlantic City either planned for or proposed gambling. Although gambling and its social and economic effects were hotly contested topics in the early 1990s, analyst Sheldon Grodsky wryly told the *Cleveland Plain Dealer*'s Bill Lubinger that "This is what they do, whether they do it with gambling-related property or retail or mixed use or apartments—that's real estate development.'' Clearly, Forest city and the Ratner family had long been winners at the real estate game, and there was no reason to believe that a losing streak was at hand.

Charles A. Ratner, son of Max, became president and chief operating officer that same year, and assumed the chief executive office in 1995. That year, which marked the company's 75th anniversary, the new CEO revealed a strategic plan that outlined financial goals and the strategies necessary to reach them, a mission statement, and a set of core values. The new CEO hoped that these guidelines would help Forest City continue to increase its revenues and net income, which had grown from $499.6 million and $6.8 million, respectively, in fiscal 1995 (ended January 31) to record-setting $506.9 million and $13.5 million in fiscal 1996.

### Principal Subsidiaries

Forest City Finance Corporation; Forest City Trading Group, Inc.; Forest City Capital Corporation.

### Principal Divisions

Forest City Commercial Group; Forest City Residential Group; Forest City Land Group; Forest City Trading Group.

### Further Reading

Bullard, Stan, "Forest City Finds Amigo to Build Malls in Mexico," *Crain's Cleveland Business*, May 17, 1993, pp. 3, 25.
——, "Forest City's Miller Likes Privacy, Power," *Crain's Cleveland Business*, August 2, 1993, pp. 13, 15.
Chatman, Angela D., "Ohio Companies Among Tops in Multifamily Units," *Cleveland Plain Dealer*, April 1, 1995, p. 9SU.
Clark, Sandra, "Putting Projects on Hold," *Cleveland Plain Dealer*, January 16, 1992, p. 1D.
DeWitt, John, "Halle's Building Splendid Again," *Cleveland Plain Dealer*, December 11, 1985, p. 7D.
Gerdel, Thomas, "Forest City Goes Full Speed on Its Development Course," *Cleveland Plain Dealer*, July 31, 1990, pp. 1D, 8D.
Gleisser, Marcus, "Close Family Enterprise," *Cleveland Plain Dealer*, January 15, 1987, p. 2C.
——, "Business Leader Max Ratner Dies," *Cleveland Plain Dealer*, June 2, 1995, pp. 1A, 12A.
——, "Forest City Named Developer for Project in NYC's Times Square," *Cleveland Plain Dealer*, September 8, 1995.
"Hurting Balance Sheet Helps Firm Build Assets," *Engineering News Record*, October 11, 1979 p. 23.
Karle, Delinda, "Forest City Ends Home Improving," *Cleveland Plain Dealer*, January 15, 1987, pp. 1A, 17A.
Koshar, John Leo, "Ambitious Projects Fill Forest City's Drawing Boards," *Cleveland Plain Dealer*, July 1, 1984, p. 1G.
Lubinger, Bill, "Forest City Forges Gambling Ties," *Cleveland Plain Dealer*, July 10, 1996, pp. 1C, 3C.
Phillips, Stephen, "Forest City Betting on Projects," *Cleveland Plain Dealer*, July 1, 1994, pp. 1C, 2C.
Rudnitsky, Howard, "Survivor," *Forbes*, June 8, 1992, p. 48.
Sabath, Donald, "Forest City to Celebrate Nate Shafran's 50 Years," *Cleveland Plain Dealer*, June 13, 1989, p. 4D.
Sartin, V. David, "Tower City Project is Scrapped," *Cleveland Plain Dealer*, August 31, 1984, pp. 1A, 10A.
——, "Save Tower City, Kucinich Demands," *Cleveland Plain Dealer*, September 1, 1984, pp. 1A, 11A.
Sullivan, Elizabeth, "Hilton, Forest City Sign Deal on Downtown Hotel," *Cleveland Plain Dealer*, July 27, 1983, pp. 1A, 8A.

—April Dougal Gasbarre

# FoxMeyer Health Corporation

**1220 Senlac Drive**
**Carrollton, Texas 75006**
**U.S.A.**
**(214) 446-4800**
**Fax: (214) 446-2836**

*Public Company*
*Incorporated:* 1977
*Employees:* 4,097
*Sales:* $5.17 billion (1995)
*Stock Exchanges:* New York
*SICs:* 5122 Drugs, Proprietaries & Sundries

The second-largest wholesale drug distributor in the United States, FoxMeyer Health Corporation functions through two operating units, FoxMeyer Corporation and Ben Franklin Retail Stores, Inc., a chain of general variety stores. In 1986, Fox-Meyer was acquired by National Intergroup, Inc., a holding company created by National Steel Corporation to facilitate the entry into businesses other than steel and aluminum production. During the ensuing decade, the steel and aluminum properties were divested, leaving the former steel giant with FoxMeyer as its chief revenue source. In 1994, FoxMeyer Corporation and National Intergroup, Inc. merged, creating FoxMeyer Health Corporation.

Throughout much of its first 20 years of business, FoxMeyer was a pawn, albeit an enormously large pawn, caught in the contentious corporate affairs of its parent company, National Intergroup, Inc. (NII). During the decade that spanned Fox-Meyer's conversion from an independent company to a subsidiary company to a publicly owned subsidiary, NII underwent more sweeping changes, changes that revolved around Fox-Meyer and its wholesale drug distribution business. In the years leading up to NII's purchase of FoxMeyer, NII ranked as one of the largest steel companies in the United States, then the company diversified, quickly taking on the characteristics of a conglomerate before shedding its steel and other variegated assets to emerge during the 1990s as a company reliant on one primary source of revenue: the wholesale drug business operated by FoxMeyer. Within a decade, a steel company with more than a half century of experience was transformed into a wholesale drug distributor, representing a metamorphosis that charted the rise of FoxMeyer.

## Origins

Before FoxMeyer and NII officials convened together to discuss their corporate marriage, the predecessor to FoxMeyer operated on its own for nine years, the formative years of the company's development into a national wholesale drug power-house. The company was incorporated in 1977 for the express purpose of acquiring Fox-Vliet Drug Company, a drug distributor based in Wichita, Kansas, that had first opened its doors in 1903. Fours year later, in July 1981, the company completed a major acquisition, purchasing St. Louis, Missouri-based Meyer Brothers Drug Company, the second of a series of acquisitions that would greatly amplify the company's stature. Once Meyer Brothers Drug Company was added to the fold, annual revenues nearly doubled and expansion into the midwestern United States was achieved. Following the acquisition, the company adopted a new name, incorporating the first two words of the company's first two acquisitions to create the FoxMeyer name.

FoxMeyer Corporation went public two years after the acquisition of Meyer Brothers Drug Company, making its initial public offering of stock in July 1983. After completing the conversion to public ownership, FoxMeyer was less than three years away from its acquisition by NII, but in the interim the company did not remain idle; instead FoxMeyer completed a number of acquisitions that strengthened its standing in the eyes of NII executives and engendered explosive growth. Two drug wholesalers were added to the company in fiscal 1984, Cincinnati Economy Drug Company, a $35 million-a-year business, and Lincoln, Nebraska-based Lincoln Drug Company, with $16 million in annual sales. More acquisitions followed, including Yahr-Lange, Inc., an $80 million-a-year wholesale drug distributor with facilities in Wisconsin and northern Illinois, and I.L. Lyons Ltd., a New Orleans, Louisiana drug distributor with annual sales of $90 million. In 1985, the company purchased Kansas City-based McPike, Inc., a drug wholesaler that was collecting $90 million a year in sales. FoxMeyer also purchased two computer products and service companies in the years preceding its acquisition by NII: TBL Inc. in fiscal 1994 and PharmAssist, Inc. in fiscal 1985, which together serviced nearly 2,000 pharmacies scattered across 29 states.

### National Intergroup's Emergence in the 1980s

As FoxMeyer entered 1986, it was experiencing rapid growth, growth largely realized through an acquisition program that with each passing year had significantly increased its sales volume and made the company a tantalizing asset for an interested buyer. In less than eight years, FoxMeyer had developed itself into the third-largest drug distributor in the country, becoming a flourishing and rapidly-growing company that was attracting $1.5 billion in sales by the beginning of 1986. Elsewhere, there was a company on the lookout for a thriving enterprise of FoxMeyer's type, a company that was attempting to break out of a mold formed during more than five decades of existence as a steel producer. That company was NII, and in early 1986 its acquisitive eye would stop and rest on the fast-growing wholesale drug distributor known as FoxMeyer Corporation.

NII was in many respects the creation of Howard M. Love, who would spend the 1980s as one of the most closely watched business leaders during the decade. Love was promoted in 1980 to chief executive officer of National Steel Corporation, then the sixth-largest steel company in the United States. National Steel Corp. traced its roots back to the 1929 merger of Great Lakes Steel Company, Hanna Iron Ore Company, and the Weirton Steel Company. The company operated exclusively as a steel concern following the merger that created it, remaining a one-faceted enterprise until 1964, when National Steel Corp. opened its first metal service center. Four years later, the company entered the aluminum industry, developing this new business segment into a significant contributor to its overall sales. By the end of the 1970s, steel and aluminum were driving National Steel Corp.'s growth, but in 1979 the company began to diversify beyond its two primary businesses, branching into new areas to lessen the company's exposure to the historically cyclical steel market. No individual embraced the concept of diversification more tightly than the person named as National Steel Corp.'s chief executive officer in 1980, Howard "Pete" Love.

The vehicle for Love's diversification plans was formed in 1983, a holding company that would serve as a corporate umbrella under which a variegated range of businesses would be controlled and help engender an international industrial and financial services conglomerate. That company was NII, its creation approved by National Steel Corp. shareholders in September 1983, when they agreed to receive one share of NII for each share of National Steel Corp. they held. Concurrently, National Steel Corp. became a wholly owned subsidiary of its new parent company, NII.

The push toward diversification began in earnest for the newly formed NII in 1984, just as FoxMeyer was beginning to bolster its position in the wholesale drug distribution market following its initial public offering. In September 1983, Love addressed a press conference organized to publicize the creation of NII, telling the reporters in attendance, "I don't see steel ever

being less than 50 percent of the company. It is our core business and we intend to keep it on that basis." Four months later, however, things began to change. In early 1984, NII reached an agreement in principle with the United States Steel Corporation to sell the steel giant's largest business group, National Steel Corp. Though the deal ultimately fell through, major divestitures were completed before the year was through that stripped the company of significant steel operations. NII sold Weirton Steel to Weirton Steel's employees and sold 50 percent of National Steel Corp., the company's original business, to a Japanese company, Nippon Kokan KK.

### 1986 Acquisition by National Intergroup

More changes were in the offing for NII, as Love endeavored to reposition the company to avoid the capricious steel market. In an interview with *American Metal Market,* a national trade publication, Love hinted at what the future might hold for NII, saying, "We will probably become a three-legged stool. One segment in the steel, aluminum, and distribution business, another in financial services, and the third is yet to be acquired." The third, as-yet-to-be-determined leg that NII would rest on would be FoxMeyer and eventually the wholesale drug distribution business operated by FoxMeyer would be the only leg supporting NII.

After acquiring Permian Corporation, a Houston-based oil distribution company, in 1985, NII acquired FoxMeyer in March 1986. That same month, FoxMeyer in turn acquired Ben Franklin Stores Inc., a chain of 1,300 five-and-dime stores, and then six months later the company acquired Lawrence Pharmaceuticals, a Jacksonville, Florida-based wholesaler. These two additions strengthened what already had represented a valuable asset for NII, giving the company a sturdy foundation in the wholesale distribution business. By the time NII acquired FoxMeyer, the drug wholesaler controlled 400 Health Mart drugstores, which combined with the addition of a retail chain, Lawrence Pharmaceuticals, and the $1.5 billion FoxMeyer collected sales each year, propelled Love's diversification program decisively. What looked good on paper, however, did not perform well in reality, as Love, his executives, and NII shareholders quickly discovered in the years following the acquisition of FoxMeyer.

### Lackluster Late 1980s

Before the dust had settled from the move into the wholesale drug business, NII was reeling from the affects of its far-flung and ambitious diversification program. By early 1987, the company was experiencing dire financial difficulties. Oil prices had plummeted, hobbling Permian Corporation's business, FoxMeyer had not performed up to expectations, recording a 50 percent decline in profits in 1986, and the chain of Ben Franklin stores were plagued by problems arising from its merger into FoxMeyer. Saddled with $600 million in debt, NII was floundering, raising the ire of shareholders who pointed their accusative fingers at the company's chairman, chief executive officer, and orchestrator of the diversification program, Howard Love. As the late 1980s progressed, NII's condition did not improve and by 1990 the frustration and anxiety pervading the NII organization reached a climax.

As NII entered the 1990s, the company's financial performance was woeful, a trait not developed overnight. Between 1984 and 1990, NII posted six consecutive years of net per share losses, a record that needless to say did not impress the company's shareholders. The company, by this point, had abandoned its diversification plan, opting instead to shed businesses that no longer fit with the company's future plans. In 1989, NII sold the bulk of its aluminum business, then in 1990 reduced its stake in National Steel Corp. to 13.33 percent, leaving Fox-Meyer as the source for 85 percent of the former steel company's total sales. With its fate resting primarily on FoxMeyer's business, NII appeared to be heading in one, clear direction after more than a decade of pursuing a host of eclectic business interests, but in 1990 a dissident shareholder group led by Centaur Partners, L.P., a New York investment group, won several important seats on NII's board and removed Love from command. In the wake of Centaur Partners' ascension, Permian Corporation was sold, then FoxMeyer itself was slated for divestiture, a move that would strip the company of nearly all its revenue-generating power.

### The 1990s

FoxMeyer was put up for sale in August 1990 and remained on the auction block until March 1991, but an acceptable offer never surfaced. Six months later, in August 1991, an alternative solution was found, and a public offering of a percentage of FoxMeyer's stock was put on the market. The public offering reduced NII's stake in FoxMeyer to 67 percent, lessening the nearly $3 billion-a-year drug distributor from the deleterious debt problems weighing down its parent company. After rumors of takeover of FoxMeyer in 1992 died down, the massive distributor of pharmaceutical and health and beauty aids experienced the latest in a lengthy series of major corporate changes. In October 1994, FoxMeyer Corporation merged with NII, creating a new company named FoxMeyer Health Corporation that, despite the years of turmoil surrounding it, entered the late 1990s with high expectations for future growth.

During the 1980s, the wholesale drug industry in the United States grew 300 percent, giving participating companies the opportunity to achieve robust growth. At the same time the wholesale drug industry was expanding meteorically, the number of competitors vying for a share of the ever-increasing business dropped, plunging 40 percent during the decade. Growth continued in the 1990s, with further industry-wide con-

traction expected to occur as the decade progressed. Enviably positioned as the second-largest drug wholesaler during the mid-1990s, FoxMeyer Health Corporation was expected to gain a lion's share of the wholesale drug industry's business in the years to come and put to rest the difficulties characterizing its first decade of existence.

### Principal Subsidiaries

Ben Franklin Retail Stores, Inc. (67.2%); Ben Franklin Transportation, Inc.; FoxMeyer Corp. (80.5%); FoxMeyer Realty Company; FoxMeyer Software, Inc. (80%); Intergroup Services, Inc.; M&A Investments, Inc.; National Aluminum Corporation; National Intergroup Realty Corporation; National Intergroup Realty Development, Inc.; National Magnesium Corporation; National Steel Products Company, Inc.; Natmin Development Corporation; Natoil Corporation; NII Health Care Corporation; NI World Trade, Incorporated; Oceanside Enterprises, Inc.; Riverside Insurance Co., Ltd. (Bermuda); Starcom International, Inc. (80%)

### Further Reading

Aikens, Tom, "Fate of NII's FoxMeyer Corp. Up in Air After Vote," *Pittsburgh Business Times,* July 30, 1990, p. 3.

Balcerek, Tom, "NII Bid for Drug Firm Part of Distribution Shift," *American Metal Market,* February 11, 1986, p. 2.

Bergin, Daniel M., "National Intergroup, FoxMeyer for Sale," *Drug Tropics,* September 17, 1990, p. 23.

Biesada, Alexandra, "Love's Labors Lost: Cursed Is the Son of a Famous Man Who Tries to Live Up to His Father's Image," *Financial World,* May 1, 1990, p. 30.

Golightly, Glen, "Rumors Put FoxMeyer in Takeover Spotlight," *Dallas Business Journal,* March 20, 1992, p. 25.

LaRue, Gloria T., "National: Picture Beyond Steel," *American Metal Market,* February 23, 1984, p. 1.

Mehlman, William, "Liberated FoxMeyer Refining the Identity of Drug Wholesalers," *The Insiders' Chronicle,* December 9, 1991, p. 1.

Miles, Gregory L., "At National Intergroup, the Choice May Be Love or Money," *Business Week,* July 11, 1988, p. 28.

——, "The Best-Laid Plans of Howard Love," *Business Week,* August 10, 1987, p. 74.

Ricketts, Chip, "Service Helps FoxMeyer Weather Changes," *Dallas Business Journal,* February 19, 1990, p. 5.

Teaff, Rick, "FoxMeyer President Ready for Independence," *Pittsburgh Business Times,* June 11, 1990, p. 1.

—Jeffrey L. Covell

# Frederick Atkins Inc.

1515 Broadway
New York, New York 10036
U.S.A.
(212) 840-7000
Fax: (212) 536-7029

*Nonprofit Company*
*Founded:* 1900
*Sales:* $367 million (1995)
*Employees:* 430
*SICs:* 5023 Home Furnishings; 5136 Men's and Boys'
Clothing and Furnishings; 5137 Women's, Children's
and Infants' Clothing and Accessories; 5199
Nondurable Goods, Not Elsewhere Classified; 8732
Commercial Economic, Sociological and Educational
Research

Frederick Atkins Inc. is a nonprofit marketing organization that functions as a cooperative buying office for the department and specialty stores who own it and are its members. The company also conducts retail-marketing research studies for its members. It earns revenue from fees charged to members, based on each store's sales volume, and from private-label sales of apparel and home goods. In 1993 Frederick Atkins had 30 members in the United States and four foreign affiliates. Together they were operating more than 900 stores in North America and had sales totaling an estimated $14 billion in that year.

## The Founding Father

Frederick Atkins began his business career in 1874, when at the age of 13 he went to work as a stock and general handy boy in a store for $1 a week. He opened his office as a resident buyer in New York City's Union Square in 1900. This enterprise grew to become first Atkins Mercantile Co. and later Frederick Atkins Inc. By 1938, when Atkins was honored at a testimonial dinner for his 50 years as a resident buyer in New York City, he was representing 30 department stores in the United States and

abroad and was buying goods valued at as much as $100 million a year. By the time Atkins died in 1946, his firm was owned by its member clients.

By the mid 1950s there were some 700 buying offices in the United States, of which nearly 500 were located in New York City. They not only bought merchandise but monitored supplies, prices, and fashion trends; looked for new items; and issued market reports and surveys to the stores they represented. They even served as a clearinghouse for communication between members. In 1954 Frederick Atkins had members who sold a combined $475 million worth of merchandise. The next year it picked up as a member the Philadelphia department store John Wanamaker. Like other buying offices, the company usually represented only one store in a city so that information remained confidential in any one area.

## Second Place in Its Field

Robert J. Futoran became president of Frederick Atkins in 1967. Interviewed by the *New York Times,* the new president declared that his company's members were challenged both by discount retailers and chains like Sears and Penney's. This and other major trends in retailing, he continued, were causing the independent stores to "buy more creatively and more efficiently in order to compete." Futoran went on to recommend long-term planning to his clients, including establishing a demographic outline of the customers being aimed at, the product mix, the price range, and profit and volume growth. "I'm also very high on fashion research," he added. "The central buying office . . . must stress creative market development. That means not just accepting what the market is, but also to help it creatively to design new fashion ideas."

By 1969 Frederick Atkins was second only to the Associated Merchandising Corp. among buying offices and merchandising-research centers in the United States. Its 40 members had annual sales volume of more than $1.2 billion. According to Charles W. Veysey, its incoming president in 1970, Frederick Atkins was better described not as a buying office but as "a consulting and researching organization" that helped its members generally develop their total business by keeping abreast of the market. Veysey told the *New York Times* that groups like Frederick Atkins were needed to enable independents to compete with chain stores. He also said that the trends of the future for his members, who included B. Altman in New York and Halle Bros. in Cleveland, were buying merchandise abroad and buying private-label goods, because they would provide the buyers with exclusive merchandise.

In the course of its work Frederick Atkins was keeping track of detailed sales and inventory data: for example, of the availability and disposition of 5,000 to 6,000 dress styles in 10 departments within 300 department stores in the United States. This information was entered on file cards before Atkins bought an IBM 360-20 computer and Cognitronics remote optical character-recognition scanner. By 1974, when an Atkins buyer gave an order to a vendor, the information was entered in the computer. As the merchandise was sold, stores sent in data on optical character-recognition sheets, punch cards, or magnetic tape, which the computer used to produce a midweek sales report, weekly sales summary, and vendor analysis report. "We couldn't operate the way we do without it," an Atkins executive told a business consultant. "There would be just too much to keep track of."

Frederick Atkins was also prominent in longer-range projections of consumer buying. An in-depth 1977 study of the dress business resulted in ten "educated guesses" defining what was likely to determine women's lifestyles in the 1980s. It concluded that by the early 1980s more than half of all American women would be gainfully employed, and that the majority of working women would be career- rather than job-oriented. Women would be participating equally, and often unilaterally, in making major financial decisions for the family, as well as making all financial decisions regarding their own personal needs for such things as clothing. It also concluded that non-working women of the 1980s would rather quickly accept most of the new social values, women would wait longer before marrying and starting families, there would be fewer children in the average family, sex attitudes would become more liberal, and women would, because of higher family income and greater educational levels, have the ability and interest to participate in a broad range of activities.

The implications for the retailer, according to the Atkins study, were that the market for women's clothing would be more heterogeneous to fit a variety of activities, that there would be a broader range of styles available, and that women would wear what they thought would be appropriate instead of believing they must wear certain outfits for certain occasions. It also concluded that women might need larger wardrobes to fit their growing number and variety of activities and thus would spend somewhat less for each garment. Since they would be too busy to spend much time shopping, they would seek to save time and effort and would be likely to make more impulse purchases. Retailers might have to organize clothing according to lifestyles or activities rather than by price or by separating outerwear from sportswear and dresses, the study concluded.

### Expanded Package of Services

Veysey was succeeded in 1981 as president and chief executive officer of Frederick Atkins by Fred O. Lawson, Jr. Inter-

viewed by the *New York Times,* Lawson called the term "buying office" antiquated and said of his company, "We provide marketing direction and research to try to direct our stores to the strongest possible resource structure in each classification." He predicted that in the future more and more of Frederick Atkins's member stores would have units in the same community. The firm's 50-odd members at this time included Altman's, the Broadway in Los Angeles, and D.H. Holmes in New Orleans.

Frederick Atkins in 1983 considered, but rejected, a merger proposed by Associated Merchandising that would have created a combined group with $15 billion in annual purchasing power. Both organizations were owned by their members, whereas most buying offices were representing retailers for a fee, but sources in the industry said a major difficulty was the likely reduction of as much as 30 percent of the staffs of both concerns. Another problem would have been posed in cities where the merged group would be representing major competing stores, such as Wanamaker and Strawbridge & Clothier in Philadelphia.

Many other buying offices closed or merged during the 1980s, reflecting a difficult decade for their members. Frederick Atkins, however, expanded its headquarters in the Times Square area in 1992, signing a new 15-year lease for 135,000 square feet of office space, compared to the 100,000 square feet it already occupied in the same Broadway building. After nearly two years of negotiations, the landlord agreed to upgrade as well as expand Atkins's space, exacting only a "minimal increase" in the rent per square foot. The company had been considering leaving Manhattan, in part because of the downturn in department-store business in the early 1990s.

Frederick Atkins announced plans in 1992 to raise its wholesale private-label sales from $400 million a year to $1 billion a year by 1997. Lawson, who had been promoted to chairman in 1987, told a *WWD (Women's Wear Daily)* interviewer that Atkins-developed private labels accounted for about seven percent of store inventories but that it hoped to raise this to 12 percent in five years. He said there had been particularly strong acceptance of the Clean Clothes line of all-cotton basics introduced in 1991, packaged with biodegradable materials. Atkins also was offering about two dozen labels in women's ready-to-wear and sportswear, including Silvercord, Allison Smith, and Danielle Martin, and was also developing menswear and home-goods lines.

Lawson also announced that Frederick Atkins planned to open an export office in Mexico in response to the North America Free Trade Agreement. He mentioned handbags, shoes, men's suits, and women's sportswear and dresses among the goods that could ultimately come from Mexican suppliers. The free-trade agreement, he continued, also would enhance Atkins's relationships with its Canadian and Mexican affiliates, including Toronto-based The Bay and Mexico City-based Liverpool Mexico S.A. The Mexican office would check quality control, execute letters of credit, and aid visiting Atkins product managers, operating, like its other overseas agents, on a commission basis.

Frederick Atkins, Lawson added, would continue to provide its members with a package of services, including regular meetings with the office's staff to discuss group buys, fashion overviews, catalogues, bestsellers, and office-price buys. Staff members would continue spending much time on the road to advise stores on presentation. The figure exchange would continue to allow stores to compare inventory-to-sales ratios, turnover, and margins. He noted that The Bay and Honolulu-based Liberty House had left Associated Merchandising in 1992 to join Atkins.

### Further Reading

Barmash, Isadore, "Buyers' Services Found Useful," *New York Times,* December 15, 1969, p. 77.

——, "New Atkins Chief Sounds Warning," *New York Times,* September 24, 1967, Sec. 3, p. 16.

"Frederick Atkins," *New York Times,* November 18, 1946, p. 23.

"Frederick Atkins Honored by Stores," *New York Times,* December 8, 1938, p. 42.

Giles, William E., "Big-City Agents Offer a Growing Variety of Services to Retailers," *Wall Street Journal,* June 9, 1955, pp. 1, 10.

King, Pat, " 'Modest' Computer Controls Inventory," *Administrative Management,* January 1974, p. 37.

Moin, David, "Atkins Targets Mexican Goods, Private Label," *WWD,* August 24, 1992, pp. 1, 8.

"New Chief at Atkins," *New York Times,* September 8, 1981, p. D2.

" 'New Woman's' Wardrobe to Be Varied, Voluminous: Moss," *Marketing News,* April 8, 1977, p. 7.

"2 Buyers Halt Plans for Merger," *New York Times,* March 15, 1983, pp. D1, D11.

—Robert Halasz

# Frederick's of Hollywood Inc.

**6608 Hollywood Boulevard**
**Los Angeles California 90028-6259**
**U.S.A.**
**(213) 466-5151**
**Fax: (213) 463-8847**

*Public Company*
*Incorporated:* 1962
*Employees:* 1,500
*Sales:* $142.93 million (1995)
*Stock Exchanges:* New York
*SICs:* 5632 Women's Accessory & Specialty Stores;
        5961 Catalog & Mail-Order Houses

With over 200 retail outlets in 39 states and a rejuvenated mail order business, Frederick's of Hollywood Inc. has been selling lingerie for over 50 years. Having endured its first-ever annual loss in the mid-1980s, the company underwent a thorough makeover in the later years of the decade. Under the direction of Chairman and Chief Executive Officer George W. Townson, the company transformed its product lines, remodeled its stores, and redesigned its catalogs.

## Postwar Foundation

The company is named for its founder and longtime president Frederick Mellinger, who conceived of his lingerie business while serving in the armed forces during World War II. After his discharge, Mellinger established a mail order undergarment operation in New York City. Known as Frederick's of Fifth Avenue, his shop offered racy black bras and panties embellished with lace and appliqués.

Mellinger took his fancy foundations to more permissive California in 1947, changing the name of the catalog business to Frederick's of Hollywood that same year. Tinseltown's glitz and glamour provided the perfect backdrop for the groundbreaking retailer, and a parade of starlets and models provided a ready customer base.

Mellinger, who came to be known as "Mr. Frederick" among his clientele, soon began to specialize in figure-enhancing foundations and accessories. He designed his first push-up bra, dubbed the "Rising Star," in 1948. Fanny pads, girdles, sky-high heeled shoes, hosiery, wigs, false eyelashes, even head pads to achieve the illusion of height—anything necessary to achieve "Frederick's figure balancing act"—followed in the years to come. The company even offered an inflatable bra that came complete with a "free straw." The catalogs and stores later added glamorous evening wear, much of it designed by Mr. Frederick himself. The garments featured daring necklines, high slits, and sheer fabrics intended to appeal to men as much as women. In fact, Mellinger once wrote that his goal was to offer "the most alluring, body-hugging, figure-enhancing outer fashions . . . always aimed at men."

Mr. Frederick opened his first retail stores in California in the early 1950s. The flamboyant Art Deco flagship store soon became known as "the purple palace." Mellinger also started advertising his catalog and garments in nationally-circulated magazines using saucy taglines like "Fashions Change—But Sex is Always in Style." After incorporating in 1962, Frederick's continued to expand its product offerings in the sexually permissive environment of the 1960s and 1970s. Soon pasties, anonymously-written sexual guides, and other "sexually oriented non-apparel products" appeared in the catalogs.

Although Frederick's offered its stock to the public in 1972, the Mellinger family continued to control a majority of the company's stock through the early 1990s. By the end of the decade, the chain had expanded to over 150 stores, accounting for over half of overall sales. The company enjoyed peak prosperity during the mid-1970s. Sales more than doubled, from $9.7 million in 1971 to $24 million in 1976, while net income tripled, from just under $500,000 to $1.5 million. It was to be Frederick's highest-ever profitability, as a combination of societal changes and management problems converged on the lingerie retailer.

Americans' sexual mores and their tastes in lingerie grew increasingly conservative in the 1980s. However, the septuagenarian founder and his management team were slow to realize

## Company Perspectives:

*Although Frederick's of Hollywood has changed ... to conform to the tastes of contemporary America, the company's fashions have remained distinctive. Today's fashions are romantic, feminine and quality-oriented, sometimes playful, and still sexier than anything else available on the market, but always in good taste. The company's customers are teenagers, young adults, homemakers, career women and senior citizens. Most of Frederick's customers are women, but at holiday time, Frederick's also becomes the place to shop for the men who love them.*

these trends. (Unbeknownst to the board of directors, in fact, Mellinger was afflicted with Alzheimer's disease during this time.) While company sales rose from $39.3 million in 1981 to $45.3 million in 1984, net profits slid from a high of $2.2 million to $627,000. This dramatic decline in profitability was reflected in the company's eroding stock price, which dropped from $7 in mid-1983 to less than $2 by mid-1985. By the time Mellinger retired in September 1984, his company had experienced its first-ever loss, a $148,000 shortfall on sales of about $45 million. In 1985, *Forbes* magazine's Ellen Paris speculated that Frederick's dip into the red meant that sex must be "going out of style." Nevertheless, when Mellinger died in 1990 at the age of 76, he was praised as a brave pioneer of intimate fashions and groundbreaking foundations.

Former Executive Vice-President Robert W. Hansen assumed the presidency on an interim basis while Frederick's board of directors sought a replacement for the venerable founder. In May 1985, they hired former Carter Hawley Hale home furnishings division chief George Townson to take the reigns at Frederick's. Townson brought two decades of experience in mail order retailing, although none of it was in apparel, let alone lingerie.

### From Raunch to Romance in the Late 1980s

It didn't take Townson long to pinpoint Frederick's problems. He later enumerated the shortcomings to *Direct Marketing*'s Mollie Neal: "outdated business assumptions, deteriorating conditions of our stores, ineffective management, inadequate merchandising and financial reporting systems, a dwindling core customer base, more sophisticated competition, archaic structures and antiquated policies." The new CEO immediately mapped out a ten-year plan for what he called the "desleazification" of Frederick's.

Store renovations shunned the traditional garish purples and hot pinks for more subtle lavenders and mauves, while softer lighting and new carpeting in the stores made for a more romantic, less burlesque atmosphere. The high profile, $300,000 renovation of the "purple palace" was a prime example of this physical repositioning. Not only did the company redecorate, but it also celebrated its heritage with the opening of the world's first Lingerie Museum, featuring some of Frederick's earliest designs as well as undergarments of the stars. Los

Angeles Mayor Tom Bradley declared "Frederick's of Hollywood Day" on the occasion of the grand reopening, November 8, 1989. The vast majority (80 percent) of Frederick's nearly 200 stores had been redecorated by 1991.

CEO Townson hired marketing consultant Walter K. Levy, to assess the company's product line and target audience. A new merchandising scheme emerged from his observations. Frederick's pared what had become an excessively broad and (in the eyes of many Americans) lewd line, dropping such items as explicit videos and bawdy games. Frederick's stores also stopped carrying certain lines of apparel and accessories, including wigs, sportswear, and swimwear (although these last two categories continued to be offered in mail order catalogs). At the same time, the company expanded its loungewear and men's undergarment lines.

The revamp—or, as many company observers punned, "devamp"—of Frederick's of Hollywood catalogs also focused on bringing the publication out of the fringes and into the mainstream. Even into the 1980s, the catalogs had featured explicit black and white photos interspersed with exaggerated and cartoonish line drawings. The new catalogs featured heavier paper, a new logo and motto ("An Intimate Experience"), and tasteful color photographs of models wearing Frederick's lingerie. Although catalog sales slid by about five percent with the first new issue, they quickly began to recover, with sales and profits gaining by double-digit percentages in the latter years of the decade. Frederick's move from mail-order's "red-light district" enabled it to buy mailing lists from catalogers who would have previously been embarrassed to be associated with the lingerie merchant. As a result, catalog circulation more than tripled from 7.5 million in 1985 to 26 million by 1990.

Behind the scenes, CEO Townson purged the executive ranks, bringing in 18 new managers within his first two years at the top. He also invested in a new computer hardware, including cash registers and data processing equipment and software. Frederick's retail rebirth clearly followed the lead of upstart competitor Victoria's Secret, a subsidiary of The Limited Inc. By 1988, Victoria's Secret had more than triple the annual sales volume with about the same number of stores. But while Frederick's had shed much of its most explicit merchandise and imagery, the company still managed to maintain its "naughty" cachet. Townson reflected on this factor in a 1996 interview with Marianne Wilson of *Chain Store Age Executive* magazine, noting that "Generally speaking, Victoria's Secret is more mainstream and romantic. Frederick's is fun and sexy." The new CEO's turnaround was effective and quick. Frederick's sales more than doubled from $45.2 million in 1985 to $114.1 million in 1991 and profits burgeoned to an historic high of $5.2 million.

### Furtive Growth in the Early 1990s

Sales increased from $117 million in fiscal 1992 to nearly $143 million in 1995, while profits declined from $5.1 million to a loss of $903,000 in 1994, then rebounded to $2.7 million in 1995. Townson blamed Frederick's difficulties on rising postage and paper costs, a generally soft retail environment, and increasing competition. Indeed, Townson's 1995 letter to shareholders noted that "department stores, mass merchandisers and specialty stores have significantly expanded their intimate apparel lines.'' By this time, Victoria's Secret alone had $1.8 billion sales and 600 retail outlets, and was expected to be spun off from The Limited in 1996.

In 1995, the company made its first international foray, circulating a holiday catalog in Canada. In 1996, on the occasion of the company's 50th anniversary, CEO Townson hoped to bring Frederick's of Hollywood full circle by launching its first-ever store in New York City. Given its well-established brand, reinvigorated growth, and young, savvy management team, Frederick's of Hollywood Inc. appeared poised for another 50 years of growth.

### Principal Subsidiaries

Frederick's of Hollywood Stores, Inc.; Hollywood Mail Order Corp.; Walgers, Inc.; Private Moments Inc.

### Further Reading

Caminiti, Susan, ''The Leading Man of Lingerie,'' *Fortune,* October 10, 1988, p. 163.
Cone, Edward F., ''Skimpy Garments, Big Profits,'' *Forbes,* January 9, 1989, p. 12.
Cook, Dan, ''Risque Business,'' *California Business,* May 1991, p. 21.
Edelson, Sharon, ''Getting More Intimate: 2 Key Lingerie Chains Focus on Manhattan,'' *Women's Wear Daily,* November 13, 1995, p. 1.
''Frederick's of Hollywood: A History: 1946–1996,'' Hollywood: Frederick's of Hollywood, 1996.
''Frederick's Year in Black,'' *Women's Wear Daily,* November 6, 1995, p. 16.
Ginsberg, Steve, ''Frederick's of Hollywood: A New Image,'' *Women's Wear Daily,* March 10, 1988, p. I23.
Gill, Penny, ''Desleazification Pays Off,'' *Stores,* May 1991, p. 44.
Gordon, Mitchell, ''Frederick's of Hollywood Boasts Alluring Sales and Earnings Curve,'' *Barron's,* March 1, 1976, pp. 66–67.
Gottwald, Laura, and Janusz Gottwald, *Frederick's of Hollywood, 1947–1973: 26 Years of Mail Order Seduction,* New York: Drake Publishers, Inc., 1973.
Marlow, Michael, ''Taming the Tease,'' *Women's Wear Daily,* July 8, 1991, p. 3.
Monget, Karyn, ''Frederick Mellinger Dead at 76; Rites Held,'' *Women's Wear Daily,* June 5, 1990, p. 14.
——, ''Frederick's Gets Payoff From its Cleaned-Up Act,'' *Women's Wear Daily,* January 18, 1990, p. 7.
Neal, Mollie, ''Naughty to Nice,'' *Direct Marketing,* April 1990, p. 35.
Paris, Ellen, ''Is Sex Going Out of Style?'' *Forbes,* December 30, 1985, p. 94.
Rees, David, ''Earnings Plunge Hits Frederick's Share Price Amid Upbeat Market,'' *Los Angeles Business Journal,* July 20, 1992, p. 7.
Wilson, Marianne, ''Frederick's Looks to Future With Updated Design,'' *Chain Store Age Executive,* May 1996, p. 116.
Wilson, Marianne, ''The De-Sleazification of Frederick's,'' *Chain Store Age Executive,* September 1989, p. 94.

—April Dougal Gasbarre

# *f*rontier

# Frontier Corp.

**180 South Clinton Avenue**
**Rochester, New York 14646-0700**
**U.S.A.**
**(716) 777-1000**
**Fax: (716) 325-4624**

*Public Company*
*Incorporated:* 1899 as Home Telephone Co. of Rochester
*Sales:* $2.14 billion (1995)
*Employees:* 7,837
*Stock Exchanges:* New York Boston Chicago
*SICs:* 4812 Radiotelephone Communications; 4813
    Telephone Communications, Except Radiotelephone

Confined to upstate New York for most of the century, Rochester Telephone became Frontier Corp. in 1995 and immediately began to transform itself from a provider of telephone service in specific parts of the United States to a nationwide provider of integrated communications services. By the end of the year Frontier, the 12th largest local-exchange service provider in the United States, was also the fifth largest U.S. long-distance telephone carrier. The company was providing local telephone services in 13 states and other telecommunication services, including cellular systems and voice, video, and data communications, to a much wider market. It also was selling and installing telecommunications systems and equipment. Offering itself as a one-stop telecommunications provider, Frontier had a customer base of 2.1 million and sales locations in 149 cities in the United States, Canada, and Great Britain in the mid-1990s. Its slogan was "Everything, Everywhere, for Everybody."

## *Rochester Telephone to Midcentury*

The city of Rochester, New York, first received telephone service in 1879. Although subscribers were unhappy with the rates, the local affiliate of the Bell System could not be challenged until Alexander Graham Bell's first patent expired in 1893. In January 1899 a group of Rochester business leaders incorporated the Home Telephone Co. of Rochester, which was renamed the Rochester Telephone Co. later in the year. It soon spread throughout Monroe County and neighboring counties by acquisition of other independent companies, but its subscribers also had to take Bell service to be linked to the many areas served only by Bell companies. Consequently, although in 1907 Rochester Telephone served almost 10,000 subscribers, New York Telephone Co.—the Bell company—had 14,000, despite its higher rates. Rochester Telephone, which soon raised its own rates, had net earnings of $172,417 in 1912 and $177,818 in 1920, when its assets came to $3.1 million.

The two rival telephone companies merged in 1921, forming an independent (non-Bell) company named the Rochester Telephone Corp., with local men in charge. Long-suffering customers did not celebrate the greater convenience for long because the new company introduced meters on all business phones in place of flat rates. Nevertheless, all benefited from a capital-spending program, much of it to replace open wire with underground and aerial cable. The company's 100,000th telephone was installed in 1929. It was serving 40 incorporated villages and cities in a six-county area of 2,200 square miles in western and central New York, with a population of about 500,000.

The Great Depression that followed the Wall Street crash of 1929 reached its nadir in 1932, when the number of Rochester Telephone phones in service dropped by 11,051 and the company's net income fell to $322,726, compared to $883,407 in 1929, a peak not topped until 1950. The 1930 company payroll of $2.7 million was not equaled again until 1941. In 1935 the company announced that, with some exceptions, in order to spread jobs over a greater number of families, it would no longer employ married women. Dividends, however, continued to be paid out regularly through the Depression. By 1940 earnings had almost recovered to the 1930 level, and total assets came to $23.5 million.

World War II brought a near-halt to Rochester Telephone's capital spending. In 1948 the city received its first, long-awaited dial system, although the company's costly conversion from manual switching was not completed until 1966. In 1950 Rochester Telephone earned $1.05 million on operating revenues of $12.2 million and had 184,322 telephones in service. With the

---

## Company Perspectives:

*We commit ourselves to the following values that must guide our performance each and every day. We listen and respond to customers' expectations at all times, determined to be their first choice. We conduct our business guided by the highest standards of ethics. We build a diverse team of employees, hiring and providing advancement based on individual ability and job requirements. We take every opportunity to learn. We communicate with our employees and the public in an effective, candid and timely way. We provide our owners with excellent returns.*

---

opening of new rural lines and the extension of service to new subdivisions, the number of subscribers almost doubled between 1945 and 1955. Rochester Telephone, which first offered common stock to the public in 1944, issued five more common-stock and three preferred-stock offerings in the 1950s in order to raise money for new construction. In 1959 it became the only independent, unaffiliated telephone company listed on the New York Stock Exchange.

### Sizzling Sixties, Stagnant Seventies

In 1960 Rochester Telephone enjoyed its best earnings yet, with net income of more than $3 million on revenues of nearly $27.8 million. Total assets were $105.8 million. In 1961 the ratio of telephones in service to the number of employees—the mark of efficiency in the telephone industry—increased to 121.2. The following year the number of telephones in service increased by a record 16,733 to 332,077. Another record increase of 17,167 was attained in 1963, and earnings reached new levels in both years. The 400,000th telephone in service was installed in 1966. Two years later the company reached new highs in revenues, earnings, and telephones added.

Beginning in 1969, Rochester Telephone took responsibility for handling all long-distance telephone calls originating in its territory, including long-haul toll traffic that had historically been in the hands of New York Telephone Co. Its customers were then able to dial all their long-distance calls, and over the company's own equipment. Speaking to securities analysts in 1968, Rochester Telephone's president declared, ''We are the only independent telephone company operating in a city of this size'' and predicted that the population of the Rochester metropolitan area would pass a million by 1980.

Rochester Telephone installed its 500,000th telephone in service in 1970. Its operating revenues for the year totaled $76.3 million, and its net income was $11.6 million, although there had not been a general rate increase since 1958. Dividends had been increased in every year since 1960, and the company had been able to raise the money it needed for expansion chiefly by internal cash generation. As early as 1971 Rochester Telephone became the first local carrier to let customers hook up their own terminal equipment and, in 1977, it was among the first companies to begin selling, rather than renting, telephones to customers. In 1974 Rochester Telephone acquired the Sylvan Lake

Telephone Co., Inc. as a subsidiary, extending its reach to a 275-square-mile area of eastern New York. Two years later it expanded into the Catskills, acquiring Highland Telephone Co., which was serving a 335-square-mile area in Orange and Ulster counties.

During a six-and-a-half-month strike in 1974–75 Rochester Telephone put 600 management employees to work doing the jobs of the 1,200 workers who had walked out. This experience convinced top executives that they could reduce the work force, which fell from 3,342 in 1975 to 2,858 in 1980. Rochester Telephone created a subsidiary called Rotelcom Inc. in 1978, with divisions for marketing telecommunications systems, distributing equipment and supplies, refurbishing telephone sets for resales, and providing consulting services for telephone companies and commercial organizations. In 1980 the company created a new subsidiary, Rotelcom Data Inc., to sell computer services and hardware to businesses. The Rotelcom subsidiaries, unlike the parent company, were free from rate regulation by the state Public Service Commission.

### New Markets in the 1980s

By 1980 it was clear that the Rochester area, like New York generally, was falling behind the rest of the nation in economic growth. Instead of reaching the million-mark in population, the metropolitan area only had about 840,000 people. Rochester Telephone, which was serving 621,949 telephones at the end of the year and had 4.4 million miles of wire, reported record operating revenues of $181.8 million and record net income of $29.6 million, but it was looking for ways of expanding outside its operating area. The company acknowledged that, despite an outstanding record in profit margin, its average annual revenue growth of 8.6 percent during 1976–80 compared poorly to the average annual growth in the industry of 12.2 percent.

Rotelcom was providing one important avenue of growth. By the end of 1981 it had customers in 24 states, plus Bermuda, and accounted for 15 percent of the parent company's total revenues. The breakup of the AT&T Bell System ordered in 1982 offered new opportunities for expansion. In that year the company created RCI Corp. as an intercity carrier and began work on a $80 million fiber-optic-based network for RCI, which concentrated on selling private lines to large companies. Rochester Telephone also stepped up efforts to acquire small, rural independent telephone operators, many of them highly profitable once the parent company centralized their operations. By early 1991 it owned 33 telephone operating subsidiaries providing telephone services to customers in 14 states. Rochester Telephone had total revenues and sales of $600 million in 1990, with consolidated net income of $49.7 million. During the 1990–1994 period, Rochester Telephone was among the top ten public telecommunications companies by return on equity and profit per employee.

### A Company Transformed in 1995

In 1993 Rochester Telephone made a bold proposal: it offered to become the nation's first local telephone company to let regulators open up to competition its exclusive franchise. This initiative was realized at the beginning of 1995, when Rochester became the first U.S. city since 1920 to allow residents a choice of local carriers. Time Warner Inc., with some 200,000 Rochester-area cable customers, vowed to compete for their telephone business as well. AT&T Corp. also jumped in, buying access to local lines at wholesale prices and reselling local service under its own name. Nevertheless, by April 1996 Time Warner and AT&T held only three percent of the Rochester market, and AT&T stopped marketing its local service.

In return for allowing rivals to poach on its preserve, Rochester Telephone won permission from state regulators to split into separate companies: a regulated wholesaler of telephone services named Rochester Telephone Corp. and an unregulated retailer named Frontier Communications of Rochester. This came into effect in January 1995, when a parent holding company named Frontier Corp. was concurrently created. The state Public Service Commission also agreed to free Rochester Telephone from a regulation limiting it to an annual return on equity of about 11 percent, in return for which the company agreed to a ten percent rate cut, followed by a seven-year rate freeze.

In August 1995 Frontier Corp. merged with ALC Communications Corp. in a transaction valued at $3.8 billion in stock. Along with ALC, Frontier gained Confer Tech International, the world's largest dedicated multimedia teleconferencing company. Later in the year Frontier acquired LINK-VTC, a videoconferencing-services company. A month earlier, Frontier had purchased Schneider Communications Inc., a long-distance voice and data carrier, and its 81 percent interest in LinkUSA Corp., a long-distance services provider, for $127 million. Other 1995 acquisitions were WCT Communications, a West Coast long-distance company; Enhanced TeleManagement, Inc., offering integrated telecommunications services in six states; American Sharecom, Inc., a Minneapolis-based long-distance company; and Minnesota Southern Cellular Telephone Co. Frontier also established its first international subsidiary for integrated services, London-based FronTel Communications Ltd.

In the mid-1990s Frontier was concentrating on "bundling," that is, offering one-stop shopping to customers that included local service, long distance, cellular phones, paging, videoconferencing, Internet access, and possibly cable television, all in one package, on one monthly bill. Frontier was convinced bundling would make unattractive to customers switching to suppliers of individual products offering cheaper prices. Frontier already held 25 percent of the long-distance traffic in Rochester and, through a joint venture with Bell Atlantic Nynex Mobile, half of its cellular market. It was also the largest local Internet provider, with 2,000 customers, and was set to fill orders for videoconferencing. Frontier reported that it had already made bundling a reality in Chicago, Cleveland, Columbus, Los Angeles, Milwaukee, Minneapolis, Portland (Oregon), Sacramento, San Francisco, Seattle, Syracuse, Toledo, and London, as well as Rochester.

At the end of 1995 Frontier, through 34 local telephone companies, served 950,875 access lines in 13 states. Long-distance products and services were provided to commercial and residential customers throughout the United States and in Great Britain, generally under the Frontier name. The company was managing a cellular network providing service in upstate New York and managing cellular systems in Alabama and Minnesota. It also had interests in wireless properties in five states. Long-distance communications services provided 69 percent of Frontier's 1995 revenues, while local communications services accounted for 29 percent, wireless communications services for 0.6 percent, and other services for the remaining 1.4 percent.

Frontier had revenues of $2.14 billion in 1995, up from $1.67 billion in 1994 and $978.8 million in 1990. Its net income fell from $180.1 million in 1994 to $22.1 million in 1995, principally because of a $121.2-million charge for extraordinary items, of which $78.8 million was related to acquisitions. The dividend on common stock was increased in 1995 for the 36th consecutive year.

### Principal Subsidiaries

ALC Communications Corp.; FronTel Communications Ltd.; Frontier Cellular Holding Inc.; Frontier Communications of Rochester; Frontier Network Systems; Telco Inc.; Frontier Telecommunications Inc.; Rochester Telephone Corp.; RTC Main Street, Inc.

### Further Reading

Arnst, Catherine, "The New Era Begins in Rochester," *Business Week*, February 20, 1995, p. 97.
Clifford, Mark, "Hey, This Is a Phone Company," *Forbes*, July 14, 1986, pp. 40, 42.
"Frontier Plans to Buy ALC in Stock Swap," *New York Times*, April 11, 1995, p. D2.
Hayes, John R., "The Bundler," *Forbes*, April 22, 1996, pp. 82, 84, 86.
Howe, F.L., ed., *This Great Contrivance: The First Hundred Years of the Telephone in Rochester*, Rochester, N.Y.: Rochester Telephone Corp., 1979.
McKelvey, Blake, *Rochester: An Emerging Metropolis, 1925–1961*. Rochester, N.Y.: Christopher Press, 1961, pp. 200–201, 321.
——, *Rochester on the Genesee*, Syracuse, N.Y.: Syracuse University Press, 1993, pp. 148–149, 174–175.
——, *Rochester: The Quest for Quality: 1890–1925*, Cambridge, Mass.: Harvard University Press, 1956, pp. 250–252, 340.
"More Fun, More Opportunities, More Rewards," *Telephony*, February 18, 1985, pp. 36–40, 42, 44.
"Rochester Telephone Corporation," *Wall Street Transcript*, July 8, 1968, p. 13808; September 12, 1977, p. 48138; April 5, 1981, p. 65249.
"Rochester Telephone: Long Term Appeal," *Financial World*, January 3, 1973, p. 9.
"Rochester Tel Is Going for the Growth," *Telephony*, August 4, 1980, pp. 23–27, 48.

—Robert Halasz

# FUJITSU

# Fujitsu Limited

6-1, Marunouchi 1-chome
Chiyoda-ku, Tokyo 100
Japan
(03) 3216-3211
Fax: (03) 3216-9352

*Public Company*
*Incorporated:* 1935
*Employees:* 49,000
*Sales:* ¥3.76 trillion (US$35.49 billion) (1995)
*Stock Exchanges:* Tokyo Osaka Nagoya London Zürich
    Basel Geneva Frankfurt
*SICs:* 3571 Electronic Computers; 3651 Household
    Audio & Video Equipment; 3663 Radio & TV
    Broadcasting & Communications Equipment

Perhaps the most dramatic example of Japan's ability to overcome long odds in a short space of time has been the growth of its computer industry, and the undisputed leader among Japanese computer makers is Fujitsu Limited. Ranked second in the world behind IBM, Fujitsu is very much a product of Japan's willingness to tackle large-scale industrial projects with a combination of private ambition and governmental funding. Since 1950 Fujitsu has become the Japanese government's primary weapon in its struggle to develop an indigenous computer industry in the face of IBM's superior might. Fujitsu operates within three main areas: computer systems—once predominantly mainframes, it now also includes client-server systems, personal computers, supercomputers, software, and peripherals—telecommunications systems, and semiconductors.

### Early History

Fujitsu was created on June 20, 1935 as the manufacturing subsidiary of Fuji Electric Limited and charged with continuing the parent company's production of telephones and automatic exchange equipment. Fuji Electric, itself a joint venture of Japan's Furukawa Electric and the German industrial conglomerate

Siemens, was part of Japan's attempt to overcome its late start in modern telecommunications. Spurred by Japan's expanding military economy, Fujitsu quickly branched off into the production of carrier transmission equipment in 1937 and radio communication two years later. Yet the country's telephone system remained archaic and incomplete, with German and British systems in use that were not fully compatible. World War II ruined a large part of this primitive system, destroying some 500,000 connections out of a total of 1.1 million, and leaving the country in a state of what might be called communication chaos. At the insistence of the occupying U.S. forces, Japan's Ministry of Communications was reorganized and nearly became a privately owned corporation that would have simply adopted existing U.S. technology to rebuild the country's telephone grid. A coalition led by Eisaku Sato, however, convinced the government to instead form a new public utility, Nippon Telephone and Telegraph (NTT). Created in 1952, NTT soon became a leading sponsor and purchaser of advanced electronic research, and it continued to be one of Fujitsu's key customers.

The link with NTT may well have been Fujitsu's greatest asset, but Fujitsu was only one of a series of increasingly determined government partners for the country's young computer industry. Fujitsu first became interested in computers in the early 1950s, when Western governments and large corporations began making extensive use of them for time-consuming calculations. After a number of years of experimentation Fujitsu succeeded in marketing Japan's first commercial computer, the FACOM 100.

This was a start, but the Japanese computer business was still in its infancy when IBM brought out the first transistorized computer in 1959. So great was the shock of this quantum leap in design that the Japanese government realized it would have to play a far more vigorous role if the country was not to fall permanently behind the United States. The government formulated a comprehensive plan that included restrictions on the number and kind of foreign computers imported, low-cost loans and other subsidies to native manufacturers, and the overall management of national production to avoid needless competition while encouraging technological innovation. Of equal importance, in 1961 the Japanese government negotiated with IBM

224

for the right to license critical patents, in exchange allowing the U.S. giant to form IBM Japan and begin local production.

### 1960s Computer Developments

Patents in hand, seven Japanese companies entered the computer race. All of them except Fujitsu quickly formed alliances with U.S. companies to further their research; Fujitsu, refused by IBM in a similar offer, remained the only "pure," or *junketsu*, Japanese computer firm, committed to the development of its own technological expertise. The other Japanese companies were all much larger than Fujitsu and devoted only a fraction of their energy to computers, while Fujitsu soon devoted itself to communications and computers.

Able to build on its already substantial electronics experience Fujitsu was directed by the government to concentrate on the development of mainframes and integrated circuitry, and in late 1962 it was given the specific goal of developing a competitor to IBM's new 1401 transistorized computer. The government stalled IBM's plans for local production and enlisted Hitachi, NEC, and Fujitsu in what it called project FONTAC, the first in what would become a series of government-industry drives. From the perspective of the marketplace, FONTAC was a complete failure—before it got off the ground IBM had launched its revolutionary 360 series, pushing the Japanese further behind than when they started—but as a first try at a coordinated national computer program, FONTAC proved to be extremely important. Fujitsu and the other Japanese manufacturers could afford poor initial performance, knowing that funds were available for further research and development. In particular, the Japanese government had by this time formed the Japanese Electronic Computer Company (JECC), a quasi-private corporation owned by the seven computer makers but given unlimited low-interest government loans with which to buy and then rent out newly produced computers. In effect, this allowed Fujitsu and the others to receive full payment for their wares immediately, thus greatly increasing corporate cash flow and making possible the huge outlays for research and development.

The result of JECC's largesse was immediate: in the space of a single year—1961 to 1962—Japanese computer sales in-

creased by 203 percent. In 1965 Fujitsu, relying largely on technology developed as part of the FONTAC project, brought out the most advanced domestic computer yet built, the FACOM 230. The company had quickly become JECC's leading manufacturer, supplying approximately 25 percent of all computers purchased by the firm during the 1960s. In addition, Fujitsu had continued its substantial work for NTT, with over half of its telecommunication products going to the phone company by the end of the decade. NTT remained a critically important governmental agency for Fujitsu and the computer industry, routinely shouldering research-and-development costs and paying high prices to ensure that its suppliers remained profitable. NTT also sponsored a super-high-performance computer project in 1968, similar in design and scope to one begun the previous year by the Ministry for Trade and Industry (MITI), to develop a new computer for its complex telecommunications needs. Both of these ambitious programs, were paid for by rival government ministries.

### Development of the M Series in the 1970s

Despite this concerted effort, however, by 1970 the Japanese were suffering from IBM's recent introduction of its 370 line. Worse yet, under international pressure the Japanese government had agreed to liberalize its import policy by 1975, giving the local computer industry a scant five years in which to become truly competitive. MITI responded by making computer prowess a national goal, greatly increasing subsidies, and reorganizing the six remaining companies into three groups of cooperative pairs. Fujitsu, as the leading mainframe maker, was paired with its arch-rival Hitachi and given the task of matching IBM's 370 line with a quartet of its own heavy-duty computers, to be called the M series.

The need to build IBM-compatible machines led Fujitsu to an important decision. In 1972 the company invested a small but vital sum of money in a new venture started by Gene Amdahl, a former IBM engineer who had been largely responsible for the design of its 360 series computers. Amdahl Corporation had been formed with the express intent of building a cheaper, more efficient version of IBM's 370 line, which made a joint venture with Fujitsu highly advantageous for both partners. With its strong government support, Fujitsu had access to the capital Amdahl badly needed, while the U.S. engineer was a valuable source of information about IBM operating systems. Fujitsu and Amdahl persevered in what became a most profitable sharing of technology and capital.

A key factor in the Fujitsu-Amdahl deal was the Japanese company's confidence that it could rely on NTT to pay top dollar for whatever computer evolved from the new venture. In this, as in many other situations, NTT served as a kind of guaranteed market for Fujitsu, which in turn was well on its way to becoming a world leader in telecommunication technology and hence a more valuable supplier to NTT. The Fujitsu-Hitachi M series of high-speed computers emerged in the late 1970s. With the M series, the Japanese had achieved a rough parity with the IBM systems. Fujitsu had become one of IBM's very few real competitors in the area of general-purpose mainframe computers; in 1979 Fujitsu took a narrow lead over IBM in Japanese computer sales that held through the mid-1990s.

### *New Initiatives of the 1980s*

After the watershed events of the 1970s, Fujitsu in the 1980s pushed ahead with an impressive array of projects in each of its three main marketing areas. In computers, which generated 60 to 70 percent of overall corporate revenue, Fujitsu continued the success of its M series while branching out into minicomputers, workstations, and personal computers. The company spent much of the 1980s in a legal dispute with IBM over the latter's charge that Fujitsu had improperly copied IBM's software. An arbitrator decided in 1988 that, after $833 million in payments to IBM, Fujitsu could continue to buy access to IBM software for ten years at a cost of at least $25 million a year. The agreement was meant as a spur to further mainframe competition. In the 1980s Fujitsu also became a leading manufacturer of supercomputers, with some 80 such units installed by the end of the decade. Though easily the leading mainframe maker in Japan, Fujitsu had little success exporting its products—with only 22 percent of corporate sales made overseas, Fujitsu remained overly dependent on its Japanese business. In particular, the company was unable to break into the U.S. market, where, in addition to the obvious presence of IBM, its mainframe bias was seen as somewhat outdated. The trend in large computer systems at the time was toward greater distribution of processing power, aided by individually tailored software applications—two areas in which Fujitsu was notably weak.

Fujitsu remained strong in telecommunications, however, where it continued its close relationship with NTT as well as with the newly emerging New Common Carriers. In light of its origin in the telecommunication field, it was not surprising that Fujitsu became a world leader in the development of Integrated Services Digital Network (ISDN), a convergence of data processing and telecommunications aiming to carry voice, image, data, and text all on one system. Fujitsu was also active in other improvements in telecommunications such as COINS (corporate information network systems), PBXs (private branch exchanges), and digital switching systems. The company also provided important terminal and branching equipment for the Trans-Pacific Cable #3, the Pacific Ocean's first optical submarine cable.

Fujitsu maintained a strong presence in its third product area as well, electronic devices. In 1987 the firm was prevented by the U.S. government from acquiring Fairchild Camera, a leading U.S. manufacturer of memory chips, but it still managed to sell about $2.5 billion worth of chips annually. The very fact that Fujitsu was barred from purchasing Fairchild was a testament to the company's strength in semiconductors as well as computers. In conjunction with the Japanese government and other Japanese computer firms, Fujitsu continued to refine its chip technology in anticipation of the arrival of the fifth generation of computers, proposed machines that would be able to write their own software and in some meaningful sense "think."

### *Partnering and Restructuring in the 1990s*

In the end, however, Fujitsu's 1980s activities proved unable to carry a healthy firm into the 1990s. Observers noted (in hindsight) that the company had played a mainly follow-the-leader (IBM) strategy which emphasized mainframe computers—this began to catch up with Fujitsu in the early 1990s as the shift to networked systems and client-server systems accelerated, cutting the market for mainframes dramatically. Other initiatives undertaken in the 1980s to great fanfare proved less important long-term than little-noticed projects; in telecommunications, for example, ISDN was still being touted as the system of the future as late as 1996, while Fujitsu's NIFTY-Serve online service, which debuted in 1986, was seen as the centerpiece of the company's telecommunications operation in the mid-1990s because of the emergence of the Internet (NIFTY-Serve had about 1.6 million subscribers in Japan in 1996).

The year 1990, then, became a year of transition for Fujitsu upon the appointment of Tadashi Sekizawa, a telecommunications engineer, as president. Sekizawa wanted Fujitsu to be more aggressive in its pursuit of foreign markets (80 percent of revenue in 1989 came from Japan), to become more market-driven, and to lessen the stifling bureaucracy that impeded product development.

To bolster the firm internationally, Sekizawa continued to seek non-Japanese partners for growth, wishing to utilize local experts knowledgeable about local markets. Already having a partner in the United States through its 43 percent stake in Amdahl, Fujitsu gained a major European partner in July 1990 when it spent £700 million (US$1.3 billion) for an 80 percent stake in International Computers Ltd. (ICL), Britain's largest and most important mainframe maker. Fujitsu and ICL—which had become a subsidiary of STC in 1984—had already collaborated on several projects, beginning in 1981. Fujitsu's European operations were further bolstered in 1991 when ICL acquired Nokia's data systems group, which was the largest computer company in Scandinavia. The U.S. market was further targeted as well with a $40 million investment in HaL Computer Systems, Inc., a start-up firm aiming to develop UNIX systems, UNIX being an increasingly popular operating system.

Unfortunately for Fujitsu, the Japanese economic bubble burst in 1991 just as the company was beginning to implement Sekizawa's program. As a result, profits fell 85.2 percent from ¥82.67 billion in fiscal 1990 to ¥12.21 billion in fiscal 1991; the following two years, Fujitsu posted losses—¥32.6 billion in fiscal 1992 and ¥37.67 billion in fiscal 1993. Looming over these figures was the downside of the company's huge investments of the 1980s—a US$12.4 billion debt by 1992.

The recession precluded Fujitsu from making further international moves in 1991, and capital spending was slashed one-third that year. Strategically, however, research and development spending was not cut. Since the Japanese culture prevents companies in Fujitsu's position from making large work force reductions to cut costs, Sekizawa dramatically cut the number of new hires. Meanwhile, to lessen its dependence on mainframe sales and strengthen its PC area, Sekizawa in 1992 established a cross-functional Personal Systems Business Group with the aim of speeding up product development. Also intended to improve product development speed was a restructuring that created a flatter organizational structure and lessened corporate bureaucracy.

Fujitsu's huge debt ruled out any major investments to create new products, so the company turned to partnerships to an even greater degree as the decade continued. The deals included: developing a next generation of less expensive mainframes with Siemens; establishing a joint venture with Advanced Mirco Devices, Inc. called Fujitsu AMD Semiconductor Limited to produce flash memory; creating multimedia technology with Sharp Corp.; developing microprocessors for Sun workstations with Sun Microsystems; and relying on Computer Associates to market Jasmine software in the United States.

Clearly, Fujitsu was juggling a number of initiatives as well as dealing with weakening mainframe sales and a difficult, highly competitive semiconductor market. Encouragingly, revenues rose sharply in fiscal 1994 (¥3.26 trillion) and 1995 (¥3.76 trillion), while the company also returned to profitability, posting net income of ¥45.02 billion in 1994 and ¥63.11 billion in 1995. It was too soon to know for sure whether Fujitsu had weathered the storms of the early 1990s, but under Sekizawa's forceful guidance the company seemed determined to regain its lofty position of the late 1980s.

### *Principal Subsidiaries*

Fujitsu Laboratories Ltd.; Fujitsu Business Systems Ltd.; Fujitsu Kiden Ltd.; Fuji Electrochemical Co., Ltd.; Shinko Electric Industries Co., Ltd.; Fujitsu TEN Limited; PFU Limited; Fujitsu Denso Ltd.; Fujitsu FACOM Information Processing Corporation; Fujitsu AMD Semiconductor Limited; Fujitsu America, Inc. (U.S.A.); Fujitsu Business Communication Systems, Inc. (U.S.A.); Fujitsu Network Transmission Systems, Inc. (U.S.A.); Fujitsu Personal Systems, Inc. (U.S.A.); HaL Computer Systems, Inc. (U.S.A.); Fujitsu Computer Products of America, Inc. (U.S.A.); Fujitsu Microelectronics, Inc. (U.S.A.); Fujitsu Compound Semiconductor, Inc. (U.S.A.); Fujitsu—ICL Systems Inc. (U.S.A.); Fujitsu Network Switching of America, Inc. (U.S.A.); Fujitsu Computer Packaging Technologies, Inc. (U.S.A.); Fujitsu Open Systems Solutions, Inc. (U.S.A.); Fujitsu Systems Business of America, Inc. (U.S.A.); Ross Technology, Inc. (U.S.A.); Fujitsu Canada, Inc.; Fujitsu Systems Business of Canada, Inc.; Fujitsu do Brasil Limitada (Brazil); International Computers (South Africa) (Pty) Ltd.; Fujitsu Europe Limited (U.K.); Fujitsu Microelectronics Ltd. (U.K.); Fujitsu Deutschland GmbH (Germany); Fujitsu Mikroelektronik GmbH (Germany); Fujitsu Microelectronics Ireland Limited; Fujitsu International Finance (Netherlands) B.V.; Fujitsu España, S.A. (Spain); ICL PLC (U.K.; 84%); Fujitsu Europe Telecom R&D Centre Limited (U.K.); Fujitsu Telecommunications Europe Limited (U.K.); Fujitsu Finance (U.K.) PLC; Fujitsu France S.A.; Fujitsu Italia S.p.A. (Italy); Fujitsu Microelectronics Italia S.r.l. (Italy); Fujitsu Nordic AB (Sweden); Fujitsu Australia Ltd.; Fujitsu Microelectronics (Malaysia) Sdn. Bhd.; Fujitsu Microelectronics Asia Pte. Ltd. (Singapore); Fujitsu (Thailand) Co., Ltd.; Fujitsu Australia Software Technology Pty. Ltd.; Fujitsu Australia Wholesale Pty. Ltd.; Fujitsu Australia Finance Pty. Ltd.; Nanjin Fujitsu Computer Products Co., Ltd.; Beijing Fujitsu System Engineering Co., Ltd. (China); Fujitsu Hong Kong Limited; Fujitsu Microelectronics Pacific Asia Ltd. (Hong Kong); Fujitsu India Telecom Limited; Fujitsu Optel Limited; Fujitsu ICIM Software Technologies Pty. Ltd.; P.T. Fujitsu Systems (Indonesia); Fujitsu Korea Limited; Fujitsu Component (Malaysia) Sdn. Bhd.; Fujitsu New Zealand Holdings Limited; Fujitsu New Zealand Limited; Fujitsu Computer Products Corporation of the Philippines; Fujitsu (Singapore) Pte. Ltd.

### *Further Reading*

Anchordoguy, Marie, *Computers Inc.: Japan's Challenge to IBM*, Cambridge: Harvard University Press, 1989, 273 p.

Brull, Steven V., and Gary McWilliams, " 'Fujitsu *Shokku*' Is Jolting American PC Makers," *Business Week,* February 19, 1996, p. 50.

Brull, Steven V., et. al., "Fujitsu Gets Wired: The Company Is Staking Its Future on the Still Elusive Frontiers of Cyberspace," *Business Week,* March 18, 1996, pp. 110–12.

"Company History," Tokyo: Fujitsu Ltd., corporate typescript, 1989.

*Creative Partners in Technology,* Santa Clara, Calif.: Amdahl Corporation, 1989.

Eisenstodt, Gale, "Race against Time," *Forbes,* December 21, 1992, pp. 292–96.

"Fujitsu's Sekizawa: Dealing with Changing User Requirements," *Datamation,* September 1, 1992, pp. 87–89.

Gross, Neil, and Robert D. Hof, "Fujitsu Gets a Helping Hand from an American Buddy," *Business Week,* June 28, 1993, p. 46.

Hills, Jill, *Deregulating Telecoms,* Westport, Conn.: Quorum Books, 1986, 220 p.

"Japanese Semiconductors: Flat as a Pancake," *Economist,* May 4, 1996, p. 66.

"Japan's Less-than-Invincible Computer Makers," *Economist,* January 11, 1992, pp. 59–60.

Johnston, Marsha W., "ICL Builds a Software House," *Datamation,* May 1, 1991, pp. 80–87.

Meyer, Richard, and Sana Siwolop, "The Samurai Have Landed: How the Japanese Computer Makers Slipped into Europe Almost Unnoticed," *Financial World,* September 18, 1990, pp. 46–50.

Meyer, Richard, "Japan's Brave New World: The Industry Fears the Commodity Computer. Fujitsu Prepares for It," *Financial World,* January 21, 1992, pp. 48–49.

Mood, Jeff, "Next Stop, World Markets," *Datamation,* August 1, 1989, p. 28.

Morris, Kathleen, "What IBM Could Have Done: IBM Almost Halved Its Staff, and It Still Has Problems. Fujitsu Thinks It Can Grow Its Way Out of Mainframe Dependence," *Financial World,* March 15, 1994, pp. 32–34.

Schlender, Brenton R., "How Fujitsu Will Tackle the Giants," *Fortune,* July 1, 1991, pp. 78–82.

—Jonathan Martin
—updated by David E. Salamie

# G&K Services, Inc.

**5995 Opus Parkway**
**Suite 500**
**Minnetonka, Minnesota 55343**
**U.S.A.**
**(612) 912-5500**
**Fax: (612) 912-5739**

*Public Company*
*Incorporated:* 1902 as Gross Brothers; 1934 as Gross-
Kronicks
*Employees:* 4,200
*Sales:* $262.5 million (1995)
*Stock Exchanges:* NASDAQ
*SICs:* 7218 Industrial Launderers

G&K Services, Inc. is the fourth largest, and the fastest growing, supplier of rental uniforms in the United States and Canada, with more than 30 processing plants and 51 sales and service centers operating in 28 states, as well as in Quebec and Ontario. Since the acquisition of BCP Corporation of North Carolina in 1994, G&K has also entered uniform manufacturing and direct sales and expects to make up to 50 percent of the uniforms it rents and sells. In addition to uniforms, which produce about 60 percent of company revenues, G&K rents and sells floor mats, industrial mops, towels and other linens, and soaps, cleaners, and air fresheners. In all, the company processes more than 600,000 uniforms per day. The company also operates a fleet of 800 service and delivery vehicles. G&K's $262 million in 1995 sales formed about 6 percent of the estimated $3.5 billion North American uniform leasing industry. Chief competitors include industry leader Aramark Corp., Cintas Corp., Unifirst Corp., and Unitog Co. G&K is headed by chairman and CEO Richard M. Fink.

### Early History

G&K started out as a family-owned business in the Minneapolis-St. Paul area when brothers Alexander and Morris Gross purchased a small dry cleaning and dyeing company. Renamed Gross Brothers Laundry, that business expanded to include family laundry services, becoming the largest laundry business in the Twin Cities area by the 1930s.

I. D. Fink joined Gross Brothers in 1927, as the company prepared to expand its range of services. In 1934, the purchase of a small Minneapolis-area company, Northwest Linen Co., led Gross Brothers into linen supply and textile rentals. The following year, Gross Brothers bought another local company, Kronicks Laundry, changing its name to Gross-Kronicks, which soon became known as G&K. In that year Fink along with other second-generation members of the Gross family took over operations of the company, with Fink being named president in 1939.

G&K continued to lead the local dry cleaning and laundry industry, while increasing its textile rental operations. In 1956, the company added uniform rentals. Over the next decade, leasing, especially uniform rentals, would provide the company with its greatest growth potential. For the time being, however, revenues from rentals grew only slowly. By the end of the 1960s, the G&K chain had grown to 45 retail laundry and dry cleaning stores, with annual revenues of $12 million.

The next generation was preparing to take over leadership of the company. Richard M. Fink joined G&K in 1964 and was named vice-president in 1968. The following year, as president, Richard Fink led the company into its initial public offering, changing the company's name formally to G&K Services, Inc. By then rentals, which reached $6 million in revenues, were outpacing the company's laundry operations. At the same time, the introduction of new, wash-and-wear fabrics in the clothing industry was softening the dry cleaning business, with retail revenues falling by as much as 10 percent per year. Meanwhile, the rise of the service industry, which incorporated uniforms as a means to enhance corporate identities, promised to become the fastest growing segment of G&K's operations. In the early 1970s, the company sold its laundry and dry cleaning operations, then the largest part of its business, to concentrate exclusively on leasing, emphasizing uniform rentals.

### Becoming an Industry Leader

G&K's rental operations still were limited, for the most part, to five Twin Cities locations. But in the 1970s the company moved aggressively to expand into neighboring states. Much of this expansion was fueled by a series of acquisitions, primarily of small companies, beginning with the 1971 purchases of Central Uniform Rental Co. and Southern Uniform Rental Co., both in Colorado. The following year, G&K added Service, Inc. of Utah and in 1974 acquired Illinois companies Ajax Industrial Cleaners, Inc. and Ace Launderers & Cleaners.

By 1976, G&K's revenues had risen to $16.5 million, earning the company nearly $850,000. In that year, G&K continued its acquisitions and expanded its range of leasing services with cash purchases of Peoria Apron & Towel Supply, Inc. in Illinois and Maloney's Dust Control Services, Inc. in Green Bay, Wisconsin. By the end of the decade, the company had added Service Industrial Rental Supply, for $1.7 million in 1978, and expanded into the South with the acquisition of Fort Worth, Texas-based Johnson Linen-Texas Garment Co. When I. D. Fink retired as chairman in 1977, the company's operations had expanded from a single metropolitan area into seven states.

The company slowed the pace of its acquisitions somewhat over the next decade as it dedicated itself to expanding its customer base in the fast-growing, but highly fragmented, uniform leasing industry. In the first half of the 1980s, the company acquired Willis Uniform & Linen Service and Chin Industries. The latter purchase brought G&K into Louisiana and Alabama. By 1984, revenues rose to $56 million, providing net income of more than $2 million. Yet, internal expansion was already providing the bulk of the company's growth.

Sales topped $100 million by 1989, and G&K's markets had grown to include California, and the burgeoning semiconductor cleanroom segment there, with the $3.2 million purchase of Certified Garments in 1986. Sales would continue to climb over the next decade, with a compounded annual growth rate of more than 15 percent, making G&K the industry's fastest growing company. By 1990, with a net income of more than $10 million on revenues of nearly $119 million, G&K was preparing its first international expansion.

### Trouble and Triumph in the 1990s

At the start of the 1990s, G&K was operating in 23 states, including 20 processing plants and 28 sales and service centers. In 1990, G&K moved across the border into Canada, making its largest acquisition to date, the $77 million purchase of one of that country's largest uniform-leasing companies, Work Wear Corp. of Canada, Ltd. Work Wear, with 25 percent of the Ontario

market and operations in Quebec as well, added a 50 percent boost to G&K's revenues (about $62 million in U.S. dollars) while raising the company's debt more than $90 million.

Trouble loomed, however, with the threat of an international recession, which, coupled with the economic crises brought on by the Persian Gulf War, proved to be Canada's worst since the Depression. Whereas the uniform rental business had been seen as largely immune to cyclical changes in the economy, G&K's Canadian operations were faced with increasing numbers of company failures and layoffs, driving down customer orders. G&K's U.S. operations remained steady, aided by the growing boom in service sector jobs in the 1990s. But despite revenue increases to $176 million in 1991 and to $194 million in 1992, the losses in Canada and investment in two new U.S. processing plants dragged profits down, to $7.7 million in 1991 and $8.5 million in 1992.

By 1993, however, profits were again on the rise, with the Canadian operations returning to profitability and boosting net profits to $11 million on $208 million in revenues. The company's 44 sales and service centers and 29 processing plants served more than 85,000 customers. Retention rates among G&K's customers, which included about half of the country's largest industrial corporations, typically ranged at 93 percent, with most customer losses stemming from companies going out of business or dropping uniforms to save money. By then, G&K's customer base spanned a broad range of industries, including food service companies, schools, office buildings, auto dealerships and auto repair and service centers, as well as transportation and distribution companies. An increasingly important source of new and existing customers were the pharmaceutical and semiconductor industries, with their need for special sanitary fabrics and cleaning techniques. G&K responded to this need by building a state-of-the-art processing plant in San Jose, California, the heart of the U.S. semiconductor industry.

Although major accounts were typically handled by the company's large sales force, delivery personnel, acting as local sales personnel, were also an important source of new orders. Drivers of G&K's fleet, who not only received pay based on performance, but also commissions for completing new sales, accounted for some 40 percent of the company's new accounts. G&K's share of the highly fragmented uniform rental market, with around 1,200 companies clothing about eight million uniformed personnel in the mid-1990s, was around seven percent, suggesting ample room for future growth.

Beginning in 1993, G&K moved to expand its share of the total uniform industry by offering direct sales to corporations making outright purchases of uniforms, which represented the largest segment of the uniform industry, with some 100 million uniformed personnel. The following year, G&K purchased BCP Corporation of North Carolina and that company's three uniform manufacturing plants in Mississippi and the Dominican Republic, for $7.5 million. Company expectations were to produce as much as half of its rental and direct sale uniforms by the end of 1995, increasing the company's margins while driving down costs. As G&K turned toward the next century, with 1995 revenues of $262 million and sales expected to top $300 million in 1996, the company planned to expand its operations into every market in the United States, while maintaining its leadership in Canada. The continued growth of G&K's core customer base, especially the service and distribution industries, which accounted for some 70 percent of the gross domestic product of the United States, appeared likely to drive this company's continued growth.

### Principal Subsidiaries

G&K Services Co.; Northwest Linen Co.; Gross Industrial Towel & Garment Service, Inc.; G&K Services of Canada, Inc.; 912489 Ontario Limited (Canada); La Corporation Work Wear du Quebec (Canada).

### Further Reading

Byrne, Harlan S., "G&K Services Inc. Acquisition To Boost Firm's Results," *Barron's,* October 22, 1990.
——, "G&K Services: Its Canadian Venture Is Beginning To Turn a Profit," *Barron's,* August 30, 1993, p. 43.
"G&K Services, Inc.," *The Wall Street Transcript,* December 12, 1994.
Jones, John A., "G&K Services Growing Fast in Booming Uniform Business," *Investor's Business Daily,* May 22, 1995.
Youngblood, Dick, "Fink's G&K Services Enjoys a Clean Rate of Growth," *Minneapolis Star Tribune,* October 2, 1995.

—M.L. Cohen

# Garan, Inc.

**350 Fifth Avenue**
**New York, New York 10018**
**U.S.A.**
**(212) 563-2000**
**Fax: (212) 564-7994**

*Public Company*
*Incorporated:* 1957
*Employees:* 2,600
*Sales:* $141.3 million (1995)
*Stock Exchanges:* American
*SICs:* 2321 Men's and Boys' Shirts, Except Work Shirts;
2329 Men's and Boys' Clothing, Not Elsewhere
Classified; 2331 Women's, Misses' and Juniors'
Blouses and Skirts; 2339 Women's, Misses and
Juniors' Outerware, Not Elsewhere Classified; 2361
Girls', Children's and Infants' Dresses, Blouses and
Skirts; 2369 Girls', Children's and Infants' Outerwear,
Not Elsewhere Classified

Garan, Inc. is engaged in the design, manufacture, and sale of men's, women's, and children's apparel, some of it under the Garan name. Its output includes knit shirts, sweatshirts, T-shirts, and sweaters bearing the names and insignia of professional sports teams and leagues or colleges and universities. Other articles of clothing, for children, depict Disney-produced characters, scenes, and logos. Most of Garan's output is sold to major national chain stores, department stores, and specialty stores. Garan was the nation's fifth largest children's wear company in 1995.

## 1957–1965: Eight Years of Growing Profits

Garan was incorporated in 1957 as a merger of seven companies, the first of which was incorporated in New York in 1941 as Myrna Knitwear, Inc. Its name originated from management coining ''Garantee'' as the name for a new T-shirt but instead deciding to use the first part of the word as the corporate title.

Company headquarters were located in Manhattan's garment district. Sales rose to $9.1 million in fiscal 1960 (the year ended September 30, 1960) from $3.2 million in 1957, when net income was only $47,000.

By 1961, the year the company went public, Garan was the nation's leading manufacturer of men's and boys' knitted sport shirts. It also made men's and boys' woven sports shirts, polo shirts, and boys' knitted pajamas. Knitted products were being made from cotton, acrylics, polyester and cotton blends, and textralized nylon yarn. Woven products were being made from cotton and rayon, and from cotton, acetate, and polyester blends. The materials were being purchased from a number of textile manufacturers.

More than 90 percent of Garan's sales volume of $8.8 million in 1961 came from its sports shirts, which retailed for between $1.95 and $2.95. About two-thirds of its output was being sold under private labels, with the remainder selling under the Garan name. Accounts included Macy's, J.C. Penney, Woolworth's, and Sears, Roebuck. A new plant in Lambert, Mississippi began manufacturing higher-priced Ban-Lon shirts from Garan's own knitted fabric in 1961, and another factory, in Clinton, Kentucky, also began operations that year.

Garan's first public offering, at $6.50 per share on the American Stock Exchange, raised $700,000 for the company and enabled it to finance its own receivables without factoring (hiring someone else to collect its bills). Almost two-thirds of the shares, the value of which rose as high as nearly $21 per share in 1961, remained in the hands of the officers and directors of the company, headed by the president and chairman of the board, Samuel Dorsky, and the executive vice-president and secretary, Seymour Lichtenstein, who soon advanced to president. The company's property in 1962 consisted of six leased factories in Kentucky, Mississippi, Pennsylvania, and Tennessee, and a warehouse in Tennessee. Net sales rose to $12 million that year, and net income increased to $464,703 from the previous fiscal year's $328,894. The company then declared a dividend for the first time.

Sales and net income for 1963 reached new levels of $15.1 million and $547,000, respectively. A 76,000-square-foot facility for the production of woven sports shirts opened in Kosciusko, Mississippi, in 1963, replacing two smaller units, and the company began selling Acrilon (as well as Ban-Lon) shirts for boys under its own Rhodes label. The following year Garan opened another 76,000-square-foot plant for knitted garments in Starksville, Mississippi, and a 35,000-square-foot factory for woven sports shirts in Carthage, Mississippi. The Lambert facility was doubled in size. Plans were begun to devote part of the existing Adamsville, Tennessee, facility to popular-priced, man-tailored women's blouses.

A new factory opened in Philadelphia, Mississippi, in 1965 for the manufacture of boys' jeans and slacks. Garan's net sales reached nearly $23 million that year, and its net profit increased for the eighth year in a row. Long-term debt was only $1.9 million. All nine of the company's plants were situated in the South. Penney and Sears were taking about two-thirds of total production. The company's Rhodes label, sold through department stores, was being promoted only modestly, and its own Garan label, directed at discounters and chain stores, required only minimal advertising.

The going got rougher for Garan in the next few years. Profits fell for the first time in 1966 because of inventory write-offs in velour, high in-house costs for a computer system subsequently phased out, and the costs of decentralizing company-wide operations to a divisional basis. Net income passed the million-dollar mark in 1967 and doubled in 1968 but fell to $920,000 in 1969 as the company's Ban-Lon sweaters and shirts met with increased competition. In 1970 sales fell from $45.1 million to $43.8 million, although net income rose slightly.

### The 1970s: A Wider Mix of Products

By 1972 Garan was back in stride, having topped $2 million in net income the previous year. Heightened productivity, tighter cost controls, fewer markdowns, and a wider mix of products were credited for the company's turnaround. Of its eleven factories, seven were located in Mississippi and one each was located in California, Kentucky, Louisiana, and Tennessee. The company started making men's pants in 1969, jeans for girls in 1971, and children's apparel in 1972. It also introduced a ''Jugs'' line of pants and knit shirts for girls 15 years and older. Shirts now represented only 46 percent of Garan's varied production. Roughly three-quarters of its merchandise bore the labels of its customers, and the balance was being sold under the Garan label.

By the mid-1970s Garan was a broad-based producer of knitted and woven apparel for girls (but not women), infants, and men as well as boys. Branded children's apparel was introduced in 1972 under the Garanimals label, a system of coordinating tops and bottoms with color-keyed mix-and-match animal tags and hangers. Two years later the company opened a new plant devoted exclusively to turning out knitted tops and woven bottoms for infants and toddlers. Garan also restored men's knit sport shirts as a meaningful part of its apparel mix. A licensing division established in 1975 began distributing sweatshirts, sweaters, knit shirts, and T-shirts bearing designs of professional sports leagues and teams.

There were 23 Garan plants at the end of 1977, a year in which net sales reached $122.8 million and net income rose to $7.7 million, both records. The Garanimals label accounted for 30 percent of sales volume. Sears and Penney remained the largest of Garan's more than 2,000 accounts. Long-term debt was only $1.9 million. About 44 percent of the company's shares of common stock were closely held.

### The Early 1980s: High Profits from Children's Wear

Garan averaged an excellent annual return on equity of more than 17 percent between 1979 and 1983. During this period it added the Garan Mountain Lion brand name, which along with Garanimals accounted for more than half of company sales in 1983 and also enjoyed higher profit margins than the firm's private labels. Licensed sweatshirts and T-shirts continued to be marketed through mass merchandisers, department stores, and other customers. Sales of children's clothing represented about 70 percent of the 1983 sales total. Branded and licensed apparel accounted for about two-thirds of sales, and private label and licensed business to Sears and Penney accounted for the rest.

Garan Advantage, a line of discounted men's sportswear with the same tagging system as Garanimals, was introduced in 1982. Garan Man, a sportswear line of knit and woven shirts, casual slacks, and pullover and cardigan sweaters, was unveiled the following year. Also in 1983, the company introduced Garan By Marita for women. Garan net sales reached a record $176.9 million in 1984, and net income rose to a record $22.8 million. There were 20 company plants at the end of 1985, in Alabama, Arkansas, Kentucky, Louisiana, Mississippi, Oklahoma, and Tennessee. A manufacturing facility was established in Costa Rica in 1984, and two facilities were opened in El Salvador during fiscal 1985. Long-term debt that year came to $9.9 million. By the mid-1980s Seymour Lichtenstein had succeeded Dorsky, who remained a director, as chairman and chief executive officer, and Jerald Kamiel had succeeded Lichtenstein as president and chief operating officer.

Fiscal 1985 began a tailspin for Garan: sales fell to $105 million in 1986 and earnings dropped to a low of $2.2 million the following year. A number of factors were blamed, including cheap imports, the demise of the preppy look, and the miniskirt disasters. The company cut back on branded products, which accounted for only 47 percent of sales in 1988, compared with 75 percent in 1986. It introduced Bobbie Brooks, an in-house label for Wal-Mart Stores' women's clothing, and began a licensed menswear line featuring the insignia of professional sports teams. Company plants were retooled for lower costs and greater efficiency. Sales and profits improved, reaching $145.3 million and nearly $10 million, respectively, in 1990.

### Relying on Wal-Mart in the 1990s

By 1992 burgeoning Wal-Mart was accounting for 45 percent of Garan's annual sales. A licensing agreement in 1990 gave Garan the right to carry the insignias of various colleges and universities on sweatshirts and knit shirts. In 1991 it became one of the few apparel companies allowed to use characters from Disney movies. After a strong first quarter in fiscal 1992, Garan, holding $30 million in cash with virtually no debt, declared a $1.20-per-share annual dividend on top of the quarterly payout. During 1988–1992 the company earned an annual average of almost 18 percent on equity.

Net sales came to a record $189.6 million in 1993, when net income totaled $16.8 million. The following year was not as good, with sales of $173 million and income of $9.4 million. For fiscal 1995, results were even more disappointing: only $143.3 million in sales and $5.5 million in income. The company's market value, once nearly $190 million, dipped to less than $90 million. Some analysts blamed the company's heavy dependence on Wal-Mart (accounting for 63 percent of sales during fiscal 1995). Oversaturation in licensing, rising raw material costs, and cut-throat pricing were also cited as reasons for the firm's poor performance. During 1995 Garan became the exclusive licensee of the Everlast trademark for men's, boys', and girls' activewear, and of the trademark Hang Ten for boys' sportswear.

During fiscal 1995 children's apparel accounted for 72 percent of Garan's net sales, with women's apparel accounting for 18 percent and men's apparel accounting for 10 percent. Sales of sports and colleges licensed apparel accounted for about 12 percent of sales and Garan's own label accounted for about 6 percent. The Bobbie Brooks label accounted for another 7 percent, and Disney characters, scenes, and logos accounted for about 8 percent. In addition to Wal-Mart (63 percent of sales), J.C. Penney (20 percent) was an important customer. Some 3,500 or so clients took the rest of the company's output.

Garan maintained 18 manufacturing plants in 1995, in the following locations: Haleyville, Jemison, and Rainesville, Alabama; Ozark, Arkansas; Clinton, Kentucky; Church Point, Kaplan, and Marksville, Louisiana; Carthage, Corinth, Eupora, Lambert, Philadelphia, and Starksville, Mississippi; Adamsville, Tennessee; San Jose, Costa Rica; and two in San Salvador, El Salvador. All were leased in whole or in part except for the plants in Clinton, Haleyville, and San Jose. The company

also was leasing its headquarters and showroom in New York City's Empire State Building. Seymour Lichtenstein owned 12 percent of Garan in 1995 and heirs of Samuel Drosky owned another 12 percent. Other officers and directors owned 16 percent. The long-term debt was $3.2 million in March 1995. Dividends had been paid every year since 1962.

### Principal Subsidiaries

Garan Central America Corp.; Garan Export Corp.; Garan Manufacturing Corp.; Garan Services Corp.; Garan de El Salvador, S.A. de C.V. (El Salvador).

### Further Reading

Brammer, Rhonda, "Threads and Chips," *Barron's,* October 23, 1995, p. 30.
Campanella, Frank W., "Garan Fashions Gains with Expanded Output," *Barron's,* June 5, 1972, pp. 28–31.
Furman, Phyllis, "Apparel Firm Rides Wal-Mart Juggernaut," *Crain's New York Business,* May 4–10, 1992, p. 3.
"Garan, Apparel Maker, To Sew Up Record Sales, Earnings This Year," *Barron's,* January 23, 1978, pp. 31–32.
"Garan Fashions Handsome Growth from Stress on Private Label Line," *Barron's,* March 1, 1965, p. 19.
"Garan To Button Down Higher Net on Steady Expansion of Facilities," *Barron's,* April 6, 1964, pp. 32, 59.
Lawrence, Calvin, Jr., "Garan's New Look Wows Wall Street," *USA Today,* May 23, 1989, p. 3B.
"New Streamlined Facilities Help Garan Style Operating Advances," *Barron's,* July 16, 1962, p. 18.
Rolland, Louis J., "Garan Grows," *Financial World,* November 22, 1961, p. 24.
Sparr, Susan L., "Garan Gears Up with EDI," *Bobbin,* July 1988, p. 102.

—Robert Halasz

# General Housewares Corporation

**1536 Beech Street, P.O. Box 4066**
**Terre Haute, Indiana 47804**
**U.S.A.**
**(812) 232-1000**
**Fax: (812) 232-7016**

*Public Company*
*Incorporated:* 1967
*Employees:* 845
*Sales:* $119 million
*Stock Exchanges:* New York
*SICs:* 3365 Aluminum Foundries; 3321 Gray & Ductile
    Iron Foundries; 3421 Cutlery

General Housewares Corporation is a leading manufacturer and marketer of cookware, cutlery, kitchen tools, wood products, and cutting tools for the housewares and craft/hardware markets. Its broad range of products are designed to "delight and excite" the consumer, offering both a distinctive appearance and superior quality. The company, with three factories in Indiana and Illinois, is the only domestic manufacturer of enamelware, a porcelain-on-steel type of cookware. It also enjoys a leading market share in kitchen cutlery, through its Chicago Cutlery line, which has received a top quality rating from *Consumer Reports* and is the company's foremost revenue generator. Other key businesses include OXO International, a division headquartered in New York that imports and markets ergonomically designed kitchen tools and gadgets, and the Olfa Products Group, a division headquartered in Montreal, Quebec, that imports and markets craft and industrial precision cutting tools.

### Early History

The multiproduct housewares company was founded in 1967 by Jack Muller, a then 43-year-old Harvard M.B.A. and former management trainee who wanted to leave his position as a marketing executive at General Foods to start his own company. He solicited the financial backing of Laird Incorporated, a group of investors with ties to the du Pont family, who raised $1 million in equity and borrowed another $5 million. Finding the

proper channel to direct his entrepreneurial energy and capital, however, proved to be a more difficult task. Several discussions with the Laird group had failed to produce a workable idea. "We talked about a number of categories," Muller told *Forbes* writer Laura Rohmann, "and for one reason or another we couldn't make anything work." Desperate, Muller drove to New York, seeking the solution to his problem in a Macy's department store. Eschewing the sophisticated marketing research techniques he had learned in business school, he went to the top floor of the store, vowing to find a business before he left that day. "I went all the way to the bottom, and as I came down the escalator and saw the housewares area, I said to myself, 'Well, this has got to be it,' " he explained to Rohmann.

In 1967, Muller, with $6 million at his disposal, acted on his impulse and purchased J.R. Clark, a struggling, $8 million, Minnesota manufacturer of outdoor furniture, ladders, and ironing boards. It did not take long, though, for Muller to discover the limitations of the company he had acquired. In an age where fashions were dominated by polyester, ironing had fallen out of favor with the general public. Ironing boards and ladders, then, came to "represent drudgery or work versus fun," Muller told Rohmann. The new owner quickly reasoned that such a negative product identification would prove an insurmountable obstacle to the profitability of his business. With the goal of selecting a product line that consumers would enjoy buying, Muller decided to build his company around a line of enamel cookware—the ceramic-on-steel pots and pans used by U.S. families since the 19th century. And in 1968 he purchased a manufacturer of kitchen ceramics to get him started. The following year, while making its initial public offering, General Housewares acquired an enamelware importer, adding to the base that would one day stand as the last domestic manufacturer in the industry.

Muller's initial decision to focus on cookware and table-top giftware proved to be a sound one. By 1972, his company had surpassed the $50-million mark in annual sales and was approaching $4 million in earnings. Along the way, though, he attempted to expand the business at a faster rate by diversifying into several different product lines, ranging from kitchen stools to novelty candles. Many of these products performed poorly, leading the company into a period of high-cost debt. What is more, seasonal products such as outdoor grills became costly to inventory as interest rates skyrocketed during the early 1970s. Having failed to see that the credit crunch and inflation were approaching, Muller found himself saddled with a high debt load and businesses that were unable to carry their weight. By the time the recession of 1973 and 1974 had run its course, bumping up interest rates to 17.5 percent, the company was on the verge of extinction. Earnings had eroded to losses of $1.9 million in 1973 and $7 million the following year; liabilities now outstripped assets.

To stay in business, General Housewares had to sell off parts of the company, such as its steel kitchen furniture business, to raise cash. By 1975, all that remained were a few parts of its original cookware, giftware, and furniture businesses. Although the streamlining process was painful, it did allow the company to strengthen its balance sheet. Between 1974 and 1977, the company was able to cut its long-term debt down to 50 percent of capitalization, while resuscitating income to $4.8 million. The road to recovery, though, was a slow one. The growth pattern for revenue and profits was not consistent during the remainder of the decade.

### Legislation Spurs Unprecedented Growth in the 1980s

By the time General Housewares entered the 1980s, it was the only manufacturer of enamelware in the United States. A decade of increasingly intense competition from poorer countries with duty preference had made the business an unprofitable venture. With the arrival of the new decade came an unexpected boost from the federal government. In 1980 the International Trade Commission ordered temporary trade protection for manufacturers of porcelain-on-steel cookware, and General Housewares was the only company left to enjoy the benefits. Muller quickly came up with a strategy to take full advantage of this boon. First, he implemented a cost-cutting program, funnelling half of the company's capital spending into the development of more efficient production in an attempt to reduce costs by 2 percent each year. The second, revenue-generating part of his plan called for a new emphasis on upscale cookware that would enable the company to enjoy higher profit margins.

While the company was doing its best to maximize its enamelware profits during the four-year tariff protection period, it did not neglect the other promising aspects of its business. In

1979, it introduced its Magnalite Professional line of cast aluminum and magnesium skillets and bakeware. Having invested $350,000 on an electrolytic coating that gave the pans a professional-looking satiny gray appearance, the company hoped to find a match with its more affluent customers who could afford to pay up to $130 a pot. Encouraged by an annual 50 percent growth in Magnalite Professional sales during the early 1980s, the company also developed a Chateau line of high-end enamel pots, with a European-looking bulge bottom, and a Gear country motif collection of enamelware marketed to compete favorably with comparable products such as Pfaltzgraff stoneware.

Muller's twofold strategy of cost-reduction and luxury product development enabled the company to survive and prosper during a second wave of high interest rates in the early 1980s. In June 1982, a year that saw record sales of $74.3 million and profits of $3.7 million, the company made its first appearance on the New York Stock Exchange. Spurred by the company's strong performance and demographic trends that showed strong increases in young households and disposable income, investors showed their confidence in General Housewares, more than doubling the price of the stock from $8 to $21 during its first year on the exchange.

But such high expectations for the company as it emerged from the 1981–82 recession were not fulfilled—at least in the short run. Although earnings were increasing and costs were declining, foreign competition was also on the rise. As the U.S. economy recovered and the dollar strengthened, cheap imports undercut sales and eroded profits. By 1985, the company again found itself in the red, reporting a loss of nearly $3 million. Two years later, its stock sank to a low of $6.

One of the most important steps to General Houseware's recovery was its purchase of Chicago Cutlery in 1988. Founded by Ronald J. Gangelhoff in the 1960s to supply meat-packing houses with razor-sharp knives, the company was instrumental in creating a consumer market for fine-edged knives in the United States. After his first encounter with the cancer that would take his life six years later, Gangelhoff sold Chicago Cutlery to General Housewares and accepted a position as vice chairman of the board. The acquisition of the *Consumer Reports* category winner proved to be one of Muller's wisest decisions. Not only did the addition contribute substantially to the company's attempts to market brands that "surprise and delight" the customer, but it provided a major source of new revenue and profit.

### Streamlining and Recovery in the Early 1990s

Just as it had a decade earlier, General Housewares recovered by divesting itself of its ancillary businesses to reduce debt and focus its energy and resources on its most profitable product lines, such as Magnalite cookware and Chicago Cutlery. Having lowered its debt to 30 percent of capitalization through the $15-million sale of unprofitable businesses, the company hoped to take advantage of strong growth in the gourmet cooking market, which was expanding at a faster rate than the housewares market in general.

Another segment of this streamlining strategy came in the form of a corporate headquarters relocation. In June 1990 the company moved its corporate offices from Stamford, Connecticut, to Terre Haute, Indiana. According to Paul Sexton, who took over as CEO the following year, the migration to the Midwest was undertaken to jettison the high operation costs of the East Coast. In an age of fax machines and computers, proximity to Wall Street was no longer an important component to running a profitable business. By transferring the corporate offices to the same building as one of its ceramic-on-steel factories, the company's top executives could not only have a closer link to their employees, but they could save money on rent as well.

In October 1992, a year that saw revenue jump to $79 million and profits increase to $4.4 million, the company took another step towards increasing its presence in the gourmet cooking market, purchasing OXO International, a New York-based manufacturer of a broad line of specialty kitchen tools. Known for their distinctive handles and ergonomic design, OXO tools—marketed under the brand names Good Grips, Prima, and Plus—quickly became a strong performer for the company. In the next two years, sales from the OXO Division would more than double as several new products, including a new line of Sierra Club gardening tools, were added.

While the early 1990s were marked by reasonable levels of growth—revenue increased 15 percent between 1989 and 1993—the company reevaluated its marketing strategy and made the painful decision to eliminate some of its less profitable operations to make room for growth in industries with greater potential. In 1993, for instance, it sold its stainless steel cookware operation, having lost market share due to competition from countries such as Korea, Taiwan, Mexico, and China. At the same time, though, General Housewares introduced a new line of nonstick cast aluminum cookware and strengthened its hold on the enamelware industry by acquiring the Normandy line of enamelware from its chief competitor in that segment, National Housewares Corporation. In October 1994 the company also significantly increased its presence in the $10-billion North American hobby and craft market, purchasing the Olfa Products Corporation, the exclusive distributor in the United States and Canada of precision cutting tools and accessories made by Olfa Corporation of Osaka Japan. The high-performance line of razor-sharp scissors and specialty knives was slated as one of the company's most promising businesses as it entered the mid-1990s.

### The Mid-1990s and Beyond

Driven primarily by explosive growth in its OXO and Olfa divisions, the company recorded a healthy 10 percent growth in sales in 1994. During the fourth quarter of that year, however, the company encountered customer service difficulties that prevented it from taking advantage of a 33.3 percent jump in sales from the previous year. Unprepared for such rapid growth, the company tried to catch up on orders through plant overtime and expensive air freight, used to bring in important products and components. Despite the best efforts of its employees, the company struggled to meet the challenge and saw its ability to deliver orders on time dip to as low as 50 percent, minimizing the strength of its outstanding performance in advertising, packaging, pricing, and promotion.

Factors other than successful marketing contributed to the dramatic shift in orders to the fourth quarter. As the industry became more dependent upon on the latest in information tech-

nology, many of the company's retail customers sought to ease the burden of carrying and financing inventory by developing sophisticated electronic data interchange (EDI) software. The widespread use of such technology, however, placed a greater burden on vendors such as General Housewares, requiring them to respond more quickly to orders, carry a larger inventory, and spend more money on interface software and the training needed for its employees to be able to use it.

In response to the late-1994 crisis, the company engineered a comprehensive overhaul of its supply chain the following year. Realizing that its largest customers—Wal-Mart, Kmart, Target, and Sears—were judging the company more on its ability to deliver goods to the retail shelf often and accurately than on product price and attractiveness, the company introduced a Supply Chain Management System to improve the logistics end of the business. The new, tightly controlled Production/Sales/Inventory program—billed as the single most important "New Product" in the company's history—enabled General Housewares to improve its overall 1995 service level to 88 percent. The improvement in efficiency contributed to a 22 percent increase in total revenue.

In January of the following year the company took additional measures to streamline its operations and allow for growth in its fastest growing businesses, putting its Magnalite Classic, Magnalite Professional, and Wagner 1891 Cast Iron lines of cookware up for sale. Although once among the company's strongest performers, these product lines, which accounted for about 15 percent of total revenue in 1995, lost significant market share in the face of tougher competition from domestic companies such as Calphalon and Meyer, and from Hong Kong imports. Instead of continuing to support the flagging, and expensive, cookware lines, the company opted to redeploy those resources in its four stronger performing businesses: OXO gadgets, Chicago Cutlery, Granite Ware enamel-on-steel cookware, and Olfa precision cutting tools.

### Principal Subsidiaries

Chicago Cutlery Inc.; General Housewares Corp. Sidney Div.

### Principal Divisions

Olfa Products Group; OXO International.

### Further Reading

McLoughlin, Bill, "Selling for Leverage: GHC to Put Funds into Its Cash Cows," *HFN: The Weekly Newspaper for the Home Furnishing Network,* January 15, 1996, pp. 67–68.
Murphy, Scott, "Pot Calling the Kettle Blue," *Indiana Business Magazine,* July 1991, p. 74.
Palmeri, Christopher, "Nouveau Housewares," *Forbes,* March 30, 1992, p. 19.
Paul, Cynthia A., "GHC Buys Rival's Brand," *HFD: The Weekly Home Furnishings Paper,* October 10, 1994, pp. 51–52.
Rohmann, Laura, "Lessons Well Learned," *Forbes,* April 11, 1983, pp. 100–101.
Weiss, Lisa Casey, "Someone's in the Kitchen," *HFD: The Weekly Home Furnishings Newspaper,* May 4, 1992, pp. 42–45.

—Jason Gallman

# Gibson Guitar Corp.

1818 Elm Hill Pike
Nashville, Tennessee 37210-5714
U.S.A.
(615) 871-4500
Fax: (615)889-3216

*Private Company*
*Incorporated:* 1902 as the Gibson Mandolin-Guitar
    Manufacturing Company
*Employees:* 500
*Sales:* $70 million (1993 est.)
*SICs:* 3931 Musical Instruments

Gibson Guitar Corp., one of the world's foremost manufacturers of fretted instruments, has enjoyed the respect of musicians for most of its century-long history. Its instruments have been used by some of the best guitarists known, including Chet Atkins, the Everly Brothers, Chuck Berry, Eric Clapton, Jimmy Page, B. B. King, Frank Zappa, and Joe Walsh. The company fell from its status as a premier guitar maker to near bankruptcy in the 1980s but was brought back to solvency and its former respect by new owners, Henry Juszkiewicz and David Berryman. Although best known for its acoustic and electric guitars, by the mid-1990s the company also produced bass guitars, mandolins, synthesizers, drums, amplifiers, and various accessories for its instruments.

## Early History

Orville Gibson, the company's namesake, was making his living as a salesman and clerk when he bought a small workshop in Kalamazoo, Michigan, in the 1880s to begin building mandolins. At the time, most mandolins were made by bending and forming the wood into shape. However, Gibson believed that this technique stressed the wood and resulted in inferior vibrating characteristics. He therefore developed a new technique based on violin construction that involved carving the front, back, and sides of the mandolin rather than bending the wood into shape. Gibson created the first archtop acoustics using this technique,

although he only received one patent for his designs, for a mandolin in 1898. Gibson began applying his techniques to the construction of guitars, banjos, and lutes as well.

Gibson soon earned a reputation as a maker of high-quality, custom stringed instruments. By 1896 Gibson was making instruments full time. Early in the new century, demand for Gibson's instruments outpaced his ability to meet it. In response, Gibson entered into an agreement with five Kalamazoo financiers to form the Gibson Mandolin-Guitar Manufacturing Company in 1902. According to the contract, O. H. Gibson was not a major stockholder; instead, he was given a few shares of stock and a lump sum of $2,500 for his patent and the right to use his name. Gibson sold his stock in July 1903 but remained at the company until 1904, consulting and training employees on his construction techniques. Thereafter, he received a monthly pension until he died in 1918.

From its inception, the company focused on innovation and the production of high-quality instruments, goals it became known for over the next half-century. In the company's first few years, production manager Sylvo Reams improved upon Gibson's already popular instruments, refining his construction techniques and using higher-quality materials and finishes. The product line began with six guitar models (three archtops with oval soundholes and three with round soundholes) and four harp guitars. Within the company's first decade, it had been granted patents for the elevated pickguard, the intonation-adjustable bridge, and the harp guitar and had introduced one of the first production guitars with a cutaway.

Despite these early innovations in fretted instrument design, the company made few changes to its guitar line in the 1910s. Instead, it concentrated on its mandolins, a far more popular instrument at the time and one that made up most of Gibson's sales. Through either luck or foresight, Gibson began making banjos in 1917, positioning the company to take advantage of the sudden popularity of this instrument in the early 1920s. Lloyd Loar, a well-known mandolinist and composer, added his talents as an acoustics engineer and musician to Gibson's engineering and research and development teams. He made significant contributions to the company's Master Line Master Tone instruments, including the two-footed, intonation-adjustable bridge, the f-hole design, and narrow pegheads.

### Early Innovations in Guitar Design

Guitars slowly increased in popularity in the 1920s, and Gibson responded by introducing several new models. Its first modern guitar, part of the company's Style 5 series in the Master Line Master Tone line, was introduced in 1922. One of the best known of Gibson's early acoustic guitars, the L-5 used Loar's innovations to build a specific pitch into the sound box, a radical concept at the time. Another unusual design, the flat-top guitar, had been produced by the company as early as 1918; however, it did not begin serious production of a flat-top model until 1926. In addition to several flat-top models, Gibson began production of an economy series, the Kalamazoo line, in 1929.

Despite the Depression, the market for guitars expanded rapidly in the 1930s. As they had in the past, Gibson promptly followed the trend, shifting the focus of their production and advertising from mandolins and banjos to guitars. Not only did they expand their line of archtop f-hole guitars and flat-top guitars, the company also pioneered new designs. In 1934 it created its legendary Super 400. An 18-inch wide archtop, this guitar pushed the edges of guitar design in size and established higher standards for craftsmanship and decoration. Other new guitar designs included the Jumbo, a 16-inch wide flat-top, and a Premier version of the L-5, which featured a modern-style, rounded cutaway.

Gibson's expansion stalled during World War II for several reasons. Materials that met the company's standards were hard to come by, so rather than lower the quality of their instruments Gibson discontinued several models, including the L-5 and Super 400. Other models continued to be made but at a radically slower rate. In addition, the company shifted production from musical instruments to parts useful in the war effort. In 1944, as the war neared its conclusion, the Chicago Musical Instrument (CMI) Company acquired Gibson and prepared the company to meet the pent-up demand for guitars when the war ended.

### Postwar Boom

The postwar period saw phenomenal expansion for Gibson, much of it due to the vision and leadership of Ted McCarty. McCarty joined Gibson in 1948 and served as company president from 1950 to 1966. During his tenure company sales grew from less than a million dollars a year to $15 million a year, its work force grew from 150 employees to 1,200, and its profits multiplied 15 times. McCarty also led CMI to purchase rival Epiphone in 1957, giving Gibson greater control of the market.

Underlying Gibson's vast success during this period was McCarty's ability to lead the company to fruitful innovations. Under McCarty, Gibson finally committed themselves to the electric guitar market, having squandered their early efforts in the area. Gibson had introduced an electric guitar in 1935, the aluminum-bodied Electric Hawaiian Guitar. The large, hollow-body guitar used a magnetic pickup that needed thousands of wire windings. However, when Grammy–award winning guitarist and inventor Les Paul, who had been endorsing Gibson guitars since 1928, approached the company with a solid-body electric guitar in 1941, Gibson rejected the idea outright. Paul continued to try to convince Gibson throughout the 1940s but met with little success until McCarty was at the helm. By that time, Leo Fender had developed his own highly successful solid-body electric guitar, the Fender Telecaster.

Although Gibson had missed the chance to take the pioneering role in electric guitars, McCarty made sure they did not lag in subsequent improvements to the design. The Les Paul model debuted in 1952, and Gibson continued to refine the design for decades. Also under McCarty's leadership, Gibson designers introduced the humbucking pickup, the first semi-solid guitar, and the distinctive reverse-body Firebirds. McCarty personally contributed several groundbreaking changes, including the stop tailpiece and the Tune-O-Matic bridge. Other important models were introduced during this period, such as the first thinline archtop, the Byrdland, and the commercially unsuccessful but subsequently influential solidbodies the Flying V, Explorer, and Moderne.

Although electric guitars played an increasing role in Gibson's sales in the 1960s, the company continued to introduce new acoustic models as well. The Hummingbird, Dove, and Everly Brothers models debuted at that time, as did several artist models, including the Johnny Smith and Trini Lopez. However, after McCarty left in 1966 the company released few new models, either acoustic or electric, and suffered from the loss of McCarty's perceptive assessments of the market.

### Declining Sales

In 1969 CMI merged with ECL, an Ecuadoran brewery, and the following year the two companies formed Norlin. Norlin combined Gibson guitars with Moog synthesizers and Lowrey organs and pianos to form a music division. Gibson suffered under the new management. Although a few new models were introduced in the 1970s they were not successful, such as the short-lived Mark series acoustics and the Marauder, S-1, and RD electrics. The company managed to maintain sales through most of the 1970s, but the long-term effects of absentee corporate management could be seen when sales steadily declined in the 1980s.

Although the guitar market in general suffered during the 1980s, Gibson exacerbated the problem by allowing its quality to slip and by abandoning their popular guitar models in favor of poorly conceived new models. ''Corporate bean counters from thousands of miles away started dictating to the sales department that the old stuff was stale, and that what they needed was new, new, new,'' Matt Umanov, a New York guitar retailer, told *The New York Times* in 1994. ''That led to all kinds of stupid design changes.''

In 1983 Norlin was taken over by Rooney Pace and Piezo Electric Product, Inc., and the new owners promptly put the Gibson music division up for sale. New owners did not materialize, and Gibson's bad times continued. In 1984 the company closed its Kalamazoo factory. Several new models were introduced and met with such a terrible response that they were discontinued almost immediately. Severe cuts in staff and the closing of all divisions but one line of guitars did not stem Gibson's losses. At last, enthusiastic new owners took over in 1986, Henry Juszkiewicz and David Berryman, who bought the company for $5 million.

### Turnaround under New Owners

Juszkiewicz, who took over as company chairman, was eminently suitable to reverse the company's fortunes. A long-time Gibson guitar enthusiast, he had played guitar professionally in high school and college. In addition to a musical sensibility and an appreciation for the company's products, Juszkiewicz brought an MBA from Harvard and some tough business experience to bear on Gibson's problems.

Juszkiewicz and Berryman began by firing 30 of Gibson's 250 employees, including all of the company's top management. They then began a series of acquisitions, including the purchase of Steinberger, a manufacturer of high-tech electric guitars, in 1987; Oberheim Corporation, a synthesizer manufacturer, in 1990; and Tobias, maker of handtooled professional quality basses, in 1990. When the company bought the Flatiron Mandolin Company in 1987, Juszkiewicz used the newly acquired factory in Bozeman, Montana, to establish a flat-top acoustic division, which soon won acclaim for its high-quality instruments. Mandolin production inherited from Flatiron also continued, reviving a division of Gibson that had long been closed. By the mid-1990s the Gibson and Flatiron mandolin lines included the Gibson F-5, based on a Lloyd Loar design from 1922, and Flatiron mandolins, mandolas, and octave mandolins in a wide range of styles.

Reissues of classic guitar models played an important role in refreshing the company's reputation. To re-create popular models, such as the Advanced Jumbo and the J-200, the company retooled its factories and dismantled old sound pickups to study their design. The popularity of these reissues encouraged Gibson to offer a special commemorative line of guitars for its 100th anniversary in 1994. In each month of 1994 Gibson released a different electric and acoustic model in limited runs of 100. In addition to reviving the classic Gibson acoustic and electric guitar models, the partners reestablished the company's amplifier division and expanded its line of accessories to include strings, picks, straps, pickups, and the Gibson Tourwear clothing line.

Since taking over the company the partners have made strong efforts to win back the loyalty of successful musicians. Much of the old Gibson aura could be attributed to famous musicians playing their guitars, such as Chuck Berry and his Gibson ES-350T. The company created a new operation to custom craft and hand tool instruments for celebrities. In addition, Gibson began wooing endorsements from well-known musicians by providing their guitars. Famous musicians who renewed or began endorsing Gibson included Chet Atkins, Steve Miller, and B. B. King. Many other musicians have joined the ranks of Gibson guitar users, such as Emmylou Harris, Pete Townshend, Travis Tritt, Johnny Cash, Neil Young, Peter Frampton, and Paul McCartney.

The changes instituted by Juszkiewicz and Berryman turned the company around. Juszkiewicz told *The New York Times* in 1994 that since 1986 Gibson has achieved a compound annual growth rate in sales of 30 percent. Starting with annual sales below $10 million in 1986, the company reached an estimated $70 million in sales by 1993, up from $50 million in 1992.

Gibson celebrated its 100th anniversary in 1994. Although the company proper was founded in 1902, Gibson Guitar has long cited 1894 as the earliest confirmable date of a Gibson instrument. An engraving on a mandolin states, ''Made by O. H. Gibson, 1894,'' although Orville Gibson clearly made instruments before that date. The company used the anniversary as the theme of a major international promotion. A concert in Tokyo by the heavy-metal group the Scorpions launched a series of national and international concerts and exhibits. A White House salute to Gibson, hosted by President Bill Clinton and First Lady Hillary Rodham Clinton, highlighted the year's activities.

Juszkiewicz's expansion plans proceeded steadily through the early and mid-1990s. To cover the lower end of the market Juszkiewicz and Berryman revived the lower-priced Epiphone line of guitars. Epiphone production had been moved to Asia in the 1970s, and the line had lost much of its distinction. In late 1995 Gibson returned Epiphone to the United States, moving it into its own facility in Nashville. Gibson's acquisition plans continued as well. The company purchased the Original Musical Instrument Company (O.M.I.) in 1993. Originator of the Dobro resonator guitar, O.M.I. continued to offer a full line of woodbody and metalbody resonator guitars and basses under the leadership of Gibson. In 1995 Gibson bought the Slingerland Drum Company. Slingerland adds its rich history to Gibson; founded in 1928, Slingerland was the choice of such famous drummers as Gene Krupa and Buddy Rich. When Gibson acquired the company, it had evolved into mainly an import company. With plans to revive its reputation, Gibson returned Slingerland production to the United States.

With Gibson exhibiting serious expansion goals, there was some speculation that the company might make a public offering of stock to gain additional cash for acquisitions. ''On the one hand it's appealing because it would be a quick way to do it,'' Juszkiewicz reflected in an interview with *The New York Times* in 1994. ''But then I don't know if I could operate the way I want having to answer to other people.''

### Principal Subsidiaries

The Original Musical Instrument; Epiphone; Oberheim Electronics; Steinberger; Slingerland; Tobias.

### Principal Divisions

Gibson Nashville; Gibson Montana; Gibson Custom, Art, Historic; Gibson Strings & Accessories; Gibson World Net Services; Flatiron; G-Wiz; Pro Sound.

### Further Reading

Carter, Walter, et al., *Gibson Guitars: 100 Years of an American Icon,* General Publishing Group, 1994.

Gill, Chris, "Gibson's Century of Excellence," *Guitar Player,* September 1994, pp. 33–36.

"Innovation and Quality: Gibson's Manufacturing Strategy," *Music Trades,* August 1986.

"The Leo Award," *Guitar Player,* January 1993, p. 52.

McCraw, Jim, "The Gibson Guitar," *Popular Mechanics,* December 1995, pp. 64–67, 122.

Miller, Bryan, "Saving Gibson Guitars from the Musical Scrap Heap," *The New York Times,* March 13, 1994, p. 7F.

"The Sale of Gibson," *Guitar Player,* January 1987, p. 12.

Watson, Bruce, "How to Take on an Ailing Company—and Make it Hum," *Smithsonian,* July 1996, pp. 53–62. !1L

—Susan W. Brown

# Golden Belt Manufacturing Co.

807 East Main Street
P.O. Box 2332
Durham, North Carolina 27702
U.S.A.
(919) 682-9394
Fax: (919) 688-1751

*Wholly Owned Subsidiary of B-A-T Industries PLC*
*Founded:* 1887
*Sales:* $45 million (1995)
*Employees:* 174
*SICs:* 2671 Packaging Paper and Plastics Film, Coated
and Laminated; 2752 Commercial Printing,
Lithographic; 2754 Commercial Printing, Gravure;
2759 Commercial Printing, Not Elsewhere Classified

Golden Belt Manufacturing Co. has been associated with the packaging of tobacco products since its inception in 1887 and remains one of the largest manufacturers of cigarette packs in the United States. It was also engaged in other forms of consumer-product printing and packaging in the 1990s, when its goods could be found in virtually every convenience store in the United States. The firm was operating five plants: four in North Carolina and one in Canada.

## Making Sacks for Bull Durham in the 19th Century

Golden Belt's story really goes back to the development after the Civil War of cigarette-grade "bright" or "golden" leaf tobacco in North Carolina. The firm of W.T. Blackwell & Co. established a plant in Durham for tobacco products, and Julian S. Carr, president of Blackwell's Durham Bull Tobacco Co., shrewdly promoted its wares under the Bull Durham trademark. The firm's success, however, was marred by a shortage of muslin bags, or sacks, for the loose smoking tobacco. These were being made by the women of Durham and adjoining communities, but not in sufficient quantity to meet the demand and were also not uniform in size. At best one worker could only produce 600 bags a day.

William Hall Kerr, a textile manufacturer, approached Carr in 1885 with a plan to develop a machine for manufacturing bags. Within a year he created a complicated device that, operated by a single worker, was capable of turning out 25,000 bags a day; indeed, in a public demonstration it cut and stitched 90,000 bags in a day. Kerr's machines were still in use in 1948. Carr won the rights to the invention for a royalty of ten cents for each 1,000 bags the company sold and established the Golden Belt Manufacturing Co. to produce them in the Bull Durham plant not only for the tobacco industry but also for manufacturers of sugar, salt, flour, meal, feedstuffs, and coins. The contract between Golden Belt and Durham Bull Tobacco stated that high-quality cloth sacks of different sizes "shall be perfect and such will readily pass the first inspection and certain approval of the inspector at said bag factory and such will not be twice handled or inspected by him." Soon Golden Belt was producing more than 13,000 Bull Durham sacks a day.

Commissioned by Carr and collaborating with Rufus Patterson, Kerr went on to devise a machine to stamp and label the bags. This was completed by the end of 1895—although Kerr had drowned during the summer—and was capable of weighing, packing, stamping, and labeling bags of uniform size at the rate of 25 per minute, enabling a single operator to equal the output of 42 handworkers.

Another Durham entrepreneur, however, was to reap the rewards of Carr's groundwork. Laboring in his father's tobacco factory, James Buchanan Duke used bright leaf for his first cigarette brands in 1881 and installed an improved cigarette machine three years later. Duke's output of 817 million cigarettes a day accounted for 38 percent of U.S. cigarette sales in 1889, and he subsequently branched out into the production of plug tobacco for chewing. (Cigarette consumption did not draw even with plug and smoking tobacco until 1921.) In 1890 Duke consolidated his holdings into the newly formed American Tobacco Co. At the end of 1897 he made a special trip to Durham to watch Golden Belt's Kerr-Patterson machine perform and called it the most ingenious piece of tobacco machinery he had ever seen. He purchased the Blackwell business in 1899 for almost $3 million.

### Printing and Packaging in the 20th Century

A year later, a cotton mill to supply cloth for the bags was built at the East Main Street location where Golden Belt still maintained his headquarters in the mid-1990s. When the Supreme Court broke up the American Tobacco empire into smaller units in 1911 for antitrust-law violations, Golden Belt was the only existing subsidiary allowed to remain. The company began printing labels for Bull Durham sacks and book covers for roll-your-own cigarette papers in 1923. It produced its first Lucky Strike cigarette label using the letterpress process in 1926. Golden Belt also continued to make larger cloth bags for products like salt, flour, coins, and ammunition in this period and produced hosiery from 1922 to 1946. In the mid-1930s it registered and printed the slogan "Made to Quality Rather Than Price" for its sacks. The company became the first to employ gravure printing for cigarette labels in 1949.

Before cellophane, tobacco companies depended largely on tin foil in packaging to keep their products fresh. By 1964, however, the packaging of cigarettes involved a triple wrap of aluminum foil, paper, and cellophane. Several machines were involved in the process. The first wrapped an inner layer of aluminum foil and an outer layer of paper around 20 cigarettes. A second sealed the packages in an "overcoat" of airtight, moisture-proof cellophane. After being packed ten to a carton, cigarette packs traveled to a device that packed 60 cartons into a cardboard case. Golden Belt became, in 1975, the first company in the United States to use lasers to punch tiny ventilation holes into filter paper for cigarettes. This enabled manufacturers to carefully control the amounts of tar and nicotine reaching the consumer. By 1995 almost all filter paper was being produced by this means.

A $2-million, 34,000-square-foot addition to Golden Belt's Durham factory was completed during 1966–67. This project, which included the installation of all-new equipment, enabled the company to diversify its textile production, adding single and plied yarn for sale to knitters and weavers. The yarn was manufactured and sold in its natural color, without dyeing or finishing. The firm also produced injection-molded plastic parts for a short period in the 1970s.

### Golden Belt, 1989–94

Although Golden Belt was doing work for all six major U.S. tobacco companies in 1989, its president, James Galioto, told the trade magazine *Paper, Film & Foil Converter* that the firm was "looking for accounts in other areas." He described its product line as "one-stop shopping for packaging materials," adding, "We consider ourselves a full-service production company in the printing field because of all of our unique capabilities." The firm's technical director said Golden Belt was cutting "across every printing and converting technology except screen printing." Its product line of consumer-product packaging materials included labels, closures, and inserts; cartons, cards, and tags; film, paper, and foil composites; film lamination for other printers; and point-of-sale materials. Pre-press facilities included typesetting, step and repeat, and platemaking.

The Durham printing plant was a 150,000-square-foot facility whose products included cigarette tipping papers on three gravure presses. A 160,000-square-foot installation in Reidsville, North Carolina, was specializing in large-volume production of foil and laminated gravure labels. A 28,000-square-foot specialty printing plant in Randleman, North Carolina, was producing labels, cartons, and a variety of laminations. GB Labels, a 10,000-square-foot plant in Burlington, North Carolina, was producing flexo and UV letterpress labels, hangtags, and point-of-sale materials. GB Converters, a 45,000-square-foot facility in Mississauga, Ontario, was producing cigarette tipping papers by gravure, mainly for the Canadian market.

Golden Belt's equipment at this time included five-, seven-, and eight-color gravure press units with sheeters for producing cut labels and a rewind for roll-fed labels, and two- and four-color gravure presses for producing roll-fed labels. The five- and eight-color presses were equipped with CC1 image processes for registration and quality. Golden Belt's two Heidelberg sheet-fed offset presses included a five-color one equipped with a CPC 1 control system for computerized ink and register control. Among the flexographic equipment were five label presses. An Arpeco label press was being used for the UV rotary letterpress work. There were four laminators: three for roll products and the fourth for sheets.

Golden Belt was placing more emphasis on its core business in 1994, when Galioto told a *Raleigh News & Observer* reporter, "Our roots have always been in the tobacco business. That is more true today than ever before." Although the company was making, for example, foil wrappers for Wrigley's Doublemint and Juicy Fruit chewing gum, it turned out, in 1993, more than 1.4 billion cigarette packs for all six major American cigarette producers except R.J. Reynolds Tobacco Co., which had its own in-house packaging operation. The reporter saw huge rolls of cigarette labels and foil wrapping emerging from floor-to-ceiling printing presses and laminating machines in the Durham factory. Recently installed computers and video cameras were monitoring every phase of the manufacturing process.

A spokesperson for cigarette manufacturer Liggett Group Inc. described her company as "a major customer of Golden Belt for many years," adding, "We've stayed with them because they are very competitive in both price and quality. It's an added bonus that they are located near our factory in Durham." However, Galioto said that because "things have been tightening up in the U.S. cigarette business overall," Golden Belt was "starting to look at overseas markets. We think that is where most of the future growth will be."

Golden Belt was still a subsidiary, in 1994, of American Tobacco Co., which was in turn a subsidiary of American Brands Inc. In December of that year, however, London-based B-A-T Industries PLC—which derived from a company once affiliated with American Tobacco—bought American Tobacco for $1 billion in cash and merged it with B-A-T's Brown & Williamson Tobacco Co. subsidiary. The transaction made B-A-T the third-largest tobacco company in the United States. Galioto did not expect the acquisition to have much effect on Golden Belt. "Basically, we have been allowed to operate as an independent company for many years, and that shouldn't change," he said.

### Further Reading

*The American Tobacco Story,* The American Tobacco Co., 1964.

Boyd, William Kenneth, *The Story of Durham,* Durham: Duke University Press, 1925, pp. 71–73.

Tilley, Nannie May, *The Bright-Tobacco Industry 1860–1925,* Chapel Hill: University of North Carolina Press, 1948, pp. 548–51, 577–79, 594.

Webb, Mena, *Jule Carr: General Without an Army,* Chapel Hill: University of North Carolina Press, 1987, pp. 76–77.

Williams, Bob, "Making It Big Making Small Packages," *Raleigh News & Observer,* November 12, 1994, p. D1.

Zuck, Robert A., "Technology Helps Quality Maintain Prominent Role," *Paper, Film & Foil Converter,* June 1989, pp. 84, 86.

—Robert Halasz

# Goodwill Industries International, Inc.

**9200 Wisconsin Avenue**
**Bethesda, Maryland 20814**
**U.S.A.**
**(301) 530-6500**
**Fax: (301) 530-1516**

*Private Nonprofit Company*
*Founded:* 1902
*Sales:* $1.04 billion (1995)
*Employees:* 52,500
*SICs:* 5932 Used Merchandise Stores; 7363 Help Supply
Services; 8331 Job Training and Related Services

Goodwill Industries International is the umbrella organization for independently operated, nonprofit, community-based affiliates that provide job-based and employment services for people with disabilities. In 1995 there were 186 member organizations in the United States, Canada, and the Pacific Basin. There were also 53 associate member organizations in 37 countries outside these areas. Goodwill Industries was, in the mid-1990s, North America's leading nonprofit provider of vocational services for people with disabilities and other special needs, and the world's largest private-sector employer of people with disabilities.

## The Early Decades

Goodwill Industries was founded in 1902 by the Rev. Edgar James Helms, a Methodist minister who came to head the Unitarian Church's multidenominational Henry Morgan Memorial Chapel in Boston's South End slums. At the time, the chapel's attendees were largely alcoholics and indigents lured inside by the smell of hot coffee and stew. When the chapel was full, the doors were locked and the visitors treated to a fire-and-brimstone sermon. However, Helms disapproved of this tactic for reform. Instead, he began using the baptistery tank to pipe in water to showers installed in the basement, in order to clean up his charges. Next, he made space for a nursery where working mothers could leave their children. Helms then issued an appeal for used clothing to give to the poor and hired poverty-stricken seamstresses to repair the clothing before selling it cheaply to the needy.

This self-help system expanded with the donation of 1,000 burlap bags from a coffee-importing firm and also grew to include the donation, repair, and resale of used furniture and other items. The effort became institutionalized under the name of the Morgan Memorial Industries and Stores. However, Helms drew criticism from some professional social workers of the day, who objected that Helms did nothing to check that his charity employees were the most worthy of help. Moreover, the Unitarian church eventually withdrew its support of the project. Helms subsequently found sponsorship from the Methodist Church and his next self-help effort manifested itself in Brooklyn, where the Goodwill Industries name was born.

By 1919 Goodwill Industries training shops and stores had opened in Cleveland, Denver, Los Angeles, and Brookline, Massachusetts, and the Methodists were planning to invest $305,000 for plants in New York, Buffalo, Philadelphia, Pittsburgh, St. Paul, and other cities. The plan called for 30 of these centers, training 120,000 people a year and spending $2 to $3 million annually for wages. An important new manpower supply was tapped in the numbers of disabled servicemen returning from World War I. Skilled workers taught the newcomers the best and quickest ways to repair donated materials and, when they became skilled themselves, the pupils were recommended to commercial shops and factories. The store for the sale of remade articles served a double purpose, offering training as salespersons, stenographers, and bookkeepers.

Helms took his message overseas in 1926, when he began a world tour, laying the ground for what was to become Goodwill Industries International. He traveled to Europe, the Middle East, Japan, Korea, Ceylon, and the Philippines. Organizations based on the Goodwill idea sprang up in Mexico, the Caribbean, and South America, and eventually in Asia, Africa, and Great Britain. An international department within Goodwill's corporate office was not formed until 1969, however. The Goodwill Industries International Foundation was later established in the mid-1980s to help fund special programs for Goodwill's network outside North America.

More than 60 cities in the United States and various communities in foreign countries had Goodwill Industries institutions by 1932. The Buffalo chapter, for example, paid more than $60,000 in 1930 to 100 persons for what it called "Jobs from Junk—Wages from Waste." These wage-earners were described in an article as including "men and women with nervous diseases; mental quirks, social complexes and maladjustments; paralysis victims, capable of training, maybe, in the use of feeble limbs, but who in regular business channels has time to try?"

The Great Depression changed Goodwill's direction. People with disabilities did not become the major focus of its work until the mid-1930s, when mass unemployment convinced the organization it needed to restrict its services to a smaller segment of the population. Their efforts yielded a payoff to others in need, for a woman's entire restyled outfit, including a silk dress and warm winter coat, could be purchased for $6.80, while a man's similar clothing, including suit and overcoat, cost only $8.50. A bed with springs and mattress sold for $6.50, and a reconditioned stove for $10.

### Goodwill at Mid-Century

When Goodwill Industries celebrated its 50th anniversary in 1952, there were 101 plants in the United States. In 1951 the company took in $13.6 million in revenue and paid $8.2 million in wages. Of the 17,545 handicapped men and women employed by Goodwill that year, about 30 percent had found full- or part-time jobs in private industry by May 1952. Many others had established their own shops. The Goodwill agencies were 90 percent self-supporting and completely nondenominational, although some still were receiving financial aid from the Methodists. There were another seven Goodwill agencies in Canada and seven more scattered from Shanghai to Lima, Peru.

A 1953 *Saturday Evening Post* article listed the main donations to Goodwill as consisting of clothing, shoes, furniture, repairable household appliances, toys, and books. Interesting stories began to crop up concerning Goodwill donations. In one incident, a painting donated to the Boston chapter was found to have been painted by the Venetian Renaissance master Gentile Bellini and was sold to the Museum of Fine Arts for a handsome sum. One woman who donated a gas range forgot to remove the roast she had cooked for dinner and called in to reclaim it. Farmers contributed such items as two bales of hay, a brace of rabbits, a horse, and a nanny goat, who devoured most of the fiberboard lining of the truck while in transit.

The *Post* article went on to report that the Norfolk Goodwill specialized in the acquisition and restoration of Early American antiques, the Denver agency specialized in silverware, and the Michigan affiliates excelled in furniture making. Fort Worth was outstanding for returning ranching gear to working condition. The Los Angeles chapter was the biggest operation, employing some 1,500 persons and doing more than $1 million worth of business annually. It was followed by Detroit, Boston, Chicago, and San Francisco. Milwaukee, Denver, St. Louis, and Cincinnati had the best-equipped physical rehabilitation centers. Chicago led all affiliates in securing contract work from manufacturers. The Dallas chapter, cited as representative, employed about 400 persons a year and always paid slightly more than the minimum wage. More than 98 percent self-supporting, it owned its own building, machinery, and fleet of trucks and employed a staff medical director, psychologist, and chaplain.

An accounting of the Goodwill personnel employed in 1952 found that six percent were blind, 47 percent physically handicapped in other ways, 15 percent emotionally handicapped, 19 percent aged, and the remaining 13 percent, who were not handicapped, largely consisting of supervisory and transportation workers. Some 60 Goodwill ladies' auxiliaries and service clubs like the Lions and Rotarians helped raise money through such devices as annual bazaars.

By 1968 the Goodwill Industries workshop network had reached 135, employing over a year's time a total of some 50,000 handicapped persons. A survey found that the percentage of employees with some neurological, mental, or social affliction had risen to 42 percent in 1966, compared to 32 percent in 1960. The percentage of physically handicapped persons fell from 20 to 15 percent over this period. The executive director of the Philadelphia chapter said the mentally retarded and emotionally distressed were more difficult to rehabilitate and often less productive than the physically handicapped, leading to increased costs. Some workshops said they were laying off handicapped workers because of the scheduled increase in the federal minimum wage to $1.80 an hour in 1969. Although "sheltered" workshops employing the handicapped could pay as little as half of the regular minimum wage, the U.S. Department of Labor was requiring that they match the percentage increase on all their wages.

### Aiding the Needy in the 1990s

By the 1990s Goodwill Industries was again concentrating on a wider segment of the needy population: not only the disabled but those socially and economically disadvantaged. It was, by the middle of the decade, serving people with a range of barriers to employment, including lack of education, welfare dependency, a criminal record, and advanced age. The largest single group of people served by the organization in the mid 1990s were those with vocational disadvantages such as welfare dependency, illiteracy, a history of criminal behavior, or past substance abuse. People with mental retardation made up the second-largest group of those served.

The federal-state vocational-rehabilitation system, the public welfare system, and the U.S. Department of Labor together accounted for more than half of yearly referrals to Goodwill. Other individuals were referred privately and through state mental health/mental retardation offices. Goodwill organizations in many communities established basic-skills programs offering tutoring in reading and basic math. Partnerships were formed with community organizations such as Literacy Volunteers of America.

High-tech training such as computer operation and word processing was increasingly popular in Goodwill's rehabilitation programs. The Honolulu affiliate was training individuals for work in the thriving local hospitality industry. The Iowa City, Iowa, chapter offered training for retail occupations. The New York City Goodwill was working with major banks to train people in financial-services areas. The most common types of training programs also included food service, janitorial and building maintenance, and horticulture. Training courses ranged in length from six weeks to several months. When Goodwill graduates were hired by a business in the community, Goodwill job coaches were available to provide long-term, one-on-one training and adjustment support.

Industrial and service contract work had become an increasingly important source of revenue for Goodwill Industries by 1995, when it accounted for $214 million, or more than 20 percent of combined revenues. Goodwill Industries was providing contractual services support to the following major industries: automotive, airline, aircraft, aerospace, lumber, pharmaceutical, paper manufacturing, electronics, recycling, printing, hospital, and corrugated products. Labor-intensive work included mechanical and electronic assembly, packaging, inspection, custodial services, groundskeeping, stockkeeping, data entry, and mailing. In addition, Goodwill Industries was providing custodial, groundskeeping, and food-service support to federal-, state-, and local-government agencies.

Goodwill's retail revenues continued to grow steadily. It was a full-line discount retailer with a special emphasis on clothing, but donations being sold also included linens, furniture, shoes, small appliances, hardware, housewares, collectibles, books, and recordings. In 1981 the Chicago chapter came out with its own line of designer jeans, called "Goodies." Although used, they came with a designer label and sold for $4.99, compared to $1.50 for Goodwill's other used jeans. A Denver outlet began selling used ski equipment in 1993, most of it in good shape but coming with a disclaimer for liability. Goodwill's combined retail revenues reached $513.5 million in 1995, up from $359.3 million in 1991.

Unsalable donated items were being sold as scrap material or in wholesale markets. In 1993 Goodwill Industries processed close to 700 million pounds of donated textiles, and more than 99 percent of it was sold either in Goodwill retail stores or on the salvage market for other uses. Some member organizations had become involved in materials recycling: sorting and sometimes processing materials like paper, aluminum, and glass.

Goodwill Industries of America Inc. changed its name to Goodwill Industries International, Inc. in 1994. In 1995 Goodwill employed nearly 52,500 people in its own facilities, retail stores, and industrial contract programs. Its member organizations in North America collectively served more than 130,000 people in vocational and rehabilitation programs. Of these, nearly 25,000 found competitive jobs in the community as a result of Goodwill training. There were 1,427 retail outlets in 1995. A 1994 survey found that five of every six dollars in Goodwill Industries income went for program spending, which ranked the organization in the top ten social-service charities in the United States in that category. Goodwill affiliates contributed to the parent organization on a purely voluntary basis.

### Further Reading

Calame, Byron E., "Institute Lays Off Handicapped Workers Due to Pay-Floor Hike," *Wall Street Journal,* January 23, 1968, p. 23.
"Enterprise of the Heart," *Time,* May 5, 1953, p. 96.
*Goodwill Industries,* Bethesda, Md.: Goodwill Industries International, Inc., 1995.
Keeler, Ralph Welles, "Men and Goods Repaired," *World Outlook,* May 1919, pp. 18–19.
Perry, George Sessions, "They Give Them a Second Chance," *Saturday Evening Post,* October 3, 1953, pp. 40–41, 124–25, 129.
Wattles, Janet B., "Jobs from Junk—Wages from Waste," *Scientific American,* February 1932, pp. 84–85.

—Robert Halasz

# The Great Atlantic & Pacific Tea Company, Inc.

2 Paragon Drive
Montvale, New Jersey 07645
U.S.A.
(201) 573-9700
Fax: (201) 930-8106

*Public Company*
*Incorporated:* 1902
*Employees:* 92,000
*Sales:* $10.3 billion (1994)
*Stock Exchanges:* New York
*SICs:* 2095 Roasted Coffee; 5411 Grocery Stores; 5921 Liquor Stores; 5143 Dairy Products, Except Dried or Canned Wholesale; 5912 Drug Stores & Proprietary Stores

The Great Atlantic & Pacific Tea Company is the fourth-largest operator of grocery store chains in the United States. A&P operates 1,108 stores across the United States and in Ontario, Canada, under the names A&P, Waldbaum's, Food Emporium, Super Fresh, Farmer Jack, Kohl's, Dominion and Miracle Food Mart. The company also manufactures and distributes coffee, under the brand names Eight O' Clock, Bokar, and Royale.

### Early History

In 1859, George Huntington Hartford and George Francis Gilman formed a partnership. Using Gilman's connections as an established grocer and the son of a wealthy ship owner, Hartford purchased coffee and tea from clipper ships on the waterfront docks of New York City. By eliminating brokers, Hartford and Gilman were able to sell their wares at "cargo prices." The enterprise was so successful that in 1869 Hartford and Gilman opened a series of stores under the name Great American Tea Company. The first of these soon became a landmark on Vesey Street in New York City.

The company's appeal to the 19th-century consumer was enhanced by the lavish storefronts and Chinese-inspired inte-

riors which Gilman designed: inside the Chinese paneled walls, cockatoos greeted customers, who brought their purchases to a pagoda-shaped cash desk. Outside, the red-and-gold storefronts were illuminated by dozens of gas lights that formed a giant "T," and on Saturdays customers were treated to the music of a live brass band.

Despite the company's extravagant trappings, its success was largely due to its innovative strategy of offering savings and incentives to the consumer. A&P's "club plan," which encouraged the formation of clubs to make bulk mail-order sales for an additional one-third discount, was so successful that by 1886 hundreds of such clubs had been formed. Pioneering the concept of private labels and house brands, the Great American Tea Company introduced its own inexpensive tea and coffee blends, continuing to direct its efforts at the price-conscious consumer. Today, A&P's "Eight O'Clock" blend remains a hallmark house brand.

In 1869 the company became the Great Atlantic & Pacific Tea Company, to commemorate the joining of the first transcontinental railroad and to separate its retail stores from its mail-order operations. A&P's gradual national expansion began shortly thereafter. The company established a foothold in the Midwest in the aftermath of the Chicago Fire of 1871, when A&P sent staff and food to help the devastated city, and stayed to open stores in the Midwest.

Careful thought and planning were given to A&P's expansion. New store openings were complemented by promotions and premiums. In the Midwest and the South, new stores gave away items such as crockery and lithographs in order to attract customers, and in other areas, garish "Teams of Eight" became legendary symbols of A&P. The brainchild of the flamboyant John Hartford, parades of teams of eight horses decorated with spangled harnesses and gold-plated bells drew red and gold vehicles through the towns; the person who best guessed the weight of the team was awarded $500 in gold.

In 1878, after Gilman's retirement, Hartford gained full control of the business. His two sons, George and John, were each apprenticed at the age of 16. Years later, a writer in the *Saturday Evening Post* observed that "in discussing the two brothers, tea

---

## Company Perspectives:

*The Great Atlantic & Pacific Tea Company, Inc., founded in 1859, is a company that has rededicated itself to excellence and leadership within the retail food business. This involves long-range commitments to: our shareholders, by consistently increasing the value of their investments; our customers, by satisfying their food shopping needs more effectively than the competition; our employees, by providing improved opportunities for professional growth and achievement; our communities, by acting as good citizens and contributing important value to the neighborhoods we serve. We strive to accomplish these primary goals by adhering to a simple premise that remains as vital today as it was in 1859: Keep searching for better ways to serve the customer.*

---

company employees seldom get beyond the differences between the two.'' The older brother, who became known as Mr. George, earned a reputation as the ''inside man'' due to his concern for the books, and was considered to be the ''conservative, bearish influence in the business.'' The younger, flamboyant Mr. John was described as an ''old-school actor-manager.'' He was well-suited for his responsibility for promotions and premiums and generally ensured a ''personal touch'' in each of A&P's stores, which, by the turn of the century numbered 200 and generated more than $850 million in annual sales. Mr. John was also responsible for A&P peddlers, who by 1910 were carrying A&P products along 5,000 separate routes into rural areas in easily-recognized red-and-black A&P wagons.

Responding to a dramatic rise in the cost of living in the first decade of the 20th century, when food prices increased by 35 percent, Mr. John devised the first cash-and-carry A&P Economy Store. Initially dismissed by both George Jr. and George Sr., economy stores obviated the problem of capital depletion posed by premiums, credit, and delivery. The cash-and-carry stores followed a simple formula—$3,000 was allotted for equipment, groceries, and working capital. Only one man was needed to run an economy store, and he was expected to adhere strictly to Mr. John's ''Manual for Managers of Economy Stores,'' which outlined, in meticulous detail, how to run the stores. Among other things, Mr. John insisted that all the stores have the same goods at the same location; A&P legend has it that Mr. John could find the beans in any of his stores—blindfolded.

When George Hartford, Sr. died in 1917, George Jr. became chairman of A&P, while John became president. By 1925, A&P had 14,000 economy stores, with sales of $440 million, marking one of the greatest retail expansions ever. At this point, the company's national expansion was so far-reaching that A&P had to be divided into five geographical divisions to decentralize management.

During the 1920s, A&P continued to diversify, opening bakeries and pastry and candy shops. It also expanded its manufacturing facilities to produce its own Anne Page brand products and set up a corporation to buy coffee directly from Colombia and Brazil. ''Combination stores'' added hitherto unheard-of meat counters to the grocery chain and, when lines at these counters became a problem, A&P devised a system to make prepackaged meats available to customers, who had never before been offered such a convenience. At the same time, A&P introduced food-testing laboratories to maintain quality standards in its manufactured products. When, in 1929, the stock market crashed, causing other retail companies to fold, merge, or sell out in the subsequent Depression, A&P was so firmly established and soundly managed that it was virtually unaffected. Responding to consumers' needs, A&P began publishing literature with money-saving tips and recipes. The public's reception of these publications prompted the company to begin publishing *Woman's Day* magazine in 1937, at two cents per issue.

### Mid-Century

The 1930s marked the advent of supermarkets in the United States. The Hartfords found the supermarket idea distasteful and were slow to respond to the trend, but as A&P began to lose market share, they were swayed. In 1938, supermarkets made up five percent of A&P's stores—and 23 percent of its business. By 1939, the total number of A&P stores had dropped to 9,100, of which 1,100 were supermarkets, and A&P's sales had regained the level they first achieved in 1930. However, the company's size, though smaller than the 15,000 stores it had at its height in 1934, was a distinct liability. In 1936, the Robinson-Patman Act was passed, marking the beginning of the antitrust woes which shook A&P's hegemony. Anti-chain-store legislation, passed at the instigation of small independent grocers who claimed chains practiced unfair competition, imposed severe taxes and regulations on A&P and other chains, limiting pricing and other competitive advantages afforded to them by virtue of their size and purchasing power. Restrictions were based simply on store numbers, hitting A&P particularly hard. The company sought to redeem its damaged public image by publicizing its sense of corporate responsibility to consumers, producers, and employees. The loss of a suit in 1949, however, imposed limitations on A&P's purchasing practices that were more severe than any others in the industry. With this final blow, the company's position as an esteemed industry leader disintegrated.

In 1950 Ralph Burger, who had started at A&P in 1911 as an $11-a-week clerk, became president of the company. Much of A&P's early success had been due to Mr. George and Mr. John's scrupulous attention to the business, or, in Mr. John's term, to ''the art of basketwatching.'' As the *Saturday Evening Post* article on the Hartfords had concluded in 1931, ''who will watch the baskets after the Hartfords are gone? Neither has any children and although the 10 grandchildren get their due shares of income from the family trust, the direct line of shrewd vigilance will be broken.'' Burger remained loyal to the Hartford brothers even after their deaths, John in 1951 and George in 1957. As president not only of A&P, but also of the Hartford Foundation, the charity to which the Hartfords had willed their A&P shares, Burger retained full control of A&P, running it, if not imaginatively, then at least reasonably successfully, until his death in 1969. At that point, despite its dusty image, A&P was still the grocery-industry leader, with sales of well over $5 billion a year—more than twice its closest competitor.

With the end of Burger's tenure, and the Hartford heirs' disinclination to enter business, A&P had no clear line of management succession. The "direct line of shrewd vigilance" was indeed broken, and management continued to change throughout the 1970s. The company's direction foundered so much that A&P, once an innovative industry leader, was no longer able even to follow the lead of its competitors. Failing to capitalize on suburban development and to accommodate changing consumer tastes, A&P's sales dropped and its reputation suffered serious injury. A&P's once "resplendent emporiums" were now perceived as antiquated, inefficient, and run-down.

### New Management, Renovations, and Acquisitions

In 1973, as A&P reported $51 million in losses and Safeway took its place as the largest food retailer in the country, Jonathan L. Scott was hired from Albertson's, marking the first time in history that A&P had looked outside its ranks for management. Scott's attempt to revive A&P by closing stores and cutting labor costs only resulted in more dissatisfied customers, and more losses. Finally, in 1979, the Tengelmann Group, a major West German retailer, bought 52.5 percent of A&P's stock.

The Tengelmann Group soon appointed James Wood, the former CEO of Grand Union, as chairman and CEO of A&P. Wood's reputation as a turnaround manager underwent a trial by fire, but his radical restructuring of the company—the chain was eventually reduced to 1,000 stores—was eventually lauded by analysts as "an outstanding success." By 1982, close to 40 percent of the company's stores had been shut down. Not only were 600 stores closed, but virtually all manufacturing facilities had been eliminated. Management had won labor concessions in key markets, and the company returned to profitability. Between 1986 and 1990, A&P's earnings grew an average of 27 percent annually. With a formidable cash flow, Wood initiated an aggressive capital-spending program to rejuvenate the store base, develop new store formats, and make prudent acquisitions.

While some markets were abandoned, others were the focus of store recycling and expansion. High-growth areas (such as Phoenix, Arizona and southern California) were avoided in favor of markets in which A&P's presence was firmly established amidst a stable and slow-growing population (such as Philadelphia, New York, and Detroit). Concentrating efforts in the most promising areas of its six major operating regions—the Northeast, the New York metropolitan area, the mid-Atlantic states, the South, the Midwest, and Ontario—the company had the flexibility to tailor store formats, product mixes, service, and pricing to local customer bases.

Initially, tens of millions of dollars were spent to remodel and expand 85 percent of A&P's extant stores to give them a more up-to-date presentation, rid the company of its tarnished reputation, and add service departments to accommodate consumers' changed tastes. Improved sales allowed the company to begin to undertake new-store construction by 1985: the "new" A&P aimed for an upscale, service-oriented image and catered to one-stop shoppers. Two new store formats addressed different market niches: Futurestores stressed A&P's broad variety of quality products, and Sav-A-Centers took a strong promotional approach by offering warehouse prices.

Wood also focused on growth through the purchase of regional chains, permitting A&P to establish itself as the top food retailer in certain regional markets without the risk and expense of building new facilities and establishing a market niche. Its 1986 Waldbaum and Shopwell/Food Emporium acquisitions combined to make A&P the market leader in the New York metropolitan area, where the company had its strongest presence, and its 1989 acquisition of Borman's, a Detroit-area chain, resulted in a majority share of the Detroit market.

After the company's restructuring under James Wood, operating income per store more than doubled. Emphasizing high profit margin departments—full service delis, cheese shops, fresh seafood, and floral departments, for example—the company departed radically from low-price generic product offerings. In 1988, Master Choice, a private-brand label of specialty chocolates, pastas, sauces, and herbal teas was introduced in order to compete with what industry experts considered the real competition: restaurants and fast-food chains.

In 1989 A&P made a bid for Gateway Corporation, the third-largest grocery chain in Britain. Gateway would have offered A&P a whole new arena for growth, one that was of considerable interest to Erivan Haub, Tengelmann's owner, who wished to shore up his European retailing empire in preparation for the unification of the common market in 1992. The Gateway bid ultimately failed. A&P also had trouble with another international venture, its $250 million acquisition of 70 Miracle Food Mart stores in Ontario in 1990. Ontario was soon hit by recession, as were A&P's other major markets in the United States, and sales fell in the Canadian stores by five percent the next year.

A&P's acquisitions had given the company top market share in many cities. Its 1989 acquisition of Farmer Jack in Detroit, and its earlier purchases of Kohl's in Milwaukee, and Waldbaum's in New York put it in the top spot in these major markets. But the company had trouble hanging on to its market share. Its stores averaged half the size of newly-built supermarkets, and many were old and run-down. Waldbaum's in New York was cited in 1991 as the worst of all area grocery chains for numerous problems with rodents and cockroaches. The company was slow to respond, and Waldbaum's sanitation record improved only slightly the next year. Earnings for the company dropped from $151 in 1990 to $71 million in 1991. Then sales for fiscal 1992 fell a shocking $1.1 billion, and the company was in the red, losing $189.5 million. By 1993, stores run by A&P had lost market share in six major markets. Faced with a poor economy and declining profits, the company cut back the amount it was spending on renovations.

A&P decided to focus its marketing efforts on a new store brand product line in 1993. Chairman Wood had sold or closed most of the company's store brand manufacturing plants in the 1980s, but A&P thought it was time to emphasize cost-cutting store brands again. The company consolidated nine different private labels into one—America's Choice—that would be found at all its different chains. 3,500 private label items were consolidated into 1,600 America's Choice items, which were promoted on television in major market areas.

A&P also remodeled more than 100 stores in 1993 and built 20 new ones. Analysts frequently noted that A&P could spend much more on remodeling, and on opening bigger stores. In 1994 A&P upped its capital spending 40 percent, to $340 million, and announced that it would concentrate on opening 50,000 to 60,000 square-foot stores, on par with its competitors'. But the company was still plagued with problems. Its Ontario chains, Miracle Food Mart and Ultra Mart, were closed by a strike for 14 weeks during 1993–94. A&P had attempted to lower its labor costs by cutting wages and relying on more part-time workers, setting off the strike. A&P finally settled with the unions, but the long strike had given Ontario customers plenty of time to build loyalty to competitive stores. A&P's Atlanta stores also faltered. The company bought up 40 stores in the Atlanta area in 1993 in order to fight back competitors who were opening new stores in the area. However, the Atlanta stores lost money and only began to show a profit in the fourth quarter of fiscal 1994.

In spite of its problems, A&P had plans in place for a smoother future. The company gained a new president in 1994, Christian Haub, the 29-year-old son of Erivan Haub, the principal owner of A&P's majority owner Tengelmann Group. This was the first time a member of the Haub family had direct involvement with managing A&P. Haub planned to improve the image of A&P stores by improving cleanliness, checkout service and other highly visible areas of customer service. More than this, the company opened 16 new stores in 1994–95, remodeled or expanded 55 more, and closed 87 stores. According to Haub, A&P planned to open 50 stores a year after 1996. The company put aside $1.5 billion for store development over the next five years. Problems with the Canadian stores seemed to be improving by 1996. The company had to write off charges related to an employee buy out program there in 1995, but the next year, A&P gained a $6.5 million tax-refund in Canada. This contributed to a happy fourth quarter of fiscal 1995, when profits more than quadrupled. Operating income was on the rise, and sales at stores open at least a year climbed modestly. The company was far from its heyday, when it had been the leading chain across the country, but a conservative goal expressed by Christian Haub of being the leading store in its key markets seemed not totally unfeasible.

### Principal Subsidiaries

A&P Wine and Spirit, Inc.; ANP Properties I Corp.; ANP Sales Corp.; APW Supermarket Corp.; Big Star, Inc.; Great Atlantic & Pacific Tea Co., Ltd. (Canada); Great Atlantic & Pacific Tea Co. of Canada, Ltd.; d/b/a A&P and New Dominion; Borman's Inc. d/b/a Farmer Jack; Compass Foods Inc.; Family Center, Inc.; Futurestore Food Markets, Inc.; Great Atlantic & Pacific Tea Co. of Vermont; Kohl's Food Stores, Inc.; Kwik Save, Inc.; Lo-Lo Discount Stores, Inc.; Richmond, Inc.; St. Pancras Co. Limited (Bermuda); Shopwell, Inc.; Southern Development, Inc.; Super Fresh Food Markets, Inc.; Super Fresh Food Markets of Maryland, Inc.; Super Fresh Food Markets of Virginia, Inc.; Super Plus Food Warehouse, Inc.; Supermarket Distributor Service Corp.; Supermarket Distributor Service-Florence, Inc.; Supermarket Distribution Services, Inc.; Supermarket Systems, Inc.; Transco Service-Milwaukee, Inc.; Waldbaum, Inc.; W.S.L. Corporation; 2008 Broadway, Inc.

### Principal Divisions

A&P Coffee Division.

### Further Reading

Biesada, Alexandra, "The Golden Coattails," *Financial World*, October 27, 1992, pp. 30–31.

DeNitto, Emily, "Private Labels Bounce Back into Favor at A&P," *Advertising Age*, September 27, 1993, p. 12.

Garry, Michael, "A&P Strikes Back," *Progressive Grocer*, February 1994, pp. 32–37.

Hager, Bruce, "Trouble Stalks the Aisles at A&P," *Business Week*, September 23, 1991, pp. 60–61.

Hoyt, Edwin P., *That Wonderful A&P!*, New York: Hawthorne Books, 1969.

Kansas, Dave, "A&P Seeking to Add Another Dash of Retailing Magic," *Wall Street Journal*, May 28, 1993, p. 4B.

Lazo, Shirley A., "Woes Up North Lead to an A&P Slash," *Barron's*, December 12, 1994, p. 39.

Naik, Gautall, "A&P, Hoping for a Comeback, to Stress Bigger Stores, Private-Label Promotion," *Wall Street Journal*, June 3, 1994, p. A7A.

"Rebound All Over Again?" *Forbes*, March 16, 1992, p. 172.

Schifrin, Matthew, "Too Sharp a Knife?" *Forbes*, March 1, 1993, pp. 44–45.

"Taking the Long View," *Progressive Grocer*, May 1994, pp. 131–133.

"Update: The Great Atlantic & Pacific Tea Co. 125th Anniversary Celebration," Great Atlantic & Pacific Tea Co., Summer 1984.

Walsh, William I., *The Rise and Decline of The Great Atlantic and Pacific Tea Company*, Secaucus, N.J.: L. Stuart, 1986.

—updated by A. Woodward

# Grolier Inc.

**Sherman Turnpike**
**Danbury, Connecticut**
**U.S.A.**
**(203) 797-3500**
**Fax: (203) 797-3197**

*Wholly Owned Subsidiary of Largardère Groupe*
*Incorporated:* 1936 as The Grolier Society, Inc.
*Employees:* 3,600
*Sales:* $700 million (1994)
*SICs:* 2731 Book Publishing and Printing

Grolier Inc. is a leading publisher of reference books and multimedia reference products in the United States. A wholly owned subsidiary of French media conglomerate Largardere, Grolier publishes encyclopedias, children's books, reference sets, educational materials, and electronic products. The company's best-known titles include *Encyclopedia Americana* and the *New Book of Knowledge,* a children's encyclopedia. Grolier's electronic products consist of the *Guiness Multimedia Disc of Records* and the *Grolier Multimedia Encyclopedia.* The company also manages children's book clubs.

### Early History

The company originated with the Grolier Society founded in 1895 by a group of Boston scholars. Named after Jean Grolier, a designer and collector of French Renaissance books, the Society produced deluxe editions and memoirs in elegant bindings and sold them on a subscription basis. The Society was incorporated as a business under the name ''The Grolier Society, Inc.'' on May 22, 1936, under the laws of Delaware after being purchased by one of the Society's top salesmen, Fred Murphy. In 1960, the company changed its name to Grolier Incorporated. Soon after purchasing the Society, Murphy acquired *Encyclopedia Americana,* which became one of Grolier's major products. Under Murphy, Grolier became a sales-oriented company. He divided it into discrete businesses, giving managers wide leeway to run their divisions and instituting an incentive plan providing division managers a percentage of sales and profits generated by their respective operations. The incentive plan helped to boost company morale and productivity as individuals could earn substantial money, while being given the freedom to run their areas with minimum interference.

In the beginning, Grolier worked much like a finance company, operating largely on installment sales. The company might borrow money, for example, at 4.5 percent and receive 12 or 15 percent in return on its installment accounts. Due to rapid expansion, by the late 1960s and early 1970s Grolier became the largest hardcover publisher of encyclopedias and reference books in the United States, earning about $317 million in sales. In 1969, the 74-year old publicly owned company recorded higher sales for the 30th consecutive year and held about 30 percent of the total encyclopedia market.

In the same year, the company purchased Scarecrow Press in Metuchen, New Jersey, a supplier of catalogues, anthologies, and other specialized publications to libraries and schools, and Haddon Bindery, Inc. of Camden, New Jersey, a provider of binder facilities for Grolier's single-volume publications. Western Wood Mfg., acquired in 1967, produced bookcases for Grolier's major multivolume sets. Grolier's juvenile book division also included the subsidiary Franklin Watts, Inc., a publisher of children's books. The company further pursued the educational market through another subsidiary, Grolier Educational Corporation.

While Grolier published the popular 30-volume *Encyclopedia Americana,* its best seller was the 20-volume *Book of Knowledge,* which gained wide acceptance as a basic reference work for children in middle elementary grades. Other Grolier products included the 50-volume set of the *World's Greatest Classics,* the 20-volume *Encyclopedia International,* the 20-volume *American Peoples Encyclopedia,* the 10-volume *Grolier Universal Encyclopedia,* the 10-volume *Book of Art,* the *Book of Popular Science,* the *Encyclopedia Canadiana,* and several other encyclopedias, yearbooks, and references in French, Spanish, and Japanese. In 1969, the company's subsidiary Grolier International sold these products in 40 foreign countries. Most of its revenues came from door-to-door sales by 7,000 salesmen on commission. Grolier also operated a mail-order business, accounting in 1968 for about 26 percent of the company's net income.

### Hard Times in the 1960s and 1970s

Despite these early successes and sound products, in the 1960s and early 1970s Grolier embarked on misguided diversification and expansion programs. The company borrowed heavily, becoming over-leveraged while diversifying into mostly unrelated areas, including trailer parks, water-ski manufacturing, trailer manufacturing, woodworking products, vending machines, and South American publishing. In 1973, Grolier wrote off three of its domestic subsidiaries—water ski manufacturing, vending machine financing, and book binding—for $5 million. Two years later, Grolier ended its mobile home operations, writing off another $11.9 million. In the 1960s, Grolier also expanded into the fast-growing foreign encyclopedia market, an expansion that proved ill-advised. By 1976, company losses included special charges of $25.4 million for divesting 23 foreign operations in 15 countries. In the same year, steep foreign exchange losses hit the company, amounting to $23.2 million. As a result of these missteps, between 1973 and 1976 Grolier lost nearly $160 million, about $77.8 million in 1976 alone. These losses, which showed a consolidated negative net loss of $45.5 million, prompted the New York Stock Exchange to delist the company.

During this period Grolier also saw its share of the U.S. encyclopedia market slip by 15 percent, stemming largely from the industry's image of slick, fast-talking door-to door salesman and high prices of encyclopedias at $300 to $500 a set. The industry's tarnished image was to some extent justified. In 1972, a complaint filed with the U.S. Federal Trade Commission (FTC) accused Grolier of fraudulent and deceptive practices in door-to-door and other sales techniques, recruitment of personnel, and debt collection. Encyclopedia Britannica and about 30 other companies were found to have engaged in similar practices. In 1976, an administrative law judge upheld the major provisions of the Grolier FTC complaint. Grolier appealed the decision to the FTC's five-member commission, which one year later unanimously sustained the 1976 decision. Grolier was ordered, therefore, to cease and desist all deceptive practices, and to ensure that the company's sales force properly represent the company's products.

At the same time that Grolier faced financial difficulties, its two major competitors for the encyclopedia market, Field Enterprises Educational Corporation and Encyclopedia Britannica, were experiencing substantial growth. The profitability of both companies resulted primarily from expansion into the same overseas markets that Grolier found unmanageable. While Grolier lost money in these markets, Encyclopedia Britannica alone had expanded into 150 countries, finding the foreign business enormously profitable.

### 1970s: Management Shifts and Facing Bankruptcy

In 1976, under duress from creditors, the company's board of directors demanded a change in management. Disagreement between members of the board and inside management, some of whom inherited substantial stock in the company, resulted in the selection of Robert B. Clarke to salvage the firm. Clarke was a longtime company insider who joined Grolier in 1949 as a shipping clerk. He rose through middle management before becoming head in 1967 of Grolier Enterprises, the company's profitable mail-order business. Three years after becoming division president, he relocated its operations to Danbury, Connecticut, for tax reasons from the company's New York headquarters on Lexington Avenue. Clarke had a reputation for financial discipline, and at the time of his selection, was working on evaluating the profitability of Grolier's various businesses.

Upon becoming company president on October 23, 1976, Clarke moved quickly to reorganize the company and keep creditors at bay. Grolier was already in default to several banks on more than $220 million. He relocated the corporate headquarters to Connecticut, where the local corporate court would be more sympathetic to Grolier's financial plight than the courts in New York. To restore the company's finances, he pulled out of losing ventures, cut staff, and hastily implemented cost- and cash-flow controls. He hired the investment firm Goldman Sachs to evaluate the company's financial viability. He also hired Harvey Miller, a bankruptcy expert of Weil, Gotshal to examine the bankruptcy angle. Clarke's concern was how bankruptcy would affect company relations with suppliers and manufacturers, and whether it would ruin Grolier's credit supply. Clarke was also worried that Grolier's subsidiary businesses would have to follow the parent company into bankruptcy. He knew that if Grolier declared bankruptcy, creditors would petition the courts for the liquidation of all assets, including the subsidiary businesses. Nevertheless, if one of Grolier's subsidiaries could pay creditors more than they would otherwise receive through wholesale liquidation, the courts would likely protect the business.

As a result, Grolier crafted a strategy of avoiding bankruptcy by using its most profitable subsidiary, the mail-order division, to carry the entire company and pay off creditors. The subsidiary placed all of Grolier's purchase and manufacturing orders, and paid suppliers and creditors from its own money. Nevertheless, Grolier's position was precarious at best. If creditors either severed its credit line or tightened the terms, the company would be put out of business. To avoid this scenario, the company courted its creditors, assuring them of payment and managing to assuage the concerns of 23 lending institutions to which Grolier owed substantial sums.

At the same time, Clarke maintained the support of Grolier's board of directors and launched other strategies to return the company to profitability. In 1977, he negotiated a restructuring agreement with the banks to give Grolier time to reorganize and set out to expand the company's market for encyclopedias. Despite criticism that the market lacked growth opportunity, Grolier nevertheless increased its door-to-door encyclopedia sales. In 1978, Clarke pursued telephone sales, a strategy that proved more profitable than traditional door-to-door sales. The company's use of telephone sales to reach a vast market yielded $43 million for its encyclopedias and other book products in just three years. Grolier began its telemarketing campaign by renting space in downtown Danbury, Connecticut, and hiring six women to make telephone calls. The company also developed a computer databank including the names of millions of individuals who either owed Grolier money or were buying one of its products. By expanding its market, increasing sales, and finally earning profits, Grolier managed to offset its debt payments.

In 1978, Grolier also launched a $1.3 million direct mail and television advertising campaign, representing another dramatic departure from its traditional door-to-door sales program. The campaign advertised the popular children's encyclopedia the *New Book of Knowledge* to the consumer using three direct-mail packages targeting 1.8 million U.S. families and two weeks' worth of television commercials in 28 prime mail-order television markets. At the same time, Grolier tried to enhance the marketability of the 20-volume set by reducing its price by 39 percent. The *Book of Knowledge* was first published in 1908 and then completely revised in 1966. In an interview, Grolier president and Chief Executive Officer, Robert Clarke, stated that the advertising program amounted to the largest new marketing campaign ever for a multivolume set in the mail-order publishing field. The campaign stemmed from marketing analysis showing declining encyclopedia sales due to consumer discontent over high prices, dislike of door-to-door salesman, and parental uncertainty of whether their children would make use of the reference books.

Despite Clarke's aggressive capital restructuring program, by 1983 the company continued to have difficulties. Grolier still owed 23 lending institutions $96 million. In lieu of payment in full, the banks agreed to receive $36 million in cash plus a combination of common and preferred stock and warrants worth more than $16 million. Clarke raised the cash through an $82 million bond issue, spending part of it to retire $35 million in Swiss notes. Although free of the banks and the Swiss, Grolier's load of public debt amounted to over half its total capital. Nevertheless, in 1982 the company formed a successful new subsidiary, Grolier Electronic Publishing, which in 1986 introduced the first encyclopedia in electronic format on compact-disk read-only memory (CD-ROM) under the name *Academic American Encyclopedia*. The company also introduced the product on laser videodisc. Grolier produced both products, containing the encyclopedia's entire nine-million-word text on a single disk, with Activenture Corporation, an expert in optical disk storage technology in Monterey, California. The products, establishing Grolier as the preeminent leader in the field, brought the company closer to realizing its plans of a disk-based encyclopedia encompassing audio, video, and software applications. In addition, the products positioned the company well for future developments in the expanding market for electronic information.

### Grolier Regains Financial Health in the 1980s

By the late 1980s Grolier reestablished its financial footing as a leading worldwide publisher and distributer of encyclopedias, children's books, reference sets, and educational materials. In 1987, the company also marketed health information after acquiring Krames Communications, a major direct distributer of health and medical publication materials. In addition to Grolier's operations as a primary producer and distributer of electronic publishing products and services, its other businesses included photofinishing services, educational toys, play equipment, and classroom furniture for children. The company sold these products in the U.S., Canada, and in 20 other countries through its operations in Mexico, Italy, Australia, the United Kingdom, and the Philippines.

The company's direct marketing operations constituted its principal means of sales. Grolier began direct marketing by selling annual supplements that updated previously sold encyclopedia or reference sets. The company considerably expanded these operations both internally and through new acquisitions. Most of its direct marketing sales in the U.S. and Canada came from direct-mail advertising using pamphlets, brochures, and specialty catalogs. The company continued its telemarketing program, selling certain products using trained telephone sales representatives. Under its direct-marketing system, Grolier also marketed children's and other books through book clubs, including the Beginner Reader's Program, Disney's Wonderful World of Reading, the Popular Science Book Club, and Outdoor Life Book Club.

### Hostile Takeover

In 1988, soon after returning to profitability, Grolier became a hostile takeover target. Although profitable, the company's comparatively small size made it vulnerable in an era of massive leveraged buyouts, mergers, acquisitions, hostile takeovers, and corporate restructurings. In 1986, Lewis Rabinowitz, head of the investment firm R. Lewis Securities Inc., anticipated the buyout by purchasing large sums of Grolier stock on behalf of his wealthy clients. Rabinowitz believed Grolier's book niche would appeal to large publishers seeking to expand their markets. Grolier's allure also lay in its extensive direct-marketing organization, providing access to upscale, education-oriented young families with children. Rabinowitz's prediction proved correct in 1988 when Hachette, France's largest communications company, offered $415 million in an unsolicited bid. In a prepared statement, Clarke responded that Grolier management would recommend to the board that the company pursue a course that would maximize shareholder value.

Despite public statements of a friendly offer, Hachette filed suit against Grolier in federal court in Manhattan. Hachette challenged Grolier's "poison pill" approach, adopted in 1986, making its acquisition enormously expensive unless approved by the company's board of directors. Hachette's suit also challenged Delaware's takeover statute, allowing corporations to impose difficult conditions on businesses pursuing acquisitions. In 1987, Hachette, owner of newspaper, film, television, radio, printing, and retailing operations, had $3 billion in sales, nearly one-third of these from its book publishing operation. That same year, Grolier had sales of $424 million.

In April 1988, Grolier's poison pill approach and Delaware registration failed to ward off Hachette's $450 million hostile takeover. Shortly after in 1990, Hachette made sweeping changes in Grolier's top management. Clarke was replaced by William C. Johnson as Grolier CEO, ending Clarke's 40-year career as a loyal company insider. Hachette removed other longtime executives, including Howard B. Graham, executive vice president of Grolier Incorporated and president of Grolier International, Jonathan N. Gillet, president of Franklin Watts, the adult and juvenile trade subsidiary.

After becoming CEO, Johnson divested several subsidiaries to focus on Grolier's core publishing businesses. He sold the company's educational toy maker, Childcraft Education, to Walt Disney for $52 million, and in 1992, sold Krames Communications to K-III Holdings. He subsequently reorganized Grolier's operations under four main divisions, including the direct marketing group, the publishing group, reference group, and the international group. Under each operation, Johnson appointed a senior executive to run the divisions. As a result of the reorganization, Grolier's operations generated returns on sales of 10 percent with revenues of $385 million in 1991. After the direct marketing division, the publishing group represented Grolier's largest operation with 440 employees and approximately 20 percent of total company sales. The publishing group targeted the school and library market as its core business. In 1992, the division had about 20 percent of the U.S. market for juvenile and young adult books and reference books for the school and library market. In a restructuring move, the division sought to eliminate competitive marketing between its various units by redirecting their sales strategies to differing segments of the library market. The publishing group consisted of Children's Press, Grolier Educational Corporation, Franklin Watts, Orchard Books, and Scarecrow Press.

### Post-Restructuring

Grolier quickly became a profitable U.S. affiliate of Hachette, a subsidiary of France's third-largest business empire, Lagardere. Hachette's management predicted a brighter future for Grolier after years of financial struggle. In 1994, Peter D. Nalle was named chief operating officer in charge of publishing and reference operations. Nalle was previously president of Simon & Shuster's professional information group, and earlier, president and CEO of J.B. Lippincott Co. His appointment was expected to enable Grolier to move more aggressively into key markets. In 1995, Grolier further streamlined operations by consolidating its Children's Press and Franklin Watts children's book publishing subsidiaries into the company's Danbury, Connecticut, headquarters. The consolidation resulted from management analysis of Grolier's long-term competitive position. As a result of this analysis, the company also sold educational publisher Scarecrow Press to University Press, and expanded its electronic publishing division, Grolier Electronic Publishing (GEP). GEP subsequently enhanced its multimedia activity through a strategic alliance with Metro-Goldwyn-Mayer, enabling the development and distribution of interactive multimedia games worldwide. In the late 1990s, Grolier continued to increase its focus on electronic publishing and multimedia. Among the titles the company introduced on CD-ROM were *Prehistoria,* an encyclopedia of prehistoric facts, and a 30-volume *Encyclopedia Americana.* Through these and other strategic initiatives, Grolier appeared well-positioned to remain profitable throughout the remainder of the decade.

### Further Reading

Fields, Howard, "Clarke Retires Among Top Shake-up at Grolier," *Publishers Weekly,* February 10, 1989, p. 14.

"FTC Rules Against Grolier on Unfair Practices," *Publishers Weekly,* April 17, 1978, pp. 24–26.

"Grolier: Its Encyclopedias Are Best Sellers," *Financial World,* August 6, 1969, p. 12.

"How Grolier Lost $13 a Share," *Business Week,* April 4, 1977, p. 31.

"How Grolier Turned Around," *Publishers Weekly,* April 30, 1982, pp. 26–27.

Marcial Gene G., "Why Grolier Looks Ripe for the Picking," *Business Week,* November 3, 1986, p. 128.

Milliot, Jim, "Grolier Moving Children's Press, Watts to Danbury," *Publishers Weekly,* March 20, 1995, p. 18.

Parr, Jann, "Waiting for New Hardware," *Forbes,* November 17, 1986, p. 262.

"Perpetual Comeback," *Forbes,* December 5, 1983, pp. 259, 262.

Reddish, Jeannette M., "People of the Financial World," *Financial World,* February 15, 1978, p. 4.

Reid, Calvin, "Grolier Looks Ahead After Divestitures, Reorganization," *Publishers Weekly,* March 16, 1992, pp. 9–10.

Reuter, Madalynne, ed., The Week: Grolier Unveils Unusual Selling Tactics for The New Book of Knowledge," *Publishers Weekly,* January 23, 1978, p. 287.

Reuter, Madalynne, ed., "News of the Week: Hachette Launches Bid of $415 Million for Grolier," *Publishers Weekly,* March 25, 1988, p. 10.

Spain, Tom, "Grolier Encyclopedia to Bow in New Formats," *Publishers Weekly,* August 16, 1985, p. 18.

Wagner, Susan, "Judge Upholds FTC Complaint Against Grolier," *Publishers Weekly,* November 22, 1976, pp. 19–20.

—Bruce P. Montgomery

# Hallmark Cards, Inc.

2501 McGee Street
Kansas City, Missouri 64108
U.S.A.
(816) 274-5111
Fax: (816) 274-8513

*Private Company*
*Incorporated:* 1923 as Hall Brothers Company
*Employees:* 19,600
*Sales:* $3.4 billion (1995 est.)
*SICs:* 2678 Stationery, Tablets & Related Products; 2679
    Converted Paper & Paperboard Products, Not
    Elsewhere Classified; 2771 Greeting Card Publishing
    & Printing; 3952 Lead Pencils, Crayons & Artists'
    Materials; 3999 Manufacturing Industries, Not
    Elsewhere Classified

Hallmark Cards, Inc. is the world's largest greeting card company, creating 21,000 different designs each year in more than 20 languages, and distributing them in more than 100 countries. In addition to the Hallmark flagship, the company also markets cards under the Ambassador and Expressions brand names. Over the years, Hallmark has branched out into other areas of the stationery business, including writing paper, party goods, gift wrap, and photo albums, as well as into such giftware as plush toys, mugs, jigsaw puzzles, and Christmas ornaments. The company's Binney & Smith Inc. subsidiary specializes in personal skill development products, including Crayola crayons, Magic Markers, modeling material, creativity software, model kits, and art supplies for professionals and students. Hallmark also creates family-oriented television programming through its Hallmark Entertainment, Inc. subsidiary. Even with the firm's diversification, the greeting card remains Hallmark's mainstay—so much so that often Hallmark has been mistakenly credited with inventing it.

## Early History

Hallmark was founded by Joyce C. Hall, a native of Norfolk, Nebraska, who as a teenager ran a postcard company with his older brothers. In 1910 Hall, still only 18, left the family business he had founded after a traveling salesman convinced him that Kansas City, Missouri, would serve him better as a wholesaling and distribution center. Almost immediately after arriving in Kansas City, Hall set up a mail-order postcard company in a small room at the Young Men's Christian Association, where he remained until his landlord complained about the volume of mail Hall was receiving. The new company was named Hall Brothers, a name justified the following year when Rollie Hall came to Kansas City to join his brother in the business.

At that time, picture postcards were all the rage in the United States, with the best ones imported from Europe. Very early on, however, Joyce Hall came to believe that the postcard's appeal was quite limited. They were novelty items rather than a means of communication and, with the leisure time needed to write long letters diminishing and the long-distance telephone call still a rare phenomenon, people would need a shorthand way of reaching each other by mail. Greeting cards suggested themselves as a viable alternative, so in 1912 Hall Brothers added them to its product line.

The outbreak of World War I bore out Hall's contention. The supply of postcards from Europe dried up, but domestic products were of inferior quality and their popularity waned. Greeting cards stepped into the breach. In 1914 Hall Brothers bought a small press and began publishing its own line of Christmas cards. In 1915 a fire destroyed the company's entire inventory, putting it $17,000 in debt, but Joyce and Rollie Hall rebuilt the business. In 1921 they were joined by their brother William Hall. By 1922 Hall Brothers had recovered to the point where it was employing 120 people, including salespeople in all 48 states. Also that year, it diversified for the first time and started selling decorative gift wrap.

In 1923 the company formally incorporated under the name Hall Brothers Company. Over the next two decades, it would attack its market aggressively through advertising. In 1928 Hall Brothers became the first greeting card company to advertise nationally when it took out an ad in *Ladies Home Journal.* In 1936, with the national economy emerging from the worst of the Great Depression, Hall Brothers went on the attack again, introducing an open display fixture for greeting cards that Joyce Hall had developed with the help of an architect. Previously,

---

**Company Perspectives:**

*Hallmark aspires to enrich people's lives and enhance their relationships. Beyond products and services, the company funds the Hallmark Corporate Foundation, which benefits human service, education, health and arts organizations in the communities in which Hallmark operates. In partnership with Boys & Girls Clubs of America, 4-H Youth Development Education and Girl Scouts of the U.S.A., the Foundation produces ''Talking with T.J.,'' a video series that helps youngsters develop essential social skills. Additionally, Hallmark sponsors Kaleidoscope, a creative workshop for youngsters.*

---

cards had always been kept under store counters, out of customers' sight and usually in a disorganized state. In 1938 Hall Brothers advertised in the broadcast medium for the first time when it began sponsoring ''Tony Won's Radio Scrapbook'' on WMAQ radio in Chicago.

When the United States entered World War II, the company pitched an appeal to friends and loved ones of military personnel with the slogan ''Keep 'em happy with mail.'' Hall Brothers would find its most famous and enduring slogan in 1944, however, when it started using the tagline ''When you care enough to send the very best,'' which had been suggested a few years earlier by sales and advertising manager Ed Goodman. After the war, a staff artist created the company's logo, consisting of a five-pointed crown and the Hallmark name in script letters. Hall Brothers took out a copyright on the logo in 1949.

### Expansion in the 1950s and 1960s

The company established another landmark in advertising on Christmas Eve 1951, when it sponsored a television production of Gian Carlo Menotti's opera *Amahl and the Night Visitors*. This was the first of the famous Hallmark Hall of Fame series, which two years later presented a production of *Hamlet* starring the noted British Shakespearean actor Maurice Evans. That broadcast marked the first time the entire play had ever been seen on U.S. television. As Joyce Hall himself once said, ''Good taste is good business.''

Also in the early 1950s, Hall Brothers began opening the first of thousands of retail shops specializing in Hallmark cards. In 1954 the company changed its name to Hallmark Cards, Inc., having already used Hallmark as a brand name for 31 years. In 1959 the company introduced its Ambassador Cards line to tap into the lucrative market presented by shoppers at mass merchandisers such as supermarkets, discount stores, and drugstores. The next year Hallmark introduced its own line of party decorations and began featuring characters from Charles M. Schulz's ''Peanuts'' comic strip on its products.

In 1966, Joyce Hall retired as president and CEO of the company he had founded. Handing the reins to his son, Donald Hall, Joyce Hall nevertheless remained active in company affairs as chairman until his death in 1982. Joyce Hall was not only a wealthy and successful businessman when he died, but also a member of the French Legion of Honor and a commander of the

British Empire. He had been friends with British Prime Minister Winston Churchill and with U.S. Presidents Harry Truman and Dwight Eisenhower. For the latter Hall Brothers custom-designed an official presidential Christmas card in 1953.

One of Donald Hall's first important moves as CEO of Hallmark was to acquire Springbok Editions, maker of jigsaw puzzles, in 1967. The next year, the company broke ground on the Crown Center, a $500 million retail, commercial, and residential complex intended to revitalize an area near downtown Kansas City and financed entirely with company funds. Hallmark created a new subsidiary, Crown Center Redevelopment Corporation, to oversee it.

### 1980s Acquisitions

In 1979 Hallmark acquired Georgia-based lithographer Litho-Krome Corporation. In 1981 the company formed a division, Hallmark Properties, to create and administer licensing projects. This division went on to create Hallmark's Rainbow Brite, Purr-Tenders, and Timeless Tales character merchandise, and also oversaw the company's licenses for Peanuts and Garfield cartoon characters.

After his father's death in 1982, Donald Hall added the chairmanship to his duties as CEO. In 1984 Hallmark acquired Binney & Smith, the Pennsylvania-based maker of Crayola crayons and Liquitex art materials. In 1986 Donald Hall retired as CEO and handed the post to president Irvine O. Hockaday Jr.

In 1987 Hallmark, after being a prominent advertiser in the broadcast media for many years, became an owner as well when it acquired a group of Spanish-language television stations from Spanish International Communication. The next year, it added another station purchased from Bahia de San Francisco Television. Also in 1988, Hallmark acquired a Spanish-language network, Univision, and amalgamated all of its holdings in a subsidiary, Univision Holdings. Based in New York, the subsidiary ran the nine full-power stations under the name Univision Station Group.

During the mid-1980s small greeting card companies began competing for Hallmark's market position with a diverse array of cards that became favorites. In the mid-1980s Hallmark fought back with its Personal Touch and Shoebox Greetings series. Many of these cards, however, bore a resemblance to rival designs that some found too striking. In 1986 Blue Mountain Arts, which produced non-occasion cards featuring poetry and pastel illustrations to produce a concentrated emotional effect, sued Hallmark for copyright and trade dress infringement and unfair competition. The initial decision went against Hallmark, which appealed ultimately to the Supreme Court. When the Supreme Court refused to hear the case in 1988, Hallmark agreed to discontinue its Personal Touch line. Financial terms of the settlement were not disclosed.

### 1990s and Beyond

Hallmark's biggest challenge during the early 1990s was confronting its continuing loss of market share to the number two and three companies in the greeting card industry, American Greetings Corp. and Gibson Greetings, Inc., respectively. From 1990 to 1995, it was estimated that Hallmark's market share fell from 50 to 45 percent. Some industry experts even suggested that American Greetings would overtake Hallmark sometime between 1999 and 2004.

The reason for Hallmark's decline rested in the very backbone of its empire—the specialty card and gift shops that sold the Hallmark brand, which by the early 1990s numbered more than 10,000. Over a long period, these shops had fallen victim to changing buying patterns in particular among women, who still bought 90 percent of all cards sold. Pressed for time, more and more consumers were opting to purchase cards at one-stop shopping outlets—supermarkets, drugstore chains, and large discounters—such as Wal-Mart. In the early 1970s more than half of all cards were sold in specialty shops; by the early 1990s only about 30 percent were. American Greetings and Gibson, which did not have such extensive ties to the card shops, were able to recognize the trend and shift to accommodate it. Hallmark, however, was in a bind. Continuing to rely so heavily on specialty shops would do nothing to halt its market share decline, but it could not simply abandon the shops for the discounters; doing so could bankrupt many of them, not something a company as paternalistic as Hallmark could seriously consider.

One strategy was to diversify away from greeting cards even further. In 1990 Hallmark acquired Willitts Designs, a maker of collectibles, but then sold the company only three years later. Likewise, Hallmark's venture into Spanish-language television was abandoned in 1992 at a loss of $10 million when Univision was sold to Grupo Televisa. Cable television was Hallmark's next foray with the 1991 formation of a Crown Media Inc. subsidiary to which was added Cenom Cable in St. Louis, through the purchase of a controlling interest for $1 billion. In 1994 this venture too was cast aside when Hallmark sold Crown Media to Charter Communications Inc. for $900 million.

During this period Hallmark also updated its product line, offering a more high tech approach to card purchasing. In 1991 the "Personalize it!" in-store kiosk was introduced (later called Touch-Screen Greetings), through which customers were able to create computer-generated personalized greeting cards. The following year Hallmark filed suit for infringement of its kiosk patent against American Greetings and its Creata-Card kiosk. The suit was settled in 1995 with each company receiving a worldwide, nonexclusive license to use the technology; no other details on the settlement were provided at that time.

Moreover, in 1994, Hallmark developed recordable greeting cards in partnership with Information Storage Devices. Initially retailing for $7.95 each, these cards allowed the sender to record his personal message, which would then play back each time the card was opened. The following year, Hallmark moved into the burgeoning area of online marketing by offering its greeting cards on America Online. The company planned additional such ventures for other online services.

In the face of declining profits brought on by the declining market share, Hallmark went through a series of reengineering and restructuring efforts in the early 1990s in an attempt to hold costs down. United States and Canadian operations were consolidated and a 1995 restructuring brought together for each Hallmark card brand its administrative, marketing, and product-development function.

Additional diversification moves were taken in the mid-1990s in the field of entertainment. In 1994 Hallmark acquired RHI Entertainment Inc. for $365 million. RHI was the television production company responsible for Hallmark's *Hall of Fame* productions. Hallmark thus acquired the world's leading producer of family-oriented entertainment, which it promptly renamed Hallmark Entertainment, Inc. and set up as a subsidiary of Hallmark Cards. Then in 1995, Hallmark purchased a 9.9 percent stake in European broadcaster Flextech for $80 million. Flextech and Hallmark will create a family-oriented cable television network, the Hallmark Entertainment Network, which was slated to commence operations in Ireland and the United Kingdom in 1996.

Given the uneven success of Hallmark's noncore ventures, greeting cards remained the company's most important endeavor. New promotions of Hallmark cards in the mid-1990s included a "sneak-a-peek" advertising campaign, comprising a series of commercials in which someone is caught looking at the back of the card he was just given, just to make sure it was a Hallmark. The company also announced plans to introduce a new brand name in 1997, Expressions by Hallmark. Heading into the 21st century, Hallmark was a market leader at a crossroads. According to some analysts, the company's decisions regarding its distribution options would likely go a long way toward determining future success.

### *Principal Subsidiaries*

Binney & Smith Inc.; Crown Center Redevelopment Corporation; Graphics International Inc.; Hallmark Entertainment, Inc.; Hallmark International; Halls Merchandising, Inc.; Litho-Krome Co.; Hallmark Cards Australia Ltd.; Binney & Smith (Canada) Ltd.; Hallmark Canada; Hallmark Cards Inc.-French Branch; Hallmark Cards GmbH (Germany); Hallmark Cards Ireland Ltd.; Hallmark de Mexico, S.A. de C.V.; Spanjersburg (Netherlands); Verkerke Reprodukties, N.V. (Netherlands); Hallmark Cards NZ Ltd. (New Zealand); Hallmark Cards Iberica, S.A. (Spain); Hallmark Cards Ltd., European Div. (U.K.); W. N. Sharpe Ltd. (U.K.); Valentines of Dundee, Ltd (U.K.).

### *Further Reading*

Chandler, Susan, "Can Hallmark Get Well Soon?," *Business Week,* June 19, 1995, pp. 62–63.

Fitzgerald, Kate, "Hallmark Alters Focus as Lifestyles Change," *Advertising Age,* October 25, 1994, p. 4.

"From Someone Who Loves You," *Economist,* August 10, 1991, p. 63.

Hall, Joyce C., with Curtiss Anderson, *When You Care Enough,* Kansas City, Mo.: Hallmark, 1979, 269 p.

Hirshey, Gerri, "Happy [ ] Day to You," *New York Times Magazine,* July 2, 1995, pp. 20+.

Howard, Elizabeth G., "Hallmark's $4 Billion Formula," *Kansas City Business Journal,* June 16, 1995, p. 17.

Kinni, Theodore B., "The Reengineering Rage," *Industry Week,* February 7, 1994, p. 11.

Schiller, Zachary, and Ron Grover, "And Now, a Show from Your Sponsor," *Business Week,* May 22, 1995, pp. 100–02.

Stern, William M., "Loyal to a Fault: Its Brand Name is August, Its Profits a Wow! But Hallmark Cards Had Better Get with It—Now!," *Forbes,* March 14, 1994, pp. 58–59.

Weiner, Steve, "Do They Speak Spanish in Kansas City?," *Forbes,* January 25, 1988, p. 46.

Young, Gordon, "Card Sharks," *Utne Reader,* May/June 1993, p. 132.

—Joan Harpham and Douglas Sun
—updated by David E. Salamie

# Harding Lawson Associates Group, Inc.

7655 Redwood Boulevard
P.O. Box 578
Novato, California 94948
U.S.A.
(415) 892-0821
Fax: (415) 892-0685

*Public Company*
*Incorporated:* 1959 as Harding Associates, Inc.
*Employees:* 1,045
*Sales:* $130.5 million (1995)
*Stock Exchanges:* NASDAQ
*SICs:* 8742 Management Consulting Services

A rising force in the engineering consulting industry, Harding Lawson Associates Group, Inc. provides engineering, environmental, and construction services related to the management of hazardous and solid wastes, as well as civil and geotechnical engineering services. During the mid-1990s, Harding Lawson Group served as the parent company for three subsidiaries, Harding Lawson Associates, Inc., Harding International, Inc., and Harding Lawson Associates Infrastructure, Inc., which together operated 35 offices located in 17 states, Australia, Indonesia, and Mexico. Although Harding Lawson Group celebrated its 36th year of business in 1995, the operations that constituted the company during the 1990s were largely developed during the 1980s and 1990s, when annual sales for the company increased from roughly $10 million to the $130 million generated in 1995.

## Origins

Founded in 1959, the Harding Lawson Group began business as Harding Associates, Inc., drawing its name from the then 35-year-old founder of the company, Richard S. Harding. When Harding took the helm of his small, start-up consulting and engineering firm during its inaugural year of business, he began what would become his life's work. Harding guided the company for more than three decades, stewarding its growth during its formative years as a modestly sized, privately held firm based in California, then, during the later years of his career, superintended its transformation into a much larger, more diversified company. The two periods in the corporate life of Harding Associates were distinct; one comprised nearly 30 years of subdued existence and moderate growth, while the other saw the advent of a more conspicuous player in the engineering consulting industry. Although Harding Associates' era of prominence came roughly three decades after its formation, reaching stride as Harding himself was nearing the end of his career at the company, the move toward diversification and greater growth was resolute, fueling sales increases that far outpaced the rate of growth recorded during the company's first era of business.

The company Harding helped to establish and the company of which he was later named chairman emeritus operated as a privately held company for 28 years before entering the public spotlight in 1987. The conversion to public ownership represented a turning point in the company's history, to be sure, but the signal year in Harding Associates' transformation into a more diversified and robust competitor in the engineering consulting industry occurred three years earlier, in 1984, when the company shifted its business focus and entered a substantially more fruitful field of operations.

## Defining Change in 1984

Until 1984, Harding Associates generated the bulk of its business from conducting soil and foundation analyses for commercial and industrial construction projects, competing as a firm whose specialty was geotechnical consulting. In 1984, however, the company's management, led by Harding who served as chairman, president, and chief executive officer, took notice of a burgeoning market that offered greater growth and greater rewards. In the years preceding 1984, federal, state, and local environmental regulations put into effect stringent stipulations concerning hazardous waste disposal, which, not surprisingly, created a pressing demand for hazardous waste disposal services during the early and mid-1980s. Noting the rise in demand for such engineering consulting services, the management of

Harding Associates decided a change in business emphasis was in order. From 1984 forward, waste management engineering would fuel the company's growth, precipitating a steady rise in its sales and touching off a new era in its corporate history.

After recasting itself as a provider of engineering and consulting services for hazardous waste disposal, Harding Associates entered the fast-growing market that would support the company in the years to come. Once hired for a project, the company sent its scientists and engineers to determine the nature and extent of contamination at a particular site. Using the information gathered from this initial inspection, company personnel designed a system to control or eliminate the problem, then managed the construction of the remedial system or waste disposal facility and, after that, managed its operation following the completion of construction. The foray into waste disposal engineering and consulting proved to be a boon to the company's financial condition, yielding ameliorative results and arresting a harmful slide in earnings. In 1983, one year before the entry into hazardous waste disposal services was effected, Harding Associates recorded a year-end loss of $147,000 on $16.2 million in annual sales. By the end of 1984, earnings had shot up to nearly $300,000, while revenues approached $25 million, giving management palpable evidence that the decision to revamp the company's business focus after 25 years was a prudent one.

Business steadily grew as the 1980s progressed, driving annual sales upward. Although the company's earnings fluctuated during the mid-1980s, jumping back and forth between $250,000 and $300,000, its revenues marched resolutely upward, surpassing $30 million by the end of 1986. By the following year, the company was ready to go public, making its initial public offering in August when it presented 1.3 million common shares at $12.50 a share. At the time, Harding Associates employed 450 people, most of whom were scientists and engineers. The company had expanded geographically and, during 1987, was operating 12 offices in seven states, the majority of which were located in the western half of the United States. In total, the company completed more than 2,000 projects during the year, collecting nearly $40 million from roughly 1,000 industrial and governmental clients, the majority of whom—70 percent—were involved in the private sector of the nation's economy. Perhaps more encouraging than the energetic leap in total sales for the year (an increase of nearly $10 million from 1986's total), was the prolific surge in earnings recorded by the company. In 1986, year-end profits amounted to $270,000, while 1987's total eclipsed the $1 million plateau, reaching $1.03 million.

Following the stock offering, Richard Harding, by now in his mid-60s, began to relinquish some of his control over the company so he could concentrate more fully on the strategic planning, development, and expansion of Harding Associates. In 1988, Harding vacated two of his posts, making room for Richard P. Prezio, who in addition to his role as the company's chief financial officer was named chief executive officer and president. With Harding at the top and Prezio holding the titles of chief executive officer, president, and chief financial officer, Harding Associates continued to grow throughout the remainder of the 1980s, entering the new decade as one of the strongest of roughly 15 publicly traded companies in the industry nationwide.

## Prominence in the 1990s

The company's pace of growth accelerated in the wake of its public offering, gaining momentum as Harding Associates moved past its 30th anniversary and entered the 1990s. The company's growth, which was occurring at a 30 percent annual rate, led some observers to question whether sufficient numbers of qualified personnel could be brought on board to sustain growth of such magnitude. The services provided by the company—consulting engineering, environmental, and construction services related to hazardous and solid waste management—constituted a narrow academic field, one that would have to be skillfully tapped to attract sufficient numbers of scientists and engineers to continue expanding as fast as Harding Associates was growing in the 1990s. Further, this potential impediment to growth would pose a greater threat as Harding Associates embraced a more aggressive expansion strategy in the new decade. From 1990 forward, the company's management intensified their expansion efforts, intent on using the company's business base in California as a springboard for expansion across the country.

By the end of 1991, Harding Associates annual sales volume had more than doubled in the four years since it had become a publicly traded company, rising to $98 million. Greater gains were recorded in annual net income, which had quadrupled since the 1987 public offering, soaring to $4.5 million. As sales began to stagnate in the early 1990s, the company moved forward with plans to become a more nationally oriented engineering consulting firm. In February 1993, Harding Associates acquired Pennsylvania-based EEC Environmental, Inc., a provider of environmental engineering and consulting services to private industry clients in the northeastern United States, then seven months later, in September, purchased Florida-based Cross/Tessitore & Associates, which was involved in providing services for air quality management and air pollution control. The following year, in May 1994, Harding Associates completed a pivotal acquisition when it purchased Alpha Engineering Group, Inc., a 150-person firm based in Washington with offices in Arizona, California, Colorado, and Nevada.

The acquisition of Alpha Engineering, which specialized in civil transportation and municipal engineering, represented a move toward diversification by Harding Associates, one important step in the company's plan to respond to changes within its industry. Uncertainty concerning the direction environmental statutes would take in the future had stifled Harding Associates environmental services market, hobbling sales growth as a result. In 1992, the company generated $112 million in sales, $115 million the following year, and $115 million in 1993. Diversification and a re-emphasis on traditional engineering services, Harding Associates' management hoped, would invigorate sales, enabling the company to resume the animated growth it had recorded during the late 1980s. The acquisition of Alpha Engineering, with its expertise in designing streets, highways, bridges, water and sewage systems, and storm water drainage and treatment systems, represented one such diversifying move, part of what would prove to be a busy 1994 for Harding Associates.

One month after the acquisition of Alpha Engineering, in June 1994, Richard Prezio resigned as chief executive officer and chairman (Richard Harding had since been named chairman emeritus). In Prezio's place, Richard D. Puntillo, a Harding Associates board member since 1989 and a finance professor at the University of San Francisco School of Business, was selected to lead the company, concurrent with the announcement that Harding Associates, through its Harding Lawson Associates subsidiary, would open an office in Pittsburgh. Although the company had already been conducting work in Pittsburgh through its offices in Chicago and Philadelphia, the establishment of a permanent office in Pittsburgh reflected Harding Associates plan to provide a full-range of services in the Ohio Valley, including air quality, emissions testing, engineering and hazardous waste services.

Following the change in leadership and the decision to open an office in Pittsburgh, Harding Associates next moved on the international front, acquiring a 76 percent interest in Envirosciences Pty. Ltd., an environmental consulting firm with five offices located in the major metropolitan areas of New South Wales and Queensland, Australia. Harding Associates' international presence was strengthened further when marketing activities were intensified in Taiwan, the Philippines, and in Indonesia during the year and by the establishment of a Mexican engineering company, Grupo de Ingenieria Ecologica (GRIECO), in which the company owned a majority interest.

Entering 1995, Harding Associates was coming off a year of significant changes, particularly its foray into international markets. On the heels of these sweeping changes, the company changed its name in 1995 from Harding Associates, Inc. to Harding Lawson Associates Group, Inc. to benefit from the name recognition earned by its similarly named subsidiary. Once the name change was effected, Harding Lawson Group represented the new corporate title for the parent company of three primary subsidiaries: Harding Lawson Associates, Inc.; Harding International, Inc.; and Harding Lawson Associates Infrastructure, Inc. (HLA-Infrastructure).

Through Harding Lawson Associates, Inc., the long-time subsidiary of the company, Harding Lawson Group provided its environmental and waste management services, which included selecting sites for waste disposal facilities, designing facilities, obtaining permits for them, and providing air quality management services, site audits and assessments, and regulatory compliance and environmental permitting and monitoring. HLA-Infrastructure, formerly known as Alpha Engineering, constituted the civil transportation and municipal engineering arm of

Harding Lawson Group's interests, operating as a consulting engineering firm involved in designing streets, highways, bridges, interchanges, high-occupancy-vehicle lanes, as well as several other services, including Harding Lawson Group's original mainstay business, geotechnical engineering. Complementing these two U.S.-based companies was Harding International, Inc., comprising HLA-Envirosciences in Australia and GRIECO in Mexico, which provided environmental, waste management, and water resources engineering services to international clients.

With these subsidiary firms supporting the company's position, Harding Lawson Group entered the mid-1990s pursuing a strategy of geographic growth and diversification. As the company prepared to fulfill this goal, encouragement came from the 13 percent increase in sales posted in 1995, following three successive years of lackluster performance. Although uncertainty continued to cloud the environmental regulatory picture in the mid-1990s, Harding Lawson Group was braced for changes affecting its industry, intent on putting the engineering consulting expertise its had developed during 37 years of business to work in the future.

### Principal Subsidiaries

Harding Lawson Associates, Inc.; Harding Lawson Associates Infrastructure, Inc.; Harding International, Inc.

### Further Reading

Brammer, Rhonda, ''Shopping List,'' *Barron's,* January 16, 1995, p. 17.

Brown, Katie, ''Toxic Waste Engineers Plan Public Offering,'' *San Francisco Business Times,* July 27, 1987, p. 5.

Carlsen, Clifford, ''Novato's Harding Associates Puts New Man in Charge: Announcement Comes as Company Takes Restructuring Charge,'' *San Francisco Business Times,* June 24, 1994, p. 7.

——, ''Harding's Stock Soars, Despite Insider Selling,'' *San Francisco Business Times,* April 16, 1990, p. 3,

''Harding Associates Inc. Has Acquired the Assets of Alpha Engineering Group, Inc.,'' *Pulp & Paper,* August 1994, p. 92.

''Harding's Prezio Is Named President, Chief Executive,'' *Wall Street Journal,* March 10, 1988, p. 32.

Welch, David, ''Harding Lawson Associates Seeking Niche in Local Environmental Market,'' *Pittsburgh Business Times,* June 27, 1994, p. 3.

—Jeffrey L. Covell

# Harrah's Entertainment, Inc.

1023 Cherry Road
Memphis, Tennessee 38117-5423
U.S.A.
(901) 762-8600
Fax: (901) 762-8637

*Public Company*
*Incorporated:* 1971 as Harrah's
*Sales:* $1.55 billion (1995)
*Employees:* 24,825
*Stock Exchanges:* New York Chicago Philadelphia
  Pacific
*SICs:* 7011 Hotels and Motels; 7999 Amusement &
  Recreation Services, Not Elsewhere Classified

William Harrah parlayed a Reno bingo parlor into a company, Harrah's Entertainment, Inc., consisting of Nevada casinos, hotels, and nightclubs that brought in nearly $200 million a year before his death in 1978. Harrah's later opened a casino-hotel in Atlantic City and expanded rapidly in the 1990s, as casino gambling spread to half the nation's 50 states. In 1994 Harrah's Entertainment, Inc. had the largest share—nearly eight percent—in the nation's $14-billion-a-year casino-gambling industry, and in 1995 it was operating more casinos in more markets, 15 casinos in eight states, than any other casino company in North America. The casinos were located not only in traditional land-based venues but also on riverboats and Indian reservations. In 1996 the company opened its first overseas casino operation, a joint venture in Auckland, New Zealand. Harrah's was proceeding with expansion plans and projects in nine markets and was aiming at a goal of 30 casinos worldwide by 2000.

### The Early Years

William Fisk Harrah was the son of a Venice, California lawyer and real estate operator who also had served as mayor of this seaside community. The senior Harrah went bankrupt during the Depression and was left with only one asset: a leased building on the honky-tonk Venice pier jutting into the Pacific Ocean. Here he operated a nickel-and-dime game of dubious legality, loosely based on bingo, in which players sat in a circle and rolled marbles toward a number. After Bill Harrah was caught cheating on a college chemistry exam in 1930 he went to work running the game and soon concluded he could do better than his father, who sold it to him for $500. He got rid of the shills his father had hired, refurbished the premises, and grossed as much as $50,000 a year.

In the wake of a state crackdown on gambling, Harrah moved in 1937 to Reno in Nevada, which had legalized gambling six years earlier. There he bought a bingo parlor that was located too far from the action and failed in three months. In 1939, however, he reopened in the two-block gambling heart of Reno. Three years later he opened a casino, equipping it with a blackjack and a craps table and 20 slot machines.

The enterprise flourished during the free-spending World War II years, and in 1946 Harrah's Club opened in quarters that had been expanded by the purchase of neighboring properties. Harrah added roulette to the card and dice tables and served liquor to the players. His spotlessly clean, glass-fronted, plush-carpeted casino was a contrast to the rough frontier-type betting parlors of the time and was the first to be lined with one-way mirrors so as to oversee the dealers and cashiers handling the chips and cash. By 1948 the gross annual revenue of Harrah's Club was more than $1.5 million and its net profit, after taxes, was about $100,000. This was just the start, for when Harrah swore off alcohol in 1952 (after almost losing his life driving while drunk), he turned his attention from hell-raising to a more highly focused passion for profit.

### The Reno and Lake Tahoe Casino-Hotels, 1955–1970

In 1955 Harrah bought a dingy casino—housed in a quonset hut—on the southern shore of Lake Tahoe, just east of the California state line, for $500,000. He built a false front around it and reopened it as Harrah's Tahoe. Four years later he relocated the casino across the highway, in the world's largest single structure devoted to gambling. The new casino was a highly integrated operation that included a ten-acre parking lot and an 850-seat theater-restaurant stocked with star entertainers. Blizzards habitually buried the area each winter, but Harrah assembled a fleet of snowplows to clear the mountain

## Company Perspectives:

*Harrah's Entertainment's vision is to offer exciting environments and to be legendary at creating smiles, laughter and lasting memories with every guest we entertain. The company's mission is to build lasting relationships and create A Great Time, Every Time . . . Guaranteed, by delivering comfort, action, shot to win and hospitality (C.A.S.H.)-to-the-MAX through enthusiastic, highly trained, friendly, attentive and empowered employees who have pledged to provide unsurpassed entertainment and service to every guest.*

roads, which were doubled in width at his own expense. Not averse to the low-budget trade, he established a vast bus network to bring in customers from 31 California cities and even opened a child-care center for gambling parents to park their offspring. The Lake Tahoe casino was said to have turned a profit of more than $1 million in its first year.

The annual gross from Harrah's two casinos was estimated at $40 million in 1961, and four years later William Harrah was described as the world's biggest gambling operator. With 2,500 employees, he was the largest employer in Nevada except for the Atomic Energy Commission. A lover of fast cars, he established Rolls Royce, Ferrari, and Jeep dealerships and assembled the world's largest automobile collection, which the Internal Revenue Service allowed him to write off as a business expense.

With both his casinos booming and no inclination to take on the competition in Las Vegas, Harrah next turned to the hotel business. He constructed the highest building in Reno, a 24-story hotel across the street from his casino. Completed in 1968, it cost about $7 million. Next he erected a luxurious 18-story hotel, which opened in 1973, on his Lake Tahoe property. Every room came with a view of the lake and two marble-finished bathrooms.

### Public Company in the 1970s

In part to finance these ventures and support his lifestyle (he was married six times), Harrah took his company public in 1971, raising $4 million after taxes and expenses by offering 13 percent of the stock at $16 per share. No Wall Street firm would handle the offering, but it was oversubscribed, and within a year the stock had soared to $71 per share. Overcoming the financial sector's misgivings about the gambling industry, Harrah's became, in 1973, the first casino company listed on the New York Stock Exchange.

Harrah's net sales increased from $77.9 million in 1970 to $195.6 million in 1979, and net income grew from a low of $4.3 million in 1971 to a record $16.9 million in 1978. One securities analyst called Harrah's the most tightly controlled and best managed casino company in the world. Its two casinos, operating around the clock every day of the year, accounted for about 10 percent of Nevada's gambling volume. Games of chance now included baccarat, poker, and keno, as well as the roulette, blackjack, craps, and bingo tables and 3,733 slot machines. The 1,600 seats at the theater-restaurants in Reno and Lake Tahoe

were almost always filled every night. The two hotels enjoyed a 92 percent occupancy rate. Nearly 250,000 customers came every year by bus, leading Harrah's president to acknowledge, "We are the Safeway of the industry."

By the late 1970s, however, Harrah's was beginning to encounter difficulties from the opening of competing hotel-casinos in Reno and environmental constraints on further development in the Lake Tahoe area. The company scrapped plans to open a new Reno hotel-casino just across the street from the existing one and a combination hotel-casino and theme park just outside the city. When Harrah died in 1978, he left his heirs almost six million shares of stock in his company, but no cash to pay estate taxes of $35 million or a $13 million debt to a Reno bank.

### Holiday Inns Subsidiary in the 1980s

At this point a buyer for Harrah's emerged in the unlikely form of family-oriented Holiday Inns, Inc., a Memphis-based company previously run by pious Baptists opposed to gambling. Even before Harrah's death, however, Holiday Inns executive Michael Rose was seeking his participation in a joint venture in Atlantic City, New Jersey, where gambling had been legalized in 1977. The company bought, in 1979, a stake in a casino adjacent to the Holiday Inn on the Las Vegas Strip. It was renamed Holiday Casino and, later, Harrah's Las Vegas. Holiday Inns also announced plans to build two casino-hotels in Atlantic City. In February 1980 the company acquired Harrah's, which was still about 70 percent owned by William Harrah's estate, for $310 million in cash and notes. Rose, who became chief executive officer of Holiday Inns the next year, sold most of Harrah's 1,400 automobiles for $100 million and gave the rest to a Reno museum.

Now a wholly owned subsidiary of Holiday Inns, Harrah's became the operator of a casino opened in 1980 on marshland a mile and a half north of Atlantic City's boardwalk and named Harrah's Marina Hotel Casino. It had 506 guest rooms, a casino with capacity for 6,300 patrons, and an array of other spaces, including restaurants and bars, a Broadway-sized theater, conference and meeting rooms, a high-rise garage for 2,100 cars, and a "fun" center for children and teenagers. A 264-suite tower was added later. Harrah's Marina (later renamed Harrah's Atlantic City) proved to be the most consistently profitable casino in Atlantic City. In 1985, for example, the facility earned $48.8 million before taxes, by far the best performance of any of the 11 Atlantic City casinos.

In 1984, Harrah's opened, in partnership with real estate developer Donald J. Trump, the tallest building on the Atlantic City boardwalk, the 39-story Harrah's Trump Plaza hotel and casino. The joint venture, built by the Trump Organization on Trump land but with Harrah's money, collapsed in acrimony when the competing Trump's Castle made its debut the following year right across the street from Harrah's Marina. In 1986 Trump bought Harrah's half-share in Trump Plaza (Harrah's name had been removed) for $59.1 million.

Bill's Lake Tahoe Casino was opened by Harrah's in 1987 on a 2.1-acre site adjacent to Harrah's Lake Tahoe. The following year Harrah's Laughlin was opened in Laughlin, Nevada, on a natural cove on the Colorado River, with 464 hotel rooms and 26,500 square feet of casino space. Late in 1988 a second Laughlin hotel tower was completed.

## Headlong Expansion in the 1990s

In 1989 Holiday Corp., formerly Holiday Inns, became The Promus Cos., Inc. The following year Rose sold the Holiday Inns hotel chain to Bass PLC of Great Britain for $2.23 billion. Holiday shares were then converted, on a one-for-one basis, to Promus shares, with Holiday's Embassy Suites, Hampton Inn, and Homewood Suites hotel divisions remaining as Promus units. Harrah's continued to thrive as the company's casino-entertainment division and in 1991 relocated its headquarters from Reno to Memphis.

Casino gambling had been legal only in Nevada and New Jersey until 1989, but between 1989 and 1996 it was legalized in some form in 21 additional states. In 1993 Harrah's established a new division for riverboat casinos and opened the first of these facilities along the Illinois River in Joliet, Illinois. A second Joliet floating casino opened the following year. Also during 1993–1995 Harrah's established riverboat casinos along the Mississippi River in Vicksburg and Tunica, Mississippi, the Red River at Shreveport, Louisiana, and along the Missouri River in North Kansas City, Missouri. A second Tunica riverboat opened in 1996.

Harrah's also continued to create land-based casinos in the 1990s. Eagle Gaming, L.P., one-sixth owned by Harrah's, opened casinos in the Colorado historic mining towns of Central City and Black Hawk in 1993. They were managed by Harrah's for a fee. In addition, in 1992 Harrah's announced the creation of a new division for casinos on Indian lands. Congress had, in 1988, passed a law legalizing games of chance on Indian reservations in any state where such games were allowed for churches, temples, and veterans' and other groups. By August 1993 no less than 73 tribes in 19 states were offering or would soon be offering full-scale casino gambling. Harrah's Ak-Chin, near Phoenix, opened in December 1994. A year later the Upper Skagit Indians and Harrah's opened a casino entertainment complex about 70 miles north of Seattle.

On February 1, 1996, Harrah's celebrated the grand opening of its first international casino entertainment complex, Sky City Casino in Auckland, New Zealand. This property consisted of 45,000 square feet of casino space and was also to include a hotel, theater, and 1,076-foot-high tower. The company, which held a 20 percent share in the joint venture, was to manage it for a fee.

An embarrassment for Harrah's was the failure of Harrah's Casino New Orleans, which was owned by Harrah's Jazz Co., a partnership in which a subsidiary of Harrah's Entertainment held a 47 percent interest. On the edge of the French Quarter, this temporary casino (a permanent one was under construction) opened in 1995 but closed in nine weeks, grossing less than half of its projected $33 million a month and causing the partnership to file for bankruptcy. Harrah's Entertainment wrote off $93.5 million of losses in the failed venture but was not responsible for Harrah's Jazz Co.'s $435 million junk bond debt.

In late 1995 Harrah's and Players International, Inc. broke ground on a joint riverboat casino entertainment complex in Maryland Heights, Missouri, a suburb of St. Louis. Each company was to operate two boats, connected by a shoreside entertainment mall anchored by a 291-room hotel managed by Harrah's. During 1995 Harrah's also announced plans for major expansions of its Las Vegas and Atlantic City casino properties,

including the addition of a hotel tower and additional casino space. Construction of a $78 million expansion of Harrah's North Kansas City also began that year.

In 1995, the Promus Cos. divided into two separate corporations, with the casino division becoming Harrah's Entertainment, Inc. and the hotel division Promus Hotels Corp. Rose remained chairman of both companies. By the end of February 1996, Harrah's offered 16 casinos with 592,500 square feet of space, 16,377 slot machines, 898 table games, 63 restaurants, and 21,905 parking spaces. There were 5,736 hotel rooms at the end of 1995. Gaming volume came to $20.6 billion that year, compared to $8.5 billion in 1991. Harrah's long-term debt was $753.7 million in 1995.

The riverboat division was Harrah's most lucrative in 1995, accounting for 43 percent of its $354 million operating profit, followed by Atlantic City (22 percent), Southern Nevada (18 percent), and Northern Nevada (16 percent). Of Harrah's $1.55 billion in revenues that year, the riverboat operations accounted for 38 percent, followed by Atlantic City (22 percent), Northern Nevada (20 percent), and Southern Nevada (19 percent). Net income was $78.8 million.

A key marketing tool was the Harrah's Gold Card, accepted at each Harrah's property. Its database included, in 1994, 3.2 million cardholders and 3.1 million potential cardholders who had stayed at a Harrah's property or played in one of the casinos. In addition to enabling the company to follow trends in play and the popularity of certain games, the gold card was used to gather information on guests for marketing purposes and to reward them, based on volume of play.

## Principal Subsidiaries

Aster Insurance Ltd. (Bermuda); Harrah's Operating Co., Inc.

## Further Reading

Berger, Meyer, ''The Gay Gamblers of Reno, *Saturday Evening Post*, July 10, 1948, pp. 22–23, 74, 76, 78.

Bukro, Gary, ''The Christmas Tree Is in the Mail, Really,'' *Chicago Tribune*, November 23, 1995, Sec. 2, pp. 1, 4.

Getmanikow, George, ''Holiday Inns Discards Family Image for Stake in Gambling Industry,'' *Wall Street Journal*, January 11, 1980, pp. 1, 31.

Hughlett, Mike, ''Analysts See Rosy Future for Harrah's Parent,'' *New Orleans Times-Picayune*, December 17, 1995, p. F3.

Johnston, David, *Temples of Chance*, New York: Doubleday, 1992, pp. 39+.

Land, Barbara, and Land, Myrick, *A Short History of Reno*, Reno and Las Vegas: University of Nevada Press, 1995, pp. 92–96.

''The Last Harrah,'' *Forbes*, October 16, 1978, p. 66.

''The Legacy of William Harrah,'' *Harrah's People*, Spring 1995, pp. 4–11.

McDowell, Edwin, ''Promus Proposes To Divide Its Units into Two Companies,'' *New York Times*, January 31, 1995, pp. D1, D7.

Mandel, Leon, *William Fisk Harrah*, New York: Doubleday, 1982.

Monroe, Keith, ''The New Gambling King and the Social Scientists, *Harper's Magazine*, January 1962, pp. 35–41.

''Taking the Risk Out of Gambling,'' *Time*, November 21, 1977, p. 78.

''The Two Faces of Bill,'' *Forbes*, July 1, 1972, pp. 39, 41.

Wernick, Robert, ''The World's Biggest Gambler,'' *Saturday Evening Post*, February 13, 1965, pp. 27–32.

—Robert Halasz

# Hasbro, Inc.

1027 Newport Avenue
Pawtucket, Rhode Island 02862-1059
U.S.A.
(401) 431-8697
Fax: (401) 431-8535

*Public Company*
*Incorporated:* 1926 as Hassenfeld Brothers Incorporated
*Employees:* 13,000
*Sales:* $2.86 billion (1995)
*Stock Exchanges:* American London
*SICs:* 3942 Dolls & Stuffed Toys; 3944 Games, Toys &
    Children's Vehicles, Except Dolls & Bicycles; 5092
    Toys & Hobby Goods & Supplies; 7812 Motion
    Picture & Video Tape Production

Truly successful toy companies do not just make toys; they manufacture popular culture. Hasbro, Inc., which is the second-largest toymaker in the world, behind only Mattel Inc., certainly fits that description. From America's Action Hero to a plastic anthropomorphized potato to vehicles that transform into robots to the largest bird in the world, Hasbro toys are instantly recognized by millions of Americans. Hasbro makes G.I. Joe, Mr. Potato Head, and Transformers, and owns licenses for *Sesame Street* characters. Thanks to numerous acquisitions in the 1980s and 1990s, it also makes Playskool and Romper Room preschool toys, Tonka trucks, Kenner's Nerf toys, and Cabbage Patch Kids (by way of Coleco); and has become dominant in the area of board games and puzzles through its ownership of Milton Bradley (maker of Scrabble and Parcheesi) and Parker Brothers (maker of Monopoly).

### Early History

Hasbro traces its origin to an enterprise founded in Providence, Rhode Island, in 1923 by Henry, Hilal, and Herman Hassenfeld, brothers who had emigrated to the United States from Poland. The Hassenfeld brothers engaged in the textile remnant business, selling cloth leftovers. By the mid-1920s they were using them to make hat liners and pencil-box covers. Soon, with eight employees—all family members—they began making the boxes themselves, after realizing their popularity. In 1926 the company incorporated under the name Hassenfeld Brothers Incorporated.

Hilal Hassenfeld became involved in other textile ventures, and Henry took control of the new company. Although a paternalistic employer, Henry Hassenfeld was also a tough and shrewd businessman. During the Great Depression—with 150 employees in 1929 and 200 employees in 1930—Hassenfeld Brothers commanded annual sales of $500,000 from sales of pencil boxes and cloth zipper pouches filled with school supplies. At that point, however, the company's pencil supplier decided to raise its prices and sell its own boxes at prices lower than Hassenfeld's. Henry Hassenfeld responded with a vow to enter the pencil business himself, and in 1935 Hassenfeld Brothers began manufacturing pencils. This product line would provide the company with a steady source of revenue for the next 45 years.

### Start of Toy Manufacturing in 1930s

During the late 1930s the Hassenfeld Brothers began to manufacture toys, an extension of the company's line of school supplies. Initial offerings included medical sets for junior nurses and doctors and modeling clay. During World War II Henry's younger son, Merrill Hassenfeld, acted on a customer's suggestion to make and market a junior air-raid warden kit, which came complete with flashlights and toy gas masks.

By 1942, as demand for school supplies tapered off, the company had become primarily a toy company, although it continued its large, profitable pencil business. Hilal Hassenfeld died in 1943, at which point Henry Hassenfeld became CEO and his son, Merrill Hassenfeld, became president. Also during World War II, the company ventured into plastics, to support its toy-making, and was forced, due to labor shortages, to reduce employment to 75.

After the war Merrill Hassenfeld began marketing a girls makeup kit after seeing his four-year-old daughter play with candy as though it were lipstick and rouge. In 1952, the company introduced its still-classic Mr. Potato Head, the first toy to be advertised on television. In 1954 Hassenfeld became a major licensee for Disney characters. By 1960, revenues hit $12 million, and Hassenfeld Brothers had become one of the largest private toy companies in the nation.

### Turbulent Times in the 1960s and 1970s

Henry Hassenfeld died in 1960. Merrill Hassenfeld then assumed full control of the parent company, while his older brother Harold Hassenfeld, continued to run the pencil-making operations. Merrill Hassenfeld's succession was logical given his interest and expertise in the toy business, but it also marked the beginning of an intramural rivalry between the two sides of the company; Harold Hassenfeld would come to resent the fact that the pencil business received a lower percentage of capital investment even though it was a steadier performer and accounted for a higher percentage of profits than toys.

In 1961 Hassenfeld Brothers (Canada) Ltd., now Hasbro Canada Inc., was founded. Hassenfeld Brothers seemed to defy the vagaries of the toy business in the early 1960s, when it introduced what would become one of its most famous and successful product lines. According to author Marvin Kaye in *A Toy is Born*, the company conceived G.I. Joe in 1963 when a licensing agent suggested a merchandise tie-in with a television program about the U.S. Marine Corps called "The Lieutenant." The company liked the idea of a military doll, but did not want to pin its fate on a TV show that might prove short-lived; so it went ahead and created its own concept, and in 1964 Hassenfeld unleashed G.I. Joe, a foot-high "action figure" with articulated joints. In its first two years, G.I. Joe brought in between $35 and $40 million and accounted for nearly two-thirds of the company's total sales.

The company changed its name to Hasbro Industries in 1968—it had sold its toys under the Hasbro trade name for some time—and went public. Only a small portion of Hasbro stock went on the open market, however; the majority stake remained in the hands of the Hassenfeld family. At the same time, Hasbro decided that it could no longer ignore the public's growing disapproval of war toys, which was fueled by disillusionment with the Vietnam War. In 1969 G.I. Joe, still the company's leading moneymaker, was repackaged in a less militaristic "adventure" motif, with a different range of accessories. Also in 1969, the company acquired Burt Claster Enterprises, the Baltimore, Maryland-based television production company responsible for the popular "Romper Room" show for preschoolers. Burt Claster Enterprises had also begun to manufacture a line of "Romper Room" toys. Nevertheless, a month-long Teamsters strike and troubles with Far Eastern suppliers hurt Hasbro in 1969, and the company posted a $1 million loss for the year.

The 1960s ended on a turbulent note for Hasbro, providing a foretaste of the decade to come. In 1970 Hasbro decided that it had to diversify, and it opened a chain of nursery schools franchised under the "Romper Room" name. The company hoped to take advantage of President Richard M. Nixon's Family Assistance Plan, which subsidized day care for working mothers. Running the preschools was a very big mistake. Merrill Hassenfeld's son, Alan Hassenfeld, told *The Wall Street Journal*, December 13, 1984: "We'd get phone calls saying, 'We can't find one of the kids.' The whole company would stop." Within five years Hasbro had left the day-care business. Another ill-fated diversification move was Hasbro's line of Galloping Gourmet cookware, which sought to capitalize on a contemporary television cooking show of the same name. That venture literally fell apart when termites ate salad bowls stacked in a warehouse.

In addition, two products from Hasbro's 1970 line turned into public relations disasters: Javelin Darts were declared unsafe by the government, and Hypo-Squirt, a water gun shaped like a hypodermic needle, was dubbed by the press a "junior junkie" kit. Both products were promptly removed from the market. The continuing success of "Romper Room" and its related toy line proved to be a bright spot for Hasbro, although the company came under fire from the citizens group Action for Children's Television, which accused the program of becoming an advertising vehicle for toys.

In 1974 Merrill Hassenfeld became CEO of Hasbro, while his son, Stephen D. Hassenfeld, became president. Hasbro regained its profitability but floundered once again later in the decade. Poor cash flow accounted for some of the problem, but the company's underlying mistake was casting its net too far and too wide in an effort to compensate for G.I. Joe's declining popularity. Hasbro discontinued G.I. Joe in 1975 because of the rising price of plastic, which was caused by rising crude oil prices. By 1977—the year Hasbro acquired *Peanuts* cartoon characters licensing rights—the company suffered $2.5 million in losses and carried a heavy debt. The financial situation became serious enough that Hasbro's bankers forced it to suspend dividend payments in early 1979. The toy division's poor performance fueled Harold Hassenfeld's resentment that the Empire Pencil subsidiary continued to receive a smaller proportion of capital spending to profits than did the toy division. The dam threatened to burst in 1979, when Merrill Hassenfeld died at age 61. Stephen Hassenfeld was chairman Merrill Hassenfeld's heir apparent, but Harold Hassenfeld refused to recognize Stephen Hassenfeld's authority.

The feud was resolved in 1980, when Hasbro spun off Empire Pencil, which had become the nation's largest pencil maker, and Harold exchanged his Hasbro shares for shares of the new company. At the same time, Stephen Hassenfeld became the toy company's CEO and chairman of the board, and dedicated himself to turning Hasbro around. Where it had once been overextended, the company slashed its product line by one-third between 1978 and 1981, while its annual number of new products was cut by one-half. Hasbro also refocused on simpler toys, such as Mr. Potato Head—products that were inexpensive to make, could be sold at lower prices, and had longer life cycles. This conservative philosophy precluded Hasbro from entering the hot new field of electronic games, as did the fact that it could not spare the cash to develop such toys. The decision to stay out of the market was vindicated in the early 1980s, when the electronics boom turned bust and shook out many competitors.

Perhaps the most important event in Hasbro's revival was the 1982 return of G.I. Joe. The U.S. political climate at the time made military toys popular again, and G.I. Joe was reintroduced as an antiterrorist commando, complete with a cast of comrades and exotic villains, whose personalities were sculpted with the help of Marvel Comics. Two years later, Hasbro introduced its highly successful Transformers line—toy vehicles and guns that could be reconfigured into toy robots. Transformers were tied into a children's animated TV series and proved so popular that *People* magazine asked Stephen Hassenfeld to pose with them for a cover photo.

### 1980s Acquisitions

In 1983 Hasbro acquired GLENCO Infant Items, a manufacturer of infant products and the world's largest bib producer. Hasbro also sold about 37 percent of its own stock to Warner Communications in exchange for cash and Warner's struggling Knickerbocker Toy Company subsidiary, which made Raggedy Ann and Raggedy Andy dolls. The new Warner holdings did not threaten the company's autonomy, however; the shares were put into a voting trust controlled by the Hassenfeld brothers and other Hasbro executives. In 1984 Stephen Hassenfeld turned over the position of president to his brother, Alan, while remaining CEO and chairman.

In the early 1980s Hasbro was the nation's sixth-best-selling toymaker, with revenues of $225.4 million and $15.2 million in profit. Flush with newfound strength, in 1984 it acquired Milton Bradley, the nation's fifth bestselling toymaker, and second only to General Mills's Parker Brothers subsidiary in production of boardgames and puzzles. Milton Bradley had been founded by a Springfield, Massachusetts, lithographer who set up shop in 1860 and immediately turned out a popular reproduction of a portrait of presidential candidate Abraham Lincoln. Bradley's portrait, however, showed Lincoln clean-shaven, so when Lincoln grew his beard, sales fell off. Looking for a way to stay in business, Bradley invented and produced a boardgame called The Checkered Game of Life, a distant precursor of a popular Milton Bradley game, The Game of Life, which was introduced in 1960. The game's success convinced Bradley to stay in the game business. During the Civil War he produced a lightweight packet of boardgames for the amusement of Union troops. The company had incorporated in 1882.

During the late 19th century, Milton Bradley (MB) relied mostly on such favorites as chess and checkers and traditional European games. During the 20th century, however, the company designed and marketed more original games, sometimes with great success. During the Depression, a Milton Bradley financial game called Easy Money became popular. In the 1950s, Milton Bradley pioneered games with tie-ins to television shows—Concentration was an early favorite. In 1968 MB acquired Chicago-based Playskool Manufacturing, which was noted for its preschool toys. Among Milton Bradley's later successes was the "body action" classic Twister, which was published in 1971 and became a popular prop with talk show

hosts for a while after Johnny Carson challenged Eva Gabor to a go-around on "The Tonight Show."

In 1984, however, Milton Bradley had found itself in an uncertain financial position after fending off a hostile takeover from British conglomerate Hanson Trust. In the wake of that failed bid, several unidentified parties bought up large blocks of MB stock, fueling speculation that another takeover attempt was imminent. Finally, in May 1984, MB agreed to be acquired by Hasbro for $360 million. MB's strength in boardgames and puzzles complemented Hasbro's plastic toys and stuffed animals. Milton Bradley's Playskool subsidiary provided a solid preschool line including classics such as Lincoln Logs and ABC blocks. The new Hasbro Bradley Incorporated immediately challenged Mattel's position as the nation's leading toymaker. In 1985 Hasbro Bradley became Hasbro, Inc.

If Hasbro's and Milton Bradley's product lines merged well, their chief executives did not. Stephen Hassenfeld became president and CEO of Hasbro Bradley, with Milton Bradley chief James Shea Jr. becoming chairman. After only a few months, however, Shea resigned. Stephen himself became chairman, with brother Alan Hassenfeld replacing him as president.

Hasbro surpassed Mattel to become the largest toy company in the world in the mid-1980s. Having done so, it then attempted to dethrone Mattel's Barbie, queen of the fashion doll market. In 1986 Hasbro introduced Jem, a fashion doll given the dual identity of business woman/record producer and purple-haired rock musician. While Jem posted strong initial sales, her popularity quickly faded and she was retired the following year. In 1988 the company brought out Maxie, a blonde doll scaled to match Barbie in size so that she could wear Barbie clothing and accessories. Maxie lasted twice as long as Jem and was discontinued in 1990.

In 1989 Hasbro acquired bankrupt rival Coleco Industries for $85 million, just four years after a *Toy and Hobby World* survey declared that Transformers had passed Coleco's Cabbage Patch Kids as the best-selling toy in the United States. In addition to the Cabbage Patch dolls, which had fallen from their peak of popularity during the 1985 Christmas season, Coleco also owned the rights to the classic board games Scrabble and Parcheesi. The Coleco acquisition proved to be Stephen Hassenfeld's final business triumph. In 1989, he died at age 47, having converted the relatively modest toy company that his grandfather had founded into a juggernaut at the top of its industry with 1989 sales of $1.41 billion, a huge increase over the $104 million figure of the year he took over.

### 1990s and Beyond

A new and more challenging era began when 41-year-old Alan Hassenfeld became chairman and CEO of Hasbro. The younger Hassenfeld continued the acquisition trend of the 1980s, as Hasbro acquired Tonka Corp. in 1991 for $486 million. With the deal, Hasbro added not only the Tonka line of toy trucks but also Tonka's Parker Brothers unit, the maker of Monopoly, and Kenner Products, which featured Batman figures and the Strawberry Shortcake doll. The Parker Brothers unit was merged into Hasbro's already strong Milton Bradley division. Hasbro took a $59 million charge in 1991 to cover costs of consolidating the Tonka acquisition and restructuring overall operations.

In the late 1980s, Alan Hassenfeld had spearheaded an effort to increase Hasbro's international sales, primarily by taking toys that failed in the U.S. market and remarketing them overseas at prices as high as four times their original prices. He had helped increase international sales from $268 million in 1985 to $433 million in 1988. So it was not surprising that as chairman he would push to increase Hasbro's international presence. He did just that in 1991, establishing operations in Greece, Hungary, and Mexico.

It was the Far East, however, which Hassenfeld saw as a critical market for Hasbro to develop. He gained two more distribution channels there in 1992 by purchasing Nomura Toys Ltd., based in Japan, and buying a majority stake in Palmyra, a Southeast Asian toy distributor. Thanks to these efforts, by 1995, Hasbro's international sales had reached $1.28 billion, which represented almost 45 percent of total sales, a significant increase over the 22 percent figure of 1985. More than 46 percent of the company's operating profit was attributable to operations outside the United States in 1995. One international setback came in 1993 when Hasbro lost out to arch-rival Mattel in a bid for J.W. Spear, a U.K.-based maker of games.

While international results were improving, Hasbro began to show some weaknesses on the domestic front. Much of the growth since 1980 had come from the company's various acquisitions, along with Hasbro's largely successful efforts to leverage the new assets it gained through the deals. Many new product development activities, on the other hand, were not as successful, with the exception of product lines developed to tie-in with the movie *Jurassic Park* and the popular children's television show *Barney*. As a result, domestic sales stagnated in the early 1990s, and actually fell from $1.67 billion in 1993 to $1.58 billion in 1995. And worldwide sales showed much slower growth as well. From 1991, the year of the Tonka acquisition, to 1995, sales increased only 33.5 percent, with half of the increase occurring in 1992 alone. To help improve the company's domestic performance, a reorganization was completed in 1994 that merged the Hasbro Toy, Playskool, Playskool Baby, Kenner, and Kid Dimension units into a new Hasbro Toy Group. Meanwhile, Mattel in 1993 acquired Fisher-Price and soon thereafter regained the number one spot in the toy industry.

Also contributing to Hasbro's challenges in the 1990s was its belated struggle to enter the market for electronic games. Eventually, in 1992, the company began development of a mass-market virtual reality game system. Although such a system was successfully developed, it was judged too expensive for the mass market and the project was abandoned in 1995, resulting in a charge of $31.1 million. In 1993, Hasbro bought a 15 percent stake in Virgin Interactive Entertainment, a producer of game software for Sega and Nintendo systems, with the intention of developing software based on Hasbro toys and games. Two years later, however, Hasbro dissolved the partnership and sold its stake.

A more promising venture began in 1995 with the establishment of Hasbro Interactive and the release of its first product that same year, a CD-ROM version of Monopoly. More than 180,000 units were sold in the first eight weeks following its release. Additional titles to be released in 1996 included Risk, Battleship, and Playskool-brand games.

In 1995, Mattel approached Hasbro about a possible merger of the two largest toy companies in the world. Negotiations took place in secret over the course of several months until the Hasbro board early in 1996 unanimously turned down a $5.2 billion merger proposal that would have given Hasbro stockholders a 73 percent premium over the then-current selling price. Hasbro officials expressed doubts that the merger could pass antitrust challenges and wanted a large upfront payment to help the company's performance during what would have likely been a lengthy antitrust review and to protect itself against the possibility that the merger would collapse. Mattel officials, on the other hand, maintained that the merger would have had little difficulty gaining approval, but backed away—and did not initiate a hostile takeover—when Hasbro waged a vigorous media campaign emphasizing the possible negative ramifications of such a mega-merger. Also clouding the deal was an ongoing Federal Trade Commission investigation into alleged exclusionary policies between toy manufacturers and toy retailers, involving most notably the Toys "R" Us chain.

Having maintained its independence, Hasbro adopted a multipronged strategy for reinvigorating its performance as the turn of the century approached. Its strategies included leveraging its well-known brands in new ways; stepping up efforts to market electronic versions of established games, particularly through the Hasbro Interactive initiative; continuing to grow internationally; and bolstering new product development primarily through media tie-ins. Already planned for 1997 were several promising film tie-in prospects, including the movies *Jurassic Park 2, Batman and Robin,* and *Barney,* as well as the theatrical rerelease of *Star Wars.*

### *Principal Subsidiaries*

Hasbro Foreign Sales Corp.; Hasbro International, Inc.; Milton Bradley Company; Playskool, Inc.; Romper Room Enterprises, Inc.; Tonka Corporation; Kenner Parker (Australia) Ltd.; Milton Bradley Australia Pty. Ltd.; Tonka Corp. Pty. Ltd. (Australia); Hasbro-MB S.A. (Belgium); Hasbro Canada Inc.; Kenner Parker Canada; Kenner Products (Canada) Limited (50%); Hasbro S.A. (France); Kenner Parker Toys (France; 70%); MB France S.A.; Kenner Parker Toys International (Germany); Milton Bradley GmbH (Germany); Hasbro Bradley Far East (1987) Ltd. (Hong Kong); Kenner Parker (H.K.) Ltd. (Hong Kong); Tonka Far East Limited (Hong Kong); MB Ireland; MB Italy S.r.l.; Tonka Italia S.p.A. (Italy); Nomura Toys Ltd. (Japan); Tonka Corp. (Mexico); Kenner Parker Toys (Netherlands); MB International B.V. (Netherlands); Kenner Parker (N.Z.) Ltd. (New Zealand); Milton Bradley (N.Z.) Ltd. (New Zealand); MB Espana, S.A. (Spain); MB (Switzerland) AG; Hasbro Bradley UK Limited; Hasbro Europe UK Limited; Kenner Parker Europe (U.K.); Tonka Europe, Limited (U.K.).

### *Principal Operating Units*

Hasbro Games Group; Hasbro Toy Group.

### *Further Reading*

"America's Toy Industry: Nightmare," *Economist,* December 16, 1995, pp. 58, 62.

Hammonds, Keith H., " 'Has-Beens' Have Been Very Good to Hasbro," *Business Week,* August 5, 1991, pp. 76–77.

"Hasbro, Inc.: Company History," Pawtucket, R.I.: Hasbro, corporate typescript, 1990.

Jereski, Laura, "It's Kid Brother's Turn to Keep Hasbro Hot," *Business Week,* June 26, 1989, pp. 152, 155.

Kaye, Marvin, *A Toy is Born,* New York: Stein and Day, 1973, 190 p.

Kimelman, John, "No Babe in Toyland," *Financial World,* January 4, 1994, pp. 34–36.

"Not Toying Around," *Forbes,* January 3, 1994, p. 131.

Pasztor, Andy, and Joseph Pereira, "Hasbro Remains Interested in a Merger with Mattel," *Wall Street Journal,* January 29, 1996, pp. A3, A6.

Pasztor, Andy, Joseph Pereira, and Steven Lipin, "Hasbro Faces New Struggles Post-Mattel," *Wall Street Journal,* February 5, 1996, pp. A3, A4.

Sansweet, Stephen J., "Toy Story: Mattel Offers $5 Billion in Unsolicited Bid for Rival Hasbro," *Wall Street Journal,* January 25, 1996, pp. A3, A10.

—Douglas Sun
—updated by David E. Salamie

# Hawkins Chemical, Inc.

3100 East Hennepin Avenue
Minneapolis, Minnesota 55413
U.S.A.
(800) 328-5460
Fax: (612) 331-5304

*Public Company*
*Incorporated:* 1938
*Employees:* 142
*Sales:* $83.3 million (1995)
*Stock Exchanges:* NASDAQ
*SICs:* 2819 Industrial Inorganic Chemicals, Not
    Elsewhere Classified; 2842 Polishes & Sanitation
    Goods; 5084 Industrial Machinery & Equipment

Hawkins Chemical, Inc. is a regional distributor of bulk chemicals, serving customers in the eight Upper Midwestern states of the United States. Although Hawkins's sales of $83.3 million in 1995 make it a niche player in the chemical distribution industry, the company has gained attention for its ability to generate an admirable profit margin of 5.3 percent, almost 4 percent higher than that of Univar, the nation's largest publicly traded chemical distribution company. Hawkins mixes, distributes, and markets more than 1,800 industrial and high-grade laboratory chemicals. The company's three subsidiaries and three divisions serve customers in the areas of steel manufacturing, pesticide and fungicide manufacturing, municipal water and waste treatment, and swimming pool maintenance. (Its subsidiary, the Lynde Company, is the largest distributor of swimming pool chemicals in the Upper Midwest.) Hawkins also operates two terminals along the Mississippi River, where it receives, stores, repackages, and blends various chemicals in bulk quantities. These chemicals are then distributed through the company's warehouses and subsidiary operations in Minnesota, Wisconsin, Iowa, Montana, Nebraska, Wyoming, and North and South Dakota.

## Early History

Hawkins Chemical was founded in 1938 as a partnership between two brothers, Kent and Howard J. Hawkins. According to company materials, facilities for their new chemical sales company consisted of "four desks, two chairs and 1,000 square feet of space." The brothers had a freewheeling attitude toward marketing, selling their chemicals, as they said, through a process of "carefully selected customers by looking for smokestacks." The process worked and business began to grow. In 1941, the brothers dissolved their partnership and Howard J. Hawkins became sole proprietor of the company. Soon after, Howard J. moved the business to a new facility with 1,500 square feet of operating space, 50 percent larger than the original.

In the mid-1940s, Fred Hoffman joined Hawkins Chemical as bookkeeper and office manager. Hawkins left the company he founded to serve in World War II, handing the reigns over to Hoffman. During that time, recalls Hawkins, "Fred Hoffman established many of the procedures we still use today. He ran the company while I was in the Armed Forces. I was thankful to him to have a job and a company to come back to." As the economy grew after the end of the war, so did Hawkins Chemical.

By 1948, the company had outgrown its space and moved to its present location on East Hennepin Avenue in Minneapolis. Around that time, Hawkins hired several new employees to work in sales and management. "We had a very direct method of selling in those days," recalls Norm Anderson, the company's first full-time sales representative. "We'd walk through the warehouse, list the products and then start calling people to sell what we had." Anderson and the other men hired at that time helped establish the company's reputation in Minnesota. They later became the nucleus of the company as it expanded its sales base from Minnesota to eight Upper Midwestern states.

## Vel-Tex Partnership in the 1950s

In 1952, Hawkins Chemical was restructured as a corporation. As the company expanded its sales territory, its continuous improvements of its sales and delivery network became the foundation of its growth. In 1955, Hawkins Chemical entered into an agreement to serve as sales agent for Vel-Tex Chemical, a manufacturer and marketer of industrial bleach. Hawkins was one of the region's largest suppliers of caustic soda, the basic component in bleach. Vel-Tex had perfected a method of improving the quality of bleach and "realized the need for a sales organization to support [its] manufacturing capabilities." The two developed a profitable relationship. Hawkins supplied the caustic soda, Vel-Tex manufactured the bleach, and Hawkins then sold and delivered the bleach using its already-established sales and distribution network.

In 1958, Hawkins and Vel-Tex firmly established their partnership when Vel-Tex developed a method of making bulk tank truck deliveries of liquid caustic soda and began delivering liquid caustic soda to Hawkins customers. By the end of the year, the two companies had entered into an agreement to jointly offer new bulk sales and delivery services to the Upper Midwest region. Hawkins installed its first storage tank for refrigeration grade anhydrous ammonia and, with Vel-Tex, designed a new system for packaging chlorine in 150-pound and one-ton cylinders.

Hawkins's sales growth necessitated the expansion of its warehouse facilities. In 1961, several additions were made to the company's storage facilities, including a separate storage area for flammable chemicals. Vel-Tex also moved some of its facilities to a barge terminal on the Mississippi River in St. Paul, Minnesota. In 1964 Hawkins acquired its first two long-distance semi-trailer delivery trucks. The two companies continued to work closely together, and in 1968 they jointly built the company's first 680,000-gallon storage tank for liquid caustic soda. During the period from 1958 to 1968, Hawkins's sales force grew steadily, and by the company's 30th anniversary, Hawkins's sales territory covered the states of Minnesota, Wisconsin, North Dakota, South Dakota, and Iowa.

### Growth Through Acquisition in the 1970s

In 1971 Hawkins acquired its long-time partner, Vel-Tex. The company became a wholly owned subsidiary of Hawkins and the name of its operations on the Mississippi River was changed to Hawkins Terminal No. I. Shortly after the acquisition, Hawkins added two 680,000-gallon storage tanks at the terminal and built a pumping system to transfer liquid caustic soda from river barges to Hawkins's storage tanks. Other improvements to the company's storage and delivery systems included new storage units for a variety of chemicals, new stainless steel tank trucks, and new loading bays and 500 feet of railroad tracks at its main plant.

In 1972 Hawkins Chemical made its initial public offering. That year, the company acquired two subsidiaries: the Lynde Company, a custom chemical formulator that specialized in swimming pool chemicals; and Feed-Rite Controls, Inc., a producer of water treatment chemicals and equipment that provided on-the-spot services for industrial and municipal water treatment systems. Hawkins merged sales functions for the two companies, but Lynde Company continued to blend its own chemicals. Sales in 1972 rose to a record high of $7.2 million, a 17 percent increase over 1971. The increase was attributed to improved sales to sewage treatment plants brought about by tighter water treatment standards mandated by the U.S. government and also to the company's expanded sales base in Wisconsin and Iowa, brought about by the acquisition of its two subsidiaries.

As the company expanded geographically, Hawkins continued to focus on its services, knowledge of chemicals, and delivery capabilities, believing them to be "only strengths upon which to build in [its] highly competitive business." In the early 1970s, the company established the Hawkins Chemical Sales Division to manage this process better. The company continued its slow but steady growth, keeping expenses down and increasing net income year by year. By 1977, Hawkins had 80,000 square feet of warehouse storage capacity and the capacity to store 2.5 million gallons of liquid chemicals. Sales that year reached $18.8 million, up 19 percent from 1976, and net income increased 12 percent to $585,455, boosted by strong sales in Hawkins's Lynde Company subsidiary.

In 1979, Hawkins expanded its sales into Montana and Wyoming through the purchase of Mon-Dak Chemical Inc., a regional supplier of industrial, dry cleaning, laundry, and janitorial chemicals based in Washburn, North Dakota. Two years later, Hawkins acquired Gordon Terminal, a chemical storage and transfer facility located on the Mississippi River in South St. Paul, Minnesota, and renamed it Hawkins Terminal No. II. The company continued expansion through acquisition of smaller operations. These included Dakota Chemical, Inc., a supplier of water treatment chemicals and equipment based in South Dakota, and Arrowhead Chemical, a former water treatment distributor for Hawkins with offices and warehouse facilities in Superior, Wisconsin.

From 1983 to 1987, Hawkins experienced a slow but steady annual growth of 5.7 percent. Despite its numerous acquisitions, Hawkins took a conservative management approach. Most of its growth was supported by internally generated funds as opposed to debt; in 1987, long-term debt was only 0.5 percent of long-term capitalization. Sales hit a record high of $30.9 million in 1985. The following year they slipped to $30.7 million due to an economic slump in the region, but earnings remained a respectable $1.3 million. Two years later, Hawkins celebrated its 50th anniversary with net income of $1.7 million on sales of $42 million.

Hawkins continued to focus on expanding its infrastructure, adding warehouse facilities at its Dakota Chemical operation with the goal of broadening sales in Nebraska, Wyoming, and South Dakota. In 1989, the company acquired Tessman Seed, Inc., a supplier of lawn and garden seeds, fertilizers, and chemicals to lawn and garden centers throughout Minnesota and

North and South Dakota. In 1990 revenues leapt 31 percent to $60.37 million, fueled primarily by an additional $13.1 million brought in through the acquisition of Tessman Seed. Net income that year was a record $3.16 million.

### Challenges in the 1980s and 1990s

During the late 1980s and early 1990s, a number of external factors affected Hawkins's operations, but not necessarily the company's bottom line. One major variable in Hawkins's sales was the weather. In the late 1980s, sales of caustic soda declined drastically during the summer months due to extremely low water levels on the Mississippi, which prevented barges from delivering the product to Hawkins's river terminals. The company resorted to shipping caustic soda from suppliers in Iowa, Illinois, and Wisconsin and experienced very little disruption of service.

At the same time, the company benefited from a trend among large chemical manufacturers to market their products through chemical distributors such as Hawkins. In 1990 Hawkins's internal operations underwent a slight transformation as the company adjusted to accommodate "a higher percentage of through-warehouse (as opposed to direct manufacturer-user) transactions." Management attributed the transformation to "a trend among customers to order smaller quantities more often in order to accommodate just-in-time inventory replenishment programs." Another factor that management attributed to this transformation was greater concern among its customers about the quantities of chemicals that were desirable on their premises. Hawkins welcomed the changes, stating that the situation helped create a stronger customer-supplier relationship and generate higher margin percentages, despite creating higher operating costs.

Hawkins experienced another record year in 1991, with revenues of $65.6 million and income of $3.5 million, up 11 percent from the previous year. Sales decreased the following year to $63.5 million, but net income increased 8 percent to $3.7 million. A major factor in the sales decline was the encroachment of national distributors on Tessman Seed's business. Hawkins responded by restructuring the subsidiary and reducing inventory and staff by 40 percent. Chemical treatment sales were also down by 60 percent that year, due to an unusually cool summer that adversely affected the company's water treatment business. The Lynde Company, Hawkins's swimming pool chemicals subsidiary, experienced its worst sales in 15 years.

In 1993 Hawkins acquired Industrial Chemical and Equipment, a 50-year-old company that supplied chemicals, equipment, and technical services to customers in the metal finishing and electronic industries. Severe weather affected Hawkins's operations again that year. Flooding on the Mississippi prevented the company's river-front terminals from receiving caustic soda via river barges for almost three months; the company successfully responded by transporting caustic soda via national highways from Illinois, Wisconsin, and Iowa. Continued cool weather during the summer months also affected Hawkins's swimming pool and water treatment operations. Revenues for 1993 reached $65.9 million, slightly above 1991 levels and earnings climbed to $4.4 million. Hawkins's improved profit margin was attributed to its acquisition of Industrial Chemical

and Equipment as well as to an increase in high-margin services offered to water and waste treatment plants.

### Focus on "Product Stewardship" in the 1990s

In the 1990s, as government regulation of the chemical distribution industry became more stringent, Hawkins developed a strategy of product stewardship that it believed would carry it successfully into the 21st century. "Only the strongest distributors can afford to make the investments in systems, facilities and training necessary to meet these [governmental] demands," management stated in the company's annual report. Its goal was to focus on "inheriting the markets of those who cannot or choose not to meet these challenges."

The company's model of stewardship was put to the test in early 1995 when a fire broke out at a Minneapolis office/warehouse facility used by the Lynde Company. The fire destroyed the facility, but, because of a newly constructed containment wall, the contaminated water "collected in the parking lot of the warehouse and did not flow into the streets or storm sewers that feed rivers and streams." Hawkins was able to replace lost inventory quickly and suffered only minor detrimental effects. Hawkins was not able to contain the vapors that escaped from the fire, however, and a number of residents in neighborhoods near the plant filed a lawsuit charging that the fire damaged their health and property. The company paid $335,000 in settlements and legal costs, but was still engaged in a lawsuit against its insurer who denied coverage, stating that its coverage did not extend to "bodily injury or other losses caused by a release or escape of pollutants."

Under the conservative direction of Howard J. Hawkins, Hawkins Chemical has established itself as a strong niche player in the chemical distribution industry. Although much of the company's growth has been through acquisition, Hawkins avoided the merger and acquisition craze of the 1980s by focusing on smaller, private companies that received little if any attention from Wall Street. In the 1990s, the company continued to focus on quietly improving its operations as a means to improve profits. In 1994, Hawkins completed construction of a facility for its Industrial Chemical & Equipment Division designed to improve efficiencies in transportation and communication. In addition, the company sold its Tessman Seed subsidiary "to better focus on its core businesses." Its 1995 earnings were a respectable $5.3 million on sales of $83.3 million.

Hawkins ventured into product development in the mid-1990s, which it hoped would provide a new venue for growth. In 1995, it received a patent for its Cheese-Phos liquid sodium system, which it believed could "substantially add to the profits of the corporation." Used primarily in the manufacturing of processed cheese, Cheese-Phos allows liquid sodium to be stored at room temperature, a drastic improvement over previous systems that required liquid sodium to be stored at temperatures between 130 and 160 degrees Fahrenheit.

With the approach of the 21st century would come the time that Howard J. Hawkins would probably relinquish control of the company he founded. As many of the company's board of directors and management have been with the company for decades, it may be safe to assume that the company will continue its conservative but steady growth.

### Principal Subsidiaries

Feed-Rite Controls Inc.; Mon-Dak Chemical, Inc.; The Lynde Company.

### Principal Divisions

Arrowhead Chemical Division; Dakota Chemical Division; Industrial Chemical and Equipment Division.

### Further Reading

Carideo, Tony, "Exchange Resource Is Looking Seriously at Public Market," *Minneapolis Star Tribune,* March 2, 1993, p. 2D.

DePass, Dee, "Disaster Plans Catch On, Pay Off for Some Firms Operating in State," *Minneapolis Star Tribune,* March 14, 1995, p. 1D.

Rystrom, Brent R., "Hawkins Chemical," *Corporate Report Minnesota,* September 1988, p. 174.

Weleczki, Ruth, "Hawkins Chemical Inc.," *Minneapolis-St. Paul City Business,* October 28, 1991, p. 26.

—Maura Troester

# Hyatt Corporation

**200 West Madison Avenue**
**Chicago, Illinois 60606**
**U.S.A.**
**(312) 750-1234**
**Fax: (312) 750-8550**

*Private Company*
*Incorporated:* 1957 as Hyatt Hotels Corporation
*Employees:* 47,000
*Sales:* $3 billion (1994 est.)
*SICs:* 6513 Operators of Apartment Buildings; 6519
    Lessors of Real Property, Not Elsewhere Classified;
    7011 Hotels & Motels

Hyatt Corporation is one of the leading hotel companies in North America. Owned by the Pritzker family of Chicago, Hyatt manages or licenses the management of 87 hotels and 16 resorts (with a total of 55,000 rooms) in 83 cities in the United States, Canada, and the Caribbean. In addition to its resorts, Hyatt has also developed other special hotel concepts—the Grand Hyatt, the Park Hyatt, and Classic Residence by Hyatt. Grand Hyatts are large-scale, higher priced hotels located in culturally rich cities, with three in the United States (New York, San Francisco, and Washington, D.C.). Park Hyatts are modeled after small European hotels and are located in Chicago, Los Angeles, San Francisco, and Washington, D.C. The Classic Residence by Hyatt properties offer luxury retirement apartments for rental. Starting in the mid-1990s, the company has also sought growth opportunities in franchising, time-share properties, free-standing golf courses, and casinos.

## The Founding Family

While Hyatt's history as a corporate entity dates from 1957, the Pritzker family, who built and control Hyatt, has been active significantly longer. In the late 19th century, the Pritzkers immigrated to the United States from the Ukraine. Patriarch Nicholas Pritzker led them to Chicago, and in 1902 he founded Pritzker & Pritzker (P&P), the law firm that was to evolve into a management company and the center of the Pritzkers' many and varied investments.

P&P grew, and by the late 1920s it had become a respected local firm. At that time, the Pritzkers' best client was Goldblatt Brothers, the low-priced Chicago department store chain. Through the Goldblatts, Abram (A. N.) Pritzker, Nicholas Pritzker's son, met Walter M. Heymann, then a leading Chicago commercial banker and an officer at the First National Bank of Chicago. In succeeding years A. N. Pritzker and Walter Heymann became business associates, and the powerful First National Bank of Chicago became the financial cornerstone of the Pritzker family empire.

Using a line of credit from the First National Bank, A. N. Pritzker began acquiring real estate, something he already knew about from P&P's concentration on real estate reorganization. As his and the family's investments grew, the law practice shrank, and in 1940 P&P stopped accepting outside clients, concentrating solely on Pritzker family investments. At the same time A. N. Pritzker began the family practice of sheltering his holdings within a dizzying array of interrelated family trusts.

## Hyatt Emerges in the 1950s

The story of Hyatt Corporation begins with the succeeding generation of Pritzkers. By the early 1950s, Pritzker's oldest son, Jay, had become active in the family business. Something of a prodigy, Jay Pritzker had graduated high school at 14. He finished college soon thereafter and then took a law degree from Northwestern University. During World War II he worked first as a flight instructor and later for the U.S. government agency that managed German-owned companies. In that position, he sat on corporate boards with men many years his senior. An accomplished deal-maker even in his earliest years, Jay would later become well known for his quickness at sizing up balance sheets and offering deals. Jay, beginning in 1957, made the initial deals that formed the basis for Hyatt.

Jay's youngest brother, Donald Pritzker, finished law school in 1959, whereupon he joined P&P. Meanwhile, the middle brother, Robert Pritzker, earned an industrial engineering degree at the Illinois Institute of Technology in Chicago and later he and Jay would found and manage the Marmon Group.

In 1957 Jay Pritzker bought a small Los Angeles International Airport motel named Hyatt House after its original owner, Hyatt von Dehn. Within four years, Jay expanded the single property into a chain of six hotels and brought Donald Pritzker to California as manager of operations, reporting to Jay. The two made a good team, with Jay's deal-making skills and Donald's managerial ability and gregarious personality.

Hyatt grew rapidly during its first decade, opening small motor inns on the West Coast and one outside Chicago. The fledgling company went public in 1967, but the more important event of that watershed year was the opening in Atlanta of its first hotel with an atrium tower lobby, designed by the architect John Portman. The Portman atrium was a 21-story interior courtyard, designed so that each hotel room entered off the high-rise open space, set off with a central glass elevator leading to all floors, and hanging green vines growing from each floor's balcony. The overall effect was revolutionary, because the Portman interior eliminated the impersonal hallway with rows of doors and brought to the hotel interior an open-air congeniality, with the spin-off of greater safety, feeling of security, and warmth. The Portman lobby became the hotel's signature and brought Hyatt to widespread notice for the first time, as well as advancing the concept of public space in buildings.

What became the Hyatt Regency Atlanta was part of the 15-building Peachtree Center. The developers of the large hotel property were in financial trouble and both Hilton and Marriott passed up opportunities to purchase the property before Hyatt did and finished construction. Soon after the hotel opened, its occupancy rate reached 94.6 percent.

Hyatt grew to a chain of 13 hotels by 1969. That year, the Pritzkers set up a separate company called Hyatt International Corporation to expand the chain overseas, with its first hotel the Hyatt Regency Hong Kong. In 1972, Donald died of a heart attack at the age of 39. Jay installed his brother-in-law, Hugh M. "Skip" Friend, Jr., as the new president.

### Growth in the 1970s

The company grew rapidly during the 1970s aided by the signature Hyatt design and the innovations that a young staff was able to devise. Management went awry, however, when it was discovered in 1977 that Friend had spent $300,000 of company money on personal expenses. After Jay Pritzker demoted him, Friend left the company. Jay took over the duties of president, in addition to his responsibilities as chairman and chief executive officer. He also moved corporate headquarters to Chicago, where he could more closely oversee matters. Then, Jay gradually bought back the public shares of stock, taking the company private in 1979.

### The 1980s

In 1980, Thomas Jay Pritzker, Jay's son, became president, with Jay remaining chairman and CEO. The decade started promisingly with three significant firsts in 1980: the openings of the

first Park Hyatt, the first Grand Hyatt, and the first Hyatt resort. Park Hyatts were designed as smaller luxury hotels with a European style, featuring personalized service, privacy, and elegance; the first one opened in Chicago near the Water Tower. Grand Hyatts were designed for the high-end market in culturally rich destinations, and featured sophisticated leisure, banquet, and conference facilities utilizing the latest technology. Hyatt Resorts were specially designed to reflect the local area of location and offered numerous activities and facilities for their guests; the first Hyatt resort was the Hyatt Regency Maui in Hawaii.

Then in 1981, two skywalks at the Kansas City Hyatt Regency Hotel collapsed, killing 114 people and injuring 229 in what the National Bureau of Standards called the most devastating structural collapse ever to take place in the United States. Between 1981 and 1986, more than 2,000 resulting lawsuits were settled for a total of $120 million. In June 1986, 900 individuals remaining in a federal class action suit against the hotel settled all claims for $1,000 each. Ultimately, "gross negligence and misconduct" were attributed to engineers Daniel Duncan, Jack Gillum, and their former company, G.C.E. International Inc., whose "hurry-up" design system caused them to be pouring concrete on one part of the building while finishing the design on the rest of the building. As was the case with most Hyatt hotels at this time, Hyatt was managing the hotel for its owner and builder, Hallmark Properties, so Hyatt was not held liable. Still it did not help to have the Hyatt name associated with such a disaster.

Hyatt's growth slowed somewhat as the 1980s progressed, in part because hotel property owners began to object to the high fees Hyatt (and other hotel managers) received for managing the hotels without taking on any ownership risks. In order to keep the company growing, the Pritzkers launched a separate company to develop and build hotels and resorts, with Jay's cousin Nick in charge.

During the decade, Hyatt Corporation also became involved in an indirect way in some of the Pritzkers' nonlodging activities. Most notable was the 1983 purchase of the troubled Braniff airline through Dalfort, a Hyatt subsidiary. Under Dalfort, and with Jay Pritzker taking the lead, Braniff's losses were cut. But after a proposed merger with the also troubled Pan Am Corp. failed in 1987, Braniff was sold the following year.

During this time, Darryl Hartley-Leonard was named president of Hyatt Hotels Corporation, which had been reorganized as a subsidiary of the parent Hyatt Corporation. Another subsidiary was launched in 1989 under the name Classic Residence by Hyatt, with Donald Pritzker's daughter Penny Pritzker as president. The Classic Residence properties were designed as luxury retirement centers with large rental apartments, housekeeping and gourmet meal service, and such activities as lectures by university professors. Aimed at the growing population of senior citizens, many of whom were looking for alternatives to institutional settings, Classic Residence centers opened initially in Reno, Dallas, and Teaneck, New Jersey. They were somewhat slow to fill, however, and the properties were typically half empty six months after opening.

Also in 1989, Hyatt introduced the Camp Hyatt program to attempt to attract more families to its somewhat business-oriented facilities. Under the program, Hyatt hotels began to offer numerous activities geared toward the toddler to preteen set, gave parents the option of taking a half-priced second room for their kids, and added menus and room service tailored for children.

### 1990s and Beyond

As the 1990s began, Hyatt's growth was somewhat challenged by what analysts regarded as the reluctance of some owners of new hotels to hire Hyatt as managers, given the relatively high cost of running a glitzy Hyatt hotel. In fact, Hyatt was beginning to run the risk of losing existing contracts. Seeking to streamline operations, the company laid off more than 1,000 of its work force and then embarked on a detailed appraisal of the services it was offering at its hotels. Major cost savings were realized in several ways, such as moving to a centralized purchasing system, changing the turning down of beds from an automatic service to one that a guest had to request, cutting down on the number of choices offered on restaurant and room service menus, and outsourcing housekeeping and valet parking. The company also sought ways to attract frequent business travelers by augmenting its Gold Passport frequent stayer program and by offering additional business-oriented amenities such as in-room fax machines. By 1994, Hyatt's gross operating profits had increased 45 percent from 1990 and the company was hearing fewer complaints from hotel owners about costs.

In 1994 Douglas G. Geoga, a lawyer who had served as head of development, was named president and CEO of Hyatt Hotels, with Hartley-Leonard remaining chairman. At about the same time, Hyatt began to pursue several new opportunities for growth, as competition from other chains grew fierce. Starting in 1994, the company moved cautiously into franchising for the first time. The first two franchised Hyatts were older hotels—the Hyatt Sainte Claire in downtown San Jose and the Hyatt Regency Pier Sixty Six in Fort Lauderdale. Scheduled to open in 1997 was a third franchised Hyatt, the Hyatt Regency Wichita, a new downtown convention hotel. Hyatt also entered, again cautiously, the crowded time-share property market with the opening in June 1995 of a resort known as Hyatt's Sunset Harbor Key West.

Freestanding golf courses and casinos were additional ventures Hyatt entered in the mid-1990s. In January 1995 it opened on the island of Aruba its first freestanding golf course, which was also the island's first golf course. In addition to developing freestanding courses, Hyatt also intended to manage existing golf courses near its hotels. Already involved in gaming through casinos it operated at some of its resorts, Hyatt moved into the riverboat gambling industry in 1994 with the opening of the Grand Victoria Casino in Elgin, Illinois, which generated reve-

nues of $37 million during the last three months of that year. In 1995, Hyatt joined with Players International Inc. in offering to purchase the two riverboat casinos in New Orleans that had closed not long after opening. Hyatt was reportedly also looking for a site to move into the lucrative Las Vegas gambling mecca.

In addition to its pursuit of these growth opportunities, Hyatt also strived through innovation to retain its role at the forefront of the industry. In 1994 the company tested automated check-in kiosks in a number of its hotels. The kiosks, which allowed guests to check themselves in less than one minute and even dispensed room keys, proved a success and were subsequently expanded to other Hyatts. The company also successfully introduced a telephone check-in system.

In 1995 and 1996, Hyatt spent $200 million in renovating more than 30 of its hotels in North America. Among the enhancements were the replacement of worn-out furnishings, the improvement of access for peoples with disabilities, the addition of coffee kiosks and convenience stores to hotel lobbies, and the installation of modem ports, larger desks, and better lighting in guest rooms.

In the face of a highly competitive but increasingly lucrative hotel industry in the 1990s, Hyatt was certainly not resting on its reputation. While its acumen in managing hotel properties was rarely questioned, some industry observers did raise doubts about the company's late entrance into such areas as time-shares and franchising. But with Jay and Thomas Pritzker still in charge of the parent company, the successful Pritzker track record boded well for Hyatt's future.

### Principal Subsidiaries

Classic Residence by Hyatt; Hyatt Hotels Corporation; Hyatt International Corporation.

### Further Reading

Cohen, Warren, "Hotels Check in Profits: After Years of Struggle, the Lodging Business Makes a Comeback," *U.S. News & World Report*, October 16, 1995, pp. 78–79.

Heller, Robert, "The Pritzker-Hyatt Phenomenon," *Management Today*, February 1987, pp. 72–75.

Melcher, Richard A., "Why Hyatt Is Toning Down the Glitz," *Business Week*, February 27, 1995, pp. 92, 94.

Rowe, Megan, "Hyatt Does a Reality Check," *Lodging Hospitality*, September 1994, pp. 30–34.

"The Times Have Changed," *Advertising Age*, January 11, 1993, p. 5.

Worthy, Ford S., "The Pritzkers: Unveiling a Private Family," *Fortune*, April 25, 1988, pp. 164–83.

—Claire Badaracco
—updated by David E. Salamie

# Inchcape

# Inchcape plc

St. James's House
23 King Street
London SW1Y 6QY
United Kingdom
(071) 321-0110
Fax: (071) 321-0604

*Public Company*
*Incorporated:* 1958 as Inchcape & Co. Ltd.
*Employees:* 46,137
*Sales:* £6.30 billion (US $9.76 billion) (1995)
*Stock Exchanges:* London
*SICs:* 6719 Offices of Holding Companies, Not
    Elsewhere Classified; 6799 Investors, Not Elsewhere
    Classified

In the mid-1990s, conglomerate Inchcape plc was in the process of transforming itself into a more focused group of businesses, all relating to international distribution. The company describes itself as the world's largest motor vehicle importer, distributor, and retailer and is the sole distributor for Toyota Motor Company of Japan's passenger cars in several countries, including the United Kingdom, Belgium, Greece, Hong Kong, Singapore, Guam, and Brunei. Inchcape's motors segment accounts for more than 60 percent of company profits. Inchcape also runs the world's largest shipping agency, with its shipping services segment providing about seven percent of profits. Inchcape's third segment is marketing, from which about 32 percent of profits flow. This segment includes the firm's Spinneys supermarket chain located in the Middle East, Coca-Cola distributorships, and a joint venture with Ricoh established in 1995 that oversees distribution of office automation machines such as photocopiers and facsimile machines.

### 19th Century Origins

Inchcape plc was launched as an overseas trading company in 1958, yet the origins of its constituent companies date back to the late 18th and early 19th centuries. Thus, the creation of Inchcape dates back to the early expansion of commerce with India by a group of Scottish merchants. In 1847 a meeting took place in Calcutta between William Mackinnon and Robert Mackenzie, two merchants from Campbeltown, which led to the formation of their general merchanting partnership, Mackinnon Mackenzie & Company. Realizing the benefits of combining trading with ocean transport, especially with the gold rush to Australia in 1851, the business expanded and diversified. In 1856, Mackinnon—aged 34—founded the Calcutta & Burmah Steam Navigation Company, secured from the East India Company the contract for carrying the mails between Calcutta and Rangoon, and incorporated the company in London with a capital of £35,000, of which Mackinnon Mackenzie & Company invested £7,000, becoming agents for the new shipping line. As a result of their success in carrying troops from Ceylon—now Sri Lanka—to India during the Indian Mutiny of 1857 to 1859, and through Mackinnon's contacts with the influential civil servant Sir Henry Bartle Frere, the partners obtained further contracts to support a fleet of coastal steamers carrying mails around the Indian coast with extensions to the Persian Gulf and Singapore. In 1862, C&B raised sufficient additional capital—a total of £400,000—to float the company under the new name of the British India Steam Navigation Company (BI). Mackinnon Mackenzie & Company continued to act as agents for the BI for nearly 100 years.

Sir William Mackinnon also promoted steamer traffic to the Dutch East Indies, establishing a Dutch-registered shipping line around Java, and forming the Netherlands India Steam Navigation Company in 1868. With the opening of the Suez Canal in 1869, BI ships entered the Mediterranean Sea, establishing a trunk line between London and India via the Suez Canal in 1876. In the process, Mackinnon Mackenzie & Company became one of the greatest Eastern agency houses, and the BI posed a mighty challenge to all other shipping lines operating between the United Kingdom and the East, including the giant Peninsular & Oriental Steam Navigation Company (P&O).

These events were the backdrop to the formative years of James Lyle Mackay, named Lord Inchcape in 1911. Born in 1852, the son of an Arbroath shipmaster, Mackay left Scotland at the age of 20 and worked in the customs department of Gellatly, Hankey and Sewell. Mackay, who joined Mackinnon Mackenzie & Company's Calcutta office in 1874, was to become the heir to the Mackinnon businesses after the death of Mackinnon in 1893. Mackay first became a partner after saving the BI's Bombay office from bankruptcy, and was to become president of the prestigious Bengal Chamber of Commerce a record three times between 1890 and 1893. A member of the Viceregal Council and a close friend and confidant of Lord Lansdowne, Viceroy of India, Mackay gained a knighthood for his contribution to the solution of India's currency problems and the ultimate adoption of the gold standard in India. Mackay returned to the United Kingdom in 1894 as a director of the BI, replacing William Mackinnon's nephew, Duncan Mackinnon, as chairman in 1913. Continuing his work on the Council of India, Mackay's growing reputation as an outstanding public servant led to his being offered the viceroyalty of India in 1909. Prime Minister Herbert Asquith opposed Mackay's nomination, however, on the grounds of his commercial interests in the subcontinent, and Mackay was offered a peerage in 1911 by way of compensation. He chose the name of Baron Inchcape of Strathnaver, commemorating the Inchcape Rock, located 12 miles from Arbroath, and expressing his loyalty to the clan Mackay, whose home is in Strathnaver. Between 1913 and 1932, Lord Inchcape personified Britain's shipping industry as chairman of the BI and the P&O, after effecting a merger between the two lines in 1914.

Less well known than Lord Inchcape's shipping activities is his consolidation of an extensive group of commercial interests in India and beyond. These began with his accumulation of shares in Mackinnon Mackenzie & Company. Sir William Mackinnon had no son, his nephew Duncan died in 1914, and his great-nephews were killed in World War I, so Inchcape became the sole surviving senior partner of the Mackinnon enterprise, and by 1950 the Inchcape family held a controlling interest. Inchcape's chairmanship of the BI and P&O resulted in a very close connection between Mackinnon Mackenzie & Company and the shipping line, to the extent that many observers came to believe that they were one company.

Mackinnon Mackenzie & Company spawned a variety of other enterprises to serve the BI routes. The BI originally employed small private firms in local ports of call as agents, but eventually replaced them with firms within the Mackinnon complex. These all came under the control of the senior partners and ultimately under Lord Inchcape himself. To separate the trading businesses from the shipping line, the Macneill & Barry partnership was developed to take over the extensive tea and merchanting operations that Lord Inchcape had acquired in 1915. Amalgamated in 1949, Macneill & Barry Ltd. comprised three merchant partnerships formed in the second half of the 19th century: Barry & Company, Macneill & Company, and Kilburn & Company, involved in tea, coal, jute, river steamers, and various trading enterprises. Their principals included the Assam Company, the oldest tea company in India; the River Steam Navigation Company; and the India General Steam Navigation and Railway Company. Between 1951 and 1956, Macneill & Barry took over Kilburn & Company, and the three groups set up Pakistan-based companies. In 1965 the two river steamer businesses were sold to the government of India.

In 1906, Mackay made a successful strategic acquisition, of Binny's, a south-India-based textile business. Founded in 1799, Binny's originally carried out banking and general merchanting, diversifying in the 1840s into agriculture and textiles. Indian production of textiles boomed in the 1860s, when the U.S. Civil War interrupted cotton supplies, and by the late 19th century Binny's mills managed 70,000 spindles with over 1,500 looms. Yet in 1906, with the crash of the great Arbuthnot & Company banking house with whom it was closely involved, Binny's faced bankruptcy. Its greatly undervalued assets were acquired by Mackay and a consortium of Mackinnon partners for £53,000. Binny & Company Ltd., as it had become in 1906, made record profits in World War I with the production of khaki cloth, and by 1917 was supplying over a million yards per month. Binny & Company was subsequently restructured, setting up an engineering department, and rose to greater prominence during World War II, producing one billion yards of cloth a year by 1942.

Owing to the need to supply shipping-agency services to the BI, Mackinnon group enterprises were established in east Africa, the Persian Gulf, Australia, and London. In east Africa, as Sir William Mackinnon began to open up the region to British influence, the BI operated a steam shipping service. In 1872, an agency was established by Archibald Smith, a member of the staff of William Mackinnon & Company, in Glasgow, together with a Mackenzie man from Calcutta, operating as BI agents and general traders. In 1887, Sir William won from the sultan of Zanzibar the right to administer a coastal strip of land in return for customs revenue, which led to the founding of the Imperial British East Africa Company (IBEA), partly in response to the build-up of German interests in this area. Smith Mackenzie took a stake in IBEA and acted as its agents, until the charter was surrendered in 1897. Smith Mackenzie & Company and the agency for Shell in east Africa became joint coaling agents to the admiralty during World War I and in the 1930s gained the agencies for British American Tobacco, Imperial Chemical Industries, and British Overseas Airways Corporation.

In 1862, when a contract was won to carry mails eight times a year up and down the Persian Gulf, the merchant partnership that became Gray Mackenzie & Company was formed, helping to develop navigation on the Euphrates and Tigris rivers, and establishing a diversified trading business in an area that was also facing German expansionism. In World War II, Gray Mackenzie & Company acted as agents for the British government in unloading military cargoes; the growth of its business was helped by the spectacular development of the oil industry and the rapidly growing need to service the expanding ports of the Middle East.

The Mackinnon complex also branched into Australia, with BI services at first managed by the British India and Queensland Agency Company Ltd. The Mackinnon partners invested in the formation of a major Australian shipping conglomerate in 1887, the Australasian United Steam Navigation Company (AUSN), formed with a capital of £600,000. In 1894 Mackay was appointed to the Board of the AUSN and, in 1900, spent several months in Australia successfully restructuring the business. In 1915, he created a new merchant partnership, Macdonald Hamilton & Company, formed by two trusted Mackinnon appointees, B. W. Macdonald and David Hamilton. The AUSN, which had once owned 42 steamers, declined in the face of increasing competition from railways in the 1920s, and Macdonald Hamilton & Company diversified its activities into mining, pastoral management, and operating the P&O agencies in Australia. The P&O acquired Macdonald Hamilton's P&O-related activities in 1959 and 1960.

The London partnership of Gray Dawes & Company was set up to serve the BI as a shipping and brokering agency, and eventually became a bank and a travel agency. It represented the interests of Smith Mackenzie & Company and Binny & Company in London, and set up a secretarial department to administer the estate of James Mackay, the first earl of Inchcape, after his death in 1932.

### Consolidation and Expansion: Late 1950s through 1970s

These diverse Mackinnon group interests were consolidated and reorganized during the 1950s, coming together as Inchcape & Company Ltd. in 1958 at the initiative of the third Earl of Inchcape. Tax considerations necessitated the conversion of these companies into private limited companies—whose former partners became the principal shareholders—controlled through London-based subsidiaries. Also in 1958, Inchcape & Company became a public company through a public offering of 25 percent of its equity, and starting in 1958 embarked on a program of growth and diversification, principally through acquisitions. The group today reflects the merger and acquisition activities of the last quarter century far more than it represents the original companies that came together in 1958.

The original Inchcape companies—Gray Dawes, Binny & Company, Gray Mackenzie, Smith Mackenzie; Duncan Macneill, Macneill & Barry, the AUSN, and Mackinnon Mackenzie itself—have been eclipsed in importance by the development of the companies since acquired. In India, the remaining Inchcape businesses were consolidated into the Assam Company Limited, now one of the largest tea groups in the subcontinent, and 74 percent-owned by Inchcape. The East African businesses of the group were sold due to declining profitability and political problems, but in the Middle East, Gray Mackenzie was retained. Also, Macdonald Hamilton & Company in Australia was sold, and Gray Dawes left the group. Gray Dawes Bank was sold in the early 1980s, and Gray Dawes Travel was acquired by its management in the late 1980s.

During the 1960s and 1970s, under the leadership of the third Earl of Inchcape, the company expanded to over 150 times its previous capitalization, due principally to a series of successful acquisitions, especially those of the Borneo Company in 1967, Gilman & Company in 1969, Dodwell & Company in 1972, Mann Egerton & Company in 1973, Anglo-Thai Corporation in 1975, A.W. Bain Holdings in 1976, and Pride & Clarke, which held the Toyota agency for the United Kingdom, in 1978. In this period, through several capitalization issues, 64 original shares costing £80 in total in 1958 were worth nearly £2,000 by 1975.

The merger with the Borneo Company almost doubled the size of Inchcape overnight, bringing in new interests in Canada, the Caribbean, Hong Kong, Malaysia, Singapore, Brunei, and Thailand. The Borneo Company operated jointly with Inchcape in the United Kingdom and Australia, but introduced two new activities into the group's portfolio, motor vehicle distribution and timber and construction business. This merger, in which Inchcape entered new geographical regions in familiar businesses and entered new businesses in regions that it knew well—allowing considerable local autonomy to existing local staff—established a pattern for subsequent acquisitions.

Through Peter Heath, originally a director of the Borneo Company, Inchcape acquired Gilman & Company, one of the great trading groups of Hong Kong. Gilman & Company was seeking an acquirer but did not wish to be taken over by an existing Hong Kong business. The acquisition of Dodwell & Company gave the group further interests in this region, which it maintained as quasi-independent companies, rather than forming one large entity. Dodwell & Company was founded in Shanghai in 1858, and by the 1970s had established extensive businesses in shipping, motors, and business-machine trading in Hong Kong, Japan, and many other Far Eastern ports and cities.

Mann Egerton, acquired in 1973, laid the foundations for Inchcape's now extensive motor-distribution business. Founded at the end of the 19th century in Norwich by an electrical engineer and an early motoring pioneer, Mann Egerton sold cars manufactured by de Dion, Renault, and Daimler for between £200 and £300 per car, at the turn of the century initially from branches in the eastern counties of England. By the 1970s, Mann Egerton distributed British Leyland cars, as well as an extensive range of luxury cars, but faced a possible takeover bid from an unwanted source, and felt increasingly vulnerable as a result of a wave of oil shocks.

The acquisition of Anglo-Thai Corporation involved the issue of nearly nine million Inchcape £1 ordinary shares, three times the number issued before, increasing Inchcape's market value by about 90 percent, and adding to group assets in the Far East and Southeast Asia. In one of the group's few predatory bids, valuable businesses such as Caldbeck Macgregor & Company, a well-known importer and distributor of wines and spirits, were included. In 1976, with A. W. Bain Holdings, Inchcape developed an important insurance business through a share issue second only to that involved in acquisition of the Anglo-Thai Corporation. With Pride & Clarke, the group gained the valuable concession of exclusive Toyota distribution in the United Kingdom after an issue of £1 million in £1 ordinary shares and £6.9 million in cash, in what some observers called the biggest bargain of the century. By 1989, the Motors segment contributed two-thirds of group turnover and 53.6 percent of group profits, the greater part contributed by Toyota.

### Reorganization in a Modern Era: 1980s, 1990s, and Beyond

Inchcape—reincorporated as Inchcape plc in 1981—under the chairmanship of George Turnbull in the 1980s reinforced its concentration on its core businesses. Inchcape's key businesses at that time were organized into three main areas: services, marketing and distribution, and resources. The service businesses consisted of buying, insurance, inspection and testing, and shipping. The marketing and distribution businesses covered business machines, consumer and industrial services, and motors. The resource-based businesses covered tea and timber (which by the early 1990s had been divested).

In April 1990, Toyota paid Inchcape £110 million in cash for a 50 percent stake in Inchcape's United Kingdom-based distributing business known as Toyota (GB). With this acquisition, Toyota also acquired a holding of nearly five percent in Inchcape itself.

Inchcape had a difficult time in the early 1990s during CEO Charles Mackay's tenure in part because it had in prior decades overdiversified into areas not related to its core distribution business. The company continued to expand during this period, in particular in the shipping services and insurance areas. Through a variety of acquisitions from 1990 through 1993, Inchcape expanded into or expanded its shipping businesses in China, Korea, Vietnam, Indonesia, Canada, Turkey, Ecuador, and the United States. The U.S. acquisitions were seen as particularly strategic as Inchcape was able to secure operations for the Pacific, Atlantic, and Gulf coasts of the United States, toward the goal of operating a broad shipping agency covering all three coasts.

In insurance, Inchcape's Bain Clarkson Ltd. insurance broker was bolstered through the 1994 acquisition of Hogg Group P.L.C. for £176.6 million (US $264.9 million). The newly named Bain Hogg Group instantly joined the ranks of the world's ten largest brokers, and Inchcape had gained a presence in the U.S. insurance market for the first time through Hogg Robinson Inc. Meanwhile, Inchcape's marketing operation was bolstered in a smaller way with the 1992 acquisition of the Spinneys group of companies, which ran a chain of supermarkets in the Middle East, from Bricom Group Ltd. for £32.1 million (US $57.9 million).

A combination of factors plunged Inchcape into its two most difficult years ever, 1994 and 1995. Difficult economic conditions in some of the company's key markets—particularly in western Europe and Hong Kong—dampened consumer spending, while the strength of the yen made Inchcape's Japanese products, notably the Toyota automobiles, less attractive than those of competitors based outside Japan. In certain areas such as marketing, Inchcape had also become a more bureaucratic organization than in the past, and had lost touch with some of the local markets it served. As a result, pretax profits fell 15.8 percent from 1993 to 1994 and 92.4 percent from 1994 to 1995.

The resulting plunge in Inchcape stock led not only to the company being dropped from the prestigious PT-SE 100 index in late 1995 but also to a management shakeup. First, David Plastow retired as chairman of Inchcape at the end of 1995 and was replaced by Colin Marshall, who at the same time was chairman of British Airways Plc and deputy chairman of British Telecommunications plc. Then in March 1996 Mackay stepped aside as CEO, and Philip Cushing, who was managing director, took his place.

The new management team determined that Inchcape had to focus on its core distribution business in order to turn things around. Already in the later months of 1995, unprofitable businesses had been jettisoned and the work force had been reduced by more than 2,000 people, which all told resulted in exceptional charges of £129.4 million for 1995. Management planned to make more significant divestments in 1996 including the

Bain Hogg and Testing Services operations which were both considered noncore. These actions would transform the services segment into simply "shipping services." In the motors segment, among a number of actions to be taken was the strategic one of moving into other areas related to new cars, including parts, service, accessories, and financing. Finally, in the marketing segment, Inchcape planned to relocate its management to the local markets served in the Middle East and Asia, thus relying on a leaner and faster-reacting operation.

Although a challenged group in the mid-1990s, Inchcape's long-time strength in its core distribution businesses indicated that a streamlined operation could once again generate healthy profits. Furthermore, Inchcape's new management appeared to be taking the right combination of major restructuring moves in order to turn the company's fortunes around.

### Principal Subsidiaries

Gray Mackenzie & Company Limited; Inchcape Motors International plc; Inchcape Shipping Services (Europe) Limited; MCL Group Limited (40%); MEVC Finance Limited (25%); Spinneys 1948 Ltd.; TGB Finance Limited (37.5%); Towergate Automotive Limited; Toyota (GB) Limited (75%); Wadham Kenning Motor Group Limited; Toyota Belgium NV/SA; CECAR SA (France; 33.1%); France Motors SARL (95%); Inchcape Finance SA (France; 49%); Toyota Hellas SA (Greece); Caldbeck MacGregor (Australia) Limited; Subaru (Aust.) Pty Limited; TKM Automotive Australia Pty Limited; Inchcape Pacific Limited (Hong Kong); Crown Motors Limited (Hong Kong); JDH Company Limited (Hong Kong); Mazda Motors (Hong Kong) Limited; Inchcape NRG Limited (Hong Kong; 50%); Inchroy Credit Corporation (Hong Kong; 50%); Inchcape Marketing Services (Japan) Limited; Inchcape Shipping Services (Japan) KK; Inchcape Timuran Bhd (49%); Inchcape Berhad (Singapore; 63%); Borneo Motors (Singapore) Pte Limited (63%); Inchcape Consumer Marketing Ltd. (Thailand); Inchcape Engineering Ltd. (Thailand); Gray MacKenzie & Partners (Abu Dhabi) LLC (49%); Spinneys (Abu Dhabi) LLC (49%); Bahrain Maritime & Mercantile International BSC (48%); Gray Mackenzie & Partners (Central Emirates) Private Limited (Dubai; 49%); Spinneys (Dubai) LLC (49%); Williamson Balfour SA (Chile); Inchcape Inc. (U.S.A.); SS Acquisition Corporation (U.S.A.).

### Further Reading

Canna, Elizabeth, "More Acquisitions for Inchcape," *American Shipper,* December 1991, p. 79.
Foster, Geoffrey, "Inchcape's Less Perilous Passage," *Management Today,* January 1988, p. 46.
Gillis, Chris, "Inchcape's Open Door to China," *American Shipper,* January 1996, p. 50.
Griffiths, Percival Joseph, *A History of the Inchcape Group,* London: Inchcape & Company Ltd., 1977, 211 p.
——, *A History of the Joint Steamer Companies,* London: Inchcape & Co. Ltd.
Jones, Stephanie, *Trade and Shipping: Lord Inchcape 1852–1952,* Manchester, Eng.: Manchester University Press, 1989, 222 p.
——, *Two Centuries of Overseas Trading: The Origins and Growth of the Inchcape Group,* London: Macmillan, 1986.
Ladbury, Adrian, "Bain Hogg Group," *Business Insurance,* July 18, 1994, pp. 35–36.

Lindberg, Ole, et. al., "Companies that Made Their Mark," *International Management,* January/February 1993, p. 60.

Magnier, Mark, "Inchcape Plans Expansion into 3 Asian Nations," *Journal of Commerce and Commercial,* March 19, 1992, p. 8B.

Porter, Janet, "Inchcape Grows with Purchase of Three Shipping Businesses," *Journal of Commerce and Commercial,* February 23, 1993, p. 8B.

Souter, Gavin, "Global Broker Merger: Bain Clarkson, Hogg Combination to Break into Top 10," *Business Insurance,* May 2, 1994, pp. 1, 61.

Vincent, Lindsay, "Inchcape's True Brit," *Observer,* April 4, 1993, p. 40.

Wighton, David, "Inchcape to Focus on Distribution Business," *Financial Times,* March 26, 1996, p. 24.

—Stephanie Jones
—updated by David E. Salamie

# Insilco Corporation

**425 Metro Place North, Fifth Floor**
**Dublin, Ohio 43017**
**U.S.A.**
**(614) 792-0468**
**Fax: (614) 791-3197**

*Public Company*
*Incorporated:* 1898 as International Silver Company
*Employees:* 4,923
*Sales:* $561.2 million (1995)
*Stock Exchanges:* NASDAQ
*SICs:* 2731 Book Publishing; 3469 Metal Stampings, Not
    Elsewhere Classified; 6719 Holding Companies, Not
    Elsewhere Classified

Formerly the largest silver company in the world, Insilco Corporation is no longer involved in the silver business, but lives on as a manufacturer of industrial and consumer products. Based in suburban Columbus, Ohio, Insilco operated for more than a half century as the International Silver Company before adopting the Insilco name and diversifying into a host of businesses that eventually supplanted the company's reliance on the production of silverware to sustain its existence. By the mid-1990s, Insilco was supported by three primary business segments: electronics and communications; automotive components; and office products and specialty publishing. Insilco chairman Durand B. Blatz announced to a *Forbes* reporter in the early 1980s: "I think I've created a financially harmonious company that is motivated in special niches to produce better-than-average profits and tends to balance itself." While presenting an accurate, if somewhat vague, description of Insilco's operations during the first few years of the decade, perhaps the most interesting aspect of Blatz's remark were the words "I've created." Indeed, Blatz had created a company through some highly unique measures, transforming the world's largest silver company into a completely new, modern enterprise positioned for the 21st century.

## Nineteenth Century Origins

Insilco began its existence as the International Silver Company, which traced its start in the silver business back to 1898, when it began producing silver and pewter spoons and dishes. During the ensuing 50 years, the company developed into a giant, wielding enough sway in the silver market to draw repeated criticism for operating as a monopoly. The target of trustbusters, International Silver held a resolute grip on the world's silver business, ranking as the largest silver company in the world during the first half of the 20th century. However, before the century was through both the name and the business of International Silver would be gone, and Durand Blatz would be there to witness it all.

## Initial Diversifications in the 1950s

Blatz joined International Silver in 1957, when the company still reigned supreme in the silver industry. By the time of Blatz's arrival, the company had already begun to diversify, albeit for practical rather than strategic reasons. In 1955, the company had made its first acquisition, purchasing Times Wire & Cable, a coaxial cable manufacturer.

The purchase of Times Wire & Cable, which would later become one of the Insilco's flagship enterprises as Times Fiber Corporation, did not formally mark the beginning of a diversification program. Instead, the acquisition was completed largely because Times Wire & Cable's operations could easily be moved into an empty silver factory owned by International Silver. "The empty-factory syndrome was the only reason they finally bought Times," Blatz later explained, "after having turned it down three times."

Nevertheless, Times Wire & Cable would later represent an important strategic asset for Insilco, particularly in the late 1970s, when the coaxial cable manufacturer would be merged with another acquisition, Fiber Communications, Inc. The marriage of Times Wire & Cable and Fiber Communications, a small New Jersey company led by two of the scientists who had developed fiber optics at Western Electric, would give Insilco a firm foundation in the high-technology communications field, one of the chief areas of business that would support the company once it severely restricted its involvement in the silver business. The purchase of Times Wire & Cable thus unintentionally signalled changes that would sweep through International Silver, changes made for strategic reasons once Blatz took control of the company.

### Durand Blatz Named CEO in 1966

Nine years after joining International Silver, Blatz became the company's chief executive officer. Blatz was responsible for much of International Silver's diversification away from silver, spearheading many of the more than 30 sizeable acquisitions that were completed during the 1960s and 1970s, acquisitions that increasingly placed less and less of an emphasis on the production of silverware. After changing its name from International Silver Company to the abbreviated Insilco Corporation in 1969, the company completed several acquisitions that would define its operations during the 1980s and contribute toward much of its growth during the 1970s.

One of the company's strengths during the 1970s was its modular housing group, a business area whose chief gains were realized through two acquisitions. In 1972, Insilco acquired Miles Homes, a leader in the build-it-yourself housing market. Purchased for $29 million, Miles Homes had sales of $7.8 million, which would rise to $58 million by 1980; similarly its eventual net operating earnings of $11 million increased considerably from the $1.7 million posted in 1972. Complementing this acquisition was Insilco's 1979 acquisition of Nationwide Homes, a manufacturer that constructed finished houses and shipped them in two parts from a limited area surrounding the company's base in Martinsville, Virginia.

Aside from the steadily growing housing group supporting the company and the promising Times Fiber Communications, Inc. subsidiary created through the merger of Times Wire & Cable and Fiber Communications, Insilco was supported by more than a dozen operating companies during the early 1980s, most of which were small and positioned in market segments of their own. Describing these other businesses, Blatz related, "Each is in a specific, isolated area that is more than ordinarily profitable and one that we can understand." Included within this group of companies were several strong entities that rounded out Insilco's operations, creating a well-balanced corporation with good potential for growth.

Insilco's office products group was highlighted by two new subsidiaries: Rolodex Corp., a perennial leader in the rolling-file business, and McDonald Products, a maker of expensive desktop accessories. Insilco also scored success with the purchase of Taylor Publishing Company, which published high school and college yearbooks as well as specialty books and gave the company an entry into the publishing business. The acquisition of

three paint companies, Enterprise, Sinclair, and Red Devil, added another business group to Insilco's business. Although Insilco's paint business was recording less-than-spectacular results during the early 1980s, each of the three companies was serving different segments of the market and together represented the seventh-largest concern among U.S. paint companies.

Conspicuous by its absence from the list of Insilco's major businesses during the early 1980s was the silver business, which contributed less than five percent of Insilco's nearly $650 million in annual sales at the start of the decade. International Silver Co., after more than half a century of underpinning the company's existence, operated as one small division during the early 1980s. In fact, a combination of low-priced silverware imports, inflated silver prices, and changing American lifestyles had hobbled Insilco's silver business since the 1970s, and as the years passed and the company's diversification program continued, the former mainstay business of the company withered away.

As the silver business declined, plants were shuttered and workers were laid off, but Blatz kept the tool-and-die making operations that had been developed during International Silver's decades as the preeminent silver company in the world. With these facilities, Blatz maneuvered Insilco into a new business area, converting them into production plants geared for the manufacture of precision parts for high-technology companies such a Pratt & Whitney and Sikorsky. From the early 1980s forward, Blatz would look to develop this business further, keeping his eye out for additional precision-tooling acquisitions.

After years of posting marginal profits, Insilco's silver business began losing money in 1982, slipping into the red and, as a consequence, damaging its parent company's image. By the following year Insilco had abandoned the business altogether, selling the subsidiary to Katy Industries Inc., a conglomerate based in Elgin, Illinois.

In the years following the divestiture of its silver business, Insilco stood on stable ground, supported by businesses that were recording modest growth, with its electronics and communications group representing the most promising facet of its operations. Headed by Times Fiber Communications, Insilco's electronics and communications group was complemented by a computer circuity group, which manufactured electronic components and supplied assembly services for computer companies. Elsewhere in the company's operations, Stewart Stamping also contributed meaningfully to Insilco's growth by manufacturing billions of small metal parts and electronic assemblies for companies such as North American Phillips and Western Electric.

### 1991 Bankruptcy

Not long after the sale of International Silver Co. in 1983, however, Blatz's "financially harmonious company" entered a period of drastic change and discord. In 1988 a pair of Midland, Texas, investors acquired publicly-traded Insilco and took the company out private in a leveraged buyout (LBO). The LBO was a costly affair, saddling Insilco with deleterious debt and seriously affecting its ability to operate successfully during the years immediately following its acquisition. Three years after the LBO, fettered to the suffocating weight of $800 million of debt, Insilco filed for protection under Chapter 11 of the U.S.

Bankruptcy Code, marking the inglorious end to what had been a thriving concern for nearly a century.

For those associated with the company, bankruptcy in 1991 was a regrettable development, regrettable because financial failure had occurred for reasons that had nothing to with the company's condition. Indeed, in the years leading up to bankruptcy, Insilco's subsidiaries had been performing well. However, but the debt incurred from the 1988 LBO had delivered the fatal blow, thrusting an obstacle before the company that it could not surmount, no matter the relative health of its operating subsidiaries. For a company with roots stretching back to the 19th century, the decades of work devoted to turning it into a company that could survive and grow into the 21st century appeared to be in vain. Insilco had collapsed financially just as the technology supporting the company was recording explosive growth, dashing hopes that it could reap the rewards of the three decades of diversification.

However, corporate spirit remained high enough to fuel the development of a plan to mount a revival of Insilco, keeping hopes alive that the storied firm could resume operation as a viable concern. In April 1993, that hope was made reality when Insilco emerged from under the protective blanket of Chapter 11 and once again entered the business fray. With a newly-assembled and highly experience management team led by chief executive officer Robert L. Smialek, Insilco embarked on its new era of existence focused intently on developing its core businesses.

### Rebirth in the Mid-1990s

Encouraging success was recorded quickly, as the company's three chief business groups—office products/specialty publishing, electronics/telecommunications, and automotive parts— each demonstrated quick success. The electronics and telecommunications division, referred to as the technologies group, manufactured high-technology products such as modular plugs and jacks for computer networking, cellular, and telecommunications. Through its automotive components group, the company manufactured thermal components, such as heat exchangers, steel parts, and decorative stainless steel tubing. Rounding out Insilco's operations was its office products and specialty publishing group, which was led by the company's Rolodex and Taylor Publishing subsidiaries. Each of these three business segments generated roughly one-third of Insilco's total annual sales.

As the company prepared for the late 1990s with $561 million in sales in 1995, its well-balanced, diversified businesses fueled hope that the turmoil of the late 1980s and early 1990s was completely behind the company and that Insilco employees, management, and shareholders could look forward to an era of strong financial performance. Though the 1990s version of the company bore no resemblance to the business founded nearly a century earlier, the legacy of International Silver Co. and its creation, Insilco, provided a history of excellence to guide the new concern toward a profitable future.

### Principal Subsidiaries

Stewart Connector Systems, Inc.; Signal Transformer Company; Signal Carbide, Inc.; Signal Dominicana, S.A. (Dominican Republic); Stewart Stamping Corporation; Escod Industries; Steel Parts Corporation; McKenica; Romac Metals; General Thermodynamics; Thermalex, Inc. (50%); Rolodex/Curtis; Taylor Publishing Company.

### Further Reading

Chakravarty, Subrata N., "The Neglected Parent," *Forbes*, September 28, 1981, p. 115.
"Insilco Corp. to Be Sold to Management, First Boston," *American Paint & Coatings Journal*, August 15, 1988, p. 14.
"Insilco," *Rubber World*, December 1991, p. 8.
"Insilco Sifting Bids for International Silver; Expect First Half Sale," *American Metal Market*, April 1, 1983, p. 7.
"Insilco to Sell World Tableware," *American Metal Market*, August 24, 1983, p. 6.
"Insilco: Trading Its Silver for a Future in High Tech and Housing," *Business Week*, October 3, 1983, p. 96.
Jaffe, Thomas, "Rip Van Insilco," *Forbes*, March 21, 1988, p. 207.
Mehlman, William, "Insilco's Prospects Buoyed by Fiber-Optic, Housing Plays," *The Insiders' Chronicle*, June 22, 1981, p. 1.
Robertson, Angela S., "Cable Maker's Corporate Officials Move to Myrtle Beach, S.C.," *Knight-Ridder/Tribune Business News*, June 12, 1994, p. 6.
Shook, Carrie, "Insilco Biggest Gainer for 1994," *Business First-Columbia*, January 9, 1995, p. 16.
——, "Insilco Sheds Debt, Seeks Global Presence," *Business First-Columbia*, August 29, 1994, p. 1.
"Signals," *Fortune*, September 28, 1987, p. 15.

—Jeffrey L. Covell

# J.A. Jones, Inc.

J.A. Jones Drive
Charlotte, North Carolina
U.S.A.
(704) 553-3000
Fax: (704) 553-3317

*Wholly Owned Subsidiary of Philipp Holzmann U.S.A. Inc.*
*Incorporated:* 1920 as J.A. Jones Construction Co.
*Employees:* 5,000
*Sales:* $1.5 billion (1994 est.)
*SICs:* 1541 Industrial Buildings & Warehouses; 1542
    Nonresidential Construction, Not Elsewhere Classified;
    1611 Highway & Street Construction; 1629 Heavy
    Construction, Not Elsewhere Classified

J.A. Jones, Inc. is a leading U.S. construction company. With offices throughout the world, Jones has been involved with a multiplicity of commercial, industrial, military, and government construction projects throughout its more than 100 years in business. Among the numerous high-profile projects to its credit is the tallest building in the world, which Jones was helping to build in the mid-1990s in Malaysia. In 1979 J.A. Jones merged with Germany's Philipp Holzmann AG, one of the largest construction conglomerates in the world.

### The Founder

James Addison Jones, a simple brick mason, founded in the 1890s what would become one of the most successful U.S. construction companies. Jones was born in 1869 in North Carolina. Like many Southerners, his family was impoverished as a result of the Civil War, so Jones learned to work hard and live meagerly. A classic American success story, Jones received only a few years of education in a one-room schoolhouse but went on to manage detailed, complex, multimillion-dollar construction projects. In fact, Jones was credited with helping to construct much of the Charlotte, North Carolina skyline during his time. He was also known as a civic leader, serving as a city alderman and as a member of the first City Council of Charlotte.

Jones was first exposed to construction at the age of 17 when he and some neighbor boys were hired by a builder in nearby Lexington to construct Charlotte's first cotton mill. That builder went on to erect many of Charlotte's early textile mills, with Jones among his employees. Jones started out working for a wage of 25 cents per day, plus room and board in the primitive workers' camps. He began making brick, learned to be a mason tender, and quickly worked his way up to an apprentice mason. Evidencing his characteristic boundless energy, Jones became known as the best and fastest mason within two years. Subsequent efforts quickly earned him promotions to foreman and then superintendent, where his innate leadership abilities were revealed.

Eager to branch out on his own as an independent contractor, managing his own construction jobs, Jones left his job and started looking for work. The first company to hire him was Southern Railways. Jones quickly hired four workers to help him on that job, and his company was born. He set up an office in his house and used a bicycle for transportation. As his business grew, Jones upgraded to a horse and buggy, and later to a Model T Ford. From the start, he based his business dealings on a philosophy of "honesty, a good job for the owner, developing his workers, expecting a day's work for a day's pay, and finding the talents he lacked," according to Edwin L. Jones, Jr., the founder's grandson.

Jones ran his business shrewdly and kept a tight rein on costs. He bought his first piece of office equipment (other than a desk) in 1904 when he paid $100 for a Remington typewriter. He brought his sons into the business early. Edwin L., the oldest, typed letters on the typewriter for his father when he was in the seventh grade. He also began handling payroll and learning masonry skills. For a wage of 10 cents per hour, he, with his father, worked whenever possible, including most holidays. The hard work paid off. By 1905 Jones was building most of the large structures in Charlotte and, during the next few years, constructed landmark projects including the first reinforced concrete building in the area and the 12-story Independence Building (Charlotte's first "skyscraper").

Jones continued to operate out of his home office until 1909, when he moved into a one-room office in the Independence Building. In 1913 he hired son Edwin at a salary of $50 per month to handle bookkeeping, estimating, and some job supervision. Three years later son Raymond A. joined the firm after finishing his engineering studies at Georgia Tech. Like his father, Raymond had a high energy level and, with his engineering knowledge, was a great asset to the company. Son Johnie also joined the company after studying business. He brought his father's charm and salesmanship ability to the team. Unfortunately, he died early.

### Incorporation in the 1920s

Jones incorporated his business in the early 1920s as J.A. Jones Construction Company. He, Edwin, and Raymond were listed as the three founders of the company. Throughout the 1920s the family managed to grow J.A. Jones Construction into a formidable regional construction company, working on numerous textile mills, warehouses, power plants, office buildings, and other major projects. J.A. Jones, while still in control of his firm, allowed his sons to handle projects for which they were better suited, and the threesome worked effectively as a team. The company became known as honest and dependable, and the Joneses often worked under verbal contracts sealed with no more than a handshake.

The company's growth ground to a screeching halt in 1929 following the infamous stock market crash. New construction basically halted throughout the country and many contractors simply closed their doors and went out of business. Fortunately, Jones entered the Depression with little debt on its balance sheet. Just as important, the company was able to secure a contract in January 1930 to build a new military airbase in the Canal Zone in Panama. Besides generating cash flow that helped the firm survive, the project helped Jones to secure other government projects during the 1930s. Specifically, Jones was hired to manage several large-scale public housing projects throughout the Southeast. The Panama Canal project also gave Jones what would become invaluable experience in managing foreign projects.

### Wartime Work

Jones emerged from the Great Depression as one of the largest and most respected construction companies in the southeastern United States. That status helped the company to secure several major defense contracts during World War II. Jones was asked, for example, to build the first and largest military camp, Camp Shelby in Mississippi. About a dozen other camp construction jobs followed, as well as contracts to build hospitals, giant dams and power plants, supply depots, and air bases in South America. Jones was also asked to build and operate a shipyard, which suddenly cast the company into the role of

shipbuilder for the U.S. government. Incredibly, Jones managed the construction of 212 cargo ships and tankers during the war.

Among the most important projects in which J.A. Jones Construction was involved during the war was the building of K-25 and K-27. K-25 was a gaseous diffusion plant in Tennessee, which, at the time, was the largest construction project in world history. K-27, a similar plant, followed. The plants were used to manufacture Uranium 235, used in the construction of the bomb that ended World War II. The construction of K-25 is a story in itself. The gargantuan complex was almost a mile long, six stories high, and contained hundreds of miles of piping, thousands of advanced motors, filters, and controls, and other equipment installed by Jones. Jones built K-25 under a contract that was only one page, much shorter than a contract to build a storage barn or a playground in the 1990s. A testament to the quality of J.A. Jones's work, the hastily but solidly built plant operated for 20 years, processing dangerous gases and chemicals without any leaks or defects.

### Changes in the 1950s and 1960s

Tragically, both Raymond and J.A. Jones died in May of 1950, leaving only Edwin in charge of the company. He assumed full control of the enterprise while it was in the midst of its greatest growth period. Indeed, during the postwar construction boom, J.A. Jones realized vigorous growth. Because it was positioned to compete for all types of projects, it managed to expand rapidly, setting up branch contracting offices throughout the southern United States, extending northward into Washington, D.C., and even branching westward with offices in Washington State. Throughout the 1950s and 1960s the company grew at a hurried pace and established itself as a premiere, multimillion-dollar U.S. construction concern.

The pace and scale of Jones construction projects during the 1950s and 1960s boggled the minds of engineers and managers that had been involved in the industry early in the century. Coming from an era when a 20-story building was a skyscraper, those people were finding themselves involved in projects that they would not have even been able to imagine before World War II. Examples of Jones's cutting-edge projects included missile bases, launching facilities at Cape Kennedy, missile tracking stations, atomic energy plants, huge stretches of highway, and giant skyscrapers, among others. Jones's geographical scope also broadened. After winning a contract to build a $20 million dam in 1946, Jones went on to build dam projects throughout the world, ranging from a dam at a U.S. Boy Scout camp to massive dams costing more than $100 million.

Among the engineers on staff (before he was drafted) during Jones's World War II era was Edwin Jones, Jr., the founder's grandson and the future leader of the company. Edwin, Jr. returned from the war and assumed the presidency of the company in 1960. It was largely under his tutelage that J.A. Jones expanded during the 1960s and 1970s. Besides tackling a wide variety and large number of new projects, Jones grew by acquiring competing companies that gave it new expertise. In 1961, for example, Edwin, Jr. engineered the acquisition of the Chas. H. Tompkins Co., one of the oldest and best construction companies in the eastern United States. Earlier acquisitions had included a respected highway construction company.

By the mid-1960s J.A. Jones was sporting ten branch offices, employing thousands of workers, and operating $15 million worth of equipment in projects throughout much of the United States and parts of the world. Importantly, the organization also boasted an excellent safety record. At one point in the 1960s, for example, Jones celebrated one million manhours of accident-free work. Company literature in the mid-1960s attributed the company's success to the following traits: experience, including book learning and job training; ruggedness of the men on Jones construction jobs; diversification; and personal attention given by managers to the details of every job.

Although the pace of construction slowed in the 1970s following the postwar U.S. expansion, Jones continued to increase its exposure and revenue. Under Edwin, Jr.'s leadership, in fact, the company's worth grew from about $12 million to more than $45 million as sales swelled past $1 billion. Feathers in the company's cap during the 1970s included numerous universities and colleges, giant churches, high-tech defense projects, and large commercial buildings and corporate campuses. Unusual projects included a set of 505 houses that Jones built for the U.S. Navy. Jones built the houses, complete with furniture and appliances, in Portland, Oregon, and then loaded them onto barges for shipment to Alaska. The first load of houses survived, unscathed, 100-mile-per-hour winds on the barge and a jarring 7.74 earthquake, again evidencing J.A. Jones quality.

### The Philipp Holzmann Acquisition

After operating as a family-controlled company for nearly 90 years, Jones gave up its independence in 1979 when Edwin, Jr. negotiated the sale of the company to Philipp Holzmann A.G. Holzmann was a huge construction conglomerate with businesses all over the world. Still, the merger with J.A. Jones was pivotal and represented a major addition to its organization. Thus, Edwin, Jr. became the last member of the family to control the company. By the late 1970s, though, Jones had become a widely diversified company with a range of subsidiaries and divisions, many of which operated relatively autonomously.

Jones reorganized during the construction industry slowdown of the late 1970s and early 1980s. Taking charge of the organization in the mid-1980s and leading it successfully into the mid-1990s was Charles Tompkins Davidson. Davidson had come to the Jones organization through his father's company, Chas. H. Tompkins Co., which Edwin, Jr. had purchased in 1961. Davidson had earned his degree in civil engineering in 1962 before working with the Army Corps of Engineers for four years. In 1964 he joined Tompkins, where he advanced to project manager. In 1972 Jones moved him to another of its subsidiaries, Metric Constructors, Inc., where Davidson served as vice-president until 1979. Davidson then served as president of Jones's Tiber Construction Company before becoming president of Jones in 1986.

### Change in Leadership in the 1980s

Under Davidson's leadership, the sprawling Jones organization continued to pursue an array of commercial, industrial, defense, and government projects. Davidson particularly emphasized growth overseas, where many of the fastest growing construction markets were located. For example, Jones penetrated the Japanese market with its "Robot FA Center" in Tokyo, and even started pursuing projects in former Iron Curtain countries, including Russia. By the early 1990s Jones had built projects in 60 different countries and was generating more than ten percent of its total revenue from overseas projects. "I think Americans have become aware that if we're not proactive in our interests we're going to be left at the gate," Davidson said in the September 17, 1990 *Business Journal-Charlotte*.

Although the J.A. Jones group of companies was no longer under the direct leadership of the original Jones family in the 1980s, heirs of the original founder were still active in top-level management. For example, Mark Jones (J.A. Jones's great-grandson) was serving as a senior development manager for Metric Constructors, a major J.A. Jones subsidiary. He had joined Jones's J.A. Jones Applied Research Company in 1983 as a buyer and had gradually worked his way up to a management position at Metric by the early 1990s. In that position, he had helped the company with several big projects in its original home base of Charlotte, where J.A. Jones was trying to reestablish its local dominance.

Meanwhile, with more than $1 billion in annual revenues, J.A. Jones and its subsidiary companies continued to be involved with both minor and major projects throughout the world, and in every aspect of those projects ranging from financing and design to construction and facilities management. For example, Jones was among the first big contractors to aid in reconstruction following the disastrous Los Angeles earthquake in 1994. Other projects in the 1990s included a large manufacturing plant built for Proctor & Gamble, a U.S. education center for Toyota, a cigarette plant constructed for Philip Morris, and a supply center built for the U.S. Army Corps of Engineers. The most prolific project in which the company was involved was the quarter-mile-high twin towers built in Malaysia. The 88-story buildings, scheduled for completion in the mid-1990s, became the tallest buildings in the world.

### Principal Subsidiaries

J.A. Jones, Inc.; J.A. Jones Construction Co.; Chas. H. Tompkins Co.; Crow Construction Co.; J.A. Jones Applied Research Company; J.A. Jones Environmental Services Co.; J.A. Jones Management Services, Inc.; Jones Capital Corporation; Metric Constructors, Inc.; Queens Properties, Inc.; REA Construction Company.

### Further Reading

Howard, J. Lee, "Metric Exec Builds a Name for Himself," *Business Journal-Charlotte*, July 24, 1995, p. 3.

*J.A. Jones Family Album*, Charlotte, N.C.: J.A. Jones, Inc., 1994.

Jones, Edwin L., *J.A. Jones Construction Company; 75 Years' Growth in Construction*, New York: The Newcomen Society in North America, 1965.

Martin, Edward, "Region's Growth Sends Builders Back to School," *Business Journal-Charlotte*, August 22, 1994, Section 1, p. 15.

Price, Scott, "Global Visions: J.A. Jones President Charlie Davidson— A Leader in Bringing Charlotte International Recognition," *Business Journal-Charlotte*, September 17, 1990, p. 8.

—Dave Mote

# J. R. Simplot Company

**999 Main Street**
**Boise, Idaho 83702**
**U.S.A.**
**(208) 336-2110**
**Fax: (208) 389-7515**

*Private Company*
*Incorporated:* 1955
*Employees:* 10,000
*Sales:* $2 billion (est. 1995)
*SICs:* 2037 Frozen Fruits & Vegetables; 2873
Nitrogenous Fertilizers; 2874 Phosphatic Fertilizers;
2879 Agricultural Chemicals, Not Elsewhere
Classified; 2875 Fertilizers—Mixing Only; 0219
General Livestock, Not Elsewhere Classified; 0191
General Farms—Primarily Crop

Nearly without rival in the global potato industry, the J. R Simplot Company is a diversified grower and processor of potatoes with substantial holdings in livestock, fertilizer production, and mining. The company's growth charts the rags-to-riches rise of J. R. Simplot, an Idahoan potato farmer who assembled a corporate empire around a small potato growing business to create a remarkable model of vertical integration in the agricultural industry. Few agricultural enterprises could match the self-sufficiency enjoyed by the J. R. Simplot Company during the 1990s. Nearly all of the company's raw material needs were supplied by its diversified businesses, a singular quality engendered by its founder, J. R. Simplot.

The complexion of Idaho's economy during the 1990s told much about the state's most prominent denizen. Idaho's chief manufactured good was processed foods; its largest agriculture crop was potatoes; its greatest number of livestock, cattle; its most abundant nonfuel mineral, phosphate; its principal industry, agriculture. Each of these primary segments of Idaho's economy described part of the diverse empire developed by John Richard (J. R.) Simplot, a self-described "gol-durn potato

farmer" whose life charted the remarkable progression of an eighth-grade dropout into a multibillionaire. During the course of his meteoric rise in the business world, Simplot became involved in an eclectic array of businesses, assembling a variegated corporate empire that underpinned Idaho's economy and constituted one of the great American fortunes. At the heart of Simplot's wide-ranging business interests was the J. R. Simplot Company, a corporate entity that at first blush appeared to comprise a motley, disconnected collection of businesses, ranging from mining operations to potato fields to livestock feedlots. The J. R. Simplot Company, however, was not the product of J. R. Simplot's compulsion to own everything, no matter the cohesiveness of the whole. Instead, the J. R. Simplot Company's seemingly odd mix of businesses were indicative of J. R. Simplot's intent to control all aspects related to the cultivation and processing of his potatoes. Around the business of growing and processing potatoes, a vertically integrated empire developed, the magnitude of which belied the humble origins of its creator, J. R. Simplot.

## Origins

Born in 1909, Simplot began his ascension to the top of the business world in Delco, Idaho, a small frontier town that was home to roughly ten families during Simplot's childhood. There, amid the sprawling plains stretching across the southern reaches of Idaho, Simplot got his working career off to an early start, deciding at age 14 that what lay outside the confines of the community's four-room schoolhouse held more promise than what lay inside. "I had to stop," Simplot later reflected, referring to his decision to drop out of school, "I didn't get along in school. I just didn't like it." Simplot left school and never returned, opting instead for the back-breaking field work that would fill his days for years to come, as those who knew the young Simplot discovered that whatever passion he lacked for formal education was compensated by his enormous appetite for labor.

Fortune, decisiveness, and an enviable willingness to work would characterize Simplot's resolute march from grade-school dropout to billionaire, beginning with his first job as a potato sorter for a local firm of potato brokers. During his off-hours, the 15-year-old Simplot moonlighted by shoring up the canals bringing water from the Snake River into irrigation ditches, earning extra money by "riprapping" the canal banks with rocks until he had enough money to rent 40 acres of potato land from his father and purchase several sow hogs. Simplot then constructed hog pens on the banks of a nearby creek, planted potatoes on his rented land, and fattened his hogs by feeding them an unusual hog slop that opened the doors to fortune and provided him with his first break in his fledgling business.

Instead of paying for feed grain as other livestock owners did, Simplot used what was available to him by tracking down the wild horses that still roamed the plains and combining the horse meat with discarded potatoes and a little barley. Once cooked in a huge iron vat, Simplot's hog slop represented a cheaper alternative to feed grain and, as luck would have it, the horse meat-cull potato-barley mash gave the resourceful Simplot an advantage over other pig farmers after a particularly harsh winter cut short the supply of feed grain. The following spring, when pigs were brought to market, Simplot's fat hogs stood in sharp contrast to the skinny hogs deprived of their usual amount of feed grain, enabling Simplot to reap the rewards from his unconventional hog slop.

Buoyed by the profits gleaned from the sale of his portly pigs, Simplot expanded his hog-raising operations, increasing his stock over the years until he owned roughly 500 hogs by the time he sold his spread for $7,500. With the money, Simplot purchased three teams of horses, some farm machinery, and a substantial supply of seed potatoes, then rented land and immersed himself in the business of growing potatoes. Shortly after beginning his new venture, Simplot learned of an electrically driven potato sorter that a machine shop in eastern Idaho had invented, the first of its kind in the state. Simplot visited the machine shop, took a look at the new piece of time-saving machinery, then convinced the proprietors to make a duplicate, which Simplot and another potato farmer purchased in 1932 for $254.

The electrically driven potato sorter proved to be a boon to Simplot's business, enabling him not only to sort his entire crop and his partner's crop, but also portions of other farmers' crops. Business was growing briskly and running smoothly until a feud developed between Simplot's partner and a potato broker, and Simplot and the electric potato sorter were caught in the middle. Simplot's partner had become angered when he learned that some of the potatoes sorted by the jointly-owned machine were being purchased by the broker. Irked that his property was indirectly benefitting his adversary, Simplot's partner ordered Simplot to stop, but Simplot, unwilling to limit his growing business intentionally, reportedly responded, "Let's flip for it." He won the coin toss, gaining full ownership of the electric potato sorter and full control over its future use.

Winning ownership of the potato sorter was a stroke of luck, but nearly all of Simplot's success by this point was owed to his legendary devotion to hard labor. During his first decade on his own, Simplot had relied on his indefatigable energy to create a burgeoning business, spending all his waking hours constructing hog pens, digging potato cellars, hauling sacks of potatoes, and tilling the soil, among the other endless and sundry duties required to keep his various ventures alive. That Simplot was able to withstand the debilitative effects of the Depression and prosper was a credit to his tireless efforts, but in the midst of the decade-long economic turmoil Simplot began to demonstrate another quality of character that would propel the young farmer toward the billions of dollars his business would later generate.

Federally funded programs aimed at providing relief to the economically devastated nation included the Bureau of Reclamation's prodigious work along the Snake River, which cut a swath of water across the state. To farmers working in an agriculturally intensive state, the work along the Snake River meant much, but Simplot was one of the few farmers to appreciate the ramifications such work would have on agricultural activity in Idaho. A reliable source of water would enable Simplot to diversify within and around the economy of the potato, supporting his entry into several agricultural and nonagricultural businesses that, once established, would strengthen his position considerably as a potato farmer. Though Simplot would continue to be regarded as a hard-working farmer, striving merely "to raise the average potato yield," as he put it, his foresightedness and decisive development of an interdependent collection of businesses powered his transformation from a "gol-durn potato farmer" into Idaho's preeminent industrialist and spawned one of the great American corporate empires.

### World War II Diversification

The development of Simplot's vertically integrated businesses occurred quickly, beginning with his move into onion farming in the late 1930s. From there, forays into other agricultural and nonagricultural areas followed in quick succession. By 1940, Simplot's large-scale onion growing operation had expanded to include facilities for dehydrating onions, which drew the attention of a scouting party for the U.S. Army's Quartermaster Corps the following year, as the nation prepared to enter the century's second great military struggle.

At the time of the scouting party's inspection of Simplot's onion-drying operations in the spring of 1941, vegetable dehydration was a crude science practiced by only a handful of businesses. There were only five vegetable-dehydrating factories in the country, none of which could dry and squeeze out the water from potatoes without mashing their cell structure. Spurred by the interest shown in his onion-drying facilities by the Quartermaster Corps, Simplot immersed himself and his resources into discovering a way to dehydrate potatoes, developing, after considerable experimentation, a revolutionary method to peel and dry potatoes efficiently and expeditiously. Simplot subsequently began producing dehydrated potatoes for the military on a scale that augured the beginning of the great achievements to come for the grade-school dropout. Over a three-year period between 1942 and 1945, Simplot produced an average of 33 million pounds of dried potatoes each year, or roughly one-third of the U.S. military's consumption during the war, catapulting him to the forefront of the potato industry.

As Simplot's business grew during the war, the range of his operations expanded, giving the fiercely independent Simplot the capability to fulfill his need for raw materials. When he ran short of wooden boxes for shipping his products overseas in 1943, Simplot built his own box production plant. When his box production facility was in need of a greater amount of lumber, he purchased his own lumber company. Simplot's supply of the fertilizer needed to grow his potatoes was cut off in 1944, so he decided to develop his own supply of fertilizer and paid a visit to a parcel of land owned by the Fort Hall Indian Reservation. Simplot scratched the surface with a scraper, searching for phosphate rock needed to produce chemical fertilizer, and, as he later related, "Damned if I didn't latch onto the biggest phosphate deposit west of Florida." Simplot leased the land, built a $1 million fertilizer plant with the help of a government loan, and began tapping into the largest phosphate mine in the west.

In a few short years, Simplot had branched out from potato growing and processing to cultivating and dehydrating onions, to mining, to producing fertilizer, and to logging, with each diversifying move bolstering his mainstay potato business. The sheer magnitude of his potato business led Simplot into another business area in 1945, when he built a small feedlot for cattle. The connection between cows and potatoes was the river of potato waste streaming from his processing plants, a mixture of peelings, sprouts, eyes, and other culls that Simplot mixed with alfalfa, barley, and several chemical supplements to make feed for cattle. From the potato, another Simplot business had been created, turning a farmer's modest hope of raising the average potato yield into a well-rounded, self-sufficient enterprise that had begun to take on the trappings of an agricultural conglomerate.

### Post-World War II Growth

The J. R. Simplot Company was incorporated following the diversified growth during the war years, its founding year in 1955 coming midway through the decade in which Simplot's pioneering contributions toward potato processing continued, resulting in an enormously beneficial discovery. During the 1950s, Simplot researchers developed a method to freeze potatoes, engendering frozen french fries and the new engine that would propel the J. R. Simplot Company's growth. During the 1960s, as Simplot's multifaceted agricultural and nonagricultural interests continued to flourish in the postwar era, Simplot developed a business relationship with Ray Kroc, a fast-food operator who became the single most important person in Simplot's business dealings. The fast-food chain Kroc had founded was none other than McDonald's, which had a nearly insatiable need for the frozen french fries first developed by the J. R. Simplot Company a decade earlier. Simplot would go on to become the single largest supplier of frozen french fries to the massive hamburger chain, adding another lucrative trade to the other prosperous enterprises operating under the Simplot name.

By the late 1960s, after two decades of resolute, postwar growth, Simplot's various businesses had made their creator a prominent fixture in American industry. Simplot grew more potatoes, owned more cattle, owned more land, and employed more people than any other Idahoan. He ranked as the largest potato processor in the world, the largest dryer and freezer of potatoes in the world, and owned processing plants, fertilizer plants, mining operations and other enterprises scattered across 36 states, in Canada, and overseas, making him Idaho's foremost industrialist and one of the biggest in the world. In the decades ahead, Simplot continued to demonstrate his resourcefulness and willingness to jump headfirst into new businesses. He began producing ethanol during the 1970s, using his ubiquitous potatoes to manufacture the alcohol-based fuel additive. During the 1980s, he used the waste water from potato process-ing for irrigation, he used cattle manure to help fuel methane gas plants, and he entered into various processed food niches.

By the end of the 1980s, Simplot stood atop a $1.2 billion-in-sales, privately held corporate powerhouse. In addition to five potato processing plants, five vegetable freezing plants, a major cattle-raising and meat-packing operation, and phosphate mines, Simplot was supported by his own construction company, his own finance company, his own transportation company, and his own cogeneration plants. Simplot's corporate reach, to be sure, extended far and wide, rivaling the largest, diversified conglomerates in the world and providing a firm foundation for future growth and long-term stability.

### The 1990s and Beyond

By the 1990s, Simplot was in his 80s and ready to hand over the reins of command to the next generation of Simplots. In 1994, control over the J. R. Simplot Company was devolved to an office of the chairman comprising three of Simplot's children and one grandchild, keeping management of the privately owned empire within the Simplot family. As these inheritors of the massive company chartered their course for the late 1990s and 21st century, the J. R Simplot Company stood solidly positioned in its numerous markets and pointed toward growth, its future stability predicated on the prodigious achievements of its past and the legacy of success established by J. R. Simplot.

### Principal Divisions

J.R. Simplot Company Food Group; Jr. Simplot Company, Minerals & Chemicals Group; J.R. Simplot Company—Agriculture Group; J.R. Simplot Company—Diversified Products Group.

### Further Reading

Brandt, Richard, "J. R. Simplot: Still Hustling, after All These Years," *Business Week,* September 3, 1990, p. 60.
Cohen, Barry, "J. R. Simplot Company," *Wall Street Transcript,"* July 8, 1968, p. 13,772.
Donahue, Christine, "Jacobson's Magic Turns Simplot's Idaho Spuds into Hot Potatoes," *Adweek's Marketing Week,* July 10, 1989, p. 21.
Erickson, Julie Liesse, "Simplot Wizardry Zaps Snack Market," *Advertising Age,* May 8, 1989, p. S6.
——, "Simplot Bites Back in Micro Snack War," *Advertising Age,* February 27, 1989, p. 4.
Glick, Daniel, "The Magic of 'Mr. Spud,' " *Newsweek,* November 27, 1989, p. 63.
Jones, Steven D., "First Frozen Food Barge Helps Bring French Fries to Orient," *Business Journal—Portland,* November 26, 1990, p. 3.
"J. R. Simplot Co. Acquires a Portion of Frozen Vegetable, Fruit Company," *Nation's Restaurant News,* September 21, 1992, p. 24.
Kiley, David, "Jacobson Sets a New Course for Simplot . . . Again," *Adweek's Marketing Week,* January 1, 1991, p. 7.
Murphy, Charles J.V., "Jack Simplot and His Private Conglomerate," *Fortune,* August 1968, pp. 122–172.
Portanger, Erik, "Pacific Dunlop Sells Most of Food Unit to Nestle, J. R. Simplot in Separate Deals," August 4, 1995, p. B10A.
Smith, Rod, "Simplot Buys ZX; Becomes Top Five in Cattle Production," *Feedstuffs,* January 10, 1994, p. 5.
Zuckerman, Laurance, "From Mr. Spud to Mr. Chip," *New York Times,* February 8, 1996, p. C1.

—Jeffrey L. Covell

## JM

# Johnson Matthey

# Johnson Matthey PLC

**2-4 Cockspur Street**
**Trafalgar Square**
**London SW1Y 5BQ**
**United Kingdom**
**(0171) 269-8400**
**Fax: (0171) 269-8433**

*Public Company*
*Incorporated:* 1891 as Johnson, Matthey & Co. Limited
*Employees:* 5,912
*Sales:* £2.27 billion (1995)
*Stock Exchanges:* London
*SICs:* 2752 Commercial Printing, Lithographic; 2819
Industrial Inorganic Chemicals, Not Elsewhere
Classified; 2834 Pharmaceutical Preparations; 2851
Paints, Varnishes, Lacquers, Enamels & Allied
Products; 2865 Cyclic Organic Crudes &
Intermediates, Organic Dyes & Pigments; 3341
Secondary Smelting & Refining of Nonferrous Metals;
3356 Rolling, Drawing & Extruding of Nonferrous
Metals, Except Copper & Aluminum; 3357 Drawing
& Insulating of Nonferrous Wire; 3569 General
Industrial Machinery & Equipment, Not Elsewhere
Classified; 3679 Electronic Components, Not
Elsewhere Classified; 5094 Jewelry, Watches,
Precious Stones & Precious Metals, Wholesale

Johnson Matthey PLC has been involved in the processing and marketing of precious metals since its founding in 1817. Although it is most widely known for its activities in platinum—it is a world leader in the refining, marketing, and technological development of the metal—Johnson Matthey has been increasingly positioning itself as a leader in advanced materials technology, including catalysts and pollution control systems, electronic materials, specialty chemicals, and pharmaceutical compounds. Through a joint venture with Cookson Group PLC, Johnson Matthey also manufactures decorative and specialized materials for the ceramics, plastics, paint, ink, and construction industries. The company has operations in 28 countries.

### Early History

The founder of Johnson Matthey was Percival Johnson, who in 1817 set himself up at 79 Hatton Garden in Holborn, London, as an ''Assayer and Practical Mineralogist.'' As such, he valued gold by applying chemical and physical tests to determine the exact quantity of gold in a bar. Johnson's business rapidly gained distinction when he began to offer to buy back the bars of gold that he assayed, thereby becoming the first London assayer to offer a guarantee of quality. In the early 1830s a small gold refinery was built at the Hatton Garden premises for the refining and assaying of gold bars that were then coming into London from Brazil. These were complex gold bars, containing impurities that were not easy to remove. Having successfully extracted platinum group metals from the bars, Johnson's technical prowess established the firm at the forefront of the London bullion market. The firm took full advantage of the gold rushes of California, from 1848, and of Australia, from 1851, while supplies of silver arrived throughout the 1850s and 1860s in the form of demonetized silver coinage—coinage that had gone out of circulation—from European states. A large-scale silver refinery was built at adjacent premises in Hatton Garden.

Johnson's interest in metallurgy had already brought him into contact with platinum, which had been the subject of considerable scientific interest throughout the early 19th century due to its strength and resistance to corrosive acids. He set up a small-scale refinery for the metal at Hatton Garden, with limited supplies coming from Colombia.

In 1838 George Matthey joined the company as an apprentice. Matthey's scientific talents, coupled with a shrewd business sense, was the driving force behind the company's development in the platinum industry during the second half of the 19th century. When the Great Exhibition was first proposed, Matthey persuaded Johnson to exhibit a number of platinum articles, together with specimens of other platinum-group metals: palladium, iridium, and rhodium. The display was a suc-

**Company Perspectives:**

*Johnson Matthey is a company with considerable pedigree. We have been supplying advanced materials for over 175 years. The real importance of this proud history is that it demonstrates the company's ability to maintain world leadership by adapting constantly to rapidly changing customer needs. Johnson Matthey has only maintained this position by remaining loyal to the values and beliefs which we contend are crucial to our business.*

cess, and Matthey became determined to make the company preeminent in the platinum business. He succeeded in gaining a more assured supply of the metal through direct arrangements with owners of a mine in the Ural mountains in Russia, then a newly discovered source. In the 1867 International Exhibition in Paris, the company exhibited a wide variety of platinum-manufactured goods on a scale never seen before. The exhibit was awarded a gold medal "for perfection and improvement in the working of platinum." Under Matthey's direction, platinum refining and fabricating grew from about 15,000 ounces in 1860 to about 75,000 ounces a year in the 1880s. The manufacturing of sulfuric acid boilers was the largest single use of platinum until the early 1900s.

The diversity of the company had actually been established from the beginning by Johnson. From the chemical refining of gold, Johnson produced a range of vitreous colors for the glass and pottery industries. He became the first refiner of nickel in Britain, with "nickel silver," popular as a silver plate. In 1833 production of silver nitrate began, its use being primarily for medical purposes in the form of lunar caustic. Over the following decades the development of photography generated considerable demand for silver nitrate.

By 1860, the year of Johnson's retirement, many of the company's present-day activities had been established: assaying and refining of bullion, platinum refining and marketing, the production of vitreous colors for glass and pottery manufacturers, and a constant experimentation and development of niche markets for other rare and precious metals. Hatton Garden remained the rather compact home of the refining, assaying, and experimental work so vital to the firm's future. There was, in addition, a small workshop in Clerkenwell, used for the manufacture of platinum dishes, crucibles, and other laboratory instruments. Twenty-five people were employed in 1860, with a trio of partners who dominated the firm's development over the next four decades: George Matthey, his younger brother Edward Matthey, and John Sellon—Percival Johnson's nephew. It was this trio, and their descendants, who were to dominate the company's development until the mid-20th century.

Over the next 50 years, technological and marketing progress coincided with a securing of supplies. Gold-refining facilities were improved and expanded at Hatton Garden in response to the arrival of African gold, and the silver refinery received constant supplies of demonetized coin from across Europe. The reputation of the assaying and chemical laboratories grew, and

in the mid-1880s Johnson Matthey succeeded in establishing itself as the ultimate referee of assayers and, as a certifier of ore quality, of South African Rand gold. Platinum supplies were secured from Russia through the co-operation of the metals houses of Quennessen of France and Heraeus of Germany; together the three European companies dominated the world platinum trade through control of this source, and ignored demands from the tzar for a refinery to be built within Russia. In 1894 the cartel was formalized through the creation of an association named The Allied Houses. In 1911 Johnson Matthey signed an agreement with the Nicolai Pavdinsky Company in the Urals, which gave Johnson Matthey the rights to mine a substantial body of platinum-bearing ore in return for Johnson Matthey building a local refinery. Despite World War I, and the chaos caused by the overthrow of the tzar, the plant was in full operation by 1918. However, no platinum ever reached London. During this period Johnson Matthey promoted the use of platinum as a corrosive-resistant electric conductor, and when platinum prices rose above gold for the first time in the 1900s the company encouraged the interest of jewelers. When the market for sulfuric acid boilers died at the turn of the century, fresh demand had been built up in other sectors.

In 1898 the company expanded its service to jewelers by purchasing new rolling mills in nearby Hop Gardens; here silver and gold alloys were formed into sheet, wire, and tube semi-manufactured goods. The company's interest in colors had been boosted in the late 1870s when it gained the British and Empire marketing rights to a variety of industrial glazes, stains, and enamels, including so-called rolled gold, from the Roessler company of Frankfurt. Roessler was shortly renamed Degussa; the two companies had a history of close association dating back to the 1860s. After initial skepticism, the Staffordshire potters took to the advanced colors and Johnson Matthey became an established supplier in that area. Meanwhile the company's interest in the rare and often novel metals was given a strong commercial footing with the 1870 acquisition of the Manchester-based Magnesium Metal Company. During the 40 years that followed, the Magnesium Metal Company's plant at Patricroft produced magnesium for flash photography and laboratory work, antimony for hardening bullet heads, vanadium for black dye and ink, and electrolytically-produced aluminum. It is thought that the statue of Eros in London's Piccadilly Circus—dedicated to the philanthropist seventh Earl of Shaftesbury—was made of aluminum from the Patricroft works.

In 1891 the company became Johnson, Matthey & Co. Limited, a private limited company, and during the 1890s and 1910s an increasing amount of departmentalism took place as the sons and nephews of the ruling trio took over the responsibilities, and increasingly delegated power to trusted clerks and technical experts. It was at this point that a corporate policy was adopted that remains at the heart of the company still: only to take part in activities in which the company could dominate. When a product's development fell out of the control of the company, Johnson Matthey's interests in it would be sold off.

### World War I through World War II Era

During World War I Johnson Matthey established itself as an innovative developer of strategic materials, despite significant supply disruptions affecting most of the metals that the company dealt with. The company was able to satisfy the Allied demand for products such as platinum catalysts, used to make sulfuric acid for explosives manufacturing, and magnesium powder, used to make incendiary bombs for dropping on German airships. In 1916 the company was brought under the direct control of the government, and platinum catalysts and electrical and magneto contacts for cars, airplanes, and tanks were manufactured in a modernized platinum workshop. The company expanded its production of silver nitrate to meet the demands of the photographic industry, and in 1916 began manufacturing its own liquid gold. In 1918 the colors division was given a firm production base through acquisition of the Sneyd color works at Burslem. A Birmingham branch of Johnson Matthey was established in the same year to supply the city's jewelry trade, and the Sheffield silversmith E.W. Oakes & Co. Ltd. was purchased. Despite difficulties in obtaining supplies, demands of industry were met and at the end of the war the air ministry gave an official message of thanks to the company for its supplies of high-precision equipment.

In 1918 John Sellon died. In order to secure a closer working relationship with the two South African mining houses that were of most significance to the company's gold activities, his shares in the company were offered in equal parts to Consolidated Gold Fields of South Africa Ltd. and to the Johannesburg Consolidated Investment Company. This is the origin of the controlling stake held by the Anglo American Corporation today.

During the early 1920s the company faced considerable problems due to continued disruptions in the supply of precious metals. From 1922 the South Africans refined their own gold, while regular supplies of platinum from the Urals had failed to resume after the war despite the ingenious attempts of Arthur Coussmaker. Coussmaker was a platinum expert with Johnson Matthey whose attempts to gain a secure supply of Russian platinum had involved deals with White Russian military forces and impromptu meetings with Soviet officials in western European cities. The difficulties of supply led to the early 1920s being a low point in the fortunes of Johnson Matthey. In 1924, however, Dr. Hans Merensky discovered the huge platinum-laden reef in the South African Transvaal that bears his name today. Coussmaker, by then a board member, made an immediate trip to the Transvaal where he identified the Rustenburg area as the most promising part of the reef. Consolidated Goldfields of South Africa and Johannesburg Consolidated Investments had mines in the Rustenburg district, and after an initial platinum mine boom in the mid-1920s those were the only mines operating in the slump that followed. Coussmaker persuaded the two mining houses to merge their platinum interests, and in 1931 the Rustenburg Platinum Company was formed. Johnson Matthey became a refiner and distributor for what was, and remains, the world's largest platinum mine. A smelting works and an electrolytic refinery were built at Brimsdown, in Essex, to extract the platinum metals according to a refining method established by Ernest Deering and Alan Powell of the Hatton Garden staff.

In 1919 Johnson Matthey joined N. M. Rothschild's bank and four other leading bullion brokers to form the London Gold Market, where a daily price-fixing still sets the price of gold. When gold supplies from South Africa ended, the sulfuric acid refinery at Hatton Garden was kept in operation through a constant stream of demonetized silver from central and eastern Europe. Much of this came via the Silberfeld brothers, initially based in Riga, who throughout the interwar period supplied Johnson Matthey with Russian Imperial coins and gold rubles, and with silver Maria Theresa coins from an office in Vienna. The company established branches in Warsaw and Prague, and came to own 75 percent of the Bank Powszechny Depozytowy in Poland.

Johnson Matthey's manufacturing capacity in this period was boosted by the acquisition in the early 1920s of the metal fabricating firm of R. Buckland & Son Ltd. In 1925 Johnson and Sons Smelting Works Ltd. of Brimsdown, Middlesex, was acquired. This was a sweeps, scrap, and residue refinery business that had been set up originally in the mid-19th century by a brother of Percival Johnson. During the 1930s the bullion refining and smelting operations were rationalized, the colors section was strengthened by a full-time research department, and a team of enterprising salesmen crossed Europe in motor cars.

At the outbreak of World War II Johnson Matthey was appointed government agent for the control and handling of platinum stocks, and manufactured items of the material grew in response to the rising demand. Products included electrical fine wires, electrodes, aircraft spark plugs, laboratory crucibles, and wire gauze catalysts for the preparation of nitric acid. Demand for platinum with a high iridium content led to Coussmaker's establishment of a refinery in Pennsylvania, where concentrates from Alaskan deposits were turned into contact tips for auto-magnets.

While bullion trade was severely limited by Bank of England supervision, and jewelry sales were almost forbidden, industrial demand—especially from photographic related industries—was strong for silver-based products. Some special uses of silver compounds included the manufacture of silver ball bearings for airplane engines, and desalination packs that enabled ditched airmen, or shipwrecked sailors, to survive on sea water. Bomb damage during the blitz of autumn 1940 resulted in the Brimsdown smelting works being put out of action temporarily, and the entire contents of the company museum and archive collection were destroyed.

### Postwar Expansion

With the end of the war came a period of rapid overseas growth for the company, much of it having been prepared from the early 1940s in expectation of a postwar boom. Representatives were sent around the world to study competitors, examine suppliers, and to establish new markets. Operations in North America, South Africa, Australia, and India were expanded as a result, with growth in Europe taking place later with the establishment of subsidiaries in France and the Netherlands in 1956, Italy in 1959, Sweden in 1960, Belgium in 1961, and Austria in 1962. Developments at home moved at an equally rapid pace: two colors factories in Staffordshire were opened immediately after the war, and in 1951 the colors section acquired Universal Transfers Co. Ltd. Johnson Matthey was now a market leader in the manufacture of color pigments and screen-printed transfers for the pottery and glass industries. In 1953 the Harlow Metal Co. Ltd. was formed to merge the company's mechanical production interests, and in 1957 a new platinum refinery was built at

Royston which brought together the company's refining operations. In 1954 Universal Matthey Products Ltd. was formed, to produce platinum catalysts for U.S. manufacturers of high-octane petrol. Enthusiasm by the North American auto industry for catalytic converters encouraged Johnson Matthey to conduct extensive research on the auto catalyst during the late 1950s and early 1960s. In 1962 L. B. Hunt was appointed director of research at new purpose-built laboratories at Wembley.

In 1963 Blythe Colours, based in Stoke-on-Trent, was acquired. This brought to Johnson Matthey an extended range of industrial colors, a worldwide network of agents, and a strong north European section based in the Netherlands. A consolidation of bullion activity took place during the 1950s and 1960s, culminating in the formation of Johnson Matthey Bankers Ltd. (JMB). Representing Johnson Matthey on the London gold market, JMB traded in the gold, silver, and precious metals produced by Johnson Matthey subsidiaries around the world.

A major reorganization of the company took place in 1966 and 1967, with the establishment of four divisions within which all the company's activities and subsidiaries were placed. These were the Jewelry and Allied Traders Division (JAT); the Chemical Division; the Industrial Division; and the Ceramic Division. A mechanical production unit was established to cater to the production needs of the four divisions. In 1969 expansion into Asia culminated with the establishment of Tanaka Matthey KK, a joint venture company with Tanaka Kikinzoku Kogyo KK of Japan. Japan is a major consumer of platinum jewelry, and the joint venture has enabled Johnson Matthey to dominate the market there.

### 1970s and 1980s

The 1970s were a decade of organic growth, with few acquisitions taking place. In 1980, however, a significant move into the U.S. jewelry trade—a business that was unfamiliar to the company—led to losses estimated at over £60 million and in 1981 the board looked to JMB to help make up the loss. JMB had done well from the spectacular rise in bullion activity that had accompanied the Soviet invasion of Afghanistan in 1980, and pressure was placed on the subsidiary to expand out of bullion-related loans and into high-risk lending in areas with which it was unfamiliar. The bank's loan book expanded, from £50 million at the end of 1981 to some £500 million by March 1984, with its contribution to group profits going from just under 25 percent in 1981 to more than 60 percent in 1983. By late 1983, however, the Bank of England had begun to suspect the quality of some of the loans. In the summer of 1984 their suspicions extended to cover the accounting practices of Arthur Young. In September 1984 the full extent of the bad loans taken on by JMB became apparent, and the Bank of England organized a bailout by JMB's creditors, shareholders, and U.K. clearing and merchant banks. The Bank of England purchased JMB for a token £1. The collapse of JMB was a disaster: in the words of *The Economist,* October 6, 1984, "The Johnson Matthey Parent Company lost its shirt, [and] its shareholders a lot of money." Meanwhile, in 1981 Johnson, Matthey & Co. Limited officially changed its name to Johnson Matthey Public Limited Company.

Charter Consolidated, effectively the holding company for Anglo American's interests in Johnson Matthey, found itself with a 38.3 percent stake in the group as a result of its assistance in the bailout of JMB, and sent in its own man, Neil Clarke, to become Johnson Matthey's chairman. In June 1985 Clarke appointed Gene Anderson as chief executive. Over the next five years the company was transformed, with £70 million of disposals made over the next two years, including an interest acquired in Wembley Stadium. The workforce was cut significantly while profits doubled to £64 million between 1986 and 1989. Seventy-four semiautonomous companies, loosely grouped into divisions, but many legally distinct and with their own boards, were reorganized into four operating divisions. These were the Catalytic Systems Division, which includes automotive exhaust and industrial air pollution control systems; the Materials Technology Division, which combines the group's rare-earth, pharmaceutical, and special materials interests; the Precious Metals Division, which acts as the sole marketing agency for Rustenburg Platinum and that controls the group's gold and silver marketing and refining businesses; and the Colour and Print Division that ties together the group's industrial colors and printing businesses. Investment in new plant and research was expanded, and in 1990 a new autocatalyst production plant was opened in Belgium to meet anticipated European demand. Research into the medical possibilities of platinum-based drugs was boosted, with cancer and HIV-fighting drugs developed.

In December 1989 Anderson resigned after failing to persuade the board to expand into nonplatinum areas. The proposed move would have diluted Anglo American's shareholding in Johnson Matthey through a share issue, and moved Johnson Matthey away from an increasing reliance on the Rustenburg mine. In testing the resolve of the South Africans, Anderson confirmed their control over the group. Almost immediately after Anderson resigned, Clarke also resigned. David J. Davies, Charter's deputy chairman, was transferred to become Johnson Matthey's chairman.

### 1990s and Beyond

Johnson Matthey's operating results in the early 1990s were generally positive, as the company began to see results from its late 1980s restructuring. Sales increased steadily from £1.73 billion in 1991 to £1.96 billion in 1994. Before-tax profits also increased steadily to a record £73.8 million in 1993 before declining in 1994 to £65.3 million thanks in part to the loss of a catalytic converter contract with General Motors toward the end of the year. Throughout this period, the company continued to restructure its operations, in particular in its Materials Technology Division. On the down side, the Precious Metals Division continued to provide more than 60 percent of Johnson Matthey's sales, while contributing only about one-quarter of the operating profit.

There were signs, however, that the company would be able to lessen the impact that precious metals had on its overall performance. The clearest signal came in 1993 when Charter Consolidated sold its 38.3 percent stake in Johnson Matthey for £342 million ($492 million). Although about 20 percent would remain in the indirect control of Anglo American since it was sold to Garrick Investment Holdings Ltd., a firm jointly held by Johannesburg Consolidated Investment Co. and Minorco of South Africa, both of which in turn were in the indirect control of Anglo American, the other 18.3 percent was sold to two British brokerage firms, Barclays de Zoete Wedd Ltd. and UBS Phillips & Drew Ltd, who were to sell the shares to investors, thus somewhat diluting Anglo American's control.

Anglo American remained in charge of Johnson Matthey through chairman Davies, but the next few years would see the company make its most aggressive expansion moves in years, all of which fell outside the precious metals area. In March 1994, Johnson Matthey and Cookson Group PLC, a U.K.-based metals-fabrication firm, combined their respective ceramics businesses into a 50–50 joint venture called Cookson Matthey Ceramics plc. This venture absorbed Johnson Matthey's Colour and Print Division, leaving the firm with the remaining three divisions and its share of the Cookson joint venture. Later in 1994, Johnson Matthey and Cookson entered into merger talks that would have created a global precious metals/industrial materials giant, but discussions were discontinued in November after the two sides could not come to an agreement on terms. The joint venture was not affected, however, and it subsequently posted positive results during its first two years in existence.

The Materials Technology Division was the next area to be targeted for growth with the 1995 acquisition of Advance Circuits Inc. (ACI) for £106.4 million ($170.2 million). ACI was a U.S.-based electronics industry supplier of multilayer printed circuit boards and plastic laminate packaging for semiconductors, the latter an emerging industry. The deal extended Johnson Matthey's range of products within the area of electronic materials, so much so that following the acquisition the company's divisions were restructured once more. The Materials Technology Division had two components—electronic materials and chemicals. The former, including the newly acquired ACI, would become a new Electronic Materials Division, a move that highlighted the importance of this area to the company's future. The latter was merged into an enlarged Precious Metals Division, which then consisted of platinum marketing and fabrication businesses, precious metal chemicals and platinum refining businesses, and worldwide gold and silver businesses. The new Electronic Materials Division was soon bolstered further through the early 1996 purchase from Cray Research Inc. of printed circuit board manufacturing facilities in Wisconsin. The company also planned to invest $200 million in capital expenditures from 1996 through 1998 in its newest division.

Johnson Matthey had its best year ever in 1995, with total sales of £2.27 billion and before-tax profits of £95.4 million. The initial success of its moves to lessen the importance of its Precious Metals Division bode well for the company's future as long as Anglo American's influence could be deflected enough for such moves to continue.

### Principal Subsidiaries

The Alta Group Inc. (U.S.A.); Arora-Matthey Limited (India; 40%); Cookson Matthey Ceramics plc (50%); Johnson Matthey & Brandenberger AG (Switzerland); Johnson Matthey (Aust) Limited (Australia); Johnson Matthey Catalog Company Inc. (U.S.A.); Johnson Matthey Electronics Inc. (U.S.A.); Johnson Matthey GmbH (Germany); Johnson Matthey Hong Kong Limited; Johnson Matthey Inc. (U.S.A.); Johnson Matthey Investments Inc. (U.S.A.); Johnson Matthey Japan Limited; Johnson Matthey Korea Limited; Johnson Matthey Limited (Australia); Johnson Matthey Limited (Canada); Johnson Matthey (New Zealand) Limited; Johnson Matthey (Pty) Limited (South Africa); Johnson Matthey SA (France); Johnson Matthey (Singapore) Pte Limited; Matthey Rustenburg Refiners (Pty) Limited (South Africa; 49%); Ryoka Matthey Corporation (Japan; 50%); SA Johnson Matthey NV (Belgium); Svenska Emissionsteknik AB (Sweden).

### Further Reading

Andrews, Walter, "Johnson Matthey Planning Three Acquisitions," *Electronic News,* July 4, 1994, p. 50.
"Cookson, Johnson Matthey Discontinue Merger Talks," *Wall Street Journal,* November 23, 1994, p. A11(W)/A9(E).
Dawkins, William, "Principles of a Profitable Alliance," *Financial Times,* November 6, 1995, p. 14.
Gooding, Kenneth, "Ceramics Superstars Aim High," *Financial Times,* August 18, 1995, p. 16.
"How Johnson Matthey Kept Bankers Up from Dusk to Dawn," *Economist,* October 6, 1984.
Hunt, L. B., "George Matthey and the Building of the Platinum Industry," *Platinum Metals Review,* April 1979.
"Johnson Matthey," *Investors Chronicle,* December 2, 1994, p. 70.
Levine, Bernard, "Johnson Matthey to Acquire Advance," *Electronic News,* August 21, 1995, p. 4.
McDonald, Donald, "The Rise of Johnson, Matthey & Co. Ltd.," in *A History of Platinum,* London: Johnson Matthey, 1961.

—Tom C. B. Elliott
—updated by David E. Salamie

# K2 Inc.

**4900 South Eastern Avenue, Suite 200**
**Los Angeles, California 90040**
**U.S.A.**
**(213) 724-2800**
**Fax: (213) 724-0470**

*Public Company*
*Incorporated:* 1959 as Anthony Pools, Inc.
*Employees:* 3,700 (est.)
*Sales:* $544.2 million (1995)
*Stock Exchanges:* New York
*SICs:* 3949 Sporting & Athletic Goods, Not Elsewhere
Classified; 2329 Men/Boy's Clothing, Not Elsewhere
Classified; 6719 Holding Companies, Not Elsewhere
Classified; 5091 Sporting & Recreational Goods

A thriving recreational and industrial products company, K2 Inc. owns a host of widely recognized recreational product brands, including K2, Olin, Exotech, ProFlex, Shakespeare, Hilton, Dana Design, and Stearns, and manufactures marine antennas, fiberglass utility poles, and residential insulative sheathing. For decades the company operated as Anthony Industries Inc., a company that began in the swimming pool business then diversified largely through acquisitions to become an industrial and recreational products conglomerate. During the mid-1990s, K2 Inc. derived approximately 65 percent of its sales and 60 percent of its pretax profits from recreational products, with its industrial products business accounting for the balance.

When Anthony Industries changed its name to K2 Inc. in mid-1996, the switch represented an acknowledgment by the company's management of the importance of a business acquired 11 years earlier, ski manufacturer K2 Corporation. At the time of the name change, K2 was Anthony Industries' largest division and its greatest contributor of sales, and it enjoyed brand name recognition that stretched around the globe. For these reasons alone, the name change seemed a fitting tribute to its strongest brand name, but the fact that Anthony Industries

adopted the name of one of its acquired companies also represented a fitting tribute to the importance acquisitions had played in its history.

During the two decades leading up to the symbolic name change, Anthony Industries had assumed an aggressive, yet prudent, acquisitive stance, dedicating the years to purchasing small companies with strong brand names. The result was a flourishing, ever-growing recreational and industrial products manufacturer by the 1990s, its business underpinned by a host of brand names that were driving robust growth. The company, in the years leading up to the name change, had become a conglomerate, but Anthony Industries had not always been a diversified competitor, ensconced, as the K2 name suggested, in the market for winter recreational products. For years, Anthony Industries was a one-product company, wholly concentrated on the production and sale of what perhaps represented the antithesis of winter recreation. The historical roots of Anthony Industries stretch back to the post-World War II era and to Los Angeles, where the company first began business as a manufacturer and installer of swimming pools.

## 1940s Origins

In 1946, Phil Anthony invested his entrepreneurial dreams in his new company, opening a business propitiously founded when the U.S. economy was about to embark on its historic postwar rebirth. Discretionary income levels for many Americans rose to unprecedented heights following the conclusion of World War II, as a decade-long economic depression and four years of military conflagration gave way to an era of prosperity. For Anthony, the resurgence of the U.S. economy would mean a greater demand for the sole product his new company sold— swimming pools—something only those with ample savings could afford. Located in Los Angeles, Anthony Pools, Inc., as the company was incorporated in 1959, enjoyed success as a marketer and installer of in-ground swimming pools, eventually becoming the largest builder of swimming pools in its field. Anthony's company would score its greatest success, however, under the stewardship of Bernard I. "Bif" Forester, who would lead the company toward diversification and engender the multifaceted conglomerate that thrived during the 1990s.

## Company Perspectives:

*K2 is dedicated to the continuous improvement of all products and services to meet our customers' needs, allowing us to prosper as a business and to provide an attractive return for our shareholders, the owners of our business. Improvement of products and services will be accomplished by focusing on the processes that make up our business and through the involvement of all employees to help with the improvement of these processes. We will strive to provide innovative and improved products and services to our customers by understanding their requirements and anticipating their future needs. We recognize that our people are our most valuable resource. We are committed to providing training and fostering a work environment of teamwork and shared values that will allow our objective of continuous improvement to be achieved. We will endeavor to be a good corporate citizen at all times by engaging in activities that have a positive social and economic impact on the communities in which we work and the world at large.*

Forester joined Anthony Pools in 1966, when the company still operated exclusively as a pool contractor in Southern California. Three years after Forester's arrival, Anthony Pools changed its name to Anthony Industries, Inc. Then, in 1973, Forester took charge, assuming control over a small company that had diversified once in 1969, acquiring mobile home manufacturer Explorer Motor Home Corp., but still relied overwhelmingly on one product: concrete in-ground swimming pools. Forester would waste little time in taking the company in several new directions, directing a diversification program that would have a lasting effect on Anthony Industries.

### Diversification Begins in 1974

One year after assuming leadership over Anthony Industries, Forester completed two pivotal acquisitions, as would become his habit during the ensuing two decades. In 1974, Anthony Industries acquired Chicago-based Hilton Athletic Apparel, a maker of bowling shirts and jackets, among other apparel items, and also acquired a 50 percent interest in Simplex Industries, Inc. By 1978, Anthony Industries had acquired the remaining interest in Simplex Industries, thereby gaining full control over what would become an integral part of its industrial products business. In the years ahead, Anthony Industries' Simplex division would manufacture a wide range of laminated, coated, and reinforced paperboard products, selling these products to the residential and manufactured housing industries, as well as to the container and industrial packaging industries.

Under Forester's guiding hand, Anthony Industries developed into a company supported by two main business segments: recreational products and industrial products. The acquisition of Simplex had paved the way for the future growth of the company's industrial side, while the addition of Hilton Athletic Apparel had marked the beginning of Forester's program to develop further Anthony Industries' recreational side. The company's next acquisition fulfilled both objectives, diversifying

the mix of recreational products and adding to the industrial products manufactured by Simplex. The acquisition, completed in 1980, brought the Shakespeare Company into the Anthony Industries fold, leading the Los Angeles-based swimming pool, athletic apparel, and industrial products company in four new directions. As part of the deal, Anthony Industries acquired Shakespeare Fishing Tackle, a well-known maker of fishing rods, reels, and tackle, and three businesses involved in industrial markets, Shakespeare Electronics & Fiberglass, Shakespeare Monofilament, which manufactured custom-blended extruded lines used in paper weaving and in products such as automobile tire cords, and Shakespeare Flexible Controls, which was sold in 1981.

The acquisition of Shakespeare represented a significant step in Anthony Industries' bid to become a recreational and industrial powerhouse, opening doors to each market. Meanwhile, as the company slowly began to take on the characteristics that would identify it as a conglomerate in the 1990s, a company that would play a defining role in Anthony Industries' future was enjoying booming business 1,000 miles to the north. There, on a small island near Seattle, Washington, K2 Corporation was revolutionizing the ski industry with its fiberglass skis and their hallmark red, white, and blue stripes. The company originated with the Kirschner Manufacturing Co., a small, family-owned business run by Otto Kirschner and his two sons, Don and William. Kirschner Manufacturing began operating at roughly the same time Phil Anthony started Anthony Pools, doing business during the postwar years as a designer and manufacturer of fiberglass animal splints, before broadening its business scope to include a line of ''chew-proof'' fiberglass dog cages.

The Kirschner family would record its greatest success, however, with another use for fiberglass when William Kirschner borrowed a pair of skis in the late 1950s to use as a pattern and then constructed his own pair of fiberglass skis. At the time of Kirschner's home experiments, Howard Head and his all-black Head aluminum skis had revolutionized the sport of skiing, introducing the first major technological breakthrough to sweep through the ski industry since skiing had become a popular recreational activity. A short time after Head introduced his skis in 1950, aluminum skis sold out in retail shops across the country, quickly supplanting the wood skis that had been the only choice for decades, and made Head skis the preferred choice for legions of skiers. Kirschner and his fiberglass skis would change all that, however, giving birth to K2 Corporation and creating what would become Anthony Industries' most valuable asset.

### 1967: The Founding of the ''Other'' K2

By 1964, Kirschner Manufacturing was ready to add fiberglass skis to its product line, producing 250 pairs of the revolutionary skis that year. The skis quickly sold out, and the following year 1,600 pairs were made, followed by 4,000 pairs in 1966, when William Kirschner decided the time was right to form his own company, along with his brother Don, to manufacture skis. In 1967, K2 Corporation was formed, named after the two Kirschner brothers and the world's second highest mountain, Mount Godwin Austen (K2) in the Karakoram Range in Kashmir. At the time of K2 Corporation's founding Head skis were still the most popular skis in the United States. But

Kirschner's colorful fiberglass skis eclipsed Head and all other domestic ski manufacturers by the late 1970s, propelled by strong marketing, the technological innovation the skis represented, and by affiliations with prominent ski celebrities, most notably, Jean-Claude Killy and Phil and Steve Mahre, the American twins who won the gold and silver medal, respectively, in the slalom event at the 1984 Winter Olympic Games.

As K2 Corporation grew from fledgling upstart to dominant champion, the company underwent several ownership changes, although its management remained essentially autonomous throughout the various shifts in ownership. The company's initial success during the late 1960s came too quickly, creating a sprawling enterprise that Kirschner found difficult to manage. Consequently, he sold K2 Corporation to Cummins Engine Company in 1970, when the Indiana-based manufacturing company was in the midst of diversifying into banking, ranching, and leisure goods. Six years later, Kirschner and five other partners regained control of K2 Corporation and formed Sitca Corporation as a holding company for K2 Corporation. Several seasons of low snowfall in the early 1980s, however, drained K2 Corporation's cash flow, forcing the company to seek an equity partner to ameliorate its financial difficulties. It was an opportunity Forester and Anthony Industries could not pass up.

### 1985 Acquisition of K2

Supported by an exceptionally strong brand image, K2 Corporation and the nearly $30 million the ski manufacturer generated in sales each year represented a perfect fit to Anthony Industries' operations. In 1985, negotiations were concluded, and Anthony Industries acquired Sitca Corporation and its sole asset, K2 Corporation, for $3.3 million, five years after the Shakespeare acquisition was completed. During the years immediately following the purchase of K2 Corporation, Anthony Industries continued to acquire additional companies, including Stearns Manufacturing Co. in 1988, a manufacturer of flotation devices, and Olin Corp. in 1989, the country's number two ski manufacturer behind K2 Corporation. The company's greatest surge of growth would take place during the 1990s, however, when annual sales leaped from under $300 million to more than $500 million during the first half of the decade.

### Growth in the 1990s

During the 1990s, Anthony Industries acquired several sporting goods manufacturers and diversified its existing businesses, particularly its K2 division, intent on broadening its product mix to take advantage of its existing distribution network comprising sporting goods chains and other retailers throughout the country. On the look for "companies that are the best of the class," as one company official put it, Anthony Industries would add greatly to what already stood as a solid collection of brands and companies. At the beginning of the 1990s, the company's Anthony Pools division, the progenitor of all that followed from its establishment in 1946, ranked as the largest builder of in-ground swimming pools in the United States; its Shakespeare Fishing Tackle group operated as a leading domestic producer and distributor of fishing rods, reels, and tackle; K2 ranked as the leading brand of alpine skis; and Hilton competed as the top U.S. brand of jackets, shirts, and other apparel for the advertising, specialty, and screen-print

markets. Not to be forgotten among the array of the company's recreational business was Anthony Industries' industrial products segment, which contributed a mighty 68 percent of the company's total annual profits. In all, the growing Anthony Industries empire was a solid, well-rounded enterprise, with sales spread across nine distinct product categories in the recreational segment and three distinct product groups in the industrial segment.

As the 1990s began, Anthony Industries added to its industrial products segment first by acquiring in 1990 Nymofil, Ltd., a Britain-based business that was merged into Shakespeare Monofilament. In 1991 the Stanhope decorative light pole business was acquired to strengthen the company's Shakespeare Electronic & Fiberglass business. Next, Anthony Industries moved on the recreational front, acquiring Girvin, Inc., the maker of ProFlex mountain bicycles, in 1993. Meanwhile, through its K2 division, the company had entered another fast-growing market to go along with its foray in the burgeoning market for mountain bikes, introducing a line of K2 snowboards in 1990, and then extending the K2 brand name further by launching a line of K2 Exotech in-line skates in 1994.

By 1995, nearly every Anthony Industries recreational brand was flourishing, with new brands being acquired at a consistent rate, such as the February 1995 purchase of Dana Design Ltd., a Bozeman, Montana-based maker of backpacks. The company's in-line skates, after recording $10.5 million in sales for its inaugural year, generated $38.9 million in sales in 1995, an enormous 267 percent increase. K2 snowboards were strongly positioned in a market growing 30 percent annually, enabling the company to achieve a 125 percent annual growth rate in its snowboard business between 1992 and 1995, when K2 snowboards collected $26.1 million in sales. Shakespeare Fishing Tackle recorded encouraging growth during 1995 as well, posting a nearly 25 percent increase in sales to reach $85.3 million for the year.

Against the backdrop of strong growth, there were several important decisions made during the year that prepared Anthony Industries for the years ahead. In October 1995, Anthony Industries signed a letter of intent to sell the company's Anthony Pools division, the original business established in 1946. Then, one month later, Forester announced his plans to retire as chief executive officer, a post he had occupied since 1973. Forester stayed on as chairman, but in January 1996 he passed the reins of command to Richard M. Rodstein, who would guide the company as president and chief executive officer as it entered the late 1990s. In March 1996, the sale of the Anthony Pools division was completed, with the founding business passed to the corporate hands of General Aquatics, Inc. With the Forester era brought to a close and the divestiture of Anthony Pools completed, Anthony Industries made a clean sweep of the vestiges of its past by adopting K2 Inc. as its new name in June 1996, 50 years after the Anthony name had first emerged. As the company moved ahead toward the late 1990s and the beginning of the 21st century, a substantial portion of its growth was expected to come from new products and acquisitions. In 1995, the company derived roughly a quarter of its total sales from products introduced within the previous two years. Bearing this in mind, Rodstein explained the future course of the newly named K2 Inc., stating, "Our mission is simple: To have lots of new products in the closet."

### Principal Subsidiaries

Shakespeare Company; Sitca Corporation; K2 Corporation; SMCA, Inc.; Girvin Inc.; Dana Design Ltd.

### Principal Operating Units

Active Apparel and Outdoor Group; Dana Design; Wilderness Experience; Garuda; Speed Zone Race Gear; Girvin/ProFlex; Hilton Active Apparel; K2; Shakespeare Electronics & Fiberglass; Shakespeare Fishing Tackle—Domestic; Shakespeare Fishing Tackle—International; Shakespeare Monofilament; Simplex Products; Stearns Active Water Sports Equipment.

### Further Reading

"Anthony Industries," *Sporting Goods Business,* February 1995, p. 68.

Bamett, Chris, "Anthony Industries: Combining R&D with Luck," *California Business,* January 1992, p. 12.

Byrne, Harlon S., "Anthony Industries: Manufacturer of K-2 Skis Heads for New Peak," *Barron's,* April 19, 1993, p. 46.

Cole, Benjamin Mark, "Anthony Industries Plans Secondary Offering," *Los Angeles Business Journal,* May 22, 1995, p. 5.

"K2 Can Do," *Forbes,* January 22, 1990, p. 156.

Labate, John, "Anthony Industries," *Fortune,* November 28, 1994, p. 189.

Leibowitz, David S., "Small Can Be Beautiful," *Financial World,* December 23, 1986, p. 120.

——, "Three Cheers for Eclectics," *Financial World,* November 12, 1991, p. 100.

Lubove, Seth, "Astro Chicken to the Rescue," *Forbes,* January 22, 1996, p. 68.

McEvoy, Christopher, "Acquiring Minds," *Sporting Goods Business,* August 1995, p. 44.

——, "Anthony Adds Dana Design to Its Pack of Companies," *Sporting Goods Business,* March 1995, p. 28.

Mehlman, William, "Anthony Synthesizes Winner from Pools, Skis, Industrials," *The Insider's Chronicle,* June 12, 1989, p. 1.

Paris, Ellen, "A Conglomerate That Works," *Forbes,* November 28, 1988, p. 52.

"Who's Fishing for This Tackle Maker," *Business Week,* October 3, 1988, p. 120.

—Jeffrey L. Covell

# Keithley Instruments Inc.

28775 Aurora Road
Solon, Ohio 44139-1891
U.S.A.
(216) 248-0400
Fax: (216) 248-6168
http://www.keithley.com

*Public Company*
*Incorporated:* 1955
*Employees:* 659
*Sales:* $109.58 million
*Stock Exchanges:* New York
*SICs:* 3825 Instruments to Measure Electricity; 3829
Measuring & Controlling Devices, Not Elsewhere
Classified

Celebrating its 50th anniversary in 1996, Keithley Instruments Inc. is one of the world's leading manufacturers of specialty electronic testing and measurement devices. While its sales are just a fraction of its primary competitor, multi-billion-dollar Hewlett Packard Co., Keithley Instruments has carved out a niche for itself in the high-margin, high-tech end of the electronic monitoring industry. The company's award-winning products are sold in more than 40 countries around the world and its stock began trading on the New York Stock Exchange in 1995. Under the direction of Joseph P. Keithley in the mid-1990s, Keithley Instruments shifted its primary focus to the fast-growing semiconductor testing market. This change in strategy was expected to rejuvenate the company's growth, which had stagnated in the early 1990s.

### Postwar Origins

Keithley was founded in 1946 by Joseph F. Keithley, who graduated from the Massachusetts Institute of Technology with a master's degree in engineering in 1937. After working for Bell Telephone Laboratories in the late 1930s, Keithley served at the U.S. Naval Ordnance Laboratory during World War II. At the war's end, he moved to Cleveland to take a job with Massa Labs. But when the company relocated in 1946, Keithley elected to stay on in Cleveland and establish his own company.

His first product, the "Phantom Repeater," amplified low-level electric signals so that they could be measured by more standard equipment. The device was used by physicists, chemists, and engineers in the development of hearing aids and amplifiers, for example. Keithley later noted that the Phantom Repeater was only "a reasonable success," but it did win him a cost-plus fixed-fee contract with the U.S. Navy.

Keithley worked alone, assembling mostly outsourced components until 1950, when he hired his first employee. Keithley added to its product line that year as well. On the advice of war buddy and Bryn Mawr head of physics Dr. Walter Michels, Joseph Keithley developed a "high input impedance DC voltmeter." Dubbed the "Model 200," this device provided researchers with a convenient way to test and measure the performance of electrical insulators—the plastic covering on a copper wire, for example. *Barron's* writer William M. Alpert later explained that the Model 200 could measure "how good [an insulator] was at keeping the electrical juice from spilling into where it did not belong." Keithley later told Jeff Dorsch of *Chilton's Electronic News* that the machine brought his young company "reasonable prosperity."

Over the course of the 1950s, Keithley developed three primary lines of highly sensitive instruments: general purpose electrometers, microvolt meters, and picoammeters. Picoammeters, which measure electric currents in terms of picoamperes, provide a good example of the sensitivity of Keithley's devices. One picoampere equals a millionth of a millionth of an ampere, or a millionth of a millionth of the amount of current it takes to power a 100-watt light bulb.

Fueled indirectly by hefty governmental expenditures on research during the Cold War era, Keithley enjoyed 30 percent to 40 percent annual sales growth in the 1950s, surpassing $268,000 in annual sales in 1956 and $1 million in 1960. Keithley incorporated in 1955.

### Product and Geographic Expansion During the 1960s and 1970s

During the 1960s, Keithley shifted its focus somewhat to the development of products for America's growing space program, with a special emphasis on satellite research probes. These efforts evolved into Keithley's special products division, which served such diverse disciplines as oceanography, biomedicine, nuclear energy, geophysics, and analytical chemistry, as well as industrial quality control. The company's product line grew and evolved throughout the decade, adopting digital display, for example.

Keithley undertook foreign growth relatively early in its history. Having placed sales representatives throughout Europe by 1963, Keithley established its first overseas office in Lausanne, Switzerland. The company founded assembly and repair operations in Munich in 1966 and created a British subsidiary, Keithley Instruments, Ltd., in 1967.

Keithley made an initial public offering in 1964 and moved to a purpose-built headquarters in Solon, a suburb of Cleveland, in 1967. Sales increased from $1.3 million in 1960 to $4.9 million in 1970.

The company began to apply its expertise to the development of testing and measuring devices for medical and industrial applications in the 1970s. At the same time, Keithley devices were evolving to incorporate newly developed technologies like integrated circuits and micro-processors.

In 1973, a 58-year-old Joseph Keithley set his long-term plan for transfer of corporate leadership into motion by promoting Thomas G. Brick to president. Keithley retained the chair and chief executive office. The end of the decade brought a major transformation of Keithley's corporate culture. Indeed, the company's rapid growth had spawned several problems, including excessive labor expenses, a high rate of in-warranty repairs, and poor employee relations. Worse, some managers felt that the company was not prepared for the possibility of future growth. In order to combat these interrelated problems, the company adopted a "team manufacturing approach," forming 12-person squads of employees responsible for the production of specific devices from start to finish. This strategy, which was fully implemented by 1982, reduced in-warranty repairs by 15 percent, lowered absenteeism by 75 percent, increased employee productivity by 90 percent, and helped resolve labor-management relations.

### Acquisitions in the 1980s

This fundamental culture shift set the stage for continued growth in the 1980s, fueled in part by acquisitions and overseas expansion. Keithley broadened its global reach with the creation of subsidiaries and sales offices in Austria, Switzerland, Hong Kong, and Japan during the decade. By 1988, the company had eight overseas subsidiaries and 23 international representatives, and foreign revenues constituted nearly half of annual sales. The decline of the U.S. dollar in the 1980s made Keithley's international operations evermore vital during this period of domestic recession. While much of the electronics industry suffered through one of its most difficult decades, Keithley's

annual sales increased from $27.8 million in 1980 to $45 million in 1985 and $88.7 million in 1989. Profits more than quadrupled, from $1 million in 1980 to a high of over $5.4 billion in 1988.

During the mid- to late 1980s, Keithley paved the way to what would become a key avenue of growth. In 1983, the company created a joint venture with Boston's Data Acquisition Systems, Inc. to computerize data collected by Keithley instruments. Keithley acquired the remainder of the venture in 1984 and merged it into itself as the data acquisition and control division. Having accumulated $9 million in cash by early 1987, Keithley acquired three companies with interrelated products through 1989. That year the company merged these three firms—Adaptable Laboratory Software, Inc., Macmillan Software Co., and MetraByte Corp.—as the Keithley MetraByte division. This division created software and hardware that converted raw data into easily read and interpreted graphics and charts. Keithley MetraByte also made highly durable "field PCs" that could endure impacts of up to 100 times the force of gravity. According to Reed Abelson of *Fortune* magazine, by 1989 Keithley boasted "the broadest product line in personal computer hardware and software to collect and analyze scientific and engineering information."

The combination of acquisitions and internal growth more than doubled sales from $45 million in 1985 to over $100 million in 1990. But at the same time, profits peaked at $5.4 million in 1988, then started to slide in the waning years of the decade as defense and research cutbacks decimated the budgets of Keithley's primary customers. Annual sales eroded from $100.6 million in 1990 to $94.7 million in 1992, and net income plummeted to a loss of $12.5 million. With its core market declining, Keithley reduced its work force from 716 in 1991 to 625 in 1993. It seemed only a glitch among the mega-downsizings of the early 1990s, but put a significant damper on morale nonetheless.

### Change in Leadership and Change in Direction in Early 1990s

In 1991 Joseph F. Keithley conferred voting control and the chairmanship over to his son, Joseph P. Keithley. The elder Keithley continued to work at his namesake firm under the simple title of "founder." He was widely recognized as "a pioneer in high-precision instrumentation." In 1992, he was inducted into the National Academy of Engineering, and in 1996 the American Physical Society created a cash award in honor of his contribution to the field of measurement and testing.

Realizing that he could not rely on defense and research budgets for long-term corporate growth, the younger Keithley sought a new direction for his company. He found it in Keithley's own systems division, a business segment that had developed and manufactured Automated Parametric Testers (APT), devices that examined semiconductor chips for quality control, since the early 1970s. The semiconductor production process involved the creation of eight-inch wafers, each of which held about 300 individual computer chips. APTs tested the chips near the end of the production process with sensitive electrical measurements.

In 1994, Keithley augmented that business with the $3.5 million acquisition of a new semiconductor testing technology from IBM. This new device, dubbed the Quantox Oxide Monitoring System, improved on older quality control methods on several levels. Quantox was designed to be implemented early in the production process, allowing for the disposal of inferior product before the manufacturer had invested too much in it. The device also reduced inspection time from up to five days to 15 minutes. And since it was a "contactless" process, it did not require the destruction of every wafer tested. In 1996, Joseph F. Keithley told *Cleveland Magazine* that "Every [integrated circuit] fabrication line in the world can benefit from this." Keithley agreed to pay IBM a royalty on each of the $500,000 machines.

The CEO made it clear that semiconductor process monitoring would become a key aspect of Keithley's future strategy. In 1994 alone, the company invested over $1 million in development of the new device. Chairman Keithley told *Crain's Cleveland Business* that he expected Quantox and similar devices to become the company's most important products, bringing in $10 million to $20 million in annual sales by the end of the decade. In 1995, products sold to semiconductor manufacturers constituted one-fourth of Keithley's sales. Although Keithley enjoyed a technological edge in the realm of semiconductor process monitoring, it faced a formidable competitor in Hewlett Packard, which controlled an estimated 66 percent of the global parametric testing market.

Investor confidence in the proprietary Quantox technology boosted Keithley's stock from less than $10 in the early 1990s to over $30 in 1995. But the stock was thinly traded; the family still owned a large proportion of the equity, and Keithley Instruments only had about 600 stockholders. In order to draw the attention of institutional investors and obtain access to more credit, the firm distributed two shares to each of its employees and encouraged existing shareholders to give their shares to a spouse in order to increase the company's float. In 1995, Keithley's shares earned a spot on the New York Stock Exchange.

Quantox wasn't the only promising development at Keithley in the mid-1990s. By this time, the company's MetraByte division had become a key player in the emerging market for "virtual instruments:" computer components that could measure current and/or voltage, then quantify the resulting data. *Individual Investor's* David Sterman called MetraByte a "golden goose" at Keithley. Even the venerable instruments division bounced back, registering double-digit sales growth in 1995.

Analyst Kevin Morrow of the Ohio Co. credited Joseph P. Keithley, who had assumed the additional responsibilities of president and chief executive officer upon the early retirement of Thomas G. Brick in 1994, with the company's newfound success. He told David Prizinsky of *Crain's Cleveland Business* that "There was no sales growth until J.P. took over the company a year ago. He lit a fire under everyone." That conflagration helped boost revenues to a record-high $109.6 million in 1995, when net income reached a near-record $4.9 million.

## Principal Subsidiaries

Keithley International Investment Corp.; Keithley Foreign Sales Corp.; Keithley Instruments SARL (France); Keithley Instruments GmbH (Germany); Keithley Instruments Ltd. (U.K.); Keithley Instruments SRL (Italy); Keithley Instruments Far East KK (Japan); Keithley Instruments BV (The Netherlands); Keithley Instruments SA (Switzerland).

## Principal Divisions

Test Instrumentation Group; Keithley MetraByte Division; Radiation Measurements Division.

## Further Reading

Abelson, Reed, "Keithley Instruments," *Fortune,* July 31, 1989, p. 108.

Alpert, William M., "High-Tech Niche Picker," *Barron's,* January 18, 1988, pp. 18, 20.

Bottoms, David T., "J.P. Keithley Eyes the '93 Test and Measurement Market," *Electronics,* January 11, 1993, p. 14.

Brick, Thomas G., "How to Succeed in Exporting," *Industry Week,* November 7, 1988, p. 14.

Card, David, "Why Keithley Instruments Hides in the Shadows," *Electronic Business,* October 15, 1988, pp. 82, 84.

Dillon, Nancy, "Field PC Stands Up to Harshest Environments, but at a Price," *InfoWorld,* January 9, 1995, p. 42.

Dorsch, Jeff, "Keithley Founder Exiting Post, Not Firm," *Chilton's Electronic News,* February 4, 1991, p. 22.

Gerdel, Thomas W., "Firm Focuses on Electronic Future," *Cleveland Plain Dealer,* June 19, 1984, p. 9E.

———, "Keithley's Comeback," *Cleveland Plain Dealer,* February 21, 1996, p. 1C.

———, "Keithley Sees New Software Keying Growth," *Cleveland Plain Dealer,* July 20, 1987, p. 5B.

"Ingredients for Innovation," *EDN,* October 4, 1990, p. 44.

"Keithley, IBM in Wafer Test Pact," *Electronic News,* May 30, 1994, p. 4.

"Keithley Profit, Sales Dip in '94," *Electronic News,* December 12, 1994, p. 20.

"Keithley, UTI End Acquisition Deal," *Electronic News,* February 6, 1995, p. 52.

King, Michael L., "Semi-Tough," *Cleveland Magazine,* January 1996, pp. 19–20, 29–30.

Livingston, Sandra, "Purchase of MetraByte to be Keithley's Largest," *Cleveland Plain Dealer,* December 14, 1987, p. 9E.

Long, Karen R., "Two Ohioans to Enter Engineering Hall of Fame," *Cleveland Plain Dealer,* May 9, 1992, pp. 1E, 3E.

Maturi, Richard J., "Taking Measure: It Pays Off Handsomely for Keithley Instruments," *Barron's,* May 18, 1987, p. 103.

Pascarella, Perry, "'Change Champion' Builds Teamwork," *Industry Week,* March 19, 1984, p. 61.

Prizinsky, David, "Keithley Finds New Direction," *Crain's Cleveland Business,* July 31, 1995, pp. 3–4.

"Profile: The First 50 Years at Keithley Instruments, Inc.," *Measurements & Control,* February 1996.

Sterman, David, "Keithley's Key," *Individual Investor,* January 1996.

Talbott, Stephen, "Keithley on Growth Search," *Cleveland Plain Dealer,* February 12, 1987, p. 8C.

—April Dougal Gasbarre

# ❋ Kimberly-Clark

# Kimberly-Clark Corporation

P.O. Box 619100
Dallas, Texas 75261-9100
U.S.A.
(214) 281-1200
Fax: (214) 281-1289

*Public Company*
*Incorporated:* 1880 as Kimberly & Clark Company
*Employees:* 55,341
*Sales:* $13.79 billion (1995)
*Stock Exchanges:* New York Midwest Pacific
*SICs:* 2297 Nonwoven Fabrics; 2381 Dress & Work
    Gloves, Except Knit & Leather; 2621 Paper Mills;
    2676 Sanitary Paper Products; 3841 Surgical &
    Medical Instruments & Apparatus; 4581 Airports,
    Flying Fields & Airport Terminal Services

With its 1995 merger with Scott Paper Co., Kimberly-Clark Corporation solidified its position as the number two player in the paper products industry and aimed its sights on number one, Procter & Gamble. The combined Kimberly-Clark and Scott operations created a giant, with manufacturing operations in 33 countries; the company includes more than 150 countries in its sales efforts. In addition to its powerful consumer paper products business, which includes market leaders in tissues and feminine-, child-, and incontinence-care products, Kimberly-Clark also continues to operate pulp and newsprint operations (the company's original areas of operation) and an aircraft services and air transportation unit, headed by Midwest Express Airlines.

### Early History

Kimberly, Clark & Company was founded in Neenah, Wisconsin, in 1872 as a partnership of four men: John A. Kimberly, Charles B. Clark, Frank C. Shattuck, and Kimberly's cousin, Havilah Babcock. The company began the first paper mill in Wisconsin. Its initial product was newsprint made from linen and cotton rags. Within six years the company expanded by acquiring a majority interest in the nearby Atlas paper mill, which converted ground pulpwood into manila wrapping paper. The business was incorporated in 1880 as Kimberly & Clark Company, with John Kimberly as president. In 1889 the company constructed a large pulp- and paper-making complex on the Fox River. The community that grew up around the factory was named Kimberly, in honor of John Kimberly.

Among the company's early innovations was the paper used for rotogravure, a procedure for printing photographs with a rotary press. In 1914 researchers working with bagasse, a pulp by-product of processed sugar cane, produced creped cellulose wadding, or tissue. During World War I this product, called cellucotton, was used to treat wounds in place of scarce surgical cottons. At that time field nurses also discovered that cellucotton worked well as a disposable feminine napkin. The company later recognized the commercial potential of this application and, in 1920, introduced its Kotex feminine napkin.

In 1924 the company introduced another disposable tissue product, Kleenex, to replace the face towels then used for removing cold cream. A survey showed, however, that consumers preferred to use Kleenex as a disposable handkerchief, prompting the company to alter its marketing strategy entirely. Nationwide advertisements promoting Kleenex for its current use began in 1930, and sales doubled within a year. Uncomfortable marketing such personal-care items as feminine napkins, Kimberly & Clark had created a separate sales company, International Cellucotton Products, which it contracted to manufacture Kotex and Kleenex.

### Expansion from 1920s to 1960s

During the 1920s the company built a Canadian pulp mill and power plant called Spruce Falls Power and Paper Company in Kapuskasing, Ontario. In 1925 the company formed what would become Canadian Cellucotton Products Limited, for marketing cellucotton products internationally. The following year Kimberly & Clark, in partnership with the New York Times Company, added a newsprint mill to the Spruce Falls complex and expanded its pulping capacity.

The company was reorganized and reincorporated in 1928 as Kimberly-Clark Corporation. That same year, as shares of Kimberly-Clark were being traded on the New York and Chicago stock exchanges for the first time, John Kimberly died. He was 90 years old and still president at the time of his death.

In the 1930s Kimberly-Clark concentrated on marketing its new products. During World War II the company devoted many of its resources to the war effort. The company also contracted Margaret Buell, creator of the cartoon strip "Little Lulu," to promote Kleenex. Buell and Little Lulu continued to promote Kleenex for Kimberly-Clark into the 1960s.

After the war, Kimberly-Clark initiated a growth program to handle revived consumer product demand. Facilities were built or acquired in Balfour, North Carolina, and Memphis, Tennessee, in 1946, and in Fullerton, California, and New Milford, Connecticut, in the late 1950s. Pulp production at Terrace Bay, Ontario, was launched in 1948, and in 1949 the company, along with a group of investors and newspaper publishers, began the large Coosa River Newsprint Company in Coosa Pines, Alabama. Kimberly-Clark acquired the Michigan-based Munising Paper Company in 1952, Neenah Paper Company in 1956, Peter J. Schweitzer, Inc.—which had mills in France and the United States—in 1957, and the American Envelope Company in 1959. International Cellucotton Products Company formally merged with its parent company in 1955, as did Coosa River Newsprint Company in 1962.

Throughout the 1960s the tampon, first manufactured by Tampax, gained favor among women and ate into Kotex's market share. Kimberly-Clark turned its attention to new products. In 1968 the company introduced Kimbies, a disposable diaper with tape closures. Initial sales were strong despite competition from Procter & Gamble's Pampers. While Kimberly-Clark tended to its diverse operations, however, it failed to keep up with early disposable diaper improvements and market innovations. As a result of continued poor sales and leakage problems, Kimbies were withdrawn from the market in the mid-1970s. Competition in the infant-care product industry caused Kimberly-Clark to reevaluate the balance between its consumer products and lumber and paper products divisions.

### Restructuring in the 1970s

Darwin E. Smith, who was elected president of Kimberly-Clark in 1971, took on Procter & Gamble's challenge. Smith decided that to compete properly in consumer product markets Kimberly-Clark had to prune its coated-paper business. Within one year of taking control of the company, Smith initiated changes that included the sale or closure of six paper mills and the sale of more than 300,000 acres of prime northern California land. With cash reserves of more than $250 million, primarily from the land sale, Smith then inaugurated an aggressive research campaign. He assembled a talented research and development team by hiring specialists away from competitors. The company's advertising budget was increased substantially, and plans were made for the construction of additional production facilities.

Marketing was central to Smith's strategy for growth, as Kimberly-Clark emphasized its commitment to consumer products. Research and development efforts enlarged the company's technological base from traditional cellulose fiber-forming technologies to lightweight nonwovens utilizing synthetic fabrics.

A new premium-priced diaper in an hourglass shape with refastenable tapes was introduced in 1978 under the name Huggies. By 1984, Huggies had captured 50 percent of the higher quality disposable diaper market. The sudden popularity of the product caught Kimberly-Clark by surprise, and it was forced to expand production to meet consumer demand.

### Diversification in the 1980s

Facial tissue and feminine-care products were also part of Kimberly-Clark's growing consumer product operations. In 1984, it was estimated that the company's Kleenex brand held 50 percent of the tissue market. A chemically treated virucidal tissue called Avert was test-marketed that same year, but the higher price and limited utility of the product prevented it from gaining widespread popularity. Aimed at health care institutions and at companies as a product to reduce absenteeism, Avert never really got off the ground, and in 1987 Kimberly-Clark decided not to mass market the product.

The 1980 toxic shock syndrome scare caused a slump in tampon sales. Kimberly-Clark began an aggressive advertising campaign on television for Depend incontinence products in the early 1980s. At the time, incontinence products were as unmentionable as feminine-care products had been some 60 years earlier. The promotion resulted in Depend gaining a profitable share of the incontinence products market, and it quickly became the best-selling retail incontinence brand in the United States. In an effort to broaden its position in therapeutic and health care products, Kimberly-Clark acquired Spenco Medical Corporation in Waco, Texas, that same year.

Although sales from primary growth operations—personal-care products—were increasing, approximately 25 percent of Kimberly-Clark's sales continued to come from the pulp, newsprint, and paper businesses. The company further diversified its operations in 1984 by converting its regularly scheduled executive air-shuttle service into a regional commercial airline.

The company's foray into aviation was initiated by the purchase of a six-seat plane in 1948 to shuttle executives between company headquarters in Wisconsin and Kimberly-Clark factories around the country. With six planes in 1969, Smith, then an executive vice-president for finance, suggested that company air travel be converted from a "cost center into a profit center" by offering corporate aircraft maintenance services. K-C Aviation, as the subsidiary was called, later remodeled three DC-9s and in June 1984 initiated flight service between Appleton and Milwaukee, Wisconsin; Boston; and Dallas, Texas. The fledgling airline, operated under the name Midwest Express, got off to a rocky start with a 1985 crash in Milwaukee, planes flying 80 percent empty, and large operating losses. By 1989, however, the operation was in the black, with planes at 66 percent capacity; a $120 million expansion increased the number of destinations to 15 cities and the airline boasted a fleet of 11 DC-9s.

In 1985, stating that the state had a bad climate for business, Smith relocated Kimberly-Clark's headquarters from Wisconsin to Texas. Just before this move Kimberly-Clark was sued by Procter & Gamble, who claimed that Kimberly-Clark had unlawfully infringed on its patented disposable diaper waistband material. Huggies had increased its market share to 31 percent, upsetting Procter & Gamble's Pampers. After nearly two years of litigation, a federal grand jury ruled against Procter & Gamble. Kimberly-Clark enjoyed further successes in its ongoing diaper rivalry with Procter & Gamble later in the decade when it introduced the extremely popular Huggies Pull-Ups disposable training pants in 1989. This product extension helped Kimberly-Clark trim Procter & Gamble's market share lead, as well as propel Huggies into the number one position in the disposable diaper market.

### 1990s and Beyond

Starting in the late 1980s, Kimberly-Clark began another diversification program—this time geographically, targeting Europe—although the company's largest international growth would come in the early and mid-1990s. To keep the company growing at a healthy pace, Smith began to increase Kimberly-Clark's presence in Europe in 1988. From that year to 1992, the company invested nearly $1 billion in European plants. Although revenues from its European operations increased steadily, the huge investments (totaling $700 million in 1993 alone) and restructuring charges that went along with them began to affect the company's profits. Net income of $435.2 million in 1991 fell to $150.1 million in 1992 before recovering slightly to $231 million in 1993.

Meanwhile, the company further reduced its commodity papers operation in 1991 when it sold Spruce Falls Power and Paper. The following year, Smith, the architect of Kimberly-Clark's restructuring and diversification efforts since 1972, retired as chairman and was succeeded by Wayne R. Sanders. The new chairman had worked his way up the ranks and had spearheaded the risky endeavor of developing Huggies Pull-Ups. The year 1992 also saw the introduction of Huggies Ultra Trim diapers.

Under Sanders's leadership, it appeared as if the company would divest itself completely of its commodity papers roots. Kimberly-Clark announced in late 1994 that it would explore the sale of its North American pulp and newsprint operations. The following year, however, the company decided not to sell because pulp and newsprint prices rose so high it no longer made economic sense to do so. Kimberly-Clark did divest its cigarette papers business in mid-1995 by spinning it off into a company called Schweitzer-Maudit International Inc. after shareholders initiated a proxy fight in 1994, concerned about the potential costs of liability lawsuits against tobacco, which were then beginning to gain strength.

In 1995 Sanders engineered the deal that would usher in a new era for the company: the merger of Kimberly-Clark with the Scott Paper Co. The deal was the logical culmination of Kimberly-Clark's international expansion, since Scott was globally strong and held the number one position in tissue in Europe. The $9.4 billion deal led to a 1995 charge of $1.4 billion for Kimberly-Clark to consolidate the merger, which led to the layoff of 6,000 workers and the sale of several plants. To pass antitrust muster, Kimberly-Clark had to sell the Scotties facial tissue operation, two of four tissue plants in the United States, and its Baby Fresh, Wash-a-Bye Baby, and Kid Fresh brands (which it sold to Procter & Gamble).

The late 1990s would be a period of transition for Kimberly-Clark as it worked to integrate the Scott Paper operations into its own. The company hoped that its newfound international clout, however, would make it a more formidable rival of the industry leader, Procter & Gamble, for years to come.

### Principal Subsidiaries

Avent, Inc.; Carlton Paper Corporation Limited (South Africa; 50%); Chengdu Comfort & Beauty Sanitary Articles Co., Ltd. (China; 98.1%); CPM Inc.; Handan Comfort & Beauty (Group) Co., Ltd. (China; 90%); Housing Horizons, LLC; Kimberly-Clark Inova a.s. (Czech Republic); K-C Aviation Inc.; Kimberly-Clark Argentina S.A. (51%); Kimberly-Clark Benelux Operations B.V. (Netherlands); Kimberly-Clark Canada Inc.; Kimberly-Clark de Centro America, S.A. (El Salvador, 75%); Kimberly-Clark Costa Rica, S.A. (75%); Kimberly-Clark Far East Pte. Limited (Singapore); Kimberly-Clark GmbH (Germany); Kimberly-Clark International, S.A. (Panama); Kimberly-Clark Limited (U.K.); Kimberly-Clark Malaysia Sendirian Berhad (51%); Kimberly-Clark Peru, S.A. (68%); Kimberly-Clark Philippines Inc. (87%); Kimberly-Clark Puerto Rico, Inc.; Kimberly-Clark Sopalin, S.A. (France); Kimberly-Clark Thailand Limited; Kunming Comfort & Beauty Hygienic Products Co., Ltd. (China; 97.9%); Nanjing Comfort & Beauty Sanitary Products Co., Ltd. (China; 97.9%); Scott Continental N.V. (Belgium); Scott GmbH (Germany); Scott Iberica, S.A. (Spain; 99.7%); Scott India; Scott Japan Limited; Scott Limited (U.K.); Scott Paper Indonesia; Scott Paper B.V. (Netherlands); Scott Paper Limited (Canada; 50.1%); Scott Paper Company; Scott Paper Company de Costa Rica, S.A. (51%); Scott Paper Company - Honduras, S.A. de C.V.; Scott Paper GmbH (Germany); Scott Paper (Guangzhou) Limited (China; 75%); Scott Paper (Hong Kong) Limited; Scott Paper (Malaysia) Sdn. Bhd.; Scott Paper Portugal Lda.; Scott Paper (Shanghai) Co., Ltd. (China; 56%); Scott Paper (Singapore) Pte. Ltd.; Scott S.N.C.

(France); Scott S.p.A. (Italy); Taiwan Scott Paper Corporation (66.7%); Thai-Scott Paper Company Limited (Thailand; 99.6%); Venekim, C.A. (Venezuela; 60%); YuHan-Kimberly, Limited (South Korea, 60%).

### *Principal Operating Units*

Health Care and Nonwovens Sector; Household Products Sector; International Consumer & Service Sector; Logistics Sector; North American Pulp & Paper Sector; Personal Care Sector; Service & Industrial Sector; U.S. Pulp and Newsprint.

### *Further Reading*

Byrne, John A., and Weber, Joseph, ''The Shredder: Did CEO Dunlap Save Scott Paper—Or Just Pretty It Up?,'' *Business Week,* January 15, 1996, pp. 56–61.

Forest, Stephanie Anderson, and Maremont, Mark, ''Kimberly-Clark's European Paper Chase,'' *Business Week,* March 16, 1992, pp. 94, 96.

Freeman, Laurie, ''Kimberly Holds Its Own Against Giants,'' *Advertising Age,* November 19, 1984.

Glowacki, Jeremy J., ''Kimberly-Clark Corp.: Accelerates Global Expansion with Scott Merger,'' *Pulp & Paper,* December 1995, pp. 34–35.

Hackney, Holt, ''Kimberly-Clark: No Escaping a Messy Diaper (Business),'' *Financial World,* April 27, 1993, p. 16.

Ingham, John N., ed., ''Kimberly, John Alfred,'' in *Biographical Dictionary of American Business Leaders,* Vol. II, Westport, Conn.: Greenwood, 1983.

Murray, Matt, ''Kimberly-Clark To Take Charge of $1.4 Billion,'' *Wall Street Journal,* December 14, 1995, pp. A3, A8.

Narisetti, Raju, ''For Sanders, Getting Scott Is Only the Start,'' *Wall Street Journal,* December 5, 1995, pp. B1, B12.

——, ''Kimberly-Clark Will Cut Staff 15% in Europe,'' *Wall Street Journal,* January 29, 1996, p. B2.

Star, Marlene Givant, ''Proxy Fight at Kimberly-Clark: Investors Request Tobacco Spin-Off,'' *Pensions & Investments,* March 6, 1995, pp. 2, 41.

—Carol I. Keeley
updated by David E. Salamie

# Kinko's Inc.

**255 West Stanley Avenue**
**Ventura, California 93002-8000**
**U.S.A.**
**(805) 652-4000**
**Fax: (805) 652-4142**

*Private Company*
*Incorporated:* 1970 as Kinko's Copies Corp.
*Employees:* 20,000
*SICs:* 2759 Commercial Printing, Not Elsewhere
　　Classified; 4899 Communications Services, Not
　　Elsewhere Classified; 7334 Photocopying and
　　Duplicating Services

Kinko's Inc. was, in 1995, the leading retail provider of document copying and business services in the world. With more than 830 outlets in early 1996, located in every state of the union and four foreign countries—Canada, Japan, South Korea, and the Netherlands—it was providing photocopies, quick printing and finishing services, electronic document distribution and production, mailing services, and time rentals on personal computers, usually at any hour of the day or night. About 145 locations had a special room for conducting videoconferences. A private company, Kinko's does not release its sales figures.

### Serving College Campuses in the 1970s

Kinko's Copies Corp. was founded in 1970 by Paul Orfalea, a young man of Lebanese ancestry who gave the company the nickname given him for his curly red hair. Self-described as mechanically inept and dyslexic, he was a "C" student at the University of Southern California, from which he graduated with a degree in finance in 1971. By then Orfalea had observed, "If you can't fix things and can't read things, then you can't get a job," but in fact he apparently never looked for one, for he had already concluded, as he later told a *Forbes* interviewer, "I'm sort of unemployable. I'm basically a peddler."

Seeking something to sell, Orfalea fixed his eye one day on the copy machine in the university library. Applying what he had learned from a marketing course that studied product life cycles, he decided, "This thing here is going to go for a long time." With funds from a $5,000 loan in 1969 from the Bank of America, cosigned by his father, he leased an 80-square-foot former hamburger stand in Isla Vista, near the campus of the University of California at Santa Barbara, and rented a small Xerox copier, charging customers four cents a page. He and a few friends also sold about $2,000 a day worth of notebooks and pens out of the makeshift store, wheeling the copier out on the sidewalk when the premises became too crowded. He supplemented his income by going from one dormitory room to another in the evenings, hawking his wares from a knapsack.

When this business proved a success, Orfalea decided to open other stores on other college campuses. Since he did not have funds to finance them and did not want to franchise them, he formed partnerships with owner-operators, retaining a controlling interest in each. These partners were other students who scouted locations along the West Coast, sleeping in their Volkswagen buses or fraternity houses. Publicity consisted of flyers stuffed in mailboxes; orders were taken and delivered personally.

Some of these Kinko's pioneers still were owner-operators many years later. Jim Warren was a surfer who met Orfalea at a keg party and was persuaded to take the enterprise to the Southeast. He and his wife rented a small storefront near the University of Georgia in 1978, where they kept a fire extinguisher handy because the copier they leased tended to burn paper. By 1995 Warren was president of Southeast Kinko's Inc. and a part-owner in about 120 Kinko's from Delaware to Florida. Tim Stancliffe opened the first Midwest Kinko's in a 175-square-foot space near the University of Colorado. In 1995 he was president of K-Graphics Inc., which owned and operated 90 Kinko's outlets in Colorado, Iowa, Kansas, Michigan, Missouri, Nebraska, New Mexico, South Dakota, and Wisconsin.

By the mid-1970s Kinko's was providing custom publishing materials for colleges, an innovation extremely popular with college professors. The company had 80 stores, averaging 400

## Company Perspectives:

*Our primary objective is to take care of our customer. We are proud of our ability to serve him or her in a timely and helpful manner, and to provide consistency and high quality at a reasonable price. We develop long term relationships that promote mutual growth and prosperity. We value initiative, productivity and loyalty, and we encourage independent thinking and teamwork.*

square feet in space and located primarily near colleges and universities, by the end of the decade.

### Reaching Out to Small Businesses in the 1980s

By the early 1980s Kinko's Copies was no longer content simply to copy documents for students. "At the time, no one was offering a low-end alternative to typesetting in the document duplication market," a marketing executive for Kinko's Service Corp., the chain's support arm, told a *Computer World* reporter in 1987. To exploit this emerging business opportunity, the company began to install typewriters in its shops.

This decision was soon rendered obsolete by the spread of personal computers. Kinko's then considered buying IBM PC clones but opted instead, in 1985, for Apple Computer's Macintosh as easier to use by customers who wanted to create documents without help from Kinko's employees. Another Macintosh advantage was that the documents created could be reproduced on Apple's high-quality Laserwriter printer. By mid-1987 almost one-third of Kinko's roughly 300 outlets were offering desktop-publishing services. Kinko's also began selling university-developed educational software for the Macintosh and Apple II computers in 1986.

In 1989 Kinko's Graphics Corp., operator of about 100 of the chain's copy shops, was slapped with a copyright-infringement lawsuit by eight textbook publishers for copying book segments of as long as 110 pages without permission. A federal judge found the company guilty in 1991 and assessed $1.9 million in damages and court fees. Kinko's Service Corp. then agreed that none of the stores would photocopy textbook anthologies in the future without permission for all copyrighted material.

Kinko's opened its first 24-hours-a-day, seven-days-a-week, outlet in Chicago in 1985. According to the president of Kinko's of Illinois, the company made this decision when people "started knocking on the glass" after hours, "begging us to let them in." Soon more of Kinko's stores—which numbered 420 at the end of the decade—were operating around the clock to accommodate people who had to get it done right away, whatever "it" was: manuscripts, screenplays, opera librettos, resumes, posters, fliers, wedding invitations. A 24-hour Kinko's was installed in the lobby of Chicago's Stouffer Renaissance because foreign executives staying at the hotel wanted to communicate across time zones with headquarters at home.

The late-night manager of a Long Beach, California, store told about a man having a heart attack in his shop, a woman

screaming for help with a copy job at three A.M., and a gang shooting in front of the store that left a man dead. By mid-1994 almost all Kinko's shops were open all the time. Manhattan's five stores filled at night with students and business people who rubbed shoulders with punk rockers and anarchists designing, copying, and faxing posters. Each of the five had its own cat as a mascot and dispensed coffee from a machine at no charge.

### "Your Branch Office" in the 1990s

The Kinko's of the 1990s had graduated beyond a low-tech service for college students. The company began opening stores averaging 7,000 square feet in size in suburbs and business areas to attract small-business owners seeking more advanced document copies, sometimes oversize or in color or bearing sophisticated graphics. In a nationally advertised television campaign begun in 1992, small-business people were urged to use Kinko's as "your branch office."

By 1994 Kinko's had added sophisticated color copiers, high-speed, high-volume laser printers, and facsimile machines, leasing rather than buying in order to conserve cash and avoid commitment to equipment that rapidly became outdated. Kinko's shops also began leasing conference rooms. In 1995 only 15 percent of Kinko's sales were still believed to be college-oriented, with large corporations accounting for another 15 percent, miscellaneous community retail use for 10 percent, and small or home-based businesses for 60 percent. The number of Americans estimated to be working from home in 1995 was 40 million, up from about 28 million in 1989. The number of businesses employing between five and 100 persons grew by almost 40 percent between 1980 and 1994. Typically, such customers prepared documents in their offices, then brought them to Kinko's for the professional look possible only by using quality printing equipment.

In 1993 Kinko's introduced videoconference rooms to 100 of its 725 outlets. Bidding for trade from entrepreneurs, telecommuters, traveling business people, and local representatives of corporations based elsewhere, the company was expecting to invest $20 million in videoconferencing. For $150 an hour, customers were offered a room with a large-screen television monitor, a videocassette recorder, a camera with wide-angle and zoom capabilities for focusing on a group or individual, and a device resembling an oversized television remote control. U.S. Sprint provided the equipment and high-speed telephone lines for the voice-picture-data network. Kinko Service Corp.'s president said he believed that families might take advantage of a half-price holiday promotion to use such facilities for video "reunions."

In 1995 new Kinko's stores were, on average, four times larger than the ones they replaced, in order to find space for the equipment needed for updated services. (The Xerox 5090, for example, a high-speed color-printing machine, nearly filled an entire room.) The company was seeking more business from large corporations, adding a sales force dedicated exclusively to seeking corporate accounts. It also installed Kinkonet, a system enabling companies to send in orders by computer over modem lines, with Kinko's distributing the finished product, such as a training manual, to points all over the United States. Internet service was expected by the end of 1996, with some stores able to help business customers establish home pages on the Internet's World Wide Web. Test stores in Seattle, Houston, and Philadelphia were enabling patrons in 1996 to send and receive graphics over the global network. Kinko's own award-winning Website was introduced in January 1996.

A Kinko's outlet typically offered the following services in 1996: full and self-service copying, including four-color copies; desktop publishing, including laser typesetting and printing; onsite Macintosh and IBM computer rentals; office supplies and stationery; finishing services such as folding, binding, collating, and stapling; custom printing services; facsimile transmission; and mailing, pick-up, and delivery service. Some locations also offered one-hour photo service. Kinko's considered customer service of such importance that each location was being "mystery shopped" on a regular basis, with anonymous shoppers grading the store on 29 different points of customer service and store atmosphere.

Kinko's was sponsoring an annual five-day meeting for its international network of managers in order to enable them to interact on a professional, social, and recreational level. It offered its employees (whom it called "co-workers") a wealth of career opportunities, with an emphasis on promotion from within the company. A series of comprehensive management training courses were being held at the company's central office to help them develop skills necessary to success in management positions.

Of the 830 or so Kinko's in March 1996, which were said to average $750,000 a year in sales, about 100 to 110 were solely owned by Orfalea's Kinko Graphics Corp. He also had a stake—sometimes said to be a controlling stake—in all the others, which were in essence joint ventures held in partnership with one or another of 127 owner-operators. It was rumored, however, that Kinko's would be going public later in the year.

Described as reclusive, Orfalea allowed *Forbes* to interview him in 1995, but only by videoconference. The bylined story by Zina Moukheiber reported that he "looks and sometimes talks like a rebellious student despite his 47 years." Orfalea was maintaining his links to the past by teaching a class in business on Mondays at the University of California at Santa Barbara, where he opened his first store.

### Principal Subsidiaries

G & S Corp.; K-Graphics Inc.; Kinko's Graphics Corp.; Kinko's Northwest LP; Kinko's of Illinois; Kinko's Service Corp.; Southeast Kinko's Inc.

### Further Reading

Apodaca, Patrice, "Kinko's Gambles on High-Tech Services," *Los Angeles Times,* October 7, 1994, pp. D2–D3.
Beeler, Jeffry, "Firm Taps Mac for Strategy Move," *Computer World,* February 16, 1987, p. 69.
Cox, Meg, "Kinko's, Publishers Reach Settlement of Copyright Suit," *Wall Street Journal,* October 18, 1991, p. B6.
Fierman, Jacyln, "It's 2 A.M. Let's Go to Work," *Fortune,* August 21, 1995, p. 85.
Flynn, Laurie, "Kinko's Adds Internet Services to Its Copying Business, *New York Times,* March 18, 1996, p. D5.
Kempner, Matt, "Surf's Up for Ever-Changing Kinko's," *Atlanta Constitution,* July 6, 1995, p. E1.
Moukheiber, Zina, "I'm Just a Peddler," *Forbes,* July 17, 1995, pp. 42–43.
Parker, Penny, "Partnership Hopes to Copy Success," *Denver Post,* May 24, 1995, pp. 1C, 3C.
Szabo, Julia, "Copy Shop Stitches the Urban Crazy Quilt," *New York Times,* July 3, 1994, p. 31.

—Robert Halasz

# KOMATSU

## Komatsu Ltd.

2-3-6, Akasaka
Minato-ku, Tokyo 107
Japan
81-3-5561-2616
Fax: 81-3-3505-9662

*Public Company*
*Incorporated:* 1921
*Employees:* 28,040
*Sales:* 918.9 billion (US$10.6 billion) (1995)
*Stock Exchanges:* Tokyo Osaka Nagoya Luxembourg
    Frankfurt
*SICs:* 3531 Construction Machinery & Equipment; 3541
    Machine Tools, Metal Cutting Types; 3561 Pumps &
    Pumping Equipment

An international leader in the manufacture of construction equipment and industrial machinery, Komatsu Ltd. is the second-largest manufacturer of construction tractors and earth movers in the United States, after Caterpillar. The company's products include forklift trucks, dump trucks, bulldozers, hydraulic excavators, road surface survey vehicles, and rough-terrain cranes. Komatsu also has a major division devoted to the production of electronics. This business includes production related to semi-conductors and computer technology for use in factory automation. Komatsu divisions produce a wide variety of other products, including plastics injection molding machinery, electronic parts, optical tablets, laser machines, armored cars for the military, small-diameter pipe jacking systems, machine tools, diesel engines, and hydraulic presses. Komatsu also has a growing division producing equipment for the recycling and incineration business.

While its main manufacturing operations are in Japan, Komatsu owns production plants and sales and service units in other countries, mainly in the United States, Canada, the United Kingdom, Mexico, and Indonesia. Other operations with foreign partners are located in India, New Zealand, Malaysia, China, the Republic of Korea, Turkey, Germany, and Italy.

### 19th-Century Origins

Komatsu had its origins in 1894 when the Takeuchi Mining Company was founded. A major expansion occurred in 1917, during World War I, when the Komatsu ironworks was established to manufacture mining equipment and machine tools to expand the mining operations. The name Komatsu came into existence in 1921 when the ironworks separated from the mining company to become Komatsu. Tashiro Shiraishi, an engineer, was the founder and first president, serving until 1925. In the 1920s and 1930s the firm grew as a major manufacturer of machine tools and pumps, including development of a metal press in 1924 and the firm's first farm tractor in 1931. Production of steel materials began in 1935.

By 1929 the number of employees had risen to 742, from its original 1921 work force of 121 employees, but during the depth of the Great Depression in 1933 it dropped to 505 workers. The firm soon increased production and by 1936 increased its staff to 601. Mitsugi Nakemura served as president during the Depression and war years, from 1934 to 1946.

During World War II the firm expanded by supplying the navy with antiaircraft artillery shells and bulldozers. Komatsu's first major product after the war was a redesigned bulldozer, which came off the assembly line in 1947. One year later diesel engines were produced. From 1947 to 1964 President Yoshinari Kawai provided key leadership in rebuilding the company and making it a global multinational corporation.

The Korean War gave the Japanese economy a boost with orders from the United States to supply its troops in Korea. At that time the firm had plants in Awazu, Osaka, Kaweasaki, Himi, and Komatsu, Japan. Production of forklift trucks, dump trucks, armored cars, and shell mold castings were added to the line. By 1959 defense production included armored personnel carriers and self-propelled cannons.

International activities increased in 1955 when both construction equipment and presses were shipped outside the country. In 1958 operations began in India with an agreement between the firm and the Indian government to manufacture tractors. Another license agreement was signed with a U.S.

---

### Company Perspectives:

*In order to ensure its future growth as the most reliable partner for its customers, the company is doubling its efforts to reciprocate customer trust with new concept-driven products and services. Made with leading-edge engineering insights, these products will reflect the creativity of Komatsu people worldwide coming together under the new corporate motto of "Work for the World. Care for the Community."*

---

manufacturer, Cummins Engine Company, to make and sell diesel engines.

### 1960s: Sights on Caterpillar

By the early 1960s the firm had grown to the point where a new headquarters was needed, and the Komatsu Building was constructed in Tokyo. In 1964 the firm received the Deming Prize for quality, named after William Edwards Deming, the American quality guru whose writings on quality control between 1950 and 1952 became the bible of Japanese manufacturing.

Ryoichi Kawai became president in 1964. The 1960s saw an economic build-up for Japan as a result of the Vietnam War, and Komatsu's expansion continued at a rapid pace. In the latter part of the decade a new engine plant began production in Japan, a radio-controlled bulldozer was introduced, and a technical research center was established. President Kawai articulated the company's goal as "surpass Caterpillar." Each year, Kawai presented his managers with a clear set of priorities modeled after Caterpillar's performance. The yearly priorities were then worked into detailed plans of action, known as Plan, Do, Check Act (PDCA). Kawai's growth strategy was clearly successful. Over the next twenty years, Komatsu grew from a small local manufacturer to a serious competitor in the global construction market. As a result, Komatsu's management style became widely studied and emulated.

### Global Expansion, 1970s and 1980s

In 1970 the firm began its first direct investment in the United States, with the establishment of Komatsu America Corporation. Other foreign operations soon followed, in Singapore, Australia, Mexico, Brazil, and China.

In 1981 Komatsu was awarded the Japan Quality Control Prize, to honor the company's outstanding production quality. The following year Shoji Nogawa became president. The 1980s brought expansion of global operations. In 1985, after a number of incentives from the state of Tennessee, Komatsu purchased a 55-acre empty plant in Chattanooga, a purchase that reflected a decision by the firm to challenge its principal rival, Caterpillar, in its home market. Canadian operations expanded as well, as two plants were built in Quebec and Ontario. European operations included an interest in the West German construction firm of Hamomag AG, a licensing agreement with FAI of Italy, and a plant in the United Kingdom.

The year 1987 marked expansion in other areas, such as the establishment of two financial subsidiaries in Europe, the marketing of plastics injection molding machinery, and the development of a telephone with a data terminal. At the same time, the construction market was changing, and Komatsu's sales began to slump. From 1985 to 1987, construction equipment sales dropped each year. As a result, the company president, Shoji Nogawa, was dismissed by Chairman Ryoichi Kawai, and changes were instituted. In 1988 an international business division was set up in the Tokyo headquarters. The division had three regional groups which were the main focus of the firm's international business operations: the Americas, Europe, and Japan. The goals of the division included development of joint ventures around the world and overseas purchase of parts.

In 1988 the company established a new subsidiary, Komatsu Trading International, to increase imports to Japan, in response to the Japanese government's commitment to reduce its trade surplus by importing more foreign products. As a result, logging machinery from Canada, backhoe loaders from Italy, and high-powered motor boats from Norway were brought into Japan for sale in the domestic market under importer agreements between Komatsu and companies in the respective countries.

Also in 1988, Komatsu sharpened its competitive edge in the U.S. market by forming a joint venture with Dresser Industries, Komatsu Dresser Company. This combination of a major U.S. producer with a major Japanese global player, Komatsu, added considerable research-and-development resources to the U.S. firm. Furthermore, the combination enabled Komatsu to move assembly of its construction equipment to the United States, using Dresser plants that were running at 50 percent capacity while Komatsu was unable to fill all of its orders.

### New Targets, 1990s

A new president, Tetsuya Katada, took over in 1989. Katada decided that Komatsu's management had been hampered to some extent by the company's goal of catching Caterpillar. While this strategy had worked remarkably well in expanding the company while the global market was growing, now that worldwide demand for construction equipment was down, Komatsu did not have the flexibility to adapt. Katada believed that the creativity of Komatsu's middle managers had been sacrificed while everyone was concentrating on Caterpillar, and that managers had grown afraid to question the direction of the company. Katada's solution was to stop comparing Komatsu to Caterpillar. He encouraged managers to think of Komatsu as a "total technology enterprise," and to find new products and markets that fit the wider definition of the company. Komatsu's new goal became the somewhat broader "Growth, Global, Groupwide," with a more concrete aim to double sales by the mid-1990s.

Katada's success became clear quickly. Sales had been declining since 1982, but after Katada initiated the new business strategy, sales began to climb again. Komatsu's non-construction business grew by 40 percent between 1989 and 1992. Nevertheless, the Komatsu Dresser Company lost money, due to deteriorating markets for heavy equipment and to problems with the merger. The Dresser and Komatsu product lines were to remain distinct under the merged company, but this resulted in dealers within the company directly competing with each other. Dresser managers also reported problems communicating with their Komatsu counterparts. This was to some extent remedied when Komatsu began bringing its American employees to Japan to learn more about Japanese culture and work. Steep appreciation of the Japanese yen also ate into Komatsu's profits. In 1993 Komatsu introduced cost-cutting measures, including some cuts in its work force and streamlining of its manufacturing facilities in Japan.

The firm had shown a quick response to the 1992 integration of Europe by the European Common Market. British operations included purchase agreements with the British firm of Perkins Engines Ltd. for diesel engines to power Komatsu excavators. The U.K. plant in Birtley was the main production facility for European construction equipment. Other parts came from Spain, France, Belgium, and Germany. An additional agreement with the Italian firm of FAI to manufacture under license mini-hydraulic excavators added to a strong European presence. Komatsu also began expanding its production of large trucks in the U.S. and Brazil in 1993, and increased its imports of parts from Brazil, South Korea, Indonesia and China.

A key to Komatsu's continued growth was its diversification into new markets, including non-construction businesses. Electronics became Komatsu's second most important business area. To increase its presence in this area, Komatsu made a strategic alliance with Applied Materials, Inc., a U.S. manufacturer of computer display panels, in 1993. Komatsu invested tens of millions of dollars in a 50 percent share of a new joint venture with the American company, renamed Applied Komatsu Technology Inc. (AKT). By 1995 AKT had become a competitive force in the Japanese market for computer liquid crystal displays.

Komatsu also began to focus more on business ventures related to recycling. In 1994 the company began a joint venture with Japan Samtech Co. Ltd., a leading Japanese maker of incinerators. And in 1995 Komatsu entered an agreement with a leading plastics recycler in the United States, Pure Tech International, to begin building and marketing recycling plants in Japan. Komatsu also continued to press for an expansion of its core construction business worldwide in the mid-1990s. Construction in Komatsu's domestic market boomed in 1995 and 1996, sadly due to the massive Kobe earthquake in January 1995. Around the world, Komatsu had 15 plants in 10 countries outside Japan as of 1995, and the company entered new joint ventures in Thailand, Vietnam, and China in that year.

### Future Plans

And Komatsu had concrete plans for the future of its business. Satoru Anzaki became the new president of Komatsu Ltd. in June 1995, and former president Kataka became chairman. Under this new leadership, the company aimed to continue diversifying its business through new joint ventures, and to localize control of many of its overseas subsidiaries to make them more competitive in their own regions. Komatsu also planned to become the world's number one maker of hydraulic excavators—the kind of clear goal Komatsu has excelled at meeting in the past.

### Principal Subsidiaries

Komatsu Dresser Company (U.S., 50%); Komatsu UK Ltd.; Dina Komatsu Nacional S.A. de C.V. (Mexico, 68.4%); P.T. Komatsu Indonesia (55%); Komatsu Dresser Brazil (50%); Komatsu America Industries Corp. (U.S.); Komatsu Europe International N.V. (Belgium); Komatsu Baumaschinen Deutschland (Germany); Komatsu Singapore Pte. Ltd; Komatsu Australia Pty.; Komatsu Overseas Finance PLC (U.K.); Komatsu Finance (Netherlands) B.V.

### Further Reading

*Fact Book '89*, Komatsu, Tokyo: Komatsu Ltd., 1989.
Kelly, Kevin, ''A Dream Marriage Turns Nightmarish,'' *Business Week,* April 29, 1991, pp. 94–95.
''Komatsu Plans to Trim Jobs in Revamping,'' *Wall Street Journal,* September 17, 1993, p. A7B.
Pollack, Andrew, ''Applied Materials Plans Venture with Komatsu,'' *New York Times,* June 18, 1993, p. D3.

—Joseph A. LeMay
Updated by Angela Woodward

# Ahold

# Koninklijke Ahold N.V. (Royal Ahold)

**Albert Heijnweg 1, Zaandam**
**P.O. Box 33, 1500 EA Zaandam**
**The Netherlands**
**31(0) 75 59 5720**
**Fax: 31(0) 75 59 8360**

*Public Company*
*Incorporated:* 1948 as Albert Heijn N.V.
*Employees:* 119,027
*Sales:* $18 billion (1995)
*Stock Exchanges:* Amsterdam Zurich Brussels New York
*SICs:* 6719 Holding Companies, Not Elsewhere
    Classified; 5411 Grocery Stores

Koninklijke Ahold N.V. (known outside the Netherlands as Royal Ahold) is the world's tenth-largest grocery chain. Royal Ahold operates more than 1,500 supermarket or specialty stores in the Netherlands, making it Holland's largest food retailer. Its Albert Heijn, Alberto, and Etos units are familiar names throughout the country. The company also operates several retail chains overseas, where growth potential is much greater. The company operates stores in Portugal, Spain, Belgium, and the Czech Republic, and is beginning to expand into Southeast Asia.

Ahold is also one of the largest grocery chain operators in the United States. Well over half the company's total sales come from its six U.S. chains—Tops, Finast, Edwards, Bi-Lo, Giant Food Stores, and Stop & Shop. Royal Ahold also operates food production facilities, producing and processing coffee, tea, wine, bread, meat and other food products, mainly for sale in its Albert Heijn stores. The company has an institutional food supply business, supplying restaurants, hotels, and other large institutional kitchens. In the Netherlands, Ahold operates wine and liquor stores, a chain of confectioners, a wholesale pharmaceutical company, health and beauty care stores, and is a major share-holder in Schuitema, a leading Dutch grocery wholesaler and supplier.

## Early History

In 1887, Albert Heijn and his wife opened a small grocery store in Oostzan, the Netherlands. Holland was in the midst of an economic boom sustained by its colonial network. Heijn's grocery store prospered and soon became a chain, under the name Albert Heijn. By the end of World War I, Heijn was running a bakery and a confectionery to help supply his chain of 50 grocery stores.

Steady growth continued throughout the 1920s, as the company added new stores each year. In 1923 Heijn branched into the restaurant trade, providing his company with a new source of income. By the end of the decade, Albert Heijn was in a very solid position. As a result, the company was able not only to weather the worldwide Depression of the 1930s, but even to grow.

In 1941, the Nazi occupation of the Netherlands brought economic turmoil to the country. Dutch wealth was drained to fuel Germany's war machine. But, as during the Depression, the nature of the food business insulated Albert Heijn from the ruin faced by companies in other industries throughout Holland. By the end of World War II the chain had nearly 250 stores in operation.

In 1948, the company went public in preparation for the challenges of the postwar era. Self-service shopping was clearly the trend. In 1952 the company opened its first self-service store, followed three years later by its first supermarket. Albert Heijn emerged from the 1950s as a leader in its industry, and expansion continued in the 1960s through diversification and the addition of new stores. In 1966 Albert Heijn acquired the Meester meat-packing plant, which produced a wide variety of processed meat products, delicatessen items, and sausages, among other things. In 1969 the company opened the first of its Alberto liquor stores.

## Expansion in the 1970s

As the company began the 1970s it had a firm grip on about 20 percent of the Dutch market, and was poised to expand. In 1971 Albert Heijn opened the first Miro hypermarket. A year later the company acquired the Simon de Wit chain, bringing

**Company Perspectives:**

*The success of Ahold comes from its overall strategy to operate modern, competitive stores under their own name, management and local identity; invest substantially in supermarket technology and training, with strict quality standards and efficient operations; and reach the highest possible number of customers by providing high quality products and services in attractive and friendly shopping environments.*

137 new supermarkets under the Albert Heijn banner. In 1973, the company changed its name to Ahold N.V. It also entered the health and beauty care market that year with the purchase of the Etos chain.

A number of adverse conditions combined to slow growth just as Ahold digested its new acquisitions: the energy crisis of 1973 softened consumer demand somewhat, labor costs rose considerably, and the government removed artificial price supports. Ahold's management, accustomed to the often cyclical nature of the food retailing industry, rode out the storm. The company stepped up discount store activities and its roadside restaurant operations. By 1975 Ahold was enjoying rapid growth once again, and was poised to make a major thrust overseas.

After carefully researching European markets, Ahold decided to establish a chain of supermarkets in Spain. Spain had a relatively undeveloped industry and Ahold believed its expertise would go the farthest there. In 1976 the company opened the first Cadadia store near Madrid. Ahold planned to develop a major chain in the country, but the Spanish subsidiary got off to a sluggish start, hindered in part by a slow-moving Spanish bureaucracy and a depressed economy.

In 1977 Ahold made a major purchase in the United States when it acquired the Bi-Lo chain for $60 million. Bi-Lo operated 98 stores throughout North and South Carolina and Georgia. The Bi-Lo chain got off to a strong start within the Ahold group, returning a 3 percent profit margin, compared with 1.7 percent for Ahold's Dutch operations. Ahold retained Bi-Lo's management in the belief that local autonomy would best serve the company's interests. In 1981, however, the president of Bi-Lo resigned when the chain followed its competitors and began selling beer and wine.

Ahold continued its program of diversification when it purchased ten restaurants from the struggling Jacques Borel group of Belgium in 1978. The acquisition strengthened Ahold's network of AC restaurants, located on roadsides throughout Europe. Ahold's Ostara holiday parks in West Germany and Holland provided strong earnings outside of the retail food sector for the company in the late 1970s.

In 1978 the company set up a foundation to hold Dfl 100,000 in preferred stock as protection against hostile bids, after watching a number of hostile takeover attempts, including a particularly bitter battle between Heineken and Lucas Bols. To the company's relief, no hostile bids for Ahold actually materialized.

### International Growth in the 1980s

In 1981, Ahold made its second major U.S. purchase: the Giant Food Stores chain, of Carlisle, Pennsylvania, for $35 million. Giant had 29 stores, mostly in Pennsylvania, and Ahold planned to add four or so new stores each year. As with the Bi-Lo purchase, the company's management remained autonomous.

That same year Ahold bought 50 percent of the Spanish sherry producer Luis Paez. By the end of the decade Ahold was producing one-third of all sherry sold in the Netherlands. In addition, the company's Alberto liquor store unit had grown to 89 stores in its first 20 years, and continued to improve its share even in a shrinking market.

Ahold recorded vigorous profits in the early 1980s largely on the strength of its American operations. Growth slowed a bit around 1984, as vicious competition in the Netherlands shaved already thin margins and the Spanish chain Cadadia reported a loss. In 1985 the company sold the 38 Cadadia stores to the British Dee Corporation (now Gateway), having decided not to undertake a major expansion in Spain. It kept its winery holdings, however. The company also acquired the Van Kok-Ede company, a major wholesale foods supplier in Holland, in 1985.

Ahold purchased 80 percent of the American First National Supermarkets chain in 1988, an acquisition which doubled the size of its U.S. operations. First National ran the Finast, Pick-n-Pay, and Edwards Food Warehouse chains. The deal gave Ahold a footing in New England, Ohio, and New York. Ahold slowed the expansion of its Giant and Bi-Lo chains in order to concentrate its resources on the First National stores.

Meanwhile Ahold increased its holding in the Dutch supplier Schuitema to 55 percent. Schuitema, Holland's largest supplier of independent supermarkets in the country, gave Ahold an even stronger grip on the industry in Holland.

Ahold had always been committed to using the latest technology in its stores. In the late 1980s the company piloted a program which allowed customers to self-scan the items they wish to purchase. At the Albert Heijn store in Tilberg, the Netherlands, customers were offered the choice of self-scanning or traditional shopping. Self-scanning shoppers selected a cart equipped to scan each item before they put it in the cart; the scanner also kept a running total on an electronic readout. When customers were finished shopping, they proceeded to a special line, where the cashier entered the data from the cart's scanner into the register. Customers liked the shorter lines at the checkout and the idea of a running total displayed at all times. But self-scanning was still considered experimental through the early 1990s, and was not tested at one of Ahold's U.S. supermarkets until 1995.

In 1989, Pierre J. Everaert, formerly head of the company's overseas operations, replaced Albert Heijn, grandson of the company's founder, as president of Ahold. Heijn had reached the company's mandatory retirement age of 62, and so the company passed out of the direct control of the Heijn family for the first time in three generations.

Ahold was well-positioned for the integration of European markets in 1992. The company enjoyed substantial market share in the Netherlands and in 1991 it founded a food retail and distribution company in the Czech Republic, called Euronova. Ahold bought 49 percent of a Portuguese food retailer in 1992. By 1995, Ahold ran four ''supercenters'' or ''hypermarkets'' in Portugal—70,000 square foot stores selling groceries and other household goods.

But Royal Ahold's expansion into the American market was its most dramatic. After acquiring Finast in 1988, Ahold purchased the Buffalo, New York-based Topps Markets in 1991. The chain had 168 stores, and sales of $1.6 billion. Three years later Ahold purchased the smaller Red Food Stores chain, based in Chattanooga, Tennessee, for about $125 million. Red Food had sales of $400 million, and 55 stores. Ahold quickly merged Red Food into its larger Bi-Lo chain. The acquisition gave Ahold more than 600 food stores in the United States. Sales from its American group were $6.6 billion before the purchase of Red Foods, making Ahold the ninth-largest grocery operator in the United States. And when Ahold bought the Tennessee chain, the company announced its ambitious plan to become the biggest supermarket group on the East Coast within 10 years.

Though its U.S. chains retained separate management, the Ahold group was able to work as a unit and cut costs. The different chains cooperated with joint buying and distribution departments in some cases, and management shared marketing strategies and information systems. To some extent different chains shared advertising campaigns. But Ahold wanted its chains to keep their own identity. Each benefitted from economies of scale and sharing of resources, but regional differences persisted, as local managers tailored their stores to unique customer needs. Royal Ahold was content to let its American firms run in American ways, and not hold them to Dutch models. This contributed to the great success of Ahold's U.S. acquisitions, according to Robert Zwartendijk, president of Ahold USA. He noted in a 1995 interview in *Advertising Age* that other European supermarket companies had entered the U.S. market and then withdrawn. Applying European formulas to the highly competitive U.S. market did not work. But Ahold did not operate that way.

Ahold did work to build up sales of private label items at all its stores. Private labels saved the company money. So when approximately 15 percent of sales at its American stores were of private label products by 1995, the company estimated it was able to lower prices overall by 7 percent. Sales at Ahold's Dutch supermarkets were close to 40 percent private label goods, and increasing the private label share at its American markets was one way Ahold brought its European experience to bear on the American market. But for the most part, Ahold left management

of its U.S. chains in local hands. In fact, Ahold USA, as the company's American division was called, had 65,000 employees in 1995, but only two were Dutch.

In accord with its U.S. growth plan, Ahold bought a New Jersey chain, Mayfair supermarkets, in 1995. Mayfair operated 28 stores, with sales of $575 million. This purchase made Ahold the third-largest Eastern chain, close behind second-place Winn Dixie. Ahold was bringing in $8.3 billion in 1995 from its 650 stores. The next year, Ahold made its largest purchase in the U.S. when it bought Stop & Shop Companies Inc., the largest supermarket chain in New England. Stop & Shop had 1995 sales of $4.1 billion, brought in from its 116 Superstores, 43 Stop & Shop supermarkets, and 17 Mel's Foodtown supermarkets. The company also owned another chain of 28 Purity Supreme supermarkets and 64 convenience stores called Li'l Peach. The acquisition of Stop & Shop made Royal Ahold one of the top five supermarket operators in the U.S. Ahold was very close to attaining its goal of being the largest supermarket operator in the East.

## Principal Subsidiaries

Albert Heijn; Albert Heijn Franchising; James Telesuper; Alberto; Etos; Albro Bakkerijen Zwanenburg; Marvelo; Meester Wijhe; AC Restaurants; AC Restaurants (Belgium/Germany); Grootverbruik Ahold; Ahold Recreational Activities; Ahead Advertising; Pensioenfonds Ahold; Ahold Financieringsmaatschappij, Curacao (Netherlands Antilles); Luis Paez (Spain); Ahold USA Inc.; BI-LO Inc. (U.S.); Giant Food Stores Inc. (U.S.); FNS Holding Company Inc. (U.S.); First National Supermarkets, Inc. (U.S.); J.M.R.-Gestâo de Empresas de Retalho (Portugal, 49%); Stop & Shop Companies, Inc. (U.S.); ABS Development Company (U.S.).

## Further Reading

*Ahold Corporate Profile,* Zaandam, The Netherlands: Koninklijke Ahold N.V., 1993.
Bowes, Elena, ''Applying the Dutch Touch to Running U.S. Chains,'' *Advertising Age,* May 8, 1995, p. S-8.
Browning, E. S., ''Ahold's Supermarkets 'Go Native' to Succeed in U.S.,'' *Wall Street Journal,* October 4, 1994, p. B4.
Coupe, Kevin, ''Innovation Is the Key,'' *Progressive Grocer,* January 1995, pp. 29–33.
Rosner, Hillary, ''Dutch Retailer Ahold's U.S. Masterplan Unfolds,'' *Brandweek,* July 17, 1995, p. 5.

—Tom Tucker
—updated by A. Woodward

# Lattice Semiconductor Corp.

**5555 N.E. Moore Court**
**Hillsboro, Oregon 97124-6421**
**U.S.A.**
**(503) 681-0118**
**Fax: (503) 681-3077**

*Public Company*
*Incorporated:* 1983 as Lattice International, Inc.
*Employees:* 438
*Sales:* $144 million (1995)
*Stock Exchanges:* NASDAQ
*SICs:* 3674 Semiconductors & Related Devices; 3679
Electronic Components, Not Elsewhere Classified

Lattice Semiconductor Corp. designs and markets programmable logic semiconductor devices and contracts other companies to manufacture those chips. After struggling through the late 1980s, the company grew rapidly beginning in the early 1990s, particularly after it moved into the market for more advanced, high-density semiconductors.

### 1980s Startup

Management novices Rahul Sud and Raymond Capece started Lattice in the early 1980s, when the market for semiconductors was red hot. Sud, a native of India, had worked as a chip designer at both Inmos and vaunted Intel. Capece had gained experience raising capital through his job with venture capitalist Ben Rosen. Although neither partner had experience managing a company, they believed that Sud's ideas and Capece's ability to raise investment capital were a winning combination. The pair formed Lattice International Inc. in April of 1983 with the help of C. Norman Winningstad, the founder of the successful Floating Point Systems, a maker of computers and peripherals.

Winningstad was integral to Lattice's startup because he and several of his friends in the Portland business community fronted much of the initial investment capital. They invested in the company partly because they believed that Lattice's success would help Portland become a U.S. technology center. Winningstad helped Sud and Capece to raise about $19 million. But that sum paled in comparison to Sud's grandiose business plans. Sud decided that the fledgling Lattice should immediately begin construction of a $100 million, cutting-edge manufacturing facility. Scheduled for completion by 1986, the facility would, according to Sud and Capece, churn out high-tech chips designed by the semiconductor-industry superstars who would comprise Lattice's work force.

Sud's and Capece's vision never materialized. Part of the problem was that semiconductor markets slumped in 1985. But even before the industry tailspinned Lattice was clearly headed in the wrong direction. Sud and Capece did lure some top chip-design talent to their company, but they managed the company poorly. The most glaring flaw was their unwise use of the company's cash. Rather than carefully investing the maximum amount of capital in research and development, they squandered money, leasing an extravagant 140,000-square-foot building, and catering expensive breakfasts for the employees. One worker was even given a Porsche for Christmas. The company's posh, fake-marble lobby was enough to turn one investment banker on his heels.

Moreover, Lattice's production schedule began to slide and the company started losing huge sums of money. Lattice's first product had been a promising high-speed memory chip. But the device was introduced early in 1985, in the midst of the industry slump, when few buyers were willing to risk the switch to a new chip design. Also in the works was a high-performance programmable memory chip. But that product ultimately posed too great a challenge for Lattice's design team and was never introduced in finished form. To help buoy lagging sales, Sud decided to try selling different versions of the memory chip. To that end, he hired a giant 65-member sales and marketing team (for a company that was generating sales of only $1.5 million per quarter).

Sud was perplexed by his company's inability to make money. During a trip to the Far East, he became convinced that lazy employees were the problem. In the Fall of 1985, therefore, he moved Lattice to a six-day work week, similar to that in Japan and Korea. "We were working seven days a week," recalled David Rutledge, product development director, in *Forbes,* "and then they mandated six days." Lattice lost $7 million in 1986 from sales of the same amount. Despite that deficit, it looked as though the company's fortunes might be changing. Sales of a version of its programmable memory chip were surging and overall revenues were climbing. But that temporary boon was squelched when Monolithic Memories, a Silicon Valley chip maker, filed suit against Lattice claiming patent infringement. Sales of Lattice's promising chip quickly dried up and the company found itself back at square one.

By 1987 Lattice was on the ropes. Desperate, Sud scrambled to raise $10 million in venture capital to keep the enterprise afloat. Just one year earlier he had explained to *The Oregonian* that Lattice would succeed because there were no semi-conductor-industry venture capitalists involved to "force-feed the company with their conventional wisdom." Not surprisingly, Sud was unable to secure financing. Some of Lattice's employees paid for critical supplies out of their own pockets and went without paychecks to keep the venture moving. The company was dealt a nearly lethal blow when Seiko, of Japan, stopped producing Lattice's chips. Lattice's board of directors finally sent Sud packing (Sud later filed for wrongful discharge, but settled out of court after Lattice countersued). They brought in Winningstad to try to turn the company around, but it was too late. In July 1987 Lattice filed Chapter 11 bankruptcy to get protection from its creditors.

### Renewal

Lattice posted a net loss of $8.5 million for the year, and many analysts wondered if the company was worth saving. Winningstad believed it was. He realized that Lattice possessed some great talent and had developed some promising technology, but it lacked management expertise. By selling stock to an insurance company, he raised $7.5 million to help pay some bills. He also quickly lowered company overhead by slashing the work force, moving to lower-cost facilities, and eliminating other unnecessary expenses. After getting creditors to restructure the company's debt, Lattice emerged from bankruptcy after only 88 days.

Having kept the company from going under, Winningstad now faced the formidable task of making Lattice into a profitable competitor in the semiconductor industry. Success hinged on the company's ability to parlay its technology into products that it could market. When Winningstad took the helm, Lattice was trying to support five product lines. He decided to dump all except the most promising one; General Array Logic (GAL) devices. Lattice's GAL devices were low-density chips used primarily to link other microprocessors in consumer electronics and computers. Lattice's GAL chips were low-tech in comparison to some of its other products. But insufficient capital would force Lattice to shelve work on more advanced technology, such as its electrically erasable memory chips and digital signal processing devices.

Winningstad's most pivotal move at Lattice came in 1989, when he convinced Cyrus Tsui to become president of the company. Tsui was a native of China. He left Shanghai in the 1960s to attend the University of Southern California, from which he graduated in 1968. He worked a brief stint at semicon-

ductor powerhouse Fairchild Semiconductor before getting Masters degrees in electrical engineering and business at Stanford. He eventually went to work at Advanced Micro Devices (AMD), a chip-technology leader in Silicon Valley in the mid-1970s. He bounced from AMD to Monolithic Memories and back to AMD during the 1980s before he was offered the top job at Lattice. Tsui initially rejected Winningstad's offer, but reconsidered.

### A New Direction

By the time Tsui assumed the presidency, Lattice had already achieved an impressive recovery from its 1987 low. Sales had grown from $14 million in 1988 and would hit $21.5 million in 1989. More importantly, the company was generating positive cashflow and would record its first surplus in 1989, when it netted income of $2.2 million. But Lattice was still depending on a relatively limited product line and was in need of a long-term growth strategy. To that end, Lattice went public with stock offerings late in 1989 and in mid-1990 that raised about $40 million. Tsui planned to invest that cash in the research and development of new technology, prompted by Advanced Micro Devices' announced plan to target Lattice's niche in low-density programmable logic devices that incorporated cutting-edge complimentary metal oxide silicon (CMOS) technology.

Tsui focussed Lattice on the market for high-density programmable logic devices. The market for high-density chips was growing in the wake of the introduction and popularity of more complex computing and telecommunications devices. High-density chips were used for data-intensive applications that often required reprogramming of the chip. The greatest barrier to entry to the growing industry niche was technology. But Tsui believed that Lattice possessed the technical acuity to excel in the high-density arena, and that success would mean significantly greater sales and, possibly, much higher profit margins.

Relying on sales of its low-density chips, Lattice managed to increase revenues to $38.9 million in 1990 and then to $64.5 million in 1991 (year ended March 1991). Net income, meanwhile, rose to more than $10 million in 1991, providing a much needed boost to the company's bottom line. Then, in March of 1992, Lattice introduced its first high-density devices. The company unveiled a family of eight high-density programmable logic devices along with software tools that chip designers could use to integrate the semiconductors into their systems. The chips were introduced three months ahead of schedule, and Lattice's stock price had grown more than 70 percent since January in anticipation of the success of the new line.

Lattice's new line of high-density devices was well-received, and helped to establish Lattice as a technological contender in that market segment. Bolstering the success of that new line in 1993 was Lattice's $19 million purchase of Quick-Logic Corp., a Santa Clara, California, designer and marketer of field-programmable gate arrays (FPGAs). FPGAs were a rapidly growing segment of the semiconductor industry that complemented Lattice's drive into high-density programmable logic devices. FPGAs were more versatile and generally more powerful than high-density programmable logic devices and were typically used in the most demanding military, aerospace, and industrial applications. The merger worked well because Tsui had worked with the founders of QuickLogic when he was with Monolithic Memories.

Lattice managed to boost sales of both its high-density and low-density devices during the early 1990s. Importantly, it advanced in the high-density market rather quickly. That speedy progress was largely attributable to an important advantage; unlike its competitors' high-density programmable chips, Lattice's semiconductors could be reprogrammed without unplugging them from the systems in which they had been installed. As competitors hustled to copy the innovation, Lattice worked to pioneer new advances. Lattice continued to trail industry-niche leaders Advanced Micro Devices and Xilinx (in terms of sales volume), but it made big gains and was closing in on those opponents by the mid-1990s.

Lattice's sales reached $100 million in 1993 and then climbed to $144 million by the fiscal year ending March, 1995. Net income tracked those gains, rising to $27 million in 1995 and then to $41.8 million in 1996 (from sales of nearly $200 million). By 1996 Lattice was employing about 500 workers, serving more than 400 customers, and supporting offices in Europe and Asia. In 1994, in fact, Tsui had connected with his native country, China, when he opened a Lattice research and development center in Shanghai. Tsui planned to target China for expansion because of his intimate knowledge of the country. Going into 1996, Lattice continued to act primarily as a development and marketing company, but was moving to add manufacturing operations in Taiwan.

### Further Reading

Anthony, Joseph, "Cheating Defeat: It Looked Bad for Lattice," *Oregon Business,* February 1994, p. 20.

Barnett, Jim, "The Chip Boom Has a Downside for Hillsboro's Lattice Semiconductor, Which Learns that Its Manufacturer Might Not Be Able to Meet Its Needs: Pushing the Limit," *Oregonian,* August 15, 1995, p. 14B.

Francis, Mike, "Lattice Takes Another Bow, Prepares for Next Leap," *Oregonian,* October 25, 1992.

——, "Profiles in Perseverance: Cyrus Tsui," *Oregonian,* October 6, 1992.

Manning, Jeff, "Growing Lattice Swings $19 Million Deal," *Business Journal-Portland,* September 27, 1993, p. 1.

——, "Humbled Lattice Finds Smaller Office," *Business Journal-Portland,* October 5, 1987, p. 7.

——, "Lattice Betting Its Chips on High-Density Semiconductors," *Business Journal-Portland,* March 9, 1992, p. 4.

——, "Lattice Climbs to Success with Two Public Stock Offerings," *Business Journal-Portland,* August 6, 1990, p. 4.

——, "Lattice Tries to Stave Off Chapter 11," *Business Journal-Portland,* June 29, 1987, p. 1.

Marks, Anita, "Lattice Dials Growth Market," *Business Journal-Portland,* April 14, 1995, p. 1.

——, "Lattice Set for Next Market Twist," *Business Journal-Portland,* June 9, 1995, p. 1.

Rice, Valerie, "Once Bankrupt, the Good Times Come Back to Lattice," *Electronic Business,* November 27, 1989, p. 38.

Weigner, Kathleen K., "How Lattice Almost Went Under," *Forbes,* December 12, 1988, p. 238.

Wilkerson, Jan, "For New Lattice Leader, More Risk Takes Priority," *Business Journal-Portland,* April 24, 1989, p. 10.

——, "Lattice Leaves Troubles Behind, Pushes into Black," *Business Journal-Portland,* June 27, 1988, p. 6.

—Dave Mote

# LCI International, Inc.

8180 Greensboro Drive, Suite 800
McLean, Virginia 22102
U.S.A.
(703) 442-0220
Fax: (703) 448-6792

*Public Company*
*Incorporated:* 1983 as LiTel Communications, Inc.
*Employees:* 1,400
*Sales:* $600 million (1995)
*Stock Exchanges:* NASDAQ
*SICs:* 4813 Telephone Communications Except
  Radiotelephone; 6719 Holding Companies, Not
  Elsewhere Classified

LCI International, Inc. is a long-distance telephone and telecommunications company, originating and placing telephone calls throughout the continental United States and placing calls in more than 200 countries worldwide. Based in Virginia, LCI offers a wide variety of domestic and international voice and data services to commercial and residential markets. The company experienced rapid growth in the late 1980s and early 1990s, largely a corollary of deregulation of the U.S. telecommunications industry during the 1980s. Such deregulation made it possible for companies like LCI to compete for a piece of the mammoth U.S. long-distance services pie.

### Origins in the Break Up of AT&T

LCI was formed in 1983, the same year the vaunted divestiture of American Telephone & Telegraph Co. became effective. The enterprise was incorporated as LiTel Communications, Inc. by nine investors and telecommunications industry veterans. Spearheading the venture was 45-year-old Lawrence McLernon, a New Jersey native who had spent the past two decades working for different telephone companies. He was joined by Alan Ashworth, Ron Crammer, Richard Hicks, Mike Morris, Ghanshyam C. Patel, Jill Risch, James E. Sobwick, and Larry Wolfe.

McLernon and his eight associates hoped to get in early on opportunities created by telecommunications deregulation and to quickly stake out some of the market share ceded by AT&T. Specifically, they hoped to develop a cutting-edge fiber-optic cable network in the Midwest that could efficiently handle high volumes of telephone calls and digital communications, primarily for business customers. The founders first set up shop in a small office above a beauty salon near Milwaukee, Wisconsin. Less than a year later, however, they moved the company's headquarters to a small office park near Columbus, Ohio. McLernon was attracted to the high-tech business environment that Columbus was trying to cultivate through, among other lures, various tax incentives for companies willing to locate there. "Governor [Richard] Celeste called me personally and asked me to come to Ohio," McLernon recalled in the August 1990 *Business Cleveland*. "He was the only governor to do that," he added.

Celeste's interest in attracting LiTel to Columbus reflected the company's great growth potential. LiTel had managed to attract a significant amount of startup capital, boasted a solid management team, and had an impressive business plan. It seemed entirely possible at the time that LiTel could be one of the major players in the future telecommunications industry. LiTel did achieve impressive gains during the late 1980s, building and expanding its fiber-optic network throughout several midwestern states. By the early 1990s, in fact, LiTel (LCI) would be known as one of the leaders in the second tier of the telecommunications industry, the top tier consisting of telecommunication giants AT&T, MCI, and Sprint.

LiTel's gains, however, came at a high price. The cost to lay a single mile of fiber-optic cable was approximately $100,000, and LiTel was effectively starting from scratch. It initially planned to develop a 1,300-mile, $85 million network stretching from New York to Illinois and south into Kentucky. To that end, LiTel began acquiring other companies with operations and infrastructure that complemented this goal. The company also started laying its own fiber-optic cable. The ambitious endeavor was financed by several investors, among the largest of which were Alltel Corp., Centel Corp., and Pirelli Societe Generale of Switzerland. In addition, LiTel borrowed heavily to

318

finance new construction, which was initially centered primarily in its local Ohio market.

Through a combination of acquisitions and new construction, LiTel managed to quickly exceed its original goals. Importantly, the company won a $14 million contract in 1987 to provide the Ohio state government with long-distance service. By late 1987 the company was operating a fiber-optic network with about 1,500 miles of cable serving more than 10,000 customers. More than 20 percent of those customers were located in the company's core Columbus market. LiTel focused on serving businesses, which were more willing to pay for the quality of service made possible by fiber-optic technology. But in the long term, LiTel planned to branch out into other market segments, and McLernon hoped to become one of only four or five major companies serving the entire U.S. long-distance market.

### Increased Competition in the Late 1980s

Throughout the late 1980s, LiTel scrambled to rapidly get its telecommunications network in place and secure market share. Meanwhile, the competition intensified, and LiTel found itself under increasing pressure to grow rapidly. The company borrowed heavily to fund new construction and sustain its acquisition drive, buying up both smaller and larger companies in an effort to stay ahead or get control of its competitors. Notable among its acquisitions was the 1990 buyout of Indianapolis-based Once Call Communications Inc., which boosted LiTel's customer base by more than 30 percent. The purchase was LiTel's third in less than seven months, contributing to a total customer base of more than 70,000 by late 1990. LiTel's revenues increased accordingly, to nearly $200 million in 1989 and then rising to $260 million in 1990.

By 1990, LiTel was considered among the ten largest of about 250 companies still competing in the long-distance services industry. Despite huge increases in both sales and customers, however, LiTel remained unprofitable into the early 1990s. The lack of a surplus was mostly the result of the massive capital investments required for growth. Indeed, by the early 1990s LiTel was sitting on a mountain of debt that had been used to fund growth and to pay off some of the original investors in the company. Unfortunately, income and cash flow had failed to keep pace with debt growth. The end result was that LiTel, still under the direction of McLernon, was unable to meet its debt service and was even having trouble paying its suppliers. Demise was imminent unless management could engineer a quick turnaround.

### Shake-Up in the 1990s

Impatient with what it viewed as mismanagement, LiTel's biggest investor, E.M. Warburg, Pincus & Co., stepped in and forced a shakeup at LiTel beginning in 1990. Specifically, Warburg and other LiTel investors felt that McLernon and other top executives had failed to properly integrate acquisitions, which had resulted in the loss of both salespeople and customers. They also felt that, among other mistakes, LiTel had unwisely neglected the massive residential market, while at the same time pouring resources into experimental markets such as video conferencing. To whip the organization into shape and give it a new direction, Warburg brought in H. Brian Thompson, a former MCI executive, to act as chief executive. Thompson eliminated several of LiTel's executives and brought in a new team made up largely of former MCI associates.

Thompson immediately went to work, engineering a successful turnaround that had LiTel generating profits by 1994. In an effort he referred to as "triage," Thompson quickly shut down and eliminated unnecessary business, fired sales managers who weren't performing adequately, and laid off much of the company's bloated marketing force. In total, he laid off nearly 25 percent of the entire 1,000 member work force. Importantly, he shifted the company's focus from business customers, who were accounting for about 70 percent of LiTel's business in 1990, to the residential market, which was much more price competitive but made up about 94 percent of all long-distance telephone customers. Thompson also initiated an aggressive drive into international business. To reflect the changes, the company changed its name in 1992 to LCI International.

The changes at LCI quickly showed up on its bottom line. Total debt was steadily slashed (from about $220 million in 1990 to about $120 by the mid-1990s), and profits began to rise. The debt drain was alleviated in 1993 when LCI went public with two stock offerings, spaced 90 days apart, which raised about $200 million. At the same time, Thompson and fellow executives managed to continue growing the company at a rapid pace. While revenues initially dropped as management jettisoned poorly performing operations, they soon climbed, growing from about $260 million in 1992 to $341 million in 1993 and then to about $463 million in 1994. The company showed its first positive net income, of about $7 million, in 1994.

LCI's recovery was conducted without the help of the company's founders. Since LCI's start in 1983, almost all of the members of the original team had departed, and several of them went on to become major players in the telecommunications industry. Ghanshyam C. Patel, for example, went on to become the chairman and chief executive of ConQuest Telecommunication Services Inc., a competing long-distance carrier, and James E. Sobwick became president at ConQuest. Larry Wolfe went to work with Smart Talk Network, Inc., a Canadian telecommunications concern. After resigning from his LCI post in 1991, McLernon devoted his attention to McLernon Enterprises, a launching pad for various technological ventures. Meanwhile, Thompson staffed LCI's management ranks with many outside telecommunications industry veterans.

### Economic Turnaround and Hope for the Future

In a period of three years LCI's new management team increased the company's net worth from less than zero to more than $800 million. That figure still made LCI a very minor player in the multi-billion-dollar telecommunications industry, in which three companies controlled a giant 85 percent of the market. LCI controlled less than one percent, but had big plans for growth. In fact, Thompson had made a point of only hiring executives "who think in terms of billions of dollars," he said in the July 18, 1994 *Washington Post*. "I am trying," he observed, "to build a world class enterprise here that is capable of taking on the best in the business." Among other changes, Thompson moved LCI's corporate headquarters to McLean,

Virginia, reflecting its geographic diversity. The core of company operations, however, remained in Columbus.

Although the majority of LCI's revenues still came from business customers going into 1995, the company was rapidly growing its residential and international businesses in its pursuit to become a fully integrated service provider. In addition to its various long-distance pursuits, LCI started gearing up to compete in the market for local telephone services, which was opened through further deregulation in the mid-1990s. Going into 1996, LCI was employing about 1,200 workers and generating roughly $600 million in revenues annually, and management expected sales to top $1 billion in 1996. LCI continued to pursue rapid growth through acquisitions—such as the October 1995 buyout of US Signal Corp.'s long-distance division—and by expanding existing operations.

### Principal Subsidiaries

LCI International Management Services, Inc.; LCI International Telecom Corp.; LCI Telecom South, Inc.; Ontario Inc.

### Further Reading

Bowen, Mark, "US Signal to Sell Teledial America Inc. to LCI," *PR Newswire,* October 25, 1995.

Byron, Nancy, "Telecommunications Boom: All Paths Linked to LCI," *Small Business News-Columbus,* February 1995, p. 16.

"Columbus Connects to Fiber Optics," *Columbus Business Journal,* June 1985, Sec. 2, p. 12.

Dooms, Tracey M., "LiTel Continues Expansion With One Call Purchase," *Indianapolis Business Journal,* July 16, 1990, p. 5A.

Fette, Jim, "LCI International to Inaugurate Breakthrough 'Simple, Fair and Inexpensive'," *PR Newswire,* July 9, 1992.

Foster, Pamela E., "LiTel Battles Its Way Into the Future," *Business-First Columbus,* April 8, 1991, p. 25.

Gordon, Paul, "Firm Trumpets No-frills Approach to Long Distance," *Peoria Journal Star,* January 19, 1993.

——, "New LiTel Chief Shifts Focus From Going Public," *Business First Columbus,* July 29, 1991, p. 4.

Heschmeyer, Mark, "Worthington Phone Firm Buys Hudson Carrier," *Business First-Columbus,* May 6, 1985, p. 3.

Leger, Michelle, and Ann Hollifield, "LiTel Talking With Buyer, Sources Say," *Business First-Columbus,* October 12, 1987, p. 1.

Lietzke, Ron, "LCI Expects to See Profit Next Year," *Columbus Dispatch,* October 22, 1992, Bus. Sec.

——, "LCI Plans 2nd Customer-service Center," *Columbus Dispatch,* November 15, 1995, p. F1.

——, "LiTel Takes on New Name, New Mission," *Columbus Dispatch,* January 14, 1992, Bus. Sec.

"LiTel: A Heart of Glass," *Business Cleveland,* August 1990, p. 76.

Mills, Mike, "LCI's Multilevel Approach to Marketing," *Washington Post,* September 18, 1995, Bus. Sec., p. 10.

——, "Placing the Right Call with LCI International," *Washington Post,* July 18, 1994, Bus. Sec., p. 5.

Mougey, Susan, "LiTel Registers $140 Million in Floating and Fixed Notes," *Business First-Columbus,* October 8, 1990, p. 4.

Shook, Carrie, "LCI Bets Flat-rate Fees Will Connect with Customers," *Business First-Columbus,* October 31, 1994.

Truck, Julie, "LCI Wants to Ring Up Sales in Home Market," *Business First-Columbus,* March 16, 1992, p. 4.

Wahl, Melissa, "Hotels Are Dialing 'O' for ConQuest Service," *Business First-Columbus,* November 9, 1992, p. 18.

Walpert, Bryan, "The Fall and Rise of LCI International," *Small Business News-Washington,* August 1995, p. 16.

—Dave Mote

# Lear Seating Corporation

21557 Telegraph Road
Southfield, Michigan 48034-6817
U.S.A.
(810) 746-1500
Fax: (810) 746-1524

*Public Company*
*Incorporated:* 1917 as American Metal Products Company
*Employees:* 25,000
*Sales:* $3.15 billion
*Stock Exchanges:* New York
*SICs:* 2531 Public Building & Related Furniture, Seats for
Automobiles; 3465 Automotive Stampings; 3495 Wire
Springs.

Using a strategy of acquisition and geographic expansion, Lear Seating Corporation moved into a leading position among the world's independent (i.e., not owned by an automaker) suppliers of automotive seats in the early 1990s. By 1995, the company held just over one-third of the North American seat market and nearly 20 percent of Western European auto seat sales. The company's more than 100 locations around the world design and manufacture automotive seat frames, covers and components, as well as complete seats and other interior features. More than two-thirds of the company's sales were made in North America, and the remainder were generated in Europe. Although Lear relied on two clients, carmaking giants General Motors Corp. and Ford Motor Co., for more than two-thirds of its sales, the company's seats can be found in more than 80 different car models from automakers worldwide. Following a management-led leveraged buyout in 1988, Lear's sales grew from less than $200 million to more than $4.5 billion by 1995, as the company broadened its geographic reach and expanded its product line to include a wider variety of interior automotive features.

## Establishment and Postwar Growth

Although Lear Seating and its predecessors have always made auto seat components, the company did not make a finished car seat until the mid-1980s. In the near seven-decade interim, it produced everything from plumbing fixtures to office furniture. The business was founded in 1917 as American Metal Products Company (AMP), a manufacturer of tubular, welded, and stamped steel seat frames. Its close proximity to Detroit helped it forge close ties with major auto manufacturers General Motors Corp. and Ford Motor Co. AMP incorporated in 1928 and had broken the $1 million sales mark by the late 1930s. Wartime contracts swelled its annual sales to $11 million by 1944.

AMP's revenues declined sharply in the immediate aftermath of World War II, to $7.7 million in 1945, but postwar demand for automobiles combined with a series of acquisitions to usher in a decade of mounting sales and profits. In 1954, AMP acquired Tube Reducing Corp., a New Jersey manufacturer of specialty hydraulic and aircraft parts. A Canadian producer of metal automotive springs was purchased that same year. In 1955, AMP diversified into plumbing and porcelain bath and kitchen fixtures with the acquisition of AllianceWare, Inc. Burroughs Mfg. Co., a producer of office furniture and storage units, was also added to the corporate roster during this period. Revenues nearly quadrupled to $30.7 million by 1950, then doubled to $63.5 million over the next five years. Net income kept the pace fairly well, jumping eightfold from $346,000 in 1945 to $3 million in 1950, then increasing to $4.3 million by mid-decade. AMP went public at the dawn of this period of dramatic growth in 1946 with a $2.25 million stock offering.

This era of prosperity reached its summit in 1957, when sales and profit peaked at $72.5 million and $4.7 million, respectively. Revenues slid by 36 percent the following year to $46.4 million and net income plunged to $1.6 million. Although AMP's revenues began to recover, rising to $64 million in 1963, its profit level hovered between $1.5 and $2 million.

## Acquisition by Lear Siegler in the Late 1960s

By the time it was acquired by and merged into the Lear Siegler conglomerate in 1966, AMP had amassed an array of businesses with products and competencies that would later be combined in the production of a finished automotive seat. General Spring Products and, later, the No-Sag Spring Co., supplied the springs. The Burroughs Division and Middletown Manufacturing Co., Inc. (acquired in 1965) were already making durable metal office furniture, and AMP itself had long made seat components for cars. While AMP was under Lear Siegler's wing, the parent company acquired Central Foam Corporation, making it a sister division. But nearly two decades would pass before Lear combined these disparate functions to manufacture a complete auto seat.

Lear Siegler was a widely diversified producer of aerospace electronics, climate control devices, and plastics. In fact, AMP (renamed the Automotive Group) was one of more than three dozen acquisitions made by Lear Siegler from 1955 to 1970. With the support of this large parent company, the Automotive Group built its first outsourced passenger car seat in 1984 and set up its first just-in-time plant near a General Motors facility soon thereafter. By 1983, the Automotive Group's annual sales had reached $160 million.

### Management Buyout in Late 1980s Sparks Rejuvenation

The late 1980s ushered in challenges and opportunities that would transform the Automotive Group from a bit player in automotive components to one of the industry's top stars. In spite of anti-takeover measures, Lear Siegler was acquired by the Forstmann Little & Co. investment firm in a $2.1 billion leveraged buyout. Determining that the parts were worth more than the whole, Forstmann Little soon began spinning off Lear Siegler's disparate business segments.

Kenneth L. Way, then corporate vice-president of the Automotive Group, led a leveraged buyout of the division in 1988. Way, who had joined the company in 1966, was able to convince Kidder, Peabody to finance the $500 million deal (more than $400 million of it borrowed) that launched Lear Siegler Seating Corporation. (The "Siegler" has since been dropped.) He became the company's chairman and CEO in 1988 and continued in that position through the mid-1990s.

Once it had gained its independence, Lear Seating grew rapidly by embracing several important industry trends: outsourcing, just-in-time, and globalization, among others. Outsourcing, or contracting parts of the manufacturing process to independent businesses, took the auto industry by storm in the late 1990s. Carmakers found that they could save money and often obtain a better product by putting discrete components up for competitive bid. In the seat segment, for example, Lear and Johnson Controls Inc. competed for the top market share. Knowing this, a given carmaker could negotiate for better

prices, improved features, and higher levels of efficiency than it could gain by keeping production in-house.

Under Way, Lear strove for excellence on all of these fronts. The company had begun to adopt just-in-time (JIT) manufacturing, which emphasizes inventory reduction through efficient and timely production and delivery, in the early 1980s. By 1988, 12 of Lear's American plants were operating on a JIT basis. By locating its production facilities near its clients, Lear cut both storage and shipping costs. In the early 1990s, it added "sequencing" to the JIT equation by integrating its computers with those of its customers. A 1995 *Forbes* article told how Lear's Romulus, Michigan plant is linked to Chrysler's "Dodge City" factory. "When a pickup starts down 'Dodge City's' line, an electronic message calling for the particular seats for that truck is flashed to Romulus, which can produce the seats and deliver them to Chrysler in 90 minutes." Lear was so enamored with the just-in-time process that in 1993 it made "JIT" a part of some divisions' names, as in "Opel/Eurostar JIT."

Lear also began to apply its specialized expertise to the design of auto seats. As a result, the company has a number of industry "firsts" to its credit, including the patented Sure-Bond process, which adheres seat covers directly to the foam padding inside. This process cuts down on labor and waste and broadens the range of design options. During the early 1990s, Lear's innovations included the development of the first child-restraint seat, integration of the seat belt into the seat (instead of the traditional door mounting), and development of a side-impact seat with an airbag. Lear also employed sophisticated computer-aided design and manufacturing systems, utilized in-depth consumer comfort surveys, and conducted numerous safety and durability tests. These efforts resulted not only in growing sales, but also in awards for excellence from customers, including General Motors, Ford, Chrysler, Saab, and Mazda.

Within just a few years of its management buyout, Lear Seating's sales had multiplied nearly eight times, from around $150 million to $1.24 billion in 1990.

### Acquisitions Fuel Continued Growth in Early 1990s

Lear undertook a concerted acquisition strategy in the early 1990s, focusing strongly but not exclusively on the international market. The ongoing outsourcing trend allowed Lear to purchase the seat and interior component divisions of several major original equipment manufacturers, diversifying geographically in the process. In 1991, the company acquired Saab's Swedish and Finnish interior operations. Volvo's interior business came next, in 1992. In 1993 Lear bought Ford Motor Co.'s North American seatmaking operations (Favesa, S.A. de C.V., headquartered in Mexico) for $173.4 million in cash, thereby becoming Ford's seatmaker of choice. Fiat's seat operations (SEPI S.p.A.) were added in 1994, and in 1995 Lear formed a joint venture with Spain's Inespo (a foam manufacturer) to supply seats to Volkswagen in Brazil. By the mid-1990s, Lear had plants in North and South America, Europe, Thailand, Indonesia, and Australia. At that time, more than one-fourth of Lear's sales were generated outside North America.

Fueled in large part by these acquisitions, Lear's sales and earnings multiplied dramatically in the early 1990s. Sales increased at a 34.9 percent average annual clip, from $1.4 billion in 1991 to $4.7 billion by 1995. Earnings grew from a $22.2 million deficit to a $91.6 million profit during the same period.

Lear went public in 1994 with an offering of 14 percent of its equity. The $103 million raised was applied to Lear's long-term debt, reducing it by about 25 percent. It apparently freed up just enough credit to allow the company to make the biggest acquisition in its history. In 1995, Lear purchased Automotive Industries Holding Inc. for $626 million and made it the AI Division. According to the company's 1995 annual report, AI added more than $300 million in sales and doubled Lear's potential market to about $22 billion. The acquisition boosted Lear's product line to what it called "full interior systems," including door panels, headliners, and instrument panels, but not airbags and electronics.

The purchase also seemed to indicate that Lear concurred with industry analysts and executives who felt that outsourcing of complete seat systems had reached its peak and would begin to decline in the late 1990s. As a consequence, Lear expected to maintain its double-digit rate of annual sales increase through research and development of new products, maintenance of a low cost structure, and strategic acquisitions. With more than eight decades of experience and a ranking among the global automobile industry's top ten independent suppliers, Lear Seating Corp. appeared well-positioned to attain that goal.

## Principal Subsidiaries

LS Acquisition Corp. No. 14; Lear Seating Holdings Corp.; LS Acquisition Corporation No. 24; Fair Haven Industries, Inc.; Lear Plastics Corp.; Lear Seating Sweden AB; Equipos Automotrices Totales A.A. de (Mexico); Central de Industria S.A. de C.V. (Mexico; 59.6%); Lear Seating Canada Ltd.; Lear International Ltd. (Barbados) Lear Industries Holdings B.V. (Netherlands); Interim S.A. de C.V. (Mexico; 99.5%); NS Beteiligungs GmbH (Germany); Lear Seating Autositze GmbH (Austria); No Sag Draftfedern GmbH (Germany; 99.8%); Lear Seating GmbH (Germany); Lear France E.U.R.L. (France); Societe No Sag Francaise (55.8%); Souby S.A. (France); Spitzer GmbH (Austria; 62%); Lear Seating (U.K.) Ltd.; Lear Seating Australia PTY. Ltd. (99.9%); Favesa S.A. de C.V. (Mexico); Lear Seating Italia S.r.l. (99%). [principal affiliates] General Seating of Canada Limited (35%); General Seating of America (35%); Industrias Cousin Freres, S.L. (Spain) 49%); Markol Otomotiv Yan Sanayi Ve Ticart (Turkey; 35%); Lear Seating Thailand Corp. (Thailand; 49%).

## Further Reading

Flint, Jerry, "King Lear," *Forbes,* May 22, 1995, pp. 43–44.

Hampton, Bill, "Kenneth L. Way," *Chief Executive,* May 1995, p. 32.

"King Lear: How Competitors View Lear/Automotive Industries Deal," *Ward's Auto World,* August 1995, p. 17.

Kisiel, Ralph, "Buyout Positions Lear as Complete Interior Provider," *Automotive News,* July 24, 1995, p. 14.

Krebs, Michelle, "Integrated Interiors," *Automotive News,* February 27, 1989, p. E20.

Phelan, Mark, "Rocking Around the Clock," *Automotive Industries,* October 1995, p. 129.

Plumb, Stephen E., "Lear Expansion Jumping into High Gear," *Ward's Auto World,* December 1991, p. 63.

——, "Scrambling for Seats: Outside Vendors Offer Complete Seating Systems," *Ward's Auto World,* August 1989, p. 51.

Rivard, K.A., "Lear Seating Corporation," *Investext,* Robert W. Baird & Co., Inc., November 30, 1995.

Sawyer, Christopher A., "Can't Sit Still," *Automotive Industries,* February 1994, p. 68.

Simmons, Jacqueline, "Lear Seating To Sell Shares in Public Offer," *Wall Street Journal,* March 14, 1994, p. A8.

Sorge, Marjorie, "Do Seats Flog Your Fanny?," *Ward's Auto World,* November 1993, p. 44.

——, "Lear Gets Behind Outsourced Seating Plan," *Ward's Auto World,* February 1995, p. 50.

"Southern Exposure," *Automotive News,* December 27, 1993, p. 8.

Winter, Drew, "Growing Modular," *Ward's Auto World,* January 1996, p. 57.

—April Dougal Gasbarre

# Levi Strauss & Co.

**1155 Battery Street**
**San Francisco, California 94111**
**U.S.A.**
**(415) 544-6000**
**Fax: (415) 544-1693**

*Wholly Owned Subsidary of Levi Strauss Associates Inc.*
*Incorporated:* 1890
*Employees:* 37,648
*Sales:* $6.7 billion (1995)
*SICs:* 2325 Men's/Boys' Trousers & Slacks; 2321 Men's/
   Boys' Shirts; 2331 Women's/Misses' Blouses &
   Shirts; 2339 Women's/Misses Outerwear, Not
   Elsewhere Classified

Levi Strauss & Co., the world's largest brand-name apparel manufacturer, gave the world blue jeans and grew enormously rich on this piece of U.S. culture. Indeed, around the world the name of the company's founder has grown to be synonymous with the pants he invented: Levi's. Levi Strauss markets apparel in more than 60 countries, and it has 53 production facilities and 32 customer service centers in 49 countries. The company operates wholly owned businesses in most European countries, in South Africa, Australia, Japan, Hong Kong, India, The Philippines, Malaysia, New Zealand, South Korea, Taiwan, Brazil and Argentina, and operates through joint ventures and licensing agreements in a host of other countries. Besides its well-known Levi's brand products, the company markets clothing and accessories under the brand names Dockers, Britannia, and Slates.

### Early History

Levi Strauss, born in Bavaria in 1829, emigrated to the United States with his family in 1847, at the age of 18. In New York, he was met by his two half-brothers, who had already established a dry-goods business. A year later, he was dispatched to Kentucky to live with relatives and walk the countryside peddling his brothers' goods.

While Levi Strauss was still traveling about the hills of the South, his older sister's husband, David Stern, established a dry-goods store in San Francisco, California, in the wake of the 1849 California gold rush, and the company that would come to bear Levi Strauss's name dates its beginning to this 1850 founding. Three years later, Strauss made the arduous sea journey around Cape Horn to join his brother-in-law. San Francisco at the time was a booming frontier town, and the opportunity was ripe for a well-run business to flourish. Strauss and Stern set up their small store near the waterfront, where they could easily receive shipments of goods from the Strauss brothers back east.

Jeans, which would become the staple of the family business, were invented when Levi Strauss, noting the need for rugged pants for miners, had a tailor sew pants from some sturdy brown canvas he had brought with him on his journey. Once the supply of canvas was exhausted, Strauss turned to a thick fabric made in the French town of Nimes, known as serge de Nimes, which would be shortened to denim. The denim pants, dyed with indigo to make them blue, sold quickly, and the business of Levi Strauss & Co. expanded rapidly, moving three times to new and expanded quarters in the next 13 years. In 1866 the company moved to a luxurious new location on Battery Street, only to have the building cracked from roof to foundation in an earthquake two years later.

In 1872 the proprietors of Levi Strauss & Co. received a letter from Jacob Davis, a tailor in Nevada, offering them a half interest in the patent on a technique he had invented for strengthening the seams of pants by fastening them with rivets. In return, they would pay the cost of obtaining the patent. The cost was negligible, and Strauss and his brother-in-law quickly took the tailor up on his offer. The following year, the company was granted a patent on the use of rivets to secure pocket seams, and also on the double-arc stitching found on the back pockets of its pants.

At first, the company had the pants sewn by tailors working individually at home, in the same way that the Strauss brothers in New York manufactured goods. Soon, however, the demand for the new pants became too great, despite the economic depression that had struck California in 1873, and the company collected its stitchers under one roof, in a small factory on

Fremont Street, which was managed by Davis, the tailor from Nevada. Such remarkable success brought envious competitors, and Levi Strauss & Co. filed its first lawsuit for patent infringement against two other makers of riveted clothing in January 1874. On the second day of that month, the founder of the San Francisco concern, David Stern, died. About two years later, Strauss's two oldest nephews, Jacob and Louis Stern, entered the firm with their uncle.

In 1877, in a climate of dire economic conditions, mobs attacked San Francisco's Chinatown, sacking and burning shops and homes in a three-day riot. White men, unable to find work, took out their frustrations on the Chinese, who had been willing to work for lower wages. In the wake of this event, Levi Strauss & Co. solidified its policy of courting its customers' goodwill by relying exclusively on white women as seamstresses. Because this entailed paying higher wages, the company had to charge higher prices for its products, and thus find ways to deliver higher-quality goods.

In 1877 the Levi Strauss & Co. factory expanded, and the notable features of Levi's pants—the dark blue denim, the rivets, the stitching, the guarantee of quality—became further standardized. By 1879 the pants were selling for $1.46, and they had become widely worn in the rough-and-tumble mines and ranches of the West. The firm also continued to sell other dry goods, chalking up sales of $2.4 million in 1880, and it prospered throughout the 1880s.

In 1886 the "Two Horse Brand" leather tag, showing a team of horses trying to pull apart a pair of pants, began to be sewn into the back of the company's "waist-high overalls," the term Levi Strauss preferred to "jeans." In 1890 the firm assigned its first lot numbers to its products, and the famous number "501" was assigned to the riveted pants. In that year as well, Levi Strauss & Co. was formally incorporated and issued 18,000 shares of stock in the company to family members and employees.

In September 1902, the patriarch of the company died. In his later years, Levi Strauss had entrusted the business more to his four Stern nephews, who inherited the firm, in order to devote his energy to charitable and civic causes. Four years after Strauss's death the company endured another shock, when the

Great San Francisco Earthquake and Fire of 1906 struck. Both the company's headquarters building on Battery Street and the factory on Fremont Street were destroyed. Along with the rest of the city, Levi Strauss & Co. rebuilt, but the ensuing years were difficult. In 1907 a financial panic, which started in New York and crept westward, caused a slowdown in business, and the company began to streamline the merchandise it sold, relying more and more on its own products. Overall, however, sales were flat, and the four Stern brothers had drifted into a pattern of hands-off management.

In 1912 the company introduced its first innovative product in decades, Koveralls, playsuits for children designed by Simon Davis, the son of tailor Jacob Davis, who had followed his father into the business. Advertised widely, Koveralls became the first Levi Strauss & Co. product to be sold nationwide, helping the company to eventually break out of its regional market. The coming of World War I, and the boom in production for the war, had little or no impact on Levi Strauss & Co., since the company held no government contracts. Its riveted denim goods were sold only to the western laborers for whom they had originally been manufactured, and resale of eastern goods accounted for twice the sales of goods made at the San Francisco factory. Slowly, under the hands of the aging Stern brothers, who were resistant to change, Levi Strauss & Co.'s enterprise was losing ground.

### New Leadership

In 1919 Sigmund Stern, who would take over the presidency of the company from his brother, Jacob, in 1921, brought aboard his son-in-law, Walter Haas, to give new blood to the leadership of Levi Strauss & Co. The Haas family, part of the Stern and Strauss clans by marriage, would continue to lead the company into the early 1990s. Walter Haas had little background in the family business, but one of the first changes he made was to update the company's inefficient system of keeping financial records. Despite Haas's attempts at efficiency, the company was battered in the early 1920s by a steep drop in the cost of cotton, the primary raw material for its products, that allowed competitors from other parts of the nation to undercut its prices. Company profits fell by one-third in 1920. In addition, Haas discovered that Levi Strauss & Co. was losing $1 on every dozen Koveralls sold. After a brief internal struggle, the price of Koveralls was adjusted, and steps to increase overall productivity, including the implementation, at this late date, of the assembly-line system, were taken.

The company began attaching belt loops to its basic denim pants in 1922, in addition to the traditional suspender buttons. Throughout the 1920s, Levi Strauss & Co. did business at a profit under the direction of Haas and his brother-in-law Daniel Koshland, a banker, whom he had brought into the firm to assist him. The firm found itself relying increasingly on the pants it manufactured, rather than the other dry goods it wholesaled, for the bulk of its profits. By 1929, 70 percent of the firm's profit derived from its sale of jeans.

### The Great Depression and Thereafter

With the stock market crash in 1929, and the subsequent Great Depression, Levi Strauss & Co. fell on hard times. The widespread unemployment that swept the country throughout the 1930s hit the manual laborers who bought the company's pants particularly hard. By 1930 the company's profits had vanished, and it posted a loss on sales that had fallen one-sixth. Unwilling to cut back production by firing workers, the company amassed a large backlog of unsold products, and then put its employees on a three-day work week. By 1932 company sales had dropped to half their 1929 level. With the coming of the next year, however, the Depression had started to lessen, and sales of Levi's pants slowly began to pick up.

In the economic turmoil of the 1930s, the growing U.S. union movement gained a new stronghold in San Francisco. Although workers in the Levi Strauss & Co. factory had not joined a union, organized labor's insistence that union workers wear union-made clothes sharply limited the company's sales in the heavily unionized San Francisco area. In 1935 Levi Strauss & Co. employees joined the United Garment Workers with management's acquiescence, thereby averting a strike and ending the virtual union boycott of Levi Strauss & Co.'s products.

The Depression and subsequent farm failures of the 1930s eventually worked in the company's favor, enabling it to break out of the relatively small market it had served since its inception. Western ranchers, unable to support themselves through agriculture, turned in the mid-1930s to tourism, inviting easterners to visit "dude ranches," where they were introduced to the cowboy's habitual garb, Levi's jeans. In addition, the advent and growth in popularity of Hollywood western movies further spread the word about Levi's jeans. In its advertising the company had always emphasized durability, but now it also stressed a certain western mystique. To capitalize on its growing brand identification, the company added the trademarked red "Levi's" tab to the back pocket of its pants in 1936, the first label to be placed on the outside of a piece of clothing. As demand increased, the vast stockpile of denim pants accumulated during the early years of the 1930s became depleted, and the factory returned to normal operation.

By 1939 the Levi Strauss & Co. blue denim "waist overall" had just begun to be popular outside the world of blue-collar workers. College students in California and Oregon adopted them as a fad, and slowly this humble item of clothing began to take on a status all its own. After the United States entered World War II, the government declared the jeans an essential commodity for the war effort, available only to defense workers. This restricted distribution made them an even more coveted item, and contributed, in the long run, to the brand's success. In the short run, however, wartime price restrictions cut into the company's profits.

With the war's end, the company was well-situated to prosper. Demographic shifts had brought a large number of potential new customers to the West Coast, and Levi Strauss & Co. now operated five jeans factories, in a futile effort to keep up with demand. The immediate postwar years brought a significant production shortage, and the company instituted a strict program of allocation, favoring retailers that were long-time customers. By 1948 company profits for the first time topped $1 million on sales of four million pairs of pants.

In the booming postwar economy of the 1950s, Levi Strauss & Co. underwent the most significant transition in the company's history. Taking advantage of demographic trends, the company began to focus its marketing efforts on young people, members of the "baby boom," who would wear its pants, now known colloquially as "Levi's," for play, not work. Targeting this new market involved widening the company's sales force to a truly nationwide scope, and shifting its emphasis from rural to more urban areas. As a sign of the company's future, Levi Strauss & Co. closed down its business wholesaling others' merchandise in the early 1950s.

Once again, in the 1950s Hollywood gave the company a large boost in its efforts to sell jeans to young people, when actors such as Marlon Brando and James Dean appeared in *The Wild Ones* and *Rebel without a Cause*, personifying youthful rebellion, and wearing jeans. The pants were losing their status as a symbol of the rugged frontier, and becoming instead a symbol of defiance toward the adult world. Levi's were on their way to becoming the uniform of an entire generation.

In 1954 the company branched out from denim to the sportswear business, launching Lighter Blues, a line of casual slacks for men. The following year the company added jeans with zipper flies, as opposed to the traditional five-button fly, in an attempt to woo customers in the East, where the pants, relegated to department store bargain basements, lagged in popularity. By the end of the decade, Levi Strauss & Co. was selling 20 million pieces of clothing a year, half of them jeans. The company was growing fast, and profits were robust.

### Product Development in the 1950s and 1960s

In the late 1950s and early 1960s, Levi Strauss & Co. experimented with different products and lines of clothing in an effort to build on its reputation and diversify its offerings. In 1959 the company introduced "Orange, Lemon and Lime," pants in six bold colors, which were a short-lived hit. The following year, white Levi's were introduced, a duplicate of traditional jeans, but made in beige twill. Also in 1960, the company introduced pre-shrunk denim jeans, in an effort to overcome the objections of eastern customers, who were uncomfortable with shrinking pants. In 1963 stretch denim and corduroy Levi's joined the fold.

In 1964, after an arduous and expensive process of development, Levi Strauss & Co. introduced Sta-Prest permanent-press pants. Although the product was an initial sales success, problems with the chemical process that created a crease resulted in a large number of defective pants, and it was only later that the pants were perfected. The following year, the company expanded its international division to cover Europe, relying on Europeans to manage company operations in their home countries.

Throughout the 1960s, the company profited from movements in U.S. society, such as campus rebellions and the counter-culture, in which jeans became a uniform. The company's growth was mind-boggling. New manufacturing facilities were added steadily, but demand for jeans still outstripped supply. In the mid-1960s, sales doubled in just three years to $152 million in 1966. That year, the company negotiated a $20 million loan to finance further expansion. Two years later, the company reorganized, establishing a division to produce and market women's clothing. By 1968 the company had grown to become one of the six largest clothing manufacturers in the United States, with sales nearing $200 million.

### Global Expansion in the 1970s

In 1971 Levi Strauss & Co.'s long-standing status as a wholly family- and employee-owned enterprise came to an end, when the company sold stock to the public for the first time. Denim jeans, Levi's in particular, had transcended the status of a mere product to become a worldwide social and cultural phenomenon, and the company could no longer raise enough capital privately to pay for needed expansion. The craze for jeans continued to grow, with seemingly no end in sight. The company coped with a constant shortage of denim. Levi Strauss & Co.'s existing, heavily centralized structure became inadequate, and operations were broken into four divisions: jeans, Levi's for women, boys' wear, and men's sportswear.

The company's phenomenal growth caught up with it in 1973, when its European division found itself with huge supplies of jeans in an outmoded style—straight-legged, as opposed to flared, or bell-bottomed—with more of the same on order. The problem was the culmination of years of undermanagement, and cost the company $12 million as it tried to unload the overstock. For the first time since the Depression, Levi Strauss & Co. announced a losing quarter, and the company's stock price fell dramatically. The following year, European operations were reorganized, and the company moved its headquarters from the site it had occupied on Battery Street for 108 years to new quarters. Seven years later, the company would move again to Levi's Plaza, a newly built complex.

Despite the sobering demonstration in Europe of the company's fallibility, by 1974 sales of Levi Strauss & Co. products had reached $1 billion. The following year the company was once again reminded of the hazards of operating in the murky waters of international business when it was revealed that Levi Strauss & Co. employees in international locations had bribed foreign officials on four separate occasions. When the incidents were discovered by the home office in San Francisco, the practice was immediately terminated. In addition, the company ran into trouble domestically in 1976 when the Federal Trade Commission accused it of price-fixing and restraint of trade because it prohibited retailers from discounting its products. The company reached an agreement with the government in 1977 in which it did not admit wrongdoing, but gave up suggested pricing, retaining the freedom not to sell to certain retailers. In the next several years, the company settled several suits, brought in nine states that charged illegal price-setting practices. The 1970s also saw the formation of the company's community-affairs department, which is Levi Strauss & Co.'s philanthropic arm, and of community-involvement teams, which are company-funded employee groups that participate in projects in communities in which Levi Strauss & Co. does business.

By 1977 Levi Strauss & Co. had become the largest clothing maker in the world. In addition to its original products, the company had grown through acquisitions, and also licensed its name to be used on other products, such as shoes and socks.

Sales doubled in just four years, to hit $2 billion in 1979. Purchases such as Koracorp Industries Inc., a large maker of men's and women's sportswear, in 1979, and Santone Industries Inc., a menswear manufacturer, in 1981, prepared the ground for further growth.

The company, now an industry behemoth, ran into difficulties in the early 1980s, however, as the demand for denim stabilized, and its profits flattened. Attempting to increase its distribution, the company reached agreements with several mass merchandisers, including J.C. Penney and Sears, to market its products. Nonetheless, earnings dropped by nearly 25 percent in 1981, and the company undertook another reorganization, which included the elimination of one level of corporate management. Profits continued to plummet in 1982, and the company shut down nine plants, eliminating 2,000 jobs.

Levi Strauss & Co.'s fortunes made a short recovery in 1983, and the company planned a $40 million promotional tie-in with the 1984 Olympics to promote its relatively new active-wear division. Nevertheless, during the year of the Olympics, in which the firm dressed more than 60,000 participants in the games, profits were down again, and the company undertook a major retrenching, closing many factories and eliminating thousands of jobs. Faced with a demographic trend that showed the baby boomers outgrowing jeans, the company began heavy advertising campaigns, allied itself with designer Perry Ellis in an attempt to move into the high-fashion market, and continued its plans to retrench, as profits dropped by 50 percent.

### A Private Company

In 1985, as Levi Strauss & Co. continued to restructure and cut back, the company was taken private in a leveraged buy out for $1.45 billion by the Haas family, descendants of its founders and long-time company leaders. Several other officers and directors also were members of the buy out group, Levi Strauss Associates Inc. The following year the company introduced a successful upscale men's pants line, Dockers, and, with increasing demand around the world for U.S. jeans, and with the addition of innovative finishes, such as bleaching or stone-washing, 1990 sales reached $4 billion.

Dockers was one of the most successful brand launches in the history of the American apparel industry. The cotton pants appealed to older customers, whose expanding waistlines didn't fit into traditional jeans any more. Sales of Dockers alone came to $1 billion by 1994, and Dockers represented almost 30 percent of Levi's domestic sales. However, this was only one part of the success of the newly private company. CEO Haas, along with Thomas Tusher, head of Levi's foreign operations, transformed the company's overseas markets. In the 1980s, Levi's had diversified its product in Europe into dozens of unrelated lines. Foreign operations accounted for only 23 percent of sales in 1984. Tusher and Haas moved to concentrate foreign sales on the classic 501 jeans, and positioned the pants as a high-priced, prestige product. The company began selling its jeans at posh boutiques in Europe and Japan, at prices more than double the U.S. price. By 1992, foreign sales represented close to 40 percent of the company's revenues, and over 50 percent of profits.

Levi Strauss also tried to upgrade the image of its pants in the U.S., with great success. Levi Strauss spent $230 million on advertising in 1992, in a campaign to add glamour to its old stand-by. Levi's jeans, which were being sold at lower-end department stores like J.C. Penney and Sears, Roebuck began to appear in Macy's, with a considerably higher price tag. The company also began to open its own stand-alone jeans boutiques. The flagship store in Manhattan opened across the street from Bloomingdale's in 1993. Standard 501 jeans there cost $47. Macy's charged $42, and J.C. Penney $29.99. Of course in Europe, the price could be over $80. The same pair of pants retailed at these drastically different prices depending on where it was bought. Not surprisingly under these circumstances, the company's profits soared. Earnings were $155 million on the average in the 1980s. By 1990, earnings stood at $251, and the next year increased to $361. The next two years each added a hundred million also, until by 1995 the company earned over $700 million.

By 1996, Levi Strauss was virtually free of debt, and the company announced it would undertake a second leveraged buy out later in the year, to concentrate its stock in fewer hands. The company made plans to spend $90 million to open stand-alone Levi's stores, Dockers stores, and discount stores for both brands in the United States. Levi Strauss continued to expand its foreign markets, moving into Eastern Europe and expanding sales in India, for example. The company believed that the American market would continue to grow as well. The trend toward casual dress by office workers seemed to be increasing—according to one study, 90 percent of U.S. office workers were allowed to wear casual clothes to work on Friday by the mid-1990s. As jeans became more accepted in the white-collar world, the market for Levi's was expected to widen.

### Further Reading

Cray, Ed, *Levi's: The "Shrink to Fit" Business That Stretched to Cover the Whole World*, Boston: Houghton Mifflin Company, 1978.

*Everyone Knows His First Name*, San Francisco: Levi Strauss & Co., 1985.

Lenzner, Robert, and Johnson, Stephen S., "A Few Yards of Denim and Five Copper Rivets," *Forbes*, February 26, 1996, pp. 82–87.

Mitchell, Russ, "Managing by Values," *Business Week*, August 1, 1994, pp. 46–52.

Munk, Nina, "The Levi Straddle," *Forbes*, January 17, 1994, pp. 44–45.

Teitelbaum, Richard S., "Companies to Watch," *Fortune*, February 8, 1993, p. 127.

—Elizabeth Rourke
—updated by A. Woodward

# Lewis Galoob Toys Inc.

**500 Forbes Boulevard**
**South San Francisco, California 94080**
**U.S.A.**
**(415) 952-1678**
**Fax: (415) 583-4996**

*Public Company*
*Incorporated:* 1968
*Employees:* 241
*Sales:* $220.0 million (1995)
*Stock Exchanges:* New York
*SICs:* 3944 Games, Toys & Children's Vehicles; 3942
    Dolls & Stuffed Toys

Lewis Galoob Toys Inc. is among the ten largest toy companies in North America. This California-based company produces and distributes a variety of promotional toys and games including the Micro Machine line of toy vehicles and Sky Dancer dolls.

## Company Origins

Lewis Galoob Toys was founded in 1957 by Lewis and Barbara Galoob as a small distributor of toys and stationery; the company was incorporated in 1968. Galoob's first toy success was the reintroduction of a battery-powered Jolly Chimp that banged cymbals and nodded his head when activated. This classic toy, along with such stationery items as photo albums and calendars, brought in modest but steady annual sales in the low six figures during the 1960s and early 1970s. In 1970 company founder Lewis Galoob became too ill to continue as president, and his 21-year-old son, David, dropped out of the University of Southern California to take over the family business. David Galoob, whose previous business experience had consisted of selling waterbeds from the back of a truck, began to look for products with the potential to transform the small firm into a top toy producer. In partnership with his brother, Vice-President Robert Galoob, David aggressively pursued new product development, and thereby transformed the company into a $1 million business by 1976.

## First Growth in the 1970s

Lewis Galoob Toy's first breakthrough product was introduced in 1976 when the company purchased the rights to an inexpensive line of radio-controlled, battery-operated cars and trucks. In the era of the "monster truck" rally and the revival of stunt driving, the toy vehicles charmed American kids, and the line of products became one of the company's mainstays for the next twenty years. By 1978 these sturdy little cars had generated sales of nearly $5 million. During the mid 1970s product licensing became an important factor in the toy business as producers sought new ways to predict and harness the desires of young consumers. Galoob made its first major entry into this market when the company bought the license to manufacture Smurf toys. These elfin creatures made popular by an animated television series served as Galoob's main entry into the girl's toy category during the 1970s and early 1980s.

The late 1970s were a time of experimentation for Galoob, as management sought the direction that would allow the company to break into the top echelon of toy producers. "We kept trying to get a handle on the company," David Galoob told *Forbes* in a 1985 interview. After a number of unsuccessful products, including an electronic crap game called "Strobe-Dice," Galoob found its entry into the mainstream through the unlikely medium of a toy license for a television phenomenon called "Mr. T." A bejewelled strong man and his crime-fighting cohorts, the A team, Mr. T had inexplicably captured the imagination of kids around the world, and in 1983, thanks almost exclusively to Mr. T dolls, Galoob posted sales of $28 million. The Galoob brothers decided that Mr. T sales provided the capital they needed to become a major factor in the toy industry, and in 1984 they took the family business public with an IPO of 1.25 million shares.

## Major Successes in the 1980s

With the large influx of capital from Mr. T and the public offering, Galoob was able to expand its own new toy line and to intensify advertising and marketing efforts. In spite of a complete collapse in sales of the fad-driven Mr. T toys, total sales nearly doubled in 1984. With such products as The Animal, an off-road vehicle with claws to climb over rugged terrain, and Sweet Secrets, the first girl-oriented transformable toys, Galoob sales

---

**Company Perspectives:**

*The Company's strategies in selecting and developing products are to focus primarily on lower priced, extendable product lines, to capitalize on current trends in the toy industry and popular culture, and to expand and diversify its product categories.*

---

broke the $100 million mark by 1985. One of the most promising toys of the 1985 line-up became a debacle in the following year as Baby Talk, an electronic talking doll, was one of many casualties of the electronic toy glut of 1987. These high-tech toys had seemed to be the wave of the future in the mid-1980s as toy companies scrambled to compete with Nintendo video games. High costs and technical glitches, however, disenchanted parents and kids alike, and electronic toys led an industry-wide slump in 1987. Galoob's entries into this category included a number of talking dolls as well as a $125 talking board game called Mr. Game Show, whose snide patter and high price tag became a symbol of the unmarketability of these products. The failure of Galoob's electronic toys, as well as serious production delays caused by the shift of toy production to the People's Republic of China, caused sales to decline 40 percent in 1987, and the company posted a net loss of almost $25 million.

The boom and bust cycle experienced by Galoob is inherent in a fad-driven industry like toys, but, where established companies like Mattel could fall back on such long-time favorites as Barbie or Hot Wheels, Galoob was faced with continually developing new hit products just to stay in business. It was clear that the company had to produce a toy with staying power if investors were to be wooed into sticking with the company. Although 1987 was a disastrous year financially for Galoob, it also marked the introduction of the product that was to stand the best chance of becoming a perennial favorite. From the company's first success in the mid 1970s, the toy vehicle category had produced results more often than any other type of toy, and Galoob looked to this category for a new hit. In the early 1980s Galoob purchased the license for a line of miniature toy vehicles from a Wisconsin lawyer-cum-toy-inventor who had tinkered with the idea in his garage. Dubbed "Micro Machines," these cars were modeled on a much smaller scale than traditional toy vehicles, while retaining much of the detail that boys looked for in these toys. Although industry buyers were sceptical, a tremendously successful advertising campaign featuring fast-talking actor John Moschitta came through for Galoob, and the smallest-ever line of toy vehicles became Galoob's best-selling product in its 30-year history. By 1988 sales of Micro Machines contributed $60 million to Galoob's $140 million in revenues; the following year the line's sales had climbed to $135 million out of $228 million in total revenues.

With the spectacular results from Micro Machines, as well as a very successful line of crawling baby dolls called Bouncin' Babies, by the end of 1989 Galoob seemed poised to enter the next decade as one of the premier toy producers in the country. Net income had risen to a record $18.9 million, with cash on hand of over $25 million. In spite of these impressive statistics,

Galoob was unable to escape the boom and bust cycle that is the scourge of the toy industry. 1990 proved to be the worst year that the toy industry had seen in over a decade. With the country in economic recession, consumers were unwilling to spend as much on toys, and nervous retailers began to cancel orders. Galoob's Micro Machines were already overstocked at many retailers because of smaller than expected sales in the 1989 Christmas season, and buyers balked at ordering more inventory. Bouncin' Babies sales had also all but dried up, and none of the newly introduced girl's toys provided comparable financial returns. By the end of the year Galoob had posted a disastrous net loss of $29 million, and development costs of unsuccessful products had eaten up most of the 1989 surplus. To make matters worse, the Federal Trade Commission charged Galoob with making deceptive advertising claims about a number of its toys, and although Galoob denied any wrongdoing, a settlement was reached with the FTC and the ads were pulled.

### Recovery in the 1990s

Faced with plummeting share prices, and with no hit product in the wings, Galoob management was quick to implement a long-term recovery plan with 1994 targeted as the earliest date by which the company could return to profitability. Crucial to this strategy was the development of core brands that could be extended and renewed each year and thereby provide a steady and reliable source of income. In addition, new product development costs were to be reduced in order to lower the break-even point for products, as well as to cushion the company from the effect of unsuccessful introductions. Following the predominant corporate trend of the 1990s, Galoob also undertook considerable reduction of personnel costs by laying off 17 percent of its workforce. In 1991, in what some analysts called a forced ouster, David Galoob resigned, leaving Lewis Galoob Toys with no Galoob in management and ending an era for the family business. Mark Goldman, who had been the company's Chief Operating Officer since 1987 and who was perceived to have a more cautious management style, took over the presidency of the troubled firm.

Micro Machines, Galoob's most successful product to date, was chosen as the key brand to be developed under the new management plan. In the course of the next four years, the Micro Machines concept was extended to five independently marketed thematic playsets featuring more than 155 vehicles in 40 collections. In addition, licensed entertainment properties such as the Power Rangers and Star Wars were applied to the Micro Machines vehicle lines and playsets. Annual sales of Micro Machines, which had dropped to only $43 million in 1991, climbed steadily back up, reaching $113 million by 1994.

Entertainment licensing was vigorously pursued by Galoob in the early 1990s in an attempt to ensure a continuous flow of toy lines based on entertainment properties. Already in control of the valuable Star Wars and Star Trek licenses, Galoob also acquired the rights to Starship Troopers and Jonny Quest, and signed an ongoing agreement with Twentieth Century Fox for new entertainment licenses.

Galoob's first serious entry into the video game market contributed significantly to the company's recovery in the early 1990s. The Game Genie, an adaptor for the Nintendo video game system, allowed players to manipulate attributes in a game that did not normally have built-in variability. Players could give certain characters extra lives, extra strength, speed, or weapons and move from one level to another more easily. Galoob had purchased the rights to the Game Genie from a Canadian inventor in 1990, but before major production could begin, Nintendo of America sued the company for copyright infringement, claiming that the adaptor would make their games less challenging and thereby reduce sales. Nintendo was successful in obtaining a preliminary injunction preventing Galoob from selling the product while the lawsuit was in litigation, but Galoob ultimately won the suit as well as a $16 million settlement for lost sales. The Game Genie was an initial, though transient, success, bringing in $65 million in 1992. This revenue was critical in easing the difficult transition of the early 1990s, but the rapid pace of change in the video game market made such a product inherently unstable and sales dropped to only $4 million by 1994.

Although the development of the Micro Machines brand, the Game Genie, and a lower-risk management style were instrumental in restoring Galoob to fiscal health, it was ultimately another runaway hit toy that propelled Galoob back into the favor of Wall Street. In 1993 Galoob purchased the rights to a flying doll from AGE Entertainment, and the following year the company introduced Sky Dancer, a fairy-like doll whose styrofoam wings lofted her into the air when propelled from a pull-string launcher. Sky Dancer was one of a handful of new girls' toys to be introduced by Galoob that year, and Galoob management was optimistic about the doll's potential. "If it brings in $25 million in 1995, as I expect it will, that'll be a big percentage of our business," CEO Mark Goldman said in a Christmas 1994 *New York Times* article on the doll. By the following month the company had raised this estimate to $40 million, and by April 1995 Sky Dancer had become the No. 1 selling girls' toy in America, with final sales for 1995 topping $70 million. Galoob's stock price, which had been mired at around $6 for over a year, more than doubled over the last half of 1995 thanks in large part to the excitement generated by the Sky Dancer phenomenon.

A renewed Micro Machines line and soaring Sky Dancer sales pushed Galoob's 1995 net income to $6 million on sales of $220 million. In addition, international sales, which had been slowly gaining momentum through the 1990s, now took off, rising 35 percent in just one year. With Galoob firmly in recovery, analysts began to speculate about the company as a candidate for acquisition. As Lewis Galoob Toys entered the last few years of the century, the company appeared to have transformed itself from a hit-dependent young toy company to a more solidly based mainstay of the industry. The toy business and its young customers, however, are notoriously fickle, and it remained to be seen if Galoob could continue to satisfy their ever changing appetite for new toys.

### Principal Subsidiaries

Galco International Toys N.V. (Hong Kong).

### Further Reading

Carlton, Jim, "Who's News: David Galoob Quits Toy Maker Started by His Parents," *Wall Street Journal,* July 1, 1991, p. B6.

King, Thomas R., "FTC Cites Galoob and Its Ad Agency on Toy Claims," *Wall Street Journal,* December 7, 1990, p. B6.

Marcial, Gene G., "A Knock at the Toy Shop Door?" *Business Week,* January 22, 1996, p. 83.

Pereira, Joseph, "Shares of Lewis Galoob Toys Fail to Get a Lift as Its Sky Dancer Doll Flies off Store Shelves," *Wall Street Journal,* April 27, 1995.

Sella, Marshall, "Can a Flying Doll . . . Fly?" *New York Times Magazine,* December 25, 1994, pp. 20–25, 40–45.

Slutsker, Gary, "Good-Bye, Mr. T," *Forbes,* March 25, 1985, pp. 198, 202.

—Hilary Gopnik

# Linear Technology, Inc.

**1630 McCarthy Boulevard**
**Milpitas, California 95035-7487**
**U.S.A.**
**(408) 432-1900**
**Fax: (408) 434-0507**

*Public Company*
*Incorporated:* 1981
*Employees:* 1,350
*Sales:* $265 million (1995)
*Stock Exchanges:* NASDAQ
*SICs:* 3612 Power, Distribution & Specialty
Transformers; 3674 Semiconductors & Related
Devices; 3679 Electronic Components, Not Elsewhere
Classified; 3699 Electrical Machinery, Equipment &
Supplies, Not Elsewhere Classified

Linear Technology, Inc. develops, manufactures, and markets an array of high-performance linear integrated circuits (linear circuits use analog waves, as opposed to binary digits, to measure physical properties such as sound, pressure, weight, and light). The company's products include audio amplifiers, voltage regulators, power management products, and other electronic devices. Other manufacturers incorporate those devices into computers, telephones, satellites, automobiles, and other end-user products.

## The Making of a CEO

Linear Technology is the progeny of engineer and semiconductor industry pioneer Robert Swanson, who founded the company in 1981. With three former coworkers, Swanson built the fledgling Linear into a $100 million company in the span of a decade, and established Linear as a technological leader in its niche. A self-proclaimed goof-off, Swanson nevertheless displayed his desire, early on, to succeed at what interested him. He lettered in football, baseball, and hockey at his western Massachusetts high school during the 1950s, for example, and

spent his summers as a lifeguard. It was during high school, in fact, that Swanson became intrigued with the burgeoning technology of semiconductors.

Swanson graduated from Northeastern University in 1960 with a degree in industrial engineering. Most colleges at the time were still teaching vacuum-tube technology, and semiconductors were in many ways considered to be experimental. But Swanson was fascinated by the promise of the technology. He started hunting for a job in the field, walking into prospective employers' offices in Boston without a resume and asking for work. He turned down a $100-per-week offer from Polaroid to take a job with Transitron, then the nation's second-largest chip manufacturer. It happened to be a great opportunity, as Transitron became a leader in military semiconductor applications. Swanson quickly became involved in a number of high-tech, high-profile projects, including the Polaris Missile program.

After three years at Transitron, Swanson yearned to move to California, where Silicon Valley was emerging as the center of the expanding semiconductor universe. After receiving a call from one of the soon-to-be famous founders of then-unknown Fairchild Semiconductor, he moved west. Swanson worked for chip pioneer Fairchild from 1963 to 1968 before joining National Semiconductor. He spent ten years at that company, helping it grow into one of the largest and most successful players in the chip business. But as National Semiconductor made the transition from a smaller, more entrepreneurial company to a big corporation, Swanson lost interest. "For 13 of 14 years at National, I was a gung-ho guy," Swanson said in the May 13, 1991 *Business Journal-San Jose.* "Then, the company started to get big. I kept looking at all the companies whose butts we'd been kicking. And then National started organizing itself like them. It was frustrating."

Swanson was eager to jump ship and start his own company. He saw the opportunity to do that in the traditional analog chip industry. By the early 1980s the semiconductor industry was beginning to focus heavily on newer digital chips, which offered greater speed and power than traditional analog chips. But Swanson believed that, despite new technology, demand for analog chips would continue to grow. Importantly, analog chips were better than digital chips at measuring real world properties like pressure and temperature, and digital chips required support from analog chips in many applications. Swanson reasoned that, as digital chips increased the potential applications for semiconductors, demand for analog chips would continue to grow despite the fact that they would represent an increasingly smaller share of the overall semiconductor market.

### 1980s: The Startup

Swanson finally left National Semiconductor, and in 1981 formed Linear Technology. His goal was to develop analog chips, and to eventually profit from the growth in new applications created by digital chip technology. He took three fellow executives from National with him, and secured $5 million in venture capital funding. They subsequently hired away several of National's most talented minds. Swanson's former boss at National, Charlie Sporck, was furious that his former coworkers were now going to compete with his company. He tried to squelch the venture with lawsuits, claiming that Linear had stolen technology developed at National. "We did choose to compete against them, and they accused us of misappropriating trade secrets, or stealing," Swanson told the *Business Journal-San Jose*. "But I'll tell you, for every guy we hired away from National, ten applied."

The tiny Linear Technology started out developing and supplying popular analog devices like voltage regulators. It initially found its niche as a second-source supplier, providing chips to buyers whose main suppliers failed to fill an order. By filling that role, Linear was able to get its foot in the door and show the marketplace that it could provide semiconductors that were cheaper, more reliable, and had more features than those provided by the competition. The second-source strategy was particularly effective during the chip boom in 1983 and 1984, when big suppliers reached capacity and equipment manufacturers had to turn to Linear to fulfill their analog semiconductor needs.

During the early 1980s, Linear used the cash flow from its successful, but relatively low-tech, line of analog chips to fund research and development of more advanced linear devices. The company's goal was to become a leader in developing, making, and marketing advanced, high-profit analog chips that could be used in new applications made possible by digital technology. Such applications included miniature battery-powered devices, like cellular phones and portable computers, that required analog technology to, for example, regulate voltage or interpret analog sound waves. The challenge was to design analog chips that were simultaneously more powerful, more efficient, and smaller than those currently in use.

### A Successful Strategy

Linear's legal battles with National Semiconductor turned out to be its greatest challenge during its startup. National filed a series of lawsuits as part of an effort to quash Linear and reduce its competitiveness. But Swanson's bet on the analog chip market paid off big, allowing Linear to overcome huge legal bills that might have ruined most startup companies. In fact, even when the overall semiconductor industry tailspinned in 1985, Linear was able to double revenues in the wake of surging demand for its analog chips. Linear's success was due in part to its growing reputation for quality products and good customer service.

As important as its service and quality focus, though, was the simple fact that Linear was the biggest of only a handful of U.S. companies that had targeted the analog market instead of chasing digital technology. Furthermore, the analog chip industry differed from the digital sector in that the chips Linear produced were typically customized, and did not lend themselves to mass production. One important corollary of that attribute was that Linear was effectively excluded from the rash of Japanese competition that battered U.S. digital chip producers during the mid-1980s. Another advantage that Linear, as an analog chip company, enjoyed was a diversified customer base. That diversity reduced the risk many large digital chip manufactures faced in relying on a few major industries to buy its products.

A final boon for Linear was that it could rely on relatively old technology to produce its chips, while digital chip makers had to stay on the cutting edge to remain competitive. That allowed Linear to post big profit margins once it had successfully developed more advanced analog chips. "The digital guys have to constantly stay on the cutting edge," Swanson said in *Financial World*. "They're lucky if $1 of capital spending yields $1.50 of revenues. For us, $1 will generate $4 of sales." Proof of that statement was eventually supplied by Linear's bottom line. Linear invested heavily and posted net losses throughout the early 1980s. But, as annual sales rose past $20 million, Linear showed its first net income (of $1.17 million) in the fiscal year ending June 30, 1986, and would continue to boost profits every year into mid-1990s.

Linear went public with a May 1986 stock offering to raise expansion capital. During the next 12 months, its sales shot up 60 percent to $35 million, about $3.3 million of which was netted as income. To bolster its manufacturing side and keep up with increasing demand, Linear entered into an important partnership in June of 1987 with Texas Instruments. The deal gave Linear access to Texas Instruments' advanced chip processing technologies and low-cost assembly and test facilities in Taiwan. In return, Texas Instruments was allowed to use several of Linear's proprietary chips for relatively negligible royalties. That expanded production capacity helped push Linear's sales to $51 million in 1988 and then to $65 million in 1989, by which time Linear was generating nearly $16 million in annual profits.

### Growth in the 1990s

After wowing investors with big gains during the mid- and late 1980s, Linear went on to achieve even greater growth and profitability during the early 1990s. Linear's engineers and marketers attacked almost every niche of the semiconductor market, producing specialized, high-tech analog chips that were incorporated into automobiles, cellular telephones, computer peripherals, satellites, medical instruments, and many other electronic products. "They're basically in anything that has a switch," said semiconductor industry analyst Carolyn Rogers in a 1992 *Business Journal-San Jose* article. Linear's sales increased to $119 million in 1992, while net income rose to $25 million. Investors made the company a Wall Street darling, pushing its stock price to record highs quarter after quarter.

Going into 1993, Linear's war chest was brimming with $100 million in cash that was waiting to be invested in new projects. And the company's long-practiced strategy was still producing big profits. Indeed, by the mid-1990s Linear was the largest of only two big companies competing in the high-end analog circuit business. And foreign competition was still negligible, as Linear sold small volumes of specialized chips to American buyers, a market of little interest to Japanese producers of low-cost, mass-market chips. To take advantage of ongoing market growth, Swanson announced plans in 1993 to build a semiconductor wafer fabrication plant in Camas, Washington. Scheduled for phase-one completion in 1996, the plant was expected to consume up to $85 million in capital over a six to ten year period.

Linear sustained its rampant growth into the mid-1990s, increasing revenues to $150 million in 1993 and then to $201 million in 1994. Meanwhile, net income rose to $36.5 million and then to $56 million, evidencing the huge profit margins generated by Linear's premium chips. Its performance earned it a reputation as one of the hottest prospects in Silicon Valley, and one of the best-managed companies in America. For the first five years of the 1990s, in fact, Linear was named to *Forbes* magazine's Best 200 Small Public Companies. Likewise, in 1995 *Business Week* listed it as the 557th most valuable company in America. Semiconductor industry watcher *In-Stat* declared that Linear Technology Corp. was "the best financially managed manufacturer in the semiconductor industry."

Linear boosted sales to $265 million in 1995, an impressive $84.7 million of which was netted as income. With sales continuing to surge in 1996, Linear remained focused on its strategy of developing and producing high-performance analog circuits for almost any application, ranging from factory automation and avionics to satellites and automobiles.

## Principal Subsidiaries

Linear Semiconductor Sdn. Bhd.

## Further Reading

Coghlan, Paul, "Linear Technology Corporation to Build Wafer Fabrication Facility in Camas, Washington," *PR Newswire*, July 29, 1993.

Goldman, James S., "Bob Swanson: Hard-driver Focuses on Low-tech Chips," *Business Journal-San Jose*, May 13, 1991, p. 12.

Goldman, James S., "Linear Technology Profits in Manufacturing Analog Chips," *Business Journal-San Jose*, October 19, 1992, p. 5.

Jones, Stephen, "Linear Tech Projects New Growth in Analog Chip Market," *Business Journal-San Jose*, June 22, 1987, p. 9.

Plansky, Paul, "Reading Between the Headlines of Gloom & Doom," *Santa Clara County Business*, November 1986, p. 15.

Twitty, Roy, "New Generation Multiple-output DC/DC Converters Power Notebook Computers at Constant Frequency," *Business Wire*, January 31, 1996.

Wrubel, Robert, "Back to the Future," *Financial World*, April 19, 1988, p. 48.

Yanish, Donna Leigh, "Linear Tech Seeks at Least $11 Million in Offering," *Business Journal-San Jose*, April 21, 1986, p. 39.

—Dave Mote

# Lionel L.L.C.

50625 Richard W. Boulevard
Chesterfield, Michigan 48051
U.S.A.
(810) 949-4100
Fax: (810) 949-3340

*Wholly Owned Subsidiary of Wellspring Associates L.L.C.*
*Incorporated:* 1900 as Lionel Manufacturing Company
*Employees:* 600
*Sales:* $55 million (1992)
*SICs:* 3944 Games, Toys & Children's Vehicles

Lionel L.L.C. is the world's leading manufacturer and marketer of model and toy trains. With almost a century of experience by the mid-1990s, Lionel held an established and respected name in the toy industry. Although the company suffered serious problems from the late 1950s through the 1960s, including bankruptcy proceedings, it recovered and regained much of the ground it lost by the 1990s. With 350 products and seemingly stable sales growth, Lionel enjoyed a resurgence of model train enthusiasm in the mid-1990s.

Joshua Lionel Cowen, born in New York City on August 25, 1877, did not set out to create the electric model train or to found one of the most successful 20th century toy manufacturers in the United States. Cowen dropped out of Columbia University and began work as an assembler at an electric lamp factory. However, Cowen's natural skill with electric devices and his desire to innovate led him to conduct electrical experiments after hours at work. About 1898 Cowen's tinkering led to his development of a fuse for igniting magnesium powder for photographers. The U.S. Navy heard about the invention and contacted Cowen to build fuses to be used for exploding mines. Cowen gained $12,000 from his subsequent contract with the Navy, which he used to open a small shop in New York City in 1900. The new enterprise, christened the Lionel Manufacturing Company, produced fuses, low-voltage motors, and electrical novelties. Cowen continued to experiment with electricity, and in 1900 he developed the first dry cell battery.

## Early Electric Trains

In 1901 Cowen created a window display for his shop that would change the direction of his company. To showcase one of his small electrical motors, he placed one in a model railroad car and ran it on a track in his shop window. Cowen had hoped the train would grab the attention of passers-by, and they would stay to buy his products. The train did indeed attract the attention of people, but what they wanted to buy was the train! Cowen was soon selling the trains to individual customers and other stores. Within two years, the Lionel Manufacturing Company was issuing catalogs for the trains. The first catalog, in 1903, featured $2\frac{7}{8}$-inch gauge trains and track. The gauge refers to the width between the rails of the track. In addition to locomotives, the catalog offered a steel derrick car and a gondola car. A particular train in this catalog, a steel reproduction of a Baltimore and Ohio R.R. locomotive powered by a wet cell battery, initiated a demand for small scale reproductions of real trains. Designing and manufacturing reproductions for those interested in this new hobby would become a staple for Lionel.

Business grew rapidly. In 1905 Cowen hired Mario Caruso, a young engineer, to help with manufacturing. Soon a strict division of labor developed: Cowen handled the marketing of the trains, and Caruso ran the manufacturing plants. Caruso remained with the company until 1945. Production quickly outgrew the company's New York manufacturing plant, and in 1910 Lionel moved to a new factory in New Haven, Connecticut. In addition to an increase in the sheer number of trains produced, the selection expanded rapidly as well. The 1906 catalog offered a single locomotive, two electric trolley cars, two passenger cars, and seven freight cars, which included an oil tank, a coal car, a cattle car, a box car, a gondola, and a caboose. In contrast, the 1910 catalog offered several different locomotives, an increased number of freight and passenger cars, and eleven trolley cars. The company had also introduced tin lithograph stations and small human figures to aid in the creation of realistic scenes.

## Company Perspectives:

*Lionel has so much to offer everyone. But what may even be more important than the products offered, is the American family tradition that Lionel represents. Lionel model railroading is not just a hobby, it's an American institution which dates back nearly 100 years. From the time Joshua Lionel Cowen placed the first electrically-powered car on a circle of track, individuals, fathers and sons, and entire families have joined together to experience the "magic" of Lionel model railroading. Whether placed in large public displays, in living rooms, in basements, or around the family Christmas tree, a Lionel train truly has something special to offer everyone.*

A couple of important changes occurred in Lionel train design in the first decade of the century. First, the increasing number of homes wired for electricity meant that the trains no longer had to be powered by dry cell batteries. Cowen developed a transformer that reduced household current to a safe level for use with Lionel trains. Second, Lionel introduced in 1907 a three-rail track that measured 2⅛ inch between rails. This gauge became so popular in the United States it was soon known as "standard gauge."

Gauge became an important marketing factor when Lionel competitor Ives Trains introduced the "O" gauge train in 1910. Smaller than the standard gauge train, the "O" gauge had only 1¼ inches between the rails. The gauge's popularity led Lionel into that market in 1915, when the company introduced 9 sets of "O" gauge trains. At the time, Lionel offered 17 sets of trains in standard gauge.

### Rapid Growth

The company, which changed its name in 1918 to the Lionel Corporation, continued to experience rapid growth through the 1920s. Increased production again forced the company to move to larger facilities, this time to a plant in Irvinton, New Jersey. Lionel also increased its size and market share by acquiring its biggest competitor, Ives Trains, in 1928. Initially Lionel bought the company in partnership with the model train company American Flyer Trains, and both companies supplied some parts for Ives trains through 1929 and 1930. However, Lionel bought out American Flyer's interest in Ives at the end of 1930. Lionel then closed the Ives plant in Bridgeport, Connecticut, and transferred the operations to its New Jersey facility.

The demand for reproductions of real trains grew through the 1920s. Throughout this time Lionel produced several sets of highly authentic trains as part of its numerous offerings of locomotives and train cars. During this "classic period" for Lionel, the company created model cars and engines with an astonishing attention to detail, including many models with brass and nickel trim. For example, the powerful 408E twin-motored engine featured six running lights, operating pantographs, and all brass detail. Lionel sets from this time, which included highly detailed passenger cars in addition to the loco-

motives, became valuable collectors' items, sought after by collectors and train enthusiasts through the end of the century.

### Depression Product Lines

The Depression forced a slight change in focus at Lionel. Sales dropped for the toy manufacturer early in the Depression, and the company responded by shifting production to lower-cost items, particularly to the smaller "O" gauge trains. Customers reacted favorably, and by 1939 Lionel had completely discontinued production of its standard gauge, three-rail trains. Despite the focus on lower costs, Lionel continued to introduce new models. The company's first steam-type "O" gauge locomotive debuted in 1930; within five years, Lionel made eight different "O" gauge steam engines. Streamlined passenger trains were introduced in the middle of the decade, as was the first steam whistle. Some demand for high-priced reproduction models remained, and Lionel filled it with its exact scale "O" gauge Hudson steam locomotive in 1937, which cost $75 at the time.

However, low-priced items were a staple in the company's sales during the Depression. One new line in particular helped buoy company sales. In collaboration with the Walt Disney Company, Lionel created a Mickey Mouse hand car in 1934. A single car that was wound by hand, the one-dollar toy enjoyed a vast popularity. Its success engendered a whole line of similar toys, including a Santa Claus hand car, introduced in 1935; Donald Duck and Peter Rabbit "chick mobiles," which came out the following year; and the Mickey Mouse Circus Train. Mickey, as the conductor of the tin locomotive, led the train filled with Disney passengers past a cardboard backdrop of a circus.

In 1938 Lionel introduced its first "OO" gauge train, a scale model of the Hudson engine with a tender and four freight cars. An immediate success in the "OO" gauge market, the Hudson model was the first of several that Lionel designed in the late 1930s. However, Lionel stopped production of toy trains in 1942 to join the war effort and never resumed its line of "OO" trains, even after the war ended.

Lionel's adjustments to the Depression market appeared successful. In 1937 the company employed 1,000 people and produced approximately 40,000 model train engines, 1.2 million railcars, and more than a million sets of track. That year Lionel offered stock to the public for the first time. With the entrance of the United States into World War II, Lionel suspended its model train production and began manufacturing navigation and communication equipment for the armed forces.

### Postwar Growth

Toy train production resumed in 1945 under the direction of Lawrence Cowen, the son of Joshua Lionel Cowen. Having assumed the presidency that year, Lawrence remained at the head of the company until its sale in 1959. He oversaw the introduction of the company's all-time top-selling train engine, the Santa Fe Diesel, in 1948. Not only did Lionel begin producing diesel engines in 1948, it used plastic in its trains for the first time. The year of its fiftieth anniversary, 1950, Lionel unveiled Magne-Traction, a system designed to increase the pulling power of the locomotives. By inserting permanent magnets into the locomotive driving axles, a magnetic attraction was induced between the wheels and the steel track, enabling the locomotives to pull more cars and work better on steep grades.

Pent-up demand for consumer goods after the war led to some of Lionel's best years. By 1953 Lionel was the largest toy manufacturer in the world and employed 2,000 people. Mismanagement and a shrinking market, however, reversed the company's fortunes. In the mid-1950s Lawrence Cowen attempted to diversify Lionel's products and holdings, perhaps in response to decreasing interest in model trains from the public. In 1957 the company began marketing "HO" gauge trains, licensed first from Rivarossi and later from Athern, but the line didn't sell and was dropped in 1967. Cohen also introduced a stereo camera and acquired Airex Corporation, a fishing reel manufacturer, but both ventures proved unprofitable. Labor disputes added to the company's misfortunes, disrupting production at the New Jersey plant with strikes. In 1958 Lionel lost $470,000 on sales of $14.5 million, the company's first yearly loss since the Depression.

The next year, 1959, Lawrence Cowen sold Lionel to a group of investors, sparking almost three decades of shifting ownership. Roy Cohn, Joshua Cowen's great nephew and head of the investors, hoped to gain government missile contracts by acquiring electronics firms. Cohn placed John Maderis, a former major general, at the head of Lionel but replaced him in 1962 with Melvin Raney. Not only did government missile contracts fail to appear, but sales remained stagnant as well. Cohn sold Lionel at a significant loss in 1963 to financier Victor Muscat, who resold the company later the same year to a group led by A. M. Sonnabend of the Hotel Corporation of America. Sonnabend died the next year, and Robert Wolfe, a former toy company executive, was named president.

Wolfe took over a company that had suffered at the hands of its numerous leaders in the previous decade. Employees had been let go, and high-quality product lines had been discontinued in order to cut costs. Efforts to diversify the company's product line, including ventures into microscopes, science labs, and tape recorders, had only served to blur the company's focus. Wolfe was determined to return Lionel to its traditional niche as a high-quality toy train manufacturer. However, even with the company's focus back on producing high-quality electric trains, Lionel continued to lose money. Its 1967 purchase of American Flyer Trains, its largest competitor, did nothing to stem the tide.

### Bankruptcy and Reorganization

In 1969 the company was forced to reorganize by a bankruptcy proceeding. General Mills, Inc., bought the rights to the Lionel name and all of the company's manufacturing equipment. What was left of the original Lionel Corporation emerged as a holding company for toy stores and hobby shops. Before resuming production of Lionel trains, General Mills moved the company's manufacturing equipment from New Jersey to Mt. Clemens, Michigan. Fundimensions, a division of General Mills Fun Group, assumed responsibility for the Lionel train production and revitalized the ailing brand.

In 1973 Fundimensions attempted to revive the Lionel "HO" gauge line, manufacturing the trains in Mt. Clemens and the Orient. However, the line once again failed to sell and was discontinued five years later. In 1979 Fundimensions reintroduced the American Flyer S Gauge trains as part of the Lionel line. In general, Lionel trains regained its health in the 1970s, enjoying increasing sales through the decade. However, in 1983 General Mills combined its toy manufacturing, including the production from Fundimensions, Kenner Toys, and Parker Brothers Games, and moved it all to Mexico. The new plant had a difficult time maintaining the quality of Lionel products and frequently missed delivery dates to retailers, injuring the reputation of the brand. When Kenner-Parker Toys, Inc., spun off from General Mills in 1985, Lionel went with it as one of its divisions. That year Lionel moved its train production back to Mt. Clemens.

In 1986 Richard P. Kughn, a Detroit real estate developer, formed a corporation with a group of investors in order to purchase Lionel Trains. After paying an estimated $25 million, the group incorporated the enterprise as Lionel Trains, Inc. Kughn, who took over as the company's chairman, was an avid model train collector and, when he became interested in purchasing Lionel, already owned thousands of trains in a collection whose worth was estimated at nearly $1 million. Within two years of the purchase, Lionel's sales rose 150 percent, to $50 million a year, and market share reached 60 percent. Both the Collector and Traditional lines of trains showed record sales that year.

Kughn, with his background as a model train collector, saw a market for reissues of classic Lionel trains. He initiated a new line in 1988, Lionel Classics, that directly reproduced the metal Lionel trains of the 1920s and 1930s. However, Kughn also encouraged innovation, particularly in the development of state-of-the-art technological features. RailScope, a locomotive with a miniature video camera in the nose, was introduced in 1988 to give railroading enthusiasts a chance to see the ride as an engineer would. The following year RailSounds debuted in the Pennsylvania B6 Scale Switcher engine and the Reading T-1 Northern Locomotives. The micro-electronic sound chip placed inside the engines held an exact sound recording from full-size trains. In 1994 Lionel incorporated a high-tech remote control device into a new series of trains. Through a joint venture with Lionel called Liontech, the rock singer Neil Young developed the TrainMaster in order to share his passion for model railroading with his son Ben, a victim of cerebral palsy. Easier to use than a traditional transformer, the hand-held controller uses on-board electronic processors to move the train via electronic signal and incorporates digital sound to more closely reproduce such sounds as engines churning or cars uncoupling.

Completely new product lines also expanded Lionel's offerings during the late 1980s and early 1990s. Ready-to-run sets of trains with an "O27" gauge, slightly smaller than the "O" gauge, were first offered in the late 1980s. A new line of trains that were 1/24th the size of real trains was introduced in 1987. Roughly twice the size of the "O" gauge trains, the Lionel Large Scale was made of weather resistant plastic to allow their use indoors or out. In collaboration with the Smithsonian Institution, Lionel created a collection of museum-quality "O" gauge engines. An exact replica of the 1938 New York Central Dreyfuss-Hudson locomotive, the first engine produced, was offered in a limited edition run of only 500.

### New Owners in the 1990s

Neil Young's interest in Lionel expanded in 1995 when he joined with former Paramount Communications chairman Martin Davis to purchase Lionel from Kughn. The purchase was friendly, with Kughn remaining as chairman emeritus and retaining a minority share in the renamed Lionel L.L.C. Wellspring Associates L.L.C., an investment firm started by Davis, held Davis's majority share. As part of the deal, Lionel became the full owner of Liontech, the joint venture with Young.

The increasing popularity of model trains in the mid-1990s boded well for Lionel. With 350 products and several years of steady growth, Lionel had a sturdy base from which the new owners could work. Davis and Young hoped that incorporating new technology into the company's traditional train sets would draw even more enthusiasts into the Lionel fold. "[Lionel's] technology is now the leading technology in toys," Young was quoted as saying in *Fortune* in 1995. "The overall goal is to make an advanced toy that brings families together in a way videogames don't."

### Further Reading

"Developing a New Train of Thought: Rocker Helps Lionel Make a Better Toy," *Crain's Detroit Business,* December 5, 1994, p. 1.

McComas, Tom, and James Tuohy, *Lionel: A Collector's Guide and History,* Wilmette, Ill.: TM Productions, 1978.

"Neil's Wheels," *Time,* October 9, 1995, p. 91.

"Rocker, Partner Buy Lionel," *Crain's Detroit Business,* October 2, 1995, p. 33.

Serwer, Andrew E., "An Odd Couple Aims to Put Lionel on the Fast Track," *Fortune,* October 30, 1995, p. 21.

"Toy Train Fanciers Team Up to Acquire, Modernize Lionel," *Wall Street Journal,* September 26, 1995, p. 9B.

Treece, James B., "The Little Train Company That Could," *Business Week,* December 26, 1988, pp. 70–71.

—Susan W. Brown

# Liqui-Box Corporation

6950 Worthington-Galena Road
Worthington, Ohio 43085
U.S.A.
(614) 888-9280
Fax: (614) 888-0982

*Public Company*
*Incorporated:* 1920 as Corrugated Container Co.
*Employees:* 818
*Sales:* $147.8 million (1994)
*Stock Exchanges:* NASDAQ
*SICs:* 3565 Packaging Machinery; 3089 Plastics
Products, Not Elsewhere Classified

Liqui-Box Corporation pioneered the use of bag-in-box packaging in the United States in the 1960s and continued to lead that market into the mid-1990s. The company's specialty packaging and the filling and dispensing systems that compliment it are used in the processed food and beverage, pharmaceutical, and specialty chemical industries. Liqui-Box's strong rate of return and steady growth won it recognition as one of *Forbes* magazine's "Best Small Companies in America" throughout the 1980s and into the 1990s. Liqui-Box had the U.S. aseptic packaging market to itself for most of its history, but by the mid-1990s, its domestic competitors included Combibloc Inc., Thermoforming USA, and Asepak Corp., all of Ohio. In many respects, however, the firm's biggest rivals are the manufacturers of metal, paperboard, and glass containers. Members of the Davis family, including Samuel B., his sister Jane D. Ferger, and mother Jeanette A. Davis, continued to control at least 25 percent of the company's equity through the early 1990s.

## Origins and Early History

Liqui-Box traces its origins to Corrugated Container Company, incorporated in 1920 in Columbus, Ohio. The firm's first generation in business appears to have been rather uneventful; by 1945, when it was acquired by Sam S. Davis, the company had only 25 employees and $250,000 in annual sales. The new owner invested heavily in production and warehouse space, opening a box assembly plant in West Virginia in 1953 and more than tripling the headquarters operation from 1945 to 1962. By 1960, annual sales had grown to $6.8 million, with net income of about $213,000. The business became so vital to its community that the city of Columbus named the street it occupied "Corrugated Way" during the 1960s.

### Pioneers in Aseptic Packaging during the 1960s

Corrugated boxes would not be the company's longstanding claim to fame, however. In 1960, Corrugated Container pioneered the production and use of aseptic packaging in the United States. Originally developed in post–World War II Europe, aseptic packaging marries the product (usually a liquid) with the packing process in a totally sterile environment. The package's best-known incarnation in the United States is the drink box, but by the early 1990s consumers could find aseptically packaged wine, tomato products, and soy milk on their supermarket shelves. Aseptic packages enjoy several advantages over their more traditional glass, metal and rigid plastic counterparts. When packaged aseptically, foods, beverages, and other perishables have a longer shelf life and don't need to be refrigerated until the package's seal is broken. The packages usually weigh less, generating savings on shipping costs, and constitute less solid waste. The concept has been widely known and employed in Japan and Europe for decades but was prohibited in the United States for many years.

Spearheaded by Robert S. Hamilton and Bob Curie, Corrugated Container developed the bag-in-box liquid packaging system around the aseptic idea. Liqui-Box Corporation was created in 1961 as a subsidiary of Corrugated Container. Although company executives were convinced that their new product was superior to many of the liquid packaging systems then available, they were faced with two primary obstacles. First, as the founders of the industry in the United States, they were obliged to design and manufacture the equipment needed to manufacture and fill the plastic bags as well as the closures that would make the packages practical. Second, the company needed to win converts to their newfangled packages. Although Liqui-Box has obviously enjoyed a measure of success in both these

---

**Company Perspectives:**

*The availability, formability and recyclability of the raw materials common to our products—and the cost savings afforded customers by our products over other packaging materials—have led to continued acceptance of our products in established markets. These same elements are permitting us to pursue new, attractive opportunities as we increasingly view established markets from a global perspective.*

---

areas, the company has continued to develop new products and cultivate new markets throughout its history.

Largely out of necessity, Liqui-Box quickly became vertically integrated, manufacturing and selling the machines that filled, sealed, put a closure or tap in each bag, and simultaneously enclosed the bag in a box. By 1973, the company had even added a plastic extruding subsidiary that made the plastic film for shrink-wrapping and trash-can liners as well as the bags in bag-in-box.

Liqui-Box initially marketed its bag-in-box package to dairies as a replacement for the typical metal five-gallon milk can. According to a case study on Liqui-Box published in a 1990 marketing textbook, "dairies were so enthused with the bag-in-box that within six years of introduction, 95 percent of dairies had converted to the bag-in-box packaging concept for institutional size packaging of fluid milk."

In 1968, Liqui-Box developed a ten-quart, rigid polyethylene bottle originally intended for home delivery of milk. The blow-molded package featured the "Handi-tap closure," a proprietary toggle valve that made the package easy to use. When home delivery of milk declined, Liqui-Box marketed its package to the bottled water industry. By the early 1990s, Liqui-Box's Handi-tap dominated the bottled water category. A company video proudly proclaimed that the closure used on the container was "never successfully duplicated."

Within a decade of the Liqui-Box launch, Corrugated Container's sales multiplied more than fourfold, from $6.8 million in 1960 to over $33.5 million by 1972. Profits more than sextupled, from $213,000 to $1.4 million during the same period. The company's corrugated business continued to expand during this period, with the addition of a joint-venture paper mill in 1967 and the acquisition of box manufacturers in Kentucky and Michigan in the late 1960s and early 1970s. A name change, to Corco, Inc. in 1968, reflected the company's diversification. The corrugated operations were moved to a new, larger facility in nearby Delaware, Ohio, in 1974. Liqui-Box was spun-off as a separate company in 1977, when Corco merged with longtime affiliate Willamette Industries. Samuel S. Davis remained with Liqui-Box.

### Expansion in the 1970s and 1980s

Representing the second generation of the Davis family to bring change to Corco, Sam B. Davis joined the company as vice-president for corporate growth in the mid-1970s. In 1975, he adapted General Electric's Lexan brand polycarbonate plastic for use in the bottled water industry. The substance's light weight, resistance to breakage, and lack of taste transfer made it an ideal replacement for the heavy, five- and 10-gallon glass bottles traditionally used for office-style water coolers. Dubbed "unglass" by Liqui-Box's marketers, the clear plastic container eventually earned the company a leading position in the corporate and residential markets for replacement bottles for water coolers.

Over the course of the 1970s and 1980s, Liqui-Box expanded the potential applications for its bag-in-box packaging from its base in dairy products. The company had the most success marketing its unique packaging to bulk producers and institutional food servers. By the late 1980s, they had adapted the technology to package concentrated mixes and flavorings, condiments, wine, chemicals, and liquid detergents. Liqui-Box's development of dispensing systems around the bag-in-box helped make the transition from traditional packages easier for potential customers. For example, the company created portioning devices that connected easily with its condiment packages. This commitment to research and development won converts in the fast food industry, where strict cost controls and efficiency are paramount.

Although the company wasn't particularly successful at marketing its packaging for retail consumption, beverages in pouches were better-received at the single-serving level. Such institutional meal servers as schools and hospitals began adopting the package in 1971, when some beverage producers began offering milk and juice in eight-ounce pouches to schools. The packaging offered up-front savings as well as real economies in the areas of waste reduction (at 80 percent less than the familiar paperboard containers) and storage space.

Liqui-Box's sales more than doubled, from $29.1 million in 1977 to $63.9 million by 1985, and its net income quadrupled from $1.1 million to $4.6 million during the same period. The company was listed on *Forbes*'s roster of the "200 Best Small Companies in America" five times from 1980 to 1990, and made the "Honor Roll" of companies with a return on equity of more than 17.2 percent from 1985 to 1990.

Liqui-Box's 1989 acquisition of B-Bar-B Corp. of New Albany, Indiana, helped push annual revenues over $100 million that year. The new affiliate brought valuable sales and marketing skills to compliment Liqui-Box's well-established expertise in research, development and manufacturing. Executive Vice-President Peter Linn told the *Columbus Dispatch* that the merger would make Liqui-Box the world's largest producer among bag-in-box manufacturers in terms of units and dollars.

### Acquisitions in the 1990s

Acquisitions fueled geographic and product diversification in the early 1990s. In 1991, Liqui-Box purchased Inpaco for $312,000, adding specialty capabilities in wholesale food and pharmaceutical packaging. Two years later, Liqui-Box paid $14.85 million to acquire liquid packaging plants in California and England from Sonoco Products Co., consolidating its European production capacity at Sonoco's headquarters in Romiley, England. By 1994, international sales—both direct and via licensees and distributors—contributed between 10 and 15 percent of Liqui-Box's total annual sales. The company made a logical—and admittedly "defensive"—diversification into bottled water production in 1991, launching its own "Alaskan Falls" brand that year.

Annual sales grew by over 38 percent, from $113.1 million in 1990 to $156.4 million in 1995, and net income grew by over 22 percent, from $9.9 million to $12.1 million, during the same period.

Although American consumers remained suspicious of unrefrigerated (aseptically packaged) milk, Liqui-Box began to penetrate the retail packaging segment in the early 1990s. Via warehouse stores the company began to offer milk and juice in the 2.5 gallon Handi-tap container traditionally used for bottled water.

In 1993, Liqui-Box inked a 10-year contract with Perrier Corporation of America to manufacture 2.5-gallon and larger containers for the company. While CEO Samuel B. Davis touted the long-term commitment, sales to Perrier totaled over 15 percent of Liqui-Box's total annual revenues in 1994 and 1995.

Liqui-Box appeared to be firmly ensconced in several growing markets in the mid-1990s. Consumption of bottled water, through both office-style water coolers and retail outlets, enjoyed double-digit annual growth in the early 1990s, and that trend was expected to continue through the remainder of the decade. Liqui-Box's persistent efforts to penetrate the retail market through supermarket and warehouse packages should also pay off, as consumers become more accustomed to aseptic packages. In the long term, the company's commitment to research and development combined with its sharp marketing and promotions capabilities seemed likely to keep it at the forefront of this emerging segment of the packaging industry.

### Principal Subsidiaries

Alaskan Falls Bottling Company; LB Communications, Inc.; LB Development Corp.; LB Investments, Inc.; LB Acquisition Corp.; LB Europe Limited (England); Inpaco Corporation; Commander Systems, Inc.; Liqui-Box International, Inc., Liqui-Box Europe, SA (England); Liqui-Box of Canada, Ltd.; Corporate Design, Inc.

### Further Reading

Bacha, Sarah Mills, "Box Company Adding Water to Its Package," *Columbus Dispatch,* October 19, 1991, p. 1E.
——, "Liqui-Box Links Growth to Perrier Deal," *Columbus Dispatch,* April 23, 1993, p. 2E.
——, "Liqui-Box Pins Growth on Overseas Market, New Products," *Columbus Dispatch,* April 28, 1994, p. 1D.
Blackwell, Roger D., et. al., *Cases in Marketing Management and Strategy.* Chicago: Dryden Press, 1985, pp. 151–160.
——, *Contemporary Cases in Consumer Behavior.* Chicago: Dryden Press, 1990, pp. 165–177.
Candisky, Catherine, "Liqui-Box Accused of Sexual Harassment," *Columbus Dispatch,* February 10, 1993, p. 3D.
Foster, Pamela E., "Liqui-Box Bags New Markets with Inpaco Acquisition," *Business First-Columbus,* January 14, 1991, p. 3.
"Liqui-Box Deal Makes It Largest," *Columbus Dispatch,* July 7, 1989, p. 1E.
Moore, Richard N., "Corco Division Introduces Giant Plastic Water Bottle," *Columbus Dispatch,* June 26, 1975, p. 4C.
Turner, Mike, "Boxy Beverages Carve a Niche," *Grand Rapids Business Journal,* May 4, 1987, p. 1.
Wagman, David, "Combibloc's Aseptic Packaging Making Inroads," *Business First-Columbus,* August 25, 1986, p. 6.
Wasnak, Lynn, "Good Old Factory Cooking," *Ohio Business,* November 1985, p. 36.
Wolf, Barnet D., "Liqui-Box Increases Its Shares," *Columbus Dispatch,* April 27, 1990, p. 2E.
——, "Liqui-Box Striving for Excellence," *Columbus Dispatch,* April 30, 1992, p. 2B.

—April Dougal Gasbarre

THE LOEWEN GROUP INC.

# The Loewen Group, Inc.

**4126 Norland Avenue**
**Burnaby, British Columbia V5G 3S8**
**Canada**
**(604) 293-6447**
**Fax: (604) 473-7330**

*Public Company*
*Incorporated:* 1985
*Employees:* 10,000
*Sales:* $599.9 million (1995)
*Stock Exchanges:* Toronto and NASDAQ
*SICs:* 7261 Funeral Services & Crematories; 6311 Life
Insurance; 6531 Real Estate Agents & Managers

The Loewen Group, Inc. is a funeral service corporation located in British Columbia, Canada. The largest funeral service corporation in Canada and the second largest such firm in North America, The Loewen Group owns and operates 847 funeral homes, 23 cemeteries, 12 crematoria, and 3 ambulance companies in Canada, the United States, and Puerto Rico. With more than 10,000 employees, the company provides a full range of funeral services, including prearrangement, family consultation, the sale of caskets and related funeral items, the preparation of the body and removal of the remains, the use of a funeral home for both visitation and worship, various transportation services, and, in addition to the traditional burial items, a cremation service.

### Early History

The roots of The Loewen Group can be traced to A. T. Loewen, the director of a small funeral home in Steinbach, Manitoba. Opening his business in 1961, Loewen operated a highly successful, but small-volume, operation in a rural area in one of the great western provinces of Canada. When A. T. Loewen fell sick and was unable to continue as director of the funeral home, his son Ray assumed control of the entire business. Ray Loewen had just completed his degree in theology from Briercrest Theological College located in Saskatchewan. He had not intended to follow in his father's footsteps; given the circumstances, however, Ray dutifully continued what his father had begun.

Not satisfied with the state of funeral care and services in Manitoba, Ray Loewen came up with an idea to create a chain of funeral homes that would arrange to share resources such as hearses and services such as body preparation. Unfortunately, not many people were won over by his idea. The young entrepreneur could not find many funeral homes that were willing to become part of a national chain, and the idea of economies of scale was alien to him. Part of Loewen's initial difficulties in establishing a funeral home chain was the result of unusually high barriers to entering the funeral home business. Because of the long-standing reputations and recognition of family-run funeral homes within individual communities, it was almost unheard of for an outsider to arrive in a small town and suddenly open a funeral home. Therefore, the resistance to the idea of establishing a funeral home chain was disappointing to Loewen, but not altogether surprising.

Unable to fulfill his dream, in 1969 Loewen decided to move his family to British Columbia, where he operated a funeral home, but also delved into real estate and transportation businesses. Although he was able to acquire a number of funeral homes during this time, Loewen became increasingly disillusioned with the funeral home industry. In 1975, Loewen abruptly turned over all responsibility and management of his business holdings to one of his most trusted managers and campaigned successfully as a member of the Conservative Party for a seat in the provincial legislature of British Columbia. Loewen served as a member of the legislature for a period of four years and was much admired by his fellow Conservative Party colleagues for his trustworthiness and knowledge of the political issues of the day. In 1979, Loewen left the political arena as abruptly as he had entered it and set up a major real estate development and management company. When the real estate market began to suffer during the early 1980s, Loewen thought he would take another chance at fulfilling his dream of building a chain of funeral homes.

## Company Perspectives:

*Funeral service is an old and honorable profession. The people of The Loewen Group are proud to stand as champions of this noble calling. Our commitment is to help families through one of the most difficult times humankind endures.*

### Creating a Company During the Mid-1980s

Loewen had more luck the second time around. In the United States, Houston-based Service Corporation International was in the process of an aggressive acquisitions campaign, buying up funeral homes at a rapid pace across the country. When Service Corporation International entered the Canadian market, funeral home owners in Manitoba, British Columbia, and other provinces began to think about selling their businesses. Suddenly, Loewen found himself flooded with acquisition opportunities primarily consisting of "mom and pop" family-run funeral homes in small communities that preferred to sell their business to a large Canadian consolidator.

Incorporated as The Loewen Group, Inc., in October of 1985 and encompassing funeral services, real estate, and insurance, in two brief years the company was operating 45 funeral homes throughout the western provinces of Canada. Loewen had also learned the meaning of economies of scale, and he had centralized the firm's purchase of such items as embalming fluid, coffins, advertising, and other essential ingredients to the funeral service industry. During the late 1980s, Loewen's wide range of funeral service offerings, his ability to create economies of scale, and his successful advertising resulted in a phenomenal 65 percent increase in revenue for each funeral service conducted under the auspices of his growing company.

In 1987, The Loewen Group reported earnings of $786,000 on revenues of approximately $14 million. Yet this was not enough capital to expand the company as rapidly as Loewen wished. So the founder decided to sell 10 percent of the company to the public and, as a result, raised $4.6 million to fund his ever-growing list of acquisitions. As it happened, however, the year reflected a very mediocre performance for the worldwide stock exchanges, consequently diminishing the inflow of capital that Loewen initially had expected. His ability to make acquisitions was curtailed, and, as he experienced unexpected difficulties turning around the acquisitions he had recently made, Loewen arranged a management conference in Vancouver to discuss the direction of the company. At the conference, Loewen asked how many of the former funeral home owners who were now within The Loewen Group had previous experience managing their business within the framework of a budget. Out of a total of 160 former owners, only 4 people had such experience. Loewen immediately initiated a comprehensive plan to teach each funeral home director the intricate details of balancing a budget. Loewen's commonsense strategy was that it was much easier to teach a funeral home director how to do accounting than it was to teach an accountant how to treat grieving relatives of the deceased.

### Acquisition and Expansion During the Late 1980s

At the beginning of fiscal 1988, The Loewen Group owned and operated 98 funeral homes and 5 cemeteries. One year later, that number had risen to more than 120 funeral homes and 10 cemeteries. The focus of Ray Loewen's acquisition strategy during these years, a strategy that has remained relatively unchanged, was his concentration on small, family-operated funeral homes and cemeteries. Loewen's modus operandi was to acquire a funeral home or cemetery, keep the existing management in place, retain the name of the acquired funeral home, and provide funeral directors with generous stock options in the company.

Loewen's unique strategy of "regional partners" also proved highly successful. Regional partners were the leading operators of acquired businesses who were allowed to strike a formal affiliation with The Loewen Group and were permitted to retain an interest of approximately 10 percent in the future appreciation of the company's entire regional operation. This arrangement gave the regional partner the ability to benefit from The Loewen Group's financial support, while the parent company benefited from the regional partner's involvement in the local community and ability to identify potential candidates for acquisition. Loewen's "regional partner" strategy worked so well that within two years nearly 30 percent of all company acquisitions of family-run funeral homes had been identified by regional partners.

The Loewen Group was also able to take advantage of the stability of what had come to be called the "death care provider" industry. From 1983 onward, demographic statistics showed that not less than two million people in North America would die each year. And as baby boom survivors reached the age of 65, it was projected that the annual death rate would surpass three million. Thus, regardless of economic conditions, the death rate assured the industry of a regular customer base. By continuing its strategic acquisition policy of "mom and pop" family funeral homes and capitalizing on the gradual rise in death rates across North America, by the beginning of 1990 the company had acquired almost 300 funeral homes and approximately 25 cemeteries.

### Growth During the 1990s

In April 1991, to accommodate the growth of the company and the expansion of its administrative offices, The Loewen Group moved its headquarters to a large, three-story building in Burnaby, British Columbia. Always cognizant of the welfare of its employees, during this period of time the company established an employee share ownership program for both full-time and eligible part-time employees. By the end of fiscal 1993, The Loewen Group had acquired an additional 83 funeral homes and 33 cemeteries; by the end of fiscal 1994, the company had acquired another 108 funeral homes and 46 cemeteries. The total number of funeral homes and cemeteries owned by The Loewen Group on September 18, 1995 was 764 and 172, respectively, an astounding six-fold increase since 1989.

Along with this phenomenal period of acquisition and expansion, however, came an event that threatened the very existence of the company. The Loewen Group, in the course of its expansion strategy, acquired several local funeral homes in the immediate area of Biloxi, Mississippi. Valued at a cost of $8.5 million, two of the funeral homes belonged to Jerry O'Keefe, a former mayor of the city of Biloxi. The purchase ended O'Keefe's exclusive arrangement to sell his own insurance in the funeral homes that The Loewen Group had purchased. Therefore, O'Keefe decided to sue The Loewen Group for the right to sell his own insurance. Rather than litigate over what management at The Loewen Group regarded as a minor issue, the company agreed to combine funeral-insurance operations in the funeral homes purchased from O'Keefe.

When The Loewen Group backed out of the agreement, O'Keefe returned to court and sued the company for fraud and antitrust violations. O'Keefe had hired an extremely enterprising lawyer who convinced the local jury to award his client between $100 and $400 million in compensatory and punitive damages. These amounts would have wiped out the net worth of The Loewen Group, and the company decided to appeal the verdict. To make matters worse, however, the Mississippi judge ruled that The Loewen Group would have to post 125 percent of the award within one week, a total of $625 million, if the company wished to continue with the appeal. Company management was understandably stunned. They considered a range of alternatives, from borrowing the money for the bond to declaring bankruptcy under Chapter 11. At the eleventh hour, after endless meetings and sleepless nights, management at the company's headquarters in Burnaby, British Columbia finally agreed to settle out of court for $240 million.

Although the company's stock fell from a high of $41 per share to an all-time low of $8 during the litigation, Ray Loewen was determined not to let this episode prevent him from forging ahead. In early 1995, Loewen acquired the Osiris Holding Company for $103.8 million. Located in Philadelphia, Pennsylvania, Osiris owned and operated 22 cemeteries and 4 combination funeral home/cemetery facilities, all of the properties within the United States. In August of 1995, the company purchased MHI Group, Inc., an operator of 13 funeral homes, 4 cemeteries, and 3 crematories in the state of Florida, and 5 additional properties in Colorado. One of the most significant properties involved in this transaction was the Star of David funeral home/cemetery facility that served a large Jewish community in Fort Lauderdale, Florida. During late 1995 and early 1996, the company concluded two more major acquisitions, including the Shipper Group and Ourso Investment Corporation. Shipper Group owned and operated a total of 7 cemeteries in the New York/New Jersey area, including Beth Israel Cemetery in Woodbridge, New Jersey. Beth Israel Cemetery was the largest cemetery serving the Jewish community in the state of New Jersey. Ourso Investment Corporation, located in Louisi-

ana, was the owner of 15 funeral homes, 2 cemeteries, and a growing life insurance business. With annual revenues of more than $70 million, The Loewen Group expected high returns from Ourso within a very short time.

In addition to its aggressive expansion of its network of funeral homes and cemeteries in North America, in the early 1990s the company established The Loewen Children's Foundation, a not-for-profit organization to promote and support hospice care for terminally ill children in both Canada and the United States. The company was also a founding sponsor of Canuck Place, the first free-standing hospice facility to care for terminally ill children and the needs of their families in North America.

The Loewen Group became the second largest provider of death care services in North America, ranked along with the leader in the industry, Service Corporation International, and third-placed Stewart Enterprises. These three companies, however, represented less than 8 percent of the industry's total properties and less than 15 percent of its total revenues. With more than 85 percent of the funeral homes within the United States still family-owned or under private ownership by the mid-1990s, The Loewen Group felt confident that there would be ample opportunity to continue its growth through acquisition strategy.

### Principal Subsidiaries

Loewen Group International, Inc.; TLGI Management Corporation.

### Further Reading

Bohner, Kate, "Tasteless," *Forbes,* July 3, 1995, p. 18.

Carlisle, Tamsin, "Loewen To Settle Provident Lawsuit for $30 Million," *The Wall Street Journal,* February 13, 1996, p. A8(E).

"Crisis for a Funeral Giant," *MacLean's,* February 5, 1996, p. 40.

Day, Eileen, "Beyond Breaking Records," *Vision, The Loewen Group, Inc.,* November 1995, p. 5.

Hyndman, Peter, "Closure in Mississippi," *Vision, The Loewen Group, Inc.,* March/April 1996, p. 8.

"Loewen Group," *The Wall Street Journal,* November 7, 1995, p. B4(E).

"Loewen Group Buys U.S. Firm," *The Wall Street Journal,* March 20, 1995, p. B4(E).

McMurdy, Deirdre, "Mississippi Blues," *MacLean's,* February 12, 1996, p. 50.

Olsen, Walter, "A Small Canadian Firm Meets the American Tort Monster," *The Wall Street Journal,* February 14, 1996, p. A15(E).

"Undertaker Lives On," *MacLean's,* February, 12, 1996, p. 68.

—Thomas Derdak

# LONG ISLAND BANCORP INC

# Long Island Bancorp, Inc.

201 Old Country Road
Melville, New York 11747
U.S.A.
(516) 547-2000
Fax: (516) 547-2631

*Public Company*
*Incorporated:* 1867 as Long Island City Savings Bank
*Employees:* 1,341
*Total Assets:* $4.93 billion (1995)
*Stock Exchanges:* NASDAQ
*SICs:* 6035 Savings Institutions, Federally Chartered

Long Island Bancorp, Inc. is the holding company for The Long Island Savings Bank, FSB, which converted from a mutual to a stock form of organization in 1994. The Long Island Savings Bank was one of the ten largest thrift institutions in the New York metropolitan area in the early 1990s and ranked second in deposits in Long Island's Suffolk County in 1994. In 1995 it had 36 full-service bank offices: 19 in Suffolk County, 11 in Nassau County, and 6 in Queens County (New York City's borough of Queens). The bank also operated 16 regional leading centers along the eastern seaboard.

## 19th Century Beginnings

The bank was founded as the Long Island City Savings Bank in 1876. Long Island City, which was incorporated as a municipality in 1870 and became the county seat of Queens in 1872, was larger than the present-day neighborhood of that name; it took in all of Queens's East River shoreline and included the communities of Astoria, Steinway, Ravenswood, Sunnyside, and Hunter's Point. Even so, Long Island City had only about 20,000 residents in 1876. It was still rural except along the riverfront. Here the southern part was filling with factories, and the northern part held a number of large suburban homes. Long Island City could only be reached from New York City (which then consisted of Manhattan and the southern Bronx) by ferry.

The Long Island City Savings Bank opened its doors in a building on Jackson Avenue and Third Street in Hunter's Point. Its first president, Sylvester Gray, owned a nearby refrigeration factory and was politically well connected, having served as chairman of the local board of education and as excise commissioner. J. Harry Smedley, superintendent of a nearby lard-oil factory, was the bank's secretary and served in that post for 36 years. Long Island Savings was a mutual savings bank, owned by its depositors. Since there was no commercial bank in the area, a special act of the state legislature gave it permission to establish a checking department, but this act was soon repealed.

The first years of the Long Island Savings Bank were difficult ones. Smedley later recalled that in addition to serving as secretary, he was also the bank's cashier, bookkeeper, janitor, and office boy. Because of the small salary he also took a job with the Standard Oil Co., which gave him leave for the two hours a day that the bank was open. About 1885, however, John H. Thiry, another member of the board of education, initiated the idea of teaching children thrift by having them establish bank accounts. A special legislative act authorized teachers to collect pupils' savings and turn them over to the principal, who opened an account as trustee for the children. By 1925 the bank had 22,000 children, attending 27 schools, as depositors.

The school children of Long Island City were credited by Smedley with saving the bank, however unwittingly. In 1883 total deposits, from 705 accounts, came to only $51,300. Ten years later, when the Long Island City Savings Bank was still one of only two banks in western Queens, the number of its accounts had grown to 6,232, with deposits totaling $553,846. The last decade of the 19th century also saw other significant changes. The bank moved to a new Jackson Avenue building in 1893. William J. Burnett, a physician, succeeded Gray as president in 1896, and Queens became a borough of New York City in 1898. The Long Island Savings Bank made many mortgage loans to homeowners and was described in a book published during this period as "the poor man's best friend" in Long Island City. At the end of 1902 the bank had 8,157 accounts and deposits of $2.35 million.

345

---

**Company Perspectives:**

*We build lifelong relationships by listening to our customers and fulfilling their changing financial needs.*

---

### Continued Growth to Mid-Century

The next great event in Queens history was the opening of the Queensboro Bridge, linking Long Island City to midtown Manhattan, in 1909. Three years later the bank moved its quarters to the Queens Court Plaza building by the bridge, using wagons to haul millions of dollars in cash and securities to the new offices during the Labor Day holiday lull. In 1920 the bank moved into its own building on Bridge Plaza North. A branch was opened in Astoria the following year.

By 1928 the Long Island Savings Bank had 64,874 depositors and deposits of $51.7 million. Its earnings that year came to nearly $3 million. Of its assets, $35.3 million was held in bonds and mortgages. With not only the bridge but railway and rapid transit service reaching western Queens from Manhattan, the area grew quickly in population. Around 1920 most Long Island City lots could be purchased for between $3,000 and $5,000, compared with $8,000 to $15,000 in the Bronx and Brooklyn. Real estate investment jumped from $35 million in 1920 to $157 million in 1924. With more than 1,600 factories, Long Island City also had become one of the largest manufacturing centers in the United States.

Savings banks weathered the Great Depression better than commercial banks or fellow thrift institutions like savings and loan associations. Commercial banks were at greater risk than thrifts because of their high proportion of demand deposits. Savings banks had substantially higher reserves than savings and loans, made shorter-term loans, and had portfolios with lower loan-to-value ratios. The Long Island Savings Bank never had annual net earnings in this decade below the $195,827 recorded in 1935. With $63.2 million in deposits in 1939, it ranked 27th among U.S. savings banks. There were 102,525 depositors at the end of 1940.

### Expansion Eastward into Suburbia in the 1950s

The Long Island City Savings Bank added a Jackson Heights branch in 1948 and in 1951 had assets of $179 million and more than 112,000 depositors. More than $1 million was in children's accounts. A Rego Park branch was opened in 1956. At the end of 1960 the bank had $329.3 million in deposits from 193,479 depositors and net earnings of $1.7 million for the year. By this time the bank, like many of its customers, was looking eastward to suburbia. It opened a branch in the Nassau County community of Syosset in 1962 and changed its name from the Long Island City Savings Bank to the Long Island Savings Bank in 1966.

In 1970 the Long Island Savings Bank had assets of $690.3 million and deposits of $632 million, with 184,113 depositors at the end of the year. During the 1970s the bank opened branches in Astoria, Flushing, Long Island City, and Whitestone in Queens, Huntington, Merrick, and Seaford in Nassau County, and West Islip in Suffolk County. In 1976, its centennial year, the bank moved its headquarters from Long Island City to Syosset.

### The 1980s: Growth by Acquisition

The Long Island Savings Bank had nearly $1.2 billion in assets in 1980. By the end of 1982 it was the largest savings bank on Long Island, and the following year it switched from a state to a federal charter. In 1983 the bank acquired, with federal aid, a troubled thrift institution, Suffolk County Federal Savings and Loan Association, which had 36 offices and $2.7 billion in assets. It was made a subsidiary and renamed the Long Island Savings Bank of Centereach.

The Long Island Savings Bank added, in 1986, another ailing thrift institution, the Flushing Federal Savings & Loan Association. In agreeing to acquire this institution, which had eight offices and $467.5 million in assets but a negative net worth of $7 million, the bank received a commitment of $60.8 million in assistance from the Federal Savings and Loan Insurance Corp. Long Island Savings, with $5.2 billion in assets and 55 branches, now was the seventh largest mutual savings bank in New York. It slimmed down again, however, in 1993, when it sold branches with deposits of about $950 million to Home Savings of America for an undisclosed sum.

### A Broader Range of Products and Services in the 1990s

In 1990 the bank established the Long Island Savings Agency ("LISA") as a wholly owned service corporation to offer nontraditional, fee-based products to its customers. At first LISA sold single-premium deferred-annuity products. It was expanded in 1993 to offer a broader range of financial products and services, including an expanded line of annuities and other investment products, by marketing a line of mutual funds with a variety of investment objectives.

Ranking seventh among lenders on Long Island in 1994, the Long Island Savings Bank was seeking to enter the top three by turning as many depositors as possible into borrowers and increasing its purchases of new loans from other lenders. The bank was buying loans on a wholesale or correspondent basis in New Jersey and Connecticut as well as New York. Its methods of getting the word out to potential retail customers included targeted mailings, advertising on radio and television, and a prospective point-of-sale lending program in the offices of real estate agents.

The Long Island Savings Bank converted from mutual ownership—ownership by its depositors—to a stock form of ownership in December 1993. The restructuring involved the creation of a Delaware-incorporated holding company, Long Island Bancorp, Inc., with the bank as its subsidiary. Long Island Bancorp completed a common stock offering in April 1994, raising $296.9 million in net proceeds by selling 26.8 million shares of stock at $11.50 per share. Long Island Bancorp then purchased all of the capital stock of the Long Island Savings Bank for $164 million. Traded on the Nasdaq stock market, Long Island Bancorp shares rose almost immediately after issue and closed at $24.50 a share at the end of 1995.

The bank's principal business continued to be attracting deposits from the general public and investing these deposits and other funds primarily in single-family, owner-occupied residential mortgage loans. It was also investing, however, in higher-yielding mortgage-backed and asset-backed securities and, to a lesser extent, in multifamily residential mortgage loans, commercial loans, consumer loans, and other marketable securities. The bank's main sources of funds, in addition to deposits, were borrowings under reverse repurchase agreements and principal and interest payments on loans and mortgage-backed securities. It was also offering investments, life insurance, homeowners' insurance, mortgage life insurance, and other products. In 1995 the bank introduced its first credit card program, featuring Visa and MasterCard with low introductory rates and no annual fees.

During fiscal year 1995 Long Island Bancorp acquired the lending operations of Entrust Financial Corp. and Developer's Mortgage Corp. The acquisitions of these mortgage bankers enabled the bank to open retail offices in Pennsylvania, Delaware, Maryland, Virginia, and Georgia as well as New York, New Jersey, and Connecticut. As a result, the bank closed more than $1 billion in mortgage loans in fiscal 1995, compared with $435 million in fiscal 1994. The bank also had correspondent loan agreements with select mortgage bankers originating loans throughout the United States.

At the end of 1995 Long Island Bancorp had assets of $4.93 billion and deposits of $3.6 billion. Of its net loan portfolio of $2.1 billion, one-to-four-family real estate loans formed 81 percent of the total in fiscal 1995 and all real estate loans accounted for 94 percent of the total. Nonperforming loans came to $63.8 million, or 1.2 percent of total assets. Net income was $43.5 million in fiscal 1995. Management and employees held about 13 percent of Long Island Bancorp's shares.

Long Island Savings Bank moved its executive offices in 1988 from Syosset to a building on a 682,000-square-foot plot in Melville. This property had a book value of $46.1 million in 1995, when Long Island Bancorp owned 24 and leased 12 of its branches. Its regional lending centers were being leased.

### Principal Subsidiaries

Long Island Savings Agency; Long Island Savings Bank, FSB; Mortgage Headquarters Inc.

### Further Reading

Easton, Nina, "Long Island Savings Bank Buys Ailing Flushing Federal Thrift," *American Banker,* May 1, 1986, p. 2.

"From Yesterday to the World of Tomorrow," *QueensBorough,* November 1939, pp. 6, 18.

Hazelton, Henry Isham, *The Boroughs of Brooklyn and Queens, Counties of Nassau and Suffolk,* Vol. 4, New York and Chicago: Lewis Historical Publishing Co., 1925, pp. 391–392.

Kelsey, J.S., *History of Long Island City, New York,* Long Island City: Long Island Star Publishing Co., 1896, pp. 123, 165, 167.

Queensborough Chamber of Commerce publication, January 1925, p. 64.

Roosevelt, Phil, "Long Island Savings Taking on the Big Players in Its Market," *American Banker,* February 25, 1994, p. 10.

Stahl, David, "Getting Your Fair Share," *Savings & Community Banker,* May 1994, pp. 34–37.

"Thrift Unit Rescued in L.I. Merger," *New York Times,* August 18, 1983, pp. D1, D4.

—Robert Halasz

Maine Central
Railroad

# Maine Central Railroad Company

**Ironhorse Park**
**North Billerica, Massachusetts 01862**
**U.S.A.**
**(508) 663-1129**
**Fax: (508) 663-1143**

*Wholly Owned Subsidiary of Guilford Transportation*
  *Industries, Inc.*
*Incorporated:* 1862
*Employees:* 600
*Sales:* $50 million (1995 est.)
*SICs:* 4011 Railroads, Line-Haul Operating

Maine Central Railroad Company is a private subsidiary of Guilford Transportation Industries, Inc., one of the largest and most successful transportation firms operating in the northeastern section of the United States. Maine Central Railroad hauls thousands of tons of freight per year, mostly in Maine and New Hampshire.

### Early History

The beginning of Maine Central Railroad dates to the early and mid-19th century when small railroad lines were established to haul lumber from inland mills to seacoast ports. Because of the large amount of timber that required transportation, numerous railroad firms sprang up throughout the New England region, especially in the dense wooded areas in Maine. Firms like the Calais Railroad Company and the Piscataquis Canal and Railroad Company owned and operated small tracks, consisting of anywhere between two- and 12-mile rail lines. One of the most important of these companies, the Whitneyville and Machiasport Railroad Company, had constructed an eight-mile rail line to ship lumber from the burgeoning mills in Whitneyville to the shipping facilities at Machiasport. Like many other small railroad lines, the Whitneyville and Machiasport would soon become part of the Maine Central Railroad.

By the early 1860s, there were so many small railroad companies hauling lumber over relatively short distances that competition began to drive out some of the firms. To increase their chances of survival and ensure their companies of being able to take advantage of the coming boom in railroad traffic, the Androscoggin and Kennebec Railroad Company decided to arrange a merger with the Penobscot and Kennebec Railroad Company. This merger, finalized in Waterville, Maine on October 28, 1862, resulted in the formation of the Maine Central Railroad. Just one year later, the newly formed company reported gross revenues of approximately $350,000. Having consolidated its operations and administration, management at Maine Central decided to purchase or lease a significant mileage of rail lines to prepare for the future.

One of Maine Central Railroad's most important leases, concluded in 1882, involved the connecting line for transatlantic liners between Halifax and St. John, Canada, and New York City. The arrangement stipulated that the Canadian Pacific Railroad would operate the section of the line that ran from St. John, across the international bridge between Canada and the United States, to Vanceboro, Maine. The Maine Central Railroad leased and would operate 163 miles of railroad track from Vanceboro to Bangor, Maine. Although the track of the Whitneyville and Machiasport was sold during the 1890s because of the decline of the lumber business in the state of Maine, additional acquisitions and leases of rail lines led to a continued expansion of Maine Central Railroad operations.

During the early years of the 20th century, Maine Central Railroad played a leading role in the development of Maine as a holiday state. Affluent families from farther south on the eastern seaboard, stretching from New Jersey to Massachusetts, chose Maine as their vacation spot. The company's parlor cars and coaches were full of visitors destined for luxury hotels operated by enterprising individuals and many of the railroads themselves. By 1910, because of the influx of ever-larger numbers of annual summer visitors, Maine Central Railroad created a fleet of steamships that extended the company's services far beyond the final destinations of its rail lines.

In 1917, Maine Central Railroad stretched across three states, including Maine, New Hampshire, and Vermont, with a total of 1,358 miles of rail lines within its continually increasing transportation system. Before the car began to alter the method of transportation in the 1920s throughout America, people were almost entirely dependent upon public transport, especially relying on the railroads to traverse long distances. Companies such as Maine Central Railroad connected larger metropolitan areas with smaller rural communities and encouraged the development of industry along the rail lines. With the resurgence of the lumber and paper industry in Maine during the 1920s, Maine Central Railroad provided access to forested land that seemed to be, at the time, an inexhaustible supply of timber for the paper mills.

The high point for Maine Central Railroad and, indeed, for the American railroad industry occurred in 1929. The company operated nearly 1,500 miles of track and reported 1,659,000 freight train miles, with 78 locomotives in service. Nearly 500 miles of rail lines were operated through leases that cost the company more than $800,000 in annual rentals. In 1929, operating revenues reached a total of slightly more than $20 million, $5 million of which was derived from passenger train and boat service revenues for transporting approximately 1,397,000 passengers.

### The Great Depression

When the stock market crashed in the autumn of 1929, the company was dealt a severe financial blow. Hauling of freight over the company's rail lines decreased dramatically, and the annual visits by summer vacationers all but ended. To compensate for the loss of passenger revenue, Maine Central Railroad reduced its passenger rail service and began to lay off railroad employees. Many of these same employees were rehired, however, when the company created the Maine Central Transportation Company, a bus passenger service. This subsidiary was formed for the purpose of substituting less costly bus transportation for railroad passenger service on minor and less frequented tracks. Fortunately for Maine Central Railroad, the new subsidiary acquired both interstate and intrastate rights over its routes and, during the entire decade of the 1930s, brought in handsome profits to its parent company.

The 1940s were difficult years for Maine Central Railroad. Net income amounted to only $360,000 in 1940, but shot up dramatically with the start of World War II. Both freight and passenger revenues reached their highest point since 1930, accounting for a net income of $1,165,000. But this was the end of the good news for Maine Central Railroad. In early 1943, the company began to fall into arrears, primarily from the increase in annual leasing fees for rail lines. A lack of sound decision making by company management exacerbated the railroad's deteriorating financial condition, and Maine Central Railroad was on the verge of bankruptcy by the end of the war years.

### The Postwar Period

Immediately after World War II, the company invested heavily in the future of passenger rail service by purchasing eight of the most modern streamlined coaches and two deluxe dining cars. High-speed round trips were initiated between Bangor, Maine and Boston, Massachusetts to infuse enthusiasm for the company's passenger rail service. Unfortunately, overall revenues continued to fall, with passenger revenues declining precipitously in 1948 and 1949. By the beginning of 1950, Maine Central Railroad management had decided to begin selling some of its track in both Maine and New Hampshire.

Maine Central Railroad entered the 1950s heavily in debt. An attempt by company management to refinance its growing financial problems failed in 1953. Making matters worse, in 1954 one of the most devastating storms ever to hit the northeastern United States, Hurricane Edna, brought the entire operation of Maine Central Railroad to a grinding halt. Tracks were washed away, and the loss of both passenger and freight traffic was incalculable. Repair costs were enormous. Realizing that money for repairs must come from somewhere, management decided to sell the Maine Central Transportation Company, its bus passenger service, to the Greyhound Bus Company during the same year.

Troubles piled upon troubles during the mid- and late 1950s for Maine Central Railroad. In 1956, losses from the company's passenger service exceeded the net income of the entire railroad. In an attempt to rectify a rapidly declining situation, management decided to discontinue the Farmington train in 1957, eliminate the Bangor-Calais train during the same year, and cease operations for the scenic trip to St. Johnsbury in 1958. By the end of the decade, with a decline in passenger travel of more than 65 percent between 1949 and 1958 and disappointing earnings of only $754,000 in 1958, Maine Central Railroad terminated passenger service on all Maine Central Railroad routes.

In the early 1960s, the company barely avoided deficit spending on operations, and average net income during these years was a disappointing $600,000. In December 1965, prospects for the company seemed to brighten with the construction in Maine of a new pulp and paper manufacturing facility by International Paper Company. International Paper Company soon became Maine Central Railroad's largest customer, and by 1966 the company's net income jumped to more than $1.1 million. Yet operating costs continued to surpass income, despite the financial windfall from the arrangement to transport lumber for International Paper Company, and the railroad was forced to sell many of its long-held branch lines.

### The 1970s and 1980s

The years 1973 and 1974 were arguably two of the best in the company's history. Net income had risen to more than $6 million during 1974, the highest in the company's entire existence. But high debt still plagued management at Maine Central Railroad. To sustain profitable railroad operations, company management chose to abandon or sell many miles of unprofitable rail lines. Some of these abandonments included the 57-mile run from Quebec Junction, New Hampshire to Beecher Falls, Vermont, once one of the railroad's most profitable lines. The company's 16-mile Farmington branch was also abandoned at the same time. In 1976 a 16-mile stretch of the North Anson to Bingham branch was abandoned, and the Eastport branch was abandoned in 1978.

During the late 1970s and throughout the 1980s there was a concerted attempt to revive the fortunes of railroad companies through a process of merger and consolidation. The majority of railroads across the United States had ceased passenger service altogether, having been forced by economic necessity to concentrate their operations on hauling freight. Yet with the construction of modern and convenient superhighways, the trucking industry began to take over a large part of hauling freight, which had always been the mainstay of the railroads. One of the most important mergers to occur during these years was the arrangement among Great Northern, Northern Pacific, and the Burlington to merge and consolidate their operations into the Burlington Northern. These three railroads, with extensive rail lines in the western and northwestern areas of the United States, decided the merger was in their combined interest, since the elimination of duplicate services, the lowering of freight charges, and the pooling of resources and personnel to repair locomotives, for example, improved the financial condition of the newly formed Burlington Northern.

Maine Central Railroad was not immune from the movement toward merger and consolidation within the industry. On January 5, 1984, Maine Central Railroad was purchased by Guilford Transportation Company, a large and extensive transportation firm with holdings throughout the northeastern section of the United States. Along with Maine Central, Guilford Transportation also purchased two other major northeastern railroads, including the Boston and Maine Corporation and the Delaware and Hudson Railway Company. The ostensible purpose of the acquisitions was to coordinate the operations of the three railroads and thereby heighten their efficiency through the consolidation of equipment and facilities, the sharing of data, the improvement of freight car utilization, and the use of run-through train services. Such a combined system would lower costs and expedite the handling of freight.

Yet there was more to the merger than a consolidation of railroad operations and services. Management at Guilford Transportation anticipated a comprehensive regeneration in the economic activity of the northeast. The combination of the three railroads, therefore, was intended to create a highly competitive railroad system within the northeastern transportation market. With greater viability working together rather than as indepen-

dent operations, the new rail system would provide quick, efficient service to those companies wishing to haul freight, as well as maximizing the long-term profitability of the combined system. Together the railroads either owned or leased more than 4,000 miles of rail lines, stretching from Montreal, Canada to Washington, D.C., and from Calais, Maine to Buffalo, New York. With a combined work force of about 4,500 employees, and with approximately 400 locomotives and 12,000 freight cars, the new system would result in an improved opportunity to haul and route more freight more easily than ever before.

Throughout the late 1980s and mid-1990s, management at Guilford Transportation was proved correct. The combined operations and services of the three railroads, under the administration and direction of Guilford Transportation, developed into a highly successful regional railroad system that attracted significant amounts of new traffic with each passing year. By the mid-1990s, Guilford Transportation had achieved the goals of the merger: the railroad system had grown large enough to establish a strong presence in the northeastern market for hauling freight, in spite of the difficulties brought on by deregulation within the industry, yet remained small enough to provide the kinds of services usually reserved for small local railroad companies.

### The 1990s and Beyond

By the mid-1990s, Maine Central Railroad was thriving under the management of Guilford Transportation. Profits and earnings continued to increase in the extremely competitive market of handling and hauling freight. Although Maine Central Railroad had not resumed passenger service in the mid-1990s, it continued to hope that passenger service would once again develop into an economically viable form of transportation.

### Further Reading

"Guilford Express," *Company Newsletter,* Fall 1989.
"Guilford Express," *Company Newsletter,* Fall 1993.
"Guilford: The New Rail Alternative," company document, 1984.
Miller, E., Spencer, *Maine Central Railroad 1940–1978,* Newcomen Society: New York, 1978.

—Thomas Derdak

# MALDEN MILLS

# Malden Mills Industries, Inc.

46 Stafford Street
Lawrence, Massachusetts 01841
U.S.A.
(508) 685-6341
Fax: (508) 975-2595

*Private Company*
*Incorporated:* 1906
*Employees:* 3,200
*Sales:* $425 million (1995 est.)
*SIC(s):* 2221, Broadwoven Fabric Mills (Manmade Fiber
   & Silk); 2257, Weft Knit Fabric Mills; 2258, Lace &
   Wrap Knit Fabric Mills; 2262, Finishing Plants
   (Manmade Fiber & Silk Fabrics); 2297, Nonwoven
   Fabrics; 3086, Plastics Foam Products

Although Polartec lightweight fabrics are recognized worldwide for their moisture resistance and thermal qualities, few know this extraordinary product is the creation of Malden Mills Industries, Inc. of Massachusetts. Family-run and -operated, Malden Mills quietly grew by 200% in the 1980s and 1990s as Polartec and a line of high-performance jacquard velvets for home furnishings generated a $3 billion market. Yet what put Malden Mills firmly in the international spotlight was a devastating fire in December 1995 that destroyed much of the factory and injured 33 employees. Rebuilding immediately, Malden not only assured workers of their jobs but paid full salaries to those unable to work during reconstruction. In an era of massive layoffs and closings, Malden Mills's dedication to the industry, its employees, and the community was a welcome anomaly in the fractured business world of the mid-1990s.

### Wool and Woolies, 1906 to the 1960s

Henry Feuerstein came to America in the 1890s from Hungary and found work in New York City sewing blouses. After losing his job twice, Feuerstein turned to selling dry goods across the state. From small push cart to factory to wholesale outlets, young Henry prospered and soon lived among the well-heeled in Manhattan's Upper East Side. When his real estate investments went awry, Henry answered a classified ad and spent the remainder of his fortune, $50,000, on a small mill in Malden, Massachusetts in 1906.

Malden Knitting produced wool "workman's" sweaters and bathing suits. Under Feuerstein's leadership, the company flourished and created Malden Spinning and Dyeing in 1923 to keep up with demand, much of which was producing uniforms for the U.S. Army during World Wars I and II. By the end of World War II, Malden Knitting was experimenting with various fabrics and applications to broaden its production capacity and to anticipate the ever-changing needs of American families. By this time, Henry Feuerstein's son Samuel had taken charge of Malden Knitting and his teenaged grandson, Aaron, also worked in the family business. Beginning with school vacations and then becoming full-time after graduation from Yeshiva University in 1947, Aaron was appointed factory supervisor and began a long and distinguished career at Malden.

By 1956 Malden Mills achieved what the industry called "vertical" continuous production with dyeing, printing, and finishing all completed within one facility. This year also marked the company's relocation to Lawrence, Massachusetts, 35 miles north of Boston, and into the historic Arlington Mill complex built before the turn of the century. One former employee of the mill wrote a poem about it, entitled "A Lone Striker"; the poet's name was Robert Frost.

In 1962 Malden opened a new knitting mill in Bridgton, Maine, and four years later again branched out, this time by dabbling in synthetic fabrics for the upholstery market. With Samuel Feuerstein nearing retirement, Aaron's role was increasingly important at Malden. Under his tutelage, Malden became more automated and, unlike other textile manufacturers, stayed in Massachusetts rather than relocating to the South or the West Coast where land and labor were cheaper. Instead, Malden relied on the company's proximity to Boston for the area's skilled work force and high-tech breakthroughs.

### The Fake Fur Faux Pas: the 1970s, and the Early 1980s

As the 1960s came to a close, Aaron Feuerstein took full control of Malden and bet big on fake fur products by pouring

## Company Perspectives:

*Malden Mills has spent the past quarter-century building one of the top textile research and development teams in the world. On the premise that customer interests are best served by continual innovation in both manufacturing and product design, the firm's skilled chemists, engineers, and textile designers constantly explore new ways to improve fabrics—making them warmer, stretchier, more comfortable, more moisture-resistant, easier to clean, and more durable.*

$20 million into specialized equipment and opening mills in Hudson, New Hampshire, and Barre, Vermont. "I thought there would be unbelievable growth because of the fur activists," Feuerstein later told *Forbes* magazine, yet despite capturing 25 percent of the U.S. market, fake fur demand never blossomed and began declining. Opening still another factory in North Berwick, Maine, in 1976, Malden tried to make ends meet by selling both upholstery fabrics and fake fur products, while continuing to pour funds into researching a synthetic, lightweight, thermal fabric. Though Malden's fake fur market share grew to 50 percent, Feuerstein realized this was not the huge opportunity he had originally believed it would be.

To head off falling sales Malden started producing velvet upholstery for home furnishings, but not in time. Forced into Chapter 11 bankruptcy in 1981, the company laid off hundreds of employees, and Feuerstein vowed to make it up to them some day. Salvation came soon in the form of Polarfleece, which revolutionized the fabric industry. Debuting in 1979, Polarfleece was 100 percent polyester, capable of drawing moisture away from the body while providing warmth; it became the fabric of choice for high-performance athletic and aerobic apparel. Among Malden's first major customers was Patagonia, which produced outerwear for mountain climbers and hikers. Thoroughly impressed with the unique shearling knit, Patagonia used Polarfleece for a variety of garments, buying "every yard we could make as fast as we could make it," Vice-President Henry Ackerman told the *Wall Street Journal*. Polarfleece was not only a huge success for Patagonia, which expanded into several related apparel lines, but put Malden on the map for a variety of other outdoor clothing manufacturers. By 1982, Polarfleece pushed sales to $5 million and helped pull the company out of bankruptcy in 1983.

### Polartec—"The Ultimate Answer"— Mid-1980s to Early 1990s

Capitalizing on the incredible popularity of Polarfleece, Malden produced several new lines of high-performance, technically advanced fabrics to service the outdoorsy set. Yet Malden stayed ahead of its many imitators with constant innovation and by producing customized lots of varied colors, thicknesses, and textures so each of its customers could market their own blend. By 1986 overall sales had grown to about $150 million, and Malden began investing $10 million per year in state-of-the-art research, design, and production equipment to keep up with the ever-growing demand for its products. As Polarfleece continued to gain prominence, Malden's upholstery

fabric sales had increased substantially and by 1988 accounted for more than $105 million in revenue. Polarfleece raked in a respectable $69 million. The end of the 1980s also marked Malden's expansion into Europe, where its nylon velvet and warp-knit upholstery fabrics were especially popular, helping total sales climb to $200 million in 1989.

As the 1990s approached, Malden was a dinosaur in the New England area. The few textile manufacturers who remained either went out of business or were plagued by the state's harsh environmental laws and ever-increasing labor costs. Yet Malden demonstrated its commitment both to the area and to protecting and preserving the environment by building a water treatment plant to restore the Spicket River systems encompassing the company's mills. The treatment plant conserved energy and reduced waste, air emissions, and the amount of chemicals necessary to produce its many fabrics.

In 1991 Polarfleece products were trademarked as Polartec Climate Control Fabrics available in light-, medium-, and heavyweight thicknesses with more than 100 different styles (from underwear, bike shorts, and sweatshirts to jackets, wet suits, and gloves) available in 5,000 colors and 1,000 patterns. Polartec remained the industry leader because of its stretch, fast wicking, easy dyeing, and durable, nonpilling finish. Clients like Eddie Bauer, Land's End, L.L. Bean, Ralph Lauren, and others often based their entire outdoor or athletic lines on Polartec fabrics, which in turn supported 1991's strong sales of $250 million.

### Polartec and Eco-Velvet: 1992 and Beyond

Malden established the Glenn Street Studio in 1992 to develop and produce natural jacquard velvets. This sturdy, stylish cotton adorned a wide array of products from elegant, vibrantly colored furniture to vehicle upholstery and infant carseats. By this time Malden's home furnishings were sold in Australia, Canada, the Middle East, New Zealand, and South Africa, with such customers as Al Janoub, Carina Polstermobel, Ian Walker, Rexmore, and the Steinhoff Group. In the United States, Malden was a regular supplier to Action, Klaussner, and La-Z-Boy, and was also selling to Century, Frederick Edwards, Hickory Chair, and Southwood Furniture. This year, 1992, also marked the initiation of the Polartec Performance Challenge to sponsor and support outdoor adventures like the Trango Towers Expedition in Southern Pakistan, a 7,000-mile yacht trip around Europe, and a 4,000-mile trek of China's centuries old Silk Road. Another first was Malden's sponsorship of the 1992 Winter Olympics by providing Polartec fabric for the official garments worn by U.S. athletes.

In another environmentally conscious move in 1993, Malden debuted a new line of upholstery (including cotton novelty prints in botanical, floral, and jungle motifs) and clothing fabrics made from recycled fibers. By the end of the year Polartec fabrics contained up to 15 percent recycled fibers, a figure Malden hoped to raise when availability increased and costs of recycled products were less prohibitive. Overall sales for the year climbed to $340 million, with Polartec and upholstery each accounting for half of Malden's sales, but Polartec pulling in most of its $10 million in profits. New products included undergarments for NASA's astronauts, booties for sled dogs racing in Alaska's Iditarod, and hopes for new-fangled diapers.

In 1994 Malden hired a former leader of the state's Fish and Wildlife Commission to spearhead their continuing environmental efforts. The company reduced consumption and added further reuse and recycling programs and was recognized by the American Textile Manufacturers Institute (ATMI) for environmental ''excellence'' and leadership in the textile industry. Exports to 60 nations worldwide now accounted for 20 percent of Malden's revenues, with total weekly fabric production exceeding 1.6 million yards. Annual research and development investments had risen to $20 million, with another $20 million spent on new computer-directed textile machinery, including looms and weaving equipment to keep operations steady and competitors at bay.

Unforeseen by Feuerstein and the staff at Malden Mills, 1995 would be a year of banner success and shocking tragedy. In February, Dakotah, a popular apparel manufacturer, was given exclusive license to launch and produce a new home accessories line of pillows and throws made from Polartec. Next came the first of a series of blows when the U.S. Consumer Products Safety Commission televised segments in March of fleece fabrics catching fire. Though the products shown on the air were made by Coville Inc. (which later recalled more than 150,000 fleece products), consumers began returning Polartec garments for fear of their flammability. Malden immediately sought damage control by launching a $8.5 million advertising campaign, stressing the company's rigid standards and the repeated passing of inflammability tests conducted by the government.

By May the company introduced Eco-Velvet, a new upholstery fabric made from recycled soda bottles, and most of its Polartec products now contained from 80 percent to 100 percent recycled fiber. For environmentally conscious consumers, Malden Mills's fabrics were both a fashion statement and a political statement. In August, Malden announced several changes in the company: first, restructuring with newly appointed CEO Howard Ackerman (formerly vice-president) taking responsibility for running daily operations; second, integrating the home furnishings and apparel divisions to streamline production and share marketing and research and development staffing; third, funding additional promotion of Polartec fabrics (with projected sales hitting or surpassing $225 million for 1995); and fourth, building an $80 million European textile manufacturing plant in Gorlitz, Germany, as a companion to the company's distribution plant in Rotterdam by the end of the year.

The Gorlitz factory was expected to employ 150 and support extensive international sales to such companies as Berghaus, Jack Wolfskin, Lower Alpine, Schoffel, Silvy, and Japan's Asics, Goldwin, and mont-bell, while cutting down on slow turnaround and the expensive tariffs placed on goods imported from the United States. The implemented changes were designed to make Malden Mills, with total sales exceeding $400 million in 1995, a billion-dollar company within five years. ''There's no reason why we shouldn't hit $1 billion by the end of the century,'' Ackerman told the *Wall Street Journal* in November 1995. Unfortunately, something could keep Malden

Mills from reaching its goals—a catastrophe that rocked the company a few months later.

On the evening of December 11, 1995, while Aaron Feuerstein was celebrating his 70th birthday among family and friends at a Boston restaurant, there was an explosion at Malden Mills. The explosion sparked a fire that swept through three of the company's nine buildings, injuring 33 night shift employees and causing an estimated $500 million in damages. Feuerstein rushed to the scene, refused to lose his composure, and vowed to rebuild. Three nights later, Feuerstein announced that Malden Mills would reopen on January 2, that he would pay all employees their regular salaries (at a cost of $1.5 million per week) for the next 30 days, possibly more, and that he would continue health benefits for 90 days. Several companies and local organizations, hearing of Malden Mills's plight, immediately sent contributions to help rebuild and to support employees. Other responses ranged from U.S. President Clinton's invitation to attend the State of the Union Address, to comparisons with George Bailey from ''It's a Wonderful Life,'' and the repeated use of words such as ''hero'' and ''mensch'' (a Yiddish term for a person of unquestionable honor and integrity).

Feuerstein hoped to have Malden Mills fully operational within 90 days and to have his diverse workforce (of British, Canadian, French, German, Irish, Israeli, Italian, and Portuguese men and women) back to their posts as soon as possible. Within days of his ''full-pay'' announcement, 80 percent of the Polartec division was on-line. By February, Feuerstein was still paying all employees and vowed to continue until at least the end of the month. With more than 70 percent of the workforce back on the premises, Feuerstein also announced that the construction outfit building the new Polartec facility was giving ''first preference'' to Malden's idle employees.

As the 1990s progressed, Malden Mills's comeback was assured and many wondered if there would be a changing of the guard. Although Aaron Feuerstein said he planned ''to guide the company into the 21st century with success'' and ''work until the last minute of the last day,'' he had, characteristically, laid the groundwork for his two sons, Daniel and Raphael, to succeed him.

### *Further Reading*

Curley, Tom, ''Mill Owner's Heart Is Fabric of Mass. Town,'' *USA Today,* January 29, 1996, n.p.

Diesenhouse, Susan, ''A Textile Maker Thrives by Breaking All the Rules,'' *New York Times,* July 24, 1994, p. F5.

Jerome, Richard, and Sawicki, Stephen, ''Holding the Line,'' *PEOPLE Weekly,* February 5, 1996, pp. 122, 123–125.

Lee, Melissa, ''Malden Looks Spiffy in New England Textile Gloom,'' *Wall Street Journal,* November 10, 1995, p. B4.

''Malden Unveils New Fleece Categories,'' *Sporting Goods Business,* March 1992, p. 11.

''Performance Fleece Fabrics Force New Insulating Frontiers,'' *Sporting Goods Business,* September 1991, pp. 46–47.

''P.R. for Polartec,'' *Wall Street Journal,* March 7, 1995, p. B9.

Rotenier, Nancy, ''The Golden Fleece,'' *Forbes,* May 24, 1993, p. 220.

Witkowski, Tim, ''The Glow from a Fire,'' *TIME,* January 8, 1996, n.p.

—Taryn Benbow-Pfalzgraf

# The Marmon Group

225 West Washington Street
Chicago, Illinois 60606
U.S.A.
(312) 372-9500
Fax: (312) 845-5305

*Private Company*
*Incorporated:* 1953 as The Colson Company
*Employees:* 30,000
*Sales:* $6.08 billion (1995)
*SICs:* 2381 Dress & Work Gloves, Except Knit &
Leather; 3199 Leather Goods, Not Elsewhere
Classified; 3351 Rolling, Drawing & Extruding of
Copper; 3354 Aluminum Extruded Products; 3432
Plumbing Fixture Fittings & Trim; 3452 Bolts, Nuts,
Screws, Rivets & Washers; 3493 Steel Springs, Except
Wire; 3494 Valves & Pipe Fittings, Not Elsewhere
Classified; 3523 Farm Machinery & Equipment; 3672
Printed Circuit Boards; 3711 Motor Vehicles &
Passenger Car Bodies; 3714 Motor Vehicle Parts &
Accessories; 3715 Truck Trailers; 3841 Surgical &
Medical Instruments & Apparatus; 4741 Rental of
Railroad Cars; 5051 Metals Service Centers & Offices;
6719 Offices of Holding Companies, Not Elsewhere
Classified; 7359 Equipment Rental & Leasing, Not
Elsewhere Classified

The Marmon Group, one of the largest privately owned organizations in the United States, is in essence a holding company for more than 60 autonomously operated manufacturing and service companies. A small central office in Chicago manages and invests the financial resources of member companies, and aids and advises them on accounting, legal, tax, finance, personnel, and other matters. Owned by entities that are owned indirectly by the Pritzker family of Chicago, Marmon companies consistently achieve high returns from low-technology, low-glamour industries. Marmon has repeatedly bought and turned around troubled "smokestack" companies. With more than 400 facilities in more than 30 countries, the Marmon Group today earns about half of its revenues from service companies and about half from manufacturers. The major sectors represented by Marmon companies are: agricultural, industrial, and medical equipment; automotive equipment; building and commercial products; consumer and health care products; industrial materials and components; marketing, finance, and information services; mining equipment; railway equipment; and water treatment products. Recent trends have shown an increasing interest in international expansion.

## Pre-Founding Background

Marmon's history as a corporate entity dates from 1953, but the Pritzker family, who built and control the massive conglomerate, has been active significantly longer. In the late 19th century, the Pritzkers immigrated to the United States from the Ukraine. Patriarch Nicholas Pritzker led them to Chicago, and in 1902 he founded Pritzker & Pritzker, the law firm that was to evolve into a management company and the center of the Pritzkers' many and varied investments.

Pritzker & Pritzker grew, and by the late 1920s it had become a respected local firm. At that time, the Pritzkers' best client was Goldblatt Brothers, the low-priced Chicago department store chain. Through the Goldblatts, Abram (A. N.) Pritzker, Nicholas Pritzker's son, met Walter M. Heymann, then a leading Chicago commercial banker and an officer at the First National Bank of Chicago. In succeeding years A. N. Pritzker and Walter Heymann became business associates, and the powerful First National Bank of Chicago became the financial cornerstone of the Pritzker family empire.

Using a line of credit from the First National Bank, A. N. Pritzker began acquiring real estate, something he already knew about from Pritzker & Pritzker's concentration on real estate reorganization. As his and the family's investments grew, the law practice shrank, and in 1940 Pritzker & Pritzker stopped accepting outside clients, concentrating solely on Pritzker family investments. At the same time A. N. Pritzker began the family practice of sheltering his holdings within a dizzying array of interrelated family trusts.

The story of Marmon, however, begins with the generation of Pritzkers following A.N.'s. By the early 1950s, Pritzker's oldest son, Jay, had become active in the family business. Something of a prodigy, Jay Pritzker had graduated high school at 14. He finished college soon thereafter and then took a law degree from Northwestern University. During World War II he worked first as a flight instructor and later for the U.S. government agency that managed German-owned companies. In that position, he sat on corporate boards with men many years his senior. An accomplished deal-maker even in his earliest years, Jay would later become well known for his quickness at sizing up balance sheets and offering deals.

While Pritzker was beginning his career as a deal-maker, his younger brother Robert Pritzker was finishing advanced training in industrial engineering at the Illinois Institute of Technology in Chicago. Robert Pritzker, A. N.'s second son, was the family's only engineer. During the 1950s and later, his interest in industrial processes, both theoretical and practical, led the family into manufacturing and later enabled him to turn around a staggering array of troubled companies.

The relationship between Jay Pritzker, the lawyer/deal-maker, and Robert Pritzker, the engineer/manager, became the basis for the continuing operations of The Marmon Group. Their youngest brother, Donald Pritzker, would later become the force behind Hyatt Hotels before dying suddenly at the age of 39 in 1972. Jay would buy troubled companies, usually for less than 80 percent of their book value. Then Robert would nurse the companies back to health, finding their real profit-making potentials and with Jay's help exploiting any tax advantages a company's previous losses might produce.

### Early Activities: 1950s and 1960s

Their first venture was the acquisition of Colson Company in 1953. Colson, a money-loser, was a small, $8 million in sales, manufacturer of casters, bicycles, navy rockets, and wheelchairs. In Colson, Jay Pritzker saw a company that had some profit-making potential but whose assets could nevertheless be liquidated at a price higher than what the family had paid for it.

After Jay completed the deal, Robert Pritzker, went to Ohio and took over the running of Colson. He began by eliminating unprofitable lines. Bicycles went first. He knew he could not compete with cheaper European bikes, so he dropped them. To improve production of U.S. Navy rockets, Pritzker instituted modern statistical quality controls. Cost-cutting steps paid for most of Colson. When the program ended, he discontinued military production. This left him with casters and wheelchairs, products he was able to promote and sell successfully.

Over the next several years, the Pritzkers acquired several more manufactures of small metal products. Chief among these was the L.A. Darling Company of Bronson, Michigan, a maker of merchandising display equipment and retail fixtures; it also operated a plastics division and a foundry division. To achieve economies of scale, the Pritzkers combined and affiliated their new companies with Colson and, in a typically adept financial move, made Colson a subsidiary of L.A. Darling.

It was not until ten years after acquiring Colson that the Pritzker brothers made their next major acquisition. In 1963 the Pritzkers acquired the Marmon-Herrington Company, successor to the Marmon Motor Car Company. The way Jay Pritzker structured the deal, the L.A. Darling Company, which was headed by Robert Pritzker, paid approximately $2.7 million for 260,000 shares of Marmon-Herrington's 580,000 outstanding shares of stock. This acquisition gave the Pritzkers's industrial holdings their permanent name, The Marmon Group. Marmon discontinued the company's production of heavy-duty tractors, transit vehicles, and bus chassis. The most significant addition to the Pritzker holdings was the Long-Airdox Company, a division of Marmon-Herrington that added a broad range of coal mining equipment to Darling's display equipment and fixtures, and its foundry operations; and to Colson's casters, institutional housekeeping trucks, and hospital equipment. The acquisition was also indicative of the complex, interlocking ways that the Pritzkers owned their companies. Sales grew quickly, and in 1965 Marmon topped $51.8 million in total revenues.

In 1966 Marmon merged with publicly held Fenestra Incorporated, a maker of architectural steel doors and leaf springs for trucks. As the deal was structured as a stock swap, Marmon itself became a public company, The Marmon Group, Inc., and for the first time, the Pritzkers' industrial empire was exposed to the scrutiny of shareholders.

Shy of the public eye and jealous of their controlling interest, the Pritzkers soon moved to take greater control of The Marmon Group. In a complicated stock transaction of October 1967, Jay Pritzker had Fenestra, which was technically controlled by a subsidiary of The Marmon Group, Inc., acquire both The Marmon Group, Inc., and Boykin Enterprises, another newly acquired Pritzker company, that produced and exported agricultural equipment. At the end of the deal the Pritzkers owned more than 84.3 percent of voting stock of Fenestra and had changed Fenestra's name to The Marmon Group, Inc.

In 1968 Marmon acquired Triangle Auto Springs Company, a manufacturer of flat-leaf truck springs for the replacement market. Triangle's line of springs fit in well with the products Marmon was already making at Fenestra's Detroit Steel Products subsidiary.

In 1969 Marmon further consolidated its role in the parts replacement business by buying Lowell Bearing Company, a distributor of replacement parts to truck, bus, and trolley fleets in the United States and around the world. The same year, the L.A. Darling plant was moved from Michigan to Paragould, Arkansas. Also in 1969, the company acquired the rights to the Universal Track Machine, a machine that Marmon had previously manufactured under contract. It performed mechanized maintenance on the nation's railroad tracks and railroad rights-of-way. Rising labor costs had made this robotic maintenance device a highly desirable product.

By the end of 1969, Marmon had become a diversified industrial company supplying low-tech goods in noncompetitive fields not vulnerable to changes in consumer tastes. About 39 percent of sales came from automotive replacement parts; 30 percent came from building materials, hardware, and retail fixtures, much of which was sold by the L.A. Darling Fixture division. Mining equipment supplied by Long-Airdox and Pickrose & Co., of England, accounted for 25 percent of sales; and agricultural, irrigation, and animal husbandry equipment by Jamesway Company Limited, now Jamesway Incubator Corporation, of Canada, and the AMISA export arm accounted for the remaining 6 percent of sales.

### Acquisition of Cerro Corporation in the 1970s

The year 1970 was a time of internal investment and growth. Sales climbed from $77 million to $87 million. Triangle Auto Springs and Jamesway each made additions to its physical plant. The Darling Store Fixtures division was in the process of building a new plant in Corning, Arkansas. New plant equipment was bought for Fenestra, Detroit Steel Products, and Darling. Finally, in December of 1970, Marmon paid $6 million for Keystone Pipe and Supply Company, a nationwide supplier of pipes and tubes based in Butler, Pennsylvania. In succeeding years, Great Lakes Corporation, which was owned by Marmon Holdings, which was itself owned by the Pritzkers, bought up outstanding shares and converted preferred stock to voting stock. In 1970 sales topped $100 million, and by 1971 The Marmon Group was again private.

Marmon's largest and most successful acquisition of the 1970s was Cerro Corporation, with $800 million in sales, a company that the Pritzkers gradually acquired between 1973 and 1976. Cerro's operations included mining, manufacturing, trucking, and real estate. Like many Marmon acquisitions, the Cerro deal was financed through the First National Bank of Chicago. The relationship between the Pritzkers and First Chicago had remained strong since their initial contacts in the late 1920s.

Cerro was a typical, if much larger than previous, Marmon acquisition. It was rich in assets and selling at far below book value. In fact, Cerro was atypical only in that it was publicly held and that the Pritzkers ousted the current management and installed Jay Pritzker as chief executive officer and Robert Pritzker as president.

Soon after taking a controlling interest in Cerro, Robert Pritzker began commuting to Cerro's New York headquarters, where he oversaw its industrial processes and worked at freeing up the somewhat tense corporate culture. Robert Pritzker told the *Wall Street Journal*, of March 27, 1975, that "Cerro is one of those typical, highly structured big companies. . . . We think that loosening it up will make people there feel better and perform better, too." By 1977, Marmon had the Cerro acquisition under control. It sold Cerro's trucking subsidiary, ICX, for $22.6 million, and it was also dealing with Cerro's troubled Florida real estate venture, Leadership Housing Incorporated.

During the same period in which Marmon was acquiring Cerro, it bought the Hammond Corporation. Completed in 1977, the acquisition of the organ manufacturer was neither as successful nor as canny as the Cerro acquisition had been. The Pritzkers bought Hammond just as a recession struck and the decline in the economy caused a slump in organ sales. The one bright spot of the deal was Hammond's work gloves subsidiary, Wells Lamont. Using these facilities as a basis, Marmon has gone on to become a leading manufacturer of gloves and other apparel items.

In 1978 Marmon paid $27.3 million for American Safety Equipment Corporation, a maker of seat-belt systems for cars

and aircraft, with $48.1 million in sales and owner of Kangol Limited, a British headwear manufacturer. Marmon also in 1978 divested itself of Leadership Housing, by distributing as dividends its investments in the company.

Between 1970 and 1980 Marmon's sales grew from $103 million to $1.9 billion, and during the same period profits rocketed from $5 million to $79 million. Marmon had expanded from five basic product groups to a much larger cluster of companies making pipe and tubing, wire and cable, automotive products, other metal products, apparel accessories, mining and agricultural equipment, and musical instruments. Services such as metals trading and coal mining were becoming increasingly important elements of the business.

Some of Marmon's successes of the 1970s can be attributed to the advantages of a privately owned company whose owners get on well. In a March 27, 1975, interview with the *Wall Street Journal* J. Ira Harris, then a Chicago-based partner of Salomon Brothers, said that the Pritzkers' ability to work together "gives them the kind of flexibility that doesn't exist elsewhere at their level of operations. They've closed a lot of important deals because they were able to move faster than the competition."

The ability to move fast also helped Robert Pritzker deal effectively with Marmon's divisions. Normally a manager who allows Marmon's component companies substantial autonomy, he was able to make necessary decisions on a person-to-person basis without expensive and time consuming studies. The Marmon Group's board of directors, headed by Jay Pritzker, rarely met, and the corporate office was sparsely staffed. The divisions themselves spent little on advertising and less on their offices.

While Robert Pritzker ceded authority to managers, he kept the accounting tight. Divisional controllers reported not only to their general managers but also to a corporate controller in Chicago. Robert Pritzker often left final decisions to local managers. Marmon's commitment to capital investment and drive to be the low-cost producer allowed local managers to make the large investments that stand-alone companies could never make. After buying Midwest Foundry Company in 1960, for example, Marmon's capital commitment led the company to expand tenfold in 20 years. During the same period, 40 percent of all gray-iron foundries in the United States shut down. In the early years of the 1980s, Midwest Foundry was returning 40 percent on Marmon's investment.

### Further Growth in the 1980s

In September 1980, Marmon announced the proposed acquisition of Illinois-based Trans Union Corporation for $688 million. Trans Union was a $1.1 billion conglomerate whose businesses included rail car and general-equipment leasing by its Union Tank Car Company subsidiary; credit information services; international trading by the subsidiary Getz Corporation; and the manufacture of waste and water treatment equipment.

Completed in 1981, the Trans Union acquisition was unusual in that it was both huge and expensive. Jay Pritzker had been attracted by Trans Union's large accumulation of investment tax credits and federal tax deferrals, which Marmon could use to offset taxable income. Further, once bought, Robert Pritzker found a series of unexpectedly profitable components within the larger Trans Union. A case in point is the Getz Corporation, a San Francisco-based Pacific trading company that grossed over $600 million in 1989. When Marmon acquired Trans Union, Getz was failing. Within a few years, Robert Pritzker had solidified Getz's management and was exploiting Getz's untapped potential as a travel agency and its experience as a player in the expanding market of the Pacific Rim. Getz deals in a wide array of automotive, industrial, and food products—from farm tractors in Thailand to powdered milk in Taiwan.

In January 1984 Marmon purchased Altamil Corporation and thereby acquired the Fontaine Trucking Company, manufacturer of truck and trailer couplers, trailers and special purpose truck bodies; Aluminum Forge Company, a producer of precision aluminum forging for aerospace industries; and American Box Company, producer of wirebound boxes and crates, which later was sold.

Between 1980 and 1989 revenues jumped from $1.9 billion to $3.9 billion. During the same time earnings swelled from $84 million to $205 million. At the start of the decade, Marmon's average return on equity, profits as a percentage of the company's total worth, ran 19.1 percent, a full five points higher than the median of the *Fortune* 500, and in 1989 that proportion reached 26.3 percent, more than ten points higher than the median of the *Fortune* 500.

### 1990s and Beyond

Starting in the late 1980s and into the early 1990s, much of Marmon's expansion came through member companies themselves making acquisitions, such as the early 1990 acquisition of the medical products division of the National Standard Corporation by Marmon's Microware Surgical Instruments Corporation. The same was also true of Marmon's increasing growth outside the United States. Marmon/Keystone Corporation, a Pennsylvania-based distributor of steel pipes and tubing, was particularly active outside the United States, with a 1993 acquisition of the Canadian distributor Lyman Tubeco; the 1994 purchase of Specialty Steels, another Canadian distributor; the establishment of a sales office in Mexico in 1994; and the acquisition in 1995 of The Anbuma Group, a tubing distributor based in Belgium.

During the late 1980s Marmon had grown to such an extent that some observers had begun to question the ability of its corporate structure to handle its holdings, which were becoming increasingly diverse, both technically and geographically. An example of a high-tech firm that failed under Marmon leadership was Accutronics Inc., a maker of printed circuit boards, which Marmon shut down in 1994, selling its assets. The president of Accutronics, while praising Marmon's financial and management skills, blamed the inability of Marmon to deal with a non-low-tech business for the failure.

Marmon also struggled to turn around some of the low-tech firms it made its name on. For example, in early 1995 it closed Fenestra Corp., a manufacturer of steel and fiberglass doors and door frames, which had lost money for the previous four years. Robert Pritzker blamed the closure on Marmon's own "lousy management" of the company as well as the difficulties of strained relations between management and the unionized workers at Fenestra's plants.

Such failures, however, seem inevitable for a company that had taken on as many troubled firms as Marmon had. Through 1995, Marmon continued to grow to record levels, with revenues increasing from $3.85 billion in 1990 to $6.08 billion in 1995. Meanwhile, earnings jumped from $125.1 million to $306.9 million.

From a small company making casters and wheelchairs, The Marmon Group grew through acquisition and internal reinvestment into a diversified manufacturing and services conglomerate with an increasingly global reach. With an experienced management team in place, and a new generation of Pritzkers entering the business, Marmon's future looked bright as it moved closer to its 50th anniversary.

### *Principal Subsidiaries*

Alaron Inc.; Albion Industries, Inc.; Amarillo Gear Company; Am-Safe, Inc.; Anderson Copper and Brass Company; Atlas Bolt & Screw Company; Cerro Copper Products Co.; Cerro Metal Products Company; Cerro Sales Corporation; Cerro Wire & Cable Co., Inc.; Colson Caster Corporation; L.A. Darling Company; Detroit Steel Products Co., Inc.; Eagle-Gypsum Products; Ecodyne MRM, Inc.; EcoWater Commercial/Industrial Systems, Inc.; EcoWater Systems, Inc.; Fontaine Industries, Inc.; Getz Bros. & Co., Inc.; Graver Chemical Company; The Graver Company; Great Lakes Consulting Group, Inc.; Harbour Industries, Inc.; Huron Steel Company, Inc.; Long-Airdox Companies; MarCap Corporation; Marmon/Keystone Corporation; Medical Device Technologies, Inc.; Meyer Material Co.; Micro-Aire Surgical Instruments, Inc.; Miles Metal Company; National Mine Service, Inc.; Pan American Screw; Penn Aluminum International, Inc.; Perfection Hy-Test Company; Rochester Instrument Systems, Inc.; The Rockbestos Company; Shepherd Products U.S. Inc.; Solidstate Controls, Inc.; Sound Enhancements, Inc.; Spectrum Labs, Inc.; Trackmobile, Inc.; Trans Union Corporation; The Triangle Group; Union Tank Car Company; Webb Wheel Products, Inc.; Wells Lamont; Ecodyne Limited (Canada); Jamesway Incubator Company Ltd. (Canada); Procor LPG Storage Inc. (Canada); Procor Limited (Canada); Procor Sulphur Services Inc. (Canada); Robertson Whitehouse Inc. (Canada); Shepherd Hardware Products Ltd. (Canada); Shepherd Products Inc. (Canada); Sterling Crane (Canada); Kangol Limited (U.K.).

### *Further Reading*

Cuff, Daniel F., "A Pritzker 'Hobby' Is Expanding Abroad," *New York Times,* September 1, 1989, p. C3, D3.

Elstrom, Peter J. W., "How Bob Pritzker Does It: At Marmon, A Light Touch Yields Profits," *Crain's Chicago Business,* May 22, 1995.

"The Hustling Pritzkers," *Business Week,* May 5, 1975.

Klein, Frederic C., "Family Business: The Pritzkers Are an Acquisitive Bunch Which Pays Off Well," *Wall Street Journal,* March 27, 1975.

Worthy, Ford S., "The Pritzkers: Unveiling A Private Family," *Fortune,* April 25, 1988, pp. 164–82.

—Jordan Wankoff
—updated by David E. Salamie

# /V/AXI/V/

# Maxim Integrated Products, Inc.

120 San Gabriel Drive
Sunnyvale, California 94086
U.S.A.
(408) 737-7600
Fax: (408) 737-7194

*Public Company*
*Incorporated:* 1983
*Employees:* 1,550
*Sales:* $250 million (1995)
*Stock Exchanges:* NASDAQ
*SICs:* 3629 Electrical Industrial Apparatus, Not
    Elsewhere Classified; 3674 Semiconductors & Related
    Devices; 3679 Electronic Components, Not Elsewhere
    Classified; 3699 Electrical Machinery, Equipment &
    Supplies, Not Elsewhere Classified

Maxim Integrated Products, Inc., is a leading developer, manufacturer, and seller of linear as well as mixed (linear and digital) signal integrated circuits for the analog market. Analog devices process signals that represent real-world phenomena such as temperature, pressure, sound, or speed. Maxim's products include circuits used in data converters, power supplies, battery chargers, amplifiers, switches, and other mechanisms produced by the instrumentation, control, communications, and data processing industries. More than half of Maxim's sales in the mid-1990s were overseas.

## New Technology, New Markets

Maxim was founded in 1983 by a group of ten coworkers, several of whom had formerly been employed by Intersil Inc. Intersil was the General Electric Co. subsidiary that developed and manufactured linear circuits. Linear, or analog, circuits measure physical properties by means of analog waves. They differ from digital circuits in that digital devices operate using a binary language based on ones and zeros (rather than analog waves). Various characteristics make digital circuits preferable

for advanced logic-based applications, such as processing data and controlling computers. Linear circuits, in contrast, are favored for some jobs that require the interpretation of varying physical properties like temperature and pressure.

By the early 1980s, digital technology was rapidly supplanting traditional analog technology. In fact, the general consensus was that digital circuits would eventually replace analog circuits in almost all applications. Many companies began heavily emphasizing the development of digital technology, and most universities eliminated many of their analog technology courses and replaced them with digital-related curricula. In part as a result of this trend, the coworkers at Intersil banded together to launch their own venture. Indeed, that group believed that linear circuits would continue to be important in applications for which digital technology was inferior. They felt that Intersil (and other semiconductor companies) were failing to take advantage of opportunities related to linear technology.

Several Intersil employees, led by Intersil executive Jack Gifford, left the General Electric subsidiary in the early 1980s and joined with a few other entrepreneurs to incorporate Maxim Integrated Products in April 1983. Gifford, the leader of the group, was a chip industry veteran who had started his career in 1965 with industry pioneer Fairchild. He had held several senior management positions before becoming chief executive of Intersil, and had founded a number of high-technology concerns. Interestingly, he was also a member of the UCLA Baseball Hall of Fame. Gifford planned to pool his team's brainpower to develop a range of linear chips. He hoped to benefit from huge growth in the semiconductor industry, which was being driven by new digital technology, by offering linear chips that would complement digital devices.

Specifically, Gifford and his co-founders saw an opportunity to make advanced analog chips that could interpret real-world physical properties (like temperature, voltage, and sound) and then transfer that information to a digital chip for processing. For example, linear circuits could be used in new telecommunications equipment like cellular phones, because phone systems still used analog waves to communicate. Linear circuits could also be used in the growing array of handheld battery devices, which utilized the advantages of analog circuits to measure voltage. Furthermore, linear technology still played an important role in many broad applications; for instance, it was used to manage various computer functions like printing.

### Getting Started

Maxim spent its first two years trying to develop marketable chips. Aside from the problems typically related to a small business startup, such as a lack of investment capital and low cash flow, Maxim had to deal with a lawsuit filed by General Electric's Intersil. Intersil filed suit shortly after Maxim was incorporated, claiming that Gifford and other former employees were infringing on its trade secrets. In fact, the former Intersil workers had brought with them much of the proprietary knowledge that they had developed while employed by Intersil. The suit was resolved in 1984 when Maxim agreed to let Intersil choose up to ten of its products (by July 1989) to manufacture and sell free of royalties. In exchange, Intersil agreed to grant Maxim the right to specific trade secrets, products, and patent rights.

Proponents of digital technology were correct in predicting that digital circuits would quickly overshadow analog circuits and replace the older technology in most applications. In fact, during the 1980s the analog share of the circuit market shrank to represent less than 20 percent of industry sales. But Maxim's founders were also correct in guessing that aggregate sales of analog chips would rise in the wake of huge chip industry growth. Because Maxim was one of the few companies targeting the sector, it benefitted greatly and even outperformed most of the companies competing in the digital arena. The company posted net losses during its first few years in business because of startup and research and development expenses. But sales rose rapidly, to $4.6 million by 1985 and then to nearly $16 million in 1987. It was in 1987 that Maxim posted its first net surplus (of $340,000).

Maxim's gains during the mid-1980s were the result of a savvy, multifaceted strategy. Importantly, from the start Gifford chose to emphasize overseas sales, where markets were realizing the fastest growth. By 1987 Maxim was shipping well over 50 percent of its output abroad. Gifford also chose to target the high end of the analog market, using Maxim's respected brain trust to chase the high-profit segment of the business. To that end, Maxim focused on developing high-tech analog chips for new applications, such as miniature handheld electronic devices and cutting-edge telecommunications equipment. That segment represented about 20 percent of the chip industry, and

consisted primarily of circuits that operated at high speeds and at very low power levels.

Among other advantages, Maxim's contrarian product strategy (i.e., building analog circuits while the rest of the industry moved toward digital chips) allowed it to keep production costs relatively low. While manufacturers of cutting-edge digital chips often had to invest in expensive new manufacturing facilities, Maxim was able to produce most of its circuits and products using somewhat dated manufacturing facilities. To keep costs low, Maxim began developing the chips, contracted production to domestic manufacturers, and hired Asian companies to package the goods. Late in 1989, though, Maxim became a manufacturer when it bought a wafer fabrication plant from the bankrupt Saratoga Semiconductor. Maxim paid only $5 million for the plant, which had relatively little value to manufacturers of high-end digital semiconductors.

### The Late 1980s

Maxim's move into manufacturing followed its transition to a public company early in 1988. The initial public offering represented a big risk for Maxim, because it was the first initial public offering made by a technology company following the stock market crash of 1987. Maxim was dubbed a "polar bear" by the investment community, because it was the first high-technology enterprise to "break the ice" with an initial public offering since the crash. Nevertheless, the offering was a big success and brought a hefty $16 million into Maxim's coffers. For the 1988 fiscal year (ended June 30, 1988), Maxim recorded sales of $28.3 million, about $3 million of which was netted as income. Within a year of the offering, Maxim's stock price had increased nearly 40 percent to about $7.5.

Despite an ugly semiconductor industry downturn during the early 1990s, Maxim continued to prosper, and seemed immune from industry turbulence. In fact, the company made news during the summer of 1991. While almost two dozen of Silicon Valley's biggest chip makers shut down operations during the week of July Fourth in response to economic recession, Maxim not only remained open, but sustained its round-the-clock manufacturing shifts. Meanwhile, it continued to enjoy marked sales and profit gains: revenues increased to $42 million in 1989 and to $74 million in 1991, while net income rose from $7.6 million to $13.7 million during the same period. "We're open 24 hours a day, every day [including Christmas]," explained a company spokesman in the December 23, 1991, *Business Journal-San Jose.* "That's where the big profitability numbers come from."

As important to Maxim's success during the 1980s and 1990s as its product strategy was its management philosophy. The company was largely employee-owned, for example, and was known as a well-managed, good place to work. Maxim was also known for high-quality products and good customer service. It was only one of a handful of companies, for instance, that was named to *Business Week*'s Top 100 Small Companies and *Forbes*'s Top 200 in both 1991 and 1992. In addition, in 1993 *Forbes* named Maxim one of the 13 "best-of-the-best" small companies in the United States. Among its greatest strengths was its research and development team. In 1992, for example, Maxim churned out a total of more than 70 new products (14 more than it had introduced the previous year).

### The Mid-1990s

Maxim continued to benefit from industry trends into the mid-1990s as demand for new miniature electronic devices surged. The number and type of wireless communications devices, for example, was growing rapidly. And entirely new product categories—such as portable notebook computers and handheld electronic testing devices—that had emerged since the early 1980s were thriving. Maxim prospered by developing specialized chips, many of which incorporated both analog and digital technology and worked in conjunction with digital semiconductors. By 1993 Maxim had introduced more than 600 new chips and was selling its goods to more than 10,000 customers around the world, including International Business Machines, Motorola, and Hitachi.

By the 1990s, Maxim was vying for market share in its high-end, linear-technology niche with only one major competitor: Linear Technology Corp. As markets continued to rise, so did Maxim's (and Linear's) sales. Indeed, Maxim's revenue climbed to $87 million in 1992 and grew to more than $150 million by 1994. More importantly, profits climbed to about $14 million before increasing to $24 million in 1994. Those gains helped push Maxim's stock price up to more than $50 early in 1994 (from less than $10 in 1988). In 1994 Maxim brought out 140 new products, and the company planned to increase that number every year throughout the mid-1990s.

Maxim diversified its operations late in 1994 when it purchased the integrated-circuits division Tectronix. The move reflected Gifford's intent to move into the wireless and fiber-optics communications businesses, which depended on complementary linear technology. It also brought additional manufacturing facilities to Maxim's pressured production arm. With new production facilities, the only major hindrance to Maxim's growth was a shortage of chip designers that were schooled in linear technology, as many universities had almost abandoned the technology. To that end, Maxim devised a mentoring program that was designed to turn entry-level engineers into senior chip designers in a span of only five years.

Maxim posted consecutive sales and profit gains every year after it was incorporated in 1983, and continued to do so into the mid-1990s. At the same time, its growth highlighted the company's chief constraint: a lack of analog-engineering talent, which Maxim was trying to address through its own training program. Aside from that limitation, there was relatively little hindering Maxim's potential to sustain gains into the late 1990s.

### Principal Divisions

Maxim North.

### Further Reading

Croughan, Lore, "Rearguard Action: Sometimes Betting on Yesterday's Technology Pays Off in Spades," *Financial World,* July 18, 1995, p. 53.

Francis, Mike, "High-Tech Help Wanted," *Oregonian,* February 1, 1996, p. B1.

Goldman, James S., "Saratoga Semiconductor Liquidating Assets," *Business Journal-San Jose,* December 11, 1989, p. 1.

——, "Maxim Workers 'Scrooged,' " *Business Journal-San Jose,* December 23, 1991, p. 1.

Hayes, Mary, "Linear and Maxim Look to the Future with an Older Technology," *Business Journal-San Jose,* February 7, 1994, p. 6.

Koland, Cordell, and Guy Lasnier, "Maxim Tests Stock Market with Offering," *Business Journal-San Jose,* January 25, 1988, p. 1.

Labate, John, "Maxim Integrated Products," *Fortune,* December 13, 1993, p. 172.

Lasnier, Guy, "Warm Market Reception for 'Polar Bear' Maxim," *Business Journal-San Jose,* August 8, 1988, p. 18S.

Slater, Richard, "Maxim Reports Net Income," *Business Wire,* August 11, 1992.

—Dave Mote

# Metallgesellschaft AG

Reuterweg 14
D-60271 Frankfurt am Main
Germany
(69) 159-0
Fax: (69) 159-2125

*Public Company*
*Incorporated:* 1881
*Employees:* 23,378
*Sales:* DM 17.64 billion (1994/95)
*Stock Exchanges:* Berlin Düsseldorf Frankfurt Hamburg
  Stuttgart
*SICs:* 1081 Metal Mining Services; 2899 Chemicals &
  Chemical Preparations, Not Elsewhere Classified;
  3089 Plastic Products, Not Elsewhere Classified; 3433
  Heating Equipment, Except Electrical & Warm Air
  Furnaces; 3494 Valves & Pipe Fittings, Not
  Elsewhere Classified; 3567 Industrial Process
  Furnaces & Ovens; 3714 Motor Vehicle Parts &
  Accessories; 4412 Deep Sea Freight Transportation-
  Foreign; 5051 Metals Service Centers & Offices; 8712
  Architectural Services

Metallgesellschaft AG (MG), based in the heart of Frankfurt since its foundation, is a conglomerate providing raw materials and technological services. It is divided into five branches: trade, finance, engineering and contracting, chemicals, and building technology. On the brink of bankruptcy in early 1994 because of huge losses incurred from oil-futures and derivatives trading, MG bounced back to profitability in the 1994/95 fiscal year but still faces an uncertain future.

### Early History

"The trade in and manufacturing of metals and metal oxides" were the business aims of the firm according to its articles of association. The company was founded on May 17, 1881, by the Anglo-German merchant Wilhelm Merton and his two part-ners, Leo Ellinger and Zachary Hochschild, with a share capital of 2 million marks. It had its roots in the firm of Philipp Abm. Cohen, already established some 150 years previously, with its headquarters in Hanover. Initially this company was involved in banking, then increasingly in metal trading, and was incorporated in Frankfurt in 1821. In 1856, Cohen entrusted his business interests to his son-in-law Ralph Merton, who had emigrated from London to Frankfurt. One of Ralph Merton's sons, William, born in 1848 and later to change his name to Wilhelm, became an associate partner in 1876, having worked for many years both in London and in Frankfurt. Close business as well as personal ties were formed with the firm of Henry R. Merton (HRM), the metals trading firm of the English branch of the family, named after another of Ralph's sons.

MG, with 40 employees and one telephone—the first telephones were installed in Frankfurt in 1881—at the outset traded in copper, lead, and zinc, later diversifying into nickel and aluminum. The firm Philipp Abm. Cohen had also been involved in silver trading, but abandoned this line in 1872, leaving the way open for the founding of the Deutsche Goldund Silber-Scheideanstalt (Degussa).

Since the domestic mines could not satisfy the country's metal requirements, the company rapidly developed extensive relations abroad and within a short time MG was represented in such cities as Basel, Amsterdam, Milan, Brussels, Stockholm, St. Petersburg, Moscow, Vienna, and Paris. Within a few years, therefore, a network of subsidiaries spanned the globe. In 1887, the American Metal Company was founded in New York; in 1889, the Companhia de Minerales y Metales in Mexico; and in 1889 the Australian Metal Co. The last was the result of an expedition the company organized together with HRM and Degussa into the ore-rich Broken Hill district, where lead and lead concentrates were produced in vast quantities. This constituted the start of MG's trading in ore, which would assume greater and greater importance in the future.

From 1889, these ores were analyzed and tested by the specially created technical department. This technical department was to be the seed from which grew the largest enterprise that MG has ever created; from it arose in 1897 the Metall-urgische Gesellschaft Aktiengesellschaft, a fully owned MG

## Company Perspectives:

*The 12 Guiding Principles of Metallgesellschaft: 1. We increase our earning power and financial strength through market orientation and cost-consciousness. 2. We increase the value of our company for our shareholders. 3. We concentrate on our core business areas. 4. We act according to our objectives within the scope of our strategic orientation. 5. We want to be among the leaders in our international markets. 6. Our customers pay our wages and salaries. Therefore we place them at the centre of our thoughts and actions. 7. We promote the ideas and initiative of all our staff. 8. Our objective is constant quality improvement. 9. We desire effective communication and welcome objective criticism. 10. We develop our staff and executives in accordance with our corporate commitment. 11. We are active innovators while preserving meaningful traditions. 12. We are a company which is aware of its responsibilities in our society and to the environment.*

subsidiary, to look after MG's industrial and technical interests. Under the abbreviation it uses for telegrams, LURGI, this enterprise has become known as a leading worldwide engineering business. The appointment of the scientists Clemens Winkler and Curt Netto to the supervisory board was clear evidence of the importance technological skills had acquired for MG.

MG developed and flourished in the generally favorable climate of the late period of the *Gründerjahre*—the period, beginning in 1871, of rapid industrial expansion in Germany. In the company's first ten years, its capital was raised to 6 million marks and the dividend payments were between 7 and 33 percent. From the outset MG had proved exemplary in its social provisions. For example, a pension fund was established for employees long before this became a legal obligation. The founder of MG's social policy was legendary. He founded numerous institutions, using the anonymity of the holding company, the Institut für Gemeinwohl, which were concerned with research into social questions and with providing practical assistance. The feeling that those involved in the business world generally lacked grounding in academic background knowledge in commerce, economics, and social sciences led him to found the Akademie für Sozial-und Handelswissenschaften. The University of Frankfurt would emerge from this academy, once again backed by Wilhelm Merton's strong personal and financial involvement.

### Early 20th Century

By 1906, the year of its 25th anniversary, MG was a steadily growing, prosperous concern, involved in many sectors, and active internationally in trading and engineering technology, in the fields of mining and metallurgy. In the same year, Wilhelm Merton brought about the long-envisaged creation of a separate finance company and a broader financial base for the group through the founding of the Berg- und Metallbank. This was merged with the Metallurgische Gesellschaft in 1910, after it was realized that a precise division between the industrial

business and its financing was creating unnecessary duplication of work and was not economically favorable to the group.

Although Wilhelm Merton is recorded in autobiographical notes as saying of MG that: "Our trading company will not be involved in any kind of advertising" and is credited with the remark that it would be far more pleasant "to be able to pursue one's business without the need of the stock exchange, the public or the press," he broke fundamentally with his principles in one important way—the publication *Metallstatistik,* which had appeared annually since 1892, giving an overview of metal production, consumption, and prices worldwide, made MG's name, to quote Wilhelm Merton again, "known, and I might add, respected." In general, however, Wilhelm Merton strongly objected to any interest in the firm which he considered to be excessive.

World War I hit MG hard. The good relations established abroad were broken off, imports of raw material dried up, the sister company HRM fell under the British Non-Ferrous Metals Industry Bill of November 1917, designed to eliminate enemy influence and control over the British ore and metal trade, and the deliveries of Australian ore failed to appear. This meant MG had to obtain its metal supplies from neutral countries for as long as possible and eventually to use up domestic sources or intensify their exploitation. Three aluminum works were built, in conjunction with the firm Griesheim Elektron: in Horrem, close to Cologne; in Berlin-Rummelsburg; and in Bitterfeld near Halle.

In the middle of World War I, on December 15, 1916, Wilhelm Merton died suddenly on a business trip to Berlin. His partner Hochschild had died in 1912 and Ellinger had died in the summer of 1916. This meant none of the founders were left. Wilhelm had prepared his sons to continue the businesses and Richard and Alfred took on the top management positions in MG and in Metallbank.

After the war, they were faced with three main tasks: overcoming the consequences of inflation; reestablishing ties abroad; and adjusting MG's organization to the altered circumstances. Representation abroad was cautiously and gradually reestablished, and a cooperation agreen.·nt was signed and shares exchanged with the successor to HRM, which had gone into liquidation during the war.

MG was reorganized into four and later five constituent parts between 1919 and 1922, reflecting its different areas of activity. Through the acquisition of water transport companies (Schleppschiffahrtsgesellschaft Unterweser in 1919 and Lehnkering AG in 1926); a land transport company (Kommanditgesellschaft S. Elkan & Co., Hamburg in 1922); and the founding of a land transport company, Montan Transport GmbH, MG created its own transport services. In 1928, MG and the group Berg -und Metallbank and Metallurgische Gesellschaft which had merged in 1910 were brought together with the aim of operating more efficiently. In the field of metal working, the Vereinigte Deutsche Metallwerke AG (VDM) was founded in 1930 through mergers and partnerships. MG had the majority shareholding.

In the 1920s, the company's constant efforts to reestablish contacts abroad, especially through Richard Merton's strong personal involvement, bore fruit. Together with the already mentioned exchange of shares with the British Metal Corporation is the example of the takeover by MG in 1926 of the Ore and Chemical Corporation (OCC), founded in 1923, in New York. In 1922 MG's stock was changed from registered shares to bearer shares; it was consequently registered on the Frankfurt stock exchange in 1922 and on the Berlin exchange in 1926.

After the battle against inflation had been won, MG would only have a few years to benefit from a peaceful and favorable business environment, as the world Depression and political changes would once more affect the group badly. At the time of MG's 50th anniversary, the company's 18 board members and 500 employees faced a gloomy future.

### The World War II Era

After the National Socialists had seized power in 1933, MG became an object of desire for the new dictatorship, which viewed it as an important enterprise for armaments and later for war. This meant in the first instance that it became the object of Aryanization—between 1935 and 1938, eight out of the 11 directors on the board of management were dismissed from their posts for being Jewish or having Jewish connections. Alfred Merton had emigrated in 1933 for political reasons. Richard Merton, however, tried to keep his position for as long as possible. Forced to resign from his post as head of the board, he was arrested during the November pogrom and transported to a concentration camp for several weeks, but in spring 1939 managed to escape to England. Richard was automatically made a British subject as his father had retained his British nationality.

During the reign of the Merton brothers, a four-man central committee had been formed in 1932 from among the board members and invested with extended powers. Its original members were Alfred Merton; Rudolf Euler, Zachary Hochschild's son-in-law; Alfred Petersen; and Julius Sommer. In 1938 the Nationalsozialistische Deutsche Arbeiterpartei (Nazi Party) succeeded in establishing R. W. Avieny, the choice of Gauleiter (or regional Nazi administrator) Sprenger, on the board of MG. He also became a member of the central committee, together with R. Kissel and F. Traudes. The last took on the role of general manager until 1940. There was no chairman of the board of directors in this period until Avieny was elected in 1940 to this position, which he held until April 1945. The death in 1939 of the then-chairman of the supervisory board, Ernst Busemann, brought about the appointment of Carl Lüer, president of the board of trade of the Rhein-Main-Wirtschaftsraum, the regional economic council. Astonishingly, the two English members of the supervisory board, Oliver Lyttelton and Walter Gardner, still occupied their posts after World War II had begun. It was only at the sitting of the board in October 1940 that they retired from their positions.

In March 1944 the MG head office was severely damaged by bombing which killed some two dozen employees. Toward the end of the war the administrative offices and production sites were moved out of Frankfurt. After Frankfurt had been taken by U.S. troops in April 1945, the latter established their administrative headquarters in the MG complex. Almost all the leading management posts were filled by new people after the end of the war. Petersen, who had been held in detention for some time by the Nazis, took the position of chairman of the board of directors and Rudolf Euler that of chairman of the supervisory board until Richard Merton returned in 1947 from his exile in England. Merton remained chairman until his death in 1960.

### Postwar Restructuring

The situation facing the company in 1945 was somewhat worse than it had been in 1918. Many of the domestic companies lay in ruins and the mining and production works beyond the Elbe had to be given up. After the war, MG's main business for a time was in rubble—Trümmer-Verwertungs-Gesellschaft, in which MG was one of three shareholders, was concerned with recovering rubble, with demolition work, and with recycling rubble—and the manufacturing of roofing felt and jam substitute based on turnips.

Denazification courts—set up by the Allied victors to dismantle all Nazi organizations and get rid of Nazis from key positions as quickly as possible—and decartelization proceedings resulted in major changes to MG's board of directors and supervisory board by 1948. Shortly before this, on the occasion of the German currency reform, MG had lowered its capital, by a ratio of ten to eight, to DM 56 million.

For the company's 75th anniversary, the American military authorities returned to MG the building which they had used as their administrative headquarters for 11 years. Under Alfred Petersen, the firm's technical adviser, the emphasis was put on consolidating and extending the group's technical capabilities. LURGI's research laboratories were expanded. The company pursued its own development program and adopted new processes and areas of work. Lurgi Paris S.A., founded in 1960, was the first branch to be established abroad.

Under the leadership of Hellmut Ley, likewise a technical expert, MG once again acquired an international presence between 1961 and 1973. Ley's name is associated with the extension of the company's smelter capacities. MG subsidiaries or affiliates involved in many of the projects included Ruhr-Zink, Datteln, and "Berzelius" Metallhütten Gesellschaft in Duisburg.

In these years of strong economic growth, MG saw its work force climb to 30,000 in 1961, expanded its business in the transport sector, and became involved in exploratory navigation. In the processing sector, piston manufacturing installations were established in South Africa and in Brazil.

The second half of the 1960s saw MG turn its attention more to publicity. Together with the *Metallstatistik* and the regular publication of scientific research essays in *Mitteilungen aus dem Arbeitsbereich,* the journal *MG Information* came into existence in 1966 and appeared in English for several years.

The "disorganized giant," as the *Financial Times* once called MG, referring to the lack of organizational and divisional structures which the rapid diversification of the group would seem to have necessitated, underwent significant changes in 1971. All MG enterprises and subsidiaries were divided into five divisions: metals processing, plant construction, chemicals, transport, and communications. A functional reorganization also took place in the three central fields of finance, staff and administration, and technology. This structure would last almost 20 years.

In the same year, MG became the first non-British company to be admitted to the London Metal Exchange. The company MG Ltd. was founded for this purpose and the company's historical connection with England was reestablished.

### Karl Gustaf Ratjen Era, 1973–84

Ley died suddenly at the end of the year 1973 and with the appointment of Karl Gustaf Ratjen as chairman of the board, the group found itself with a lawyer and banker at the helm. Ratjen's decade of leadership was marked by strong growth in MG's international activities. In Germany, this period was characterized by recession. In the mining sector, the group ventured into large projects, some in distant locations, such as northern Canada, Thailand, and Papua New Guinea, where copper, lead, and zinc deposits were opened up by group companies, often in conjunction with international partners. The year 1978 saw the founding of Metallgesellschaft of Australia (Pty) Ltd., followed by Metallgesellschaft Corporation in the United States in 1978. The LURGI companies won large contracts from China and the USSR in the 1970s to build petrochemical plants.

The introduction of the codetermination law in 1978 led to the election of employee representatives to the supervisory board. W. Guth of the Deutsche Bank succeeded Hermann Richter after almost two decades as the head of this board. Guth was initially appointed for one year, and later for a further five. Between Guth's two periods in office, H. Friderichs presided for five years. Kuwait Petroleum Company became an MG shareholder in 1980–81 with a 20 percent holding.

In 1981, MG's centenary year, Ratjen defined the company's new aims as increased involvement in raw materials and an accompanying increase in trading activity, engineering services, and specialty chemicals for processing industries. MG made several divestments, including that of VDM. The closure of the Heddernheim works followed in 1982.

### Dietrich Natus Era, 1984–89

Dr. Dietrich Natus, from LURGI, succeeded Ratjen as chairman of the board of directors in 1984. Directly before this, he had turned the combined LURGI operations into a private limited company, and LURGI had moved its new offices to VDM's former site. These offices became the most extensive in Germany.

During Natus's five years as chairman, the company concentrated on strengthening its productivity and financial basis. After several years of low dividend payments, MG's dividends returned to a satisfactory level. MG severed its ties with peripheral and problematic commitments and concentrated its strength on its core activities. Of particular note were the launch onto the stock exchange of motor vehicle distributor Kolbenschmidt, in which MG had a 62.5 percent holding (later reduced to 50.5 percent); the beginning of MG's cooperation with and shareholding in the Canadian mining concern Cominco; and the founding of the mining company Metall Mining Corporation in

Toronto, measures that signaled recovery for the long-ailing mining division.

### Heinz Schimmelbusch Era, 1989–93

In 1989 Natus passed on the chairmanship of MG to Dr. Heinz Schimmelbusch, at 44 the youngest chairman of the board in the history of the group. An economics graduate, Schimmelbusch had been in charge of the raw materials division and had distinguished himself in the previous few years as a member of the board with his innovative and creative ideas and concepts. He immediately set about giving MG a new, flexible managerial and organizational structure. Under Schimmelbusch the raw materials and technological services division concentrated its efforts on the increasingly important domain of environmental technology. Ultramodern plants—for example, a copper electrolysis plant of the Norddeutsche Affinerie and a zinc electrolysis plant for "Berzelius" in Duisburg—were built and fell under the legal emission limits. With the launch onto the stock exchange of Berzelius Umwelt-Service (BUS), MG created a company that would complete the industrial circle— BUS disposed of problematic industrial waste and recycled valuable materials back into the production circuit.

The aim and result of Schimmelbusch's reforms was an harmonious triangle consisting of plant construction, trade in raw materials, and financial services—conducting universal banking operations on behalf of clients inside and outside the group— which worked synergistically within a net that pulled together the most varied sectors of the market. This structure reduced MG's very great dependence on the prices of raw materials and shifts in exchange rates. MG's range of activity was at the same time widely diversified and closely bound together; it covered the discovery, development, and processing of ores together with the processing of the resulting concentrates and the marketing of the processes developed, including the increasingly important field of recycling methods and furthermore encompassing the finance, transport, and marketing sectors.

A constituent part of MG's entrepreneurial philosophy was to give the individual sectors independence as soon as they reach their respective targets for production volume and sales. In short, the group was being divided into separate units that also act efficiently together.

In 1990, MG employees were given the opportunity for the first time to buy staff shares in the company. Connected with this was the latest rise in the company's capital, in which the company's stock capital was increased by more than DM 100 million within two years to DM 381.74 million. In 1991, LURGI acquired Davy McKee AG, a plant-building enterprise with 600 employees, formed out of Zimmer AG and Davy Bamag GmbH.

In June 1991 MG acquired for $706 million (U.S.) the nonpaper division of Dynamit Nobel AG, whose activities included heating and materials technology and explosives and complemented the group's corresponding core activities. In connection with this, the share capital was once more raised, this time by DM 60 million to DM 441.74 million. This takeover raised the number of employees in the MG group to 52,000.

Overall, Schimmelbusch had embarked on a huge acquisitions spree, which through 1991 had cost more than $2 billion (U.S.) and had created a global conglomerate of 258 companies loosely based around environmental services and materials technology. That year, he was named manager of the year by the German magazine *Manager*.

MG's weaknesses in its core metals operations, however, had been exacerbated by the flood of cheap imported metals that began to flow from Eastern Europe following the end of the Cold War in 1989. MG's environmental operations that created recycled metals—on which large sums of development money had been spent—were hurt by the depressed prices before these nascent businesses had barely gotten off the ground. By 1992 these difficulties were compounded by the German economic recession.

As one way of countering these problems, Schimmelbusch entered the American oil business through MG's U.S. financial subsidiary Metallgesellschaft Corp. and its MG Refining and Marketing (MGRM) business. MGRM offered gasoline stations and other small businesses long-term (up to ten-year) contracts to buy fuel at a fixed price. In offering this unique arrangement, MGRM quickly gained two percent of the oil-products market.

### 1993 and Beyond

Meanwhile, MG's cash position was eroding in part because of the large debt the company had accumulated through its huge acquisitions. In February 1993 Schimmelbusch began a divestment program aiming to generate $600 million (U.S.) in cash. MG's financial picture had been further placed in jeopardy, however, by oil-futures hedging positions taken to guard against a rise in oil prices; if oil prices did rise, MGRM would be forced to pay more for the fuel it needed than it would receive from its contractees who were locked into fixed prices. This derivatives strategy was undermined when oil prices, instead of rising, fell starting in the fall of 1993. As a result, on paper at least, the losses were potentially in excess of $1 billion (U.S.). Schimmelbusch needed more cash in order to sustain this strategy until the paper losses evaporated. He sought capital from Deutsche Bank, who then discovered the mounting paper losses, leading to Schimmelbusch's ouster by MG's chairman Ronaldo H. Schmitz, who happened also to serve on Deutsche Bank's board.

Schmitz quickly pulled the plug on the derivatives strategy turning paper losses into real ones—MG subsequently posted a 1992/93 fiscal year loss of DM 1.97 billion ($1.06 billion U.S.). The company's debt then stood at $4.9 billion (U.S.).

Some derivatives experts have claimed that Schmitz and the MG board were too hasty in their abandonment of what the experts saw as a sound hedging strategy. By continuing to roll over the futures contracts until the long-term oil contracts expired, MGRM might have actually profited from its strategy—provided it was given enough money to continue underwriting the futures contracts. Schmitz had in fact said that MG could not afford the interest payments it would have had to pay to continue the derivatives strategy. Such issues were still being debated in the press and the courts into mid-1996.

In any event, along with Schimmelbusch, four other members of MG's management board were fired by Schmitz, who brought in corporate rescuer Kajo Neukirchen to save the company from what would have been Germany's largest post-World War II bankruptcy. He did so first by quickly pulling together a $2.06 billion (U.S.) bank bailout. He then began a $1.63 billion (U.S.) cost-cutting program which included slashing 7,500 jobs and cutting inventory and materials. Neukirchen also started in 1994 to sell off noncore businesses, hoping to raise $600 million (U.S.) in the process.

MG suffered another huge loss—DM 2.63 billion—in fiscal 1993/94. By early 1996, however, Neukirchen could boast of having returned a much-smaller MG to modest profitability in fiscal 1994/95—DM 118 million in net income on revenue of DM 17.64 billion (down from the peak of DM 26.09 billion in fiscal 1992/93). Nearly all of the bailout money had by then been paid back; MG was able in mid-1995 to secure DM 1.26 billion in new credit that provided it with flexibility for future initiatives.

Having already abandoned the fixed-priced contracts that had led MG to the brink of ruin, the company completely exited the U.S. oil marketing business early in 1996. This was perhaps an important symbolic move, since MG was still dealing with numerous lawsuits relating to the derivatives fiasco (including ones filed by and against Schimmelbusch). It will likely take several more years before this chapter in MG's history is complete, at which point the future direction of the company should be clearer.

### Principal Subsidiaries

Cometal SA (Spain); Compania General de Carbones S.A. (Spain); Dynamit Nobel AG; Lentjes Aktiengesellschaft; Lurgi AG; The Metal and Commodity Company Ltd (U.K.); Metallbank GmbH; Metall Capital S.A. (Spain); Metallgesellschaft Capital Corp. (U.S.A.); Metallgesellschaft China Limited; Metallgesellschaft Corp (U.S.A.); Metallgesellschaft do Brasil Ltda. (Brazil); Metallgesellschaft Far East Ltd. (Hong Kong); Metallgesellschaft (France) SA; Metallgesellschaft Handel & Beteiligungen Aktiengesellschaft; Metallgesellschaft Hong Kong Limited; Metallgesellschaft Italiana S.r.l. (Italy); Metallgesellschaft Ltd (U.K.); Metallgesellschaft of Australia (Pty) Ltd.; Metallgesellschaft (South Africa) (Pty) Ltd.; MG Chemiehandel GmbH; MG Erz- & Metallhandel GmbH; MG Metallgesellschaft AG (Switzerland); MG NE-Produkthandel GmbH; MG Refining and Marketing Inc. (U.S.A.); MG Stahl & Recycling Beteiligungen GmbH; MG Terminal Gent N.V. (Belgium); Nihon Metallgesellschaft KK (Japan); The Ore & Chemical Corporation (U.S.A.); Rheinzink GmbH; Zimmer AG.

### Principal Divisions

Trade; Financial Services; Plant Engineering and Contracting; Chemicals; Building Technology.

### Further Reading

Achinger, Hans, *Richard Merton,* Frankfurt am Main: Verlag Waldemar Kramer, 1970.

——, *Wilhelm Merton in seiner Zeit,* Frankfurt am Main: Verlag Waldemar Kramer, 1965.

"Answering Back," *Economist,* October 15, 1994, p. 104.

Däbritz, Walter, *Fünfzig Jahre Metallgesellschaft 1881–1931,* Frankfurt am Main: Metallgesellschaft, 1931.

"Dreaming of Butterflies," *Economist,* June 26, 1993, pp. 65–66, 71.

Edwards, Franklin R., and Michael S. Canter, "The Collapse of Metallgesellschaft: Unhedgeable Risks, Poor Hedging Strategy, or Just Bad Luck?," *Journal of Futures Markets,* May 1995, pp. 211–64.

"Germany's Corporate Whodunnit," *Economist,* February 4, 1995, p. 71.

Glasgall, William, and Karen Lowry Miller, "Executive in Exile: Metallgesellschaft's Heinz Schimmelbusch Speaks Out," *Business Week,* March 21, 1994, pp. 52–54.

"Gunning for Metall," *Economist,* October 1, 1994, p. 96.

Merton, Richard, *Erinnerswertes aus meinem Leben,* Frankfurt am Main: Fritz Knapp Verlag, 1955.

"MG 100 Jahre," *MG Information,* Sonderausgabe: Metallgesellschaft, No. 1, 1981.

Miller, Karen Lowry, " 'I Came, I Saw, I Conquered': Metallgesellschaft's Neukirchen Is Making Waves, but Getting Results," *Business Week,* July 4, 1994, pp. 58, 60.

"Not So Clever," *Economist,* January 15, 1994, p. 83.

Phelps, Richard W., "Metallgesellschaft," *Engineering & Mining Journal,* October 1993, p. 18.

"Revolution at Metallgesellschaft," *Economist,* December 25, 1993–January 7, 1994, p. 90.

"Schadenfreude," *Economist,* January 22, 1994, p. 83.

Schares, Gail E., "The Meltdown at Metallgesellschaft . . . ," *Business Week,* January 24, 1994, pp. 48–49.

"Smoking," *Economist,* January 8, 1994, p. 66.

Sommer, Julius, *Die Metallgesellschaft,* Frankfurt am Main: Metallgesellschaft, 1931.

"A Waste of Resources?," *Economist,* September 24, 1994, p. 85.

—Hannelore Becker-Hess
translated from the German by Philippe A. Barbour
—updated by David E. Salamie

# MicroAge, Inc.

2400 South MicroAge Way
Tempe, Arizona 85282
U.S.A.
(602) 804-2000
Fax: (602) 929-2444

*Public Company*
*Incorporated:* 1976
*Employees:* 1,900
*Sales:* $2.9 billion (1995)
*Stock Exchanges:* NASDAQ
*SICs:* 7373 Computer Integrated Systems Design; 6794
   Patent Owners & Lessors

MicroAge, Inc., a *Fortune 500* company, is one of the nation's largest resellers of computer equipment and systems. Offering customers over 20,000 products from more than 500 vendors—including such leading manufacturers as Compaq, Hewlett-Packard, IBM, Apple, and Microsoft—the company is one of the oldest distributors in the computer industry and is one of only two companies in the entire technology industry that has retained the leadership of its founders. In addition to its headquarters in Tempe, Arizona, the company has two distribution facilities—in Tempe and Cincinnati, Ohio—that together incorporate more than 700,000 square feet, making it one of the largest and most comprehensive technology centers in the industry. Having survived the rapid technological changes that have defined the computer business throughout its history, the company has long played a major role in the evolution of information technology. Through its MicroAge Infosystems Services (MIS) branch network, the company provides large organizations throughout the world with systems integration services and distributed computing solutions—involving servers, desktops, notebooks, software, memory, and peripherals. Other services include integration, project management, global support and service, system installation, help desk services, software licensing and upgrades, Internet access, CD-ROM publishing, and financing programs.

## Early History

MicroAge was founded in 1976 by a pair of Arizona bankers with an avid interest in the budding field of computer technology, Jeffrey McKeever and Alan Hald. Having taken computer classes—then called "numerical analysis"—while at the University of Arizona, McKeever ran the Air Force's largest computer center in the Far East for three years, before taking a job with Southern Arizona Bank, where he met his future partner. After earning degrees from Rensselaer Polytechnic Institute and Harvard University, Hald also spent time in the military before moving to Arizona and entering the banking industry. The impetus for the company that would take just 16 years to surpass the $1 billion mark in sales came from a 1975 article in the computer magazine *Byte,* which described the latest in microcomputer "kits," as they were known at the time. As the two put together their own microcomputer, they shared their vision of creating a business that would sell the machines. The following year, convinced that there was money to be made in the technology that was familiar to only a small number of hobbyists like themselves, they pooled their "pocket capital" and opened up a small store in Tempe called The Byte Shop, where they assembled and sold Norstan computer kits.

Although conventional business wisdom suggested that the hobby-computer store surge would be short-lived, the two sold enough of their $691 kits to generate $1.5 million in revenue that first year and expand to four locations. Having entered the market in its infancy, the founders of Arizona's first computer company took full advantage of the public's growing interest in the rapidly developing technology. They renamed their firm MicroAge and quickly established mail-order and wholesale divisions, while achieving sales of $8 million in their second year and $15 million their third. By 1979, the company had expanded to several stores and had grown to become the largest computer retailer-wholesaler in the United States.

Two years later, the computer distributor attempted to accelerate its growth by launching a franchise program. Their plans for continued national and international expansion, however, collided with the onset of a recession and a financially debilitating combination of high interest rates, increasing competition, and increasingly complex corporate structure. And in 1982, the

---

**Company Perspectives:**

*Our mission is to develop satisfied clients by providing quality sales and services of information technology solutions through an international network of franchised, company-owned and affiliated reseller locations. MicroAge values: add value to everything we do; respect our relationships; act with integrity; make things happen; do it right the first time; have fun.*

---

company was forced to regroup, filing for reorganization under Chapter 11 of the U.S. Bankruptcy Code. Ten months later, the company successfully exited bankruptcy and was ready to rebuild, having learned to temper its entrepreneurial zeal with a larger degree of fiscal responsibility.

### Reemergence and Record Growth in the Mid-1980s

As MicroAge set out to rebuild its operation, it benefited from the increasing popularity of the IBM Personal Computer (PC). Introduced to the market in the early 1980s, the IBM PCs inspired confidence in the microcomputer as a powerful new tool for personal and business productivity. Realizing the tremendous potential of this rapidly evolving technology, the company began negotiating strategic partnerships with first-rate computer vendors such as Hewlett-Packard, sharing resources and ideas in an attempt to provide better products and services to its customers.

Such partnerships became increasingly important as the magnitude and scope of computer use entered a new era in the mid-1980s. At this point, individual PC "islands" began to appear frequently in the business environment, enabling people to discover the advantages of linking computers together, sharing ideas, information, and resources. This phenomenon spawned the next generation of computer technology: the PC local-area network (LAN). Together, MicroAge and Hewlett-Packard began developing products and services to help businesses and organizations use this technology to improve the efficiency and lower the costs of their operations.

MicroAge demonstrated its position of leadership in LAN technology by launching an aggressive new marketing strategy in 1985. Having grown to a 149-store computer chain, the company established an industry first by opening up an 8,000-square-foot test store in Tempe that was equipped and wired to demonstrate networks, multiuser systems, and the latest in telecommunications technology. The new facility—which included products such as multiuser systems, personal computers, voice/data workstations, and telecommunications products—gave MicroAge the ability to let customers see for themselves how various systems operate, instead of just listening to the claims of a salesperson.

That same year the company, in an attempt to keep pace with the rapid development of technology, became the first computer retailer to initiate an in-store satellite television network. Designed to keep its employees abreast of the latest information on advanced technology, the satellite TV service, called the MicroAge Communications Network (MCN-TV), became an easily accessible and cost-effective medium for both employees, through training seminars, and for customers wishing to learn more about various computer systems. What is more, leading vendors such as IBM, AT&T, and Compaq strongly supported the new communications channel, recognizing it as a viable way to provide information to MicroAge technicians and salespeople.

Innovations such as these, combined with the exponential expansion in the market for computers, proved to be a favorable combination for the company. Between 1984 and 1985, the number of MicroAge stores skyrocketed from 36 to 178, while sales more than tripled, from $42 million to $142 million, and profits jumped from $804,000 to $3.8 million.

While the company continued to enjoy considerable success through the remainder of the decade, it did so in the face of an increasingly competitive computer industry that quickly evolved into one of the highest velocity and thinnest margin businesses around. As McKeever told Leslie Brokaw of *Inc.* magazine, "If you don't figure out how to improve what you do each year, you're going to be out of business fairly quickly." Operating in an environment that saw gross profits dwindle to 5 percent, MicroAge found it necessary to come up with a new strategy for growth to continue—even if that meant replacing its own ideas.

Until as late as 1989, MicroAge operated its franchises on a royalty system, requiring each franchise to pay a percentage of its total sales to the company. Under the royalty program—one of the most expensive in the industry—store owners purchased products from the company at cost plus a markup of approximately 5.9 percent and then paid the corporation an additional 5 percent of all revenues, with 1 percent earmarked for advertising. With the rapid growth of the competition, especially from resellers such as Connecting Point of America and Intelligent Electronics who were offering their dealers less expensive rates through a cost-plus program that allowed dealers to pay a markup only on the equipment and services they bought, MicroAge decided to make a change. In one fell swoop, the company eliminated its royalty franchise system, eliminating the source of approximately half of its gross margins and forfeiting $100 million in outstanding royalty payments, simply to change to a cost-plus program. Under the new system, called MicroAge 2000, storefront owners paid MicroAge a mark-up fee of between 3.9 and 8.5 percent, an enticing offer for many independent stores. With the new franchise model in place, MicroAge became the first cost-plus reseller authorized by the top three PC makers: IBM, Apple Computer Inc., and Compaq Computer Corporation. And it was now able to compete for new franchises more competitively and enjoy more rapid growth. In just over three years, the company expanded from 600 to 1,500 locations, while seeing its revenue jump from $364 million to over $1 billion.

### The 1990s: Meeting the Needs of the Information Superhighway

As MicroAge entered the new decade, it also found itself in a new era of technology, with the LAN giving way to the information superhighway. No longer was it enough for companies to move information to various places within a company, it now became necessary for information—more information—to be moved over a wider geography, and to diverse populations of users using different computer systems. MicroAge's continued success would thus be dependent upon its ability to integrate these converging technologies. In 1990, the company attempted to better serve this need by initiating its Quality Integration Center (QIC), a systems integration facility that takes "raw materials"—servers, workstations, software, and other components—and creates specialized, network-integrated solutions for businesses and organizations. With the ability to integrate more than 500 different vendor products, the QIC has earned the highest international quality standard—the ISO 9002—a certification vital to high-quality computer manufacturers such as Compaq.

Although sales for the nation's oldest major reseller continued to grow steadily, the company experienced a drop in earnings during the early 1990s. As more and more smaller manufacturers entered the computer industry, offering lower-priced PC clones, the sale of brand-name PCs declined, weakening business for traditional resellers such as MicroAge. Finding itself shipping more boxes but making less money, the company reported a drop in profits for the first time in several years in 1991. The company also suffered from a boom in the mail-order computer and computer superstore industry, which significantly altered the market share distribution of the computer business. While retailers, such as MicroAge, controlled 60 percent of the market during the 1980s, their share dropped to 30 percent by 1992.

Beginning in 1993, though, corporate computer buyers, which benefited from price wars and reduced prices by the big three—Apple, IBM, and Compaq—again turned to brand-name retailers for their computer solutions. MicroAge, having developed a specialized business networking division, called MicroAge Infosystems Services (MIS), in 1992, did its best to take full advantage of this shift in the market. The highly regarded MIS division helped the company to answer the increasingly complex networking needs of Corporate America and return the company to the path of record growth. And in 1993, the company generated more than $1.5 billion in sales and, more importantly, $10.5 million in profits, a twofold increase from the previous year.

### The Mid-1990s and Beyond

In 1994, in anticipation of future changes in the industry, the company reorganized itself into separate businesses to better meet the diverse needs of its customers. MicroAge Computer Centers and MicroAge Technologies were established to serve franchised resellers and market to Value Added Resellers (VARs), respectively. MicroAge Product Services was given the responsibility of distribution, logistics, technical, and outsourcing services, while MicroAge Channel Services was set up to provide purchasing and marketing services for resellers and vendors. Finally, MIS retained the duties of coordinating and servicing large-account marketing in conjunction with franchised resellers.

Operating in an industry marked by constant flux and ever-increasing competition, MicroAge attempted to diversify its operations in the mid-1990s to separate itself from its smaller

competitors with less resources. Taking advantage of its size and low-cost structure, the company began placing more emphasis on its outsourcing business—that is, performing duties such as technical service, inventory management, and logistics management for other resellers and vendors. Such opportunities have enabled the company to further leverage its low-cost structure and further expand its business. As the winner of several service awards from *Computerworld* and *Datamation* magazines, the company, which was one of only five chosen to support the nationwide introduction of Windows 95, has developed the reputation for excellence and the economies of scale needed to make such ventures profitable.

After having posted 36 consecutive profitable quarters and nearing the $3 billion mark in sales, MicroAge looked toward the second half of the decade and the dawn of the 21st century, hoping to benefit from several new developments in the industry. First, the corporate demand from information technology appeared to be strengthening as companies made plans to upgrade their existing systems to take advantage of new 32-bit operating systems and applications. Second, manufacturers such as IBM have suggested that they will outsource more joint manufacturing and light assembly work, representing the potential for more work for the company's 133,000-square-foot Quality Integration Center, which has tested and configured more than 10,000 complete systems each month. Finally, MicroAge, as one of only four suppliers chosen to participate in IBM's Electronic Purchasing Service Program, has expected to derive much of its future business through electronic linkages with its customers. With its balance sheet as strong as it has ever been, the company claims to be in a favorable position to "navigate the next wave" of the Information Age and add to its streak of profitability along the way.

### Principal Subsidiaries

MicroAge Computer Centers, Inc. (MCCI); MicroAge Infosystems Services, Inc. (MIS); MicroAge Solutions, Inc. (MAC).

### Principal Divisions

MicroAge Channel Services (MCS); MicroAge Computer Centers (MCC); MicroAge Data Services (MDS); MicroAge Logistics Services (MLS); MicroAge Technologies (MAT).

### Further Reading

Arnst, Catherine, Joseph Weber, and Kathy Rebello, "A Surprise Lift for Computer Retailers," *Business Week,* October 19, 1992, pp. 63–64.

Brokaw, Leslie, "Flexible Fliers," *Inc.,* December 1995, pp. 82–85.

Faletra, Robert, "MicroAge Replacing Royalty Plan with Cost-Plus Franchise Program, *PC Week,* June 12, 1989, p. 74.

——, "PC Service from Third Parties Is on the Rise," *PC Week,* November 13, 1989, p. S19.

Fisher, Susan E., "Reseller Outlook Remains Gloomy," *PC Week,* October 21, 1991, p. 243.

Humphrey, Charles, "MicroAge's Apple Affiliates Program Changes All the Rules," *PC Week,* April 17, 1989, p. 92.

Kuzela, Lad, "Alan Hald Mixes Dreams, Reality," *Industry Week,* March 31, 1986, p. 84.

Littman, Jonathan, "MicroAge Wires Store to Demonstrate LANs, Other Multiuse Systems," *PC Week,* July 16 1985, p. 112.

Loge, Peter, ''Hald's Vision Kicked Off MicroAge,'' *The Business Journal-Serving Phoenix & the Valley of the Sun,* June 16, 1995, p. 18.

Luebke, Cathy, ''MicroAge's Jeffrey McKeever Thrives on Role as Innovator,'' *The Business Journal-Serving Phoenix & the Valley of the Sun,* May 6, 1991, pp. 28–29.

Whitmore, Sam, ''MicroAge to Broadcast PC-Related TV Shows in Retail-Chain Stores,'' *PC Week,* September 10, 1985, pp. 139–40.

—Jason Gallman

# Micro Warehouse, Inc.

## Micro Warehouse, Inc.

535 Connecticut Avenue
Norwalk, Connecticut 06854
U.S.A.
(203) 899-4000
Fax: (203) 899-4203

*Public Company*
*Incorporated:* 1992
*Employees:* 3,100
*Sales:* $1.31 billion (1995)
*Stock Exchanges:* NASDAQ
*SICs:* 5961 Catalog & Mail-Order Houses

Micro Warehouse, Inc. is a leading direct marketer of Macintosh and IBM-compatible personal computers, software, accessories, and peripheral equipment. The company markets its products primarily through a telemarketing sales force and color catalogs, which it was shipping to 15 countries in 1995. Micro Warehouse achieved rampant growth during the late 1980s and early 1990s by acquiring other companies and boosting its mail-order sales.

### Focusing on the Apple Macintosh

Founded in 1987 as Mac Warehouse, Micro Warehouse grew from a small direct marketing company to one of the largest computer equipment retailers in the world in fewer than ten years. Driving that growth was an explosion in mail-order computer sales combined with a savvy business strategy employed by the company's founders: Peter Godfrey, Robert Bartner, and Felix Dennis. The three entrepreneurs had already achieved impressive success with another computer-related venture before starting the company that would become Micro Warehouse. In 1985 they had launched a magazine dubbed *Mac User,* which had quickly gained a wide readership among owners of the popular Apple Macintosh computer. Moreover, the publication became an important marketing medium for sellers of Macintosh products and related peripheral devices.

Godfrey, Bartner, and Dennis were among the first to realize the potential of the growth in computer-related publications and the burgeoning mail-order market for computer gear. Prices for PCs and peripherals (printers, monitors, disk drives, etc.) were rapidly falling in the mid-1980s as the cost of the technology dropped. As prices became increasingly attractive to individuals and small business owners, a massive market was rapidly building. It was at that segment of that rapidly growing computer crowd that *Mac User* was targeted. The magazine kept buyers abreast of new products and developments related to their Macintosh systems and gave computing hints and advice to loyal Macintosh users, a market segment largely ignored by publications aimed at owners of IBM-compatible PCs.

*Mac User*'s readership rapidly soared, and the magazine became an important advertising channel, particularly for companies trying to sell their goods by mail-order. The rapid success of the new magazine attracted the interest of publishing giant Ziff-Davis, which believed that it could use its deep pockets to grow the publication even faster. In 1987, just 16 months after they had launched the periodical, the three founders of *Mac User* sold their magazine to Ziff-Davis for $23 million. *Mac User* went on to become a dominant periodical in the Macintosh market, while Godfrey and his associates started looking for a new venture in which to invest their cash.

Shortly after they sold *Mac User,* Godfrey, Dennis, and Bartner launched another publication. Titled *MacWarehouse,* the new "magazine" was effectively a catalog of Macintosh software, supplies, and equipment. Rather than proffering value-added information to readers, *MacWarehouse* simply provided an inventory of available products. The concept was a corollary of the rapidly emerging market for mail-order equipment. Indeed, as computer users at home and at small and mid-size businesses were becoming more comfortable with PC technology, they were increasingly willing to purchase software and equipment through the mail without the aid of a salesperson. By cutting out the middle man, mail-order buyers enjoyed much lower prices, as well as the ability to shop and compare prices from their desk or sofa.

Like *Mac User, MacWarehouse* was an instant success. The company generated $18.4 million in 1988, its first full year of operation, and was chalking up steady gains going into 1989. New products were added to the catalog, telephone operators were added to the company's order-taking team, and the company's warehouse was expanded to hold more inventory.

### Diversification into the IBM-Compatible Market

Buoyed by the quick success of *MacWarehouse,* Godfrey and his associates decided to broaden their scope. Rather than targeting the relatively tiny niche of Macintosh buyers, they decided to chase the much larger pool of owners of IBM-compatible devices. Toward that end, they launched *Micro Warehouse* in 1989, which offered IBM-compatible machines along with a range of complementary peripheral devices and software.

The *Micro Warehouse* catalog was a big success. Sales through both catalogs rose to $52.56 million for 1989 before more than doubling to $123 million in 1990. The company posted its first net surplus in 1990, of $1.4 million. Godfrey and fellow executives scrambled to increase sales capacity to keep pace with surging order volume. The company opened a second distribution center, giving it warehouse facilities in New Jersey and Ohio. It also added new phone operators and aggressively increased distribution of its full-color catalogs. As a result, sales increased to $163.6 million in 1991 before climbing to $270 million in 1992. By that time, the organization's net income was approaching $10 million annually. Despite those gains, growth during the next few years would dwarf the company's early rise.

### Phenomenal Growth in the 1990s

Micro Warehouse's growth during the late 1980s and early 1990s was funded largely by the founders' investment and by cashflow from operations. By 1992, however, those sources had become insufficient to finance the kind of expansion that the company's leaders hoped to achieve during the remainder of the decade. In October 1992, therefore, Godfrey and fellow managers took the enterprise public with a NASDAQ stock offering that raised more than $50 million. The cash was used to pay back about $14.1 million that had been invested by the founders, reduce other debt obligations, and to fund various growth initiatives. It was at the time of the offering that the company was incorporated under the new name of Micro Warehouse, Inc.

The success of the stock offering—the stock price settled at about $23 within one month of the initial public offering—evidenced investors' faith in Micro Warehouse's operating strategy. By the time of the stock offering, in fact, Micro Warehouse was handling 10,000 phone calls per day and shipping its IBM-compatible and Macintosh products throughout North America. To accomplish that feat in so short a time period, management had adeptly built an efficient marketing and distribution network that was among the most respected in the industry. Indeed, despite rapid growth Micro Warehouse had managed to retain its reputation for prompt and reliable service. The efficiency of its operations had also made it known in both the commercial and consumer marketplaces as a price leader in the industry.

Micro Warehouse's sales strategy was relatively simple. The company churned out thousands of eye-catching, full-color catalogs, which were delivered monthly to prospective customers. Because it purchased in bulk and ran low-cost operations, the company was able to offer the goods in its catalogs at cut-rate prices. Customers scanned the catalogs to find the products they wanted, called a toll-free number, and then ordered the item from one of Micro Warehouse's hundreds of sales and customer representatives and support staff. Workers manned the phones 24 hours per day, seven days each week. And all customer orders were shipped for next-day delivery. The emphasis was on customer service, and the company's loyal customer base was much of the reason that Micro Warehouse was able to so quickly increase its sales and profits during the mid-1990s. In 1993, in fact, Micro Warehouse boosted revenue nearly 70 percent to about $450 million, $15 million of which was netted as income. Furthermore, the company went into 1994 with virtually no long-term debt on its balance sheet.

Not satisfied with the company's blistering growth rate, Godfrey (the company's chairman, chief executive, and president) launched a number of new expansion initiatives in 1993 and 1994. In 1993 he started four new catalog publications: *Data Comm Warehouse* (for the network and data communications market); *Micro Supplies Warehouse; Paper Design Warehouse;* and *CD-ROM Warehouse.* Then, in 1994, the company started distributing *Home Computer Warehouse* and *Micro Systems Warehouse. Paper Design Warehouse* and *CD-ROM Warehouse* soon folded, but the other three publications became profitable additions to the organization's marketing program. They helped push 1994 sales and profits to $776 million and $28 million, respectively. In 1994, in fact, *Micro Warehouse* fielded a whopping seven million telephone calls and was serving a customer base of more than 900,000 people.

Perhaps more important than Micro Warehouse's new catalogs during the early and mid-1990s was its aggressive drive to expand overseas. Micro Warehouse first tested the waters in the United Kingdom, where it started a full-service catalog and mail-order operation in 1991. In 1992, the company began similar operations in France and Germany, and then moved into the rest of Europe, Japan, Canada, Mexico, and Australia, before entering into licensing agreements with international partners in several other countries. Micro Warehouse moved into many of those countries by purchasing existing businesses already operating in those markets. In 1993 the company purchased businesses in Denmark, Norway, and Sweden, and added eight more new enterprises to its fold in 1994 in Europe, Mexico, and Canada. It bought eight more foreign businesses in 1995, confirming the company's intent to establish a global direct marketing network.

Micro Warehouse received a big boost in 1994 when several major manufacturers began authorizing direct marketers like Micro Warehouse to sell their goods. In the past, big computer and peripheral makers such as IBM and Apple had shunned such arrangements. By the mid-1990s, however, there was no denying the power of such direct marketers as Micro Warehouse to reach the swelling home and home business PC market. Micro Warehouse jumped on the opportunity and was soon selling brand name goods in its catalogs from such mass sellers as Compaq, IBM, Apple, and Hewlett Packard. The development was a boon for Micro Warehouse, which by 1994 had jumped to the top of the global PC direct marketing industry. Indeed, after boosting sales at a rampant pace for years, Micro Warehouse nearly doubled revenues to $1.31 billion in 1995 and increased net income to $45 million.

Going into 1996, Micro Warehouse was offering more than 20,000 products through several catalogs in 15 countries and employing more than 3,000 workers worldwide. Most of its sales were to small and mid-size businesses, and about 25 percent of shipments were to overseas buyers (up 150 percent from 1994 to 1995). Its core catalogs included *Micro Warehouse, Mac Warehouse,* and *Data Comm Warehouse,* but it also sold gear through *Micro Systems Warehouse* and *Mac Systems Warehouse.* All of the catalogs were full-color, ad-packed, and focused on cutting-edge technology and equipment.

In January 1996 Micro Warehouse made a substantial addition to its business with the purchase of Inmac, Inc., a leading international direct marketer of computer desktop and networking products. Inmac brought more than $350 million in revenues to Micro Warehouse's sales base, while also adding operations in North America and five countries in Europe. In the long term, Micro Warehouse planned to sustain its rapid expansion by acquiring other companies and by growing its catalog and mail-order business with the addition of new computer-related and electronic information-related products.

### Principal Subsidiaries

Inmac Corp.; Micro Warehouse, Inc.; Micro Warehouse, Inc.; Micro Warehouse Limited (United Kingdom); Microwarehouse France SARL; Micro Warehouse (Deutschland) GmbH (Germany); Micro Warehouse, Sweden AB; Micro Warehouse, Denmark APS; Micro Warehouse, Norway AS; Micro Warehouse, Finland OY; Micro Warehouse Holding B.V.; Micro Warehouse, Japan KK; Micro Warehouse Canada Limited; Micro Warehouse, S.A. (Mexico); Micro Warehouse (Australia) Pty Ltd.; MacWarehouse (Belgium).

### Further Reading

Comte, Elizabeth, "From Chips to Porn," *Forbes,* November 23, 1992, p. 20.

Croghan, Lore, "Micro Warehouse CDW Computer Centers; The Endless Wave?," *Financial World,* June 20, 1995, p. 18.

*Micro Warehouse, Inc. Company Update,* New York: Prudential Securities, February 29, 1996.

*Micro Warehouse, Inc. Company Update,* San Francisco: Montgomery Securities, March 12, 1996.

Pandya, Mukul, "Micro Warehouse's Giant Deal Brings A Building Back to Life," *Business News New Jersey,* September 20, 1995, p. 32.

Roberts, Jim, "Investors Welcome Micro Warehouse, United Waste IPOs," *Fairfield County Business Journal,* December 28, 1992, p. 1.

Scussel, Patricia, "Catalog of the Year," *Catalog Age,* September 15, 1995, p. 69.

Teitelbaum, Richard S., "Micro Warehouse," *Fortune,* February 22, 1994, p. 91.

*U.S. Research Micro Warehouse, Inc.,* New York: Goldman Sachs, February 14, 1996.

—Dave Mote

# *MORGAN STANLEY*

# Morgan Stanley Group Inc.

1585 Broadway
New York, New York 10036
U.S.A.
(212) 761-4000
Fax: (212) 761-0086

*Public Company*
*Incorporated:* 1935 as Morgan Stanley & Co.
    Incorporated
*Employees:* 9,238
*Total Assets:* $143.75 billion (1995)
*Stock Exchanges:* New York Boston Pacific Midwest
*SICs:* 6211 Security Brokers, Dealers & Flotation
    Companies; 6799 Investors, Not Elsewhere Classified

Morgan Stanley Group Inc. is one of the world's top investment banking firms. Since 1935 it has been underwriting, managing, and distributing corporate and governmental securities issues. By 1995, it was ranked the top mergers and acquisitions adviser worldwide and was the number three global underwriter. In step with the deregulation of the financial markets which began in the 1980s, Morgan Stanley diversified its range of financial services. In the mid-1990s, it operated in three core businesses: investment banking, asset management, and sales and trading. The late 1980s also began a period of aggressive international expansion, which led by 1996 to a network of 27 principal offices in 19 countries—mainly European nations and the emerging states of Asia.

## *Investment Banking in the 19th and Early 20th Centuries*

The story of Morgan Stanley begins long before it was incorporated in 1935. The company's roots may actually be traced to 1860, when J. P. Morgan founded the world's first international banking concern, Drexel, Morgan & Company. Morgan's financial empire became legendary, as large industrialists turned to Morgan and his colleagues when they wanted to raise capital. By 1895, the firm had become J.P. Morgan and Company, and by the turn of the century Morgan was a premier agent for large quantities of securities, selling them both at home and abroad.

At this time, investment houses began to join together in syndicates to share the responsibilities and risks of financing to better serve the mushrooming capital requirements of American industry. They also affiliated themselves with large, prestigious banking syndicates to provide credibility and value to the issue of borrowers' securities. Syndicates could often broaden the geographic scope of a company's investors, which was the reason Boston-based American Telephone and Telegraph granted leadership to Morgan's New York firm in 1906 to underwrite $100 million of a $150 million bond issue, although it retained Kidder, Peabody as its principal banker.

As industry depended on the banks for capital, and banks depended on the revenue created by generating that capital, it became very common for bankers and businessmen to serve on each others' boards. These interlocking directorships eventually became a primary concern of the U.S. House of Representatives Banking and Currency Committee, which decided to investigate. Its findings led to the Federal Reserve Act of 1913 and the Clayton Antitrust Act of 1914, which ended reciprocal directorships.

Regulation of investment banking remained an area of public concern throughout the first few decades of the century. Kansas was the first state to regulate all securities offered for sale to its citizens, a trend that spread across the nation. By 1933 every state but Nevada had enacted legislation to protect investors from fraud.

During World War I, investment bankers coordinated the sale of more than $2.2 billion in French and British bonds and the resale of more than $3 billion in American securities held in Europe. The house of Morgan accounted for more than $2 billion of that total. By serving in this capacity, investment bankers played a vital role in transforming the United States from a debtor to a creditor nation and in making New York the financial capital of the world.

## Company Perspectives:

*Why do clients choose Morgan Stanley? They can depend on us to put our clients first, to focus the efforts and talents of the entire firm on each assignment. They recognize that we build enduring relationships and consistently take the long-term view in an industry in which change is the only constant.*

### Company Founding and Early History

The disastrous business practices of banks during the decade before the stock market crash on October 29, 1929 provided the real impetus for the birth of Morgan Stanley. During these years, commercial banks speculated with their depositors' money—borrowed money—and played the market on margin. The frenzy escalated as hundreds of issues, many of them worthless, flooded the market and fueled the speculation. The market's plummet devastated margin players on all levels. Upon taking office, President Franklin D. Roosevelt initiated a number of investigations, and Congress enacted legislation to prevent a recurrence of the events that caused the crash.

The Banking Act of 1933, better known as the Glass-Steagall Act, affected the investment banking industry more significantly than any other piece of legislation by requiring the separation of commercial and investment banks. Deposit business went to commercial banks, and underwriting and syndication went to investment banks, thus making the average depositor's money unavailable for speculation. The act became law June 16, 1933, and banks were given 12 months to comply.

J.P. Morgan and Company chose to pursue deposit banking. Within a year and a half of this decision, three of its partners organized Morgan Stanley & Co. Incorporated to enter the investment banking business. The new company was incorporated on September 16, 1935 and claimed some of the most experienced men in investment banking as assets. Harold Stanley, at age 42 one of the youngest J.P. Morgan and Company partners, was president. Henry Morgan, grandson of J. P., was secretary-treasurer. Morgan would play an integral role in the firm for more than 40 years.

The extensive experience of Morgan Stanley's leadership was one key to the company's immediate success. Another was the firm's ties to J.P. Morgan and Company and the corporate connections that came with them. Personal endorsements carried a great deal of influence during this period. Morgan Stanley chose syndicate partners based on ''historical affiliations,'' meaning those that had been in place before Glass-Steagall.

During its first month alone, the new investment bank handled three major underwritings, including $43 million for AT&T; Morgan Stanley was blue chip from the start. It was also one of a select group that managed underwriting syndicates and handled wholesaling. It rarely participated in originations directed by another firm. Morgan Stanley's clients included nearly half of the largest 50 companies in the nation, among them Exxon, General Motors, and General Electric. By the end of its first full year of operations, Morgan Stanley had acquired a 24 percent market share of negotiated corporate and foreign issues, and by 1938, Morgan Stanley led all New York investment firms in original bond issues.

Throughout the 1930s, investment banking was dominated by a relatively small number of firms, and by the end of the decade, the government had again taken an interest in the affairs of investment houses. Morgan Stanley's quick success made it a particularly visible target. The Temporary National Economic Committee was formed to investigate monopolies in big business. In 1939, the committee called a number of investment bankers to testify in order to determine how much power investment banks held over industry through their control of the access to long-term capital markets. A key issue during the hearings was whether the negotiation of prices between corporations and securities underwriters infringed upon free trade. Many investment bankers, most notably Harold Stuart of the Chicago investment bank Halsey, Stuart & Company, were in favor of the competitive bidding system. Under this system, securities were auctioned off to the highest bidder. Morgan Stanley, which benefited immensely from its strong personal connections throughout the business community, was fiercely opposed to mandatory competitive bidding. The government, however, leaned in favor of the sealed bid system.

In 1941, the SEC required all public utilities companies to issue securities by public sealed bidding. Public utilities made up a substantial portion of the domestic market; between 1935 and 1939, they accounted for 13 percent of all U.S. common stock offerings. In addition, the Federal Communications Commission urged AT&T to use the competitive bidding system for its issues. Many investment banks feared the nature of their business would be drastically changed. In anticipation of the changes, Morgan Stanley decided to branch into the brokerage business. On November 28, 1941, in order to meet the criteria for membership on the New York Stock Exchange, Morgan Stanley liquidated its stock and reorganized as a partnership.

World War II brought the securities business to a virtual halt. Morgan Stanley survived on brokerage commissions, consulting fees, and a small number of private placements. Founding partner Henry Morgan joined the navy, where he served on the Joint Army and Navy Munitions Board and as a commander attached to the Naval Command Office of Strategic Services. Other high-ranking Morgan Stanley officers also entered the service in various capacities, including partner Perry Hall, who served as executive manager of the War Loan Committee of the Second Federal Reserve District. After the war, the company quickly reestablished its business relationships.

Government allegations of monopoly continued to plague Morgan Stanley in the late 1940s. In 1947, the Justice Department filed suit against Morgan Stanley and 16 other investment banking firms accusing them of conspiring to monopolize and restrain the securities industry. In forming syndicates, the government charged, investment bankers practiced both collusion and exclusion. After three years of pretrial hearings, proceedings opened in the Circuit Court of New York on November 28, 1950. On September 22, 1953, three years after its introduction in court and six years after the suit was filed, Circuit Judge Harold R. Medina concluded that none of the 17 investment banks named in the suit were guilty of any of the charges brought forth by the government. ''What is now taking shape,'' Medina wrote, ''is not a static mosaic of conspiracy but a constantly changing panorama of competition among the 17 defendant firms.'' The antitrust storm had finally passed.

### Prosperity of the 1950s and Early 1960s

In 1951, Harold Stanley took a back seat in the operations of the company and Perry Hall, another of Morgan Stanley's founding partners, took his place. Hall remained managing partner until 1961. The 1950s were a prosperous time for Morgan Stanley, and the firm grew steadily throughout the decade. In 1954, Morgan Stanley managed a $300 million bond issue for General Motors. It was at the time the biggest securities issue ever underwritten in the history of investment banking. At the time Perry Hall commented to *The New Yorker,* with the nonchalant confidence typical of Morgan Stanley, ''After the G.M. deal was cooked I went down to South Carolina for a week's shooting. Shot two wild turkeys while I was down there. First time I ever got turkey. Generally got quail before. Come to think of it I got quail this time, too—fifteen of them.''

As the bull market of the 1950s continued into the 1960s, Morgan Stanley remained a leader in institutional investment banking. The company consistently ranked in the top five firms managing new issues. In its first 30 years Morgan Stanley had managed or comanaged more than $30 billion in public offerings and private placements.

In the late 1960s, the firm expanded its base. In 1966, together with the Morgan Guaranty Trust Company, it established a French subsidiary to broaden its international operations. The new Morgan & Cie International S.A. managed and participated in underwritings of foreign securities. In 1967, Morgan Stanley moved its headquarters to 140 Broadway from its old home at No. 2 Wall Street in deference to the need for more space. In 1969, Morgan Stanley plunged deeper into real estate financing when it bought a controlling interest in Brooks, Harvey & Company, Inc., which had been in the business of advising and financing real estate developments for more than 50 years.

### Volatility and Transitions of the 1970s

The 1970s, however, were a more volatile time for Morgan Stanley. Early in the decade, the company went through a major corporate restructuring, reverting to incorporation from a limited partnership. The trend in investment banking was toward full service. Morgan Stanley, like other large investment banks, entered retail markets, added venture capital units, and aggressively sought foreign customers. In 1971, Morgan Stanley moved its headquarters for the second time in five years, to the Exxon Building in Rockefeller Center, in order to be nearer its corporate clients' midtown headquarters. Samuel Payne was the reorganized company's first president. He was soon followed by Chester Lasell, and in 1973, by Robert Baldwin.

The company created a mergers and acquisition department in 1972 to help its clients find and evaluate appropriate acquisition targets and to provide strategic planning to complete the deals. It also broadened its real estate activities with the creation of Morstan Development Company, Inc. In 1973, Morgan Stanley opened a research department and entered the equity markets full-scale. Morgan Stanley's asset management division, which began in 1975, became a strong revenue producer. Morgan Stanley began to offer individual investment services to wealthy individuals and to smaller institutional investors in 1977.

Not only did the scope of Morgan Stanley's business shift during the 1970s, but the style of its leadership did too. In 1973, Frank Petito became chairman of Morgan Stanley, the year Robert Baldwin became president. Petito, and to an even greater extent Baldwin, represented the new breed of investment bankers. While Morgan Stanley had until now depended heavily on relationships and personal affiliations, the revamped company, following the general trend in big business, concentrated on the bottom line. Under its new leadership, Morgan Stanley grew rapidly. Paid-in capital mushroomed from $7.5 million in 1970 to $118 million in 1980, and the staff swelled from fewer than 200 to 1,700 in the same period.

Growth did not come without setbacks, however. IBM abandoned its long-term relationship with the firm when Morgan Stanley refused to share managership with Salomon Brothers on a $1 billion note issue. Olincraft, Inc. sued Morgan Stanley for divulging confidential information for use by another client in a hostile takeover, and Occidental Petroleum filed a separate suit on similar grounds that was later dropped.

The court ruled in favor of Morgan Stanley in the Olincraft case, stating that ''Olincraft's management placed its confidence in Morgan Stanley not to disclose the information. Morgan Stanley owed no duty to observe that confidence.'' Not surprisingly, despite winning the suit, Morgan Stanley was subsequently viewed in a different light by corporations and by its competitors. The firm's reputation, commonly referred to as ''the franchise,'' was not as pristine as it once had been.

Another setback occurred in 1981, when it came to light that two former employees of Morgan Stanley had passed on inside information during the mid-1970s to a number of outside traders in return for a share of the resulting profits. Information on at least 18 acquisitions was leaked between 1974 and 1978. The incident focused a great deal of attention on insider trading, and the business community called for harsher penalties for violators.

### Survival During the Highly Competitive 1980s

As the firm entered the 1980s, competition in investment banking was as fierce as ever. Although Morgan Stanley continued to grow at a considerable pace, it was outperformed by its rivals. While investment bankers such as Salomon Brothers and Goldman, Sachs began trading in commercial paper, mortgage-backed securities, and foreign currencies early in the decade, Morgan Stanley, fearful of overextending itself, dragged its feet in these areas. The company also lagged behind in leveraged buyouts and the explosive municipal bond market.

In 1984, leadership passed to an even more aggressive team. S. Parker Gilbert, the stepson of Harold Stanley, became chairman, and Richard Fisher became president. The company had set out to fill the gaps in its financial services in 1983 by hiring an aggressive staff. By the time the new management team was in place, the firm was making headway in a number of key areas.

Throughout the 1980s, the U.S. government deregulated financial markets, allowing increased competition across the board. Commercial banks began to operate in the capital markets for the first time since the Glass-Steagall Act. Competition, both at home and abroad, increased as financial services companies expanded the range of services they offered. In 1986, seeking to meet the demands of the increasingly complex marketplace, Morgan Stanley went public in order to broaden its capital base.

By the end of the 1980s, Morgan Stanley had regained its position. Indeed, the company was the only New York investment bank to increase its profits in the crash year of 1987. Its activities in leveraged buyouts were exceptionally profitable; the company's first leveraged buyout fund earned more than 25 times the original investment. By the end of the decade, Morgan Stanley's long-term equity investments were worth more than $7 billion. Unlike other Wall Street firms, Morgan Stanley's position in the late 1980s was strong enough (its average return on equity over a seven-year period during the decade was twice that of its competitors) that it did not have to lay off any employees.

### 1990s and Beyond

The firm's ascendancy was short-lived, however. Corporate leadership again changed hands in the early 1990s. Fisher took over the chairmanship in 1990 from the retired Gilbert, while the presidency passed first to Robert Greenhill (who defected to the Travelers's Smith Barney in 1993) and then to another aggressive manager and former bond trader, John J. Mack. At that point, Morgan Stanley faced a backlash from its heady days of the 1980s in the form of numerous lawsuits relating to its leveraged buyout and merger and acquisition activities. As a result of a 1991 jury award, the company had to pay $16 million to investors for its part in the failure of First RepublicBank Corp. In 1995, the state of West Virginia won a lawsuit stemming from more than $32 million in pension fund losses from the 1987 crash, with Morgan Stanley being ordered to reimburse the state for its loss.

The company lost market share in the early 1990s in part because of such lawsuits and also as a result of the defections of key managers including Greenhill, one of the top investment bankers in the field. These years also saw the firm's return on equity fall from the 30 percent average achieved during the late 1980s to just under 17 percent for 1990 through 1995.

Another part of the reason for the decline, however, lay in Fisher and Mack's aggressive plan to diversify Morgan Stanley both operationally—especially in the area of asset management—and geographically. Major expansions were undertaken throughout Europe and the Third World as the historically conservative company adopted Mack's admonition to "grow or die." From 1990 to 1995, the number of Morgan Stanley employees in Europe increased 43 percent, while the Far East operations posted a 39 percent increase. Company management

was essentially sacrificing the short-term in order to invest heavily in Morgan Stanley's future.

Although Great Britain was a particular focus of the company's European expansion, Morgan Stanley's growth was slowed in late 1994 when a proposed merger with merchant banker S. G. Warburg Group fell apart. Warburg's asset management subsidiary, Mercury Asset Management, had demanded a higher price than Morgan Stanley was willing to pay. Although this chance to augment its asset management sector failed to materialize, less than a year later Morgan Stanley was able to announce the successful acquisition of Miller Anderson & Sherrerd LLP, a Philadelphia-based asset-management partnership, for $350 million in cash and stock. The purchase, finalized in January 1996 after which Miller Anderson became a Morgan Stanley subsidiary, added $33 billion in assets under management to Morgan Stanley's total, an increase of 66 percent. Just as importantly, Morgan Stanley's domestic asset management operations—which had not been as strong as those overseas—were significantly bolstered.

By the mid-1990s, Morgan Stanley was generating more than half of its revenues outside the United States. In addition to its focus on Europe, the company also targeted other emerging economies. For example, a $200 million investment in hotel development in Mexico was announced in January 1996, a brave move as it was the first deal by an American company since the Mexican market collapsed in 1994. In the Far East, Morgan Stanley invested $35 million in late 1995 to help form China International Capital Corp., China's first international investment bank. Morgan Stanley held a 35 percent stake in the new bank as a result. And in Malaysia the company set up a joint venture company in early 1996 to offer fund-management services.

Morgan Stanley withstood many changes from its founding during the Great Depression to the frenzied period of global competition of the 1990s. It continued to adapt to the volatile capital markets and made aggressive moves in the 1990s to position itself as a global leader in its core areas, while anticipating major trends such as worldwide economic and financial deregulation, strong growth in developing countries, and increasing demand for asset management services. Morgan Stanley's international expansion in the 1990s was both risky and filled with potential, as the company's leaders were well aware; Fisher told *Business Week* in early 1996: "I think we have the most resources and the most conviction. We could be wrong. We won't know for five years whether we are right."

### Principal Subsidiaries

Miller Anderson & Sherrerd, LLP; Morgan Stanley & Co. Incorporated; Morgan Stanley Asset Management, Inc.; Morgan Stanley Capital Group Inc.; Morgan Stanley International Inc.; Morgan Stanley Realty, Inc.; Morgan Stanley Australia Ltd.; Morgan Stanley do Brasil Ltda.; Morgan Stanley Canada Ltd.; China International Capital Corp. (35%); Morgan Stanley Asia Ltd. (China); Morgan Stanley SA (France); Morgan Stanley Bank AG (Germany); Morgan Stanley Asia Ltd. (Hong Kong); Banca Morgan Stanley Spa (Italy); Morgan Stanley India; Morgan Stanley Japan Ltd.; Morgan Stanley Bank Luxembourg; Morgan Stanley México Casa de Bolsa, S.A. de C.V.;

Morgan Stanley (Europe) Ltd. (Russia); Morgan Stanley Asset Management (Singapore) Pte. Ltd.; Morgan Stanley South Africa (PTY) LTD; Morgan Stanley & Co. (South Korea); Morgan Stanley & Co. Ltd. (Spain); Bank Morgan Stanley AG (Switzerland); Banque Morgan Stanley SA (Switzerland); Capital International Perspectives S.A. (Switzerland); Morgan Stanley Asia (Taiwan) Ltd.; Morgan Stanley UK Group.

## *Further Reading*

Barnathan, Joyce, "Morgan Stanley's Chinese Coup," *Business Week,* November 7, 1994, pp. 50–51.

Berman, Phyllis, and Roula Khalaf, "A Game of Chicken," *Forbes,* May 28, 1990, pp. 38–40.

——, "A Sweetheart of a Deal," *Forbes,* September 3, 1990, pp. 39–40.

"Best of a Breed," *Economist,* September 30, 1989, p. 86.

Carosso, Vincent P., *Investment Banking in America: A History,* Cambridge, Mass.: Harvard University Press, 1970, 569 p.

Carosso, Vincent P., with Rose C. Carosso, *The Morgans: Private International Bankers, 1854–1913,* Cambridge, Mass.: Harvard University Press, 1987, 888 p.

Chernow, Ron, *The House of Morgan: An American Banking Dynasty and the Rise of Modern Finance,* New York: Atlantic Monthly Press, 1990, 812 p.

Corey, Lewis, *The House of Morgan: A Social Biography of the Masters of Money,* New York: AMS Press, 1969, 479 p.

Ferris, Paul, *The Master Bankers: Controlling the World's Finances,* New York: William Morrow, 1984, 285 p.

Hoffman, Paul, *The Dealmakers: Inside the World of Investment Banking,* Garden City, N.Y.: Doubleday, 1984, 230 p.

Jackson, Stanley, *J. P. Morgan: A Biography,* New York: Stein and Day, 1983, 332 p.

Kahn, Joseph, "Morgan Stanley Joins Chinese Bank to Form Beijing Investment Company," *Wall Street Journal,* August 11, 1995, p. A4(E), A6(W).

*Morgan Stanley: The First Fifty Years,* New York: Morgan Stanley Group Inc.

Raghavan, Anita, and Robert McGough, "Morgan Stanley to Buy Miller Anderson for $350 Million in Cash, Stock Accord," *Wall Street Journal,* June 30, 1995, p. B4(E), A7(W).

Schifrin, Matthew, "Bull in Morgan's China Shop," *Forbes,* February 19, 1990, pp. 94–98.

Sinclair, Andrew, *Corsair: The Life of J. Pierpont Morgan,* Boston: Little, Brown, 1981, 269 p.

Spiro, Leah Nathans, "Cut, Slash, Slice, Trim, Chop," *Business Week,* January 14, 1991, p. 117.

Spiro, Leah Nathans, et. al., "Global Gamble: Morgan Stanley Is Charging into the Third World. Will It Get Burned?," *Business Week,* February 12, 1996, pp. 63–72.

Stevenson, Richard W., "Financial Merger Is Scuttled: Morgan Stanley and Warburg Part Ways," *New York Times,* December 16, 1994, pp. D1–D2.

—Tom Tucker
—updated by David E. Salamie

# National Auto Credit, Inc.

**30000 Aurora Road**
**Solon, Ohio 44139**
**U.S.A.**
**(216) 349-1000**
**Fax: (216) 349-0203**

*Public Company*
*Incorporated:* 1971
*Employees:* 1,000
*Sales:* $219.2 million (1995)
*Stock Exchanges:* New York
*SICs:* 6140 Personal Credit Institutions

National Auto Credit, Inc. is a "new" company with a 25-year heritage. In 1994, the firm shifted its focus from the insurance-replacement segment of the auto rental industry to used car sales and financing. Its initial establishment as Agency Rent-A-Car in 1971 formed the foundation of the insurance-replacement segment of the auto rental industry, consisting of companies that rented cars to victims of accidents or thefts (as opposed to vacation or business rentals). Agency's growth was the bellwether of that business, and its decline signaled the segment's maturity. In the early 1990s, when the market began to show signs of saturation and Agency's revenues and profits took a precipitous slide, founder, president, and majority owner Samuel Frankino restructured the company to focus on used car sales and financing and named it for National Auto Credit, Inc., the financing subsidiary.

## Foundation and Growth in the 1970s and Early 1980s

Incorporated by Sam Frankino in 1971, National Auto Credit's genesis actually came in 1969. At the time, Frankino was a real estate agent and landlord. One day, an insurance agent and tenant mentioned that a client of his needed a car on a short-term loan. Frankino stepped in, offering to rent the man his daughter's Chevrolet Impala. He charged $9.50 per day; it was the most the insurance company would pay, but signifi-

cantly less than the standard rate. By the time the first client was through with the car, the insurance agent had lined up another taker. Frankino later reflected, "My daughter never did get that Impala," in a 1985 interview with Jay McCormick of *Forbes*.

That first rental signaled the dawn of the insurance-replacement segment of the auto rental industry. Frankino incorporated the service under the blasé, but straightforward, Agency Rent-A-Car name in 1971, maintaining it as a private concern. He attracted business by keeping his rates low and made money by keeping his cars on the road. The company's daily rental cost about half as much as the going rate of traditional auto rental companies, which, not coincidentally, was about as much as insurance companies would reimburse their customers. Agency kept its overhead low by maintaining low-rent offices and offering free delivery of its cars to incapacitated clients. And the fleet's typically low-mileage use resulted in less wear and tear.

Although it eschewed the commercial rental market, Agency maintained the car rental industry's highest utilization rate, at more than 90 percent, compared with a 65 percent to 75 percent industry average. Frankino did not advertise, either. Instead, he hired salesmen to promote the service to insurance agents and adjusters. *Forbes's* McCormick credited Agency's success to "a little hustle and a lot of service." This fairly simple formula kept the company's operating margins high. At 20.5 percent, they were more than twice as high as those of Avis, Inc., at 7.8 percent, and quadruple Hertz's 3.5 percent.

Frankino had modest aspirations for his sideline, hoping eventually to build the enterprise up to 50 or 60 cars. In fact, he kept up his real estate business throughout Agency's first decade and did not pay himself a salary until after he took the company public. He was especially adamant about avoiding debt; in October 1985, Frankino proudly told Delinda Karle of the *Cleveland Plain Dealer* that, "For the first nine or ten years each piece of equipment was free of debt."

Agency clearly exceeded all of Frankino's expectations; it had a fleet of 9,800 vehicles and annual revenues of about $60 million by 1983. Frankino took the company public that year, raising $30 million with a minority stake. As if that payoff was not enough of a reward, the businessman also won the Harvard

Business School Alumni Association's George S. Dively Entrepreneur Award. Sales doubled, from less than $60 million in 1983 to $118.3 million in fiscal 1986 (ended January 31, 1986), and net income nearly tripled from about $5 million to $14 million during the same period. Agency's success inspired awe and imitation.

### The Industry Matures

Frankino and Agency began to feel the effects of steadily increasing competition in the late 1980s, much of it from Agency expatriates. A 1974 mutiny led to the formation of Adjusters Auto Rental Inc., later known as Jiffy Auto Rental. Agency president Russell A. Smith and three other executives left the company to launch a competitor in 1983 and had built up a 3,900-car fleet by 1986. Agency's success also inspired Robert Birrer, owner of a suburban Chrysler-Plymouth dealership from which Frankino had leased 300 cars, to found Replacement Enterprises Inc. in the late 1970s. (Agency acquired Replacement, called a "friendly rival" in a *Crain's Cleveland Business* article, for $9.6 million in cash and stock in 1988.) Agency's biggest competition, however, came from St. Louis's privately held Enterprise Rent-A-Car, which had built up a 30,000-plus fleet by 1986. These new rivals exerted downward pressure on rental rates, while low used car prices had a correspondingly bad influence on the amount Agency made when it sold its cars on the wholesale market.

Thus, although Agency's revenues and net income continued to increase in the late 1980s, its profitability shrunk. Sales nearly doubled, from $118.3 million in fiscal 1986 to $227 million in fiscal 1989, but net income only increased by 65 percent, from $14 million to $23.5 million during the same period. The gap grew wider as Agency entered the 1990s. Although revenues increased to $331.7 million by fiscal 1993, profits shrunk to $16.8 million. It was readily apparent that the segment of the rental business that Agency had founded was maturing and that prospects for a rebound were slim.

### A New Avocation Emerges

Luckily for Frankino and company, other aspects of Agency's business were gathering steam during this same period. The firm's auto sales and financing business evolved out of the natural "recycling" of Agency's fleet. Cars were typically rented for 24 to 30 months, then auctioned at wholesale. By 1985, the company was operating three car dealerships, which economized on both new car purchases and used car sales. Executive Vice-President Peter Zackaroff described the evolution of this sideline in an interview with Donald Sabath for the *Cleveland Plain Dealer*. In 1988, Agency found itself stuck with several of Chrysler Corp.'s K-cars, which were notorious for rapid depreciation. The crisis, which cost the company $5.6 million that year, compelled Agency to diversify its selection of cars and to retain more of the yield from its used car sales. This well-timed move coincided with the growth of the used car market overall. By 1992, Agency had 18 retail operations nationwide.

This operation spawned another business, auto financing, which was formally organized as Agency's National Auto Credit, Inc. (NAC) subsidiary in 1992. NAC provided financing services to Agency and other dealers, garnering a roster of 750 dealers, four branch offices, 11,000 retail installment loans, and $80 million in receivables by the end of 1993. NAC focused on the "alternative financing market," targeting "customers who have limited access to consumer credit."

As Agency's insurance-replacement business declined, both in terms of gross revenues (down from almost $300 million in 1993 to $132.1 million by 1995) and percentage of sales (down from about 85 percent to less than 35 percent during the same period), the financing segment grew. By mid-1994, NAC boasted 1,150 dealers and $132 million in receivables. The potential was even higher; Agency estimated that only 5 percent of the nation's $100 billion used car financing market went to alternative financers like NAC.

### A New Business for the 1990s and Beyond

Financing became so significant and renting so competitive that in 1994 Frankino and Agency's board elected to divest the original rental business to concentrate on the financing operation. That June, the firm formally changed its name to National Auto Credit, Inc. One year later, NAC announced that its fleet of rental cars (which had shrunk from a high of 45,000 vehicles in 1992 to just 8,000 cars by 1995) was on the auction block. The company sold its rental operations to Avis, Inc. in August 1995.

The firm's transformation from renting to financing made for a rough ride, for both stockholders and company executives. The company's stock started its roller coaster ride in 1988, when operating margins began to erode. Rumors that Sam Frankino was gearing up to sell his majority stake in Agency fueled run-ups throughout the late 1980s and into the early 1990s. The stock started at about $14.60 in the beginning of 1989, rose to $24 (in spite of lukewarm operating results) after Frankino publicly revealed that he was in negotiations to sell mid-year, then plunged to $10 by February 1990 when the sale was not forthcoming. Frankino continued to hold about 55 percent of the firm as of 1995. NAC's stock price stood at about $10.50 early that year.

Agency's upper echelon was plagued with high turnover throughout its history, and this trend intensified in the late 1980s and early 1990s. From 1988 to 1994 alone, the company had five different presidents; Frankino served the longest in this capacity during this period. Vincent T. Garrenton, Jr. advanced from executive vice-president (a position he had held since 1974) to president and chief executive officer in 1987, only to resign in October 1988. He was replaced by Kenneth J. Lorek, who served less than a year in his new role. The 64-year-old Frankino resumed the presidency in August 1989, holding Agency's three top offices until June 1992, when Terry W. Holt was elected president and CEO. But Holt's reign under Chairman Frankino also proved short-lived. He resigned in March 1994, when it became clear that NAC would be changing its focus. Holt was succeeded by Chief Financial Officer Robert J. Bronchetti. McDonald & Co. Securities analyst Robert C. Damron judged this last appointment logical, noting that, "It is important to have someone with a finance background at the top," in a 1994 *Crain's Cleveland Business* article.

Regardless of the executive shakeups, NAC's fiscal performance undoubtedly improved following its transformation. Although annual revenues declined from $303.2 million in fiscal 1994 to $219.1 million in fiscal 1995, its profits surged from $18.2 million to $22.4 million, nearing fiscal 1989's record high of $23.5 million.

### Principal Subsidiaries

Agency Chrysler Plymouth, Inc.; Agency Ford, Inc.; Agency Rent-A-Car, Ltd.; National Motors, Inc.; NAC, Inc.

### Further Reading

Baird, Kristen, "National Auto May Scrap Fleet of Rental Cars," *Crain's Cleveland Business,* February 20, 1995, pp. 3, 26.

Barker, Robert, "Smashing Success: Agency Rent-A-Car's Growth Is No Accident," *Barron's,* July 28, 1986, p. 13.

Canedy, Dana, "Agency Changes Name To Reflect Major Focus," *Cleveland Plain Dealer,* May 12, 1994, p. 1C.

Casey, Mike, "Agency Buys Friendly Rival Replacement," *Crain's Cleveland Business,* April 11, 1988, pp. 3, 19.

Edgerton, Jerry, and Jordan, E. Goodman, "Profiting from Pilferage," *Money,* June 1987, p. 8.

Freeh, John, "Advisers Like Consistency of Car Rental Firm," *Cleveland Plain Dealer,* June 22, 1987, p. 10C.

Gleisser, Marcus, "Revenue of Car Rental Agency Hits High," *Cleveland Plain Dealer,* November 27, 1984, p. 5D.

Jaffe, Thomas, "Two for the Stocking," *Forbes,* January 11, 1988, p. 266.

Karle, Delinda, "Agency Chief Clams Up on Sale Rumors," *Cleveland Plain Dealer,* June 15, 1989, p. 7C.

——, "Agency Rent-A-Car Chief Leaves Wall Street in the Dark on Sale," *Cleveland Plain Dealer,* June 14, 1990, p. 10C.

——, "Agency Rent-A-Car Sale Afoot," *Cleveland Plain Dealer,* March 25, 1989, p. 1C.

——, "Agency Strays Off Course," *Cleveland Plain Dealer,* December 26, 1988, p. 4C.

——, "Auto Leaser Aims To Stay at Top by Keeping Debt at a Minimum," *Cleveland Plain Dealer,* October 27, 1985, p. 3D.

——, "Resale Crunch Helps Depress Agency Rent-A-Car Earnings," *Cleveland Plain Dealer,* June 13, 1989, p. 1D.

Marcial, Gene G., "Is Someone Tailing Agency Rent-A-Car?," *Business Week,* February 26, 1990, p. 92.

McCormick, Jay, "Hot Wheels," *Forbes,* May 20, 1985, p. 118.

Sabath, Donald, "Agency Rent-A-Car Boosting Revenues with Retail Sales," *Cleveland Plain Dealer,* September 15, 1992, p. 1F.

——, "Agency Rent-A-Car Changes Name to National Auto Credit," *Cleveland Plain Dealer,* June 23, 1994, p. 1C.

——, "Agency Rent-A-Car Income Plunges," *Cleveland Plain Dealer,* April 20, 1991, p. 1D.

——, "Agency Rent-A-Car Rolling Merrily Along," *Cleveland Plain Dealer,* December 10, 1993, p. 2E.

——, "National Auto Credit To Cease Renting Cars," *Cleveland Plain Dealer,* June 22, 1995, p. 2C.

——, "National Auto Disposes of Its Rental Fleet," *Cleveland Plain Dealer,* August 3, 1995, p. 1C.

Solov, Diane, "New Chief Executive Takes Driver's Seat at Agency," *Cleveland Plain Dealer,* June 26, 1992, p. 3G.

Thompson, Chris, "Agency Rent-A-Car Shifts Focus to Financing," *Crain's Cleveland Business,* March 14, 1994, p. 5.

Willke, Jeanne, "Frankino Replaces President Who Quit at Agency Rent-A-Car," *Cleveland Plain Dealer,* August 29, 1989, p. 3C.

Yerak, Rebecca, "Agency Stock Rises on Rumors," *Cleveland Plain Dealer,* December 22, 1989, p. 11B.

—April Dougal Gasbarre

# National Presto Industries, Inc.

**3925 N. Hastings Way**
**Eau Claire, Wisconsin 54703**
**U.S.A.**
**(715) 839-21210**
**Fax: (715) 839-2122**

*Public Company*
*Incorporated:* 1929 as National Pressure Cooking Co.
*Employees:* 700
*Sales:* $128 million (1994)
*Stock Exchanges:* New York
*SICs:* 3634 Electrical Housewares and Fans

National Presto Industries, Inc., based in Eau Claire, Wisconsin, is a leading manufacturer of small, electric kitchen appliances and pressure cookers. An aggressive advertiser, National Presto markets its products through national discount chain stores, including Wal-Mart and Kmart, which account for nearly 70 percent of sales. Although traded on the New York Stock Exchange, the company is essentially family owned; in the mid-1990s, the family of chairman Melvin Cohen controlled more than 45 percent of the stock. In 1994, the company had earnings of $21.5 million on sales of $128 million, and 1995 marked the 51st consecutive year the company paid a dividend to shareholders.

### Early 20th-Century Origins

Best known since the 1970s for its innovative, sometimes quirky kitchen gadgets, National Presto can trace its history to the 1905 founding of the Northwestern Iron and Steel Works in Eau Claire, Wisconsin, as the Northwestern Iron and Steel Works for the production of cement mixers. By 1908, however, the company had settled into manufacturing 50-gallon retorts, or steam pressure cookers, for the canning industry. The company also made 30-gallon retorts for hotel use, and in 1915, installed an aluminum foundry for manufacturing ten-gallon pressure cookers for home use.

Two years later, the U.S. Department of Agriculture reported that using steam-pressure cookers was the safest way to eliminate the bacteria that cause botulism when canning low-acid foods, including meats and most kinds of vegetables. Business boomed for Northwestern Iron and Steel, whose pressure cookers, sold under the brand name of National, were already well known among home canners. In 1929, the company, which also manufactured a line of cast-aluminum cookware, further capitalized on its market niche by changing its name to the National Pressure Cooking Co. By 1930, annual net income had surpassed $1 million on revenues of more than $12 million.

### Innovations in Pressure Cooking in the 1930s

By 1935, in the midst of the Great Depression, the National Pressure Cooking Co. was selling 60,000 pressure cookers annually, mostly for home canning by farm households. But these were still miniature versions of the complex, large-scale commercial retorts the company made. Then in the late 1930s, a company engineer, E.H. Wittenberg, developed an easier sealing mechanism with a rubber gasket clamped between upper and lower handles. Wittenberg's "home-ec seal" meant that pressure cookers, which provided the fastest as well as the safest method of preparing food, could be used for everyday cooking.

In 1939, the company also introduced the first saucepan-style pressure cooker for home use, which it marketed under the trade name "Presto." The demand for the new Presto cooker, which became virtually synonymous with pressure cooking, was so great that by 1940, despite a decade of economic depression in the United States, sales had doubled to $2 million.

### Wartime Production Shake-Up

But in 1941, as the United States prepared to enter World War II, government restrictions on the use of aluminum in domestic products sharply curtailed production, and National Pressure Cooker, which had invested heavily to increase its manufacturing capacity, was forced to lay off most of its employees. Everett R. Hamilton, then president and majority owner of the company, managed to land a $3 million government contract to make artillery fuses, but Hamilton died of a heart attack in February 1942, before the conversion to defense work could be completed. An editorial in the *Eau Claire Leader* noted that Hamilton "had the satisfaction of knowing that it would be only a matter of months before employees laid off by priorities would be back on the job and that perhaps in the not too distant future the National Pressure Cooker company might be Eau Claire's most important industry."

However, despite the defense contract, by the summer of 1942, National Pressure Cooker was reportedly on the verge of bankruptcy and unable to meet its payroll. To save the company, Lewis E. Phillips, an Eau Claire businessman, together with his brother Jay, bought controlling interest in the company from Hamilton's widow. The brothers also owned Ed Phillips and Sons, a wholesale distributor of liquor, tobacco, and candy, with operations in Wisconsin and Minnesota. Lewis Phillips became president of National Pressure Cooker and ultimately managed to right the company by negotiating additional government defense contracts. In fact, National Pressure Cooker eventually received five Army and Navy E Awards for its contribution to the war effort, including about 500,000 "victory pressure canners" at the request of the Department of Agriculture.

## Post-War Diversification

The company resumed production of cookware after the war, introducing a 16-quart canner and a four-quart Presto saucepan pressure cooker in 1945. The company also acquired the Century Metalcraft Association in Los Angeles, which gave it access to West Coast markets, and the Lakeside Aluminum Co. in Menomonie, Wisconsin.

In 1946, the National Pressure Cooker Co. also formed a subsidiary, the Martin Motors Division, to manufacture outboard motors developed by George W. Martin, a former professional outboard-racing champion. The *Aluminator,* National Pressure Cooker's company newspaper, touted Martin's innovative design, noting that "this type of motor once in use would give a great new thrill, and unlimited pleasure, to the vast throng of outdoor living people who find so much peace and relaxation on the many waterways of America." A year later, the company moved its outboard-motor operations and its research and development operations to a 348-acre, former government ordnance site near Eau Claire that it had purchased from the War Assets Administration for $350,000. The site became known as Presto, Wisconsin.

However, National Pressure Cooker faced stiff competition in the postwar leisure boating market from Outboard, Marine

and Manufacturing, the Illinois-based company later known as the Outboard Marine Corporation, which made both the popular Johnson and Evinrude-brand outboard motors. In 1948, Outboard, Marine and Manufacturing introduced the first outboard motor with a separate fuel tank and a shift lever that allowed the operator to select forward, reverse, or neutral. Outdoor Marine also began manufacturing fiberglass motorboats that were sold through the same network of dealers and distributors that handled Evinrude and Johnson motors. In the early 1950s, National Pressure Cooker filed a complaint with the Federal Trade Commission alleging that Outboard, Marine and Manufacturing was pressuring dealers not to carry its Martin outboard motors. The company liquidated the Martin Motor Division in 1954, before the case was resolved.

In 1949, the company also introduced its first electric appliance, a steam iron with the Presto brand name that could use tap water instead of distilled water. By 1950, National Pressure Cooker had introduced the Presto Automatic Dixie-Fryer, a thermostat-controlled deep-fryer for home use that presaged many of the company's later innovations. In a "Talk of the Town" column in a November 1950 *New Yorker* magazine, company spokesman Russell Bloomberg remarked on the versatility of the deep-fryer: "The Fryer fills a much needed want for Mrs. Housewife. It does the same work as the expensive commercial kettle. It can take very mediocre leftovers, such as cold mash potatoes and chicken wings, and convert them into delicious croquettes. With it you can glorify corn-meal mush by frying it along with ten per-cent ground-up leftover cheese. Mrs. Housewife can use the fat over and over again, with no interchange of taste. I spent a month frying doughnuts in it eight hours a day, just to determine the absorption of fat. Its entertaining possibilities are endless. Suppose your husband, after a fishing trip, brings home a tiny trout. You can cook it with bread crumbs."

As the company began introducing more consumer products under the Presto brand name, including an automatic coffee maker, the stockholders voted at the 1953 annual meeting to change the corporate name to National Presto Industries, Inc.

## Defense Contracts in the 1950s and 1960s

A few months after changing its name to emphasize its consumer products, National Presto announced that it had signed a multimillion dollar contract with the U.S. government to produce artillery shells. The company immediately began converting its Eau Claire manufacturing facilities, including the former ordnance plant purchased at the end of World War II, to defense work, and announced that its consumer-products division would move to Jackson, Mississippi, where a subsidiary, the Century Manufacturing Co., was building a new facility.

In 1955, National Presto expanded its defense work to include airplane components for the U.S. Air Force. At the time, the company employed about 2,000 defense workers in Eau Claire and about 650 consumer-products workers in Mississippi. In a press release, Phillips noted that the "new contract represents a diversification of our Eau Claire production, and if all concerned extend their full support, this new contract should aid not only in increasing local employment generally, but in stabilizing our employment at a higher level."

However, by 1958, the government had cut back sharply on orders for artillery shells, and employment at Presto in Eau Claire had fallen to about 500. Moreover, National Presto's remaining defense workers went out on strike for 60 days in the summer of 1958. When the strike ended, Phillips issued a warning: "The future of this company in Eau Claire and hence the security of our jobs here, is now almost wholly dependent upon defense contracts awarded by the U.S. Government. Our Government is rapidly moving toward a policy of granting or renewing contracts only where the supplying company has established and is maintaining a reputation for efficiency and quality in production, competitive prices, and above all, reliability and dependability as a supplier."

Phillips' concern was borne out a year later. In 1959, the Army Ordnance Corps abruptly cancelled its contract with National Presto for artillery shells. In a tersely worded statement, Phillips announced, "This cancellation is indeed an unfortunate turn of events for Presto and its manufacturing employees here at Eau Claire. With little or no notice, this Government decision has forced us completely out of the manufacturing business here in Eau Claire."

National Presto shut down its defense operations in Eau Claire in 1960 but contracted with the government to maintain the manufacturing equipment in a state of semi-readiness. The tide would soon turn again as the company resumed production of artillery shells in 1964, as U.S. ground troops were being sent to Vietnam, and between 1966 and 1975, National Presto produced more than 92 million 105-millimeter artillery shells. It also produced two million eight-inch artillery shells between 1967 and 1971. At the height of U.S. involvement in Southeast Asia, employment at the defense plant in Eau Claire reached 3,000, a figure that fell off dramatically after the United States withdrew from Vietnam in 1973. The defense plant was again closed in 1980, two years after Phillips' death, but the government continued to contract with National Presto to keep the plant on stand-by through the 1990s. Defense requirements were eventually ceased in 1993, and in the mid-1990s, the company was planning on how best to dispose of the special purpose manufacturing equipment.

Lewis Phillips served as company president until 1960 and chairperson until 1966. An important contributor to his community, he created the Presto Foundation and L.E. Phillips Charities, and upon his death in 1978 was memorialized in Eau Claire by the numerous educational and health-care facilities that bore his name.

### Focus on Consumer Products

While the company's success in defense production through military contracts was erratic, the postwar economy was ripe for new consumer product introductions, as American housewives in particular were encouraged to purchase appliances that would make their lives easier. During the 1950s, Presto's consumer products division had introduced the first in a line of immersible electric cooking appliances. The cookware, including an electric skillet, griddle, and coffee maker, featured a removable "Master Control" heat unit, allowing the appliance to be washed safely in water. Over the next dozen years, National Presto also introduced popular models of toasters, egg cookers,

hair dryers, and electric toothbrushes. A second manufacturing plant for consumer products was built in Alamogordo, New Mexico, in 1971.

In the mid-1970s, National Presto began introducing kitchen appliances designed for a changing American lifestyle, starting in 1974 with the PrestoBurger, an electric hamburger cooker that broiled a single patty of meat in less than three minutes. The PrestoBurger was followed by the electric Hot Dogger in 1975 and the Fry Baby, a single-serving, deep-fat fryer, in 1976. As Melvin S. Cohen, Lewis Phillips' son-in-law and then-chairman of the board, told *Forbes* in 1977, "we were the first in our industry to recognize a fundamental change in American society." Cohen referred to demographic changes, noting that "the Census Bureau says 51% of all U.S. households now consist of singles and doubles, not the traditional family group. They have informal, casual lifestyles and money to spend. Yet everybody designs appliances for that old, traditional 5.8-member family. Well, we started designing for singles and doubles."

The company continued to expand its product line. Cohen told the *Wisconsin Business Journal* in 1984: "Our life-blood is new products. And we must constantly be turning them out and developing new ones. We also recognize that to some extent they're in the nature of yo-yos—that they'll be faddish in nature, they'll enjoy a brief popularity and then virtually disappear from the scene, either by virtue of loss of consumer interest or because it is so widely copied it is no longer attractive." While National Presto was unable to guarantee that every one of its products would catch on with consumers—for example, an electric, vibrating hairbrush was a flop—it aggressively tried to defend its successes from copycat competition through patents and litigation.

### Competition in the Late 1980s and 1990s

In 1988, National Presto introduced the SaladShooter, an electric slicer/shredder. Hamilton Beach Corp. and Black & Decker Corp. introduced similar products the same year, and National Presto, which had patented the mechanical features of its SaladShooter, filed suit against both competitors. Two years later, Hamilton Beach settled by agreeing to destroy its remaining inventory and withdrawing from the slicer/shredder market. In 1992, a federal district court jury found Black & Decker guilty of infringing on National Presto's patent and awarded the company $2.35 million in damages.

In 1991, National Presto introduced the Tater Twister potato peeler. The same year, the West Bend Co. introduced a similar product. The two companies sued each other, and again National Presto prevailed. In 1993, a federal jury found West Bend guilty of patent infringement and awarded National Presto $230,000 in damages. Indeed, National Presto was becoming a formidable name in the industry; also in 1993, the Dazey Corp. agreed to withdraw from the deep-fryer market after being sued by National Presto. In the company's 1994 annual report, management noted: "Hopefully, this Company's competitors are now convinced that it will not brook copying, and will aggressively seek injunctive and/or damages relief when infringements occur."

Despite costly involvements in litigation, increased competition from other manufacturers, the permanent closing of its defense operations, the negative effects of new inventory practices at such retailers as Kmart and Wal-Mart, and some criticism from shareholders, National Presto was experiencing improved sales and earnings as it moved into the mid-1990s. Consolidated net sales rose to $128 million in 1994, up from $118 million the year before, while consolidated net earnings reached $21 million, up from $18 million in 1993.

The company attributed its success largely to its product innovations. Research and development resulted in new versions of National Presto pressure cookers, griddles, and deep fryers, as well as new electric knives and sharpeners, coffee pots, and electric can openers. The company also experienced success with its line of popcorn poppers, including the Orville Redenbacher air popper and the Presto PowerPop microwave corn popper. In the 1990s, National Presto began aggressively introducing new products shortly before the Christmas shopping season, supporting such introductions with national television advertising campaigns. In 1994, for example, the company's "featured product" was the Presto PowerPop, and the company estimated its advertising reached 98 percent of all U.S. households an average of 36 times, making for about 3.3 billion "consumer impressions." With such efforts, the company might expect to garner a greater share of the American market for electric housewares in the 21st century and could assuredly be proud of its long history as an innovator in the industry.

### Principal Subsidiaries

Presto Manufacturing Co.; Presto Products Manufacturing Inc.; Jackson Sales and Storage Co.; Canton Sales & Storage Co.; National Holding Investment Co.; National Defense Corp.

### Further Reading

Brammer, Rhonda, "Gizmo King: And National Presto is a Veritable Bank, to Boot," *Barron's,* May 10, 1993, p. 14.
Hamel, Mark, "National Presto: The Corporate Kitchen Magician," *Wisconsin Business Journal,* December 1984, pp. 20–30.
"The History of National Presto Industries, Inc.," Eau Claire, Wisc.: National Presto Industries, Inc., 1996.
Linquist, Eric, "Empty Plant Awaits Uncle Sam's Call," *Eau Claire Leader-Telegram,* July 19, 1987, p. D1.
——, "Presto Keeps Cash on Hand, Seeks 'Friendly' Acquisition," *Eau Claire Leader-Telegram,* June 19, 1989, p. D1.
"National Presto Industries Plant Humming with Activity with 3,000 Employed in Manufacture of Shells," *Eau Claire Daily Telegram,* March 30, 1968, p. C2.
"National Presto Is Prospering by Thinking Small in Appliances," *Barron's,* August 22, 1977, pp. 30–31.
"Presto Changeo!," *Financial World,* April 15, 1980, pp. 50–51.
"Presto Grew with Pressure Cooker," *Eau Claire Leader-Telegram,* July 28, 1972, p. E9.
Purpura, Linda M., "B&D, Presto Salad Shootout: File Shredder Patent Suits," *HFN—The Weekly Home Furnishings Newspaper,* June 25, 1990, p. 1.
Rublin, Lauren R., "Pot Full of Cash: National Presto's Beautiful Balance Sheet," *Barron's,* October 24, 1988, pp. 38–42.
"Talk of the Town," *The New Yorker,* November 25, 1950, p. 30.
"Tom Swift And His Electric Hamburger Cooker," *Forbes,* October 15, 1977, p. 112.
"What Took the Steam Out of National Presto," *Business Week,* April 3, 1978, pp. 29–30.

—Dean Boyer

# National Sanitary Supply Co.

**2900 Chemed Center**
**255 East 5th Street**
**Cincinnati, Ohio 45202-4729**
**U.S.A.**
**(513) 762-6500**
**Fax: (513) 762-6644**

*Public Company*
*Incorporated:* 1983
*Employees:* 1,715
*Sales:* $308.28 million (1994)
*Stock Exchanges:* NASDAQ
*SICs:* 5113 Industrial & Personàl Service Paper; 5169
    Chemicals & Allied Products, Not Elsewhere
    Classified; 5087 Service Establishment Equipment;
    5112 Stationery & Office Supplies

National Sanitary Supply Co. is the world's largest distributor of janitorial supplies, but its name is more indicative of its goal than its actual status in the mid-1990s. For although National Sanitary led its industry, its operations were limited to 18 western, southern and midwestern states. Privately owned and operated for over 50 years, the company was acquired by Cincinnati-based Chemed Corporation and taken public in 1986. Chemed continued to hold a controlling 83 percent share of National Sanitary Supply through the mid-1990s.

Using an acquisition strategy to gain critical mass in its highly fragmented industry, National Sanitary Supply experienced an astonishing average annual sales growth rate of 44.85 percent from 1984 to 1994. In fact, the business boasted an unbroken record of 65 years of rising sales from 1929 to 1994. While the company operates in one business segment, its products can be grouped into three main categories: paper goods (about 60 percent of annual sales); industrial cleaners and chemicals (25 percent); and housekeeping goods like mops and brooms (15 percent). National Sanitary Supply manufactures some of its own branded paper goods, cleaners, and chemicals and distributes a broad variety of cleaning supplies ranging from paper goods to waste receptacles and cleaning equipment. The company's clientele includes the industrial market, schools, hotels and motels, retailers, and hospitals.

## Early History

National Sanitary Supply Co. (NSS, also known as Nat San) was founded in Los Angeles, California, in 1929 as a private distributor of hand soap to industrial and institutional customers. This company later achieved a measure of vertical integration by affiliating with Sanichem Manufacturing Company and La-Ru Truck Rental Company, Inc. Over the years, Sanichem earned a reputation for innovation in the field of industrial chemicals. This segment of NSS produced specialty cleaners and polishes for particular applications and surfaces, like the marble and composite floors in schools, restaurants and shopping centers. The trucking company, whose fleet numbered nearly 200 trucks by the early 1990s, gave Nat San delivery capabilities. Over the years, the company's line of proprietary and distributed products grew to fulfill virtually every janitorial need, including garbage bags, brooms and mops, buckets, paper goods like toilet tissue and paper towels, and even big-ticket items like ladders, pressure washers and carts. This comprehensive catalog would become a key aspect of NSS's rapid growth in the 1980s.

## Postwar Growth

National Sanitary Supply grew slowly in its early decades and didn't establish its first sales office outside Los Angeles until 1957. NSS expanded outside California in 1971 with the acquisition of a small janitorial supply company, but didn't establish another regional center until 1981, when it created one in Las Vegas. Although its geographic growth during this period wasn't particularly earth-shattering, NSS did develop a sales culture focused squarely on gross profits. The company's sales force, which numbered over 700 by the mid-1990s, was considered a key to its ongoing success. Their efforts to saturate the western United States helped multiply sales more than 2.5 times, from $12.8 million in 1975 to $34.6 million in 1980.

---

**Company Perspectives:**

*National's business is meeting housekeeping and building maintenance needs. This sole focus, however, leads to multi-dimensional service for customers. National starts with a vision to supply the best combination of quality, dependability, and economy possible. This leads to seeking out and providing many innovative cleaning products. Knowledgeable sales people and efficient distribution systems add value to each customer relationship.*

---

## Acquisitions in the 1980s

This impressive growth increased after 1983, when NSS was acquired by Chemed Corporation, a diversified manufacturer of specialty chemicals. Chemed, which also owns Roto-Rooter plumbing service, put its significant financial weight behind NSS, and the combined effort quickly bore fruit. Over the course of the decade, NSS purchased companies in New Mexico, Utah, Washington, and Colorado. One of the most significant of these was San Francisco's Paul Koss Supply Co. Chemed took NSS public that same year, selling 17 percent of the company's equity to raise $8.3 million for debt reduction, capital improvements and new acquisitions. A year later, National Sanitary acquired the janitorial supply business of Calgon/Vestal Laboratories, a division of Calgon Corp. The new operation's St. Louis location became NSS's first significant office east of the Rocky Mountains. The company added a subsidiary, Century Papers, Inc., in the fall of 1988.

The acquisitions doubled its sales offices from 13 to 25 and widened its distribution reach from three centers in three states to nine outlets in eight states. For the eight years prior to the acquisition, National Sanitary's sales had been steadily advancing an average of 33.6 percent each year. However, in the six years after the change in corporate ownership, sales increased at an average annual rate of 76 percent, and nearly tripled from $92.6 million in 1987 to $262.4 million in 1989. By 1990, NSS's gross profit exceeded 1986's total sales.

NSS's dramatic growth has been compared to that of Sysco Corp., which blossomed from a regional food distributor into a multibillion-dollar national company in less than 10 years. Like that company, NSS operated in a very fragmented, highly competitive industry—the $7.7 billion sanitary supply business had about 7,000 participant companies in the mid-1980s and enjoyed a healthy eight percent annual growth rate. National Sanitary's dominance has been credited to its comprehensive product line; its large, proficient sales force; and its dedication to customer service. The company's full-service approach, incorporating regulatory advice, just-in-time delivery, and technical support for its 10,000-product line, has won it almost 120,000 customers across the country.

## The 1990s and Beyond

Nat San inched closer to a coast-to-coast reach in the early 1990s, adding operations in Ohio, Washington, Michigan and Texas. Financial growth slowed from the breakneck pace of the 1980s but still surpassed the industry average. Sales increased only 16 percent, from $265.42 million to $308.28 million, and after slumping a bit during an early 1990s recession, profits increased apace, from $4.1 million to $4.75 million.

The sanitary supply distribution industry remained fragmented into the mid-1990s. In fact, although National Sanitary Supply was the clear leader of the category, it had only captured about 10 percent of overall sales and served less than 40 percent of the American population. The company still wasn't "the first coast-to-coast supplier of quality sanitary supplies," but it enjoyed a significant head start over all its competitors.

Robert B. Garber, son-in-law of one of the company's co-founders, remained president and chief operating officer of Nat San for nearly a decade after its acquisition by Chemed, bringing a measure of continuity to the takeover. The second founding family was represented by Charles Lane and Thomas Lane, who served in executive capacities through the mid-1990s. In 1992, Chemed exerted closer control over its major investment, installing Paul C. Voet, an Executive Vice-President of Chemed, as Nat San's president and CEO. Chemed Chairman and CEO E. L. Hutton became NSS chairman in 1993. Garber and the Lane brothers continued to work at their fathers' company, albeit in lesser roles.

National Sanitary Supply expected to post record sales and income for 1995 in spite of the loss of about 15 percent of its annual sales when a major customer, fast-food restaurateur Sonic, Inc., defected. The company hoped to use computerized ordering, alternative marketing and sales techniques, intensified research and development, and joint ventures to fulfill the promise its name has held for more than 65 years.

### Principal Subsidiaries

Century Papers, Inc.; National Sanitary Supply Development, Inc.

### Further Reading

Larkin, Patrick, "Client Loss Won't Hurt Year for Sanitary Firm," *Cincinnati Post,* November 23, 1995, p. 11B.

Lundegaard, Karen M., "National Sanitary Forms Partnership with Distributor," *Cincinnati Business Courier,* March 28, 1994, p. 3.

"Marketing to the Janitorial & Sanitary Supply Market," *Spray Technology and Marketing,* December 1994, p. 34.

Mehlman, William, "National Sanitary Asserting Janitorial Group Leadership," *The Insiders' Chronicle,* September 14, 1987, p. 1.

"Nat San to Open Fairfield Center for Distribution," *Cincinnati Business Courier,* June 20, 1994, p. 3.

"National Sanitary Supply Co.: Restaurant Chain to Stop Buying from Firm in 1996," *The Wall Street Journal,* November 27, 1995, p. 3B.

Newberry, Jon, "Chemed Spinoff Prelude to Further Expansion," *Cincinnati Business Courier,* May 19, 1986, p. 12.

—April Dougal Gasbarre

# Noodle Kidoodle

**105 Price Parkway**
**Farmingdale, New York 11735**
**U.S.A.**
**(516) 293-5300**
**Fax: (516) 420-8738**

*Public Company*
*Incorporated:* 1931
*Employees:* 595
*Sales:* 32.1 million (1996)
*Stock Exchanges:* NASDAQ
*SICs:* 5945 Hobby, Toy & Game Shops

Noodle Kidoodle operates a chain of education-oriented toy stores with outlets in New York, New Jersey, and Illinois. Formerly known as Greenman Brothers Inc., this New York–based company has a long history in the toy wholesale and retail business.

## Company Origins

Greenman Brothers was founded as the Star Trading Company in 1931 by the Greenman family. Star Trading was a modest wholesaling concern that distributed a variety of goods, including toys and housewares, from a small warehouse in Manhattan's Lower East Side. In 1946, management of the firm was handed over to the second generation, Bernard, Nathan and Sidney, and the company was renamed Greenman Brothers Inc. Greenman Brothers continued to operate on a modest scale through the 1950s, during which time the company headquarters and warehouse were moved from Manhattan to Hicksville, New York. The previously mixed inventory became centered on toys and related goods including sporting equipment and juvenile furniture.

## First Growth in the 1960s

By the early 1960s analysts were predicting that toy wholesalers would become obsolete. The growth of larger retail outlets as well as the consolidation of the toy manufacturing industry meant that retailers were increasingly dealing directly with manufacturers and bypassing brokers like Greenman Brothers. It became clear to the small New York wholesaler that it must diversify and provide a new type of service if it were to continue in business. Greenman undertook two major initiatives in the 1960s to help achieve these goals. The first was the opening of a number of leased retail outlets in discount stores. Bernard Greenman, who had assumed the presidency of the company on the retirement of brother Sidney in 1964, commented on this development in a 1969 article in *Investor's Reader*: "With our knowledge of the toy business, we can operate these departments better than the stores themselves. They afford us another outlet for our wholesale toy inventories, enable us to experiment with hobby and sporting goods lines and help us to spot the fashion changes in toys at the retail level quickly."

The second crucial move for Greenman was to take the company public in 1967. The injection of cash made available by this step allowed the company to expand and upgrade its warehouse facilities as well as to purchase expensive computer equipment. The new computerized inventory system played a significant role in the preservation and growth of their customer base by allowing the company to offer such services as price ticketing, inventory control and automatic reorder services. By 1969, these innovations had increased the number of the company's retail customers to 450 ranging from such large Manhattan department stores as Macy's to small local toy stores. Greenman's own retail operations had grown to 24 leased toy departments in a variety of discount stores in New York and New Jersey. Total sales had reached $21 million.

## National Expansion in the 1970s

In spite of the growth of the 1960s, Greenman Brothers operations had remained essentially a local concern with distribution confined to a 300-mile radius of the Hicksville, New York, warehouse. The first step in transforming Greenman into a national company was taken in 1969 with the purchase of Watson-Triangle, a Florida-based toy wholesaler. This was quickly followed by the acquisition of a number of wholesale toy and housewares companies, including H. Berlind Inc., Hudson Housewares Corp., Associated Sales Agency and L. & H. Sales Co. With these acquisitions the wholesale network of Greenman Brothers included warehouses in New York, Florida, Alabama, and Washington, D.C., and distribution extended over almost the entire Eastern seaboard. In addition, the company opened 24 additional retail outlets as leased toy departments in discount stores in Georgia, Maryland, Florida and Virginia. Within four years of the company's first out of state expansion, sales had almost tripled to $60 million with a net income of $1.7 million.

An important part of this expansion was the diversification of Greenman's wholesale product line to include housewares and stationery. It was hoped that this diversification would provide increased stability to the company's wholesale business and provide a balance to the extremely seasonal and volatile toy market. By 1976 housewares accounted for 29 percent of total sales.

Greenman also looked to a new direction in its retail market during the 1970s. In 1972 the company acquired seven free-standing stores in New York which would become the Playworld chain of toy stores. Playworld stores pioneered the supermarket format similar to the one Toys 'R' Us would later use to build the world's largest toy store chain.

### Wholesale Consolidation in the Early 1980s

Although Greenman Brothers originally intended to expand the initially successful Playworld chain at a fairly rapid pace, sales bogged down in the mid-1970s, and the total number of Playworld outlets peaked in 1977 at 15 stores. With increased competition from the seemingly unstoppable Toys 'R' Us, Greenman was faced with either diverting considerable capital into its Playworld concept, or ceding the field to the larger competitor and falling back on the company's core wholesale business. In the late 1970s Greenman began to close Playworld outlets, and by 1984 only six Playworld stores remained in operation.

The leased departments in discount stores that had served as Greenman's main retail presence throughout the 1960s and 1970s were also under duress during the late 1970s. A realignment of the oversaturated discount department store segment saw the closing of many of the small chains that had leased to Greenman, and the larger chains that emerged from the shake-out preferred to operate their own toy departments. Only six of

Greenman's 45 leased departments that had operated during the 1970s remained in business by the end of the decade.

In spite of troubles in the retail market, the early 1980s was a period of consolidation and growth of Greenman Brothers' wholesale business. In 1981 the company purchased Martin Zippel Co., a Phillipsburg, New Jersey, toy wholesaler that contributed $13 million to overall sales in the first year of its acquisition. With the addition of Martin Zippel, and the consolidation of its other distribution facilities, Greenman's wholesale operations were run out of three warehouses in Farmingdale, New York, Phillipsburg, New Jersey, and Miami, Florida. By 1982, Greenman's wholesale business was contributing 75 percent of the company's $96 million in sales and 94 percent of its $2 million in profits. Housewares contributed a substantial 29 percent of sales, but toys still made up the bulk of the company's wholesale product selection. During this period Greenman Brothers was the leading toy distributor in the eastern United States and the only toy wholesaler with a presence in more than one metropolitan area. New in the 1980s was the addition of electronic products to the toy category, with personal computers and video games appearing to be the hot growth prospect of the decade.

### Return to Retail in the Mid-1980s

In spite of a steady performance in Greenman's wholesale business, profit margins of only about 3.5 percent were not likely to impress investors. In addition, growth opportunities were limited because increasingly large retailers like Toys 'R' Us tended to bypass brokers and buy directly from toy producers. Greenman Brothers began to look once again toward the retail market to provide a better return on investment and more growth potential. In late 1982 Greenman acquired the Playland chain of toy stores. Playland, a customer of Greenman's wholesale business, was a Georgia-based chain with 31 units in the southeastern United States. Playland stores were located in malls and, at 4,000 square feet, were much smaller than the supermarket format Playworld or Toys 'R' Us stores. Mall-based stores were attractive to Greenman because they offered a niche that was not in direct competition with the giant Toys 'R' Us. Playland was also distinguished from its main mall competitor, Kay-Bee Toys, because of an emphasis on upscale rather than discount merchandise. President Bernard Greenman felt that the company's experience in the toy industry would enable them to offer product selection that would be attractive to the casual shopper offered by mall traffic. In addition, start-up costs for mall-based stores were much lower than for the toy supermarkets that the company had been forced to close in the 1970s.

Greenman Brothers originally intended to slowly expand the number of Playland units, but in 1985 when Rite-Aid's Circus World came on the market, Greenman jumped at the chance to acquire the 189-store chain. Although Circus World had been only marginally profitable under Rite-Aid's management, Bernard Greenman was convinced that his company's buying expertise could convert the national chain into a toy powerhouse. Greenman Brothers merged the Playland and Circus World chains and began a process of renovation and upgrading of existing stores as well as opening new units. By the close of

1985, Greenman was operating 310 toy stores in 26 states, with annual retail sales of over $49 million for the retail chain alone.

From the perspective of the mid-1980s prospects looked good for Greenman Brothers. Sales for Circus World stores were up 26 percent, and wholesale sales jumped an impressive 49 percent in a single year to $125 million. By 1986 total sales had reached $218 million with net income over $7 million. Analysts were predicting continued sales and earnings growth into the 1990s. However, cracks began to appear in the Greenman plan in 1987 when record sales of $244 million failed to produce a profit, and the company recorded a net loss of $3 million. Improvements in Circus World merchandising and distribution had taken longer and had required more capital than was predicted. In addition, the toy industry, which had been prospering for a number of years, entered a slump, affecting both Greenman's wholesale and retail divisions. To make matters worse, Watson-Triangle, the company's wholesale housewares division in Miami, also saw an 11 percent sales drop, and the decision was made to close the facility. While overall sales continued to grow, thanks mainly to new store openings, same store sales were flat and in 1988 Greenman Brothers, now under the management of Bernard Greenman's son Stanley, recorded another net loss of almost $3 million.

Circus World had failed to distinguish itself from competitor Kay-Bee Toys, and the larger and older Kay-Bee chain had already seized many of the best mall locations. Greenman Brothers had a difficult time convincing mall owners that their malls could support two very similar toy stores, thereby limiting the number of new units that could be opened. While Kay-Bee also underwent some lean years in the late 1980s, its parent, the retail giant Melville Corp., could afford to carry the chain and had capital to invest in store restructuring. By 1990, Greenman Brothers found itself with growing debt, flat sales and tough competition in a recessionary economy. Circus World stores were back in the black, but with net profits of only $2 million and no improvement in sight, Greenman management decided to cut their losses and in August of 1990 agreed to sell its 330 Circus World stores to competitor Kay-Bee.

### Noodle Kidoodle

With the sale of Circus World, Greenman was left with a profitable but stagnant wholesale business and a handful of Playworld toy stores in the New York area. After the discontinued Circus World operations left the company with a net loss of over $14 million in 1991, even the modest net income of $3.5 million in 1992 could not instill much confidence in investors. It was clear that the company had to take a new direction to regain the sales and profits of the mid-1980s. The toy retail industry had been totally transformed since the early days of Greenman's leased departments. Toys 'R' Us now controlled more than 20 percent of the retail market in the United States with no serious competitor in sight. Huge discount chains like Wal-Mart and Target also had a significant presence mostly because they could afford to take very low mark-ups and offer prices on standard, mass market merchandise that no small competitor could match. With almost 1000 units in malls across the country Kay-Bee was in firm control of that segment of the toy market. Greenman Brothers CEO, Stanley Greenman, began to search for an opening in this tightly controlled industry.

Greenman Brothers looked first at the upscale, specialty toy market which was not being fully served by mass-market outlets. The company opened two higher end toy stores in New York under the name Toy Park, but the merchandise mix offered in these stores did not present sufficient differentiation from the large chains to permit substantial growth. Market research revealed that one under-represented segment in the toy industry lay in educational and creative toys, which tended to be sold in specialty stores like Toy Park but which did not have a broad distribution channel. Greenman Brothers decided that these toys represented a potential niche with room for significant growth, and in 1993 the company opened its first Noodle Kidoodle store in Greenvale, New York.

The Noodle Kidoodle concept was to take the supermarket approach of a Toys 'R' Us and marry it with the specialty boutique quality of the Toy Park stores. Noodle Kidoodle would steer clear of the mass-marketed, television-inspired toys and offer instead a mix of creative and education-oriented toys, books and computer software. Noodle Kidoodle stores would be large at 10,000 square feet, but aisles would be spacious, thematic areas well marked with colorful, child friendly signs, and areas would be available for kids and parents to try out merchandise. The layout of these stores would be designed to circumvent the warehouse atmosphere that tended to frustrate parents and exhaust children in most toy superstores. Merchandise categories included science and nature, arts and crafts, games and puzzles, infants and pre-school, electronic learning and computer software. Each store would also include a small theater area with a stage and large screen television for video and live performances. Noodle Kidoodle promotion and advertising, directed almost exclusively toward parents, would stress the educational yet fun nature of the merchandise.

From the start, Noodle Kidoodle was conceived of as a retail chain with units across the country. After the first store in Greenvale showed decent sales in its first year of operation and customer reviews were favorable, the decision was made to go ahead with new store openings. Over the course of the next two years 20 Noodle Kidoodle units were added to the Greenman Brothers roster, and by 1995 it became clear that Noodle Kidoodle had become the driving force of the company. Wholesale sales continued to contribute the bulk of Greenman Brothers sales, but with profit margins diminishing and no prospect for growth in sight, the decision was made to sell the wholesale business and to expend all resources in furthering the Noodle Kidoodle concept. In December 1985, Greenman Brothers officially changed its name to Noodle Kidoodle, bringing a close to its 60-year-old family wholesale business.

By 1996, Noodle Kidoodle was operating 21 stores in New York, New Jersey, Connecticut and Illinois with plans to open at least 15 more stores in the following year and "several hundred" by the end of the decade. Sales had reached $32 million, but the large costs associated with new store openings resulted in a net loss of $14 million for fiscal 1996. In February 1996 the company completed a common stock offering of two million shares in order to finance the rapid expansion. In an industry with tough competition and a fashion-driven customer base, it remained to be seen whether Noodle Kidoodle would be able to bring the Greenman family business into the 21st century.

### *Further Reading*

Bernstein, James, ''Using Their Noodle,'' *Newsday,* March 11, 1996, pp. 1C, 6–7C.

Dunkin, Amy, ''Greenman Bros. Is No Babe in Toyland,'' *Business Week,* August 26, 1985, pp. 75–76.

Gordon, Mitchell, ''More Than Santa,'' *Barron's,* August 13, 1984, pp. 71–72.

''Greenman Brothers, Toy Distributor,'' *Investor's Reader,* November 19, 1969, pp. 17–18.

Lilly, Richard M., ''Greenman Brothers Inc.'' *Wall Street Transcript,* February 25, 1985, pp. 77,032–77,034.

''Space Age Santa,'' *Barron's,* October 18, 1982, pp. 53–54.

—Hilary Gopnik

# Norstan, Inc.

605 North Highway 169
Twelfth Floor
Plymouth, Minnesota 55441
U.S.A.
(612) 513-4540
Fax: (612) 513-4537

*Public Company*
*Incorporated:* 1961 as Norstan Research and
    Development Company
*Employees:* 3,100
*Sales:* $323 million (1996)
*Stock Exchanges:* NASDAQ
*SICs:* 5065 Electronic Parts and Equipment, Not
    Elsewhere Classified; 5046 Commercial Equipment,
    Not Elsewhere Classified

---

Norstan, Inc. has gained a strong position as a "one-stop" provider of communications solutions in the United States and Canada. Norstan offers consulting, sales, and support services for best-of-breed telephone systems, videoconferencing equipment, long-distance services, call transaction processing, intelligent cabling services, and network integration. Increasingly, Norstan's focus has been on becoming a full-service communications systems integrator of voice, video, data, and image communications solutions. Norstan has formed strategic alliances and distributor relationships with many of the top makers of communications equipment and software, including Siemens ROLM, Aspect Telecommunications, Chipcom, Compression Labs Inc., Lotus, Microsoft, Novell, Sprint, Northern Telecom, Synoptics, and others. With revenues expected to reach $323 million in 1996, sales of telephone systems account for about one-third of Norstan's business, and recurring revenues from services provide another 32 percent. By the year 2000, however, the company expected its integration and cabling services, accounting for about 9 percent of its revenues in the mid-1990s, to grow to about 33 percent of its business. In 1995, Norstan's clients numbered more than 13,000, principally in the West, Southwest, and Midwest regions.

## First Steps

Although Norstan was founded as Norstan Research and Development Company in Minnesota in 1961, it operated as a shell company until it was purchased by Sydney R. Cohen in 1970. At the same time, Cohen bought Summit Gear Company, a maker of gears, gear trains, and other precision parts for the aerospace and defense industries. For the next several years, the company achieved modest sales and earnings, posting $1.8 million in revenues by 1973 and a net income of $11,000. During this initial period, Norstan attempted to enter the pollution control business, acquiring the marketing and manufacturing rights to the Westcreek Afterburner system for burning animal wastes. But it was another early venture that would drive the company's future direction and growth.

Telephone equipment was controlled entirely by the Bell System until the 1960s, when it lost its monopoly. In 1973, Norstan co-founder Paul Baszucki, together with several partners in the company, formed a wholly owned subsidiary, Norstan Communications Systems, Inc. (NCS), with the intention of entering the nascent telecommunications equipment and service industry. Norstan secured a distributor agreement with Siemens ROLM of Germany for ROLM's private-branch exchange (PBX) equipment. The PBX computer managed private telephone networks and featured corporate switchboard functions and cost-monitoring systems.

NCS recorded early successes, and by 1975 it was handling 75 percent of the private telephone networks operating in Norstan's Minneapolis-St. Paul base. The acquisition of Allcom of Minnesota, a distributor of PBX systems, in 1975 expanded the company's reach through Minnesota and into other midwestern states. Norstan went public, and revenues rose to $2.8 million in 1975. The following year, Norstan signed an exclusive distribution agreement with ROLM, becoming the sole reseller of ROLM equipment in its territory. By 1977, with customers including the operation of Harley Davidson's toll-free Hog line, Norstan's sales neared $5 million. In that year, Norstan discontinued its Westcreek operations. NCS and Allcom were merged together, and Norstan changed its name to Norstan, Inc. Two years later, Norstan reorganized as a holding company for its telecommunications and Summit Gear subsidiaries.

The PBX sales of the 1970s and early 1980s continued to drive the company's growth. Norstan's agreements with ROLM expanded to include most of the Midwest. Norstan typically entered smaller cities, avoiding the higher competition and costs of larger cities, such as Chicago. By 1979, Norstan's sales topped $10 million; two years later, revenues reached $25 million, earning a $1.8 million net profit. By then, Norstan was preparing new additions to its portfolio.

### Becoming a $100 Million Company

In 1981, Norstan formed its Norstan Financial Corp. subsidiary to assist in the lease financing of its PBX sales. At the same time, the company attempted to enter the young information processing market, forming a new subsidiary, Norstan Information Systems. Norstan posted a second public offering of 1.1 million shares at $14 per share to finance these ventures. In the meantime, sales and service contracts for its PBX products continued to increase revenues.

The deregulation of the telephone industry in the 1980s added fuel to Norstan's growth. With traditional Bell leasing arrangements coming to an end, large numbers of corporations turned from leasing to purchasing the equipment for their private telephone networks. Meanwhile, technology had outstripped the Bell System's analog technology, and digital systems, such as ROLM's products, became the PBXs of choice. The resulting boom in PBX purchases lasted into the mid-1980s, with hundreds of start-ups, both manufacturers and distributors, competing for market share.

By the mid-1980s, however, the PBX boom had faded, and many of the start-up manufacturers and distributors disappeared. Several factors were responsible for these companies' failures. Manufacturers tended to sign distribution agreements with several vendors in the same region. This competition forced vendors to cut prices, usually below cost. The distributors expected to make up these negative margins by selling support services at inflated prices. An array of third-party service providers sprang up, however, undercutting the distributors' service charges. When the PBX market stalled later in the 1980s, most of the distributors and many manufacturers went out of business.

Norstan, however, prospered during this period, with sales rising to $54 million in 1985 and to $106 million by 1989. Important for Norstan's growth was the company's relationship with ROLM, which provided for not only steady increases in territory, but also exclusive distribution agreements in each new area, a relationship that continued despite ROLM's several changes in ownership. During the 1980s, Norstan continued to specialize in ROLM products, selling these more expensive PBXs at a profit and acting as the sole independent distributor of

ROLM PBXs in Iowa, Michigan, Minnesota, Nebraska, and the Dakotas. Norstan added new territories with a number of acquisitions, including Electronic Engineering Co. in 1985, which brought Norstan into Kentucky and Ohio, and Communications Consultants, Inc. in 1988, which brought the company to Arizona and New Mexico. In that year, Norstan also signed an exclusive contract with ROLM as the reseller of refurbished ROLM equipment, which was becoming an increasingly important market.

Equally important for Norstan's growth was its growing reputation as a strong, and ethical, service provider. With customer satisfaction and retention levels running above 90 percent, Norstan was able to fight off attempts of third-party providers to take away the company's service contracts. As Norstan's installed base grew, these service contracts provided a steady source of revenue, even as the end of the PBX boom put many of Norstan's competitors out of business. By the late 1980s, Norstan's focus was changing. Whereas sales of ROLM PBXs had accounted for 50 percent or more of the company's revenues in the first half of the decade, by 1990, more than two-thirds of Norstan's revenues came from service, support, and upgrades. The company's acquisition of Solsound Industries for $5.5 million in 1986 further strengthened its communication capabilities.

Norstan was less fortunate in its attempts to diversify beyond communications. In 1985 the company formed a new subsidiary, Norstan Software Systems, in an attempt to develop proprietary software systems for the IBM PC-type computer market. Yet combined sales with Norstan Information Systems were only $12 million for 1985, and, after posting a loss of $1.5 million in 1986, Norstan Information Systems was discontinued. Meanwhile, the company's Summit Gear subsidiary was also in trouble, with sales stagnating around $8 million per year during the mid-1980s and losses mounting to $2.6 million in 1986, causing the first net loss in Norstan's history. In 1987, Norstan sold Summit Gear for $11.4 million and dedicated its focus to telecommunications.

### Positioning for the 1990s

Within the first five years of the new decade, Norstan, under leadership of CEO Paul Baszucki, would reinvent itself from essentially a reseller of a single product to a vendor of diversified telecommunications solutions. At the start of the decade, Norstan worked with about 8,000 clients, including major corporations such as Land O'Lakes and First Interstate Bank of Arizona, and many others with long-term relationships with the company. Norstan moved to offer a broader range of products and services, adding the products of Aspect, a San Jose-based company created by former employees of ROLM, long-distance services through Sprint, and other products, such as cabling and voice messaging, that would allow it to become a provider of vertical integration solutions, from telephone equipment to personal computer networks.

The expansion of its product portfolio came at the right time, as consolidation of the PBX industry was rapidly limiting Norstan's potential growth in that area. In 1991, agreements with ROLM brought Norstan into eight more states, bringing the number of states in which Norstan operated to a total of 18. The acquisition of ROLM offices from Centel and of Tel Plus Communications, both in 1992, expanded Norstan's territories in the Midwest, South, and Southwest. Consolidation of the industry, however, made expansion into other territories in the United States unlikely. In an important move, Norstan purchased IBM's struggling ROLM subsidiary in Canada in 1992. In that year, as well, the company won distribution rights for the videoconferencing products made by Compression Labs Inc., while becoming a direct reseller of Sprint network products and signing distribution agreements for Octel Communications voice information processing equipment and Siemens HCM 200 PBX equipment.

Revenues soared, from $142 million in 1992 to nearly $196 million in 1993. Earnings could not keep pace, however, because of the company's aggressive expansion and losses from its Canadian operations. Nevertheless, net income grew to $5.1 million for 1993, and the Canadian subsidiary turned a profit by 1995.

Further agreements added Novell, Microsoft, Intel, Hewlett Packard, and Lotus products to Norstan's growing capacity. In 1995, Norstan strengthened its consulting arm with the acquisition of Toronto-based Renaissance Connects, which specialized in consulting, design, and engineering of wide-area and local-area networks (WANs and LANs). Outsourcing, by which Norstan contracted to design, install, and staff a corporation's communications systems, was also a rising source of revenue, boosted by a five-year, $12 million contract with British Petroleum, which included the purchase of their physical plant, to provide telecommunications over British Petroleum's 10,000-line PBX system. Meanwhile, sales of PBX systems began to pick up again, after a ten-year lull, driven by corporations moving to replace their outdated equipment.

Yet Norstan's strongest growth was expected to come from several newly developing areas, including videoconferencing and networking and, especially, communication systems integration. Both markets were expected to take off in the latter half of the 1990s, and Norstan was positioned well to play a major role in the coming boom. Norstan made a strategic move in 1995 with the appointment of Max Mayer, former vice-president and CEO with Digital Equipment Corp.'s computer systems division, as Norstan's president, bringing in Mayer's experience with electronic communications. With 1995 revenues reaching $285 million, 1996 revenues forecasted to rise to $332 million, and forecasts calling for the company to top $500 million by 1998, Norstan was poised not only to remain one of the largest independent telecommunications providers in the United States, but also to become a major player in the communications integration industry.

## Principal Subsidiaries

Norstan Communications, Inc.; Norstan Canada Inc.; Norstan Network Services, Inc.; Norstan Financial Services, Inc.; ROLM Resale Services; Norstan Resale Services; Norstan Integration Services.

## Further Reading

Browder, Seanna, "A Skeleton in the Closet," *Corporate Report Minnesota,* October 1990, p. 79.

Byrne, Harlan S., "Norstan: Dialing the Right Numbers for Stronger Performance," *Barron's,* October 18, 1993, p. 35.

Gross, Steve, "Norstan Looks North," *Star Tribune,* March 18, 1992, p. 1D.

Labate, John, "Norstan," *Fortune,* May 1, 1995.

"Norstan, Inc.," *Minneapolis St. Paul Citybusiness,* September 22, 1995.

Powers, Glenn T., "Norstan, Inc.," *Research Report/Dan Bosworth Incorporated,* March 1, 1995.

Rinkoff, Rick, "Don't Hang Up," *Twin Cities Business Monthly,* March 1996.

—M.L. Cohen

**ONEX** corporation

# Onex Corporation

P.O. Box 153
**Toronto**
**Ontario M5L 1E7**
**Canada**
(416) 362-7711
Fax: (416) 362-5765

*Public Company*
*Incorporated:* 1984
*Employees:* 34,000
*Sales:* $6.5 billion
*Stock Exchanges:* Toronto Montreal
*SIC:* 6719 Holding Company

Onex Corporation is not only one of the largest and most successful of all the holding companies in Canada, it is also one of the youngest. A highly diversified firm that is comprised of autonomous subsidiaries, associated companies, and strategic partnerships, Onex Corporation posted revenues of $6.5 billion in fiscal 1995, an astounding increase of 86 percent over the previous year. The company's operations include: Sky Chefs, the largest in-flight caterer to both domestic and international airlines in the world; ProSource Distribution, the largest foodservice systems distributor in the continental United States; Dura Automotive, the biggest North American supplier of parking-brake systems; and Tower Automotive, one of the leading North American manufacturers of structural-metal stampings. The company also has significant holdings in such businesses as Phoenix Pictures, a newly formed entertainment company, and Purolator Courier, the leading overnight courier service in Canada.

### Early History

The history of Onex Corporation is actually the biography of one man, Gerald Schwartz. A young man with ambition and bold ideas, Schwartz graduated from the University of Manitoba with degrees in commerce and law. Upon graduation, he headed for Harvard University and earned a degree in business administration in 1970. Schwartz then took a job in Europe,

working for Bernard Cornfield, a rather eccentric and flamboyant international financier based in Switzerland. When Cornfield's company, Investors Overseas Services, was investigated for fraud and then collapsed in 1973, Schwartz moved on to the United States, seeking work in the financial caverns of Wall Street in New York City. Hired by Bear Stearns & Company, Schwartz learned the intricacies of hostile takeovers and corporate mergers. Two of his most renowned and notorious colleagues included Henry Kravis and Jerome Kohlberg.

After a stint of four years in America, Schwartz decided to return to his hometown of Winnipeg. There, he formed a partnership with a lawyer, Israel Asper, an astute and driven entrepreneur, and together they founded CanWest Capital Corporation, the forerunner of CanWest Global Communications Corporation, which would own numerous broadcasting businesses throughout western Canada. The partnership first acquired several small to mid-sized Canadian firms during the late 1970s and early 1980s, and seemed to be heading in a promising direction. Yet Schwartz and Asper began to quarrel about strategic issues surrounding acquisitions, venture capital, and timing, and before long decided to end their partnership.

### A New Company in the 1980s

In 1983, Schwartz relocated to Toronto and, with the financial backing of former investors at CanWest, formed Onex Capital Corporation, which he intended to use as a holding company for widely diversified acquisitions. The first such acquisition was Onex Packaging, the Canadian subsidiary of the American Can Company based in Connecticut. With a purchase price of approximately $220 million, the acquisition was the largest leveraged buyout in the history of Canada.

Schwartz was not afraid of debt and had learned his lessons well while working at Bear Stearns in New York. His *modus operandi* was to use debt or other innovative financing to purchase undervalued companies, and then initiate a comprehensive restructuring of the company purchased. He would then sell either parts of the company or the whole at a profit. Onex Packaging, a manufacturer of rigid packing materials, offered an initial public sale of its stock in 1987, to cover the costs of the

---

## Company Perspectives:

*Onex Corporation is a diversified company that operates through autonomous subsidiaries and strategic partnerships. Our long-term objective is to maximze the value of Onex Corporation for its shareholders by: acquiring high-quality companies at reasonable prices; creating value through the entrepreneurial management of these companies; redeploying assets at opportune times.*

---

restructuring and to raise additional funds for the expenses incurring in modernizing the company. Unfortunately, by 1987, Onex Packaging was losing money and Schwartz decided to take the company private once again. Not long afterwards, he sold Onex Packaging for less than he had originally anticipated.

Having learned a hard lesson about economies of scale in the North American market with Onex Packaging, Schwartz wasn't about to make the same mistake twice. During 1987, as Onex Packaging began to flounder, Schwartz acquired both Norex Leasing, a leading leasing company owned and operated by Citibank, and Purolator Courier Ltd., the leading overnight delivery service in Canada. At the same time, Schwartz made a conscious decision to make more acquisitions in the United States and began to decrease his holdings in Canada, although his company would always remain based in his native country. This strategy led him to one of the most important acquisitions during the late 1980s: the purchase of the airline catering company called Sky Chefs.

### Growth Through Acquisition in the 1990s

One of the first huge successes of Schwartz's acquisition strategy was Beatrice Foods Canada, Ltd. Purchased in 1987 when its parent firm was in the course of being dismantled in Chicago, Schwartz paid a bargain-basement cash price of $21.9 million for the company, although it was valued at a purchase price of just over $300 million. In 1991, the entrepreneur resold the company at a cost of $475 million, after a complicated but productive restructuring plan that involved merging Beatrice Foods Canada with two other Canadian dairy firms. Additional acquisitions followed at a quick pace, including ProSource Distribution, a foodservice distributor in both the United States and Canada, and Dura Automotive Systems and Tower Automotive, two high-quality automotive parts manufacturers.

Schwartz's goal with Sky Chefs was to transform it into a leader in the in-flight catering industry. The first step in this direction was an alliance formed between Sky Chefs and LSG Lufthansa Service in 1993. The alliance was formed to give Sky Chefs access to international airline customers that it did not previously have. Revenues for Sky Chefs remained relatively the same from 1991 through 1994, hovering around $470 million annually. During this time, however, Sky Chefs was transformed into the leading low-cost producer of in-flight meals for the airline industry. A policy of cycle-time reduction was implemented in 1992 and resulted in a 30 percent labor production increase over a three-year period.

Although many innovative alliances and policies had been implemented at Sky Chefs during the early 1990s, it wasn't until 1995 that the company developed a worldwide reputation. Much of this was due to the takeover of Caterair International Corporation, one of the preeminent in-flight catering companies. Funded entirely by third-party lenders, the acquisition of Caterair International propelled Sky Chefs to the top of the industry with just under 50 percent of the American domestic airline catering market and 30 percent of the international airline catering market. The acquisition of Caterair International and the earlier alliance with LSG Lufthansa gave Sky Chefs access to airline customers around the world, including new contracts in Central and South America, as well as in Australia. As the consolidation of in-flight catering services continued through 1995, additional contracts were signed with British Airways, Delta Airlines, USAir, and Midway. By the end of fiscal 1995, Sky Chefs counted more than 250 airline customers located in every part of the world, while revenues shot up to $739 million, an increase of 58 percent over the previous year.

ProSource, Onex Corporation's foodservice distributor for restaurant chains, was the largest in North America. Starting in 1992 with a single customer, Burger King, the company expanded to provide services for over 22 different types of restaurants and fast-food establishments. In 1993, ProSource acquired Valley Food Services, and in 1994 Malone Products, but the most significant addition was the acquisition of the National Accounts division of the Martin-Brower Company in 1995. These three acquisitions expanded and diversified the ProSource Distribution customer base, so that instead of relying exclusively on quick-serve restaurants, there was more of a balance, with distribution to quick-serve establishments comprising 75 percent and distribution to casual dining restaurants totaling 25 percent of ProSource business. Revenues in 1995 for ProSource were reported at $3.5 billion, compared to the 1994 figure of $1.6 billion. Much of the increased revenue was derived from the acquisition of the National Accounts division of Martin-Brower, but a significant portion of the increase was due to implementing highly successful cost-effective distribution techniques. One such technique involved "rolling shelving," wherein carts used by ProSource delivery trucks could also be used for instant in-store shelving at restaurants. Another cost-effective distribution method involved the company's electronic ordering system, which reduced time and effort. These innovations helped ProSource develop into one of the leading-edge distributors in the food service industry.

Hidden Creek Industries was formed as a partnership by Onex Corporation to manage the operations of Dura Automotive and Tower Automotive. Dura Automotive, purchased in 1990, became the largest supplier of parking-brake systems to original equipment manufacturers (OEM) in North America. In 1994, Dura acquired the Orscheln Company, to increase its market share of the parking-brake systems industry. With the purchase of Orscheln, Dura achieved its goal; revenues increased 34 percent from 1994 to 1995, jumping from $189.7 million to $253.7 million. Tower Automotive was purchased in 1993 and was transformed by management into one of the leading developers and manufacturers of structural metal stampings and various other assemblies for original equipment manufacturers. In 1994, Tower purchased Edgewood Tool and

Manufacturing, as well as Kalamazoo Stamping and Die, and the following year added the Trylon Corporation to its holdings. These acquisitions not only increased revenues from 1994 to 1995 by 35 percent, but complemented Tower Automotive's already existing line of products. While Dura Automotive's major customers included Ford, Chrysler, General Motors, and Toyota, Tower Automotive negotiated lucrative contracts with Ford and Honda motor companies.

As a holding company, one of Onex Corp.'s top priorities was to enhance the value of shareholder equity. During 1995, this goal was pursued by a number of strategic investments, made primarily under the direction of Gerald Schwartz. Onex invested $20 million in Phoenix Pictures, a brand new film production company owned by Onex, Sony Pictures Entertainment, and Britain's Pearson PLC. The company also purchased Vencap Equities Alberta, Ltd., a promising venture capital fund located in western Canada. And finally, management at Onex formed Rippledwood Holdings, an acquisition fund developed to hold the 52 percent of the company's interest in Dayton Superior Corporation. Other continuing strategic investments included a 19 percent share of Purolator Courier (down from majority ownership a few years earlier), 16 percent of Scotsman Industries (a manufacturer of ice machines, freezers, food preparation workstations, and refrigerators), and an 8.1 percent share in Alliance Communications, the leading producer and distributor of television entertainment in Canada.

## Looking Toward the Future

In the spring of 1995, Gerald Schwartz decided to launch a $2.3 billion hostile takeover of John Labatt Ltd., one of the most prominent brewers in Canada. Located in Toronto, Labatt had a long and distinguished history that started as a brewer of fine beers in London, England in 1847. Controlling approximately 45 percent of the Canadian beer market in North America, second only to Molson, by 1995, Labatt had also diversified into businesses unrelated to the brewing industry. At the time of Schwartz's attempted takeover, Labatt owned The Sports Network, Le Reseau des Sports, an 80 percent interest in The Discovery Network, a 42 percent interest in Toronto's Sky-Dome, and a 90 percent stake in the Toronto Blue Jays baseball team.

Unwilling to join the Onex Corporation holdings, management at Labatt began looking for a "white knight" to foil the hostile takeover attempt. After meetings with a number of possible suitors, Labatt finally arranged a deal with Interbrew S.A., a Belgian-based brewery that had been attempting to break into the North American beer market for years. Interbrew cooked up a deal that amounted to $2.7 billion, successfully outbidding Onex Corporation for control of Labatt. After the acquisition was finalized, Interbrew began to sell off Labatt's non-brewing operations, which had been the sole purpose of Schwartz's attempted takeover of the company.

Although Schwartz was frustrated in his attempt to acquire Labatt, he continued to seek out undervalued companies for acquisition. And though committed to running his company from Canadian headquarters, he was reportedly increasingly interested in looking south towards the United States in order to expand his operations.

### Principal Subsidiaries

Sky Chefs, Inc.; ProSource Distribution, Inc.; Hidden Creek Industries, Inc.; Norex Leasing, Inc.; ONEX Food Services, Inc.; Purolator Courier, Inc. (19%); Scotsman Industries, Inc. (16%); Alliance Communications (8.1%).

### Further Reading

Dalglish, Brenda, "A Private Play: Onex Bids $2.3 Billion To Take Over Labatt," *MacLean's,* May 29, 1995, p. 44.

De Santis, Solange, and Martin Du Bois, "Labatt Agrees To White Knight Deal With Belgium's Interbrew, Foiling Onex," *The Wall Street Journal,* June 7, 1995, p. A3(E).

"Holding Company Agrees To Buy Vencap Equities," *The Wall Street Journal,* October 26, 1995, p. A19(E).

McMurdy, Deirdre, "Predators On Parade," *MacLean's,* May 29, 1995, p. 49.

——, "Sacred Pensions In Play," *MacLean's,* June 12, 1995, p. 36.

——, "Southern Accent," *MacLean's,* August 2 1993, p. 26.

"Onex Corporation," *The Wall Street Journal,* May 11, 1995, p. C18.

Willis, Andrew, "Eye For The Prize," *MacLean's,* May 29, 1995, p. 46.

——, "The Winning Brew," *MacLean's,* June 19, 1995, p. 44.

—Thomas Derdak

# Owens & Minor, Inc.

**4800 Cox Road**
**Glen Allen, Virginia 23060**
**U.S.A.**
**(804) 747-9794**
**Fax: (804) 273-0232**

*Public Company*
*Incorporated:* 1927 as Owens & Minor Drug Company,
 Inc.
*Employees:* 3,350
*Sales:* $2.97 billion (1995)
*Stock Exchanges:* New York
*SICs:* 5047 Medical & Hospital Equipment; 5122 Drugs,
 Proprietaries & Sundries

The second-largest wholesale distributor of medical and surgical supplies in the United States, Owens & Minor, Inc. owns distribution centers across the nation that serve hospitals, primary care facilities, healthcare systems, and group purchasing organizations. Originally founded as a wholesale drug company in 1882, Owens & Minor first entered the medical and surgical supply business in 1966 and then, through a series of acquisitions completed during the ensuing three decades, entrenched its position in its new business, divesting its wholesale drug business in 1992 to operate exclusively as a medical and surgical supply distributor during the mid-1990s.

### Origins

The corporate history of Owens & Minor charts the history of the Minor family, tracing the roots of a family tree that stretch back more than a century before the company was founded. Four generations before a Minor family member founded the company that would employ generations of Minors, Dr. George Gilmer spent his life working as an apothecary-surgeon, attending to patients in colonial Williamsburg until his death in 1751. Dr. Gilmer was the first in a long line of family members who would spend their professional careers working in the pharmaceutical or medical fields, beginning a legacy that would continue on two centuries later and inspire his son to enter the medical profession as well.

Dr. Gilmer's son and namesake followed his father's footsteps and received training in the medical field. The younger Gilmer, who would earn distinction as Thomas Jefferson's personal physician, practiced medicine in Charlottesville, Virginia, working there as a doctor before and after the Revolutionary War. His sister, Lucy Gilmer, lived in Charlottesville as well, where she married Dr. Peter Minor, also a Charlottesville physician. The married couple's son, George Gilmer Minor, took to the seas and studied medicine abroad, then returned to the United States and began practicing medicine in New Kent County, not far from Williamsburg. Following the conclusion of the Civil War, George Gilmer Minor, the first of many generations to bear that name, moved his family to the newly reconstructed and burgeoning city of Richmond, Virginia, where his son, George Gilmer Minor, Jr., cofounded what would become one of the oldest family-operated companies in the country. It was in Richmond and through the efforts of George Gilmer Minor, Jr., that Owens & Minor was first established.

Before entering into the business world on his own, George Gilmer Minor, Jr., worked as a salesman for a Richmond wholesale drug firm called Powers Taylor Drug Company. The introduction to the wholesale drug business would have a lasting effect on the youngest of the Minor family, as would the fortuitous meeting between Minor and another salesman, Otho O. Owens. Owens, who worked for a rival drug company named Purcell Ladd and Company, and Minor presumably met through the course of their business, as each plied his trade in and around the Richmond area. Any competitive fire between Owens and Minor was forever snuffed in January 1882, when the two salesmen entered into business together and established a company that a century later would dominate its industry as Owens & Minor, Inc.

The company was founded as Owens & Minor Drug Company and operated as a wholesale and retail business, with the wholesale side of the enterprise conducted behind the retail

## Company Perspectives:

*Owens & Minor's mission is to provide our customers and suppliers with the most responsive, efficient and cost-effective distribution system for the delivery of healthcare products and services in the markets we serve; to earn a return on our invested capital consistent with being an industry leader; and to manage our business with the highest ethical standards in a socially responsible manner with particular emphasis on the welfare of our teammates and the communities we serve.*

space that faced Richmond's Main Street. From these quarters, Owens & Minor sold patent medicines, cosmetics, prepared prescriptions, and a wide range of other goods, including window glass, paints, oils, and dyes. Otho Owens served as the company's president, heading the operation for the first five years, until Owens & Minor Drug Company was reorganized as a limited partnership comprising 24 investors, and for the ensuing 19 years, until his death in 1906. George Gilmer Minor, Jr., then took the reins of command, picking up where Owens left off and guiding the company for five years until his death in 1911.

The next leader of the company came from neither the Owens nor the Minor family, but instead from inside the organization itself. Conway M. Knox, a former stock boy for the company who had worked his way up Owens & Minor's ranks, received the ultimate promotion in 1911, when he succeeded George Gilmer Minor, Jr., as president. Under Knox's watch, Owens & Minor moved to a larger location, occupying in 1913 what would serve as the company's headquarters for more than the next 50 years. Knox superintended the company's fortunes for a commensurate amount of time, serving as the president from 1911 to 1941, successfully bringing the company through one world war, a devastating, decade-long economic depression, and to the dawn of World War II. During his tenure at Owens & Minor, Knox was assisted by two sons of the company's founder, George Gilmer Minor, III, and William Y. Minor, who were with the company when it was incorporated in 1927, the year the Owens family sold their stake in the company and brought to an end a 45-year business relationship between the two families. George Gilmer Minor, III, succeeded Knox as president of the company in 1941, but his term was cut tragically short, ending just 15 months after it began with his death in 1942.

To fill the leadership void, the company once again turned to someone outside the Minor family, naming James B. Bowers president in 1942. Bowers had joined the company in 1902 and served as its president for five years before retiring in 1947, ending his career after 50 years of involvement with Owens & Minor. The next Minor to take charge of the company would be the company's most influential leader in its first century of business, a man who represented the third generation of the Minor family to head Owens & Minor and who would direct the company into a new line of business that would predicate its existence during the 1990s.

In 1934, George Gilmer Minor, IV, joined the family business directly from the Virginia Military Institute, starting with Owens & Minor as an office boy and eventually gaining experience in every facet of the company's operations before succeeding Bowers in 1947. Grandson of the company's founder, George Gilmer Minor, IV, would play as pivotal a role in the company's history as his grandfather had played, and like his grandfather, he went by the name George Gilmer Minor, Jr.

In a presidency that would span 29 years, George Gilmer Minor, Jr., waited until 1955 to make his first major move. At the time, the number of competitors in Richmond's drug wholesale business community had been whittled down to three major companies: Bodeker Drug Company; Powers Taylor, which had purchased Purcell Ladd in 1910, the company Otho Owens had worked for; and Owens & Minor. In 1955, however, that number was reduced to two when Owens & Minor acquired the accounts and the name of Bodeker Drug Company. Bodeker Drug Co. was well-known to generations of Richmond citizens, having been established in 1846, nearly two decades before Owens & Minor Drug Co. was founded. Bodeker Drug was also twice as large as its new owner, giving Owens & Minor a considerable boost to its business and lending the company a new name: Owens, Minor & Bodeker Drug Co.

### 1966 Entry into a New Business

In the wake of the 1955 acquisition of Bodeker Drug Co., the company expanded, establishing its first distribution center outside of Richmond in 1959 in Wilson, North Carolina, and another in Norfolk, Virginia, in 1962. The company's acquisitive pace picked up under George Gilmer Minor, Jr.'s presidency as well, accelerating Owens, Minor & Bodeker's growth appreciably. The company completed ten acquisitions between 1964 and 1981, but none was as important as the purchase of A&J Hospital Supply in 1966. From 1966 forward, Owens, Minor & Bodeker would gradually become a different kind of company entirely.

Up until 1966, the company had always operated as a wholesale drug firm, devoting 84 years to the sale of pharmaceutical goods, but with the acquisition of A&J Hospital Supply, Owens, Minor & Bodeker Drug Co. entered the medical and surgical distribution business for the first time. The move into a new business area, a move spearheaded by George Gilmer Minor, Jr., began to steer the company in a new direction, one that would completely reshape the company and define its existence during the 1990s. From 1966 forward, all major acquisitions would add to the company's presence in the medical and surgical distribution field, not its storied wholesale drug business. Owens, Minor & Bodeker Drug Co. did not abandon the wholesale drug business by any means, but it would be another 18 years before the company acquired a company whose business was related to the wholesale drug business.

Further acquisitions in the medical and surgical distribution business followed the 1966 purchase of A&J Hospital Supply, as the company, with George Gilmer Minor, Jr., still leading the way, strove to expand its new business. In 1968, the company acquired the Richmond, Norfolk, and Washington, D.C., operations belonging to Powers & Anderson, Inc., then the following year purchased Powers & Anderson's operations in Charleston,

South Carolina. With the properties gained from this two-year buying spree, Owens, Minor & Bodeker gained strategically valuable product lines for the medical and surgical distribution market. Next, in 1970, the company acquired Augusta, Georgia-based Marks Surgical, another strategically important move that helped Owens, Minor & Bodeker eclipse $20 million in sales by the end of the year and widen its geographical scope to comprise a four-state territory.

### Growth in the 1970s

The company went public the following year, in 1971, offering stock for the first time on the over-the-counter exchange, then embarked on another acquisition spree, entrenching its position in the medical and surgical distribution market. In 1972 the company acquired Murray Drug, based in Norfolk, Virginia, then two years later purchased White Surgical of Knoxville. In 1976 the company increased its geographic territory, gaining four locations in Texas and Louisiana through the acquisition of Southern Hospital, and securing a foothold in Florida fours years later with the purchase of Jacksonville, Florida-based Medical Supply.

These acquisitions were completed during a decade that saw Owens, Minor & Bodeker Drug Co.'s sales volume increase sixfold and its geographic scope broaden considerably. The company entered the 1970s generating slightly more than $20 million a year, and exited the decade with annual sales exceeding $130 million. Geographically, the acquisitions completed by Owens, Minor & Bodeker helped extend its service territory from six to ten states during the 1970s, as year by year the magnitude of the company's medical and surgical distribution business grew.

Aside from exponential growth, the 1970s also marked the end of an era when George Gilmer Minor, Jr., ended his nearly 30-year presidency in 1976. George Gilmer Minor, Jr., who had been instrumental in the company's diversification into the medical and surgical distribution business, stayed on as chairman and chief executive officer after 1976, but from that year until 1981 another individual from outside the Minor family, William F. Fife, assumed the duties of president. When Fife, in turn, vacated the post of president in 1981, the next Minor in line, George Gilmer Minor, III, stepped in, beginning a term of office that would carry the company through the mid-1990s and would span the complete transformation his father had initiated in 1966.

George Gilmer Minor, III, fifth by generation and the fourth Minor to head the company, joined the family business at age 15, beginning his career as a schoolboy before assuming a more influential role in the company's operation after his graduation from Virginia Military Institute in 1963 and his graduation from the Colgate Darden School of Business Administration at the University of Virginia in 1966. Following his education, George Gilmer Minor, III, went on to become the division manager of the company's wholesale drug division and general manager of all three drug divisions. Continuing his rise through the company's ranks, George Gilmer Minor, III, eventually was named vice-president of operations for Owens, Minor & Bodeker, gaining more and more responsibility until he was ultimately selected as the company's president in 1981, a year

during which he had played a leading role in the company's acquisition of eight locations belonging to the Will Ross division of G.D. Searle, the second-largest distributor of medical and surgical supplies in the country.

In January 1982, at the beginning of the company's centennial year, a name change was effected and Owens, Minor & Bodeker Drug Co. became Owens & Minor, Inc. Acquisitions continued to drive the company's growth during the 1980s, including the purchase of Oklahoma City-based S&S Hospital Supply in 1983, a year in which medical and surgical supplies as a percentage of total sales doubled. Florida Hospital Supply was purchased the following year, representing the first wholesale drug acquisition in nearly two decades, but the most momentous development in 1984 occurred in Owens & Minor's other business segment. For the first time, medical and surgical sales eclipsed the total generated by the company's 102-year-old wholesale drug business, marking a milestone in Owens & Minor's history that foretold the direction the company was headed toward.

Sales reached $367 million in 1985, the year George Gilmer Minor, III, announced his ambitious goal of reaching $1 billion in sales by 1990. Toward this lofty goal, the company made an important step in 1985 when it signed a three-year contract with the Voluntary Hospitals of America, the largest nonprofit hospital system in the United States, which was renewed in 1988 in perpetuity. The company expanded beyond the Sunbelt in 1987 with the acquisition of Bridgeton, New Jersey-based Leon Stotter Company, then expanded westward in 1989 through the purchase of National Healthcare, which operated in California, Arizona, Texas, Oregon, Utah, and Colorado.

### 1992 Divestiture of Wholesale Drug Division

In 1990, the year George Gilmer Minor, III, had hoped to reach $1 billion in sales, Owens & Minor recorded $1.2 billion in sales, exceeding earlier expectations. Two years later, after 110 years in the business, Owens & Minor exited the drug wholesale trade, divesting nearly all the assets composing its drug wholesale division. From 1992 forward, Owens & Minor executives would focus exclusively on the business the previous generation had first entered in 1966, devoting their energies and resources toward positioning the company as one of the country's preeminent surgical and medical supply distributors. In 1994, two years after selling its drug wholesale business, Owens & Minor completed a gigantic leap toward becoming one of the country's elite medical and surgical supply competitors when the company acquired $890 million-in-sales Stuart Medical, Inc., the third largest distributor of medical and surgical supplies in the nation.

On the heels of this major acquisition, Owens & Minor recorded $2.4 billion in sales, then the following year, in 1995, generated $2.97 billion in sales, more than eight times the figure posted 10 years earlier. Owens & Minor was growing at a robust pace during the 1990s, and as management, with George Gilmer Minor, III, leading the way, looked toward the late 1990s and the beginning of the 21st century, further acquisitions in the medical and surgical supply field were expected. In the years ahead, Owens & Minor would build on the business established by George Gilmer Minor, Jr., the founder, and George Gilmer

Minor, Jr., who led the company into the medical and surgical supply business in 1966.

## Principal Subsidiaries

A. Kuhlman & Co.; Koley's Medical Supply, Inc.; Lyons Physician Supply Company; National Medical Supply Corporation; Owens & Minor Medical, Inc.; Owens & Minor West, Inc.; Stuart Medical, Inc.

## Further Reading

Campanella, Frank W., "Wholesale Health," *Barron's,* October 7, 1995, p. 57.

Gold, Jacqueline S., "Owens & Minor: No. 2 in Health—and Loving It," *Financial World,* May 11, 1993, p. 20.

Larson, Julie, "Distributor Buys Into Market for Columbia," *Denver Business Journal,* May 26, 1995, p. 3C.

Lee, Carrie, "Owens and Minor: Heal Thyself," *Financial World,* November 7, 1995, p. 18.

*Owens & Minor, Inc. 1882 and Beyond,* Glen Allen, Va.: Owens & Minor, Inc., 1992.

Rublin, Lauren R., "For Whom Old Age Is More Than a Consolation," *Barron's,* December 7, 1987, p. 70.

Stanley, Bonnie Newman, "Richmond-Based Owens & Minor Inc.," *Richmond Times-Dispatch,* May 1, 1996, p. 50.

—Jeffrey L. Covell

# Oxford Health Plans, Inc.

**800 Connecticut Avenue**
**Norwalk, Connecticut 06854**
**U.S.A.**
**(203) 852-1442**
**Fax: (203) 851-2464**

*Public Company*
*Incorporated:* 1984
*Employees:* 4,400
*Sales:* $1.77 billion (1995)
*Stock Exchanges:* NASDAQ
*SICs:* 6324 Hospital & Medical Service Plans; 6321
　　Accident & Health Insurance

Operating in five northeastern states, Oxford Health Plans, Inc. is a leading provider of health benefit plans. The company primarily offers health maintenance organization (HMO) plans, but also provides dental, Medicare, and Medicaid plans and related products and services. The company has grown rapidly since the mid-1980s by acquiring competitors and increasing enrollment in its cost-efficient health plans.

### The Company's Founder

Oxford Health Plans is primarily the creation of Stephen F. Wiggins, who founded the company in 1984. Wiggins was only 28 years old at the time, but had already gained valuable experience in the health care industry. A native of Minnesota, Wiggins had earned his bachelor's degree at Macalester College in St. Paul before tagging on a Harvard MBA. He started his career in 1976 with Health Central, Inc., a company that owned and operated several midwestern hospitals. After fewer than three years with Health Central, Wiggins followed his entrepreneurial calling and started his own company, Accessible Space, Inc. (ASI). ASI was a nonprofit health care organization that provided long-term care for handicapped and brain-injured people.

ASI would eventually grow to a leading midwestern provider of long-term care for the handicapped, with more than 15 facilities in five midwestern states by the mid-1990s. Although

Wiggins remained executive director of the company, he remained in day-to-day operating control of ASI just long enough to get it started. Within a few years, in fact, he was engrossed in other health care ventures. For example, he founded Grasslands Housing, Inc., Osborne Apartments, and St. Marys Senior Housing, Inc., which were all nonprofit health care organizations that owned and operated housing for handicapped and/or elderly residents. Also during the early and mid-1980s, Wiggins became involved in various health care investment ventures through two New York venture capital firms.

Wiggins' efforts during the early and mid-1980s exhibited his unbound optimism and empathy for health care consumers, as well as his forward-thinking, innovative nature—traits that would help to make Oxford Health Plans so successful. A major impetus for Wiggins to start ASI, for example, was his best friend in college, who had been paralyzed in a driving accident; observing the treatment his friend received, Wiggins found that existing care for handicapped people was of poor quality. Among other innovations, ASI's facilities were managed by the residents themselves, which helped them to regain their feeling of independence and worth. Another example of Wiggins' experimental spirit was Grasslands Housing, which was the largest earth-sheltered housing project in the United States when it was built.

Driving Wiggins' will to succeed in business was, in part, his experience with his family's business as a youth. While still in high school, Wiggins had helped to close down his family's struggling office supply store. He vowed to be a success after the humiliating experience. "I still remember hanging up the going-out-of-business sign," Wiggins said in the March 21, 1994 *Fortune*. It was that desire to succeed, combined with his interest and experience in the health care field, that led to the formation of Oxford Health Plans. Wiggins incorporated the company on September 17, 1984, and Oxford began operations late in 1986. In less than a decade, Oxford would be generating nearly $2 billion annually in revenues as a leading provider of health care in the northeastern United States.

### Company Origins in the 1980s

Wiggins teamed up to launch Oxford with Dr. Benjamin Safirstein. Their plan was to bring health maintenance organizations (HMOs) to New York. The HMO concept was becoming popular in the United States at the time as an affordable, efficient alternative to traditional health insurance and health care delivery plans. In short, HMO (or managed care) plans reduced health care costs by more closely managing each patient's care, rather than simply paying medical bills as do traditional insurance companies. Doctors joined the HMO to gain access to, among other benefits, a large base of clients, while patients joined the HMO plan to receive lower health insurance premiums. HMOs and similar managed care options first became widely popular during the 1980s, when health care costs were spiraling at double-digit rates.

Despite their success in other areas, HMOs had been slow to catch on in New York (particularly New York City), reportedly because residents in that state feared that managed care would diminish the overall quality of their health care. Recognizing the potential of the largely untapped New York market, Wiggins and Safirstein decided to implement an HMO plan that would appeal to the New York market. To that end, Wiggins worked to form an HMO that included high-quality doctors and leading hospitals. He also implemented a number of innovative cost-reduction and efficiency measures that helped to make the plan attractive to companies seeking lower health insurance rates for their workers. By 1987, its first full year of operation, Oxford generated premiums of about $5.6 million.

Oxford would sustain meteoric growth throughout the late 1980s as membership in its HMO plans spiraled. Importantly, Wiggins developed a number of key innovations that not only contributed to the success of Oxford, but influenced and changed the entire managed care industry. Most notable was an option that Wiggins dubbed the Freedom Plan. The Freedom Plan overcame the common objection to HMOs that members were limited to using only the doctors who belonged to the HMO network. Through the Freedom Plan, Oxford allowed members to use their own doctors outside of the HMO network in exchange for higher deductibles and copayments. The innovation was a major hit and allowed Oxford to quickly overcome its competitors in the New York market and to sign up some high-profile accounts that would have otherwise never joined an HMO.

Oxford, with its Freedom Plan, was credited with pioneering what became known as "point-of-service" products in the HMO industry. The invention allowed tiny Oxford to compete with such deep-pocketed players in the insurance industry as Prudential and Aetna. Indeed, Oxford's revenues rose to $25 million in 1988, $45 million in 1989, and then to $61.4 million in 1990, when it showed its first profit. In 1990, in fact, Oxford was the second most profitable HMO in New York. During the year, the company's HMO membership climbed more than 80

percent in New York City and about 17 percent in the metropolitan area for a total subscriber base of nearly 65,000. Wiggins boldly predicted that Oxford would have 500,000 members by 1995.

As surprising as Oxford's success during the late 1980s was the fact that it had even survived as an independent company. Throughout the late 1980s and into the early 1990s, many of Oxford's startup HMO peers had been acquired by big insurance companies looking for a route into the growing managed care business. Oxford shunned takeover attempts, however, and was able to establish a presence. The company raised $11.2 million through a private stock placement in 1988 and used the money to beef up its sales force, to increase advertising and promotions, and to scout for some acquisitions of its own to bolster its product offerings. Meanwhile, Wiggins continued to try to innovate and stay ahead of the competition. "The reason I'm still alive is because I change with the marketplace, and we give the most innovative products," Wiggins said in the October 1, 1990 *Crain's New York Business.*

Among Oxford's innovations were new ways to deliver cost-effective care to patients with asthma and other chronic conditions. In addition to those improvements, the company developed a reputation as a provider of high-quality care and good customer service. "More than health care. HumanCare," became the company's slogan. In fact, Oxford was ranked tops in customer satisfaction surveys of HMO members and was also regarded by many health care organizations as one of the easier health plans with which to work. Its reputation helped it to enroll impressive clients such as the respected Fried Frank Harris law firm and the venerable Columbia-Presbyterian Medical Center. The company's membership ranks rapidly swelled past 100,000 in the early 1990s and then toward the half-million mark.

### Continued Growth and Some Challenges in the 1990s

Many critics doubted Oxford's ability to profit and sustain growth in the early 1990s. By then, managed care had become an accepted means of insurance, and other managed care providers had implemented their own point-of-service options. Furthermore, Oxford was still operating at a distinct disadvantage to well-heeled companies that had huge war chests of capital to dump into aggressive HMO sales and marketing programs. Nevertheless, Oxford managed to rapidly grow its membership base, sales, and profits, and boasted the fastest growing stock price in the entire U.S. managed care industry between 1990 and 1995. Wiggins' greatest problem, in fact, became keeping up with a growth rate of more than 50 percent annually.

Wiggins' concern about keeping up with growth intensified going into the mid-1990s. After jumping from $95 to $156 million between 1991 and 1992, Oxford's sales more than doubled in 1993 to $311 million. Revenues more than doubled again in 1994, moreover, to $721 million. Net income rose during the same period from about $3.6 million (1991) to nearly $28 million. By early 1994 Oxford was boasting a roster of about 250,000 members. That number increased rapidly during 1994 and 1995, as Oxford acquired other companies and added members to existing plans. Furthermore, Oxford was offering other plans and services including Medicare and Medicaid plans, and an administration services division that helped other companies manage their plans. By late 1995, Oxford was serving a base of about one million customers and annualized sales had surpassed $1 billion.

Oxford's rampant gains came at a price. With the sudden surge in members, the company's infrastructure became overburdened. Some of its computer systems, for example, became bogged down by overuse. "You'd press a button and wait 20 seconds for it to respond," said Robert M. Smoler, Oxford executive vice-president, in the August 28, 1995 *Crain's New York Business*. "You can't process a claim like that," he observed. The growth also put a strain on employee morale. The overall result was a perceived decline in quality of service, high standards for which had been Oxford's hallmark for nearly a decade. Some critics and customers feared that Oxford was finally delivering the inadequate service that had kept New Yorkers away from managed care for so long. "Customers saw the highest-level service in the industry slip off," Smoler explained, adding "a lot depends on how quickly we recover."

Much of Oxford's growth in 1995 was attributable to its purchase of OakTree Health Plan Inc., a Pennsylvania managed-care provider. That important buyout extended its reach to Pennsylvania and bolstered its presence in what had by 1996 become a five-state region including New York, New Jersey, Connecticut, New Hampshire, and Pennsylvania. During 1995, Oxford added about 25,000 physicians and about 200 hospitals to its network to serve a clientele of more than one million, or nearly double the members that Wiggins had predicted in 1990 that the company would have by 1995. Sales for the year grew to nearly $1.8 billion. Meanwhile, Oxford continued to scramble to absorb the additions, control growth, and maintain its service level.

For the mid- and late 1990s, Wiggins and fellow managers were focusing on whipping Oxford's operations into shape as part of an effort to minimize costs, improve service, and continue positioning Oxford for future changes in the marketplace. They were also working to sustain rapid growth as part of their plan to become a dominant provider of managed care and related products and services in the Northeast United States.

## Principal Subsidiaries

Oxford Health Plans (NY), Inc.; Oxford Health Plans (NJ), Inc.; Oxford Health Plans (CT), Inc.; Oxford Health Plans (NH), Inc.; Oxford Health Plans (PA), Inc.; Oxford Health Insurance, Inc.

## Further Reading

Agovino, Theresa, "Innovative Oxford Finds HMO Cure," *Crain's New York Business,* October 1, 1990, p. 3.

Benson, Barbara, "Growth Causes Pain for the Industry Star," *Crain's New York Business,* August 28, 1995, p. 19.

Dentzer, Susan, "Inside the World of Managed Care," *U.S. News & World Report,* April 15, 1996, p. 56.

Dumaine, Brian, "America's Smart Young Entrepreneurs," *Fortune,* March 21, 1994, p. 34(9).

Fleischer, Jo, "Oxford Needs More Room As Torrid Growth Continues," *Fairfield County Business Journal,* March 3, 1996, p. 1.

Hollreiser, Eric, "New CEO a Foot Soldier for Oxford Health Plans," *Philadelphia Business Journal,* February 23, 1996.

Kenkel, Paul J., "Stephen F. Wiggins, 36," *Modern Healthcare,* October 26, 1992, p. 48.

"Oxford Health Inc. Tabs New President," *Fairfield County Business Journal,* May 25, 1992, p. 17.

"Oxford Health Plans, Inc.," *The Wall Street Transcript,* December 19, 1994, pp. 116,865–952.

Wiggins, Stephen F., "New Ways to Create Lifetime Bonds with Your Customers," *Fortune,* August 21, 1995.

—Dave Mote

# Parametric Technology Corp.

128 Technology Drive
Waltham, Massachusetts
U.S.A.
(617) 894-7111
Fax: (617) 891-1069

*Public Company*
*Incorporated:* 1985
*Employees:* 2,200
*Sales:* $394.3 million (1995)
*Stock Exchanges:* NASDAQ
*SICs:* 7372 Prepackaged Software

Less than ten years after introducing its first products, Parametric Technology Corp. had established itself as a leader in the computer-aided design (CAD), computer-aided manufacturing (CAM), and computer-aided engineering software markets. Incorporated in 1985, Parametric Technology Corp. developed and started selling software that engineers use to design products ranging from tires and toys to engines and buildings in 1988. The company has profited by developing high-performance software that, among other benefits, reduces the amount of time necessary to take a product from the conceptual stage to manufacturing.

## Coming to America

Parametric's swift success was largely attributable to the efforts of Russian immigrant and mathematics genius Samuel P. Geisberg. Geisberg, a math professor in Leningrad, fled the Soviet Union and moved to the United States in 1974. He took his 11-year-old son with him, but was forced to leave his wife, Mira, and their six-year-old daughter behind; Soviet officials refused to allow Mira to leave until the late 1970s because she had worked as an electrical engineer on several defense-related projects. Despite his lack of familiarity with American culture, Geisberg's sheer intellect allowed him to quickly find work as a software designer. Indeed, Geisberg soon became recognized as a mathematics and software prodigy.

Geisberg worked for software-design firms Applicon and Computervision during the late 1970s and early 1980s. His stint at Computervision briefly overlapped with that of his brother, Vladimir, who had emigrated from the Soviet Union in 1980. Vladimir would also go on to start his own software firm, and would be a major impetus for the creation of Parametric Technology. In fact, it was Vladimir who suggested that Samuel speak with an attorney named Noel Posternak about setting up and financing his own company. Samuel had spent nearly ten years designing computer-aided design and computer-aided manufacturing (CAD-CAM) software, and he was ready to start developing and selling some of his own ideas.

Posternak helped Geisberg round up about $150,000 in seed money, which he used to develop a prototype of his own CAD-CAM software package. Geisberg, suspicious that Posternak might be trying to take advantage of him, would accept only $125,000 of the $150,000 that was offered. He asked Posternak to contribute the other $25,000 out of his own pocket. "I think he wanted 150 percent effort from me," Posternak recalled in the August 29, 1993 *Boston Globe*. "I think that having come from Russia, Sam wasn't sure who his friends were and who his allies were . . . he felt that if I had some money up, I would fight even harder for him."

## The Startup

Geisberg incorporated his company as Parametric Technology Corporation in May of 1985. He spent the first few years developing a new CAD-CAM program, and then looking for venture capital to help market and distribute his software. Geisberg—short, rumpled, demanding, and with a thick Russian accent—was turned down by a number of venture capital firms. He was finally able to get Charles River Ventures and two other venture capital companies, along with some individual investors, to provide a total of $4 million to launch his new CAD-CAM product. Parametric had burned through more than $2 million by 1988, when the company began selling its first products.

Parametric was jumping into the CAD-CAM industry relatively late in the game. CAD-CAM technology had been introduced in the late 1960s, and by the 1980s the industry was dominated by a handful of players. In essence, CAD-CAM software allowed engineers to create three-dimensional, to-scale computer models of almost anything ranging from bolts and carburetors to golf clubs and truck tires. By the 1980s the technology had advanced to the point at which it offered important advantages over traditional paper-and-pencil design techniques. For example, engineers could transpose imaginary layers over a computer drawing, thus allowing them to make additions or deletions to a design. The technology could view three-dimensional drawings from different angles by rotating them.

Geisberg's software brought an important innovation to the CAD-CAM world that even his competitors conceded was revolutionary. His software could recognize a change in a single variable of a design and adjust the rest of the model accordingly. For example, a person designing a plane could change the length of the wings, and Geisberg's CAD-CAM software would indicate what implications that change would have on the rest of the plane. The innovation sped up the design process and made it much easier for engineers to experiment with new ideas. Parametric's breakthrough software, dubbed Pro/Engineer, was quickly accepted by the marketplace. Sales topped $3 million in 1988 before rising to $11 million in 1989. Parametric became profitable in 1989 with a net income of more than $1.5 million.

### The Late 1980s and Early 1990s

Parametric spent the late 1980s and early 1990s parlaying its cutting edge mechanical design software into commercial success. The company went public with a stock offering in 1989 to raise expansion capital. With the extra capital, Geisberg increased Parametric's offerings to include a number of different versions of the Pro/Engineer software developed to operate on various operating systems and to complement different technical applications. Many engineers quickly recognized the software's advantages and purchased it. By the early 1990s Parametric was controlling about ten percent of the entire CAD-CAM market and was aggressively boosting that share every quarter. By 1991, in fact, Parametric was generating $45 million in sales and netting more than $10 million in annual income.

Parametric's success surprised many observers who had previously believed that the CAD-CAM industry was mature and offered little growth potential. By the time Parametric came along, big companies like IBM and EDS were entrenched in the niche, which amounted to roughly $1 billion each year in total sales. Seeing little opportunity for expansion, those companies had produced few new major products in a number of years. And few doubted the viability of a new startup in the industry. But Parametric's Pro/Engineer system destroyed the old paradigm. Besides breaking into the industry and stealing customers from established competitors, Parametric was able to broaden the reach of the industry by appealing to electrical engineers, a group that had not used much CAD-CAM technology in the past.

As important as Parametric's technology to its success during the late 1980s and early 1990s was its stellar marketing and sales team. Indeed, Parametric became known within the indus-

try as much for its aggressive sales strategy as its Pro/Engineer software. The sales effort was directed by Steven C. Walske, the man who would eventually head the entire company. Walske had been coupled with Geisberg early in the startup by Charles River Ventures. The pair was a good match. Geisberg was happy to spearhead technical advances, but, largely because of his accent, was publicity shy and disliked the limelight. The gregarious Walske, on the other hand, was happy to assume a high profile.

A 1978 Harvard Business School graduate, Walske joined Parametric at 35 years old. He quickly assembled a crack marketing and sales team at the company, and, with the help of Dick Harrison, managed to whip them into a fervor. Its enthusiastic sales force earned the company a reputation as the "Mary Kay of the CAD-CAM industry." But Parametric's sales force also managed to ruffle the feathers of some of its potential customers. The company was known, for example, for going behind some of its prospects' backs and trying to get their superiors to pressure them into buying Parametric software. Walske made no apologies for his aggressive tactics, believing that his sales force's siege mentality was necessary to overcome entrenched, status-quo competitors like IBM and Computervision.

Its advanced software and assertive sales initiative allowed Parametric to land major manufacturing clients like Ford Motor Company and Caterpillar Inc. Just as important, the company was able to secure a very high portion of new entrants into the CAD-CAM market, because those buyers were not already accustomed to using a specific software system. By 1993 Parametric's share of the CAD-CAM market was approaching 20 percent. As sales flourished, so did Parametric's operations. By 1992 the company employed a work force of 300. But that number rose to more than 800 by the end of 1993. Likewise, annual revenues doubled in both 1992 and 1993, rising to $163 million. Net income for 1993 hit $43 million, securing Parametric's claim to one of the highest profit margins in the industry.

Parametric's success during the early 1990s and going into the mid-1990s continued to be based on its core Pro/Engineer CAD-CAM software systems. The packages sold for between $1,500 and $9,500 each, but were often sold in sets of six to eight for workstations at a price of roughly $18,000. Relying on the innovative software, Parametric was able to place among the top five in the *Boston Globe* 100 survey of best-performing public companies in Massachusetts for five straight years between 1989 and 1993. By 1994, moreover, Parametric was the second-largest seller of CAD-CAM software in the world, trailing only IBM.

Geisberg moved aside during the early 1990s and let Walske and other executives assume more control of Parametric. He finally cashed out in 1992, taking a payout of $13.7 million in cash and stocks with him. Although he continued to be involved with Parametric's research and development arm, he left his management posts to devote more time to his Geisberg Foundation, which was dedicated to the research of diabetes and arthritis. Walske became chairman and chief executive, and Harrison moved to the president and chief operating officer slots in 1994; Harrison had helped direct Parametric's sales and marketing arm since 1987.

### The Mid-1990s and Beyond

Although it continued to be the technological leader, by the mid-1990s Parametric was facing greater competition from companies that were beginning to offer similar features in their CAD-CAM packages. In an effort to bolster its product offerings and exploit the respected Parametric name, the company began looking for new avenues for growth. To that end, Parametric purchased Conceptual Design and Rendering System's software business in April of 1995. The acquisition brought new industrial design and visualization software products and technology to Parametric, thus bolstering its ability to appeal to conceptual designers who used free-form shapes.

Shortly after that purchase, Parametric paid about $180 million for Rasna Corp. software, which had a breakthrough innovation that allowed mechanical engineers and analysts to simulate the real-life operation of products. Although several companies had developed similar technology, Rasna was among the leaders in that burgeoning market. The purchase was a welcome boost to Parametric's older Pro/Engineer line of software. The new line of products were called Pro/Mechanica. Parametric integrated some of its proprietary technology used in the Pro/Engineer software to significantly speed up and improve the Pro/Mechanica line. It then introduced the Pro/Mechanica products with its proven sales and distribution mechanism.

The Rasna buyout helped Parametric to increase sales from $244 million in 1994 to $394 million in 1995, while net income moved toward the $100-million mark. Going into 1996, Parametric was the leading global supplier of CAD/CAM/CAE software. It employed a work force of 2,200 people in 140 offices in 26 countries in North America, Europe, and the Far East, and its customer base had swelled to about 9,000 companies. For the mid-1990s, Parametric planned to focus on international growth and the development of new products.

### Principal Subsidiaries

PTC International, Inc.; PT Technology Scandinavia AB.

### Further Reading

Crosariol, Beppi, ''Parametric, California Firm in $180M Deal,'' *Boston Globe,* May 31, 1995, p. 39.

Hudson, John W., ''Parametric Technology Corp. Ships Pro/Mechanica Release 8.0,'' *Business Wire,* October 4, 1995.

Knell, Michael E., ''Parametric Technology to Purchase Software Company,'' *Boston Herald,* May 31, 1995, p. 33BUS.

Krassner, Jeffrey, ''Customers Find Parametric Hard to Ignore,'' *Boston Herald,* January 25, 1994, BUS.

McCright, John S., ''Parametric Boom Shows No Signs of Slowing Down,'' *Boston Globe,* p. 5.

Pham, Alex, ''Overall Performance—The Globe 100: Parametric Technology Corp.,'' *Boston Globe,* May 17, 1994, Section 1, p. 34.

''Software Company Growth Continues,'' *Boston Herald,* May 10, 1993, BUS.

Upendra, Misra, ''Parametric Seeks More Space,'' *Boston Business Journal,* July 14, 1995, p. 5.

Volpe, Louis J., ''Parametric Technology Corp. Announces Promotions, New Responsibilities for Members of Its Senior Management,'' *Business Wire,* August 19, 1994.

Zitner, Aaron, ''Parametric Progression: Parametric Technology Has a Reclusive Russian Founder the State's Highest-Paid CEO, and a Stock Price That's Gone Through the Roof,'' *Boston Globe,* August 29, 1993, p. 75.

——, ''Seventh Annual Globe 100—The Best of Massachusetts,'' *Boston Globe,* May 23, 1995, p. 34.

—Dave Mote

# Peavey Electronics Corporation

P.O. Box 2898
Meridian, Mississippi 39302-2898
U.S.A.
(601) 483-5365
Fax: (601) 486-1278

*Private Company*
*Incorporated:* 1965
*Employees:* 2,200
*Sales:* $210 million (1993)
*SICs:* 3651 Household Audio & Video Equipment

The Peavey Electronics Corporation, founded in 1965 by Hartley Peavey, is a major manufacturer of guitars, amplifiers, speakers, electronic keyboards, and other electronic audio-enhancement equipment. In 1993, the company, solely owned by Hartley, then chairman, and Melia Peavey, his wife and president of the company, had sales estimated at $210 million. Exports to more than a hundred countries accounted for an estimated 40 percent of sales. Peavey Electronics, with more than 1,600 different products, is also the tenth largest manufacturer in Mississippi, with more than a million square feet of warehouse and manufacturing space in east-central Mississippi, including a 40-acre headquarters site known as Peavey City in Meridian. The company also has manufacturing operations in Foley, Alabama, and in Corby, England, and distribution centers in The Netherlands and Canada. Its chief competitor is Yamaha, the Japanese conglomerate. Founder Hartley Peavey, whose "hometown boy makes good" story made him a local legend in Mississippi, has been the recipient of numerous awards for entrepreneurship, including the "E Star" award for success in international markets from the U.S. Department of Commerce. He was also inducted into Hollywood's "Rock Walk of Fame" in 1990 for his contributions to rock 'n' roll music.

### Musical Ambitions in the 1950s

Hartley Peavey grew up in Meridian, Mississippi, and had early aspirations of becoming a rock 'n' roll guitar player. As a teenager in the late 1950s, he worked in the Peavey Melody Music Store, owned by his father, J.B. "Mutt" Peavey, and tinkered with building amplifiers for local musicians. When, as he once confessed to *Inc.* magazine, he turned out to be a "pretty lousy guitarist," Peavey decided his future was in making amplifiers.

In 1965, after graduating from Mississippi State University with a degree in marketing and management, Peavey, then 23, took the remaining $8,000 in his college fund and formed Peavey Electronics, working out of his parents' basement. As he later recalled in "Music and Sound's Greatest Hit," published by Peavey Electronics for its 25th anniversary: "I would build one (amplifier) a week, go out and sell it, come back and start on another one." The amplifiers were inscribed with the lightning bolt logo that Peavey had designed as a college freshman.

A year later, Peavey moved the business from the family's basement to an attic in the building that had housed his father's music store. By then, his father had sold the music store but still owned the building. Peavey also hired his first employee, a salesman, so he could concentrate on building amplifiers.

In the mid-1960s, however, there were many larger, better-known companies making amplifiers, and Peavey soon expanded into building public address systems to keep his young business afloat. In the company's 25th anniversary retrospective, Peavey explained that as "I traveled and talked to music dealers, I realized there was no shortage of instrument amplifiers. But if you wanted a PA system there were essentially only two available and both were expensive systems. . . . Most folks think I got into the music business with guitar amps. Not necessarily so!"

### Staying in Meridian

By 1968, business was good enough that Peavey decided to borrow $17,500 to build a small "factory" in Meridian. Over the next five years, Peavey Electronics enlarged the building seven times, and having grown to more than 150 employees, in 1973 the company began construction on Plant #3, which would become its main manufacturing facility. To hire enough skilled employees, Peavey Electronics established training courses at Meridian Community College.

Over the years, Peavey was often asked about his decision to keep the company in Meridian. In 1985, he told *Inc.* that Mississippi "unfortunately runs dead last in everything. You don't have the skilled people you need, you don't have the suppliers, you don't have the access to the freight network. . . . Back in 1965, when I got into this, I was too damn dumb to know it couldn't be done." He went on to say that he had "lost count" of how often he wished he had built Peavey Electronics somewhere else. In a later interview with his hometown newspaper, *The Meridian Star,* Peavey explained, "What I tried to say in the *Inc.* article was that Mississippi presented many difficulties in starting a high-tech business. And some of these difficulties exist to this day." In 1982, the City of Meridian honored its hometown industrialist by proclaiming April 21 as Hartley Peavey Day.

In the late 1980s, when the company was considering building its first U.S. manufacturing facility outside of Mississippi, then-Governor Ray Mabus worked with Peavey Electronics and Meridian Community College to create The Meridian Partnership, the first private-sector use of the Job Skills Education Program, a technology and basic-skills program originally developed by the U.S. Army. In the early 1990s, Peavey Electronics opened a 58,000-square-foot training center, complete with its own recording studio, for its employees and more than 1,200 dealers. In 1993, Peavey told *The News* in Boca Raton, Florida, where he and his wife had a second home, "People ask me why Mississippi and I say, "Where do you think rock 'n' roll was born?""

### Vertical Integration in the 1970s

It was in the early 1970s that the company began the vertical integration that would make it unique among major electronic musical equipment manufacturers. Unable to purchase reliable speaker components for its high-power amplifiers, Peavey Electronics began making its own loudspeakers. Eventually, Peavey Electronics would build everything it needed for its musical instruments, from cabinets and metal work down to making its own circuit boards and running its own advertising agency.

In 1990, Peavey explained, "If somebody local had been able to subcontract for me the things I needed to build amplifiers, I would probably still be using subcontractors. We had to learn to make our own chassis, our own circuit boards, and eventually everything 'in-house.' And while we thought it was a tremendous disadvantage, and in many ways it was, we discovered that it was the best thing that could have happened."

In the mid-1970s, Peavey Electronics also began manufacturing electric guitars, again more from necessity than design. Several leading electronic instrument companies were gobbled up by conglomerates during the 1960s, including Fender Musical Instruments, which was purchased by CBS in 1964. These companies, with their immense marketing power, began encouraging dealers to sell their guitars and amplifiers as a package deal, cutting into sales of Peavey amps.

As he had when he adopted solid-state components for his first amplifiers, Peavey embraced state-of-the-art technology to produce guitars at lower cost, becoming the first manufacturer to use computer-controlled machinery to turn out guitar bodies and precision parts. Years later, Peavey recalled, "When we announced that we were making guitar bodies on computer-controlled machinery, some of the most prominent names in the industry said, 'Impossible. Everybody knows you can't make guitars with a computer.' That was a rather simplistic attitude, we thought, because, in fact, we weren't making guitars on computers. We were using . . . computer-controlled machines to make precision guitar parts to tolerances that heretofore manufacturers couldn't even think about approaching. Guitar makers are always talking about handcraftsmanship. What handcraftsmanship is, in many instances, is the ability to fit together parts that are produced with a lot of 'slop' in them."

In the early 1990s, Peavey Electronics would establish a Computer-Integrated Manufacturing (CIM) system to link and track all aspects of its manufacturing, and increasingly the company was using robotics in its assembly processes. The company, however, had an unofficial no-layoffs policy and employees whose jobs were eliminated by technology were retrained for other positions. In 1994, Jere Hess, then director of public relations, told *The Meridian Star,* "No one in this company has ever lost their job because of automation."

### Twenty-Fifth Anniversary

When Peavey Electronics celebrated its 25th anniversary in 1990, *The Meridian Star* published a 40-page special edition to honor the company that had become the area's largest employer. The newspaper noted that Peavey Electronics created more than 1,000 new jobs in east-central Mississippi between 1980 and 1989, including more than 850 in the Meridian area, and 73 percent of all new manufacturing jobs in Lauderdale County. Among those saluting the company was Mayor Jimmy Kemp, who said, "Of course the obvious things you think about when somebody in your community employs 1,850 people is the enormous impact it has on your city, which is fantastic. I'd hate to think what we'd do without Peavey Electronics as far as our city is concerned." Peavey Electronics was then the tenth largest manufacturing employer in the state.

In 1991, Peavey Electronics was one of 20 companies selected by the U.S. Department of Commerce to participate in a five-year program designed to stimulate export of U.S. products to Japan. As part of the program, the Department of Commerce arranged meetings between heads of the U.S. companies and Japanese officials, including Prime Minister Toshiki Kaifu and Minister of International Trade and Industry Eiichi Nakao. Peavey Electronics, which first entered the Japanese market in the mid-1970s in a short-lived relationship with industrial giant

Yamaha Corporation, also agreed to participate in at least one trade show a year in Japan. Although the company contracted with other distributor, Japan was never a significant market.

In 1991, President George Bush chose Peavey Electronics as the site to give a speech on economic growth. *The Meridian Star* noted, "Hoping to pump fresh air into his sagging popularity, President Bush hailed the success of Meridian's Peavey Electronics Co. as proof that Americans can excel in a worldwide economic battle." The newspaper also quoted Peavey as stating that the company's "one real goal, perhaps unreachable, is to become a $1 billion company." At the time, Peavey Electronics was reported in the local media to have sales approaching $500 million a year, although company executives said that figure was greatly exaggerated. As a matter of policy, the privately held company did not release financial information, but annual sales in the mid-1990s were generally believed to be about $200 million to $220 million.

### *Principal Subsidiaries*

Peavey Amplification Ltd. (U.K.).

### *Further Reading*

Armbruster, William, "US Guitar Maker Hopes For Big Hit in Japan," *The Journal of Commerce and Commercial,* June 3, 1991, p. 1.
Hallam, Linda, "Building Business on Caring," *Southern Living,* July 1991, pp. 67–68.
Moulden, Philip, "Bush, Peavey Harmonize on Economy," *The Meridian (Miss.) Star,* December 4, 1991, p. 1.
"Music and Sound's Greatest Hit," Meridian, Miss.: Peavey Electronics Corporation, 1990.
"Peavey 25th Anniversary Souvenir Edition," *The Meridian (Miss.) Star,* June 14, 1990.
Rodgers, Johna, "President's Visit Amplifies Peavey's Success," *The Meridian (Miss.) Star,* December 4, 1991, p. 5A.
Sheffield, Skip, "Chilling Out in Boca," *The Boca Raton (Fla.) News,* April 4, 1993., p. E1.
Slaughter, Jeff, "Peavey Electronics: 'Tenacious, Innovative, Responsive'," *Mississippi Business Journal,* August 1, 1994, p. 24.
Torgerson, Stan, "Peavey Grows with Automation," *The Meridian (Miss.) Star,* August 7, 1994, p. B1.
Wojahn, Ellen, "Homegrown: Peavey Electronics Does it All—Better and Cheaper—in Meridian, Miss.," *Inc.,* May 1985, p. 136.

—Dean Boyer

# Peebles Inc.

1 Peebles Street
South Hill, Virginia 23970-5001
U.S.A.
(804) 447-5200
Fax: (804) 447-5302

*Private Company*
*Incorporated:* 1891
*Employees:* 2,213
*Sales:* $176 million (1995)
*SICs:* 5311 Department Stores; 6719 Holding Companies, Not Elsewhere Classified

With 65 stores in ten Mid-Atlantic states ranging from South Carolina to New York, Peebles Inc. is one of the oldest and most successful department store chains in the United States. The company specializes in brand-name and private-label family clothing and home furnishings, but aims to offer its customers a broad array of merchandise priced for average shoppers—the "Ford and Chevrolet" customers, in the words of William S. Peebles, Jr., who served as the firm's vice-president from 1931 to 1973. Indeed, Peebles has carved a distinct market niche that caters to middle-income Americans in small- to mid-sized markets located in underserved rural areas and on the distant outskirts of growing metropolitan areas.

Throughout most of its history, Peebles has been a closely associated group of individually managed stores owned and operated by Peebles family members and their friends. "Most of the business," wrote Peebles historian Howard E. Covington, Jr., "was tied up in W. S. Peebles & Co., but all the stores were part of a corporate network [that ultimately consisted of] nearly twenty privately held corporations." By the late 1980s, however, that ceased to be the case. Two leveraged buyouts by Wall Street investors that decade shook up the company's management structure and culminated in a corporate restructuring of the firm to Peebles Inc. in 1992. The company is still privately held, but increasingly has taken on the characteristics of a public concern, disclosing, for example, financial information that had previously gone unreported.

Although disruptive and troubling, especially to a company with more than 100 years' history behind it, these management shake-ups proved remarkably successful, as they established a sound basis for rapid, long-term growth. The number of stores in operation increased by a net 30 percent from 1990 to 1995, while total sales during that same time period increased by more than 26 percent, from $138.7 million in 1990 to $176 million in 1995. By the mid-1990s Peebles ranked as one of the most profitable retailers in the country, even outperforming retail giant Wal-Mart in gross operating margin.

### Local Beginnings, 1890s

Peebles Inc. dates its origins to the establishment of the Peebles and Green clothing store in rural Lawrenceville, Virginia, in 1891. Named after its two founders, William S. Peebles and Arthur S. Green, the store was renamed the Peebles and Purdy Co. in 1907 when Green decided to leave the clothing business to become a food retailer. Peebles took on another business partner, Leonard Purdy, and together the two headed up what Covington described as "one of the major mercantile businesses in Lawrenceville, [then] a thriving county seat community with a population of 2,000."

As the town and surrounding Brunswick County grew, so did Peebles's ambition, and he invested $26,000 of his own money in a new retail business, W. S. Peebles & Company. His cousin, W. B. Mitchell, joined him with a $6,000 investment, signing on as vice-president of the firm. Peebles's four sons also were brought on board, as stockholders and, later, as company officers and executives.

The year was 1923. Four years later, Peebles open a second department store in South Hill, Virginia. In 1929 a third store, in Emporia, Virginia, was added. "By 1930," wrote Covington, "Peebles enterprises were among Lawrenceville's brightest success stories."

Like many companies, the firm suffered during the Great Depression, with retail sales in 1930 dropping to 40 percent of what they had been the year before. During this period William S. Peebles died. His eldest son, John Isler Peebles, became company president, only to pass away himself six months later.

### The Next Generation of Leadership, 1930s

Peebles's other sons stepped into the breach, assuming leadership of the company with dedication and commitment. Wesley became president and treasurer, William vice-president, and Marion secretary. Under their leadership, Peebles soon recovered from its difficulties. In 1934 stockholders began to receive a dividend on their investment, and bonuses were given out to employees. In 1935 a fourth store was opened (in Clarksville, Virginia), and, two years later, two additional stores in southeast Virginia were opened, making Peebles the largest retail merchandiser in the Lawrenceville area.

During the next 40 years Peebles expanded steadily throughout the region, adding stores in North Carolina (1938), South Carolina (1950), Delaware (1960), and Maryland (1967). In 1943 it entered into a partnership with businessman E. B. Kimbrell and opened a Peebles-Kimbrell department store in Forest City, North Carolina, which was the first of three highly successful joint ventures between the two companies. Twenty years later there were 26 Peebles or Peebles-Kimbrell stores in four states.

Throughout this period, Peebles distinguished itself from rival competitors in a number of ways. First, it sought to sidestep competition by locating in small communities of between 10,000 and 30,000 households—places typically not served by such larger department store chains as Sears, Macy's, Levitz, and Kmart. In this way, Peebles usually was able to establish itself as a community's dominant retail department store.

Second, individual store managers were given broad latitude to run their stores as they saw fit, with little or no interference from centralized management—provided, that is, they were profitable, which most were. Merchandising, staffing, training, expansion, customer credit, salaries, and compensation were the responsibility of the individual store managers. This system allowed the stores the flexibility they needed to succeed in distinct and competitive markets.

### Postwar Changes

In the aftermath of World War II, however, as the U.S. economy witnessed unprecedented growth and prosperity, the old ways of doing business no longer proved adequate, and American business became more centralized and hierarchical. Peebles began to make significant changes, sometimes in anticipation of its need to do so, and other times in response to sudden and painful realities.

For example, in 1952 Peebles began coordinating bulk purchases for the firm's growing number of stores. At the same time, Peebles began promoting itself and its products via direct mail marketing, which was then a novel business practice. In 1956, in Lawrenceville, Virginia, it opened its first "supermarket," also a novel move for the time. In 1958 the company took another dramatic step forward when it opened its first store in a

major metropolitan area, in Manassas, Virginia, on the outskirts of suburban Washington, D.C.

The move marked a significant change with past company policy, which had been to open stores in the central business districts of rural America. Such a policy became increasingly difficult to maintain, however, as economic growth bypassed these areas and became concentrated instead in the suburbs surrounding major American cities.

Although the Manassas store quickly became profitable, Peebles did not take immediate steps to build on its success. As late as 1968, in fact, two-thirds of its business still took place in the company's traditional small-town department stores. Peebles was changing, but not fast enough, it seemed, to keep pace with the times. Indeed, many of its stores in older and more rural towns were losing money or barely breaking even. And newer stores in metropolitan Washington, D.C., were too few in number for the company to take full advantage of their profitability.

### Leveraged Buyout, 1960s

Leadership of the company was split, moreover, between the older generation of Peebles, who sought to stay the course, and the younger generation of Peebles, who were pushing for more rapid change. Wesley Peebles, Jr., son of the president and company secretary, was the main catalyst pushing for change, and in December 1968 he finally won out, as Peebles began merger discussions with a New York investment banking firm. Peebles eventually reached an agreement with another firm, and Wesley and his cousins agreed to divide the company.

As a result, Peebles's books were opened up to outside analysis for the first time ever, and the firm was found to be worth close to $3.7 million. After a leveraged buyout was executed, Wesley, Jr., left the day-to-day operations of Peebles, and his cousin Bill (William Peebles, III) became defacto chief executive officer (the first in the history of the firm).

Despite its financial strength, Peebles was facing significant challenges. The rise of suburban shopping malls or strip centers and heightened competition from discount retailers like Kmart, Grant's, and Roses were rendering many of its traditional stores obsolete and unprofitable, while the average lead time on a new store was two years. Management turnover was a growing problem, and it was becoming increasingly difficult to find young managers to replace those who were departing.

Progress was slow but steady. In 1972 Peebles began using computers to record, track, monitor, and centralize its system of charge accounts, which previously had been done by individual store managers in hand-written entries. Not long thereafter Peebles moved to a centralized buying and distribution system, which also was made possible through computerization. Still, it was not until 1985 that the firm completed its transition to centralized buying, and not until 1988 that all in-house credit operations were done electronically.

In October 1972, Peebles opened a second 30,000-square-foot store, in Waldorf, Maryland, a southeastern suburb of Washington, D.C. A year later, William S. Peebles, III, formally replaced his uncle, Wesley S. Peebles, as president. In September 1978, Peebles held its first annual management meeting, and, one month later, the company completed its purchase of eight Southern Department Stores, an established department store chain in Virginia specializing in cosmetics, the purchase of which proved immensely profitable. The company now had 37 stores in four states.

### Continued Growth and Modernization, 1980s and 1990s

Thirty-one new locations were added in the 1980s as the process of modernization continued. Downtown stores in declining or stagnant rural areas were closed, but the conservative management style and close customer contact developed there was maintained in the chain's rapidly growing suburban stores.

In 1984 Peebles joined the prestigious New York-based Frederick Atkins buying office, a move which, according to one former merchandise manager, "put us into the major leagues of retailing." In 1984 Peebles also acquired The Collins Company, a regional department store group based in Charlotte, North Carolina, thereby giving the firm its first locations in America's increasingly popular shopping malls. In 1985 Peebles moved its corporate offices from Lawrenceville to South Hill, Virginia, and, in 1986, opened its first centralized distribution center.

Peebles considered going public in the mid-1980s, but was effectively precluded from doing so by virtue of the fact that, despite real progress at modernizing, it still was a network of interlocking companies rather than a single corporate entity with an exclusive balance sheet. Management worked through this problem and decided that it would be substantially more profitable for them to sell Peebles to the highest bidder than to go public. The firm put itself on the market in June 1986 and was bought out in October of that year by Investcorp, an investment group based in Bahrain, for $77.6 million.

In January 1988, Peebles celebrated $100 million in annual sales. That same year, Mike Moorman became the first non-family member to run the Peebles business. A lifelong company employee who began his career at Peebles as a manager trainee in 1964, Moorman remained CEO well into the next decade, despite further shakeups at the firm. In 1989, for instance, Peebles was the beneficiary of an immensely profitable leveraged buyout by an investment group headed by PaineWebber Inc., which paid $152 million for Peebles and its 48 stores in seven states. Also that year the National Retail Merchants Association named Bill Peebles its "Independent Retailer of the Year," in honor of his lifelong service to the industry.

In the 1990s, in an effort to stay ahead of the competition and avert the intense competitive pressures plaguing many other retailers, Peebles modernized and streamlined its operations still further. In 1992, the year it renamed itself Peebles Inc., the company cut the lead time that it needed to open a new store from one to two years to only six weeks. The number of Peebles stores thus grew dramatically in the 1990s, as did the number of states in which they were located. In 1996 alone, eight stores were slated to be built in two new states, Alabama and Ohio, further solidifying the company's strength in its core market.

### Further Reading

Covington, Howard E., Jr., *Peebles: A Retail Tradition Begins Its Second Century,* South Hill, Va.: Peebles Inc., 1993.
Reed, Vita, "Peebles Keeps Chain Growing by Sticking to a Simple Plan," *Charlotte Observer,* November 15, 1993, p. 2D.
Richards, Geoffrey, "Peebles Capitalizes on Its Rural Retail Heritage," *Shopping Center World,* June 1995.
Stoughton, Stephanie, "Peebles: A Retail Tradition's Next Step," *Virginia-Pilot and the Ledger-Star,* December 26, 1994, pp. 1, 8–9, 11.
Stowe, Michael, "Peebles Chairman Knows Employees, Customers Alike," *Roanoke (Virginia) Times & World News,* September 12, 1993, pp. F1–F2.
——, "Peebles Counters Department Store Moves," *Roanoke [Virginia] Times & World-News,* September 12, 1993, pp. F1–F2.

—John R. Guardiano

# Philip Environmental Inc.

100 King Street West
P.O. Box 2440 LCD 1
Hamilton, Ontario
Canada L8N 4J6
(905) 521-1600
Fax: (905) 521-9160

*Public Company*
*Incorporated:* 1990
*Employees:* 3,166
*Operating Revenues:* US$732 million (1995)
*Stock Exchanges:* Toronto NASDAQ
*SICs:* 8742 Waste Management Consulting Services;
4953 Waste Disposal Services; 4959 Waste Recovery
Services

Philip Environmental Inc. is one of the most innovative and fastest-growing environmental firms in Canada. The company is involved in by-products recovery, metals recovery, environmental consulting and engineering, solid waste management, and municipal utility management. With revenues approaching the $1 billion mark, since 1990 the company has grown nearly 40 times its size at that time—an astounding accomplishment by any standard. Although the company's headquarters are based in Hamilton, Ontario, more than 60 percent of its income is derived from business operations in the United States, and expansion into Alaska and South America will increase the amount of revenues garnered from foreign operations.

## Early History

In 1965 Enzo Fracassi and his family arrived in Hamilton, Ontario, from Italy. The new immigrant, an enterprising and ambitious businessman, started a small firm that hauled sand and scrap out of local steel mills and foundries. The company also began trucking sand and gravel for the heavy-construction firms in and around Hamilton. His two sons, Allen and Philip, joined him as soon as they were old enough, fixing tires, clean-

ing tools, and fueling trucks during weekends and holidays. By the late 1970s, however, due to the effects of a worldwide recession, the business faltered. To help turn the company around, Allen left his job in real estate and Philip returned home from college, but it was too late and the family firm went into receivership.

Undismayed by the failure of the family business, Philip and Allen borrowed money to purchase a few dump trucks and started a new company. At first the two brothers hauled sand from a foundry owned by Canron Inc., in Hamilton. Ordinarily used to make ingot molds for steel mills, foundry sand is peppered with scrap iron. After the workday was over, Philip and Allen would dump the last truckload of sand in their own backyard, then pick out the scrap iron before reloading the sand and driving it to a nearby landfill. Since the brothers had no landfill of their own, they had to pay a fee to dispose of the sand. The less they took to the landfill, the lower their cost of operation, and the more scrap iron they could resell, the greater their own revenue. This approach to doing business was the beginning of Philip and Allen's success as entrepreneurs.

## A New Company Is Born

Owned and managed jointly by the two brothers, the company was known as Philip Enterprises, Inc., throughout the 1980s. During these years the company grew slowly but steadily, essentially combing sand and trash for valuable morsels that could be reworked into more valuable materials. In 1990, however, the company underwent a drastic and fundamental change. Philip and Allen Fracassi sold the entire firm to Lincoln Capital Corporation, a merchant bank with a solid reputation in Ontario. The Fracassi brothers sold their company on the condition that they would remain on board both as managers and as major shareholders.

The purchase of Philip Enterprises by Lincoln Capital was a success from the very beginning—yet few people anticipated the magnitude of the success the company would eventually experience. One of the reasons Lincoln Capital purchased Philip Enterprises was to merge it with Taro Landfill, located near Stoney Creek, Ontario. The Fracassi brothers were the most important customers of the Taro landfill site, making the combination of their business and the Taro landfill a natural fit. Initially called Lincoln Waste Management Inc., the name was changed to Philip Environmental Inc. one year later at the request of the Fracassi brothers, who wanted to rename the firm in honor of their grandfather, Philip Fracassi.

Shortly after the acquisition was completed, St. Lawrence Cement, Inc., purchased a 13 percent interest in the company, which was worth approximately $25 million. Another $65 million was raised when Philip Environmental made a public offering of its stock. This influx of money transformed the company from a regional family operation to a business that had the capital to expand throughout North America. Allen Fracassi became the company's president and chief executive officer, while his brother Philip assumed the position of chief operating officer. In command of the company and its direction, with more than adequate funds available to implement a continental acquisitions strategy, the two brothers began buying companies as quickly as they could.

### Growth through Acquisition

The three most important acquisitions came in 1993, when Philip Environmental bought I. Waxman & Sons, Ltd., Burlington Environmental Inc., and Nortru Inc. Also based in Hamilton, Ontario, Waxman & Sons, a leader in the ferrous and nonferrous scrap processing industry, reported sales of approximately $200 million. When the purchase was completed, the Fracassi brothers hired Robert Waxman to serve as head of Waxman Resources, with the explicit purpose of forming a company to carve out a large market share in the burgeoning field of resources recovery. Waxman immediately began to

initiate new ways to recycle all the metals and plastics that worked their way through Philip Environmental.

Burlington Environmental Inc., based in Seattle, Washington, was involved in environmental engineering consulting and chemical waste management. The purchase of Burlington by Philip immediately increased its chemical waste operations by 35 percent and, as the Fracassi brothers were always thinking of expansion, provided significant access to markets in the northwestern part of the United States. Nortru Inc., located in Detroit, Michigan, was a medium-sized, diversified, hazardous waste management and recycling company with revenues of just over $34 million. The acquisition of Nortru gave Philip Environmental access to markets across the midwestern United States. Other important acquisitions during the early 1990s included Recyclage Cote Nord Inc. and Recyclage d'Aluminum Quebec Inc., both recyclers of aluminum based in Quebec.

With these purchases, Philip Environmental doubled its size within a few months. According to the Fracassi brothers' strategic plan, the acquisitions resulted in a better variety of services, increased revenues, and geographical diversity. Philip Environmental had grown from its modest beginnings into one of the largest companies in the industry, providing such services as solid waste management, including commercial, municipal and industrial waste hauling and disposal; hazardous waste recycling, including oil, paint, and contaminated soil recycling; resource recovery, including aluminum dross and scrap-metal recycling; and a host of environmental services such as industrial cleaning and vacuuming, consulting, and environmental auditing.

### Vertical Integration in the 1990s

The other key to Philip Environmental's success, in addition to its acquisition strategy, lay in what has been described by the Fracassi brothers as "cross selling." Allen and Philip became masters in arranging to cross-sell the services of each Philip company to the growing client list of all the rest. In this way, the company provided comprehensive environmental services to its customers. For instance, Waxman Resources sent the tin-plated copper scrap that it retrieved from its brass-mill customers to another Philip-owned subsidiary for de-tinning. The aluminum scraps Waxman Resources retrieved were sent to another Philip company, Recyclage Cote-Nord Inc. This strategy of "crossselling" resulted in two significant advantages for the company. First, cross-selling was a useful marketing tool the Fracassi brothers used to convince their customers that Philip Environmental could provide them with all the services they required. Second, cross-selling was enormously profitable. In his capacity as president and CEO, Allen Fracassi studied a number of companies that had implemented the cross-selling strategy. He discovered that once the plan was initiated, the companies reported an increase in sales of approximately 50 percent, and pretax profits jumped an impressive 110 percent.

When the strategy of cross-selling was combined with the strategy of management retainment, revenues at Philip Environment rocketed upward. A good example of this policy was the acquisition of Intersan Inc. during the early 1990s. In 1966 Intersan was a small firm that operated four trucks and had one contract to haul garbage in a Montreal suburb. By 1990 Intersan owned three landfills, operated more than 150 trucks, and managed the largest waste-transfer facility in Canada. The owner of Intersan, Lucien Remillard, realized that the time of the small, independent operator was a thing of the past in Canada, and that the only way for his business to survive was to make a deal with a larger, more established, and competitive company. Yet at the same time, Remillard, like many entrepreneurs who started a company out of nothing, didn't relish the thought of relinquishing control. The Fracassi brothers purchased Intersan with the understanding that Remillard would remain to manage that company that he had built. When the signatures of agreement were finally placed on the dotted line, all the parties involved were satisfied. An integration committee was then established to coordinate and consolidate Intersan into the Philip Environmental family and train its managers in the cross-selling strategy.

### Competition in the Mid-1990s

The largest of the integrated waste management companies operating on the North American Continent included WMX Technologies Inc., based in Chicago, Browning-Ferris Industries, Inc., located in Houston, and Laidlaw Inc., a Canadian firm, and Philip Environmental was not close to breaking into the ranks of the big three. At approximately the same time, competition within the industry increased dramatically due to excess capacity, falling prices, and shrinking margins. WMX was forced to lay off 1,200 employees and take an after-tax writedown of $363 million, while Laidlaw was forced to take special charges of $225 million that reflected changes in legislation covering waste recovery and disposal. Much of Philip Environmental's stiffest competition was coming from customers themselves. Many of the companies contracted by Philip Environmental began to change their raw materials or retool their manufacturing procedures in order to lessen the amount of waste generated as byproducts. The less waste, the less money spent paying companies like Philip Environmental for their services.

### The Mid-1990s and Beyond

Yet through the mid-1990s Philip Environmental remained highly successful in a remarkably competitive industry. By the end of 1994 the company had acquired more than 20 firms, adding to both the comprehensive services it provided to customers and to its own revenues. Revenues grew rapidly to $253 million in 1993, $570 million in 1994, and $732 million in 1995. Philip Environmental had also successfully expanded its network of facilities throughout North America. In 1992 approximately 90 percent of the company's revenue came from its operations in Canada and only 10 percent from the United States; by the end of fiscal 1995, however, 40 percent of its

revenues came from Canada and 60 percent from the United States. In 1995 the company's by-products recovery operation accounted for 27 percent of all revenues, while metals recovery accounted for 42 percent, environmental services 14 percent, and solid waste 17 percent.

In one of the most important developments at the company, in 1994 the Fracassi brothers formed a utilities operation to design, build, operate, and manage both industrial and municipal water and wastewater treatment facilities. One year later Philip Utilities Management Corporation had landed six highly lucrative contracts from both industrial and municipal sources. In January 1995 the company began operating and managing water and wastewater treatment plants for the municipality of Hamilton-Wentworth, a region of 500,000 people in southern Ontario. In November of the same year, Philip Environmental purchased Thorburn Penny Ltd., an engineering firm that developed and installed a highly sophisticated computerized system that allowed numerous water and wastewater facilities to be integrated and operated from a centralized location. The Fracassi brothers believed that this technology was one of the most significant developments in the utilities industry and would garner ever increasing revenues in the years to come.

### Principal Subsidiaries

Burlington Environmental Inc.; Delsan Environmental Group Inc.; I.W.& S. Ferrous Limited; Nortru, Inc.; Philip Enterprises Inc.; Philip Environmental Services Corporation; Philip Environmental (Quebec) Inc.; Philip Utilities Management Corporation; Waxman Resources.

### Further Reading

"Philip Buying Waste Management, Recycling Companies in Expansion," *American Metal Market,* October 13, 1993, p. 9.

"Philip Completes Acquisition of Consulting Firm, Recycler," *American Metal Market,* December 29, 1993, p. 10.

"Philip Purchases Selsan Soil-Treatment Company," *American Metal Market,* November 22, 1994, p. 6.

"Philip Pushes Takeover Plan," *American Metal Market,* April 18, 1995, p. 7.

Stevenson, Mark, "Waste Not," *Canadian Business,* January 1994, pp. 20–27.

"Waxman's Buyout Sets off a Lawsuit," *American Metal Market,* November 2, 1993, p. 2.

Worden, Edward, "Philip Enters Canadian Scrap Mart with Waxman Purchase," *American Metal Market,* September 24, 1993, p. 10.

——, "Philip Puts Waxman in Charge of Its Resource Recovery Unit," *American Metal Market,* October 18, 1993, p. 10.

——, "Zinc Recovery Venture Formed," *American Metal Market,* March 14, 1995, p. 6.

—Thomas Derdak

# Radius Inc.

**215 Moffett Park Drive**
**Sunnyvale, California 94809**
**U.S.A.**
**(408) 541-6100**
**Fax: (408) 541-6150**

*Public Company*
*Incorporated:* 1986
*Employees:* 237
*Sales:* $308 million (1995)
*Stock Exchanges:* NASDAQ
*SICs:* 5054 Computers & Computer Peripheral
Equipment & Software; 7373 Computer Integrated
Systems Design

Radius Inc. designs, manufactures, services, and sells computer peripheral devices and various accessories that enhance power and graphics capabilities. Examples of products include video-editing systems and software, high-resolution video displays, high-quality color printers, and graphic accelerators that facilitate the creation and manipulation of graphic images. Since its start in 1986, Radius has achieved dramatic growth through product innovation and by purchasing other companies and technology.

### A New Idea

The success of Radius Inc. was built on the success of Apple Computer Inc., the maker of the famous Apple and Macintosh personal computer systems. In fact, the company was founded by several former Apple employees, including Andy Hertzfield, Mike Boich, Alain Rossman, and William Carter. Heading up the effort was Burrell Smith, the lead designer at Apple who had helped design the electronics for the first Macintosh computer and the popular LaserWriter printer, among other credits. Eager to flee the corporate world and launch his own enterprise, Smith took a leave of absence from Apple in the mid-1980s and spent his leave designing a breakthrough Macintosh-compatible video display.

The advantage of Smith's new display was that it offered full-page viewing, which contrasted with the much smaller display built into Macintosh units at the time. Smith decided to take a permanent leave of absence in 1986. By that time, he had let some of his associates in on his backroom project. Leaving with him was Andy Hertzfield, who had helped design the systems software for Apple's vaunted Macintosh. Exiting Apple's management ranks from the marketing side to help start Radius were Mike Boich, a Macintosh marketing wizard who had spurred Smith to launch the new venture, and Alain Rossmann, one of Apple's marketing and sales executives. Together, the team of former Apple managers launched Radius Inc., which was incorporated on May 19, 1986.

### Success in the Late 1980s

At Radius, Smith and his cofounders sought to construct a culture that mimicked that of the early, entrepreneurial Apple Computer. "We tried to recreate what we really liked at Apple," Rossmann recalled in *Business Journal-San Jose*. "We tried to achieve a very informal environment where people can create. We certainly pay as much attention as we can to treating people well. That's what Steve [Jobs, Apple's founder] used to do. . . ." Such a culture helped Radius, like Apple, grow rapidly. Starting with just a handful of employees, Radius quadrupled in size in its first year to a team of 30. In 1987 they moved Radius' operations to a 35,000-square-foot facility to keep pace with growth.

The foundation of Radius' growth during that first year was its hugely successful Radius Full Page Display. Designed as a peripheral device to accompany the popular small-screened Macintosh SE and other Macintosh systems, the monitor was a huge success. It was a gray-scale, high-resolution monitor, much like the one sold with the integrated Macintosh computer unit. But it was a full six inches larger than the Macintosh SE's 13-inch screen, thus increasing the viewing area more than threefold. Furthermore, it was designed to accelerate the speed of the graphics process by 400 to 600 percent on different Macintosh systems. The screen initially sold for a list price of $1995. Radius sold the complementary accelerator, which sped up the graphics process, for $995. "The thing we try to do is

417

turn the Macintosh into a graphics workstation,'' Boich said in *Business Journal-San Jose.* ''Our concentration is on high performance graphics systems.''

In 1987 the Radius monitor was voted by readers of *Macworld* as the most promising hardware product. They also voted it the best display device for a Macintosh by a margin of three-to-one. The high-performance monitor and accelerator allowed Radius to quickly snare a full 36 percent of the entire market for Macintosh graphics subsystems (peripheral monitors), with about 8,000 units shipped during Radius' first full year of operation. The company's sales shot up from almost nothing in 1986 to more than $7 million during its first full year of operation. In 1988, moreover, Radius' revenues vaulted to nearly $33 million. Radius achieved profitability after its first nine months of operation, and would continue to post successive profit gains throughout the 1980s.

Radius managed to establish itself in the computer peripherals market quickly and with a low investment compared to many of its competitors. The company was originally funded privately, largely by its founders. But only nine months after its founding, venture capital investors—including Kleiner, Perkins, Caufield & Byers, InterWest Partners, and Associate Venture Investors—injected $3 million into the company in return for about 34-percent ownership. Radius kept costs low by having its units manufactured by contractors and purchasing its video displays overseas. It distributed the products through a dealer channel that, by mid-1989, reached 1,500 retail outlets in 17 countries. The displays and accelerators were originally purchased primarily by graphics and design departments of large corporations, although that market broadened in the 1990s.

### Trouble in the Early 1990s

The success of Radius' Macintosh peripherals allowed it to post impressive revenue increases, to $82 million in 1989 and then to $111 million in 1990. Meanwhile, net income grew to more than $6 million annually. Radius scrambled to expand its facilities and bolster its work force to more than 300 employees by 1990. Confident of future growth, Radius went public in August of 1990 with a stock offering at $10 per share. Unfortunately, that public offering signaled an end to Radius' rapid rise and successive profitability. By the end of 1990, in fact, Radius' stock price had plummeted by nearly 50 percent after the company announced its first quarterly loss.

Radius' problems late in 1990 evidenced underlying weaknesses in the company's overall strategy. Radius had profited during the late 1980s by chasing the largely untapped market for high-end Macintosh add-on monitors and graphics accelerators. By the early 1990s, Radius was relying on sales of Macintosh-related products for roughly 90 percent of its sales. Personal computer markets began to change in the late 1980s and early 1990s, though, and Radius failed to adapt. Importantly, Radius' management didn't recognize the importance of Apple Computer's shift toward the low-priced segment of the hyper-competitive personal computer industry. When Macintosh introduced the highly successful, low-priced ''Macintosh LC'' model, Radius was caught off guard. Radius had to scramble to develop products that could work with the LC, as a large

proportion of its sales was dependent on the Macintosh SE, which Apple discontinued in the wake of the LC's success.

To make matters worse, Radius suffered several minor blows, such as the loss of a potentially lucrative contract to supply its products to the exclusive Apple federal government reseller. Furthermore, Apple Computer itself was struggling to retain market share and the personal computer industry had become fiercely price-competitive. Radius executives recognized the need to emphasize products for the IBM-compatible PC market, but had been slow to move. Critics at the time derided management for being arrogant and myopic, and for replaying the Apple Computer mistake of spending too much money on personnel and marketing. They argued that although Radius had achieved important innovations, such as the world's first pivoting monitor that could operate in portrait or landscape mode, it had also missed some important opportunities. Regardless of the cause of its problems, Radius suffered a dive in net income to just $3.7 million in fiscal year 1991 from sales of $118 million.

Even before Radius posted its 1991 decline the company's board had shaken up the management ranks. In March, Boich lost his titles of president and chief executive to Barry Folsom, although Boich retained his role of chairman. Folsom had held various marketing and development positions at Sun Microsystems Inc., Digital Equipment Corp., and Data General Corp. before moving to Radius. He was known as a scrappy, hard-charging executive. ''I'm a can-do, make-it-happen kind of person,'' Folsom declared in a 1991 *Business Journal-San Jose* article. Those prophetic words were followed by Folsom's resignation just 17 months later.

Folsom did make progress at Radius. He reduced the company's work force and lowered overhead, for example, and dispatched several key executives. Among other efforts, he worked to reduce infighting between the engineering and marketings factions of Radius. Folsom also oversaw the opening of a new Japanese subsidiary (Radius K.K.), and initiated a drive to more aggressively develop products for the giant IBM-compatible segment of the market. Furthermore, under his tutelage, Radius managed to boost sales to $160 million and nearly double annual profits in 1991. But critics feared that Radius was losing it direction under Folsom, and that the company lacked a clear strategy for long-term growth.

Perhaps more surprising than Folsom's resignation was the reappointment of Boich as president and chief executive officer. ''I learned a lot watching another person do the job,'' Boich said in *Business Journal-San Jose,* ''and I also learned that I could do a lot better job than I gave myself credit for.'' In fact, Boich was grossly mistaken. Radius took an ugly dive after he recaptured the helm; sales slipped to $134 million in 1993 and the company posted an embarrassing net deficit of $18 million. That decline occurred as Radius' core Macintosh product line languished in the face of increased competition and sluggish Macintosh sales.

### A New Direction for the Mid-1990s

Before he could drive the company into the ground, Boich left Radius and was replaced in March of 1993 by Charles W.

Berger. Berger had previously served as a vice-president at Apple and as president of Sun Microsystems, gaining experience in all facets of the computer business. He launched a number of initiatives at Radius, the most notable of which revolved around diversifying the company's product line and developing and introducing new technology. Importantly, in 1994 Berger helped to engineer the buyout of Radius' key competitor, SuperMac Technology Inc. The move reflected Radius' goal of becoming the dominant player in the digital-video desktop PC market.

SuperMac brought an array of new products and technologies to Radius. Importantly, it promised to give Radius the leverage it needed to become a major player in the emerging desktop video-editing industry, which Berger believed would offer massive growth potential reminiscent of the switch from professional to desktop word processing in the 1980s. But SuperMac also burdened Radius with 500 new employees, a bloated inventory, and numerous overlapping departments and functions. Adding to the fray was Radius' buyout of the much smaller VideoFusion, Inc., a leader in video desktop technology. Radius scurried to absorb SuperMac and VideoFusion during 1994 and 1995, and to prop up its existing lines of graphics peripherals, "Radius Rocket" accelerators, and other products.

As a result of the merger with Supermac and VideoFusion, Radius' revenue base more than doubled to $324 million in 1994. But the company also recorded a net loss of about $77 million. The company's financial health continued to suffer through 1995, when sales slipped to about $308 million and gross losses increased about two percent. Management remained optimistic, however, believing that the company's move to dominate the video-editing/production/playback market and to concentrate on high-end digital video and graphics customers would pay off big in the long-term.

Late in 1995 and early in 1996, Radius sold off its color server and systems businesses, helping to reduce its payroll to less than 250 employees. Furthermore, management renewed its effort to divest mass-market and other low-value-added business. The company planned to use the cash from these sales to pursue markets related to high-end color publishing and video-editing and production, and to fund new projects. Most notable among Radius' new projects in the mid-1990s was its System 100. Introduced in 1995, the System 100 was the first-ever Macintosh clone. The product signaled Radius' jump into the market for complete, high-end PC systems. However, mediocre results from the effort persuaded Radius to sell the Macintosh clone division in January of 1996. Meanwhile, analysts were waiting to see if Radius could pull out of its downward spiral and regain profitability.

### Principal Subsidiaries

Radius France S.A.; Radius S.A.R.L.; Radius K.K. (Japan); Nihon SuperMac K.K. (Japan); SuperMac Asia Pacific (Hong Kong); Radius UK Ltd. (United Kingdom); SuperMac Technology Europe; Radius GmbH (Germany); Radius FSC Inc. (Barbados); Radius Pty. Ltd. (Australia); Radius Canada.

### Further Reading

"Ahoy, Mate!" *PC Week,* January 22, 1996.

Gengo, Lorraine, "Rapidly Rising Radius Moving into Its Second 'Mansion,'" *Business Journal-San Jose,* September 5, 1988, p. 9.

Hamm, Steve, "Refilming Radius," *PC Week,* September 12, 1994, p. A3.

Harter, Jeneane, and Maria Gagliardi, "Radius Establishes Japanese Subsidiary," *Business Wire,* November 11, 1991.

Krey, Michael, "Radius, Facing Losses, Trims Staff," *Business Journal-San Jose,* March 11, 1991, p. 1.

Matsumoto, Craig, "Long-Awaited Macintosh Clones Ready," *Business Journal-San Jose,* April 3, 1995, p. 9.

Picarille, Lisa, "Radius' Woes Proliferate, 'Significant' Loss Expected," *Computerworld,* September 4, 1995, p. 32.

——, "Yin and Yang of Mac Clone Makers," *Computerworld,* January 29, 1996, p. 32.

"Radius," *Computer Pictures,* May–June 1994, p. 83.

Saltmarsh, Robert, "Radius Acquires VideoFusion Inc.," *Business Wire,* July 19, 1994.

Shafer, Richard A., "Radius: Facing Growth Challenges," *Personal Computing,* March 1989, p. 41.

Swartz, Jon, "Ailing Radius Struggles to Come Out of Its Slump," *Business Journal-San Jose,* July 22, 1991, p. 1.

"Taiwan's UMAX Buys a Fellow Mac Licensee," *Electronic News,* January 15, 1996, p. 16.

Toothman, Dina, "Radius Delivers True Value in New Display," *Business Wire,* June 12, 1995.

Weisman, Jonathan, "Revolving Door Continues to Spin for Top Executives at Radius," *Business Journal-San Jose,* September 21, 1992, p. 3.

Young, Margaret, "Mac Peripherals Open Doors for Radius," *Business Journal-San Jose,* August 10, 1987, p. 1.

—Dave Mote

# ɹ randstad
## staffing services®

# Randstad Holding n.v.

<table>
<tr><td>

**P.O. Box 12600**
**1100 AP Amsterdam-Zuidoost**
**The Netherlands**
**020-5 69 59 11**
**Fax: 020-5 69 55 20**

*Public Company*
*Incorporated:* 1960 as Uitzendbureau Amstelveen
*Employees:* 4,200
*Sales:* NLG 3.76 billion (1994)
*Stock Exchanges:* Amsterdam London
*SICs:* 7363 Temporary Help Services; 7361 Employment
Agencies; 7349 Building Maintenance Services, Not
Elsewhere Classified; 7381 Detective & Armored Car
Services; 7372 Prepackaged Software

</td></tr>
</table>

Randstad Holding n.v. thrived in the era of widespread corporate staff reductions and outsourcing, supplying other businesses with labor, management, and professional talent as needed. Its fourth decade was marked by expansion into what could prove to be the Dutch company's largest and most lucrative market: the United States. In 1994, a half million people received paychecks from Randstad, the largest temporary services agency in the Benelux countries and the fifth largest in the world, with annual sales of $1.7 billion. Randstad estimated the total global potential of its markets at NLG 500 billion.

## Beginnings and Early Success

In 1960, Frits J. D. Goldschmeding was working on a thesis for a master's degree at Amsterdam's Vrije Universiteit. His topic: temporary employment. He subsequently started his own temporary services agency, known as Uitzendbureau Amstelveen, from his dorm room. Soon he had more than three dozen employees. Goldschmeding is said to have conceived the idea after reading a Citroën annual report.

The company was renamed Randstad Uitzendbureau in 1964. (The Randstad is a very densely populated region in the

western Netherlands made up of cities, towns, and villages which encircle an area of woods and lakes.) The next year, the company's first international branch, Interlabor, opened in Belgium. In 1968, new offices in Germany followed. The 32 offices in the three countries brought in more than NLG 47 million of revenues in 1970. Three years later, Randstad broached the French market.

In 1974, a contract cleaning division was established in Germany. These services were initiated in Belgium the next year, and Belglas was acquired. Contract cleaning services were expanded to the Netherlands in 1976, and Korrekt Gebäudereinigung was acquired in Germany. Randstad cleaned or serviced a variety of different things, including planes, trains, and buildings. According to the company, this revenue source grew consistently because businesses believed in the motivational benefit of a clean working environment while at the same time they preferred to delegate non-core activities. Randstad supported the formation of objective quality standards in the cleaning industry and has proudly displayed its ISO certification in this area since 1992.

In 1978, the corporate name was changed to Randstad Holding n.v. The next year, the company opened its 100th office and achieved a net income of more than NLG 10 million.

Group revenues surpassed NLG 500 million in 1980. The decade began with the formation of Randon, the security division, which opened in the Netherlands. Besides guard and surveillance services, Randstad provided a home security alarm system through Randon Meldkamer. The company felt its insistence on professionalism made it attractive to this market.

In 1983, the company continued its expansion in the Dutch staffing market with the purchase of a mid-sized Dutch temporary services agency, Tempo-Team, which specialized in industrial and technical services, as did two other of Randstad's Dutch offices, Werknet and Otter-Westelaken. Belgium followed with training services in 1988, when automation services were added to the company's repertoire in the Netherlands. This profitable venture eventually had six offices. Software and hardware sales to financial, distribution, and transport companies added to the revenues of AICA, the computer services bureau, which also developed accounting systems.

Revenues exceeded NLG 1 billion in time for the company's 25th anniversary in 1985. Over 1,300 staff and a daily average of 36,000 temporary employees then worked for Randstad's 257 offices in four countries. In addition, Lavold, a cleaning services company, was bought, adding to Randstad's capacity in the Netherlands and Belgium.

Randstad began training cashiers, computer operators, and telemarketers, and other personnel for its Dutch clientele in 1986. The Randstad Training Center consisted of fourteen offices in 1994; Randstad also conducted these activities on-site for client companies.

Offices were opened in Great Britain in 1989, when group revenues exceeded NLG 2 billion. By 1993, the Randstad Employment Bureau there had seven offices. Randstad entered the Spanish market late in 1993, as the one-office firm Randstad Trabajo Temporal.

In the 1990s, Randstad began offering higher-trained technical staff in the Netherlands, Belgium, and Great Britain through nine specialized companies (Randstad Interim Techniek, Randstad Research & Development Services, Inter Techniek, Polydesign Nederland, Polydesign België, Interdesign, Randstad Inter Engineering, Randstad Specialist Engineering, and Technisch Bureau Visser). Randstad's technical services division was active in the machinery, transport equipment, electronics, hospitality, insurance, petroleum, and construction industries, among others.

### Industry Liberalization in the 1990s

Since the 1960s, the Netherlands had an ideal environment for temp agencies. In the early 1990s, it was estimated that two percent of Dutch workers were temps, more than four times the ratio found in Germany. A third of all Dutch workers had worked for a temporary services agency at some time in their careers. In 1994, the company had 408 offices overall in the Netherlands.

The bugbear for Randstad in Europe, like that for many other companies with international aspirations, was the restrictive attitude of certain governments, particularly Germany, Spain, and especially Italy. In these countries, temporary employment agencies were seen as a threat to the job security of long term employees. The "Doppeleinsatz" requirement in

Germany, where Randstad Zeit-Arbeit had 31 offices, mandated temporary agencies provide two successive temporary positions for every worker. After a group of temp agencies filed a complaint with the European Commission in 1992, Spain and Germany liberalized their markets somewhat; the "Doppeleinsatz" rule was waived for hard-to-place workers in Germany in 1994, and workers were allowed to work nine months as temporaries, rather than six months. A class action was filed against Italy, ultimately to be decided by the European Court of Justice. In areas where public and private sectors controlled labor supply, Randstad foresaw government agencies focusing on gathering candidates, while temporary agencies concentrated on matching the candidates to the most appropriate jobs. In 1994, legislation was passed allowing Belgians to work as long as six months as temporaries, compared to three months previously. Randstad operated under the names Interlabor Interim, Randstad Interim, and Flex Interim in Belgium.

After determining that many of its clients were seeking long-term solutions, Randstad set up several new programs. Vendor-on-Premise placed a Randstad staffing manager to support company management. Facility Staffing handled large-scale, long term staffing needs. Outsourcing gave Randstad functional responsibility for an entire department, process, or function. Other solutions were labeled "Vectoring" and "Temp-to-Hire."

### Preparing for a New Century

Randstad termed its processes "social technology." ISO certification gave Randstad the opportunity to highlight its systematic approach. These international quality guidelines, originally applied to manufacturing industries, were extended to service industries in 1992 in the Netherlands. Soon, Randstad had picked up a series of certifications—first as a specialist cleaning company, later, in 1993, as the first international temporary employment agency to receive the appellation.

In 1994, Randstad operated 780 offices in seven countries, including Belgium, Germany, France, Great Britain, and Spain. Nevertheless, the Netherlands hosted the majority—495—of the company's offices, where it had a 37 percent market share. Thirty-five percent of revenues were earned outside the Netherlands. On the average day, nearly 100,000 were employed by Randstad. This figure had tripled from 36,000 in 1985. Most (86 percent, or NLG 3.2 billion in 1994) of the firm's income came from Temporary Services.

The company's French operations, Flex and Randstad, were integrated in 1994 under the name Randstad Intérim. This move, which reduced the number of offices in France from 94 to 75, resulted in some loss of market share but also more efficiency and greater revenues.

The acquisition of Temp Force in 1993 allowed Randstad entrée into the world's largest temporary services market, the United States. Randstad limited itself exclusively to the Southeast, a region where growth in temporary services consistently exceeded 10 percent annually and in which relatively few worked as temporaries. In spite of Randstad's tradition of hiring workers with higher than average educational backgrounds— more than sixty percent had attended post-secondary schools—

they reported no problems regarding worker skills in the South, which had long had a spotty reputation for education. Randstad acquired 12 Atlanta offices with the Temp Force purchase, and instantly became the city's largest temporary employer. Nashville's Jane Jones Enterprises, Tennessee's largest independent staffing service, was bought the same year, giving Randstad a total of 25 U.S. offices. Nearly 40 new offices were opened in the next two years; by 1995, the company had over 70 in the United States. Erik Vonk, a newly hired banker who specialized in mergers and acquisitions, led U.S. operations for Randstad Holding n.v.; Randstad's U.S. presence was named Randstad Staffing Services.

As had been its custom elsewhere, the company actively managed its U.S. acquisitions, to the chagrin of many existing managers—fewer than half stayed with the new owner more than two years. A chasm existed in most temporary agencies between recruiting temps and marketing to clients; however, Randstad managers were responsible for both areas. The company also prided itself on its decentralized organization.

Randstad supported its risky American start-up with an audacious marketing strategy. While bidding to supply employees for the 1996 Olympic Games, the company elected to become an official sponsor—an unprecedented position for a staffing service. The challenging contract reportedly gave the company a loss on some of its assignments but allowed it instant name recognition and a chance to display its skills. Part of the job included finding over 4,000 bus drivers for the public transportation system.

Company managers were expecting 1995 to be Randstad's first profitable year in America. In 1996, Randstad aimed to expand beyond its single office in Greenville, South Carolina, to become a key player in the Carolinas and beyond.

### Principal Subsidiaries

Randstad Uitzendbureau b.v.; Tempo-Team Uitzendbureau b.v.; Tempo-Team Beheer b.v.; Werknet Uitzendbureau b.v; Uitzendbureau Otter-Westelaken b.v.; SAVAZ Uitzendzorg; Lavold Schoonmaak b.v.; Lavold-IDG b.v.; Randon Beveiliging b.v.; Randon Meldkamer b.v.; Randon Services b.v.; Randstad Opleidingscentrum b.v.; Randstad Automatiseringsdiensten; AICA b.v.; Randstad Interim Kader; Randstad Interim Techniek; Tempo-Team Projecten; Inter Techniek Rotterdam b.v.; Polydesign b.v.; Technisch Bureau S. Visser b.v.; Randstad Research & Development; Maxon Project Support; Randstad Automation Center b.v.; Randstad Automatiseringsdiensten b.v.; Randstad Contracting b.v.; Randstad Dienstengroep Nederland b.v.; Diemermere b.v.; Randstad Interim (Belgium); Interlabor Interim (Belgium); Flex Interim België (Belgium); Lavold Nettoyage/Lavold Schoonmaak (Belgium); Interlabor Training & Services n.v. (Belgium); Polydesign België n.v. (Belgium); Interdesign s.a. (Belgium); Randstad Intérim s.a. (France); Randstad Organisation für Zeit-Arbeit GmbH (Germany); Korrekt Gebäudereinigung (Germany); Randstad Employment Bureau (Great Britain); Randstad Inter Engineering (Great Britain); Randstad Specialist Engineering (Great Britain); Randstad Empleo, Empresa de Trabajo Temporal s.a. (Spain); Randstad Interim (Switzerland); Randstad Staffing Services LP (USA).

### Principal Divisions

Temporary Services; Cleaning Services; Security Services; Automation Services; Technical Services; Training; Interim Management; Transport and Logistics Services.

### Further Reading

Bueno, Jacqueline, "Shortage of Bus Drivers Has Put Organizers of Olympics in a Jam," *The Wall Street Journal,* October 25, 1995, p. 4S.

DeChant, Meredith, "Atlanta's Top 20 Employment Agencies," *Atlanta Business Chronicle,* June 23, 1995, p. 10B.

DeLavan, Joanne, "Temping Appeals to a Wide Range of Workers," *Atlanta Journal-Constitution,* September 10, 1995.

DeMarco, Edward, "Randstad Will Try to Boost U.S. Temp Use," *Atlanta Business Chronicle,* May 7, 1993, p. 10A.

"Frits Goldschmeding, Eredoctor University of Rochester," Amsterdam: Randstad Holding n.v., n.d.

Laster, Kasee, "Changes in Temping Industry Varied, But Needed," *Business Ledger,* June 13, 1995, p. 14.

Pousner, Howard, "Welcoming the World," *Atlanta Journal-Constitution,* May 9, 1995.

Salwen, Kevin G., "How a Bold Temp Agency Took Gambles—and Won," *The Wall Street Journal,* July 5, 1995, p. 1S.

Turner, Melissa, "Randstad Signs on as Olympic Sponsor, Will Handle Hiring," *Atlanta Journal-Constitution,* September 8, 1994.

Van de Krol, Ronald, "The Netherlands' Invisible Army," *International Management,* March, 1993, pp. 44–45.

Vance, Nick, "Many Ways to Work Temp," *Atlanta Employment Weekly,* June 18–24, 1995.

—Frederick C. Ingram

# Repsol S.A.

**Paseo de la Castellana 89**
**28046 Madrid**
**Spain**
**+34 1 348 81 00**
**Fax: +34 1 314 28 21**

*Public Company*
*Incorporated:* 1987
*Employees:* 19,632
*Sales:* US$18.20 billion (1994)
*Stock Exchanges:* Madrid New York
*SICs:* 1311 Crude Petroleum & Natural Gas; 2869
    Industrial Organic Chemicals, Not Elsewhere
    Classified; 2911 Petroleum Refining; 3559 Special
    Industry Machinery, Not Elsewhere Classified; 4925
    Mixed, Manufactured or Liquefied Petroleum Gas
    Production and/or Distribution; 5169 Chemicals &
    Allied Products, Not Elsewhere Classified

Repsol S.A. is Spain's largest industrial company and is the sixth-largest oil company in Europe in terms of sales. Formed in 1987 by the merger of state-controlled oil sector companies, Repsol is now more than 90 percent privatized thanks to four separate share offerings from 1989 to 1996. The company controls about 60 percent of the refining market in Spain and has a 45.5 percent stake in Gas Natural, which dominates the Spanish natural gas market. Repsol is Spain's first integrated international company in a national oil industry that, although dating back centuries, was relatively small and unimportant until recent times.

### Early History

In 1539, the Spanish ship *Santa Cruz* transported the first transatlantic oil shipment when it carried a barrel from Venezuela to Spain. It was thought the dark fluid had properties to relieve the gout of King Charles I. History does not record whether he found it to be an effective remedy.

State monopoly and control, a characteristic that persisted in the Spanish industry, was established at the end of the 18th century when King Charles III declared all mining deposits, whether they were of a commercial character or not, to be the property of the crown. Only the crown would have the right to grant exploration or development concessions.

As 19th and 20th century Spain fell into a long period of decline and lagged behind the rest of Europe in industrial development, the country failed to develop a strong domestic oil industry. By the mid-1920s only a few unsuccessful attempts at oil exploration had taken place. No refineries were built. The country was heavily dependent on imported foreign oil, supplied by Shell and other major multinationals and distributed through an inadequate and fragmented network.

Spain was forced to spend valuable foreign exchange to import expensive refined oil. The corrupt dictatorship of Primo de Rivera, which governed the country between 1923 and 1930, realized that this state of affairs could not continue if Spain were to industrialize. The problem haunted successive Spanish governments and later it became more important as living standards and the number of motor vehicles rose in the period of rapid economic growth that followed World War II. By 1980, 65 percent of Spain's oil was still imported. Rivera's solution was to return to the tradition of state monopoly, a policy that was followed in modified forms by all successive Spanish governments up to 1986. In 1927, the dictator issued a decree expropriating all foreign and domestic oil sector companies and placing them under the control of a state agency. Administration was entrusted to Compañia Arrendataria del Monopolio de Pétroleos Sociedad Anónima (CAMPSA), which had the sole rights to purchase oil from producers at state-controlled prices.

Ironically, the country's first refinery was built in the Canary Islands by Compañia Española de Petróleos S.A. (CEPSA), a private company, in 1930. The islands had been specifically excluded from the decree. Today CEPSA remains an important Spanish oil company. Three state-owned refineries were built prior to the disruptions of the 1936–39 Spanish civil war and the Franco dictatorship's diplomatic isolation and armed neutrality during World War II.

In July 1941, CAMPSA undertook the country's first major exploration, the "Tudanca" survey of the northern Burgos region, with negative results. Foreign exchange pressures and CAMPSA's continued failure to discover oil on Spanish territory led the Franco regime to relax rules on foreign participation.

A 1947 law left CAMPSA in control of marketing and distribution, but enabled the government to authorize private and public companies to develop a wide range of activities in trade, industrial handling—especially refining—storage, research, and exploration for production of oil and gas fields.

In practice, the government usually required foreign companies to work under joint participation schemes with CAMPSA or other state-controlled entities. A requirement that both private and public refineries had to sell to CAMPSA continued, and in 1957 it was extended to gassified petroleum products.

### The State Monopoly in the 1960s and 1970s

In 1963, the government announced the National Combustibles Plan and it asserted direct control of sales, imports, and production of oil products. The government would determine each refinery's contribution to the national supply. Each refinery had to offer its product to CAMPSA, which then sold to consumers through its monopoly distribution network. To protect the balance of payments, refineries had to purchase a set percentage of their crude requirements from the Spanish government. This was known as the "Government Quote" and reached a height of 50 percent in 1980, then declined until it was removed in 1985.

After 169 wildcat failures, an association of Caltex and CAMPSA made the first discovery of oil in the "la Lora" concession and produced small amounts of low-grade crude oil in 1964. In 1965 offshore drilling began, and ten years later joint ventures discovered substantial quantities off the Mediterranean coast. By the early 1990s five offshore producing fields were in operation.

The rapid expansion of the Spanish economy created a 15 percent increase in annual oil consumption. In 1965, the government founded Hispanica de Petróleos (Hispanoil) as a state-owned company charged with spearheading exploration and development efforts in Spain and elsewhere.

When the share of imported crude reached 73 percent of the country's total supply share in 1973, the government initiated a policy of encouraging more foreign participation to build refineries. It hoped to offset the costs of imported crude with exports of refined products. Shortly afterward, it attempted to cushion the shock of the first Arab oil boycott and OPEC-induced price rises by lowering taxes on products, with the result that only some of the costs were passed on to consumers.

In June 1974, the government announced the merger of the three refineries in which the state had a controlling interest: REPESA, ENCASO, and ENTASA. The state retained 72 percent of the shares. The new company, Empresa Nacional del Petróleo (ENPETROL) was also given the task of coordinating efforts to secure crude supplies through direct bargaining with producing states. An attempt to develop the First National Energy Plan was soon abandoned in 1976 and the country was without a coordinated energy plan until 1979. Authority for the use and production of energy was dispersed among different agencies, departments, and public companies.

### Transition to Privatization in the 1980s

Francisco Franco died in 1975 and Spain passed into a new democratic era. In October 1977, the Spanish government and political leaders signed the Pacts of Moncloa, which attempted to establish a consensus for political and economic change. Included were provisions for the reorganization of the energy sector.

The Second National Energy Plan, introduced in July 1979, laid the groundwork for the formation of Repsol. According to the plan, a reorganization of public entities was required because exploration had failed to develop. The structure of the industry was fragmented and lacked vertical integration. CAMPSA, the Spanish banks, and the Department of Finance continued to resist moves toward integration. the second oil crisis and moves toward joining the European Community (EC), however, forced the logic of integration and the creation of Instituto Nacional de Hidrocarboros (INH), Repsol's direct predecessor. On December 18, 1981, all public participations in the oil sector were brought together in one holding company: INH. Minority foreign shareholders in Spanish public oil companies were gradually bought out.

During the 1983–86 negotiations for Spain's entry to the EC, it became increasingly clear that Spain would have to dismantle its formal government monopoly in marketing. CAMPSA shares were split among the refineries, with INH retaining the majority of the shares. Negotiators hoped to avoid a situation in which the EC would require CAMPSA to offer its distribution network and services to every interested foreign company. The refineries agreed to continue to sell products destined for the domestic market to CAMPSA.

In 1985, Hispanoil took over ENIEPSA, a public company formed in 1976 to engage in exploration. Shortly afterward, INH was reorganized into a divisional structure: Hispanoil exploration, Enpetrol refining, Alcudia petrochemicals, Butano liquefied petroleum gas, and Enagas natural gas distribution. In September 1987, all these divisions, except Enagas, were incorporated into the new Repsol S.A., a company then 100 percent-owned by the Spanish state. The name Repsol, formerly a trademark for lubrication products, was chosen after extensive marketing research because it was short, widely recognized in Spain, and easy to pronounce in other languages. It was envisaged that Enagas would be added to Repsol at some future point. The time was not yet appropriate because it had an ambitious investment program, which would generate insufficient immediate returns. Otherwise, Repsol retained the INH divisional structure but Hispanoil became Repsol Exploración, Enpetrol was renamed Repsol Petróleo, Alcudia became Repsol Química, and Butano became Repsol Butano.

### Repsol's Initial Years

In 1986 Spain joined the EC under a phased plan to enable the country's protected industries, including the oil industry, to adapt to EC regulations. With the creation of Repsol, the government hoped to create an integrated national oil company that would be able to compete successfully in the post-1992 single European market. By changing the structure from that of a government agency to a company in which the government retained a majority stake through INH, an arm's-length relationship was established that might satisfy critics of the Spanish government's close involvement with its oil industry. The INH also wanted to have a strong domestic oil company able to develop an overall strategy including exploration, production, refining, and distribution.

The EC Commission was reluctant to accept Repsol's dominant role in CAMPSA because Article 37 of the Treaty of Rome declared that member states should adjust commercial monopolies to the extent that all discrimination in trade between citizens of member states disappeared. Also, Article 48 of Spain's treaty of adhesion to the EC required Spain to open up its frontiers to the importation of oil products originating from the EC. In December 1987, the EC Commission warned Spain that it would be taken to the European Court if it did not take further steps to liberalize the market.

A decision had already been made to sell 26 percent of Repsol to the public, both in Spain and abroad. Repsol and the government were impressed with similar privatizations in the United Kingdom. It was believed that a partial flotation would not only raise money and make it easier for the company to secure private sector finance, but also introduce a private sector discipline and increase the international stature of the company. INH would continue to hold a two-thirds share to ensure government control.

The May 1989 share issue, on the Madrid and New York stock markets simultaneously, was successful beyond expectations. The initial offering of 40 million shares was heavily oversubscribed and a further issue equivalent to ten percent of the original had to be made. Overall, the equivalent of more than US$1 billion was raised and the company had 400,000 new shareholders (to date this was the largest share offer ever for a Spanish firm and largest of 1989 worldwide). The issues were so attractive that at least three brokerage firms were later successfully prosecuted for irregularities in the flotation by the Comision Nacional de Valores (CNV), the Spanish stock market supervisory body.

At the beginning of 1989, Repsol acquired the Naviera Vizcaina shipping company to increase its own marine fleet and avoid rising charter rates. Later that year, Repsol took over the 34 percent interest of Petróleos Mexicanos (Pemex), the Mexican state oil company, from the Spanish Petronor refinery company in exchange for a three percent interest in Repsol. The deal included a five-year supply contract by Pemex and envisaged cooperative ventures in Mexico. It brought Repsol to a holding of 90 percent in Petronor and 70 percent in CAMPSA. In August of that year, Repsol purchased Carless Refining & Marketing and Carless Petroleum from Kelt Energy, the U.K. oil independent. Repsol intended to develop a market for its products in the United Kingdom through the Carless chain of 500 service stations.

## 1990s and Beyond

By 1990, Spain still had only 5,000 service stations. The United Kingdom, by comparison, had 20,000. Foreign companies had only opened seven in Spain, and Repsol's Spanish competitors had opened only 180. In November 1989 Leon Brittan, the EC Competition Commissioner, attacked Spain for failure to open markets in heating oils and liquefied petroleum gas (LPG). With 13 million customers, the subsidiary Repsol Butano had 100 percent of Europe's largest market for butane. But prices for liquefied petroleum gas were soon to liberalized.

Brittan warned that the commission would keep a close watch on Spanish interpretations of regulations, the dominant position of Repsol in CAMPSA, and the slow development of independent outlets. He said the commission would reexamine a possible court action against Spain if the Spanish market were not fully opened up to foreign competitors.

In 1991 Repsol refined more than 60 percent of all the crude processed in Spain, distributed all liquefied petroleum gas, and produced half the petrochemical and oil products. Partially in response to EC criticism, Repsol and the other CAMPSA shareholders decided that CAMPSA's 3,800 service stations and some other retail assets would be divided between Repsol and the CAMPSA minority shareholders—CEPSA, Petromed, and Ertoil. In 1991 the division took place, with Repsol gaining about two-thirds of the stations as well as the use of the service station brand name Campsa (the company continued to also use the Repsol and Repshop brands). CAMPSA continued as a distribution and transportation company, with Repsol in control of the majority of the shares.

Market liberalization continued in Spain into the mid-1990s, resulting in increased competition for Repsol and the loss of some of its clout, such as from the dissolution of CAMPSA. Competitors entering the Spanish market included British Petroleum which took over Petromed, a small refiner, and the French oil powerhouse Elf which bought a stake in CEPSA, the largest private refiner in the country. Altogether about 40 different petroleum companies had been allowed into the Spanish market by the end of 1995.

In response to the growing competition, Repsol pursued an increasingly international strategy of seeking both sources of crude and markets for its products abroad. The company successfully discovered oil in the North Sea, Colombia, Angola, and Egypt and was awarded new exploration areas in Argentina, Angola, Algeria, Dubai, Egypt, and Vietnam. In 1990, it began explorations in Soviet Turkmenistan and agreed to explore in other Soviet areas in cooperation with Total and Petrofina.

Overseeing Repsol since its founding in 1987 was chairman and chief executive officer Oscar Fanjul-Martin. A former economics professor and technocrat, he was instrumental in the negotiations that led to Spain's entry into the European Union. In the early 1990s, Fanjul-Martin succeeded in his efforts to significantly expand Repsol's natural gas operations. In 1992, Repsol and La Caixa, a Spanish bank, merged their natural gas operations to form Gas Natural, with Repsol holding 45.5 percent of the new gas utility. The following year, Repsol gained an even stronger position in natural gas when Gas Natural purchased 91 percent of the Spanish state-owned Enagas, giving Gas Natural a near-monopoly on natural gas on Spain. By 1995, Repsol's natural gas and bottled-gas businesses contributed about 25 percent of company earnings, compared to just nine percent in 1987.

Fanjul-Martin also had the difficult task of guiding Repsol through the oil downturn of 1993, when prices plunged. The company's strengths—such as having much stronger downstream operations than such price-sensitive areas as exploration—were clearly in view, however, and by instituting a vigorous cost-cutting program, Repsol was able to increase profits more than 11 percent, outperforming most of its competitors.

The mid-1990s were marked by a significant reduction in the government ownership of Repsol. Share issues in 1993, 1995, and early 1996 reduced INH's stake in the company to 40.5, 21, and about ten percent, respectively. Each of the issues proved extremely popular in Spain, elsewhere in Europe, and in the United States, testifying to Repsol's strong position.

Repsol headed into the end of the century almost fully privatized and with enviable strength in oil and gas in its home market. The company showed considerable resilience in the face of generally difficult conditions in the oil industry and increased competition. Repsol's diversification into natural gas would likely prove extremely important, as the Spanish market for natural gas was only in its infancy in the mid-1990s.

### Principal Subsidiaries

CLH; Gas Natural (45.5%); Petronor EE. SS., SA (86.58%); Repsol Butano, SA; Repsol Comercial de Productos Petroliferos SA (96.93%); Repsol Derivados, SA (99.96%); Repsol Distribución, SA (99.96%); Repsol Exploración; Repsol Naviera Vizcaína, SA (99.54%); Repsol Petróleo (99.96%); Repsol Química SA; Repsol S.A., Repsol Quimica; Repsol Oil International Ltd. (Channel Islands); Repsol Petroli S.p.A. (Italy); Gaviota Re, S.A. (Luxembourg); Repsol S.A. de C.V. Mexico; Carless Refining & Marketing BV (Netherlands); Repsol Intl. Finance BV (Netherlands); British Solvent Oils (U.K.); Repsol Petroleum Ltd. (U.K.); Repsol (U.K.) Ltd.; Repsol Oil, U.S.A.

### Further Reading

Calian, Sara, and Carlta Vitzthum, "Demand for Repsol Shares Outstrips Supply in Offering as Investors Expect to Strike Oil," *Wall Street Journal,* January 31, 1996, p. C2.

Correlje, A. F., *The Liberalization of the Spanish Oil Sector: Strategies for a Competitive Future,* Rotterdam: The Centre For Policy Studies, Erasmus University, 1990.

Correlje, Aad, *The Spanish Oil Industry: Structural Change and Modernization,* Amsterdam: Thesis Publishers, 1994, 349 p.

Irvine, Steven, and Elisa Martinuzzi, "Repsol Guarantees Satisfaction," *Euromoney,* September 1995, p. 258.

Kielmas, Maria, "Ole Repsol! The Spanish Oil Company Sets a Swift Pace," *Barron's,* August 7, 1989, p. 15.

"Oscar Fanjul-Martin: Repsol," *Financial World,* July 19, 1994, p. 46.

"Profits from Adversity," *International Management,* January/February 1994, pp. 36–41.

Santamaria, Javier, *El petroleo en Espana: del monopolio a la libertad,* Madrid: Espasa Calpe, 1988, 210 p.

—Clark Siewert

—updated by David E. Salamie

# Revell-Monogram Inc.

**8601 Waukegan Road**
**Morton Grove, Illinois 60053**
**U.S.A.**
**(708) 966-3500**
**Fax: (708) 967-5857**

*Wholly Owned Subsidiary of Hallmark Cards Inc.*
*Incorporated:* 1945 as Monogram Models, Inc.; 1955 as
    Revell Inc.
*Employees:* 500
*Sales:* $100 million (1995 est.)
*SICs:* 3944 Games, Toys and Children's Vehicles

Revell-Monogram Inc., a wholly owned subsidiary of Hallmark Cards Inc.'s Binney & Smith unit, is the largest plastic model kit manufacturer in the world. Formed in 1986 with the merger of one-time arch-competitors Revell Inc. and Monogram Models, Revell-Monogram boasts brands and products that have dominated the model industry for generations. In addition to the company's leading position in the American industry, Revell-Monogram's German subsidiary, Revell A.G., provides a strong entry into the European market.

## Company Origins

Monogram Models was founded in Chicago in 1945 as a manufacturer of balsa wood model kits. The company's first kits reproduced World War II ships and airplanes and provided the first inexpensive yet accurate wartime models for beginner builders. Monogram's kits featured better quality balsa wood, wider subject selection and more precut and preshaped parts than other kits on the market at the time and were largely responsible for a postwar surge in model building in America. Meanwhile, across the country in California, a small toy manufacturer named Revell Inc. took advantage of the post war boom in cheap plastic to introduce scale models made entirely of the newly available synthetic compounds. Good quality, inexpensive plastic revolutionized the toy industry in the early 1950s by providing a versatile, light construction material at a fraction of

the cost of wood or metal. Plastic's ability to be molded quickly and cheaply in a huge variety of shapes was particularly attractive to the growing modeling industry, which relied on exploiting emerging fads in a timely fashion. In addition, plastic models were easier to build and could include more detail than their wooden counterparts. Plastic kits quickly became so popular with consumers that by the mid-1950s all other materials had been virtually eclipsed in the modeling industry.

Revell's first big success came in 1951 when it introduced a scale replica of the luxury Maxwell car made famous by the immensely popular radio comedian Jack Benny. Encouraged by the success of the Maxwell, Revell quickly brought out a fleet of vintage car models called "Highway Pioneers." This new line of models proved so profitable that Revell soon dropped all the other toys in its line to concentrate exclusively on plastic model kits. Chicago-based Monogram Models, whose balsa wood models of World War II airplanes had popularized model building in America, quickly jumped on the plastic model bandwagon by introducing a bright red plastic model race car called the Midget Racer. Revell and Monogram soon became fierce competitors in the plastic model industry, each company racing to introduce more intricate and innovative model designs.

## Growth in the 1960s

The 1950s baby boom and postwar prosperity saw record sales in toys of all kinds and both Revell and Monogram Models were able to capitalize on the growing generation of underage consumers. The American love affair with the automobile that reached a peak during the 1950s also contributed to the growth of the modeling industry as Revell and Monogram sought both to capitalize on current trends in automobile design and to develop "fantasy" collectible model cars. In the early 1960s Revell signed an agreement with custom show car designer Ed Roth to produce miniatures based on actual show cars as well as vehicles created exclusively for Revell. Among the memorable models produced by Roth was the "Surfite" single seater beach car, equipped with a surfboard instead of a passenger seat, whose real life duplicate was popularized in the teen movie "Beach Blanket Bingo." Not to be outdone, Monogram hired designer Tom Daniel to create a series of exclusive "fun cars,"

---

**Company Perspectives:**

*Revell-Monogram will be the best model hobby company in the world. We will protect, grow and leverage our proud heritage. We will also use our expertise to capture a leading position in hands-on products which build upon the enduring values of modeling . . . the building experience, fantasy and collectibility.*

---

models based not on actual vehicles but on vintage and contemporary fantasy automobiles. Among Monogram's original creations in the early 1960s was the Li'l Coffin show rod model kit complete with skeleton which was to become one of the company's bestselling kits ever and which was re-released in 1995 to mark Monogram's 50th anniversary.

### Public and Private Ownership in the 1970s

Although the history and growth of these two leading model companies closely paralleled each other through the 1950s and early 1960s, their paths would diverge in the mid-1960s. In 1965 Revell went public with an initial public offering of 150,000 shares. By this time annual sales for the California company had reached $12 million with profits of $1.19 per share. Although Revell's primary products remained automotive, naval, and military model kits, the company also began to experiment with a variety of new merchandise. In addition to capitalizing on such fads as the Beatles by producing three-dimensional model figures, Revell introduced a Lego-like block toy, n-scale trains, and racing car sets. Although each of these products enjoyed initial success, invariably their faddish appeal would wane and Revell would fall back on their core model business. Towards the mid-1960s one of these transient fads, slot-car racing, would land the company in serious financial difficulties. Revell entered this field in 1965 with the acquisition of International Raceways, a small company that had initiated the slot-car racing phenomenon. These scaled up racing cars required large, elaborate track layouts and "commercial" slot-car racing centers began to spring up across the nation to service enthusiasts. In spite of initial enthusiasm about this new form of entertainment, the notoriously fickle teen customers that the racing cars appealed to quickly turned to other amusements and, in 1967, Revell was left with a large inventory of unsaleable slot-car paraphernalia and a $438,000 net loss.

While Revell was going public and diversifying its product line, Monogram maintained a more conservative and focused approach to growing their core business. After revolutionizing the military model industry in the early 1960s with a line of intricately detailed model airplanes at a new scale of $\frac{1}{48}$, Monogram chose to develop its adult modeling business as well as building on its line of youth-targeted miniatures. An important innovation in the children's modeling industry came in 1968 when Monogram introduced the first snap-together models that required no messy and potentially toxic glue for assembly. Parental concerns over glue fumes had become a public relations problem for the modeling industry and the glueless model went a long way towards reviving parents' trust in model

building as a safe and educational experience. This new "snap-tite" brand would become one of Monogram's top selling categories for the next 30 years.

The late 1960s were banner years for the toy industry as the baby boom generation reached prime toy-buying age and American incomes were on the rise. Among the many toy companies that peaked during this period was toy giant Mattel whose Barbie and Hot Wheels brands were bringing in record sales and profits. The booming company began a program of acquisitions in an attempt to grow its share of the toy market. Monogram, which would provide an entry into the model category for Mattel, became the target of interest by the huge toy firm in the summer of '68 and by Christmas of that year Monogram was acquired in full by Mattel. Under Mattel, Monogram continued to produce traditional military and automotive models but also began to expand into licensed properties such as Superman and Snoopy.

### International Expansion for Revell in the 1970s

Through the late 1960s and 1970s Revell also continued to experiment with new products, branching out into educational aids such as filmstrips and scientific models intended for the institutional market as well as expanding their own licensed product line. The company, whose products had traditionally had an almost exclusively male market, now also introduced a girl-oriented craft line featuring fabric art and other craft kits. Most importantly, this was a time of significant international expansion for the growing California firm as the company opened subsidiaries in Germany, Great Britain, Australia, and Switzerland. The annual Revell sweepstakes became the company's most important marketing tool during this period. Prizes such as around-the-world trips and motorcycles were intended to raise awareness of Revell models among boys aged eight through 15. The sweepstakes were tremendously successful and continued to be a crucial component of Revell marketing policy into the late 1970s. The 1970s were a decade of substantial growth for Revell with sales rising from $16 million in 1969 to $47 million in 1978. Nonetheless, the company encountered difficulties turning sales into profits in the late 1970s and in 1978 Revell recorded a net loss of $2.5 million.

### Changing Ownership in the 1980s

Faced with this debilitating loss and with family management undergoing changes, Revell decided to accept an offer by the leading French toy company, Generale du Jouet, to buy out the California firm. Revell's already strong presence in the European market through its British and German subsidiaries facilitated the merger of the company into Generale du Jouet's marketing structure but Revell nevertheless continued to flounder. Not only were overall sales of model kits diminishing at an alarming rate but Revell's share of this market, although still over 50 percent, started to erode in the early 1980s. In addition, parent Generale du Jouet ran into serious difficulties itself because of overexpansion in the late 1970s and in 1982 the French toy giant was faced with a loss of over 50 million French francs. Bailed out by the Edmond de Rothschild financial firm, Generale du Jouet undertook a massive reorganization in 1983 which included a selloff of Revell to American investors.

The toy slump of the early 1980s was as damaging in the United States as it was abroad. Mattel had overextended itself on the development of videogames and, when toy sales dropped in 1984, the huge company posted a net loss of almost $400 million. Like Generale du Jouet, Mattel was forced to undertake a massive reorganization that included selling all of its non-toy divisions. Monogram Models was acquired by a group of investors that included former company president Thomas A. Ganon.

### Joining Forces in the late 1980s

With the two largest model companies now under independent ownership, and with the model kit market under duress, it did not take long before the advantages of joining forces became overwhelming. In 1986 the two longtime competitors, Revell Inc. and Monogram Models, were merged to form the largest model kit company in the world, Revell-Monogram. Although the joining of the two companies was officially termed a merger, the operations of Revell were essentially brought to an end with all molds, tooling, and designs transferred to the offices of Monogram in Illinois.

The newly revitalized company began to see a renewal in the modeling industry, which had taken a hard hit from the video games that had become the new obsession of pre-teen boys. By 1989 sales had risen to $88 million and, with the addition of a line of science toys and die-cast replicas, Revell-Monogram had regained much of the market lost to videogames. In 1991, under CEO Timothy Cawley, Revell-Monogram was brought public with an initial public offering of 1,825,000 shares. Profits that year were a comfortable $2.6 million on $106 million in sales and analysts were positive about Revell-Monogram's prospects. As the company entered the 1990s a new form of competition for the attention of eight- to 14-year-old boys came in the form of the CD-ROM-based computer game and Revell-Monogram felt that an entry into this market would help maintain its presence among this traditional modeling customer base. The company invested about $4 million into the development of an interactive CD-ROM racing car game called Power Modeler that would be sold together with plastic model kits for the featured vehicles. The idea was to encourage collectibility and to give youngsters a new vision of the excitement inherent in the Revell-Monogram models. The hefty retail price of about $70 per kit, however, discouraged parent shoppers who were not sure if they were buying a model or a game. After a year on the market Power Modeler had sold fewer than 50,000 units and the

project was scrapped, leaving Revell-Monogram with a $4 million loss in fiscal 1993. Newly appointed CEO Theodore J. Eischeid commented on the failure of the Power Modeler in *Advertising Age*: "Our idea was the model makes the game better and vice versa. In this particular case, the experiment didn't quite work the way we hoped it would."

### Acquired by Hallmark in 1994

In spite of the Power Modeler debacle, Revell-Monogram's domination of the modeling industry made the company an attractive target for acquisition and, in 1994, Hallmark Cards Inc. purchased the model-kit maker and its foreign affiliates for $85 million. Revell-Monogram became part of Hallmark's Binney & Smith division, which also distributed Crayola crayons around the world. Although the exact nature of the company's products might change, it seemed clear that the youthful urge to build in miniature would carry Revell-Monogram into the 21st century.

### Principal Subsidiaries

Monaco Hobby & Toys (HK) Limited (Hong Kong); Revell AG (Germany); Revell Ltd. (Great Britain); Revell Monogram (Australia) Pty. Ltd.

### Further Reading

Borden, Jeff, "Revell-Monogram Rebuilding After CD-ROM Disaster," *Crain's Chicago Business,* June 27, 1994, p. 26.
"Christmas in July," *Barron's,* July 10, 1967, pp. 15–16.
"La compagnie Generale du Jouet recevra 170 millions de francs," *Le Monde,* March 24, 1983, p. 39.
"Fantasy Figures for Fun and Profits," *Sales and Marketing Management,* June 6, 1983, pp. 23–24.
"Hallmark Cards Inc.," *The Wall Street Journal,* September 28, 1994, p. A6.
"Mattel Inc. Completes Sale of Monogram Models Unit," *The Wall Street Journal,* March 27, 1984, p. 62.
"Play's the Thing," *Barron's,* May 3, 1965, p. 5.
"Revell Completes Merger," *The Wall Street Journal,* August 27, 1979, p. 18.
"Revell Must Stretch Promotion Dollars," *Advertising Age,* December 16, 1968, p. 36.
Wallace, David J., "Toy Cars, Multimedia Make for a Poor Fit," *Advertising Age,* September 26, 1994, p. 18.

—Hilary Gopnik

# Roadmaster Industries, Inc.

## Roadmaster Industries, Inc.

---

**250 Spring Street NW**
**Atlanta, Georgia 30303**
**U.S.A.**
**(404) 586-9000**

*Public Company*
*Incorporated:* 1925 as Anderson and Vail Stamping
  Company
*Employees:* 5,700
*Sales:* $730.9 million (1995)
*Stock Exchanges:* New York
*SICs:* 3751 Motorcycles, Bicycles & Parts; 6719 Holding
  Companies Not Elsewhere Classified

---

Roadmaster Industries Inc. is one of the largest manufacturers of bicycles and a leading producer of fitness equipment and toy products in the United States. The company's major product lines, some of which date back to the 19th century, include bicycles for the adult, teen, and juvenile markets; fitness equipment, including stationary aerobic equipment, multi-station weight systems, and benches; toy products, such as tricycles, wagons, toy horses, bulk plastic toys, sleds, and swings sets; and team sports equipment. The winner of several Vendor of the Year awards in the 1990s, the company sells its products to leading mass merchandisers, such as Toys "R" Us, Wal-Mart, and Target. Some of its better known brand names include Roadmaster, Vitamaster, Flexible Flyer, DP, Hutch, Mac-Gregor, and American Playworld.

### Early History

The origins of the Roadmaster product family can be traced to a small metal factory located in Harvey, Illinois, where its proprietor, Brett Anderson, began making four-inch wheel disks for toy manufacturers in 1925. The following year, he moved his business, now known as the Anderson and Vail Stamping Company to Hammond, Indiana. As the decade progressed, the fledgling company, which changed its name to Junior Toy in

1929, began manufacturing the metal tricycles and little red wagons that would become a familiar part of the American childhood experience. Noted for their dependability, these toys were often passed down from one generation to the next.

Just as the company was starting to establish itself as a reputable toy manufacturer, it found itself in the midst of the Great Depression. While the stock market crash of 1929 and the precipitous decline of the American economy may have spelled the end for many businesses—especially those engaged in the production of such nonessential items as toys—Anderson's company managed to survive. In fact, during the 1930s, the company actually managed to double sales each year as it was able to turn out a line of toys that fell within the budget of average Depression-era wage earner. Its most popular item during the period, a sidewalk bicycle with a stamped metal frame, carried an affordable one-dollar price tag. In 1935, the Junior Toy company began marketing this line of metal framed bicycles and tricycles under the Roadmaster label. The increasing popularity of the products suggested that the name was quickly gaining a reputation for high quality and value.

### Peaks and Valleys: 1950s–1960s

After more than a decade of strong growth, Junior Toy and its Roadmaster line, now under the control of the privately held Cleveland Welding Company, were acquired by AMF Wheel Goods. The 1951 purchase began an era of peaks and valleys for the Roadmaster line. The booming economy of the 1950s and the explosion in the number of births during the postwar era provided a favorable environment for the bike maker. Taking advantage of the increase in its target markets, the company was able to diversify its product line, adding exercise equipment under the brand name Vitamaster in 1950. As the "baby boom" population continued to expand, the company found the need for a new manufacturing facility to keep up with demand. In 1962, the company moved its operations to Olney, Illinois, where it built a new factory on the 122-acre site in southern Illinois that would remain the company's principal bicycle manufacturing location into the 1990s.

After two decades of consistent growth, however, the AMF Wheel Goods Division stalled under the long-distance management of a parent company bogged down in layer after layer of bureaucracy. By the late 1970s, the bicycle division had fallen on hard times. The absence of stable management—the company had seven presidents between 1972 and 1982—and the inability of AMF to run the division efficiently from its headquarters in White Plains, New York, contributed to a steady decline in sales and profits. In the late 1970s and early 1980s, for instance, the company lost an average of $8 million a year. Moreover, the quality of the Roadmaster line—once its hallmark—had fallen to an all-time low. Bicycles made at the Olney plant, according to Judith Vandewater's article in the *St. Louis Post-Dispatch,* were manufactured so poorly that some bike shops in the area refused to repair them, claiming that the bikes would not stay fixed no matter how much labor and effort was put into them.

### The 1980s: Birth of the Roadmaster Corporation

In February 1982, AMF hired a new division president, George C. Nebel, a 47-year-old former Naval officer and vice-president of Milton Bradley Electronics, who was given the challenge of resuscitating the dying bike maker. The deteriorating performance of the Olney plant, however, proved to be too much for AMF executives, who announced their decision to sell the Wheel Goods Division six months later.

During his short tenure as an AMF executive, Nebel had discovered enough potential in the layers of corporate inefficiency to take a chance on the struggling company. He called in Robert O. Zinnen, a 56-year-old lawyer and certified public accountant with whom he had worked at Milton Bradley, to help him survey the company. Six months later, the two, convinced that the labor force in the impoverished agricultural Richland County area would not let them down, completed a leveraged buyout of the company, relying heavily on the assets of the company to finance the deal.

After renaming their new company the Roadmaster Corporation, the two men implemented an aggressive plan for recovery. "We did all the things that were necessary to turn a big ship around," Zinnen told Vandewater. Not only did they cut out waste and reduce inventory to a manageable level, but they launched a more aggressive sales campaign and added new product lines to offset the losses resulting from increasingly strong foreign competition. They expanded the children's product division with a new toddler line, while adding three new divisions: Healthmaster home fitness equipment; Arrow bicy-

cles, a higher-end line designed to boost Roadmaster's reputation with bicycle shops; and a contract manufacturing business that would bid on Defense Department contracts.

To improve sales on their core bicycle business, the newly-formed Roadmaster began more aggressively courting such major retailers as Sears, Penney's, Kmart, and Venture stores, attempting to carve a profitable niche in the popularly-priced segment of the market. While boosting sales 40 percent in its first two years, the company also managed to make large cuts in overhead, reducing the number of administrative employees from 260 to 130, eliminating a variety of corporate perks, and hiring an auditing firm to improve inventory counts. Other improvements included the conversion to "cell manufacturing"—a system under which only one group of employees was responsible for processing raw materials into finished components instead of several throughout the plant, cutting down significantly on the number of times parts had to be moved—and an incentive wage system based on workmanship rather than total output.

While such measures succeeded in making the company profitable within a few years, the gains were only temporary. During the first half of the 1980s, lower-priced imports swallowed up more than one-third of the six U.S. bicycle manufacturers market share. By 1985, domestic companies controlled only half of the $9–$10 million U.S. bicycle market. Such competition forced low-end producers such as Roadmaster to sacrifice profit margins to stay in business.

Competition also forced Roadmaster, the largest employer in southern Illinois at the time, to cut its work force by more than 50 percent in less than four years and to cut the wages of the 460 hourly workers who remained in 1986. That same year, the company imposed a wage agreement on employees that stripped them of their health insurance and lowered wages to below $4 per hour. These draconian measures, while viewed by management as essential to the company's continued existence, precipitated a bitter labor dispute that saw hundreds of employees quit, claiming they could make more from unemployment than from Roadmaster.

Adding to this list of difficulties were a series of lawsuits and Federal Trade Commission investigations concerning the questionable use of the American flag stickers on Roadmaster bikes. According to some employee charges, the company imported bicycles manufactured in Taiwan, fixed the flaws in the bicycles, and then replaced "Made in Taiwan" stickers with American flag stickers.

### The Late 1980s and Early 1990s: New Ownership and Expansion

In spite of such difficulties, Roadmaster managed to sell $55 million worth of bicycles, tricycles, and exercise equipment in 1987. The company's heavy debt load and nagging labor problems prevented it from earning more than $457,000, however. In June of that same year, a new group of owners took on the challenge of making the company profitable over the long run. Henry Fong, head of Denver investment firm Equitex Inc., engineered a $27 million leveraged buyout of the company, which he renamed Roadmaster Industries and took public in

January 1988. Headquarters for the new holding company were established in Colorado.

With Fong at the helm, Roadmaster now had the entrepreneurial drive and, perhaps more important, the financial backing needed to expand the company and turn a sizable profit. The first step in Fong's aggressive growth strategy was the August 1988 acquisition of Ajay Enterprises Corporation, a manufacturer of fitness equipment and sports accessories, with a sports division in Delavan, Wisconsin, and plants in Mexicali, Mexico; Sun Valley, California; Tyler, Texas; and Reading, Pennsylvania. This purchase doubled the size of the company and helped to boost 1988 sales to $109 million, nearly triple that of the previous year, largely as a result of the addition of Ajay's line of treadmills, exercise benches, and free weights. The following year, which saw the company further diversify its product line with the acquisition of Hamilton Lamp, Roadmaster achieved another sales record of $189 million.

This purchase and the series of acquisitions that would follow during the early 1990s helped the company to take advantage of the growing emphasis placed on physical fitness by the American public. As the "baby boom" generation moved into their 30s and 40s, the number of adults conscious about their health and physical appearance reached an all-time high. Bicycling, long one of the most popular leisure and exercise activities in the United States, benefitted from this trend. Roadmaster, while continuing to offer a diverse line for children and teens, did not fail to capitalize on this development in the adult market, quadrupling its sales of bicycles between 1989 and 1993.

By 1990, Roadmaster Corporation, the Illinois-based sporting goods arm of Roadmaster Industries, had grown to become the 44th largest sporting goods company in the nation, on sales of $72 million, 42 percent of the company's total revenues. That figure would quickly expand as Roadmaster Industries acquired Diversified Products, a $215 million sporting-goods manufacturer based in Opelika, Alabama, known for its "DP/Fit for Life" brand name of fitness equipment. The consolidation created a $400 million, 4,500-employee conglomerate that quickly became one of the nation's largest sporting goods companies. Later that year, Roadmaster added size—and prestige—to its bicycle line by acquiring the 113-year-old Columbia Manufacturing Company, a Westfield, Massachusetts, bicycle company.

Having dramatically increased the size and the scope of company operations since his arrival, Fong, along with his co-president and chief executive officer, Edward Shake, had the clout to expand contracts with several of the nation's largest and fastest growing retail chains. While in 1990 one retailer accounted for a large percentage of total sales, by 1992 three retailers—Wal-Mart, Toys "R" Us, and Sears—contributed approximately 50 percent of sales. That same year, Roadmaster launched an aggressive marketing strategy emphasizing what the company believed a unique combination of quality and value. Pointing to products such as mountain bikes that featured racing-quality components at a mass merchandiser price, the company attempted to win retailers and customers over with upscale features at a "best value" price.

As the decade progressed, Roadmaster, along with other U.S. bicycle manufacturers, benefitted from the strengthening of Asian currency and the modest decline in foreign competition that followed. Doing its best to increase market share while trade conditions were favorable, the company engineered one of its most successful product launches in its history, introducing in 1992 the Motocycle, a bicycle made to look like a motorcycle for ten- to 14-year-olds. A concentrated marketing effort that included print advertisements in *Good Housekeeping, Parenting,* and *Family Circle,* as well as television spots on the youth-oriented cable channel "Nickelodeon," enabled the company to sell out its inventory in just five months, on the way to totaling $226.2 million in sales, another record performance.

### The Mid-1990s and Beyond

Roadmaster added to the momentum brought on by its success in the early 1990s with several key acquisitions that helped to diversify the company's interests and significantly boost its sales potential. In September 1993, the company purchased the century-old Flexible Flyer company, maker of the legendary steerable wooden snow sled. The acquisition not only complemented Roadmaster's line of classic toys but helped to moderate the seasonal fluctuations that had previously hurt the company. Flexible Flyer's line of swing sets, for instance, traditionally performed well in the first six months of the year, in contrast to many traditional Roadmaster products, which enjoyed greater sales volume during the Christmas season.

In 1994, the same year that the company began trading on the New York Stock Exchange and moved its corporate headquarters to Atlanta, Georgia, Roadmaster made one of its largest acquisitions to date, as it purchased the Actava Group's four sports subsidiaries: Diversified Products; Nelson/Weather-Rite, a leading supplier of outdoor and camping equipment to mass merchandisers; Hutch Sports U.S.A, a national marketer and distributor of products for team sports with the official license for The National Football League, The National Basketball Association, The National Hockey League, Major League Baseball, and several colleges; and Willow Hosiery Company, a national distributor of socks for the NFL and several collegiate teams. Added sales from the $120 million deal, as Fong told Don Knox of *The Rocky Mountain News,* helped to "accelerate" the company's plans to become the "leading producer" in several segments of the sporting goods industry.

As Roadmaster entered the second half of the 1990s, having increased it sales 377 percent to $730.9 million in the past five years, it expected to continue its strategy of steady growth by improving and expanding its existing product lines. With the foreign market share in the bicycle industry down to 45 percent, the company expected to take advantage of its added size and economies of scale to strengthen its position as a leading bicycle manufacturer for mass merchandisers. As Roadmaster maneuvered to position itself as a low-cost producer in several segments of its business, however, it had to face the pressures resulting from higher than expected increases in the cost of materials such as plastics, cardboard, and steel. Just how well the company would respond to such challenges would play a significant role in its ability to market "best value" products in the future.

## Principal Subsidiaries

Roadmaster Corporation; Roadmaster Limited; Diversified Products Corporation; Hutch Sports, U.S.A. Inc.; Willow Hosiery Company; Nelson/Weather Rite, Inc.

## Principal Divisions

American Playworld; Flexible Flyer.

## Further Reading

Block, Toddi Gutner, ''CEO of the Year,'' *Forbes,* November 7, 1994, pp. 57–58.
Dubroff, Henry, ''Blinder Reaps Profits from New Underwriting,'' *Denver Post,* January 24, 1988.
——, ''Denver Firm Buys No. 1 Tricycle Maker,'' *Denver Post,* August 15, 1987.
Graham, Judith, ''Roadmaster, Diversified Products Merging in $60 Million Deal,'' *Denver Post,* August 8, 1991, p. C2.
Knox, Don, ''Roadmaster to Buy Four Actava Companies,'' *Rocky Mountain News,* June 1, 1994, Bus. Sec., p. 51A.
Marcial, Gene G. ''Roadmaster Goes Freewheeling,'' *Business Week,* November 28, 1994, p. 108.
McKenna, Jon, ''Actava Spin-off to Move Here,'' *Atlanta Business Chronicle,* June 3, 1994.
Rossi, Cathy, ''Columbia's Uphill Climb Ends with Purchase by Roadmaster,'' *Metalworking News,* April 23, 1990, pp. 5–6.
Scaggs, Jim, ''U.S., Illinois Officials Probe Roadmaster,'' *Evansville (Indiana) Courier and Press,* September 21, 1986.
Vandewater, Judith, ''Bike Maker Is on the Road Again,'' *St. Louis Post-Dispatch,* July 7, 1985.

—Jason Gallman

# BOSCH

## Robert Bosch GmbH

**Robert-Bosch-Platz 1**
**Postfach 10 60 50**
**D-70049 Stuttgart**
**Germany**
**(07 11) 811-0**
**Fax: (07 11) 811-6630**

*Private Company*
*Incorporated:* 1886
*Employees:* 158,372 ·
*Sales:* DM 35.84 billion (1995)
*SICs:* 3089 Plastic Products, Not Elsewhere Classified;
3262 Vitreous China Table & Kitchen Articles; 3546
Power Driven Hand Tools; 3663 Radio & TV
Broadcasting & Communications Equipment; 3714
Motor Vehicle Parts & Accessories; 3829 Measuring
& Controlling Devices, Not Elsewhere Classified;
6719 Holding Companies, Not Elsewhere Classified

One of the ten largest companies in Germany, Robert Bosch GmbH is best known as a worldwide supplier of automotive equipment, with world leadership in fuel injection systems and antilock brakes. The company has also developed into a world leader in various other areas, including communications and radio technology, traffic management systems, power tools, household appliances, kitchen and bathroom furniture, thermotechnology, automation technology, and packaging machines. Bosch has operations in more than 128 countries, including the stakes it holds in 42 joint ventures worldwide. Since 1964, 92 percent of the company has been owned by the Robert Bosch Foundation (the Bosch family owns the remaining eight percent), which runs the company on the basis of nonprofit principles and uses its share of company profits to fund various philanthropic programs.

### Early History

The company was founded in Stuttgart in 1886 by a highly motivated, self-educated electrical engineer named Robert Bosch. More talented as an administrator than as an engineer, Robert Bosch gained a reputation for innovation in industrial relations. He instituted an eight-hour work day (which was uncommon at the time) and paid employees at a higher standard rate in the belief that superior working conditions would encourage better employee performance. Bosch readily acknowledged ability and creativity in his employees, assigning the most talented among them to positions in the most promising areas. He also recognized the need for a diverse, high-quality product line as the most direct means to growth.

Bosch entered the automotive industry in the early 1890s, when the company introduced a hand-crank motor starter. Near the turn of the century, on the strength of the growing American automobile market, Bosch became the world leader in ignition systems. By 1914, 70 percent of the company's sales were in the United States. The outbreak that year of World War I resulted in an American trade embargo against Germany. Bosch was prevented from doing any more business in the United States and forced to rely solely on European sales under a wartime economy.

When the war ended in 1918, the German economy was in a state of complete disarray. The nation fell into a serious economic depression during the 1920s, which caused many businesses to fail. Bosch, however, managed to remain in business, partly as a result of its diversification and good management. As the economic situation stabilized, public discontent in Germany began to rise. Bosch, which expanded modestly during this period, purchased the radio manufacturer Blaupunkt-Werke in 1933. That same year, the Nazis under Adolf Hitler seized power and initiated a new economic order characterized by industrial growth and rearmament.

The company enjoyed several periods of strong growth during the 1930s, primarily due to strong demand from German industry and the military for electronic and mechanical products. The company's growth necessitated a new form of organization, and in 1937 it was incorporated as a private limited company. German military adventurism and territorial expansion precipitated World War II which again eliminated foreign markets for companies such as Bosch. Robert Bosch died in 1942, during the height of Germany's success in the war, and was succeeded by Hans Walz. As outlined in Robert Bosch's

## Company Perspectives:

*We want satisfied customers. That is why the highest quality of our products and services is one of our major corporate objectives. This also applies to the quality of the work carried out in our name by our trading partners, and in their sales and service organization.*

will, ownership of the company eventually—in 1964—was transferred in large part to the Robert Bosch Foundation, with the balance remaining in the hands of the Bosch family.

### Postwar Rebuilding

For Germany, the remainder of the war was characterized by severe shortages of all kinds and extensive war damage. At the end of the war Germany was partitioned into occupied Soviet and Western Powers zones (later East and West Germany). The more heavily industrialized western zone, where Bosch was located, was in ruins. Bosch reorganized and its factories were rebuilt. The American market, however, remained closed to Bosch after the war, again forcing the company to strengthen its connections with smaller European manufacturers. New efforts were made to develop more advanced products, and by 1949 Bosch perfected a mechanical fuel injection system.

West Germany was "readmitted" to the world market system in the early 1950s, during which time Bosch became a major supplier of automotive products to foreign manufacturers. During the 1950s the consumer automobile market experienced strong growth, due this time to an expanding world economy and new levels of prosperity.

Also during the 1950s, Bosch began a cautious program of long-term diversification. For example, household appliances were added to the company's product line in 1952 with the introduction of Bosch kitchen appliances. In 1958 washing machines were added, then dishwashers in 1964. In 1952 Bosch also began to manufacture hydraulic equipment and do-it-yourself power tools.

Hans Walz retired in 1962 after 20 years as the company's chief executive. He was replaced by Hans Merkle, a self-taught and apprenticed engineer and businessman, known for his ability to predict changing market conditions. Merkle recognized pollution control and fuel economy as key factors in future automobile sales. Under Merkle's leadership, Bosch began to devote more of its resources to the development of electronic products, and later produced a new fuel injection system that promoted a smoother running engine and reduced fuel consumption.

Potential competitors of Bosch, including Siemens and Bendix, largely ignored the potential of fuel injection systems while Bosch continually perfected new and better versions. When strict new antipollution regulations were enacted in the United States, automobiles equipped with Bosch fuel injectors, such as the Volkswagen Beetle, became extremely popular. Soon afterwards, other European manufacturers, including Daimler-Benz and Volvo, decided to integrate the Bosch system into their product line. When the 1973 OPEC oil crisis caused dramatic increases in the price of petroleum, the highly efficient Bosch fuel injection systems became virtually indispensable.

### Expansion and Diversification in the 1970s and 1980s

Throughout the 1970s, Bosch made moves to expand its operations overseas, moving into Japan and Malaysia in 1972, Turkey in 1973, and Spain in 1978. By the mid-1970s, Bosch had made strong progress in regaining its prewar market share in the United States. Bosch purchased a plant in Charleston, Virginia, in 1974 to produce fuel injection systems in the United States. The company also acquired a 25 percent share of American Microsystems, a manufacturer of integrated circuitry, and a 9.3 percent stake in Borg-Warner, which was well-established in the area of microcircuitry. Bosch planned to apply technologies developed by these two companies to produce even more advanced automotive systems.

The Charleston plant was subsequently expanded three times. Through the late 1970s fuel injection systems, Bosch's primary product, became the most important electronic component to automobile manufacturers. By 1984, nearly half of the cars sold in the U.S. were equipped with fuel injection systems.

In the early 1980s, several other manufacturers initiated efforts to reduce Bosch's share of the worldwide automotive components market. Marcus Bierich, who was named chief executive officer of Bosch in 1984, reacted quickly to these threats by expanding the company's product line and diversifying its operations.

One of the most important products to emerge from this new initiative was ABS, the antilock braking system. This device prevented brakes from locking by means of an electronic gauge wired to the brake pedal. In addition to being an important safety feature, it made a number of other wires and cables redundant, allowing physical space for "cruise control" and other features. By 1985, the Bosch ABS system was standard on many European automobiles and had also been introduced on American luxury cars. Despite competition in this area from Alfred Teves (a subsidiary of ITT) and Honda, Bosch developed additional facilities to build ABS system in order to meet the anticipated increased demand.

Following up on the success of ABS, Bosch was also involved in the development of electronic traction control, which involved sensors to measure wheel speed and adjust the speed as necessary to keep the car under control. Bosch began production of its first traction control system in 1986.

As car features grew more sophisticated, Bosch continued to develop systems to aid the driver. A new device called the digital trip meter calculated the course and direction of a car by measuring heat levels of the terrain and posting a computerized map on the driver's dashboard. In addition to making the driver aware of the most efficient available routes, the meter could also detect traffic jams. The product was introduced in 1989 as the Travelpilot navigation system. A more sophisticated version using CD-ROMs and providing data to the driver via voice and symbols was later introduced in 1995 on luxury-model Japanese vehicles.

Fierce competition and a 1984 metalworkers strike seriously affected the company's production for several months and weakened its lead over competitors. For virtually the first time, clients were forced to evaluate alternative suppliers.

The 1980s also saw Bosch enter the telecommunications market through the acquisition of or the purchase of stakes in various companies involved in the manufacture of equipment and the development of systems, including Telefonbau und Normalzeit, a German telecommunications company, and Telenorma, the exclusive supplier of communications systems to Bundespost, the national postal and telecommunications group. In 1989, these various activities were consolidated with the creation of the Bosch Telecom Business Sector.

### 1990s and Beyond

In addition to expansion into the newly merged areas of the former East Germany, Bosch continued to expand internationally in the early 1990s. The newly opened markets of Eastern Europe were one targeted area, as marketing operations were established in Poland, Hungary, and the Czech Republic in 1992; in Bulgaria, Croatia, Latvia, Russia, Slovenia, Ukraine, and Belarus in 1993; and in Romania in 1994. On the manufacturing side, two Czech Republic-based joint ventures were formed in 1992 to produce automotive equipment. In the Asia-Pacific region, Bosch entered into a joint venture to form Korea Automotive Motor Corp. in South Korea in 1993; was involved in another South Korean joint venture the following year, Korea Mechanics and Electronics Corporation; established a sales company in the Philippines in 1995; and entered into no less than six joint ventures in China also in 1995. Finally, in the United States in 1992, Bosch joined Penske Transportation in setting up a joint venture called Diesel Technology Company to develop and produce injector technology for diesel engines used by heavy-duty commercial vehicles.

Bosch continued to refine its electronic automotive components in the 1990s, introducing the Vehicle Dynamics Control system in 1994, designed to improve the stability of vehicles in critical situations by detecting all rotational movements of the car around its vertical axis. The company also entered into the increasingly lucrative market for airbags through a joint venture with Morton International called United Airbag Systems. Bosch was contributing its expertise in electronic components by developing the triggering devices for side-impact airbags the venture was developing.

Despite continuing its long tradition of innovation, Bosch entered a difficult period in the early 1990s under the combined pressure of depressed markets for automobiles and increased competition. Although known for the high quality of its products, Bosch had also over the years developed a reputation for high prices and inflexibility in its relations with its clients. Auto makers were increasingly turning to other cheaper and more cooperative suppliers for parts they used to purchase from Bosch or manufacturing the parts themselves. The latter occurred in 1991 when General Motors suddenly cut in half what was previously a standing order for fuel-injection parts. Also contributing to Bosch's difficulties was its telecommunications business which, although profitable and already contributing nearly a quarter of overall sales, was finding it increasingly difficult to compete against the giants of the industry—Siemens, Alcatel, and Northern Telecom.

In response to these challenges, Bosch in late 1991 instituted a cost-cutting program and process improvement initiative, and also cut its work force by about 8,000. The company continued to struggle, however, as market conditions failed to improve, leading in 1993 to the company's first sales decline since 1967. At the same time, net income fell every year from 1989 to 1993, overall going from DM 626 million in 1989 to DM 426 million in 1993. Further moves were taken in 1993 to turn the company around, including the elimination of 13,000 additional jobs and the institution of team-oriented work groups.

The next two years showed modest improvements for Bosch as sales increased 6.2 percent in 1994 and four percent in 1995, while net income increased to DM 512 million in 1994 and DM 550 million in 1995. Even if not completely recovered, the company was feeling healthy enough by early 1996 to make a $1.5 billion acquisition of Allied Signal Inc.'s hydraulic- and antilock-braking business for light vehicles. The purchase enabled Bosch for the first time to provide its customers with complete brake systems, and as one of the world's leaders in the field to boot.

The size of this latest acquisition confirmed Bosch's commitment to its core automotive components business and also raised the question of whether the company might divest itself of some assets in order to invest further in the core. The most likely candidate was the telecommunications technology sector, given its struggle to establishment itself. Even if it retained its diversified portfolio, Bosch's future, like its past, would certainly be tied most closely to automobile components.

### Principal Subsidiaries

Blaupunkt-Werke GmbH; Bomoro Bocklenberg & Motte GmbH; Bosch-Siemens Hausgeräte GmbH (50%); Bosch Telecom GmbH; Bosch Telecom Radeberg GmbH; MotoMeter GmbH; Robert Bosch Electronik GmbH; Robert Bosch Elektrowerkzeuge GmbH; Robert Bosch Fahrzeugelektrik Eisenach GmbH; Signal Huber AG; VB Autobatterie GmbH (35%); Robet Bosch AG (Austria); Robert Bosch Produktie NV (Belgium); Robert Bosch spol. sr.o. (Czech Republic); Bosch Diesel spol. sr.o. (Czech Republic; 76%); Robert Bosch (France) SA; Rober Bosch SpA (Italy); Robert Bosch Verpakkingsmachines BV (Netherlands); Blaupunkt Auto-Rádio Portugal Lda (70%); Vulcano Termo-Domésticos SA (Portugal); Robert Bosch España SA (Spain); Robert Bosch España Fábrica Madrid SA (Spain); Robert Bosch España Fábrica Treto SA (Spain); Robert Bosch AB (Sweden); Robert Bosch Internationale Beteiligungen AG (Switzerland; 90%); Scintilla AG (Switzerland; 85%); Bosch Sanayi ve Ticaret AS (Turkey); Robert Bosch Ltd. (U.K.); Worcester Group plc (U.K.; 69%); Robert Bosch Ltda (Brazil); WAPSA Auto Peças Ltda (Brazil); Robert Bosch SA de CV (Mexico); Robert Bosch Corporation (U.S.A.); S-B Power Tool Company (U.S.A.; 50%); Vermont American Corporation (U.S.A.; 50%); Motor Industries Co Ltd (India; 51%); Bosch KK (Japan); Nippon ABS Ltd (Japan; 50%); Doowon Precision Industry Co Ltd (South Korea; 20%); KEFICO Corporation (South Korea; 25%); Robert Bosch (Malaysia) Sdn Bhd; Robert Bosch (South East Asia) Pte Ltd (Singapore; 70%); Robert Bosch (Pty) Ltd (South Africa; 64%); Robert Bosch (Australia) Pty Ltd.

### *Further Reading*

Blau, John R., "As Bosch Gets Tougher, Will Customers Get Going?," *Electronic Business,* January 8, 1990, pp. 81–85.

"Braking," *Economist,* April 25, 1992, pp. 75–76.

Brooke, Lindsay, "No Strong Recovery," *Automotive Industries,* December 1991, pp. 36–38.

Fuhrman, Peter, "Euro-Thrash," *Forbes,* July 22, 1991, pp. 66–67.

Heuss, Theodor, *Robert Bosch, His Life and Achievements,* New York: Henry Holt, 1994, 612 p.

"Knowing Who's Bosch," *Economist,* February 27, 1993, p. 61.

Kobe, Gerry, "Robert Bosch Corp. Automotive Group," *Automotive Industries,* February 1990, pp. 69–70.

Naj, Amal Kumar, "Allied Signal Selling Piece of Auto Unit," *Wall Street Journal,* March 1, 1996, pp. A3, A4.

Plumb, Stephen E., "All Quiet on the Eastern Front? Not at Bosch," *Ward's Auto World,* July 1993, p. 104.

Reier, Sharon, "Components: Robert Bosch," *Financial World,* April 14, 1992, p. 56.

"Success by Stealth," *Economist,* July 9, 1988, p. 69.

Schroter, Harm G., "The German Question, the Unification of Europe, and the European Market Strategies of Germany's Chemical and Electrical Industries, 1900–1992," *Business History Review,* Autumn 1993, p. 369.

Way, Arthur, "A Mark of Respect for German Supplier," *Financial Times,* July 12, 1994, p. FTS3.

—updated by David E. Salamie

# Roberts Pharmaceutical Corporation

**6 Industrial Way West**
**Eatontown, New Jersey 07724**
**U.S.A.**
**(908) 389-1182**
**Fax: (908) 389-1014**

*Public Company*
*Incorporated:* 1983 as VRG International
*Employees:* 348
*Sales:* $112.2 million (1994)
*Stock Exchanges:* NASDAQ
*SICs:* 2834 Pharmaceutical Preparations

A small yet fast-growing pharmaceutical company, Roberts Pharmaceutical Corporation licenses or buys drugs that are nearing completion of the federal approval process, operating not as a manufacturer of medications, but as a purchaser, developer, and marketer of products that have already been subjected to preliminary research by larger drug concerns. One of the pharmaceutical industry's elite group of small-sized competitors, Roberts Pharmaceutical was founded in 1983 by Dr. Robert A. Vukovich, who led the company from a one-man operation to the rousing success it had become by the mid-1990s, with roughly 350 employees and more than $100 million in annual sales. During the mid-1990s, the company marketed its pharmaceutical products in seven countries and maintained operating subsidiaries in the United States, Canada, and the United Kingdom.

### The Pharmaceutical Industry in the 1980s

As the 1980s were winding down, a trend within the pharmaceutical industry was picking up speed. Increasingly, as the decade was drawing to a close, drug companies were seeking the benefits of consolidating their operations with other drug companies, touching off a spate of mergers among the largest pharmaceutical concerns that divided the multibillion dollar market for prescription and nonprescription drugs into increasingly bigger slices. One after another, one large drug company merged with another large company, combining the already prodigious assets owned by each to create a cadre of industry titans who held sway over drug research and manufacturing. In the space of a few short years, behemoth drug conglomerates were created as industry stalwarts joined forces: SmithKline merged with Beecham, Rhone-Poulenc merged with Rorer, Bristol-Myers merged with Squibb, Marion Laboratories merged with Merrell Dow, and American Home Products merged with A.H. Robins. Ironically, as the big merged with the big, the same trend that tightened the grip these massive pharmaceutical corporations held on the drug market also benefited a much smaller breed of pharmaceutical competitors. One such company was Roberts Pharmaceutical.

For large national and international drug companies, merging yielded instantaneous benefits, combining the might of two competitors into one appreciably more powerful corporation. Once the agreement to merge was signed, the company created through the consolidation enjoyed increased marketing strength, a broader product line, and, of particular importance in the pharmaceutical industry, greater financial resources to devote to the research and development of pharmaceutical products. There was, however, a price to be paid for the advantages of large size. Large pharmaceutical companies needed to realize large profits to maintain their stature, a circumstance of their magnitude that forced the bigger drug companies to eschew involvement with products that had little hope of generating sufficient sales or profits to contribute to their growth. As a result, there were numerous, potentially profitable drugs that large pharmaceutical companies were forced to pass over, a condition of their operating strategies that created opportunities for small drug companies willing to market what industry giants could not afford to do.

Although the rash of mega-mergers widened the gap separating what large and small drug companies considered to be financially viable drugs to market, the disparity had existed for decades before consolidation became a pervasive trend during the late 1980s and early 1990s, something one employee of a large pharmaceutical corporation noted during his career. Robert A. Vukovich, the founder of Roberts Pharmaceutical, had spent much of his professional life working for several of the most prominent drug companies in the world, serving in various research and management capacities at Warner-Lambert, Squibb, and Revlon. Vukovich spent five years at Revlon and another ten years at Squibb, noting during his tenure at each company that corporate strategy precluded the development of certain drugs. "There would be many product opportunities that would be passed up," Vukovich later remembered in an interview with the *Business Journal of New Jersey*, "We would pass up on products all the time that didn't meet certain strategies or didn't have [potential] third-year sales of $50 million." Vukovich's observations had a definitive effect, sparking his interest in forming his own small drug company that could develop those drugs the billion-dollar pharmaceutical corporations passed up.

### Early 1980s Company Origins

After spending years working for others, Vukovich decided to set out on his own, resolving to establish his own small pharmaceutical concern and vie for the business eschewed by large corporations in the industry. Knowing, as he succinctly put it, that "big companies need big drugs to deliver big growth," Vukovich entered the pharmaceutical fray with his mind set on obtaining the rights to drugs with licensing opportunities, hoping to build his business on the business cast aside by his larger pharmaceutical counterparts. In 1983, he formed VRG International, a contract testing laboratory that soon shifted its focus and then began its meteoric rise in the pharmaceutical industry, recording exponential growth before adopting the Roberts Pharmaceutical name in 1988.

A one-man operation, VRG International represented a modest beginning for Vukovich, giving the former pharmaceutical researcher and manager nowhere to go but up. In this direction, Vukovich and his fledgling enterprise moved with resolute speed, registering startling growth in an industry dominated by entrenched giants. To operate successfully within the shadow of these recognized world leaders in drug research, manufacture, and marketing, Vukovich employed a strategy he coined "search and develop," an approach tailor-made for a small, resourceful, and under-financed company such as Roberts Pharmaceutical. While the huge corporations spent millions of research and development dollars, Vukovich spent his time and limited financial means searching for, rather than researching, product opportunities that, as he termed it, "may not fit the big company mold." Using the numerous contacts he had developed within the pharmaceutical industry during his career, Vukovich scoured the world to find drugs that, typically, were undergoing Food and Drug Administration (FDA) scrutiny and then acquired the rights to such drugs, avoiding the costly, time-consuming, yet conventional research and development approach used by large pharmaceutical corporations.

### Rapid Growth During the Late 1980s

The strategy worked, fueling the company's growth and drawing the attention of industry observers and the business press. By 1985, two years after the company was founded, VRG International's annual sales reached $200,000, a respectable but otherwise unremarkable total for a small pharmaceutical firm. From 1985 forward, however, the pace of growth increased considerably, as Vukovich's business flourished during the lat-

ter half of the 1980s. The $200,000 generated in sales in 1985 quintupled the following year, reaching the $1 million mark, then nearly quadrupled in 1987. At the end of 1988, by which time VRG International had been renamed Roberts Pharmaceutical, Vukovich was sitting atop a firm that was drawing praise from both those within and outside the pharmaceutical industry. Over a four-year period, the company's annual sales had increased an incredible 3,350 percent, enough to make it the fastest growing private company in New Jersey and silence any speculation that small drug companies were a dying breed.

Roberts Pharmaceutical's energetic sales growth during the second half of the decade had been highlighted by the establishment of a 20,000-square-foot headquarters facility in Eatontown, New Jersey in 1986 and by the opening of a 26-bed clinical research facility at Riverview Medical Center in Red Bark, New Jersey in 1988. The company had also broadened its geographic scope considerably in 1988, forming two subsidiaries, Monmouth Pharmaceuticals Ltd. in Great Britain and Roberts Pharmaceutical in Canada, to bolster its search and development activities.

By the end of the 1980s, the conditions in the pharmaceutical industry were becoming increasingly better for Vukovich and his fast-growing company. While Vukovich was employed by Revlon, Squibb, and Warner-Lambert, operating strategy had stipulated that a drug must have potential third-year sales of at least $50 million. By the end of the 1980s, as Roberts Pharmaceutical was growing by leaps and bounds and as large drug corporations were consolidating, the projected three-year minimum had grown to $250 million, creating, theoretically, more opportunities for a small drug company that did not require huge, money-generating medications to sustain its existence. In the years ahead, this fundamental difference in the operating strategies between the industry stalwarts and Roberts Pharmaceutical would enable Vukovich to secure a firmer grip on his company's markets and ensure that the future for small drug companies would be filled with numerous prospects.

Another fundamental difference separating the way Vukovich's business and large drug corporations operated was that, unlike its much larger competitors, Roberts Pharmaceutical did not manufacture the medications it marketed. Instead, the company contracted out the production of its pharmaceutical products to roughly two dozen manufacturers, relying on a number of strategic alliances to license and produce its products. By the end of the 1980s, Roberts Pharmaceutical had affiliations with nonprofit, academic, and corporate organizations. The company was involved in research activities with eight universities, the National Cancer Institute, the U.S. Army, and the U.S. Department of Energy, among others. Licensing agreements had been struck with some of the most prominent drug and scientific concerns in the world, including Bayer AG, Dupont, Johnson Matthey, and Chemie Linz. Further, manufacturing contracts joined Roberts Pharmaceutical with industry leaders such as Squibb (the former employer of Vukovich), Ben Venue Laboratories, and Pace Pharmaceuticals. With these strategic alliances in place by the end of the decade, Roberts Pharmaceutical entered the 1990s as a fast-rising company, one of the elite of a burgeoning breed within the pharmaceutical industry.

### 1990 Public Offering

About the only obstacle blocking the company's growth as it entered the 1990s was a shortage of cash. Although product opportunities were abundant, to acquire the rights to drugs undergoing exhaustive FDA approval trials, Vukovich needed money. He helped to resolve this problem by taking his company public as the new decade began. In 1990, two million Roberts Pharmaceutical shares went on the market at $16 per share, giving Vukovich a quick infusion of cash to purchase the rights to pharmaceutical products. The initial public offering in 1990 helped the company assume a more aggressive acquisitive stance, as it began buying both established and development-stage compounds. As part of the expansion program that took place during that year, Roberts Pharmaceutical acquired, in January 1990, IV Therapy Associates, which distributed high-cost biotechnology pharmaceuticals for use in physicians' offices on a prescription basis. In September 1990, the company acquired the rights to a group of 16 over-the-counter products from UpJohn, including Cheracol, a line of cough medicines, Haltran, for menstrual pain, and Pyrroxate, for allergies.

Additions to the company's product line continued in 1991, when four prescription products from the Norwich division of Procter & Gamble were acquired in March, the same month Roberts Pharmaceutical secured the rights to three nonprescription products from a joint venture involving Johnson & Johnson and Merck. On the heels of these acquisitions, another public offering was completed in June, when 2.3 million shares were sold for $10.25 per share, providing the resources for further acquisitions.

By the end of 1991, Roberts Pharmaceutical was marketing 38 pharmaceutical products, with eight additional products in the later stages of development and another dozen undergoing pre-clinical testing. The company's strategy of buying or licensing drugs on which larger pharmaceutical corporations had conducted preliminary research was proving to be a boon to its growth, eliminating some of the significant developmental risks associated with bringing a drug to market yet positioning it to reap the financial rewards once the drug was granted FDA approval. Of the company's six drugs undergoing advanced clinical testing at the end of 1991, each, according to Vukovich's projections, were capable of eventually generating $100 million in annual sales, which represented enormous potential growth for a company that was anticipating $12 million in annual sales by year's end.

From the early 1990s to the mid-1990s, Roberts Pharmaceutical enjoyed robust growth, as it continued to add to its product line by acquiring pharmaceutical products undergoing FDA scrutiny. Annual sales soared from roughly $10 million at the beginning of the decade to more than $100 million by 1995, drawing the attention not only of those in New Jersey but of investors and industry observers throughout the country. Roberts Pharmaceutical was ranked during this period of strong growth as one of the 50 fastest growing companies by *Fortune* magazine, as one of the 100 fastest growing companies by *Inc.* magazine, and as one of *CEO* magazine's "top 50 companies." As the company moved forward from the mid-1990s and prepared for the latter part of the decade and the future ahead, Vukovich hoped to keep his company's name among the nation's elite and continue the pace of growth that had transformed his fledgling, one-man operation into a flourishing international enterprise.

### Further Reading

"Climbing Quickly," *Business Journal of New Jersey,* September 1989, p. 46.
Peaff, George Jr., "On the Fast Track," *Business Journal of New Jersey,* September 1989, p. 43.
Savitz, Eric J., "Who Needs R&D," *Barron's,* October 28, 1991, p. 16.

—Jeffrey L. Covell

# SAP AG

Neurottstrasse 16
69190 Walldorf
Germany
(+49) 6227/34-0
Fax: (+49) 6227/34-1282
Internet site: http://www.sap-ag.de

*Public Company*
*Incorporated:* 1976
*Employees:* 6,857
*Sales:* 2.70 billion DM (1995)
*Stock Exchanges:* Berlin Bremen Düsseldorf Frankfurt
    Hamburg Hanover Munich Stuttgart Geneva
*SICs:* 7372 Prepackaged Software; 7373 Computer
    Integrated Systems Design; 7389 Miscellaneous
    Business Services

SAP AG is the fifth largest independent software producer worldwide and the largest producer of standard enterprise-wide business applications for the roughly $9 billion global client-server software market. The company's principal business activities are the development and marketing of an integrated line of prepackaged computer software for over 1,000 predefined business processes, from financial accounting, human resources, and plant maintenance to quality assurance, materials management, sales and distribution, and business workflow. Its two major products, the R/2 and R/3 suite of business software applications, are used by over 4,000 companies in the oil and gas, banking, insurance, utilities, telecommunications, pharmaceuticals, consumer products, automotive, retail, health care, chemicals, and high tech and electronics industries. Through its 28 international subsidiaries, led by its U.S. subsidiary SAP America, SAP AG markets its software and consulting, training, and support services in more than 50 countries.

### 1970s Founding

SAP AG was founded in 1972 by five German engineers with IBM in Mannheim, Germany; interestingly four of the founders—Hasso Plattner, Dietmar Hopp, Klaus Tschira, and Hans Werner Hector—were still with SAP in early 1996. When an IBM client asked IBM to provide enterprise-wide software to run on its mainframe, the five began writing the program only to be told the assignment was being transferred to another unit. Rather than abandon the project altogether, they left IBM and founded SAP in Walldorf, near Heidelberg. While the company originally took its name from the abbreviation for *Systemanalyse und Programmenentwicklung* (systems analysis and program development), SAP eventually came to stand for *Systeme, Anwendungen, und Produkte in Datenverarbeitung* (systems, applications, and products in data processing).

Without the benefit of loans from banks, venture capitalists, or the German government, SAP began fashioning its software business gradually through the cash flow generated by an ever-growing stable of customers. Working at night on borrowed computers to land their first contracts, Plattner and colleagues built SAP's client list with German firms in its region, beginning with a German subsidiary of the global chemical company ICI and later adding such major German multinationals as Siemens and BMW.

Operating in a corporate computing climate in which business programs were designed to provide only specific, isolated solutions with no relevance to a company's other applications—let alone any outside company's needs—the idea of a fully integrated software product that could be tailored to any company's business proved a hard sell at first. However, because SAP produced software, a non-labor-intensive product, it was able to avoid the labor agreements and high costs that dog many German manufacturing startups. In 1976 SAP declared itself a GmbH (*Gesellschaft mit beschränkter Haftung*) corporation, or limited company, and by 1978 it was selling its financial accounting software to 40 corporate customers.

### R/2 in the Late 1970s

In 1978 SAP began developing, and the following year released, R/2 (R for "real-time"), a mainframe-based, standard business software suite in which integratable modules for accounting, sales and distribution, and production enabled customers to consolidate their financial and operational data into a single database and eliminate costly paperwork and data entry. Because the modules were self-standing, businesses could select only those they needed, which could then be further customized to their unique requirements. The promise of real-time integration of mission-critical corporate data, viewable through the spreadsheet-like windows of specialized software, offered the potential for uniform data flow, streamlined business operations, and centralized decision-making.

Relying on word of mouth filtering through the overseas branches of its German customers, SAP soon began selling its software outside Europe. With corporate giants like Dow Chemical and Bayer already running R/2, SAP could rely on the fear of obsolescence of its customers' rivals to sell its software to the major competitors in each industry. Among the large corporations who began to adopt R/2 were Dupont, General Mills, Goodyear Tire and Rubber, Heinz, and Shell Oil, as well as 80 of the 100 largest companies in Germany, such as Hoechst, Daimler Benz, and BASF. By 1991 R/2 had gone through four releases or versions and had established itself as the standard for integrated corporate business software in Europe. By 1994, SAP could claim more than 1,400 R/2 installations worldwide.

### R/3 Development in the 1980s

As R/2's potential began to peak in the mid-1980s, Plattner and company's former employer, IBM, announced a new "system applications architecture" (SAA) technology in which all IBM operating systems and platforms would be fully harmonized such that code written for one product would work with any other. Seeing the ramifications of such integratability for its own products, in 1987 SAP began developing R/3 for use in the decentralized, non-mainframe computing environment known as client-server. In client-server arrangements, data is processed not by a single costly mainframe but by many cheaper networked "server" computers, which display their data on flexibly arrangeable PCs called "clients." While R/2 focused on providing data processing solutions for static, individual functions of business operations, such as inventory tracking or shipping, R/3 was designed to allow a business to view its entire business operation as a single integrated process in which data entered into any single application in the system would simultaneously be registered in every other. In theory, a company's entire data network would now be a cohesive, interpretable whole that would enable management to more efficiently allocate resources, develop products, manage inventory, forecast trends, streamline manufacturing processes, and automate routine operations.

R/3 itself consisted of IBM's OS/2 operating system as its "front end" or user interface, IBM's DB2 program as its database component, and SAP's own proprietary application component, which was based on AT&T's Unix operating system because it offered the greatest functionality with other vendors' systems. Thus was created the three-tiered architecture—interface or desktop + database + application—on which all later versions of R/3 would be based.

By 1987 SAP had grown to 450 employees and boasted sales of DM150 million. And although no less than 27 percent of this was plowed back into research, in 1988 SAP GmbH formally converted itself to a publicly traded *Aktiengesellschaft* (AG) to raise even more capital for research and development. SAP had established its first operations outside Germany in the mid-1980s, but it was not until the creation of a Swiss-based subsidiary, SAP International, in the late 1980s that it began the expansion that would make it a truly international player in the global client-server software market. In 1988, it established SAP America in Philadelphia, staffing it initially with transplanted German managers. SAP executives soon realized, however, that an American team was more likely to be able to maneuver through the idiosyncrasies of the U.S. software market and soon began hiring U.S. professionals. One not unimportant result was the abandonment of traditional German business practices in favor of a more American approach: lifting limits, for example, on how much salesmen could earn in commissions and submitting budgets in which fully one-third of all annual resources were devoted to product marketing. Fueled by the release of R/3 in 1992, SAP America began to grow into SAP AG's most profitable subsidiary, expanding from two U.S. offices to twenty between 1992 and 1995 alone.

### Introduction of R/3 in the 1990s

After five years in development, R/3 had been launched with the expectation that it would complement R/2's multinational-oriented niche by extending SAP's reach into the mid-sized, less mainframe-dominated business software market. Unexpectedly, however, R/3's release coincided with a growing trend toward corporate downsizing, and even SAP's largest customers began eyeing R/3 as a less labor-intensive replacement for R/2. As a result, in the space of one year (1992–93), the percentage of SAP America's total revenue generated by R/3 catapulted from five to 80 percent, and R/2's status as SAP's flagship product dwindled from 95 percent of revenues to only 20 percent. R/3 was suddenly hot, and virtually overnight SAP had translated its reputation as Germany's *wunderfirma* to the global stage.

On the strength of R/3's rocketing sales, by the mid-1990s SAP had traveled from the relative anonymity of 1992 to the business applications vendor of choice for nine of the ten largest U.S. corporations, one-third of the *Fortune* 500, seven of the ten largest *Business Week* Global 1000, and 80 percent of the *Fortune* 100 companies in software, computers, peripherals, and semiconductors. Total sales revenues had nearly tripled between 1991 and 1995 to DM 2.7 billion and had increased 66 percent between 1993 and 1994 alone. Such major corporations as Apple, Chevron, Colgate-Palmolive, Digital Equipment, and Polaroid were jumping on the R/3 bandwagon, and by September 1995 SAP could claim over 1,100 installations of R/3 for companies with $1 billion or more in sales (in addition to 700 R/2 installations) and more than 1,300 installations in smaller companies (with 800 R/2 installations). SAP's share price had in the meantime grown 1,000 percent since its introduction on the German stock exchange in 1988, and by 1996 it ranked as the highest valued company in Germany.

## Foreign Markets in the 1990s

Two years into the R/3 boom, SAP's sales to German companies, once its sole market, had fallen to 37 percent; North American sales accounted for one-third of all revenues; and the Asia-Pacific market was expected to reach the same level by the year 2000. With two-thirds of all sales revenues now coming from its foreign subsidiaries, in 1996 SAP relocated most of its marketing operation to its Wayne, Pennsylvania, complex. Between 1992 and 1996, it opened subsidiaries in South Africa, Malaysia, Japan, the Czech Republic, Russia, mainland China, and Mexico among others, and was making R/3 available in 14 foreign languages including Russian, Mandarin Chinese, and Thai.

As SAP's global market share in client-server applications began to climb toward 30 percent, new versions of R/3 were released to enhance customizability, reduce installation time, and extend the number of business processes the product addressed. Version 3.0, released in 1995, offered modules in four basic business areas: financial, sales and distribution, manufacturing and logistics, and human resources. A complete R/3 system involved more than 75 modules, 7,000 tables controlling over 3,000 processes, as many as 17 million lines of code, and an installation time of seven to nine months. While individual modules were priced at about $100,000 each, the total installation tab for the average customer (excluding consultants' fees) amounted to $1 million. Complete installations, however, including software, hardware, and system integration, were known to climb as high as $30 million.

If the corporate world's sudden enthusiasm for the R/3 solution at times resembled a religious conversion, there was never a scarcity of heretical dissent. Some customers began to complain of the extreme complexity of R/3's structure, which forced users to search through several layers of menus before finding the application they wanted to run. Configuring the product to conform to the highly particular needs of corporate clients took months, and sometimes over a year, to complete, and the third-party consultants hired to guide clients through the installation ordeal often had little practical experience or abandoned customers for more lucrative projects midway through. Moreover, the rule of thumb that corporations should prepare to spend one dollar on consultants for every dollar spent on software became an object of nostalgia as consultant-to-software expense ratios for R/3 installations rose to four and even ten to one. As SAP began to enjoy the monolithic status of Microsoft and IBM it was also accused of arrogantly forcing its system on customers who could not use R/3 unless it was modified to conform to their unique business practices. Finally, some corporate information technology managers, taking the dictum "You don't get fired for buying SAP" too close to heart, were convincing their companies to invest in R/3 without examining whether they really needed so robustly featured a system or whether it could create, for them, the efficiencies that would justify its cost.

## Competition and Other Challenges

SAP's two major competitors, Oracle Systems (United States) and Baan (the Netherlands), were meanwhile making inroads into SAP's market share. Although Oracle's database product was the program most often used as R/3's database component—making SAP the largest value-added reseller of Oracle products—in 1995 Oracle announced it would overtake SAP as the world's leading provider of industry-specific software within three years. Baan, though dwarfed by SAP in sales and customers, scored major coups in the mid-1990s when both Boeing and German giant Siemens Nixdorf rejected R/3 in favor of Baan's quick-installing business software package. SAP boardmember Henning Kagermann dismissed the setbacks, telling the Deutsche Presse Agentur, "If SAP wins a large order, it's accepted as natural. When we lose a potential customer, immediately it's a big headline." SAP management also dispelled the severity of the threat posed by Oracle, pointing out that it in head-to-head competition SAP still won the contract 80 percent of the time.

Two public relations disasters in the mid-1990s suggested not only the extent of the controversy that had begun to surround R/3 but also SAP's saavy in handling criticism. In March 1995 the German business magazine *Wirtschaftswoche* published an article accusing SAP of accepting commissions from hardware vendors for computers sold to SAP customers and quoting several users' disparaging remarks about the expense and installation time required by R/3. As share prices nosedived, SAP lashed back. Its hardware partners unanimously denied any kickback arrangement with SAP, and SAP itself took out a court order on the magazine for inaccuracy and deliberate misquotation and ran four-page ads in major German print outlets in which the article's sources claimed they were misquoted and expressed satisfaction with R/3.

Then, in early 1996, U.S. computer industry analyst Forrester Research published a study in which it argued that SAP's R/3 was based on an obsolete architecture that could not keep pace with the open, nonproprietary architecture increasingly favored by the software industry. SAP, Forrester claimed, knew that R/3 would be obsolete by 1997 and secretly planned to foist a brand new "object-based" system called R/10 on its customers in 1999, masking its deployment through a series of add-ons to R/3. All SAP customers, Forrester advised, should minimize their dependency on R/3 and prepare "exit strategies" to avoid being trapped into an expensive installation of a new SAP product.

SAP reacted by prematurely releasing quarterly financial figures showing that R/3 sales had not in fact peaked and by vehemently denying that it was planning to abandon R/3. It further vowed to spend DM3 billion on R&D over the next five years and announced plans for new versions of R/3 that reflected its willingness to make the product, which was based on its own proprietary programming language, more open to integration with other vendors' products. SAP, moreover, signaled it was embracing the Internet-driven trend toward "object-oriented" software in which applications could be embedded with other vendors' mini-programs (called "objects" or "applets"). The strategy worked, and Forrester Research was soon announcing that SAP was "leading in the new Internet game."

## The Future

In the mid-1990s industry observers agreed that SAP's continued dominance of the client-server business software market rested on its ability to stay ahead of the breathtaking pace of change in the global software market. In the mid-1990s, for example, SAP was directly affected by the rise of the "intranet," a microcosmic version of the Internet created by companies as in-house data networks, mirroring the structure and appearance of the World Wide Web but protected from the cybersurfing public by so-called firewalls. By seeming to offer the potential to perform many of the same business applications and data processing features of R/3, such intranets represented a plausible threat to SAP's market leadership. SAP responded by announcing new features that would turn R/3 into an Internet-capable tool. Using a browser connected to the Web, for example, two companies with R/3 installed in their systems could process orders in real time over the Internet, while consumers could order products electronically from a company's online catalog and be confident the order was registered immediately in the company's R/3 system.

SAP's ability to sustain its success also depended on its willingness to continue working, à la Microsoft, with its hundreds of strategic partner firms throughout the computer and services industries. SAP's Platform Partners program, for example, had enabled it to cooperate with computer manufacturers such as Compaq and IBM in tailoring SAP products to new hardware developments. And its partnership program with such Big Six accounting firms as Arthur Andersen and Price Waterhouse had spawned a lucrative new subindustry of R/3 consultants whose institutional independence from SAP enabled it to focus more of its resources on improving its product. Finally, SAP's participation with other software vendors in industry-wide initiatives (such as the Open Application Group) to determine standards for new technologies demonstrated its willingness to cooperate with potential competitors to ensure the continued functionality and influence of its products.

Significantly, in 1994 SAP formed an alliance with America's software giant Microsoft to make SAP software integratable with such Microsoft products as Windows NT, an operating system for networked computers, and SQL Server, a database product. In 1995, Microsoft returned the favor by selecting R/3 for its global finance and accounting data system. In early 1996, Microsoft founder and chairman Bill Gates paid a symbolic visit to SAP AG's German headquarters to talk up the two megacompanies' budding relationship. "We love SAP," he said. "SAP has had more impact on our general product direction than any other software company we have worked with. . . . [Microsoft and SAP] are the two best companies to be in."

By learning how to quash media and public relations flare-ups and better market its products, by continuing to modify R/3 to capitalize on new technologies like the Internet, and by encouraging third-party vendors to develop specialized add-on applications to extend the number of business areas in which R/3 could be used, SAP appeared to have positioned itself to remain a formidable presence in the global business software market.

## Principal Subsidiaries

SAP America Inc., SAP (Schweiz) AG, SAP France S.A., SAP Canada, SAP (UK) Limited, SAP Japan Co. Ltd., SAP Italia S.p.A., SAP Asia Pte. Ltd. (Singapore), SAP Hong Kong, SAP (Beijing) Software System Co., Ltd., SAP Aktiengesellscaft (Moscow), SAP Nederland B.V., SAP Österreich GmbH (Austria), SAPSA (PTY) LTD. (South Africa), SAP Australia PTY LTD, SAP Mexico, S.A. DE C.V., SAP-M GmbH, STEEB-CAS Informationstechnik GmbH.

## Further Reading

Edmondson, Gail, "America's Latest Software Success Story Is German," *Business Week,* August 8, 1994, p. 46.

Fondiller, David S., "Client Serving," *Forbes,* July 4, 1994, p. 130.

"The Prudent Approach to R/3," *The Forrester Report,* April 1996.

Hamm, Steve, "All Abooarrrd!: SAP America and SAP AG Gain Momentum," *PC Week,* July 17, 1995, p. A1.

Lieber, Ronald, "Here Comes SAP," *Fortune,* October 2, 1995.

Nee, Eric, "Hasso Plattner and Klaus Besier: An Interview with Eric Nee," *Upside,* December 1995.

Ricciuti, Mike, and J. William Semich, "SAP's Client/Server Battle Plan," *Datamation,* March 15, 1993, pp. 26–32.

Saltz-Trautman, Peggy, "Creating an Industry," *International Business,* February 1996.

*SAPInfo: The Magazine of the SAP Group,* Walldorf, Germany: SAP AG.

"SAP Responds to Media Slaying," *IBM System User International,* http://apt.usa.globalnews.com/ibmsu/iss6/sap.htm

Steinmetz, Greg, "German Firm Grows, Silicon-Valley Style," *Wall Street Journal,* April 11, 1995, p. A16.

Zeitz, William A., "SAP R/3: Dream or Nightmare?" *ComputerWorld,* January 29, 1996.

—Paul S. Bodine

# Sbarro, Inc.

763 Larkfield Road
Commack, New York 11725
U.S.A.
(516) 864-0200
Fax: (516) 462-9058

*Public Company*
*Incorporated:* 1977
*Employees:* 9,100
*Sales:* $319.2 million (1995)
*Stock Exchanges:* New York
*SICs:* 5812 Eating Places; 6794 Patent Owners & Lessors

Sbarro, Inc. operates and franchises an international chain of family-oriented Italian restaurants under the "Sbarro," "Sbarro The Italian Eatery," and "Cafe Sbarro" names. Most of these are buffet and cafeteria-style restaurants located in food courts in shopping malls. Others are found in airports, toll-road rest areas, sports arenas, hospitals, universities, and downtown locations. The Sbarro menu offers pizza, pasta, hot and cold Italian entrees, salads, sandwiches, cheesecake, and other desserts at a modest price with fast service. As of April 1, 1996, there were nearly 800 Sbarro restaurants, located in 47 states, the District of Columbia, Puerto Rico, Canada, England, Belgium, Australia, Kuwait, Chile, France, Qatar, Saudi Arabia, Israel, Lebanon, and the Philippines. Three-fourths of these were company-owned and operated; the others were franchised. The Sbarro family owned 49 percent of the stock.

### Early History

In 1956, Gennaro Sbarro (pronounced zah-BAHR-ro) and his wife Carmela emigrated from Naples, Italy, to Brooklyn with their three young sons, Joe, Mario, and Anthony. The Sbarros wanted to open a salumeria—a gourmet Italian delicatessen—like the one they had back in Italy. To earn the money to do so, Carmela worked as a seamstress and Gennaro, Joe, and Mario worked in various delis in the city.

In 1959, the Sbarros opened their salumeria in the Bensonhurst section of Brooklyn, offering sandwiches, pasta dishes, and homemade cheesecake. The deli was a hit, and by 1964 the family had opened three more. Working behind the counters, the Sbarros noticed fewer customers were "taking out" their purchases. Instead, they were eating the deli food before they left the store. "Customers were standing at the counter eating pasta," Mario Sbarro told *Business Week* in 1987. "We knew we were on the threshold of something different." Responding to customers' needs, the Sbarros put in some chairs and tables and started offering hot food, such as pizza and lasagna.

### Expansion in the 1970s and 1980s

By the early 1970s, the Sbarros found themselves owning four popular restaurants. At that point the family had to decide how to expand but keep standards high. Gennaro Sbarro did not want to franchise his operation. Instead, he opened 12 new restaurants in the New York area, and had all the food made daily at the original deli. Eventually Sbarro and his sons established a formula that gave productive managers 15 percent of a restaurant's net profits but kept the ownership of the restaurants in the family. Under the growth plan, Carmela still produced all the cheesecakes, while other ingredients were all purchased through one wholesaler. In 1977, the family incorporated its various food and restaurant businesses as Sbarro, Inc.

As the Sbarros were developing their growth strategy, real estate developers were building shopping centers at a furious pace to serve the expanding suburban customer base. In the 20 years from 1970 to 1990, the number of shopping centers nationally grew from about 10,000 to 37,000, according to the International Council of Shopping Centers. Shopping at malls became a leisure-time activity, and mall developers incorporated food courts into their plans to keep customers within the facility. For the Sbarros, food courts appeared to offer the perfect opportunity to combine their dine-in focus with quick service while reaching a dependable flow of customers, and they took it.

Under the food court concept, shoppers were able to select their meal from a variety of restaurants and take the food to an

---

**Company Perspectives:**

*The Mission of Sbarro, Inc. is to deliver high quality, affordably priced Italian food products to a wide range of consumers. We will serve our guests in attractive, distinctively designed, strategically located restaurants, wherever the demand for our products exists. We are committed to excellent service, dedicated to achieving Company objectives and maintaining profitability through the pride and commitment to excellence by our people. We create new guests through entrepreneurial-minded people who operate their restaurants with the Sbarro passion for guest satisfaction and maximum profit.*

---

open, common dining area. Sbarro's food court restaurants were small, occupying about 500 to 1000 square feet, and contained only enough space for kitchen and service areas. The menu was more limited than at the larger, sit-down units, and there were fewer staff, usually between six and 30 employees. The decor of all Sbarro units incorporated the green, white, and orange of the Italian flag, and many had replicas of cheeses, salamis, and prosciutto hams hanging from the ceiling, harking back to the company's origin as a delicatessen.

At the time of Gennaro Sbarro's death in 1984, the company had 97 stores grossing $20 million. Mario headed the company as chairman and CEO. Tony became president and chief operating officer, and Joe was named senior executive vice-president. Carmela was vice-president and continued to make her cheesecakes. The following year Mario opened 36 more restaurants and took Sbarro public, raising $8 million on the American Stock Exchange for 30 percent of the equity. Mario used the money to pay down bank loans made to finance the expansion and to develop the franchising side of the business.

By mid-1987, Sbarro had grown to 157 company-owned restaurants and 63 franchises, with units in the United States, Puerto Rico, and Canada. *Business Week* ranked Sbarro 21st on its list of America's 100 hot-growth companies, and the company agreed to let Marriott Corp. open 20 franchises on selected highways, testing the Sbarro concept beyond the shopping mall. Sales for the year rose 70 percent over 1986, to $58.5 million, and profits jumped 43 percent, to $4.8 million.

The company was opening between 65 and 70 restaurants a year. Wanting to increase the number of franchise operations, Mario started a program in 1989 offering managers with three years' seniority the opportunity to buy their own franchise with 100 percent company financing. During the first year, four managers took advantage of the program. Company revenues for 1989 reached $149 million, a 27 percent increase over 1988, and profits reached $14.5 million.

### 1990 to 1994

In 1990 the first Sbarro restaurant opened in Europe, in the London suburb of Woking. The move was made through a joint venture with a British partner, Forte PLC (formerly Trusthouse

Forte), and was part of Mario's plan to achieve system-wide sales of $500 million.

The company was growing by nearly 16 percent a year but was still operating much as it had 20 years earlier. When a problem arose at any outlet, the manager could pick up the phone and call Tony. The brothers needed better information systems and operating controls for the more than 300 restaurants the company owned if they were to reach their goal. They hired several computer specialists familiar with the restaurant industry to set up new information systems. To improve operations, they established a new regional and district structure and brought in 20 managers from such larger chains as McDonald's and Roy Rogers.

Problems quickly developed as resentment grew among longtime Sbarro managers and employees towards new forms and rigid rules. Sales per restaurant began to drop. Earnings for the first quarter in 1992 were one-third lower than expected. The Sbarros realized they had made a mistake going outside and not promoting their own employees. "Many of our own people had the qualifications to do the job," Mario told Robert La Franco in a 1994 *Forbes* article. "It was a case of 'the grass always looks greener'."

Mario and his brothers corrected the situation; during the second quarter of 1992 they fired 14 of the new managers and began promoting Sbarro managers to district and regional positions. By the fall, sales and earnings were improving. The company ended the year with 587 restaurants (131 of them franchises) and revenues up 13.2 percent to $237.5 million.

Employees at Sbarro units prepared the food fresh daily, according to special recipes developed by the family. John Bowen, one of Sbarro's early franchisees, explained in a June 1995 article in *Inc.,* "I lean upon the operations manual. They are successful procedures. If you are going to make a cake—in our case, a pizza—and you don't follow that recipe, it's going to turn out a little different every time." Restaurants bought pastries locally, but in 1996, Carmela Sbarro was still overseeing the preparation of the company's cheesecakes in the kitchen of the original Sbarro's in Brooklyn.

During 1993 and 1994, Sbarro continued to open new restaurants and franchises, though at a slower rate of about ten percent a year. Sales from company-owned restaurants increased by more than 11 percent annually, well ahead of the average for the pizza restaurant industry. In 1993 the company began paying quarterly cash dividends which have increased approximately 20 percent each year. By the end of 1994, Sbarro had 729 restaurants. Of these, 162 were franchised. Host Marriott Services Corp., with 19 units, and Concession Air, with 11 units, were among Sbarro's biggest franchisees, with units at airports and at travel plazas on toll roads. In September 1994, Sbarro moved its stock listing to the New York Stock Exchange.

Pizza, sold primarily in individual slices, accounted for about half of Sbarro's sales. The pizza restaurant industry, structured into several tiers, was highly competitive. In the mid-1990s, three giant chains led the industry. Pizza Hut, with 9,566 restaurants in the United States and 2,989 international units, had sales of $6.9 billion in 1994. Domino's Pizza (5,100 domestic restaurants and 860 overseas) reported sales of $2.5 billion. Little Caesar had sales of $2 billion from its 4,600 locations in the United States, Canada, Puerto Rico, Guam, and the Czech and Slovak Republics.

The second tier of pizza chains included Papa John's International (730 restaurants in 21 states), with reported sales of $297.6 million for 1994; Sbarro, with $296 million; and Show-Biz Pizza Time (327 units) with $267.8 million. Round Table, a private company with 560 locations, was believed to have sales in that range, and Pizza Inn reported sales of about $218 million from its 485 restaurants. Chains with 1994 sales between $100–$200 million comprised a third tier, and included Uno Restaurant Corp., Shakey's Pizza, and Bertucci's Brick Oven Pizzeria.

In 1994 the $20 billion pizza business grew at a rate of two percent, below the overall restaurant industry's rate of 4.1 percent. That figure was skewed by relatively flat sales for the big three companies; the gourmet and casual dining segments grew faster as evidenced by Sbarro's growth. However, pizza operators were taking steps to expand their business in the face of competition. For some it meant more international operations; others added new menu offerings such as buffalo wings, stuffed crust or deep dish pizza, roasted chicken, and pastas. Some chains beefed up delivery services and moved into nontraditional locations. Little Caesar, for example, opened pizza restaurants with some seating in 561 Kmart stores and began delivery service.

### 1995 and Beyond

In the mid-1990s Sbarro too was looking at ways to remain competitive. During 1995 the company explored new growth opportunities through joint ventures with other restaurateurs. The first of these, Boulder Creek Steaks & Saloon, a steakhouse, had two restaurants opened by early 1996. The second, BICE Med Grille, was a moderately priced, casual-dining restaurant featuring Italian and Mediterranean food. The third new opportunity was a family restaurant concept, Umberto's of New Hyde Park Pizzeria. This offered both sit-down and takeout service, and featured pizza and other Italian-style food. The initial locations of these two ventures opened in April 1996, with more planned for later that year.

Within its existing units, the company began testing a buffet format in 45 of its restaurants. Sbarro also expanded abroad, with franchise restaurants opening in Israel, Lebanon, and Saudi Arabia in 1995. As in the United States, overseas Sbarros were located primarily in malls and airports. In England they were also found at service areas along major motorways. At home, company-operated restaurants continued moving into locations other than shopping malls, such as the Balboa Naval Hospital in

San Diego, Florida State University in Tallahassee, St. Joseph's Hospital in Towson, Maryland, and Hofstra University Student Union, in New York City. Sbarro also operated restaurants in downtown areas of major U.S. cities, including New York, Boston, Chicago, and Philadelphia. By the end of 1995 the company had 771 restaurants in 14 countries on six continents. Of these, 200 were franchised. Company revenue grew seven percent to $319.2 million for the year. Sales system-wide, including franchised units, increased eight percent to $416.3 million.

Despite the growth in sales, the company had a rough 1995 financially, with net income down. After taking various steps to control costs, profits for the last half of the year were above those of 1994. In December 1995, the company announced plans to close 40 underperforming locations and to open about 80 new units during 1996, half of which would be company-operated.

In the mid-1990s Sbarro was strong financially. It paid quarterly cash dividends of $.19 per share in 1995; in March 1996, the company increased quarterly dividends to $.23 per share. The company also was debt free, paying for its expansion with cash from existing operations. With the third generation of Sbarros involved in managing the company, Sbarro appeared poised to continue its pattern of growth toward reaching Mario's goal of $500 million in sales system-wide.

### Further Reading

Brumback, Nancy, "Market Report: Pizza, Foreign Service," *Restaurant Business,* August 10, 1995, pp. 122–141.

Burns, Greg, "All Together Now: 'Make That to Go'," *Business Week,* January 8, 1996.

——, "Restaurants: Bye-Bye to Fat Times?" *Business Week,* January 9, 1995.

Garrett, Echo Montgomery, "Franchise Inc.: The Many Faces of Franchising," *Inc.,* June 1995, pp. 98–106.

La Franco, Robert, "Promote from Within," *Forbes,* February 28, 1994, pp. 86–87.

McCoy, Frank, "Sbarro's Juicy Slice of the Fast-Food Market," *Business Week,* September 7, 1987, pp. 72–73.

Pressler, Margaret Webb, and Steven Pearlstein, "Growing Out of Business: The Shakeout Has Just Begun in the Overbuilt Retail Industry," *The Washington Post,* February 22, 1996, pp. A1, A8.

"Sbarro to Shutter 40 Units by March," *Nation's Restaurant News,* January 1, 1996, p. 2.

Slovak, Julianne, "Corporate Performance: Companies to Watch," *Fortune,* May 7, 1990, p. 114.

Stark, Ellen, "Small-Stock Outlook: Sbarro," *Money,* March 1995, p. 62.

Therrien, Lois, "The Upstarts Teaching McDonald's a Thing or Two," *Business Week,* October 21, 1991, p. 122.

—Ellen D. Wernick

# Sir Speedy

## Sir Speedy, Inc.

**26722 Plaza Drive**
**P.O. Box 9077**
**Mission Viejo, California 92690-9077**
**U.S.A.**
**(714) 348-5000**
**Fax: (714) 348-5066**

*Wholly Owned Subsidiary of KOA Holdings, Inc.*
*Incorporated:* 1968
*Employees:* 8,000 (est.)
*Sales:* $400 million (1995)
*SICs:* 6794 Patent Owners and Lessors; 7334
    Photocopying and Duplicating Services; 7379
    Computer Related Services, Not Elsewhere Classified

Sir Speedy, Inc. is one of the world's largest franchisors of printing, copying, and digital-network centers. In 1995, the Sir Speedy network comprised more than 800 centers operating under the Sir Speedy name and over 40 centers under the Copies Now name. These centers were located throughout the United States and in 16 foreign countries, including Canada, Brazil, Mexico, Taiwan, Saudi Arabia, and elsewhere.

### Birth, Bankruptcy, and Sale

Sir Speedy was founded in 1968 by James A. Merriam. It leased facilities in Newport Beach, California, licensing quick-print shops under the name Sir Speedy Instant Printing Centers. The company lost $190,000 on revenues of $765,000 in 1970 and lost $75,000 on revenues of more than $1 million in 1971. In 1972 it had net income of $277,000 on revenues of $4.5 million.

By late 1974 Sir Speedy was the nation's largest instant-printing franchise chain, with 350 outlets, many of them in southern California. As a consequence, however, of the recession of the early 1970s, business dropped off, and the company found itself unable to meet lease payments. In October 1974 Sir Speedy filed papers in federal bankruptcy court, going into Chapter 11 receivership.

Sir Speedy was still the third-largest franchiser of quick-print stores when Kampgrounds of America, Inc. (later KOA Holdings, Inc.) acquired a controlling interest in the company in 1977 for $1.3 million. At that time there remained more than 235 Sir Speedy Instant Printing Centers, located primarily in major metropolitan markets. Under its new ownership, Sir Speedy saw as its major strength its concentration on professional management techniques at the store level. It provided a number of support services for its franchised shops, including market research, advertising and promotion, research and development, quality controls, technical services, franchisee training, and long-range planning. It also saw as a selling point its ability to purchase printing supplies, film, inks, and other supplies for the franchisee at volume discount with no markup. Franchisees also received help in finding a location and in negotiating and setting up a lease, and two weeks of full-time support by a service representative.

The Sir Speedy franchise price was $48,000 in October 1978, which included a $10,000 franchise fee, a build-up fee for training, and $27,000 for an equipment package. Sir Speedy also received 5 percent of gross income from its franchisees, returning royalty rebates once a store reached a certain volume of sales. Store owners were at the time averaging gross revenue of about $14,000 per month, of which 25 to 35 percent was profit. Sir Speedy had sales of $2.2 million in 1978, or about 15 percent of the parent company's total. Its earnings that year came to about $138,000, or some 6 percent of KOA's earnings.

The quick-print industry was then specializing in short-run, one- or two-color printing jobs for customers ranging from a neighborhood church, local law firm, or wholesale distributor to the overflow from a big corporation's in-house print shop. It was filling a wide range of needs for graphic printed materials that fell between the office duplicator and the commercial printer. Sir Speedy generally was serving organizations that required 100 to 10,000 copies of a single sheet or simple brochure or pamphlet.

### Focusing on Small and Midsized Businesses in the 1980s

When Don Lowe became president of Sir Speedy in 1981, there were 320 franchisees in the network, with combined sales of some $50 million a year. One of the first things he did was to order a survey to get a better understanding of who Sir Speedy's clients were. The company thought it was running neighborhood copy shops, but Lowe found, to his surprise, that nine out of ten of the customers were businesses. Accordingly, he put the store owners to work making presentations to business clients and created a four-point marketing plan to sell to this market segment. Lowe had the company logo and store layouts redesigned and launched a new advertising campaign to position Sir Speedy as a business printer.

Lowe also commissioned focus groups that found most of Sir Speedy's order placers worked in businesses with fewer than 50 employees and that most of them were low-level buyers. Further research revealed that for every business customer Sir Speedy saw, there were scores of other prospects who didn't have the time or staff to get out of their offices. Lowe then held a series of regional "town meetings" in which he implored franchisees to get out in the field in order to hunt down clients. This was not easy: one store owner recalled that it took two hours for him to work up the courage to make a sales call, after which he was "drenched with sweat." Follow-up calls, Lowe stressed, were also necessary, noting 80 percent of the company's accounts came only after six contacts.

Building on this basis, Sir Speedy became, in 1985, the first franchise network to advertise and market nationally as business printers specializing in graphic design, printing, and copying for small and midsized businesses as well as corporate communications departments. These were customers whose needs were beyond what most quick printers could provide, yet too limited for commercial printers. By 1995, 90 percent of Sir Speedy customers fit this description, comprising a business market estimated at $20 billion to $25 billion, compared to the traditional quick-printing market, valued at about $9.5 billion.

During the 1980s Sir Speedy moved from photocopying to offset printing and electronic services. By late 1987 Sir Speedy had moved to second place in its industry, with about 800 stores. Now based in Laguna Hills, California, the Sir Speedy chain was expected to show a pretax profit of $4.4 million for the year on revenues of $220 million. Also in 1987, the company launched FastFax, a facsimile network that initially included not only 600 Sir Speedy shops in the United States but also franchises in Canada, Great Britain, and Hong Kong. Franchisees were able to lease a fax machine from headquarters for $12 a week.

### New Electronic Services in the 1990s

Continuing their phenomenal growth, quick-printing and copying franchises had estimated sales of $1.9 billion in 1991, compared to only $9 million in 1969. Sir Speedy's sales reached $320 million in 1990, by which time it was offering computer-enhanced graphic design, layout, typography, black-and-white and full-color printing, binding, photocopying, and electronic publishing. In that year the company introduced Digital Quick-

color, Inc., the first completely digital full-color printing operation in the world. This wholly owned subsidiary operated as a wholesale production facility and a research and development arm of Sir Speedy. In 1991 Sir Speedy was named the nation's best-managed printing franchise in a study conducted by the accounting firm Arthur Andersen and Co.

Sir Speedy's strategy now was to acquire and convert smaller franchised print shops, adding to his 875-member chain. Unlike newcomers, converted franchisees, Lowe told a *Nation's Business* reporter, "understand the business, and they also understand the benefits of belonging to a franchise organization." Sir Speedy also preferred owner-operated franchises to units owned by absentee investors, feeling that they would provide more personalized and detail-oriented service to business clients. The start-up cost for a franchise now had reached $120,000, of which the initiation fee came to $40,000.

By April 1993 Sir Speedy was operating in eight countries, dealing only with entrepreneurs willing to buy the franchise rights for an entire country and to develop a region by subfranchising to owner-operators. The company also insisted that its foreign franchisees be bilingual. International franchisees were invited to participate in the two-week training sessions offered to American store owners. Among Sir Speedy's star franchisees in 1993 was Ken Mathes and his wife, Cookie, who were doing more than $1 million a year in sales with two franchises in Long Beach, California. Rod Rodenmeyer, owner of five Sir Speedy printing centers in Memphis, had no printing experience but attributed his success over the past four years to 18 years with companies in which growth dominated thinking at every level. The average sales volume for a Sir Speedy center was more than $450,00 in 1994. The top 25 franchisees averaged more than $1 million each in gross sales.

Sir Speedy in 1994 became the first service provider for distribution of Eastman Kodak Co.'s Photo, Portfolio and Writable CD system, which stored photos on compact disks so they could be viewed and edited on television sets and computers. Sir Speedy offered this system, for use in pamphlets and brochures, initially in 40 percent of its 885 stores. (By now Copies Now had been established as a Sir Speedy subsidiary specializing in electronic imaging.) A Photo CD could hold the equivalent of 100 color photographs, 500 floppy disks, or 250,000 pages of text. The Sir Speedy and Copies Now franchisees would now be able to create affordable multimedia presentations for customers, including photos, graphics, text, and sound on a computer, a television monitor, or a CD-I, a playback unit developed by Kodak for the Portfolio CD. "We are positioning ourselves as being not only in the printing business but also in the business of information distribution," Dave Collins, director of franchise development, told *Nation's Business*. "And CD technology is a natural extension, he added."

In 1994 the company established Sir Speedy Net, a national online electronic bulletin-board service to communicate with the 350 or so franchisees equipped to receive it. The system provided a message service, operating manuals, repair advice, and clip art. Text and graphics could be downloaded to the local units' personal computers at no charge. The following year the company established Sir Speedy Online. This allowed customers to send electronic files via modem to individual centers for printing or copying around the clock, every day in the year. Also in 1995, Sir Speedy became the first franchised printing company to develop a home page on the Internet's World Wide Web. Its installed base of more than 1,000 computers was the largest in the quick-printing industry.

The company already was offering discounts ranging from 10 to 30 percent on computers and software for its franchisees. "Every Sir Speedy is different," one affiliate told the trade magazine *CIO*. "There are those of us who are on top of things electronically and those who are in the Dark Ages." He said he made most of his purchases through company headquarters because "The royalty you pay is offset by what you can save because they can negotiate better pricing for us."

### Aiming at the Fortune 1000 and Home Markets

Interviewed by *Franchising World* in 1995, Lowe saw Sir Speedy's digital network as enabling the company to broaden its customer base to serve Fortune 1000 companies as well as small and midsized local businesses. Instead of printing documents in large quantities, carrying them in inventory, and then mailing or shipping them, Sir Speedy's network enabled documents to be sent over telephones lines in electronic form and then printed in the location and quantity needed, saving storage and shipping costs. "While traditional offset printing and production copying will continue to generate the majority of revenue in the immediate future," said Lowe, "we are prepared to take full advantage and be a major player in the digital-technology revolution."

Sir Speedy also saw digital technology as expanding its client base downward, taking in the small-office, home-office, or telecommuting customer. Research suggested that 41 million Americans were working out of their homes, up from 27 million in 1990. Another potential customer was the digital-information and communication specialist, including graphic designers, large corporate communications departments, and others sophisticated in digital technology who had access to state-of-the-art equipment.

Lowe said that, in order to be successful, every Sir Speedy center should have the following minimum services: graphic design; color printing in one, two, or four colors; copying in black and white, color, and oversized; folding, collating, laminating, die cutting, embossing, binding, and other finishing services; and mailing and shipping services. In addition, minimum digital services should include CD-ROM, computer disks, fax, and Sir Speedy Online.

In 1995 Sir Speedy was charging a franchise fee of $17,500, with $120,000 in start-up investment and $60,000 in working capital required to operate a unit. One of the company's model franchisees was Bill Tallent, who opened a Nashville store in 1991 and soon topped the company's growth chart, recording sales increases of greater than 30 percent for 21 consecutive months. He expected to gross $1.6 million in 1995 for his two stores, nearly twice the industry average. Tallent, who told *Inc.*,

"I didn't get into this business to get ink under my fingernails," was reinvesting 80 percent of his earnings in new technology. He also served on an "image redesign" task force that recommended a more up-to-date logo and colors for the company.

At the beginning of 1996 Sir Speedy announced that it would purchase for an undisclosed sum MultiCopy International, B.V., the largest full-service quick-printing franchiser operating in continental Europe, from Moore Corp. Ltd. of Toronto. Included in the purchase were 19 company-owned locations in France, Austria, and the Netherlands, and 78 franchise locations in the Netherlands. In addition to the United States and Puerto Rico, Sir Speedy at this time was also operating centers in Argentina, Brazil, Canada, Colombia, Costa Rica, El Salvador, Guatemala, Indonesia, Mexico, Peru, Saudi Arabia, and Taiwan.

In 1996 Sir Speedy centers provided a full range of black-and-white and color professional printing and copying services for business applications, including letterheads, business cards, brochures, newsletters, business forms, catalogues, and manuals. It also offered the latest in digital services, such as networking, computer-disk transfer and conversion, digital storage capability, electronic original transmission, and "on-demand printing." Copies Now centers specialized in high-speed copying, color copying, and reproduction of special format work, such as engineering drawings. Both Sir Speedy and Copies Now centers offered graphic design and typography by electronic publishing. Each also offered facsimile transmission and reception through the Sir Speedy FastFax network, a full range of finishing and bindery services, and even direct-mail fulfillment.

### Principal Subsidiaries

Digital Quickcolor, Inc.; Comprehensive Business Services, Inc.; MultiCopy International, B.V. (Netherlands).

### Further Reading

Cole, Patrick E., "Your Friendly Neighborhood Fax Shop?" *Business Week,* November 9, 1987, p. 138A.
Finegan, Jay, "The Smartest Franchisers in America," *Inc.,* November 1995, pp. 54, 58.
"Kampgrounds of America, Inc.," *Wall Street Transcript,* October 23, 1978, pp. 52,254–256.
"KOA: Cold Nights on the Campground," *Dun's Review,* August 1979, p. 18.
Matusky, Gregory, "Going Global," *Success,* April 1993, pp. 62–63.
——, "Power Partnerships," *Success,* October 1993, pp. 60, 62–63.
Sanderson, Rhonda, "Staying One Step Ahead," *Franchising World,* July/August 1995, pp. 22, 24.
"Sir Speedy Sees Fast Chapter 11 Recovery," *Los Angeles Times,* October 23, 1974, p. 12.
Whittemore, May, "Quick Printing Turns High-Tech," *Nation's Business,* April 1991, pp. 63–64.
Williamson, Mickey, "Franchise Players," *CIO,* February 1, 1995, pp. 46, 48–49.

—Robert Halasz

# Smart & Final, Inc.

**4700 South Boyle Avenue**
**Los Angeles, California 90058**
**U.S.A.**
**(213) 584-9850**
**Fax: (213) 589-4283**

*Public Company*
*Incorporated:* 1871 as Hellman-Haas Grocery Co.
*Employees:* 4,293
*Sales:* $1.2 billion (1995)
*Stock Exchanges:* New York
*SICs:* 5141 Groceries, General Line; 5411 Grocery Stores

Smart & Final, Inc. operates the United States' largest warehouse grocery chain, with more than 140 nonmembership stores in California, and more than 20 stores in Arizona, Nevada, Florida, and in Mexico. Smart & Final stores average 17,000 square feet of selling space, stocking 11,000 items, which range from canned goods to freezer-deli, dairy, produce, paper products, and janitorial supplies, all of which are sold in large institutional sizes and quantities. About 10 percent of this assortment is made up of Smart & Final's Iris, Montecito, Table Queen, and Smart Buy private labels, which together produce nearly one-fourth of annual sales. Small businesses, especially restaurants, and clubs and organizations account for nearly two-thirds of Smart & Final sales, with the remainder contributed by consumer purchases. Smart & Final also operates as a foodservice distributor in its West Coast and Florida markets under its Henry Lee Company and Port Stockton subsidiaries, which together accounted for nearly $250 million of Smart & Final's $1.2 billion in 1995 sales.

### Grocery Pioneers

Los Angeles was a dusty town of unpaved streets and wood or adobe buildings when Hellman, Haas & Co. opened as a wholesale grocer in 1871. Founded by Abraham Haas, who had arrived from Bavaria at the age of 16, along with brother Jacob Haas and partners Bernard Cohn and Herman Hellman, the two-story brick building provided bulk staple items such as flour, brown sugar, salt, rope, chewing tobacco, gunpowder, patent medicines, and shepherding supplies to the town's 6,000 residents.

The small store played an important role in the early growth of Los Angeles, adding items catering to the town's many ethnic populations, including Native and Mexican Americans, and a growing Chinese community. As the town grew, Hellman, Haas & Co. grew with it; in 1880, the store was listed among the seven names in Los Angeles's first phone directory. The partners played a role in the area's growth as well. Herman Hellman would later head the Farmers and Merchants Bank and join in the founding of the University of Southern California. Abraham Haas branched out into the flour milling and cold storage businesses and was among the founders of southern California's first gas and electric companies.

In 1889, Jacob Baruch bought Hellman's interest in the company, and the company's name changed to Haas, Baruch & Co. The store continued to prosper and, in 1895, began selling canned tomatoes under its own Iris brand name. Sales by that year had reached an impressive $2 million. By the turn of the century, Haas, Baruch was the leading grocer in a town that, over the next two decades, would swell to a population of nearly one million. Abraham Haas left Los Angeles during this period, opening a successful wholesale operation in San Francisco. Haas's son, Walter, worked in the family business, but later left to join a small clothing company, Levi Strauss, where he would serve as president for the next 30 years. Haas, Baruch continued to thrive; in 1948 the company opened its own 3.5-acre warehouse in Vernon, California.

Meanwhile, J.S. Smart, a banker from Saginaw, Michigan, arrived in California in 1914, where he purchased a small feed and grain supplier, the Santa Ana Wholesale Company, which had been founded two years earlier. Smart was soon joined by H.D. Final, and the partners moved their business to San Pedro, renaming the company Smart & Final Wholesale Grocers. By the end of the decade, the company's sales reached $10 million.

Competition among the area's wholesalers intensified over the next decade. The grocery industry itself was changing, as more and more retailers began purchasing directly from the manufacturers, bypassing the wholesalers altogether. But Smart, on a trip to Ohio, discovered the latest trend in grocery sales—that of allowing the customer to choose their purchases, rather than having the grocery's clerks gather the items. In 1923, Smart brought this innovation to the West Coast, and Smart & Final became the first in the area to offer the "cash and carry" concept. Another key to the company's survival and success was its practice of locating its stores close to the businesses they served, instead of requiring customers to travel to remotely located warehouses.

Smart & Final was helped by the outbreak of the Second World War, winning supply contracts to support the military effort. After the war, the company expanded its customer base to include churches and local clubs and organizations and, by the beginning of the 1950s, had grown to a chain of 65 stores. New changes were occurring in the grocery industry, as improved cold storage and refrigeration techniques were making possible an expanding assortment of foods. A new type of store, the supermarket, became popular during this time, placing still more pressure on the wholesalers. In 1953, Smart & Final acquired Haas, Baruch, adding the latter's popular Iris brand to the Smart & Final name. The new company, Smart & Final Iris Co., moved its headquarters to Haas, Baruch's Vernon warehouse site. Two years later, however, Smart & Final was bought by the Thriftimart supermarket chain, founded by Roger M. Laverty.

Laverty had been active in the grocery trade since 1930, when he bought the small, Los Angeles-based chain Fitzsimmons Stores Inc. In 1947, Laverty acquired Thriftimart Inc., also based in Los Angeles, merging the two chains under the Thriftimart name. The addition of Smart & Final's warehouse stores boosted Thriftimart's sales to $168 million by 1960. When Laverty died in 1969, he was succeeded by his son, Roger Laverty II.

### Toward the 1980s

Under Thriftimart, the Iris brand name was expanded to include hundreds of frozen food products, paper and canned goods, and janitorial supplies. The chain of Smart & Final cash and carry stores, which averaged from 4,000 to 10,000 square

feet, grew to 86 stores by the 1980s. Together with Thriftimart's 41 supermarkets, sales passed $250 million by the early 1970s and climbed to $500 million by the early 1980s.

Despite this growth, however, Thriftimart struggled for profitability. After posting an $822,000 loss on sales of $260 million in 1972, the company climbed back into the black, only to post a $5.4 million loss on $343 million sales in 1976. Thriftimart fared better in the second half of that decade, rebuilding its bottom line to a $4.5 million net income on sales of $368 million in 1979. The following year, net income rose to a high of $7.2 million, with sales climbing to $431 million. But the growth of warehouse clubs such as Price Club and Costco began to pressure the supermarket industry. By 1982, when Thriftimart's sales peaked at $506 million, its net income fell to $4.8 million. Thriftimart moved to divest its struggling supermarket division, selling 23 California supermarkets to Safeway Stores, Inc. in 1983. By 1984, with sales just under $500 million, net income had dropped to $1.5 million.

In that year, Roger Laverty II, his brother Robert, and their sister Nancy Harris, who together owned 85 percent of Thriftimart's stock, sold their interest in the company to Casino USA and its parent, Etablissements Economiques du Casino Guichard-Perrachon et Cie, a $3 billion French-based operator of supermarkets, convenience stores, restaurants, and food production and processing facilities. Laverty II retired after the sale of the company, and Robert Emmons was named chairman, president, and CEO in 1984.

Thriftimart's 17 remaining supermarkets were liquidated after the Casino acquisition, and the focus was shifted to Smart & Final's 86-store cash and carry operations, which had remained profitable throughout the Thriftimart period. As Smart & Final, Inc., the company moved to refocus, modernize, and expand the chain. The new management, which included Roger Laverty III, developed the strategy that would take the company into the next decade. This strategy targeted smaller, independent foodservice and related businesses with a redesigned store concept offering a product assortment adapted to this market's needs. At the same time, the company moved to modernize its stores, closing a number of its aging stores while relocating dozens more stores to locations featuring parking, convenient access to customers, and larger size (over the next ten years, store size would more than double to an average 17,000 square feet).

### Evolving into the 1990s

By 1988, the Smart & Final chain had been pared down to 72 modern stores. Until then, the chain had served exclusively the southern California market. In the late 1980s, Smart & Final began an aggressive expansion into northern California, Nevada, and Arizona. Sales, which dropped to $335 million in 1986, rose to $498 million by 1989. One year later, sales neared $560 million, generating a net income of $9.4 million.

As the country slipped into the recession of the early 1990s, Smart & Final's growth continued. The drop in real estate prices in its core California market proved a boon to the expanding company, which numbered 99 stores by 1989 and 135 stores by 1993. In 1991, with sales of $663 million, Smart & Final went public again, with Casino maintaining a 53 percent share of the company's stock. In that year, Smart & Final expanded into foodservice distribution with the purchase of northern California-based Port Stockton Food Distributors, Inc. The company next launched its Casino Frozen Foods, Inc. subsidiary as distributor both to its own stores and to independent customers. By 1993, that business expanded beyond frozen foods to supply delicatessen and other products as well. In that year, Roger Laverty III was named the company's president and CEO.

While Smart & Final continued to increase its presence in California, growing to 140 stores in 20 counties by the end of 1995, the company began to eye other markets. Encouraged by the passage of the North American Free Trade Agreement, and joining a growing trend among U.S. retailers, in 1993 the company formed a joint venture with Central Detallista, S.A. de C.V. to bring Smart & Final stores into Mexico. The first stores opened in Baja, Mexico, with plans for nine stores by 1995 and as many as 50 stores in the near future. The company next prepared to enter the Florida market, which, with its large Hispanic population, fit well with its Californian customer base. In 1994, Smart & Final added the Henry Lee Company, which served the Florida, Central and South American, and Caribbean markets, to its distribution business. The acquisition of Henry Lee, which ranked among the largest foodservice distributors in the country, paved the way for the expansion of Smart & Final's cash and carry operations into Florida. In early 1996 the company opened its first six Dade and Broward county stores, with plans to grow to as many as 40 stores in Florida by the end of the century.

In Florida, Smart & Final continued its policy of opening stores in inner city areas typically shunned by other grocers—after the 1992 riots, for example, Smart & Final opened 11 stores in Los Angeles—while providing a product assortment geared to its customers' cultures and needs. The company, which boasted of being "125 years old but 12 years young," maintained as well its strategy of updating its stores, so that, of the 161 stores in its chain in 1996, 136 stores were built in the past decade. With revenues soaring to $1.2 billion in 1995, Smart & Final appeared to have many more years of growth to come.

## Principal Subsidiaries

Henry Lee Company (90 percent); Port Stockton Food Distributors, Inc.

## Further Reading

Brooks, Nancy Rivera, "Growth Market: Smart & Final Celebrates 125 Years in a Big Way," *Los Angeles Times,* March 4, 1996, p. D1.

Coupe, Kevin, "Smart & Focused (& Growing Fast)," *Progressive Grocer,* September 1994, p. 44.

Goodman, Cindy Krischer, "Smart & Final Bulk Grocery Chain Targets Florida Inner Cities," *Miami Herald,* December 14, 1994.

Taylor, John H., "Niche Guys Finish First," *Forbes,* October 26, 1992, p. 128.

—M.L. Cohen

# Sport Chalet, Inc.

920 Foothill Boulevard
La Canada, California 91011
U.S.A.
(818) 790-2717
Fax: (818) 790-1134

*Public Company*
*Incorporated:* 1960
*Employees:* 1,303
*Sales:* $133.7 (1996)
*Stock Exchanges:* NASDAQ
*SICs:* 5941 Sporting Goods & Bicycle Shops

A leading operator of full service, specialty sporting goods superstores, Sport Chalet, Inc. operates exclusively in Southern California, where the 18 stores comprising the company's retail chain in 1996 were located. A small business for decades, Sport Chalet began expanding rapidly during the late 1980s, quickly establishing its superstores throughout five counties in Southern California. The company's stores stock a full line of traditional sporting goods, as well as thousands of products for nontraditional sports such as downhill skiing, bicycling, mountaineering, scuba diving, and kayaking. In 1996, seven of the company's 18 stores featured swimming pools for scuba diving and kayaking instruction and promotion.

### The Founder and Early Company History

No figure looms larger in Sport Chalet's history than Norbert J. Olberz, the company's founder, chairman, and guiding hand during its evolution from a one-store enterprise to an 18-unit chain of sporting goods superstores. Olberz superintended Sport Chalet's development over a four-decade span and was still in command as his company entered the late 1990s and he was in his early 70s. Olberz's tenure at Sport Chalet may be divided into two eras of the company's history, the first consisting of 20 years during which Sport Chalet operated as a modestly-sized business, and the second consisting of another two-decade period during which Sport Chalet rapidly grew into a

chain of sporting goods superstores, becoming one of the leading sporting goods chains in the United States. Through the slow years and the years of animated growth, Olberz held sway over Sport Chalet's operation, guiding the company from his office in La Canada, California.

Olberz founded Sport Chalet in 1959 and opened the first Sport Chalet store in La Canada in June of the following year. From the company's inaugural year forward, it would remain headquartered in La Canada, its geographical scope would be limited to Southern California, and Olberz would serve as chairman. However, little else would remain the same by the 1990s.

During these early years of Sport Chalet's history, Olberz, then in his early 30s, lived in a small house several blocks away from the site of his original store, which was located along Foothill Boulevard as it passed through La Canada. The first store measured 2,000 square feet and focused on the sale of skiing gear, as the company's name suggested. Merchandise moved quickly enough, however, to enable Olberz to expand the scope of his business not long after opening the first store.

Shortly after the grand opening of the first store, Olberz branched out and moved across the street to a 25,000 square-foot facility. Though the move represented a giant leap for the start-up, the expansion did not signal continued rapid growth. Rather, Olberz and his retail business assumed a stable position in the Southern California sporting goods retail community, not mounting any aggressive assault on neighboring sporting goods retailers until the 1980s.

### Expansion Begins During the 1980s

Sport Chalet had already celebrated its 20th anniversary by the time it began to show intentions of capturing the lion's share of the sporting goods retail sales in Southern California. In fact, the bid to become big began exactly 21 years after the first store was opened, when Olberz established a Sport Chalet in Huntington Beach in June 1981. Another Sport Chalet was opened in June 1983, followed by the August 1986 establishment of a Sport Chalet in Mission Viejo. Stores in Point Loma and Santa Clarita were opened in 1987, and the pace of expansion picked up considerably. Olberz spearheaded the establishment of two stores in 1989 (Beverly Hills and Marina del Rey), and another two in 1990 (Brea and Oxnard), none of which were smaller than 30,000 square feet, widely considered the minimum size for a superstore.

During the latter part of the decade in particular, Sport Chalet began to take on the trappings of a retail powerhouse. Aside from the ambitious store expansion, the company upgraded its accounting and inventory systems and opened a 116,000 square-foot warehouse in Montclair, part of which would later be devoted to retail space for another Sport Chalet store.

### Going Public in the 1990s

Following the establishment of the stores in Brea and Oxnard in 1990, both of which featured indoor pools, Olberz opened the largest Sport Chalet at the time, a 44,000-square-foot store complete with indoor pool that opened in June 1991 in West Hills. A slightly larger store was opened a little more than a year later, when customers first walked through the 45,000-square-foot Sport Chalet in Burbank in August 1992.

The two months that followed the Burbank grand opening were the last months of Sport Chalet's existence as a private company. Competition among Southern California sporting goods superstores was intensifying with each passing month, as mammoth retail outlets proliferated throughout the area. In 1992 alone, three sporting goods superstore retailers—Atlanta-based Sportstown; Tampa, Florida-based Sports & Recreation; and Niles, Illinois-based Sportmart—had completed initial public offerings to fund store expansion. By November 1992, its was Sport Chalet's turn. Olberz at the time was hoping to open nine to 12 Sport Chalet stores during the ensuing three years, a plan that would require at least $2 million per store opening. Consequently, in November Olberz put roughly 25 percent of his 13-store company on the market, then used the money gained from the public offering to help finance the Sport Chalet's expansion.

The conversion to public ownership led to the first disclosure of Sport Chalet's financial figures in the company's 32-year history. Between 1988 and 1992, as documents filed with the Securities and Exchange Commission revealed, Sport Chalet had recorded a robust 24.9 percent annually compounded growth rate, achieving enviable sales growth during its rise to superstore chain status. Fiscal 1991's totals reached $79.2 million in sales and $344,000 in net income, figures easily eclipsed by the totals generated in fiscal 1992, when Sport Chalet collected $94.8 million in sales and $1.85 million in net income.

Propelled by the momentum of solid financial growth, Sport Chalet entered the public spotlight in November 1992, then proceeded to implement its ambitious expansion program that called for the establishment of three to four stores per year. Two stores were opened in November 1993, one in Torrance and another in Glendora, each of which measured 40,000 square feet. The addition of these two stores followed the announcement of 1993's financial figures, which elevated Sport Chalet past the $100 million-in-sales plateau for the first time. For the year, the company generated $106.3 million in sales and earned more than $2 million in net income, fueling confidence that

Sport Chalet had successfully withstood the deleterious affects of a national economic recession.

During the early 1990s, Sport Chalet stores stocked merchandise that the company categorized in nine product groups, giving each store a full spectrum of products. In addition to selling downhill skiing equipment and apparel, which had contributed the largest percentage of store sales since 1960, Sport Chalet stores stocked camping, backpacking, and mountaineering merchandise, including camping equipment rentals, and scuba gear, including air compressors to refill dive tanks. Rounding out the company's merchandise lines were fishing gear, cycling gear, including bicycle repair service, general sporting goods, shoes and in-line skates, racquet sports, and water sports, including swimwear, water skis, and kayaks. Of the company's total sales, winter-related merchandise represented Sport Chalet's largest sporting goods category, accounting for nearly 30 percent of annual sales. In ranking order, general sporting goods and water sports represented the second-largest category, contributing nearly 25 percent of the company total sales, followed by the 15 percent derived from outdoor gear, the 13 percent grossed from the sale of shoes and in-line skates, and the nine percent contributed by scuba equipment.

The stores by this point were huge, generally containing more than 30,000 square feet each and one—the Sport Chalet in Marina del Rey—as large as 42,000 square feet. Despite their size, Sport Chalet stores avoided the trappings typically associated with massive retail stores, featuring carpeted floors and standard retail gondolas and fixtures instead of warehouse racking structures and concrete floors. Sport Chalet stores were upscale rather than spartan, and several of the company's largest stores were outfitted with glass-walled pools for scuba and kayaking instruction and promotion.

Sport Chalet opened two more stores in 1994, one in June in Rancho Cucamonga and another in August in El Cajon, but the continued expansion of the company's retail units was the only bright spot in an otherwise dismal year. For the first time in its history Sport Chalet lost money, generating $122.2 million in sales but posting a $111,127 loss. The recession was partly to blame, but Sport Chalet executives also attributed the loss to an earthquake that temporarily closed five of the company's stores as well as below-average snowfall in Southern California. Sales of winter-related merchandise in Sport Chalet stores fell 8.7 percent during the year, while the company's other merchandise categories registered a six percent increase, pinning Sport Chalet's anemic profitability on its dependence on skiing equipment and apparel sales.

### The Mid-1990s and Beyond

In the wake of 1994's loss, Sport Chalet intensified efforts to reduce its reliance on winter-related merchandise, striving to lessen its exposure to the vagaries of snowfall by expanding into other areas such as bicycling and in-line skating. In November 1995, when it opened a store in Irvine, Sport Chalet climbed out of the red and posted $292,000 in net income on $134.7 million in sales, but the return to profitability was short-lived.

In 1996, as Sport Chalet executives were charting the company's course for the future, warm and dry weather contributed to another year of below average snowfall, causing the company's winter-related merchandise sales to plummet 31 percent. As a result, total sales for the company fell .7 percent, slipping to $133.7 million, and net income plunged precipitously, cascading to a $1.3 million loss. With these financial totals hanging over company executives, Sport Chalet prepared for the late 1990s, hoping for steady snowfall in the years ahead and a revival of a sluggish California economy.

### *Further Reading*

Brooks, Holly, "Looking in on California," *STN,* December 1992, p. 21.

Cole, Benjamin Mark, "Sport Chalet Sporting Good Chain Will Take Plunge into Stock Market," *Los Angeles Business Journal,* October 26, 1992, p. 1.

Lee, Louise, "More Closings in Store for Retailers in '96," *Wall Street Journal,* December 27, 1995, p. 2.

Sims, Burt, "Shows Kick Off Southern California Ski Season," *STN,* January 1994, p. 14.

——, "Sport Chalet Reports Loss," *STN,* October 1994, p. 11.

"Sport Chalet Announces Year End Results," *PR Newswire,* June 7, 1996, p. 60.

"Sport Chalet Files Public Offering," *Discount Store News,* November 16, 1992, p. 6.

—Jeffrey L. Covell

# The Sports Authority, Inc.

**3383 North State Road 7**
**Fort Lauderdale, Florida 33319**
**U.S.A.**
**(305) 735-1701**
**Fax: (305) 484-0837**

*Public Company*
*Incorporated:* 1987
*Employees:* 9,000
*Sales:* $1.04 billion (1995)
*Stock Exchanges:* New York
*SICs:* 5941 Sporting Goods & Bicycle Shops

The Sports Authority, Inc. is the world's largest full-line sporting goods retailer. From its 136 stores, which are located in 26 states and in Canada, the company sells sporting goods in over 1,200 merchandise categories. Its large format stores, virtually all of which exceed 40,000 square feet, carry more than 900 brand names, including Adidas, Asics, Coleman, K2, Nike, Prince, and Starter. Over half of the company's annual revenue is generated from the sale of hard lines—equipment for team sports, fitness, hunting, fishing, camping, golf, racquet sports, cycling, water sports, marine, snow sports, and general merchandise. Soft lines—apparel and footwear, its most profitable product—make up the rest. The first comprehensive sporting goods store to top $1 billion in sales, The Sports Authority competes in a $35 billion market that includes traditional and specialty sporting goods retailers, as well as large format sporting goods retailers and mass merchandisers.

### Early History

The idea behind the company that would grow to become the nation's largest sporting goods chain in just five years came from Jack Smith, a former CEO of Herman's World of Sports, who opened the first Sports Authority store in Fort Lauderdale, Florida, in 1987. While at Herman's, Smith tried unsuccessfully to bring the same comprehensive megastore concept that had fueled the tremendous growth of Toys "R" Us and Home

Depot to the sporting goods industry. With the backing of a group of venture capitalists, he got another chance and set out to build his own sporting goods giant. By 1990 he was running eight megastores, mainly in Florida, and while his company had yet to turn a profit, the then 55-year-old fitness enthusiast was convinced he could make the idea work if he could obtain the capital to fund full-scale expansion.

Joseph Antonini, then chairman of Kmart Corporation, shared Smith's confidence and acquired the sporting goods minichain for $75 million in March of that same year. With the financial backing of the multi-billion-dollar retail giant, Smith now had the resources he needed to implement his plans fully and begin an expansion program that would see The Sports Authority grow to 100 stores four years later. In 1990, the company more than doubled its size to 19 stores. While such rapid growth was accompanied by proportional gains in total revenue, it did not yet translate well onto the balance sheet. At the end of the fiscal year, the company reported a loss of $3.3 million, its fourth consecutive year in the red.

Although the company was unable to realize a profit during these developmental years, it succeeded in building the technological infrastructure needed to support more important long-term growth. At the expense of short-term profits, the experienced sporting goods executive had the foresight to invest heavily in state-of-the-art computer systems that closely monitored inventory. Not only would this give Sports Authority an early technological edge on the competition; it would enable the company to keep its shelves stocked without the use of a distribution facility. The accuracy and availability of information housed in the company's extensive computer system would allow vendors to ship directly to individual stores.

### Early 1990s Growth

In 1991, as revenue rose to $240 million, the company enjoyed its first profitable year of operation, reporting an operating income of $3.3 million. With financial support from Kmart, it was also able to again more than double the size of its operations, building 11 new stores and taking over six existing stores. The company's 36 stores now occupied a total of more

---

**Company Perspectives:**

*Our mission is simple—create a shopping experience establishing The Sports Authority as the first choice for the sports, leisure and recreational customer. Our strategy to achieve this goal is offer our customers: an extensive selection of quality brand name merchandise; powerfully merchandised megastores that provide ease of shopping; competitive prices that create value; premium customer service and product knowledge; and convenient locations throughout our markets.*

---

than 1.5 million square feet. Although the company at this time had not yet won over many of the major brand names in the industry, such as Nike and Starter, its strong growth suggested that Smith's version of the sporting goods superstore was quickly gaining in popularity. One of the key factors to its success was its ability to combine the best features of the small specialty sporting goods store and the large discount store. While other companies preceded Sports Authority in introducing the public to the idea of a sporting goods megastore, their stores quickly gained a reputation for being warehouse type operations that offered poor service and an unpleasant shopping environment. What Smith contributed to the field were significant improvements on both counts. He made merchandise displays more attractive, investing in high-quality displays that added to the shopping experience, and staffed his stores with enough well-trained employees to give customers the type of service they might receive at a specialty store. In short, he was able to make the "big box" of the superstore workable.

The company's rapid expansion program unfolded at an even faster rate over the next two years. In 1992, sales climbed more than 70 percent while income more than tripled as 20 new stores were opened. The following year, sales increased 50 percent as earnings doubled and 24 new stores entered the fold. Again, Sports Authority followed its simple, time-honored retailing philosophy, described by Smith in *Discount Store News* as "the simple blocking and tackling of retail": keeping shelves stocked, keeping stores clean, and providing good service. Patterned after category killers such as Home Depot and Toys "R" Us, the company did not attempt to beat the competition by undercutting their prices; instead, it tried to win customers over with shelves so densely stocked that virtually anyone would have a difficult time leaving the store empty-handed. The company's receipts at the cash register, in keeping with its policy of "consistent everyday fair pricing," would likely fall somewhere between those of specialty sporting goods retailers and mass merchandisers. And while the company tried to keep its prices comparable to other sporting goods superstores, it did not—unlike many of its competitors—take temporary price reductions to promote product sales. It simply relied on the product quality strength of its ever-increasing stable of brand names.

By the start of 1993, Sports Authority had become less dependent on Kmart and had gained enough financial strength to fund the opening of 10 new stores on its own during the first six months of the year. As intense competition from Wal-Mart threatened Kmart's future ability to support the expansion of its top subsidiaries, Sports Authority's increasing sense of autonomy became an even more important factor. At this time, the company also stepped up its bid to increase its share and presence by opening up multiple stores in major markets. This growth strategy—known as "cannibalizing" because new stores sometimes "eat up" sales from existing stores in an attempt to capture a dominant overall market share—enabled the company to take advantage of economies of scale in advertising and promotion in Florida locations such as Dade and Broward counties, where it had 10 stores by the end of the year. The company also attempted to make a strong entrance in major markets such as Seattle and New York City, where it opened 15 stores.

### Initial Public Offering

Just as Sports Authority was fast becoming the largest sporting goods store in the nation, its parent company, Kmart, the second largest retail company in the United States, struggled in the face of increasing competition from Wal-Mart, Target, and other top retailers. In August 1994, following a record $974 million loss the previous year, Kmart made the decision to take its three most successful specialty shops public to fund the renovation of its older stores and the introduction of Super Kmart Centers. Sports Authority, along with OfficeMax and Borders-Walden bookstores, were subsequently approved for initial public offerings with the hope of raising more than $1 billion. Kmart's loss, however, proved to be a boon for Smith and Sports Authority. On November 18, 71 percent of the company was sold to the public for around $270 million. Although Sports Authority had always essentially run its own business, its growth would no longer be hindered by the retail giant.

That same year Sports Authority opened its 100th store as it recorded another record-breaking performance: sales increased to $838 million, up 38 percent from the previous year, and earnings rose to $16.9 million, a 33 percent jump. While growing at such a rapid rate, the company managed to maintain a strong balance sheet and cash flow. With equity in excess of $250 million, cash and cash equivalents of around $37 million, and—most notably—no long-term debt, the company placed itself in a favorable position to continue its aggressive national expansion program, focusing its growth on the New York metropolitan area, where it opened six stores, and Chicago, where it opened four. In addition to opening 12 stores in existing markets, the company entered several new markets, including Anchorage, Seattle/Tacoma, Sacramento, and Tucson.

The Sports Authority complemented its efforts toward dominating the domestic sporting goods market by also launching an international program in 1994. Its first movement outside of the United States' borders consisted of a plan to open five new stores in Toronto. Not only did Canada offer the company a market with characteristics and dynamics similar to those in the U.S., but it also featured an easily accessible supply line from existing vendors, most of whom already had Canadian operations. That same year the company also laid the groundwork for overseas expansion, signing a joint venture agreement with JUSCO Co., Ltd, to operate Sports Authority stores in Japan. The country's third-largest retailer, JUSCO brought to the table a wealth of experience in property management and retail sight selection as well as broad experience in working with other western based retailers. With an estimated size of $16 billion, the Japanese sporting goods market presented the opportunity to tap a densely populated market with high disposable income, a strong attraction to branded products, and a commitment to sports and leisure activities.

Perhaps the most visible sign of the company's arrival, though, was the addition of one of the most popular vendors in the industry, Nike. After seven years of refusing to sell to The Sports Authority, the footwear and apparel giant began selling to the fast-growing chain, paving the way for a number of upscale brands to enter the fold. Starter apparel, Timberland, and Teva quickly followed suit, adding significantly to the company's bid to offer its customers the most comprehensive array of products in the industry.

### Breaking the Billion-Dollar Barrier: 1995 and Beyond

In its first full year of operation as a publicly traded company, Sports Authority became the first full-line sporting goods retailer to top $1 billion in sales. The now 136-store chain also proved to its investors that such unprecedented growth did not come without a concomitant boost in earnings, which increased 32 percent. A number of strategic moves contributed to the record-breaking success of the company and provided a foundation for continued growth over the long run.

Although the company had long earned high marks for its extensive product line, its reputation for customer service had not been as strong. In an effort to set itself apart from other large-format sporting goods retailers and other mass merchandisers, Sports Authority launched a company-wide initiative to enhance customer service in each one of its stores. Known as TSA 2000, the new standard tried to address the most common complaint against the company: employees too busy stocking shelves to devote full attention to the needs of customers. TSA 2000 attempted to eliminate this problem by moving receiving and stocking duties, as well as other non-selling functions, to the hours immediately prior to opening or shortly after closing, enabling associates to place a greater emphasis on listening to customers and providing information about products.

In keeping with the year's focus on improving the environment of its stores, the company also invested $4 million in new "ladder-style" apparel fixtures designed to display and coordinate merchandise in a more user-friendly manner. Installed to replace conventional gondolas, the in-house designed ladder fixtures enabled stores to combine graphics and coordinate presentations on the same fixture to make a more powerful impression on the customer and save store space at the same time. Another significant merchandising presentation innovation implemented that year was the use of "statement shops"— designated areas located near the front of the store that feature specialized footwear and related apparel from top manufactures. A New Jersey store, for instance, created a Rugged Apparel shop—complete with a wooden sign with carved letters outlined in green—that featured hiking boots as well as shirts, shorts, and winter flannel apparel from upscale vendors such as Woolrich, Columbia, and Jansport.

As Smith looked forward to the second half of the decade, he predicted that by the year 2000 his company would reach $5 billion in annual sales and expand to 500 stores in the United States alone. His strategy for achieving that goal did not promise to deviate from the "simple blocking and tackling" business fundamentals that allowed for its rise to the top of the industry. Setting a market share goal of 35 percent in each of its markets, the company intended to continue its practice of cannibalizing existing store sales to take business away from mass merchandisers and traditional sporting goods retailers. It planned to finance further expansion—at least 30 stores were scheduled to open in 1996—with proceeds from the $160 million sale of the remaining 29 percent of the company.

According to analysts' long-term predictions, the sporting goods industry as a whole should continue to expand as baby boomers gain more disposable income and leisure time, and as increasing numbers of people take up some form of exercise. The Sporting Authority, with its strong financial base, economies of scale, and technological edge, expects to lead the competition in taking advantage of these trends. Whether or not it will reach the goals of its energetic and ambitious founder remains to be seen.

### Further Reading

Book, Esther Wachs, "Here Comes a Cat Killer," *Forbes,* April 22, 1996, pp. 49, 52.

Boyd, Christopher, "Agassi Vs. Courier," *Florida Trend,* October 1993, pp. 60–64.

"Chains Square Off to Take Manhattan," *Sporting Goods Business,* December 1994, p. 10.

Gaffney, Andrew, "Jack Smith," *Sporting Goods Business,* June 25, 1995, pp. 62–63.

Halverson, Richard, "Sports Authority Aims for $5B in Sales, 500 Stores by Year 2000," *Discount Store News,* July 17, 1995, pp. 15–16.

"Image, Presentation Key to Merchandising," *Discount Store News,* July 17, 1995, pp. 19–20.

—Jason Gallman

STERLING CHEMICALS

# Sterling Chemicals, Inc.

**1200 Smith Street, Suite 1900**
**Houston, Texas 77002-4312**
**U.S.A.**
**(713) 650-3700**
**Fax: (713) 654-9551**

*Public Company*
*Incorporated:* 1986
*Employees:* 1,197
*Sales:* $1.03 billion (1995)
*Stock Exchanges:* New York
*SICs:* 2819 Industrial Inorganic Chemicals, Not
    Elsewhere Classified; 2821 Plastics Materials,
    Synthetic Resins & Nonvulcanizable Elastomers; 2865
    Cyclic Organic Crudes & Intermediates & Organic
    Dyes & Pigments; 2869 Industrial Organic Chemicals,
    Not Elsewhere Classified; 2899 Chemicals &
    Chemical Preparations, Not Elsewhere Classified

Sterling Chemicals, Inc. was, in 1995, a major producer of seven petrochemical products. Its Canadian subsidiary was a major producer of sodium chlorate for the pulp and paper industry and the leading supplier of large-scale chlorine dioxide generators for this industry. Although not yet a decade old, the company had experienced a roller-coaster ride typical of enterprises engaged in the volatile, energy-related petrochemicals field. It was put up for sale in early 1996.

### Early History

Sterling Chemicals, Inc. was founded in 1986 to acquire and operate Monsanto Co.'s petrochemical plant in Texas City, Texas. The purchase was completed on August 1, 1986. The cost, $213 million, was financed partly by a syndicate of banks led by Chase Manhattan Bank, which provided a public offering of $120 million of subordinate notes and $140 million in credit.

The Texas City facility was on a 250-acre site on Galveston Bay, about 45 miles from downtown Houston, where Sterling Chemicals established its corporate headquarters. Production from the plant consisted of acrylonitrile, styrene monomer, lactic acid, acetic acid, tertiary butylamine, and plasticizers. These chemicals, through intermediate products, became integral elements in finished goods such as synthetic fibers, coatings and adhesives, plastics, and synthetic rubbers used in many household and industrial applications.

Sterling Chemicals was founded on the premise that there was a "window of opportunity" for the chemicals produced at the Texas City complex because of rising demand and no new manufacturing capacity in the offing. Gordon A. Cain, leader of Sterling Group Inc., the investor group that founded the chemical company and chairman of Sterling Chemicals' board, was a retired chemical-industry executive who acquired several chemical complexes from major companies during the recessionary period of the early 1980s. He owned 10.8 percent of the stock at the end of 1994; J. Virgil Waggoner, president and chief executive officer of the company from its inception, owned 8.2 percent.

"As long as oil was selling for $30 a barrel," Cain told a *Houston Post* reporter, "there was a trend to build plants like this in Saudi Arabia." But, he continued, as a result of lower oil prices, which even fell below $10 a barrel in 1986, "There's no incentive to build competing plants in that part of the world." Cain also foresaw that the new venture would benefit from the lower cost of petroleum feedstocks (because of the lower price of crude oil) that served as Sterling Chemicals' raw material and from a weakening dollar, which would make the company's products more competitive in the world chemical markets.

Contributing to Sterling Chemicals' low costs was a small corporate staff with minimum layers of management and a cooperative work force. Company officials established an employee stock-ownership plan and later, a profit-sharing plan, in order to gain greater productivity from a highly unionized labor force with strict work rules and a long history of adversarial relations with management. About 12 percent of the common stock was held by employees in 1988. The company was contributing, in 1990, 60 cents for every dollar employees put into the stock-option program.

The new company had an anchor client in Monsanto, which was paying Sterling Chemicals a fee and a share of the profits to convert its petroleum feedstocks. The Texas City facility was the only one in the United States producing synthetic lactic acid, a preservative, and tertiary butylamine, used significantly by Monsanto in rubber production. Within a year of Sterling Chemicals' founding, the prices of its two main products—styrene monomer and acrylonitrile—had risen. For its first fiscal year (ended September 30, 1987), the company reported revenues of $413.2 million and net income of $47.4 million. The long-term debt of $187.3 million had been reduced to $116 million. Total common stockholders' equity had increased from $5.1 million to $52.4 million. Results were so good in Sterling Chemicals' initial year that its board approved a voluntary distribution to its employees that came out to be about $2,500 each.

### Success Leads to Expansion

Fiscal 1988 was a year of spectacular success for Sterling Chemicals. The company reported revenues of nearly $699 million and a whopping net income of $213.1 million. Long-term debt dropped to $86.3 million, while stockholders' equity rose to $90.6 million. Sterling Chemicals ranked first for the year among all Fortune 500 companies in return on assets and second in return on sales. The company attributed its outstanding performance to a favorable supply/demand situation, availability of raw materials at reasonable costs, the relatively weak dollar, lack of easily substitutable materials, and a healthy world economy. Shortly before October 1988 Sterling Chemicals became a publicly traded company, its stock listed on the New York Stock Exchange. Stockholders sold 12.65 million shares (more than 20 percent of the stock outstanding) at $16 a share in the initial public offering.

A program of expansion also was under way. BP Chemicals America Inc., a U.S. subsidiary of British Petroleum Co., was working with Sterling Chemicals to increase its acrylonitrile capacity by 55 percent and its acetic acid capacity by a minimum of 100 million pounds a year. A sodium cyanide facility also was being constructed at the Texas City site, by E.I. du Pont de Nemours and Co. Sterling Chemicals reported that much of its production was committed through long-term contracts with companies like BP Chemicals and Du Pont, enabling it to lower working-capital requirements for raw materials and inventories and to lower its overhead by dispensing with the need for a sales force and many other staffers. A company executive told *Barron's* that its selling and administrative costs were only one-quarter those of most competitors. In 1990 the company had an entire corporate staff of only 22 and a marketing department of only six.

Revenues fell to $580.8 million in fiscal 1989, and net income to $103.9 million. During the year available supplies of styrene monomer (Sterling Chemicals' major product) and acrylonitrile increased while demand weakened, resulting in price declines from what had been unprecedented levels. The dollar strengthened appreciably, reducing demand for Sterling Chemicals' product line overseas. There was a general slowdown in the housing and automobile industries, and fashion changes

resulted in decreased demands for acrylic fibers. Sterling Chemicals' income-to-sales ratio of 18 percent remained enviable, and its stock reached a record high, exceeding $18 a share. However, the company was entering a downward spiral that would not end until 1994.

### Setbacks in the Early 1990s

During fiscal 1990 Sterling Chemicals' revenues fell to $506 million and its net income to $59.1 million. A severe freeze along the Texas Gulf Coast in December 1989 resulted in a two-week shutdown of the company's production and some degree of impairment for up to two months. The Iraqi invasion of Kuwait in August 1990 disrupted the styrene market as prices for raw materials escalated rapidly. The worldwide market for acrylonitrile continued to be affected adversely by the weakening in the East Asian market for synthetic fiber, particularly acrylic fiber. However, Sterling Chemicals announced completion of three projects: the modernization of its styrene monomer plant, an increase in the capacity of the acrylonitrile plant, and expansion of the acetic acid facility. By August 1990 Sterling Chemicals had spent about $150 million to upgrade its production facilities.

During fiscal 1991 revenues rose to $542.7 million, but net income dropped to $36.8 million. Management cited oversupply in the petrochemical industry, including the opening of new styrene plants in the Far East, and declining demand as the reasons for lower profitability. A cogeneration project was under construction as a joint venture with a subsidiary of Union Carbide Industrial Gases, Inc., in order to provide added supplies of steam and electricity. This facility was completed in 1992.

Sterling Chemicals suffered a loss of $5.9 million in fiscal 1992, its revenues plummeting to a five-year low of $430.5 million. Management cited worldwide oversupply of styrene monomer and a shutdown of acrylonitrile production for routine maintenance. It also reported that a profit would have been earned except for a one-time charge for prior years recognizing liability for post-retirement benefits.

In August 1992 Sterling Chemicals purchased the pulp-chemical division of Albright & Wilson, a division of Tenneco Canada, Inc., for about $302 million. The acquisition included four Canadian facilities for the production of sodium chlorate, used in the bleaching of pulp for the manufacture of paper. It also included ERCO Systems Group, which was licensing and constructing large-scale generators to convert the sodium chlorate into chlorine dioxide as an environmentally preferred alternative to elemental chlorine in pulp bleaching. In making this purchase Sterling Chemicals raised its long-term debt from $72.6 million to $300.2 million.

Sterling Chemicals increased its fiscal 1993 revenues to $518.8 million because of $119.3 million from the newly acquired pulp-chemical business. The company suffered its second consecutive annual loss, ending $5.4 million in the red. Its stock sank to a record low of $3.50 a share during the year. Management noted that, with three styrene monomer plants being constructed in East Asia and one in Europe, supply for the chemical seemed likely to exceed demand for several more years. It also said demand for acrylonitrile from export customers had weakened. The pulp-chemicals business was profitable despite lower demand than forecast, attributed to the recessionary North American economy.

### Market Improvement in the Mid-1990s

The fortunes of Sterling Chemicals turned around in 1994. Revenues increased to a solid $700.8 million, and net income was $19.1 million. The company said that demand for its petrochemical products, including styrene monomer, had grown significantly during the year, primarily because of a healthier world economy. Sterling Chemicals' pulp-chemical plants were operating near full capacity at the end of the fiscal year. Eight ERCO Systems generators started up in 1994, and several more were under construction in China.

Sterling Chemicals' pride in its impressive environmental and safety record was shaken in May 1994, when an ammonia leak in one of its Texas City plants sent nearly 1,400 people to a local hospital for treatment. Eight of them were hospitalized. Officials determined that the leak was caused by a worker mistakenly turning a valve that controls hot-water flow to an ammonia vaporizer.

In the best performance by Sterling Chemicals since it became a public company, revenues reached a record $1.03 billion in fiscal 1995, and net income came to more than $150 million. Strong worldwide demand and market growth from global economic expansion benefitted sales of both styrene monomer and acrylonitrile. High North American demand led to record production and sales volume of chlorine dioxide, derived from sodium chlorate. Royalty revenues from installed generator technology also grew. During the fiscal year the company's major customers were British Petroleum and its subsidiaries, accounting for 16.5 percent of revenues, and Mitsubishi International Corp., accounting for 12.6 percent. Revenue from exports came to nearly 52 percent of the total, with Asia accounting for 64 percent and Europe for 36 percent.

During the fiscal year Sterling Chemicals reduced its long-term debt by $89 million, to $103.6 million. The company obtained a $275-million bank-credit facility, and the pulp-chemicals unit received a separate $60-million credit facility. Most of this new financing was earmarked for a three-year, $200-million capital-spending program. Under construction at Texas City in 1995, in conjunction with BP Chemicals, was an expansion of acetic acid capacity and a world-scale unit for the production of methanol. About half the methanol would be used as a raw material for the production of acetic acid, with the rest available to BP. A partial-oxidation unit by Praxair, Inc. would refurbish Sterling Chemicals' existing synthesis gas reformer, freeing it for methanol production. This unit also would convert natural gas into carbon monoxide and hydrogen for use in the production of acetic acid and plasticizers.

Also under construction in 1995 was Sterling Chemicals' first sodium chlorate plant in the United States. The 110,000-ton-per-year facility in Valdosta, Georgia, would be the company's second largest for this purpose and would increase its capacity to produce this chemical by 30 percent. Production was scheduled to begin in December 1996.

Sterling Chemicals announced on January 29, 1996, that it had entered discussions with a number of third parties with respect to the possible sale of the company in a single transaction or a series of related transactions. Shares of the stock immediately rose 35 percent, from $9.25 to $12.50 a share. Employees and directors owned about 30 percent of the stock in 1995.

### Operations in the Mid-1990s

At the end of fiscal 1995 Sterling Chemicals' 290-acre facility in Texas City included one of the world's largest units for the production of styrene monomer, with an annual capacity of more than 1.5 billion pounds. This unit accounted for more than one-third of the company's total chemical production capacity and for about 11 percent of total domestic capacity of this chemical. Derivatives of styrene monomer, a raw material, were being used in the production of foam products such as ice chests, residential sheathing, egg cartons, insulation, and protective packagings; housings for computers, telephones, videocassettes, small home appliances, and automotive parts; and for tableware, luggage, packing, toys, textile products, and synthetic rubber products.

Sterling Chemicals' annual production capacity of acrylonitrile was in excess of 700 million pounds. It was the second largest domestic producer of the chemical, with about 31 percent of total domestic capacity. Produced using ammonia, air, and propylene as raw materials, it was being used in synthetic fibers for apparel, rugs, and blankets; in polymer products for casings for ice chests, hard luggage, calculators, telephone handsets, and computers; in automotive parts; and for synthetic rubber products.

Sterling Chemicals' share of domestic capacity for acetic acid production came to 13 percent and was scheduled to reach nearly 800 million pounds annually with the completion of the expansion of the unit. Produced using methanol and carbon monoxide as raw materials, its largest use was in the production of vinyl acetate. BP Chemicals was marketing the unit's production. The company's plasticizer capacity was about 280 million pounds a year. Its plasticizers were being used in producing flexible vinyl plastics for consumer products and building materials. BASF Corp. was marketing Sterling Chemicals' plasticizers.

Sterling Chemicals was the only domestic producer of synthetic lactic acid, with an annual capacity of 19 million pounds. It was being used as a preservative for food products, for the manufacture of acrylic enamel, for silk finishing, and in intravenous solutions. The company was also the only U.S. producer of tertiary butylamine, and one of only three worldwide, with an annual capacity of 21 million pounds. This chemical was being used for silicone caulk, in tires and hoses, and as a chemical intermediate. It was being purchased and resold by Flexys, a joint venture of Monsanto and Akzo Nobel N.V. The company's annual capacity of sodium cyanide was 100 million pounds. It was being used for electroplating and to enhance the recovery of precious metals. The unit was operated by Sterling Chemicals but owned by Du Pont, which marketed its output.

Sterling Chemicals' revenues from pulp chemicals came to $143.95 million, or 14 percent of the company total, in fiscal

1995. Its net income came to $9.7 million, or 6.4 percent, of the company total. Sterling Pulp Chemicals, Ltd. was the second-largest supplier of sodium chlorate to the North American pulp and paper industry, with about 20 percent of the market. It had headquarters in Toronto and held four manufacturing plants: at Buckingham, Quebec; Grand Prairie, Alberta; Thunder Bay, Ontario; and Vancouver, British Columbia. These plants had a combined capacity of about 350,000 tons. The Georgia facility under construction would increase capacity by more than 30 percent. The Buckingham facility also was producing small amounts of sodium chlorite, using sodium chlorate as a raw material. Sodium chlorite was being used as an antimicrobial agent in water treatment, as a disinfectant for fresh produce, for treatment of industrial waste water, and for oil field microbe control.

Sterling Pulp Chemicals' ERCO Systems Group was licensing, designing, and overseeing construction of large-scale generators at pulp-mill sites. These generators were converting sodium chlorate to chlorine dioxide for the bleaching of kraft pulp. ERCO had supplied about two-thirds of the generators in use worldwide.

### Principal Subsidiaries

Sterling Pulp Chemicals, Ltd.

### Further Reading

Brammer, Rhonda, ''Sterling Value?'' *Barron's,* October 9, 1995, p. 17.

Byrne, Harlan S., ''Sterling Chemicals Inc.,'' *Barron's,* March 13, 1989, pp. 45–46.

Fletcher, Sam, ''Oil Slump Helps Monsanto Sale,'' *Houston Post,* August 20, 1986, p. 1E.

——, ''Sterling Chemicals Able to Beat Highs and Lows of Price Extremes,'' *Houston Post,* August 6, 1990, p. 4C.

Wruck, Karen Hopper, and Jensen, Michael C., ''Science, Specific Knowledge, and Total Quality Management,'' *Journal of Accounting & Economics,* 18 (1994), pp. 247–287.

—Robert Halasz

# Storehouse PLC

**Marylebone House**
**129-137 Marylebone Road**
**London, NW1 5QD**
**United Kingdom**
**(44) 171 262 3456**
**Fax: (44) 171 262 4740**

*Public Company*
*Incorporated:* 1986
*Employees:* 19,086
*Sales:* £1.08 billion (US$1.7 billion) (1995)
*Stock Exchanges:* London
*SICs:* 5311 Department Stores; 5621 Women's Clothing
  Stores; 5611 Men's and Boys' Clothing Stores; 5712
  Furniture Stores; 2511 Wood Household Furniture

With its British Home Stores (Bhs) and Mothercare chains, Storehouse PLC ranks among the United Kingdom's top ten retail holding companies. The firm's 142 company-owned and 51 franchised Bhs department stores sell apparel, housewares, and giftware under the Bhs, Universal, and The One and Only trademarks. The 263 company-owned and 109 franchised Mothercare stores constitute Britain's largest retailer of clothing and housewares for mothers and their young children. The chains have international franchisees throughout Europe, the Middle East, and Asia. Led by CEO Keith Edelman in the mid-1990s, Storehouse appeared to have rebounded from an abrupt decline in the late 1980s.

## Creation and Development in the 1960s

Storehouse was created through the 1986 merger of Habitat/Mothercare PLC and British Home Stores PLC. The brainchild of designer Terence Conran, this union created Great Britain's eighth-largest retail entity. It was to have been the crowning achievement of Conran's acclaimed career, but instead was his dénouement.

Trained as a textile designer, Conran had launched his own line of furniture in 1960. Dissatisfied with the retail atmosphere in which his goods were sold, Conran opened his first Habitat store in London's Chelsea district in 1964. The reasonably-priced, Bauhaus-inspired furniture was an instant hit and soon came to represent the epitome of British taste. It didn't hurt that the styles were adopted by royalty as well as such pop stars as the Beatles. Fifteen years and 52 stores later, Habitat easily qualified as, in the words of *Forbes'* Jeffrey Ferry, "a British institution." In 1983, Prime Minister Margaret Thatcher knighted Conran "for services to British design and industry."

Emboldened by his sweeping success in the United Kingdom, Conran expanded into the United States in 1977. Since the Habitat name was already owned by a New York furniture store, the American units became known as Conran's. Fierce competition and discrepancies between British and American sizing methods (i.e., comforters too short for U.S. beds), however, made for a rocky start; Conran's didn't break even until 1983.

## Expansion through Acquisition in the 1980s

Back at home, it seemed that Conran was on a roll. He embarked on a program of expansion and diversification through acquisition in the early 1980s. With help from British investment banker Roger Seelig of Morgan Grenfell, Conran took Habitat public in 1981. The following year, Habitat acquired the 360-store Mothercare chain for £50 million. Founded in the early 1960s by Selim Zilkha, this retailer specialized in maternity apparel and childrenswear, and had operations in the United States as well as the United Kingdom. Habitat took a 65 percent stake in France's Maison la Redoute retail chain in 1982 and 48 percent of ladies' apparel chain Richard Shops Holdings Inc. the following year. Conran also created a teen fashion and menswear chain called NOW during this period.

Conran's marketing savvy appeared boundless. During this period he wrote several successful design and decorating how-to books, launched his own publishing company (Conran Octopus), founded a trendy London restaurant, and established a "town-planning firm."

The early 1980s acquisition spree appeared to have been a retail coup. Sales had grown from £67.2 million in fiscal 1981 to £446.7 million (US$634 million) in 1984, and pre-tax profits grew from £4 million to £35.6 million (US$52 million) during the same period. The company's stock price multiplied more than four times by mid-1985, leading *Management Today* to declare the Habitat/Mothercare merger "a clear success" in a February 1986 article.

### British Home Stores Merger

That year Conran made what was to have been his crowning achievement, merging his chains of boutiques with British Home Stores. The addition of this 130-unit department store chain more than doubled sales to over £1 billion (US$1.47 billion). The newest member of Conran's coterie was also the oldest, having been established in 1928 as a variety store along the lines of Woolworth's.

By the early 1980s, British Home Stores ranked a distant second among the country's mass retailers and struggled with a "dowdy" image. Although it boasted efficient back office operations and had invested £100 million on store and merchandise renovations in 1984 and 1985, the company suffered from unflattering comparisons with Britain's leading retailer, Marks & Spencer. Conran hoped that the merger would exploit the best characteristics of its key components: Habitat/Mothercare could benefit from British Home Store's strict controls, while British Home Stores could achieve the marketing flair it lacked.

A new holding company, Storehouse PLC, was formed, and although British Home Stores owned a controlling 55 percent share and Habitat/Mothercare the remaining 45 percent, the charismatic Conran was elected chairman and CEO of the parent company. With over six million square feet of selling space, Britain's eighth-ranking retail holding company featured seven chains: British Home Stores, Habitat, Mothercare, Richards, NOW, Heals, and Conran's. By the time of the merger, the company's over 200 Conran's and Mothercare stores in the United States were contributing 17 percent of annual sales. Relatively small acquisitions in 1987 and 1988 added France's Jacadi, an upscale childrenswear chain, and the six-store Blazer chain, which sold high-end menswear designed in-house.

Conran embarked on what was expected to be a three-year period of transition from which Storehouse's subsidiaries would emerge reformed in each other's image. British Home Stores' repositioning focused on three areas—merchandise, store design, and image—with the primary goal of appealing to the younger, more affluent consumers to whom Habitat had traditionally catered. Storehouse closed the company's embattled food departments and updated its apparel lines with trendier, more youthful styles. Store renovations begun in the early 1980s continued through the decade. The chain's image makeover included a rather idiosyncratic logo change known as "the flying h," in which a lowercase "h" replaced the middle initial in the corporate insignia. The "s" was later lowercased as well. An increased advertising budget promoted the "Conranization" of Bhs. At the same time, Storehouse was trying to apply Bhs's operational know-how to Habitat/Mothercare. Storehouse also launched a group chargecard in 1986 and a home-shopping joint venture in 1987.

### Late 1980s Decline

But as the British retail environment began to sour in the late 1980s, Storehouse's efforts to achieve marketing and operational excellence fell short. Retail analysts and takeover artists began to opine that Storehouse's parts were worth more than the whole, and at one point, Conran himself appeared to agree with them. In mid-1987, he apparently opened negotiations with Mountleigh PLC, which planned a leveraged buyout and spinoff of the individual retail chains. Mountleigh's £4.45 per share bid pegged Storehouses' value at £1.7 billion (US$3 billion).

Conran changed his mind, however, and that September he publicly declared his loyalty to the unified group, shunning the buyout. It was, ironically, the wrong choice. The stock market crashed in October, and Storehouse's share price dropped to less than £3. That's when Benlox Holdings PLC joined the fray with a £1.93 billion (US$3.42 billion) takeover bid. Institutional investors frustrated with Conran's apparent inability to manage a £1 billion holding company told him that they would throw their support to Benlox unless Conran agreed to immediately relinquish the chief executive office and retire from the chairmanship in 1991. Hoping to save face and Storehouse, Conran acquiesced. *Forbes'* Jeffrey Ferry observed that "It [was] all a rather tarnished ending to an otherwise brilliant career."

In June 1988, Storehouse's board of directors brought in 49-year-old Michael Julien to replace Conran as CEO. Although Julien had no retail experience, he had a strong financial background.

As Storehouse struggled to right itself, group pretax profits plunged from about £130 million in 1987 to £11.3 million in 1989. All the primary business segments were in trouble, in part because of Britain's retail slump. Mothercare's British market share slid from 11 percent to nine percent, Habitat UK suffered its first-ever loss, a £10 million shortfall, and Bhs's operating profits declined by over 40 percent.

### Early 1990s Turnaround

Following a review of Storehouse's operations, Julien reorganized the company into three primary divisions: Specialty Retail, comprising Mothercare, Richards, Blazer, Anonymous, and Jacadi; Home Furnishing, including Habitat, Heals, and the Conran Shop; and Bhs. Julien then made a three-pronged effort at cutting costs, which were rising twice as fast as sales. A centralization of Storehouse's distribution system allowed for the closure of one warehouse and eliminated several hundred employees. A rationalization of the group's computer systems made four of the company's six data processing centers redundant. Inventory reductions and £49.4 million worth of write-offs for unsalable goods and unusable store furnishings were completed early in 1989. In an interview with the *Financial Times* that year, Julien commented that "the provisions we are making today are really only those that should have been made at the time of the merger in 1986."

In 1989, Julien began a second, more drastic effort to turn Storehouse around, divesting noncore interests to focus squarely on Bhs and Mothercare UK. That year, the company raised over £140 million through the sale of partial stakes in FNAC SA and Great Savacentre Ltd. The 1990 spin-off of Jacadi Childrenswear brought in Ffr136.6 million (US$28.2 million). In 1991, Storehouse sold Mothercare Stores, Inc., the U.S. arm of its maternity chain, to American investment company Bain Capital Inc., taking a £7.5 million (US$13.5 million) loss on the transaction.

Michael Julien retired in mid-1992 due to health concerns, and David Dworkin advanced from chairman and CEO of Bhs to succeed him. Dworkin continued Julien's divestment strategy. Spin-offs of Richards, Habitat Europe, and Conran's that year raised over £150 million. The proceeds were invested in renovations of Mothercare UK and Bhs, as well as advertising campaigns that publicized the changes.

After less than a year in Storehouse's top spot, Dworkin quit to become president and CEO of Carter Hawley Hale Stores in April 1993. After a four-month search, Storehouse hired 42-year-old Keith Edelman to fill the vacant slot. Despite the frequent changes in top management, the overriding strategy of divestment to focus primarily on Bhs and Mothercare began to bear fruit in the mid-1990s. Group sales remained flat, at just over £1 billion, but profits rose from £46.6 million in fiscal 1993 to nearly £109 million by fiscal 1996.

## Principal Subsidiaries

Bhs PLC; Bhs (Jersey) Ltd.; TCR Properties Ltd.; Mothercare UK Ltd.; Storehouse Finance PLC; Storehouse Properties LTD.; Davenbush Ltd.

### Further Reading

Bidlake, Suzanne, "City Jitters Persist in Wake of Storehouse Loss," *Marketing,* June 8, 1989, p. 13.
——, "Storehouse Seeks to Thwart Bidders," *Marketing,* March 16, 1989, p. 13.
——, "Storehouse Stays Divided," *Marketing,* May 3, 1990, p. 1.
Britton, Noelle, "Armchair Shopping Takes on Fresh Look," *Marketing,* November 5, 1987, p. 15.
——, "Storehouse Link Opens Door to Home Shopping," *Marketing,* October 29, 1987, pp. 1, 60.
"Conran Gets Down to the Roots of Decline," *Marketing,* June 9, 1988, p. 17.
"Edelman Named Chief Executive Storehouse PLC," *Daily News Record,* July 1, 1993, p. 10.
Fallon, James, "Storehouse Moves Into Men's Wear With Purchase of Blazer Chain," *Daily News Record,* December 23, 1987, p. 7.
——, "Bain Capital Acquires Mothercare for $11M," *Women's Wear Daily,* March 20, 1991, p. 12.
——, "Storehouse Eyes Conran's Sale to Traub Group in 30 Days," *Women's Wear Daily,* October 27, 1992, p. 17.
Ferry, Jeffrey, "Another Bloody Nose for Asher?" *Forbes,* November 27, 1989, p. 184.
——, "Broken By the Bottom Line," *Forbes,* November 1989, p. 180.
Grimm, Matthew, "He'll Get Rid of the Sand Pits and Take Conran's Habitat National," *ADWEEK's Marketing Week,* October 30, 1989, p. 8.
Moin, David, "Traub Group Agrees to buy Conran's Habitat," *Women's Wear Daily,* November 17, 1992, p. 10.
Nicholas, Ruth, "Storehouse Set to Build up Bhs," *Marketing,* March 3, 1994, p. 2.
"Storehouse PLC Born of Uk Retailers' Merger," *Daily News Record,* January 8, 1986, p. 17.
Warnaby, Gary, "Storehouse," *International Journal of Retail & Distribution Management,* May–June 1993, pp. 27–34.
Whelan, Sean, "Battered Storehouse Tightens Up Its Act," *Marketing,* December 8, 1988, pp. 13–16.

—April Dougal Gasbarre

# StrataCom, Inc.

1400 Parkmoor Avenue
San Jose, California 95126
U.S.A.
(408) 294-7600
Fax: (408) 999-0464

*Public Company*
*Incorporated:* 1986
*Employees:* 997
*Sales:* $331.74 million (1995)
*Stock Exchanges:* NASDAQ
*SICs:* 3661 Telephone and Telegraph Apparatus

StrataCom, Inc. is a worldwide leader in networking technology, producing frame relay and asynchronous transfer mode (ATM) communications switches, access devices, and support services for the fast-growing wide-area network (WAN) market. Its revenues doubling in both 1994 and 1995, StrataCom dominates the worldwide frame relay market, with a commanding 41.1 percent share, and holds a strong second position in the WAN ATM market, with more than 16 percent behind the leader Newbridge's nearly 32 percent. StrataCom's product portfolio includes its IPX cell switch, the Integrated Gigaswitch (IGX), the BPX ATM switch, and its family of FastPacket networking systems. Together these products boosted StrataCom's 1995 revenues to $331 million, in markets estimated to near $3 billion by the turn of the century. Top StrataCom clients include its exclusive vendor agreement with AT&T, which provided approximately 40 percent of StrataCom's revenues, as well as LDDS WorldCom, Inc., CompuServe, some 40 public phone companies, and more than 450 private companies, such as Air France, Daimler Benz, Lufkin and Jenrette, Motorola, and the Securities and Exchange Commission.

## The Frame-Relay Innovation

A group of venture capitalists led by Anthony Sun formed StrataCom in 1986 to develop new networking technologies being pioneered by Charles Corbalis (later StrataCom's vice-

president of engineering) and others. Richard M. Moley, formerly of ROLM, a maker of telecommunications switches, was hired to head the new company as chairman and chief executive officer. Moley's task was to convince the international market of the need for StrataCom's ATM technology.

ATM represented a break from the traditional circuit switching that had for years been a mainstay of the telecommunications industry. Circuit switching, or time-division multiplexing (TDM), set up a circuit for a certain amount of time through which data, such as a voice in the typical telephone call, flowed from one end of the circuit to the other. The advent of networking, and especially WANs, however, placed an extreme burden on the circuit. With only a limited bandwidth through which data could move, network communications could easily bog down, particularly when a large amount of data was being sent. WANs, which were set up over existing phone carrier lines, were also expensive to maintain: companies would typically rent a dedicated amount of bandwidth from a phone carrier. Even with the advent of T1 connections, with bandwidths capable of sending 1.5 million bits of information per second, networks were still hampered by the existing circuit switches. A data-intensive transmission, such as video or a large database, could easily slow down the entire network.

StrataCom's ATM technology provided the innovation to transform communications and launch the 1990s boom in private networking. Rather than opening a continuous circuit, ATM broke up the transmission into identically sized cells or ''packets'' of information. Each cell held the address for the transmission's destination. But instead of flowing in a continuous stream, each cell traveled individually through the telecommunication channels, essentially finding openings in the traffic, and thus preventing the traffic from becoming clogged. Once the cells reached their destination, they could be reassembled in their original configuration.

This process could be likened to a department store's escalator. A department store outfitted following traditional TDM switching would have a separate escalator leading to each department. Cell switching, or frame relay, adopted an approach similar to the typical department store's escalator, that is, instead of many escalators, a department store normally featured a

## Company Perspectives:

*Stratacom's mission is to develop, deliver and support the best fastpacket networking systems in the world by sustaining profitable growth; delivering innovative, high quality products and services; being a valued business partner; and being a great place to work.*

single escalator system. Each cell of the several or many transmissions being sent over a frame relay-based network took its own step on the elevator; the cells of the various transmissions then sorted themselves out at the appropriate department, or destination.

ATM permitted more efficient use of a network's dedicated bandwidth or rented T1 connection. In addition, companies were no longer dependent on month-by-month rentals of guaranteed bandwidths or T1 connections. Adoption of the technology could achieve significant cost savings, up to 50 percent of a company's network transmission costs, especially as it allowed companies to pay for transmissions only during the actual transmission. In 1988, StrataCom incorporated and introduced its first product, the IPX switch, a narrowband ATM system that supported voice, video, and data transmission at speeds up to 2 million bits per second (bps). Sales were slow at first as StrataCom faced a market that had already invested heavily in the existing technology. Corporations were reluctant to scrap their investments for StrataCom's ATM devices. First year sales reached $17.8 million, with a net loss of nearly half a million dollars. The following year, StrataCom shipped its 500th IPX, for sales of nearly $24 million but a loss of more than $3.3 million.

StrataCom's losses continued into 1990, doubling over the previous year to $6.8 million, on revenues that had barely climbed to $25.8 million. Until 1990, the company's sales had gone entirely to corporations setting up their own networks. But 1990 marked StrataCom's turning point.

### The Frame-Relay Standard

In October 1990, StrataCom became the first to offer frame relay capabilities, by mapping frame relay onto an ATM infrastructure. One month earlier, StrataCom had joined with Northern Telecom, Digital, and Cisco Systems to form the Frame Relay Forum, constructing international standards for the new technology and for its application to local-area networks (LANs) and WANs.

Frame relay permitted companies not only to use T1 connections for their networks more effectively, but also to abandon the T1 connection altogether. Networks could be returned to public, long-distance networks. Over the next several years, frame relay posed a growing threat to the T1 market, which would grow to an $8 billion business by 1995. In response, phone companies and public carriers moved to offer frame relay services to take up the slack from shrinking T1 revenues.

One of the first public carriers to offer frame relay was Wiltel Network Services, later renamed LDDS Worldcom, Inc. The March 1991 launch of Wiltel's frame relay services, using StrataCom products, provided StrataCom with its first major entry into the public carrier market. As Richard Moley said to the *Wall Street Journal*, "Wiltel was absolutely seminal" for StrataCom. Frame relay quickly became a standard for networking transmissions, and StrataCom's role as innovator of the technology placed it in the prime position to gain a dominant place in the market.

StrataCom made further inroads in 1991. CompuServe announced its own public frame relay service, to be based on the IPX, in January 1991. In March, Europe's largest company, Daimler Benz, chose StrataCom as the vendor for its own company network. Later in 1991, StrataCom entered a worldwide reseller agreement with British Telecom, which would base its own international high-speed frame relay service on the IPX early the following year. One of StrataCom's most important sales occurred in November 1991, when AT&T announced its own IPX-based public frame relay service. This endorsement of the IPX by AT&T, known for its preference for providing its own internally developed equipment, placed StrataCom at the forefront of frame relay technology.

In 1991 StrataCom showed its first earnings, $53,000 on nearly $40 million in revenues. By 1992, with revenues climbing past $55 million, StrataCom posted a net income of $4.5 million. In July of that year, StrataCom went public, offering 2.5 million shares at $7 per share; by the end of 1992, StrataCom's stock had already topped $19 per share.

ATM and frame relay quickly became worldwide standards in data transmission. More and more corporations began to adopt the new technologies for their private LANs and WANs. StrataCom soon faced competition from other vendors, chiefly Cascade Communications Corp. of Massachusetts, which had been founded in 1990 and rapidly seized a strong 15 percent share of the market. StrataCom's portfolio grew to include the IPX 8, IPX 16, and IPX 32, offering coverage from small network sites to larger, traffic-heavy sites. The company next turned to development of broadband systems, spending from 18 percent to 20 percent of revenues on research and development efforts.

### The 1990s: Becoming a Multiband Vendor

By January 1993, StrataCom was ready to announce its high-speed, broadband switch, the BPX. Aimed at the public carrier market, the BPX provided a high-performance, multiservice 9.6 gigabyte per second (Gbps) crosspoint switch capable of data transmission up to 20 million bps. Next, StrataCom formed a partnership with AT&T and Cisco Systems, Inc. to produce AT&T's Network Systems GCNS-2000 and InterSpan Data Communications Services, a network providing support for multimedia and distributed data applications. StrataCom's 1993 revenues grew to $74.4 million, with a net income of $7.5 million.

Shipments of the BPX system helped to double StrataCom's revenues in 1994. Sales reached $154 million, and income grew by 163 percent to near $20 million. Revenues were split almost evenly between the public carrier channel, which grew by 159 percent from 1993 to 1994, and the private WAN channel, which brought in about $72 million of 1994 revenues. International sales also strengthened, rising from $22 million in 1993 to $64 million in 1994. Importantly, StrataCom stepped up its research and development efforts, doubling expenditures in 1994 to more than $29 million.

Until 1994, StrataCom had remained a one-product company. But in the first quarter of 1994, StrataCom introduced a line of multimedia access products, the FastPAD multiplexers, which integrated slower-speed voice and data transfers into an IPX network. Frame relay was emerging quickly; by 1994 the market for frame relay products had grown to $293 million and public carriers revenues from frame relay had reached $234 million. In October 1994, with stock reaching a 52-week high of $49.25 per share, StrataCom filed a second public offering of $1.5 million, for $62 million earmarked for research and development. In November 1994, StrataCom announced a two-for-one stock split.

StrataCom introduced a number of new products in 1995, including support for its BPX switch with AXIS, a product that created 53-byte cells from low-speed traffic that could be integrated into a BPX network, providing significant cost advantages over an IPX network. In June 1995, StrataCom launched a mid-range ATM system, the IGX, filling out its line of switches. Positioned between the IPX and the BPX, the IGX was targeted at mid-sized corporate network users and smaller service providers. By the end of 1995, StrataCom had shipped 200 IGXs. Its IPX presence grew to 4,000 IPXs worldwide. Revenues more than doubled again, to $331.7 million, including $100 million from a newly signed multiyear, exclusive-vendor contract with AT&T.

StrataCom's future was seen as being strongly linked to its research and development efforts, which received 18 percent of revenues in 1995. As ATM and frame relay became the world-wide standard, competition intensified; AT&T also announced plans to enter the ATM equipment market. StrataCom faced a problem common in the computer industry: the rapid advances in technology quickly made products obsolete. The IGX, for example, was expected to cannibalize IPX sales. StrataCom's product line also faced pressure from the latest advances in networking technology, particularly the announcement of StrataCom's Fulcrum Intelligent Network Server (INS) system, which would reduce the vulnerability of single-server systems. With reliance on ATM systems expected to continue through the end of the 1990s, however, and StrataCom's strong commitment to research and development as well as its renowned customer support efforts, the company appeared to be well-positioned to maintain its industry dominance into the next century.

### Principal Subsidiaries

StrataCom Ltd. (U.K.); StrataCom GmbH (Germany); StrataCom China Limited (Hong Kong); StrataCom Korea, Inc.; Nihon StrataCom K.K. (Tokyo); StrataCom SARL (Paris); StrataCom Srl (Italy); StrataCom de Mexico S.A. de C.V.); StrataCom Australia Pty. Ltd.; StrataCom Pte Ltd. (Singapore); StrataCom BV (The Netherlands); StrataCom do Brasil Ltda.

### Further Reading

Bank, David, ''New Technology Spurs High Growth for Silicon Valley's StrataCom Inc.,'' *San Jose Mercury News,* July 9, 1995.

Choron, Olivia, Maier, Ursula, and Coons, John, ''StrataCom Inc.,'' *Dataquest,* May 22, 1995.

Clark, Don, ''StrataCom Flourishes as Computer Networking Leader,'' *Wall Street Journal,* June 12, 1995, p. B4.

Hostetler, Michele, ''StrataCom Spies Niche To Fill for Techno-Weary Companies,'' *San Jose Business Journal,* June 19, 1995.

Wiegers, Alex, ''StrataCom in Stratosphere This Summer,'' *San Jose Business Journal,* September 12, 1994.

—M.L. Cohen

STUART ENTERTAINMENT, S.A. DE C.V.

# Stuart Entertainment Inc.

3211 Nebraska Avenue
Council Bluffs, Iowa 51501
U.S.A.
(712) 323-1488
Fax: (712) 323-3215

*Public Company*
*Incorporated:* 1948
*Employees:* 1,325
*Sales:* $109.9 million (1995)
*Stock Exchanges:* NASDAQ
*SICs:* 3944 Games, Toys & Children's Vehicles; 3999
Manufacturing Industries; 3951 Pens and Mechanical
Pencils

Stuart Entertainment Inc. is the world's leading supplier of bingo products. The company's two major subsidiaries, Bingo King and Bazaar & Novelty, distribute the majority of all bingo paraphernalia in the United States and Canada. Founded as Bingo King in 1949, Stuart Entertainment has grown from a small, mail-order supplier of fund raising equipment to a multinational company that distributes all types of bingo-related products, from the ink used to mark bingo cards to computerized electronic bingo games.

## Company Origins in the 1940s

The game of bingo was introduced in the mid-1920s by a toy salesman named Edwin Lowe. Lowe had seen a version of the game of chance, then called "beano," being played for small prizes at a local carnival and decided to try to market a home version of the game. After an enthusiastic but tongue-tied winner yelled out "bingo" instead of "beano," Lowe realized that this was the perfect name for the simple but addictive game. Lowe never bothered to copyright the name and bingo became the generic name for the increasingly popular pastime. Although commercial bingo was prohibited by most state gambling laws, during the 1930s and 1940s the playing of bingo to raise money for churches had reached huge proportions. It is estimated that by 1934 there were 10,000 weekly public bingo games throughout the country. Under heavy pressure by anti-gambling forces, legislation was eventually passed in most states that either limited the size of prizes or outlawed bingo playing outright. By 1949 bingo in anything but a very limited form was legal in only four states. It was in this highly regulated atmosphere that Bingo King was founded in Colorado in 1948 as a small distributor of bingo cards to various fund raising organizations.

In the 1950s and 1960s, Bingo King was one of many small distributors of bingo products throughout the country. Most of these companies were limited by region because of varying regulations from state to state. Bingo King operated primarily on a mail-order basis and provided advice on how to organize and set up games in addition to selling the cards, markers, and "blowers" that randomized number selection. Through the building of a close relationship with many large charities Bingo King was able to extend the reach of its distribution system. By the late 1960s, with a 15 percent market share, Bingo King had become one of the top five distributors in the country and the only large distributor that did not operate out of the New York area.

During the 1970s anti-bingo legislation began to be repealed in many states. Under growing pressure from nonprofit organizations, for which more traditional sources of funding were drying up, as well as with an increased cultural tolerance for gambling in general, politicians started to cede ground to bingo enthusiasts. In addition, law enforcement agencies were finding it increasingly difficult to get convictions on bingo charges laid against institutions like the Elks Club or the March of Dimes. By 1979, bingo had been legalized in some form in all but 12 states. In most states, however, bingo was still restricted to charitable organizations, using volunteer labor. Only Nevada and Maryland permitted fully commercial bingo. It was in this atmosphere of increased liberalization of bingo laws that Bingo King was acquired in 1971 by a growing conglomerate, Standex International Corp.

## New Parentage in the 1970s

Standex was a corporation with a long and profitable history of acquiring diverse companies. Standex Chairman Daniel Hogan sought for acquisition private companies that he felt were in

## Company Perspectives:

*While many bingo players will say luck is at the heart of their game, the bingo industry recognizes that its luck is the product of hard work and good business practices. For Stuart that translates to attention to its market, outstanding relationships with its distributors, production savvy that enables it to be a low-cost producer, flexibility to keep the game fresh, the capability to remain a dependable, flexible, innovative bingo supplier, and the ability to deal with change in this fast-moving world.*

a growth position, had a history of profitability, and were located away from business centers like New York. The nature of the company's business was less important than these factors, although Standex tended to "stay pretty much with companies that manufacture useful articles and sell them," Hogan said in a 1979 interview in *Forbes*. Bingo King was renamed the Norbro Corporation and incorporated into Standex's mail-order division along with a mail-order grapefruit distributor and a mail-order colonial furniture manufacturer.

Under Standex, Bingo King, now operating as the Norbro Corporation, began to de-emphasize its connection to bingo products. Although bingo paraphernalia remained the backbone of the company's business, Norbro began to distribute other products related to fund raising to nonprofit organizations, including churches, lodges, hospitals, and nursing homes. In 1974 the company moved its headquarters and main manufacturing plant into a new 30,000-square-foot plant in Littleton, Colorado, as well as opening a new plant in Mexico. Norbro soon became the star performer of Standex's mail-order division and, by the mid-1970s, the company had opened distribution centers in Texas, Florida, and Nevada. In addition to distributing fundraising supplies, Norbro also began offering seminars at their new headquarters for nonprofit organizations demonstrating the best methods of setting up large fund-raising activities like bingo that by law required a volunteer labor force. By 1980, in spite of a marked economic downturn, Norbro was turning in record performances and capturing a larger share of the growing bingo market.

The early 1980s were a difficult time for Standex. Faced with a deep recession and high interest rates, Standex's earnings were at a record low and the pattern of acquisitions that had defined the conglomerate was put on hold. Instead, Standex management decided to divest by spinning off some of the company's divisions to raise both capital and visibility. Norbro was the prime candidate for such a spin-off both because of its impressive performance even during poor economic times and because Standex was leery of the potential bad publicity entailed by the company's affiliation with bingo. In 1979 a *Forbes* exposé of the bingo trade and its association with organized crime had cited Standex's Norbro division as a leading supplier of bingo equipment. Although no wrongdoing was implied, Standex's largest unit was a religious publishing company and management was ambivalent about being involved with the gaming industry. "Standex had mixed feelings about the industry," Bingo King Chairman Robert Jacob said in a

1984 article in *Forbes*. In 1981, Norbro, now once again under the Bingo King name, was spun off to Standex shareholders.

### A Public Company in the 1980s

As Bingo King became a fully independent public company the bingo industry was flourishing. By 1984, bingo was the fourth largest form of legal gambling in the country, with a total of about $4 million being spent on the game annually. In addition to the liberalization of bingo laws in many states, Native American-run bingo had become a major new factor in the industry. Court decisions that affirmed Native Americans' rights to certain sovereign powers had allowed Native American tribes to circumvent state gambling laws that limited the size of bingo jackpots. With these "super" jackpots Native American-run bingo parlors attracted a new, more spendthrift clientele. Although nonprofit organizations still made up the bulk of Bingo King's business, Native American bingo became a large and growing customer for the company's products.

Freed from the constraints of corporate ownership and faced with an expanding market, Bingo King set out to grow its own market share through acquisitions. By 1984, Bingo King had acquired three small companies, Precision Games, Western Bingo, and Jack Frain Enterprises. Within three years of the spin-off the company's market share had grown from 15 percent to 25 percent and revenues had doubled to almost $14 million. In addition to a program of acquisitions, Bingo King set out to revamp its distribution system. Under Standex, Bingo King had operated primarily on a mail-order basis, but this had allowed competitors to undercut listed catalog prices. The company now opened its own retail distributorships, permitting more flexible pricing and a quicker response to market demands.

In spite of a growing bingo market, Bingo King ran into trouble in the mid-1980s as the company was unable to manage the pace of growth that it had set for itself. In 1985, in what was expected to be a banner year for the firm, sales grew to an impressive $18 million but costs involved in opening new distributorships and merging the operations of acquisitions saw Bingo King ending the fiscal year with a net loss of more than $1 million. Enter Leonard Stuart. Stuart was the owner and president of Canada's leading bingo equipment supplier, Bazaar & Novelty, which controlled well over 50 percent of the bingo market in that country. Bazaar & Novelty's U.S. division was the leading supplier of disposable bingo cards to Bingo King, and when that company had trouble paying its bills Stuart moved in and assumed control of the floundering firm. In 1988, Bazaar's U.S. division was merged with Bingo King, with Stuart retaining control of 53 percent of the merged company's stock. In 1991 the combined operations of the two companies were officially renamed Stuart Entertainment Inc.

Stuart's success in Canada had been in large part due to his promotion of disposable bingo cards as a replacement for the traditional reusable boards that had been used since the game was introduced in the 1920s. With traditional bingo boards players marked called numbers using beans or plastic disks that required a certain, albeit limited, degree of dexterity to place on the boards. The new disposable cards were marked with specially designed inked markers, also sold by the bingo supply companies, that permitted players to play a much larger number of games at one time. This meant that players played more games in an evening and spent considerably more money doing so. Players were happy with the added convenience, bingo hall operators were happy with the added income, and Bazaar & Novelty was happy with the orders for thousands of bingo cards used in any one session. Stuart had managed to persuade almost 90 percent of Canadian bingo halls to switch to the disposable cards and was convinced that American operators would do likewise.

In addition to promoting disposable bingo cards and the markers that went with them, Stuart reorganized Bingo King's distribution system, which had required a continual influx of capital to maintain. The bulk of U.S. bingo was still being run by amateurs, and maintaining a good relationship with these operators was critical to the company's sales. Stuart felt that local independent distributors would do a better job serving this clientele than a centrally run network, in addition to relieving Bingo King of the burden of running a retail operation. By 1991, Bingo King, now named Stuart Entertainment, had sold all of its retail distributors to independent operators, although the company continued to nurture a close relationship with these dealers through seminars, workshops, and a variety of marketing services.

### The 1990s and Beyond

By 1992 Stuart Entertainment's share of the U.S. bingo market had climbed to more than 50 percent, with annual sales of $52 million and income of $1.7 million. Disposable cards had become the norm and Stuart was now exploring the possibilities of electronic video bingo terminals, opening a wholly owned subsidiary called Video King to promote these new electronic products. The early 1990s saw Stuart Entertainment making the first forays into the international market and, by 1993, the company had opened a manufacturing facility in Mexico and a manufacturing and marketing subsidiary in England. In addition, Stuart began an intensive marketing campaign to sell its electronic bingo products to casinos worldwide, striking deals with gaming organizations in South Africa, Peru, and Venezuela. The pace of international expansion was slowed when the company's British subsidiary was unable to turn a profit. By 1994 this subsidiary was draining funds from its parent at an alarming rate, leading the company to a $1.6 million loss and forcing closure of Stuart's manufacturing operations in England.

In spite of losses incurred by the company's British subsidiary, Stuart Entertainment entered the last half of the 1990s with a growing market, increased sales, and a healthy income of $786,000. In 1995 the decision was made to merge Leonard Stuart's privately held Canadian company, Bazaar & Novelty, with Stuart Entertainment, thereby creating the largest bingo supply company in the world. Operating out of a central office in Council Bluffs, Iowa, and with nine manufacturing facilities in the United States, Canada, and Mexico, the now multinational Stuart Entertainment seemed well poised to take advantage of a growing and seemingly insatiable appetite for playing bingo.

### Principal Subsidiaries

Video King Gaming Systems Inc.; Bingo Press and Specialty Limited (Canada); Stuart Entertainment, S.A. de C.V. (Mexico); Stuart Entertainment Limited (England).

### Further Reading

Byrne, H. S., "Stuart Entertainment, Bingo! Low Rollers Keep It in the Chips," *Barron's,* September 28, 1992, p. 36.

Cook, James, "Bingo!" *Forbes,* August 6, 1979, pp. 37–45.

——, "Bingo!" *Forbes,* November 25, 1991, pp. 177–178.

——, "Haphazard Conglomerate," *Forbes,* March 19, 1979, p. 38.

Curtis, Carol E., "Filling the Bottom Line," *Forbes,* July 2, 1984 pp. 84–86.

Kaye, Marvin, *The Story of Monopoly, Silly Putty, Bingo, Twister, Frisbee, Scrabble, Et Cetera,* New York: Stein and Day, 1973, pp. 51–56.

—Hilary Gopnik

# S SUDBURY, INC.

## Sudbury Inc.

**30100 Chagrin Boulevard, Suite 203**
**Cleveland, Ohio 44124**
**U.S.A.**
**(216) 464-7026**
**Fax: (216) 464-4614**

*Public Company*
*Incorporated:* 1983 as Sudbury Holdings Inc.
*Employees:* 2549
*Sales:* $305 million (1995)
*Stock Exchanges:* NASDAQ
*SICs:* 2992 Lubricating Oils and Greases; 3321 Gray &
Ductile Iron Foundries; 3322 Malleable Iron
Foundries; 3363 Aluminum Die-Castings; 3364
Nonferrous Die-Castings, Except Aluminum; 3479
Coating, Engraving, & Allied Services, Not Elsewhere
Classified; 3492 Fluid Power Valves & Hose Fittings;
3531 Construction Machinery & Equipment; 3541
Machine Tools, Metal Cutting Types; 3545 Cutting
Tools, Machine Tool Accessories, & Machinists'
Precision Measuring Devices; 3559 Special Industry
Machinery, Not Elsewhere Classified; 3713 Truck &
Bus Bodies

Sudbury Inc. manufactures and sells a broad range of industrial products, including: iron, aluminum, and zinc castings; coating applications; cranes, truck bodies, and related equipment; and oil and chemical industry services like storage and processing. In the mid-1990s the company operated through six subsidiaries with operations throughout much of the United States and parts of Canada. Sudbury emerged from bankruptcy in the early 1990s and began posting profits in 1994.

Sudbury Inc. was incorporated in 1987 as a subsidiary of a company called Sudbury Holdings Inc. Sudbury Inc. subsequently purchased its parent company as part of a plan to reorganize Sudbury's diverse group of more than 30 companies that had been assembled since the early 1980s. Indeed, after incorporating in 1983, Sudbury Holdings pursued an aggressive growth strategy that propelled it from a small, defunct meat packing company to a diversified conglomerate with more than a half-billion dollars in revenues.

Sudbury Holdings Inc. was founded in 1983 by a group of businessmen that included founders of Alco Standard Corp., a hugely successful manufacturing and distribution conglomerate. Leading the start-up venture were Tinkham Veale II, a founder of Alco, and Charles W. Walton. Their goal was to build a conglomerate similar to Alco using a relatively simple strategy. They would purchase small and medium-sized companies involved in industrial products and services industries. They would then allow the companies to continue operating relatively autonomously, but would take over routine corporate and administrative tasks. By consolidating and streamlining administrative and recordkeeping tasks of several subsidiaries, Sudbury's founders hoped to achieve economies of scale that would boost overall profitability.

The start-up venture's first purchase was American Beef Packers, Inc. Sudbury's founders acquired the company in August 1983 and changed its name to Sudbury Holdings Inc. American Beef Packers was a relatively small and basically defunct beef and pork business that had been incorporated in Iowa in 1965. The business clearly did not complement Sudbury's goal of buying industrial businesses, rather, it was purchased for its tax credits. Walton and Veale quickly parlayed that modest beginning into a sizable enterprise with a rapid spate of acquisitions during the next few years. Between 1984 and 1988, in fact, Sudbury borrowed about $200 million to acquire more than two dozen companies. The companies were involved in industrial industries ranging from coatings (e.g., paints) and machine tools to rubber manufacturing and chemical processing.

Sudbury bought most of the companies in its portfolio during the mid-1980s through arrangements that involved both cash and profit-sharing. For example, Sudbury might pay the owner $15 million for a company that was valued at $20

473

---

## Company Perspectives:

*The mission of Sudbury's companies is to build profitable and solid businesses based on customer satisfaction, people involvement and constant process improvements. The companies are managed locally with support from the corporate staff, under operating plans designed to help them achieve their fullest potential.*

---

million. But the owner would be able to earn as much as, say, $10 million more if his company met certain performance objectives. Thus, in that example, if the owner met his goals he could end up with $5 million more than the actual worth of his business, while Sudbury would benefit from higher income from the subsidiary. Using that acquisition strategy, Walton, Veale, and other executives at Sudbury Holdings managed to add 28 companies to their roster by 1988.

Sudbury sustained a relatively laissez-faire operating strategy. Sudbury managers required subsidiary heads to provide periodic reports, but basically allowed them to operate independently. "We get the managers together twice a year, with each discussing past performance and future goals," Chief Executive Walton said in the February 15, 1988 *Industry Week*. "They don't like to stand up at two meetings in a row and tell their partners they didn't do very well." Sudbury also tried to provide technical, administrative, and marketing support to its companies. The goal was to create a "synergy" that made Sudbury greater than the sum of its parts.

The acquisition and operating strategy of Sudbury Holdings appeared to be highly effective during the mid-1980s, allowing it to post gains reminiscent of the success enjoyed by its model Alco Standard Corp. Following Sudbury's restructuring in 1987, to become Sudbury Inc., company sales rose to an impressive $531 million for the 1988 fiscal year from $200 million in 1986. Meanwhile, net income grew to $5 million in 1986 and, along with sales, more than doubled by 1988 to about $11.3 million. By mid-1988, Sudbury was operating about 30 companies grouped under six divisions: auto and truck parts, solid waste and material-handling equipment, steel tubing, machining, lubricants, and miscellaneous companies.

"We have built Sudbury around a core of hard-working dedicated entrepreneurs who are free to run their businesses in the efficient, profitable manner which made them successful," Walton proclaimed in the *Industry Week* article. Indeed, heading into the late 1980s it appeared as though Sudbury was on the fast track to success. But those were some of Walton's last words as chief executive of Sudbury. In reality, the strategy pursued by Walton, Veale, and fellow executives culminated in an unmitigated disaster that ultimately cost investors millions of dollars.

Sudbury's underlying problems began to emerge in 1988 when the automobile industry, in particular, faltered. It soon became apparent that Sudbury's ability to remain profitable during the mid-1980s, despite a massive debt load incurred

during its acquisition campaign, was largely the result of strong markets in its core businesses. In fact, the synergy and economies of scale touted by Sudbury's executive team never fully materialized. The company had become a loose conglomeration of subsidiaries that lacked direction and, in some cases, discipline and operating efficiency. As the economy began to plunge into a recession, Sudbury began to fall apart.

Walton resigned as president and chief executive in the summer of 1988. Veale, Sudbury's chairman, replaced him with Douglas F. Johnston, a seasoned corporate executive who had served in top posts with several smaller and mid-sized corporations. Veale described Johnston as the "best businessman in America" at Sudbury's 1988 annual meeting. Johnston, however, did not live up to this praise. His new strategy was two-pronged; he planned to jettison several of Sudbury's companies in an effort to pare its staggering debt load and, at the same time, implement new electronic information systems and management controls that would boost operating efficiency. Although the tactic pleased investors, Johnston did not produce. Sudbury's board sent him packing in 1990.

Johnston had made some progress, however. He reorganized Sudbury into a simpler structure, for example, with just two divisions: Industrial Products Group and Equipment and Systems Group. Johnston also succeeded in selling some of Sudbury's companies and reducing its debt. Still, Sudbury was sporting an embarrassing debt ratio of 3.5 to 1 by mid-1990. Furthermore, the company had posted a net loss of $11 million in 1989. In 1990 Sudbury's board hired Ross Lake as chief executive to speed up debt reduction and improve financial performance. Lake had formerly served as executive vice-president and chief operating officer.

Lake had hoped to divest many of Sudbury's businesses quickly. Unfortunately, the recession during 1990 and 1991 squelched that effort. He was also unable to improve the overall operating performance and cash flow from Sudbury's operating companies. Sudbury desperately reshuffled management in an attempt to avert disaster, but failed. Unable to meet its debt obligations, Sudbury filed for Chapter 11 bankruptcy protection on January 10, 1992. Many investors and the former owners of some of Sudbury's subsidiaries were outraged. The former owners of Wagner Castings Company and Galbreath Escott, for example, filed suit against Sudbury executives, claiming that they had misrepresented Sudbury's financial condition before cutting their acquisition deals.

With the battered Sudbury on the ropes and gasping, creditors brought in former Goodyear executive Jacques Sardas to clean up the mess left by Veale and other managers. The 62-year-old Sardas had recently retired from the number two position at Goodyear, but he was already bored and looking for a challenge. "It was not merely a challenge—it was a disaster," he would later recall in the October 20, 1993 *Knight-Ridder/Tribune Business News*. A week after Sudbury filed for bankruptcy, Sardas accepted the chief executive post and launched an aggressive reorganization initiative. Creditors gave the go-ahead to a plan that would rapidly jettison 20 of Sudbury's companies and pay off $70 million of bank debt. Sardas went to work slashing overhead, selling subsidiaries, and reducing Sudbury's debt.

Within nine months Sardas succeeded in selling 15 companies, or all but 6 of Sudbury's subsidiaries. He also slashed the headquarters staff in Cleveland down to just 9 from 28, and he was able to get creditors to renegotiate some of the company's debt. Importantly, Sardas convinced BankAmerica Business Credit to renegotiate a new credit line that allowed Sudbury to retain 3 subsidiaries that it otherwise would have been forced to sell. Sudbury posted sales of $222 million in 1993 and a net loss of $56 million (following a net loss of $64 million in 1992), which was largely the result of restructuring charges. But the company was poised for gains in the mid-1990s. "This has probably been one of the most successful turnarounds that I've seen in my 20 years in banking," said Patrick Costello, a banker involved with Sudbury's debt restructuring, in the May 10, 1993 *Crain's Cleveland Business*.

By 1993 Sudbury Inc. consisted of six companies that manufactured and sold a range of industrial products, roughly half of which were purchased by automobile and truck industries. Its three main companies were Wagner Castings Company, Iowa Mold Tooling Co., Inc., and Industrial Powder Coatings, Inc. Wagner, which alone accounted for nearly half of Sudbury's entire revenue base, designed and manufactured engineered iron castings for automobile and commercial products industries. Iowa Mold Tooling designed and built service vehicles and related equipment for tire, mining, forestry, and other industries. Industrial Powder Coatings made coatings for automobile, appliance, and other industries. Sudbury's three smaller units were the following: Frisby P.M.C. Incorporated, a maker of precision machine parts and components; South Coast Terminals, Inc., a provider of storage and processing services for oil and chemical industries; and Cast-Matic Corporation, a manufacturer of precision aluminum and zinc die castings. Those three companies generated combined sales of about $50 million in 1994.

Recovering markets and savvy management sustained Sudbury's rebound in 1994 and 1995, allowing it to increase sales from its six companies to $250 million in 1994 and then to $305 million in 1995. Meanwhile, net income climbed to $6.8 million in 1994 and then to a respectable $13.6 million in 1995, as the company's debt load shrunk significantly. In late 1995 Sardas declared that Sudbury's recovery, repair, and renewal phase was complete and that the company was ready to begin growing. "As we say in Texas, you haven't seen anything yet," Sardas said in the September 28, 1995 *Knight-Ridder/Tribune Business News*. His plan was to grow the company through selective acquisitions that complemented existing operations and by expanding internal operations.

## Principal Subsidiaries

Wagner Castings Company; Iowa Mold Tooling Co., Inc.; Industrial Powder Coatings, Inc.; Frisby P.M.C. Incorporated; South Coast Terminals, Inc.; Cast-Matic Corporation.

## Further Reading

Bishop, Floyd J., and Eaton, Henry E., "Sudbury, Inc. Announces Top Management Changes," *Business Wire*, August 31, 1988.

Denney, Jon E., "Sudbury Inc. Financial Results," *Business Wire*, August 11, 1988.

Drown, Stuart, "Cleveland's Sudbury Finishes Restructuring: Ready To Grow," *Knight-Ridder/Tribune Business News*, September 28, 1995.

——, "Akron, Ohio Executive Ends Early Retirement To Turn Sudbury Around," *Knight-Ridder/Tribune Business News*, October 20, 1993.

Farrar, Mary C., "Sudbury Extends Contract of Chairman, Chief Executive Officer and President Jacques R. Sardas," *PR Newswire*, July 31, 1995.

Gerdel, Thomas W., "Positive Thinking Pays at Sudbury," *The Cleveland Plain Dealer*, September 1, 1993.

——, "Sudbury Inc. Keeps an Eye on Past for Future Growth," *The Cleveland Plain Dealer*, October 11, 1994.

Jenke, Anita C., "Sudbury Gets New Top Execs in Debt Clash," *Metalworking News*, July 16, 1990, p. 4.

Modic, Stanley J., "Money Talks in Motivating 'Acquired' Execs," *Industry Week*, February 15, 1988, p. 26.

Prizinsky, David, "Sudbury Aims To Divest, Trim Its Long-term Debt," *Crain's Cleveland Business*, October 31, 1988, p. 3.

——, "Sudbury's Up and Running," *Crain's Cleveland Business*, May 10, 1993, p. 6.

Shingler, Dan, "Changing Times: Tight Financing Makes It Tougher To Pull Off Business Acquisitions," *Crain's Cleveland Business*, October 8, 1990, p. 3.

——, "Roulston Ups Ante: Partnerships Already Show Sudbury Investment Gains," *Crain's Cleveland Business*, February 1, 1993, p. 1.

Stoyer, Lloyd, "Sardas Beats the Odds a Second Time," *Modern Tire Dealer*, October 1993, pp. 30–32.

"Sudbury Responds Well Under Sardas," *The Beacon Journal*, September 19, 1994.

Suttell, Scott, "Sudbury CEO Insists There's More To Be Done," *The News-Herald*, October 14, 1994.

Thompson, Chris, "Fast Sudbury Action Saved Cash: $3.7-million Bill Illustrates High Cost of Going Chapter 11," *Crain's Cleveland Business*, January 18, 1993, p. 4.

——, "Judge Decrees Sudbury Can't Shield Principals," *Crain's Cleveland Business*, August 10, 1992, Section 1, p. 3.

——, "Sudbury Fees Top $5MM," *Crain's Cleveland Business*, April 6, 1992, p. 3.

Winter, Ralph E., "Sudbury Progresses with Reorganizing, Its President Says," *The Wall Street Journal*, November 13, 1992.

—Dave Mote

# SUTTER HOME®

## Sutter Home Winery Inc.

P.O. Box 248
St. Helena, California 94574
U.S.A.
(707) 963-3104
Fax: (707) 963-2381

*Private Company*
*Incorporated:* 1874
*Employees:* 335
*Sales:* $140 million (1995 est.)
*SICs:* 2084 Wines Brandy & Brandy Spirits; 0172 Grapes

Sutter Home Winery Inc. is one of the leading producers of premium varietal wines in the United States. The company is perhaps best known for originating a light, slightly sweet, lower-alcohol type of wine known as white Zinfandel, which became the nation's most popular premium wine in the 1980s and spawned an entire new market of emulative "blush" wines. The owner of more than 3,500 vineyard acres in California, Sutter Home manufactures a wide range of red wines under the brand names California Zinfandel, Amador County Reserve Zinfandel, Cabernet Sauvignon, and Soleo. Its white wines include Chenin Blanc, Sauvignon Blanc, Chardonnay, and Muscat Alexandria.

### Early History

The founder of the company was a Swiss-German immigrant named John Thomann, who established a small winery and distillery in California's Napa Valley in 1874. After Thomann died in 1900, his heirs sold the winery and the Victorian home he had built to another Swiss family, the Leuenbergers. The new owners rechristened the estate Sutter Home, in honor of Lina Leuenberger's father, John Sutter. For the next half century, the Leuenberger family maintained control of the modest winery.

In 1947, John and Mario Trinchero, two Italian immigrant brothers whose family had been involved in the wine business in Italy for six generations, purchased the dilapidated winery.

When the Trincheros took over, the Napa Valley region was a long way from becoming the thriving tourist attraction it is today: prunes, tomatoes, and walnuts were, in fact, more plentiful than wine grapes. Having emigrated to the United States in the 1920s, the aspiring winemakers moved their families from New York City to test their fortunes in a California rural area that seemed to be populated by as many cattle as people.

During the early years, the fledgling winery operated strictly as a "mom-and-pop" operation. Almost two-thirds of the wine sold was purchased at the front door. As Mario Trinchero's son Bob, who was only 12 years old when the family settled in St. Helena, recalled, "If you could carry or roll a container through the door, we'd fill it for you." In those days, during the 1950s, the company struggled to break even, and as the elder Trinchero neared retirement, the future of the wine business did not look favorable. Despite the tireless efforts of the Trincheros, their operation failed to turn a profit, and by 1960 they were in desperate need of a loan to keep the winery afloat.

When Mario Trinchero retired that same year, he managed to convince his son Bob—who had left at 18 for a four-year stint in the Air Force, vowing never to return to the Napa Valley region again—to carry on the family business and buy out his uncle's half share. However, before Bob could comply he first had to acquire the capital needed to rebuild the company. Bank of America, the only bank in town at the time, turned the company down for a loan, and the Trincheros were forced to put the winery on the market. To their good fortune, they found no takers at their asking price, and a new bank moved into town that was willing to loan them the money they needed. With their bills now paid and $5,000 in fresh capital, the Trincheros were ready to rebuild their winery and their product.

### First Signs of Success in the 1960s

Although Bob learned the art of winemaking from the ground up, handling such duties as barrel washing and pomace shoveling during his teenage years, he had no formal training. His efforts to improve the quality of the wine would be a matter of trial and error. While he was working on upgrading his product—he later told Robyn Bullard of *The Wine Spectator* that the wine was "actually drinkable by the late 1960s"—he made a discovery that would give him a secure foothold in the industry. In 1968, he paid a visit to Sacramento retailer Darrell Corti, who insisted that he try a homemade Zinfandel produced from grapes grown in the Sierra foothills' Amador County, an historic grape-growing region that had lain dormant since Prohibition. Immediately taken by the wine's intensity of flavor, Trinchero, who owned no fields of his own, contacted the grower and immediately contracted to purchase grapes from him the following year. Not only would the change enable him to avoid the high cost of Napa Valley grapes, but he would finally get an opportunity to make his mark on the industry.

Trinchero's first experience with the Amador County grapes suggested that he had made a wise decision and that his wine-making skills were improving. The 1968 vintage of Amador County Zinfandel, produced from the century-old vines grown at the Deaver Ranch Vineyard in Amador's Shenandoah Valley, earned Sutter Home its first accolades and paved the way for future recognition.

### The 1970s: A New Product for the American Palate

Encouraged by the critical success of his Amador Zinfandel, Trinchero looked for ways to make the wine more robust and more appealing to a wider market. In 1972, while experimenting with his Zinfandel, he made a serendipitous discovery that would one day make him a multimillionaire and change the face of the American wine industry at the same time. Immediately after crushing a batch of Zinfandel grapes, he drained some free-run juice from the must (the juice pressed from grapes before it has been fermented) in an attempt to increase the ratio of skins, which impart most of a red wine's color and body. Modeling his creation after the French roses he greatly admired, Trinchero then fermented the drawn-off juice like a dry white wine. Just for fun, he bottled 220 cases of the pale pink elixir after a period of barrel-aging and offered the novel "blanc de noir" table wine to his tasting room clientele as a curiosity item.

The wine was originally called "Oel de Pedrix" (eye of the partridge), but the Bureau of Alcohol, Tobacco and Firearms insisted that there be an English translation on the label. Trinchero reluctantly complied with the government's request and provided his customers with an easier name to remember, white Zinfandel. As Trinchero told *The Wine Spectator,* "It was white, and it was Zinfandel, and if anyone wants to know where the name came from, it was from the BATF forcing me to do it."

Although Trinchero's novelty item created some interest in his tasting room, enough for him to increase production the following year, its popularity was not widespread. It would take another "accidental" adjustment to the recipe for that to occur.

In 1975, while working on a batch of 1,000 gallons, he discovered that the wine had stopped fermenting—a phenomenon known in the industry as a "stuck fermentation." Not knowing what else to do and busy with other more pressing concerns, Trinchero simply topped the tank and put his new concoction aside for a few weeks. When he returned to the tank to sample what he had produced, he noticed that the wine was a bit pink, taking on a kind of blush hue. The critical difference, Trinchero would later discover, lay in the two percent residual sugar the wine contained, which gave it a slightly sweeter flavor.

At this point, Trinchero's white Zinfandel was a long way from becoming America's most popular wine. For a few years, the wine remained little more than a novelty item; most of it was sold in the Sutter Home tasting room on Napa Valley's Highway 29. What is more, he had plans to convert the entire 7,000-case production into his more established product, red Zinfandel. Fortunately, the process that may have brought an end to the promising new wine was not occurring rapidly.

By the late 1970s, Trinchero, along with his younger brother, Roger, realized that a new marketing strategy was needed. Despite their efforts, the company was struggling to survive while the rest of the industry seemed to be booming. After one particularly difficult day, the two sat down to discuss their predicament over a couple of glasses of wine. The conclusion they reached, as Bob later told Bullard, was a simple one: "It seemed the consumer wanted something besides what we were giving them." Searching for a way to rectify this problem, the two took an inventory of all the wines they were making and discovered that the experimental wine they called white Zinfandel was the only wine in short supply.

### The 1980s: A New Strategy Vaults Sutter Home to the Top

Going against the rest of the industry, which was dominated by jug wines, the Trinchero's channelled their efforts and resources on the product that seemed most in line with their customers' taste preferences. They doubled the production of their white Zinfandel, hoping that the strawberry fruitiness of the product would appeal to the American masses. Their gamble paid off: they were forced to double production the following year, and again the next. By 1981, the Trincheros, while fine-tuning their white Zinfandel over several vintages, had escalated production to 25,000 cases a year. Four years later, that number would jump to 850,000.

The explosive growth in white Zinfandel production and the expansion of the California wine industry made the task of maintaining an adequate supply of grapes a major concern for the first time, and the company's longheld dependence on outside vineyards in the Napa Valley region no longer viable. In 1984, having strengthened its financial base through white Zinfandel sales, the company made its first purchase: a 300-acre vineyard in Lake County, located to the northeast of Napa Valley. Although the Trincheros initially planned to graft the vineyard entirely to Zinfandel, they decided to retain the existing varieties—Sauvignon Blanc, Chenin Blanc, and Cabernet Sauvignon—after discovering their high quality. This decision would provide Sutter Home with a base for future expansion of its line of premium varietal wines. Other purchases in the

Sacramento Valley and the Sacramento Delta added another 2,500 acres by the end of the decade, bolstering the production capability for white Zinfandel and other premium wines.

Sutter Home's decision to focus its energies on varietal wines helped to both redefine the American wine industry and prosper during the remainder of the decade. As late as 1980, the market was dominated by what was known in the industry as "The Gang of Five"—Gallo, Almaden, Masson, Inglenook, and Taylor, all of whom sold primarily generic wines simply by color and in 4-liter jugs. But Sutter Home's introduction and successful marketing of white Zinfandel—and the host of other wineries who later came up with their own—played a significant role in changing the dynamics of the industry. While jug wine sales dropped from $930 million in 1980 to $840 million in 1990, varietal wine revenue skyrocketed from $22.4 million to $1.4 billion over the same period.

A number of factors were responsible for this dramatic shift in the industry and for Sutter Home's tremendous success in the 1980s. First, according to Bob Trinchero, the enormous popularity of his white Zinfandel lay in its ability to break down the "wall of intimidation" that kept many Americans from drinking wine. Realizing that many people were apprehensive about ordering sophisticated, hard-to-pronounce wines in restaurant, the Trincheros attempted to develop a product that appealed to the majority of wine-drinking Americans who are not connoisseurs. Accordingly, instead of tailoring their wines to fit their own tastes, they asked their customers for their advice. "If you think all you've got to do is make a good wine to have people line up at the door," Roger, who takes care of sales and marketing, told Bullard, "you're kidding yourself."

White Zinfandel, an affordable varietal wine characterized by its light, slightly sweet taste and visually attractive pink hue proved to be a perfect match. By 1989, it had become, on sales of 2.9 million cases, the most popular wine in the United States.

### The 1990s and Beyond

As Sutter Home entered the 1990s, it found itself in the face of increasingly strong competition. Its unprecedented success with white Zinfandel had spawned a host of emulative "blush" wines, many of which helped to turn around the struggling wineries that produced them. An extremely cost-effective product, white Zinfandel is easy to manufacture and requires very little aging, enabling wineries to generate revenue just a few months after the harvest. While Sutter Home remained at the top, it needed to diversify its marketing strategy for growth to continue into the new decade.

Again, Sutter Home focused its attention on the majority of American wine drinkers rather than on the exclusive tastes of the elite. This time, however, the innovation came in the form of a package instead of a new wine. In April 1989, the company introduced the "Classic Single," a 187 ml single service wine packaged in a bordeaux-style bottle. The brainchild of Roger Trinchero, the Classic Single package was designed to take advantage of a "less but better" market trend, the result of the country's growing health consciousness and its emphasis on moderation. The smaller-portion size was also targeted to the increasing population of Americans who live alone, or with a

companion whose beverage preferences differ. Sales of over a million cases of Classic Single bottles of white Zinfandel, Cabernet Sauvignon, Sauvignon Blanc, and Chardonnay in 1990 and two million the following year suggested that the company had again correctly read the preferences of the American wine consumer.

In 1992 Sutter Home again led the industry on sales of 5.2 million cases, or $145 million. The company and the entire premium wine industry benefitted from several reports from the medical community, publicized most notably on a "60 Minutes" special, that praised the possible health benefits of drinking red wine in moderation. That same year the company tried to further capitalize on the good news for the wine industry by introducing a new chillable premium red wine, Soleo, a proprietary blend combining Zinfandel, Barbera, Pinot Noir and Napa Gamay. The light, fruity, easy-drinking wine was designed for white-wine drinkers seeking the lower cholesterol levels promised by red wines.

That same year, Sutter Home made its boldest attempt yet to lead the industry in meeting the needs of the health-conscious consumer. Going against the conventional wisdom of the industry, the Trincheros became the first major winery to introduce a non-alcoholic wine. The innovative product, called Fre, was developed primarily by Bob Trinchero's daughter Gina and received accolades for its resemblance in taste to wine rather than grape juice. Produced using an Australian-developed de-alcoholizing process that retains more of the wine's essence instead of adding water, Fre proved to be another successful innovation for the company. In 1993, for instance, sales jumped to 200,000 cases, a fourfold increase from the year of its release.

As Sutter Home entered the second half of the decade, it remained in 100 percent control by the innovative Trinchero family, who built the company into a $140 million operation. It looked to maintain its position of leadership in the industry by continuing to increase its diverse complement of wines. Increased competition in the premium wine market has made the company more dependent on its non-alcoholic wines, competitive pricing, and aggressive advertising in supermarkets. Vowing to "never stop experimenting," the Trincheros hoped to fuel future growth with the same type of innovative products and marketing strategies that allowed for their expansion during the past four decades.

### Further Reading

*A Brief History of Sutter Home Winery,* St. Helena, Calif.: Sutter Home Winery, Inc., 1995.

Bird, Laura, "Scanner Data Sauvignon: The American Palate is Changing," *Adweek's Marketing Week,* August 19, 1991, pp. 18–19.

Bullard, Robyn, "The House That White Zinfandel Built," *The Wine Spectator,* May 15, 1994, pp. 52–60.

Campanelli, Melissa, "Going for the Gold," *Sales and Marketing Management,* June 1992, pp. 160–61.

Graenbner, Lynn, "Sutter Home Buys 400 Acres," *The Business Journal Serving Greater Sacramento,* October 23, 1995, p. 4.

Vizard, Frank, "Grapes Without Wrath," *Popular Mechanics,* March 1993, pp. 29–32.

—Jason Gallman

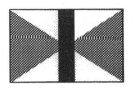

# Swire Pacific Ltd.

Swire House
9 Connaught Road
Central
Hong Kong
+852 840 8888
Fax: +852 810-6563

*Public Company*
*Incorporated:* 1866 as Butterfield and Swire
*Employees:* 35,000
*Sales:* HK $47.6 billion (US $6.1 billion) (1994)
*Stock Exchanges:* Hong Kong
*SICs:* 6719 Offices of Holding·Companies, Not
　　Elsewhere Classified

Swire Pacific Ltd., which came to prominence as one of the 19th-century British-owned trading houses based in Hong Kong, is today a diversified firm with interests in aviation, real estate, beverage bottling and foods, and insurance, as well as the traditional shipping and trading operations. Part of the larger London-based Swire Group, Swire Pacific also remains located in Hong Kong despite the prospect of Chinese rule. In fact, in the years leading up to 1997, the company has strengthened its ties to Hong Kong and expanded in a major way into China itself.

### Early History in the 19th Century

In Britain during the early 1800s a canal was built that linked the seaport of Liverpool to Halifax, a city in the northeastern county of Yorkshire. The canal introduced international trade to Halifax and in the process seriously damaged local industries that could not compete with cheaper imports. John Swire, the patriarch of the Swire family, moved from Yorkshire to Liverpool, where in 1816 he established a general trading house with primary commodities being American cotton from New Orleans and cheese, pork, and wine from Boston and New York. John Swire died in 1847, leaving the business to his two sons, John Samuel Swire and William Hudson Swire.

The John Swire & Sons, Ltd. trading company grew steadily during the next decade. It established interests in a number of Liverpool shipping companies and opened a branch office in Manchester. In 1855 John Samuel Swire traveled to the former British penal colony of Australia. He opened an office in Melbourne to handle Australian imports of his company's cotton. As soon as the business was operating successfully, he turned it over to a local agent and returned to England. His brother William was forced to retire from the company because of persistent ill health. From that time onward, John Samuel Swire was left to run the operation alone.

In 1861 the American Civil War destroyed Swire's cotton trade. Determined to reassert its position in the textile market, the company turned to the more stable markets of the Far East, where it was already engaged in the trade of tea. Swire became displeased with the performance of his agents in the Far East and decided that the company should run its own affairs there. He traveled to Shanghai in 1866 and later formed a partnership with Richard Shackleton Butterfield of the Butterfield Brothers firm in Bradford, Yorkshire. In 1867 they opened an office together in Shanghai under the name of Butterfield & Swire. The company adopted a Chinese name, *Taikoo,* meaning "great and ancient." Although the partnership was dissolved within two years, the Shanghai office continued to be called Butterfield & Swire.

The company's business in Asia benefited greatly from Japan's restoration of the Meiji leadership in 1868. Under the Meiji, Japan became a modern industrial state. Butterfield & Swire, which had opened an office near Tokyo in Yokohama the previous year, was ideally situated to take advantage of the growing strength of the Japanese economy.

By 1871 Swire's headquarters had been moved from Liverpool to London, and a third Far East office was opened in the British Colony of Hong Kong. The company expanded its interest in shipping when it became the Shanghai agent for the Blue Funnel Line. In 1872 Swire created its own shipping concern, the China Navigation Company, which served ports on the Yangtze River and along the Chinese coast. China Navigation's primary competitor on the waterways was another Hong Kong firm called Jardine Matheson & Company. In 1873 Swire established an office in New York, where the company had already been handling American imports of tea from Yokohama for several years.

Swire further diversified its business in 1884 when it created the Taikoo Sugar Refinery in Hong Kong with the intention of breaking Jardine Matheson's monopoly on sugar. The two companies competed in a fierce but gentlemanly manner for many years. According to John Samuel Swire, "Don't fight. But if you do fight, go in sharp and win."

In 1866 the Yokohama office, which for years had been dependent on the textile trade, began importing large quantities of sugar from Hong Kong and Taiwan in addition to soya beancake from China. Swire also handled Japanese exports of rice to Australia. In 1887 the company opened a second Japanese office in Kobe. In 1900 Butterfield & Swire founded the Taikoo Dockyard Company in Hong Kong. With expanded commercial interests in China, the company also opened a paint factory in Shanghai and a tugboat and barge company in Tianjin. The red, white, and blue Swire flag was seen flying over China Navigation ships plying waterways across China and throughout East Asia.

### Early 20th Century

John Samuel Swire died in 1898. His company passed to a third generation of Swires under the direction of his son John. Despite some disruptions of business in China during the Boxer Rebellion in 1900 and the Republican Revolution in 1911, Swire's interests in China, Japan, Australia, and Southeast Asia continued to prosper and expand. John Kidston Swire, grandson of John Samuel Swire, succeeded his father as director of the company in 1920.

Swire's operations were paralyzed in 1937 when Japan launched its war of expansion against China. The company's interests in northern China and Shanghai were closed. Japanese landings on either side of the Hongkong peninsula isolated the colony from the nearby Chinese city of Guangzhou (Canton), forcing Swire to curtail virtually all of its trading operations with the mainland. On December 1, 1941, six days before the attack on Pearl Harbor, Japanese troops invaded Hong Kong. During the Japanese occupation all of Swire's Far Eastern activities were suspended. By the time of the Japanese surrender in September 1945 more than half of Swire's ships, the sugar refinery, and dockyard had been destroyed.

As soon as World War II ended a civil war erupted in China between the Communists and the Nationalists. The war was won in 1949 by the Communists, who renounced all agreements concluded by the Nationalist government. This included Swire's business arrangements with Chinese partners and the Chinese government. In addition, Swire's extensive properties in China were nationalized without compensation. In only a few short years Swire's financial empire had nearly been ruined.

### Post-World War II Rebuilding and Diversification

Butterfield & Swire focused attention on rebuilding its operations in Hong Kong. The shipping facilities were rebuilt and new ships were ordered. John Kidston Swire became interested in diversifying his company's transportation interests in the Far

East. In 1948 Butterfield & Swire purchased a controlling interest in Cathay Pacific Airways, a small Hong Kong-based airline company with a fleet of two DC-3s.

The company's shipping and airline activities grew rapidly during the 1950s. Shipping offices in Japan were reopened, and new connections in Papua New Guinea, Australia, and Korea were established. Cathay Pacific absorbed its local competitor, Hong Kong Airways, purchased newer aircraft, and opened new routes to Singapore, Manila, Bangkok, and Saigon. Butterfield & Swire's involvement in Cathay Pacific led it to invest in a number of other businesses related to aviation, including the Hong Kong Aircraft Engineering Company, which operated a virtual monopoly on aircraft maintenance in the colony.

During the 1950s and 1960s the company's expansion was well planned and largely uneventful, and its name was changed from Butterfield & Swire to Swire Pacific Ltd., with the company going public in 1959. On occasion, however, profits became depressed when regional or international economic recessions lowered demand for shipping services. Because of the fact that the shipping business was so closely linked to the volatile economic cycles of Pacific nations, Swire Pacific began to diversify its operations. It became interested in property ownership in Hong Kong, where the supply of land was limited and demand was becoming acute. In 1965 Swire Bottlers Limited became the franchised bottler of Coca-Cola and its allied brands in Hong Kong.

Additional diversification occurred in the areas of shipping and warehousing services, agriculture, trucking, canning, magnetic tape, and high technology components. Cathay Pacific was continuing to grow at an annual rate of 22 percent (doubling its size every four years) and began handling air freight. As a result, Cathay Pacific became Swire's most popular subsidiary and was quickly gaining a reputation as "Hong Kong's airline."

John Kidston Swire retired as director of John Swire & Sons in 1968, leaving the company in the care of his two sons, named John and Adrian. The fifth generation of Swires oversaw most of the company's diversification and growth, especially in Hong Kong. When John Kidston Swire died in 1983, the parent company of the Swire financial empire, John Swire & Sons, Ltd., remained a privately owned family concern based in London. Meanwhile, Hong Kong, where the dynamic Swire Pacific subsidiary was located, became the subject of an international debate.

### Transition to Hong Kong's Integration into China

After a series of negotiations the governments of Great Britain and the People's Republic of China agreed in 1984 to end British colonial authority over Hong Kong on July 1, 1997. This placed into doubt the future of all capitalist enterprises operating in Hong Kong, including Swire Pacific. Jardine Matheson promptly responded by relocating its legal address and much of its business to Bermuda. In an effort to forestall the exit of more companies, the Chinese promised to preserve the unique economic character of Hong Kong after they take control of the territory. In 1987, when Swire Pacific, which was the only publicly traded Swire company, announced that it was reducing its share of ownership in Cathay Pacific, a Chinese government investment company in Hong Kong, Citic Pacific, purchased 12.5 percent. The Chinese investment in Cathay Pacific was regarded as evidence of China's sincerity in maintaining the prosperity of Hong Kong.

For its part, Swire Pacific determined early on to cast its future with China, although its vast property holdings in Hong Kong and its dependence on Cathay Pacific for most of its profits (70 percent in 1990) gave it little choice (Cathay's route rights were nontransferable, so the airline could not be moved out of Hong Kong). Even so, Swire Pacific did not have as much reason for alarm as its rivals, given that it had already established an excellent relationship with the Chinese, which promised to be advantageous when the Chinese economy developed further and selected foreign companies were invited to participate. Although the Tianamen Square massacre of June 4, 1989 gave cause for further alarm, Swire stayed on its course, committed to Hong Kong's (and its own) future. Symbolic proof of its commitment came when Cathay Pacific painted over the Union Jack on its planes.

In fact, Swire Pacific was able to profit from others' fears in the late 1980s and early 1990s by picking up numerous additional Hong Kong real estate properties at bargain prices. Real estate subsequently recovered after the peak period of fear passed, leaving Swire with an even more lucrative portfolio.

In the early 1990s the company and Cathay Pacific strengthened their relationships and position within China itself. In 1990 Swire and Cathay bought Dragon Airlines (or Dragonair), the foreign airline with the most routes to mainland China and preferred by most business travelers over China's domestic airlines because of its superior safety record. To bolster Dragonair, Cathay transferred its routes to Shanghai and Beijing to Dragonair. Swire Pacific also tied Dragonair's future to China's by selling a majority interest in the airline to Citic Pacific.

Further forays into China came in late 1993. In November, John Swire & Sons returned to China after a more than 30-year absence by reopening its Shanghai office. Also that month, Swire Pacific purchased a 25 percent stake in Shekou Container Terminals, located near Hong Kong in the Chinese city of Shekou, for HK $308 million (US $40 million). Most important, in another alliance with Citic Pacific, in December Swire bought 55 percent of BC Development, a major Coca-Cola bottler in China. Swire's partnerships with Citic Pacific were seen as particularly strategic—win-win deals where Swire gained influence in China at the same time China (through Citic Pacific) acquired a greater and greater stake in Hong Kong's future.

Although Cathay Pacific ran into trouble in the early 1990s because of increasing competition, delays in the construction of a new Hong Kong airport, and a 1993 flight attendants strike, Swire Pacific had managed to lessen its dependence on the airline and thus weathered Cathay's difficulties. By 1993, only 51 percent of operating income was derived from aviation, with real estate coming in a close second at 41 percent. Swire had begun to leverage its vast Hong Kong real estate holdings into lucrative rental properties. The most impressive development was Pacific Place, transformed by Swire from the army barracks it purchased in 1984 into a glittering complex of three fully

occupied skyscrapers with 400 apartments, three first-class hotels, nearly 200 stores and restaurants, four theaters, and hundreds of thousands of square feet of office space. The company estimated that three other major projects would bring in more than US $1 billion in profits annually starting in 1996.

Without a doubt, Hong Kong in the late 1990s was a risky place to stake one's future, but the Swire family had survived the Boxer Rebellion, two world wars, and a civil war. Their three-pronged Hong Kong/China strategy focusing on aviation, real estate, and bottling operations not only was diversified but also featured prime franchises in each case. With the still largely untapped Chinese market literally waiting at the door, Swire Pacific hoped the huge risks it was taking would be paid off in a likewise huge fashion.

### *Principal Subsidiaries*

Carol Reed International Ltd. (70%); Cathay Pacific Airways Ltd. (51.8%); German Hotel Experts Ltd. (90%); Guangmei Foods Co. Ltd. (China; 51%); Reebok Hong Kong Ltd. (70%); Swire & MacLaine Ltd.; Swire Aviation Ltd. (66.7%); Swire Bottler Holdings Ltd.; Swire Insurance Holdings Ltd.; Swire Loxley Ltd. (66.7%); Swire Pacific Offshore Maritime Ltd.; Swire Pacific Ship Management Ltd.; Swire Properties Ltd.; Swire Properties Management Ltd.

### *Principal Divisions*

Aviation Division; Property Division; Industries Division; Trading Division; Marine Services Division; Insurance Division.

### *Further Reading*

Clifford, Mark, "Back to China," *Far Eastern Economic Review,* January 27, 1994, pp. 38–40.

——, "Cathay Pacific: It's Time To Buckle Up," *Business Week,* October 9, 1995, p. 146L.

"The Dragon's Embrace," *Economist,* August 26, 1989, pp. 51–52.

Edelstein, Michael, *Overseas Investment in the Age of High Imperialism: The United Kingdom 1850–1914,* New York: Columbia University Press, 1982.

Kennedy, Carol, "Can Two Hongs Get It Right?," *Director,* February 1996, pp. 34–40.

Marriner, Sheila, and Hyde, Francis E., *The Senior John Samuel Swire, 1825–98: Management in Far Eastern Shipping Trades,* Liverpool: Liverpool University Press, 1967.

Meyer, Richard, "Hostage: Why the Taipan at Hong Kong's Biggest Public Company Is Chained to His Post," *Financial World,* September 18, 1990, pp. 22, 25–27.

Morris, Kathleen, "There's No Place Like Home: Jardine Matheson's Grip on Hong Kong Has Been Slipping, But Swire Pacific Is Doing Just Fine," *Financial World,* August 2, 1994, pp. 36–38.

"The Noble Houses Look Forward," *Economist,* October 1, 1994, pp. 77–78.

Sender, Henny, "Fixed Assets: British Hongs Still Tied to the Colony," *Far Eastern Economic Review,* July 8, 1993, p. 22.

Silverman, Gary, "Hong Kong: Look British, Think Chinese," *Far Eastern Economic Review,* December 28, 1995/January 4, 1996, pp. 64–65.

"Thin Ice?," *Economist,* September 23, 1995, p. 58.

—updated by David E. Salamie

Industries

# Talley Industries, Inc.

**2072 North 44th Street**
**Phoenix, Arizona 85008**
**U.S.A.**
**(602) 957-7711**
**Fax: (602) 852-6978**

*Public Company*
*Incorporated:* 1960 as Talley Defense Systems
*Employees:* 2417
*Sales:* $249.2 million (1994)
*Stock Exchanges:* New York Boston Philadelphia
   Chicago
*SICs:* 2879 Pesticides & Agricultural Chemicals, Not
   Elsewhere Classified; 3264 Porcelain Electrical
   Supplies; 3312 Steel Works, Blast Furnaces
   (Including Coke Ovens), & Rolling Mills; 3483
   Ammunition, Except for Small Arms; 3489 Ordnance
   & Accessories, Not Elsewhere Classified; 3519
   Internal Combustion Engines, Not Elsewhere
   Classified; 3548 Electric & Gas Welding & Soldering
   Equipment; 3589 Service Industry Machinery, Not
   Elsewhere Classified; 3621 Motors & Generators;
   3625 Relays & Industrial Controls; 3714 Motor
   Vehicle Parts & Accessories; 3764 Guided Missile &
   Space Vehicle Propulsion Units & Propulsion Unit
   Parts; 3812 Search & Navigation Equipment; 3965
   Fasteners, Buttons, Needles & Pins; 6552 Land
   Subdividers & Developers, Except Elsewhere
   Classified

Talley Industries Inc. is a diversified manufacturer of a wide range of proprietary and specialized products sold to defense, industrial, and commercial markets. Its offerings include mini-mill steel products, ceramic insulators, vehicle air bag components, welding equipment, electronic assemblies, rocket propellants, insecticides, air fresheners, and metal buttons. The company also derives income from real estate investments as well as royalties from licensing its vehicle air bag technology. Talley restructured during the late 1980s and early 1990s, following a series of setbacks, and returned to profitability in 1994. The company's curious history is punctuated by unique and diversified ventures.

## Origins and Early History

Talley began in 1960 as a tiny aerospace engineering firm in the desert north of Mesa, Arizona. The company was founded by German-born engineer Franz G. Talley and an experienced group of his associates who were also engineers. The venture, which was backed by some technically oriented investors, began with the specific purpose of developing various solid-propellant actuated devices and systems that could be used to help pilots and their crews escape from military aircraft in emergency situations. Talley prospered throughout the decade by developing advanced solid-propellant mechanisms and gas generators, which were purchased by the U.S. military and incorporated in numerous machines. Talley's sales rose from $1.2 million in 1960 to $16.7 million by 1967.

By the early 1970s Talley Industries had grown to become a Fortune 500 company, but the organization didn't achieve that status through sales of its propulsion devices. Instead, it grew rapidly during the late 1960s and 1970s largely by acquiring other companies, many of which operated in industries completely unrelated to Talley's core defense operations. Franz Talley initiated the growth strategy as a means of diversifying away from the defense sector. His ultimate goal was to reduce the company's dependence on military products to less than 50 percent of sales within three years. At the same time, he wanted to boost Talley's total sales volume to $100 million. Both of those objectives were accomplished within two years, vaulting Talley into the Fortune 500.

Among the first acquisitions was the 1968 buyout of The Waterbury Companies, a diversified manufacturer whose products ranged from metal buttons to insecticides. Then, in 1969, Talley added Adorence to its portfolio. Adorence was an importer of lower-priced women's and men's apparel. The acquisition that put Talley Industries on the map, however, was the

1970 takeover of General Time Corporation. General Time was a large manufacturer and marketer of clocks and timing devices, among other products. Venerable brand names assembled under the General Time umbrella included Westclox Seth Thomas. The merger was achieved as the result of a protracted proxy battle that angered many of General Time's shareholders. In fact, the Securities and Exchange Commission later sued to force Talley to pay those stockholders more money. The important result for Talley Industries, however, was that its revenue base was tripled as a result of the merger.

Thus, in the span of just a few years, Talley had grown from a relatively small defense products supplier to a diversified, multinational corporation with annual sales of nearly $300 million per year. That growth reflected a trend during that period toward the creation of multinational conglomerates. The thinking at the time was that, by combining diverse operations, a corporation could realize various benefits related to, for example, economies of scale and decreased vulnerability to business cycles in specific industries. However, Talley gagged on its acquisitions in the early 1970s, and its organization began to become unwieldy, so it postponed its rapid growth campaign for a few years, streamlined its holdings, and jettisoned some nonperforming divisions.

### Continued Growth through Real Estate and Acquisitions

Franz Talley resumed the conglomerate strategy in 1973, when he became involved in real estate investing and development. Talley Industries jumped into the real estate business with the acquisition of the renowned Arizona Biltmore hotel and more than 1,000 surrounding acres. The sale included the 53,000-square-foot Wrigley mansion, which had been built in 1931 and was owned by the Wrigley (chewing gum) family until the 1970s. After the purchase, Talley hired a team of land planners and real estate professionals who expanded the hotel and developed a master-planned community around it. Throughout the 1970s Talley sold off chunks of the property to developers and even sold the Biltmore Hotel itself in 1977. The project was ultimately a success.

Meanwhile, Talley Industries continued to grow internally and to acquire new companies. Importantly, in 1976 Talley purchased Sencel Aero Engineering Corporation, a designer, tester, and manufacturer of aircraft ejection seats and air crew escape systems. The purchase was an obvious complement to Talley's original propulsion business, which was still marketing cutting-edge solid-propellant-activated devices in the mid-1970s. Those operations, combined with Talley's other diverse holdings, pushed the company's revenues past $400 million by

1977 (fiscal year ended March 1978), as profits rose to a record $16.7 million. Shortly after posting those record results, Franz Talley died suddenly of a heart attack at the age of 59.

### Surmounting Difficulties in the Late 1970s

Franz Talley's death signaled the start of a serious decline in Talley Industries' financial performance. Indeed, the global recession of the late 1970s hammered several of Talley's key industries. Just as important, though, Talley's rapid expansion and simultaneous inattention to operating efficiency was hurting its bottom line. Talley's board brought in B. Paul Barnes to try to turn the lagging company around, but the problems just got worse. In fact, the company lost money in 1978 and continued to do so for four straight years. Frustrated, the board dismissed Barnes in 1981 and hired Bill Mallender to head the company. Mallender returned Talley to profitability and maintained leadership of the organization into the mid-1990s.

Prior to joining Talley in 1973, Mallender had practiced law in New York for nine years. He met Franz Talley in the 1960s, when Talley hired the Wall Street firm for which Mallender was working at the time. Mallender was putting together a mutual fund in Florida when Talley lured him away to join Talley Industries. Mallender initially served as general counsel and did much of the legal work related to the disposition of the Biltmore property. Talley respected his insight, though, and Mallender eventually became intimately involved in the company's key decisions.

### The 1980s: A New Era

Mallender moved quickly after accepting the head post at Talley. Within three weeks he eliminated half of the company's 104 headquarters employees. Within 12 months, moreover, he sold off eight companies that were engaged in industries ranging from heating and cooling to specialty plastics and apparel, and reorganized other subsidiaries. Although he kept some parts of Talley's clock division, he began to restructure it to compete in the new business environment. Indeed, the clock industry, like many other consumer products segments, was under increasing pressure from low-cost Asian manufacturers. Within 15 months Mallender had reduced long-term debt by 38 percent and had restructured some of the company's other obligations. Sales declined to $264 million in 1982 as a result of his efforts, but the company finally posted a positive net income of $8.2 million.

Having restored the health of Talley's balance sheet, Mallender and fellow executives resumed the company's acquisition drive in 1983. Their plan, though, was to purchase smaller companies in growing industries. Among Talley's first purchases was a California manufacturer of automated welding systems. Talley also jumped into a promising stainless steel minimill venture. Late in 1983, moreover, the company added to the still-intact real estate division with the purchase of a 66-acre parcel in Phoenix that included a large mall. By 1985 Talley was generating $316 million in annual sales and $12 million in earnings, and employing a work force of about 4,300 people. Government and technical sales accounted for about 50 percent of that sales volume, while realty made up roughly 25 percent and commercial goods and apparel accounted for about 20 percent and five percent, respectively.

Talley continued to buy and liquidate businesses going into the late 1980s. Importantly, the company jettisoned its apparel and clock divisions, giving it an emphasis on real estate and technical products (including many defense-related goods) by the late 1980s. Talley also made some odd moves, such as the purchase of the East-West Federal Bank, a $300-million (assets) savings bank and mortgage lender that served the Chinese-American community in Southern California. Despite the turbulence, Talley's revenues hovered around the $350-million-mark throughout most of the late 1980s and early 1990s.

### Profits from Air Bag Technology in the Late 1980s

The most important development for Talley during the late 1980s was its success in the vehicle air bag business. Demand for air bags by vehicle manufacturers throughout the world began to surge during the late 1980s, signaling the development of a giant new industry. Interestingly, Talley was poised to become a leader in the rapidly growing niche. Talley had been involved in the industry since its inception and was considered a pioneer of safety air bags. The company had started working on air bags in 1967 when Chrysler Corporation sought Talley's help in developing a compound to inflate its experimental air bags.

Talley's designers tried gunpowder and freon, but the result was a poisonous gas. After other failed efforts, they finally devised a workable system that utilized a sodium azide propellant. Talley patented the system, but Chrysler had lost interest by then, so Talley approached General Motors (GM). During the mid-1970s GM ordered 22,000 air bags from Talley that it installed in Buicks, Cadillacs, and Oldsmobiles. After that, the air bag movement lost momentum as federal regulators and automakers squabbled. Meanwhile, Talley integrated the technology into its defense-related products and set the vehicle air bag on the back burner. Finally, the Department of Transportation ordered all carmakers to equip their cars with air bags by the late 1980s. Talley was suddenly positioned to significantly influence a soon-to-be-giant industry.

Talley toyed with the idea of manufacturing its own air bags. It was obvious to Talley executives, though, that they would have trouble competing with massive automobile manufacturers and suppliers that would inevitably compete against them. Rather than try to compete as a manufacturer, Talley decided in 1989 to license its patented technology to TRW Inc. In a huge transaction, Talley agreed to let TRW use its technology for 12 years. In return, TRW paid Talley nearly $100 million in cash and agreed to pay Talley about $1.15 for every air bag system that it sold, and about half that amount for every air bag sold by companies that it allowed to use Talley's technology. Talley expected to receive a total of $200 million to $300 million throughout the term of the agreement.

Talley's air bag deal occurred at a pivotal time, just as other of Talley's operations were beginning to plummet into economic turmoil. Importantly, the bottom dropped out of the commercial real estate market in the late 1980s and early 1990s. Talley, which had bet heavily on future gains from its real estate

investments, was left sitting on acres of devalued land and property. At the same time, an economic recession was battering some of the company's smaller markets for goods like insecticides and buttons. Although Talley's defense and technical products division remained relatively healthy, the net result was that the company became strapped for cash and was forced to default on some of its major loans.

### Overcoming Financial Difficulties in the Early 1990s

Talley was able to restructure its debt during the early 1990s and to pay down some obligations by selling off its bank and an advertising subsidiary. Still, the company posted a string of ugly losses: $50 million in 1990, $43 million in 1991, and about $20 million in 1992 and 1993 combined. Fortunately, its technical products and defense-related operations continued to profit from demand for rocket motors, propellants, and other high-tech devices, and its steel operations and other industrial businesses remained strong. Income from those segments, combined with a slowly growing air bag royalty income, helped Talley avert bankruptcy and even return to profitability by the mid-1990s.

Talley narrowly escaped bankruptcy in the early 1990s. The company, still under Mallender's direction, scrambled to streamline and reorganize. By 1994 all of its divisions were producing profits except for the real estate business, which Talley was in the process of exiting. Importantly, in 1994 Talley enjoyed more than $17 million in royalties (pure earnings) from its air bag business, making that segment one of the company's most profitable. Its government products and services division contributed about $18 million in profits, while the industrial and specialty products divisions earned about $7.5 million and $5 million respectively.

Talley continued to report earnings gains in 1995 from its operations. In addition, the company received a substantial boost when a jury decided to make TRW pay Talley $138 million for failing to live up to its end of their original air bag agreement. Satisfied with the verdict, Talley forged ahead with its plan to reenter the air bag industry by teaming up with a division of General Motors to develop a more environmentally safe air bag. Talley also landed a major contract with the U.S. Navy in 1995 worth about $190 million. With its debt under control and improvements in key markets, Talley was positioned to boost earnings through the mid-1990s.

### Principal Subsidiaries

Amcan Specialty Steels, Inc.; Rowe Industries, Inc.; Waterbury Companies, Inc.; Electrodynamics, Inc.; John J. McMullen Associates, Inc.; Dimetrics, Inc.; Diversified Stainless Steel of Canada, Inc.; Universal Propulsion Co., Inc.; Talley Defense Systems, Inc.; Talley Metals Technology, Inc.; Talley Real Estate Co., Inc.

### Principal Operating Units

Government Products and Services; Air bag Royalties; Industrial Products; Specialty Products; Realty.

### *Further Reading*

Chadwell, Teena, and Cathy Luebke, "Talley Stockholders Blast Executive Compensation," *Business Journal-Phoenix & the Valley of the Sun,* May 6, 1994, Section 1, p. 4.

Fehr, Kerry, "Talley Forsaking Realty Market," *Phoenix Gazette,* March 10, 1993, p. 5D.

——, "Talley Still Counting on Air bags," *Phoenix Gazette,* May 5, 1993, p. 1C.

——, "Tallying Pluses, Minuses: Talley Industries Aims to Overcome Setbacks," *Phoenix Gazette,* April 10, 1992, p. 10C.

Fiscus, Chris, "Hormel Heir Grabs Old Wrigley Mansion," *Phoenix Gazette,* June 30, 1992, p. 5B.

Gilbertson, Dawn, "Talley, GM Unit Team up to Make Air bags," *Arizona Republic,* April 6, 1995, p. 1C.

——, "Talley Industries Stock up 8 Percent after Securing Navy Contracts," *Arizona Republic,* July 12, 1995, p. 1D.

——, "Talley Wins Air-Bag Battle with TRW," *Arizona Republic,* June 8, 1995, p. 1E.

Gray, Michael, " 'Bagging' Corporate Profits," *Arizona Business Gazette,* April 4, 1988, p. 1.

Moulton, Kristen, "A Conglomerate and Proud of It," *Arizona Trend,* November 1987, p. 46.

Mullen, Daniel R., "Talley Industries Completes Largest Transaction in Its History," *Business Wire,* April 21, 1989.

Ryan, Rick, "William Mallender: Lawyer Turned Corporate Manager Thrives at Helm of Restructured Talley Industries," *Business Journal-Phoenix & Valley of the Sun,* June 26, 1989, p. 14.

Webster, Guy, "Talley, Lenders in Accord," *Arizona Republic,* November 21, 1992, p. 1E.

—Dave Mote

# THERMOS.

## Thermos Company

**1555 Route 75 East**
**Freeport, Illinois 61032**
**U.S.A.**
**(815) 232-2111**
**Fax: (815) 233-6377**

*Wholly Owned Subsidiary of Nippon Sanso Corp.*
*Incorporated:* 1907 as American Thermos Bottle
   Company
*Employees:* 1,400
*Sales:* $200 million (1995 est.)
*SICs:* 3631 Household Cooking Equipment; 3086 Plastics
   Foam Products

Although Thermos Company may be best known for its line of vacuum-insulated bottles and lunch boxes, the Illinois-based manufacturer is also a leading maker of barbecue grills, coolers, carafes, and other household products based on its thermal technology. In fact, the largest portion of Thermos's estimated $200 million in annual sales is thought to come from its gas and electric barbecue units, which generally sell at the midrange and premium price categories. Thermos continues to dominate the U.S. lunch kit market, holding onto about 50 percent of the approximately $39 million spent on lunch kits each year. As part of the worldwide Thermos Group of Products under parent company Nippon Sanso Corp. of Japan, the company combines award-winning product designs, such as its electric barbecue grill introduced in 1993 and its thermal cooker introduced in 1994, with one of the United States' oldest brand names.

### Early History

Vacuum insulation, a technology that allows hot things to stay hot and cold things to stay cold, was invented in 1892 by the English scientist James Dewar. Dewar was studying the properties of liquid gases, that is, gases held below the temperature at which they become liquid, and he needed a way to keep the gases cold enough to remain in their liquid form. Dewar discovered that sealing one glass bottle inside another and removing the air between the two bottles gave him the temperature retention he sought. He named this discovery vacuum insulation and his device the vacuum bottle. Dewar did not patent his device, however.

Commercial development of Dewar's invention came at the turn of the century. The German company, Burger and Aschenbrenner, became the first to adapt the vacuum bottle for commercial purposes, forming Thermos GmBH in 1904. The name Thermos came as a result of a contest; it was submitted by a resident of Munich, Germany who derived the term from the Greek word "therme," or heat. In 1905, a British company, A. E. Gutman, was given United Kingdom distribution rights; the following year, Gutman registered the Thermos name as a trademark in England and, by 1907, had registered the Thermos trademark throughout the United Kingdom and in other countries around the world. In that year, William Walker founded the American Thermos Bottle Company in Brooklyn, New York, acquiring the German company's patent and taking over its U.S. business. Sales in 1907 reached $115,000.

### Becoming a Household Word:
### The Early 20th Century

American Thermos set out to popularize the Thermos name as a synonym for the vacuum bottle. By 1910, the company could claim in its catalog that Thermos had become a "household word," using the word Thermos not as an adjective for the company's vacuum bottles, but as a noun signifying the vacuum bottle itself. This marketing strategy would indeed create a household name for Thermos but would later come to haunt the company. Sales had tripled to $381,000, however, by 1910. In 1913, American Thermos moved its headquarters to Norwich, Connecticut.

The Thermos name continued to gain in popularity, and the company continued to encourage identification of the Thermos name with the product itself. By 1917, the company could assure its retailers that the public's use of the word Thermos when referring to vacuum bottles was worth three to four million dollars in free advertising. Thermos products were already becoming part of history, traveling with Robert Peary on his discovery of the North Pole, and forming part of the equipment of such aviation pioneers as the Wright Brothers and Count Zeppelin.

The terms "aspirin," "escalator," and "cellophane" also began as trademarks, but quickly passed into generic use. American Thermos soon faced a similar problem. As early as 1922, the company brought suit against W. T. Grant Co. for using the word Thermos to describe the latter company's own vacuum bottles. In that case, American Thermos won on a technicality: in its defense, it neglected to claim that Thermos had become a generic word. The decision rendered by the U.S. District Court in Massachusetts, however, stated that "there is no evidence that Thermos means to the public vacuum bottles produced by the plaintiff."

With sales nearing $1.5 million by 1923, American Thermos set out to protect its trademark, including registering its logo, adding the words "vacuum bottles" or "vacuum jugs" to its advertising, and raising the prominence of the trademark symbol beside its name. During the 1920s, the company also acquired two of its competitors, the Icy Hot Bottle Company in 1925 and the Keapsit Company in 1929. The company also acquired the majority interest in the Thermos company established by Gutman in the United Kingdom.

American Thermos succeeded in gaining recognition for its trademark in the industry, and it actively protected the trademark against commercial infringement. From 1935, the company employed a clipping service to seek out unauthorized references to the Thermos name in the trade and in advertising. Yet the word Thermos continued to be used as a generic word by the general public; it even began to appear in some dictionaries. Thermos protested these uses when it discovered them, but many hundreds of instances escaped the company's attention. At the same time, the company's protests were largely ignored by the nontrade users of the thermos term, and the company generally made no further attempts to enforce compliance.

Sales in 1936 topped $2.5 million and would double again by 1945. But the company continued to be aware of the threat to its trademark. In a 1940 memorandum, company officials raised concerns about the addition of the word "thermos" to many dictionaries, arguing that "this undoubtedly would be cited against us in a lawsuit to defend the trademark. The best we can do is to try to 'purify' the definition of the word." Yet the company let enforcement of the trademark slip during World War II, fearing negative publicity. After the war, American Thermos attempted to reinforce its trademark among the trade and advertisers. By 1952, however, the company feared that pressing a trademark infringement suit would result in losing Thermos's trademark status. Meanwhile, the company enjoyed the benefits of the strength of its name. As the market for vacuum products grew in the years following the war, Thermos's sales grew as well, from $5.3 million in 1945 to more than $13 million by the end of the 1950s.

A boost to company sales came with the introduction of its first licensed lunch kits. Prior to 1953, Thermos had been selling comparatively drab, green-painted tin lunch boxes. But, in that year, the company produced a lunch kit featuring popular performers Roy Rogers and Dale Evans painted on the box and bottle. More than 2.5 million of the Rogers-Evans kits were sold, and an American school tradition began. During the 1950s, as well, the company attempted to separate the Thermos name from the vacuum bottle itself by broadening its production to include tents, bottle openers, firelighters, lanterns, camping stoves, and other products, each bearing the Thermos name. In 1954, the company's name was changed to American Thermos Products Company to reinforce Thermos as a brand name, not a specific product.

### Losing the Trademark in the 1950s

American Thermos stepped up its efforts to protect the Thermos name in the late 1950s. The company's protests rose from less than 200 in 1957 to nearly 1,200 in 1961. But these efforts were too little, too late. Inevitably, another company would attempt to market its own vacuum bottles as thermos bottles.

That company was Aladdin Industries, which introduced its own vacuum bottles in 1945, with sales growing from $560,000 in that year to nearly $7 million by 1960. In 1958, Aladdin announced its intention to market a line of vacuum bottles as "thermos bottles." American Thermos sued Aladdin for trademark infringement in that year.

In 1962, Judge Robert Anderson rendered his decision: "thermos" was indeed a generic word. According to Anderson's decision, American Thermos, which by then had been acquired, along with its Canadian and British subsidiaries, by King-Seeley and renamed King-Seeley Thermos Company, had itself contributed to the popularization of the word thermos as a synonym for vacuum bottles, while failing in its diligence to enforce its trademark rights. Aladdin was granted the right to add the word "thermos," in lowercase only, to its thermos bottles. Thermos retained its "Thermos" brand name.

### Expanding the Company

Despite this setback, Thermos remained one of the most popular brand names in the United States and continued to hold the lead in thermos sales. In 1965, King-Seeley Thermos acquired Structo Manufacturing Company, which had been founded in 1907 as Thompson Manufacturing Company in Freeport, Illinois. Structo, which manufactured children's toys for most of its history, added production of barbecue grills in 1960. Three years after the Structo purchase, King-Seeley Thermos was itself acquired by Household International as a subsidiary.

In 1969, King-Seeley Thermos acquired the Halsey Taylor Company, a maker of drinking fountains and water coolers. Six years later, Structo dropped its other products to focus on making barbecue grills exclusively, becoming a leader in that market. The following year, Structo was consolidated into King-Seeley Thermos, which took over production of barbecues under the Structo name.

By the beginning of the 1980s, the Thermos division was producing the bulk of Household International's $125 million in consumer products sales. Sales of its glass-lined thermos products were under pressure, however, as the rise of coffee makers and other appliances began to replace the need for thermoses and as new, more durable stainless steel thermoses began to eat into the sales of glass-lined thermoses. The company introduced new products, including glass-lined carafes, to take up slumping thermos sales. In 1984, Thermos shut down its Norwich, Connecticut operations and moved the company's headquarters to Illinois. Two years later, Household International, by then renamed Household Manufacturing, finally merged Thermos and Structo, forming the Thermos Company. The combined companies would reach $188 million in sales by 1988.

By the end of the 1980s, however, Household moved to exit manufacturing, reforming as Household Finance. Thermos was sold to Nippon Sanso Corp. of Japan for $134 million in 1989. Sanso, a leading maker of industrial gases and other products, also manufactured its own premium-priced thermoses, which would later be sold under the Nissan Thermos brand name. In 1990, Monte Peterson, formerly with Coleman Co., was named president and CEO of the new subsidiary.

### Restructured for the 1990s

Through the 1980s, Thermos's sales stagnated. Its share of the thermal-insulated market, worth about $150 million in 1989, had dropped to one-third. By then, however, the company's barbecue grills were driving the company's growth, representing more than 60 percent of annual sales. Under Peterson, Thermos set out to improve its position by coming up with new product designs. Peterson reformed the company from its former bureaucratic structure, in which the company was organized by function, into an interdisciplinary team structure. This allowed Thermos to create and begin to market its new Thermal Electric Grill in less than two years. The grill would go on to win several new product awards, and it produced strong immediate sales.

Thermos also worked to reinvent the lunch box. After a failed attempt at a reusable lunch bag (children complained because their food would get crushed), Thermos introduced several new designs, including a rock-shaped "Flintstones" lunch box, purse-style lunch kits, and futuristic lunch box styles that allowed it not only to maintain its popularity among younger children, but also to increase its share of the older children's market. The company also presented its SoftThermos, a collapsible cooler. Licensing arrangements for such characters as the Teenage Mutant Ninja Turtles, the perennial bestseller Barbie, Batman, and Pocahontas helped the company maintain its leadership in the lunch box market through the first half of the 1990s, a market estimated at around $40 million per year.

Peterson left the company in 1995 and was replaced by Douglas Blair. In 1995, Blair stated his intention to build up the company's marketing efforts and redirect sales efforts from its premium-priced line to the company's mid-priced products. Growth at Thermos, however, seemed to be slow over the past decade, with sales in 1995 estimated to have reached only around $200 million. With strong competition from Weber, Sunbeam, and others in the more than $1 billion barbecue market, further growth for Thermos appeared most likely in developing new products using its thermal insulation technology and ever-popular brand name.

### Further Reading

*American Thermos Prod. Co. v. Aladdin Industries, Inc.,* 207 F.Supp. 9 (1962).

Buursma, Bruce, "Pursuing Air-Tight Strategies," *Chicago Tribune,* June 3, 1990, Bus. Sec., p. 3.

Diamond, Sidney A., "Thermos' Trademark Passes into the Language," *Advertising Age,* August 13, 1962, p. 56.

Dumane, Brian, "Payoff from the New Management," *Fortune,* December 13, 1993, p. 103.

Mandernach, Mark, "Thermos Box Packs a Punch with Lunch," *Chicago Tribune,* October 22, 1995, Tempo Sec., p. 1.

"Modern Problems Spur Changes at Thermos," *New York Times,* October 22, 1984, p. D1.

Murphy, H. Lee, "Hot Stuff: Thermos Deal Creates U.S.-Japan Giant," *Crain's Chicago Business,* July 17, 1989, p. 29.

Stankevich, Debby Garbato, "Making Thermos Hotter," *HFN: The Weekly Newspaper for the Home Furnishing Network,* May 29, 1995, p. 31.

Warner, Fara, "Message in a Bottle: Thermos Updates Its Image," *Brandweek,* January 31, 1994, p. 32.

—M. L. Cohen

# Tonen Corporation

**Palaceside Building**
**1-1, Hitotsubashi 1-chome**
**Chiyoda-ku, Tokyo 100**
**Japan**
**(03) 3286-5110**
**Fax: (03) 3286-5120**

*Public Company*
*Incorporated:* 1939 as Towa Nenryo Kogyo Co. Ltd.
*Employees:* 2,187
*Sales:* ¥438.3 billion (US$4.22 billion) (1995)
*Stock Exchanges:* Tokyo
*SICs:* 2911 Petroleum Refining; 5172 Petroleum &
      Petroleum Products, Not Elsewhere Classified—
      Except Bulk Stations & Terminals—Wholesale

Tonen Corporation specializes in oil refinery operations, importing, manufacturing, and selling petroleum and petrochemicals. Exxon and Mobil, each of which holds a 25 percent stake in Tonen, supply the majority of the crude oil that Tonen uses. Tonen operates two main refineries in Kawasaki and Wakayama, which together can process 406,000 barrels of crude oil per day. The refineries utilize advanced technology to produce a range of value-added oil products, including gasoline, naphtha, kerosene, gas oil, heavy fuel oil, lubricants, liquified petroleum gas, paraffin, asphalt, sulfur, and natural gas. These products are then sold by the Japanese subsidiaries of Exxon and Mobil, under their own brand names. The gasoline produced by Tonen's refineries hold a 15 percent market share in Japan.

### Early History

In July 1939, Towa Nenryo Kogyo Co. Ltd.—the company name was changed to Tonen Corporation in July 1989—was established as a partnership of ten Japanese oil-related companies: Nippon Sekiyu, Kokura Sekiyu, Chosen Sekiyu, Aikoku Sekiyu, Sayama Sekiyu, Mitsubishi Sha Holdings, Mitsubishi Shoji Trading, Aratsu Sekiyu, Maruzen Sekiyu, and Mitsubishi Mining Co., with a capital of ¥50 million and 59 employees under the guidance of the Ministry of Defense and the fuel department of the Ministry of Commerce and Industry. Keizaburo Hashimoto, president of the Nippon Sekiyu Co. Ltd., was appointed chairman of the board, and Fusazo Kokura, president of Kokura Sekiyu Co. Ltd., became president. The larger corporate investors dispatched managerial officers to the company.

At the start of the refinery operation, sales and the procurement of crude oil and finance were supported and ensured by the Japanese Ministry of Defense. However, the choice of an industrial site and the question of which technologies to adopt for the refinery operations were major concerns. As the result of cooperative discussions among shareholders, a research and development center was located at the Shimizu plant site in the Shizuoka prefecture, and the refinery facilities were located in the Wakayama plant site in the Wakayama Prefecture.

In September 1939, the production and distribution of oil products in Japan fell under the influence of the national policy promoted by the fuel department of the Ministry of Commerce and Industry. All Japanese oil companies' independent business activities were severely restricted. However, the effects of the national policy were limited in the case of Towa Nenryo (Tonen), which was heavily engaged in munitions production.

In 1941, normal-pressure distillers began to operate in the Wakayama refinery and successfully produced engine starter volatile oil, airplane fuels, automobile gasoline, mineral turpentine, solvent, kerosene, light oils, and heavy oil. From 1941 to 1945, the Wakayama refinery processed 842,000 kiloliters of crude oil, 53 percent for munitions and 47 percent for civilian use. In 1943, a crude oil heating distillery was built at the Wakayama refinery and processed 86,000 kiloliters of crude oil before the end of World War II—77 percent for munitions and 23 percent for civilian use.

On the Shimizu site, research and development activities started as a result of the serious shortage of natural resources caused by the war. The major projects at the research and development center were the substitution for petroleum products of other materials, such as high-octane gasoline developed from artificial oil and lubricants made from raw natural rubber; and the processing of heavy tar oil produced in Southeast Asia and volatile oil, made from pine-tree gum. The construction of the Shimizu refinery was hindered by the shortage of materials under wartime conditions and was not realized on a large scale until 1950.

### Postwar Restructuring and Expansion

After the war ended, Tonen experienced a considerable fall in sales when the need for airplane fuel for munitions use ceased abruptly. Three-quarters of Tonen's 2,600 employees were dismissed in 1945. The major board members, including chairman and president, were banned from public duties by the Supreme Commander for the Allied Powers (SCAP) because of their involvement in Japan's war effort, and they were obliged to resign from the company. Nobuhei Nakahara became president. SCAP prohibited crude oil imports to Japan and banned refinery operations on the Pacific coast site. Tonen almost ceased to operate until 1947.

In December 1948, Tonen cooperated with the Standard-Vacuum Oil Company (Stan-Vac), which intended to reenter the Japanese market. To start up its refinery business again, Tonen needed a crude oil supply, distribution outlets, and technical and financial support for production facilities, and a tie-up with Stan-Vac was thought to be indispensable. To acquire the highest production technology from Standard Oil Development Company (SOD), later renamed Exxon Research and Engineering Company, Tonen transferred 51 percent of its ownership to Stan-Vac. In July 1949, oil refining on the Pacific coast site was again permitted by SCAP, and Tonen started operations in 1950.

In the 1950s, Tonen pursued two basic strategies. First, the expansion of production facilities had to take place as quickly as possible to enable Tonen to take advantage of domestic market opportunities. As the strategic importance of its Pacific coast location increased, the Shimizu refinery's production capacity had to increase very quickly. Second, using advanced technology licensed from SOD, the quality of products and the efficiency of refinery processes had to be improved. As the motorization of Japan was expected to take place in the near future, the development of high-octane gasoline and high quality lubricants was necessary. The establishment of production methods was of great importance to Tonen.

In November 1954, fluid catalytic cracking (FCC), a refinery method using catalysts to make fuel oil, was introduced in the Wakayama refinery, processing 4,700 barrels per day. In 1953, Tonen's refining capacity reached 28,500 barrels per day. The Wakayama refinery processed 21,000 barrels per day of crude oil, and the Shimizu refinery processed 7,500 barrels per day, at that time the largest refinery operations in Japan.

Expansion projects continued after this period. In 1955, a new 36,000-barrel-per-day refinery was completed, and another 10,200-barrels-per-day FCC refinery was built in 1956. In 1957, after the completion of alkylation equipment, production volume of airplane fuels reached 90,000 barrels per year, almost equal to the annual airplane fuel consumption of the country. Tonen almost monopolized the airplane fuel market in Japan.

From 1949 to 1957, Tonen's investment in production capacity expansion amounted to ¥12.2 billion. The company made seven issues of stock to finance its expansion. Consequently, the company's equity grew 84 times in this period, from ¥37.5 million in 1950 to ¥3.159 billion in 1955.

### 1960s Vertical Integration

Tonen's aim in the 1960s was vertical integration into oil-related fields, including transportation of crude oil, new product development, diversification into petrochemicals, and alliance with other industrial enterprises. These changes were achieved in several stages. Tonen founded Toa Tanker Co. Ltd., with a capital of ¥1 billion. Minao Furihata, vice-president of Towa Nenryo, became Toa Tanker's president and in 1961 the company's name was changed to Tonen Tanker Co. Ltd. In the 1960s, transportation costs represented a relatively large proportion of the total cost of crude oil. To bring down crude oil prices, the reduction of transportation costs was essential.

Tonen decided that its technological dependence on SVOC had gone too far, and that independence in research and development activities had to be regained. In 1961, Tonen acquired a 25-acre site, and spent ¥800 million on establishing a research and development center.

Under the policy for promoting Japan's petrochemical industry, enacted by MITI—the Ministry of International Trade and Industry—Tonen diversified into petrochemicals. In 1960, Tonen founded Tonen Sekiyukagaku (Petrochemical) Co. Ltd, with capital of ¥4 billion. Tonen's president Enpei Nakahara was also president of this new company. Steam-cracking and oxyalcohol plants were built in the Kawasaki refinery, and production of ethylene, propylene, and butane began.

In 1958 two joint ventures were established: General Sekiyu K.K., capitalized at ¥1 billion and owned on a 50–50 basis with General Bussan Kaisha, Ltd., which became General Sekiyu Seisei Co. Ltd. in 1967; and Nichimo Sekiyu Co. Ltd., equally owned with Nippon Gyomo Sengu Co. Ltd. By entering into joint ventures, Tonen was able to operate at higher capacity and thus benefit from economies of scale. To finance its expansion the company made seven new stock issues between 1956 and 1962, when it was capitalized at ¥8.9 billion, having grown almost three times over this period.

The next decade, from 1962 to 1972, saw further continuous growth at Tonen. This intensive growth was stimulated by a reorganization of the parent company. In 1962 Standard-Vacuum Oil was split in two and the resulting companies integrated, respectively, with Mobil Oil Corporation and Esso Standard Eastern—now Esso Eastern. Tonen's arrangement with SVOC was transferred to these two companies. Consequently, SVOC's stake in Tonen was split into two stakes of 25 percent each. Both companies supplied crude oil to Tonen and distributed its products under their own brand names and through different marketing channels. Competition between Esso Standard Sekiyu K.K. and Mobil Sekiyu K.K. in the Japanese market gave impetus to the company's growth.

At the Wakayama refinery, the first stage of the expansion project in the Ogake area was completed in 1965, and the second expansion project in the area in 1968. This made the refinery the newest and the largest in Japan. The first stage of the expansion project at the Kawasaki Refinery was completed in 1970. Equity participation in Kygnus Sekiyu K.K. in 1972 boosted the Kawasaki refinery's economy of scale. By 1969, Tonen's total assets reached ¥73.2 billion, and the company was capitalized at ¥14.3 billion.

### Challenges in the 1970s and 1980s

In the 1970s, during the two oil crises and severe recession in the Japanese economy, Tonen reduced excess production capacity, cut its costs, and stopped new employment to adjust to slower economic growth. During the oil crisis Tonen recognized that the oil industry in Japan had already matured, and that new fields of business had to be developed. Tonen Technology K.K., established in 1971 as a crude oil reserve company, diversified into computer sciences. In 1977, Tonen Energy International Corporation was established, with its headquarters in New York and a branch in London, to obtain finance for the crude oil transactions of the company.

In 1981 the price for Arabian light oil amounted to $34 per barrel, and the total annual deficit of Japanese oil industry amounted to almost ¥350 billion. Tonen concentrated its efforts on the rationalization of production. Through the successful development of energy-saving technologies, Tonen achieved a saving of almost 220,000 kiloliters—¥10 billion annually compared with the 1973 level. As a result of improvements in its production process and management system, Tonen's business situation gradually improved. From 1984 through the end of the decade, the company's financial statements showed a profit each year. The long-term orientation of management policies resulted in the improvement of Tonen's equity ratio to 60 percent in 1989, among the highest in the Japanese oil industry.

Tonen aimed to develop an intelligent refinery by employing the most advanced information technology and operation backup systems. In terms of new product development, Tonen chose to focus on new energy sources, new materials, life sciences, and information technology. Tonen's major development in the field of new energy was an efficient, low-cost amorphous silicon for electricity, and a clean combustion system—supersonic fuel injection—used in the F3000 racing car. In the field of new materials, Tonen developed and patented a high quality pitch-based carbon fiber with a host of applications in airplane bodies, automobile frames, and mechanical parts. In the field of life science, Tonen established a reputation as a pioneer in genetic engineering and cell technology, including a leukemia vaccine, which enabled a double-digit increase in the general potency of a wide variety of vaccines. In the field of information technology Tonen benefited from years of experience in computerized operational control and plant maintenance systems. For this purpose, Tonen System Plaza Inc. was established in 1985.

### 1990s and Beyond

The 1990s have been a more troubled time for Tonen. In addition to a February 1994 fire at the Kawasaki refinery which cut into the company's 1994 earnings, its safety record was further tarnished by a May 1995 gas leak at the same refinery.

Most importantly, however, behind-the-scenes clashes between Tonen's management and its Exxon and Mobil major shareholders came to light in the early 1990s that raised doubts about Tonen's future.

According to an article in *Tokyo Business Today,* the roots of the conflict were found in Tonen's diversification efforts and conservative management philosophy. Tonen had entered a period of slow growth in the 1980s because of the mature nature of the refinery business. Under President Nobuyuki Nakahara, the company began to build up larger cash reserves to save for future investments in new growth areas. But Nakahara began to be stymied in his efforts to diversify by Exxon and Mobil, as these shareholders pressured him for higher dividend payouts, which in turn started to draw down Tonen's cash reserves. According to some analysts, the oil giants in addition to wanting a higher return on their investment also wished to keep Tonen from diversifying into areas where it would compete with them.

From 1988 into the mid-1990s, Tonen had in fact invested little in its existing facilities or in developing new ones, with its late 1994 decision to add an H-Oil hydroconversion unit to its Kawasaki refinery—the first such unit in Japan—being one of the exceptions. Meanwhile, Tonen's dividend payout ratio, historically in the 30 to 40 percent range, exceeded 90 percent from 1988 to 1991, then surpassed 100 percent starting in 1992. Nakahara reportedly fought over the increased dividends, but to no avail, and was eventually pressured to resign early in 1994.

Nakahara's successor—Tamehiko Tamahori, who had been president of Tonen Tanker K.K.—developed a new corporate strategy to become a "World-Class Refiner." Therein he outlined four challenges for the company: attaining global cost-competitiveness through reengineering, employing world-class technology such as the H-Oil unit, offering "full cooperation" with Exxon and Mobil, and pursuing growth opportunities after "carefully evaluating the business risks." It appeared then to some analysts that Tamahori intended to be even more cautious about diversification and would work more closely with Exxon and Mobil than his predecessor.

Japan began to deregulate the oil industry in the mid-1990s, which posed additional dilemmas for Tonen as it headed toward the end of the century. Deregulation would mean increased competition, which might depress the company's earnings even further. Clearly, the company faced further diversification moves if it were to survive the competitive climate, but the question of whether Exxon and Mobil would allow such movement remained unanswered. Nevertheless, it was reported in early 1996 that Tonen was considering a move into the power generation industry, an indication that it was beginning to seek growth areas that would not compete with Exxon and Mobil interests.

### Principal Subsidiaries

Kygnus Sekiyu K.K. (50%); Kygnus Sekiyu Seisei K.K.; Tonen Chemical Corp.; Tonen Tanker K.K.; Tonen Properties Inc.; Tonen Sogo Service Co. Ltd.; Tonen System Plaza Inc.; Tonen Technology K.K.; Tonen Energy International Corp. (U.S.A.).

### *Further Reading*

Asai, Hideki, "*Gaiatsu* in the Boardroom: U.S. Oil Companies Run Tonen as They Like," *Tokyo Business Today,* May 1994, pp. 22–24.

*The Course of Tonen's History,* Tokyo: Tonen Corporation, 1980.

Hardy, Quentin, "Tonen President's Resignation Reflects Culture Clash Between Japan, U.S. Firms," *Asian Wall Street Journal Weekly,* January 24, 1994, p. 3.

Park, Christopher, "Uncertain Start to Japan's Deregulation: Refiners Look to Diversify," *Platt's Oilgram News,* April 2, 1996, p. 1.

Sterngold, James, "Lesson in Shareholder Power for Japanese Refiner," *New York Times,* January 17, 1994, p. C2(N), p. D2(L).

*Thirty Years of Tonen: From 1939 to 1969,* Vols. 1–2, Tokyo: Tonen Corporation, 1971.

—Kenichi Yasumuro
—updated by David E. Salamie

# Trek Bicycle Corporation

801 West Madison Street
P.O. Box 183
Waterloo, Wisconsin 53594
U.S.A.
(414) 478-2191
Fax: (414) 478-2774

*Wholly Owned Subsidiary of Intrepid Corporation*
*Incorporated:* 1976
*Employees:* 1,600
*Sales:* $327 million (1995 est.)
*SICs:* 3751 Motorcycles, Bicycles & Parts

Trek Bicycle Corporation is the world's largest manufacturer of bicycles sold by specialty retailers. Founded in 1976, the company sells close to a million bikes a year, as well as full lines of bicycle accessories and clothing. In addition to bicycles bearing the Trek brand name, the company also markets a line of mountain bikes named after Gary Fisher, one of the inventors of the mountain bike, and a line of bikes named for racing star Greg LeMond. Trek has several European subsidiaries, and its equipment is distributed in over 60 countries across the globe. In the United States, Trek maintains five Wisconsin manufacturing plants and four distribution centers. In addition to its manufacturing operations, Trek sponsors a number of racing teams, an on-site repair program, and an annual fund-raising ride for Midwest Athletes Against Childhood Cancer.

## Early History

Trek was established in 1976, at the peak of the 1970s bicycle boom. Its founders were Dick Burke, president of Milwaukee-based appliance and electronics distributor Roth Co., and Bevill Hogg, the proprietor of a chain of bike stores, one of which was located in nearby Madison. With financial backing from Roth's parent company, the Brookfield, Wisconsin–based Intrepid Corporation, Burke and Hogg launched Trek in an old warehouse in Waterloo, Wisconsin, located halfway between Milwaukee and Madison. With a work force of about

five, the company began making high-quality, lightweight steel bicycle frames by hand.

From the outset, Trek committed itself to selling bicycles primarily through specialty bicycle stores, rather than through general retail outlets. This decision helped the company to maintain its image as a supplier of equipment for serious bicycling enthusiasts. Trek quickly became a favorite brand among that connoisseur market, and independent bicycle shops have remained Trek's most important outlet.

Competing primarily against European and Japanese manufacturers, Trek began to have an impact quickly, gaining industry attention both for the quality of its bikes and for being an American company. Trek bicycles were especially popular in the Midwest, the company's own backyard. By 1978, however, Trek was distributing to both coasts, as well as to other bicycling hotspots, such as Colorado. After only three years in business, the company's annual sales had grown to $750,000.

By 1980, Trek had outgrown its original plant. The company moved to a new facility in Waterloo, and there it began mass-producing bicycles. Sales were so brisk that Trek also contracted a Taiwanese firm to produce some of the company's bikes. Among bicycling enthusiasts, Trek was quickly gaining a reputation as a producer of the very highest caliber of bicycles available, and its sales reflected that reputation. During the early 1980s, sales virtually doubled each year.

## The Age of Mountain Bikes

In 1983 Trek became a fairly early entrant into the mountain bike market, with the introduction of its 850 model. Developed in California in the late 1970s, mountain bikes featured more comfortable seats, fatter tires, and more gears than the ten-speed road bikes that dominated the market at the time. Fueled largely by the surging popularity of mountain bikes, Trek sold more than 45,000 bikes in 1984. The company also launched its Trek Components Group that year.

During the 1980s, Trek was one of the very few American companies that stood in the way of an all-out takeover of bicycle manufacturing by Taiwanese factories. Although even

493

## Company Perspectives:

*The Trek philosophy is to produce a quality product for a competitive value, deliver it on time and in a positive environment.*

Trek continued to import some of its bikes from Taiwan, the company found that it was able to offset the somewhat higher costs associated with manufacturing in America by saving on ocean shipping and cutting out other middlemen. Even labor costs proved to be a relatively minor problem, since making bikes was seen by young employees, many of them avid bicycling hobbyists themselves, as a fairly glamorous job, and those employees were therefore willing to work for rather modest wages. As Trek expanded its facilities over the next several years, it was able to rely less and less on imports.

After a conflict with cofounder Burke, Hogg left Trek in 1985 to start his own bicycle company in California. In spite of the changes, Trek continued to grow at an impressive rate. In 1985 the company introduced its first aluminum road bike, Model 2000. Its first carbon composite road bike, Model 2500, hit the market the following year. By 1986 sales had soared to $16 million, and surging demand led to the addition of 75,000 square feet to the company's Waterloo manufacturing facility.

### A New Philosophy for the Late 1980s

Ten years of startling growth did not come without problems, however. As Burke explained in a 1996 *Capital Times* (Madison, Wisconsin) interview, "In all fairness, Bevill [Hogg, company cofounder] was more of a dreamer than a manager." Although sales remained solid, Trek began to experience difficulties in a number of areas. Unsold inventory began to pile up, and as a result the company was losing money. With morale nearing rock bottom, Burke decided to take over the day-to-day management of the company. He instituted a "back to basics" approach, emphasizing sensible business practices and quality service. His new mission statement had four components: "Produce a quality product at a competitive price, deliver it on time in a positive environment."

Burke's new approach began to pay off quickly. Improved efficiency and marketing, combined with Trek's ongoing reputation for turning out quality products, breathed new life into the company's sagging bottom line. Sales doubled in each of the next three years. In 1987 Trek successfully introduced a new line of mountain bikes, and their popularity helped the company sell a total of about 100,000 bicycles in 1988.

Trek continued to find innovative ways to make money during the last years of the 1980s. In 1988 the company introduced a line of bicycling apparel. The following year, Trek entered the stationary bicycle market with Trek Fitness bikes. In 1989 the Jazz line of children's bicycles were introduced, and the company opened subsidiaries in Great Britain and Germany. Within five years, international sales accounted for about 35 percent of the company's business. By 1990 mountain bikes made up nearly half the bicycles sold in the United States, and Trek was prepared to claim a strong share of those sales. The company sold 350,000 bikes altogether that year. Trek's sales grew to about $175 million for fiscal 1991, and the company had about 700 employees by that time.

### The High-Tech 1990s

During the first part of the 1990s, Trek remained at the technological forefront among bicycle manufacturers. Throughout the 1980s, the company had succeeded in developing advanced materials that enabled it to maximize the lightness and strength of its bicycle frames. These breakthroughs led to the 1992 development of the Optimum Compaction Low Void (OCLV) carbon fiber lamination process. Using the OCLV process, Trek was able to make the lightest production frames in the world, weighing in at a mere 2.44 pounds. Trek's first OCLV carbon road bike, Model 5500, was introduced in 1992, and its first OCLV carbon mountain bikes, Models 9800 and 9900, were unveiled a year later.

Meanwhile, another expansion project took place at Trek's Waterloo plant, which now measured 140,000 square feet. During the early 1990s, the bicycle industry in the United States experienced a bit of a sales slump. To compensate, Trek looked to boost its sales in other areas. The company continued to emphasize international growth during this period. Sales in Japan, for example grew by about 40 percent per year from 1991 through 1993. Trek also concentrated more on sales in Europe, where it was gaining a solid reputation among bicycle buyers who had long thought of American bikes as heavy, clunky monsters built for kids.

In addition, the company began to focus more on the sale of bicycling accessories. Beginning in 1992, Trek assembled helmets at a new plant in Oconomowoc, Wisconsin, out of parts purchased from other companies. By 1993 the plant was making helmets at a rate of about half a million a year, double its total from 1992. Trek also launched a small line of tandem bikes in 1992. Although a relatively small market, the tandem bikes proved popular among family fitness buffs.

In 1993 Trek acquired the Gary Fisher Mountain Bike Company, the company founded by and named for the originator of the mountain bike. Gary Fisher's sales increased tenfold in its first year as part of the growing Trek empire, from $2 million to $20 million. Altogether, company sales reached $230 million for 1993, a $20 million increase from the previous year. That modest increase was impressive considering that it came during a period so difficult for bike makers that it saw longtime industry giant Schwinn sink into bankruptcy. Having passed competitors Specialized and Cannondale, Trek was now the clear market leader in specialty bike shop sales. By this time, exports generated $80 million of Trek's sales, and the company maintained seven overseas distribution operations—one in Japan and the other six in Europe.

Trek passed the $250 million mark in sales in 1994. By that time, the company was manufacturing 65 different models in its Wisconsin plants, including road bike, mountain bike, hybrid, and tandem styles. Trek expanded its children's bicycle business that year with the introduction of a line called Trek Kids. A number of major developments took place at Trek in 1995. That year, the company opened a new state-of-the-art manufacturing facility in Whitewater, Wisconsin. The Whitewater plant, capable of producing 3,000 bicycles a day, dwarfed the company's other factories.

### Acquisitions in the Mid-1990s

Trek also bought out two smaller niche-market competitors in 1995—Bontrager Bicycles, based in Santa Cruz, California; and Klein Bicycles of Chehalis, Washington. Those companies' plants remained in operation after the purchases. On top of those additions, Trek also signed a ten-year licensing deal with bicycle-racing superstar Greg LeMond to use his name on a line of road bikes. Additionally, the company introduced a new line of mountain bikes featuring an innovative Y-shaped frame. Trek's Y-frame received an "Outstanding Design and Engineering Award" from *Popular Mechanics* magazine, and the U.S. Secret Service even bought a few Y-frame bikes for patrolling the grounds of the White House.

Largely on the continuing strength of mountain bike sales, Trek's revenue grew to $327 million in 1995, a jump of nearly 19 percent. In early 1996, the company announced plans to add another 45,000 square feet to its Oconomowoc distribution center. It also announced its intention to build a distribution center in Atlanta to go with its existing centers in New Jersey and Southern California. Around the same time, Trek revealed that it was joining forces with Volkswagen of America to form a professional mountain bike team. The Trek/Volkswagen alliance went further yet, with the introduction of the Volkswagen Jetta Trek, a car that comes equipped with a mountain bike and rack.

In 1996, Trek also began planning a retail "superstore" on the west side of Madison, Wisconsin. The announcement did not sit particularly well with the specialty retailers already selling Trek bikes in the area. Although the company had dabbled in retail operations before—Trek has another retail store already operating in Madison, and flirted briefly with part ownership of a chain of stores in northern California—Burke insisted that it was not about to plunge into retail as a major part of their operation.

Meanwhile, Trek continued to beat out much of the competition in terms of quality and service, as it sought to solidify its position at the front of the high-end bicycle pack. Its ability to thrive during a period in which the bicycle industry as a whole was more or less stagnant suggests that Trek is poised to maintain its dominant position.

### Principal Subsidiaries

Fahrradhandel Gesellschaft GmbH (Austria); Bikeurope BV (Netherlands); Trek Denmark; Trek Bicycle GmbH (Germany); Trek Japan; Bike USA S.L. (Spain); Trek Fahrrad AG (Switzerland); Trek UK.

### Principal Operating Units

Klein Bicycle Corporation; Greg LeMond Bicycles; Fisher Bicycle; Bontrager; Matrix.

### Further Reading

Fauber, John, "Riding a Profitable Cycle," *Milwaukee Journal,* September 15, 1991.
——. "Riding Up in a Down Market," *Milwaukee Journal,* October 24, 1993.
Gribble, Roger A., "Trek Builds Worldwide Reputation," *Wisconsin State Journal,* February 14, 1993.
Holley, Paul, "Trek Bicycle Plans Addition in Oconomowoc," *Business Journal of Milwaukee,* February 3, 1996, p. 4.
Ivey, Mike, "Trek Cycles to the Top," (Madison, Wis.) *Capital Times,* March 29, 1996, p. C1.
Schubert, John, "Trek Is Going Strong," *Bicycling,* March 1984, p. 137.
"Trek Bicycle Corporation Reinvents the Wheel," Waterloo, Wis.: Trek Bicycle Corporation, 1995.

—Robert R. Jacobson

**Union Bank**

# Union Bank of California

350 California Street
San Francisco, California 94104
U.S.A.
(415) 705-7000
Fax: (415) 705-7335

*Public Subsidiary of Bank of Tokyo Ltd.*
*Incorporated:* 1883
*Employees:* 6,923
*Total Assets:* $16 billion
*Stock Exchanges:* NASDAQ
*SICs:* 6022 State Commercial Banks

In late 1995, it was announced that Union Bank of San Francisco planned to merge with the Bank of California in order to form the largest foreign-owned bank in the United States. The merger was brought about by the merger of the Bank of Tokyo Ltd., which owns Union Bank, and Mitsubishi Bank Ltd., which owns the Bank of California. The combination of Union Bank and the Bank of California creates a company whose share of the financial services market will be the fourth largest in the state of California. Union Bank of California offers numerous customer services, including ATM/Debit Cards, home mortgages, supermarket branches, real estate financing, asset-based finance and leasing, import/export financing, electronic letters of credit, trust and money management, and many, many more.

### Early History of Union Bank of San Francisco

The founder of Union Bank, Kaspare Cohn, was a highly successful businessman in the wool-growing industry in the state of California. During the late 19th century and early years of the 20th century, California was still a pastoral state, with huge tracts of land upon which cattle and sheep used to graze. During one period of the state's history, over seven million sheep roamed the California landscape. In his capacity as a wool merchant, Kaspare Cohn worked with Basque shepherds who supplied him with the wool for his business. Since these shepherds tended their sheep far from the city of Los Angeles, they were naturally inclined to ask Cohn, with whom they had developed a close working relationship, to safeguard the proceeds of their wool sales until there came a time when the money was needed. Occasionally, when one shepherd needed an advance to help him during a financially difficult time, or another needed credit to improve or add to his flock of sheep, Cohn would provide the necessary funds.

When the California Banking Department became aware that Cohn was functioning like his own bank, namely, accepting deposits from customers and arranging loans, the state authorities gave him the choice of either formalizing his activities by creating a bank or desisting from any further financial transactions. Cohn, already a wealthy man from his various investments in land and vineyards, decided that he had all the contacts necessary to establish and organize a bank. In 1914, he founded the Kaspare Cohn Commercial & Savings Bank. Some of the more important decisions Cohn made while serving as president of the bank included the financing of the San Gabriel Light & Power Company, and another small natural gas company that ultimately became part of Pacific Lighting Corporation.

Kaspare Cohn died in 1916 and was followed by Ben Meyer as president of the bank. Just before America's entry into World War I, the city of Los Angeles and the state of California were starting their long period of growth and development. Businesses, restaurants, and civic organizations were being created all over the state, and many of these enterprises were founded by people who had just arrived. The search for capital was at an all time high, yet risks were understandably great, and the banking community was conservative in its loan policies. A new bank like Kaspare Cohn Commercial & Savings Bank saw an opportunity to manage customer deposits by providing exceptional service. In addition, under the direction of Meyer, the bank began to garner a reputation as an astute lender. Meyer had an uncanny ability to provide loans to those entrepreneurs who not only were successful in their business endeavors, but were also able to promote the development of the city of Los Angeles.

In 1918, the name of the bank was changed to Union Bank & Trust Company. In 1922, the bank was growing at such a fast

## Company Perspectives:

*At Union Bank, we are building on our strengths. We appreciate our customers' business and work hard to maintain their loyalty. We believe that we stand out from our competitors because of our highly professional staff and superior service.*

rate that it opened a new headquarters on Eighth and Hill Streets and, just five years later, the bank's continued growth required an enlargement and significant improvement of these facilities. Much of the bank's business during this time was based on the civic leadership and personal qualities of Ben Meyer. As president of Cedar Hospital, Meyer visited the hospital every morning, greeting both staff and patients. While attending a ballet one evening at the Hollywood Bowl, Meyer discovered that the performance was in danger of being canceled since the stagehands had not been paid their wages. Meyer went backstage, presented the stagehands with a personal check for what they were owed, and the show was performed.

During the entire decade of the 1920s, Meyer presided over Union Bank's period of uninhibited growth. Deposits were increasing, the loan department was successful in its choice of entrepreneurs, and assets continued to rise at an astounding rate. Like every bank across the nation, however, Union Bank was affected by the stock market crash of 1929. Yet the bank survived the crash and the worst of the Great Depression. After Franklin Delano Roosevelt's Bank Holiday Proclamation in 1933, Union Bank was one of the banks allowed to reopen for business. The deft management of the bank's assets and business activities during this time was largely due to the talent of Ben Meyer.

### Expanded Services in the 1940s, 1950s, and 1960s

The early 1940s were disruptive for the entire United States since men of all ages were involved in the military conflicts of World War II. Yet even below normal staff levels, Union Bank continued to expand its services and extend its asset base. The bank was the first bank throughout the entire western part of United States to implement a program known as "bank-by-mail service." This program involved free postage both ways for customers doing banking business. Since the bank had a policy of not opening branch offices, the nearby mailbox was a highly successful substitute. Union Bank was also one of the first banks throughout the western United States to provide its customers with "lock-box banking," a new development for collecting payments. During the latter part of the decade, Union Bank's slogan became, "The Bank of Personal Service."

Ben Meyer retired in 1950, and Herman Hahn, an executive with 20 years service in Union Bank, became president. Hahn was an energetic leader and active in many civic groups in the Los Angeles area. Within the bank, he had built a reputation for his ability to structure complex loans and had thereby brought a good deal of visibility to the loan department. Unfortunately, Hahn unexpectedly died in 1954, and the bank was forced to

look for a successor. Meyer came out of retirement to temporarily assume the responsibilities of president, as the bank's board of directors searched for a new candidate. In 1957, the bank appointed Harry J. Volk to serve as president. Volk brought with him extensive experience from the insurance industry, having left a job at The Prudential Insurance Company to accept the presidency at Union Bank. Two months following Volk's appointment, Ben Meyer died.

Soon after Volk became president, he assembled his staff and members of the bank's board of directors to discuss the changes in the banking industry and how Union Bank should respond to the challenges ahead. The overwhelming response was that the bank had to take advantage of as many growth opportunities as possible. As a result, management decided to expand its presence throughout the state of California, but rather than imitate the branch banking system of most retail banks, Union Bank decided to organize semi-autonomous offices staffed with senior bank officers that would provide all the services normally available at the bank's headquarters on Eighth and Hill Streets in San Francisco. The bank adopted the phrase, "Regional Banking," in order to describe this comprehensive, yet highly innovative, banking system.

Over the next decade, Union Bank opened 16 regional head offices, including facilities in major areas such as Beverly Hills, Sacramento, and San Diego. Along with its development of regional offices, Union Bank acquired Occidental Bank, located in the heart of the San Fernando Valley. This was Union Bank's first acquisition. While concentrating on expanding geographically, the bank also initiated new, and highly creative, customer services. The bank was the first financial institution to calculate a daily compounded interest rate on individual savings accounts, the first to introduce savings statements for customers that were computer generated, and the first to introduce original techniques for interim construction financing.

### A New Concept in Banking

The year 1967 was one of the most important years in the history of Union Bank. The bank was the first major bank in the United States to form and establish a one-bank holding company. This new concept in banking completely transformed the banking industry. The holding company, Union Bancorp (subsequently changed to Unionamerica, Inc. in 1969) was formed to assume the ownership of Union Bank and to create new opportunities for expanding into diversified areas of financial services. The day after the formation of the bank holding company, Union Bank acquired one of the largest mortgage firms in the United States, Western Mortgage Corporation.

When the Bank Holding Company Act was passed in 1970, describing strict limitations on the activities of bank holding companies, and requiring that some of these activities be divested under the Bank Holding Company Act, Unionamerica changed its name back to Union Bancorp, and reorganized its operations, including the operations of all its subsidiaries. The company's new headquarters on Bunker Hill were occupied by this time, and new acquisitions of banks were made in Oakland, San Francisco, Palo Alto, and Long Beach. By 1972, the bank's deposits in its Northern California regional office were greater than those of the entire bank. It was during this period that the bank entered the field of international banking and opened offices in Rio de Janeiro, Tokyo, and London.

### Ownership by the Bank of Tokyo

The late 1970s, and the entire decade of the 1980s, were highly profitable years for the bank. Under astute management, the bank continued to improve upon its already-attractive customer services. Most important, however, the bank continued to expand throughout the state. Not content with regional offices anymore, management decided to go into branch banking. By the mid-1980s, Union Bank had an extensive network of branch locations up and down the coast of California. One of the surprises within the state banking industry occurred when the Bank of Tokyo, a Japanese-based bank holding company, purchased Union Bank in October of 1988. Although Union Bank was performing admirably, the acquisition by the Bank of Tokyo signaled that the bank's board of directors was willing to use the resources of its Japanese parent to grow even larger.

Under the direction of the Bank of Tokyo, Union Bank continued its expansion program, and the result was an impressive increase in the assets of the bank. By the mid-1990s, assets had grown to approximately $18 billion. In addition to its ever-increasing asset base, however, the bank built its branch network to include a total of over 200 offices in the state. Union Bank was widely regarded as one of the financial institutions with the best customer services on the west coast.

### Merger with the Bank of California in 1996

In 1995, the Bank of Tokyo and Mitsubishi Bank Ltd., also a Japanese-based bank holding company, agreed to merge in order to create the world's largest bank. The two financial titans arranged to established a private bank whose assets totaled approximately $820 billion. At the same time, the Bank of Tokyo and Mitsubishi Bank Ltd., agreed to merge their two most prominent subsidiaries, Union Bank and the Bank of California, and call it Union Bank of California. The Bank of California was less than half the size of Union Bank, with only $7 million in assets and 46 branch offices in Washington, Oregon, and California. Effective April 1, 1996, the merger between the two subsidiaries forms the fourth-largest bank in the state of California, with over $25 billion in assets. The combined resources of Union Bank and the Bank of California meant improved services in such areas as commercial markets, specialized lending, trust services, private banking, treasury services, retail markets, and international banking.

Union Bank of California will continue a number of the more important strategies management at Union Bank was working on at the time of the merger. Union Bank had a long-established policy of providing support services to individual entrepreneurs and businesses from Asia and the Pacific Rim that wanted to establish themselves in the United States. At the time of the merger, Union Bank was helping over 1,200 Japanese corporations with their operations in California. Union Bank of California plans to continue assisting these business pioneers by offering such services as cash management, pension plans, investment products, wire transfers, expedited loan approvals, and general financial advice. Another policy likely to continue at Union Bank of California is the bank's commitment to community involvement. In the past, Union Bank has sponsored 5K runs for charity, funded the construction of low-income family dwellings in Los Angeles, and contributed $150,000 to the brand new San Francisco Main Library.

The merger between Union Bank and the Bank of California has provided a wider range of financial services, including trust and investment services, retail banking, private banking, business banking, and international banking. One of the top 25 banks in the United States in terms of total assets, Union Bank of California will serve as a key ingredient in the success of its Japanese parent institution.

### Principal Subsidiaries

Bankers Commercial Corporation; Cal First Properties, Inc.; SBS Realty Inc.; Stanco Properties, Inc.; U.B. Equities, Inc.; UB Investment Services, Inc.; UB Leasing, Inc.; UB Mortgage Corporation; Union Bank Realty Company; Union Commercial Funding Corporation; Union Venture Corporation; and Unionbanc Leasing Corporation.

### Further Reading

Clark, Don, "Union Bank to Buy Bank of California as Parents Merge," *The Wall Street Journal,* September 29, 1995, p. A7(E).
Crockett, Barton, "Bank of California, Union Bank Put Merger Savings at $90 Million," *American Banker,* September 29, 1995, p. 4.
——, "Japanese Giants' California Jewels Are Seen as Takeover Target," *American Banker,* August 28, 1995, p. 4.
"Japanese Megamerger to Create California Giant," *American Banker,* May 30, 1995, p. 26.
Kraus, James, R., "Japan Likely to Create the Biggest Foreign-Owned Bank in the U.S.," *American Banker,* March 30, 1995, p. 1.
Monahan, Julie, "Union Bank of California Plans to Speed New Accounts Using the Local Area Net," *American Banker,* March 22, 1995, pp. 10A–11A.
Pesek, Jr., William, "Union Bank Rings up Retail Profits with Phone-Based System," *American Banker,* May 24, 1993, p. 8A.
"Union Bank Purchase of Branches Approved," *American Banker,* May 29, 1992, p. 8.
Volk, Harry J., *Union Bank,* Newcomen Society: New York, 1974.

—Thomas Derdak

# United Dominion

# United Dominion Industries Limited

**2300 One First Union Center**
**Charlotte, North Carolina 28202-6039**
**U.S.A.**
**(704) 347-6800**
**Fax: (704) 347-6900**

*Public Company*
*Incorporated:* 1882 as Dominion Bridge Company Ltd.
*Employees:* 10,666
*Sales:* $1.81 billion (1995)
*Stock Exchanges:* New York Montreal Toronto
*SICs:* 3441 Fabricated Structural Metal; 3599 Industrial
Machinery, Not Elsewhere Classified; 3569 General
Industrial Machinery, Not Elsewhere Classified; 3541
Machine Tools—Metal Cutting Types

United Dominion Industries Limited once provided extensive manufacturing, engineering, and construction services to customers around the globe, but in the mid-1990s the company resolved to focus its vast resources on the design and sale of proprietary engineered products for industrial and construction customers. With 60 primary operating locations selling to 120 countries, United Dominion divided its operations into two principal business segments: Industrial Products and Building Products. Industrial products included market leaders BOMAG/HYPAC (compaction equipment for asphalt, soil, and sanitary landfills); Fenn Manufacturing (new and overhauled aerospace parts and industrial equipment); Flair (industrial equipment and filters to dehydrate, filter, and purify air); the Marley companies and Weil-McLain (engineered equipment and services for heat exchange, heating applications, and fluid handling including cast iron boilers, submersible pumps, and water cooling towers); and Waukesha Cherry-Burrell (pumps and food processing equipment). The Building Products division manufactured an array of mostly nonresidential construction products, produced by Ceco/Windsor (commercial, industrial, and residential doors); Robertson (architectural panels for roofs and walls); Serco (loading dock equipment); and Varco-Pruden (pre-engineered metal building systems).

## United Dominion's Roots, 1882–1950s

United Dominion was originally incorporated in 1882 as Dominion Bridge Company, Limited, and reincorporated in 1912 under the Companies Act of Canada. As the name suggested, Dominion Bridge was primarily engaged in building bridges, specifically the bridges required for the completion of the 2,600-mile Canadian transcontinental railroad. From these beginnings, the company diversified in the early 1900s into more of a general engineering firm, capable of handling most types of structural steel work. By the beginning of the 1930s, Dominion Bridge had either formed or acquired several companies. Among these were the National Bridge Company of Canada, Ltd., founded in 1910; Riverside Iron Works, Ltd., of which Dominion Bridge acquired controlling interest in 1928; and Dominion Hoist & Shovel Co., a joint venture with American Hoist & Derrick Co., which was launched in 1931.

By 1934 Dominion Bridge's plants had an annual capacity of 200,000 tons of bridge and structural work. In addition to steel and iron bridges, the company was producing boilers and electric- and hand-powered traveling cranes, among other things. The company's headquarters and main works were located in Lachine, Quebec, where it had connections with important railways including the Canadian Pacific. Branches were also operating in Ottawa, Winnipeg, and Toronto, as were fabricating plants in Vancouver, Amherst (Nova Scotia), and Calgary. The company remained primarily a structural steelmaker and construction outfit, with nearly all of its properties located in Canada, through the first half of the 20th century. In fact, Dominion Bridge quickly became Canada's largest steel distributor, as well as its leading structural steel company.

## Change and Growth, 1960s and 1970s

In 1961 Dominion Bridge acquired the Runnymede Construction Co. and all of its assets. That year, the company also absorbed its former subsidiaries Manitoba Bridge and Engineering Works Ltd. (acquired in 1930), and Manitoba Rolling Mill

499

**Company Perspectives:**

*Vision '99 is a strategic plan designed to take United Dominion to a new growth plateau. Its strategies: increase profitability through strategic acquisitions; pursue international growth; improve margins through intensive operating focus; capitalize on natural synergies of building products mosaic; accelerate internal development of engineered products.*

Ltd. Another of the company's subsidiaries, the majority-owned Dominion Engineering Works Ltd., was sold to Canadian General Electric Co. in 1962, while in 1964 its Robb Engineering Works subsidiary was merged into the company. Another acquisition, the Crane division of Provincial Engineering Ltd., was finalized in 1967.

As the 1960s drew to a close, a long-term decision was made at Dominion Bridge's executive offices to move the company— by this time based in Montreal and controlled by Algoma Steel (with 43 percent ownership)—into the United States. Management determined that the company had to diversify beyond the structural steel market, and at the same time escape the uncertainties associated with both the capital goods market and labor situation in Canada. Over the next several years, many of the company's Canadian holdings were sold to raise money for the purchase of U.S. firms. This move across the border was spearheaded by Kenneth Barclay, then vice-president of finance who became CEO a few years later. A ten-year plan was put into effect, with the goal of reaching $1 billion in sales by the end of the 1970s.

Dominion Bridge's first significant incursion into the United States was the 1971 acquisition of Varco-Pruden, Inc., of Pine Bluff, Arkansas, by Dominion Bridge's U.S. subsidiary, Dombrico, Inc. Varco-Pruden, which made pre-engineered metal buildings, was purchased from Fuqua Industries, Inc., and had annual sales of about $25 million.

Barclay set up shop in Hanover, New Hampshire, which served as a base of operations for Dominion Bridge's U.S. expansion program. Meanwhile, the acquisitions continued in rapid succession: in 1973, the Dombrico subsidiary purchased Priggen Steel Building Co. of Holbrook, Massachusetts; two other companies (Wiley Manufacturing Co., a maker of vehicular tunnel tubes, and Clyde Iron Works, which produced Whirley cranes) were also purchased from Microdot Inc. that year. When he became chief executive the following year, Barclay gradually began to relocate the company's corporate headquarters to Hanover rather than return to Montreal.

A year later in 1975, another shopping spree commenced, including Morgan Engineering Co., an industrial crane manufacturer based in Alliance, Ohio, purchased from United Industrial Syndicate; Cherry-Burrell, a maker of processing and packaging equipment, purchased from Paxall, Inc.; the Indianapolis-based Insley Manufacturing Co.; and Chicago's DESA Industries, which manufactured construction equipment like chain

saws, power tools, and excavating machines. The purchases were once again made by the company's U.S. subsidiary, which by this time had been renamed AMCA International Corporation. Between 1970 and 1978, Dominion Bridge purchased and absorbed a total of 12 businesses. During roughly the same period, ten major plants and properties that were no longer in the company's long-term plan were sold, as was its $12 million interest in Canadian General Electric, to raise money for Barclay's acquisition program.

As a result of the extensive acquisition program, Dominion Bridge's sales grew from $168 million in 1970 to $521 million by 1977. That same year, Barclay added chairman of the board to his list of titles. His mentor during this period of diversification and expansion was Royal Little, who had orchestrated a similar process at Textron Inc. over a decade earlier. Little, along with his partner Lon Casler, sought out companies for Dominion Bridge to consider as potential acquisition targets. Another company whose agenda for growth had been guided by Little was Amtel, Inc., which was founded by Little after he left Textron. In 1978 Dominion Bridge acquired Amtel, a diversified steel products and energy services company, for $80 million. Amtel, which had sales of over $250 million, was the company's most important acquisition of the decade, with 33 percent of Dominion Bridge's $886 million in sales for 1978 contributed by Amtel.

Yet the company didn't stop its quest for growth after the Amtel purchase. In 1979, Dominion Bridge formed a subsidiary to explore business possibilities in the Far East. The same year the company geared up for another major acquisition by selling a fabricating facility in Quebec and various debt issues to raise $200 million in cash in its bid for control of the Cleveland-based Warner and Swasey Co., only to be narrowly beaten by the Bendix Corporation.

### A Second Ten-Year Plan and a New Name, 1980–89

In 1980 Dominion Bridge embarked on a second ten-year plan, this time to reach sales of $5 billion by 1989. The first move toward the new goal was the $140 million acquisition of the Koehring Company, a Wisconsin-based manufacturer of construction equipment, which increased Dominion's sales by about 50 percent. In the long run, however, the acquisitions of the 1980s did not achieve the unqualified success of those of the 1970s. In order to simplify, in 1981 Dominion Bridge changed its name to a slight variation of its U.S. subsidiary and officially became AMCA International Ltd.

The newly renamed company soon had to deal with the souring of the 1982 purchase of Giddings & Lewis Inc., a Wisconsin machine tool company with sales of nearly $400 million. AMCA paid $310 million for Giddings, which at the time was the fifth-largest company in its industry. Although Giddings & Lewis had always been a strong performer compared to other machine tool operations, it didn't survive the beating the entire American tool industry took in the 1980s, mainly at the hands of competitors from Germany and Asia. By 1987, AMCA was ready to write off much of its investment in Giddings, and the company was spun off to the public two years later.

AMCA purchased Chemetron Process Equipment, Inc., a subsidiary of Allegheny International, Inc., in 1983. A manufacturer of food and chemical processing equipment, Chemetron was integrated into AMCA's Cherry-Burrell division. The following year, the company's Dominion Bridge operating unit shared a contract with a British firm for the construction of a special coal harbor in Indonesia, at the island of Sumatra's southernmost point. By 1985 AMCA had sales of $1.6 billion, but overall the company was losing money. Between 1983 and 1987 AMCA lost $285 million, including the write-off for Giddings & Lewis. William Holland took over as president and CEO in 1986, with Barclay continuing as chairman.

Holland embarked on a mission to pare the company back down to its core engineering-related businesses, eliminating many of the other enterprises that held the company's earnings down. This restructuring, AMCA announced, would amount to some $500 million, or about one-third of the company's total assets. Yet unable to find a buyer for the company's construction products business, Holland ended up closing it down and taking a write-off that erased 20 percent of AMCA's revenue for 1986. By this time, Canadian Pacific had bought out Algoma Steel's 34.5 percent holding in AMCA, bringing its own interest in the company to just over 50 percent.

In 1987 Holland became chairman in addition to his duties as CEO, with Barclay remaining a director. That year AMCA reported a net loss of $188 million on sales of $974 million, but the company finally rebounded to profitability in 1988 with $25 million in earnings on sales of nearly $1.3 billion. The company had also succeeded in raising $261 million in 1988 through two offerings of common stock. Another important development was the reconsolidation of BOMAG, the company's West German subsidiary and a world leader in landfill compaction equipment. AMCA had been trying unsuccessfully to sell BOMAG since 1986. The failure to find a buyer, however, proved fortunate, as BOMAG's business improved significantly in 1989, bringing in $240 million in sales and a record $25 million in pretax profits.

### Another Name Change and a Five-Year Plan, 1990–95

Eager to shake things up after a decade of disappointments, AMCA moved its headquarters from Hanover to Charlotte, North Carolina, in 1989. Moreover, the company succeeded in going public with its shares in Giddings & Lewis, which had accounted for $168 million of the company's sales the year before. By 1990 the company underwent another name change to United Dominion Industries in homage to its strongest subsidiary. A new five-year plan was initiated, whose goals included doubling the company's 1989 net income, producing at least a 15 percent after-tax return on common equity, and keeping net debt at or below 30 percent of total capital. This was to be accomplished by concentrating on fewer and larger businesses that were leaders in their markets, or which served a very specific market niche.

For 1990 United Dominion earned $26 million on sales of $1.4 billion and returned to its acquisition mode. Among its purchases was AEP-Span, a producer and distributor of architectural metal roofing and composite wall products for nonresi-

dential construction uses. In 1991 United Dominion combined the operations of units Varco-Pruden and Stran (purchased in 1983), which both produced pre-engineered building systems and acquired the Blaine Construction Company. Although sales dropped off a bit to $1.35 billion in 1991, net income actually increased, to $37 million. More acquisitions followed at the beginning of 1992. Most important among these was the Robertson-Ceco Corporation, which included Ceco Door and Robertson Building Products. Bredel Exploitatie B.V., a pump manufacturer in the Netherlands, was also acquired, prompting a jump in sales to $1.7 billion. Also contributing to the increase was Litwin Engineers & Constructors, whose sales grew by $200 million from the previous year.

In May 1992 United Dominion made an offering of 6.5 million shares of common stock (which reduced Canadian Pacific's ownership to 45.4 percent interest). At this time, the company announced a realignment of its management structure to decentralize decision-making and increase the autonomy of each business unit. Then, in one of Holland's more inspired moves, United Dominion agreed to purchase the Marley Co. from Kohlberg Kravis Roberts for $356 million, an acquisition that proved nearly priceless in the years to come.

At the beginning of 1994, United Dominion ended talks with the Manson Group of Montreal and instead moved to the Cedar Group Inc. of Conshohocken, Pennsylvania, selling an 85 percent stake in Dominion Bridge for less than $20 million, which was a sad end for the venerable subsidiary. That year also marked the appointment of Jan Ver Hagen, formerly vice-chairman of Emerson Electric, as United Dominion's new president and chief operating officer. Serco Doors, a loading dock manufacturer, was then purchased, and a stock offering of another three million shares in September was quickly snapped up by mostly Canadian investors. The public offering again lowered Canadian Pacific's ownership in United Dominion (to 41.2 percent), yet Canadian Pacific was immersed in a restructuring plan and was more concerned with its core assets.

Year-end 1994 brought United Dominion's sales to just short of $1.6 billion, with net income up by 56 percent to $62.1 million; the recently acquired Marley companies contributed 43 percent to these earnings. During the year, four more companies were purchased: Flair Corp. (air-drying and purification equipment and filters), McKee Door, Inc. (garage and rolling steel doors), Puriti S.A. de C.V. (a pump manufacturer from Mexico), and Davenport International (a European cooling tower company). On the international front, Varco-Pruden formed a joint venture (30 percent stake) with the Bao Steel Group of Shanghai and the International Steel Company of Taipei to build China's first pre-engineered metal manufacturing facility, and signed a licensing agreement with Dongbu Steel for manufacturing in South Korea. Marley Cooling Tower also established a joint venture in China, to produce fiberglass HVAC towers. International sales for 1994 reached 15 percent, a slight downturn from 1993, but rallied again in 1995 to 19 percent of United Dominion's revenues.

Though growth through acquisition seemed unabated, Ver Hagen and Holland had successfully reduced debt and increased sales to $1.8 billion and net income (by 26 percent) to $78.5 million in 1995. Unfortunately, much of the trimming came from the divestiture of the company's construction units Aneco, Blaine Construction, and JESCO, as well as the Litwin Companies. ''While these units are fundamentally good businesses,'' Holland announced at the time, ''they no longer fit our strategic focus on manufacturing proprietary engineered products.''

### Streamlined, Independent, and Ready for the Future, 1996–2000

United Dominion seemed to have regained the footing it had lost during the previous decade. By narrowing the focus of its growth to include the acquisition of only companies among the top handful in their specific markets, the potential for problems such as those experienced with Giddings & Lewis had been sharply reduced. Having pulled itself together during a period in which the manufacturing and building products industry wasn't particularly strong, United Dominion's future seemed secure for the late 1990s and beyond. Additionally, United Dominion was finally free of its former parent company, Canadian Pacific, which divested the remainder of its controlling interest in August and December of 1995. And while U.S. investors didn't generally associate United Dominion with its internationally known, top-notch subsidiaries like BOMAG, Marley, Varco-Pruden, and Waukesha Cherry-Burrell, a February 1996 stock offering of nearly 5.2 million shares was quickly picked up by mostly North American investors. With another five-year plan in place, United Dominion hoped to double earnings to $3.10 per share and raise revenues to $3 billion by the end of the decade.

### Principal Subsidiaries

AEP-Span; BOMAG; Ceco Door Products; Compaction America; Davenport International; Fenn Manufacturing Company; Flair Corp.; Marley Cooling Tower Company; Marley Electric Heating Company; Marley Pump Company; McKee Door, Inc.; Puriti S.A. de C.V.; Robertson Building Products; Varco-Pru-den Buildings; Waukesha Cherry-Burrell; Weil-McLain; Windsor Door Products.

### Further Reading

''Company Agrees to Sell 85% of Dominion Bridge Unit,'' *Wall Street Journal,* February 1, 1994, p. C21.
Cook, James, ''Crossing the Border,'' *Forbes,* November 15, 1977, pp. 85–88.
''Dominion Bridge Co.'s AMCA Unit Increases Stake in Amtel to 96%,'' *Wall Street Journal,* January 6, 1978, p. 18.
''Dominion Bridge Plans Growth,'' *New York Times,* August 12, 1980, p. D1.
''Dominion Bridge: Poised for a Big Buy,'' *Business Week,* September 24, 1979, pp. 73–77.
Freeman, Alan, ''AMCA Posts Loss of $178.5 Million for Fourth Quarter,'' *Wall Street Journal,* February 8, 1988, p. 41.
Greenberg, Larry M., ''United Dominion to Acquire Flair for $126 Million,'' *Wall Street Journal,* May 9, 1995, p. A14.
Litvak, I. A., and Maule, C. J., *The Canadian Multinationals,* Toronto: Butterworth & Co. Ltd., 1981, pp. 22, 34.
''Picking up the Pieces at United Dominion,'' *Business North Carolina,* January 1991, pp. 57–59.
Reingold, Jennifer, ''Haste Makes . . . ,'' *Financial World (FW),* April 25, 1995, pp. 38, 39, 42.
''United Dominion to Acquire Marley for $207 Million, and Assume Its Debt,'' *Wall Street Journal,* July 22, 1993, p. B4.
''Warner-Swasey Takeover Fight's Stakes Increased,'' *Wall Street Journal,* December 17, 1979, p. 4.
Weinberg, Neil, ''Staying Power,'' *Forbes,* August 14, 1995, pp. 96, 98.
Wessel, David, ''AMCA Will Shed Units Representing a Third of Sales,'' *Wall Street Journal,* July 22, 1986, p. 38.
Williams, Winston, ''A Giddings Takeover Likely,'' *New York Times,* July 12, 1982, p. D1.

—Robert R. Jacobson
Updated by Taryn Benbow-Pfalzgraf

# UNITRIN

## Unitrin Inc.

One East Wacker Drive
Chicago, Illinois 60601
U.S.A.
(312) 661-4600
Fax: (312) 661-4690

*Public Company*
*Founded:* 1990
*Employees:* 7,600
*Operating Revenues:* $1.45 billion (1995)
*Stock Exchanges:* NASDAQ
*SICs:* 6311 Life Insurance; 6331 Marine & Casualty
   Insurance; 6361 Title Insurance

Although Chicago-based Unitrin has only existed as a stand-alone company since 1990, when it was spun off from conglomerate Teledyne Inc., the firm has become a leader in the insurance industry, providing auto, casualty, property, life, and health policies to individuals and groups, as well as offering an array of consumer financial services. Rated by A. M. Best in the top 100 largest insurance providers in the United States, Unitrin's capital and surplus have placed it as high as No. 28 among its competitors. Unitrin's success in the home service market and consumer finance, coupled with a strong, conservative management, made it a major takeover target in the 1994. Yet Unitrin rallied to its own defense—adopting a poison pill strategy and repurchasing enough of its own stock to fend off takers then and in the future. Determined to maintain its independence, Unitrin not only retained control of its considerable assets but strengthened its bottom line at the same time.

### Teledyne Gives Birth to Unitrin, 1990

Unitrin was founded as a subsidiary of Teledyne Inc. Best known for the Water Pik dental aid and ubiquitous Shower Massage, Teledyne began business in 1960 as a semiconductor manufacturer. Before the decade was over, Teledyne began acquiring undervalued companies of various sizes; pursuing this strategy aggressively into the 1970s and 1980s, Teledyne be-

came one the most successful and recognized corporations in the United States under the leadership of legendary entrepreneur Henry E. Singleton.

By the late 1980s Singleton began to break up his extensive and increasingly unwieldy empire. In 1986 he spun off the Argonaut Group Inc., a worker's compensation insurance provider, with great success: Argonaut's original $20 per share stock appreciated 240 percent by 1990. Shortly before Unitrin's slated debut, Teledyne (with $4.6 billion in revenue for 1989) treated stockholders to a five-for-one stock split in March 1990. Believing Unitrin could duplicate Argonaut's good fortune, Singleton (who remained chairman of both new ventures) spun Unitrin off to shareholders in April 1990 at $31.25 per share, trading on NASDAQ. Beginning its independent corporate life as a holding company for several insurance carriers, Unitrin divided its business into three major categories: life and health insurance; property and casualty insurance; and consumer finance, which covered a variety of services including automobile and industrial loans.

### Unitrin's Insurance Divisions

Unitrin's life and health division comprised three large wholly owned subsidiaries: United Insurance Company of America, rated A + by A. M. Best; Union National Life Insurance Company, also rated A + by Best; and the Pyramid Life Insurance Company, rated A − by Best. In addition to its high industry ratings, Unitrin differentiated itself from a slew of health and life insurance carriers (which numbered about 1,800 in the United States by 1995) not by offering an unusual mix of products, but instead by providing typical policies with an unusual method of marketing these products. Life insurance policies were offered in standard increments of up to $250,000 for individuals and groups (such as employees of large companies and credit unions) in permanent and term policies; health insurance was sold to both individuals and groups on either a limited-benefit or major medical coverage basis with a maximum risk of $500,000 in any one calendar year.

Yet what drew many customers to Unitrin's insurance packages was the old-fashioned concept of selling services door-to-door with some 4,000 sales representatives (out of a total of 5,300 in the division), who visited middle- and lower-income suburban and rural communities. As a convenience, agents then returned monthly to pick up premium payments, omitting postal services and delays. Although there were two-and-a-half dozen competitors in the "home service" market, Unitrin carved out a comfortable niche in 26 states and the District of Columbia, and within five years this segment generated almost 80 percent of the life and health insurance division's premiums.

Unitrin's second major insurance segment in property and casualty policies covered automobiles and motorcycles, homes, watercraft, and commercial businesses from fire, theft, and other property damage. Worker's compensation policies were also available to small and medium-sized companies. The property/casualty division worked through five subsidiaries: Financial Indemnity Company, rated A+ by Best; the Milwaukee Insurance Companies (including Alpha Property & Casualty, Milwaukee Guardian, and Milwaukee Safeguard Insurance companies—all part of a 1995 merger), rated A−; Trinity Universal Insurance Company, rated A++; Union National Fire Insurance Company, rated A; and United Casualty Insurance Company of America (rated A+ by Best) with 1,700 divisional employees and approximately 15,000 independent agents across the nation. Premium sales were concentrated in the South (predominantly Louisiana, with six percent of the division's sales), Midwest (especially Illinois, Minnesota, and Wisconsin for a combined total of 19 percent), Texas (32 percent), and California (12 percent of premiums). Geographic hazards included hurricanes in the South (generally worse in the fall), windstorms, tornadoes, and flooding in the Midwest (in the spring), and fires in the West. Much like the weather, profitability in the casualty and property insurance companies tended to be cyclical and easily riven by pricing competition and a flooded marketplace.

Unitrin's consumer finance division, which conducted business through the Fireside Thrift Co., located in Newark, California, was chiefly involved in financing used automobiles from dealerships. Fireside also sold consumers personal loans using automobiles as collateral, and offered timely service and flexible terms to win clients over its competition. Fireside's activities were financed by thrift investment certificates (ranging from 31 days to five years), money market accounts, and IRAs, products routinely offered by banks, savings and loans, and other industrial loan providers.

### Dollars and Cents: The 1990s

Following its earlier success while still part of Teledyne, Inc., Unitrin posted sales of $1 billion from premiums and consumer finance loans in its first independent year. Total revenue was over $1.25 billion for 1991, with net income of $136 million. The following year, premiums and consumer finance services increased to $1.1 billion and total revenues to $1.36 billion, but net income fell to $123 million due to a one-time accounting charge of $40 million.

By 1993 the life and health insurance segment generated about half of Unitrin's revenues ($688 million), property and casualty brought in $570.8 million, and consumer finance $81.3 million. The following year (1994) consumer finance performed

better than its siblings, climbing more than 12 percent to $91.4 million, while property/casualty was up 10 percent to $575.6 million, and the life/health division fell to $667.6 million due to a lower sales volume, except in individual traditional life insurance, which increased in volume. Operating profits dropped for property/casualty, falling from 1993's $76 million to $65.5 million, but the other two segments saw healthy increases: consumer finance rose from 1993's $25.8 million to $31 million, and life/health reached $68.7 million from 1993's $54.5 million—all this despite a serious threat to the company's well-being by a hostile takeover attempt.

### Fighting off an Unwanted Suitor, 1994–95

Unitrin spent the second part of 1994 fending off a $2.6 billion takeover bid by American General Corp., an insurance carrier headquartered in Houston, whose business was very similar to its own. Though American General said it originally broached the subject of a merger to Unitrin's management in January 1994, the aggressor went public with its intentions in early June. Hoping to swallow Unitrin's home service business, American General was also attracted to Unitrin's $1.4 billion in excess capital and undervalued assets (major shares in Litton Industries Inc., Curtiss-Wright Corp., and Western Atlas Inc.) which were listed on Unitrin's books at cost rather than stock value. If the takeover succeeded, American General stood to gain combined assets of $50 billion with a customer base over eight million.

On June 26th Unitrin unequivocally rejected the $50.38 per share offer and adopted a poison pill defense. Despite American General's hints of sweetening the offer or paying with stock instead of cash (for shareholder tax purposes), Unitrin remained steadfast and initiated a stock buyback plan of ten million shares, or 19 percent of its stock (51.8 million shares outstanding), to placate frustrated shareholders and increase the board's controlling interest. American General then took Unitrin to court and argued that such a repurchase plan would prove harmful to shareholders of both companies, as Unitrin's board could effectively block any acquisition regardless of shareholders' best interests. A Delaware Chancery Court judge agreed and issued a restraining order against Unitrin's proposed stock buyback until September 27, 1994.

Having gained the advantage and still hoping Unitrin's board would reconsider, American General extended its merger offer from October through November 30th, then again to February 7th, 1995. Unitrin continued to resist, and on December 13th the Delaware Supreme Court overturned the lower court's injunction, freeing Unitrin to repurchase its stock. As the tumultuous 1994 ended, Unitrin's total revenues climbed to $1.37 billion, just slightly over the previous year's $1.36 billion. Yet the big news was in net income: 1993's figure of $95 million was surpassed by a whopping $148 million for 1994.

As Unitrin entered its fifth year of independence, the company continued buying back its stock to keep American General and other rumored suitors at bay. Unitrin's maneuvers paid off: American General's takeover bid quietly expired on February 7th and was not renewed. During the time Unitrin was facing off against American General, former parent Teledyne Inc. underwent a similar battle with WHX Corp., run by Ron LaBow, previously of junk bond haven Drexel Burnham Lambert. That two of Henry Single-ton's companies were waging a fierce battle for survival struck many Wall Streeters as the ultimate irony. Many analysts believed that it was only a matter of time before Singleton's other spin-off, the Argonaut Group Inc., became a takeover target.

### Staying Strong and Looking to the Future, the Late 1990s

The remainder of 1995 brought several highs for Unitrin, including an agreement between subsidiary Financial Indemnity Company and Allstate of California to market Unitrin automobile insurance policies throughout the state. In a move Unitrin's management found "too good a business fit to pass up," Uni-trin's wholly owned subsidiary, Dallas-based Trinity Universal Insurance Company, merged with the Milwaukee Insurance Group, Inc. ($186 million in 1994 for net premiums written), for $92.6 million in cash. Milwaukee Insurance, rated B + + at the time of acquisition due to some recent financial difficulties, nicely complemented Trinity's property and casualty operations (the only state in which the two companies were in direct competition was Illinois) and was a holding company of Milwaukee Mutual Insurance Company, a venerable family-owned business founded in 1917 to fill the needs of new auto owners and drivers.

By the end of 1995, Unitrin had bought back 8.7 million of its shares for $416 million, raising the total number of repur-chased shares from August 1994 to 13.5 million or $661 mil-lion, in hopes of preventing future hostile takeover attempts. Year-end total revenues were $1.45 billion ($649.7 million from the life and health division, $631.5 million from property/casualty, and $106.5 million from consumer finance). With over five million policies in force across the United States, $5 billion in assets, and a growing number of consumer finance clients (100,000 in 1995), Unitrin had proved its mettle to both the insurance industry and the enclaves of Wall Street.

### Principal Subsidiaries

Fireside Thrift Co.; Financial Indemnity Company; Milwaukee Insurance Group, Inc. (Alpha Property & Casualty Insurance Company, Milwaukee Guardian Insurance, Inc., and Milwau-kee Safeguard Insurance Company); Pyramid Life Insurance Company; Trinity Universal Insurance Company; Union Na-tional Fire Insurance Company; Union National Life Insurance Company; United Casualty Insurance Company of America; United Insurance Company of America (United Insurance's Home Service Division and Worksite Marketing Division).

### Further Reading

"American General Gains against Unitrin Buyback," *Wall Street Jour-nal,* October 14, 1994, p. A4.

Buckler, Arthur, and Scism, Leslie, "Unitrin Counters American Gen-eral on Takeover Bid," *Wall Street Journal,* August 5, 1994, pp. A2, A10.

"Divorce Singleton Style," *Forbes,* June 25, 1990, p. 142.

"Judge Temporarily Blocks Unitrin from Buying Back 19% of Stock," *Wall Street Journal,* August 29, 1994, p. B6.

Lazo, Shirley A., "Unitrin Increases Its Quarterly by 25%," *Barron's,* February 6, 1995, p. 37.

Mullins, Robert, "In Unitrin Deal, Milwaukee Insurance Chose Partner Carefully," *Business Journal,* July 15, 1995, pp. 2A, 3A.

Rees, David, "Events Swirling around Teledyne Intrigue Analysts," *Los Angeles Business Journal,* March 26, 1990, p. 9.

Scism, Leslie, "American General Corp. Seeks to Buy Life Insurance Unit of American Brands," *Wall Street Journal,* November 29, 1994, p. A3.

——, and Buckler, Arthur, "American General Makes Bid for In-surer," *Wall Street Journal,* August 4, 1994, p. A3.

——, and Steinmetz, Greg, "Famed Conglomerate Builder Singleton Plays a Key Role in Battle for Unitrin," *Wall Street Journal,* August 9, 1994, p. A3.

——, and Arthur Buckler, "Unitrin Clears Buyback of 19% of Stock; American General Files to Raise Its Stake," *Wall Street Journal,* August 15, 1994, pp. A2, A6.

Sloan, Allan, "Teledyne's Henry Singleton Finds Takeover Shoe on the Other Foot," *Washington Post,* January 24, 1995, p. D3.

Veverka, Mark, and Gornstein, Leslie, "How Insurer Plans to Battle for Its Life," *Crain's Chicago Business,* August 8, 1994, pp. 4, 45.

—Taryn Benbow-Pfalzgraf

# Value Line, Inc.

220 East 42nd Street
New York, New York 10017-5891
U.S.A.
(212) 907-1500
Fax: (212) 818-9748

*Public Company*
*Incorporated:* 1931 as Arnold Bernhard & Company
*Employees:* 375
*Sales:* $79 million (1995)
*Stock Exchanges:* NASDAQ
*SICs:* Miscellaneous Publishing; 7372 Prepackaged
   Software; 6282 Investment Advice; 6289 Security and
   Commodity Services, Not Elsewhere Classified

Value Line, Inc. is perhaps best known for publishing *The Value Line Investment Survey,* the most widely used independent investment service in the world. With more than 100,000 subscribers and approximately half a million readers, the company's flagship weekly periodical, which provides comprehensive information on more than 1,700 stocks, is generally considered to be the bible of Wall Street. Long known for its strong and consistent record, the 60-year-old information service is regarded by many as the world's best-performing financial newsletter. Since 1980, the *Investment Survey* has been ranked No. 1 by the *Hulbert Financial Digest.* Other publications bearing the venerable company name include the *Value Line Mutual Fund Survey,* which provides full-page profiles of more than 1,500 mutual funds, and the *Value Line No-Load Fund Advisor,* a monthly newsletter covering no- and low-load funds. The company also serves as an investment adviser for the Value Line Family of Mutual Funds, a diverse group of 15 investment companies, and manages investments for private and institutional clients, while also furnishing financial database information through various on-line computer services.

## Early History

Value Line was founded in 1931 by the legendary financier Arnold Bernhard. Following a brief stint as a reporter and playwright, the would be "Dean of Wall Street" made his entry into the business world as a trainee in the Railroad Department of Moody's Investment Service during the late 1920s. The neophyte investor, like the rest of the Wall Street community, was ill prepared for the disastrous events to come. The Great Crash of 1929 and the ensuing collapse in the early 1930s, however, proved to be the catalyst for his entrepreneurial drive.

Having realized that not even Moody's, one of the most respected sources of financial opinion in the world, had been able to predict the impending collapse of stock values to come, Bernhard concluded that what his investors needed was a standard of normal value that would signal when stocks were overvalued and when they were undervalued. Instead of accepting the conventional wisdom of the time, that the value of a stock is revealed completely in its market price, he began examining the correlation between the monthly price of stocks and such factors as annual earnings and book values over twenty-year periods.

Bernhard's new ideas, along with the continued decline in the market in the early 1930s, did not sit well with one of his clients who suffered heavy losses during the period and eventually brought suit against Moody's for allowing Bernhard to manage his account. In 1931, the young investment counselor was fired. The apparent catastrophe, though, proved to be a blessing: not only did many of his clients retain his services, but he now had the freedom and the time to work on his Ratings of Normal Value.

By 1935, Bernhard had worked out equations for 120 individual stocks, assigning each a rating based on the charting of prices and earnings over time. He bought a multilith press and printed 1,000 copies of the book, which he called the *Value Line Ratings of Normal Value,* setting the price at $200 each. "It was hard for me to realize how little the world would be interested," Bernhard said 50 years later in a speech before the Newsletter Association of America. His numerous calls to banks and other financial institutions resulted mostly in polite stares and only one sale, to a skeptical portfolio manager.

With an embarrassingly large inventory of 999 books in his office and much of his time and energy diverted from his investment counsel accounts, Bernhard was paid a visit by

Major L.L.B Angas, the publisher of an enormously influential financial newsletter. Although Angas refused to purchase a copy of the book, he agreed to review it in the forthcoming edition of his bulletin. A few days later, Angas made good on his promise, advising his readers that they "should own" a copy of the "young fellow's" book; however, the price had been lowered to $55. Not only was Bernhard's inventory reduced by nearly 75 percent overnight, but he received a bill for $800 from the Major to cover the cost of printing the bulletin in which the endorsement appeared. The recommendation, though, proved to be a worthy investment: 60 checks for $55 appeared on Bernhard's desk shortly after the publication of the newsletter.

The lesson Bernhard had learned from the crafty publisher would guide his future marketing strategy. Instead of relying merely on personal representation, Bernhard channelled his resources into print advertisements to build the circulation of his fledgling newsletter. He invested $70 in a two-week advertisement in *Barron's* for $5 samples of *The Value Line Ratings of Normal Value*. Although the two ads brought in only nine leads and a $45 initial return, follow-up letters that included more information about the ratings resulted in the sale of three books at $55 each. Once again, what appeared to be a setback turned out to be a blessing.

### Postwar Growth and Innovation

For the first decade, Bernhard's formula for rating stocks consisted of simply tracking a security's past price and earnings history and projecting that into the future by multiplying a percentage of the company's book value by a conservative multiple of anticipated earnings per share. This relatively simple equation underwent a significant revision with the hiring of Samuel Eisenstadt, who brought his extensive knowledge of statistics theory to the company upon his arrival in 1946. Among the more sophisticated measuring instruments he helped to introduce included the use of "multiple regression analysis"—the simultaneous comparison of a number of variables. The added complexity to Bernhard's basic formula did not, however, significantly improve the accuracy of the ratings. As Eisenstadt recalled in *The Wall Street Journal,* Value Line's predictive performance during this period was "ho-hum—just a little better than average."

The availability of computer technology in the 1960s enabled Bernhard and his chief statistician to add the missing variable to their formula. Using the computer's power to measure each stock's price and earning characteristics against the comparable characteristics of all other Value Line stocks, they developed what became known as a "cross-sectional" method of analysis. In April 1965, they introduced what would become

the hallmark of the Value Line rating system: the "timeliness" ranking, whereby all stocks in the survey receive a ranking of 1 to 5 based on the computer-aided analysis of several variables of financial strength and a prediction of investment suitability over the next twelve months. Despite widespread skepticism among mainline sources of financial opinion, the new methodology proved successful almost from the start. Value Line's team of statisticians noticed immediately that on average the top 100 stocks—those that received a Group 1 rating—performed better than their counterparts in other categories, rising more in strong markets and declining less in weak ones.

### Challenges of the 1970s

During the late 1960s and early 1970s, the stock market experienced a period a strong growth. Value Line fund managers, according to Tim Metz's profile in *The Wall Street Journal,* however, maintained a conservative outlook and were slow to react to the bullish market. When the company finally did take a more aggressive course, the market declined, causing some investors to lose money and confidence in the Value Line system.

A number of wide-ranging investigations by the Securities and Exchange Commission (SEC) provided other obstacles for the company during this period. In the late 1960s, the SEC accused Bernhard and another company official of taking fees in connection with two company funds without informing investors in the fund prospectus or remitting the funds. The agency also charged some company analysts of withholding information from Value Line subscribers and shareholders regarding their agreements to serve as financing or acquisition finders for companies they were following. Without admitting or denying the SEC charges, the defendants consented to a 1971 federal-court injunction against future securities-laws violations.

In 1974, new scandals emerged that threatened to further tarnish the esteemed Value Line reputation. A former editor was accused of accepting a $15,000 bribe from two brokers in 1972 in exchange for writing bullish recommendations on two selected stocks. The 1971 injunction and the charges against the editor generated a host of civil lawsuits. While Bernhard denied the charges, they remained a hindrance throughout the decade, costing the company more than $500,000 in out of court settlements.

### Recovery and Growth in the 1980s

Consistent with its proven ability to turn adversity into growth, Value Line did not fail to learn from its mistakes. By tightening investment standards and improving the methodology behind its stock rankings, the company succeeded in doubling subscriptions to the then $365-a-year *Value Line Investment Survey* between 1978 and 1983, while boosting annual revenues to approximately $40 million. Meanwhile, profits increased more than 80 percent, to $6.7 million, between 1980 and 1983. First, in an attempt to make its forecasts more objective by further removing the "human element," the company ended a three-year "experiment" that allowed the analysts' judgment factor to account for 20 percent of the weight in its stock rankings. The company also stopped its earlier practice of purchasing unregistered "letter stock" for which there was not yet a public market. In addition to boosting subscriptions, such policies contributed to the strong performance of the flagship Value Line Fund, which demonstrated average annual returns of nearly 33 percent between 1974 and 1981.

By 1983, the 375-employee firm had expanded its survey to include ratings on 1,700 stocks, while controlling $1.2 billion in assets through its six mutual funds. The success of the "timeliness" rankings, well publicized in such popular magazines as *Time* and *Newsweek,* contributed to the excitement surrounding Bernhard's decision to make a public offering of 19 percent of his company in April 1983. Widespread interest in new issues and stock investments in general at the time brought the selling price to $17 a share and helped the price to climb to a record high of $40 by the summer of 1984.

The company, aided by the more than $30 million brought in by the public offering, grew steadily during the latter part of the decade, boosting revenue to nearly $70 million by 1987, largely on the strength of the *Investment Survey*'s 30 percent to 35 percent operating margins. Although cautious with his approach to new ventures, Bernhard worked to expand the company by diversifying profitably into the money-management business, adding several new publications, and entering the investment software market.

In the midst of this period of expansion, though, the company also had to overcome a new challenge: a transition in leadership brought on by the death of its founder and leader, Arnold Bernhard. Although Bernhard's son, Van, who had worked for the firm for several years, seemed the probable successor, he declined the job, and his sister, Jean Buttner, who joined the company in 1982, was appointed CEO and given the task of leading the company through the challenges of a recessionary economy and a new era in technology. Although the company enjoyed record total revenue and profits during the first year of Buttner's tenure, it suffered from a general malaise in the investment market following the stock market crash of 1987 and the ensuing recession of the late 1980s. Value Line, like many other businesses in the field, saw its pattern of vibrant growth come to a halt at the close of the decade.

### The 1990s and Beyond

With the new decade came the start of market recovery and a concomitant increase in the *Investment Survey*'s circulation. In 1992, Value Line saw its revenue return to near-record levels and profits climb to an all-time high of $26 million. Despite the strong balance sheets, Buttner drew criticism for what *Business Week*'s Anthony Bianco described as an "autocratic" style of leadership that lowered employee morale. The company, long known for its ability to hold down costs and a forerunner of the downsizing trend, reduced its work force from approximately 425 to 325 during this period, largely through resignations and firings that some believed threatened the stability of the company.

Despite drawing heavy criticism from disgruntled former employees and the media for her management techniques, Buttner, who has been named one of the top 50 businesswomen by *Working Mother* magazine, led the company to three straight years of record earnings, building on the growth that led *Forbes*

magazine to name Value Line the best small company in America, based on return on equity. She is also credited with updating the company to the demands of the Information Age, initiating and expanding the "Value/Screen" electronic database/software service, which covers 1,600 stocks, and DataFile, the institutional equity database covering 5,200 U.S. and foreign companies.

A number of new publications and features have also been added to the *Value Line* fold during her tenure. The company has more than doubled its coverage of the market by providing investors with *The Value Line Investment Survey—Expanded Edition,* which reports on 1,800 stocks not included in the flagship publication. Moreover, it has added a separate 16-page newsletter called "Selection & Opinion," which highlights individual stocks, reports general market and interest-rate conditions, and offers three different model portfolios of 20 stocks to suit different types of investors. In 1993, the firm added mutual funds to its survey through the introduction of *The Value Line Mutual Fund Survey,* a biweekly publication that covers more than 2,000 funds. In 1995, the company also offered its first online service, negotiating a deal with CompuServe through which subscribers can access both *The Value Line Investment Survey* and *The Value Line Mutual Fund Survey* and can view individual company and industry reports. Whether or not Value Line can continue to hold its position as the top-rated investment newsletter may depend largely on its ability to adapt to the demands of the computer age.

### Principal Subsidiaries

Value Line Securities, Inc.; Vanderbilt Advertising Agency, Inc.; Compupower Corp. (99.9%); Value Line Publishing, Inc.

### Further Reading

Baldwin, William, "Paying the Piper," *Forbes,* October 19, 1987, p. 208.

Bianco, Anthony, "Value Line: Too Lean, Too Mean?" *Business Week,* March 16, 1992, pp. 104–106.

"Coming Out: A Top Stock Picker Goes Public," *Time,* April 25, 1993, p. 98.

Curran, John J., "Value Line's Winning Way," *Fortune,* April 18, 1983, pp. 131–132.

Hulbert, Mark, "Tweaking the Numbers," *Forbes,* February 13, 1995, p. 214.

"In Memoriam: Arnold Bernhard," Value Line, Inc., 1988.

Kahn, Virginia Munger, "Nice Try," *Financial World,* March 14, 1995, pp. 77–80.

Metz, Tim, "Better Days," *The Wall Street Journal,* January 14, 1981, pp. 1, 19.

——, "Value Line Plans to Sell 19% of Concern to Public for as Much as $34.2 Million," *The Wall Street Journal,* April 8, 1983, p. 13.

Miller, Annetta, and Spragins, Ellyn E., "Family Values," *Newsweek,* October 10, 1994, pp. 48–50.

Vartan, Vartanig G., "The Downturn at Value Line," *The New York Times,* August 28, 1995, p. D6.

Weiss, Gary, "Arnold Bernhard Is a Tough Act to Follow," *Business Week,* January 25, 1988, pp. 93–94.

—Jason Gallman

# Vans, Inc.

2095 Batavia
Orange, California 92665-3101
U.S.A.
(714) 974-7414
Fax: (714) 998-6564

*Public Company*
*Incorporated:* 1966 as Van Doren Rubber Co.
*Employees:* 1,621
*Sales:* $88 million (1995)
*Stock Exchanges:* NASDAQ
*SICs:* 3021 Rubber & Plastics Footwear; 5661 Shoe Stores

Vans, Inc. is a manufacturer and retailer of casual footwear in men's, women's, and children's styles. Vans also makes footwear for the specialty athletic market, leading the skateboard and BMX bicycle markets and holding a strong third place with its two-year-old line of snowboarding shoes. The majority of Vans' more than 60 styles of shoes, offered in the wide-ranging assortment of colors and patterns that has become the company's hallmark, are produced by third-party manufacturers in South Korea; however, the company maintains a 90,000-square-foot, state-of-the-art facility in Vista, California, which boasts a three-week order-to-delivery turnaround time.

In May 1995, Vans closed its larger Orange, California, plant, which brought the company a $37 million loss in restructuring and write-off charges on revenues of $88 million. The largest portion of Vans' sales are through the company's chain of 81 retail stores and factory outlets. Vans shoes are also sold through larger department and specialty store channels such as Nordstrom's, Sears, JC Penney, and Footlocker, and through independent distributors to more than 30 countries. Vans is led by Walter Schoenfeld, who founded Brittania Sportswear in 1971 and later sold that company to Levi Strauss in the early 1980s. In 1995 Schoenfeld's son, Gary Schoenfeld, joined the company as executive vice-president and CEO. Revenues for 1996 are expected to reach $118 million, with net earnings of $4 million.

## Birth of a California Style

Paul Van Doren gained experience manufacturing shoes on the East Coast in the early 1960s. By 1965, Van Doren had developed the idea to start up his own plant. But instead of selling his shoes to retailers, Van Doren decided to take on retailing activities as well and to sell the shoes he manufactured directly to the public.

Van Doren, together with partners Serge D'Elia, an investor based in Japan, and Gordy Lee, who also had shoe manufacturing experience, moved to Southern California, building a factory and opening a first 400-square-foot retail store in Anaheim in March 1966. The company was incorporated as the Van Doren Rubber Company, and Van Doren's shoes came to be known simply as Vans. Later, Van Doren's younger brother, James Van Doren, joined the company. Paul Van Doren and D'Elia owned the majority of the company; James Van Doren and Gordy Lee each were given a 10 percent stake.

As the company itself tells it, the opening of its first store was inauspicious. Vans offered three styles, priced from $2.49 to $4.99, but on the day the store opened for business, the company had only made display models. The store racks were filled with empty boxes. Nevertheless, 12 customers came into the store and chose the colors and styles they wanted. The customers were asked to come back in the afternoon, while Van Doren and Lee rushed to the factory to make their shoes. When the customers returned to pick up the shoes, Van Doren and Lee realized that they had neglected to have money available to make change. The customers were given the shoes and asked to return the next day to pay for them. All 12 customers did.

Over the next year, the company opened a new retail store almost every week. A pattern developed in which Paul Van Doren scouted locations on Monday, signed a lease on Tuesday, remodeled on Wednesday, added shoe racks on Thursday and displays on Friday, hired a store manager on Saturday, and trained staff on Sunday. Retail operations would generate the bulk of Van Doren's early sales; the stores also enabled the company to get close to its public. Complaints over the early design of the company's rubber soles, which featured a diamond pattern that cracked too easily along the ball of the outsole, led to the addition of vertical lines to the ball area. The new design was patented as Vans' waffle sole.

A new type of customer boosted the company's fortunes in the early 1970s. The skateboarding craze, an outgrowth of California's surfing culture, provided an opportunity for Van Doren to prove its flexibility. When skateboarders began requesting new colors and patterns, the company responded by offering the Era, a red-and-blue shoe designed by professional skateboarders. Vans quickly became the skateboard shoe of choice, beginning the company's long, and devoted, association with the sport. Many more color combinations and patterns were added in the 1970s. A new style, the slip-on, was introduced in 1979, and it became the rage of Southern California.

In 1976, ownership of the company was equalized among the four original partners, and James Van Doren was given control of the company's direction. The younger Van Doren set out to expand the company. He was helped by the latest sports craze sweeping California, the BMX bicycle: Vans became the shoe of choice among the young BMXers. But it was a movie that gave Vans a national market.

### From Dude to Dud in the 1980s

The 1982 hit film, ''Fast Times at Ridgemont High,'' featured the California surfer dude Jeff Spicoli, played by Sean Penn, wearing a pair of Vans checkerboard slip-ons. The film made a star of Penn and launched Vans nationwide, bringing the company's shoes into department stores and independent retailers. With sales skyrocketing, James Van Doren boosted production capacity, moving the company to a new 175,000-square-foot plant in Orange, California in 1984 and raising the number of employees to more than 1,000. The Vans slip-on craze spawned a variety of licensing agreements, including items such as sunglasses and notebooks. Van Doren also pushed the company deeper into specialty sports footwear, developing baseball, football, umpiring, basketball, soccer, wrestling, boxing, and skydiving shoes. Most companies had already begun to move manufacturing to Asia, where labor costs were lower and environmental regulations were less restrictive, but Vans remained dedicated to domestic production, while expanding product offerings to include widths from EEEE to AAAA.

Faced with high labor costs, absorbing expansion costs, and the expense of maintaining the breadth and depth of its line, Van Doren was soon hit by a flood of competitors selling cheap imitations and knockoffs. In response, Van Doren was forced to drop its prices below manufacturing costs. Adding to the company's troubles was a 1984 raid by federal immigration officials, which resulted in the arrest of nearly 150 suspected illegal workers. And then the bottom dropped out of the slip-on craze.

Over 21 months, Van Doren lost some $3.6 million, building up a total debt of $12 million. When the company's bank demanded payment on a $6.7 million note in 1984, the company was forced to declare bankruptcy. Conditions for its Chapter 11 bankruptcy reorganization called for the ouster of James Van Doren. Paul Van Doren returned to lead the company out of bankruptcy, which was accomplished in 1986.

### From Leveraged Buyout to Initial Public Offering

Demand for Vans shoes continued to be strong and, by 1987, with two million pairs of shoes manufactured at its Orange plant bringing in $50 million in sales, Van Doren returned to profitability. International sales, particularly to Mexico and Europe, were also growing strongly, accounting for 10 percent of company sales. A third of the company's business went to custom-designed shoes. In a time when almost all of the major sneaker makers had shifted production to South Korea, Vans clung to its tradition of domestic production, boasting order-to-delivery times for its catalogue items of five days, compared with an industry average of nine months.

In 1988, Paul Van Doren, explaining that he was tired of overseeing the company's day-to-day operations, agreed to sell the company in a leveraged buyout organized by the San Francisco-based venture banking firm McCown De Leeuw & Co. The leveraged buyout, worth $74.4 million including the assumption of existing liabilities, left Paul Van Doren in place as chairman and Gordy Lee as vice-chairman. Richard Leeuwenberg, formerly with Boise Cascade Corp., was brought in as president and CEO for the company, now renamed Vans, Inc.

In 1989, raids by U.S. and Mexican officials shut down several counterfeit operations that had flooded the market with cheap Vans imitations. Despite losses to counterfeits, Vans sales topped $70 million in 1990, with international sales rising to 25 percent of sales, and special orders continuing to play a strong role in revenues. The following year, Vans went public, with an initial public offering of 4.1 million shares, at $14 per share. Paul Van Doren, while retaining shares in the company, stepped down from the board.

By 1992, however, the recession of the early 1990s, and especially poor earnings performances among the major footwear producers, forced Vans's share price down to $7. Yet, revenues from the company's 70 retail stores and 4,500 independent outlets grew to $91 million, raising net income to $6.5 million in 1992. By then, more than 32 percent of sales came from international exports. But on the domestic front, Vans was losing ground.

Vans's production techniques had changed little in the past two decades. Although its catalogue offerings swelled to more than 200 different styles, its original canvas-and-rubber shoe continued to provide roughly half of its sales. But sport shoe fashions had changed in the 1990s, with new materials and styles eroding Vans's market. The other manufacturers were producing their shoes in Asia, where labor costs were as low as 14 cents an hour. Foreign production allowed manufacturers to use solvents and other materials that were closely controlled by California's environmental regulation.

Vans clung to domestic production, spending $5 million to build a state-of-the-art plant in Vista, California. But sales and earnings were slipping, down to $86.5 million and $2.7 million, respectively, in 1993, and to $80.5 million and $1.4 million in 1994. In 1993, the company again ran afoul of immigration laws; 300 employees were deported and the company was fined $400,000.

### Enter Walter Schoenfeld

By 1993, Vans sought to replace Richard Leeuwenberg. Gary Schoenfeld, then a partner at McCown De Leeuw suggested his father, Walter Schoenfeld. In the late 1960s, the senior Schoenfeld had joined his father's company, a small maker of ties. In 1971, Schoenfeld launched a new division, to be called Brittania Sportswear, with $1.5 million raised equally among himself, two investors, and a bank. Brittania married the burgeoning blue jeans trend with coordinated jackets, sportshirts, and sweaters. Sales took off from $100,000 in 1973 to more than $50 million in 1975, and Schoenfeld Industries revenues increased to more than $300 million by 1981. In the early 1980s, Schoenfeld sold Brittania to Levi Strauss and retired.

Brought out of retirement to head Vans, Schoenfeld acted to expand the Vans product line, going overseas for the first time to manufacture a new line of shoes in step with the current fashion. Schoenfeld also addressed the company's troubled chain of retail stores, which had been hit hard by California's continued recession, closing some stores and converting others as factory outlets to siphon off misfired shoes and excess inventory. Schoenfeld sought to boost the company's marketing efforts, hiring new designers and marketing staff. In 1994, with revenues and profits on the rise again, Schoenfeld retired again, bringing in Christopher G. Staff, former president and CEO of the Speedo and Action Sports divisions of Authentic Fitness Corp.

Sales of Vans's foreign-made ''international collection'' took off and soon accounted for as much as 75 percent of the company's revenues. Domestic production, however, had become a drag on the company's profits. Sales were falling, inventory was climbing, and Vans stock dropped to a 3⅛ low.

To stem problems, the company laid off 300 workers, then idled their plants for two weeks in March 1995. In May 1995, Schoenfeld came out of retirement again, resuming leadership of the company.

In July 1995, the company closed its Orange plant, firing nearly all of the 1,000 workers there. Restructuring and write-off charges from the plant closing created most of the company's $37 million loss on its $88 million in 1995 revenues. The Vista plant continued operations, but most of Vans' production was now contracted through a dozen or so factories in South Korea.

Importantly, Schoenfeld worked to change the focus of the company. From a company rooted in manufacturing, Vans would become far more market-oriented, that is, producing what will sell, rather than selling what it produces. The introduction of the Vans line of snowboarding boots in 1995 added $7 million to gross sales and within one year gained the company the number three position among the leaders in that market. Deeper expansion into women's and children's lines also produced strong successes. With analyst estimates of revenues climbing to $118 million, with earnings reaching to $4 million, and with its stock rebounding to 11 in early 1996, Vans appeared finally to be on a steady course for the future.

### Further Reading

Ferguson, Tim W., ''Grandpa to the Grunges,'' *Forbes,* February 12, 1996, p. 88.

Granelli, James S., ''Little Leverage in Shoemaker's Buyout,'' *Los Angeles Times,* April 4, 1989, Sec. 4, p. 9F.

Lee, Don, ''Sneaker Maker Had—Till Now—Bounced Back,'' *Los Angeles Times,* June 1, 1995, p. D1.

Maio, Patrick J., ''Kicking,'' *Investor's Daily,* January 31, 1996, p. A4.

McAllister, Robert, ''Vans Optimistic With Schoenfeld at the Helm,'' *Footwear News,* August 9, 1993, p. 108.

Paris, Ellen, ''As the Twig Is Bent,'' *Forbes,* April 27, 1981, p. 131.

Vans, Inc., ''Company Profile,'' Vans, Inc. World Wide Web Site, April 1996.

—M.L. Cohen

# Varlen Corporation

**55 Shuman Boulevard**
**Naperville, Illinois 60566-7089**
**U.S.A.**
**(708) 420-0400**
**Fax: (708) 420-7123**

*Public Company*
*Incorporated:* 1969
*Employees:* 3,200
*Sales:* $386.99 million (1995)
*Stock Exchanges:* NASDAQ
*SICs:* 3743 Railroad Equipment; 3714 Motor Vehicles
Parts and Accessories; 3821 Laboratory Apparatus
and Furniture; 3469 Metal Stampings, Not Elsewhere
Classified

The Varlen Corporation is a continuously evolving diversified manufacturing company. Founded in 1969 as a railway holding company, Varlen has expanded through a carefully managed program of acquisitions and divestitures. Although the exact nature of the products manufactured by Varlen subsidiaries has changed repeatedly through time, the company has maintained a continuous emphasis on industrial products aimed at specialized "niche" markets as well as an ongoing relationship with the railroad industry.

## Company Origins

Varlen was founded in 1969 by the Dyson-Kissner investment firm as a railroad holding company. The company's first president and CEO, John A. Moran, came up with the name "Varlen" as a combination of "various" and "lines," reflecting the intention of running the company as a diversified manufacturing firm. From the outset, Varlen's main emphasis was on the railroad industry, with its two founding subsidiaries Unit Rail and Chrome Crankshaft both predominately serving this market. Unit Rail, spun off by Dyson-Kissner as the seed company for the new enterprise, consisted of two smaller companies: Hubbard Manufacturing, which made the forged steel anchors that hold rails in place, and Beall Manufacturing, a producer of agricultural implements, washers, and fasteners. Chrome Crankshaft, acquired from outside interests, used a specialized chrome plating process to remanufacture crankshafts for railroad and other diesel engines. In 1970, the company's first full year of operation, Varlen acquired its first non-rail related enterprise, the Stanlift Corporation, a distributor of material handling equipment. Sales surpassed $10 million in 1970 setting the company off on a promising start.

## Growth in the 1970s

Varlen continued pursuing acquisitions through the 1970s incorporating each new company into the corporate structure while at the same time reconfiguring this structure to fit the companies acquired. In 1971 Varlen purchased the Loose Leaf Metals Company from private interests for $1.9 million and Varlen stock. Loose Leaf was a leading independent producer of ring and post binders for loose leaf notebooks and pads, selling to most of the major stationery manufacturers. With annual sales of about $5 million Loose Leaf would provide a sizable boost to Varlen's total sales while extending its market to consumer related products.

The following year Varlen further extended this segment with the purchase of National Metalwares one of the largest manufacturers of custom steel tubular components in the U.S. National Metalwares' products were used in furniture manufacture, child car seats, playpens and other consumer items. With these additions the common ground of Varlen's subsidiaries switched from railroad products to metalworking and Varlen began positioning itself as a metalworking specialist.

In 1973 Jack Connor, a mechanical engineer and former executive with the American Can Company, took over the presidency of the growing firm, bringing with him a commitment to metalworking technology and a definitive plan as to how to grow a diversified company like Varlen. In an article in *Management Review,* Connor outlined the principles that Varlen would use to manage its diverse subsidiaries in the company's program of "controlled diversification." Connor

**Company Perspectives:**

*Varlen's primary objective is to increase the long term value of its shareowners' investment. This will be achieved by building upon our employees' creativity and their commitment to serving customers better and more efficiently than our competitors do in the markets where Varlen chooses to compete. Varlen will invest resources in selected industrial markets where it has, or can obtain, a leadership position; we will redeploy resources from markets where we cannot. We will continue to enhance our global presence. Varlen's engineered products for the niche markets in which it participates are characterized by differentiable process technology employed in their manufacture and/or superior performance attributes. Our dedication to continuous improvement will be unrelenting.*

insisted on the need for a common technology amongst corporate divisions so that corporate management could concentrate on a limited range of expertise yet he also encouraged the servicing of a variety of markets to limit the damage if a given market turned soft. Although in succeeding years Varlen would diversify into more widely distinct technologies, the company maintained the notion of preserving an underlying commonality of interest amongst its subsidiaries to avoid the hazards of a highly disparate conglomerate.

Under Connor, Varlen also established a decentralized management style that emphasized decision making on a local level. Incentives based on return on investment were used to encourage performance by division managers rather than imposing solutions from the corporate office. (The head office itself was moved from New York to Illinois in order to be closer to more Varlen facilities.) In fact, throughout its history Varlen maintained a very small corporate staff whose primary responsibilities were overall fiscal management and the overseeing of acquisitions and divestitures. Although the fundamental basis of Varlen's corporate plan was to grow through acquisitions, the company's approach to this process was relatively cautious, avoiding acquisition prospects that would not fit with other Varlen interests or that would require massive reorganization to turn a profit. At the same time Varlen was committed to selling off companies on a timely basis whose performance did not match expectations or that had become marginal to the corporation's main goals. The final principle established early in Varlen's corporate history was to borrow heavily for acquisitions but to pay off the debt quickly even if this meant temporarily reducing earnings. This studied approach to corporate growth has seen Varlen through almost 30 years of operation with only one non-profitable year and an almost unbroken string of sales increases.

By the mid-1970s Varlen was characterizing itself as an "industrial metalworking company serving a wide spectrum of markets." With the acquisition of Webco Tank Inc. and Keystone Industries, and with the sale of the ill-fitting material handling distributor Stanlift Corp, the company was now divided into six business segments: railroad industry products,

including track anchors, locomotive component rebuilding, freight car cushioning, and gates for hopper cars; agricultural products; tubular metal products; loose leaf metal products for the bindery industry; large industrial applications, including steel storage tanks, heat exchangers, grain oil extraction equipment, and metal columns and towers; and specialized industrial bolts and fasteners.

Sales climbed to $103 million and earnings to a record $5 million in 1978. Over half of these profits were provided by the railroad industry which, despite analysts' scepticism in the early 1970s, had shown steady growth through the decade. Once thought to be a dying or at least sickly industry, rail transportation had increased during the energy crisis of the 1970s. In addition, the 1976 Federal Railroad Revitalization and Regulatory Reform Act promised billions in loans and grants for rolling stock and trackbed improvements, both of which were key markets for Varlen's railroad products.

### Reorganization in the 1980s

While Varlen's first decade of operation had shown steady and impressive sales and earnings growth, the company was to encounter its first stumbles in the recession plagued 1980s. During the early 1980s Varlen extended its locomotive engine rebuilding capabilities, which had been part of the company's operations from its inception, to heavy duty industrial diesel engines with the purchase of S-G Diesel Power Inc. and Forsyth Engineering. At the same time the company shed its agricultural products segment, which had not been performing well, with the sale of its Union Iron Works and Beall Manufacturing subsidiaries, announcing plans to divest its tank fabrication companies, Sapulpa Tank and Webco Tank.

By 1984, under the management of new company president, Richard L. Welleck, Varlen was divided into three operating segments: remanufacture and fabrication of large industrial processing machinery and diesel engine components (S-G Diesel and Forsyth Engineering); railroad products (Unit Rail Anchor, Keystone Railway Equipment, Chrome Crankshaft and Chrome Locomotive); and metal products (National Metalwares, Loose Leaf Metals, and Rockford Bolt and Steel). Annual income had topped $6 million on sales of $137 million.

The company's railroad products segment was augmented in 1981 with the acquisition of the locomotive, locomotive parts, and locomotive rebuilding facilities of the defunct Rock Island Railroad. Although this purchase would make Varlen one of the world's largest independent rebuilders of locomotives, it would also ultimately result in a $6.9 million inventory write-down and a $3.3 million net loss in 1985, the company's only non-profitable year.

The railroad products boom of the late 1970s softened in the early 1980s as high interest rates, a recessionary economy, and unfavorable tax laws discouraged railroads from making the capital improvements that Varlen products served. In spite of the new acquisition, Varlen's railroad segment dropped to only 31 percent of profits in 1984 and metal products, particularly tubular steel products and loose leaf binders, became the top money maker for the diversified firm.

By 1986, it became clear that the remanufacturing segment was not adding substantially to earnings; S-G Diesel was sold and the segment eliminated. In its place, Varlen entered the automotive components field with the purchase of Means Stamping Industries, composed of four companies manufacturing precision metal components for auto parts makers.

Over the course of the next few years Varlen began to reposition itself away from an emphasis on metalworking and focused instead on building a reputation as a manufacturer of precision industrial components for niche markets. The purchase in 1988 of Precision Scientific, Inc., a $30 million manufacturer of research laboratory and petroleum analysis equipment, moved the company more firmly in this direction and created a fourth operating segment.

The year 1989 was a watershed for Varlen as management decided to divest some of the subsidiaries that had been mainstays of the company since its founding in order to consolidate operations and divert assets to its new core precision components industries. Loose Leaf Metals, Rockford Bolt and Steel, Jackson Screw Company, Chrome Crankshaft, Chrome Locomotive, and Forsyth Engineering were all sold in the course of this reorganization. The company's auto parts business was enlarged with the acquisition of Consolidated Metco, Inc., an Oregon-based manufacturer of tight tolerance aluminum castings and structural foam plastic parts for heavy duty trucks and trailers.

In spite of an overall slowdown in the auto industry in the late 1980s, Varlen's auto components sales rose thanks to the company's emphasis on trucks and vans, which were the one growth segment in the industry. The 1989 reorganization of Varlen saw the company's operations consolidated into two operating segments: Transportation Products (Consolidated Metco, Keystone Railway Equipment, Means Industries, and Unit Rail Anchor) and Laboratory and Other Products (Precision Scientific and National Metalwares). With sales of $226 million and earnings of over $10 million it appeared that Varlen was moving in the right direction with the restructuring of its core industries and the company was named one of the top 200 small companies in America by *Forbes* in 1989.

### International Expansion in the 1990s

The recession of the early 1990s had a damaging effect on all of Varlen's product segments but was particularly hard on the railroad and research laboratory products subsidiaries. Earnings were halved to only $5 million in 1990, and the company began to look towards other markets to improve performance. Increasingly in the 1990s, American business began to think globally, trying to compete in the international marketplace. An international presence became necessary for industrial component manufacturers like Varlen not only to increase markets but because American industries were looking for suppliers that could serve their growing foreign operations.

In keeping with this trend, in 1990 Varlen purchased Walter Herzog GmbH of Germany, the leading manufacturer of auto-

mated equipment for petroleum analysis, a sector that was growing worldwide. Varlen's railroad equipment sector was strengthened in 1994 with the purchase of Aciéries de Ploërmel, a French manufacturer serving the passenger and freight car markets in Europe. In the same year, Varlen acquired an American firm Prime Manufacturing Corp., a manufacturer of heating and air conditioning systems which, two years later, would capture an important contract for locomotive air conditioners in the People's Republic of China. By 1996, international sales accounted for 19 percent of Varlen's revenues.

By the mid-1990s Varlen had shed its last original metalware company with the sale of National Metalwares, the tubular steel manufacturer acquired in 1972, whose products had boosted sales in the 1980s when railroads were in a slump but which had lost major markets in the early 1990s. Varlen's operations were now divided into two sectors: Transportation Products, including railroad and automotive equipment, and Analytical Instruments, including research laboratory and petroleum analysis equipment. The first of these segments accounted for over 80 percent of earnings, and Varlen announced plans to divest its research laboratory equipment companies that had been suffering from declining government funding for scientific research.

The company's railroad equipment sales, which had risen by 42 percent form 1994 to 1995, received a potentially substantial boost in 1996 when the company entered into a definitive agreement to acquire Brenco Inc., a leading manufacturer of tapered roller bearings for freight cars. This acquisition had the potential to increase Varlen sales, which had reached $387 million in 1995, to about $500 million. With the Brenco acquisition Varlen was poised to enter the last half of the 1990s in a strong position to meet their corporate goal of maximizing shareholder investment.

### Principal Subsidiaries

Aciéries de Ploërmel (France); Alcor Petroleum Instruments, Inc.; Chrome Crankshaft Companies; Consolidated Metco, Inc.; Walter Herzog GmbH (Germany); Keystone Railway Equipment Company; Means Industries, Inc.; Precision Scientific Petroleum Instruments Company; Prime Manufacturing Corporation; Unit Rail Anchor Company; Varlen Instruments, N.A.

### Further Reading

Byrne, Harlan S., "Varlen Corp." *Barron's,* May 15, 1989, p. 110.
Cathey, Paul J., "How to Effectively Manage Metals Acquisitions," *Iron Age,* February 10, 1975, pp. 40–42.
Connor, Jack, "Secrets of Controlled Diversification," *Management Review,* October 1974, pp. 4–9.
Gordon, Mitchell, "Making Tracks," *Barron's,* August 13, 1979, pp. 30–31.
Rolland, Louis J., "Varlen Vista," *Financial World,* January 5, 1972, p. 20.
"Smoother Ride: Varlen Corp. Steams Ahead After Two-Year Slump," *Barron's,* September 17, 1984, pp. 58–59.

—Hilary Gopnik

# Vencor

## Vencor, Inc.

3300 Capital Holding Center
400 West Market Street
Louisville, Kentucky 40202
U.S.A.
(502) 569-7300
Fax: (502) 569-7499

*Public Company*
*Incorporated:* 1983 as Vencare, Inc.
*Employees:* 4,040
*Sales:* $400 million (1994)
*Stock Exchanges:* New York
*SICs:* 8062 General Medical & Surgical Hospitals; 8069
    Specialty Hospitals Except Psychiatric

Vencor, Inc. is one of the largest diversified health care providers in the United States. Entering 1996, the company's 38-state network encompassed 35 long-term acute care hospitals, 311 nursing centers with 42,000 beds, 23 retirement communities, and a chain of 55 retail and institutional pharmacies. Vencor more than tripled in size in 1995 when it acquired Hillhaven Corp., a leading national operator of nursing centers.

### William Bruce Lunsford: Early Career

Formed in 1985, Vencor rapidly grew into a leading U.S. health care company within a span of less than ten years. A driving force behind that rampant expansion was William Bruce Lunsford, chairman, chief executive, president, and cofounder of the company. Lunsford grew up on a 120-acre midwestern farm and decided early that farming wouldn't be his future. He attended the University of Kentucky, where he was known as an above average student and a natural leader. After completing an accounting degree, Lunsford joined the Cincinnati accounting firm of Alexander Grant & Co. in 1969. He also went to night school and earned a law degree at the Salmon P. Chase College of Law. In 1974 Lunsford left the accounting firm and joined Keating Muething & Klekamp, a law firm based in Cincinnati. As an accountant and attorney, Lunsford counseled about 40 business clients. It was through his work with the numerous business owners he advised that Lunsford became interested in starting his own enterprise.

Lunsford's last career jaunt before starting Vencor was in the political arena. In 1979 Lunsford accepted an invitation to join John Y. Brown, Jr.'s campaign for the governorship of Kentucky. Within little more than two months Lunsford found himself the treasurer of the State Democratic Party. In 1980 he left his law practice to join Brown's administration as deputy commerce secretary. Within a month after Brown was elected, he asked Lunsford to head his legislative team. Shortly thereafter, at the age of 33, Lunsford was cast into Brown's inner-circle when Brown made him his youngest cabinet member.

As commerce secretary and a cabinet member, Lunsford suddenly found himself in charge of 2,000 employees and a $150 million budget. Unfortunately, Kentucky's economy crumbled under Brown's administration. The state unemployment rate doubled, in fact, and the number of jobs in Kentucky declined under Brown's leadership. However, Lunsford's job put him in daily contact with business leaders and investors, some of whom would later play an important role in the formation of Vencor. They would also inspire him to make the jump into business. "I was around a lot of people like Frank Metts and W. T. Young who had successfully started several companies from scratch," Lunsford remembered in the January 1992 *Louisville.* "I love the law, but (they) made being an attorney and accountant seem pretty insignificant."

### A Niche in the Health Care Industry

Lunsford eventually teamed up in an investment venture with associate Gene Smith, a wealthy veteran of the Brown administration. Lunsford was basically seeking business opportunities at the time. The chance that he was looking for finally came when he was approached by Michael Barr, a respiratory therapist. Barr recognized an unmet need for long-term hospitals to house patients who were dependent on ventilators. That group was only marginally profitable for typical hospitals at the time, because those patients didn't require much high-cost treatment. Barr thought that a hospital geared primarily to critically

## Company Perspectives:

*We believe healthcare is moving toward patient-focused care provided in a variety of sites based on the acuity of a patient's condition. This framework is designed to ensure that the level and cost of the care provided to a patient best meet that patient's specific needs. Our vision is for Vencor to develop such a network for patients with cardiopulmonary disorders.*

ill, long-term patients could profit by tapping Medicare and private insurers for reimbursements. Importantly, such a facility would benefit from lower operating costs because it wouldn't need to financially support the expensive, high-tech equipment that general-purpose hospitals needed.

Lunsford had barely considered getting into the health care industry, and he didn't know the first thing about ventilators, long-term care, or operating a hospital. But, after some cursory research, Lunsford realized that it was a growth industry and that Barr had what might be a great idea. Lunsford and Barr, with financial backing from Smith, quickly put a deal together. They incorporated the venture in 1983 as Vencare, Inc., and began looking for a hospital that they could purchase and convert as a sort of test for Barr's concept. After searching for several months, the fledgling start-up spent $3 million to purchase LaGrange Community Hospital, a 62-bed money-losing facility in northern Indiana.

When Vencare bought LaGrange Community, the hospital was losing roughly $60,000 each month. Lunsford and Barr's team quickly eliminated about 18 percent of the hospital's staff, improved the facility's layout and appearance, changed the layout to improve efficiency, and hired some new doctors. They also installed 20 new beds specifically for ventilator patients. Within three months the hospital was turning a profit. Soon thereafter Vencare leased space for 28 beds in another hospital outside of Chicago. The beds filled up quickly, and Lunsford knew that he was working with a viable concept.

### Development and Expansion

During the next few years Vencare bought several more hospitals and turned them around, and in the process gained valuable experience that Vencare management used to continually improve operations and profit margins. In 1986 Vencare leased a wing of the Parkway Medical Center in Miami, and in 1988 it moved into Tampa and Fort Lauderdale before jumping into ventures in San Antonio and Dallas in 1989. By 1989 Vencare owned or leased space in seven hospitals, and had 421 beds in four states; Indiana, Illinois, Florida, and Kentucky. As a result, the company's revenue base rose from $703,000 in 1985 to $27.4 million in 1988, and then to $54.26 million in 1989. During the same period, net income increased from a net loss of $71,000 to more than $1 million annually.

Vencor's (the company changed its name from Vencare in 1989) success during the late 1980s was the result of a changing health care industry and Vencor's ability to adapt to those

changes. Paramount in the industry was a trend toward increasing pressure to reduce costs. Vencor reduced costs associated with caring for chronically ill patients by getting them out of the expensive general-hospital environment. It placed them in a more efficient long-term care situation, but gave them more care than they would get at a typical nursing home, for example. Vencor kept care prices down by, among other efforts, centralizing paperwork and administrative functions at its Louisville headquarters.

The result was that Vencor was able to treat patients for a fraction of what it would cost to treat them in a traditional hospital environment. Furthermore, Vencor claimed to provide better care for its patients because its facilities were geared specifically for the typical long-term acute care patient. Most of its patients were over the age of 65 and were dependent on a ventilator. Vencor was able to design a treatment system geared for that population. ''We look at all of the patient's needs holistically,'' Barr said in the *Louisville* article. ''We look at all of the patient's needs . . . we work to stimulate the patient as much as possible.'' An important advantage of Vencor's treatment method was that it got patients off of their ventilators more quickly, thus further reducing overall care costs.

Encouraged by rising demand for its services, Vencor management continued to pursue growth, but at a much more rapid pace. The company added nearly 150 beds in 1990 when it opened four new facilities in Texas, Arizona, Colorado, and Georgia. It followed that growth in 1991 by tagging on 400 beds in Michigan, Illinois, Texas, and St. Louis. Going into 1992, Vencor was operating 17 hospitals in 11 states, employing 2,500 people, generating more than $10 million annually in net income, and carrying less than $1 million in long-term debt. Furthermore, the potential for growth was huge, with a seemingly limitless number of areas in which Vencor could expand. Indeed, although the possibility of competition was ever-present, Vencor had effectively created a niche in which it was the only serious player.

### Continued Growth and the Addition of the Vencare Program

Vencor added about 400 more beds to its network in 1992, with new facilities in California, Missouri, Florida, and Arizona. Then, in 1993, Vencor added nearly 700 beds in facilities in Oklahoma, Tennessee, and North Carolina, among other places. By the end of the year the company was operating 29 facilities across much of the United States. In addition, Vencor initiated its Vencare respiratory care program in 1993. Through that operation, Vencor began helping some nursing homes to set up their own acute care facilities. Vencare effectively provided a comprehensive package to such clients, helping them to set up a program that included licensed therapists, equipment, and management expertise.

Vencor's revenues increased to $282.2 million in 1993, a record $22.9 million of which was netted as income. By then, Lunsford had grown rich and was becoming relatively well-known in Louisville, where his company was headquartered. Lunsford darted around town in a Porsche 911 with VENCOR vanity license plates and was known as a hard-driving businessman with diverse interests including horse breeding and politics. "Within four hours he'll buy a horse, buy a hospital, hire somebody, and hold a meeting on an under-performing unit," said former law partner Dennis Doyle in the February 5, 1995 *Courier-Journal*. Lunsford was also known as a capable and respected manager, and, despite the cash windfall from Vencor, he and his family continued to live in the same home they had purchased before he started the company.

Vencor continued to add facilities to its network and to expand and diversify its successful Vencare unit in 1994. Sales for the year increased to nearly $400 million while net income grew to $31.42 million. By the end of the year the company was operating 34 facilities in 15 states. Furthermore, the Vencare effort had taken off and had managed to capture more than 600 nursing home contracts in 22 states in little more than one year of operation. At the same time, Vencor continued to strive for greater efficiency in an effort to retain control of its niche. To that end, Vencor introduced its ProTouch clinical information system, which, when installed in its facilities, would allow the company to further reduce labor and overhead costs.

### Merger with Hillhaven Corp.

Vencor continued to acquire and open new acute care facilities in 1995 and to pursue new contracts through Vencare. Of import, though, was a striking maneuver that changed the complexion of the entire company. In September 1995, shareholders voted in favor of a proposed merger of Vencor and The Hillhaven Corp. In effect, Vencor was acquiring Hillhaven (in a transaction valued at about $1.9 billion), and the companies were being merged under the Vencor name. Surprisingly, Hillhaven was a much larger enterprise with a revenue base of about $1.8 billion. It was primarily a nursing home operator, with about 310 facilities under its control, but it also brought to Vencor a chain of nearly 60 pharmacy outlets as well as a group of 23 retirement communities.

The giant Hillhaven merger instantly made Vencor one of the largest long-term health care providers in the United States. Lunsford's idea with the merger was to begin positioning Vencor as a single source for employers and health-plan companies seeking long-term health care solutions, serving patients ranging from the chronically ill to less-care-intensive nursing home residents. "We're trying to position this company as the pre-eminent long-term health care company in America," Lunsford said in the April 29, 1995, *Courier-Journal*.

### Principal Subsidiaries

Hillhaven Corp.; Vencor Hospitals South, Inc.; Vencor Hospitals California, Inc.; Vencor Investments, Inc.; Ventech Systems, Inc.; Candle Subacute Services, Inc.; Vencare Kentucky, Inc.

### Further Reading

Benmour, Eric, "Thriving Vencor Has Cornered Its Market," *Business First-Louisville*, January 6, 1992, Section 2, p. 3.
——, "Vencor Stock Split Will Be Third One in Five Years," *Business First-Louisville*, October 10, 1994, p. 11.
Hershberg, Ben Z., "Hospital Firm Has Niche in Long-Term Care," *Courier-Journal Louisville*, April 16, 1990, p. BUS1.
Meeks, Fleming, and R. Lee Sullivan, "If at First You Don't Succeed . . . ," *Forbes*, November 9, 1992.
Reichert, Walt, "High on Health Care," *Louisville*, January 1992, p. 11.
Song, Kyung M., "Acquiring Four Firms Expands Vencor Territory," *Courier-Journal Louisville*, June 16, 1995, p. 1C.
——, "Vencor Stock Falls over Merger Worries," *Courier-Journal Louisville*, April 1995, p. 14B.
Ward, Joe, "Vencor-Hillhaven Merger Approved," *Courier-Journal Louisville*, September 28, 1995, p. 10B.
Wolfson, Andrew, "Health Care Titan: Lunsford Claims His Success Is Due to Luck as Much as Pluck," *Courier-Journal*, February 5, 1995, p. 1A.

—Dave Mote

# VLSI Technology, Inc.

**1109 McKay Drive**
**San Jose, California 95131**
**U.S.A.**
**(408) 434-3000**
**Fax: (408) 263-2511**

*Public Company*
*Incorporated:* 1979
*Employees:* 2,738
*Sales:* $719.92 million (1995)
*Stock Exchanges:* NASDAQ
*SICs:* 3674 Semiconductors & Related Devices; 5054
Computers & Computer Peripheral Equipment &
Software

VLSI Technology, Inc. is known as a pioneer in ASIC technology. It designs, manufactures, and sells customized integrated circuits called application-specific integrated circuits (ASICs) and application-specific standard products (semi-custom chips designed for a particular market application). In addition, the company has become a leader in the chipset business through its personal computer division, where it develops and manufactures computer peripheral devices.

### Starting Out

VLSI Technology was started in the late 1970s by Douglas Fairbairn, Jack Balletto, Dan Floyd, and Gunnar Weslesen. The latter three had been friends at California Institute of Technology before getting together in Los Gatos, California, to start VTI, the company that would soon become VLSI. Fairbairn met VTI's founders in 1979 when he interviewed them for an article in his semiconductor magazine. The three were so impressed that they offered Fairbairn a job. Shortly thereafter, the company was incorporated as VLSI Technology, Inc.

The name VLSI was taken from the acronym for "very large scale integration." Semiconductors from earlier years had been dubbed SSI (small scale integration) and then MSI (medium

scale integration), before progressing to LSI (large scale integration). That progression tracked the increasing numbers of transistors that were being placed on single chips, culminating in VLSI, which came to describe chips with more than 100,000 transistors. VLSI started out offering software design services that helped semiconductor manufacturers develop and produce advanced integrated circuits.

VLSI pioneered the development of some design technology related to ASICs. Prior to ASICs, chips were designed to be mass produced and utilized in a broad range of applications. ASICs allowed manufacturers to tailor chips to perform a specific job. VLSI's first major innovation was a workstation system that allowed semiconductor engineers to effectively design and tailor their own chips. Introduced into the burgeoning market in the early 1980s, the invention helped VLSI boost its revenues from less than $20 million to more than $100 million within four years.

Fairbairn received much of the credit for the development of VLSI's ASIC technology and the creation of the workstation. In fact, Fairbairn lead VLSI's ASIC and chip-design tool division into the 1990s as the only remaining founder of the company. Fairbairn was known as a highly intelligent workaholic. Born in 1948, he grew up in a suburb of Los Angeles where he delivered newspapers and worked for his father selling seeds. His technological skills surfaced early. After watching the Soviet Union's 1957 launch of Sputnik, the nine-year-old Fairbairn, built his own model rocket, complete with fuel and an electrical system that deployed a landing parachute. By the time he was 15 he was building ham radios out of trashed electronic gear.

Fairbairn enrolled at Stanford in 1966, where he studied electrical engineering and worked part-time for Hewlett-Packard. He started his career in 1972 in Silicon Valley, working with a number of legendary inventors and on several groundbreaking projects including the first personal computer ("Alto") and the first laser printer. It was in 1976 that Fairbairn, after listening to a speech by technology guru Carver Mead, decided to design software that would allow engineers to design their own integrated circuits. He teamed up with Mead's prize pupil, Jim Rowson, to start developing his software. In-

## Company Perspectives:

*Customer satisfaction is fundamental to our business. Their success is the basis of our success and their perception of our service is reality. Our people are our most valuable resource. We encourage mutual trust, integrity and open communication throughout the organization. We strive for technical excellence through the development of innovative products. Our goal is to achieve consistent profits to ensure continued prosperity for all who depend on us. Through our Customer Excellence philosophy, we strive to inspire those with whom we work. We foster an environment where teamwork, risk taking, and willingness to change define our culture. We are pledged to continuously improve, to create a challenging and rewarding work environment, and to be good world citizens.*

vesting only $20,000, Fairbairn simultaneously launched *Magazine Lambda,* a slick periodical developed specifically for semiconductor engineers.

It was through *Magazine Lambda* that Fairbairn came into contact with the progenitors of VTI. Fairbairn sold *Magazine Lambda* in 1979 (to a big publisher, and at a large profit), and quit his part-time job at Xerox so that he could devote his energy to the VLSI venture. Rowson went with him, and would remain his right-hand man into the 1990s. When VLSI hit the jackpot with its innovative workstation, the founders' took the company public in 1983 to raise expansion capital. That move allowed VLSI to expand from a developer of chip-design systems to a manufacturer of chips. "The software and design system was only meant as a way of getting into the silicon business," Fairbairn explained in *Financial World.* In fact, VLSI often sold its design software at a loss as a way to establish a presence with its customers.

### A New Direction for the Mid-1980s

To shepherd VLSI into the role of chip manufacturer, the company's board brought in semiconductor industry veterans Al Stein and Henri Jarrat. Stein, who became chairman and chief executive of VLSI, had served in key executive positions at Texas Instruments and Motorola. Jarrat, who became president and chief operating officer, had also worked at Texas Instruments and then with Stein at Motorola. Together, they planned to lead VLSI into the semiconductor manufacturing industry. Meanwhile, Fairbairn and Rowson remained in charge of the company's ASIC and chip-design tools division, helping to develop new technology and products that complemented VLSI's manufacturing initiatives.

By mid-1985, VLSI operated chip design centers and sales offices in San Jose, Irvine, Boston, Dallas, and Chicago, as well as overseas in Germany, Paris, and the United Kingdom. Through those centers, VLSI worked with clients to design chips for specific applications. It could also produce ASICs, as well as more conventional chips, through its high-tech foundry (wafer processing facility). Indeed, VLSI became a sort of one-stop shop for companies that needed semiconductors; it helped its customers design application-specific chips using its proprietary design technology, manufactured the chips, and then helped the customer employ the chips.

VLSI's advantage came through its ability to help clients quickly develop advanced chips at a minimum cost. Indeed, VLSI gained a reputation for being able to design and produce high-quality ASICs as fast as any company in the industry. Its reputation allowed it to land some of the biggest buyers in the market, such as Apple, which used VLSI's chips to give its successful Macintosh computers many of their distinctive features. By 1985 VLSI was employing more than 600 workers and generating sales of nearly $80 million annually. Despite a general slowdown in the semiconductor industry during the mid-1980s, VLSI continued to post successive revenue gains; sales grew to $112 million in 1986 and then to $171 million in 1988.

Despite VLSI's technology prowess and reputation for excellent customer service, profits remained elusive throughout the 1980s. Revenue growth was huge, but the company posted meager and inconsistent net income figures. Between 1985 and 1989, for example, VLSI's total net income amounted to less than $3 million from a total of more than $800 million in sales. That shortfall was hardly the result of VLSI's failure to compete technologically. Instead, the failure was linked to problems with its manufacturing operations.

The problem stemmed primarily from management's decision during the industry slowdown of the mid-1980s not to expand production facilities. In 1987 Stein decided not to build a $70 million production facility, but to wait one year and see if demand picked up. Until then, he would contract production to outside foundries, if necessary. Unfortunately for VLSI, semiconductor demand ballooned in 1987 and the company was swamped with orders which it didn't have the manufacturing capacity to fill. Furthermore, it had trouble finding outside contractors that could handle its orders. In its race to get its production facilities up-and-running, VLSI bobbled many of its customers' orders and lost sales and profits. "VLSI has been a disappointment," Shearson Lehman analyst Tom Thornhill said in *Financial World.* "They found out they had to be good at a lot more than design."

### The 1990s

VLSI increased sales to $288 million in 1989, but profits remained evasive. However, going into the 1990s its manufacturing facilities were up-and-running at full capacity and the company seemed positioned to profit from ongoing growth in demand, particularly for its ASIC chips and technology. At the same time, VLSI was branching out into other niches. It had begun targeting the market for application-specific standard products, which are semi-custom chips designed for a particular market application and can be used by several different customers. It also began focusing on the computer products industry during the early 1990s, developing personal computer peripheral devices that utilized its proprietary semiconductors.

By 1990, Fairbairn had become disenchanted with the direction in which VLSI was moving. Furthermore, the ASIC division, which he headed, was accounting for less than 50 percent of VLSI's sales and the original chip-design tools business was only contributing about ten percent. Stein wanted to let VLSI focus on manufacturing chips and spun off the chip-design software and tool division, as Compass Design Automation, in 1990. Before that move was completed, however, Fairbairn left VLSI. Rowson went with him, as did Dan Yoder, director of corporate strategic planning for VLSI. Together, the three founded a new company called Redwood Design Automation to focus on chip- and software-design tools.

Meanwhile, VLSI, still under the direction of Stein, sustained its drive to establish itself as a leading manufacturer of ASIC semiconductors, and to branch into complementary market niches. In mid-1992, for example, the company announced that it would be working with Intel Corp. to manufacture chips that would enable computer manufacturers to build powerful handheld computer devices. Intel agreed to provide proprietary chip technology to VLSI, which would produce the microprocessor cores (or chipsets) for the devices. This "chipset" business would quickly grow to become a significant portion of VLSI's revenue base.

As it had since its inception, VLSI increased revenues throughout the early 1990s. Sales grew to $324 million in 1990 and rose to more than $428 million in 1992. But poor profit numbers continued to plague VLSI. Partly to blame was a temporary industry slowdown in the early 1990s, which caused many chip manufacturers to decrease output significantly. VLSI managed to recover from the slowdown in 1993, when big sales gains were mirrored by a rise in net income to about $16 million. That success was diminished in December of 1993, however, when Apple Computer decided to cancel a large portion of its chip orders from VLSI. The announcement sent VLSI's stock tumbling 30 percent in a single day.

Despite the setback with Apple, VLSI managed to increase sales in 1994 to $587 million, a record $31.7 million of which was netted as income. That success was underscored by IBM's decision in October of 1994 to use VLSI as the chipset supplier for its Pentium-based desktop computers. That development highlighted the growing importance of VLSI's chipset business. By the mid-1990s VLSI had become a recognized leader in the chipset business, designing and building the chips that were the core logic components in computers and linked microprocessors with various peripheral devices. Largely as a result of its

surging chipset business, VLSI boosted sales to $720 million in 1995. Going into 1996 it was employing 3,000 workers throughout North America, Europe, and Asia.

### Principal Subsidiaries

Compass Design Automation.

### Principal Divisions

VLSI Products Division; Personal Computer Division.

### Further Reading

Avalos, George, "VLSI Bucks Semiconductor Industry Turndown," *Business Journal-San Jose,* October 21, 1985, p. 10.

Davis, Don, "VLSI Technology Unveils Its Next-Generation DECT Protocol Engine," *Business Wire,* February 29, 1996.

Goldman, James S., "Douglas Fairbairn: Sputnik Spawned More Than Space Race," *Business Journal-San Jose,* November 25, 1991, p. 12.

——, "Three Former VLSI Managers to Start a New Firm," *Business Journal-San Jose,* December 17, 1990, p. 5.

——, "Three Top VLSI Officials Leave to Start Own Outfit," *Business Journal-San Jose,* December 3, 1990, p. 3.

Hayes, Mary, "VLSI Technology Loses $20 Million Chip Order," *Business Journal-San Jose,* December 13, p. 1.

Herr, Jeff, "VLSI Technology Chips Away at Quality," *Arizona Business Gazette,* May 20, 1993, Section 2, p. 3Q.

Hutchison, G. Dan, "Corporate Profile for VLSI Research," *Business Wire,* June 5, 1992.

Johnson, Sally, "VTI . . . Expanding the VLSI Horizon," *Silicon Valley,* April 1985, p. 5.

Lasnier, Guy, "Former VLSI President Jarrat Eyes Start-up or Venture Hel," *Business Journal-San Hose,* January 11, 1988, p. 10.

Luebke, Cathy, "Team Builder Leads Tempe Technology Firm," *Pittsburgh Business Times & Journal,* October 21, 1994, p. 24.

Mensheha, Mark, "VLSI Technology Expanding Local Production, Work Force," *San Antonio Business Journal,* August 18, 1995, p. 1.

Moore, Paula, "Local VLSI Plant to Make Newest Chip," *San Antonio Business Journal,* November 7, 1988, p. 1.

Pollace, Pam, "Chips for Emerging Handheld Market," *Business Wire,* July 8, 1992.

Schneider, Paul, "VLSI Wins Supply Deal with IBM," *Arizona Business Gazette,* October 20, 1994, p. 1.

Wrubel, Robert, "Not Guts, Not Factory," *Financial World,* April 4, 1989, p. 88.

—Dave Mote

# Wachovia Bank of Georgia, N.A.

**191 Peachtree Street, N.E.**
**Atlanta, Georgia 30303**
**U.S.A.**
**(404) 332-5000**
**Fax: (404) 332-5919**

*Wholly Owned Subsidiary of Wachovia Corporation*
*Incorporated:* 1929 as the First National Bank of Atlanta
*Assets:* $8 Billion (1995 est.)
*Employees:* 730
*SICs:* 6712 Bank Holding Companies; 6021 National
Commercial Banks

A leader in Southern banking, Wachovia Bank of Georgia, N.A. is one of the three banks that constitute the Wachovia Corporation, along with the Wachovia Banks of North and South Carolina. Wachovia Bank of Georgia, the pre-eminent bank within the Peanut State, was one of the country's early leaders in providing highly sophisticated cash management services to businesses and corporations throughout the southern part of the United States, including such technologies as automated lockbox centers to process receivables. Wachovia Bank of Georgia was the first bank holding company in the state to list its stock on the New York Stock Exchange, and was in the vanguard of American banks that encouraged and assisted domestic companies with the growing volume of international trade during the 1960s and 1970s. As a subsidiary of Wachovia Corporation since 1985, the bank's asset base continues to grow at an impressive rate.

## Following the Fortunes of the South

The beginning of the most important bank in the state of Georgia was tied to the fortunes and talents of Alfred Austell, a native of East Tennessee born in 1814. Raised on a farm and taught in a field school, Austell worked his way to Atlanta, Georgia, where he worked in various businesses as clerk and cashier, and as a planter. As a successful businessman, Brigadier General of the Georgia Militia, and a civic leader, he established the Bank of Fulton, and worked as its cashier. The

bank soon garnered a reputation as one of the most trustworthy financial institutions within the state.

Unfortunately, with the advent of the Civil War in 1861 the city of Atlanta, along with all its financial institutions, fell on hard times. At the time of Georgia's secession from the United States in January of 1861, Atlanta was one of the most illustrious and charming cities in the nation. As the cornerstone of the Confederate war efforts, Atlanta became the target of the Union army's wrath and was in ruins by the end of the war. The Bank of Fulton, having dealt in Confederate currency during the war, was left insolvent by the demise of the Confederacy.

Despite these setbacks, Alfred Austell was determined to use his own personal resources to redeem every one of the bank's Confederate notes held by loyal customers. Austell reimbursed all the bank's customers in gold and then, with his fortune depleted, headed north to New York to explore the possibilities of revitalizing the financial community in Atlanta. Using his network of Northern contacts, Austell was able to procure a federal charter for a bank that he named the Atlanta National Bank. The first such national bank in the Southeast, the Atlanta National Bank opened for business on December 19, 1865, in Austell's home. Capitalized at $100,000, and with Austell as president, the new bank grew quickly. Within eight months, the bank had moved to permanent offices on Alabama Street in the heart of downtown Atlanta, had gained more than $300,000 in new deposits, and had made loans surpassing $100,000. After its first full year in operation, the Atlanta National Bank was operating at a profit.

By the time Alfred Austell died in 1881, the Atlanta National Bank had developed into one of the premier financial institutions in the state of Georgia. The bank had loaned the city of Atlanta funds for reconstruction activities, and continued to do so throughout the remainder of the 19th century. As the city grew, the bank issued bonds to fund public services such as street construction, school building, water supply, and the creation of fire and police departments. Atlanta National Bank was also one of the first banks in the South to provide its customers with individual bank accounts where checks could be written in order to draw on their deposits.

## The 20th Century

By the turn of the century, the Atlanta National Bank was one of the most successful and most stable in the entire South. Largely due to its financial stability, the bank was able to take advantage of the Panic of 1903 and purchase some of its local competitors, such as the Capital City National Bank. As a federally chartered national bank, Atlanta National Bank was required to become a member of the regional Federal Reserve Bank, created by the Federal Reserve Act of 1913. This federal legislation required member banks to keep a portion of their reserves on deposit with the local Federal Reserve Bank, and allowed the member bank to borrow from the pool of money collected. Atlanta National Bank again capitalized on this opportunity to expand its activities by acquiring some smaller banks and enlarging its offices. During the First World War, the bank was highly successful in promoting the purchase of Liberty Bonds to finance the American military effort in Europe.

State law prohibited Georgia banks from expanding their services through branch banking outside the city limits within which they originally operated. The only other method to expand their presence in communities and towns other than their own was to pursue a strategy of merger and acquisition. Thus in 1916, Atlanta National Bank merged with American National Bank, and in 1923 Atlanta National merged with the Lowry Bank and Trust Company of Georgia. In 1929, the mergers were brought to their culmination when Atlanta National Bank merged with the Fourth National Bank, also located in Atlanta. The merger created the largest bank in Georgia and the oldest national bank in the southeastern section of the United States. With approximately $58 million in assets, the newly formed First National Bank of Atlanta was the largest financial institution south of Philadelphia, Pennsylvania, and ranked among the top 15 in the nation.

## The Great Depression and World War II

By the time Franklin Delano Roosevelt was sworn in as president of the United States on March 4, 1933, the Depression was in full force across the country. The Stock Market crash of 1929 brought with it widespread panic in financial circles, and many banks were forced into bankruptcy when they were unable to meet the demand to return the deposits of their customers. Upon assuming office, Roosevelt declared a national Bank Holiday which closed all American banks. With the passage of the Emergency Banking Bill less than one week after his inauguration, banks were subjected to strict financial guidelines before they could reopen. First National Bank of Atlanta was one of the first banks in the South to reopen for business after the Bank Holidays.

Through its conservative investment policies and astute financial management, First National Bank of Atlanta weathered the difficult years of the Great Depression. By the end of the 1930s, the bank had regained its depositors and had implemented new loan programs that stabilized the finances of many commercial firms in the city. When America entered World War II in December of 1941, the revitalization of industry required to sustain the war effort did more than anything else to lift the country out of the Great Depression. First National Bank of Atlanta was at the forefront of mobilizing all its resources to support America's involvement in World War II. The bank assumed a leading role in financing those companies in the South that retooled their manufacturing facilities to produce ammunition, and also provided many loans to textile firms making clothing for soldiers serving overseas. The U.S. Treasury Department requested banks to join its campaign selling war bonds in order to finance the massive expenditures required by the American military effort, and First National Bank of Atlanta responded enthusiastically. Setting an example, the bank purchased many war bonds and, by the end of the war in 1945, was one of the banks whose commercial assets were mostly in the form of government bonds.

## Postwar Years

When U.S. soldiers returned home from the battlegrounds of World War II, First National Bank of Atlanta was ready to meet their needs as consumers. As the demand for housing, automobiles, appliances, and other consumer goods increased, the bank established such services as installment loans for the purchase of a wide variety of items. With a new emphasis on corporate lending, the bank initiated a program designed to provide companies in the Southeast with the capital required to convert their manufacturing facilities from wartime to peacetime production. Continuing a practice established at the turn of the century, First National Bank of Atlanta also financed the construction of schools and local roads by issuing bonds. One of the most important services that the bank provided during the 1950s involved retirement plans set up for elderly citizens through the trust department. From 1945 to 1960, the number of employees belonging to their company's private pension plan more than tripled, and the First National Bank of Atlanta provided consulting services to individuals and companies seeking advice on pension management and investments.

The decade of the 1960s was one of the most prosperous periods for First National Bank. During the early part of the decade, the bank established an international department to assist domestic companies in the Southeast that wished to expand their presence in Europe and Asia. Although the bank's deposits began to decline, its mortgage lending program and loans to small and mid-sized companies brought in significant revenue. In 1965, First National Bank of Atlanta began construction on a 41-story headquarters tower, one of the most impressive of the new buildings that adorned downtown Atlanta. In 1969, the bank's management decided to form First National Holding Corporation, a holding company for its banking operations, in order to take advantage of the many benefits involved in such a reorganization.

## Expansion and Consolidation

During the 1970s, First National opened its first foreign office in London, and implemented a strategic policy to expand its presence overseas. When the state of Georgia relaxed its requirements for banks to open branch offices, First National immediately initiated an aggressive acquisitions policy and acquired 13 banks during the mid- and late 1970s, including the prominent First Bank of Savannah. Through these acquisitions, First National rapidly extended its services to 17 counties throughout the state of Georgia. In 1978, the bank was one of the first in the South to support the Community Reinvestment Act, legislation passed by the U.S. Congress which detailed the financial responsibilities of banks to serve the needs of lower-income communities and neighborhoods. In 1979, the bank renamed itself the First Atlanta Corporation.

First Atlanta was a leader in innovative banking technology. The bank's tape-driven computers were replaced rapidly by electronic computers; its automated teller machine, *Tillie The All-Time Teller,* was one of the first in use throughout the South; and the electronic transfer of funds and point-of-sale devices were welcomed by an enlightened management that wanted to increase the convenience of the bank's customer services. These new developments in technology allowed First Atlanta to expand its overseas network of offices and simultaneously concentrate on new and increasing domestic opportunities such as corporate business lending and development, mortgage lending, and the burgeoning field of credit card operations.

Yet even with such a bright future, management at First Atlanta arrived at the conclusion that the bank would be better prepared for the competition of the future if it merged with another large banking institution. In the mid-1980s, First Atlanta entered into merger negotiations with Wachovia Bank Corporation, located in North Carolina. Having already rejected another offer from a southeastern bank, management at First Atlanta felt that Wachovia was the perfect match. Throughout the late 1980s, teams were set up by both banks to plan, arrange, and implement the consolidation of the separate operations and staff.

### The 1990s and Beyond

By 1993, the merger between First Atlanta and Wachovia had been completed. Joined by South Carolina National Corporation, the three banks formed one of the largest and most impressive financial institutions in the United States. By 1994, total assets had doubled to $36 billion, deposits had climbed from $12 billion to $23 billion, and trust assets had increased from $38 billion to $92 billion. Under the Wachovia name, new offices were opened in London, Tokyo, New York City, and Chicago, and an extensive network of new branch offices in the Southeast was in the planning stage. To reflect its involvement with and commitment to its new partners, First Atlanta decided to adopt the Wachovia logo and change its name to Wachovia Bank of Georgia, N.A.

### *Principal Subsidiaries*

First Bank Building Corporation; First Atlanta Services Corporation; Wachovia Auto Leasing Company of Georgia; WMCS, Inc.

### *Further Reading*

Bronstein, Barbara, ''Big Georgia Banks Win Branching Battle,'' *American Banker,* January 30, 1996, p. 7.

Gordon, Noel, ''Homes for Orphans,'' *The Banker,* January 1996, p. 3A.

Harker, Patrick J., and Kathleen C. McClave, ''Inconsistent Decisions Undermine Value of Technology Spending,'' *American Banker,* February 7, 1996, p. 14.

*A History of Banking And Wachovia,* Winston-Salem, N.C.: Wachovia Corporation, 1994.

Moore, Michael, ''Wachovia Doubling Its Staff for Branch Fund Sales,'' *American Banker,* January 10, 1996, p. 4.

Rhoads, Christopher, ''Georgia Regulator Comes Out for Intrastate Branching,'' *American Banker,* December 22, 1995, p. 6.

Tracey, Brian, ''Reopening the Door to Outsourcing: Eased Rules on Subsidiary Operations May Bring Banks Back,'' *American Banker,* December 27, 1994, p. 15.

—Thomas Derdak

# WACHOVIA

## Wachovia Bank of South Carolina, N.A.

Palmetto Center
1426 Main Street
Columbia, South Carolina 29226
U.S.A.
(803) 765-3000
Fax: (803) 771-3472

*Wholly Owned Subsidiary of Wachovia Corporation*
*Incorporated:* 1929 as South Carolina National Bank
*Assets:* $7 billion (1995 est.)
*Employees:* 4,113
*SICs:* 6712 Bank Holding Companies; 6021 National
Commercial Banks

Wachovia Bank of South Carolina, N.A. is one of the three banks that constitute Wachovia Corporation, along with Wachovia Bank of North Carolina and Wachovia Bank of Georgia. Each of these three banks has a distinguished history, but the South Carolina Bank subsidiary's heritage goes back the furthest. Wachovia Bank of South Carolina has been at the forefront of the state's financial community since its inception, and offers customers the entire range of financial services, including conveniently located automated teller machines (ATMs), mortgage services, real estate advice, and insurance programs to fit every need.

### Early History

Wachovia Bank of South Carolina was chartered by the state as the Bank of Charleston in 1834, but its roots go back to the very beginning of banking in the United States. Following the ratification of the U.S. Constitution in 1789, the newly established First United States Bank opened a branch in Charleston in 1792. When the charter for the First United States Bank lapsed in 1811, the Second Bank of the United States was chartered in 1816. Yet there was intense disagreement among those people in the new capitol of Washington, D.C., over the issue of whether state chartered banks were preferable to na-

tional banks. This disagreement finally resulted in a veto of the bill to recharter the federal bank in 1832. Consequently, the branch office of the Second United States Bank in Charleston was forced to close, and the city was left without any financial institution.

Realizing that their city was in need of a bank, and determined to maintain control of its operations, the city fathers convinced the South Carolina state legislature to charter the Bank of Charleston on December 17, 1834. Located in the same office as the national bank, and operating with almost the same staff, the Bank of Charleston was capitalized at $2 million and reported its first dividend only six months after it had opened for business. During the 1830s and 1840s, the bank was involved in highly successful domestic and international currency exchange. One of the methods that the bank used to increase its profitability was to issue and circulate its own notes. By exchanging its own bank notes for drafts on banks located in the North, and subsequently "discounting" that commercial paper, the Bank of Charleston reaped large profits. By 1845, the bank had also established an agency network that extended the length of the eastern seaboard and into some western states. The bank had initiated and established close working relations with 123 banks and agencies in states such as Georgia, Florida, Louisiana, and Kentucky to help the wholesale merchants in Charleston fill the orders of store owners in such budding American towns as Apalachicola, Florida, and Macon, Georgia.

### The Civil War and Reconstruction

The Bank of Charleston had over $6 million in assets at the start of the Civil War in 1861, reported profits of $275,000, and had paid semi-annual dividends for 25 consecutive years. At the forefront in asserting the issue of states' rights against the U.S. Federal Government, South Carolina was one of the leaders in forming the Confederacy and seceding from the Union. In late 1860, the Bank of Charleston loaned the state legislature $100,000 to carry out the beginning of its secession policy. In early 1861, the bank made loans and donations to help supply and equip the Beauregard Light Infantry and the Charleston Riflemen. Just before the fall of Fort Sumter, situated in the city's thriving international harbor, the Bank of Charleston provided a $200,000 loan to the Confederate Treasury.

In 1862, under the threat of advancing Union troops, the bank was forced to relocate all its records and currency to Columbia, South Carolina, the state's capitol. In 1863, the bank donated its old ledgers to be made into cartridge paper by the Charleston Arsenal. A short time later, the bank donated $2,000 in silver coins, a valuable currency in the Confederacy during the Civil War, to make silver nitrate, a chemical used as an antiseptic to treat wounded soldiers.

Robert E. Lee, the general in charge of the Confederate forces fighting the Union Army, was unable to stave off defeat. Charleston harbor had been isolated due to a successful Union blockade, and business had all but come to a standstill. When Sherman marched through Georgia and South Carolina, cutting the Confederacy in two with a large Union Army, the days of secession were all but numbered. As the Union Army advanced on Columbia, the Bank of Charleston transferred its records and assets to Greenville, South Carolina, for the remainder of the war. When the war formally ended with Lee's surrender to General Grant, head of all the Union forces, at Appomattox, Virginia, the south was in ruins. The Bank of Charleston, with almost all of its assets, notes, and securities in worthless Confederate currency, found itself insolvent.

The only antebellum bank in South Carolina to survive the Civil War and the difficult years of the Reconstruction, the Bank of Charleston relocated from Greenville back to Charleston and opened its doors for business in 1872. Under new federal laws, the bank was converted into a national bank. During this time, the officers of the bank worked hard to reduce the bank's liabilities incurred before the war, and re-establish its reputation and credibility. By the end of 1880, the bank was able to declare a divided of three cents on all outstanding shares. As the 19th century drew to a close, the revival of economic activity in Charleston, due largely to the resurgence of the city's harbor facilities and the growth of the phosphate industry, directly affected the financial welfare of the Bank of Charleston.

### The 20th Century

By the summer of 1905, the Bank of Charleston had fully recovered and reported assets of approximately $3 million. Yet the bank's growth was severely limited due to the restrictions on national banks. Nationally chartered banks were not allowed to engage in branch banking, so the Bank of Charleston could not expand its services to customers other than at its central office on the corner of Broad and State Streets. At the same time, however, state banks which were not restricted by the legislation expanded throughout the state of South Carolina.

The Bank of Charleston joined the Federal Reserve System in 1914, and profited by borrowing money from the federal reserve district office located in Richmond. Able to establish branch offices under new federal legislation, the bank expanded quickly around Charleston and throughout the state. With America's entry into the First World War in 1917, the Bank of Charleston sold Liberty Bonds to support the country's war effort. The rapid expansion of the nearby United States Navy Yard, which built warships for the Navy and poured $15 million

into improving dock facilities, prompted management at the bank to establish the Charleston Trust Company, a state-chartered bank which conducted business almost exclusively with the U.S. Navy and the shipbuilding companies surrounding North Charleston.

During the 1920s, the Bank of Charleston prospered. In one of management's most important decisions involving the future of the bank, the Bank of Charleston consolidated its operations with two other banks, the Carolina National Bank and the Norwood National Bank, in order to form the brand-new South Carolina National Bank. Carolina National Bank, created in 1868, and Norwood National Bank, founded in 1907, were financial institutions located in rural areas of the state. The merger involved a unique diversification: the demand for loans in rural areas served by Carolina National and Norwood National occurred at opposite seasonal times as the demand for loans in the city of Charleston. Thus the creation of South Carolina National Bank would benefit from both urban and rural customers seeking loans. Finalized in 1926, the merger resulted in a bank with resources over $25 million, making South Carolina National Bank the largest in the state.

### The Great Depression and World War II

After the stock market crash in the fall of 1929, many banks could not meet their customers' demands to redeem deposits. In 1933, as the financial situation worsened across the country, newly elected president Franklin D. Roosevelt sought to protect banks from bankruptcy and restore credibility to the U.S. banking system by declaring a Bank Holiday. Roosevelt also asked Congress to pass the Emergency Banking Act, which described the conditions under which banks could reopen for business.

The decline in deposits prevented South Carolina National Bank from reopening on an unrestricted basis. When the bank was finally allowed to reopen for business under the Emergency Banking Act, a reorganization of the nationally chartered bank was necessary, along with constant supervision by federal bank examiners. Slowly but certainly, South Carolina National Bank restored its credibility, and gained public confidence with its conservative yet stable financing policy through the remainder of the decade. One of the bank's most impressive efforts involved the use of a plane to assure adequate amounts of currency at all its branch locations across South Carolina.

When World War II began and America entered the global conflict at the end of 1941, South Carolina National Bank again sold War Bonds to support the country's military effort. During the same time, the bank reaped more business through increased activity at the North Charleston Navy Yard. The bank opened a new branch located at Camp Jackson near the Navy Yard, and by the end of 1943 had transacted millions of dollars of business with companies involved in the varied activities of supplying war materials to the United States Navy. At the end of the war in 1945, South Carolina National Bank had established itself as one of the most successful banks in the southeastern part of the nation.

### Postwar Prosperity

In 1951, the bank instituted its first drive-in teller window in the back of the Broad Street location in Charleston, initiated an installment loan policy for the purchase of automobiles, and provided customers with long-term credit services by implementing a Sure Credit Plan which gave an approved line of credit for an individual's personal use. As the bank grew in assets during the 1950s, its loan portfolio shifted from the agricultural to the industrial sector.

In 1957, South Carolina National Bank merged with the First National Bank of Greenville. This merger expanded the presence of South Carolina National in many smaller towns within the state, and brought the number of bank offices to a total of 33 in 20 towns and cities across the state. During the same year, the bank installed up-to-date automated bookkeeping equipment, and many other technological innovations during the rest of the decade that would forever change the nature of the banking industry.

During the 1960s, South Carolina National Bank experienced its most profitable period to date. By 1962, consumer lending was one of the fastest growing segments of earnings within the bank, and auto loans became an increasingly important factor in its profitability. By the end of 1964, through numerous mergers and branch openings, the total number of offices reached 64. In 1967, the bank organized an international division to deal with the growing commerce in international trade brought into the state through the harbor in Charleston. In 1968, South Carolina National Bank reached an agreement with BankAmericard to become one of its licensees, and a BankAmericard Center was established at the office in Columbia, South Carolina.

### Transition and Expansion in the 1970s and 1980s

In 1971, management at the bank decided to centralize its operations and formed a holding company, South Carolina National Corporation. One year later, the company acquired Provident Financial Corporation, a large and highly successful firm which owned numerous finance companies spread across Virginia, South Carolina, and North Carolina. Management at South Carolina National Corporation reorganized these companies into five subsidiaries, including SCNC Advisory Corporation, SCN Services Corporation, SCN Leasing Corporation, August Kohn and Company, and SCNC's mortgage lending subsidiary. The bank also made a commitment to improving its customer services by purchasing 11 automated teller machines, which were soon integrated into the TouchMatic system, providing around the clock access to customer account information and readily available cash.

During 1983, South Carolina National Corporation moved its corporate offices from Charleston to the Palmetto Center, a modern office complex located in Columbia. One year later, the bank made two of its most important acquisitions: First National Bank of South Carolina and First Bankshares Corporation of South Carolina. These two acquisitions significantly increased the assets of South Carolina National, and resulted in an even greater

influence within the financial community of the Southeast. By the mid-1980s, South Carolina National Corporation operated more than 160 branch offices in the state, and more than 100 TouchMatic automatic teller machines. By joining Relay and CIRRUS a few years later, the bank was able to offer its customers access to quick cash and account information at over 5,000 automated teller machines across the United States.

### The 1990s and Beyond

In order to consolidate its holdings, expand its presence in new markets, and enhance its standards of customer service, management at South Carolina National Corporation decided to merge with Wachovia Corporation of North Carolina. With over $7 billion in assets and a network of 164 offices spread throughout the state, South Carolina National became a wholly owned subsidiary of Wachovia Corporation on December 6, 1991. In May of 1994, the bank assumed the name Wachovia Bank of South Carolina, N.A., and adopted the distinctive blue Wachovia logo for all its operating offices.

The merger of South Carolina National Bank with Wachovia Corporation, along with the additional merger of First Atlanta National Bank in 1993, resulted in combined assets of approximately $36 billion by the end of fiscal 1994. With offices in New York City, Chicago, London, and Tokyo, Wachovia Bank of South Carolina has become part of one of the largest and most respected financial institutions not only in the Southeast but in the world.

### Principal Subsidiaries

Wachovia Insurance Services of South Carolina, Inc.: First National Properties, Inc.: South Carolina OREO, Inc.

### Further Reading

Dillon, Edward, "A Better Gauge of Merger Success: Looking at Net Operating Expenses," *American Banker*, December 8, 1993, p. 4.
Fickenscher, Lisa, "Wachovia Says It May Attract $1 Billion in Card Balance Transfers This Year," *American Banker*, May 11, 1994, p. 16.
*A History of Banking and Wachovia*, Winston-Salem, N.C.: Wachovia Corporation, 1994.
Lindley, James, *The South Carolina National Bank*, New York: Newcomen Society, 1985.
Marjanovic, Steven, "Major Investments Expected in New-Product Development," *American Banker*, September 21, 1994, p. 12.
Seiberg, Jaret, "Fed Allows Bank Holding Companies to Link Units' Services for Pricing," *American Banker*, July 28, 1994, p. 2.
Smith, Franklin, "Wachovia Bank S.C. President Is Now Chief Executive Too," *American Banker*, August 25, 1995, p. 5.
"South Carolina Bank to Use Check Imaging," *American Banker*, July 6, 1993, p. A16.
"Three Regional Execs Named for Wachovia South Carolina Bank," *American Banker*, August 4, 1995, p. 5.

—Thomas Derdak

# Watson Pharmaceuticals Inc.

311 Bonnie Circle
Corona, California 91720
U.S.A.
(909) 270-1400
Fax: (909) 270-1906

*Public Company*
*Incorporated:* 1985 as Watson Laboratories, Inc.
*Employees:* 554
*Sales:* $153 million (1995)
*Stock Exchanges:* NASDAQ
*SICs:* 2834 Pharmaceutical Operations

Watson Pharmaceuticals, Inc. develops, manufactures, and sells off-patent, or generic, pharmaceutical products. In 1996 it was selling more than 80 different products throughout the United States and parts of the world. Formed in 1985, Watson was still working in the mid-1990s to become a fully integrated pharmaceutical company, one that also researches, develops, and markets proprietary drugs and related delivery systems.

Watson Pharmaceuticals was launched in the mid-1980s, when the market for generic drugs was blooming. Generic drugs are off-brand drugs that are chemically the same as their brand-name cousins. When a pharmaceutical company develops and patents a new drug, the patent protection typically allows the inventor to sell the drug (at a premium) for several years free from direct competition. Once the patent protection terminates, however, other companies are free to copy and produce the same drug. The generic drug industry began to emerge as a force in the early 1980s, when many pharmaceutical goods that had been developed in the 1970s lost their patent protection. When the manufacturers of those propriety products continued to charge high prices, generic drug makers jumped into the game, offering drugs that were identical in effect but much lower in price.

## Coming to America

Enter Taiwan native Allen Chao. Chao had left Taiwan in 1968 to study pharmacy sciences in the United States. After

only five years, Chao earned his doctorate in industrial and physical pharmacy at Purdue University. He then took a job with pharmaceutical developer and manufacturer G. D. Searle & Co. There, in a span of five years, he rose from a position as researcher to the director of new product and new pharmaceutical technology development. After a few years in that post, however, Chao was restless. He wanted to strike out on his own and build a pharmaceutical company from scratch.

Chao's motivation to start his own enterprise came partly from his parents: "You know, you'll never win the Nobel Prize," Chao's mother told him after he went to work with G. D. Searle, according to *Forbes*. In fact, Chao's parents had originally hoped that their son would return to Taiwan to run the family pharmaceuticals manufacturing business. When Chao's father realized that his son was going to begin a career in the United States, he sold the business and he and his wife moved to California to retire. Throughout his career at Searle, Chao's mother prodded him to start his own company. She got her wish in 1983, when Chao left G. D. Searle and launched the venture that would become Watson Pharmaceutical.

## Getting Started

Chao's long-term goal was to build a fully integrated pharmaceutical company that, like Searle, developed and marketed its own drugs. Such a venture, however, typically required massive sums of money to fund the research and development of new drugs. Of import were the huge costs and risks related to getting a new drug approved for market by the Food and Drug Administration (FDA); if a proposed drug failed to receive FDA approval, which was often the case after months or years of FDA studies, a larger company could suffer greatly and a startup company would likely be destroyed. Lacking the resources needed to launch a fully integrated drug company, Chao decided to start with generics.

The chief appeal of the generic segment of the pharmaceutical industry for Chao was that drug approval was much less complicated; the FDA had already accepted the original drug and had only to complete cursory research to ensure that the generic counterpart was safe. Although generic drugs didn't offer the huge profit margins intrinsic to patented products, many generic producers were able to profit handsomely. Success in the industry depended largely on the generic drug producer's ability to move quickly to fill a void in the marketplace, but also on its ability to minimize overhead costs related to production, packaging, marketing, and distribution.

Joining Chao in the startup was David S. Hsia, who started out as vice president of product development and would later become senior vice-president of scientific affairs. Although the generics strategy reduced their capital requirements, Chao felt that they still needed about $4 million to develop their first generic drug, and possibly as much as $2 million more to achieve FDA approval. Few investors were interested. Venture capital companies snubbed the entrepreneurs, and the banks in Chicago (where Chao originally wanted to locate the company) wouldn't even loan him money against the family's personal property in California.

Unable to find startup capital from conventional sources, Chao returned to California and tapped his connections in the Taiwanese community. Family members and friends eventually contributed nearly $4 million, which helped the founders to land another $1.5 million from U.S. venture capital firms. All the while, Chao and Hsia scurried to develop the company's first drug, Furosemide, a treatment for high blood pressure. Chao and Hsia incorporated their venture in January of 1985 as Watson Laboratories, Inc. The name was an amalgamation of ''Hwa,'' Chao's mother's maiden name, and ''son,'' Americanized into ''Watson.'' By the end of 1985 Watson Pharmaceuticals had received FDA approval for Furosemide, which it began selling almost immediately.

### Developing a Formula for Success

Watson was able to turn a profit in its first full year of sales. The company used cash flow from that first drug to fund the development of other generics, or off-patent drugs. Watson survived a period of more than two years in the late 1980s during which it received no new drug approvals from the FDA. Despite that hindrance, however, Watson continued to profit and to research a string of new generics. Sales rose to about $13.25 million in 1988 as net income inched up to $259,000. Despite heavy investments in ongoing research and development, Watson managed to boost profits to $1.26 million in 1989, from sales of nearly $21 million.

Watson's successful development efforts following the introduction of Furosemide provided the formula for its work on Loxapine, a tranquilizer used to treat schizophrenia. Chao began developing a generic substitute for the original patented product in 1986, and it eventually won the FDA's blessing. At that time, the market for the drug was only $10 million. Soon the sales volume of the drug more than doubled and Watson was able to capture a full 50 percent of the market. By 1996, Watson was still the only pharmaceutical company selling a generic version of the original drug.

Loxapine was a good illustration of Watson's unique operating stratagem. It was true that Chao was competing in the typically low-margin generics industry. But his company had managed to avert many of the downsides of generics manufac-

turing by pursuing a singular market approach. Rather than target the markets for big drugs that were coming off patent, such as Tagamet and Valium, Chao decided to chase smaller market segments that were of less interest to the big generics manufacturers. Watson was willing to chase drugs with markets of less than $30 million annually, while its bigger competitors often ignored drugs with less than $150 million in annual sales.

Watson was able to profit, though, because it was often the only company competing in its selected niches. The big drugs, in contrast, were often copied by as many as ten or more generics manufacturers that competed fiercely on price. In addition to pursuing smaller market niches, Watson focused on developing drugs that were difficult to duplicate. That tactic allowed the company to utilize its advanced research and development arm to generate relatively high profit margins, even in the generics industry. To find those high-margin, small-market drugs, Watson's researchers regularly plied public records, searching for little known drug prospects with big potential.

### Imitation Leads to Innovation in the 1990s

Success at developing generics for niche drug markets allowed Watson to post steady gains in the early 1990s. Sales increased from $23.4 million in 1990 to $34.7 million in 1992, while net income more than quadrupled during the same period to about $2.4 million. In 1993, moreover, sales nearly doubled to $67.6 million, a hefty $12.2 million of which was netted as income. The big jump in 1993 was the result of several new drug introductions. By late 1993, in fact, Watson had the exclusive right to produce 17 generic products, and was also making about 40 drugs for other companies. It also had about a dozen new products in its research and development pipeline that were awaiting FDA approval.

Bolstering its niche market strategy in this period were Watson's efforts to develop proprietary value-added delivery systems that enhanced its generics and gave it an edge in the marketplace. For example, Watson would develop a generic substitute for a drug that was typically administered to the patient through a syringe by a trained professional. Watson might then create a new dose delivery system—such as a patch worn on the skin or a device that administered the drug through the nose or mouth—that allowed the patient to administer the drug. Not only would Watson benefit from revenue from the new delivery technique, but it would profit from an often significantly expanded market for the drug.

To take advantage of rising sales, Chao and fellow executives pursued an aggressive plan to expand Watson's manufacturing operations. To that end, they had taken Watson public in February of 1993 with a stock sale that raised $25 million. A subsequent offering brought a total of more than $100 million to Watson's war chest. The cash was used to add manufacturing capabilities. For instance, Watson purchased the patent on an injection-molding technology that would let Watson make suppository products that were less waxy and messy. The money was also used to fund research and development of new generics and delivery systems. Importantly, Watson's cash surplus allowed Chao to move closer to his initial goal of making the company a fully integrated pharmaceutical firm.

### Toward Full Integration

Watson's revenues rose to $87 million in 1994 as it introduced new drugs to market. The company followed those gains early in 1995 with the acquisition of Circa Pharmaceuticals, another maker and marketer of generics. Circa had formerly operated as Bolar Pharmaceutical Co. before being disgraced in a fraud and bribery scandal. In 1989, in fact, the FDA announced that several of its employees had accepted bribes from various generic drug makers. Watson wasn't involved in the scandal. Bolar, on the other hand, ultimately lost nearly all of its government drug approvals and was fined $10 million (the largest penalty ever levied against a generic drug maker). In addition, several Bolar executives went to jail.

By 1995 Circa, after changing its name from Bolar, was staging a recovery. Chao saw an opportunity to buy the company at a reasonable price and add a number of drugs and related proprietary products to its own portfolio. Watson paid the equivalent of about $600 million for the company. Management at the two companies planned to work together to create a global, one-stop shop pharmaceutical company that sold both generic and proprietary products. After the merger was complete, Watson's product line had grown to include more than 80 different drugs (variations of 30 major pharmaceutical products). Sales for 1995 increased to $153 million, reflecting the merger as well as revenue growth related to new and established products.

Despite the challenges presented by such rapid growth, Chao remained focused on his goal of making Watson a fully integrated, global pharmaceutical company. To that end, Watson entered two joint ventures with Chinese companies that would allow the company to begin manufacturing and marketing its products to Chao's native region. The company was also working to develop its own patented drugs through joint ventures and partnerships with other drug makers.

### Principal Subsidiaries

Circa Pharmaceuticals, Inc.; Somerset Pharmaceuticals, Inc. (50%); Watson Laboratories, Inc.; Watson Pharmaceuticals (Asia) Ltd.

### Further Reading

"Watson Pharmaceuticals Inc. and Mylan Laboratories Inc. Announce Management Promotions at Jointly-Owned Somerset Pharmaceuticals," *PR Newswire,* August 9, 1995.

Darlin, Damon, "Still Running Scared," *Forbes,* September 26, 1994, p. 127.

McAuliffe, Don, "Corona Drug Company Plans 1994 Expansion," *Press Enterprise,* October 14, 1993.

——, "Corona Drug Firm Capitalizes on New Technology," *Press Enterprise,* August 2, 1993.

——, "Stock Selloff Puzzles Watson as Plant Expansion Continues," *Press Enterprise,* February 24, 1994.

——, "Watson Pharmaceuticals' Profit Slips Because of Acquisition Cost," *Press Enterprise,* November 3, 1995, p. 9E.

Sanchez, Jesus, "Deal Would Create a Generic Drug Giant," *Los Angeles Times,* March 31, 1995, p. 2D.

Unger, Michael, "Circa Pharmaceutical to Merge," *Newsday,* March 31, 1995, p. 69A.

—Dave Mote

# WAVERLY

# Waverly, Inc.

351 West Camden Street
Baltimore, Maryland 21201-2436
U.S.A.
(410) 528-4000
Fax: (410) 528-4414
http://www.wwilkins.com

*Public Company*
*Incorporated:* 1892 as the Williams & Wilkins Co.
*Sales:* $156.07 million (1995)
*Employees:* 440
*Stock Exchanges:* NASDAQ
*SICs:* 2721 Periodicals Publishing; 2731 Book
   Publishing; 2741 Miscellaneous Publishing; 5192
   Books, Periodicals and Newspapers

Waverly, Inc. is a leading worldwide publisher of books, periodicals, and electronic media in the fields of medicine, allied health, and related disciplines. In 1995 it was publishing, under the trade name Williams & Wilkins, 48 periodicals for medical and scientific societies, with which it shared certain editorial responsibilities, as well as 26 periodicals it owned directly. It was also publishing and distributing more than 1,300 book titles, principally under the Williams & Wilkins name in the United States. In addition, Waverly was turning out about 400 electronic-media products under various trade names. Its products were being sold in more than 50 countries, and its subsidiaries included a German-language publisher.

## Under Private Ownership Until 1972

Waverly, Inc. owes its beginning to John Williams, who started a small printing press in his Baltimore attic in 1890 with $600 in funds. Shortly after, Harry Wilkins and John and Robert Garrett provided the fresh infusion of money needed to form the Williams & Wilkins Co. printing firm. One of its early employees was Edward B. Passano, who joined the firm in 1897 as a $75-a-month salesman. After a downtown fire in 1904 de-

stroyed the company's premises, Passano borrowed $12,000 from the Garretts to salvage the business. The plant was moved to the Waverly neighborhood, and the company was renamed Waverly Press. Passano became its sole owner in 1907.

Waverly Press, which specialized in printing medical and scientific material, began, in 1909, publishing its first scientific periodical, *The Journal of Pharmacology and Experimental Therapeutics.* By 1924 the company was publishing 18 journals and 50 books. It split the next year into two divisions: Waverly Press for printing scientific and technical literature, and Williams & Wilkins for publishing scientific and medical books and journals. In 1932 it made its first acquisition, Wm. Wood & Co., a New York City publisher and distributer of medical books. This immediately added 386 titles to the Williams & Wilkins list, and by 1940 book sales had increased fourfold since the acquisition.

Waverly probably never had a year in which it did not make money. During the Great Depression no employees were laid off, and no rates of pay were cut. Printing-plant employees worked six hours a day, six days a week, and there were four shifts a day. During World War II Waverly Press printed a large amount of classified material, especially for the Navy. Passano, who died in 1946, was succeeded as president by his elder son, William M. Passano. He became chief executive officer of Williams & Wilkins in 1963, when his brother Edward M. Passano succeeded him as president of Waverly Press.

## Steady Growth in the 1970s

When Waverly Press went public in 1972, it owned four properties in Baltimore, including a printing plant, and also a larger printing plant in Easton, Maryland, that opened in late 1949. Net sales totaled $16.7 million in 1971, up from $12.5 million in 1967, and net income rose from $827,000 to $1,128,000 in this period. Current assets came to $9.7 million in mid-1972, and there was no long-term debt. William M. Passano, Jr., became president and chief executive officer of Waverly Press in 1972. The initial public stock offering was held in April of that year. In 1996 members of the Passano family still held 59 percent of the company's common stock.

530

Publishing and printing each accounted for roughly half of company sales in 1972. In the publishing division, operating under the Williams & Wilkins trade name, periodicals contributed 55 percent of revenue in 1971, books, 38 percent, and services, 7 percent. About three-quarters of the revenue from its 31 periodicals came from journals owned either wholly by the company or jointly with a major scientific society. The company also was earning income from publishing services for 40 other periodicals. Two-thirds of book revenues came from the company's own books, with almost all of the rest from sales of books imported from foreign publishers. About 1,700 titles were being offered, including staples like *Stedman's Medical Dictionary,* which went through 25 editions between 1911 and 1989, and *Grant's Atlas of Anatomy,* first published in 1943.

Waverly's printing division was printing all of the material published by the company and also books and periodicals published by unaffiliated customers. About 130 periodicals were being printed for professional societies, commercial publishers, and academic institutions. Booklets, pamphlets, and promotional literature were also being printed. About 65 percent of all the books published by Waverly and a majority of those printed by Waverly were being sold to medical students. In 1972 the company produced an audiovisual tape cassette accompanied by an instructional medical manual, its first venture outside traditional publishing.

Net sales for Waverly Press continued to rise in the 1970s, reaching nearly $38 million in 1979. Net income grew at a slower pace, reaching nearly $1.9 million in 1979. By this time books had become as important to the publishing division in revenue as periodicals, with more than 669 titles published and offered for sale by the company.

### Diversifying in the 1980s

Of 531,941 books sold by Waverly Press in 1980, about 84 percent were in the medical field, with the rest in related fields. Of the 39 periodicals, 12 were owned by the company and 27 published for major scientific societies and institutions. Printing operations changed little in the decade, except that there were significant increases in pamphlets, booklets, and direct-mail promotion material for other clients.

Partly because of a drop in medical school enrollment, Waverly Press became seriously engaged in diversifying by the mid-1980s. In 1983 it began selling software teaching programs run on personal computers and visual teaching aids on videocassettes. Armed with $14 million in cash from periodical subscriptions paid in advance, the company also began making acquisitions, buying Nurseco Inc., a small nursing publishing firm, in 1985. The printing division also had been diversifying, turning out such nonscientific journals as *Foreign Affairs* and *Wilson Quarterly.*

Although earnings remained at a comfortable level, major efforts were made at Waverly Press to contain costs. When the labor-intensive, but nonunionized, printing division began lagging in profits, the company in 1986 changed medical carriers, eliminated automatic annual bonuses, cut back vacations, and raised the work week from 38 to 40 hours without an increase in pay. Waverly officers, many of them relatives, lost the right to buy company cars at after-tax cost because they were ordering Jaguars and BMWs. "We have an independent board of directors that passes on my salary and all major capital expenditures," William Passano told a *Barron's* reporter in 1987.

Among these expenditures was the purchase, in 1988, of Rynd Communications, Inc. for $1.6 million and MedDeck, Inc. for more than $2.2 million. Two years later Waverly Press acquired Urban & Schwarzenberg GmbH, a German publisher of medical books with a U.S. subsidiary publishing English-language medical books, for cash and stock valued at about $13 million. Later in 1990 it bought most of the assets of Harwal Publishing Co., a publisher of review books for medical students, from John Wiley & Sons Inc. for $8 million. In 1991 the company acquired Lea & Febiger, L.P., another medical publisher, for about $10 million.

### Printing Division Sold in 1993

Waverly Press, Inc. changed its name to Waverly, Inc. in 1988. Interviewed in 1990 by *Wall Street Transcript,* Passano said that publishing now accounted for two-thirds of Waverly's revenue and that the company increasingly saw its future in publishing rather than in its printing operations, which had suffered in morale, performance, and profits ever since the 1986 crackdown on labor costs. He called Waverly, with 35 software programs, a leader in electronic publishing. A greater effort also was being made in marketing abroad, since foreign customers were now accounting for 45 percent of publishing revenues. By 1992 the company had formed joint ventures with local partners to sell medical books in Australia, Hong Kong, and Japan, and to print them in Poland.

In 1990 Waverly's net sales jumped to $121.7 million and its net income to almost $4 million. The following year Edward B. Hutton, president of the company since 1988, became its chief executive officer, the first from outside the Passano family. Sales that year rose to $147.3 million, but earnings per share fell from a record $1.01 to 78 cents because of the need to pay for the recent acquisitions, which had caused Waverly to take on long-term debt for the first time in history. In 1992 the company earned nearly $2.8 million from continuing operations but had a net loss of $108,000 after taking a $4.9-million charge to reflect the adoption of new rules covering the accounting treatment for post-retirement medical benefits.

In October 1993 Waverly sold its printing division to Cadmus Communications Corp. for between $14.5 million and $20 million. Waverly Press had accounted for about 22 percent of the parent company's revenues of $161 million in 1992.

Waverly, Inc. ended the year with a net loss of $2 million, which it attributed to declining sales to the pharmaceutical industry and one-time charges related to its relocation within Baltimore. Just before Christmas 1993 Waverly agreed to become the first commercial tenant of the city's Camden Yards warehouse, leasing 72,400 square feet of space. It moved its corporate headquarters to this location in June 1995.

Waverly responded to a drop of 11 percent in book sales during 1993 by cutting its workforce by about ten percent and eschewing bonuses for top executives. As part of the restructuring, the Harwal and Lea & Febiger imprints were consolidated under new management and principally put under the Williams & Wilkins name. The company made further acquisitions during the year, however, buying 235 computer programs from Medi-Sim for $1.9 million, *Hearing Journal* for $970,000, and Editions Pradel, a French medical- and science-book publisher, for $600,000.

The 1993 debacle, retrospectively attributed by Waverly to uncertainty in the health-care industry over President Clinton's proposed program, was followed by record sales of $131.9 million and record income of $4.7 million in 1994. During the year the company made further acquisitions, purchasing Betz Publishing Co. for about $2.2 million and various electronic media, book, and periodical publishing properties for a total of about $1.4 million. Urban & Schwarzenberg acquired Muller and Steinicke, a Munich medical bookstore, for about $2 million, and certain medical-book titles for $1 million.

In 1995 Waverly had record sales of over $156 million and record net income of $5.3 million. The United States accounted for 58 percent of revenues and Europe for 36 percent, while the remaining sales were generated in the Far East and elsewhere. After six years of stagnant stock prices, Waverly shareholders were rewarded in 1995, when the price of a share nearly doubled in value. About 45 percent of the shares were owned by the Passano family, which was said to control another 15 percent held by insiders. Long-term debt had been reduced to $3.7 million at the end of the year, compared to $12.2 million at the end of 1991. Waverly's total assets were valued at $128.2 million at the end of 1995.

In addition to its Williams & Wilkins imprint, Waverly was using among its book-publishing trade names Lea & Febiger, National Medical Series, and Stedman's World Series in the United States and Urban & Schwarzenberg in Germany. About 400 of its approximately 1,300 book titles were in German rather than English. The English-language books were being marketed and distributed overseas by a separate division with offices in London, Paris, Buenos Aires, Hong Kong, and Bangkok, as well as Baltimore. Waverly also was a partner in distribution companies located in Tokyo and Sydney, Australia.

A direct-mail-order firm in Munich was promoting and distributing the German-language books. Waverly also operated a publishing firm in Wroclaw, Poland, to translate its books into the local language and was participating in a number of joint ventures with foreign publishers to translate its English-language titles into local languages.

Waverly's periodicals had a paid subscription base of about 385,000 at the end of 1995. Its electronic products were being sold in various formats, including computer software, interactive videodiscs, and CD-ROM, and were being marketed under various trade names, including Williams & Wilkins, Medi-Sim, Stedman Words, and de'MEDICI.

### Principal Subsidiaries

Editions Pradel (France); Med-Pub, Inc.; Oscar Rothacker Verlagschuchandlung, GmbH (Germany); Urban & Partner (Poland); Urban & Schwarzenberg GmbH (Germany); Urban & Schwarzenberg Ges.m.b.H. (Austria); Urban & Schwarzenberg Verlag fur Medizin GmbH (Germany); Waverly Europe Ltd. (UK); Waverly Info-Med Ltd. (Hong Kong); Waverly Info-Med Ltd. (Thailand); Waverly Sales, Inc. (U.S. Virgin Islands); Williams & Wilkins Sales, Inc.

### Principal Divisions

Professional Learning Systems Division; Waverly International; Waverly North America; Williams & Wilkins Book Publishing; Williams & Wilkins Periodical Publishing.

### Further Reading

*A Century of Progress: 1890–1990,* Baltimore: Waverly, Inc., 1989.

"E.B. Passano Dies Suddenly," *Baltimore Sun,* June 14, 1946, pp. 12, 28.

Hinden, Stan, "Publisher Waverly Inc.'s Prescription for Success," *Washington Post,* May 1, 1994, Bus. Sec., p. 31.

Mahar, Maggie, "Just What the Doctor Ordered," *Barron's,* June 1, 1987, pp. 18, 20.

Milliot, James, "Waverly Agrees to Sell Printing Division," *Publishers Weekly,* October 11, 1993, p. 8.

——, "Waverly Expects Slow Rebound from Poor 1993," *Publishers Weekly,* June 6, 1994, p. 16.

Mirabella, Lorraine, "Waverly to Remain in the City," *Baltimore Sun,* December 24, 1993, pp. 7C, 14C.

Savitz, Eric J., "On the Mend," *Barron's,* June 29, 1992, pp. 22, 36.

"Waverly Press, Inc.," *Wall Street Transcript,* October 2, 1972, pp. 30145–30146; May 4, 1981, p. 61506; May 5, 1986, p. 81782; June 11, 1990, p. 97519.

"West German Firm Bought by Publisher," *Washington Post,* March 12, 1990, *Washington Business,* p. 12.

—Robert Halasz

# WestPoint Stevens Inc.

**507 West Tenth Street**
**P.O. Box 71**
**West Point, Georgia 31833**
**U.S.A.**
**(706) 645-4000**
**Fax: (706) 645-4068**

*Public Company*
*Incorporated:* 1880 as West Point Manufacturing
    Company
*Employees:* 16,560
*Sales:* $1.65 billion (1995)
*Stock Exchanges:* NASDAQ
*SICs:* 2211 Broadwoven Fabric Mills Cotton

WestPoint Stevens Inc. is America's largest manufacturer and marketer of bed and bath textile products. It is also, through its Alamac subsidiary, a leading producer of knitted sportswear fabric. The company, whose southern roots date back to the early 19th century, operates 33 manufacturing facilities located in Alabama, Georgia, North Carolina, South Carolina, Maine, Florida, and Virginia. The textile giant markets bed, bath, and related accessory products under the well-known brand names of Martex, Unitica, Lady Pepperell, Stevens, and Vellux. Its licensed designer names include Ralph Lauren and Julie Ingleman.

### Early History

WestPoint Stevens owes its present structure to three textile leaders founded in the 19th century: the West Point Manufacturing Company, the Pepperell Manufacturing Company, and J.P. Stevens & Company. The oldest strand of the lineage dates back to 1813 when Nathaniel Stevens began producing woolen broadcloth in a converted grist mill located in Andover, Massachusetts. The company, under the direction of three generations of the Stevens family, grew to become the nation's second-largest publicly traded textile producer by the time it was acquired by WestPoint Pepperell in 1988. Pepperell, which merged with Westpoint in 1965, owes its inception to Sir William Pepperell, who began exporting cloth to the Orient from his Biddeford, Maine, mill in 1851. While the rich individual histories of each of the three companies are important in WestPoint Stevens's current identity and all are represented in the corporate logo, the company—at least through most of the 20th century—has been most easily identified by its West Point heritage and the Lanier family, who incorporated the West Point Manufacturing Company in 1880 and maintained leadership through the late 1980s.

The textile mills that would become the West Point Manufacturing Company originated in West Point, the antebellum cotton center of east central Alabama and west central Georgia, shortly after Appomattox and the end of the Civil War. In 1866, two separate groups of local planters and merchants, their plantations and businesses ruined, pooled enough resources to build two cotton mills in the valley of the Chattahoochee River. The mills had the advantage of being located in the midst of cotton fields and would not have to pay the high freight rates for the long haul to the East. They also benefitted from a large supply of water power and labor. However, the fledgling operation suffered from a shortage of capital and experienced management. During the Panic of 1873, both mills were forced to shut down.

It was during the Panic that two young Confederate veterans, Lafayette Lanier and his older brother, Ward Crockett, sons of a successful antebellum copper miner, began purchasing stock in the idle mill. The Laniers, along with a new president, John D. Johnson, revitalized the enterprise by investing in new equipment and securing the services of William Lang, an experienced cotton mill manager from England, to help direct the rebuilding and reorganization effort. Realizing that the company had been losing money by manufacturing osnaburgs, a type of coarse cloth used in local markets, Lanier converted the mills to flat duck, a canvas-type fabric used for tents and covered wagons that was in heavy demand along the frontier.

Under Lang's efficient management and the Laniers' strong business sense, the company prospered, supplying millions of yards of duck needed to provide shelter for railroad workers during the building of the five transcontinental lines between 1865 and 1893. By 1880, the Laniers owned 70 percent of the stock in the Chattahoochee mill and reorganized the business as

**Company Perspectives:**

*We are focused on being the premier consumer products company in the home fashions industry with the strongest brands and licenses. We intend to increase our market share by offering a broad product line through all major channels of distribution. We are committed to supporting our products through innovation, styling, and consumer advertising.*

the West Point Manufacturing Company. The new company was incorporated in both Alabama and Georgia, with eight stockholders and a capital of $107,000.

Disaster struck eight years later. The mill burned to the ground, completely destroying the Laniers' manufacturing business. The company was saved, however, by its selling agency in Boston, N. Boynton & Co., a sail manufacturer that depended on West Point to outfit its clipper ships, who provided the financial support for the rebuilding. The Eastern money enabled the company to diversify its line of duck fabric into heavier fabrics and take full advantage of the increasing demand for textiles brought on by the development of the West during the 1880s and 1890s. Before the close of the century, the company made its first expansion, building a new mill on a large tract of partially cultivated land lying along the Alabama bank of the Chattahoochee next to West Point. In honor of the two men who conceived the idea, Lanier and Theodore Bennett, an N. Boynton salesman, the new mill and surrounding village were named Lanett.

### Early 20th-Century Expansion

As a testament to its financial stability, West Point, which had added a bleachery and dye works facility and a railway, initiated a second major plan of expansion during the Panic of 1907. Under the direction of Lafayette Lanier's son, George, the company constructed a new mill and village in the Valley region named Shawmut. Modelling the design of Washington, D.C., Lanier hired a landscape architect to build the town after the pattern of a wheel with streets radiating from the hub. Like his father, who had established a school, library, and nursery school for the Valley, the progressively minded Lanier exercised a strong commitment to the social development of the community. Under his tenure, the company abolished child labor, funded the construction of modern schools, and supplemented state teacher salaries, while also erecting public libraries, gymnasiums, churches and community centers.

By the close of the Great Depression and the more prosperous 1940s, West Point had completed a third phase of expansion. It purchased mills in the Southeastern states and bought its selling agency. Through the implementation of multiple shifts, the company was able to keep its mills operating around the clock, enabling the same number of spindles to produce a much larger volume of goods. This strategy made it more profitable for West Point to purchase existing mills rather than build new ones. Other significant developments during this phase of rapid growth included the acquisition of a tufting company and the institution of a research division.

### Postwar Growth

By 1954, West Point Manufacturing Company had grown to include 12,000 employees, with annual sales of more than $125 million. Meanwhile, Pepperell Manufacturing and Stevens, both of which had—along with West Point—won Army-Navy "E Awards" for their support of the war effort, were growing steadily. Pepperell, having just constructed a new plant in Abbeville, Alabama, was fast becoming a leader in the sheet and pillow case industry. J.P. Stevens, having consolidated its nine mill companies and sales operation, had expanded to include 29 manufacturing plants and was becoming a leader in the production of sheets, bedroom accessories, towels, and carpet.

### The 1960s and 1970s: Growth through Merger and Acquisition

In March 1965, West Point joined forces with Pepperell Manufacturing, creating the fourth-largest publicly held textile company in the United States at the time. Joe Lanier continued as chairman and CEO, leading the new entity into an era of continued growth and product development. Two years after the merger, WestPoint Pepperell introduced the revolutionary Vellux blanket, which offered the highest warmth-to-weight ration of any brand and was able to withstand laundering and retain its colorful appearance. That same year the company opened up the newly constructed Lanier Mill and Carter Mill in one new modern facility located in the Valley.

In 1968, the company extended the geographical borders of its operations further, purchasing Alamac Knitting Mills, Inc., with locations in Massachusetts, North Carolina, and New York City, while strengthening its base in the South, through the construction of a new chemical plant in Opelika, Alabama.

With the new decade, came the end of Lanier's tenure as chief executive and the ascension of son, Joe Jr., to the position held by his family for nearly a century. During the early 1970s, the company broke ground on its first WestPoint Pepperell store in the Valley, while making plans to build a new Alamac facility in Elizabethtown, North Carolina. Channelling much of its energies into the profitable knitted sportswear division, the company further expanded its Alamac facilities through the remainder of the decade. In 1978, WestPoint Pepperell doubled the Elizabethtown operation through new construction, while further expanding the Alamac division through the purchase of two North Carolina plants.

### New Challenges of the 1980s

WestPoint Pepperell's expansionary efforts during the 1970s paved the way for record growth in the early years of the next decade. Despite recessionary conditions, marked most notably by 17.5 percent interest rates that put a crunch on the home-buying industry, WestPoint Pepperell's business remained upbeat. In 1980, the company generated sales of $1.25 billion and earnings of $42.5 million—a 55 percent jump from the previous year, and while the vast majority of textile companies struggled through the recession of the early 1980s, the doyenne of the industry continued to grow, adding a new bed products facility in 1983.

New challenges, however, threatened to flatten the growth of the company that had grown to 41 manufacturing plants in eight states by 1985. Now the third-largest publicly held textile company in the United States, WestPoint Pepperell, along with the rest of the industry, faced increasingly strong competition from foreign clothmakers: cheap-labor manufacturers in Asia and South America now supplied more than 25 percent of the U.S. market. What is more, the company—with some of its mills more than a century old—was caught in the midst of a revolution in information technology and needed to invest heavily to survive.

The company installed its first computers well ahead of most of the competition, building its own units for machine monitoring as early as 1978. The initial applications developed by the company's team of electrical engineers were used to collect and calculate the complicated data needed to measure the performance of plant machinery and workers. Because profitability in the textile industry is primarily a function of plant efficiency, such monitoring was fundamental to the company's continued success. With the advent of computer technology, the company was able to improve product quality and reduce waste, largely by paying its workers based on their output. During the mid-1980s, the company also began reducing its clerical expenses through investments in personal computers for sales and marketing purposes, saving millions of dollars in reduced inventories.

### The Turbulent Late 1980s

As the decade drew to a close, WestPoint Pepperell attempted to offset the growing force of foreign competition through expansion. Looking specifically to strengthen its presence in branded textiles, the company began negotiating the acquisition of one of its chief competitors, J.P. Stevens, then the second-largest publicly traded textile producer in the United States. In May 1988, after obtaining antitrust clearance from the Federal Trade Commission, WestPoint Pepperell took over the top spot in the $1.2 billion bed-linen business by acquiring the bed and bath operations of Stevens. The $1.2 billion deal, which included the acquisition of facilities in New York City, North Carolina, South Carolina, and Virginia, also elevated the company to a number two position in the towel market, behind Fieldcrest Cannon.

Just a year after the acquisition was finalized, WestPoint Pepperell itself became the target of a takeover, as it faced a challenge at least as threatening as the fire that demolished its mills a hundred years earlier: a hostile takeover attempt by corporate raider William Farley, the high-profile ''Fruit of the Loom'' underwear king. After several battles with WestPoint Pepperell chairman Joseph L. Lanier, Jr. and the Georgia legislature, Farley, with junk-bond financing from Drexel Burnham Lambert's Michael Milken, managed to purchase 95 percent of WestPoint Pepperell's stock at $58 a share, or an estimated $1.7 billion—20 times earnings and 2.2 times book value. The company's sluggish performance, however, prevented Farley from raising the money to buy the remaining shares. With WestPoint Pepperell's bank covenants protected, West Point Acquisition Co., the vehicle for the takeover, which had borrowed heavily to finance the purchase of the stock, defaulted on its own debt.

Arguing that Farley's acquisition company was obligated to purchase all of the shares, a group of WestPoint shareholders, including Lanier, filed suit, exacerbating Farley's problems.

Although Farley promised that he would add jobs and expand the business, he was forced to lay off several hundred employees and sell off some of the company's assets in a desperate attempt to raise the funds needed to purchase the remaining shares, but he was unable to do so. In 1991, the West Point Acquisition Co. finally gave up and sought Chapter 11 bankruptcy court protection from the angry shareholders who had tried to force Farley into involuntary bankruptcy. In September of that same year, the bankruptcy court approved a reorganization plan that eliminated all but five percent of Farley's company holdings. A year later, and hundreds of millions of dollars poorer, Farley resigned.

### A Return to Stability: The 1990s and Beyond

With the chaos of the failed takeover beyond it, WestPoint Pepperell, now controlled by Valley Fashions Corp., the group of investors that acquired Farley's shares under the bankruptcy agreement, looked to regain stability. Holcombe T. Green, an Atlanta financier, was named CEO. Joe Jennings, a 20-year veteran in the textile industry, and a member of the Lanier family, was named president and given the responsibility of managing the company's daily affairs. The strategy unveiled by the new management team included the consolidation of company brands and a $200 million investment in mill equipment and in computer equipment for customer links, internal operations, and design.

In December 1993, the company acquired the remaining five percent of WestPoint Pepperell through refinancing and merged with several of its subsidiaries to form WestPoint Stevens, Inc. Over the following two years the company engaged in an aggressive plan to increase its market share in the home fashions industry in an increasingly competitive retail market through the introduction of several new products. Examples included the creation of wrinkle-free cotton sheets and the introduction of new border treatments for towels developed with new, computerized looms. In February 1995 the company launched an unprecedented advertising campaign for its Martex line of bed and bath products. The award-winning campaign, entitled ''The Bare Necessities,'' helped to boost revenue for the third consecutive year. With innovations such as these, continuing measures to ensure low-cost production through technology, and a move toward employee-ownership through stock matching programs, WestPoint Stevens approached the late 1990s with the hope of improving its leadership position.

### Principal Subsidiaries

WestPoint-Pepperell Enterprises, Inc.; J.P. Stevens & Co., Inc.; WestPoint Stevens (Canada) Ltd.; Productos Textiles Mision Viega S.A.; Chattahoochee Valley Railway Co.; WestPoint Stevens Stores Inc.; Alamac Knit Fabrics, Inc.; WPS Receivables Corp.

### Principal Divisions

Home Fashions; Alamac.

### *Further Reading*

Barrett, Joyce, "Takeover of WestPoint Seen Damaging to Textile Industry," *Daily News Record,* February 28, 1989, p. 15.

Egan, Jack, "Farley Gets a Workout: A Big Buy Out Could Cost the Fruit of the Loom King His T-Shirt," *U.S. News & World Report,* March 12, 1990, pp. 57–58.

Lanier, Joseph L., *The First Seventy-Five Years of West Point Manufacturing Company 1880–1955,* New York: The Newcomen Society in North America, 1955.

McNamara, Michael, "WPP's Jennings: Off and Running," *WWD,* February 9, 1993, p. 14.

Ruby, Daniel, and Call, Barbara, "Micros at the Mill," *PC Week,* December 24, 1985, pp. 25–29.

Schwartz, Donna Boyle, "Sharp Point: WestPoint Pepperell Hones Its Strengths," *HFD—The Weekly Home Furnishings Newspaper,* June 21, 1993, pp. 24–26.

Taub, Stephen, "WestPoint-Pepperell: Life after Farley," *Financial World,* March 17, 1992, p. 14.

*WestPoint Stevens: Heritage from Three,* West Point, Ga.: WestPoint Stevens, 1995.

—Jason Gallman

# WINDMERE®

## Windmere Corporation

5980 Miami Lakes Drive
Miami Lakes, Florida 33014
U.S.A.
(305) 362-2611
Fax: (305) 364-0635

*Public Company*
*Incorporated:* 1963 as Save-Way Barber and Beauty
 Supply, Inc.
*Employees:* 12,000
*Sales:* $181.11 million (1994)
*Stock Exchanges:* New York
*SICs:* 3999 Manufacturing Industries, Not Elsewhere
 Classified; 3634 Electric Housewares & Fans

Windmere Corporation is a leading manufacturer and distributor of personal care and seasonal products, such as hair dryers, curling irons, mirrors, and electric fans. The company is perhaps best known for introducing the American public to gadgets ranging from hair crimpers to lint removers. With more than 20 percent of the $800 million annual personal care hair appliances market during the early 1990s, the company made a name for itself by making specialized hair dryers and curling irons, once found only in beauty and barber shops, available to the general public at a low price. Nearly all of its products are manufactured by Durable Electrical Metal Factory, Ltd., the company's wholly owned Chinese manufacturing subsidiary, which employs more than 8,000 people and occupies more than one million square feet of space. One of the nation's largest suppliers of hair care appliances to the U.S. salon industry, marketing products under brand names such as Curlmaster, Gold'n Hot, and Pro Star, the company also sells to national retailers such as Wal-Mart, Kmart, Target, and Sears. In addition to selling products under the Windmere name, the company also markets under a number of private labels and derivative brand names developed for retailers requiring their own brand.

### Early History

Windmere Corporation was founded in 1963 by Belvin Friedson, a longtime operator of five barber colleges in down-town Miami. With an initial capital investment of $45,000, the former college dropout launched Save-Way Barber and Beauty Supply, Inc., selling various hair-care products on a cash-and-carry discount basis to both professional shop owners and consumers. In 1964, Friedson opened his first store, in North Miami Beach, and generated $2 million in sales, quickly taking advantage of the contacts he had acquired during his career in the barber and beauty shop industry.

In his fourth year of operating the company, Friedson took it public to raise funds for his rapidly expanding business. The $450,000 generated from the initial public offering of common stock not only stood as a visible sign of the promise shown by the young company, but it provided the capital for product diversification. Backed by this financial support, Save-Way's early success continued in the late 1960s as Friedson began marketing women's wigs and hairpieces nationwide.

With the new decade came the first serious test for the company. The market for beauty and barber supplies virtually dried up, forcing Friedson to focus on a new market. And in 1972 he switched to the product line that would soon become the company's backbone: hair dryers, curlers, and other personal care accessories. That same year, he enlisted the services of Durable, a Chinese manufacturing company that would later become a subsidiary, to supply Save-Way with appliances. And to handle the distribution of the new product line, Friedson established the Windmere Products division.

The new strategy showed early signs of success. By 1975 revenues had grown to $9 million, and Save-Way had landed its most important sales contract to date, entering into an agreement with Eckerd Drugs, a nationally known retailer which would remain one of its largest customers through the 1990s.

During the mid-1970s, the Windmere division quickly rose to the forefront of the company. Under the direction of Friedson's son David, who took over as the division's national sales manager in 1976 after he himself dropped out of college, Windmere sales would increase five-fold over the next eight years, jumping to $35 million in 1983, 70 percent of the entire company's revenue.

The rapid expansion of Windmere products was fueled primarily by what Toni Mack of *Forbes* has called an "unabashed copycat'' strategy. Instead of developing its own products, the company attempted to reproduce gadgets that others had made successful. For instance, when an industry leader such as Bristol-Myers' Clairol was successful with an innovative curling iron or hair roller set, Windmere would quickly join forces with Durable, which became a 50 percent joint partner in 1979, to produce a replica of the product at a considerably lower cost. Taking advantage of cheap labor costs in Durable's Hong Kong factories, Windmere was able to pass the savings along to its customers and become the low-cost producer in the industry.

### Explosive Growth in the 1980s

Having completed a second public offering that raised an additional $1 million, the company entered the 1980s with a sound balance sheet and momentum from a year that saw revenues increase by 50 percent to $41.8 million and net profit more than double to $4.6 million. Such rapid growth, however, was temporarily checked in the early 1980s by a shortage of labor in the company's Hong Kong factories that made getting products out the door on time a difficult task. To fix the chronic problem, Friedson and Durable established manufacturing operations in China, where the labor supply was abundant and half as costly. Although the decision proved to be sound in the long run, immediate gains were negated by high set-up costs that resulted in three years of slow growth.

A new marketing strategy, though, would serve as another catalyst for the company's strong growth in the mid-1980s. Having adopted the corporate name Windmere in 1983, making Save-Way Industries Inc. a division, the company attempted to increase its presence in the hair care products market and jumpstart its profit margins through an aggressive mail-in rebate campaign. Hair dryers and curling irons, for instance, were advertised at an outrageously low "final cost"—usually below $5 and sometimes even free. Consumers had only to follow the rebate form correctly and mail it in with their coupon and sales receipt to take advantage of the savings. Although the company would, of course, lose money on consumers who were so diligent, Friedson wagered that most would not, after leaving the store, take the time to follow the correct procedure.

The former philosophy major's views on human nature proved correct; on average, only one out of every four buyers went to the trouble to claim his money. And the cost of paying off that 25 percent, according to Friedson, did not come close to offsetting the increase in sales volume—at no additional cost—that the rebates generated. One product alone, the VIP Pro hair dryer, advertised at just $4.88 after rebate, netted a profit of $6.5 million, a large contribution to a 30 percent climb in total earnings in 1983.

While this rebate gimmick provided a needed boost during a down period in the personal care appliance market, it could not sustain long-term growth. That would depend on the company's ability to add reputable brand names to its stable through acquisition, while at the same time adapting rapidly to the trends in the volatile hair care appliance industry.

To meet the first of these two marketing objectives, Windmere acquired a 44 percent interest in Extron International Inc. in 1983 and the remaining 56 percent the following year. The purchase of the Texas-based private corporation gave Wind-

mere the licensing rights to the trade names Fabergé, Brut, and Grand Finale.

Six months after signing the deal, Windmere acquired an exclusive license to market four lines of Ronson electric shavers and other small consumer appliances. By June 1984, the company had contracted Japanese and Austrian firms to manufacture rotary electric and rechargeable razors and was selling them by as much as $20 less than the competition. Six months later, Windmere controlled five percent of the national electric razor market. Licensing established product names such as these proved a more cost-effective strategy for expanding the company. Not only did the company save on research and development expenses, but it did not have to invest heavily in the expensive advertising campaigns needed to introduce a new product to the market.

Much of the company's growth in the mid- and late 1980s, however, was the direct result of the strong performance of its own products. From its earliest days, the company had attempted to develop the Windmere product line by introducing products used in beauty salons to the general public. In the 1970s, for instance, Windmere began manufacturing and selling a pistol-grip hairdryer based on a model from its professional line.

The company tried to make the same profitable transition a decade later with a product designed to make hair wavy, known as the Crimper. Although retailers initially showed little interest in the hair-crimper when it was introduced in 1987, once it became popular in trend-setting Hollywood, it became a huge success. A similar type of curling iron, the Waver, introduced that same year, along with the Clothes Shaver, a device that removed fuzz and fabric pills from clothing, helped to give Windmere instant brand recognition, something it had struggled 12 years to achieve.

As young women across the country snatched up the new-fangled curling irons in hopes of achieving the "in" look, Windmere revenues and profits soared to record levels. By 1987, the performance of the company had exploded to record-breaking levels. Sales climbed to $145 million and earnings had risen to $11.9 million, increases of 54 percent and 120 percent, respectively, from the previous year. The momentum from these new products led the company to another year of torrid growth in 1988, as sales rose to $193 million and earnings more than doubled to $32.6 million. Meanwhile its stock jumped from $11 a share to high of $27 per share.

### Late 1980s Setbacks

While most outward signs suggested that Windmere had finally arrived as a major player in the personal appliances industry, a number of obstacles surfaced in the late 1980s that brought growth to a near standstill. In May 1989, the first sign of trouble appeared. Sales of hot products such as the Crimper fell victim to changing fashion trends, leading to an 11 percent decline in earnings and an alarming build-up of inventory. Moreover, products designed to fill the void performed poorly, exacerbating the problem. And in November Friedson sold $2.9 million worth of company stock shortly before another quarter of disappointing financial results was released. As Windmere stock plummeted, revenues—which had been predicted by some analysts to exceed $285 million—dipped to $178 million and earnings fell to $7.6 million.

Perhaps the most serious threat to the stability of the company, however, came from China (the site for 90 percent of Windmere's manufacturing operations) and the 30-cents-an-hour labor that made the company the low-cost producer in the industry. In June 1989 a series of student-led protests and period of political unrest temporarily slowed down production and jeopardized the future of Windmere's manufacturing operations. Although the turmoil in China directly affected the company for only four to six weeks, it posed a serious threat to the company's debt financing. With virtually all of the company's manufacturing equipment based in the tumultuous area, the violence in Tiananman Square, in the view of the financial community, made Windmere a risk. For the next three years, the company would be forced to take out unsecured loans on a 60–90 day basis.

### Early 1990s Recovery

Windmere's downward spiral continued into the new decade. It failed to come up with a new premier product that could pick up the slack left by declining sales of the Crimper, the Waver, and the Clothes Shaver. The company's entrance into the health-related products industry, through the introduction of an electric rotary toothbrush called Plak-Trak, did not live up to the high expectations suggested by a $3 million advertising campaign. Furthermore, an ongoing unfair competition and patent infringement lawsuit with North American Philips regarding Windmere's rotary electric shaver, initiated in 1984, continued to divert much needed resources and energy from the development of a viable management strategy for renewal.

In 1990, however, Windmere emerged from the lawsuit victorious and was awarded an $86.9 million judgement, and two years later, the company collected $57 million in full settlement from Philips. The decision not only gave the company a financial shot in the arm—a net gain of $29 million after legal fees, taxes, and other expenses—but it enabled Friedson and his managerial team to focus on reshaping the business.

Between the time of the decision and the time of the final settlement, Windmere devoted its attention primarily to reorganization and restructuring. The company cut costs at its Durable manufacturing facilities, reducing the break-even point by more than one-third, largely by reducing its work force by 30 percent, down to 7,000. At the same time, the company worked to reduce its inventories and tighten up its balance sheet. Not only did the company trim its inventories by more than 16 percent, but it used the money from the lawsuit to pay off debts.

A favorable ruling from President Bill Clinton the following year, retaining China's status as a most favored nation, added to the positive momentum of the lawsuit. If duties had been imposed, Windmere would have had to raise prices and most likely would have lost its advantage over such competitors as Conair, Bristol-Myers Squibb and Helen of Troy, all of whom manufactured in Costa Rica or bought from the Far East, locations that all had higher labor and manufacturing costs.

### The Mid-1990s and Beyond

As Windmere celebrated its 30th anniversary in 1993, it showed several visible signs of recovery. Total revenues, for the second straight year, approached the record levels of 1988. More significant, the company attained the strongest financial position in its history, with $146 million in equity, $25 million in cash, and virtually no debt. An aggressive television and print campaign to support new lines of hair and curling irons, combined with completely redesigned packaging represented the company's renewed commitment to its core business. The following year, the company strengthened its presence by acquiring the licensing rights to the Helene Curtis Salon Selectives brand name for a line of personal hair care appliances, opening the way for a new line of hair dryers, curling irons, hair setters, combs, and brushes.

As Windmere entered the second half of the 1990s, it looked to distance itself further from the 1990–1991 decline and regain the respect of its stockholders and the financial community. While continuing to improve the efficiency of its operations, the company has also hoped to develop a gadget that would do for the 1990s what the Crimper and the Clothes Shaver did for the 1980s. In a June 1996 meeting with shareholders, Friedson unveiled one of the leading candidates: the Litter Maid, a computerized cat box billed as the "pooper scooper" for the Internet Age. Friedson planned an extensive marketing campaign, including infomercials and adding specialty retailers to market the companies latest gadget to the 65 million cat owners in the United States. Whether or not the product that used infrared signals to activate an automatic raking system would enjoy widespread use depended largely on the company's ability to make the space-age invention affordable—the same type of manufacturing challenge the company has faced throughout its history.

### Principal Subsidiaries

Durable Electrical Metal Factory, Ltd.; Paragon Industries (50%); Salton/Maxim Housewares Inc. (50%)

### Further Reading

DeGeorge, Gail, "Windmere Tries to Comb Out the Kinks," *Business Week,* July 24, 1989, p. 44.

Fields, Gregg, "Florida-Based Windmere Has High Hopes for Self-Cleaning Cat Box," *Miami Herald,* June 14, 1996.

Fogarty, Fred E., "Work Is a Family Affair for Windmere Executive," *South Florida Business Journal,* June 22, 1987, p. 28.

Hagy, James R., "Windmere to Wall Street: Take Us Back," *Florida Trend,* June 1992, pp. 29–32.

Mack, Toni, "Rebate Madness," *Forbes,* February 13, 1984, p. 76.

Oakes, David L., "New Windmere President Carves Own Niche," *South Florida Business Journal,* February 11, 1985, p. 3.

Phillips, Dana, "Under Heat, Windmere Stock Turns On," *South Florida Business Journal,* April 5, 1996, p. 1A.

Seemuth, Mike, "Florida's CEOs: Life at the Top," *Florida Trend,* June 1994, pp. 50–54.

Turner, Alison, "Windmere Rally More Than Hot Air," *South Florida Business Journal,* July 23–29, 1993, pp. 1, 18.

—Jason Gallman

# Witco

## Witco Corporation

**One American Lane**
**Greenwich, Connecticut 06831-2559**
**U.S.A.**
**(203) 552-2000**
**Fax: (203) 552-2010**

*Public Company*
*Incorporated:* 1920 as Wishnick-Tumpeer Chemical
    Company
*Employees:* 8,053
*Sales:* $1.98 billion (1995)
*Stock Exchanges:* New York Frankfurt
*SICs:* 2819 Industrial Inorganic Chemicals, Not
    Elsewhere Classified; 2842 Specialty Cleaning,
    Polishing & Sanitation Preparations; 2851 Paints,
    Varnishes, Lacquers, Enamels & Allied Products;
    2869 Industrial Organic Chemicals, Not Elsewhere
    Classified; 2911 Petroleum Refining; 2992 Lubricating
    Oils & Greases; 5169 Chemicals & Allied Products,
    Not Elsewhere Classified

Witco Corporation is one of the world's leading manufacturers of specialty chemicals. In the mid-1990s, more than 75 percent of the company's revenues came from its specialty chemicals operations, a significant shift from the much more diversified Witco of the 1970s and 1980s. The company still manufacturers specialty petroleum products, but announced in late 1995 that it would divest its lubricants business. In the 1990s, Witco not only committed to a future as a specialty chemicals company but also expanded internationally, deriving about one-third of its revenues from outside the United States.

### Company Roots and Founding

The company was founded as Wishnick-Tumpeer Chemical Company by Robert I. Wishnick in association with the brothers Julius and David Tumpeer. Wishnick was president, owning 51 percent of the company's shares, and was chairman emeritus of

Witco until his death in 1980. It was Wishnick who shaped the company's growth and direction for over half its life. His two original partners, who together owned only 20 percent of the company's shares, sold their interest shortly after World War II.

Born in Koltchina, Russia, in 1892, Robert Wishnick came to the United States to join his father and oldest brother in 1896. At age seven he lost his right arm at the elbow after breaking it badly in a fall. This childhood accident seems only to have hardened Wishnick's determination to make something of himself. He put himself through school, earning one of the first degrees in chemical engineering from the Armour Institute of Technology, now the Illinois Institute of Technology. Then, employed days as a chemist, he worked toward a law degree, which he received in 1917 from Kent College of Law.

His first job with the American Magnesium Products Company brought near disaster to his employers, but ironically foretold the successful business strategy Wishnick would follow to bring Witco to its present position in the chemical industry. His company sold a floor wax which complemented its product line of magnasite floor materials. Wishnick, however, thought that the company should produce its own floor wax, rather than reselling floor wax originally purchased elsewhere. He had his own mixture of wax and turpentine on a burner when the telephone rang and drew him away. In his absence, the mixture boiled over and set the entire factory on fire, burning it to the ground. This may not have been the most auspicious of beginnings, but it demonstrated clearly Wishnick's drive for independence. From that time Wishnick continually strived to push Witco to self-sufficiency through manufacturing its own products.

### Early History

In 1920 after working as a sales representative with A. Dager & Company for two years, Wishnick, with Julius Tumpeer, set up Wishnick-Tumpeer as a chemical distributing concern on East Illinois Street in Chicago. The company's largest market was in carbon black and various other coloring agents needed by Chicago's vigorous printing industry. Before the company was a year old, however, a recession set in and

## Company Perspectives:

*Central to Witco's ongoing success is serving our customers well. We continually strive to bring our customers the very best products and attendant technical service in ways that truly satisfy each of them. Creative, open communication amongst our employees will always be focused on how we can best help our customers succeed in their businesses. Witco's long-term profitability depends on an increasingly global outlook and strong international expansion. Success in the global marketplace will be driven by ongoing reevaluation of our methods and processes, focused research and development, and an ever-present spirit of innovation. The fulfillment of this vision of Witco depends on the commitment of our valued employees and their commitment to the total quality management process that pervades our organization. Welcoming change, teamwork, and individual achievement will be hallmarks of our workplace environment where each employee can make a contribution. We will provide our employees with training and resources for career development, and will be committed to recognizing and rewarding significant contributions to achieving corporate objectives.*

sales declined considerably. Wishnick responded by cutting costs wherever possible. He reduced his own salary, cut the company's profit margin then worked to increase volume. These measures have been consistently successful for Witco and have been used to great effect whenever the company suffered from changes in the market. It also helped the company record a profit during its first year, despite the recession.

In 1922 the company was able to buy a 20 percent interest in a carbon black plant in Swartz, Louisiana. Witco then marketed the product on a commission basis in its own area. In 1923 Wishnick felt it was time to expand further and asked Julius Tumpeer to head the company's first New York office, though Wishnick later replaced him.

Also in 1924, Wishnick-Tumpeer purchased its first manufacturing concern, Pioneer Asphalt Company in Lawrenceville, Illinois. By 1926 so much of the company's business was in asphalt products that the board elected to drop Chemical from the company name, making the new name simply Wishnick-Tumpeer Incorporated. The steady growth that had marked the company from its beginnings continued through the 1920s until the crash of 1929.

Once again, Wishnick and his company implemented cost-cutting measures. Wishnick reduced wages, salaries and, of course, margins. This strategy worked again and the company managed to turn a profit in each year of the 1930s. During this time, cash flow was a severe problem, but Wishnick had a unique solution. Most of the company's cash flow problems were caused by its customers' late bill payments. Each month Wishnick made a special trip to the accounts payable departments of the company's major accounts. There he left a small gift of candy or flowers with the secretaries and politely sug-

gested that his bill be moved from the bottom of the pile to the top where it could be paid as soon as possible.

In 1933 the company acquired another carbon black plant which, after additional negotiations, led to Wishnick's formation of Continental Carbon Company in association with Continental Oil Company and Shamrock Oil and Gas Company. These two other concerns supplied the needed natural gas for carbon black production and Wishnick-Tumpeer became the exclusive sales agents for the new company.

In 1935 Witco's first overseas operation was created in Britain: the company acquired an interest in Harold A. Wilson & Company, a supplier of pigments to the United States. Eventually, the entire company was bought by Wishnick. This effort was only the beginning of what are today extensive overseas holdings.

The company's last important move before World War II was to build its first chemical plant in Chicago to produce industrial chemicals and asphalt products. The war brought large amounts of business for Wishnick-Tumpeer, but it also led to problems of shortages and rationing. Most of the company's business was still in distribution, and at times Wishnick's suppliers were unable to deliver what was needed.

### Postwar Transition to Manufacturing

As the war was ending, annual sales were at approximately $7.8 million. The company was larger than ever before, but its future was uncertain. Many of the larger chemical companies Wishnick was accustomed to buying from were developing their own competing sales forces. In 1944 Wishnick changed the name of his company to Witco Chemical Incorporated. Then, in 1945, the board of the new company made official its plans to move as quickly as possible into manufacturing and to leave the distributing business.

Soon thereafter, the Chicago plant was expanded to include the production of metallic stearates, and then a number of new companies were acquired. Franks Chemical Products Inc. was purchased and then moved to less expensive quarters in Perth Amboy, New Jersey. A Los Angeles plant was bought from the India Paint and Varnish division of American Marietta, and new equipment was ordered for the plant to begin production of stearates. In 1954, by the time sales had grown to nearly $20 million, a British stearate plant was also purchased. This steady and extended expansion was not without difficulties, however. There were recurring operating problems in the Perth Amboy plant, some of which William Wishnick, the president's son, was asked to help solve. There was also a major fire in the Chicago plant, and then in 1953 the first strike in Witco's history took place in the Lawrenceville plant.

None of this weakened William Wishnick's resolve, however. In 1955 the decision was announced to end the company's distributing business altogether and to begin moving toward complete self-sufficiency. Witco sales were as high as $30 million, but over a ten-year period only 35 percent of that was from its own manufacturing operations. Some major acquisitions were on the horizon, but not until after a management reorganization. The Tumpeer brothers were no longer with the company (Julius had retired in 1947 and David had died in

1951). It was then, in 1955, that Robert Wishnick became chairman of the board, and Max Minnig, a long-time senior employee, became president. At that time, William Wishnick rose to the executive vice-presidency from his position as vice president and treasurer.

In keeping with its new corporate strategy, Witco spent the next two years making acquisitions and expanding operations. Sales rose to $40 million, 40 percent of which came from Witco manufacturing facilities. Then, in 1958 Witco went public and sold 150,000 shares of common stock. This expansion continued unabated through the mid-1960s. In 1960 the Sonneborn Chemical and Refining Company was acquired, bringing sales up to the $100 million mark. International expansion accelerated as well, with new acquisitions in Belgium, France, and Canada.

## Expansion in the 1960s and 1970s

In 1964 further administrative changes led the way for even greater expansion. Robert Wishnick became chairman of the finance committee as well as managing director of international activities. Robert's son, William, succeeded him as chairman of the board, and Max Minnig became chief executive officer while maintaining his position as president. As chairman, William initiated the greatest growth period in Witco's history. He began with the 1966 acquisition of Argus Chemical Company at a price of $22 million. This provided Witco with a new plastics operation and one of its senior managers, Bill Setzler. The younger Wishnick also spent considerable sums on plant modernization and research and development. This tendency toward reinvestment of generated capital was to characterize the next two decades of Witco growth. In the period from 1966 to 1975 William Wishnick increased the company's sales by 250 percent. During this period he also assumed the duties of president and chief executive officer after Max Minnig's retirement in 1971.

In fulfillment of Robert Wishnick's dream, Witco became a firm devoted exclusively to manufacturing chemical products when its 1933 agreement with Continental Carbon Company expired. Witco kept its 20 percent interest in the company, but did not renew its licensing contract with the company. Witco now sold only Witco-manufactured products.

The recession in 1974 brought the traditional cost-cutting measures at Witco. The recession also brought a fourth-quarter drop of 50 percent in sales compared to the previous quarter. In addition, there was a sharp earnings drop in early 1975. By the end of 1975 matters had returned to normal, but there was still an overall drop in operating earnings of 23 percent. Despite this, Witco continued to expand, albeit more slowly. The Waverly Oil Works was purchased and a new $10 million hydrogenation plant was built in Pennsylvania.

The year 1975 witnessed additional administrative changes as highly talented managers from acquired companies rose to executive levels. Henry Sonneborn, brought in when his company was purchased in 1960, assumed the presidency and also became chief executive officer while William Setzler of the Argus division was appointed to the board of directors. William Wishnick returned to the position of chairman and his father

Robert was appointed chairman emeritus, a position he held until his death in 1980.

## Acquisitions and Divestments in the 1980s

The period from 1975 to 1986, half of it spent without the founder's presence, was characterized by a somewhat haphazard approach to acquisitions. Under William Wishnick's guidance, the new administration made several purchases, such as the $38 million deal with Kraft in 1980 for Humko Chemical, a manufacturer of oleochemicals which are used in a variety of industries. But other acquisitions made during the period diversified Witco away from its core specialty chemicals and petroleum businesses. This was particularly true of the 1982 purchase of The Richardson Company for $62.6 million. Although the company was a market leader, Richardson's variety of products—including battery casings, conveyor belts, and offset plates for printing—had little in common with Witco's product lines.

At this same time, Witco and the U.S. chemical industry in general was hit hard by the "double-dip" recession of the early 1980s, which had been brought on by the oil shock of 1979. The company's numerous acquisitions of the 1970s and 1980s had created not only a much larger company but also a more unwieldy one with 18 operating divisions. Wishnick was forced to launch a divestment program to improve earnings. From 1981 through 1985, a variety of operations were sold, including a detergent business, urethane systems operations, Richardson's offset plates business, and Pioneer Asphalt's Lawrenceville plant (which had been Witco's first manufacturing facility). Witco also sold off some of its oil reserves since petroleum prices were falling rapidly. Coupled with the divestments, Wishnick also began to invest more heavily in the company's existing operations, in particular upgrading aging facilities; by 1985, 75 percent of the $70 million used for reinvestment went to plant modernization.

Although the company's growth was slowed during this retrenchment—sales only increased to $1.35 billion in 1986 from the $1.2 billion posted in 1980—net income of $65.2 million was a company record. Further, Witco's 1986 profit margin of 4.8 percent was the best in 18 years.

In October 1985 "Chemical" was again dropped from the company name, making the new company name Witco Corporation. At that time lubricants and specialty petroleum products made up 53 percent of the company's business, while specialty chemical products accounted for only 41 percent. The remaining six percent consisted of a variety of engineered materials for special applications.

In 1986 Thomas J. Bickett took over as president and chief executive officer from the retiring William J. Ashe, who had occupied the job since Henry Sonneborn retired. In 1978 Bickett had been asked to join Witco while working for an accounting firm contracted by Witco. His appointment to the position came after he had been with the company for 12 years, serving for much of that time on the board of directors. Although Bickett was considered a possible heir apparent to Wishnick, who was nearing retirement, Bickett left the company in 1989 reportedly because his and Wishnick's operational styles clashed. Although Denis Andreuzzi was named president and chief operating officer following Bickett's department, it was William R. Toller whom Wishnick recommended be elected chairman upon his retirement in October 1990. Toller had joined Witco in 1984 when the company acquired Continental Carbon from Conoco.

### 1990s and Beyond

Toller inherited a company that had struggled during the latter half of the 1980s. Net sales reached only $1.59 billion by 1989, an increase of just 9.7 percent over a five-year period. The company stayed away from major acquisitions during the period, while organic growth was difficult given Witco's mature markets.

Toller knew that major changes were needed in order to get the company growing again. Just two months after gaining the chairmanship, he asserted that the company had to globalize its operations. He also set a goal of reaching $2 billion in sales and a 16 percent return on equity by 1995. In 1991, Toller's first major undertaking was to commit the company to developing a state-of-the-art information system that would help the divisions' managers run their operations more efficiently as well as provide upper management a better handle on the overall operations. The new system began operation in 1994.

Meanwhile, the shape of a future Witco began to take form as Toller slowly began to win over the company's other senior managers to his vision of a Witco dedicated to the specialty chemicals business. Although some managers recommended that the company remained diversified, Witco's largest acquisition to date propelled it into a new era. In 1992, Witco acquired the Industrial Chemicals and Natural Substances divisions of Germany's Schering AG for $440 million. The deal not only solidified the company's future in specialty chemicals—in 1993 chemicals accounted for 58 percent of Witco's sales—it also significantly enhanced the firm's global presence. A key symbol of the company's newfound international strength came in 1994 when Witco stock began to be traded on the Frankfurt Stock Exchange. Also in 1994, Witco moved its corporate headquarters from New York to Greenwich, Connecticut.

A major reorganization in 1993 did away with the divisional structure, replacing it with a structure that revolved around market-focused operating units. Initially the groups included Oleo/Surfactants, Polymer Additives, and Resins within the chemicals area; Petroleum Specialties and Lubricants within the petroleum area; and a Diversified Products Group which consisted of noncore businesses to be divested. During the mid-1990s, Witco divested itself of numerous nonchemical units and also announced in 1995 that it intended to divest its Lubricants Group as well, after which it would be almost exclusively in the specialty chemicals business (with a relatively small Petroleum Specialties Group).

Toller's goal of international expansion led to another major acquisition in 1995, which improved Witco's position in Europe but more importantly expanded the company's presence in the Pacific Rim and South America. Witco acquired OSi Specialties, Inc. in October 1995 in a $486 million deal. OSi was the global leader in silicone specialty chemicals and had significant operations in Asia, a region Witco was eager to expand in. Under Witco, OSi became one of the company's operating groups, the OSi Specialties Group.

In a few short years, Toller and his team had overseen a major transformation at Witco, one at least as important as the shift from distribution to manufacturing that occurred earlier in the century. Witco was now a major player in the international specialty chemicals industry and was more focused than ever before. In 1993, the company had already passed the $2 billion sales goal Toller had set when he took over the chairmanship, and even when the company began in 1995 to report its Lubricants Group as a discontinued operation, Witco fell just barely short of the $2 billion mark that year, thanks to its acquisition of OSi. Over the remainder of the 1990s, Witco was likely to concentrate on consolidating its 1990s acquisitions, making additional acquisitions to meet Toller's new goal of $5 billion in revenues by 2000, improving the company's earnings, and grooming a successor for the near-to-retirement Toller.

### Principal Subsidiaries

Witco Canada Inc.; Witco S.A. (France); Witco Deutschland GmbH (Germany); Witco Ltd. (Israel; 60%); Witco Italianna Srl. (Italy); Witco B.V. (Netherlands); Witco Espãna S.L. (Spain); Baxenden Chemicals Limited (U.K.; 53.5%).

### Principal Operating Units

OSi Specialties Group; Polymer Additives Group; Asia/Pacific Group; Resins Group; Oleo/Surfactants Group; Petroleum Specialties Group; Lubricants Group.

### Further Reading

"An Acquiring Lifestyle," *Forbes*, July 19, 1993, p. 230.

Brown, Alan S., *The Witco Story: Hard Work and Integrity*, Lyme, Conn.: Greenwich Publishing Group, 1995.

Fink, Ronald, "Pass the Rolaids: The Chemical Businesses Witco Has Acquired Will Sharpen Its Focus and Broaden Its Reach—If They Aren't Too Much to Digest," *Financial World*, June 22, 1993, pp. 54–55.

Freedman, William, "Witco Absorbs OSi," *Chemical Week*, September 20, 1995, p. 8.

Plishner, Emily S., "Passing the Baton: Bill Toller Has Transformed Witco into a Growing Specialty Chemical Company. Who's Next?," *Financial World*, November 21, 1995, pp. 52–53.

Protzman, Ferdinand, "Witco's Move in Europe Grows into Better-than-Expected Fit," *New York Times*, November 16, 1993, p. C6.

Stringer, Judy, "Managing Change at Witco," *Chemical Week*, June 7, 1995, pp. 44–45.

Warren, J. Robert, "Witco Has Bold Asian Goals," *Chemical Marketing Reporter*, April 17, 1995, pp. 7, 20.

Wishnick, William, *The Witco Story*, New York: Newcomen Society in North America, 1976.

—updated by David E. Salamie

# Wolverine World Wide Inc.

9341 Courtland Drive
Rockford, Michigan 49341
U.S.A.
(616) 866-5500
Fax: (616) 866-0257

*Public Company*
*Incorporated:* 1906
*Employees:* 5,586
*Sales:* $413.96 million (1995)
*Stock Exchanges:* New York Pacific
*SICs:* 3143 Men's Footwear Manufacturers Except
Athletic; 3144 Women's Footwear Manufacturers
Except Athletic; 5661 Shoe Stores; 5139 Shoes &
Footwear, Wholesalers & Manufacturers; 6794 Patent
Owners & Lessors Services

Wolverine World Wide Inc.'s success has hinged on its ability to cling tenaciously to a cache of well-known footwear brands. Family-owned from its inception in 1883 until 1965, the company and its best-known brand, Hush Puppies, struggled to compete with athletic and imported shoes in the 1970s and 1980s. A combination of shrewd marketing, fresh-yet-retro design, and pure luck contributed to the company's spectacular comeback in the early 1990s. In 1995, Wolverine World Wide capped a four-year string of rising sales and earnings with awards from *Footwear News,* whose industry poll ranked it "Company of the Year," and the Council of Fashion Designers of America, which named Hush Puppies the "Accessory of the Year." In 1995, Hush Puppies generated about 45 percent of annual sales and Wolverine brand work boots brought in another 40 percent. The remaining sales were divided among private label and licensed brand footwear and the company's tanning business.

### The Late 19th and Early 20th Centuries

Wolverine was established in 1883 by G.A. Krause and his uncle, Fred Hirth, and named the Hirth-Krause Company. The son of Prussian immigrants, Krause brought a two-century heritage of leather tanning to the enterprise. The company originally sold leather, buttonhooks, lacing, and soles at wholesale, and purchased finished shoes for retail sale.

Krause began to consolidate vertically after the turn of the century, placing his sons in independent, but related, shoe-making and leather tanning businesses. In 1903, he established a shoe manufacture in Rockford, Michigan. His eldest son, Otto, who had a degree in engineering from the University of Michigan, operated this arm of the family enterprise, which supplied finished footwear to the Hirth-Krause retail outlets. Five years later, G.A. and younger son Victor created the Wolverine Tanning Company to supply leather to the shoe-making business.

Victor, whose postsecondary education had included apprenticeships in tanning, would be a driving force behind Wolverine's establishment as a premiere American shoe company. In 1909, he traveled to Milwaukee, Wisconsin, to study a chrome tanning and retanning process developed by master tanner John Pfingsten. By 1914, Victor's own experiments had resulted in a tanning process for "shell horsehide," a cheap, durable, but heretofore unworkably stiff section of hide taken from the horse's rear. The company soon stopped using cowhide in favor of their unique new material.

Promoted as "1,000 mile shoes," sales of the heavy-duty Wolverine boots helped increase corporate earnings almost 700 percent from 1916 to 1923. A centennial company history noted that "Wolverine boots and shoes became one of rural and small-town America's most popular brands."

In 1921, Hirth-Krause and the Rockford shoe factory—which had previously merged under the name Michigan Shoe Makers—were united with Wolverine to form Wolverine Shoe and Tanning Corporation. The company acquired a glovemaking business that same year and began manufacturing horsehide work gloves. Over the course of the decade, Wolverine built its first warehouse, created an employee profit-sharing plan, launched a nationwide advertising campaign, and erected its first consolidated headquarters.

### Depression and World War Spark Innovation

Although Wolverine survived the Great Depression intact, the accelerating transition from horse-drawn transportation to gasoline-powered transport severely diminished the need for horses in America. As a result, the company was compelled to turn to less reliable international markets for its hides.

When the United States entered World War II, the federal government's War Production Board assigned Wolverine to manufacture gloves for the troops and suggested that the company try pigskin as a raw material. It seemed like a fine idea until the company discovered the inadequacy of pigskinning methods, which were not satisfactory to either the tanners or the meat processors. Not only was it difficult to remove the skin without taking some of the flesh with it, but separating all the flesh from the skin often damaged the hide. Sometimes the only useful pieces were barely large enough to make a glove. A company history quoted one employee in the project who remarked, "It looked like these pigs didn't care to be skinned." Nevertheless, Wolverine did manage to manufacture enough gloves to keep the military happy and its books in the black throughout the war years.

But when the global conflict ended, demand for pigskin gloves fizzled and Wolverine was forced to revert to cowhide, which was in steadier supply than horsehide and in more reliable condition than pigskin. Then Chairman Victor Krause was convinced that pigskin could be a viable alternative to cowhide; it was softer than either cowhide or horsehide, widely available, woefully underused, breathable, and easy to dye and clean. He became so obsessed with "the pigskin processing dilemma" that he resigned Wolverine's chairmanship to dedicate his full attention to the question. His son, Adolph, advanced to corporate leadership.

Working as an unpaid consultant, Victor Krause assembled a team of engineers who spent two years designing a device that separated the pigskin from the flesh without damaging either product. Wolverine patented the machine, which was created to fit neatly into the pig production process. By the early 1980s, Wolverine would have one of the world's largest pigskin tanneries.

When tanned, pigskin was soft and flexible, but it was not tough enough to be use in Wolverine's traditional work boots and shoes. In a radical departure from the company's historical emphasis, Krause designed a pair of casual shoes from the pigskin and presented them to Wolverine's board of directors.

The board was not particularly enthusiastic about the new product, but decided that market research would determine whether and how to proceed.

According to corporate legend, the genesis of the Hush Puppies brand name came at a southern-style fish fry where deep-fried nuggets of dough commonly known as "hush puppies" were served. When Wolverine World Wide Sales Manager Jim Muir asked his host about the origins of the strange name, he was told that farmers used the treats "to quiet their barking dogs." That conversation reminded Muir of another colloquial meaning for "barking dogs": sore feet. It occurred to him that Wolverine's new shoes worked on sore feet just like hush puppies worked on yelping dogs, so he proposed the name as a new trademark. In 1957, Wolverine President Adolph Krause, son of Victor Krause, chose the canine name and basset hound logo from a field of ten possibilities.

After a brief period of test marketing, the company launched a national advertising campaign that was unprecedented in the shoe industry. Hush Puppies proved a timely innovation in footwear. With workers moving from farms to offices and from the countryside to the suburbs, Wolverine faced a decline in the sale of heavy-duty work shoes, but looked forward to a boom in more casual shoes. Hush Puppies became the footwear phenomenon of the late 1950s and early 1960s. Wolverine took the brand international via licensing agreements, the first of which was sold to Canada's Greb Shoes, Ltd. in 1959. Renamed Wolverine World Wide Inc. in 1966, the parent company's sales nearly quintupled from 1958 to 1965, when it made its initial public offering on the New York Stock Exchange.

### Decline in the 1970s and 1980s

Hush Puppies put Wolverine at the top of the casual shoe industry, but the branded shoes could not keep it there very long. Sales flattened in the late 1960s, as Hush Puppies' core market matured and the brand failed to win younger customers. The company attempted to diversify via acquisition during this period, acquiring Bates, Frolic, and Tru-Stitch shoes and slippers. In spite of these efforts, however, Wolverine World Wide's nearly 90 years of Krause family management came to an end after the company experienced a net loss in 1972. Wolverine appeared to recover in the later years of the decade, as sales increased from about $125 million in 1975 to about $250 million in 1980.

But the new decade brought increased competition from imported and athletic shoes that seriously undermined the already-weakened business. In 1981, the Reagan administration dropped import quotas in favor of freer trade, prompting a deluge of inexpensive shoes from Asia and Latin America. Rita Koselka of *Forbes* magazine noted in a 1992 article that, "Among U.S. industries, few have been hit harder by foreign competition than shoemaking." Half of America's footwear manufacturers went bankrupt over the course of the 1980s, as the imports share of the U.S. market grew from 50 percent to 86 percent. During the same period, consumers began to turn from Hush Puppy-type shoes to athletic shoes for casual wear, further eroding Wolverine's potential market.

Unlike so many of its compatriots, Wolverine survived the 1980s, but not without its share of fits and starts. Under the direction of Thomas Gleason from 1972 to 1992, the company struggled to meet the challenge by diversifying its footwear lineup, expanding its direct retail operation, leveraging the Hush Puppies brand via licensing, and moving some production overseas.

Wolverine World Wide had launched its own chain of "Little Red Shoe House" specialty stores, which emphasized children's shoes, in 1976. Acquisitions and internal growth expanded the company's retail operation to more than 100 stores by 1983. The well-known Hush Puppies logo was licensed to manufacturers of clothing, umbrellas, luggage, hats, and handbags, and could be found in 56 countries by 1987.

From its well-established base in work shoes and "career casual" footwear, Wolverine diversified via acquisition and internal development. The company entered the athletic market with the 1981 purchase of Brooks Shoe Manufacturing Co., a struggling maker of running shoes. Wolverine acquired Town & Country and Viner Bros. shoes in 1982 and added Kaepa dual-laced, split-vamp specialty athletic shoes the following year. The company also developed its own new shoes, including the Body Shoe, which featured an ergonomic "comfort curve," and Cloud 10 shoes, with special cushioning for the ball of the foot. Wolverine hoped that its expanded line of comfortable yet fashionable footwear would attract more 30- to 45-year-olds to its stores.

But in spite of these apparently well-thought-out efforts, Wolverine's bottom line continued to show signs of stress: net income slid from $15.5 million in 1981 to $2.1 million in 1984. After a slight recovery in 1985, the company suffered a $12.6 million loss on sales of $341.7 million. The shortfall sparked a restructuring and reorganization that included the closure of five U.S. factories, the sale of two small retail chains and shuttering of 15 other outlets, the spin-off of Kaepa and divestment of a relatively new West German footwear manufacturing and 105-store retail operation. The domestic factory closings helped increase the proportion of Wolverine's shoes manufactured overseas to about 50 percent.

Analysts found plenty to blame at Wolverine. Some said that the company's new casual and career-oriented brands—Town & Country, Harbor Town of Maine, and Wimzees Casuals—were cannibalizing Hush Puppies' sales. One analyst told *Footwear News* in September 1985 that top executives "have lost their direction in recent years and can't get either manufacturing or retailing back on track." Another said the company had grown "too big to run effectively." Thomas Jaffe of *Forbes* was more direct, blaming "impulsive management, silly diversification, and finally, the flood of cheap imports that has knocked the socks off most of the U.S. shoe industry." Analyst Sheldon Grodsky told *Business Week*'s Keith Naughton, "Dullness permeated the company and they just missed the entire 1980s."

In 1987, the company hired Geoffrey B. Bloom, a marketing and product development expert with 12 years of experience at Florsheim Shoe Co., as president and chief operating officer. In the waning years of the decade, Wolverine made another attempt at revitalization. The company leveraged its basic lines of work shoes and boots, dress shoes, and casual footwear to fit the multiple fashion and function demands of younger customers.

For example, the company's 100-plus years of expertise in making durable work boots gave it insight into the development of hiking and outdoor boots. Wolverine used its own venerable brand and licensed the Coleman name for this new venture. The company hired new designers to update its athletic and casual shoes, and it even contracted with a Michigan State University laboratory for new footwear innovations.

Although Wolverine World Wide's net income rose to $7.7 million on sales of $324 million by 1988, other nagging problems stole the spotlight from this modest recovery. Most infamous of these was a 1989 lawsuit charging that Wolverine and Fred Goldston, a pigskin and cowhide broker, had conspired to steal cowhide from Southwest Hide Co. Goldston had been hired by Wolverine to raise the quantity and quality of pigskin rinds to supply the company's tannery. Southwest originally accused Goldston of exchanging their high-grade cowhides with lower-quality skins, but when Goldston went bankrupt, the plaintiff added partner Wolverine to the suit. Faced with a jury verdict of more than $39.3 million, Wolverine elected to settle the suit for $8.5 million in cash and bonds in 1992. CEO Gleason continued to assert his company's innocence in spite of the settlement, telling *Forbes'* Rita Koselka, "We were just the deep pockets around." Wolverine was also plagued with quality control and inventory problems in the late 1980s.

### Dramatic Recovery in the Early 1990s

In the fall of 1990, Wolverine announced another restructuring, including plans to scale back its retail operations, shutter a manufacturing plant, and eliminate certain shoe lines. After multiple reorganizations, infrequent profitability, and sliding market share, the company elected to divest its Brooks athletic shoe division to Rokke Group, Seattle, a U.S.-Norway joint venture, in 1992. The restructuring shrunk Wolverine's overall revenues from more than $320 million in 1990 to $282.86 million in 1992, but allowed it to concentrate on its Wolverine and Hush Puppies brands, which made near-miraculous recoveries in the early 1990s.

Wolverine's revitalization after more than a decade of lackluster performance came about through a combination of rejuvenated designs, savvy marketing, strict cost controls, and a healthy dose of good luck. From 1990 to 1995, Geoffrey Bloom, who succeeded Thomas Gleason as chief executive officer in 1993, closed more than 100 of the company's retail outlets, designating the remaining 60 as factory outlets. He also consolidated Wolverine's 16 divisions into five streamlined operating units, thereby increasing productivity (measured in revenue per employee) by nearly one-fourth from 1992 to 1994.

Taking a cue from fashion designer John Bartlett, newly-hired designer Maggie Mercado revived 1950s-era styles like the "Wayne" (nee Duke) oxford and "Earl" slip-on, offering the waterproof suede shoes in a rainbow of new colors like Pepto-Bismol pink and Day-Glo green. Both Bartlett and designer Anna Sui featured the shoes in their 1995 collections. Hush Puppies soon began to turn up on the famous feet of stars like Jim Carrey, Sharon Stone, David Bowie, Tom Hanks, and Sylvester Stallone. Hush Puppies also benefited from the trend toward dressing-down at work, filling the fashion gap between tennis shoes and dress shoes. Wolverine sent videotapes with tips for casual dressing at work to 200 businesses around America. In the ultimate retro coup, the company revived the "We invented casual" tagline that had launched Hush Puppies in 1958. By 1995, tony stores like Barneys in New York and Pleasure Swell in California struggled to keep the shoes in stock.

While its Hush Puppies conquered the world of fashion, Wolverine World Wide's work boots and hikers tackled more mundane markets. In spite of steadily declining employment in American construction and manufacturing sectors, sales of Wolverine work boots reached record levels in 1991. The high-tech, relatively lightweight footwear featured DuraShock shock absorbers and slip-resistant treads. Smart new ads told prospective customers that they could "hunt 'til hell freezes over." Coleman hiking boots gave Wolverine entree into the mass market via distribution in Wal-Mart stores.

A focus on international growth increased the geographic distribution of the company's sales to about 50 percent international by 1995. Wolverine was the only American shoemaker to achieve a comprehensive contract in Russia, it established a Hush Puppies store in China, and its branded shoes were offered in more than 60 countries around the world.

By mid-1995, *Forbes* had declared Wolverine "a dog no more." Sales had risen by more than 46 percent from $282.86 million in 1992 to $413.96 million in 1995, and net income more than tripled from $4.7 million to $24.07 million during the same period. CEO Geoffrey Bloom told *Forbes,* "For Wolverine the best is yet to come."

### Principal Operating Units

Bates; Caterpillar; Coleman; Hush Puppies; Tru-Stitch; Wolverine Boots & Shoes; Wolverine Leathers; Wolverine Wilderness.

### Further Reading

Carr, Debra, "Hot Dogs," *Footwear News,* August 7, 1995, p. 108.
"A Dog No More," *Forbes,* May 8, 1995, p. 16.
Jaffe, Thomas, "Fit To Be Tied?" *Forbes,* September 9, 1985, p. 2.

Kern, Beth Sexer, "Wolverine World Wide: Americana—A Long-Term Investment Portfolio," *Footwear News,* December 4, 1995, p. 23.
Koselka, Rita, "The Dog That Survived," *Forbes,* November 9, 1992, p. 82.
Lassiter, Dawn, "Wolverine Will Put Lock on Hush Puppies Plant," *Footwear News,* August 18, 1986, p. 4.
——, "WWW Picks Hartmax Exec as New Prexy," *Footwear News,* April 6, 1987, p. 1.
——, "WWW's Balance Sheet Shapes Up as Sales Drop," *Footwear News,* April 20, 1987, p. 4.
Miller, Cyndee, "Hush Puppies: All of a Sudden They're Cool," *Marketing News,* February 12, 1996, p. 10.
Min, Janice, "Puttin' on the Dog," *People Weekly,* December 11, 1995, p. 163.
Naughton, Keith, "Don't Step on My Blue Suede Hush Puppies," *Business Week,* September 11, 1995, p. 84.
Rooney, Ellen, "Gleason Will Drop WWW CEO Hat by '93," *Footwear News,* May 11, 1992, p. 2.
——, "Hush Puppies Seeks Fountain of Youth," *Footwear News,* May 31, 1993, p. 15.
Rooney, Ellen, and Wilner, Rich, "Norway's Rokke Dealing for the Purchase of Brooks," *Footwear News,* September 28, 1992, p. 1.
Schneider-Levy, Barbara, "New Bites and Barks from Hush Puppies," *Footwear News,* February 15, 1993, p. 27.
Sender, Isabelle, "WWW To Capitalize on Hush Puppies," *Footwear News,* April 22, 1996, p. 2.
Silverman, Dick, "Solid 1st Half Buoys WWW's Prospects," *Footwear News,* August 9, 1993, p. 28.
Weldon, Michele, "Brooks: Off and Running with Innovation," *Footwear News,* September 1983, p. 35.
——, "Hush Puppies Is Having a Facelift To Raise Sales," *Footwear News,* February 13, 1984, p. 14.
——, "Imports Won't Let Wolverine Rest on Its Laurels," *Footwear News,* May 2, 1983, p. 21.
Wilner, Rich, "Hush Puppies Out To Learn New Tricks," *Footwear News,* August 17, 1992, p. 55.
"Wolverine Plans To Restructure," *Footwear News,* October 8, 1990, p. 1.
*Wolverine Worldwide, Inc.: A Tradition of Success,* Rockford, MI: Wolverine World Wide, Inc., 1983.
"WWW Posts Record Work Boot Sales," *Footwear News,* February 3, 1992, p. 53.

—April Dougal Gasbarre

# Xilinx, Inc.

**2100 Logic Drive**
**San Jose, California 95124**
**U.S.A.**
**(408) 559-7778**
**Fax: (408) 559-7114**

*Public Company*
*Incorporated:* 1984
*Employees:* 1,144
*Sales:* $550 million (1996)
*Stock Exchanges:* NASDAQ
*SICs:* 3674 Semiconductors & Related Devices; 7372
   Prepackaged Software

Xilinx, Inc. designs, develops, and sells advanced programmable logic devices and related software development systems. It is the leading global supplier of programmable logic. In essence, the company's customized chips sequentially order the logic that tells sophisticated electronic gear the order in which its functions are to be performed. Xilinx bolted to the forefront of its industry during the late 1980s and early 1990s through breakthrough product innovations.

### 1980s Founding

Xilinx was founded in 1984 by Ross Freeman and Bernard Vonderschmitt. Freeman and Vonderschmitt were both working as chip engineers at Zilog Corp. prior to joining in the Xilinx venture. Zilog, a subsidiary of oil behemoth Exxon Corp., was a developer of integrated circuits and related solid-state devices and had numerous technological innovations to its credit. It was at Zilog that Freeman came up with the idea that would soon make Xilinx larger than Zilog. He wanted to design a computer chip that effectively acted as a blank tape, allowing the user to program the chip himself rather than having to purchase a preprogrammed chip from the manufacturer.

Freeman was on the cutting edge of changes that were beginning to occur in the semiconductor industry. Prior to the

mid-1980s, most computer chip manufacturers were interested almost solely in mass-market chips that could be produced in large volumes and sold for big profits. For several years that strategy was profitable for U.S. chipmakers, who dominated the global semiconductor market. But when low-cost foreign manufacturers, particularly in Japan, began competing for market share, traditional manufacturers, including Zilog, suffered in what eventually became a commodity industry. At the same time, chip consumers began demanding increasingly specialized chips that could be used for specific applications.

Few big chip producers were excited about the prospects of chasing the market for application-specific circuits. Serving those customers meant designing and manufacturing many different chips, each of which would be sold to much smaller markets and at a lower total profit in comparison with mass-market chips. Because of the reluctance of chip makers to cater to their needs, consumers of application-specific circuits also were frustrated. Besides having to pay a relatively high price for customized chips, they were usually forced to endure costly problems related to defects in their chips. Specifically, if the semiconductor had a flaw or if the customer's chip requirements suddenly changed, the customer would have to wait up to several weeks or even months for a new chip. Such a holdup could cost millions of dollars if an entire project was stalled while waiting for the new semiconductor.

Freeman realized that there might be a better way of meeting the need for application-specific circuits. His idea was to develop a sort of blank computer chip that could be programmed by the customer, thus minimizing risks associated with faulty chips and allowing much greater flexibility for companies designing equipment that incorporated the chips. The technology became known as "field programmable gate array," or FPGA. Freeman, who was a vice-president and general manager at Zilog at the time, approached his superiors and suggested that the development of FPGA devices could be a viable new avenue for Zilog. But Freeman was unable to convince executives at Exxon, who controlled more than $100 billion in assets, to chase a totally unexplored market that was worth perhaps only $100 million at the time.

Confident of the practicality of his concept, Freeman left his post at Zilog and began developing the first FPGA chip. He joined forces with another Zilog expatriate, Bernard Vonderschmitt. The 60-year-old Vonderschmitt also had been working as a vice-president and general manager at Zilog. Prior to that he had served 20 years at RCA, where he had headed the solid-state division. Their combined brainpower and management experience allowed them to attract several million dollars of venture capital, which they used to design the first commercially viable field programmable gate array. In 1984 they incorporated the venture as Xilinx, and in November of 1985 they began selling their first product.

Xilinx's FPGA was based on the company's patented Logic Cell Array technology. The company's system basically consisted of an off-the-shelf programmable chip and a software package that could be used to program and tailor the chip for specific needs. The technology was based on the arrangement of gates (the lowest level building block in a logic circuit) in complex formations called arrays; as the number of gates increased, the more complex were the functions that the semiconductor could perform. The advantage of Xilinx's system was that the software allowed the customer to program the gates and arrays, in a manner analogous to a connect-the-dots puzzle, to perform any number of different functions. Also integral to the success of the system was a small family of advanced standard semiconductors, which were manufactured for Xilinx under license by Seiko Epson in Japan.

Xilinx's FPGA systems ultimately lived up to Freeman's original vision, providing greater flexibility for equipment manufacturers and minimizing problems caused by traditional chip manufacturing methods. The company's first products offered less complexity (i.e., fewer gates) than non-field-programmable devices available at the time. But by late 1987, after injections of venture capital amounting to more than $18 million, Xilinx was offering a new generation of FPGA chips that, with 9,000 gates, could compete technologically with all but the most advanced non-field-programmable products. The result was that in 1987, after marketing its products for little more than one year, Xilinx was generating revenues at an annualized rate of nearly $14 million.

### Market Growth and Company Success

As Xilinx was earning respect for its FPGA technology, the market for application-specific circuits continued to grow during the late 1980s and into the 1990s. The result was that the market for FPGA chips surged, contributing to rapid revenue and profit growth at Xilinx. Indeed, sales rose to nearly $30.5 million in 1988 (fiscal year ended March 30, 1989) before rising to $50 million in 1989. Xilinx posted its first surplus—a net income of $2.92 million—in 1988 and went on to generate profits of $6 million in 1989. Unfortunately, Freeman died in 1989. Vonderschmitt took the reins as president and chief executive.

Xilinx was aided during the late 1980s by a partnership with Monolithic Memories Inc. (MMI), which in 1987 signed a deal with Xilinx that gave MMI royalties and free patent rights to manufacture Xilinx's products. In return, MMI supplied capital to Xilinx. The arrangement provided needed funding to bring Xilinx's products to market and sustain its research and development initiatives. Soon after signing the deal, though, MMI was purchased by American Micro Devices, Inc. Xilinx became uncomfortable with the new arrangement, partly because American Micro was one of its competitors. So, in 1989 Vonderschmitt convinced American Micro to buy 20 percent of the company at a ten percent premium and dissolve the original agreement. In search of new funding, Xilinx went public with a stock offering on the NASDAQ over-the-counter exchange.

With cash from the stock sale, Xilinx continued to grow. By late 1990 the company was selling its products throughout the United States, but was also shipping about 30 percent of its output overseas. More than half of its revenues were attributable to its popular XC3000 family of FPGA systems, but Xilinx had a stream of products in its development pipeline. The company sold nearly $100 million worth of its products in 1990, and its base of 3,500-plus customers grew to include big names like Apple Computer, IBM, Compaq Computer, Hewlett-Packard Co., Fujitsu, Sun Microsystems, and Northern Telecom. To keep pace with demand, Xilinx moved into a 144,000-square-foot plant in San Jose, California.

Although Xilinx rapidly increased sales and profits in the late 1980s and early 1990s, it also ceded much of its market share. Indeed, after Xilinx had invented its niche and controlled 100 percent of the FPGA market during the mid-1990s, other companies began offering competing technology that rapidly eroded Xilinx's dominance. By the early 1990s, in fact, Xilinx was controlling only about 65 percent of the total FPGA market. It had succeeded, though, in pressuring many of its earliest competitors out of the business, despite the fact that some of them had access to much more funding. By 1993 only a few companies were seriously vying for market share. The largest was Actel, which had introduced its first product in 1988 and by 1993 was serving about 18 percent of the market. The distant third-place contender was Altera, which sold technology similar to FPGA systems.

Despite loss of market share, high demand allowed Xilinx to boost revenues to $135 million in 1991 (fiscal year ended March 30, 1992) and then to $178 million in 1992. Part of that growth resulted from Xilinx's jump into the market for EPLDs (EPROM technology-based complex Programmable Logic Devices), which effectively offered higher performance and higher density per chip, and were designed to complement FPGA devices. By 1993 Xilinx was capturing more than $250 million in annual revenue and generating net income of $41.3 million.

In addition, market growth for FPGA chips was expected to intensify in the mid-1990s.

To take advantage of market expansion, Xilinx introduced a completely new line of FPGA products in 1994: the XC5000 family of FPGA chips and software. The XC5000 line was developed to cater to the market for low-end gate array products. Specifically, XC5000 chips were designed to offer a cost-effective alternative to high-volume non-field-programmable gate array products, thus giving Xilinx access to a new spectrum of the market for application-specific circuits. Xilinx followed the introduction of the XC5000 family with other new products, including the XC3100L and XC4000L. Both new families of FPGA chips were designed to complement low-power applications, which boosted Xilinx's access to manufacturers of increasingly popular low-power devices like portable computers and related peripheral devices, portable and wireless communication gear, and digital cameras.

New products and healthy demand growth for existing FPGA chips helped Xilinx to boost its sales to $335 million in 1994, a record $59.28 million of which was netted as income. Likewise, revenues rose to about $550 million in 1995 (fiscal year ended March 30, 1996). By that time, Xilinx was employing more than 1,000 workers in offices throughout North America, Asia, and Europe. The company was selling more than 40 varieties of programmable logic products and related software applications and continued to be firmly entrenched as the leader in its industry niche.

Early in 1996 Vonderschmitt stepped down as chief executive of the company he had cofounded 11 years earlier. Vonderschmitt remained as chairman of the board, but handed control of the company to Willem P. "Wim" Roelandts. The 51-year-old Roelandts had worked for 28 years at Hewlett-Packard Co., serving as senior vice-president and managing the company's Computer Systems Organization, among other posts. He was known as a seasoned high-tech industry veteran and was chosen to lead Xilinx into a "new era of growth," according to Vonderschmitt.

### Principal Subsidiaries

NeoCAD, Inc.; Xilinx K.K. (Japan).

### Further Reading

Autry, Ret, "Xilinx," *Fortune,* August 27, 1990, p. 81.

Dennis, Ann, "Xilinx Triples Three-Volt Product Offerings," *Business Wire,* December 18, 1995.

Ghosheh, Vallee, "Xilinx Targets Gate Array Market with New XC5000 FPGA Family," *PR Newswire,* November 28, 1994.

Goldman, James S., "With Just Two Xs They Pack a Punch," *Business Journal-San Jose,* August 12, 1991, p. 1.

Hayes, Mary, "Xilinx Leads, Actel Gains," *Business Journal-San Jose,* May 3, 1993, p. 1.

Koland, Cordell, "Xilinx Founder Opens "Gate" to New Chip Market Horizon," *Business Journal-San Jose,* October 19, 1987, Section 1, p. 10.

Seither, Mike, "Xilinx Appoints Hewlett-Packard Executive as New CEO," *Business Wire,* January 11, 1996.

Sutherland, Lani, "Corporate Profits for Xilinx," *Business Wire,* February 25, 1994.

——, "Xilinx Announces Record Results," *Business Wire,* October 11, 1990.

Xilinx Corp. *Xilinx; About the Company,* San Jose: Xilinx Corp., 1995.

—Dave Mote

# YAGEO

## Yageo Corporation

3F, #233-1 Pao Chiao Road
Hsin Tien, Taipei
Taiwan, R.O.C.
886-2-9177555
Fax: 886-2-9174286

*Public Company*
*Incorporated:* 1977
*Employees:* 930
*Sales:* NT$2.23 billion (US$82 million) (1995)
*Stock Exchanges:* Taiwan
*SICs:* 3676 Electronic Resistors; 3629 Electrical Industrial Apparatus, Not Elsewhere Classified; 3675 Electronic Capacitors; 3679 Electronic Components, Not Elsewhere Classified

With an estimated two percent share of the US$4 billion global market for electronic resistors, Taiwan's Yageo Corporation has earned global attention as an aggressive competitor. Barely 20 years old, the company has grown quickly in a market traditionally dominated by the Japanese. In 1995, it was one of only four Taiwanese firms to make *Forbes* magazine's list of the "100 Best Small Companies Outside of America." Despite operating in a mature, highly competitive market, Yageo has managed to capture an increasing share of domestic and global sales in its category while maintaining high profit margins. By the mid-1990s, the company ranked as Taiwan's largest independent producer of resistors, having garnered an estimated 18 percent of the domestic market. Sales quintupled from 1990 to 1995, and profits increased an estimated 13-fold, as the company sharpened its focus on high-margin products within the otherwise stagnant resistor market. Led by the Chen brothers, Wood (the company's chairman) and Pierre (CEO), the company has earned its leading position in the Taiwanese market by using a potent combination of innovation and efficiency. After going public in 1993, the company's young leaders looked to expand globally through acquisition.

Throughout its two-decade history, Yageo has been involved in the production of electronic resistors. These products are a key component of all electronic devices, from household appliances to computers. J. Ross of Hoare Govett Securities Ltd. has noted that "resistors are the most basic electronic component next to the circuit wire." These tiny parts, which often measure less than one-fourth of a square inch and cost a fraction of a cent, adjust voltage and flow of current along a circuit. In a computer, for example, some parts, such as the hard disk drive, require relatively high current (low resistance), while other more sensitive functions, like microprocessors, cannot withstand high current and therefore require high resistance. An array of different resistors permit operation of these disparate components on the same circuit. A single cellular phone can contain 150 resistors, a notebook computer up to 250.

### Early History

Yageo bridged two major phases in the evolution of Taiwan's rapidly growing economy. While Taiwan's was essentially an agrarian economy until the mid-1930s, a second phase, during which the island nation developed manufacturing and assembly operations, began to emerge and develop through the 1980s. Many of these second-phase businesses relied on Japanese technology, existing merely as manufacturing clones. Then, a third economic wave emerged in the 1980s, led by a group of patriotic, well-educated, and generally young businessmen. Instead of borrowing technology from others, these "third wave" enterprises came up with their own innovations.

Yageo founder Wood Chen was among this new breed of Taiwanese businessmen. After graduating from the National Cheng Kong University with a degree in electrical engineering, he went to work for Philips Electronics N.V.'s Taiwanese resistor division. He created Yageo in 1977 to manufacture the equipment needed in producing resistors. Younger brother Pierre joined Yageo in 1981, having graduated with a degree in computer science from Cheng Kong University the year before. The company would undertake production of the actual metal film resistor beginning in 1983.

The brothers were said to be motivated by "patriotism, as well as by personal ambition," according to a 1995 *Forbes* article. For decades, Taiwan's economy depended heavily on Japan, and to a lesser extent on the United States, for technology and components. But instead of relying upon Japanese technology, the Chens decided to develop their own processes. In 1986, they launched their own research and development effort, sending a team of researchers to California's famed Silicon Valley to brainstorm with American engineers. Their creation of the vacuum sputtering coating machine (VSCM) and laser trimming system (LTS) in 1990 made Yageo the first resistor manufacturer in Taiwan to use internally-developed production methods. In fact, Yageo was the only manufacturer in the world to combine both technologies. This highly touted "technological self-sufficiency" gave Yageo the cost advantages it needed to compete with well-entrenched Japanese rivals. By 1995, the company's strong financial commitment to research and development—which averaged from three percent to five percent of annual sales—had earned it three patents and five copyrights.

The Chens also took a unique approach to corporate culture, encouraging its workers to take the initiative. Toward that end, highly automated plants were designed to be more skill intensive than labor intensive, and the Yageo work force, whose average age was 30 and average work week was between 50 to 70 hours, was not required to punch a time clock. Moreover, manufacturing plants featured on-site exercise facilities and an audio/visual center. In short, the Chen brothers believed that such a progressive approach made for happier, more productive, and more efficient workers.

### Diversification in 1980s

Yageo continued to design, manufacture, and sell the machinery necessary in producing resistors through the early 1990s and was one of the world's few producers of high-tech laser trimming systems and vacuum sputtering coating machines. Although this segment of Yageo's business had declined to about ten percent of annual sales by the mid-1990s, it continued to provide an element of vertical integration that gave the company a significant cost advantage over its competitors.

In the 1980s Yageo shifted its focus from manufacturing production equipment to producing the resistors themselves. The company started out making thin-film resistors, a commodity-type component used in such low-tech goods as electronic toys and audio equipment. Over two-thirds of Yageo's production capacity was devoted to these relatively cheap devices throughout the 1980s.

Late in the decade, however, when the market for thin-film resistors began to mature and profit margins eroded, the company began to shift its focus to higher margin thick-film resistors. Although the name would indicate otherwise, thick-film resistors were actually smaller than thin-film resistors and were also made according to more stringent standards. Consequently, thick-film resistors, while more expensive, were in high demand for use in the ever-widening array of such highly standardized miniature devices as notebook computers and cellular phones. By 1993, thick-film resistors constituted over 60 percent of Yageo's resistor sales.

This strategy proved profitable. While the overall resistor market posted anemic average annual growth of 1.5 percent from 1989 to 1993, the thick-film segment was estimated to have grown at over 5.4 percent annually from 1991 through 1994.

### The 1990s and Beyond

Yageo worked to maintain its success by shifting to even higher margin niche resistors in the mid-1990s. In 1995, for example, the company started making high-tech chip array resistors, which featured four resistors on each chip and commanded 70 percent gross profit margins. Chip-array resistors are a fairly closely defined niche market, however, being created specifically for laptop computers.

At the same time, Pierre Chen concentrated on efficiency, reducing operating expenses from 16 percent of sales in 1992 to nine percent of sales by 1995. He increased production capacity with a new plant in Taiwan in 1995 and added a fourth shift at the company's existing plant. By the end of 1996, Yageo expected to manufacture over 3.5 billion resistors each month. The company also hopped on the just-in-time (JIT) inventory bandwagon, setting up a specialized warehouse in 1995. The new system was expected to speed order fulfillment from about one month to less than a week.

In a 1995 interview with *Forbes's* Andrew Tanzer, CEO Pierre Chen predicted that the family company would break into the thick-film resistors' global top three. Acquisition promised to be a key vehicle for growth. By way of preparation, the Chens sold all but 35 percent of their company to the public on the Taiwan Stock Exchange in 1993. The following year, they spent $3 million of the proceeds to acquire ASJ Ptd. Ltd., a Singapore manufacturer of resistors. Yageo hoped to triple ASJ's production capacity from 1994 to 1995 by applying its own efficient methods. As of late 1995, Pierre Chen expected to spend another $200 million in cash on acquisition candidates in Europe and the United States, as well as in Japan. By that time, the company had purchased minority positions in Capital Securities Corp., Hotung Venture Capital Corp., WK Technology Fund, Golden Friend Corp., and MAG Technology.

Yageo's sales nearly quadrupled in the early 1990s, from NT$419 million in 1990 to an estimated NT$1.61 billion by 1994. Net income multiplied more than sevenfold during that same period, from NT$54 million to NT$407.1 million. In 1995, net income was expected to increase to NT$701 million (US$50 million) on revenues of NT$2.1 billion (US$94 million).

As of 1995, Yageo's home market remained its most important, constituting more than half annual sales. Most of the company's exports were shipped to Asia (primarily Hong Kong and Singapore), a slightly smaller proportion went to North America, and the remainder were sent to Europe. Hoare Govett Securities analyst J. Ross expected Yageo to come out on top of a consolidation of Taiwan's fragmented resistor industry in the late 1990s. He also predicted that the company's domestic market share would grow from 18 percent in 1994 to at least 34.4 percent by 1997, and that its share of global resistor sales would top five percent by that time.

With its young, energetic leadership; dedication to research and development; significant acquisition bankroll; and emphasis on high-margin products, Yageo appeared poised to achieve its growth and profitability goals into the 21st century.

*Principal Subsidiaries*

WK Technology Fund; MAG Technology Co., Ltd.; Teapo Electronic Corporation; Chilisin Electronics Corporation; Scan Technology (Singapore) Pte. Ltd.

*Further Reading*

Ross, J., "Yageo Corp., Company Report (Hoare Govett Securities Ltd.)," *INVESTEXT,* February 13, 1995.
Tanzer, Andrew, " 'Every Day We Punch the Market'," *Forbes,* November 6, 1995, pp. 256–57.

—April Dougal Gasbarre

# YAMAHA

## Yamaha Corporation

10-1, Nakazawa-cho
Hamamatsu, Shizuoka 430
Japan
(53) 460-2850
Fax: (53) 456-1109

*Public Company*
*Incorporated:* 1897 as Nippon Gakki Co., Ltd.
*Employees:* 10,676
*Sales:* ¥446 billion (US$2.93 billion) (1994)
*Stock Exchanges:* Tokyo Osaka Nagoya
*SICs:* 3325 Steel Foundries, Not Elsewhere Classified;
3577 Computer Peripheral Equipment, Not Elsewhere
Classified; 3651 Household Audio & Video
Equipment; 3931 Musical Instruments; 6719 Offices
of Holding Companies, Not Elsewhere Classified

Yamaha Corporation, one of Japan's most diversified companies, is the world's largest maker of musical instruments. Since 1950 the company has also become a major producer of electronics, audio products, semiconductors and other computer-related products, home appliances and furniture, sporting goods, specialty metals, machine tools, and industrial robots. Yamaha also owns and operates a string of resorts located throughout Japan, and holds a 31 percent stake in the separately managed Yamaha Motor Company, Ltd. which is the world's second-largest producer of motorcycles. Yamaha Corporation foundered in the 1980s from mismanagement, but was turned around following the appointment of its eighth president, Seisuke Ueshima, in 1992.

### 19th Century Origins

Yamaha founder Torakusu Yamaha's venture reflected turn-of-the-century Japan's enthusiasm for new technologies and the ability of its middle-class entrepreneurs to develop products based on them. Raised in what is now the Wakayama Prefecture, Yamaha received an unusual education for the time from his samurai father, a surveyor with broad interests in astronomy and mechanics and a remarkable library. The Meiji Restoration, a government-subsidized effort to hasten technological development in the late 19th century, put educated people like Yamaha in a position to capitalize on the new growth.

At age 20 Yamaha studied watch repair in Nagasaki under a British engineer. He formed his own watchmaking company, but he was unable to stay in business due to lack of money. He then took a job repairing medical equipment in Osaka after completing an apprenticeship at Japan's first school of Western medicine in Nagasaki.

As part of his job, Yamaha repaired surgical equipment in Hamamatsu, a small Pacific coastal fishing town. Because of their area's isolation, a township school there asked him in 1887 to repair their prized U.S.-made Mason & Hamlin reed organ. Seeing the instrument's commercial potential in Japan, Yamaha produced his own functional version of the organ within a year and then set up a new business in Hamasatsu to manufacture organs for Japanese primary schools. In 1889 he established the Yamaha Organ Manufacturing Company, Japan's first maker of Western musical instruments. At the same time, the government granted Hamamatsu township status, which provided it with rail service and made it a regional commerce center.

Western musical traditions interested the Japanese government, which fostered and catered to growing enthusiasm for Western ideas. While Yamaha's technical education enabled him to manufacture a product, government investment in infrastructure made it possible for him to create a business. Yamaha Organ used modern mass-production methods, and by 1889 it employed 100 people and produced 250 organs annually.

During the 1890s the more inexpensive upright piano surpassed the reed organ in popularity in U.S. homes. Yamaha saw the potential of this market. In 1897 he renamed his company Nippon Gakki Co., Ltd., which literally means Japan musical instruments. He opened a new plant and headquarters in the Itaya-cho district of Hamamatsu.

In 1899 one of Yamaha's initial investors convinced other investors to pull out of Yamaha in favor of a competitor, a new organ maker that was near failure. Yamaha managed to borrow the money necessary to remain solvent and buy out his partners.

Japan's government not only supported industrialization through heavy manufacturing, but also encouraged upstart businesses to contact overseas markets directly. Expansion into pianos required more research, so the Japanese Ministry of Education sponsored a Yamaha tour of the United States in 1899. He was to study piano making and to establish suppliers for the materials needed to produce pianos in Japan. In one year Nippon Gakki produced its first piano. Governmental and institutional orders were the first filled, including some for the Ministry of Education. In 1902, with U.S. materials and German technology, Nippon Gakki introduced its first grand piano. In 1903 the company produced 21 pianos.

Nippon Gakki demonstrated its new pianos in select international exhibitions. Between 1902 and 1920, the company received awards for its pianos and organs that had never before gone to a Japanese manufacturer, for example a Grand Prix at the Saint Louis World Exposition in 1904.

### The World Wars

World War I curtailed sales by a German harmonica marker in Japan, so Nippon Gakki took the opportunity to broaden its product base and begin making and exporting harmonicas. Producing new products that share raw materials and manufacturing skills became a major operating principle for Nippon Gakki.

Yamaha died suddenly during the war. He had succeeded in introducing Western instruments and assembly techniques, but despite his assembly lines, piano making was still a craftsperson's industry at his death. Vice-president Chiyomaru Amano assumed the presidency in 1917. His political contacts had helped the company expand. He saw the company through repeated labor strife for ten years before being replaced.

World War I produced tremendous growth in Japanese industry, and Nippon Gakki grew with it, supplying Asian markets cut off from traditional sources of supply. By 1920 it employed 1,000 workers and produced 10,000 organs and 1,200 pianos a year. The sales records set during the war continued afterward, despite recession. These gains were largely due to piano sales which doubled to ¥2 million between 1919 and 1921.

The next five years nearly put the company in bankruptcy. Appreciation of the yen, which made Nippon Gakki products less competitive overseas, was part of the problem. In 1922, fire destroyed a new plant in Nakazawa and the main Itayacho plant in Hamamatsu. The next year the Great Kanto earthquake destroyed the Tokyo office and again damaged company plants. Before the company recovered, labor unions went on strike after Amano refused to negotiate. Amano gave in to the union's demands 105 days later, after the company's reserves were depleted.

Board member Kaichi Kawakami, by request of the other directors, took the presidency in 1927. A director of Sumitomo Wire Company, Kawakami made an unexpectedly nontraditional choice in accepting the position at the troubled company. Kawakami cut production costs and reorganized the company. Half of all debts were paid within 18 months of Kawakami taking over.

Between the world wars, Western imports still dominated the Japanese sales of Western instruments. Since Nippon Gakki's advantage was in price alone, Kawakami opened an acoustics lab and research center in 1930 to improve quality. He also hired advisors from C. Bechstein of Germany to improve the quality of the Yamaha piano.

The growth of the public school system of the 1930s expanded the market for Western instruments, and Nippon Gakki introduced lower-priced accordions and guitars to capitalize on the expansion.

When World War II began, Nippon Gakki plants produced propellers for Zero fighter planes, fuel tanks, and wing parts. As with expansion during World War I, these items laid the groundwork for broader diversification in the postwar years. In the meantime, Nippon Gakki had to stop making musical instruments altogether in 1945.

### Postwar Expansion

Only one Nippon Gakki factory survived the wartime U.S. bombing raids. Postwar financial assistance from the United States made possible the production of harmonicas and xylophones just two months after receipt of the funds. Within six months it produced organs, accordions, tube horns, and guitars. After the Allied powers approved civilian trade in 1947, Nippon Gakki began once again to export harmonicas.

Nippon Gakki already had experience with wooden aircraft parts dating back to 1920, but wartime activity exposed the company to new technologies. By 1947 Nippon Gakki could cast its own metal piano frames and produced its first pianos in three years. The company also produced its first audio component—a phonograph—in 1947.

Postwar growth was rapid. The Japanese government had fostered the growth of Western music in Japan since 1879, but Nippon Gakki received its biggest boost to date in 1948. That year the Education Ministry mandated musical education for

Japanese children—only encouraged before the war—and greatly expanded business.

Kaichi Kawakami's son, Gen'ichi Kawakami, became the company's fourth president in 1950. During his tenure the Japanese rebuilt their economy, and consumer buying power increased. Nippon Gakki became less reliant on institutional purchases. President for 27 years, Kawakami made more progress in popularizing Western music in Japan by beginning the Yamaha music schools in 1954 to train young musicians. With the help of the Ministry of Education, Nippon Gakki founded the nonprofit Yamaha Music Foundation in 1966 to sponsor festivals and concerts and run the music schools.

Kawakami's biggest accomplishments were in production, diversification, and the creation of foreign markets, all of which built the framework for the modern Yamaha Corporation. Kawakami toured the United States and Europe in 1953, a trip that inspired diversification into many areas unrelated to the music industry. Like Yamaha's tour of the United States in 1899, G. Kawakami's tour affected the company's product line and reputation for decades to come.

His return sparked research into new uses for materials since capital was scarce. The company researched uses for fiberglass reinforced plastics (FRP). In 1960 the company produced its first sailboat made of FRP. Later it expanded to produce yachts, patrol boats for Japan's Maritime Safety Agency, and ocean-going fishing vessels. Primarily serving the Asian market, it eventually became Japan's largest FRP boat producer. FRP capability led to introduction of other products, such as archery bows, skis, and bathtubs. Through metals research Nippon Gakki developed sophisticated alloys for electronics as well as less complex alloys for structural purposes. Nippon Gakki soon became a major producer of equipment for the household construction industry, such as boilers and central heating systems.

In its traditional line of pianos, Nippon Gakki expanded production, raised its quality standards, and cut production costs, already lower than the industry average, even further. Through a conveyer belt system and an innovative kiln drying technique that facilitated the rapid drying of wood used in pianos, Nippon Gakki decreased the amount of time required to produce a piano from two years to three months.

The first large-scale marketing drive toward the United States was not related to music at all. In 1954 the government returned the company's World War II-era metal working factory, which had been among confiscated assets. Nippon Gakki produced its first motorcycle in 1955 and established the Yamaha Motor Company Ltd., of which it was partial owner. Later it produced smaller motorized vehicles such as snowmobiles, outboard engines, and golf carts. For the next 20 years, however, it was motorcycles for which the West would recognize the Yamaha brand. Following Honda's lead, Yamaha introduced its first motorcycles in the United States in the early 1960s. Along with Suzuki, the three companies made smaller and lower-priced motorcycles and greatly expanded the U.S. market, which had been limited to large cycles for serious enthusiasts. Yamaha also marketed its motorcycles successfully in Asia.

Nippon Gakki began an ambitious drive into electronics in 1959, when it introduced the world's first all-transistor organ to replace electronic organs using vacuum tubes. Nippon Gakki's first electronic instrument represented the company's new competence in product development.

With its new variety of products Nippon Gakki began its first serious export push, establishing its first overseas subsidiary, in Mexico in 1958. In 1959 the company made a few pianos with a U.S. retailer's name on them, and in 1960 it created its own sales subsidiary in Los Angeles. Within a year Yamaha won a conspicuous contract to supply the Los Angeles Board of Education with 53 grand pianos. For the next seven years, the board annually purchased Yamaha pianos for schools in its jurisdiction. Since Nippon Gakki priced its pianos considerably lower than Western competition, this boost to its reputation for quality allowed it to bid with more success on U.S. institutional contracts.

Having worked well in Japan, Nippon Gakki sponsored overseas musical events and education beginning in 1964, when it opened the first Yamaha school in the United States. Like its Japanese counterpart, it was designed to teach music appreciation to students at an early age and create a long-term market. Financially independent of Yamaha, these nonprofit schools operate throughout Europe and the United States and have taught more than one million students.

These educational efforts were just beginning to pay off in Japan. During the 1960s Nippon Gakki's domestic market grew tremendously. Annual piano output increased from 24,000 in 1960 to 100,000 in 1966, making the company the world's largest piano maker.

In the mid-1960s, Nippon Gakki began to produce wind instruments on a large scale. In 1968 Nippon Gakki started exporting trumpets, trombones, and xylophones. Five years in development, the company produced is first concert grand piano in 1967.

U.S. instrument makers did not welcome Yamaha's growth. In 1969 U.S. piano manufacturers sought a 30 percent tariff on imported pianos, but the U.S. Tariff Commission ruled in Yamaha's favor. Nonetheless, the hearings delayed for three years a tariff reduction that had already been scheduled and established a hostile precedent for Nippon Gakki expansion in North America. In 1973 Yamaha bought its first U.S. manufacturing facility, but a strike there further delayed Yamaha's U.S. drive.

### Electronics Developments in the 1970s

Just as transistors had once replaced tubes in electronics, integrated circuits (ICs) replaced transistors in the 1970s. Because no manufacturer would develop an IC for Nippon Gakki's relatively limited demand, the company built a plant in 1971 to make its own. By developing the technology early, Nippon Gakki established itself as a serious electronics firm, better able to serve the accelerating demand for electronic keyboards and audio components.

Large-scale integrated circuits (LSIs) allowed the company to digitalize its keyboards. Nippon Gakki built an LSI plant in

1976 so it could convert all of its electronic products from analog to digital formats. LSIs also made possible Yamaha's growth as an electronics supplier and the manufacture of advanced electronic systems such as industrial robots. Nippon Gakki developed electronic components more quickly than other types of components. In its traditional line of pianos and organs, by contrast, Nippon Gakki still depended on overseas suppliers for components in the 1970s. While Nippon Gakki's sales in 1979 remained steady, a favorable exchange rate boosted earnings to a record ¥15 billion. Nevertheless, the same exchange rate hurt motorcycle sales.

### Overextension in the 1980s

The 1980s were a difficult decade for the company. While there were notable successes, Nippon Gakki was badly mismanaged in a case of imperial overreach. The company's first major blunder actually came from its affiliate, Yamaha Motor, which in 1981 unwisely tried to unseat Honda from its top position in motorcycles. Yamaha introduced new models and increased production. When Honda and other motorcycle manufacturers did the same, the industry faced overproduction. As a result Yamaha Motor posted two consecutive losses totaling US$126.1 million. A relatively small motor manufacturer, Yamaha Motor was left with an inventory of one million motorcycles and debts that approached US$1 billion. In addition, the price competition among Japanese motorcycle makers caused U.S. manufacturer Harley Davidson to request tariffs on imports, straining Yamaha's U.S. business, since it did not have any U.S. factories. Nippon Gakki remained profitable since it only owned 39.1 percent of Yamaha Motor (later reduced to 31 percent), but the debacle damaged the company's reputation and position at home.

On the positive side, synthesizers and LSIs brought the company success early in the decade. Electronics research paid off well with the 1983 introduction of the DX-7 digital synthesizer, which went on to become the best-selling synthesizer ever. The development of LSIs allowed Nippon Gakki to produce its first professional sound systems and to keep pace with the consumer audio industry during the early 1980s. In 1983 the company put its LSIs themselves on the market.

Also in the early 1980s, Nippon Gakki divided its research facilities to reflect its electronics emphasis. Research was then carried out by four sections: one on semiconductors and LSIs, a second for research applications to audiovisual equipment, a third on hall and theater acoustic design, and the fourth for products design.

While expanding its product line, Nippon Gakki also initiated a program to spread its manufacturing base overseas, adding to its network of marketing subsidiaries. Hiroshi Kawashima, former president of the U.S. subsidiary, spearheaded the U.S. drive. In 1980 Nippon Gakki opened an electronic keyboard plant in Georgia in the hope that basing this new venture in the United States would ease trade tension.

Further difficulties, however, were in store when Hiroshi, the third generation of Kawakamis, became the company's seventh president in 1983. His father, then chairman, reportedly distrusted Hiroshi and battles between the two helped lead the company astray. Hiroshi brought in outside consultants in end-runs around his father, but this only resulted in such unwise moves as building huge headquarters in London and Buena Park, California, which served simply as symbols of a global powerhouse that wasn't. The company also became notorious for moving ahead with ambitious projects after doing little, if any, market research. Before there was even the smallest market for it, for example, Nippon Gakki attempted to develop a multimedia computer in the early 1980s and probably to the company's fortune failed. Another marketing miscalculation at the other end of the decade left Yamaha with 200,000 unsold wind instruments in 1990.

Such ventures might have been perceived as noble failures if it were not for the company's increasingly troubled finances. By the end of the decade, it was seen that 1980 represented the decade's peak of profitability. Hiroshi Kawakami's attempt at a reorganization from 1985 to 1987 had failed to turn the company around. Meanwhile, to celebrate the 100th anniversary of the firm, Kawakami changed the corporate name to Yamaha Corporation in 1987.

### 1990s and Beyond

Kawakami made another attempt to resurrect Yamaha but was thwarted by a demoralized and rebellious work force. He reportedly had hoped to use early retirement as a means of reducing the company's number of employees, but the workers' labor union refused to go along with the plan and demanded that Kawakami be fired—and he was.

Taking over in 1992 was a 36-year Yamaha veteran with a marketing background, Seisuke Ueshima, who quickly moved to turn the company around. He demoted Kawakami cronies and came to an agreement with the union that retained all nonmanagerial employees but led to the elimination of 30 percent of the administrative positions in Japan along with overseas employees (notably those in the London and Buena Park headquarters). Ueshima also downsized the noncore resorts and sporting goods operations, both of which were losing money.

For the longer term, Ueshima had to change the way new products were developed and marketed. Specifically, he wanted Yamaha employees to ask "Why are we building this product?," a question rarely raised during previous decades. In the face of the maturation of some markets, Ueshima decided to go after the high-end of these markets where larger profits can be made. One example was the Disklavier series of pianos with built-in computers for recording and playing back performances; individual Disklavier models could retail for more than US$30,000.

Ueshima also pushed the company to develop innovative new products. In 1993 the Silent Piano series was introduced to great success. Costing US$7,300 each, more than 17,000 were sold in Japan in their first 12 months on the market, 70 percent above the amount projected. These pianos could either be played as regular acoustic pianos or their sound could be muted and only heard by the pianist through headphones. In 1995, Yamaha introduced a similarly functional electronic trumpet mute and sold 13,000 of them in the first few months. Other successful musical introductions of this period included the

VL1 and VP1 virtual acoustic synthesizers, which, rather than storing libraries of sounds that could be replayed, stored computer models of the instruments themselves which were then able to reproduce a wider variety of sounds and in a more authentic fashion.

Other innovations during this time included the Yamaha FM sound chip used in many sound boards that were an essential feature of multimedia computers, and a karaoke system that received music via phone lines connected to a central computer loaded with laser disks. Such successes returned Yamaha to healthy profitability: ¥6.4 billion in 1994 and ¥28.5 billion in 1995. Although the company still had some distracting noncore assets as it headed into the 21st century, the leadership of Ueshima appeared to have set it on course for a new era of musical and electronic success.

### Principal Subsidiaries

Yamaha Credit Co., Ltd.; Yamaha Plans Co., Ltd.; Yamaha Hall Co., Ltd.; Yamaha Kyohan Co., Ltd.; Yamaha Livingtec Corporation; Yamaha Motor Company, Ltd. (31%); Yamaha Recreation Co., Ltd.; Yamaha Electronik Europa G.m.b.H. (Germany); Yamaha Europa G.m.b.H. (Germany); Yamaha Music (Asia) Pte. Ltd. (Singapore); Yamaha Corporation of America (U.S.A.); Yamaha Electronics Corp. USA.

### Further Reading

Armstrong, Larry, "Sweet Music with Ominous Undertones for Yamaha," *Business Week,* November 15, 1993, pp. 119–20.

Henry, Lawrence, "Yamaha Stubs Its Imperial Toe," *Industry Week,* April 6, 1992, pp. 29–31.

Morris, Kathleen, "Play It Again, Seisuke," *Financial World,* November 22, 1994, pp. 42–46.

"Perfect Pitch?," *Economist,* February 17, 1996, p. 60.

Schlender, Brenton R., "The Perils of Losing Focus," *Fortune,* May 17, 1993, p. 100.

"Yamaha's First Century," *Music Trades,* August 1987.

*Yamaha: A Century of Excellence: 1887–1987,* Hamamatsu, Japan: Yamaha Corporation, 1987.

—Ray Walsh
—updated by David E. Salamie

# Zale Corporation

901 West Walnut Hill Lane
Irving, Texas 75038-1003
U.S.A.
(214) 580-4000
Fax: (214) 580-5336

*Public Company*
*Incorporated:* 1924
*Employees:* 9,000
*Sales:* $1.04 billion (1995)
*Stock Exchanges:* NASDAQ
*SICs:* 5944 Jewelry Stores

Zale Corporation is the largest operator of retail jewelry stores in the United States. Zale's 1,177 stores, located in 48 states, as well as in Puerto Rico and Guam, generated $1.4 billion in sales in 1995, achieving net earnings of $31.5 million and a return to profitability since the company's bankruptcy reorganization in the early 1990s. Zale stores operate within four distinct divisions: the Zales division, with 534 stores in 48 states and Puerto Rico representing 42 percent of company revenues, focuses on mainstream, middle-income consumers, and specializes heavily in diamonds; the Gordon's division is positioned as a regional retailer for the lower and middle-income consumer, with 332 stores operating primarily under the Gordon's name (14 stores operate as Daniel's Jewelers in Arizona) providing 26 percent of Zale Corp. revenues; the upscale Fine Jewelers Guild division accounts for 19 percent of company revenues and comprises 123 stores operating under the Bailey, Banks & Biddle, Zell Bros., Sweeney's, Corrigan's, and Linz trade names; the fourth division, Diamond Park Fine Jewelers, operates 188 leased jewelry departments for such leading department store chains such as Dillard's and Dayton Hudson, providing 13 percent of company revenues.

### Early Growth

Morris B. Zale, born in Russia but raised in Texas, opened his first jewelry store in Witchita Falls, Texas, in 1924. Two years later, Zale opened a second Texas store and was joined b childhood friend, and brother-in-law, Ben Lipshy. From the beginning, Zale stores offered credit, with payments typically spread out over 12 months, even to its low-income customers. It leased its first locations, a practice that placed pressure on the company, grown to three stores at the beginning of the 1930s, when the company was stuck with long-term leases fixed at high, pre-Depression rents. However, despite the Depression, the company continued to expand through the decade, opening a fourth store in Amarillo in 1934, and growing to 12 locations by 1941. In that year, the company's revenues had grown to $2.73 million. Zale avoided building long-term debt by paying modest salaries and dividends to himself, Lipshy, and other family members joining the company; instead, earnings were invested back into the company.

The years of the Second World War limited Zale's expansion of new locations but not its revenue growth. The devotion of raw materials to the war effort during this period led to a scarcity of most consumer items; jewelry, with limited strategic value, drew consumer interest. By 1944, Zale's revenues had doubled, to over $5 million. In that year, Zale acquired a thirteenth store, Corrigan's in Houston, which allowed it to move into higher-end jewelry. Two years later, revenues doubled again, passing $10 million for the year. By then, Zale had begun to operate as a big company, rather than as a collection of stores. In 1942, Zale opened a buying office in New York, which allowed the company to purchase diamonds and watches in quantity at wholesale prices. As the company grew, to 19 stores in 1946, Zale set up a central design, display, and printing operation in Dallas to service its growing chain. The company's next step toward centralization of its operations came when it opened its own shops for building store fixtures and constructing store interiors. Company headquarters were also moved to Dallas in 1946.

The postwar boom in consumer spending brought a new period of growth to Zale, which added more than 50 stores between 1947 and 1957, the year in which the company went public. That offering, of 125,000 shares, raised $1.5 million, which, according to *Fortune* magazine, "appear[ed] to have been the only new money put into the company since it was started.'' Listed on the American Stock Exchange in 1958, the company operated 102 stores, primarily under the Zale trade name. Much of this growth came through the acquisition of existing stores; stores marketing to high-end consumers generally kept their original names. Diamonds formed the largest part of company sales, with diamond rings, other diamond jewelry and diamond watches providing about 38 percent of revenues; costume jewelry and watches added to sales, while the company also sold electric appliances, silverware, dinnerware, luggage, cameras, eyeglasses, and other items.

With sales topping $37 million in 1958, Zale moved closer to complete vertical integration of the company when it was invited to purchase its diamonds directly from the Central Selling Organization, otherwise known as the diamond syndicate. Based in London and representing a group of diamond producers including the De Beers of South Africa, the diamond syndicate represented more than 80 percent of the world's supply of rough diamonds. The syndicate not only controlled the world's diamond output, but also the choice of companies allowed to purchase its diamonds, and which diamonds a company was allowed to purchase. Zale, because of its integrated operations, including cutting, polishing and setting operations in New York, and its ability to market the full scale of diamonds from the smallest to the largest, most expensive diamonds, became the only U.S. jewelry retailer invited to purchase directly from the syndicate.

### Branching Out and Buckling Under

By the mid-1960s, Zale operated the nation's—and the world's—largest retail jewelry chain. Its 403 stores produced $81 million in 1963, with a net income of nearly $5 million. Diamonds continued to represent the largest share of Zale's sales, about $27 million. Operating manufacturing plants in New York, Tel Aviv, and Puerto Rico, the company also operated a wholesale division, selling to other jewelry retailers. Zale also made and sold watches under its own Baylor's label, buying mechanisms from Switzerland.

By 1965, Zale found itself with a surplus of cash. Its business was tied up in its jewelry store operations, and the development of the first synthetic diamonds, at the time viewed as a potential replacement for real diamonds in the retail jewelry trade, frightened the company into diversifying its product base. The company decided to move into the broader retailing field, purchasing the Texas-based Skillern drug store chain. This acquisition was followed by forays into budget fashion apparel, sporting goods, shoes, furniture, and a chain of airport-based tobacco and newsstand concessions. By 1974, in addition to 956 retail jewelry stores, Zale had grown to include 351 shoe stores, 83 drug stores, 146 clothing stores, 25 sporting goods stores, 13 home furnishings stores, and 13 tobacco/newsstand concessions. Together, these divisions produced revenues nearing $600 million; half of the company's revenues, however, continued to come from its jewelry operations—with one highlight coming from the 1969 purchase of the Light of Peace diamond for $1.4 million—which also contributed three-quarters of the company's more than $30 million in 1974 profits.

Trouble began to brew for Zale in the mid-1970s. Charges that the company's chief financial officer had been embezzling

funds—the CFO was eventually acquitted—led to investigations from the Internal Revenue Service and other government agencies into alleged misappropriation of funds, including avoiding some $27 million in federal tax payments. These investigations would culminate in a $78 million tax charge brought by the IRS against Zale in 1982, and contributed to the replacement of Ben Lipshy, president of the company since 1957 and chairman of the board since 1971, by M. B. Zale's son, Donald Zale as chairman in 1980. By then, Zale's more than 1,400 stores included international operations in the United Kingdom, Switzerland, France, West Germany, Canada, and South Africa.

At the beginning of the decade, Zale abruptly began selling off its non-jewelry retail operations. Despite raising revenues, which topped $1 billion in 1980, these operations produced little of the company's profits. By then, also, the synthetic diamond scare had passed—these found industrial applications, but could not be successfully developed for retail sales, partly because of consumer insistence on purchasing real diamonds. In the space of a few weeks at the end of 1980, Zale sold off the Skillern chain to Revco, Inc. for $60 million; its 37-store sporting goods chain went to Oshman Sporting Goods, Inc. for $14 million; and its Butler Shoe division, with 385 stores, went to Sears for $100 million. Except for its newsstand/tobacco concessions, which would grow to 90 stores, and its O.G. Wilson catalog showroom division, the company had come back to its core jewelry business.

Jewelry sales slumped across the industry during the recession of the early 1980s. Worse, gold and diamond values, which had traditionally seen steady appreciation, began to fluctuate wildly. Zale saw revenues fall to $939 million in 1982. Profits slipped more drastically, from $33 million in 1981 to a loss of $6 million in 1982, the result, in part, of a $10.6 million charge brought on by the company's settlement with the IRS for its 1970s tax liabilities. The collapse of the oil industry in the Southwest, where the highest concentration of Zale stores were located, also hurt the company's sales. The company struggled to maintain its share of the jewelry market, while facing increasing competition from department stores. Zale, which had perennially relied on sales of wedding rings for its chief source of revenues, had fallen behind the times—particularly with the decline in marriages since the 1970s. Meanwhile, it saw customers departing for the larger assortments of jewelry, and especially gold jewelry, available elsewhere.

Part of Zale's troubles were blamed on the lingering influence of its old management, which had been manufacturing-oriented, rather than marketing-oriented, allowing further inroads into the jewelry market by retailers more responsive to trends in consumer demands. Breaking the hold of former management, who were still largely loyal to M. B. Zale, would take several years and eventually a relocation of the company's headquarters. Zale struggled to recover from the recession, but sales in its 1,500 stores barely budged, remaining around $1 billion.

### The Peoples' Takeover

In 1986, the company posted a net loss of over $60 million, including a restructuring charge of about $80 million as it disposed of its European retail operations, and the last of its non-jewelry divisions, and a $50 million writedown of old inventory. By that time, Zale had already rejected an attempt at a takeover by Peoples Jewelers of Canada. Peoples, led by Irving Gerstein, was looking to expand beyond its Canadian base. That company already owned 15 percent of Zale's stock, purchased for $70 million in 1980. When Zale's problems rose in the early 1980s, Peoples attempted to sell its stock back to Zale, but Zale refused to buy.

Critical of Zale's efforts to turn the company around, Gerstein became determined to take over the company. Under Texas law, however, Peoples needed approvals from at least two-thirds of Zale's stockholders to complete a takeover, and the Zale family controlled more than one-third of the stock.

In early 1986, Peoples, aided by Drexel Burnham Lambert, made offers of $420 million and $470 million to take over the company. The Zale family refused to sell. Gerstein next met with the Austrian Zwarovski company, makers of crystal and jewelry, which agreed to back Peoples in its next takeover effort. By 1988, Gerstein had constructed lending arrangements that allowed him to tender an offer of $50 per share of Zale stock—nearly double its trading price. The Zale family, under pressure from its own investment company, at last gave in and agreed to sell the company. By the end of that year, Peoples and Zwarovski, each with 50 percent ownership, took Zale private.

Gerstein moved quickly to settle some of the company's debt, selling some $700 million in junk bonds, leaving the company about $900 million in debt. His next step was to close Zale's New York and Puerto Rico manufacturing operations—instead turning to vendors for store stock—sold off the company's diamond inventory, and reduced the company's large advertising budget. With expenses reduced by $80 million, the company's net earnings rose, allowing Gerstein to declare a $5 million dividend to both Peoples and Zwarovski. The following year, the company acquired Gordon Jewelry Corporation, the nation's second largest retail jewelry chain. Three years later, Zale verged on collapse.

### Bankruptcy and Beyond

At the beginning of the 1990s, Zale, including the Gordon chain, had grown to 2,000 stores, with revenues of $1.3 billion. However, the international recession of the 1990s, the economic uncertainty produced by the Persian Gulf War, and a new luxury tax on purchases over $10,000 quickly took their toll on jewelry sales. In 1990, Zale posted a $64 million loss. The following year's losses amounted to over $106 million in the

first six months alone. By the end of the year, the company was unable to make a $52 million interest payment on its $850 million in debt.

Zale attempted to restructure the company, announcing the closing of 400 stores and a reduction of its headquarters, but its creditors began threatening to force the company into bankruptcy. By the end of January 1992, Zale joined the growing list of failing jewelry companies and petitioned for voluntary bankruptcy.

When Zale emerged from Chapter 11 in 1993, its debt was settled. With 700 fewer stores, Zale, led by former Macy's executive Robert DiNicola as chairman and chief executive officer, moved to return the company to profitability. The new management team worked to restructure the company, creating separate and independent divisions of the Zale and Gordon stores. The company also announced plans to spend more than $80 million over the next several years upgrading locations. At the same time, the company revitalized its purchasing, introducing a broader range of items to win back its customers.

By 1995, the company appeared back on the road to good health. Its revenues of that year, $1.04 billion, represented a 12.6 percent increase over the previous year's. Net income grew by 36 percent, to $31.5 million, while the company continued to shrink its total debt, down to $443 million. With a commitment to its "back-to-basics" approach, and a booming economy, the company's future looked bright. As DiNicola told the *Dallas Morning News,* "For the long term, we'll be running the No. 1 jewelry company in the country. That's what we have to look forward to."

### Principal Divisions

Zales; Gordon's; Fine Jewelers Guild; Diamond Park Fine Jewelers.

### Further Reading

Gubernick, Lisa, "To Catch a Falling Star," *Forbes,* June 2, 1986, p. 71.
Halkias, Maria, "Polishing a Gem in the Rough," *The Dallas Morning News,* December 7, 1994, p. D1.
McDonald, John, "Diamonds for the Masses," *Fortune,* December, 1994, p. 134.
Mehlman, William, "Canadian Admirer Gets Cold Shoulder from Cash-Rich Zale," *The Insiders' Chronicle,* February 2, 1981, p. 1.
Shuster, William George, "Zale Strategy: Return to Fundamentals," *Jewelers' Circular-Keystone,* September 1994, p. 140.

—M. L. Cohen

# *INDEX TO COMPANIES* ———————————————

# Index to Companies

Listings in this index are arranged in alphabetical order under the company name. Company names beginning with a letter or proper name such as Eli Lilly & Co. will be found under the first letter of the company name. Definite articles (The, Le, La) are ignored for alphabetical purposes as are forms of incorporation that precede the company name (AB, NV). Company names printed in bold type have full, historical essays on the page numbers appearing in bold. Updates to entries that appeared in earlier volumes are signified by the notation (**upd.**). Company names in light type are references within an essay to that company, not full historical essays. This index is cumulative with volume numbers printed in bold type.

# INDEX TO INDUSTRIES

# Index to Industries

## CONSTRUCTION

## CONTAINERS

## DRUGS

## ELECTRICAL & ELECTRONICS

## FINANCIAL SERVICES: NON-BANKS

## FOOD PRODUCTS

## FOOD SERVICES & RETAILERS

## HEALTH & PERSONAL CARE PRODUCTS

## HEALTH CARE SERVICES

## HOTELS

## INFORMATION TECHNOLOGY

Rengo Co., Ltd., IV
Riverwood International Corporation, 11
Rock-Tenn Company, 13
St. Joe Paper Company, 8
Sanyo-Kokusaku Pulp Co., Ltd., IV
Scott Paper Company, IV
Sealed Air Corporation, 14
Specialty Coatings Inc., 8
Stone Container Corporation, IV
Stora Kopparbergs Bergslags AB, IV
Svenska Cellulosa Aktiebolaget, IV
Temple-Inland Inc., IV
Union Camp Corporation, IV
United Paper Mills Ltd. (Yhtyneet
  Paperitehtaat Oy), IV
Universal Forest Products Inc., 10
Westvaco Corporation, IV
Weyerhaeuser Company, IV; 9 (upd.)
Willamette Industries, Inc., IV

## PERSONAL SERVICES

ADT Security Systems, Inc., 12
CUC International Inc., 16
The Davey Tree Expert Company, 11
Educational Testing Service, 12
Franklin Quest Co., 11
Goodwill Industries International, Inc., 16
KinderCare Learning Centers, Inc., 13
The Loewen Group, Inc., 16
Manpower, Inc., 9
Rollins, Inc., 11
Rosenbluth International Inc., 14
Service Corporation International, 6
Weight Watchers International Inc., 12

## PETROLEUM

Abu Dhabi National Oil Company, IV
Alberta Energy Company Ltd., 16
Amerada Hess Corporation, IV
Amoco Corporation, IV; 14 (upd.)
Anadarko Petroleum Corporation, 10
Anschutz Corp., 12
Apache Corp., 10
Ashland Oil, Inc., IV
Atlantic Richfield Company, IV
British Petroleum Company PLC, IV; 7
  (upd.)
Burlington Resources Inc., 10
Burmah Castrol plc, IV
Chevron Corporation, IV
Chiles Offshore Corporation, 9
Chinese Petroleum Corporation, IV
CITGO Petroleum Corporation, IV
The Coastal Corporation, IV
Compañia Española de Petróleos S.A., IV
Conoco Inc., IV; 16 (upd.)
Cosmo Oil Co., Ltd., IV
Crown Central Petroleum Corporation, 7
Den Norse Stats Oljeselskap AS, IV
Deutsche BP Aktiengesellschaft, 7
Diamond Shamrock, Inc., IV
Egyptian General Petroluem Corporation,
  IV
Empresa Colombiana de Petróleos, IV
Ente Nazionale Idrocarburi, IV
Enterprise Oil plc, 11
Entreprise Nationale Sonatrach, IV
Exxon Corporation, IV; 7 (upd.)
FINA, Inc., 7
General Sekiyu K.K., IV
Global Marine Inc., 9
Holly Corporation, 12
Hunt Oil Company, 7
Idemitsu Kosan K.K., IV
Imperial Oil Limited, IV
Indian Oil Corporation Ltd., IV
Kanematsu Corporation, IV

Kerr-McGee Corporation, IV
King Ranch, Inc., 14
Koch Industries, Inc., IV
Kuwait Petroleum Corporation, IV
Libyan National Oil Corporation, IV
The Louisiana Land and Exploration
  Company, 7
Lyondell Petrochemical Company, IV
MAPCO Inc., IV
Maxus Energy Corporation, 7
Mitchell Energy and Development
  Corporation, 7
Mitsubishi Oil Co., Ltd., IV
Mobil Corporation, IV; 7 (upd.)
Murphy Oil Corporation, 7
Nabors Industries, Inc., 9
National Iranian Oil Company, IV
Neste Oy, IV
Nigerian National Petroleum Corporation,
  IV
Nippon Mining Co. Ltd., IV
Nippon Oil Company, Limited, IV
Noble Affiliates, Inc., 11
Occidental Petroleum Corporation, IV
Oil and Natural Gas Commission, IV
ÖMV Aktiengesellschaft, IV
Oryx Energy Company, 7
Pennzoil Company, IV
PERTAMINA, IV
Petro-Canada Limited, IV
Petrofina, IV
Petróleo Brasileiro S.A., IV
Petróleos de Portugal S.A., IV
Petróleos de Venezuela S.A., IV
Petróleos del Ecuador, IV
Petróleos Mexicanos, IV
Petroleum Development Oman LLC, IV
Petronas, IV
Phillips Petroleum Company, IV
Qatar General Petroleum Corporation, IV
Quaker State Corporation, 7
Repsol S.A., IV; 16 (upd.)
Royal Dutch Petroleum Company/ The
  ''Shell'' Transport and Trading Company
  p.l.c., IV
Sasol Limited, IV
Saudi Arabian Oil Company, IV
Seagull Energy Corporation, 11
Shell Oil Company, IV; 14 (upd.)
Showa Shell Sekiyu K.K., IV
Société Nationale Elf Aquitaine, IV; 7
  (upd.)
Sun Company, Inc., IV
Talisman Energy, 9
Tesoro Petroleum Corporation, 7
Texaco Inc., IV; 14 (upd.)
Tonen Corporation, IV; 16 (upd.)
Tosco Corporation, 7
Total Compagnie Française des Pétroles
  S.A., IV
Triton Energy Corporation, 11
Türkiye Petrolleri Anonim Ortakliği, IV
Ultramar PLC, IV
Union Texas Petroleum Holdings, Inc., 9
Unocal Corporation, IV
USX Corporation, IV; 7 (upd.)
Valero Energy Corporation, 7
Wascana Energy Inc., 13
Western Atlas Inc., 12
Western Company of North America, 15
The Williams Companies, Inc., IV
YPF Sociedad Anonima, IV

## PUBLISHING & PRINTING

A.H. Belo Corporation, 10
Advance Publications Inc., IV
Affiliated Publications, Inc., 7

American Greetings Corporation, 7
Arnoldo Mondadori Editore S.p.A., IV
Axel Springer Verlag A.G., IV
Banta Corporation, 12
Bauer Publishing Group, 7
Berlitz International, Inc., 13
Bertelsmann A.G., IV; 15 (upd.)
Book-of-the-Month Club, Inc., 13
CCH Inc., 14
Central Newspapers, Inc., 10
Commerce Clearing House, Inc., 7
The Condé Nast Publications Inc., 13
Cox Enterprises, Inc., IV
Crain Communications, Inc., 12
Dai Nippon Printing Co., Ltd., IV
Day Runner, Inc., 14
De La Rue PLC, 10
Deluxe Corporation, 7
Dow Jones & Company, Inc., IV
The Dun & Bradstreet Corporation, IV
The E.W. Scripps Company, IV; 7 (upd.)
Edmark Corporation, 14
Elsevier N.V., IV
Encyclopedia Britannica, Inc., 7
Engraph, Inc., 12
Enquirer/Star Group, Inc., 10
Farrar, Straus and Giroux Inc., 15
Flint Ink Corporation, 13
Follett Corporation, 12
Gannett Co., Inc., IV; 7 (upd.)
Gibson Greetings, Inc., 12
Grolier Inc., 16
Groupe de la Cite, IV
Hachette, IV
Hallmark Cards, Inc., IV; 16 (upd.)
Harcourt Brace and Co., 12
Harcourt Brace Jovanovich, Inc., IV
HarperCollins Publishers, 15
Havas, SA, 10
The Hearst Corporation, IV
Her Majesty's Stationery Office, 7
Houghton Mifflin Company, 10
International Data Group, 7
IPC Magazines Limited, 7
John Fairfax Holdings Limited, 7
Knight-Ridder, Inc., IV; 15 (upd.)
Kodansha Ltd., IV
Landmark Communications, Inc., 12
Lee Enterprises, Incorporated, 11
Maclean Hunter Limited, IV
Macmillan, Inc., 7
Marvel Entertainment Group, Inc., 10
Matra-Hachette S.A., 15 (upd.)
Maxwell Communication Corporation plc,
  IV; 7 (upd.)
McGraw-Hill, Inc., IV
Meredith Corporation, 11
Mirror Group Newspapers plc, 7
Moore Corporation Limited, IV
Multimedia, Inc., 11
National Geographic Society, 9
The New York Times Company, IV
News America Publishing Inc., 12
News Corporation Limited, IV; 7 (upd.)
Nihon Keizai Shimbun, Inc., IV
Ottaway Newspapers, Inc., 15
Pearson plc, IV
Pulitzer Publishing Company, 15
Quebecor Inc., 12
R.L. Polk & Co., 10
R.R. Donnelley & Sons Company, IV; 9
  (upd.)
Random House, Inc., 13
The Reader's Digest Association, Inc., IV
Reed International P.L.C., IV
Reuters Holdings PLC, IV
Scholastic Corporation, 10
Scott Fetzer Company, 12

## WASTE SERVICES

# NOTES ON CONTRIBUTORS

# Notes on Contributors

**BODINE, Paul S.** Free-lance writer, editor, and researcher in Milwaukee, specializing in business subjects; contributor to the *Encyclopedia of American Industries, Encyclopedia of Global Industries, DISCovering Authors, Contemporary Popular Writers,* the Milwaukee *Journal Sentinel,* and the Baltimore *Sun.*

**BOYER, Dean.** Newspaper reporter and free-lance writer in the Seattle area.

**BROWN, Susan W.** Free-lance writer and editor.

**COHEN, M. L.** Novelist and free-lance writer living in Chicago.

**COVELL, Jeffrey L.** Free-lance writer and corporate history contractor.

**DERDAK, Thomas.** Free-lance writer and adjunct professor of philosophy at Loyola University of Chicago; former executive director of the Albert Einstein Foundation.

**GALLMAN, Jason.** Free-lance writer and English teacher at Ben Davis High School in Indianapolis, Indiana.

**GASBARRE, April Dougal.** Archivist and free-lance writer specializing in business and social history in Cleveland, Ohio.

**GOPNIK, Hilary.** Free-lance writer.

**GUARDIANO, John.** Director of Economic Research for the Washington, D.C.-based Center for American Eurasian Studies and Relations (CAESAR); Arlington, Virginia-based free-lance writer who writes often about business and economic issues.

**HALASZ, Robert.** Former editor in chief of *World Progress* and *Funk & Wagnalls New Encyclopedia Yearbook;* author, *The U.S. Marines* (Millbrook Press, 1993).

**INGRAM, Frederick.** Business writer living in Columbia, South Carolina; contributor to the *Encyclopedia of Business,* the *Encyclopedia of Consumer Brands,* and *Global Industry Profiles.*

**JACOBSON, Robert R.** Free-lance writer and musician.

**McNULTY, Mary.** Free-lance writer and editor.

**McMANUS, Donald.** Free-lance writer.

**MONTGOMERY, Bruce P.** Curator and director of historical collection, University of Colorado at Boulder.

**MOTE, Dave.** President of information retrieval company Performance Database.

**PEIPPO, Kathleen.** Minneapolis-based free-lance writer.

**PFALZGRAF, Taryn Benbow.** Free-lance editor, writer, and consultant in the Chicago area.

**SALAMIE, David E.** Part-owner of InfoWorks Development Group, a reference publication development and editorial services company.

**TROESTER, Maura.** Free-lance writer based in Chicago.

**WERNICK, Ellen D.** Free-lance writer and editor.

**WOODWARD, Angela.** Free-lance writer.

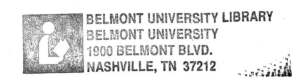